Cage, John
4′33″

Cantus firmi and counterpoint by Fux, Jeppesen, Kirnberger, and Schenker

Carter, Elliott
"Canaries," from *Eight Pieces for Four Timpani*
String Quartet No. 2, first movement

Chance, John Barnes
Variations on a Korean Folk Song

Chant
"Pange Lingua"

Chopin, Frédéric
Étude, Op. 10, No. 1
Mazurka in F Minor, Op. 68, No. 4
Mazurka in D Major, Op. 33, No. 2
Nocturne in E♭ Major, Op. 9, No. 2
Prelude in C Minor, Op. 28, No. 20
Prelude in E Minor, Op. 28, No. 4

Clarke, Jeremiah
Trumpet Voluntary (*Prince of Denmark's March*)

Clementi, Muzio
Sonatina in C Major, Op. 36, No. 1
Sonatina in F Major, Op. 36, No. 4
Sonatina in G Major, Op. 36, No. 5

Copland, Aaron
"Simple Gifts," from *Appalachian Spring*

Corelli, Archangelo
Allemanda and Sarabanda, from Trio Sonata in A Minor, Op. 4, No. 5
Preludio, from Trio Sonata in D Minor, Op. 4, No. 8
Sarabanda, from Sonata in E Minor for Violin and Continuo, Op. 5, No. 6

Corigliano, John
"Come now, my darling," from *The Ghosts of Versailles*

Crueger, Johann
"Nun danket alle Gott"

Crumb, George
"Los muertos llevan alas de musgo," from *Madrigals*, Book I

Dallapiccola, Luigi
"Die Sonne kommt!," from *Goethe-lieder*

Debussy, Claude
"La cathédral engloutie," from *Préludes*, Book I
"Voiles," from *Préludes*, Book I

Edwards, Dixon, and Williams
"Duke of Earl"

Fauré, Gabriel
"Après un rêve"

Foster, Stephen
"Camptown Races"
"Jeanie with the Light Brown Hair"
"Oh! Susanna"

Fux, Johann
Gradus ad Parnassum

Gershwin, George, and Ira Gershwin
"I Got Rhythm," from *Girl Crazy*
"'S Wonderful!," from *Funny Face*

Gibbons, Orlando
Song 46

Gilmore, Patrick S.
"When Johnny Comes Marching Home"

Goffin, Gerry, and Michael Masser
"Saving All My Love for You"

Gordy, Davis, Hutch, and West
"I'll Be There"

Gray, Jerry, and Eddie de Lange
"A String of Pearls"

Green Day
"Wake Me Up When September Ends"

Handel, George Frideric
Chaconne in G Major
From *Messiah*
"Hallelujah!"
"Rejoice greatly"
"Thy rebuke hath broken his heart"

Haydn, Joseph
Piano Sonatas
No. 9 in F Major, third movement
No. 13 in E Major
No. 53 in E Minor, second movement
String Quartet in D Minor, Op. 76, No. 2
String Quartet in F Minor, Op. 20, No. 5, first movement

Hensel, Fanny Mendelssohn
"Bitte"
"Nachtwanderer"
"Neue Liebe, neues Leben"
"Schwanenlied"

Heyman, Edward, and Victor Young
"When I Fall in Love"

Hopkins, John Henry
"Three Kings of Orient"

Horner, Mann, and Weil
"Somewhere Out There," from *An American Tail*

Hovhaness, Alan
Magnificat

Hymn tunes
"America" ("My Country, 'Tis of Thee")
"Chartres"
"Old Hundredth"
"Rosa Mystica"
"St. George's Windsor"
"St. Prisca"

Joplin, Scott
"Pine Apple Rag"
"Ragtime Dance"
"Solace"

Kern, Jerome, and Oscar Hammerstein II
"All the Things You Are"
"Can't Help Lovin' Dat Man"

Kern, Jerome, and Otto Harbach
"Smoke Gets in Your Eyes"

King, Carole
"You've Got a Friend"

Kings of Leon
"Use Somebody"

Kirnberger, Johann Philipp
"La Lutine"

Kuhlau, Friedrich
Sonatina, Op. 55, No. 1, first movement

Kuhnau, Johann
"The Fight Between David and Goliath," from *Biblical Sonatas*, second movement

(continued on back cover)

This registration code provides access to musical excerpts

and other review materials available at the

Musician's Guide to Theory and Analysis, 2E StudySpace site:

wwnorton.com/studyspace

HYSZ-MLTT

The Musician's Guide to Theory and Analysis

SECOND EDITION

W. W. NORTON & COMPANY
NEW YORK • LONDON

The Musician's Guide to Theory and Analysis

SECOND EDITION

Jane Piper Clendinning
Florida State University College of Music

Elizabeth West Marvin
Eastman School of Music

W. W. Norton & Company has been independent since its founding in 1923, when William Warder Norton and Mary D. Herter Norton first began publishing lectures delivered at the People's Institute, the adult education division of New York City's Cooper Union. The firm soon expanded its program beyond the Institute, publishing books by celebrated academics from America and abroad. By midcentury, the two major pillars of Norton's publishing program—trade books and college texts—were firmly established. In the 1950s, the Norton family transferred control of the company to its employees, and today—with a staff of four hundred and a comparable number of trade, college, and professional titles published each year—W. W. Norton & Company stands as the largest and oldest publishing house owned wholly by its employees.

Printed in the United States of America
Second Edition

The text of this book is composed in Miller Roman with the display set in Belizio.
Editor: Maribeth Payne
Developmental editor: Susan Gaustad
Managing editor, College: Marian Johnson
Emedia editor: Steve Hoge
Ancillaries editor: Courtney Hirschey
Project editor: Justin Hoffman
Editorial assistant: Ariella Foss
Senior production manager, College: Benjamin Reynolds
Proofreader: JoAnn Simony
Composition and music setting: Willow Graphics / David Botwinik
Book design: Lisa Buckley
Art director: Rubina Yeh
Manufacturing by QuadGraphics—Taunton, MA

Library of Congress Cataloging-in-Publication Data

Clendinning, Jane Piper.
The musician's guide to theory and analysis / by Jane Piper Clendinning, Elizabeth West Marvin -- 2nd ed.
p. cm.
Includes index.
ISBN 978-0-393-93081-8 (hardcover)
1. Music theory. 2. Musical analysis. I. Marvin, Elizabeth West, 1955- II. Title.

MT6.C57 2010
781--dc22 2010024272

W. W. Norton & Company, Inc., 500 Fifth Avenue, New York, N. Y. 10110
www.wwnorton.com
W. W. Norton & Company Ltd., Castle House, 75/76 Wells Street, London W1T 3QT

1 2 3 4 5 6 7 8 9 0

To our teachers, colleagues, and students—
with whom we have shared the joy of music,
and from whom we continue to learn—
and, with thanks, to our families
for their patience and support

Brief Contents

Contents

Part II Diatonic Harmony and Tonicization

Preface

Have you ever wondered what you, as a twenty-first-century musician, will need to know to prepare for a music career in the current marketplace? Perhaps you will perform music for recordings, broadcast, or podcast; write music for films, video games, web designers, or advertisers; or create new forms of jazz, rock, or electronic dance music. You might find your place in the concert hall, performing art music of the seventeenth century to today. Maybe you will become a teacher, arts advocate, or music entrepreneur. How can you prepare for such diverse opportunities? We believe the answer is to learn as much as possible, and in as many styles as possible. The more you know about many kinds of music, the better prepared you will be to perform, compose, teach, and advocate for music throughout your career.

The *Musician's Guide* series is perhaps the most comprehensive set of multimedia materials available today for learning music theory. The *Theory and Analysis* portion includes a textbook with coordinated Workbook—covering wide-ranging topics, from music fundamentals to music of today—plus an Anthology of core repertoire for study. Every work in the Anthology can be heard on the accompanying DVD set, which features many performances newly recorded for this collection by artists from the Eastman School of Music. Short musical examples in the text and Workbook are also recorded on DVDs (except where prohibited by copyright), so that you can hear an illustration of each concept as it is introduced. A coordinated website, StudySpace, allows you to experience this text in a more interactive way and to expand your learning experience beyond the printed page.

The *Aural Skills* portion of the *Musician's Guide* package, published in two volumes, is coordinated with the theory text part by part. It is organized into two volumes by skill type. One volume focuses on performance skills (sight-singing and rhythm reading, keyboard and improvisation skills). The other builds dictation skills: its DVD of recordings ranges from short chord patterns to full harmonic and melodic dictations, to contextual-listening exercises drawn from music literature in a variety of genres and ensembles.

Why Study Music Theory?

Have you ever tried to explain something without having the right words to capture exactly what you mean? It can be a frustrating experience. Part of the process of preparing for a professional career is learning the special language of your chosen field. To those outside the profession, the technical language may seem like a secret code intended to prevent the nonspecialist from understanding. For example, a medical doctor might speak of "cardiac infarction," "myocardia," or "angina" when referring to conditions that we might call (inaccurately) a heart attack. To those who know the technical terms, however, one or two words capture a wealth of associated knowledge—years of experience and books' worth of information.

Words and symbols not only let us name things, they also help us to communicate how separate elements work together and group into categories. Music theory provides useful terms and categories, but it does more than that: it also provides a framework for considering *how* music is put together, *what* musical elements are in play, *when* particular styles were prevalent, and *why* music sounds the way it does. Understanding the vocabulary for categorizing and explaining musical events will prepare you to develop your own theories about the music you are playing and studying.

The purpose of this book is to introduce you to the technical language of music. In the first part, you will learn (or review) basic terminology and notation. Mastery of terminology will allow you to communicate quickly and accurately with other musicians; mastery of notation will allow you to read and write music effortlessly. You will next learn about small- to medium-scale musical progressions and how they work. Mastery of these progressions will help you compose music in particular styles, structure improvisations on your instrument, make interpretive decisions in performance, and improve your sight-reading skills.

Later parts of the book deal with larger musical contexts, such as how sections of music fit together to make musical form. You will learn how to write in standard musical forms in differing styles, how to divide the pieces you perform into musical sections, and how to convey your understanding of form in performance. In the final chapters, we explore ways that these concepts are transformed (or abandoned) in music of the twentieth century, and consider new theories that have arisen to explain music structure in this repertoire. We will apply this information in the same ways as in previous chapters—with direct links to performance, analysis, and writing.

One of the most important things to remember about music theory is that it is all about sounds—how and why music sounds the way it does. You will be listening to music in every chapter, so that you can associate terms and notation with sounding music. We want you to make connections every day between what you are learning in this book and the music you are playing, singing, hearing, and writing. Music theory is absolutely relevant to the music making we do—whether it's performing, analyzing, or composing. You will see references in nearly every chapter to the way its content might inform your music making. Use this information! Take it to the practice room, the studio, and the rehearsal hall to make the connection between your coursework and your life as a practicing musician. We hope that the concepts you learn here will impact the ways you think about music for many years to come.

Using This Book

Each chapter includes several useful features, described below, that will facilitate your study.

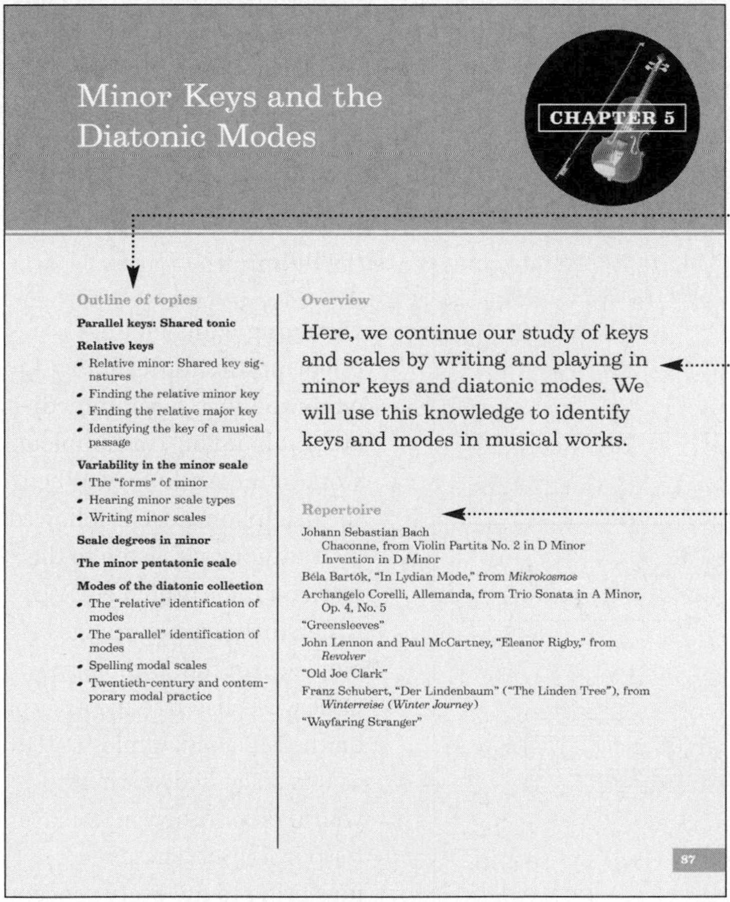
Minor Keys and the Diatonic Modes

CHAPTER 5

Outline of topics

Parallel keys: Shared tonic

Relative keys

- Relative minor: Shared key signatures
- Finding the relative minor key
- Finding the relative major key
- Identifying the key of a musical passage

Variability in the minor scale

- The "forms" of minor
- Hearing minor scale types
- Writing minor scales

Scale degrees in minor

The minor pentatonic scale

Modes of the diatonic collection

- The "relative" identification of modes
- The "parallel" identification of modes
- Spelling modal scales
- Twentieth-century and contemporary modal practice

Overview

Here, we continue our study of keys and scales by writing and playing in minor keys and diatonic modes. We will use this knowledge to identify keys and modes in musical works.

Repertoire

Johann Sebastian Bach
Chaconne, from Violin Partita No. 2 in D Minor
Invention in D Minor
Béla Bartók, "In Lydian Mode," from *Mikrokosmos*
Archangelo Corelli, Allemanda, from Trio Sonata in A Minor, Op. 4, No. 5
"Greensleeves"
John Lennon and Paul McCartney, "Eleanor Rigby," from *Revolver*
"Old Joe Clark"
Franz Schubert, "Der Lindenbaum" ("The Linden Tree"), from *Winterreise* (*Winter Journey*)
"Wayfaring Stranger"

87

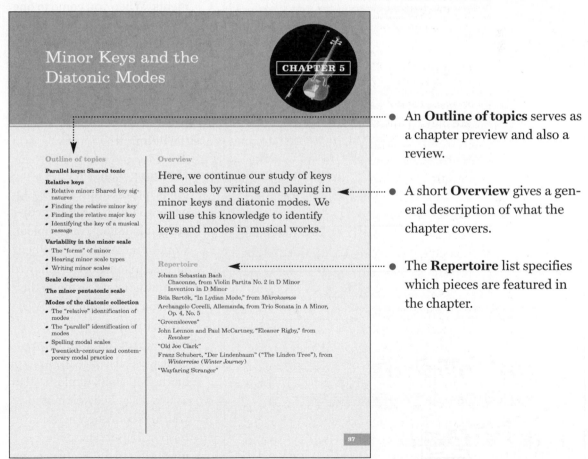

- An **Outline of topics** serves as a chapter preview and also a review.
- A short **Overview** gives a general description of what the chapter covers.
- The **Repertoire** list specifies which pieces are featured in the chapter.

Boldface signals a new and important term. Most of these terms are listed together at the end of the chapter and defined in the Glossary in Appendix 2. Definitions are also available for review on StudySpace, the companion website, in the form of interactive flashcards.

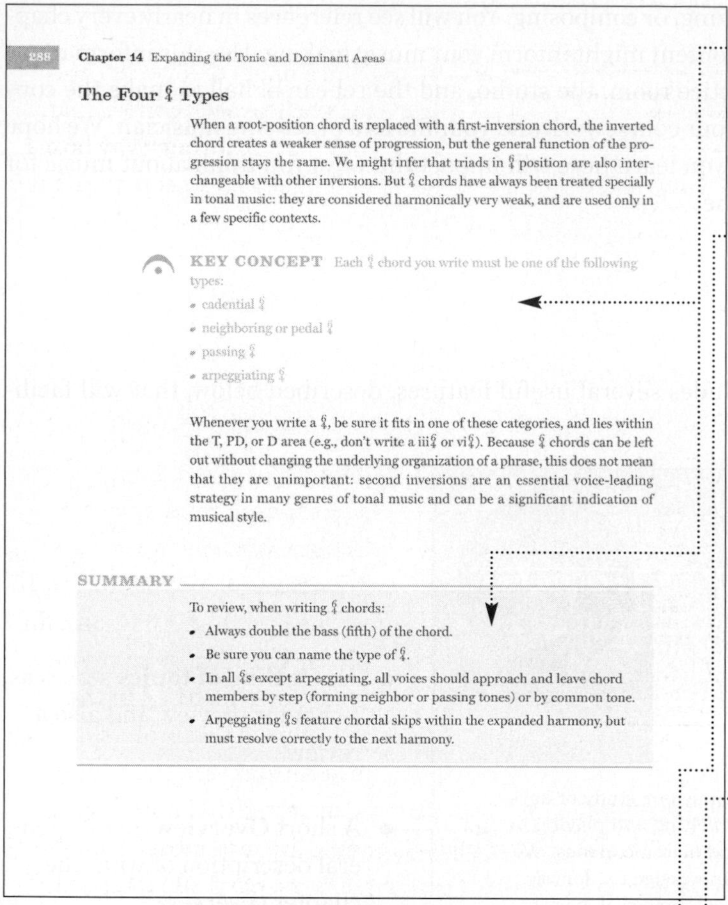
288 Chapter 14 Expanding the Tonic and Dominant Areas

The Four $^6_4$ Types

When a root-position chord is replaced with a first-inversion chord, the inverted chord creates a weaker sense of progression, but the general function of the progression stays the same. We might infer that triads in $^6_4$ position are also interchangeable with other inversions. But $^6_4$ chords have always been treated specially in tonal music: they are considered harmonically very weak, and are used only in a few specific contexts.

KEY CONCEPT Each $^6_4$ chord you write must be one of the following types:

- cadential $^6_4$
- neighboring or pedal $^6_4$
- passing $^6_4$
- arpeggiating $^6_4$

Whenever you write a $^6_4$, be sure it fits in one of these categories, and lies within the T, PD, or D area (e.g., don't write a iii$^6_4$ or vi$^6_4$). Because $^6_4$ chords can be left out without changing the underlying organization of a phrase, this does not mean that they are unimportant: second inversions are an essential voice-leading strategy in many genres of tonal music and can be a significant indication of musical style.

SUMMARY

To review, when writing $^6_4$ chords:

- Always double the bass (fifth) of the chord.
- Be sure you can name the type of $^6_4$.
- In all $^6_4$s except arpeggiating, all voices should approach and leave chord members by step (forming neighbor or passing tones) or by common tone.
- Arpeggiating $^6_4$s feature chordal skips within the expanded harmony, but must resolve correctly to the next harmony.

- **Key Concept** and **Summary** boxes in every chapter identify the most important ideas and summarize key information.
- ***Try it*** boxes, scattered through every chapter, provide immediate opportunities to practice every core concept. Many of these exercises preview upcoming Workbook assignments. When you come to one of these exercises, try it, then check your answer in Appendix 1. Only then will you know that you have understood a new concept and can apply it to your own music making.
- **Listening icons** identify opportunities for listening—either to the excerpt immediately at hand or to a complete work in the Anthology. When the headphone icon is followed by "(anthology)," listen to the work on the Anthology DVD, which includes recordings of all pieces in the Anthology. Otherwise, listen to the excerpt on the Music Examples DVD as it is discussed, or rip it to your iPod or other .mp3 player for portability. These recordings bring to life every concept under study, to help you understand it and to apply it to your own music making.

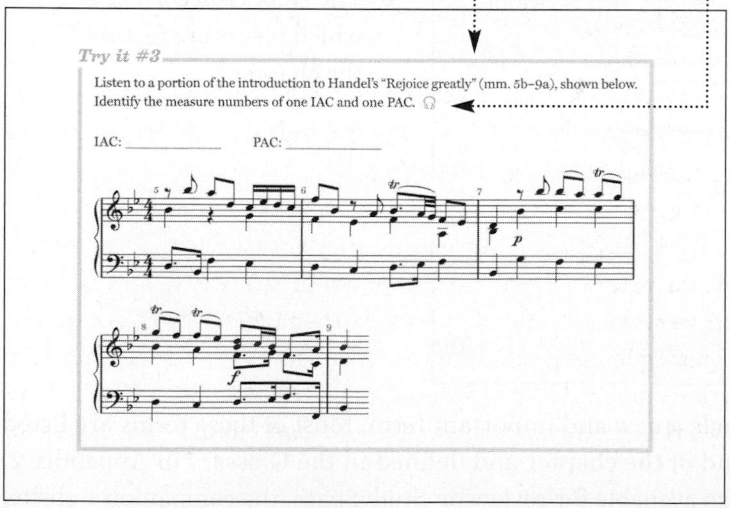
Try it #3

Listen to a portion of the introduction to Handel's "Rejoice greatly" (mm. 5b–9a), shown below. Identify the measure numbers of one IAC and one PAC.

IAC: ___________ PAC: ___________

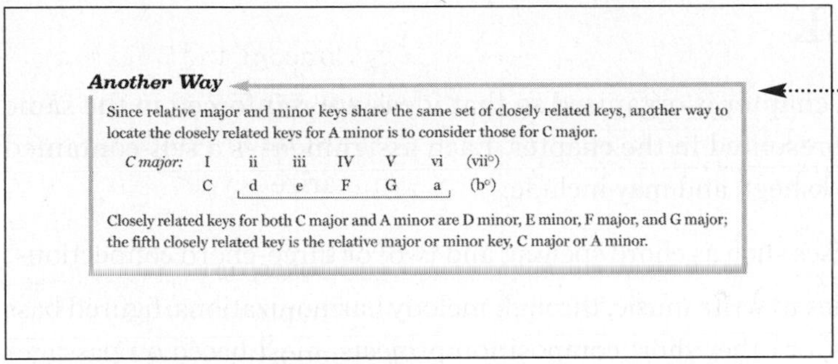

Another Way

Since relative major and minor keys share the same set of closely related keys, another way to locate the closely related keys for A minor is to consider those for C major.

C major:	I	ii	iii	IV	V	vi	(vii°)
	C	d	e	F	G	a	(b°)

Closely related keys for both C major and A minor are D minor, E minor, F major, and G major; the fifth closely related key is the relative major or minor key, C major or A minor.

Since many theory concepts can be learned in more than one way, **Another Way** boxes offer alternative explanations. Use whatever method works best for you.

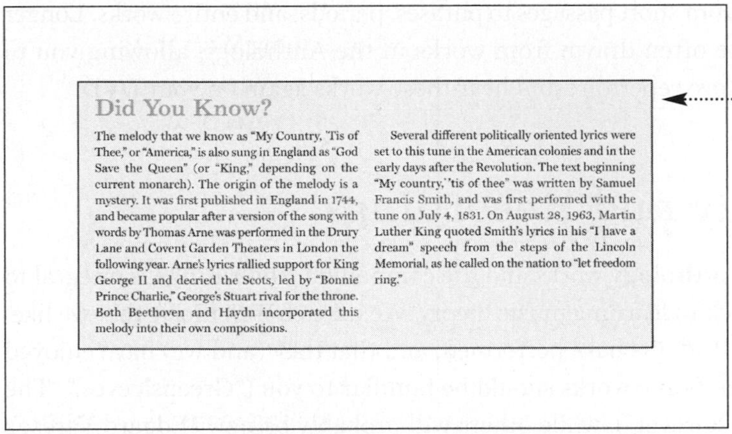

Did You Know?

The melody that we know as "My Country, 'Tis of Thee," or "America," is also sung in England as "God Save the Queen" (or "King," depending on the current monarch). The origin of the melody is a mystery. It was first published in England in 1744, and became popular after a version of the song with words by Thomas Arne was performed in the Drury Lane and Covent Garden Theaters in London the following year. Arne's lyrics rallied support for King George II and decried the Scots, led by "Bonnie Prince Charlie," George's Stuart rival for the throne. Both Beethoven and Haydn incorporated this melody into their own compositions.

Several different politically oriented lyrics were set to this tune in the American colonies and in the early days after the Revolution. The text beginning "My country, 'tis of thee" was written by Samuel Francis Smith, and was first performed with the tune on July 4, 1831. On August 28, 1963, Martin Luther King quoted Smith's lyrics in his "I have a dream" speech from the steps of the Lincoln Memorial, as he called on the nation to "let freedom ring."

Did You Know? These boxes appear at the end of each chapter and explain certain historical developments (such as the origins of notation), fill in background for composers and pieces featured in the chapter (for example, the story of a Mozart aria), or supply more advanced information (in case you're curious). These aren't required reading, but are rather a source of enrichment. They come from stories that we, as teachers, have told in class to our students.

Terms You Should Know and **Questions for Review** provide essential end-of-chapter review. In addition to the ***Try it*** **Answers** and **Glossary**, the **Appendixes** include a summary of part-writing guidelines, a summary of instrumental ranges, and a table of set classes. There are two **indexes**: one for composers and pieces studied, another for terms and concepts.

Electronic resources will help you master material in each chapter. The unique, user-friendly **StudySpace** website (www.wwnorton.com/studyspace) provides flashcards for reviewing important terms, an interactive keyboard on which you can play intervals and chords, streaming sound files for most examples in the chapter, and multiple-choice quiz items (and answers). Many of these quiz questions include short musical scores for study. In addition, you can download pages from the Workbook formatted in Finale, and submit assignments electronically.

Using the Workbook

Each **Workbook** chapter is organized so that ideas are reinforced in the same order they were presented in the chapter. Each assignment is a self-contained front-to-back worksheet, and may include:

- short exercises such as chord spelling and two- or three-chord connections;
- opportunities to write music, through melody harmonizations, figured bass realizations, or other short composition projects, most based on passages from music literature rather than author-constructed practice exercises;
- analyses—from short passages to phrases, periods, and entire works. Longer analyses are often drawn from works in the Anthology, allowing you to revisit the core repertoire and hear these works again on your DVD.

Using the Anthology and Recordings

The study of the **Anthology** works and the companion **Recordings** is integral to the book's approach to learning music theory. We have chosen music that we like, that many of our students have performed, and that they (and we) have enjoyed exploring together. Some works should be familiar to you ("Greensleeves," "The Stars and Stripes Forever"), while others will probably be new (Edgard Varèse's *Density 21.5*). There are classics of the repertoire (Mozart and Beethoven piano sonata movements, German Lieder selected from Schubert and Schumann song cycles, and groundbreaking compositions by Schoenberg and Webern); pieces for varied performing ensembles (solo flute, guitar, and violin; chamber orchestra, string quartet, and choir, among others); and pieces in contrasting musical styles—from American popular songs to French mélodie, from piano ragtime to minimalist music, from marches for band to hymns and anthems for choirs. While the Anthology includes gems of familiar repertoire, we have also included wonderful but less familiar works by women and African American composers (Fanny Mendelssohn Hensel, Scott Joplin), as well as diverse works written within the last century.

We begin every chapter by asking you to listen to one or two works from the Anthology. You will see a headphone icon in the margin or attached to the caption of a music example every time we want you to listen. Please take the time to listen and follow the Anthology score—it will increase your enjoyment of this text, make your music theory study more relevant to your performance studies, and broaden your knowledge of music literature. (If the icon is by itself, without the label "anthology," the example can be heard on the Music Examples DVD.) Our spiral-learning approach revisits the Anthology's core repertoire from chapter to chapter as you learn new concepts—thus, a single piece might be used to illustrate scales, triads, cadence types, secondary dominants, common-chord modulation, sequence, and binary form. By the third or fourth time you "visit" a particular work, it will seem like an old friend.

New in This Edition

We have worked to incorporate the ideas of many helpful reviewers, while retaining the key features of an effective pedagogical strategy. Among the biggest changes are the organization of the Workbook into front-to-back assignments and the addition of new chapters on counterpoint, art song, and popular music. The list below summarizes key new features of this edition.

- *Fundamentals:* We offer a number of new strategies for developing fundamental skills, such as interval and triad spelling, and many more basic drills in *Try its* and Workbook exercises.
- *Counterpoint:* Completely rewritten, Chapters 9 and 10 provide a focused introduction to species counterpoint, while a new chapter on chorale-style soprano-bass counterpoint (11) serves as a transition to four-part composition. A new chapter on invention and fugue (24) brings together contrapuntal and harmonic concepts to cover larger contrapuntal forms.
- *Diatonic harmony:* Comprehensively revised, expanded, and reorganized, this part of the book introduces harmonies with equivalent function more gradually, expands coverage of the basic phrase model, and introduces predominant harmony and basic embellishments earlier to allow a richer selection of examples from the literature. It treats $^6_4$ chord types together and delays the leading-tone seventh chord until students have acquired a better understanding of primary triads.
- *Chromatic harmony and form:* These chapters are expanded to incorporate new nineteenth-century repertoire, enhance coverage of chromatic harmony, and improve pacing. This section of the text features the new chapter on invention and fugue, expanded coverage of popular music and art song (now each in its own chapter), and expanded coverage of variation, recitative-aria, French mélodie, and large ternary form.

Workbook: The Workbook has been redesigned for ease of use and grading, and the Teacher's Edition has been formatted to match the Student Edition in page layout and pagination. Each chapter features:

- double-sided, self-contained worksheets, organized in chapter order;
- more basic drill-and-practice, part writing, and brief analysis exercises;
- diverse analytical examples with worksheets that capture the essential elements of each work.

Anthology: The Anthology now features over 100 scores, 40 of them new, and also

- contains more chorales and hymns, contrapuntal works, and pieces representative of nineteenth-century chromaticism and impressionism;
- adds a new chronological index and short headnotes to each score, placing works in their historical context.

The Anthology DVD recordings include alternative performances for class comparison (e.g., fortepiano and modern piano) and versions of SATB works in different textures (choral performance with text, soprano-bass and four-voice keyboard renditions).

Electronic Solutions for Students and Instructors

Students now have several ways to access the musical examples in the book: (1) via DVDs that come with the text, (2) by means of StudySpace, the student website, which contains streaming listening examples; and (3) through the eBook links to audio examples. Students can also access flashcards of each chapter's key terms, Finale-formatted worksheets from the Workbook, an online keyboard, and self-quizzes for practice and review on StudySpace.

Instructors can download free coursepacks, which include chapter-based assignments, quizzes, Finale worksheets, and an index of musical examples.

To the Instructor

The *Musician's Guide* is a comprehensive teaching and learning package for undergraduate music theory classes that integrates technological resources with a traditional textbook and recordings. Numerous support mechanisms can help you efficiently prepare for class. We know that not all theory classes are taught by professional theorists, and we have designed these materials specially with teaching assistants and performance faculty in mind.

- The **Teacher's Edition** of the **Workbook** that accompanies *The Musician's Guide to Theory and Analysis* includes answers to all exercises.
- **DVD-ROMs:** No longer will you need to plan for a trip to the library before class to find a recording of the work you will be studying; the **Anthology** that comes with this bundled package includes recordings of the entire core repertoire, and recordings are also provided of most textbook and Workbook examples, in high-quality professional performances by faculty and graduate students from the Eastman School of Music. These are formatted as .mp3 files and may be played from a computer or downloaded to any .mp3 player for use in class.
- **Highlights of the repertoire** in the Anthology/DVD set, over 100 works or movements, include the following:
    - 26 twentieth-century compositions, ranging from pre-1950 (Gershwin, Stravinsky, Bartók, Schoenberg, Webern) to post-1950 (Penderecki, Reich, Corigliano, Tavener)
    - Music by women and African American composers (Clara Schumann, Hensel, Joplin)
    - Music in popular genres (ragtime and Broadway songs by Gershwin and Willson)
    - Music for band, wind ensemble, and orchestra (Bach, Chance, Sousa, Penderecki)
    - Music for choir (Bach, Tavener, Handel, Mozart)
    - Music featuring solo instruments (flute, clarinet, trumpet, guitar, violin)
    - Keyboard performances on piano, fortepiano, harpsichord, and organ
- **Comparison performances:** Several works on the DVDs are given in two contrasting performances for comparison. These interpretations demonstrate performance-practice issues such as ornamentation, or contrast historical instruments and tunings with modern ones (Mozart, Purcell, Joplin). Bach chorales are recorded in three formats for use in class: choral performance with text, soprano-bass frameworks on organ, and full SATB texture on organ. Hymn tunes are likewise heard in soprano-bass and SATB textures.

Our Thanks to . . .

A work of this size and scope is helped along the way by many people. We are especially grateful for the support of our families—Elizabeth A. Clendinning and

Jeffrey L. Armstrong; and Glenn, Russell, and Caroline West. Our work together as co-authors has been incredibly rewarding, and we are thankful for that collaboration and friendship. We also thank Joel Phillips (Westminster Choir College) for his many important contributions—pedagogical, musical, and personal—to our project, and especially for the coordinated aural skills component of this package, *The Musician's Guide to Aural Skills*, now co-authored with Paul Murphy (State University of New York at Fredonia). While working on the project, we have received encouragement and useful ideas from our students at Florida State University and the Eastman School of Music as well as from music theory teachers across the country. We thank these teachers for their willingness to share their years of experience with us.

For subvention of the recordings that accompany the text and anthology, and for his continued support of strong music theory pedagogy, we thank Douglas Lowry (Dean of the Eastman School of Music). For performance of all the short keyboard examples in the text, we thank Richard Masters, whose sight-reading abilities, flexibility, and good grace are all appreciated. We also thank Don Gibson (Dean of Florida State University's College of Music) for his enthusiasm and unfailing support. For pedagogical discussions over the years, we are grateful to our colleagues at Florida State University, the Eastman School of Music, and to the College Board's AP Music Theory Test Development Committee members and AP Readers. Special thanks to Mary Arlin for her thorough and meticulous checking and generous help with additional workbook exercises, and to Leigh van Handel for writing the StudySpace quizzes.

We are indebted to the thorough and detailed work of our prepublication reviewers, whose careful reading of the manuscript inspired many improvements, large and small: Douglas Bartholomew (Montana State University), Rhett Bender (Southern Oregon University), Vincent Benitez (State College of Pennsylvania), Per Broman (Bowling Green State University), Poundie Burstein (Hunter College), Lora Dobos (Ohio State University), Nora Engebretson (Bowling Green State University), Benjamin Levy (Arizona State University), Peter Martens (Texas Tech University), Paul Murphy (State University of New York at Fredonia), Tim Pack (University of Oregon), Ruth Rendleman (Montclair State), Elaine Rendler (George Mason University), Stephen Rodgers (University of Oregon), Mark Spicer (Hunter College), Reynold Tharp (University of Illinois at Urbana Champaign), Gene Trantham (Bowling Green State University), Heidi Von Gunden (University of Illinois), James Wiznerowicz (Virginia Commonwealth University), and Annie Yih (University of California at Santa Barbara). We also acknowledge that the foundation for this book rests on writings of the great music theorists of the past and present, from the sixteenth to twenty-first century, from whom we have learned the "tricks of our trade" and whose pedagogical works have inspired ours.

For production of all recordings, our thanks go to recording engineers Mike Farrington and John Ebert, who worked tirelessly with Elizabeth Marvin on recording and editing sessions, as well as to Helen Smith, who oversees Eastman's Office of Technology and Music Production. We also acknowledge the strong contributions of David Peter Coppen, archivist of the Eastman Audio Archive, for his work contacting faculty and alumni for permission to include their performances among our recordings. We finally thank the faculty and students of the Eastman School who gave so generously of their time to make these recordings. The joy of their music making contributed mightily to this project.

We are indebted to the W. W. Norton staff for their commitment to *The Musician's Guide* and their painstaking care in producing these volumes. Most notable among these are Susan Gaustad, whose knowledge of music and detailed, thoughtful questions made her a joy to work with, and music editor Maribeth Payne, whose vision has helped launch each edition with great enthusiasm. We are grateful for Norton's forward-thinking technology editor Steve Hoge, who helped refine our ideas for the book's website. Justin Hoffman was invaluable in checking assignments, preparing the headnotes for the anthology, and coordinating recording logs to assist with the anthology and chapter examples. Rubina Yeh created the book's design for all parts of the *Musician's Guide* package, Courtney Hirschey project edited the Anthology, JoAnn Simony provided expert proofreading, Ariella Foss pursued copyright permissions, David Botwinik set the text and Workbook, Roberta Flechner set the Anthology, and Ben Reynolds oversaw the production of these multifaceted texts through to completion. Our gratitude to one and all.

Jane Piper Clendinning
Elizabeth West Marvin

PART I

Elements of Music

CHAPTER 1

Pitch and Pitch Class

Outline of topics

Introduction to pitch

- Letter names
- Pitch classes and pitches

The piano keyboard

- White keys
- Black keys: Flats and sharps
- Enharmonic equivalents
- Half steps and whole steps
- Double flats and sharps

Reading pitches from a score

- Staff notation
- Treble clef
- Bass clef
- C-clefs
- Naming registers
- Ledger lines
- Writing pitches on a score

Dynamic markings

Overview

When we read a page of music, we translate its symbols into sound—sung, played on an instrument, or heard in our heads. We begin our study of music theory by learning to read and write the symbols that represent pitch, one of music's basic elements.

Repertoire

Jeremiah Clarke, *Trumpet Voluntary* (*Prince of Denmark's March*)
Scott Joplin, "Solace"

Introduction to Pitch

Listen to the beginning of Jeremiah Clarke's *Trumpet Voluntary*. Follow Example 1.1, the musical notation (or **score**) of the opening. You may not have encountered some of the musical symbols, but most will become familiar in the course of this chapter.

EXAMPLE 1.1: Clarke, *Trumpet Voluntary*, mm. 1–4

Letter Names

Musical tones are named with the first seven letters of the alphabet—A, B, C, D, E, F, G—repeated endlessly.

KEY CONCEPT Imagine these seven letters ascending like stairs or arranged around a circle like a clock, as in Figure 1.1. "Count" up or down in the series by reciting the letters forward (clockwise) or backward (counterclockwise).

FIGURE 1.1: Seven letter names

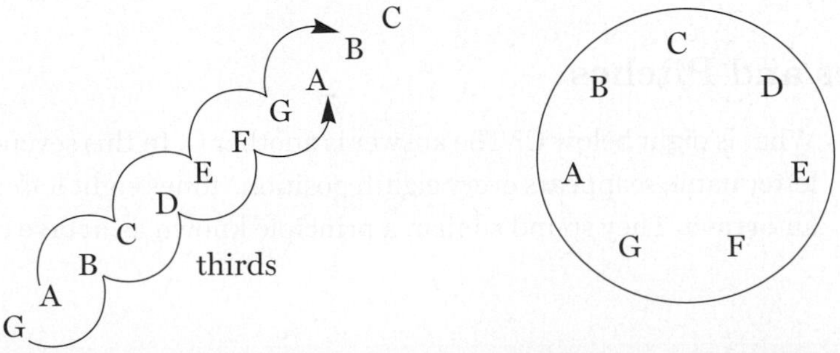

To count up beyond G, start over with A: E–F–G–A–B. . . . To count down below A, start over again with G: C–B–A–G–F–E. . . . You will read music more fluently if you also practice reading alternate letter names, as marked in Figure 1.1: A–C–E–G–B or G–B–D–F–A–C. This is called counting in thirds, because each pair of notes spans three letter names: A–C encompases A, B, and C.

Learning to count in letter names is a fundamental musical skill. Practice counting backward and forward from A to A, C to C, G to G, and so on, until you feel as comfortable counting backward as forward. Think of the movement as "upward" when you count forward, and "downward" when you count backward. For example, five above C is G: C–D–E–F–G. To find six below E, count backward: the answer is again G (E–D–C–B–A–G). When counting letter names, always include the first and last letters in the series: three above F is A, not B (count F–G–A, not G–A–B).

Try it #1

Find each letter name requested.

A. Remember to count the given note as 1.

(1) 7 above G: **F**	(6) 5 below A: _____	(11) 2 above F: _____
(2) 6 above F: _____	(7) 3 above E: _____	(12) 4 above C: _____
(3) 2 above D: _____	(8) 2 below C: _____	(13) 6 below A: _____
(4) 4 below B: _____	(9) 3 above G: _____	(14) 7 below E: _____
(5) 3 below C: _____	(10) 2 above B: _____	(15) 5 above G: _____

B. Count in thirds above the pitch given. Write one letter name in each blank.

(1) G: **B** - **D** - _____ - _____ (2) D: _____ - _____ - _____ - _____

(3) A: _____ - _____ - _____ - _____ (4) B: _____ - _____ - _____ - _____

(5) C: _____ - _____ - _____ - _____

Pitch Classes and Pitches

What is eight below C? The answer is another C. In this seven-name system, each letter name reappears every eighth position. Tones eight letter names apart make an **octave**. They sound similar, a principle known as **octave equivalence**.

KEY CONCEPT Octave-related notes belong to the same **pitch class** and have the same letter name. The pitch class D, for example, represents every D in every octave. A **pitch**, on the other hand, is a tone that sounds in one particular octave.

Listen again to Example 1.1 to hear pitch class D played in several octaves simultaneously. At the very beginning of the piece, the first two successive pitches of the lowest part (the organ pedal) sound similar because they are an octave apart. At the same time, the trumpet plays another D in a higher octave. These notes differ in octave and tone color, or **timbre** (trumpet vs. organ), but all three pitches belong to the same pitch class, D.

The Piano Keyboard

White Keys

Throughout this text, we will reinforce concepts with the help of a keyboard. As a musician, you will find keyboard skills essential, even if it is not your primary instrument. Because of the piano's great range and ability to sound numerous pitches simultaneously, keyboard skills allow you to play simple accompaniments, demonstrate musical ideas, and harmonize melodies.

The white keys of the keyboard correspond to the seven letters of the musical alphabet, as shown in Figure 1.2. Locate them in relation to the two- and three-note groups of black keys. Immediately to the left of any group of two black keys is pitch class C; immediately to the left of any three black keys is pitch class F. **Middle C** is the C closest to the middle of the piano keyboard.

KEY CONCEPT No black key appears between white keys E and F or between B and C.

FIGURE 1.2: Piano keyboard with letter names

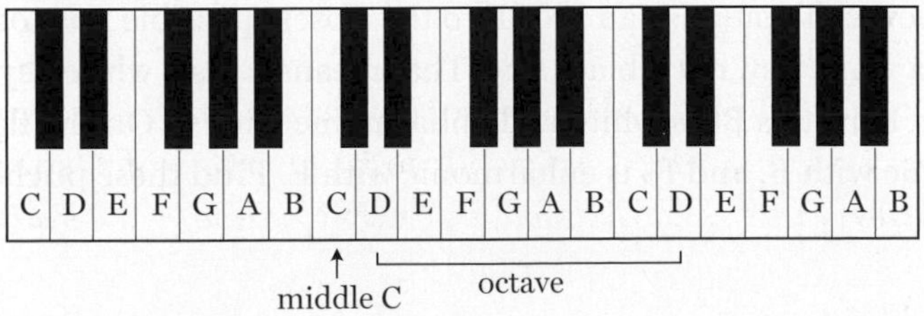

Black Keys: Flats and Sharps

The black-key pitches are named in relation to adjacent white-key pitches. The black key immediately above (to the right of) any white key gets the white note's name plus a **sharp** (♯). As Figure 1.3 shows, each group of two black keys is called C♯ (C-sharp) and D♯, and each group of three black keys is F♯, G♯, and A♯. At the same time, the black key immediately below (to the left of) any white key gets the white note's name plus a **flat** (♭). That means the group of two black keys can also be called D♭ (D-flat) and E♭, and the three black keys G♭, A♭, and B♭. Every black key therefore has two possible names: one with a sharp and one with a flat. The two names are **enharmonic** spellings.

FIGURE 1.3: Keyboard with with enharmonic pitches marked

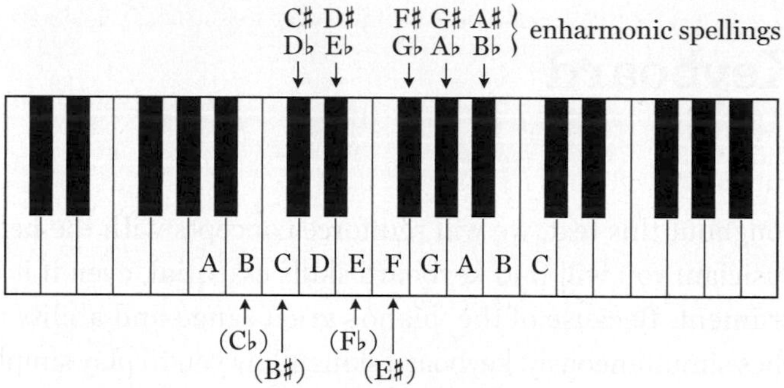

The sharp and flat symbols are called **accidentals** (although there is nothing "accidental" about their use or placement). A third common accidental, a **natural** (♮) cancels a sharp or flat. It returns the pitch to its "natural" state and to its white-key location on the keyboard.

Enharmonic Equivalents

Enharmonic pitches have the same sound but different names (B♭ = A♯); they belong to the same pitch class. Not all sharped or flatted pitches are black keys, however: if you raise an E or B to the closest possible note on the keyboard, you get a white key, not a black one. That means E♯ is a white key and is enharmonic with F, just as B♯ is white and enharmonic with C. On the flat side, C♭ is enharmonic with B, and F♭ is enharmonic with E. Find these pitches in Figure 1.3.

Try it #2

Name the enharmonic equivalent.

(1) G♭: F♯	(5) B: _____	(9) D♯: _____
(2) B♯: _____	(6) A♭: _____	(10) E: _____
(3) A♯: _____	(7) E♯: _____	(11) F♯: _____
(4) D♭: _____	(8) B♭: _____	(12) F: _____

Half Steps and Whole Steps

The distance between any two notes is called an **interval**. Two intervals that serve as basic building blocks of music are half steps and whole steps.

KEY CONCEPT A **half step** (or **semitone**) is the interval between any pitch and the next closest pitch on the keyboard, in either direction. The combination of two half steps forms a **whole step** (or **whole tone**); a whole step always has one note in between its two notes.

On a keyboard, a half step usually spans a white note to a black note (or black to white)—except in the case of B to C and E to F, as shown in Figure 1.4. Whole steps usually span two keys the same color: black to black (like F♯ to G♯) or white to white (like A to B). Again, the exceptions are the white-to-white half steps: a whole step above E is not F, but F♯; a whole step below C is not B, but B♭.

FIGURE 1.4: Half and whole steps at the keyboard

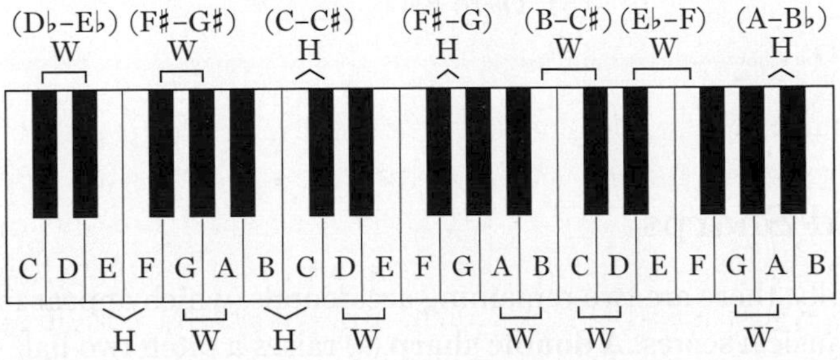

SUMMARY

1. The distance between any two notes is an interval. Two intervals that serve as basic building blocks of music are half and whole steps.
2. Half steps usually span keys of different colors: white to black or black to white.
   - The exceptions are E–F and B–C, the white-key half steps.
3. Whole steps usually span keys the same color: white to white or black to black.
   - The exceptions are E♭–F, E–F♯, B♭–C, and B–C♯.
4. Double-check the spelling of any half or whole step that includes E, F, B, or C.

Try it #3

A. Name the pitch a half step above or below the given pitch, and give an enharmonic equivalent where possible.

(1) Above G:	**G♯** or **A♭**	(5) Above D: ____ or ____
(2) Below C♯:	____ or ____	(6) Below F: ____ or ____
(3) Above E:	____ or ____	(7) Below G♯: ____ or ____
(4) Below B♭:	____ or ____	(8) Below A♭: ____ or ____

B. Identify the distance between the two notes by writing W (whole step), H (half step), or N (neither).

(1) F♯ to E:	**W**	(5) E to F:	____
(2) C♯ to D:	____	(6) F to G:	____
(3) B♭ to A♭:	____	(7) B♯ to C:	____
(4) C to B♭:	____	(8) D♭ to E♭:	____

Double Flats and Sharps

Finally, there are two remaining accidentals, which appear much less frequently in musical scores. A **double sharp** (𝄪) raises a pitch two half steps (or one whole step) above its letter name; a **double flat** (𝄫) lowers a pitch two half steps below its letter name. For example, the pitches G𝄫 and F are enharmonic, as are A𝄪 and B (Figure 1.5).

FIGURE 1.5: Enharmonic pitches on the keyboard

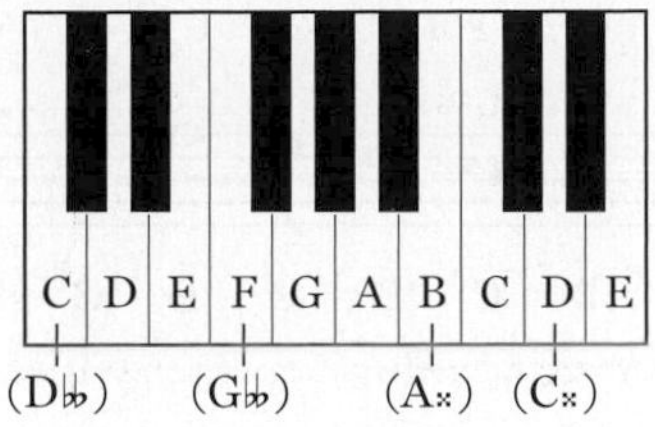

Reading Pitches from a Score

Staff Notation

Perhaps you once improvised a piece of music on your instrument, then created your own system of notation so you could remember it to play again another day. Your system may have consisted of lines slanting up or down to indicate the shape of the melody or drawings to show fingerings. These are exactly the ways that the earliest forms of Western music notation were invented: early notation of melodies merely showed rising or falling lines, and did not identify pitches by letter name. With the invention of the **staff** (the plural is staves), specific pitches could be notated by placing them on lines or spaces. The modern staff consists of five lines and four spaces, which are generally read from bottom to top, with the bottom line called the first and the top line the fifth.

FIGURE 1.6: The staff

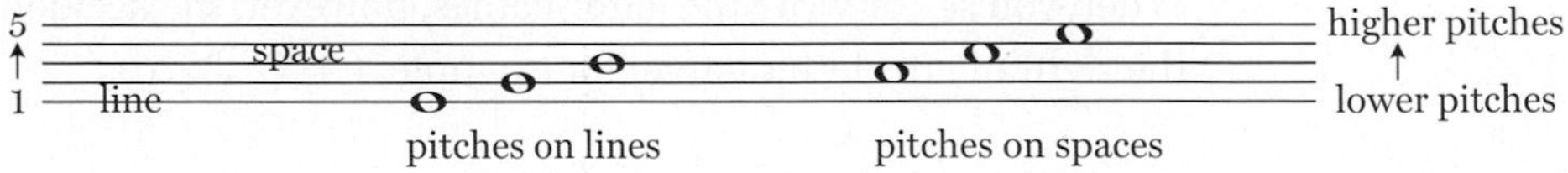

Treble Clef

To identify notes on the staff's lines and spaces, you need a **clef**, the symbol that appears to the far left of every staff. The clef tells which line or space represents which pitch (in which octave). The **treble clef** is generally used for higher notes (those played by a piano's right hand, or by higher instruments such as the trumpet in Example 1.1). This clef is sometimes called the G-clef: its shape resembles a cursive capital G, and the end of its central curving line rests on the staff line for G. Example 1.2 shows how all the other pitches can be read from G, by counting up or down in the musical alphabet: one pitch for each line and space.

EXAMPLE 1.2: Treble clef (G-clef)

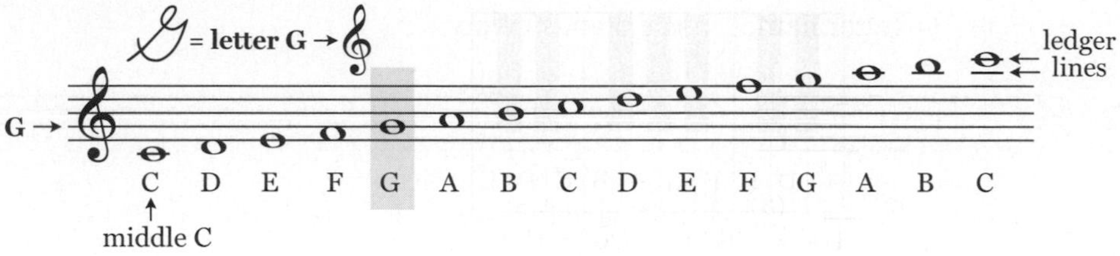

To write notes lower or higher than the staff, add short lines called **ledger lines** below or above the staff, as for middle C and the highest A, B, and C in the example. Memorize the note names for each line and space on the treble-clef staff. Learn the "line notes" together and the "space notes" together, as in Example 1.3 (these should be familiar from counting letter names in thirds). One way to memorize them is to make up sentences whose words begin with their letter names. The treble-clef lines (E-G-B-D-F), for example, might be "Every Good Bird Does Fly" or "Every Good Bond Drives Fast." The spaces of the treble clef simply spell a word: F-A-C-E.

EXAMPLE 1.3: Treble-clef lines and spaces

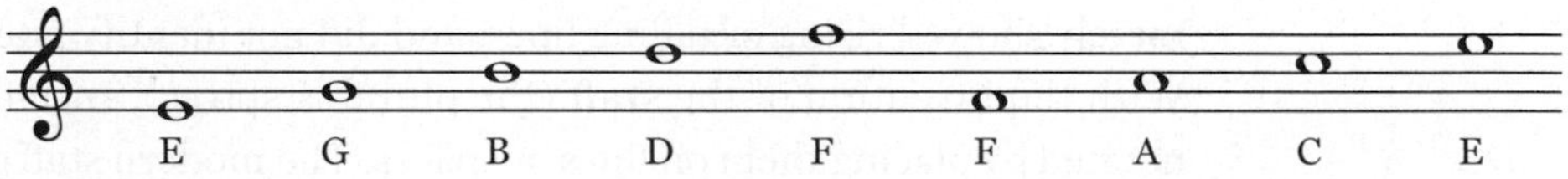

KEY CONCEPT To write pitches with accidentals on the staff, place the accidental before (to the left of) the **note head**, the main (oval) part of the note. When you say or write the letter names, however, the accidental goes after (to the right of) the letter name; for example, C♯ (C-sharp).

Example 1.4 shows various whole and half steps notated on the treble-clef staff. Play each one to hear the difference in sound between these two intervals.

EXAMPLE 1.4: Half and whole steps on a staff

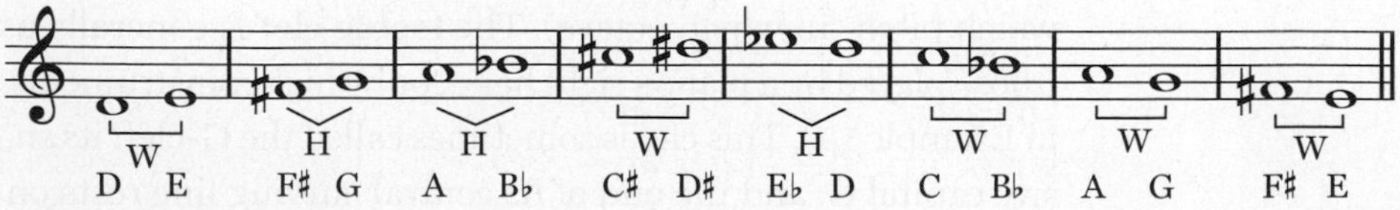

Try it #4

A. Write the letter names in the blanks below.

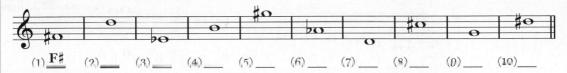

(1) F♯ (2) ___ (3) ___ (4) ___ (5) ___ (6) ___ (7) ___ (8) ___ (9) ___ (10) ___

B. Write each letter name of the melody in the blank below. (Write repeated notes twice.)

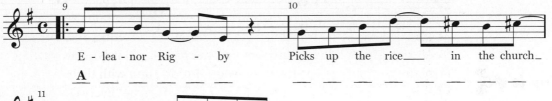

John Lennon and Paul McCartney, "Eleanor Rigby," mm. 9–11

A ___ ___ ___ ___ ___ ___ ___ ___ ___ ___ ___ ___ ___ ___

___ ___ ___ ___ ___ ___ ___ ___

C. Identify whether each pair of pitches below spans a whole step (W), half step (H), or neither (N).

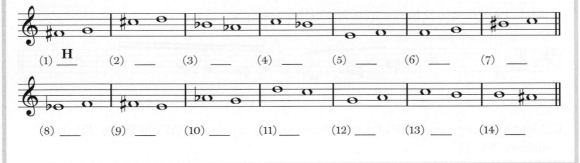

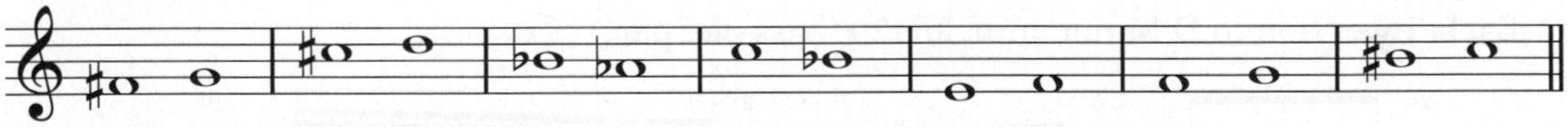

(1) H (2) ___ (3) ___ (4) ___ (5) ___ (6) ___ (7) ___

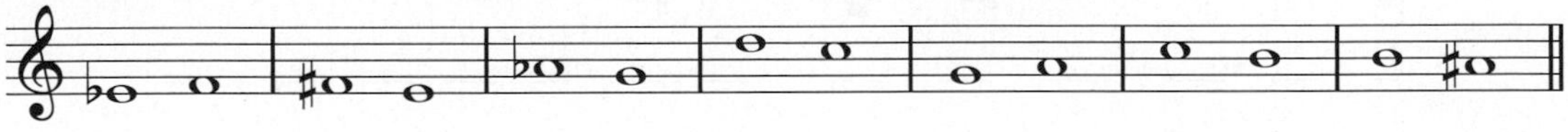

(8) ___ (9) ___ (10) ___ (11) ___ (12) ___ (13) ___ (14) ___

Bass Clef

The **bass clef** is used for lower notes (played by a pianist's left hand or lower instruments like the cello). It's also known as the F-clef: it resembles a cursive capital F. As Example 1.5 shows, its two dots surround the line that represents F. Other pitches may be counted from F or, more likely, memorized according to their position on the staff. Two ways to remember the bass-clef spaces (A-C-E-G) are "All Cows Eat Grass" or "All Cars Eat Gas." The lines (G-B-D-F-A) might be "Great Big Doves Fly Away."

Example 1.5: Bass clef (F-clef)

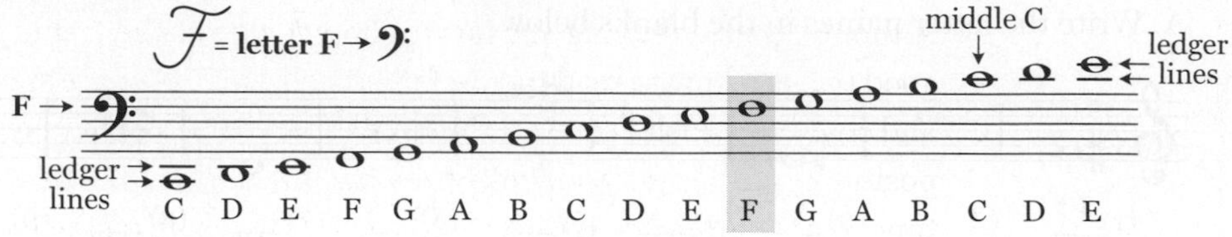

Example 1.6: Bass-clef lines and spaces

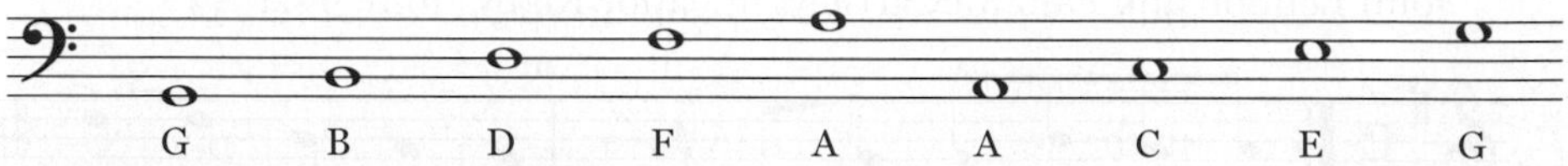

Try it #5

A. Write the letter names in the blanks below.

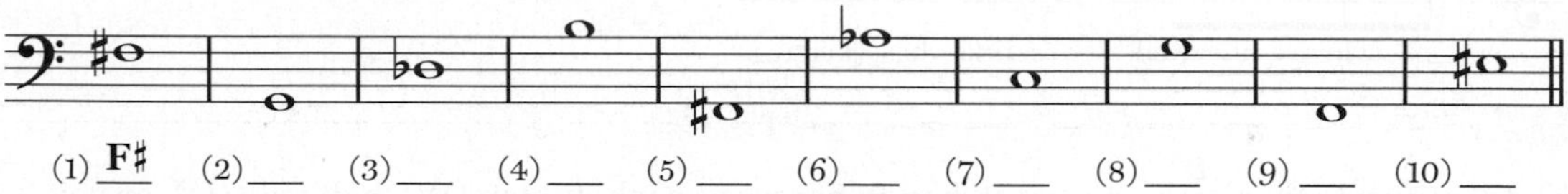

B. Write each letter name of the melody in the blank below.

Bach, Invention in D Minor, mm. 26–29 (bass-clef part)

C. Identify whether each pair of pitches below spans a whole step (W), half step (H), or neither (N).

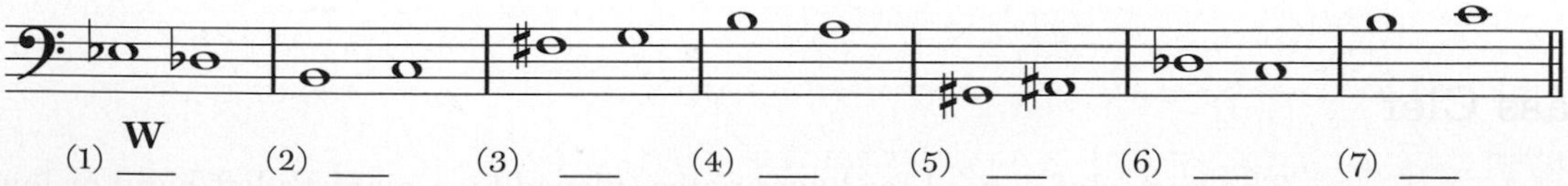

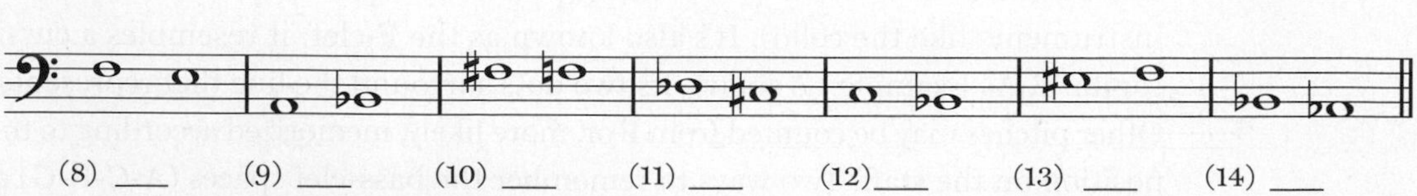

C-Clefs

Although music reading starts with knowledge of the treble and bass clefs, it is good to learn how to read the C-clefs as well, since they are standard in orchestral and chamber music scores. A **C-clef** is a "movable" clef: it may appear in different positions on the staff to identify any one of the five lines as middle C. (In Bach's time, the treble and bass clefs could move as well.) Its distinctive shape—𝄡—identifies middle C by the point at which the two curved lines join together in the middle, as illustrated in Example 1.7. Depending on its position, the clef may be called a soprano, mezzo-soprano, alto, tenor, or baritone clef. While the only C-clefs you will probably see in modern scores are the alto and tenor clefs (shaded in the example), you may come across the others in older editions. To read these clefs well, practice counting the lines and spaces in thirds, as for the other clefs, and then memorize.

EXAMPLE 1.7: Reading pitches in C-clefs

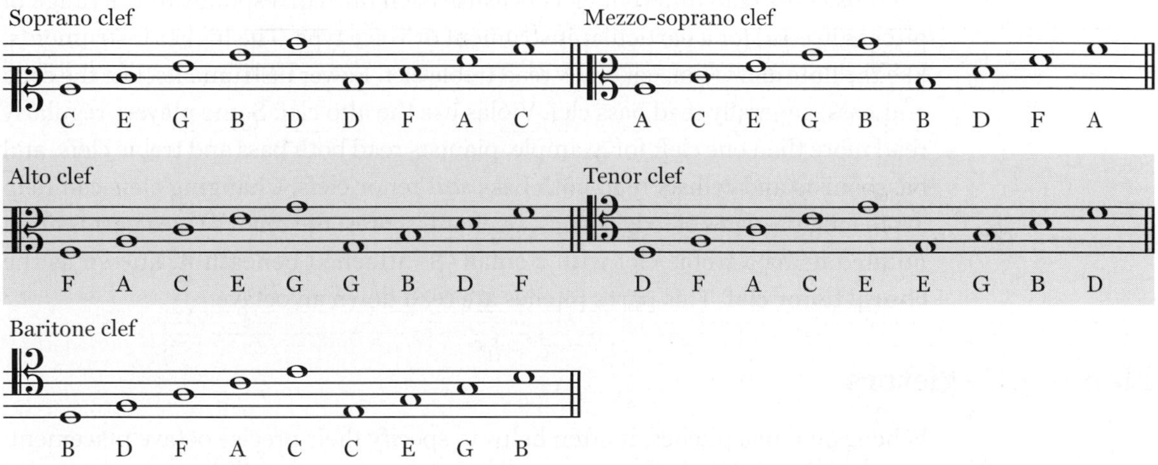

Try it #6

A. Identify the clef, then write each letter name in the blank below.

Clef: ____________________ Clef: ____________________

(1) **A** (2) ___ (3) ___ (4) ___ (5) ___ (6) ___ (7) ___ (8) ___ (9) ___ (10) ___

B. Write each letter name of the melody in the blank below.

Mozart, String Quartet in D Minor, K. 421, third movement (mm. 12–17, viola part)

E ___ ___ ___ ___ ___ ___ ___ ___ ___ ___ ___ ___ ___ ___ ___ ___ ___ ___

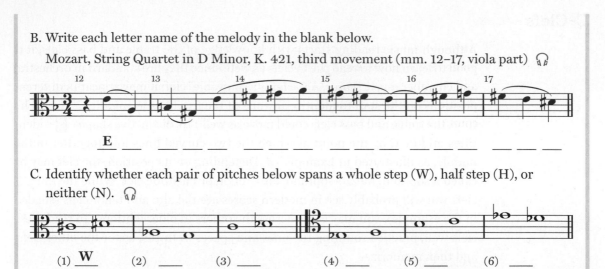

C. Identify whether each pair of pitches below spans a whole step (W), half step (H), or neither (N).

(1) W (2) ____ (3) ____ (4) ____ (5) ____ (6) ____

Musicians read different clefs because each one corresponds to the range of pitches needed for a particular instrument or voice type. The higher instruments, like the flute and violin, generally read treble clef. Lower instruments, like the cello and bass, generally read bass clef. Violas use the alto clef. Some players regularly read more than one clef: for example, pianists read both bass and treble clefs, and bassoonists and cellists read both bass and tenor clefs. Changing clefs can help avoid long passages of ledger lines. In choral scores, the tenor's voice part is often notated using a treble clef with a small "8" attached beneath it, known as the **choral tenor clef**. This part's pitches are read down an octave.

Naming Registers

When you name pitches, it often helps to specify their precise octave placement. There are several systems for doing this: we will use the numeric system shown on the keyboard in Figure 1.7. The lowest C on the piano is C1 and the highest is C8; middle C is C4. The number for a particular octave includes all the pitches from C up to the following B, so the B above C4 is B4, and the B below C4 is B3. The three notes below the C1 on the piano are A0, B♭0, and B0.

Figure 1.7: Piano keyboard with octave designations

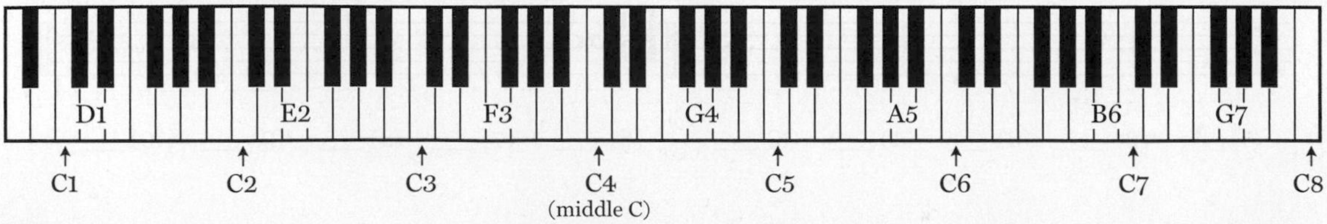

Ledger Lines

Listen to the beginning of Joplin's rag "Solace," given in Example 1.8. Like most piano music, this work is notated on a **grand staff**—two staves, one in treble clef and one in bass clef, connected by a curly brace. The shaded pitches in the example are written with ledger lines. Read ledger lines just like other staff lines, by counting forward or backward in the musical alphabet.

Example 1.8: Joplin, "Solace," mm. 1–4

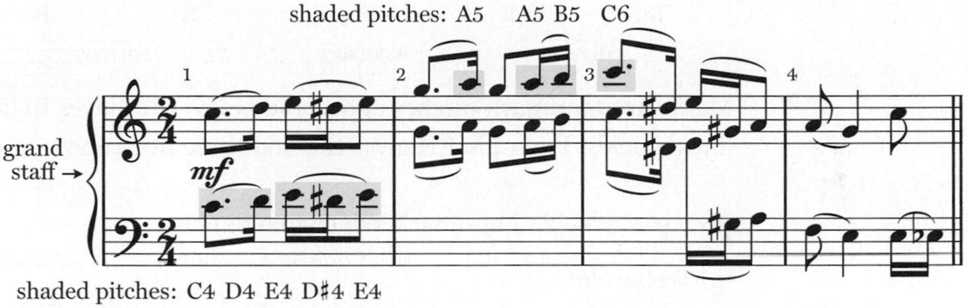

Example 1.9 consists of over four octaves of pitches, including ledger lines, on a grand staff and keyboard.

Example 1.9: Pitches on a grand staff and keyboard

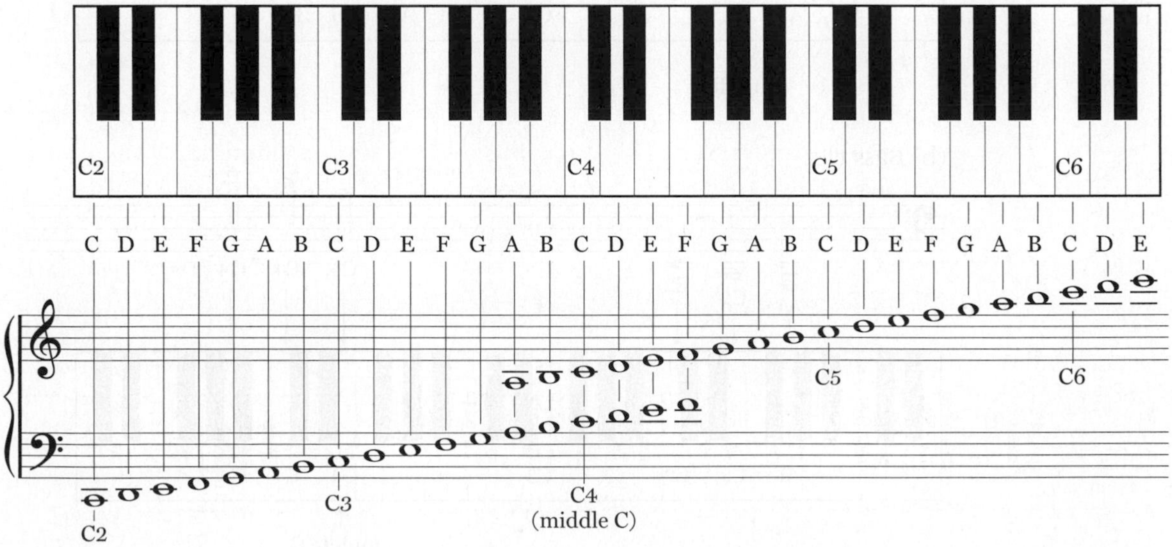

Notes higher than the staff might have ledger lines drawn through them or below them, but never above them; notes below the staff might have ledger lines through them or above them, but never below. Draw ledger lines the same distance apart as staff lines, as in Example 1.10.

Example 1.10: Correct and incorrect ledger lines

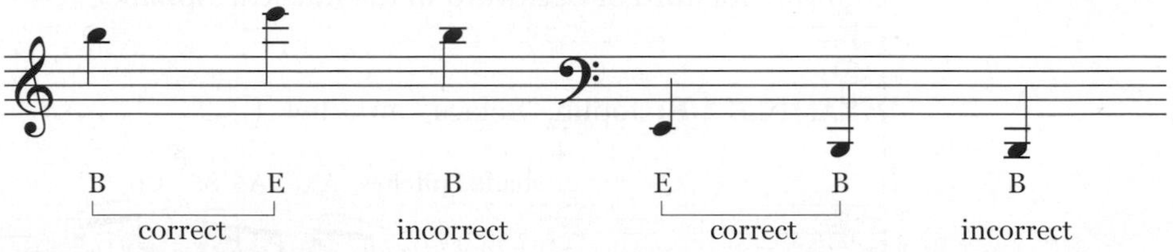

Memorize landmark pitches above and below the staves to help you read ledger lines quickly. Example 1.11 gives the first three lines above and below each staff.

Example 1.11: Landmark ledger-line pitches

(a) Treble clef

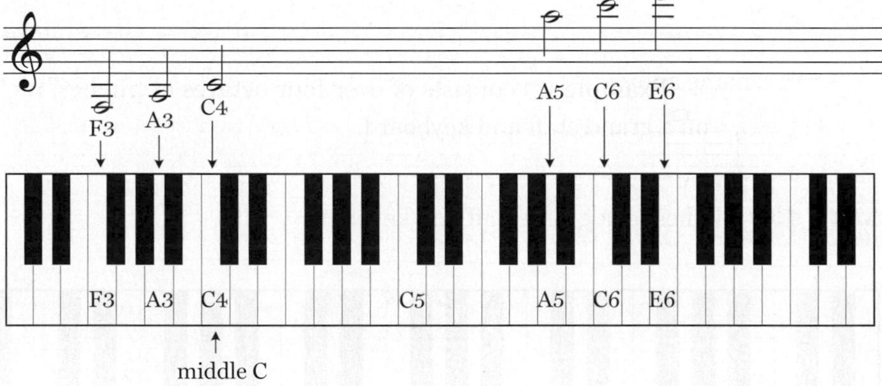

(b) Bass clef

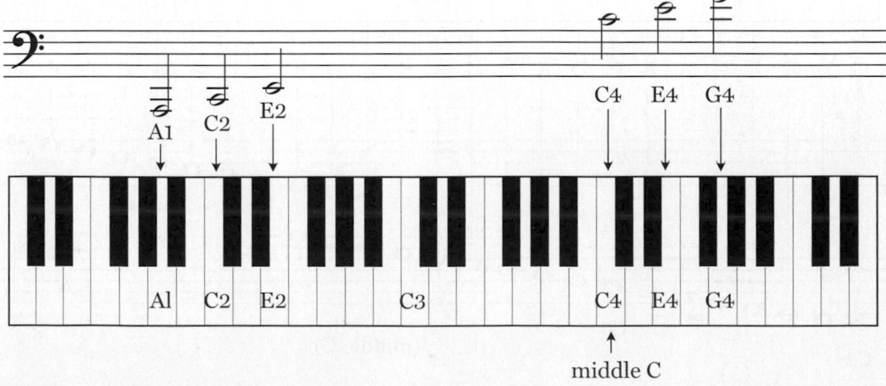

Pitches near middle C may be written between the two staves of the grand staff, as in Example 1.12 (arrows point to the equivalent ledger-line pitches in the other clef). In keyboard music, the choice of clef usually indicates which hand should play the note: bass clef for the left hand and treble clef for the right.

EXAMPLE 1.12: Ledger lines between staves on the grand staff

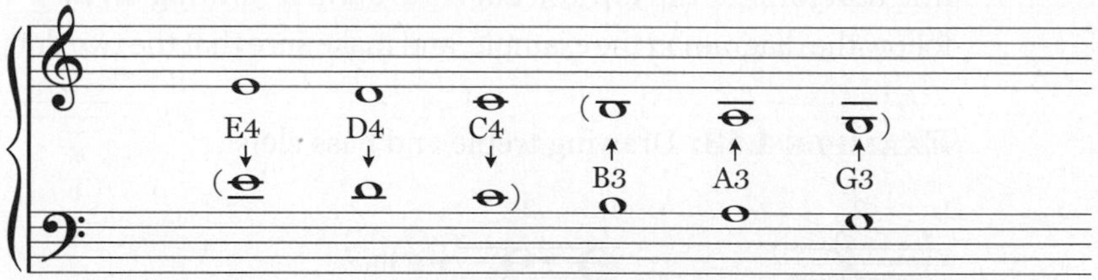

An alternative to ledger lines is the **ottava sign**. An "8va" above the staff means to play an octave higher (the "8v" stands for "octave," and the "a" stands for *alta*, Italian for "above"). An "8vb" beneath the staff means to play an octave lower (the "b" stands for *bassa*, or "below").

Try it #7

A. Write the name and octave number of each pitch in the blank provided.

(1) **G♯4** (2) _____ (3) _____ (4) _____ (5) _____ (6) _____ (7) _____ (8) _____

(1) _____ (2) _____ (3) _____ (4) _____ (5) _____ (6) _____ (7) _____ (8) _____

B. Write the name and octave number of each shaded pitch in the blank provided.

Lalo Schifrin, Theme from *Mission Impossible*, mm. 1–2

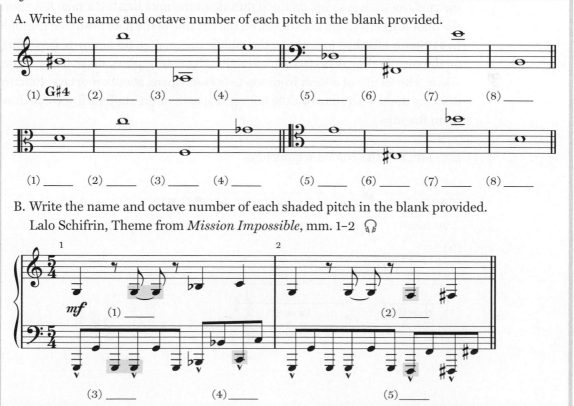

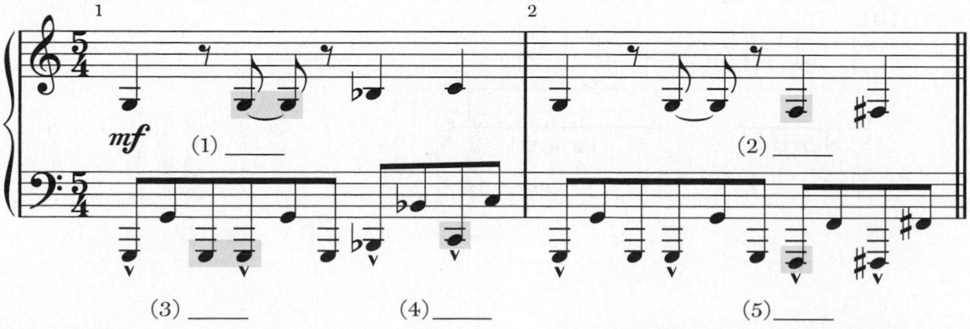

Writing Pitches on a Score

Though computer software programs for music notation are becoming more widespread, it is also important to know how to notate music correctly by hand. Draw a treble clef with a single continuous curved line, or in two strokes (Example 1.13): (1) draw a wavy line from top to bottom, like an elongated S; then (2) draw a second line that joins at the top and curves around it (ending on G4). To draw a bass clef, follow the diagram in the example, and make sure that the two dots straddle the F line.

EXAMPLE 1.13: Drawing treble and bass clefs

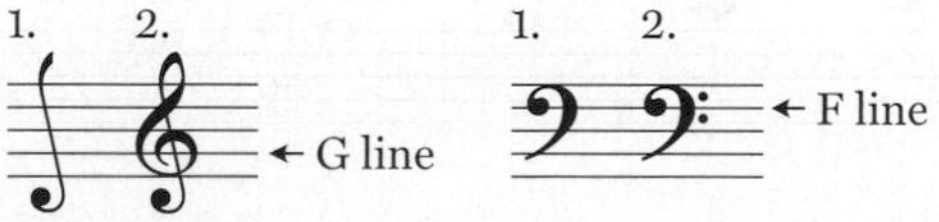

When you draw note heads on the staff, make them oval-shaped rather than round. These ovals should not be so large that it is hard to tell whether they sit on a line or space. Most notes have thin vertical lines, called **stems**, that extend above or below the note head (♩ 𝅘𝅥). Usually, if a note lies below the middle line of the staff, its stem goes up, on the right side of the note head; if a note lies above the middle line, its stem goes down, on the left side of the note head (see Example 1.14). Stems attached to notes *on* the middle line may go up or down, depending on the surrounding notes (see Chapter 2); if the note appears alone, its stem goes down. The length of a stem from top to bottom spans about an octave. Practice drawing notes with stems on the lines and spaces of the staff until you can draw them fluently.

EXAMPLE 1.14: Notation guidelines

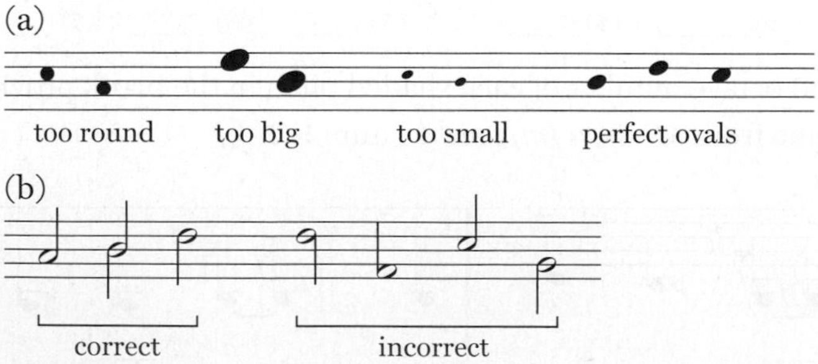

Dynamic Markings

Look again at the Clarke excerpt in Example 1.1. This passage begins with a full sound, marked with a large ***f*** in the score. This is a **dynamic** indication, which tells performers how soft or loud to play. Such markings also help musicians make decisions about the character or mood of a piece.

The ***f*** stands for *forte*, a loud dynamic marking; *piano* (abbreviated ***p***) is a soft dynamic marking. Other familiar markings are ***mp*** (for *mezzo piano*) and ***mf*** (for *mezzo forte*): *mezzo* means "half," thus indicating "half as soft" and "half as loud." Figure 1.8 shows a typical range of dynamic markings. The indication that tells you to get louder is *crescendo* (<), while *decrescendo* or *diminuendo* (>) means to grow softer. When performing, pay careful attention to these markings in the score. They will contribute greatly to shaping a musical and sensitive performance.

FIGURE 1.8: Dynamic indications from soft to loud

pp	***p***	***mp***	***mf***	***f***	***ff***
pianissimo	*piano*	*mezzo piano*	*mezzo forte*	*forte*	*fortissimo*

softest ← medium → loudest

Did You Know?

In the Middle Ages (from about 800 to 1430) and the Renaissance (roughly 1430 to 1600), musical relationships were understood in terms of a musical structure called a hexachord ("hexa-" means "six"), built in a standard pattern of whole and half steps: W-W-H-W-W. Accidentals were invented when musicians needed to transpose this hexachord's pattern of whole and half steps. The first accidental to be introduced was B♭ (with the rounded flat symbol), which allowed the hexachord on C (C–D–E–F–G–A) to begin on F (F– G–A–B♭–C–D) with the same whole- and half-step pattern.

Musicians called the hexachord beginning with C the "natural" hexachord, and the one beginning on F the "soft" hexachord. The pattern on G (G–A–B–C–D–E) was dubbed the "hard" hexachord. If a song moved from the soft to the hard hexachord, composers needed to show that B♮, not B♭, was to be played. They wrote the letter "h" to indicate B♮ (a usage that continues today in German-speaking countries), but over the years this symbol evolved into both the natural sign andthe sharp sign. After the flat and natural signs had been in use for some time to indicate B♭ and B♮, they came to be linked with other letter names as well.

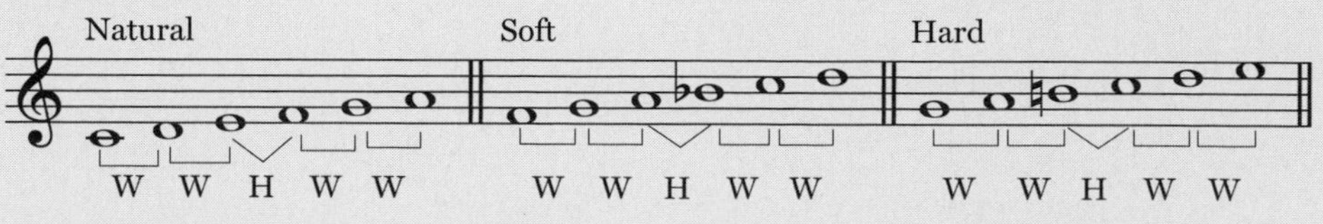

TERMS YOU SHOULD KNOW

accidental
- flat
- sharp
- natural
- double flat
- double sharp

clef
- treble clef
- bass clef
- C-clef
- alto clef
- tenor clef

counting in thirds
dynamic marking
enharmonic pitch
grand staff
half step
interval
ledger line
musical alphabet
octave
octave equivalence
pitch
pitch class
staff
whole step

QUESTIONS FOR REVIEW

1. How do the staff and clefs work together to identify pitches?
2. Starting on D, count backward for two octaves in the musical alphabet. Count forward in thirds for two octaves, starting on G.
3. What's the difference between a pitch and a pitch class?
4. What is the function of (a) C-clefs, (b) accidentals, (c) ledger lines?
5. How do the piano's white and black keys help you determine whole and half steps?
6. On a keyboard, what special relationship do B and C have? E and F?
7. Give two guidelines for notating ledger lines.
8. How are octave numbers assigned? What is the octave number for middle C?
9. Pick a melody from music in your repertoire. Identify all its pitches by octave number, and locate at least two pitches notated on ledger lines.

CHAPTER 2

Simple Meters

Outline of topics

Dividing musical time

- Beat, beat divisions, and meter
- Conducting patterns
- Tempo
- Rhythm and meter

Rhythmic notation for simple meters

- Rhythmic values
- Meter signatures

Counting rhythms in simple meters

- Beat subdivisions
- Stems, flags, and beaming
- Counting rests and dots
- Slurs and ties
- Syncopation
- Hemiola
- Anacrusis notation

Beat units other than the quarter note

Implications for performance: Metric hierarchy

Overview

We turn now to the organization of music in time. This chapter explains how beats are grouped and divided to create meter, then focuses on simple meters, whose beats divide into two parts.

Repertoire

Anonymous, Minuet in D Minor

Johann Sebastian Bach
 Chaconne, from Violin Partita No. 2 in D Minor
 Invention in D Minor

Frédéric Chopin, Mazurka in F Minor, Op. 68, No. 4

"Greensleeves"

George Frideric Handel
 Chaconne in G Major
 "Rejoice greatly," from *Messiah*

Fanny Mendelssohn Hensel, "Neue Liebe, neues Leben" ("New Love, New Life")

Scott Joplin
 "Pine Apple Rag"
 "Solace"

John Newton, "Amazing Grace"

Robert Schumann, "Trällerliedchen" ("Humming Song"), from *Album for the Young*, Op. 68, No. 3

John Philip Sousa, "The Stars and Stripes Forever"

Dividing Musical Time

Beat, Beat Divisions, and Meter

Listen to the opening of Joplin's "Pine Apple Rag" and Handel's "Rejoice greatly"—two lively works in contrasting styles. As you listen, tap your foot in time: this tap represents the work's primary pulse, or **beat**. You should also hear a secondary pulse, moving twice as fast. Tap the secondary pulse in one hand while your foot continues with the primary beat. This secondary pulse represents the **beat division**.

KEY CONCEPT Musical **meters** are defined by:
(1) the way beats are divided, and
(2) the way beats are grouped into larger recurring units.

Beats typically divide into two or three parts. In the Joplin and Handel examples, the beat divides into twos. Now listen to the English folk tune "Greensleeves." Tap your foot along with the slow beat, as before. When you add the beat division in your hand, you'll notice that the beat divides not into twos, but into threes.

KEY CONCEPT There are two principle meter types: simple and compound. Musical works in **simple meters** have beats that divide into twos. Those in **compound meters** have beats that divide into threes.

The character of these two types can be quite different: simple meters feel more even, while compound meters may sound lilting.

Try it #1

Listen to each piece below to determine the beat and its division. If the beat divides in twos, circle "simple"; if it divides in threes, circle "compound."

(a) Joplin, "Solace"	simple	compound
(b) Gilmore, "When Johnny Comes Marching Home"	simple	compound
(c) Mozart, *Variations on "Ah, vous dirai-je Maman"*	simple	compound
(d) Schumann, "Wilder Reiter"	simple	compound

Listen now to the opening of Sousa's "The Stars and Stripes Forever" and Chopin's Mazurka in F Minor. Tap the primary beat for each. In both works, the beat divides into twos: both are in simple meter. But besides dividing, primary beats also *group*—into twos, threes, or fours. As you listen to each piece, try counting "1-2, 1-2" (one number per beat); if the piece doesn't fit that pattern, try "1-2-3, 1-2-3" or "1-2-3-4, 1-2-3-4."

KEY CONCEPT When beats group into units of two, the meter type (either simple or compound) is **duple**. When they group into units of three, the meter type is **triple**; and when they group into units of four, it is **quadruple**.

The meter type for the Sousa march is simple duple, and for the Chopin mazurka simple triple. In music notation, the beat groupings are indicated by **bar lines**, which separate the notes into **measures**, or **bars**. On a grand staff like that in Example 2.1 (unlike a single-line staff), an initial bar line and curly brace connect the two staves, as does each subsequent bar line. Measures are often numbered at the top, as in the examples in this book, to help you find your place in a score. Listen again to the mazurka while following the notation in the example and the counts written beneath.

Example 2.1: Chopin, Mazurka in F Minor, mm. 1–4

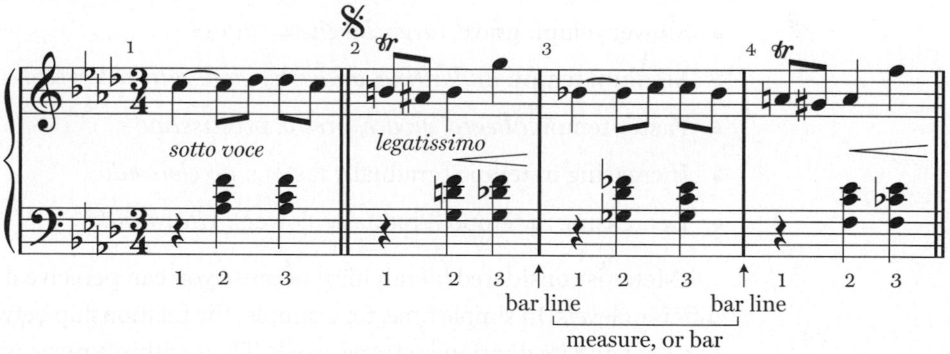

Conducting Patterns

Conductors' motions outline specific patterns for each meter to keep an ensemble playing together and to convey interpretive ideas. The basic conducting patterns for duple, triple, and quadruple meters given in Figure 2.1 are the same whether the piece is in a simple or compound meter (although the conductor may distinguish between them by subdividing the basic pattern).

As you practice each pattern, you will feel a certain physical weight associated with the **downbeat**—the motion of the hand down on beat 1 of the pattern. You will probably feel anticipation with the **upbeat**—the upward lift of the hand for the final beat. Practice these patterns until you feel comfortable with them, then use them to help you recognize meter types by ear.

FIGURE 2.1: Conducting patterns

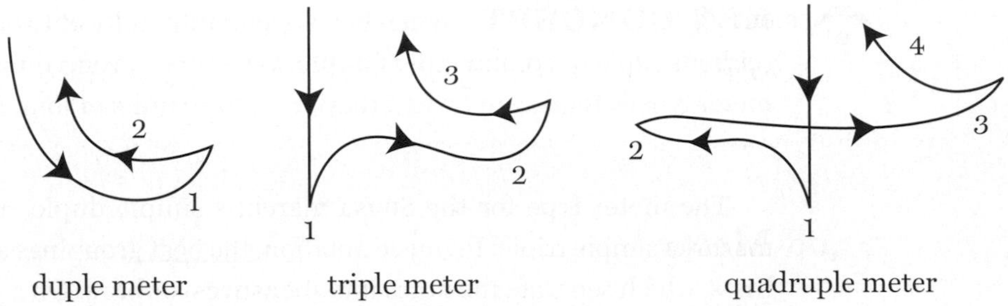

Tempo

Conductors also use conducting patterns to establish a work's **tempo**, or speed (the plural is "tempi"). The proper tempo helps to convey the character or mood of a piece. It is often indicated on a musical score with words in Italian or other languages. Following are the most common tempo indications in Italian.

- Slower tempi: grave, *largo, larghetto, adagio*
- Medium tempi: *andantino, andante, moderato, allegretto*
- Faster tempi: *allegro, vivace, presto, prestissimo*
- Increasing in tempo (gradually faster): *accelerando*
- Decreasing in tempo (gradually slower): *ritardando*

Meter is considered hierarchical because you can perceive it simultaneously at different levels. In simple time, for example, the relationship between the beginning of a beat and its division is strong-weak. Then within a measure, beats may alternate strong-weak, and at a still higher level, full measures may also alternate strong-weak. For this reason, you may sometimes have trouble hearing the difference between duple and quadruple meters by ear; you may hear one measure in quadruple meter as two bars of duple. It is also possible to hear two measures of simple triple meter as one measure of compound duple. Don't worry that you are "wrong"—you are simply identifying the meter at a different level of the hierarchy. Tempo can provide an important clue. If you perceive a very fast beat in three, for example, perhaps you are hearing the beat divisions in compound meter.

Try it #2

Listen to the beginning of each of these simple-meter compositions. Listen for the grouping and metrical accent, then circle either "duple or quadruple" or "triple."

(a) Bach, "O Haupt voll Blut und Wunden"	duple or quadruple	triple
(b) Mozart, Minuet in F Major, K. 2	duple or quadruple	triple
(c) Mozart, Piano Sonata in C Major, K. 545, first movement	duple or quadruple	triple
(d) Bach, *Passacaglia in C Minor* for organ	duple or quadruple	triple

Rhythm and Meter

Rhythm and meter are two different, but related, aspects of musical time. **Rhythm** refers to the durations of pitch and silence (notes and rests) used in a piece. **Meter** provides a framework of strong and weak beats against which the rhythms are heard.

SUMMARY

Music written in a meter has

- a recurring pattern of beats,
- perceivable divisions of beats (simple or compound),
- perceivable groupings of beats (duple, triple, or quadruple).

Rhythm consists of

- durations of pitch and silence, heard in the context of the underlying meter.

This summary applies generally to tonal music from the common-practice era, roughly 1600 through the early twentieth century. But nonmetric pieces—pieces without meter—are found in non-Western music and in Western music of the twentieth century, as you will see in later chapters.

Rhythmic Notation for Simple Meters

Rhythmic Values

The parts of a note are labeled in Figure 2.2. The wavy line attached to the stem of a single note is a **flag**, and the horizontal line connecting two or more notes is a **beam**. The **dot** (if present) is always written on a space; when you write a note on a line, the dot goes next to it on the space above, so that it can be clearly seen.

FIGURE 2.2: Parts of a note

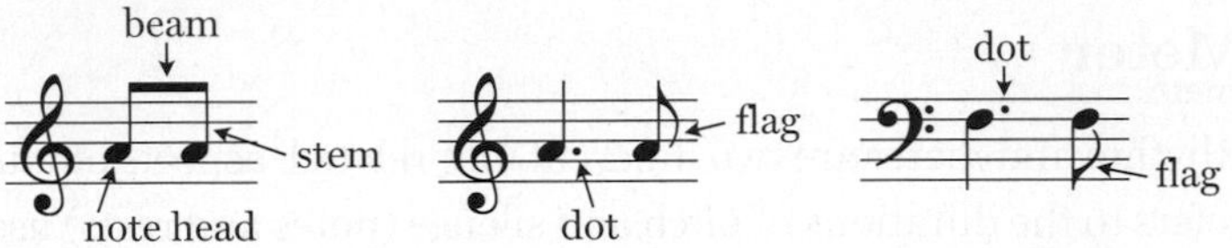

Figure 2.3 is a chart of common rhythmic values and their equivalent **rests** (durations of silence) in simple meters. The chart is organized to reflect the beat division in simple time: a **whole note** divides into two **half notes**, a half note divides into two **quarter notes**, and so on. You can create smaller note values by adding flags or beams to the stem: **eighth notes**, for example, have one beam, **sixteenth notes** two beams (a **thirty-second note** has three flags or beams, and a **sixty-fourth note** has four). In some meters, you will also see longer note values, such as the **breve** (𝅜), which lasts twice as long as a whole note; it is also sometimes written as a double whole note (𝅝𝅝).

FIGURE 2.3: Rhythmic values in simple meters

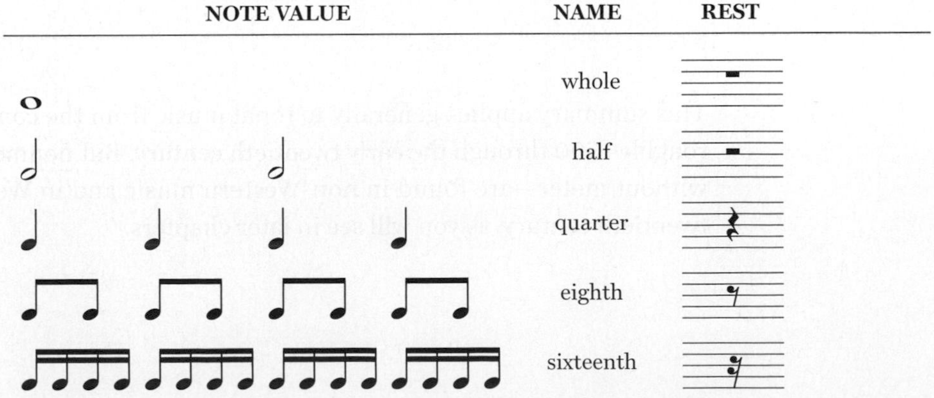

Meter Signatures

A **meter signature** (or **time signature**) at the beginning of a score establishes the meter type and **beat unit**. The meter signature in "Amazing Grace" (Example 2.2) indicates that there are three beats in each full measure, and the quarter note gets one beat.

Example 2.2: Newton, "Amazing Grace," mm. 1–4a

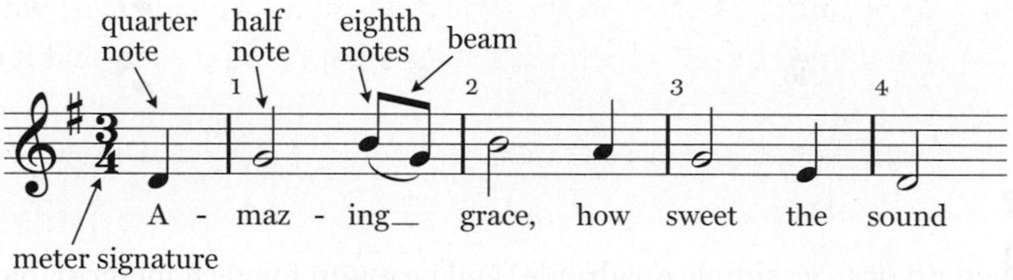

KEY CONCEPT Meter signatures are written with two numbers, one above the other. In simple meters:

- The upper number is 2, 3, or 4, to show that the meter type is simple duple, triple, or quadruple; this number tells how many beats are in each measure.
- The lower number indicates which note gets one beat (the beat unit): 2 (half note), 4 (quarter note), 8 (eighth note), or 16 (sixteenth note).

Figure 2.4 provides examples of simple meter signatures and how to interpret them.

Figure 2.4: Meter signatures

(a) Common simple meters

METER SIGNATURE	BEATS PER MEASURE	BEAT UNIT	METER TYPE
2/4	2	♩	simple duple
3/4	3	♩	simple triple
4/4	4	♩	simple quadruple

(b) Less common simple meters

METER SIGNATURE	BEATS PER MEASURE	BEAT UNIT	METER TYPE
$\frac{2}{2}$	2	𝅗𝅥	simple duple
$\frac{3}{2}$	3	𝅗𝅥	simple triple
$\frac{3}{8}$	3	♪	simple triple
$\frac{4}{8}$	4	♪	simple quadruple
$\frac{4}{16}$	4	𝅘𝅥𝅯	simple quadruple

Try it #3

Name the meter type (e.g., simple quadruple) and beat unit for each meter signature given below.

	METER TYPE	BEAT UNIT
(a) $\frac{2}{2}$	______________________________	________
(b) $\frac{3}{16}$	______________________________	________
(c) $\frac{3}{8}$	______________________________	________
(d) $\frac{4}{2}$	______________________________	________

Besides numbers, you may see other symbols in scores to represent meter signatures. For example, **c**, called "common time" (a symbol dating back to the fourteenth century), is frequently used to represent $\frac{4}{4}$, and ¢, or **alla breve** (sometimes called "cut time"), can take the place of $\frac{2}{2}$.

SUMMARY

Meter signatures you are most likey to see in simple meters include the following:

- Simple duple: $\frac{2}{2}$ ¢ $\frac{2}{4}$ $\frac{2}{8}$
- Simple triple: $\frac{3}{2}$ $\frac{3}{4}$ $\frac{3}{8}$ $\frac{3}{16}$
- Simple quadruple: $\frac{4}{2}$ $\frac{4}{4}$ c $\frac{4}{8}$ $\frac{4}{16}$

Counting Rhythms in Simple Meters

By interepreting the meter signature, we can now write counts for each beat into a score. Example 2.3 repeats the melody for "Amazing Grace," with the counts written below. Each full measure gets three beats; if no new pitch sounds on a given beat, as for beat 2 in each measure of the example, write the count in parentheses. The two eighth notes in measure 1 are written "3 &" (or "3 +") and counted aloud as "three and"; the "and" is the **offbeat**. The quarter note D preceding the first full measure is an **anacrusis** (also called an **upbeat**, or **pickup**). Count it as the final beat of an incomplete measure, as indicated by the number 3 in the example.

EXAMPLE 2.3: Newton, "Amazing Grace," mm. 1–4a

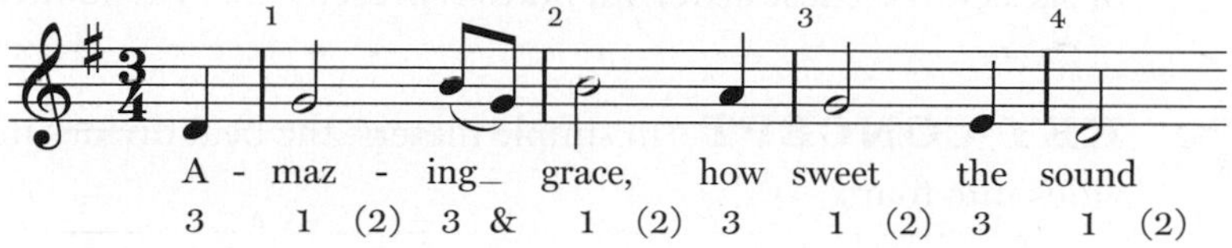

Try it #4

Write the counts beneath the following melodies. (The final measure of (c) is incomplete.)

(a) Horner, Mann, and Weil, "Somewhere Out There," mm. 40–42

(b) Anonymous, Minuet in D Minor, mm. 1–4

(c) Bono and U2, "Miracle Drug," mm. 29–32a

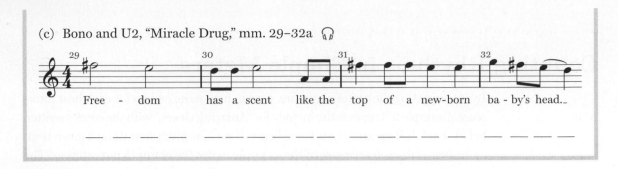

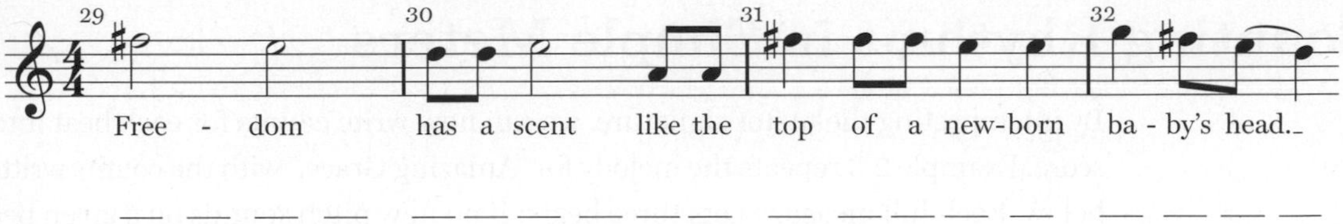

Beat Subdivisions

Now listen to Variation 19 of Handel's Chaconne in G Major, while following the score in the anthology. Here the stately melody is played in quarter and eighth notes in the right hand, while the left hand accompanies with energetic groups of sixteenths. These sixteenth notes represent the beat **subdivision**.

KEY CONCEPT In simple meters, the beat divides into twos and subdivides into fours.

Example 2.4: Handel, Chaconne in G Major, mm. 153–156

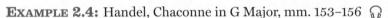

In music with a quarter-note beat, the beat divides into two eighths () and subdivides into four sixteenths (), or it may divide into a combination of eighths and sixteenths (like ).

Stems, Flags, and Beaming

Your ability to sight-read, remember, and write music will be greatly enhanced by learning the typical rhythmic patterns that can occur within a beat and notating them correctly. Look, for instance, at how stems and flags are notated in Example 2.4. In the left hand, the beams group four sixteenths into a single beat, which stands apart visually from the rest. Flags are written on the right-hand side of the stem, whether the stem goes up or down (compare the last right-hand eighth notes of measures 153 and 154). As mentioned in Chapter 1, the stems on notes below the middle line extend up, and those above it extend down. When several notes are beamed together (as in the left hand), the stem direction corresponds with the majority of the notes in the group (or with the second note, if there are only two).

Try it #5

Circle the incorrectly notated stems and flags.

Notate them correctly here.

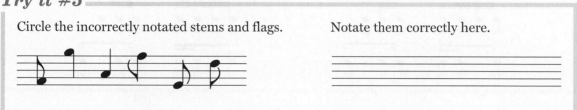

Five rhythmic patterns for the quarter-note beat unit are given in Figure 2.5: learn each pattern with its correct beaming. Familiar patterns like these can be combined and recombined in different ways in rhythms, just as words can be recombined in a sentence.

FIGURE 2.5: Five common one-beat rhythm patterns in simple meters

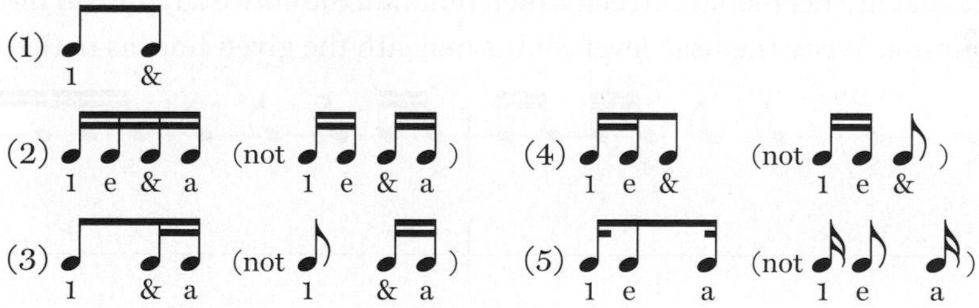

KEY CONCEPT Rhythms should be beamed to reflect the beat unit. For example, groups of eighth and sixteenth notes that span one quarter-note beat unit, such as , are beamed together.

There is one exception to the beaming guideline: in many older vocal scores, beaming corresponded with the sung syllables, rather than the beat unit. Though you may encounter the vocal notation style in scores, this text will stick with modern ("instrumental") beaming.

Another Way

Music educators may prefer other counting syllables, such as those developed by Zoltán Kodály (e.g., ta, ti-ti) or Edwin Gordon (e.g., du, du-de). Syllables for the five basic patterns in Gordon's system are on the left. A third system, which assigns every subdivision its own syllable (ta-ka-di-mi), is shown on the right.

Your memory for rhythmic patterns will be improved if you associate them with a counting system of numbers or syllables, in Figure 2.5. There are several such systems available, and each has advantages: choose one and use it consistently.

The single-line rhythms that follow in *Try it #6* and elsewhere in the book are notated with **rhythm clefs**, employed as their name suggests, to show only rhythm, not pitches. To draw a rhythm clef, write two vertical lines preceding the meter signature.

Try it #6

Circle beats that are beamed incorrectly, then renotate the entire rhythm on the second line with correct beaming. Write the beat-level counts beneath the given line, as in (a), to help you.

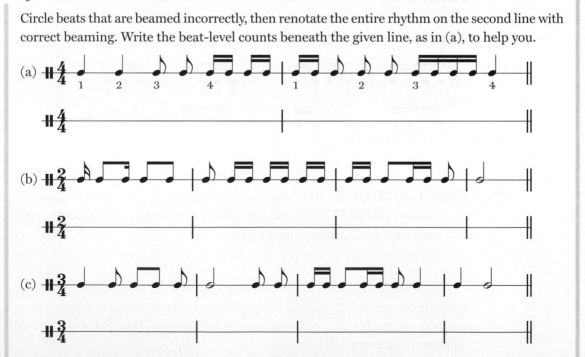

(a)

(b)

(c)

Counting Rests and Dots

Rests represent durations of silence. Each rest lasts as long as the note that shares its name (e.g., eighth rest and eighth note; see Figure 2.3). Be careful when you read and write whole and half rests, because they resemble each other. The difference is not in their shape, but in their placement on the staff: the half rest "sits" on top of the third staff line, while the whole rest "hangs" from the fourth line. (You might think of the whole rest as "heavier," and thus it has to hang from the line, while the "lighter" half rest can sit on top. Or remember that a *h*alf rest is shaped like a *h*at.)

A whole rest is sometimes written to indicate silence that lasts a whole measure regardless of how many beats are in that measure. In music with a half-note beat unit, such as $\frac{4}{2}$, you may see a double whole rest or note (breve), which lasts four half-note beats (Figure 2.6a). Finally, some scores (particularly orchestra parts where players rest for many consecutive bars) include multiple-bar rests. Here the number above the rest tells the player how many bars to rest. The rest in part (b), for example, is counted 1-2-3-4, 2-2-3-4, 3-2-3-4.

FIGURE 2.6:

(a) Breve (b) Multibar rest

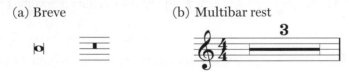

When a beat begins with a rest, write the appropriate beat number in parentheses, as in Example 2.5. This helps you count the durations of silence (or accompaniment) as accurately as the pitches.

EXAMPLE 2.5: Handel, "Rejoice greatly" (vocal part), mm. 8–11

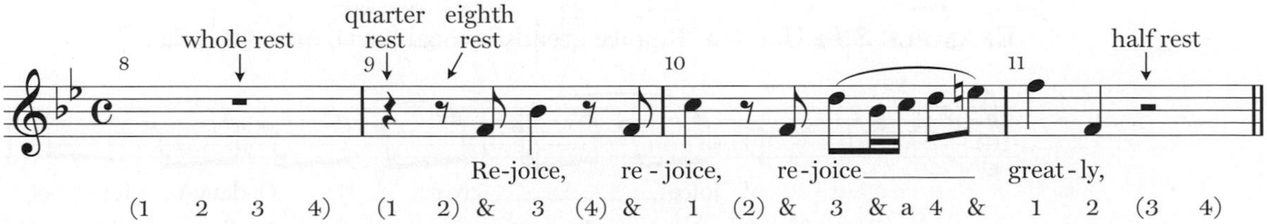

A **dot** adds to a note half its own value, as Figure 2.7a shows. That is, a dotted-quarter note equals a quarter plus an eighth, a dotted eighth equals an eighth plus a sixteenth, and so on. Dotted notes are generally paired with another note that completes a full beat or full measure. Some typical patterns are shown to the right, along with their counts in $\frac{4}{4}$. **Double dots** (more rare) add to a note half its value plus another quarter of its value (part b).

FIGURE 2.7: Use of dots

(a) Single dots

(b) Double dots

Slurs and Ties

Listen to the dotted passage from "Rejoice greatly" given in Example 2.6. The small arcs written above some of the notes in measures 92–93 are **slurs**, connecting two (or more) different pitches. Slurs affect performance articulation—bowing or tonguing, for example—but not duration: the notes encompassed by a slur should be played smoothly, or **legato**, rather than detached. For singers, slurs identify groups of pitches sung to a single syllable.

EXAMPLE 2.6: Handel, "Rejoice greatly" (vocal part), mm. 92–96a

The small arc above the F in measures 94–95, on the other hand, is a **tie**, connecting the same note. The F in measure 95 is not played again; rather the tie adds the duration of the two note values together, so "shout" lasts three and a half beats. Counts for the beats spanned by a tie are written in parentheses to show their full duration.

KEY CONCEPT Ties and dots should be notated in a way that clarifies the meter rather than obscuring it. For example, an eighth tied to a quarter would be clearer than a dotted quarter in the rhythmic context shown below, because it makes the placement of beat 3 explicit.

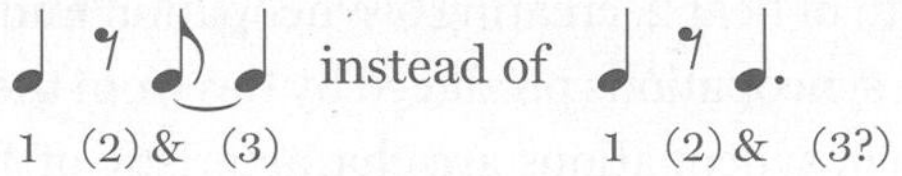

Syncopation

Syncopations are created when an expected accent is displaced or moved to another beat or part of a beat—by dots, ties, rests, dynamic markings, accent marks, or the rhythm itself. Syncopations are marked by arrows in Example 2.7. They may occur at the level of the beat (accents on beat 2 or 4 rather than 1 or 3), the division (on "&"), or the subdivision (on "e" or "a").

EXAMPLE 2.7: Syncopated rhythms

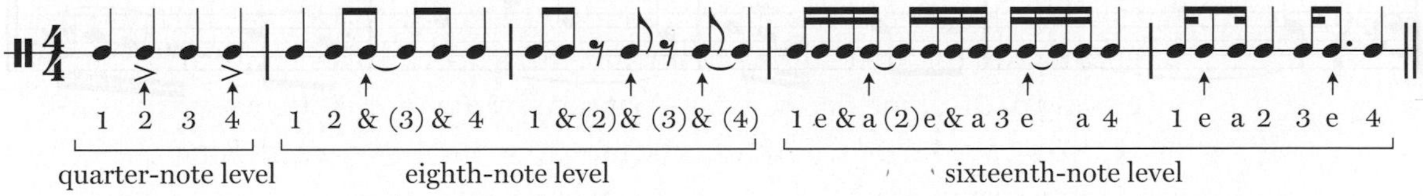

Syncopations can be found in all styles, but they appear especially frequently in popular music, jazz, and ragtime. Within a quarter-note beat, the rhythms and are the most typical syncopation patterns. In each, the longest duration of the rhythm is on the "e" of 1 e & a instead of the stronger "1" or "&."

Listen to the beginning of Joplin's "Pine Apple Rag" (Example 2.8), and locate the syncopations within the beat (mm. 1 and 3) and across the beat (mm. 2 and 4), marked by arrows. Syncopations across the beat are usually notated with ties: here, the expected emphasis on beat 2 comes earlier, on the first of the tied notes.

EXAMPLE 2.8: Joplin, "Pine Apple Rag," mm. 1–4

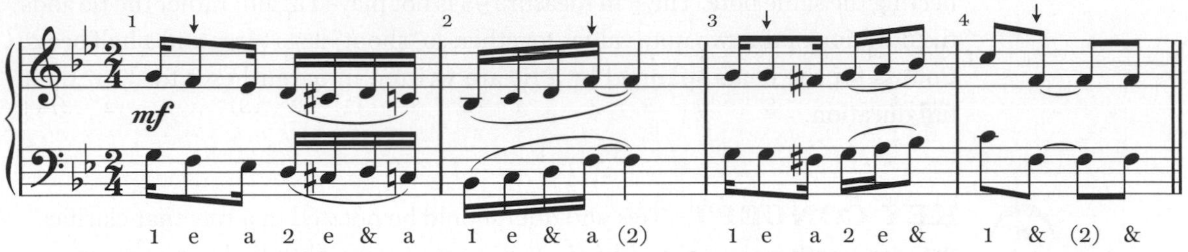

Joplin's "Solace" (Example 2.9) also includes many syncopations. Notice that every measure of the excerpt shows a tie from the last sixteenth of beat 1 to the first sixteenth or eighth of beat 2, creating a syncopation mid-measure. Measures 10 and 12 also feature syncopations produced by ties from the last sixteenth of the previous measure. Such syncopations are characteristic of Joplin rags. They are highly effective because of the steady accompaniment pattern in the left hand: syncopations can only be perceived if there is a strong sense of the underlying beat for them to play against.

EXAMPLE 2.9: Joplin, "Solace," mm. 9–12

Hemiola

Another metrical displacement pattern is illustrated in Example 2.10. Look at the beat-level counts given in level (a), and read the rhythm aloud on "tah" or counting syllables while conducting in three. As you probably felt from your performance, the rhythmic patterns and tie across the bar line in measures 3–4 temporarily disrupt the triple meter. Now read the rhythm again, while following the counts in level (b) and changing the conducting pattern as indicated. As the counts show, the beats in these measures group into twos, implying a temporary duple meter despite the overall triple meter. This type of grouping is common enough in musical practice that it has its own name: **hemiola**.

EXAMPLE 2.10: Hemiola pattern in triple meter

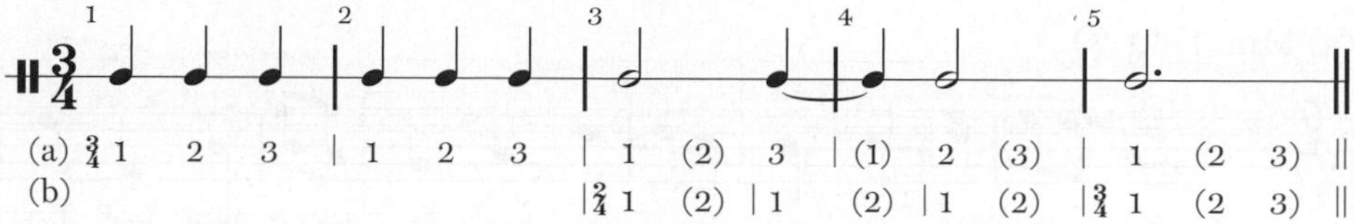

KEY CONCEPT A hemiola is a temporary duple rhythmic grouping in the context of an underlying triple meter. Typically, two measures of $\frac{3}{4}$ meter are heard as three measures of $\frac{2}{4}$ meter. A hemiola may be articulated by rhythmic durations, accents, or melodic patterns that imply duple groupings.

Measures 255–256 of Example 2.11 present a hemiola with a more complex rhythmic pattern.

EXAMPLE 2.11: Bach, Chaconne, from Violin Partita No. 2 in D Minor, mm. 251–256

We may hear a hemiola as a temporary change of meter, or as both meters (duple and triple) continuing at the same time, creating a type of syncopation. A hemiola typically appears at the end of a large section or movement as in Example 2.10, where the change in metrical feel indicates the approaching end. Hemiolas are typical of Baroque style (1600–1750), but may appear in later works (by Brahms, for example) as well.

Anacrusis Notation

In music that begins with an anacrusis, notate the last measure of the piece as an incomplete bar to "balance" the initial incomplete measure. Do this by subtracting the value of the anacrusis from the last measure of the piece. For example, in $\frac{4}{4}$ meter, a quarter-note anacrusis would be balanced at the end by a final measure of only three beats. Listen to Hensel's "Neue Liebe, neues Leben," the opening of which is given in Example 2.12a. Here the two-beat anacrusis at the beginning is balanced by a final bar in the piano postlude (conclusion of the piece) of only two beats, shown in part (b). (When numbering partial measures, call the anacrusis measure 0, and use the letters a and b to designate the first and last parts of measures.)

Example 2.12: Hensel, "Neue Liebe, neues Leben"

(a) Mm. 1–4a

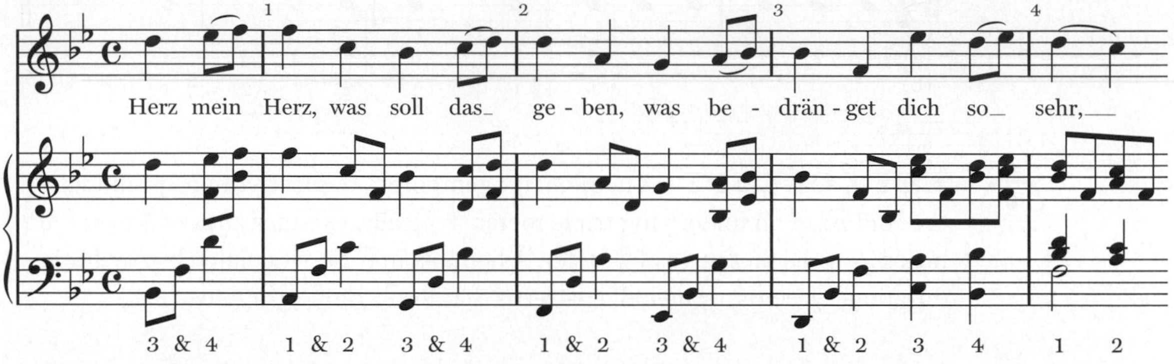

Translation: Heart, my heart, what does this mean? What is besieging you so?

(b) Mm. 73–77 (piano postlude) (anthology)

If you listen without a score, you might hear the beginning of this song as a downbeat: why might Hensel have set this text with an upbeat? Perhaps her sensitivity to the accents and meaning of the German text suggested that the second "Herz" was the more important word to set on a downbeat, as was "sehr" at the end of the phrase.

Try it #7

For each of the following melodies, identify what the duration of the last pitch (or combination of pitches and rests) of the piece should be to balance the anacrusis.

(a) Willson, "Till There Was You," mm. 1–4a (melody only)

Final note duration: ____________________

(b) Mozart, Piano Sonata in G Major, K. 283, first movement, mm. 1–4a

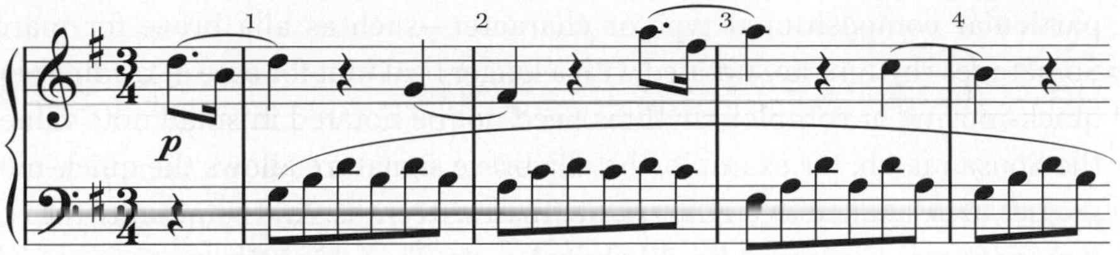

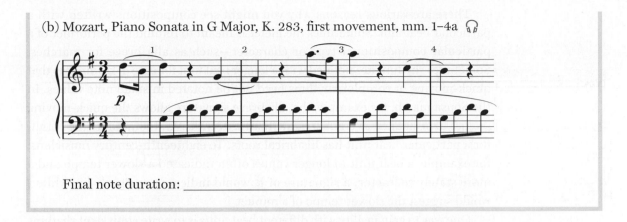

Final note duration: ________________

Beat Units Other Than the Quarter Note

The way you count the rhythm in a passage of music depends on its meter. Even the idea that "a whole note gets four beats" is correct only in certain meters, such as $\frac{4}{4}$, where a ♩ gets one beat and a 𝅗𝅥 two beats; in $\frac{4}{2}$, a ♩ gets a half beat, a 𝅗𝅥 one beat, and a two beats. Listen again to the opening of "The Stars and Stripes Forever" while following the piano score and counts in Example 2.13. The 𝄵 ($\frac{2}{2}$) meter instructs the performers to think of these measures "in two" (two beats per measure). To develop good sight-reading skills, practice reading rhythms with half-note or eighth-note beat units, as well as the more familiar quarter-note unit.

Example 2.13: Sousa, "The Stars and Stripes Forever," mm. 1–8

There are various reasons why you might see compositions written with a particular beat unit. Sometimes the meter is meant to remind the performer of a particular compositional type or character—such as alla breve for marches. Sometimes rhythms are notated with a longer beat unit for ease of reading, so that quick-moving or complex rhythms need not be notated in small note values. In the Sousa march, for example, the alla breve signature allows the quick-moving pitches to be notated as eighths rather than sixteenths. And sometimes the reason for a particular beat unit has historical roots. To eighteenth-century musicians, for example, a beat unit in longer values often indicated a slower tempo and a more stately character: a signature of $\frac{3}{16}$ would indicate a sprightly jig, while $\frac{3}{4}$ would suggest the slower tempo of a minuet.

One way to gain facility with different beat units is to write equivalent rhythms in different meters, as in Example 2.14.

Example 2.14: Equivalent rhythms notated in different meters

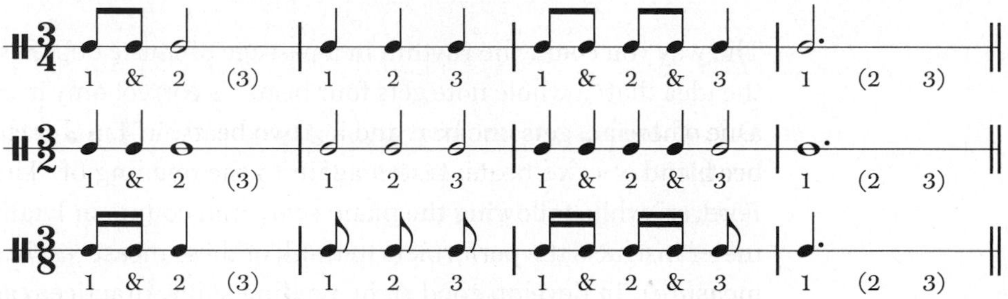

When you write in meters that are less familiar, be certain that the beaming is correct for the new beat unit. For example, in the $\frac{3}{8}$ rhythm of Example 2.14, write rather than , in order to reflect the eighth-note beat unit. (Composers are not always consistent with this guideline, as Example 2.15, in $\frac{3}{4}$, illustrates.)

Try it #8

Rewrite each rhythm below in the meter specified. Check that your beaming correctly reflects the new beat unit. Write the counts (1, 2, 3, etc.) below the new rhythms.

(a)

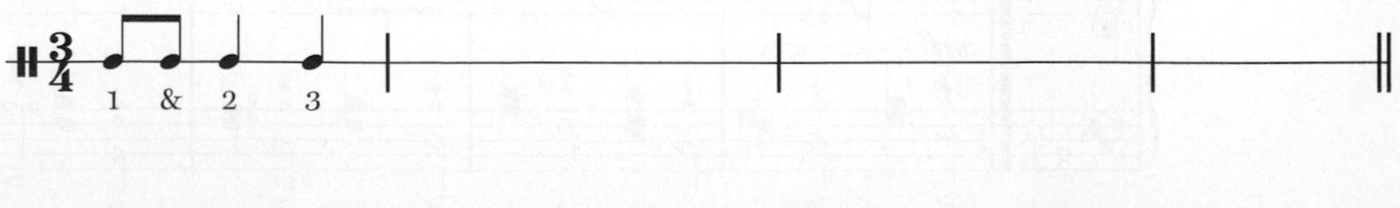

Implications for Performance: Metric Hierarchy

One of the most important concepts to remember from this chapter is that meters are hierarchical: the quicker beat division represents a low level, the beat a higher level, and the downbeat of each measure an even higher level. Within each measure, different beats carry different metric weight, with the downbeat (beat 1) the strongest. In duple meter, the beats alternate strong-weak. In triple meter, the accents are strong-weaker-weakest. And in quadruple meter, the first beat is metrically accented, but the third beat also gets a secondary accent.

This hierarchy is sometimes represented with rows of dots, as in Example 2.15, where a greater number of dots aligned vertically indicates a stronger metric position. The first beat of each measure, then, no matter the meter, receives the strongest metrical accent, and therefore the most dots.

Example 2.15: Anonymous, Minuet in D Minor, mm. 1–4

At an even higher level of the hierarchy, measures themselves typically group together in what's called "hypermeter": measures 1 and 3 are heard as metrically stronger than measures 2 and 4. This hypermetric grouping of measures is illustrated in Example 2.15 by the vertical columns of dots; in performance, think of strong and weak measures, just as you might think of strong and weak beats.

When you perform passages with continuous eighth-note motion, remember that not every eighth note is equally important. Carefully studying a work's metric and harmonic organization can help you determine the relative importance of each beat and pitch, and thus shape an effective performance. For example, listen to the opening of Schumann's "Trällerliedchen" (Example 2.16). Even though the left hand moves in continuous eighth notes, the sensitive performer will not play them all the same way.

EXAMPLE 2.16: Schumann "Trällerliedchen," mm. 1–4

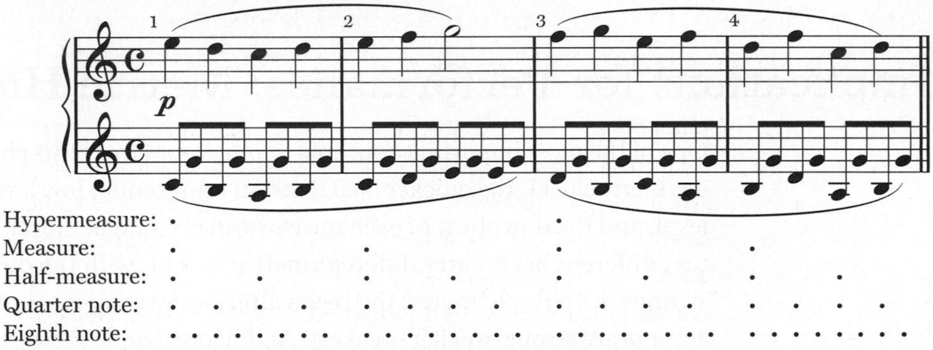

The "offbeat" eighth notes of the left hand (on "and") are weakest of all in the metric hierarchy. The downbeats of measures 1 and 3 are strongest metrically, followed by the downbeats of measures 2 and 4. Try singing or playing the right-hand melody, keeping in mind the implied strong and weak beats.

In performance, you may find it helpful sometimes to think "one to the bar" to create a large-scale hypermetric alternation between strong and weak measures. This will help contribute to a performance with broad sweep, one that is not bogged down by rhythmic detail. Try comparing several recordings of Schumann's piano work; listen for strong and weak measures, and consider whether the recordings agree in their hypermetric interpretations.

Did You Know?

Baroque musicians sometimes used motion of the hand down and up to conduct performances, but their patterns were somewhat different from those seen today. German composer and theorist Johann Mattheson (1681–1764), a contemporary of J. S. Bach, describes in one treatise the motions associated with duple and triple meters: both meters are based on a downward and upward motion of the hand, but in triple meters the up-stroke lasts twice as long as the down-stroke. Because the hand motion in triple meters was uneven, they were called "uneven" meters; duple meters were referred to as "even."

During this time, ensemble music was led by one of the players, usually the harpsichordist or organist, who signaled the first downbeat, then played with the ensemble. Sometimes opera or large-ensemble conductors indicated the downbeat by banging a large baton or staff on the floor. This proved hazardous in at least one case: Jean-Baptiste Lully, a ballet and opera composer and conductor at the French court of Louis XIV until 1687, died from an infection in his foot after energetically striking it with the conducting baton during a performance.

TERMS YOU SHOULD KNOW

- alla breve
- anacrusis
- bar line
- beam
- beat
- common time
- cut time
- dot
- downbeat
- flag
- hemiola
- measure
- meter
  - simple
  - compound
  - simple duple
  - simple quadruple
  - simple triple
- meter signature
- note head
- rest
- rhythm
- rhythmic value
  - eighth note
  - half note
  - quarter note
  - sixteenth note
  - whole note
- slur
- stem
- syncopation
- tempo
- tie
- time signature
- upbeat

QUESTIONS FOR REVIEW

1. What is the difference between (a) simple and compound meters, (b) rhythm and meter, (c) beat division and subdivision, (d) a flag and a beam, (e) a tie and a slur, (f) a syncopation and a hemiola?
2. What do the two numbers in a simple meter signature represent?
3. Provide two appropriate meter signatures each for a simple duple, simple triple, and a simple quadruple piece. Write three measures of rhythm in each meter, using rhythm clefs.
4. What are the notation rules for (a) stem direction, (b) beaming beat divisions and subdivisions, (c) upbeats?

5. How are syncopations created? Write two syncopated rhythmic patterns.
6. Find a piece of music from your repertoire in each of the following meters: simple duple, simple triple, simple quadruple. Choose at least one with an eighth- or half-note beat unit, and practice counting its rhythm while conducting the meter.
7. Choose a short passage from your repertoire. Try to perform it with equal stress on each beat. Then mark the strong and weak beats and perform again.

Pitch Collections, Scales, and Major Keys

CHAPTER 3

Outline of topics

Chromatic and diatonic collections

Scales: Ordered pitch-class collections
- Scale degrees
- Spelling major scales
- Spelling chromatic scales

Major keys
- Key signatures
- The circle of fifths
- Identifying a key from a key signature
- Writing key signatures
- Identifying the key of a piece
- Scale-degree names

The major pentatonic scale

Implications for performance

Overview

The concept of key is fundamental to Western music. In this chapter, we learn about keys by notating and playing major scales. The major key signatures and scale-degree names will serve as foundations for the study of harmony.

Repertoire

Johann Sebastian Bach, Invention in D Minor

Wolfgang Amadeus Mozart, Piano Sonata in C Major, K. 545, first movement

"My Country, 'Tis of Thee"

John Newton, "Amazing Grace"

Dolly Parton, "I Will Always Love You"

Robert Schumann, "Trällerliedchen," from *Album for the Young*, Op. 68, No. 3

Richard Sherman and Robert Sherman, "Feed the Birds," from *Mary Poppins*

John Philip Sousa, "The Stars and Stripes Forever"

Anton Webern, *Variations for Piano*, Op. 27, second movement

Chromatic and Diatonic Collections

Listen to the opening of two piano compositions written about 150 years apart: Mozart's Piano Sonata in C Major (Example 3.1) and Webern's *Variations for Piano* (Example 3.2). Below the examples, write the letter names of the pitch classes in each excerpt, writing each letter name only once, in any order. When finished, you will have written a **pitch-class collection** for each excerpt—that is, the group of pitch classes employed in the music, with no particular order and no duplications.

EXAMPLE 3.1: Mozart, Piano Sonata in C Major, first movement, mm. 1–4

Pitch-class collection: **C** ____________________

EXAMPLE 3.2: Webern, *Variations for Piano*, second movement, mm. 1–11 (anthology)

Pitch-class collection: **B♭** ____________________

The Webern passage includes all twelve pitch classes—a complete **chromatic** collection. (The word "chromatic" comes from the Greek *chroma*, meaning "color"; chromatic collections contain one of each possible pitch-class "color.") In contrast, the Mozart excerpt features only seven different pitch classes; these form a **diatonic** collection. Because no ordering guidelines were given, you could have listed C D E F G A B, or C E G B D F A, or any other order here. A diatonic collection, with seven pitch classes, is a particular subset of the chromatic collection.

Try it #1

Write the pitch-class collection for "Feed the Birds" (Example 3.3) in the blank beneath the example. Compare what you write here with the collection for Example 3.1. Do these collections differ? ___________

EXAMPLE 3.3: Sherman and Sherman, "Feed the Birds," mm. 1–4

Pitch-class collection: ______________________________________

Scales: Ordered Pitch-Class Collections

Listen again to the opening of the Mozart sonata and compare it with "Feed the Birds" in Example 3.3. Sing the pitch class in each piece that seems to be more stable than the rest. You should find that in both passages, this pitch is C. Further, it provides grounding for a special type of diatonic collection called a **major scale**.

Scales differ from collections in that they *are* ordered. When you play or sing a scale, there is a beginning pitch and an order to the remaining notes that corresponds to the musical alphabet—in this case, C D E F G A B C, the pitches of a C major scale.

When the chromatic collection is ordered, it becomes the **chromatic scale**. Because it includes all twelve pitch classes, this scale is entirely made up of consecutive half steps. Portions of chromatic scales typically appear in showy music as a decorative or virtuosic element. For an example, listen to the Trio section of "The Stars and Stripes Forever" (Example 3.4).

EXAMPLE 3.4: Sousa, "The Stars and Stripes Forever," mm. 77–84a

Try it #2

In Example 3.4, circle the longest continuous chromatic scale segment in each line. Look for numerous accidentals and consecutive half steps. Write the pitches of the scale segments below.

(a) Mm. 77–80: ______________________________

(b) Mm. 81–84: ______________________________

Example 3.5 illustrates a chromatic and a major scale, with whole and half steps identified for comparison. The chromatic scale's steps are all the same size (part a), with the pattern of continuous half steps unchanging from bottom to top. In contrast, the pattern of whole and half steps in the major scale (part b) is W-W-H-W-W-W-H; there are only two half steps. When you hear a half step in a major scale, you know it is in one of two specific locations, while in a chromatic scale the half step could be anywhere. The half step therefore helps us locate the most stable pitches in a major scale quickly.

KEY CONCEPT A major scale may begin on any pitch. It must include each of the seven pitch-class letter names, as in Example 3.5b, and follow the W-W-H-W-W-W-H arrangement of whole and half steps from bottom to top.

Example 3.5: Chromatic and major scale patterns

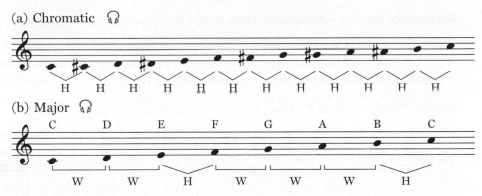

(a) Chromatic

(b) Major

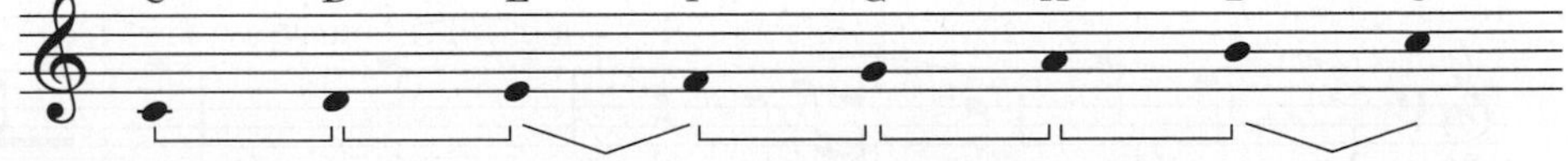

Scale Degrees

The word "scale" comes from the Latin *scalae* (or the Italian scala), meaning "stairs" or "ladder." Each pitch of the scale is a **scale degree**, or **scale step** in keeping with the stairs image. When you write or play a scale, its beginning tone—called the **tonic**—is usually repeated one octave higher at the end. The tonic scale degree (C in the C major scale) is crucial to the sound and structure of scales and musical passages. The other scale steps vary in structural weight, depending in part on the musical context.

As you begin to analyze music, you'll find it helpful to refer to specific scale degrees by number or name. Scale-degree numbers are customarily written with a caret above: $\hat{1}$, $\hat{2}$, $\hat{3}$, $\hat{4}$, and so on. Some sight-singing methods encourage singing on these numbers. Another method, **movable-do solfège**, or solfège for short, assigns each scale degree a syllable—*do, re, mi, fa, sol, la, ti, do*—as in Example 3.6a. Part (b) gives scale-degree numbers and solfège syllables for the beginning of "Twinkle, Twinkle, Little Star."

Example 3.6: Solfège syllables and scale-degree numbers

(a) Scale beginning on C

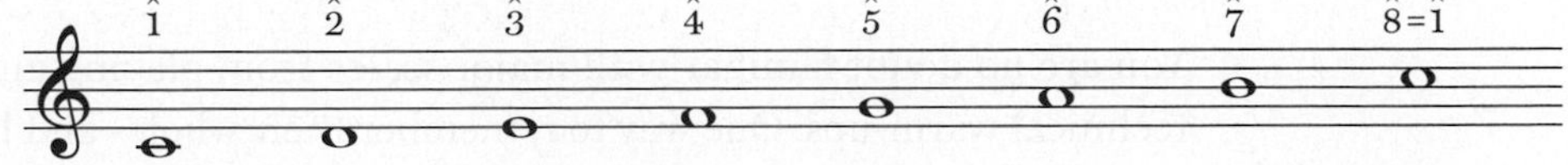

(b) "Twinkle, Twinkle, Little Star" (mm. 1–4)

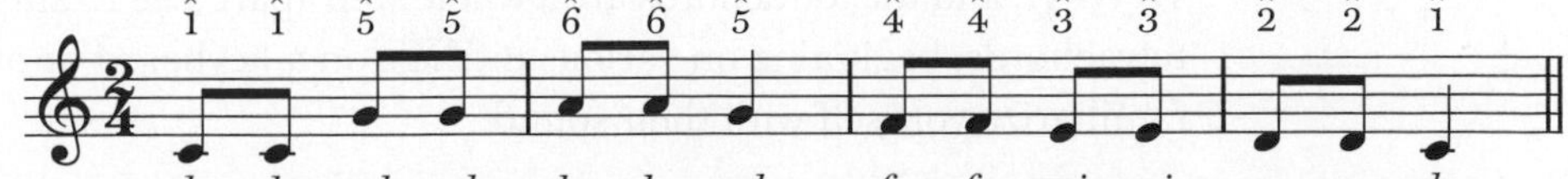

Try it #3

For practice hearing scale-degree relationships in melodies:

(a) Sing up and down a major scale on scale-degree numbers or solfège syllables beginning on any C in a comfortable range. Then write the appropriate number or syllable below each pitch of the two melodies below (assuming C is $\hat{1}$, or do).

Mozart, Piano Sonata in C Major, first movement, mm. 1–4

Sherman and Sherman, "Feed the Birds," mm. 1–4

(b) Sing the melodies above on scale-degree numbers or solfège in any octave that is comforable. After giving yourself the starting pitch, use a piano or other instrument to check your pitch only if absolutely necessary.

(c) Then compare the scale degrees for the two melodies. Draw vertical lines from the pitches in one melody to the next where you see and hear shared patterns.

(d) For more practice, sing some familiar tunes on scale-degree numbers or solfège, such as "Frère Jacques" ("Are You Sleeping?"), which starts $\hat{1}$–$\hat{2}$–$\hat{3}$–$\hat{1}$ (*do–re–mi–do*); or "Happy Birthday," which starts $\underline{\hat{5}}$–$\underline{\hat{5}}$–$\underline{\hat{6}}$–$\underline{\hat{5}}$–$\hat{1}$–$\underline{\hat{7}}$ (*sol-sol-la-sol-do-ti*). An underlined number or syllable indicates that it falls below the tonic.

Spelling Major Scales

You are no doubt familiar with major scales from playing and singing them as technical warm-ups. One way to remember their whole- and half-step pattern is to divide the scale into two four-note groups, or **tetrachords** ("tetra-" means "four"): $\hat{1}$–$\hat{2}$–$\hat{3}$–$\hat{4}$ and $\hat{5}$–$\hat{6}$–$\hat{7}$–$\hat{8}$. Each **major tetrachord** consists of the pattern W-W- H, and the tetrachords are a whole step apart (see Example 3.7). Play major tetrachords, beginning on various pitches, on a keyboard or other instrument to familiarize yourself with their sound.

KEY CONCEPT To write an ascending major scale from any given pitch:

(1) Write the given pitch (scale degree $\hat{1}$) on the staff.

(2) Write pitches with no accidentals on every line and space from that pitch, up to and including the same pitch class an octave higher (Example 3.7a).

(3) Label the space between each pair of consecutive pitches, from bottom to top, W-W-H-W-W-W-H (part b). Each *major tetrachord* is W-W-H.

(4) Add an appropriate accidental (♯ or ♭) as needed to match each whole- or half-step label (part c).

Example 3.7: Steps in constructing a major scale (D major)

(a) Note heads on staff

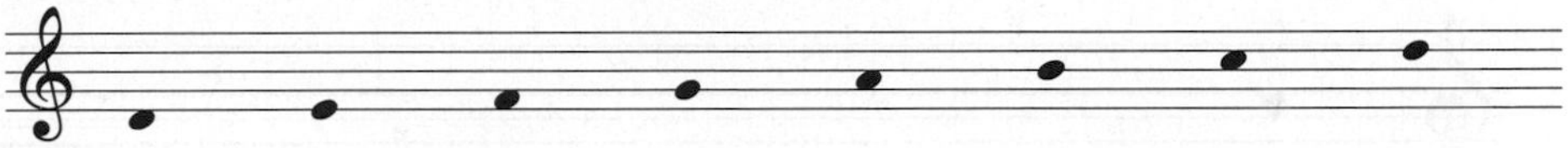

(b) Label whole and half steps

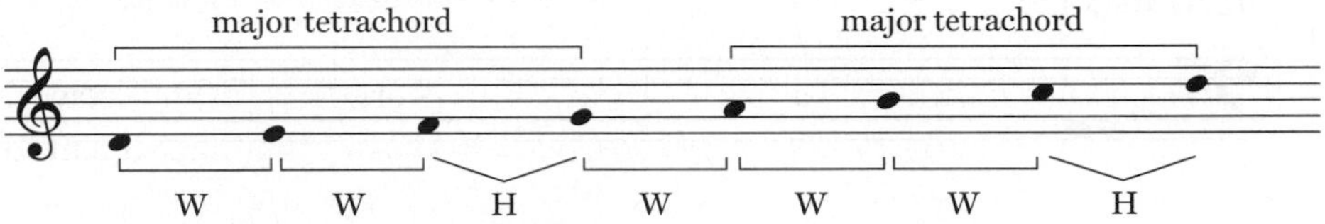

(c) Add appropriate accidentals

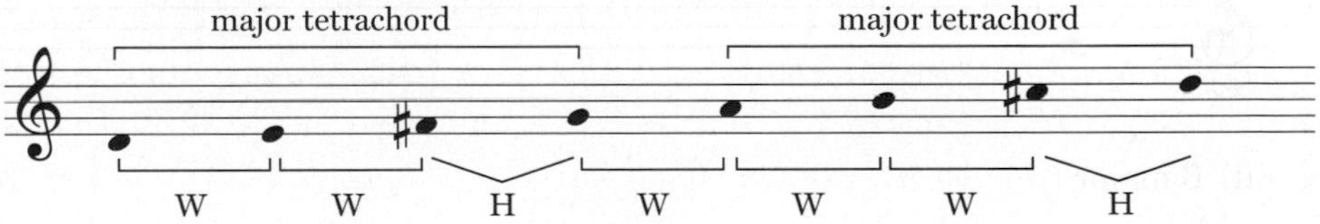

The "spelling" of a scale refers to the choice of correct enharmonic letter names for each pitch. Always write major scales with eight pitches—all seven letters of the alphabet plus the repeated tonic. Throughout the scale, accidentals should be either all sharps or all flats, not a mixture. In B♭ major, for example, it would be incorrect to write D♯ instead of E♭, as Example 3.8a demonstrates: this spelling does not include all seven letter names (there is no E), and it mixes flats with sharps. Part (b) provides the correct spelling. Finally, when spelling scales, don't change the given pitch. If your scale doesn't conform to these guidelines, go back and check your work.

EXAMPLE 3.8: Notation of the B♭ major scale

(a) Incorrect

(b) Correct

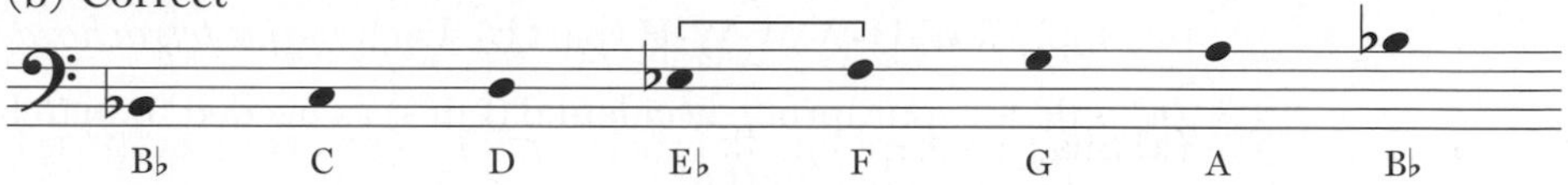

Try it #4

Follow the steps above to write a major scale from the given pitches.

(a) A major

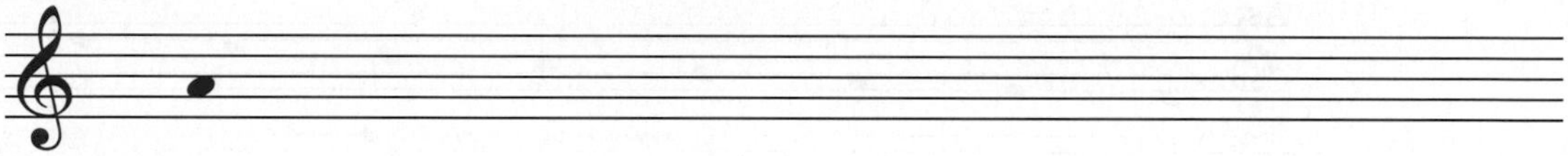

(b) A♭ major

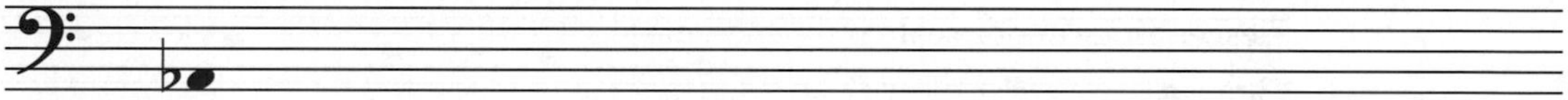

(c) G major

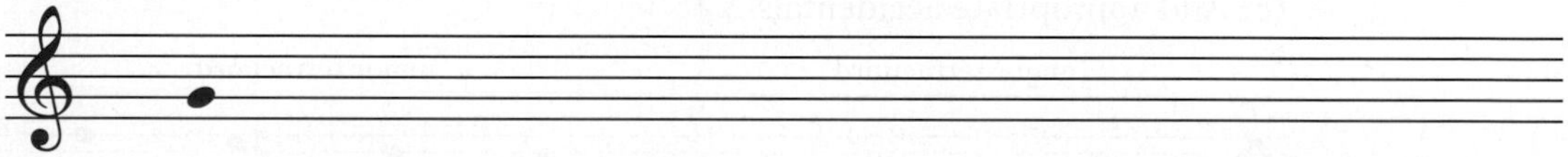

(d) B major

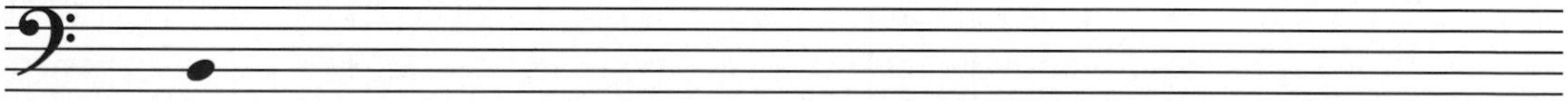

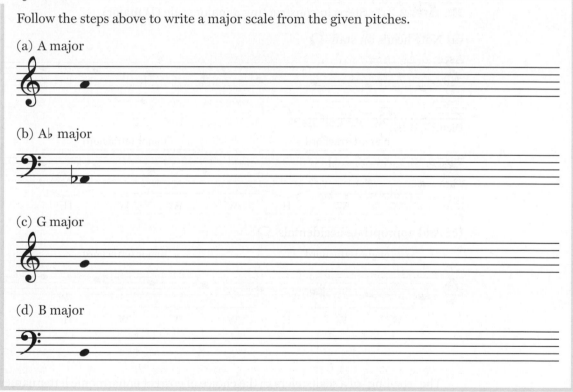

Spelling Chromatic Scales

Unlike major scales, chromatic scales include some letter names more than once.

KEY CONCEPT A half step spelled D–D♯ is a **chromatic half step**: the same letter name plus a chromatic alteration. The same half step spelled D-E♭ is a **diatonic half step**: different letter names indicating adjacent pitches in a diatonic scale.

Chromatic scales may be notated in one of two ways, depending on the context. When no key is specified or the key is unclear, simply raise notes when ascending and lower them when descending, as in Example 3.9a. (Where there are two spellings possible for a pitch, such as E♯ or F, or F♭ or E, use the simplest to read.)

Example 3.9: Two ways to notate chromatic scales

(a) Sharps ascending, flats descending (when key context is unclear)

(b) Spelling in context of major scale

Ascending (major scale in whole notes)

Descending (major scale in whole notes)

When the chromatic scale appears in the context of a major-key piece, or if a key is specified, start by writing the underlying major scale. Then fill in each whole step in the scale with a chromatic half step: raise the scale degrees going up ($\hat{1}$–♯$\hat{1}$–$\hat{2}$–♯$\hat{2}$–$\hat{3}$–$\hat{4}$, etc.), and lower them going down ($\hat{1}$–$\hat{7}$–♭$\hat{7}$–$\hat{6}$–♭$\hat{6}$–$\hat{5}$, etc.). Part (b) presents a chromatic scale in a Bb major context. Start with the Bb major scale, then raise $\hat{1}$ (B♭ to B♮), $\hat{2}$ (C to C♯), etc., going up; going down, lower $\hat{7}$ (A to A♭), $\hat{6}$ (G to G♭), etc. This results in a scale with mixed accidentals (and additional solfège syllables), but a clear underlying tonal context.

In practical terms, seeing the correct spelling helps you sight-read better. Once you are used to the look and feel of a particular key, you will find unusual spellings distracting and confusing. If you spell anything incorrectly—even if your spelling "sounds" the same—you change its musical meaning. Eventually your training in correct spelling will pay off, in both sight-reading and composition skills, and it will help others perform your music with fewer errors.

Try it #5

Write a chromatic scale (ascending and descending) beginning with the pitches shown below. Base the spelling on the corresponding major scales you wrote for *Try it #4*. Label the diatonic scale degrees, then fill in the half steps between them as appropriate. The first one has been completed for you.

(a)

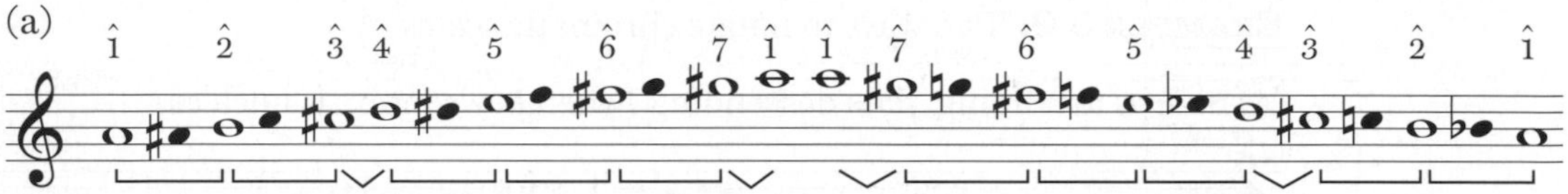

(b)

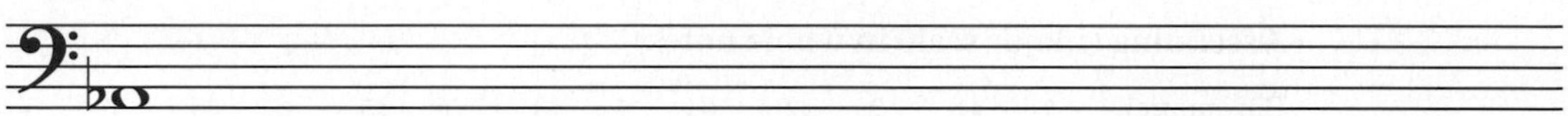

(c)

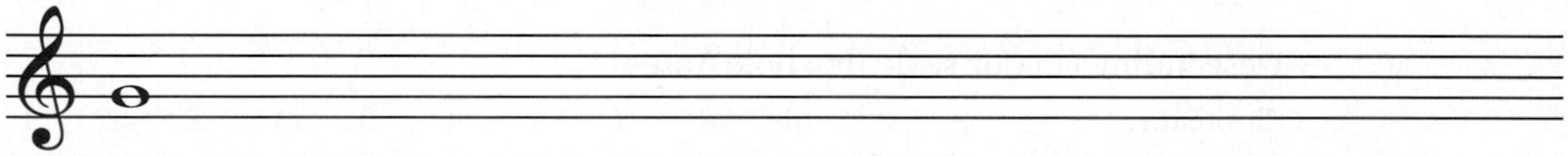

(d)

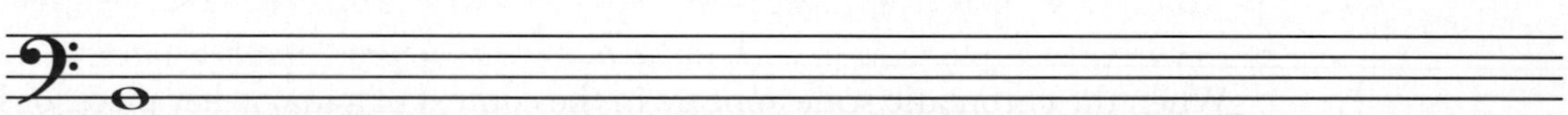

Major Keys

Key Signatures

In writing scales so far, we have placed an accidental next to any note that needed it. In tonal music, however, this type of notation is not standard practice. Look at the beginning of Parton's "I Will Always Love You," given in Example 3.10.

EXAMPLE 3.10: Parton, "I Will Always Love You," mm. 1–5a

This work is in A major, whose scale includes three sharps, yet not a single accidental is notated next to any pitch. Instead, the key signature at the beginning of each line instructs the singer to sharp every F, C, and G.

KEY CONCEPT A **key signature** shows which pitches are to be sharped or flatted consistently throughout the work. It is placed at the beginning of each line of a score, immediately after the clef. The key signature, together with the work's pitch collection and the relationships between its pitches, determine the key of the work.

To say that a piece of music is "in" a key means that its pitches are drawn primarily from a single scale, and that the pitches have predictable relationships of stability and instability in that piece. For example, the first note of the scale ($\hat{1}$) is generally the most stable (where a piece will usually end), and the others (like $\hat{7}$) have a predictable relationship to that note. Figure 3.1 presents all the major key signatures. Memorize those for treble and bass clefs (and others as assigned), since many theoretical skills you will learn in later chapters build on this knowledge.

FIGURE 3.1: Major key signatures in four clefs

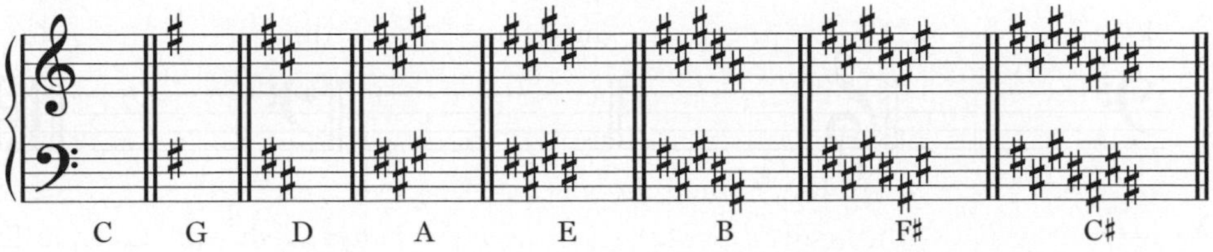

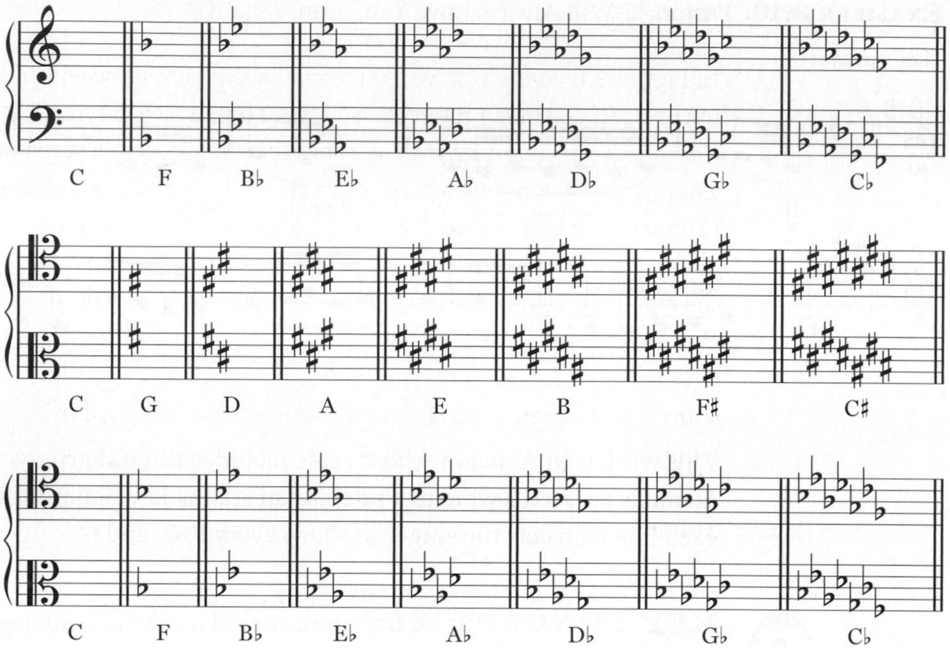

Try it #6

On the staves below, copy the major key signatures requested, taking Figure 3.1 as your model. Center each accidental on the appropriate line or space.

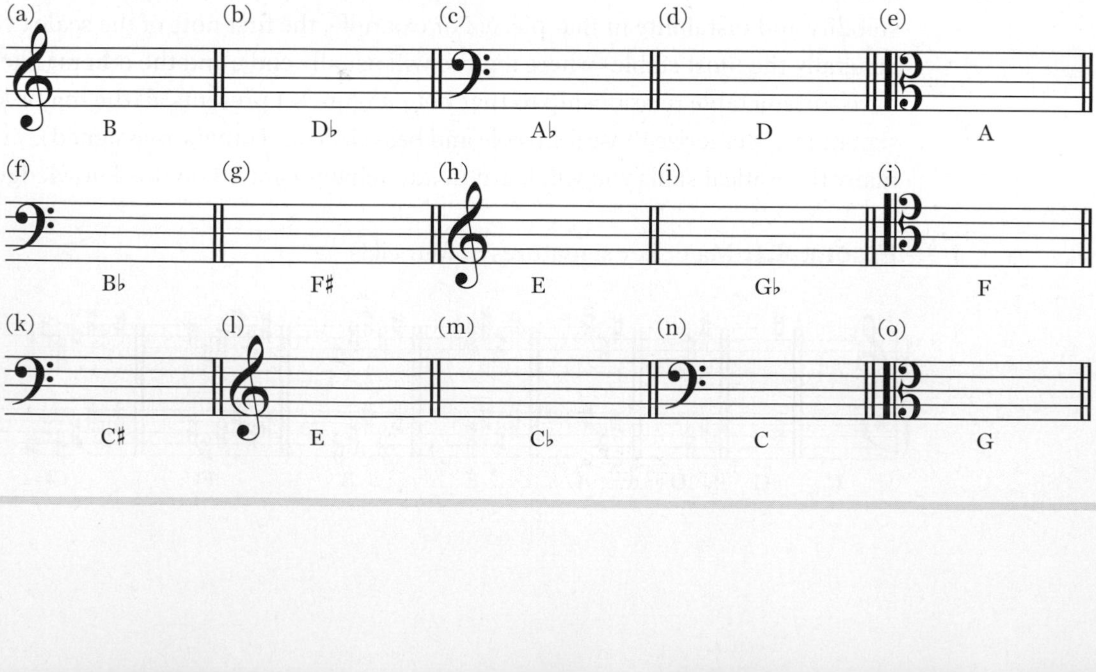

The Circle of Fifths

In Figure 3.1, you may have noticed a relationship between the successive key signatures. Each time a new sharp is added, the new key is five steps higher than the last; and as a new flat is added, the new key is five steps lower than the last. That is, C major has no sharps or flats, G major (five steps higher) has one sharp, D major (five higher than G) has two sharps, and so on. This relationship between keys is sometimes represented around a circle, like the one in Figure 3.2, called the **circle of fifths**. The keys that require sharps appear around the right side of the circle (each a fifth higher), while those that require flats appear around the left side (each a fifth lower). You may find the circle of fifths a helpful aid as you learn the key signatures. In fact, students have relied on this circle since the eighteenth century.

FIGURE 3.2: Circle of fifths

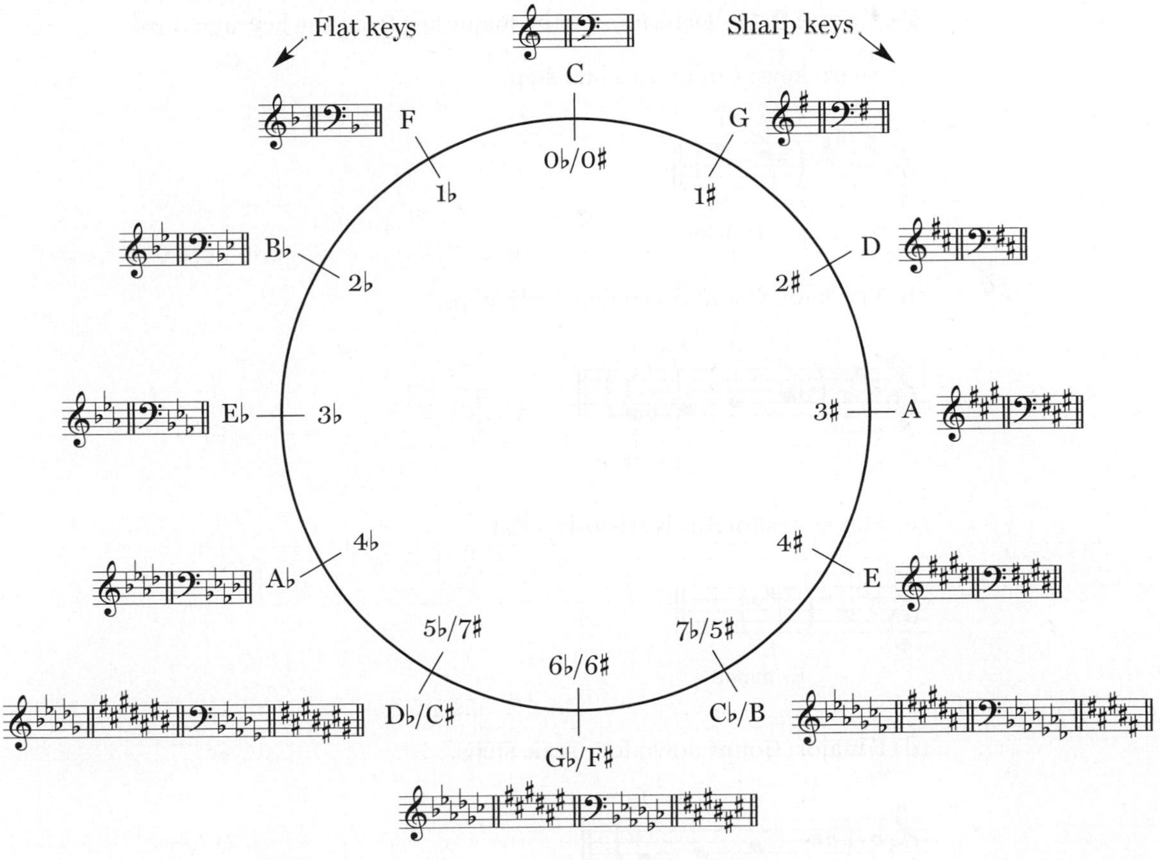

Identifying a Key from a Key Signature

Although you should memorize which key goes with each signature, you can also calculate the name of the key from looking at the signature.

KEY CONCEPT For sharp keys, imagine that the last sharp of the signature is scale degree $\hat{7}$ (or *ti*) of the key. To find the tonic ($\hat{1}$; or *do*), go up a diatonic half step (Example 3.11a)

For flat keys, consider the last flat to be $\hat{4}$ (or *fa*) of the key, and count down four diatonic steps to the tonic (part b). Shortcut: Since flats in the key signature are spaced a fourth apart, just look at the next-to-last flat of the signature, which always represents the name of the key (part c). This shortcut always works for flat keys except in the case of F major's one flat, B♭. In this case, count down four scale steps, as in part (d).

EXAMPLE 3.11: Determining the major key from the key signature

(a) Sharp keys: Count up a half step.

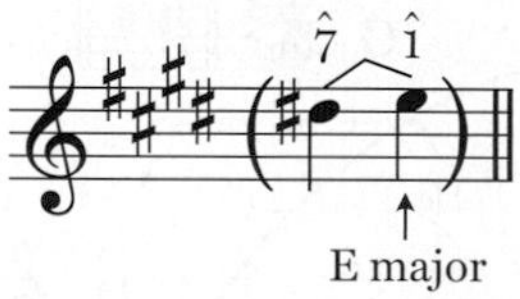

(b) Flat keys: Count down four scale steps.

(c) Flat keys shorcut: Next-to-last flat.

(d) F major: Count down four scale steps.

Writing Key Signatures

To write music that others can read easily, you need to learn the standard order, octave, and spacing for each key signature.

KEY CONCEPT The key signature is placed between the clef and meter signature. The order of the sharps is F C G D A E B; the order of the flats is the same, only backward: B-E-A-D-G-C-F.

The placement of sharps on the staff alternates directions "down-up," with a few exceptions (see Example 3.12). Because accidentals are not notated on ledger lines, the sharp on A (which would fall on a ledger line in the treble clef) is written in the lower octave, so there are two "downs" in a row. The flats alternate "up-down" without exception. In the tenor clef (Figure 3.1), the F♯ is written on the staff rather than above it (F♯3, not F♯4), and the sharps here alternate "up-down" rather than "down-up."

EXAMPLE 3.12: Order of the sharps and flats

Another Way

One fact that can help you remember the order of symbols at the beginning of the staff is that they occur in alphabetical order: clef, key, meter. A helpful mnemonic (or memory device) for the first four flats is that they spell the word "bead." A handy sentence to remember for the order of sharps and flats is "Father Charles Goes Down And Ends Battle." When you read it forward, the first letter of each word gives you the order of the sharps; when you read it backward ("Battle Ends And Down Goes Charles' Father"), it gives you the order of the flats.

When asked to write a specific key signature, you might follow the instructions for interpreting a key signature, only backward. For example, if asked to write the key signature for A♭ major, remember that the next-to-last flat is the name of the key and you therefore need to write one additional flat beyond A♭ in the standard order of flats: B♭-E♭-A♭-D♭. If asked to write the signature for B major, remember that the last sharp will be $\hat{7}$ (or *ti*) of the key. That means the last sharp is A♯. Then follow the order of sharps until you come to A♯: F♯-C♯-G♯-D♯-A♯. B major has five sharps.

Try it #7

Write key signatures for the major keys specified below from memory, in the treble and bass clefs.

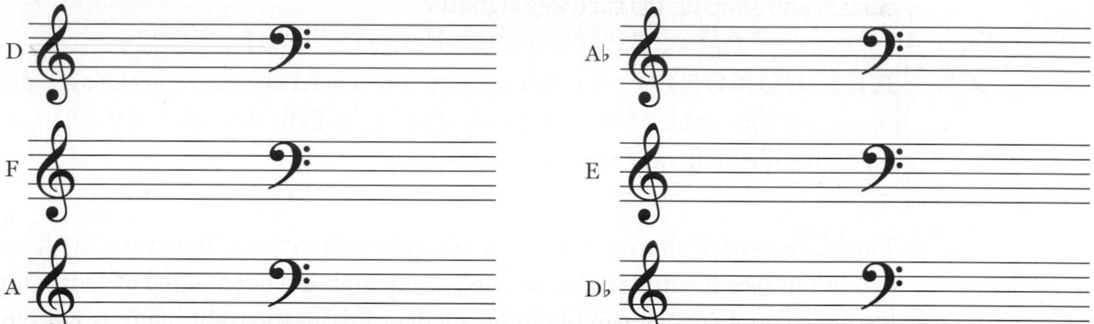

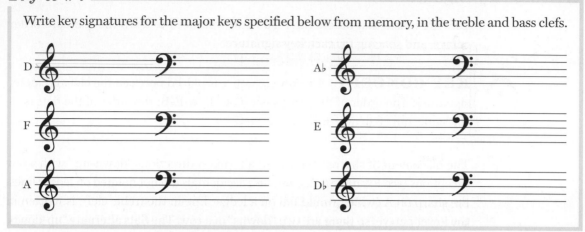

Identifying the Key of a Piece

If a piece begins with a key signature of one flat, you might assume that it is in F major. But the key signature alone is not enough to determine the key of a piece. As you will see in Chapter 5, it can indicate either a major or minor key.

KEY CONCEPT To find the key of a piece, first check the key signature, and then check the beginning and end of the piece for characteristic scale-degree patterns of the key suggested by the signature. The last note of the melody usually ends on $\hat{1}$ of the key. Typical patterns at the end are $\hat{3}$–$\hat{2}$–$\hat{1}$ in the melody and $\hat{5}$–$\hat{1}$ in the lowest-sounding voice (the bass). The most common scale degrees at the beginning of the melody and bass are $\hat{1}$, $\hat{3}$, and $\hat{5}$.

Listen to "My Country, 'Tis of Thee," and focus on the beginning and end, given in Example 3.13, to decide its key.

EXAMPLE 3.13: "My Country, 'Tis of Thee"

(a) Mm. 1–4

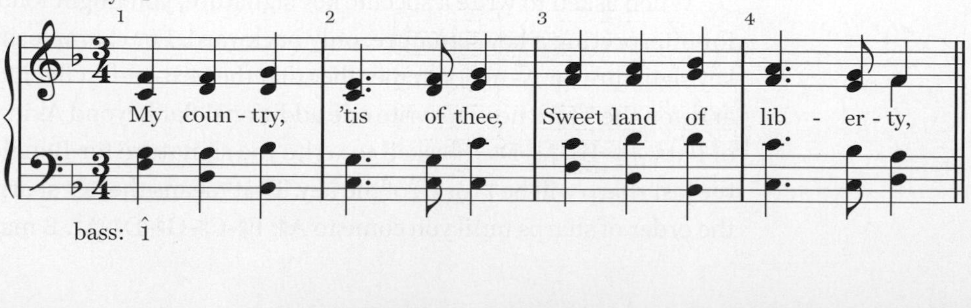

(b) Mm. 13–14

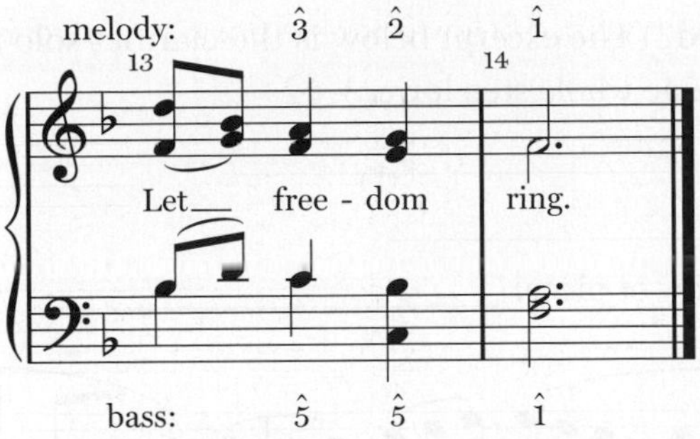

First, note the key signature of one flat, which suggests F major. Next, confirm this key by checking the beginning and end of the melody and bass line. The melody begins on $\hat{1}$ and ends with $\hat{3}$–$\hat{2}$–$\hat{1}$ in F major, while the bass begins on $\hat{1}$ and ends with $\hat{5}$–$\hat{1}$. Both clearly express the key of F major.

In contrast, look at the Bach invention excerpts given in Example 3.14. This piece also has a key signature of one flat, but the notes at the beginning and end emphasize Ds, not Fs. The melody begins in D in both voices (lines), and it ends with $\hat{3}$–$\hat{2}$–$\hat{1}$ to D in the top voice and $\hat{5}$–$\hat{1}$ to D in the bottom voice. The piece is not in F major, but in D minor (minor keys will be discussed in Chapter 5).

Example 3.14: Bach, Invention in D Minor

(a) Mm. 1–5

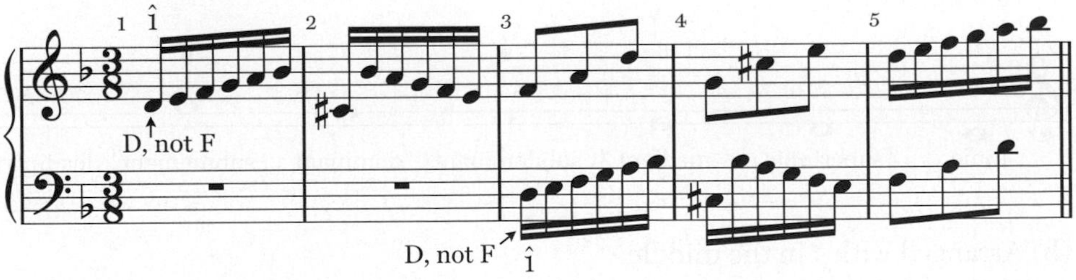

(b) Mm. 51–52

Try it #8

In what key is "Simple Gifts" notated? (The excerpt below is the clarinet solo from Copland's *Appalachian Spring*, which sounds one whole step lower.)

- Key signature suggests what key? ____________________
- First two scale degrees? ____________________
- Last scale degree? _______ Key of piece: ____________________

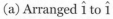

Scale-Degree Names

In addition to numbers, scale degrees also have names. These names can indicate either the scale degree itself or the harmony built on it (see Chapter 7).

Example 3.15: Scale-degree names

(a) Arranged $\hat{1}$ to $\hat{1}$

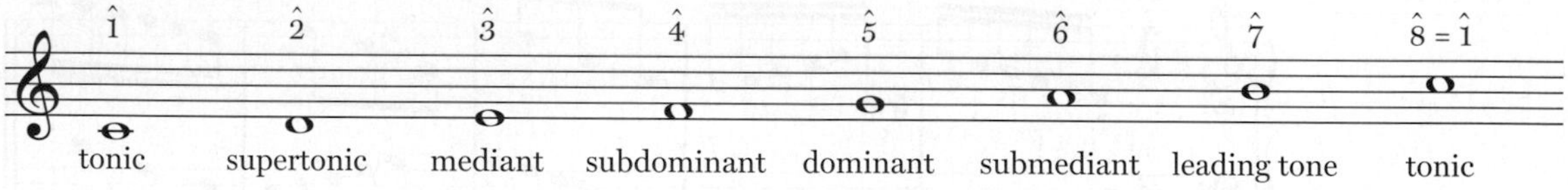

(b) Arranged with $\hat{1}$ in the middle

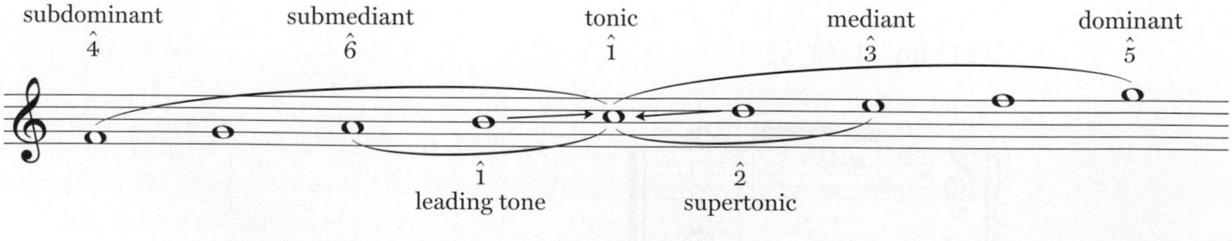

Scale degree $\hat{1}$ is called the **tonic**—it is the "tone" on which the scale is built—while $\hat{5}$ is the **dominant**: its musical function "dominates" tonal music, as will be clear in future chapters. Scale degree $\hat{3}$ is the **mediant**, since it falls in the "medial"

position midway between $\hat{1}$ and $\hat{5}$. Scale degree $\hat{2}$ is called the **supertonic**—"super-" means "above" (as in "superhuman" or "superior")—to fix its position immediately above $\hat{1}$. As Example 3.15b shows, this relationship of $\hat{2}$ above $\hat{1}$ is mirrored by $\hat{7}$ below $\hat{1}$; $\hat{7}$, the **leading tone**, gets its name from its tendency to lead upward toward the tonic. (In fact, $\hat{7}$ is sometimes called a **tendency tone** because of this strong pull.) Scale-degree $\hat{4}$ is the **subdominant**; "sub-" means "below" (as in "submarine" or "subordinate"). This label originates from the idea that $\hat{4}$ lies the same distance below the tonic as the dominant lies above. Similarly, the **submediant**, $\hat{6}$, lies three scale steps below the tonic (just as the mediant lies three scale steps above).

Try it #9

Fill in the letter name for the scale degree in each specified scale.

SCALE	SCALE DEGREE	LETTER NAME
F major	$\hat{4}$	________
G major	leading tone	________
A♭ major	$\hat{5}$	________
E major	mediant	________
B major	supertonic	________
D♭ major	$\hat{6}$	________

The Major Pentatonic Scale

Listen to Example 3.16, "Amazing Grace," or sing it on solfège or scale-degree numbers. Although the melody sounds major, it includes only a subset of the major scale: scale degrees $\hat{1}$, $\hat{2}$, $\hat{3}$, $\hat{5}$, and $\hat{6}$ (*do, re, mi, sol, la*), missing $\hat{4}$ and $\hat{7}$ (*fa* and *ti*). Because this collection features only five of the seven diatonic pitches, it is called a **pentatonic** collection ("penta-" means "five," as in the five-sided pentagon). There are a number of pentatonic collections found in folk and popular music, world music, rock, and jazz. The scale type used in "Amazing Grace" is called the **major pentatonic** collection because it begins with the first three degrees of the major scale.

Example 3.16: Newton, "Amazing Grace," mm. 1–16

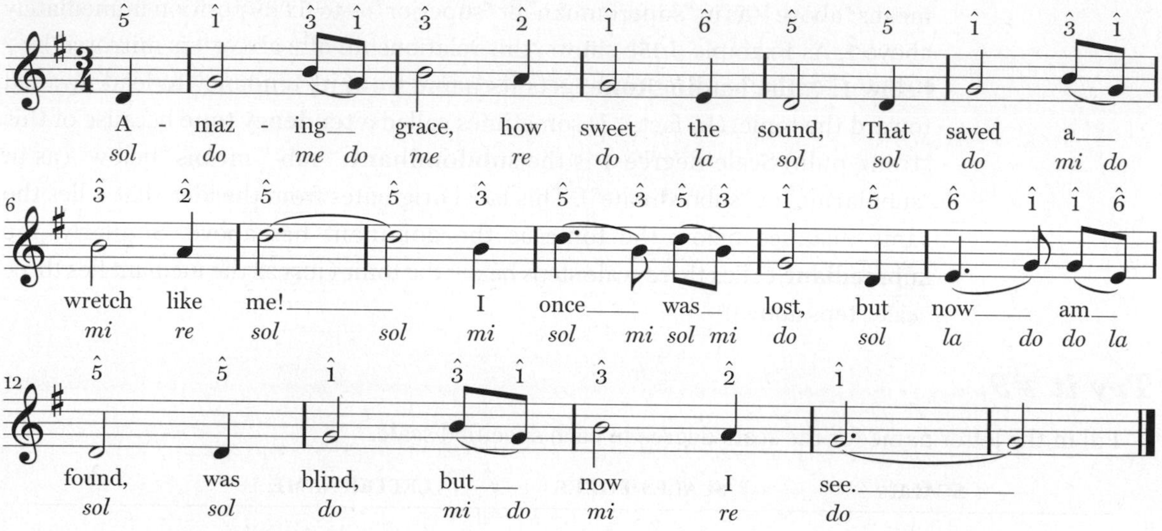

Try it #10

Write major pentatonic scales beginning on the following notes, and label the scale degrees $\hat{1}$-$\hat{2}$-$\hat{3}$-$\hat{5}$-$\hat{6}$ (or *do-re-mi-sol-la*).

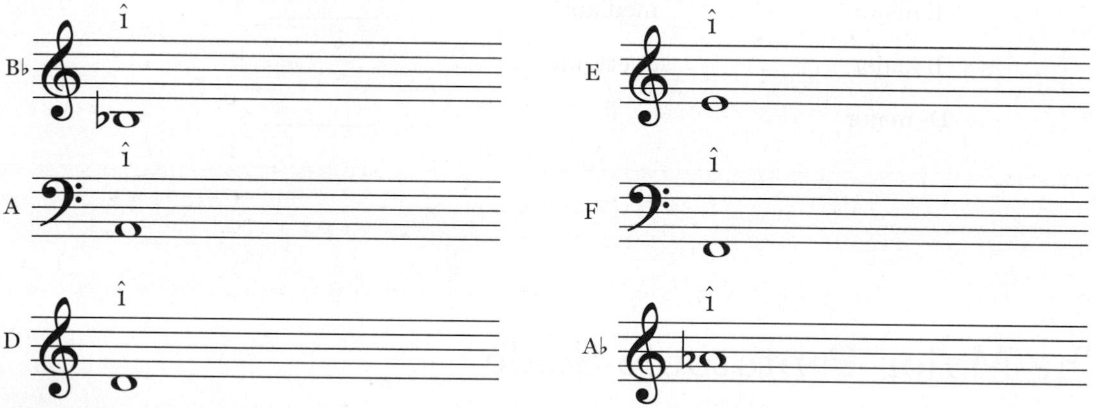

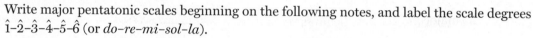

Implications for Performance

What are scales "used" for? For one thing, practicing scales on an instrument helps you gain finger facility in different keys, to prepare for the technical demands of works that include scalewise passages. It also helps you to "think" in different keys, which in turn helps with memorization and improvisation in those keys. Melodies often feature segments of the scale, such as the major tetrachord (W-W-H). Example 3.17 shows this familiar scale segment, plus another one you will encounter: the major pentachord, $\hat{1}$–$\hat{2}$–$\hat{3}$–$\hat{4}$–$\hat{5}$ (or *do-re-mi-fa-sol*; W-W-H-W).

Example 3.17: Common scale segments

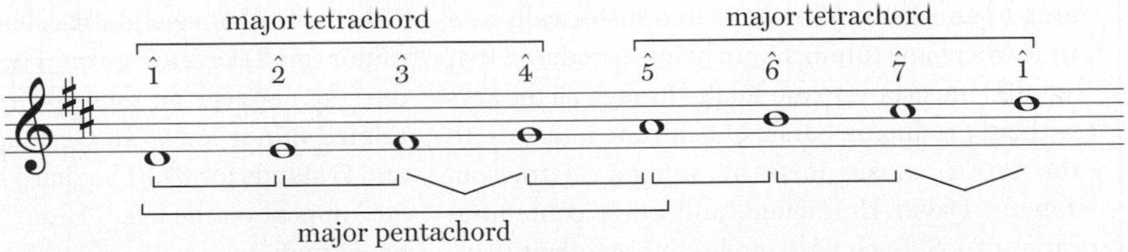

The melody of Schumann's "Trällerliedchen," as you can see in Example 3.18, features the major pentachord. Other pentachord melodies might include $\hat{1}$ to $\hat{5}$ plus a step above ($\hat{6}$), or $\hat{1}$ to $\hat{5}$ plus a step below ($\hat{7}$). If you practice playing the major pentachord in every key, you will find your sight-reading improved for melodies like this one.

Example 3.18: Schumann, "Trällerliedchen," mm. 1–8

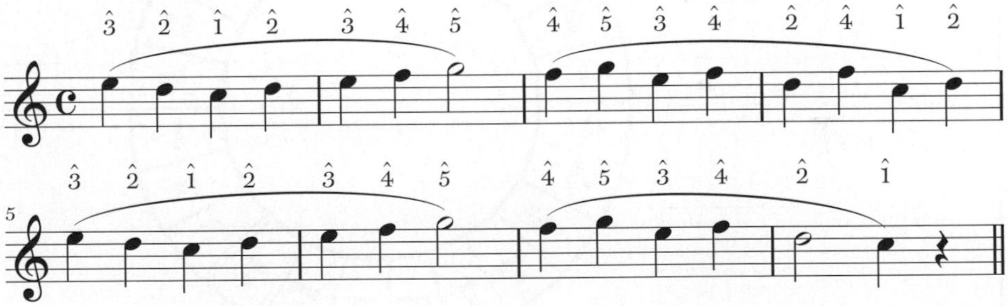

KEY CONCEPT The major pentachord is a scale segment of consecutive pitches: $\hat{1}$–$\hat{2}$–$\hat{3}$–$\hat{4}$–$\hat{5}$. Don't confuse it with the major pentatonic scale, which is made of two "gapped" segments of the major scale (it skips $\hat{4}$ and $\hat{7}$): $\hat{1}$–$\hat{2}$–$\hat{3}$–$\hat{5}$–$\hat{6}$.

Scales can also be considered an analytical tool: an abstraction from the composition that clarifies the function and relationship of pitches within it—especially the tendency tones and their expected resolutions (such as $\hat{7}$–$\hat{1}$). Eventually you may choose to bring out tendency tones and their resolutions in performance. In preparation for the analytical work in future chapters, you should be able to play all the major pentachords and major scales on a keyboard, as well as on your own instrument. Work with your performance teachers for the correct fingering and technique.

Did You Know?

Musical circles, like the circle of fifths, were typical teaching devices in eighteenth-century music theory textbooks. These circles were associated with teaching about modulation (changing from one key area to another). They appeared historically at a time when new tunings were being introduced that allowed musicians to modulate through all the keys without producing harsh, out-of-tune intervals. In the 1700s, music texts by Johann Mattheson, Johann David Heinichen, and other contemporaries of J. S. Bach used circles to teach their readers key signatures, how to move from one chord to another, and how to move from one key area to another in the proper ordering. From that time, musicians have followed their lead and looked to devices like the circle of fifths as an aid to memorization. In Heinichen's circle, both major (*dur*) and minor (*moll*) keys are given. The flat keys (F dur, B dur, etc.) appear on the right—interspersed with related minor keys. (In German, B stands for B♭ and H stands for B♮.) The sharp keys (G dur, D dur, etc.) appear on the left. ("H dur" on the left should be "H moll.")

Heinichen's musical circle of 1711 (from *Neu erfundene und grundliche Anweisung . . . des General-Basses*):

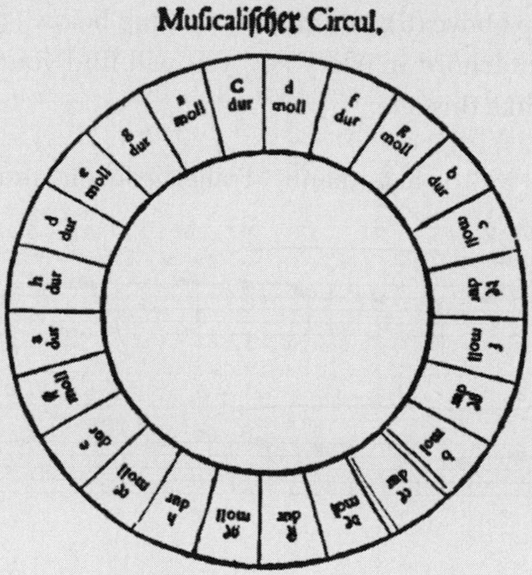

TERMS YOU SHOULD KNOW

- chromatic
- chromatic half step
- circle of fifths
- collection
- diatonic half step
- dominant
- key signature
- leading tone
- major pentachord
- mediant
- pentatonic
- scale
  - chromatic
  - diatonic
  - major
  - major pentatonic
- scale degree
- solfège syllables
- subdominant
- submediant
- supertonic
- tendency tone
- tetrachord
- tonic

QUESTIONS FOR REVIEW

1. How do the whole- and half-step patterns differ in the major and chromatic scales?
2. What are two different systems for spelling chromatic scales? How do you decide which one to use?
3. What is the interval pattern for a major tetrachord? Locate the two major tetrachords in E major.
4. How can you identify the key of a flat-key work from its key signature? a sharp-key work?
5. What is the order of the sharps? of the flats? What pattern do they follow for octave placement?
6. Name two systems for identifying scale degrees.
7. How is the circle of fifths constructed, and how can it help you learn key signatures?
8. In addition to the key signature, what other musical aspects should you check to identify the key of a work?
9. Which scale degrees form a major pentatonic scale? a major pentachord?
10. Find a passage of music for your instrument or voice that includes a portion of a chromatic scale. Do the same for a major scale and for a major pentachord.

CHAPTER 4 Compound Meters

Outline of topics

Hearing compound meters

Meter signatures

Rhythmic notation in compound meters

- The dotted-quarter beat unit
- Subdividing the beat
- Beat units other than the dotted quarter

Syncopation

Mixing beat divisions

- Triplets
- Duplets, quadruplets, and polyrhythm

Hemiola

Metrical accent and implications for performance

Overview

This chapter focuses on compound meters. We learn typical rhythmic patterns in compound meters, how to notate these patterns, and how to perform them.

Repertoire

"Agincourt Song"

Johann Sebastian Bach, Fugue in E♭ Major for Organ (*St. Anne*)

Johannes Brahms
- "Die Mainacht" ("The May Night")
- Trio in E♭ Major for Piano, Violin, and Horn, Op. 40, second movement

Frédéric Chopin, Nocturne in E♭ Major, Op. 9, No. 2

"Down in the Valley"

"Greensleeves"

John Lennon and Paul McCartney, "Norwegian Wood," from *Rubber Soul*

Smokey Robinson, "You've Really Got a Hold on Me"

Franz Schubert, "Der Lindenbaum" ("The Linden Tree"), from *Winterreise* (*Winter Journey*)

Hearing Compound Meters

(anthology) Listen to the beginning of two contrasting folk songs: "Greensleeves" (arranged for guitar) and "Down in the Valley." Tap the primary beat in each, then listen for a quick-paced secondary beat that helps establish each song's character. To determine the meter type, conduct along—"in two" for "Greensleeves" and "in three" for "Down in the Valley" (which begins with a three-note anacrusis)—while tapping the beat division. Recall that when the beat divides into twos, the meter is simple, and when it divides into threes, the meter is compound. Both songs are in compound meters: "Greensleeves" is compound duple and "Down in the Valley" compound triple. Because we associate a "lilting" quality with music in compound time, composers often choose these meters for pastoral or folk-like music, lullabies, and certain types of dances.

Meter Signatures

Compound meter signatures differ from simple meter signatures in important ways. Because the beat divides in threes, the beat unit is always a dotted note (♪♪♪ = ♩.). But the numbers in compound meter signatures, unlike those in simple meters, represent beat *divisions* rather than the beat unit: that is, a bottom number of 8 indicates the ♪ division rather than the ♩. beat.

KEY CONCEPT In compound meters:

- The top number of the meter signature is 6, 9, or 12, representing duple, triple, or quadruple meter, respectively. Divide this by three to get the number of beats per measure (two, three, or four).
- The lower number is usually 8, but can also be 4 or 16. This number shows the type of note that represents the *division* of the beat (usually ♪). Add three of these note values together to get the beat unit, which will always be a dotted note (♪., ♩., or 𝅗𝅥.).

The most common compound meters are summarized in Figure 4.1.

FIGURE 4.1: Compound meter signatures

(a) Dotted-quarter beat unit

METER SIGNATURE	BEATS PER MEASURE	BEAT UNIT	METER TYPE
6/8	2	♩.	compound duple
9/8	3	♩.	compound triple
12/8	4	♩.	compound quadruple

(b) Other beat units

METER SIGNATURE	BEATS PER MEASURE	BEAT UNIT	METER TYPE
6/4	2	𝅗𝅥.	compound duple
9/4	3	𝅗𝅥.	compound triple
12/4	4	𝅗𝅥.	compound quadruple
6/16	2	♪.	compound duple
9/16	3	♪.	compound triple
12/16	4	♪.	compound quadruple

How would you interpret the 9/8 meter signature for "Down in the Valley" (Example 4.1)? To determine the number of beats per measure, divide the top number by three: 9 ÷ 3 = 3 beats per measure. For the beat unit, add three eighth notes—from the bottom number, 8—to get a dotted quarter. The meter type is compound triple: three beats per measure with a ♩. beat unit.

EXAMPLE 4.1: "Down in the Valley," mm. 1–4a (anthology)

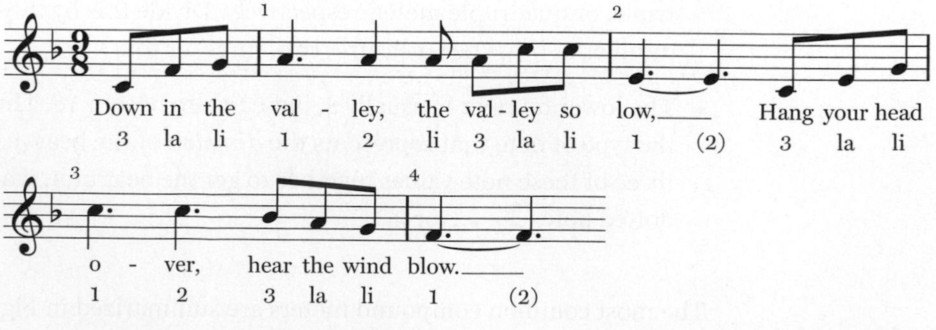

This tune begins with an anacrusis of three eighth notes, equaling one beat. As in simple meters, the final measure will be incomplete—with only two beats—to balance the anacrusis. To read rhythms in compound meters, conduct in two, three, or four, and choose a counting system that divides each beat in threes (such as 1 la li, 2 la li).

Conducting patterns remain the same for compound meters as for simple. Only in very slow tempi would the conducting pattern correspond with the upper number of the meter signature (for example, $\frac{9}{8}$ conducted "in nine"). In that case, it's considered a "subdivided" pattern.

Look now at the meter signatures of Examples 4.2 and 4.3. The $\frac{12}{8}$ meter of "Norwegian Wood" has four beats per measure (12 ÷ 3 = 4) and again a ♩. beat unit. The $\frac{6}{4}$ meter of the "Agincourt Song" has two beats per measure (6 ÷ 3 = 2) and a dotted-half beat unit (♩♩♩ = 𝅗𝅥.). At the beat level, metrical accents are the same as in simple meters: compound duple meter ($\frac{6}{8}$) is strong-weak, compound triple meter ($\frac{9}{8}$) is strong-weaker-weakest, and compound quadruple meter ($\frac{12}{8}$) alternates strong-weak, with beat 1 slightly stronger than beat 3.

EXAMPLE 4.2: Lennon and McCartney, "Norwegian Wood" (vocal part), mm. 13–14

EXAMPLE 4.3: "Agincourt Song" (England, c. 1415), mm. 1–4a

Try it #1

For each simple or compound meter in the chart below, provide the meter type (e.g., simple triple), beat unit, and number of beats per measure.

METER	METER TYPE	BEAT UNIT	BEATS PER MEASURE
9/8	compound triple	♩.	3
2/2	______________	_____	_____
12/8	______________	_____	_____
4/8	______________	_____	_____
3/2	______________	_____	_____
2/4	______________	_____	_____
6/8	______________	_____	_____

Rhythmic Notation in Compound Meters

The Dotted-Quarter Beat Unit

Figure 4.2 provides a table of note values and rests in compound meters, while Figure 4.3 shows the most common one-beat patterns in meters with a ♩. beat unit, along with one possible counting system.

FIGURE 4.2: Note values and rests in compound meters

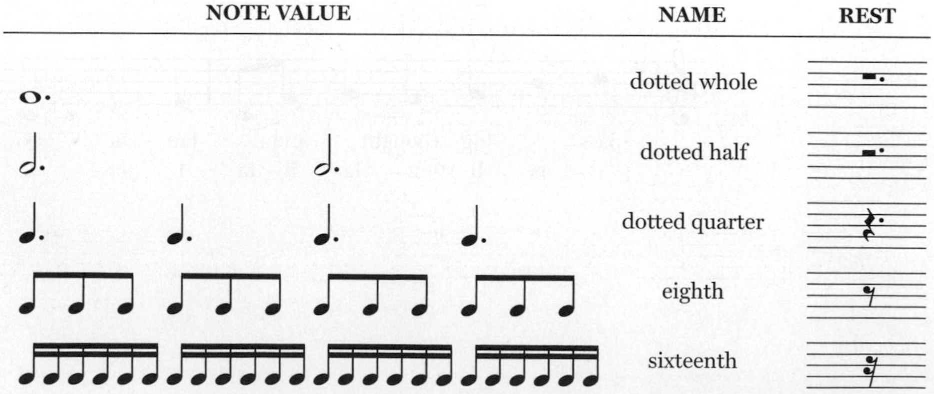

FIGURE 4.3: Five common one-beat rhythm patterns in compound meters

KEY CONCEPT As in simple meters, rhythms in compound meters should be beamed to reflect the beat unit. For example, write ♩ ♪ ♩ ♩ ♩, not ♩ ♫ ♫ (which implies simple triple meter). Rests likewise reflect the beat and its division. When two rests appear together, choose a notation that makes this clear: 𝄽. 𝄾, not 𝄼. Sometimes 𝄽. is notated 𝄽 𝄾, and 𝄽 is notated 𝄾 𝄾—both reflect the beat division.

Try it #2

Write the counting syllables for the melodies below, using Figure 4.3 as your model. Write the counts for rests in parentheses. Perform each melody; you can compare (a) and (b) with the anthology recordings.

(a) "Greensleeves," mm. 1–4a

(b) Hensel, "Nachtwanderer," mm. 3–6a

(c) Robinson, "You've Really Got a Hold on Me," mm. 6–9

Subdividing the Beat

As illustrated in Figure 4.2, an eighth note in compound meters can be subdivided into two sixteenths, which may be grouped with quarters or eighths to make additional patterns, as in Figure 4.4a. In each pattern, eighths and sixteenths are beamed together to reflect a single beat unit. Learn these patterns, together with their correct beamings and counting syllables. You can vary their sound by substituting rests—at the beginning of the beat as in part (b), or elsewhere within the beat.

FIGURE 4.4: Selected compound-meter patterns with subdivisions

(a) Without rests

(b) With rests

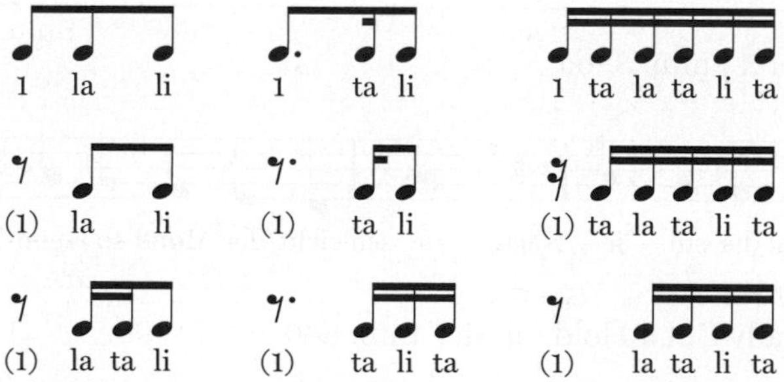

Another Way

To read rhythms with the Gordon method (which is typically used by music education students in the United States), substitute "du da di" for "1 la li." Six sixteenths are read "du ta da ta di ta." Another counting system gives each subdivision its own syllable: ♩♩♩ is "ta ki da," and ♬♬♬ is "ta va ki di da ma." If you choose not to use any syllable system, you may still find it helpful to write the number counts on the score to show where each beat begins.

Try it #3

A. Decide which of the two rhythms below is beamed correctly, and write the counts below it.

(1) 

(2) 

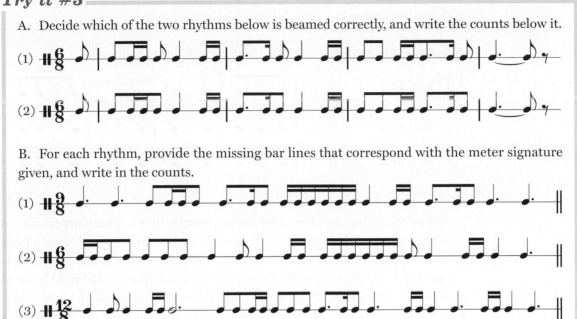

B. For each rhythm, provide the missing bar lines that correspond with the meter signature given, and write in the counts.

(1) 

(2) 

(3) 

Beat Units Other Than the Dotted Quarter

Listen again to "Greensleeves," this time comparing the alternate rhythmic notations given in Example 4.4. If performed with the same tempo for each beat unit, all three versions would sound the same, but they look quite different.

EXAMPLE 4.4: "Greensleeves," mm. 1–4a

(a) Original notation (♩. beat unit)

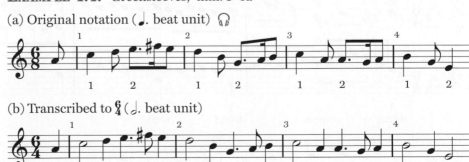

(b) Transcribed to $\frac{6}{4}$ (𝅗𝅥. beat unit)

(c) Transcribed to $\frac{6}{16}$ (♪. beat unit)

Figure 4.5 shows the five main one-beat patterns for compound meters written with the less common 𝅗𝅥. and ♪. beat units, as well as the ♩..

FIGURE 4.5: One-beat rhythm patterns with different beat units

When the bottom number of the meter signature is a 4, it becomes trickier to beam according to the beat units. To see why, look at Example 4.5, drawn from Bach's *St. Anne* Fugue. Here, the compound duple meter is 6/4, with a beat division of three quarter notes (see, for example, the top notes in the right hand of mm. 80–81). But beaming the three quarters together to reflect the beat would turn them into eighths—it can't be done without altering their duration. In this example, only the beaming of the eighth notes into groups of sixes shows the dotted-half beat unit clearly. You may find that compound meters with 𝅗𝅥. beat units are more difficult to sight-read. It is up to the performer to group the rhythms mentally to reflect the proper metrical accents. In this example, the strong-weak alternation occurs at the 𝅗𝅥. level (every half measure).

EXAMPLE 4.5: Bach, *St. Anne* Fugue, mm. 77–82a

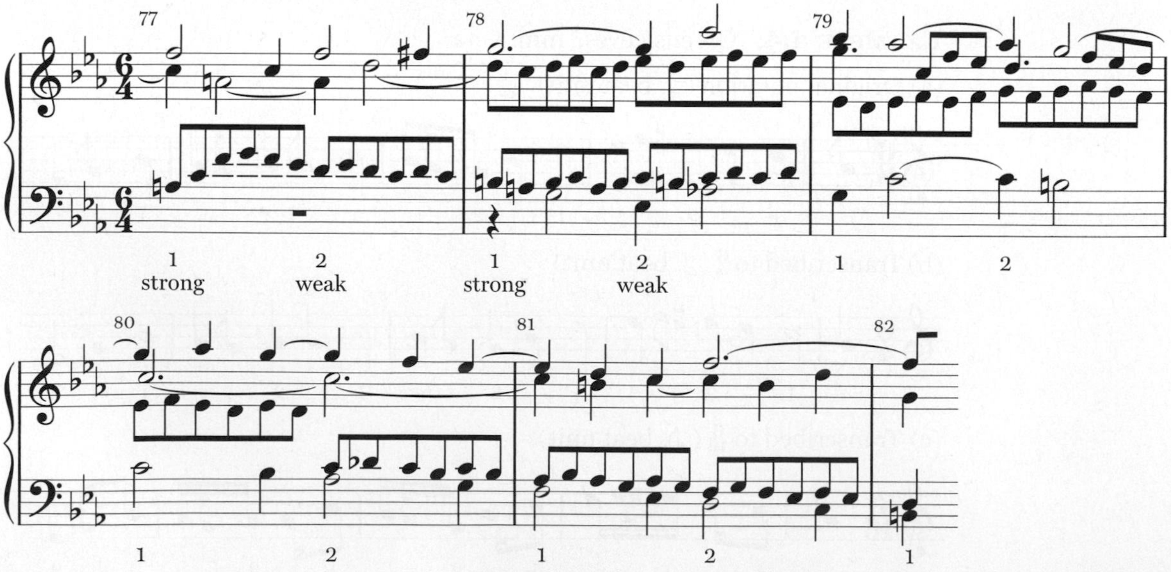

Try it #4

(a) For each rhythm below, provide the missing bar lines that correspond with the meter specified.

(b) Write the rhythm of "Home on the Range" (mm. 1–4a) in the meters specified below. Add the counts underneath.

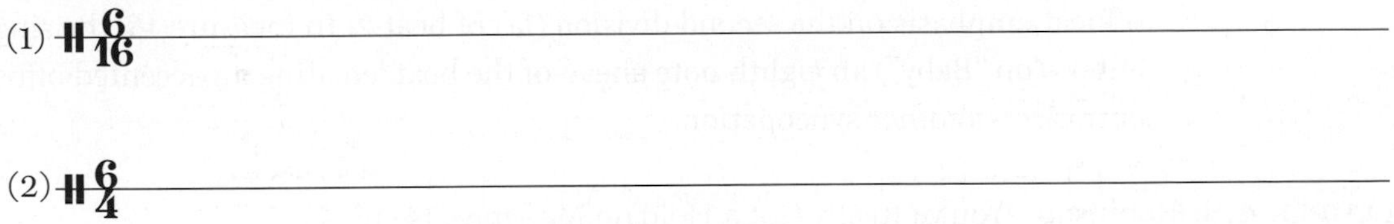

Syncopation

As in simple meters, ties and rests can create offbeat accents, or syncopations, within or across the beat.

KEY CONCEPT Syncopations are created in compound meters by placing

(1) ties from a weak part of a beat across a stronger part;

(2) an accent mark on a weak beat or the weak part of a beat;

(3) a rest on the strong part of a beat that causes a weaker part to sound accented.

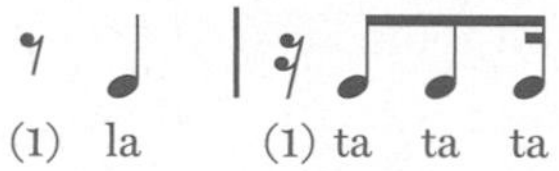

Example 4.6 illustrates syncopations in the compound quadruple melody of "You've Really Got a Hold on Me," marked with arrows. In measure 15, on "hold," the weaker third eighth note is tied across beat 2, delaying "on." This creates an offbeat emphasis on the second division (la) of beat 2. In measure 16, the singer enters (on "Baby") an eighth note ahead of the beat, creating an accented offbeat entrance—another syncopation.

Example 4.6: Robinson, "You've Really Got a Hold on Me," mm. 14–16

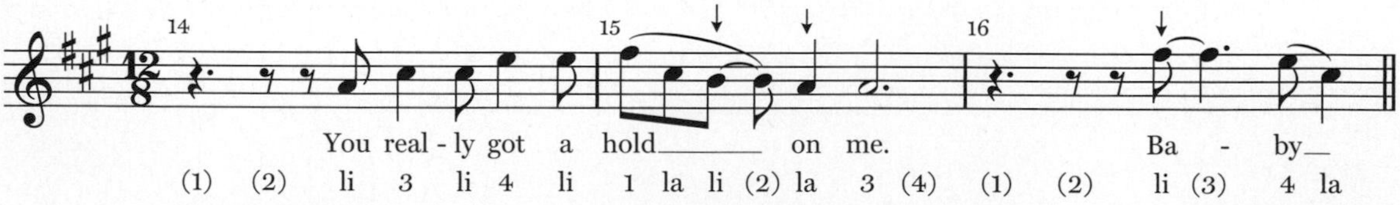

Typical syncopations within the beat are given in Figure 4.6, where the dotted-quarter note is the beat unit. As here, ties are often renotated so that an eighth note substitutes for two sixteenths tied together.

FIGURE 4.6: Typical syncopations within the beat (♩. beat unit)

Mixing Beat Divisions

Triplets

Listen to the excerpt from Schubert's "Der Lindenbaum" given in Example 4.7a. The melody moves primarily in quarter and eighth notes, except for the last beat of measure 11, which is divided into three eighth notes instead of two (indicated with a small 3 above the group).

EXAMPLE 4.7: Schubert, "Der Lindenbaum"

(a) Mm. 8b–12a

Translation: At the well in front of the gate, there stands a linden tree.

KEY CONCEPT In simple meters, the beat may occasionally be divided into three parts instead of the normal two. These beats, marked with a 3, are called **triplets**. Count triplets with syllables borrowed from compound meter (e.g., 1 la li).

Now compare part (a) with part (b), the second verse of the song. Here, Schubert has developed the triplet idea by featuring this rhythm in the piano accompaniment. In measures 29–30, the interplay of the piano's triplet division on beat 1 with the ♪. ♬ rhythms (beat 2 of the piano and beat 3 of the voice) propels the music forward and provides contrast with the more placid first verse.

(b) Mm. 28b–32a

Translation: I had to travel by it again today in dead of night.

Finally, listen to the beginning of the piano introduction to this song, given in part (c). Here the triplets are written as sixteenth notes: they divide the eighth note (rather than quarter note) into threes. The triplets create a wonderful effect, depicting the rustle of the linden tree's leaves.

(c) Mm. 1–2 (introduction)

KEY CONCEPT When notating triplets, use a note value that is one duration unit "smaller" than the beat unit it replaces (see Figure 4.7). For example, an eighth-note triplet replaces a quarter note, and a sixteenth-note triplet replaces an eighth note.

FIGURE 4.7: Notation of triplets

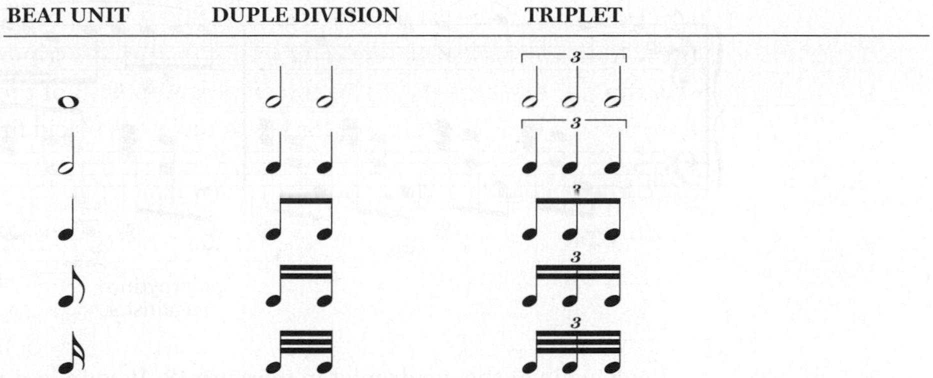

Duplets, Quadruplets, and Polyrhythm

Just as triple divisions may appear in simple meters so may duple or quadruple divisions appear in compound meters: these are called **duplets** () or **quadruplets** (). Triplets, duplets, and quadruplets are sometimes collectively called "tuplets." As an example of a quadruplet, look at measure 18 from Chopin's Nocturne in E♭ in Example 4.8. Although the piece is in compound quadruple ($\frac{12}{8}$) meter, a group of four eighth notes appears in the right hand of measure 18, with a 4 beneath. To count the quadruplet, shift from compound-meter divisions (1 la li) to simple-meter divisions (1 e & a).

Measure 16 shows a somewhat more complicated division: a *triplet* within the beat division of compound meter. On beat 2, the eighth-note division is subdivided into on the first two-thirds of the beat; on the third part, the last two of the thirty-seconds are replaced with a thirty-second-note triplet (). Other types of tuplets are possible as well, such as quintuplets (groups of five), sextuplets (groups of six), and septuplets (groups of seven). These appear most often in Romantic-era repertoire (around 1830 to 1910), such as the Chopin nocturne, where they mimic the freedom of virtuoso improvisation.

EXAMPLE 4.8: Chopin, Nocturne in E♭ Major, mm. 16–18

Look again at the quadruplet in measure 18. It sounds simultaneously in the right hand with the triple division in the left hand. This juxtaposition of two beat divisions—here, three against four—is called a **polyrhythm**.

The other polyrhythm you will typically encounter in performance is two against three, shown in Example 4.9. In this song, Brahms introduces triplets in the right hand of the piano, while the singer continues with eighth-note divisions of the beat (see mm. 33 and 34, beat 4). A typical strategy for performing such polyrhythms is to learn the composite pattern that emerges when the two rhythms are placed against each other. For two against three, for example, tap one rhythm in each hand to the words "nice piece of cake": "nice" (both hands together) "piece" (hand 1) "of" (hand 2) "cake" (hand 1) "nice" (both hands), and so on; there should be equal time between "nice," "piece," and "cake." Hand 1 will be tapping threes and hand 2 twos.

Example 4.9: Brahms, "Die Mainacht," mm. 33–35

Translation: When, O smiling image, who [shines] like rosy dawn.

Duplets and quadruplets may be found in simple triple meters as well, at the measure level rather than the beat level. The second movement of Brahms's Horn Trio, given in Example 4.10, begins with quarter-note motion in a quick $\frac{3}{4}$. Then in measures 14–16, there are two quarter-note beats per measure rather than three; these are marked with a bracket and a 2 to show the duplet. This type of "super duplet" temporarily disrupts the meter (from triple to duple).

EXAMPLE 4.10: Brahms, Horn Trio in E♭ Major, second movement, mm. 9–17a

Hemiola

Example 4.11 shows a less typical type of hemiola: this one in compound meter, where the normal three-part division of the beat is temporarily grouped in twos in the upper voice. Here it is possible to hear both meters ($\frac{3}{2}$ for the three half notes in the highest voice and $\frac{6}{4}$ in the other voices) continuing simultaneously for a measure and then realigning into the notated meter at the cadence.

Example 4.11: Bach, *St. Anne* Fugue, mm. 57–59

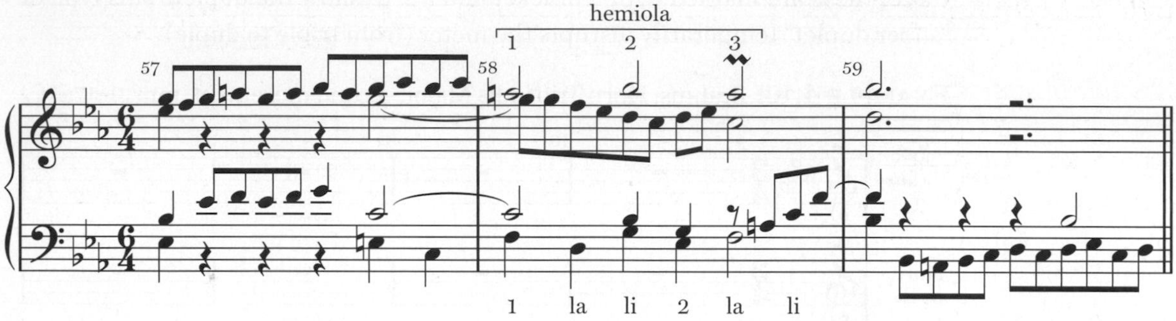

Metrical Accent and Implications for Performance

Listen again to the opening of Chopin's Nocturne in E♭ (Example 4.12) to consider ways that knowledge of the metrical hierarchy might help to shape a performance. The left-hand part consists of a repetitive rhythm that sounds on every eighth note of the 12/8 meter, but these eighths don't carry the same metrical weight, as the dots beneath the staff indicate. The pianist might want to bring out the lowest bass notes (E♭2, E♭2, D2, C2, etc.)—a melodic line whose pitches fall primarily at the measure and half-measure—and to minimize the chords on the offbeats.

Example 4.12: Chopin, Nocturne in E♭ Major, mm. 1–4

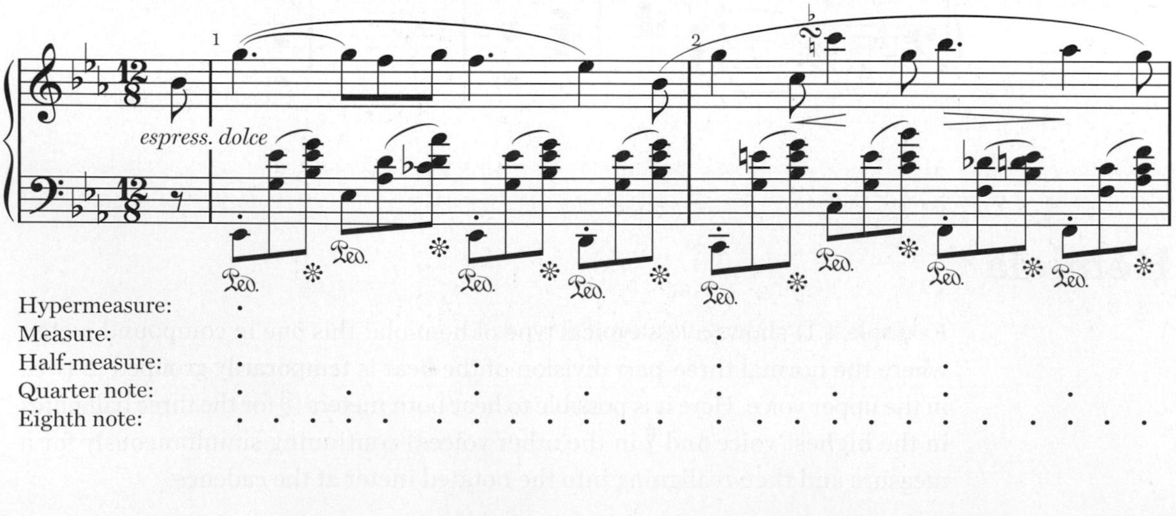

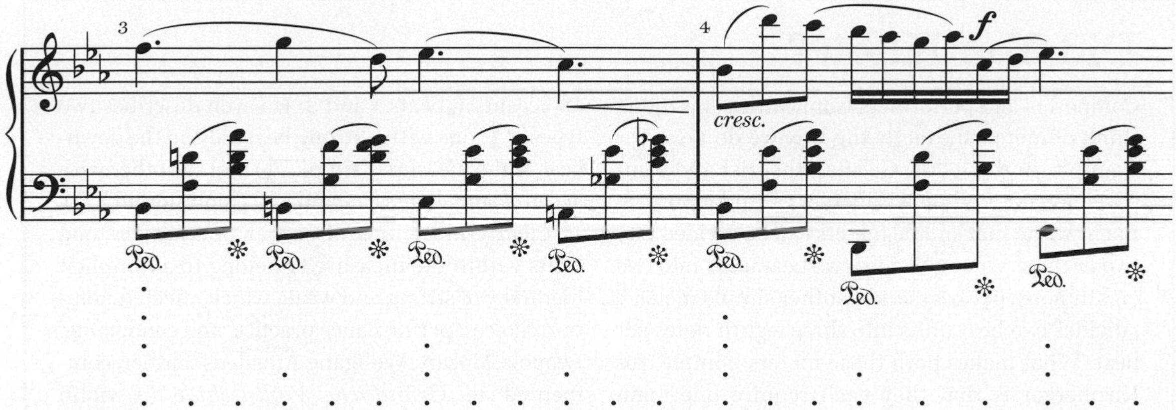

The metric analysis could also influence performance of the right-hand melodic line. For example, the pianist might want to shape the line in a pattern of strong and weak beats that corresponds to the half-measure (stronger beats on 1 and 3). Thinking in larger units sometimes raises interesting performance questions: for example, whether to aim measure 2 toward the highest pitch, C6, or beyond it to the metrically accented B♭5—while paying attention at the same time to the *crescendo* and *decrescendo* marks (crescendo and decrescendo hairpins) in the score. Such questions make the interaction of analysis and performance a fascinating topic for exploration. Compare some recordings to decide which interpretations you hear and which you prefer.

At best, rhythmic notation only approximates a truly musical performance. The performer's interpretation will usually include tempo fluctuations that speed up or slow down slightly as the work approaches an important musical goal. This type of transitory tempo fluctuation is called **rubato**.

SUMMARY

Meter is hierarchical, and implies accent patterns that are identical whether the meter is simple or compound.

- duple: strong-weak
- triple: strong-weaker-weakest
- quadruple: strong-weak-medium-weak

Did You Know?

Composers and performers from earlier eras didn't think of meter in exactly the way we do now. For example, in the 1770s, German theorist and composer Johann Philipp Kirnberger (a student of J. S. Bach) wrote that simple meters can be divided into two *or* three parts: $\genfrac{}{}{0pt}{}{2}{4}$ divides two beat units into two eighth notes per beat; and another simple meter, $\genfrac{}{}{0pt}{}{6}{8}$, divides two beat units into three eighth notes per beat. What makes both these meters "simple" for Kirnberger is that they each require one main accent, on the downbeat of the measure.

Compound meters, in contrast, are made of several measures of simple meter put together, or "compounded": for example, the compound meter $\genfrac{}{}{0pt}{}{4}{4}$ is two $\genfrac{}{}{0pt}{}{2}{4}$ measures combined, and $\genfrac{}{}{0pt}{}{12}{8}$ is two measures of $\genfrac{}{}{0pt}{}{6}{8}$. Compound meters, for Kirnberger, take an accent on beats 1 and 3. He even describes two types of $\genfrac{}{}{0pt}{}{4}{4}$: one with a strong beat only on the downbeat of the measure ("simple" $\genfrac{}{}{0pt}{}{4}{4}$) and the other with accents on beats 1 and 3 ("compound" $\genfrac{}{}{0pt}{}{4}{4}$).

Clearly musicians of earlier eras understood beats within the measure to belong to an implicit hierarchy of strong and weak, which affected notation choices, performance practice, and conducting. Leopold Mozart, Wolfgang Amadeus's father, commented in *Gründliche Violinschule* (a violin manual) that $\genfrac{}{}{0pt}{}{12}{8}$ is more suitable for a quick melody than $\genfrac{}{}{0pt}{}{3}{8}$ because the latter "cannot be beaten quickly without moving the spectators to laughter." From his remarks, Leopold presumably conducted $\genfrac{}{}{0pt}{}{12}{8}$ in four.

TERMS YOU SHOULD KNOW

anacrusis	duplet	rubato
compound duple	hemiola	triplet
compound triple	metrical accent	tuplet
compound quadruple	quadruplet	

QUESTIONS FOR REVIEW

1. How are compound meters distinguished from simple meters?
2. When reading a compound meter signature, how do you determine (a) the number of beats per measure and (b) the beat unit?
3. Provide the number of beats per measure and the beat unit for each of the following meter signatures: $\genfrac{}{}{0pt}{}{12}{4}$, $\genfrac{}{}{0pt}{}{9}{16}$, $\genfrac{}{}{0pt}{}{6}{4}$.
4. What guidelines should you follow in beaming rhythms together? What makes this difficult when the dotted-half note is the beat unit?
5. How do the guidelines for metrical accent compare in simple and compound meters?
6. If possible, find a piece of music from your repertoire in each of the following meters: compound duple, compound triple, compound quadruple. Choose at least one with a beat unit other than ♩., and practice chanting its rhythm while conducting the meter.

Minor Keys and the Diatonic Modes

Outline of topics

Parallel keys: Shared tonic

Relative keys

- Relative minor: Shared key signatures
- Finding the relative minor key
- Finding the relative major key
- Identifying the key of a musical passage

Variability in the minor scale

- The "forms" of minor
- Hearing minor scale types
- Writing minor scales

Scale degrees in minor

The minor pentatonic scale

Modes of the diatonic collection

- The "relative" identification of modes
- The "parallel" identification of modes
- Spelling modal scales
- Twentieth-century and contemporary modal practice

Overview

Here, we continue our study of keys and scales by writing and playing in minor keys and diatonic modes. We will use this knowledge to identify keys and modes in musical works.

Repertoire

Johann Sebastian Bach
Chaconne, from Violin Partita No. 2 in D Minor
Invention in D Minor

Béla Bartók, "In Lydian Mode," from *Mikrokosmos*

Archangelo Corelli, Allemanda, from Trio Sonata in A Minor, Op. 4, No. 5

"Greensleeves"

John Lennon and Paul McCartney, "Eleanor Rigby," from *Revolver*

"Old Joe Clark"

Franz Schubert, "Der Lindenbaum" ("The Linden Tree"), from *Winterreise* (*Winter Journey*)

"Wayfaring Stranger"

Parallel Keys: Shared Tonic

If all music were composed in major keys, the palette of musical colors would be very limited. Listen to two passages from Schubert's song "Der Lindenbaum" (mm. 1–16 and 25–36), and consider how they differ in color and effect. Examples 5.1a and 5.2a show the initial vocal melody and accompaniment from each passage (without the piano introduction). Part (b) of each example gives a portion of the scale—the pentachord from $\hat{1}$ to $\hat{5}$—that corresponds with the melody pitches.

Example 5.1: Schubert, "Der Lindenbaum," mm. 8b–12a

(a) Vocal line with piano accompaniment

Translation: At the well in front of the gate, there stands a linden tree.

(b) Major pentachord: Scale degrees $\hat{1}$ to $\hat{5}$ from vocal line

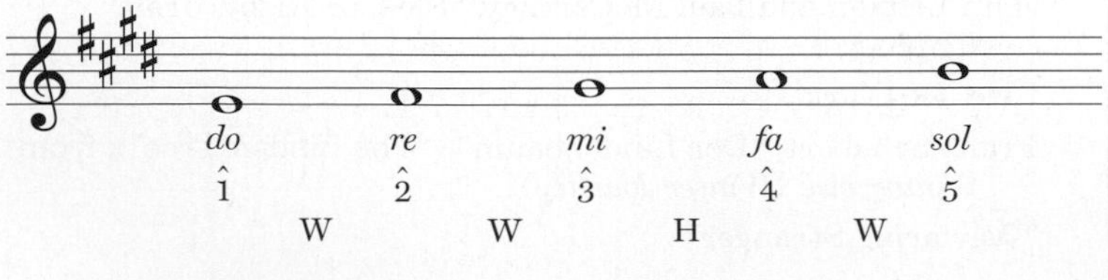

Example 5.2: Schubert, "Der Lindenbaum," mm. 28b–32a

(a) Vocal line with piano accompaniment

Translation: I had to travel by it again today in dead of night.

(b) Minor pentachord: Scale degrees $\hat{1}$ to $\hat{5}$ from vocal line

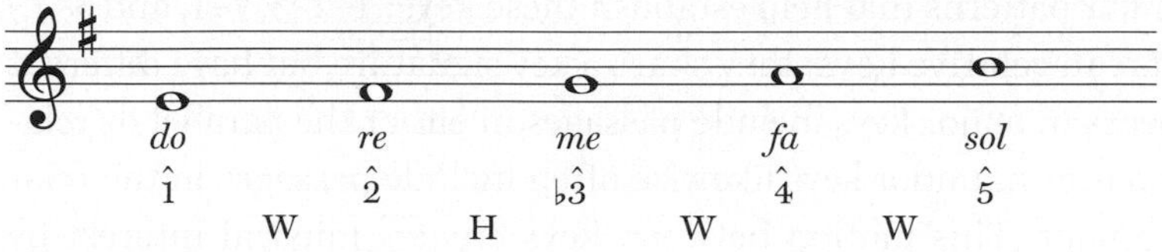

The two passages are written in **parallel keys**: E major and E minor. The major pentachord is sung as *do-re-mi-fa-sol* and written $\hat{1}$–$\hat{2}$–$\hat{3}$–$\hat{4}$–$\hat{5}$ (Example 5.1b). The minor pentachord is sung as *do-re-me-fa-sol* and written as $\hat{1}$–$\hat{2}$–$\flat\hat{3}$–$\hat{4}$–$\hat{5}$ (Example 5.2b). These pentachords differ by only one note: $\hat{3}$ (*mi*) in the major pentachord is $\flat\hat{3}$ (*me*) in the minor. Write the third scale degree of the minor pentachord with a flat sign ($\flat\hat{3}$) even when, as here, there is no flat in the key signature or by the note; the ♭ symbol simply indicates that the third scale degree has been lowered. If you prefer, you can spell pentachords with whole and half steps: W-W-H-W for the major pentachord and W-H-W-W for the minor.

KEY CONCEPT

- Parallel keys share the same tonic.
- Parallel-key pentachords share four scale degrees ($\hat{1}$, $\hat{2}$, $\hat{4}$, and $\hat{5}$).
- The third scale degree of the minor pentachord is a half step lower than in the major pentachord: $\flat\hat{3}$ (*me*) instead of $\hat{3}$ (*mi*).

Parallel keys often appear within a single piece or movement, as in "Der Lindenbaum," to reflect a change of mood. In the case of Schubert's song, the minor-key passage reflects a change in the text from daytime to a foreboding "dead of night." Parallel keys can also be used to distinguish between separate variations in a larger set or separate movements in a larger work.

Relative Keys

Relative Minor: Shared Key Signatures

Now listen to two brief passages from Corelli's Allemanda, while looking at the score excerpts given in Example 5.3. Both passages share the same key signature (no flats or sharps)—yet part (a) is in A minor and part (b) in C major. (The scale degrees written above the melody and below the bass line, the lowest-sounding part, reveal familiar patterns that help establish these keys: $\hat{1}$–$\hat{2}$–$\hat{3}$, $\hat{7}$–$\hat{1}$, and $\hat{5}$–$\hat{1}$.) These excerpts are in **relative keys**: they share a key signature but have different tonics. Many pieces in major keys include passages in either the parallel or relative minor, and pieces in minor keys likewise often include passages in the relative or parallel major. This motion between keys creates musical interest by varying the color and mood.

KEY CONCEPT Relative keys have different tonics, but share the same key signature and diatonic collection.

EXAMPLE 5.3: Corelli, Allemanda, from Trio Sonata in A Minor

(a) Mm. 1–3a

(b) Mm. 13–15a

Finding the Relative Minor Key

Example 5.4 compares the scales for two relative keys: G major and E minor. The relative minor scale is made from the same pitch-class collection as its relative major, but it begins on scale degree $\hat{6}$ of the major key.

Example 5.4: Finding the relative minor key

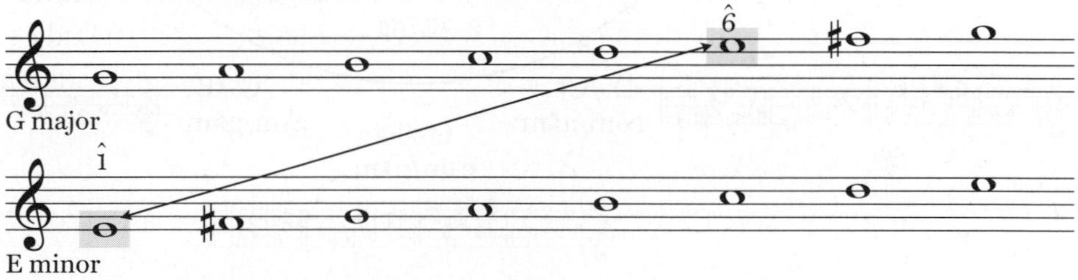

KEY CONCEPT To find the relative minor of any major key, identify scale degree $\hat{6}$ of the major scale: that pitch is the tonic of the relative minor. (Shortcut: Count down three half steps from the major-key tonic.)

With the shortcut, be careful to choose the correct spelling: it should conform to the key signature of the major key and span three different letter names. To find the relative minor of A major, for example, count down three letter names (A-G-F). Now count down three half steps: A to G♯, G♯ to G, G to F♯. The answer is F♯ minor (not G♭ minor, since A major has no flats and since that answer would span only two letter names). For speed and facility in sight-reading and analysis, memorize the minor key signatures, as well as the major. The circle of fifths, with the relative keys added in Figure 5.1, may help you. (Minor keys are labeled with lowercase letters.)

FIGURE 5.1: Circle of fifths with minor keys added

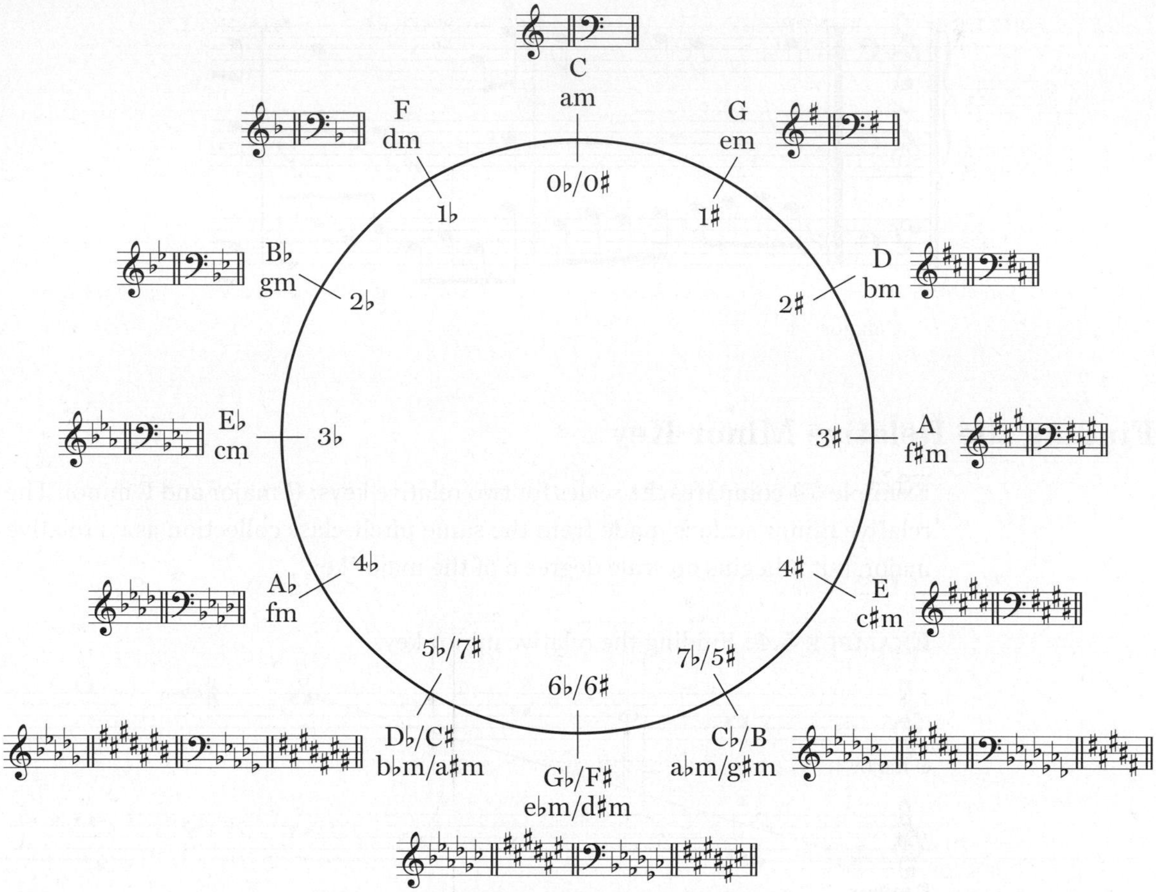

Try it #1

(a) Given the major key below, supply the name of the relative minor.

KEY	RELATIVE MINOR	KEY	RELATIVE MINOR
E major	________	A♭ major	________
D major	________	E♭ major	________
B major	________	F major	________

(b) Given the key signature below, supply the name of the minor key.

KEY SIGNATURE	MINOR KEY	KEY SIGNATURE	MINOR KEY
	____________		____________
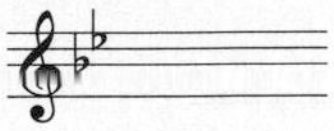	____________	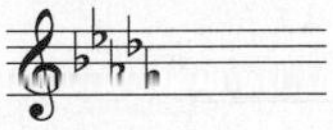	____________
	____________		____________

Finding the Relative Major Key

What if you begin with a minor key—how do you find its relative major?

KEY CONCEPT To find the relative major of any minor key, identify scale degree ♭$\hat{3}$ of the minor scale: that pitch is the tonic of the relative major (Example 5.5). (Shortcut: Count *up* three half steps from the minor-key tonic.)

Example 5.5: Finding the relative major key

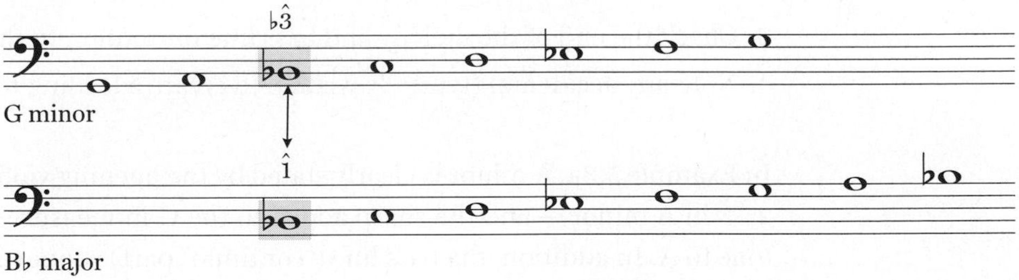

With the shortcut, again, choose a spelling that spans three letter names. For example, when finding the relative major of G minor, counting G to G♯, G♯ to A, and A to A♯ produces an incorrect answer since it does not span three letter names. The relative major of G minor is B♭ major.

Try it #2

Given the minor key below, supply the name of the relative major.

KEY	RELATIVE MAJOR	KEY	RELATIVE MAJOR
A minor	______________	C♯ minor	______________
G♯ minor	______________	F minor	______________
C minor	______________	E minor	______________
D minor	______________	B♭ minor	______________

Identifying the Key of a Musical Passage

To identify the key of a piece or passage, follow the guidelines below, as for Example 5.3.

KEY CONCEPT To identify a key:

1. Look at the key signature, and think of both the major and minor key associated with that signature.
2. Look at the beginning of the melody and bass line for motion to and from either the major-key or minor-key tonic ($\hat{1}$).
3. Check the end of the melody and bass line for motion to the tonic.
4. Note any accidental (typically written to create a leading tone in minor).

In Example 5.3a, A minor is clearly stated by the opening violin lines—A, B, C ($\hat{1}$, $\hat{2}$, $\flat\hat{3}$ in A minor)—and the sharp added to the G in measure 2 creates a leading tone to A. In addition, the bass line ("continuo" part) supports A minor: A ($\hat{1}$) on the downbeat of measure 1, and E to A ($\hat{5}$ to $\hat{1}$) at the end of the passage. In contrast, the violin melody of part (b) opens with C, D, and E ($\hat{1}$, $\hat{2}$, $\hat{3}$ in C major), and the bass line moves from G to C ($\hat{5}$ to $\hat{1}$) at the end.

Try it #3

Look at the score for each of the following pieces in the anthology to determine whether the piece is in major or minor. Then listen to the beginning of each work to check your answer by ear.

	ANTHOLOGY	KEY
(a) Joplin, "Pine Apple Rag"	p. 222	______________

	ANTHOLOGY	KEY
(b) Chopin, Mazurka, Op. 68, No. 4	p. 123	______
(c) Schumann, R., "Wilder Reiter"	p. 362	______
(d) Schumann, C., "Liebst du um Schönheit"	p. 357	______
(e) Handel, Chaconne, Variations 15–16	p. 180	______

Key signatures for parallel keys, like the E major and E minor of Examples 5.1 and 5.2, differ by three accidentals: E major has four sharps and E minor one sharp; F major has one flat and F minor four flats. Thus, to find the key signature for the *parallel* minor of a major key, you might move three "steps" counterclockwise around the circle of fifths (see Figure 5.1 on p. 92). Even D major (two sharps) and D minor (one flat) follow this rule, if you think of the three-accidental difference as three steps to the left around the circle of fifths.

SUMMARY

Parallel keys

- share the same tonic ($\hat{1}$), as well as $\hat{2}$, $\hat{4}$, and $\hat{5}$;
- have key signatures that differ by three accidentals.

Relative keys

- share the same key signature and diatonic collection;
- have tonics that differ by three half steps (and three letter names).

Try it #4

Provide key signatures (the number of sharps or flats) for these parallel keys:

	SIGNATURES		SIGNATURES
B major–B minor	5♯ – 2♯	F♯ major–F♯ minor	___ – ___
B♭ major–B♭ minor	___ – ___	A major–A minor	___ – ___
C major–C minor	___ – ___	C♯ major–C♯ minor	___ – ___

Variability in the Minor Scale

Listen to Example 5.6, a passage from Bach's Chaconne in D Minor.

Example 5.6: Bach, Chaconne in D Minor, mm. 41–47a

Try it #5

On the staff below, write the scales bracketed in measures 41 and 45. Add the accidentals, including the B♭ of the key signature if needed. How do the pitch collections differ?

m. 41

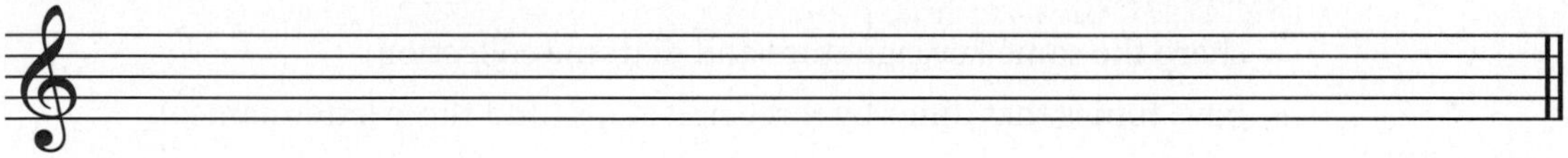

m. 45

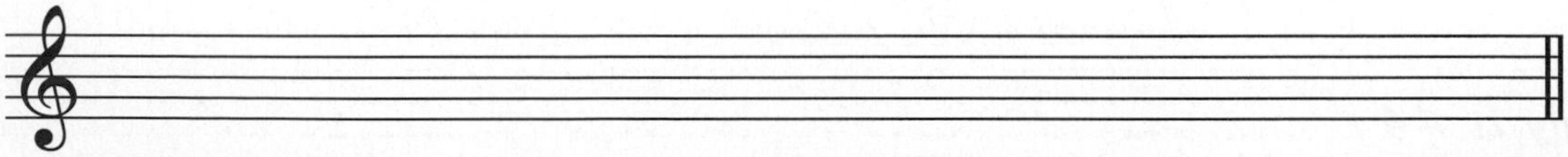

The bracketed scales in measures 41 and 45 share the same minor pentachord (D–E–F–G–A), but the upper tetrachords differ. Sing the ascending A–B♮–C♯–D from measure 41 and the descending D–C♮–B♭–A from measure 45. This variability in scale degrees is typical in minor-key compositions: $\flat\hat{6}$ or $\hat{6}$ may appear (B♭ or B♮ in D minor), as well as $\flat\hat{7}$ or $\hat{7}$ (C♮ or C♯).

Listen to Example 5.6 again, paying special attention to the sixth and seventh scale degrees, and observe which spelling Bach has chosen as the line ascends or descends. In musical contexts, rising lines are usually associated with the raised forms of $\hat{6}$ and $\hat{7}$: B♮–C♯ in measure 41. These pitches follow the tendency of the upward line toward the tonic. The A–B♮–C♯–D tetrachord is sung to the same syllables as in the parallel major, *sol-la-ti-do*, and written as scale degrees the same way as well. $\hat{5}$–$\hat{6}$–$\hat{7}$–$\hat{1}$.

Falling lines, on the other hand, are usually associated with ♭$\hat{6}$ and ♭$\hat{7}$: C♮–B♭ in measure 45. The lowered pitches here follow the tendency of the line to descend toward the tonic. The descending D–C♮–B♭–A tetrachord is sung with the syllables *do-te-le-sol*, and written $\hat{1}$–♭$\hat{7}$–♭$\hat{6}$–$\hat{5}$. Label these scale degrees ♭$\hat{7}$ and ♭$\hat{6}$ even if the actual pitches are written without a flat (here, C♮ = ♭$\hat{7}$). Think of "flat" as meaning "lowered," in comparison with the parallel major key.

The "Forms" of Minor

Because of the variability in the upper tetrachord, musicians distinguish between different "forms" of the minor scale: natural, harmonic, and melodic minor. You can write any of these forms by combining a minor pentachord with one of three different upper tetrachords, shown in Example 5.7. **Natural minor** (part a) is the scale whose accidentals exactly match the key signature of the relative major. The natural minor tetrachord is H-W-W from $\hat{5}$ up to $\hat{1}$. **Harmonic minor** (part b) raises the seventh scale degree from ♭$\hat{7}$ to $\hat{7}$ to create a leading tone. This scale has a distinctive sound, because the distance between ♭$\hat{6}$ and $\hat{7}$—here, B♭ to C♯—is larger than a whole step. It is an **augmented second** (A2), equivalent to a step and a half; the harmonic tetrachord is therefore H-A2-H.

EXAMPLE 5.7: Forms of the D minor scale

(a) Natural minor scale

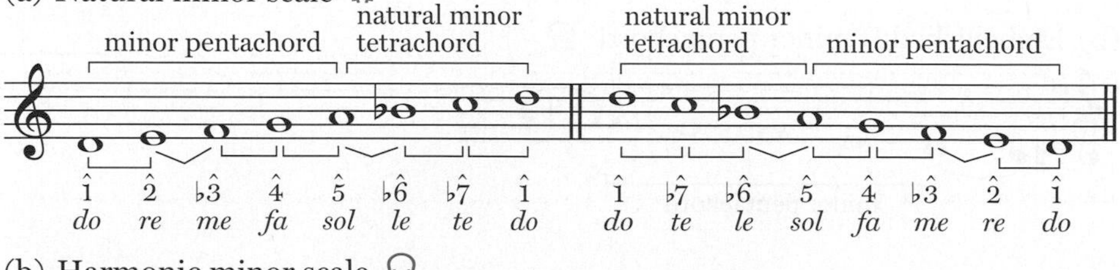

(b) Harmonic minor scale

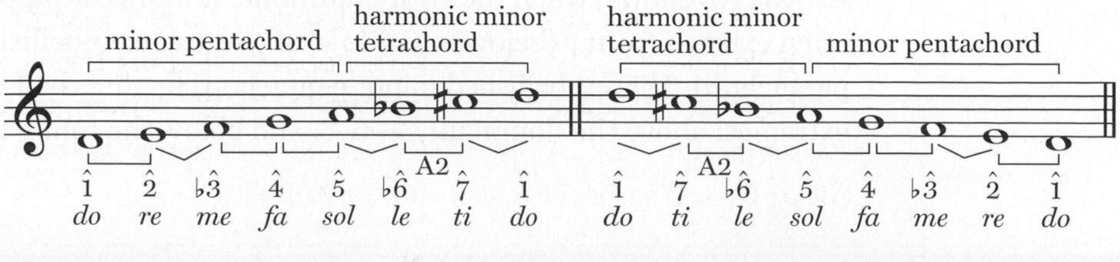

(c) Melodic minor scale

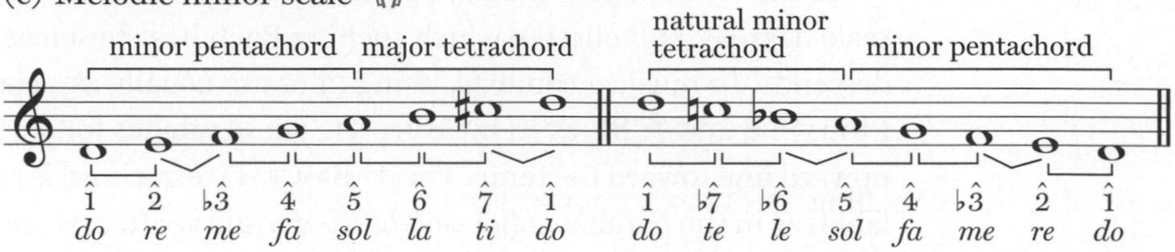

The **melodic minor** scale (part c) differs in its ascending and descending forms. Compare these scale segments with the excerpts marked in Bach's Chaconne (Example 5.6). In its ascending form, bracketed in measure 41, the minor pentachord is followed by a major tetrachord, as in a major key (W-W-H from $\hat{5}$ up to $\hat{1}$). Descending (m. 45), the major tetrachord is replaced by the natural minor tetrachord: H-H-W. Descending melodic minor is thus identical to natural minor.

One of the distinctive aural features of the natural minor scale is the absence of a leading tone, which leaves a whole step between $\flat\hat{7}$ and $\hat{1}$ (although composers typically raise $\flat\hat{7}$ to $\hat{7}$). For its part, harmonic minor poses a melodic problem, since the distinctive sound of the A2 from $\flat\hat{6}$ to $\hat{7}$ stands out from the surrounding whole and half steps. This type of minor scale is not often found as a melody in musical works; more often, the leading tone will appear as part of the accompanying harmony—a reason for this scale's name. Bach's Invention in D Minor (Example 5.8) illustrates one way this compositional problem is solved.

Example 5.8: Bach, Invention in D Minor

(a) Mm. 1–7a (right hand)

(b) Embellished D minor pentachord

As part (b) shows, when the entire harmonic minor scale appears in a melody, it often extends from $\hat{7}$ (below tonic) to $\flat\hat{6}$ above, as an embellishment of the minor pentachord. This embellished minor pentachord features half-step motion at both extremes: above the dominant, $\hat{5}$–$\flat\hat{6}$–$\hat{5}$, and below the tonic, $\hat{1}$–$\hat{7}$–$\hat{1}$.

KEY CONCEPT To change a natural minor scale to harmonic minor, raise scale degree $\flat\hat{7}$ to $\hat{7}$ (change *te* to *ti*). In harmonic minor scales, accidentals may be mixed (e.g., flats and sharps together), as in Example 5.9a, and double sharps may be necessary (part b).

EXAMPLE 5.9: Spelling harmonic minor scales

(a) Mixed accidentals in G harmonic minor

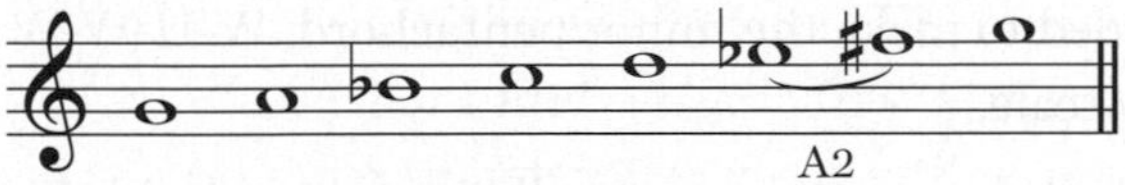

(b) Double sharp in G♯ harmonic minor

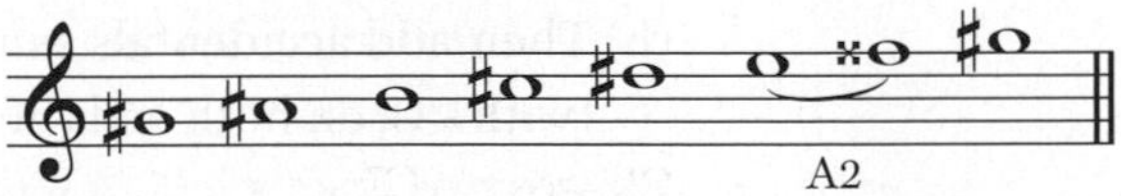

Hearing Minor Scale Types

Example 5.10 shows the C major scale and all three forms of the C minor scale, with the corresponding solfège and scale-degree numbers. To distinguish between scale types by ear, listen first for the quality of the third scale degree ($\hat{3}$ vs. $\flat\hat{3}$, *mi* vs. *me*). Then listen for the leading tone: natural minor (descending melodic minor) has no leading tone—rather, it features a whole step from $\flat\hat{7}$ to $\hat{1}$ (*te–do*). In harmonic minor, in contrast, you hear the distinctive A2 approach to its leading tone ($\flat\hat{6}$–$\hat{7}$, *le–ti*). Finally, ascending melodic minor is the only minor scale with $\hat{6}$–$\hat{7}$ (*la–ti*), the same as major, and the only one whose ascending and descending forms differ.

EXAMPLE 5.10: Scales beginning on C

(a) C major scale

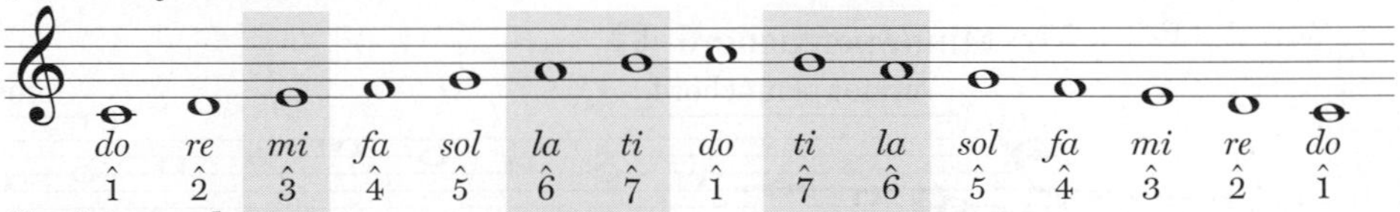

C minor scales

(b) Natural

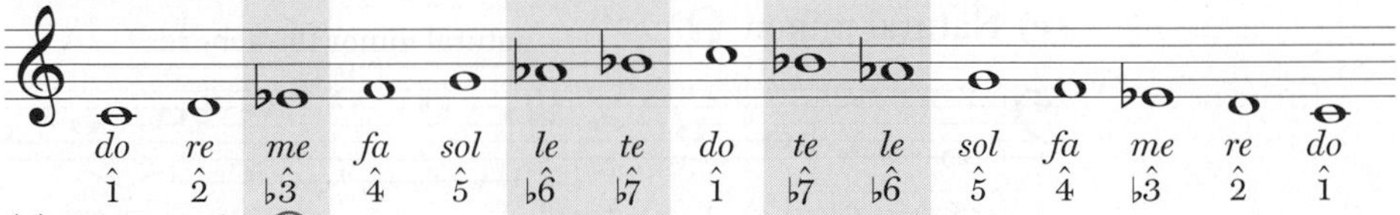

(c) Harmonic

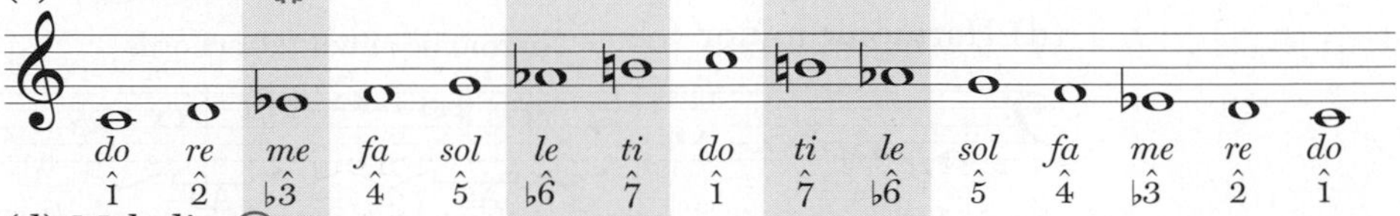

(d) Melodic

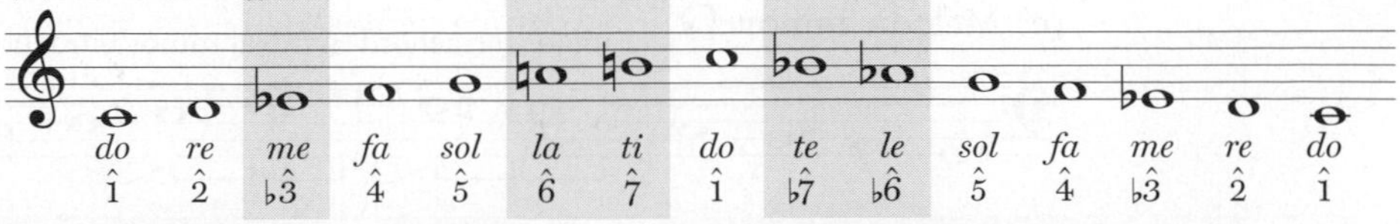

Writing Minor Scales

To write minor scales, either (1) focus on the whole- and half-step patterns in the pentachord-tetrachord structure outlined above, or (2) draw on your knowledge of key signatures. The first method is illustrated in Example 5.11, in G minor.

(a) Begin by writing pitches on the staff from tonic to tonic, ascending and descending, from G to G.

(b) Then add accidentals as needed to make the minor pentachord, W-H-W-W (with ♭$\hat{3}$), on both ends of the scale.

(c) For natural minor, add accidentals to create a natural minor tetrachord (H-W-W) on the upper part of the scale, both ascending and descending.

(d) For harmonic minor, write both E♭ and F♯ to create a harmonic minor tetrachord (H-A2-H) ascending and descending; or just add the F♯ leading tone to the natural minor scale.

(e) For melodic minor, use the major tetrachord (W-W-H) ascending; the descending form is the same as natural minor (compare parts c and e.)

Example 5.11: Writing G minor scales

(a) Note heads G to G and back

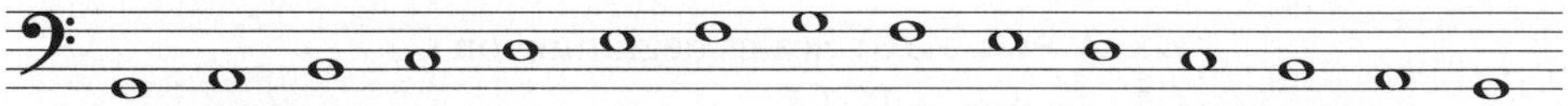

(b) Minor pentachord

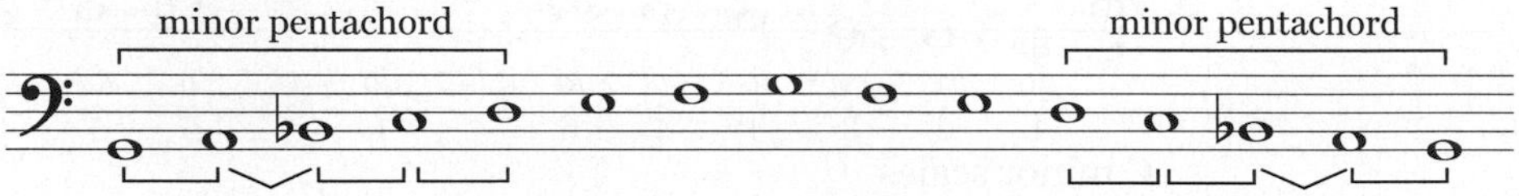

(c) Natural minor

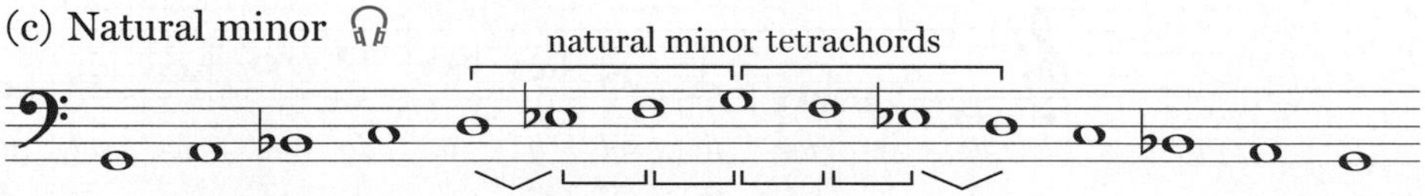

(d) Harmonic minor

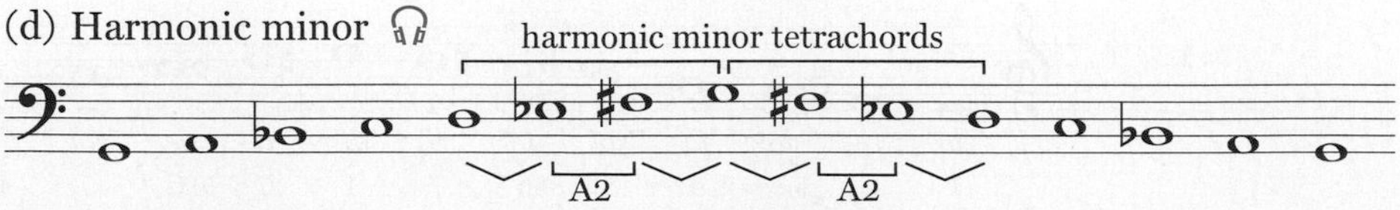

(e) Melodic minor

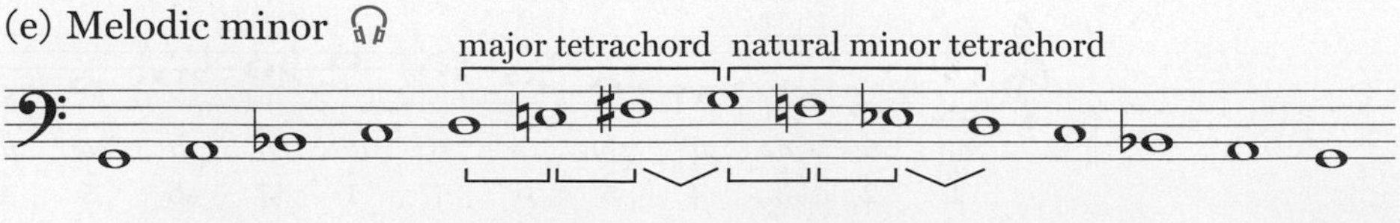

For the key signature method, begin by writing note heads from tonic to tonic as before, then determine the relative major key.

(1) Count up three half steps from the tonic, spanning three letter names: the relative major of G minor is B♭, two flats.

(2) Write in the appropriate accidentals from that key signature, and you have completed the natural minor scale.

(3) Add accidentals for the desired form of the minor scale as needed: raise $\flat\hat{7}$ to $\hat{7}$ for harmonic minor; raise $\flat\hat{6}$ and $\flat\hat{7}$ (to $\hat{6}$ and $\hat{7}$) for ascending melodic minor.

Try it #6

Write, then play, the ascending forms of the minor scales specified below, paying special attention to the spelling of the upper tetrachord.

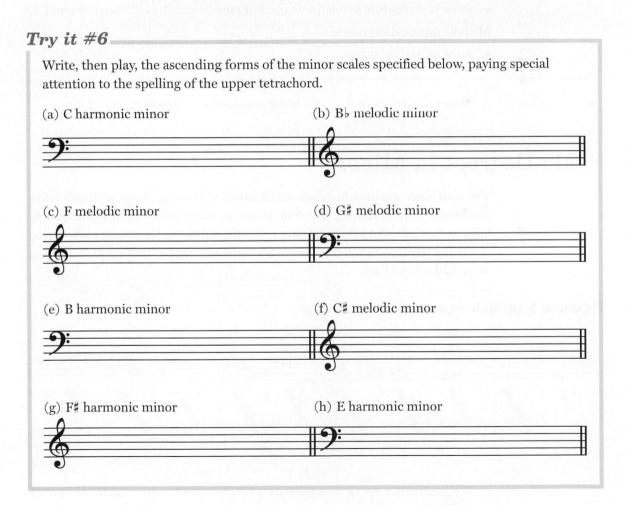

(a) C harmonic minor (b) B♭ melodic minor

(c) F melodic minor (d) G♯ melodic minor

(e) B harmonic minor (f) C♯ melodic minor

(g) F♯ harmonic minor (h) E harmonic minor

SUMMARY

Natural minor:

- Minor pentachord + natural minor tetrachord (H-W-W).
- Same key signature as relative major, no additional accidentals.

Harmonic minor:

- Minor pentachord + harmonic minor tetrachord (H-A2-H).
- Same key signature as relative major, but raise $\flat\hat{7}$ a half step to $\hat{7}$.

Melodic minor, ascending:

- Minor pentachord + major tetrachord (W-W-H).
- Same key signature as relative major, but raise $\flat\hat{6}$ and $\flat\hat{7}$ a half step to $\hat{6}$ and $\hat{7}$.

Melodic minor, descending:

- Same as natural minor.

Scale Degrees in Minor

The scale-degree names in minor are identical to those in major with only a few exceptions (Example 5.12). The $\hat{7}$ in harmonic or melodic minor is the leading tone, as in major. But in natural minor, $\flat\hat{7}$ is the **subtonic**, locating it a whole step below the tonic. When $\flat\hat{6}$ is raised to $\hat{6}$ in melodic minor, it is simply known as the raised submediant.

Example 5.12: Scale-degree names in minor keys

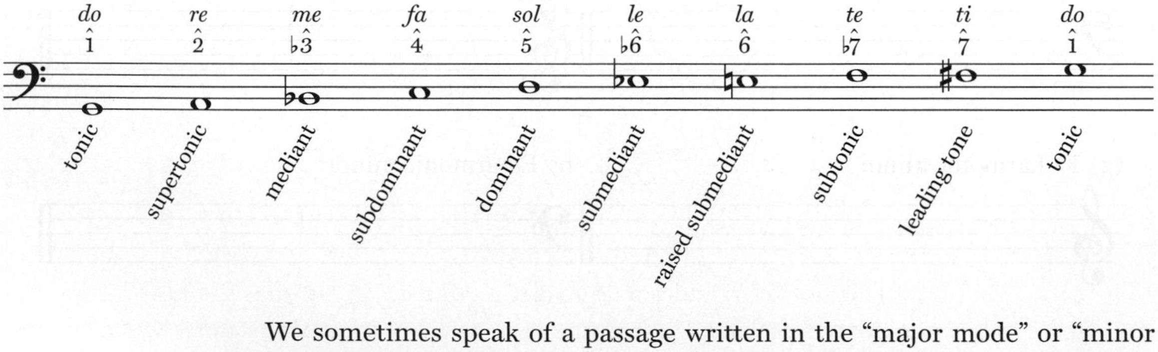

We sometimes speak of a passage written in the "major mode" or "minor mode." Because scale degrees $\hat{3}$, $\hat{6}$, and $\hat{7}$ are crucial in the distinction between major and minor, they are sometimes called the **modal scale degrees**—they create the distinctive sound of each mode. Example 5.13 highlights the modal scale degrees in the parallel keys E major and E minor.

EXAMPLE 5.13: Modal scale degrees in parallel keys

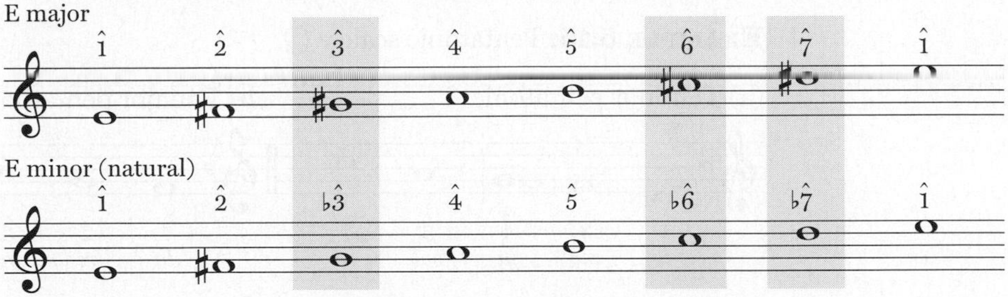

The Minor Pentatonic Scale

The natural minor scale has embedded within it a five-note scale often heard in folk melodies. For an example, sing or play through the tune "Wayfaring Stranger" (Example 5.14) on solfège or scale-degree numbers. Which scale degrees of the natural minor scale are missing?

EXAMPLE 5.14: "Wayfaring Stranger," mm. 1–8a (melody)

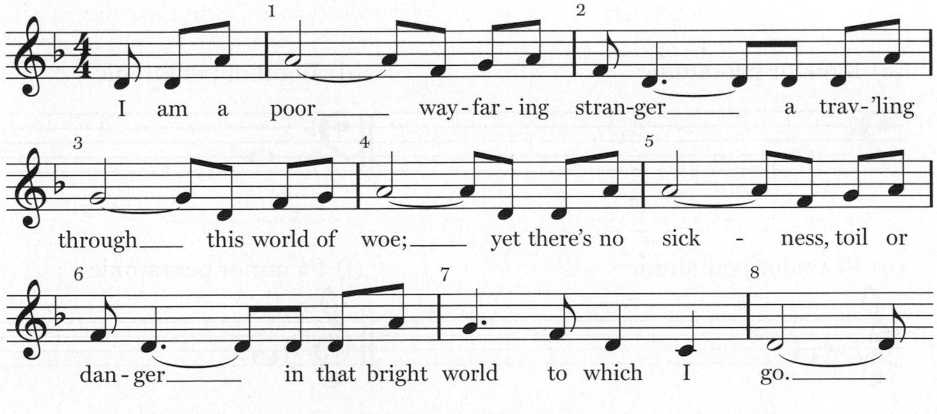

The melody includes only $\hat{1}$, $\flat\hat{3}$, $\hat{4}$, $\hat{5}$, and $\flat\hat{7}$ (*do*, *me*, *fa*, *sol*, and *te*); it is missing $\hat{2}$ (*re*) and $\flat\hat{6}$ (*le*). These pitches are written as a scale in Example 5.15a. Because it is made up of only five diatonic pitches, the scale is another of the pentatonic collections, the **minor pentatonic**: it gets its sound from $\hat{1}$, $\flat\hat{3}$, and $\hat{5}$ of the minor scale. Part (b) compares this collection with the major pentatonic (see Chapter 3), which gets *its* sound from $\hat{1}$, $\hat{3}$, and $\hat{5}$ of the major scale. The major and minor pentatonic scales are rotations of the same pitch classes, as are relative major and natural minor scales.

Example 5.15: Pentatonic scales

(a) D minor pentatonic (b) F major pentatonic

Try it #7

For each tonic pitch given, write the major pentatonic scale on the left and the minor pentatonic on the right. Think of the major and minor key signatures, and refer to the scale degrees at the top.

Major pentatonic: $\hat{1}$ *do*, $\hat{2}$ *re*, $\hat{3}$ *mi*, $\hat{5}$ *sol*, $\hat{6}$ *la*

Minor pentatonic: $\hat{1}$ *do*, $\flat\hat{3}$ *me*, $\hat{4}$ *fa*, $\hat{5}$ *sol*, $\flat\hat{7}$ *te*

(a) E major pentatonic (b) E minor pentatonic

(c) B major pentatonic (d) B minor pentatonic

(e) F♯ major pentatonic (f) F♯ minor pentatonic

(g) B♭ major pentatonic (h) B♭ minor pentatonic

Modes of the Diatonic Collection

Perhaps you know pieces whose underlying scales don't fit neatly into the major or minor scale types discussed thus far. "Greensleeves," the first half of which is given in Example 5.16, is one such melody. Sing or play it, or listen to the recording. From the melody notes, the tune appears to be in A minor, since it begins and ends on A. Yet its key signature (F♯) suggests a raised sixth scale degree. We have the same pitch collection as G major (or E minor), but with a scale that begins and ends on A.

This type of scale is neither major nor minor, but **modal**—in this case, the mode known as **Dorian**. In the arrangement of the tune that appears in your anthology, the Dorian melody is altered at the end (with an added G♯, leading tone to A) to create a tonal cadence, but the version shown in Example 5.16 is purely Dorian. Modal melodies are typically found in music of the Renaissance and early Baroque, folk and popular music of many eras, world musics, and some rock and jazz.

EXAMPLE 5.16: Dorian melody, "Greensleeves," mm. 1–8

As another example, listen to or sing through Example 5.17, "Old Joe Clark." This melody sounds somewhat major with D as the tonic, starting on $\hat{5}$, but includes a prominent lowered seventh (C♮). This mode, similar to major (with a major pentachord) but with a lowered seventh, is called **Mixolydian**.

EXAMPLE 5.17: "Old Joe Clark" (melody)

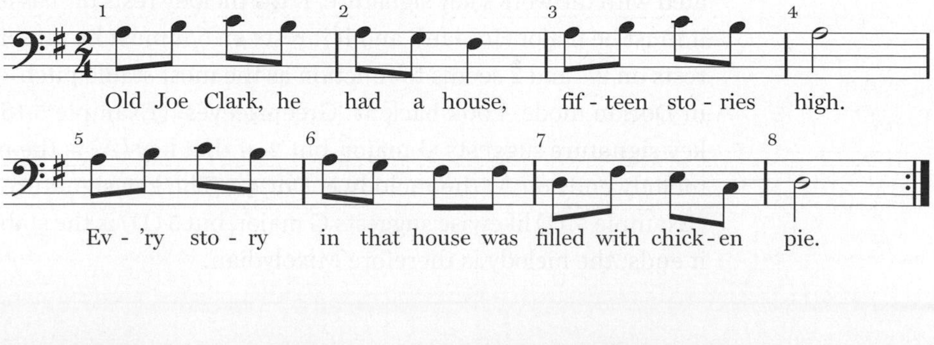

Sometimes only a segment of a mode or scale will be used, as in Bartók's piano piece "In Lydian Mode," shown in Example 5.18. In that case, the melody will inevitably feature characteristic sounds of the mode. Here, the **Lydian** mode (which sounds like a major scale but with $\sharp\hat{4}$) is identified in the title, and the melody, with F as the tonic, features a prominent downbeat on B♮ ($\sharp\hat{4}$, in m. 2). Lydian is clearly implied, even though the melody spans only five notes of the scale, F to C.

EXAMPLE 5.18: Bartók, "In Lydian Mode," mm. 1–8

The "Relative" Identification of Modes

There are six traditional **diatonic modes**, sometimes called the "church" modes because of their association with early plainsong chants sung in the Christian church. These modes share the same diatonic collection as a major scale, but each mode begins with a different starting pitch. As you listen to each mode, you will discover that the resulting new arrangement of whole and half steps gives it a distinctive sound. Sing or play the six "rotations" shown in Example 5.19.

KEY CONCEPT The diatonic collection of pitches from C to C (with no sharps or flats) may be rotated to begin with any pitch. Each rotation forms a diatonic mode. These are (in order, from C): Ionian, Dorian, Phrygian, Lydian, Mixolydian, and Aeolian (Example 5.19).

As a shortcut to learning the six mode names, think of a sentence that gives you the first letter of each mode, like "I don't particularly like magic acts."

To identify a mode with the "relative" method, think of the major key associated with the work's key signature. If the melody rests on $\hat{1}$ as its most stable pitch, it must be major (Ionian), and if it rests on $\hat{6}$ it must be minor (Aeolian). But if it rests on $\hat{2}$—and $\hat{2}$ seems to function as the most stable pitch—then the melody is in Dorian mode. Look back at "Greensleeves" (Example 5.16). The sharp in the key signature suggests G major, but $\hat{2}$ of that key (A) is the most stable and the melody ends on A: the melody is Dorian. The key signature in "Old Joe Clark" (Example 5.17) likewise suggests G major, but $\hat{5}$ (D) is the stable pitch with which it ends: the melody is therefore Mixolydian.

EXAMPLE 5.19: Modes as rotations of the C major diatonic collection

(a) Ionian (major): C to C ($\hat{1}$ to $\hat{1}$)

(b) Dorian: D to D ($\hat{2}$ to $\hat{2}$)

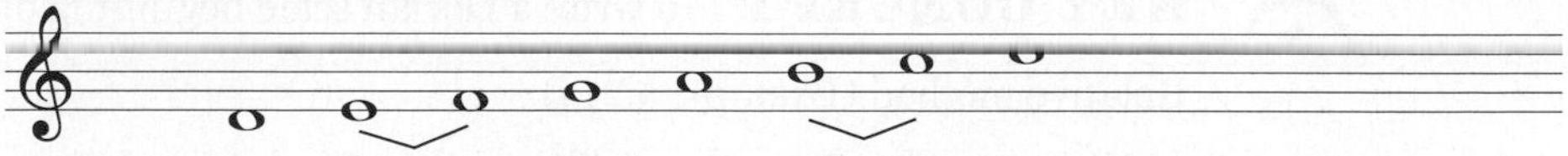

(c) Phrygian: E to E ($\hat{3}$ to $\hat{3}$)

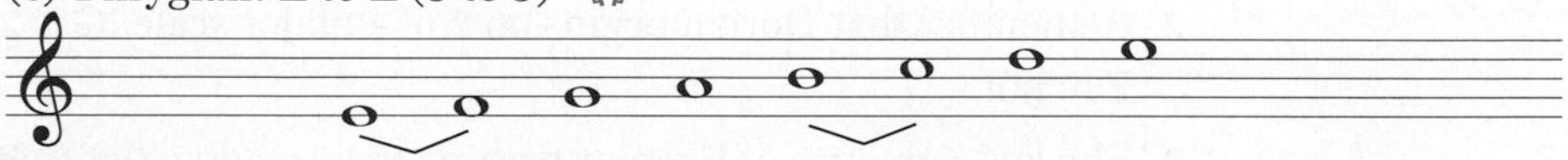

(d) Lydian: F to F ($\hat{4}$ to $\hat{4}$)

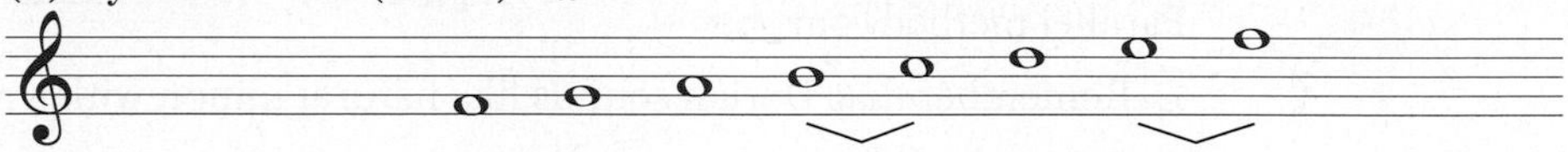

(e) Mixolydian: G to G ($\hat{5}$ to $\hat{5}$)

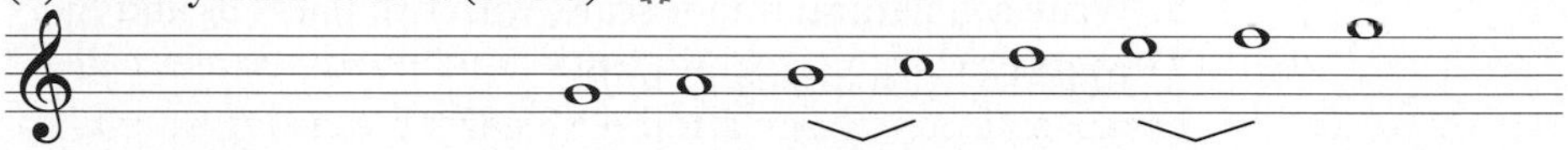

(f) Aeolian (natural minor): A to A ($\hat{6}$ to $\hat{6}$)

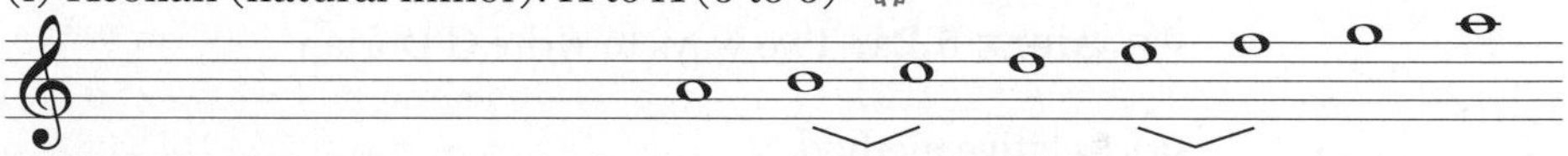

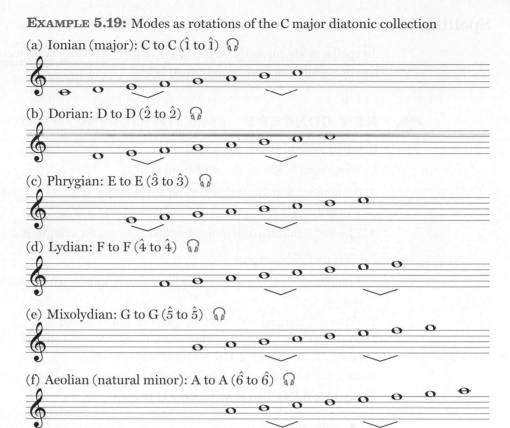

The "Parallel" Identification of Modes

Because our twenty-first-century ears are accustomed to the major and minor scales, we sometimes hear the modes as alterations of these more familiar scales. We can therefore group the modes into two families, according to whether their third scale degree comes from the major or minor pentachord. Example 5.20 summarizes this approach, with each mode beginning on C.

EXAMPLE 5.20: Modes grouped by families (on C)

(a) Based on major pentachord ($\hat{3}$)

Ionian (major)

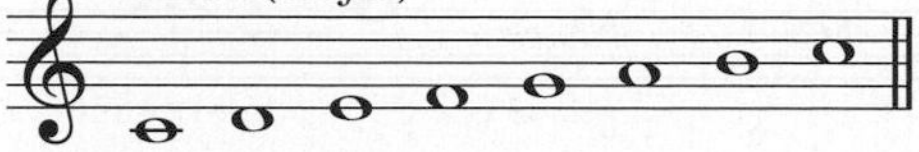

Mixolydian ($\flat\hat{7}$)

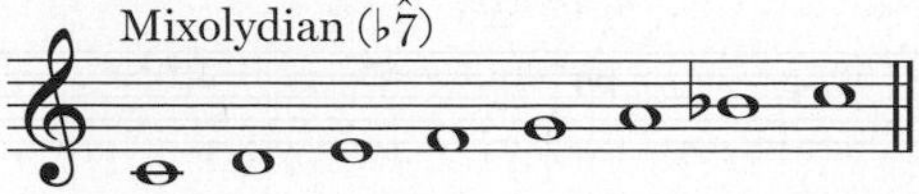

Lydian ($\sharp\hat{4}$)

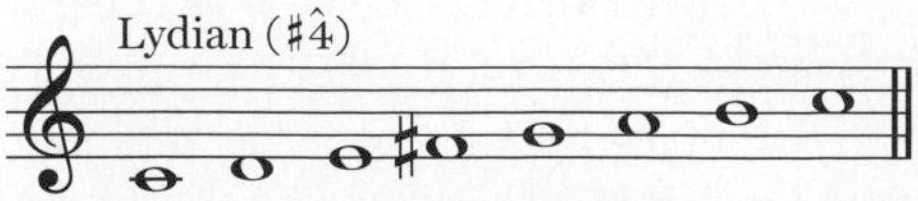

(b) Based on minor pentachord ($\flat\hat{3}$)

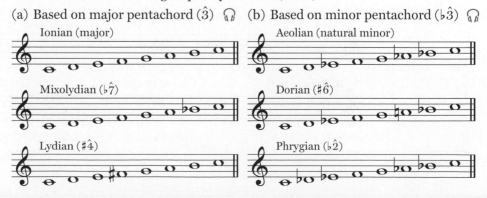

Aeolian (natural minor)

Dorian ($\sharp\hat{6}$)

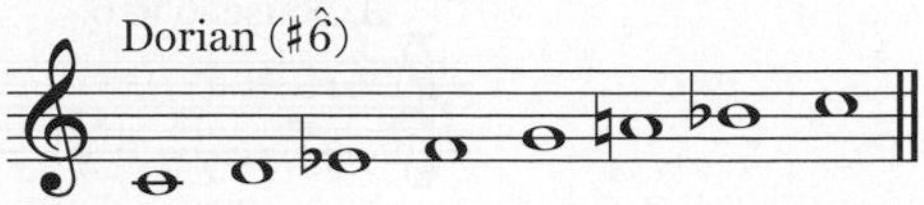

Phrygian ($\flat\hat{2}$)

Spelling Modal Scales

To spell a mode correctly, beginning on a given starting note, use either the relative or parallel method, as described below.

KEY CONCEPT To write a Dorian scale beginning on G:

Relative method (Example 5.21a):

1. Write note heads on the staff from G to G.
2. Remember that Dorian begins on $\hat{2}$ of a major scale; G is $\hat{2}$ in the scale of F major.
3. The key signature of F major has one flat, so add a flat to B.

Parallel method (part b):

1. Remember that Dorian sounds like natural minor, with a raised sixth scale degree.
2. Write a G natural minor scale, with two flats (B♭ and E♭).
3. Raise $\flat\hat{6}$ by changing E♭ to E♮.

Example 5.21: Two ways to write G Dorian

(a) Relative method

1. and 2. Write pitches G to G, and think of the scale (F major) in which G is $\hat{2}$.

3. Add accidentals from key signature of F major.

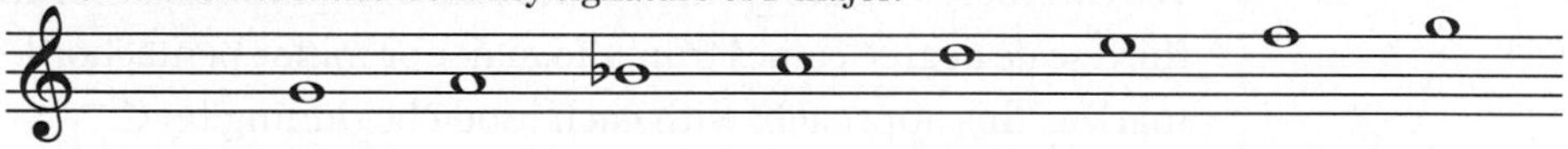

(b) Parallel method

1. and 2. Write pitches and accidentals for G natural minor.

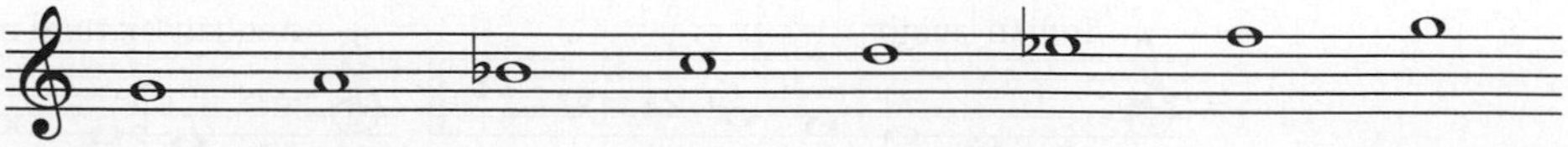

3. Raise $\flat\hat{6}$ to $\hat{6}$.

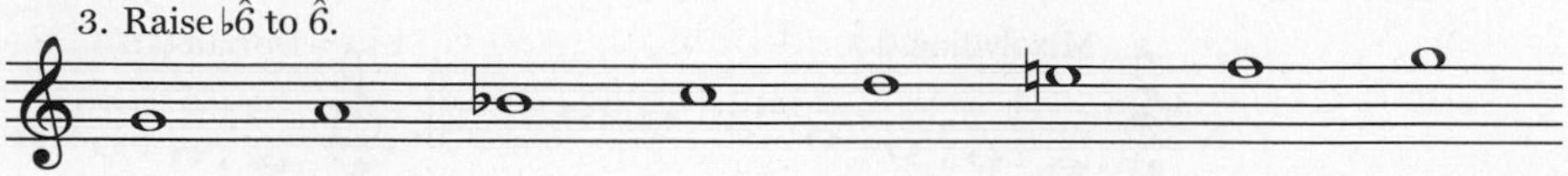

Try it #8

Use one of the methods described above to write each of the following modes.

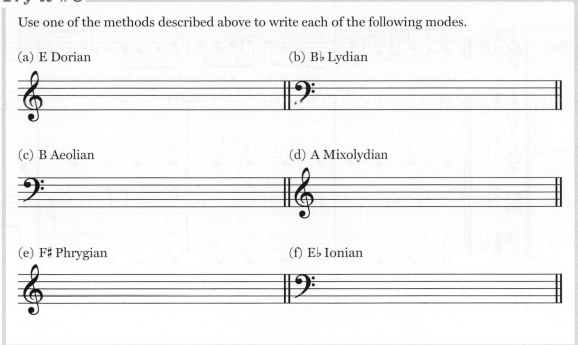

(a) E Dorian (b) B♭ Lydian

(c) B Aeolian (d) A Mixolydian

(e) F♯ Phrygian (f) E♭ Ionian

Twentieth-Century and Contemporary Modal Practice

The diatonic modes were the subject of renewed interest in the twentieth century (after years of neglect in the late eighteenth and nineteenth centuries, outside of folk music), as jazz and popular musicians—as well as classical composers—rediscovered their beauty. In modern use, the six diatonic modes can be transposed to begin on any pitch class—even so, the modes are most often seen in their white-key versions, or with one flat or one sharp. Musicians of the twentieth century occasionally drew on the **Locrian** mode—the B-to-B scale—as well, making it a seventh diatonic mode.

Just as composers mix major and minor for expressive effect, musical passages can express one mode, then shift to another. For example, consider Lennon and McCartney's "Eleanor Rigby." Its key signature of one sharp and repeated Es in the cello and second violin suggest E minor. Yet the melody of measures 9–12, reproduced in Example 5.22, features a C♯ alteration—a $\hat{6}$ that temporarily invokes the Dorian mode.

EXAMPLE 5.22: Lennon and McCartney, "Eleanor Rigby," mm. 9–12a

Did You Know?

In the seventeenth century, music teachers in France began to teach a variant of the modal system where modes might begin on a different pitch from the norm (for example, Dorian beginning on G instead of D). Such variants are called "transpositions," or "transposed modes." The first transpositions introduced B♭ and F♯ as scale tones. These transposed modes were also called "ecclesiastical," from which came our modern reference to church modes. ("Church" and "ecclesiastical" refer to the association of modes with sacred music, from the Gregorian chant of the medieval era to the modal choral works of the Renaissance.) The ecclesiastical modes traditionally included eight modes, and several of them were transpositions of Ionian and Dorian.

In the early eighteenth century (during the lifetimes of Johann Sebastian Bach, George Frideric Handel, and Joseph Haydn), writers argued over whether the old modes should be taught or whether they should be replaced by the more modern major and minor scales. Those preferring to retain the modes lamented the possible loss of their beauty and richness; those in favor of major and minor observed that the scales worked better with the functional harmonies of tonal music. You may be surprised to learn that in the early eighteenth century, the model minor scale was not our Aeolian (or natural minor) but Dorian. Manuscripts of music in minor from that time often show one less flat in their key signature than we would expect; the extra flat (for the sixth scale degree) was carefully written in every time that pitch class appeared in the music.

TERMS YOU SHOULD KNOW

diatonic modes
- Aeolian
- Dorian
- Ionian
- Locrian
- Lydian
- Mixolydian
- Phrygian

major pentachord
minor pentachord
minor scale
- harmonic
- melodic
- natural

modal scale degree
mode
parallel major
parallel minor
pentatonic scale
- major pentatonic
- minor pentatonic

raised submediant
relative major
relative minor
subtonic
tetrachord
- major
- harmonic minor
- natural minor

QUESTIONS FOR REVIEW

1. What similarities do relative and parallel minor share with major? How do relative and parallel minor differ from each other?
2. What are the differences between the three minor scale types? How are these differences reflected in the scale-degree names?
3. Given a key signature, how do you know which minor key it represents?
4. Given a minor key, how do you find the relative major?
5. How do the diatonic modes differ from major and minor scales? Describe the relative and parallel methods for identifying and spelling modes.
6. Given a pitch and a mode to build on it, what steps should you follow?
7. Find a piece, in your own repertoire if possible, with two movements related by relative or parallel keys. Find a piece written in one of the diatonic modes.

CHAPTER 6

Intervals

Outline of topics

Combining pitches

- Interval size
- Melodic and harmonic intervals
- Compound intervals

Interval quality

- Major, minor, and perfect intervals
- Inverting intervals
- Smaller intervals: Seconds, thirds, and fourths
- Larger intervals: Fifths, sixths, and sevenths
- Semitones and interval size
- Augmented and diminished intervals
- Enharmonically equivalent intervals

Consonant and dissonant intervals

- Interval classes
- Analyzing intervals in music

Overview

In this chapter, we combine pitches to form intervals. We also examine how composers use intervals to write music in different styles.

Repertoire

Johann Sebastian Bach, Invention in D Minor

George Gershwin and Ira Gershwin, "'S Wonderful!," from *Funny Face*

George Frideric Handel, Chaconne in G Major

Wolfgang Amadeus Mozart, *Variations on "Ah, vous dirai-je Maman"*

John Philip Sousa, "The Stars and Stripes Forever"

Anton Webern, *Symphonie*, Op. 21, second movement

Combining Pitches

Interval Size

Listen to Example 6.1, a passage from a keyboard composition by Handel, while focusing on the treble-clef melody. Several pairs of pitches, including whole and half steps, are bracketed in the first three measures: these are examples of intervals.

KEY CONCEPT An **interval** measures the musical space between two pitches.

Example 6.1: Handel, Chaconne in G Major, Variation 5, mm. 57–64

Intervals are named according to their size and quality. To determine the size, count the letter names (or lines and spaces) from one pitch of the interval to the other. For example, in measure 57, the interval from D5 down to C5 on beat 1 (a whole step) is a second (2: D–C); the interval from B4 up to D5 (beat 2) is a third

(3: B–C–D); and the interval from G4 up to D5 (beat 3) is a fifth (5: G–A–B–C–D). In measure 58, D5 down to E4 (beat 2) is a seventh (7: D–C–B–A–G–F–E), while D5 down to D4 in the next beat is an octave (8), and the half step D5–C♯5 is another second.

KEY CONCEPT When naming intervals, always count the first and last letter names. For example, from A up to D is a fourth (A–B–C–D); *any* A up to *any* D is some kind of fourth, no matter what the accidental. Similarly, from A down to D is a fifth (A–G–F–E–D).

Another interval with a particular name is the **unison** (from the Latin *unus*, or "one"): if two parts play the exact same pitch, this "interval"—which spans no actual space—is a unison, abbreviated U (or 1). The term may be familiar from choral singing: when all women or all men sing a line together, they are singing "in unison." (When women and men sing together, however, they typically sing in octaves.)

Melodic and Harmonic Intervals

Intervals between successive pitches, like those in the treble clef of Example 6.1, are **melodic intervals**. Listen again to the example, and now follow the bass-clef part. In measure 61, the two pitches on beat 1 sound at once: G3 and B3 (a third). Intervals between two pitches sounding simultaneously are **harmonic intervals**. Name them the same way as melodic intervals—by counting the letter names encompassed by the interval. The bass-clef part in fact features harmonic intervals in each measure; for example, in measure 57, G3-B3 forms a third, B3-D4 another third, and G3-D4 a fifth.

KEY CONCEPT Melodic intervals are formed between two successive pitches in a melodic line. Harmonic intervals are formed between two pitches sounding at the same time.

Learning to identify interval sizes quickly and accurately by eye and by ear is an essential step in reading music fluently. Example 6.2 shows all the interval sizes up to an octave. When you write harmonic intervals (part b), align the two note heads with one directly above the other; for unisons and seconds, the note heads are written side by side with the lower note of the second on the left, unless each note gets a separate stem (part c).

Example 6.2: Interval sizes up to the octave

(a) Melodic intervals

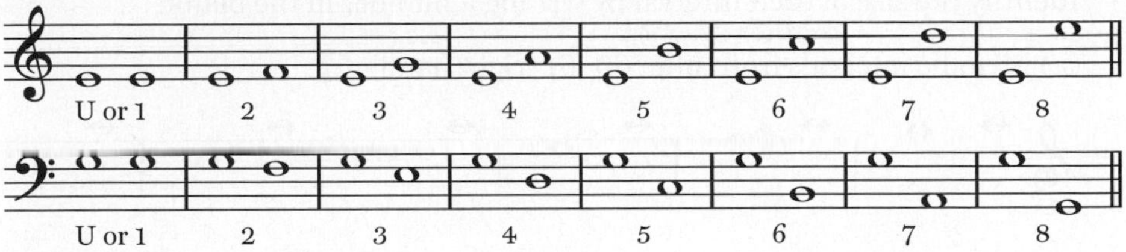

(b) Harmonic intervals

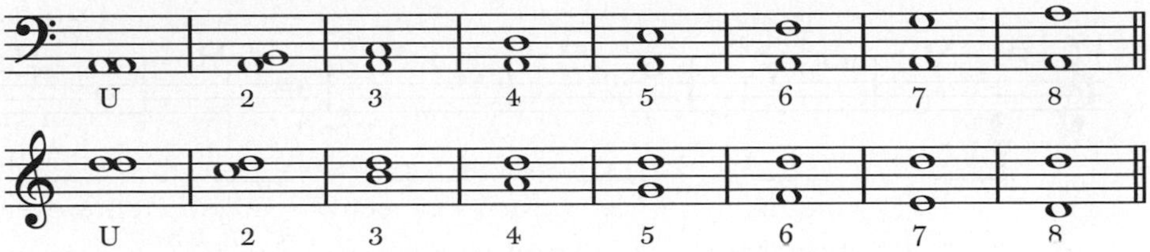

(c) Unisons and seconds with stems

KEY CONCEPT Learn these visual landmarks to identify interval sizes quickly.

Thirds, fifths, and sevenths always have both pitches on lines or both on spaces.

- For thirds, the lines or spaces are adjacent.
- For fifths, skip one line or space.
- For sevenths, skip two spaces or lines.

Seconds, fourths, sixths, and octaves always have one pitch on a line and one on a space.

Try it #1

The intervals notated below are from measures 60–64 of the Handel Chaconne in Example 6.1. Identify the size of each interval by writing a number in the blank.

(a) Melodic intervals from mm. 60–61 (right hand)

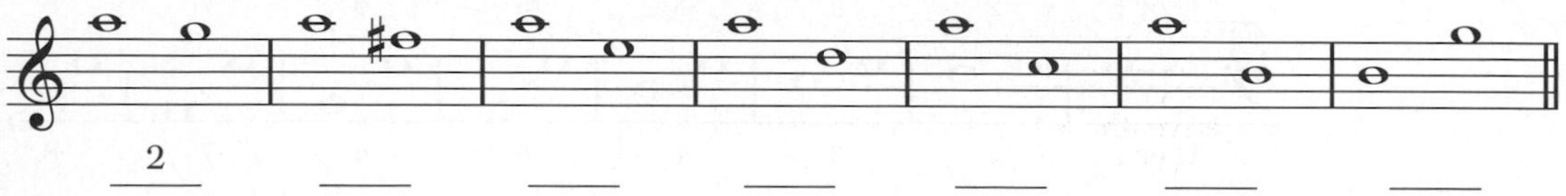

(b) Melodic intervals from mm. 61–62 (right hand)

(c) Harmonic intervals from mm. 60–64 (left hand)

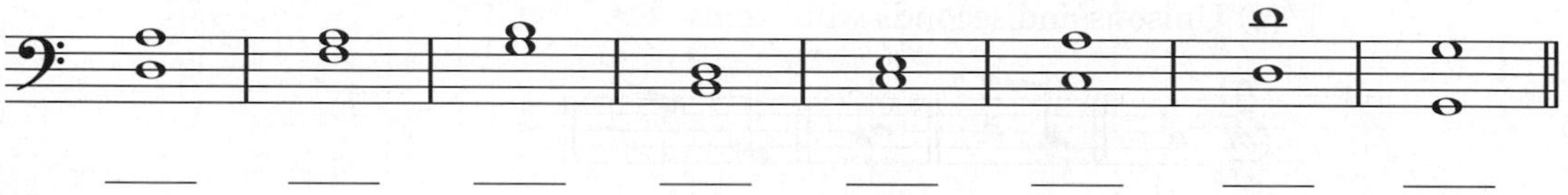

Compound Intervals

Look again at Example 6.1. In measure 63, the first interval in the treble clef (A4–B5) actually spans an octave plus a second—sometimes referred to as a ninth, since it spans nine letter names. Intervals larger than an octave are called **compound intervals**. Most common are ninths, tenths, elevenths, and twelfths—which correspond to an octave plus a second, third, fourth, and fifth. **Simple intervals** are an octave or smaller in size. Compound intervals are therefore octave expansions of simple intervals.

To name compound intervals, add 7 to the simple interval, as in Example 6.3. For example, a second plus an octave equals a ninth, and a fourth plus an octave equals an eleventh. (Add 7 rather than 8, because you begin by numbering the unison with 1 rather than 0.)

EXAMPLE 6.3: Naming compound intervals

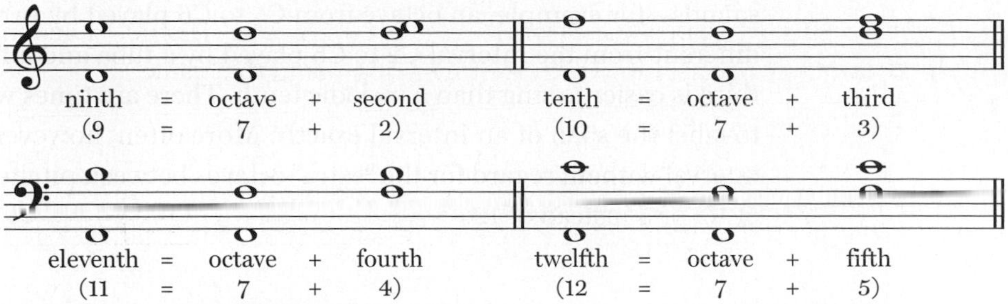

Though most melodies feature intervals smaller than an octave, some composers are known for using compound intervals in melodic lines. In Example 6.4, from Webern's *Symphonie*, the shaded large intervals are characteristic of this composer's early twentieth-century style. (Numbers refer to *Try it #2*.)

EXAMPLE 6.4: Webern, *Symphonie*, second movement, mm. 12–17

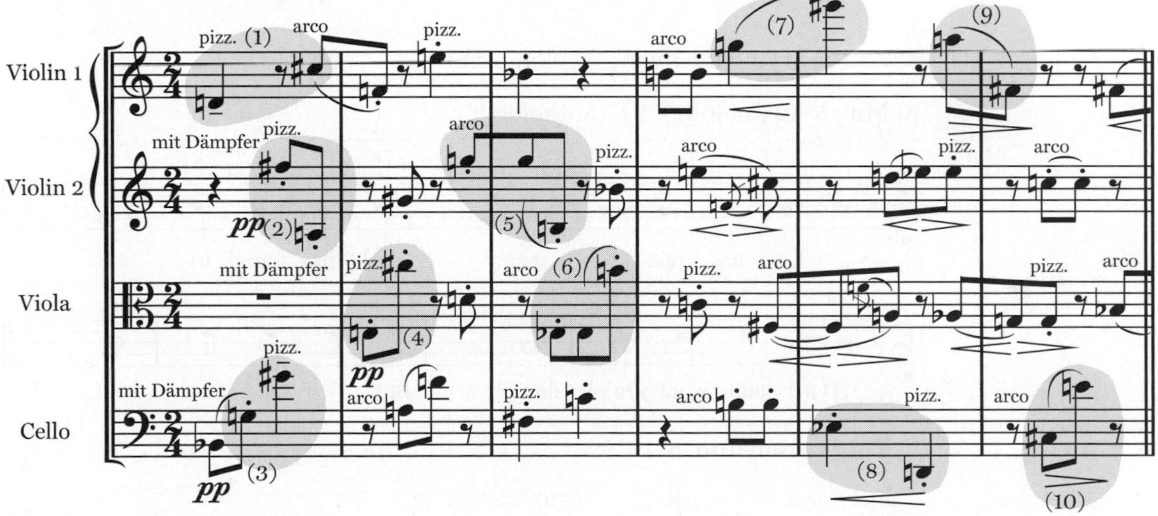

Try it #2

For each shaded interval (simple or compound) in Example 6.4, write the interval size in the corresponding blank below. If the interval is compound, also write the simple-interval equivalent in parentheses.

(1) 7	(4) ______	(7) ______	(10) ______
(2) 13 (6)	(5) ______	(8) ______	
(3) ______	(6) ______	(9) ______	

The exact musical space spanned by an interval is important to the way it sounds—for example, an octave from C5 to C6 played by two flutes sounds very different from the interval C2 to C6 played by a tuba and a flute, and a melodic third is easier to sing than a melodic tenth. There are times when it is important to label the span of an interval exactly. More often, however, you will label the interval without regard for the "extra" octaves between pitches, writing 3 instead of 10, or 5 instead of 12.

Interval Quality

Listen to the Gershwin song "'S Wonderful!" while following the score in your anthology. A portion of the melody line is given in Example 6.5a.

Example 6.5: Gershwin, "'S Wonderful!"

(a) Mm. 5–12 (melody) (anthology)

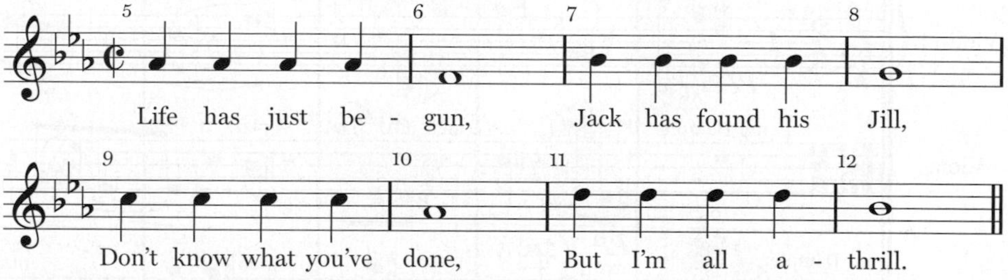

(b) Thirds from mm. 5–12

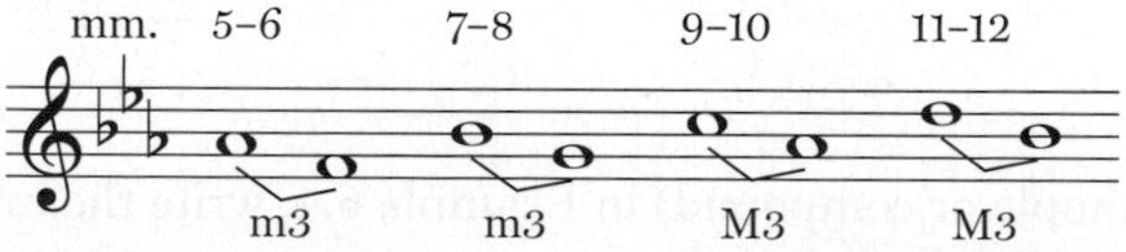

All the thirds from Gershwin's melody are isolated in part (b). If you locate these thirds on a keyboard (remember to check the key signature!) and count the half steps they span, you'll find that some of them span three half steps (in mm. 5–6 and 7–8), and some span four half steps (in mm. 9–10 and 11–12)—even though all are thirds, encompassing three letter names. The number of half steps within the interval determines the interval's **quality**.

Interval sizes—seconds, thirds, fourths, fifths, sixths, and so on—indicate roughly how large an interval is. Interval quality provides a more precise description. Intervals that span three half steps are called **minor thirds** (m3); those that span four half steps are **major thirds** (M3). Both are thirds, but their quality (major vs. minor) differs. Similarly, both half and whole steps are seconds, since both span two adjacent letter names; yet the minor second (m2) spans one half step, while the major second (M2) spans two.

KEY CONCEPT When two intervals share the same interval size but don't span the same number of half steps, they differ in quality. To find the quality of small intervals, count half steps: minor intervals are a half step smaller than major intervals.

INTERVALS	LETTER NAMES SPANNED	HALF STEPS
Minor 2 (m2)	2 letter names	1
Major 2 (M2)	2 letter names	2
Minor 3 (m3)	3 letter names	3
Major 3 (M3)	3 letter names	4

Major, Minor, and Perfect Intervals

The F major scale and its parallel minor, F minor, are given in Example 6.6. Compare scale degrees $\hat{1}$, $\hat{4}$, $\hat{5}$, and $\hat{8}$ in the two scales: they are exactly the same. The interval from $\hat{1}$ to $\hat{4}$ is known as the **perfect fourth** (abbreviated P4), from $\hat{1}$ to $\hat{5}$ is the **perfect fifth** (P5), and from $\hat{1}$ to $\hat{8}$ is the **perfect octave** (P8). From the time of the earliest writings about music, around the fifth century B.C., these intervals were considered the purest, hence the term "perfect."

EXAMPLE 6.6: Perfect intervals in major and minor scales

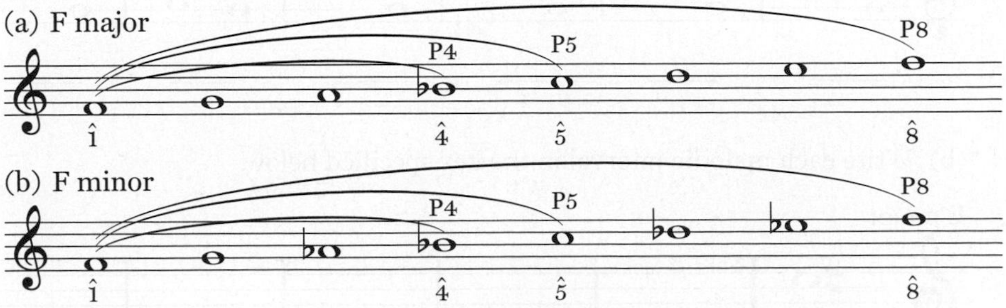

Now look at Example 6.7 and compare the intervals between $\hat{1}$ and $\hat{3}$, between $\hat{1}$ and $\hat{6}$, and between $\hat{1}$ and $\hat{7}$. In the major scale (part a), these form a major third (M3), major sixth (M6), and major seventh (M7), respectively. In the minor scale (part b), they are a minor third (m3), minor sixth (m6), and minor seventh (m7). As discussed in Chapter 5, scale degrees $\hat{3}$, $\hat{6}$, and $\hat{7}$ are sometimes referred to as the modal scale degrees because they differ between parallel major and minor keys, and the intervals they form above the tonic help give major and minor keys their characteristic sound. The third, sixth, and seventh above the tonic of a major scale are a half step larger than the corresponding third, sixth, and seventh above the tonic in a minor scale.

EXAMPLE 6.7: Major and minor intervals within scales

(a) F major

(b) F minor

Try it #3

(a) Identify the size and quality of each melodic interval in the key contexts given below.

A♭ major

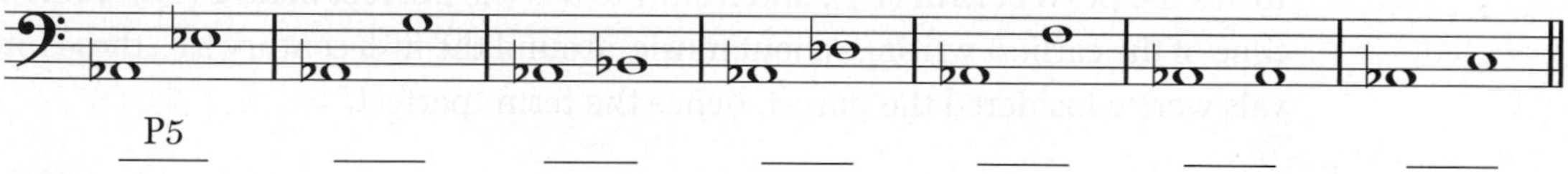

G minor

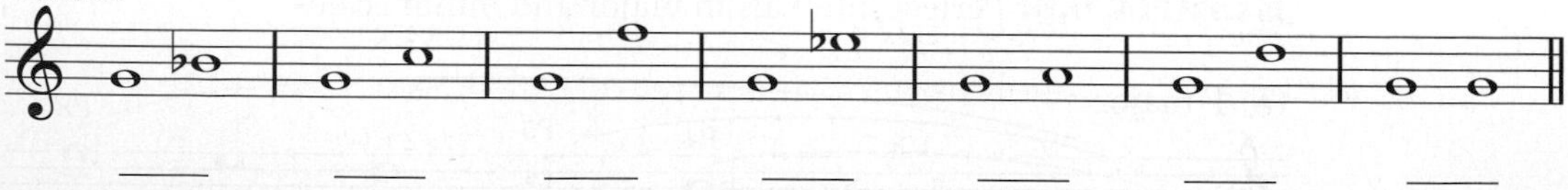

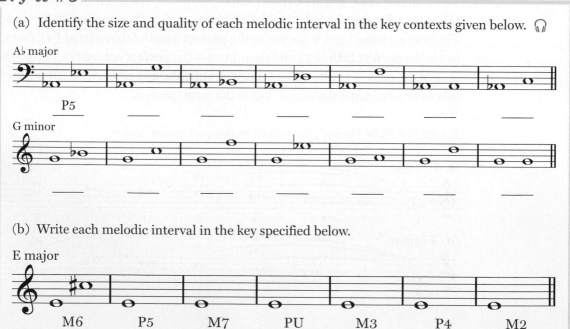

(b) Write each melodic interval in the key specified below.

E major

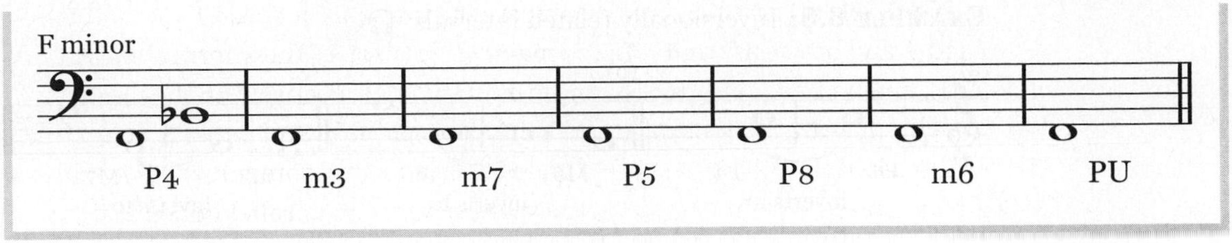

SUMMARY

Intervals may be

- melodic—measured between successive notes,
- harmonic—measured between pitches sounding at the same time,
- simple—spanning an octave or less, or
- compound—spanning more than an octave.

Intervals are labeled by their size and quality:

- Size measures the number of letter names spanned: U, 2, 3, 4, 5, 6, 7, 8.
- Intervals 2, 3, 6, and 7 may have a major or minor quality, but not perfect (e.g., m2, M3, m6).
- Intervals U, 4, 5, and 8 may be perfect, but not major or minor (P4, P5, P8).

Inverting Intervals

The interval F up to C is a perfect fifth. When the pitch classes are reversed, C up to F, the resulting interval is a perfect fourth (see Example 6.8a). Pairs of intervals like these, made from the same pitch classes but with the order reversed, are **inversionally related**. Inversion will prove helpful when you spell larger intervals, since they have a predictable relationship to their smaller counterparts. As the example shows, perfect intervals remain perfect when they are inverted. But a major interval inverts to a minor interval—for example, a M3 inverts to a m6 (part b); and a minor interval inverts to a major interval—a m2 inverts to a M7 (part c).

EXAMPLE 6.8: Inversionally related intervals

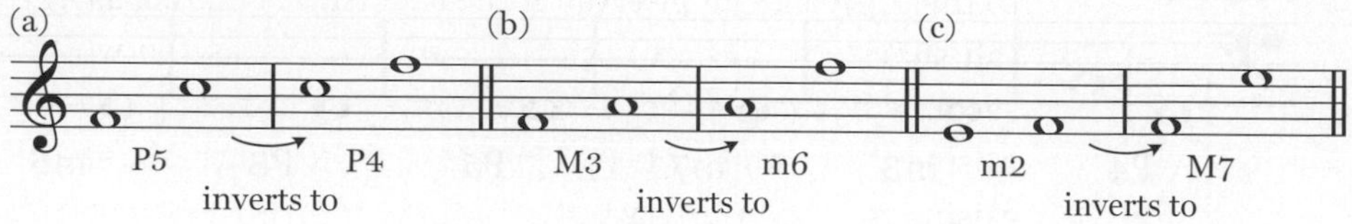

KEY CONCEPT When intervals are inverted,

- perfect intervals remain perfect,
- major intervals invert to minor,
- minor intervals invert to major,
- and the two interval sizes always sum to 9 (e.g., 1 inverts to 8, 3 inverts to 6, 4 inverts to 5).

Smaller Intervals: Seconds, Thirds, and Fourths

There are several different methods for identifying and spelling intervals. Some musicians find it quick and easy to think of the familiar "white key" intervals of the keyboard—or C major diatonic intervals on the staff—either in their original form or inverted. Memorize the size (major or minor) of the white-key seconds and thirds (Example 6.9a and b). All white-key fourths are perfect except F up to B (part c).

EXAMPLE 6.9: White-key interval qualities

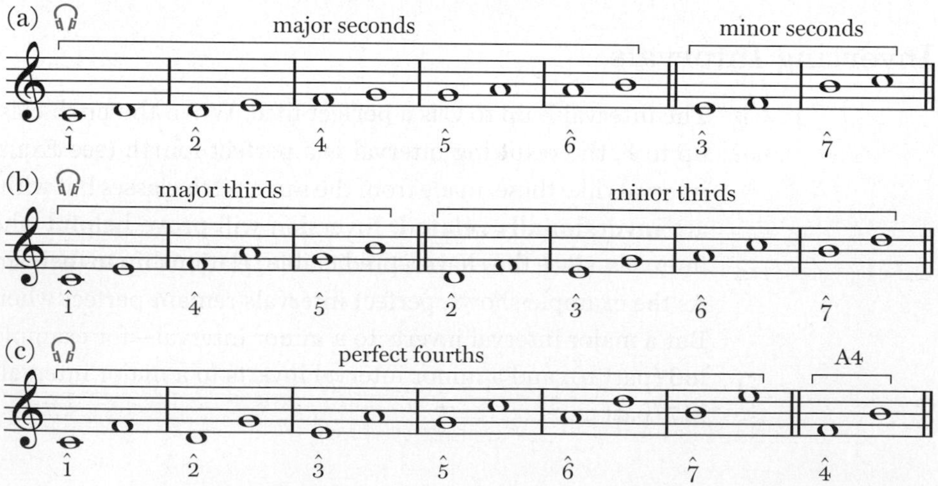

Once you know these interval qualities, all others may be calculated in relation to them. In a given interval, if the accidentals match, as in Example 6.10a and b (all sharps or all flats), it's the same quality as the white-key interval. Major seconds become minor seconds either by lowering the top note (part c) or by raising the bottom note (part e). Minor thirds are become major thirds either by raising the top note (part d) or by lowering the bottom note (part f).

Example 6.10: White-key intervals with accidentals added

(a) All major seconds

(b) All minor thirds

(c) M2 from part (a) made minor by lowering the top note

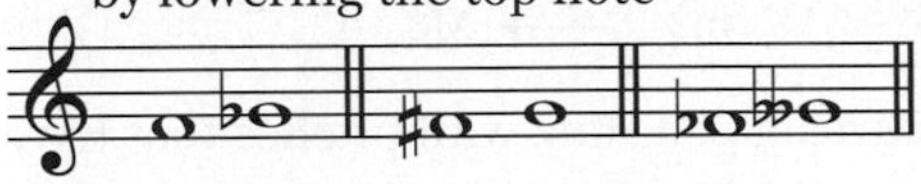

(d) m3 from part (b) made major by raising the top note

(e) M2 from part (a) made minor by raising the bottom note

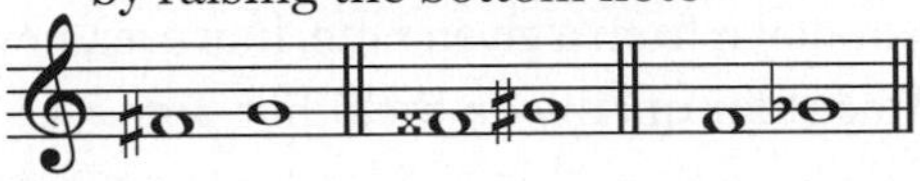

(f) m3 from part (b) made major by lowering the bottom note

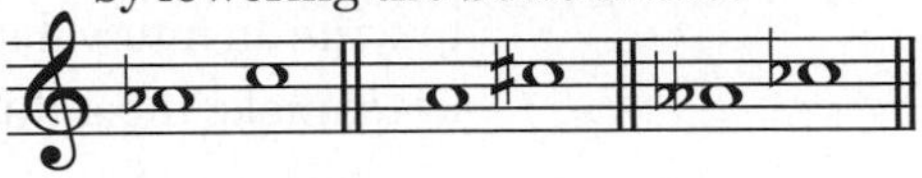

SUMMARY

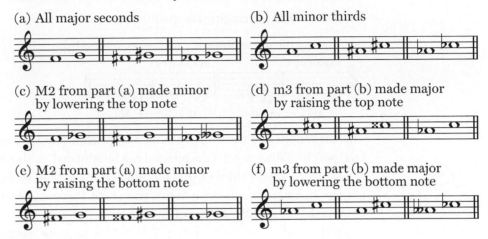

- A major interval made one chromatic half step smaller becomes minor.
- A minor interval made one chromatic half step larger becomes major.
- Perfect intervals can't be made major or minor.

Try it #4

Identify the size and quality of each second, third, or fourth below. Intervals with matching accidentals on both notes will have the same quality as their white-key counterparts.

(a)

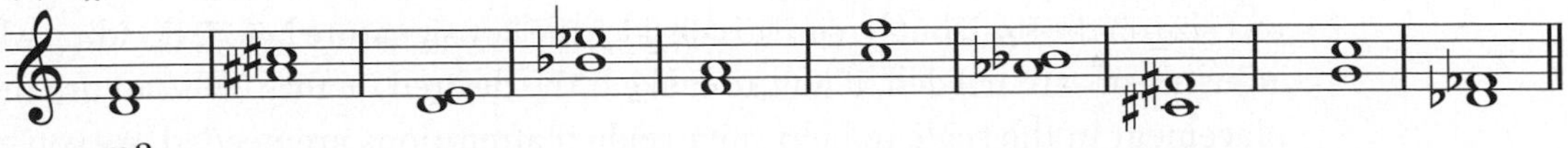

m3 ____ ____ ____ ____ ____ ____ ____ ____ ____ ____

(b)

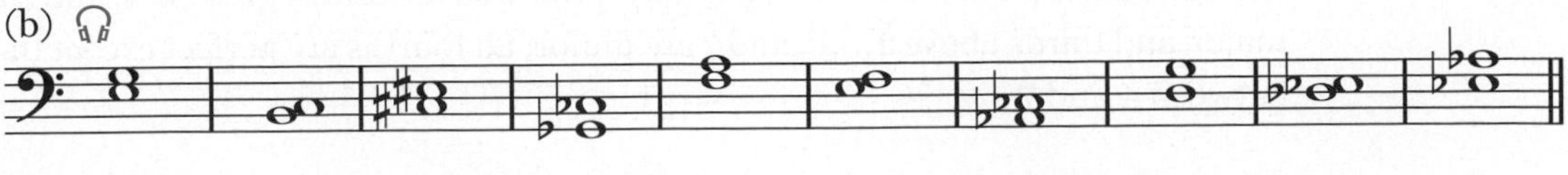

____ ____ ____ ____ ____ ____ ____ ____ ____ ____

To write isolated intervals, begin by writing the note heads for an interval of the correct size on the staff. If the quality of the white-key interval is not what you want, adjust the interval by adding a flat or sharp, as shown in Example 6.11a. For instance, to spell a minor third above C, take the major third C–E and lower the top note a half step by adding a flat to make C–E♭; to spell a major third above D, take the minor third D–F and raise the top note a half step by adding a sharp to make D–F♯.

Example 6.11: Changing the quality of intervals

(a) Altering the upper note of a white-key interval

This procedure also works if you start with pitches that have matching accidentals (part b). Either note of the interval can be adjusted, as shown in part (c): C–E can become a minor third C♯–E; D–F can become the major third D♭–F. If asked to write an interval up or down from a given note, however, never change the given note; make the adjustment for quality on the other note.

(b) Altering the upper note of an interval with matching accidentals

(c) Altering the lower note

If spelling intervals in a key context, start by writing the note heads for the correct size on the staff, but be sure to consider the key signature before deciding what adjustments are needed, if any, to make it the desired quality. You can use their placement in the scale to help you decide if alterations are needed. As you can see from Example 6.9, in any major key, thirds above scale degrees $\hat{1}$, $\hat{4}$, and $\hat{5}$ are major, and thirds above $\hat{2}$, $\hat{3}$, $\hat{6}$, and $\hat{7}$ are minor; all fourths are perfect except those between $\hat{4}$ and $\hat{7}$.

Larger Intervals: Fifths, Sixths, and Sevenths

Smaller intervals (seconds, thirds, and fourths) can help you identify their inversions (sevenths, sixths, and fifths). For example, to identify the interval D–C, think about its inversion, the second C–D (Example 6.12a). Since C–D is a M2, then D–C is a m7. This process also works if there are accidentals: since C♯–D♯ is a major second, then D♯–C♯ is a minor seventh. Follow parts (b) and (c) for the procedure for sixths and fifths.

EXAMPLE 6.12: Identifying larger intervals from their inversions

(a) Identifying sevenths by the quality of seconds

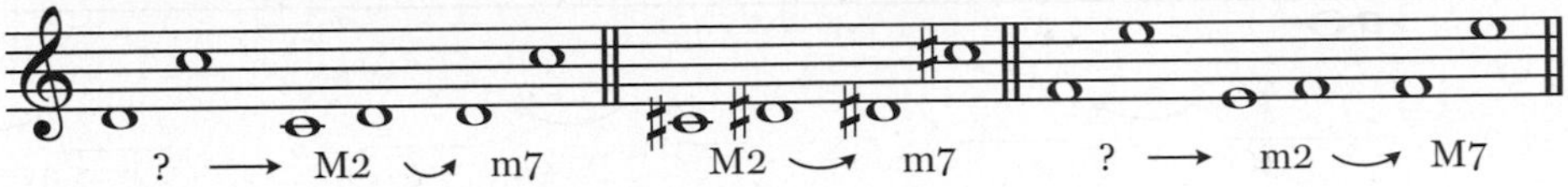

(b) Identifying sixths by the quality of thirds

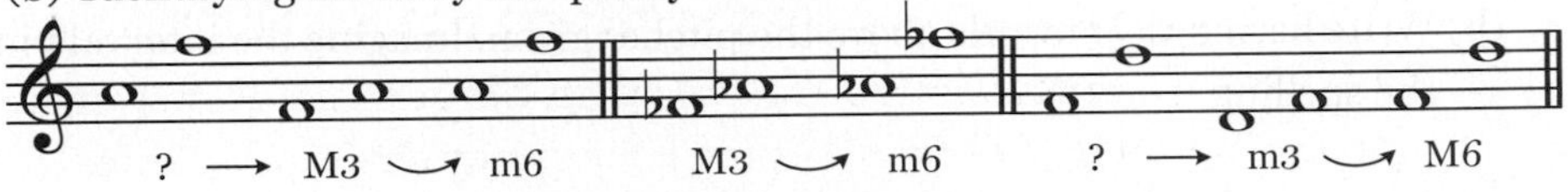

(c) Identifying fifths by the quality of fourths

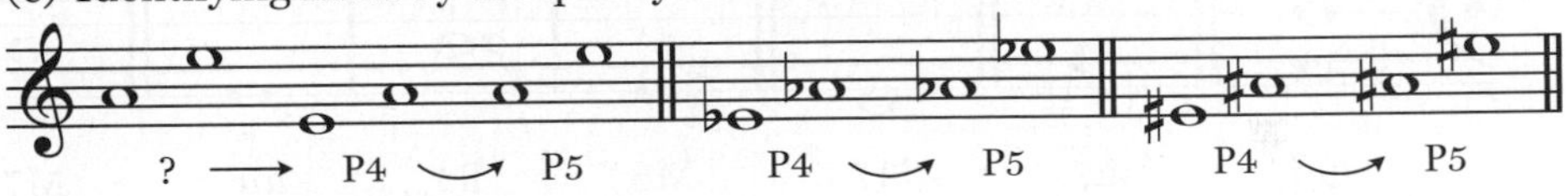

Another Way

Another way to identify sixths and sevenths is to compare them with fifths and octaves.

To spell a M6 or m6, think first of a P5 and make it larger.

- M6 = P5 + M2
- m6 = P5 + m2

To spell a M7 or m7, think first of a P8 and make it smaller.

- M7 = P8 – m2
- m7 = P8 – M2

Try it #5

(a) For each pair of pitches below, name the interval. Then write the inversion, and name the new interval.

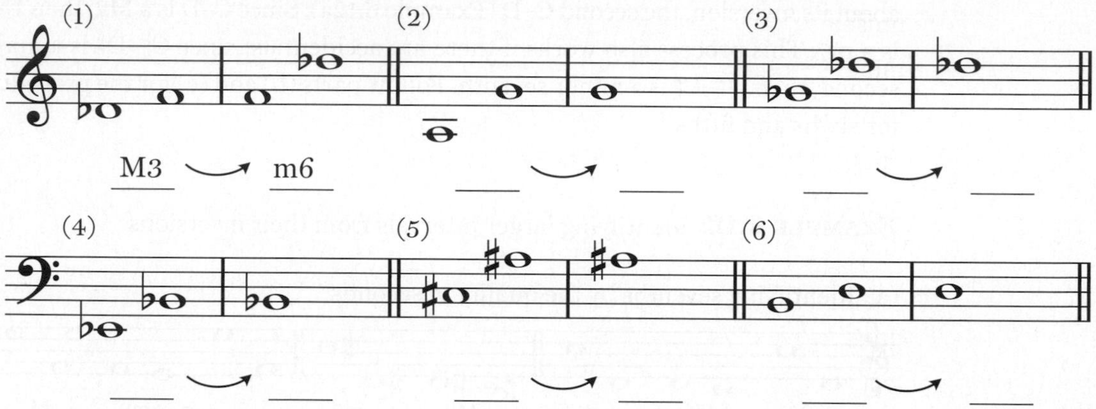

(b) Write harmonic intervals above the pitches given. Imagine the interval's inversion to check the spelling.

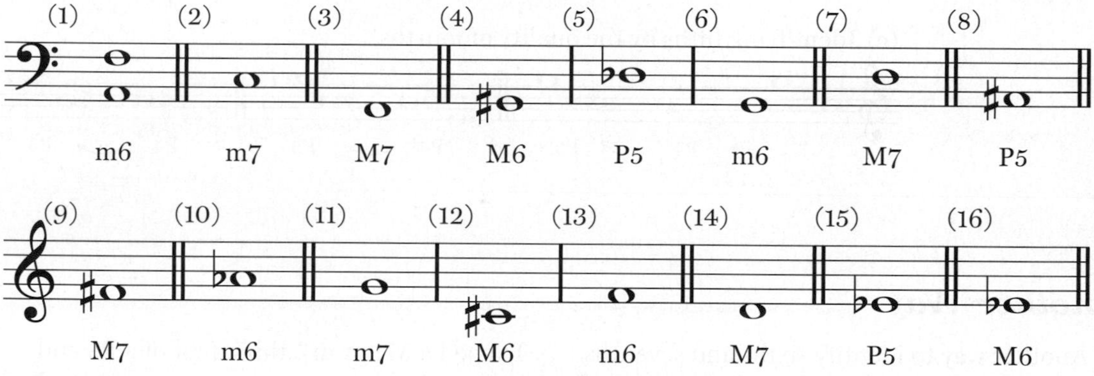

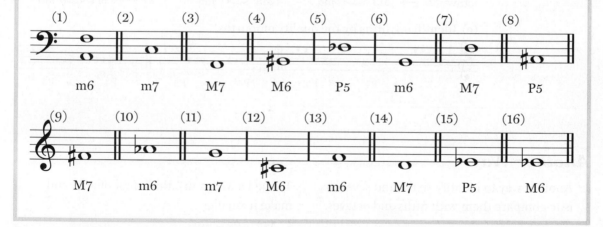

Semitones and Interval Size

You can also spell intervals by counting the scale steps from the first pitch to the second, then counting the semitones between them. Figure 6.1 summarizes this information.

FIGURE 6.1: Intervals as scale steps plus semitones

INTERVAL NAME	ABBREVIATION	NUMBER OF SCALE STEPS	NUMBER OF SEMITONES
unison	U	1	0
minor second	m2	2	1
major second	M2	2	2
minor third	m3	3	3
major third	M3	3	4
perfect fourth	P4	4	5
tritone (see p. 128)	A4 or d5	4 or 5	6
perfect fifth	P5	5	7
minor sixth	m6	6	8
major sixth	M6	6	9
minor seventh	m7	7	10
major seventh	M7	7	11
octave	P8	8	12

Augmented and Diminished Intervals

Listen to Bach's Invention in D Minor and focus on measures 1–5 of the right-hand part, shown in Example 6.13. Most of the intervals in measures 1, 2, and 5 are half and whole steps, and some of the larger intervals in measures 3 and 4 should be familiar.

EXAMPLE 6.13: Bach, Invention in D Minor, mm. 1–5

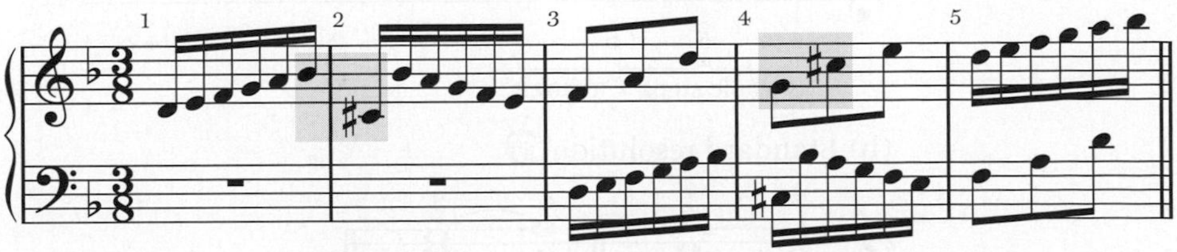

There are, however, two interval types in this passage that may be unfamiliar: the dramatic leap from B♭4 down to C♯4 and back up in measures 1–2, and the G4 to C♯5 in measure 4 (both shaded). We'll consider each in turn.

If the B♭ went down to a C♮ instead of C♯, it would be a minor seventh (m7). The interval Bach has written is a half step smaller than a m7 (but still spans seven letter names): this is a **diminished seventh** (d7). Now look at measure 4: if this interval were G4–C5, it would be a perfect fourth (P4); because it's a half step larger, it's an **augmented fourth** (A4). These striking diminished and augmented intervals are produced in this passage by the variants of scale degrees $\hat{6}$ and $\hat{7}$ that are available in harmonic and melodic minor scales.

KEY CONCEPT

- If a major or perfect interval is made one chromatic half step larger, it becomes augmented.
- If a minor or perfect interval is made one chromatic half step smaller, it becomes diminished.

The Tritone The interval between the white-key notes F and B ($\hat{4}$ and $\hat{7}$; *fa* and *ti*) may be spelled as an augmented fourth (A4) or as a **diminished fifth** (abbreviated d5), depending on where it is positioned. Just like perfect fourths, all the fifths made between pairs of white-key notes ($\hat{1}$–$\hat{5}$, $\hat{2}$–$\hat{6}$, etc.) are perfect except one: the fifth between $\hat{7}$ and $\hat{4}$ (B and F; see Example 6.14a). When $\hat{4}$ is lower than $\hat{7}$, the interval is spelled as an A4 (F–B); when $\hat{7}$ is lower than $\hat{4}$, it is a d5 (B–F). When spelled as an A4, the interval spans exactly three whole steps, from which it gets its name: the **tritone** (from "tri-," meaning "three").

EXAMPLE 6.14: The augmented fourth and diminished fifth in C major

(a) In a scale

(b) Standard resolution

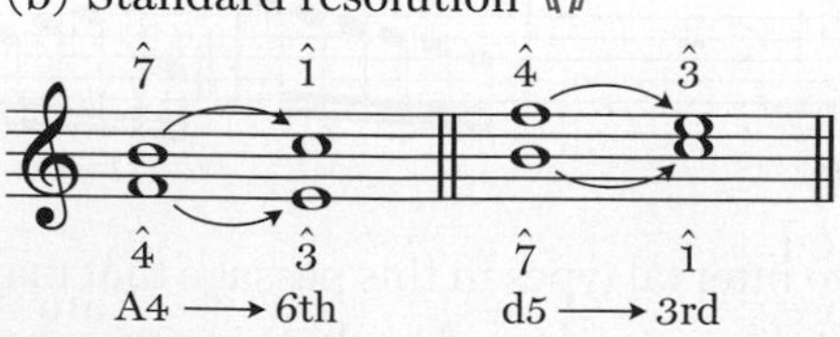

The A4 and d5 are the only inversionally related intervals that are exactly the same size in semitones: they both include six semitones, which places them between a perfect fourth and perfect fifth in size. They sound identical if not heard in a musical context; for this reason, most people use the term "tritone" for both intervals. But because of the tendency of $\hat{7}$ to move to $\hat{1}$, the two intervals **resolve** differently: augmented fourths move out, or resolve, to a sixth, while diminished fifths will move in (resolve) to a third (part b). We can thus distinguish between the sound of the two intervals—A4 and d5—by the interval to which they resolve.

Other Diminished and Augmented Intervals The A4 and d5 are the only augmented and diminished intervals that fall within the diatonic scales and modes, but others can be made by raising or lowering scale degrees by a half step. Only a few, however—including the A4, d5, A2, A6, and d7—are commonly encountered in tonal music. To spell augmented or diminished intervals, first spell a major, perfect, or minor interval, then adjust the quality, as shown in Example 6.15. Don't change the letter name of either pitch.

Example 6.15: Spelling augmented and diminished intervals

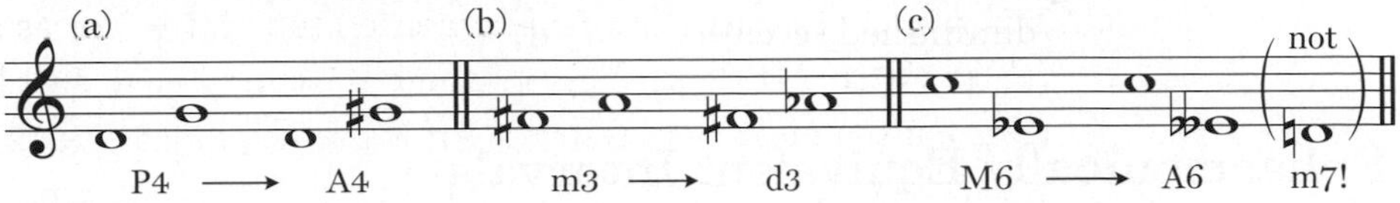

SUMMARY

FOR A	START WITH	ADD AN ACCIDENTAL TO MOVE ONE PITCH
diminished 2, 3, 6, 7	minor 2, 3, 6, 7	in one half step (makes it smaller)
diminished 4, 5, 8	perfect 4, 5, 8	in one half step
augmented 2, 3, 6, 7	major 2, 3, 6, 7	out one half step (makes it larger)
augmented U, 4, 5, 8	perfect U, 4, 5, 8	out one half step

It is also possible to make doubly augmented or doubly diminished intervals, though they are rare. They are sometimes spelled with double sharps or double flats or with one note sharped and the other flatted. If a major or perfect interval is made one whole step larger (without changing the letter names of the pitches), it is **doubly augmented**. If a minor or perfect interval is made one whole step smaller (without changing letter names), it is **doubly diminished**.

Figure 6.2 gives the number of scale steps and semitones spanned by diminished and augmented intervals. Less common intervals are marked with an asterisk. There is no diminished unison.

Figure 6.2: Augmented and diminished intervals as scale steps plus semitones

INTERVAL NAME	ABBREVIATION	NUMBER OF SCALE STEPS	NUMBER OF SEMITONES
*augmented unison	AU	1	1
*diminished second	d2	2	0
augmented second	A2	2	3
*diminished third	d3	3	2
*diminished fourth	d4	4	4
augmented fourth	a4	4	6
diminished fifth	d5	5	6
*augmented fifth	A5	5	8
*diminished sixth	d6	6	7
augmented sixth	A6	6	10
diminished seventh	d7	7	9

Enharmonically Equivalent Intervals

Intervals that span the same number of semitones but have different names are **enharmonically equivalent**. For example, the m3 F to A♭ spans three semitones, as does the A2 F to G♯. Any interval can be spelled four possible ways, all of them enharmonic. (Enharmonic intervals are similar to homonyms in language: "here" and "hear" sound the same but have completely different meanings in a sentence.) It is important to spell intervals correctly: the spelling reveals how the interval functions in the musical context.

In tonal music, intervals are usually written with pitches from the piece's major or minor key. As shown in Example 6.16, an interval spanning ten semitones spelled A♭ to G♭ (as a m7) does not resolve the same way as one spelled A♭ to F♯ (as an A6), as you will see in future chapters. The correct spelling also makes the interval easier to read for performers. Incorrect notation causes confusion and may waste rehearsal time!

Example 6.16: Resolutions of m7 and A6

Consonant and Dissonant Intervals

Over the course of music history, intervals have been characterized as **consonant** if they sound pleasing to the ear or tonally stable, and **dissonant** if they sound jarring, clashing, or as if they need to move somewhere else to find a resting point. Consonance and dissonance are relative terms based on properties of sound and on the norms of compositional practice: what sounds consonant to us today may have sounded dissonant to a Renaissance musician. As a rule of thumb, consider the following intervals to be consonant: unison, third, fifth, sixth, octave. Of these, the unison, fifth, and octave are considered **perfect consonances** because of their pure acoustic properties, while the third and sixth are **imperfect consonances**.

Dissonances include the second, seventh, and any augmented or diminished interval, such as the tritone. (Theorists in the Middle Ages considered the tritone the "devil in music" because of its dissonant sound.) The perfect fourth is sometimes grouped with the perfect consonances because of its acoustic properties, yet composers after the Renaissance tended to treat the harmonic fourth (but not the melodic fourth) as a dissonance. We will consider these properties further in later chapters on counterpoint and harmony.

To hear the difference between consonant and dissonant intervals, listen to the introduction of Sousa's "The Stars and Stripes Forever" (Example 6.17). As the introduction progresses, the intervals between the highest and lowest parts become more intense, and the music seems to push forward to the chord in measure 4. What intervals create this effect?

EXAMPLE 6.17: Sousa, "The Stars and Stripes Forever," mm. 1–4a

The first four harmonic intervals are all octaves—you can consider this passage as a single melody, but with higher and lower instruments playing the melody together (**doubled** in octaves). New harmonic intervals arrive in measure 2, beat 2, where the upper parts have an E♭ (E♭4 and E♭5) and the lower parts sound C3, E♭3, and C4. The simple interval (eliminating the octaves) between the bass part's C and the E♭ above is a m3, a consonant interval. The M6 between E♭3 and C4 is also consonant.

What about the interval from the bass's C3 to the F4/F5 at the end of measure 2? Again eliminating the octaves, this is a P4. The P4 sounds like a dissonance here, especially because it is accompaned by another dissonant interval, E♭3 to F4/F5, a major ninth. The motion from consonance to dissonance creates forward momentum into the next measure.

In measure 3, consider the intervals between the C♭ in the bass and the G♭, G♮, A♭, and A♮ in the melody: C♭–G♭ is a P5 (consonant), but C♭–G♮ is an A5 (dissonant); C♭ to A♭ is a M6 (consonant), but C♭ to A♮ is an A6 (dissonant). In addition, there is a dissonant tritone (A4) in the last chord in measure 3 between the E♭ and A♮. When the A6 and A4 connect by step to the consonant intervals of measure 4, with the A6 (C♭–A♮) moving outward to a P8 and the A4 (E♭–A♮) moving to a sixth, the tension that has built up over this passage is released. This motion from a dissonant interval to a consonant one is called its **resolution**.

One critical element that defines a given musical style is the way composers handle consonant and dissonant intervals. As you heard in examples earlier in this chapter, the dissonant interval of a seventh resolves to a consonance in the tonal music of Handel (in the first half of the eighteenth century), but does not resolve at all in the nontonal pieces of Webern (in the first half of the twentieth century).

SUMMARY

- Consonant intervals: unison, 3, 5, 6, 8
- Dissonant intervals: 2, 7, any augmented or diminished interval
- Special case: P4 (usually treated as a consonance melodically and as a dissonance harmonically)

Interval Classes

Another way to group intervals according to their sonic qualities is by **interval class**. For example, interval class 1 includes all minor seconds, their inversions (major sevenths), and the related compound intervals (minor ninths, major sevenths plus an octave, etc.). Interval class 1 also includes all intervals that are enharmonically equivalent to a minor second or major seventh, because they share the same sound. Each interval class is named for the number of semitones in the smallest representative interval of the family.

KEY CONCEPT All intervals (and their related inversions, compound intervals, and enharmonic equivalents) fall into one of these six interval-class families.

INTERVAL CLASS	BASIC INTERVALS	QUALITIES
1	m2 and M7	dissonance
2	M2 and m7	dissonance
3	m3 and M6	imperfect consonance
4	M3 and m6	imperfect consonance
5	P4 and P5	perfect consonance
6	A4 and d5 (tritones)	dissonance

Analyzing Intervals in Music

When identifying intervals in music with a key signature, consider both the key signature and any accidentals that appear in a measure. For example, if performers neglected the key signature in "The Stars and Stripes Forever" (Example 6.18), they might play the shaded notes in measures 1–2 as D–E (M2) instead of D–E♭ (m2), or as C–E (M3) instead of C–E♭ (m3). In measure 3, there are accidentals on almost every note: the natural on the second quarter note is necessary to cancel the previous G♭, and the natural on the last quarter note cancels the A♭ of the key signature. This passage ends entirely with melodic half steps—a segment of the chromatic scale.

Example 6.18: Sousa, "The Stars and Stripes Forever," mm. 1–4a

Musical scores sometimes include "courtesy" accidentals that aren't entirely necessary. For example, in measure 203 of Mozart's *Variations* (Example 6.19), flats are written in for the A♭ and E♭ on beat 2, even though those flats appear in the key signature. The E♭ is needed because the previous E in that measure has been altered with a natural sign, an accidental that would have been effective to the end of the measure. However, the A♭ in the lower voice is not really needed to cancel the A♮ of the previous *measure*, because the bar line automatically cancels it. The A♭ in measure 203 is a courtesy accidental, there to remind the performer to play the right note. Finally, the E♭ of measure 203 is tied over to the first beat of measure 204; here the accidental stays in effect through the tie (even though it crosses the bar line).

Example 6.19: Mozart, *Variations on "Ah, vous dirai-je Maman,"* Variation 8, mm. 201–208 (right hand only)

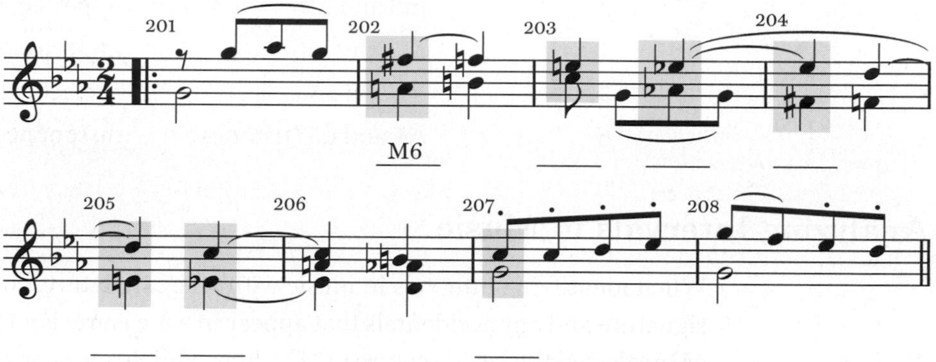

Try it #6

Listen to Variation 8 of Mozart's *Variations on "Ah, vous dirai-je Maman,"* paying particular attention to the harmonic intervals formed in the right hand of measures 201–208. On the score given in Example 6.19, analyze each shaded interval and write its name in the blank below.

SUMMARY

- Use the flats or sharps in the key signature and any accidentals marked in the score to determine the interval qualities.
- Remember that accidentals normally apply through the end of the measure unless another accidental cancels them.
- If a note with an accidental is tied over a bar line, the accidental continues in effect to the end of the tie. Courtesy accidentals may be included to remind performers that an accidental indicated in the key signature is back in effect.

Did You Know?

Many writers from the Middle Ages (c. 500–1430) and Renaissance (c. 1430–1600) attribute the characterization of "perfect intervals" to the famous Greek mathematician Pythagoras (sixth century B.C.), who was said to have discovered mathematical ratios by listening to smiths striking anvils with hammers in a blacksmith shop and noticing that when the sizes of the hammers were in a ratio of 2:1, an octave sounded. (This legend, although often repeated, is not true: the sounds produced would be determined by the size of the anvils, not the hammers.) In any case, from the time of Pythagoras, perfect intervals were considered beautiful because of their mathematical ratios, which could also be demonstrated on a plucked string. The octave described the relationship between a plucked full length of string and a plucked string divided in half (ratio 2:1). The fifth described the relationship between the full string and a string two-thirds the original length (ratio 3:2). The fourth resulted when the sound of the full string was compared with that of a string three-fourths its length (ratio 4:3). The difference between the ratio numbers in each case is 1 (2–1, 3–2, and 4–3). Mathematicians call these "superparticular" ratios. The purity of these intervals' sound and the beauty of their ratios have resulted in our term "perfect" for the octave, fifth, and fourth.

TERMS YOU SHOULD KNOW

- compound interval
- consonance
  - imperfect
  - perfect
- dissonance
- enharmonically related interval
- harmonic interval
- interval
- interval class
- interval quality
  - major
  - minor
  - perfect
  - augmented
  - diminished
- interval size
- inversionally related interval
- melodic interval
- tritone
- unison

QUESTIONS FOR REVIEW

1. What information is missing when only an interval's size is given?
2. Which interval sizes are considered consonant? dissonant?
3. What is the difference between a major and a minor interval of the same size (for example, M6 and m6)?
4. What is the interval called that is one chromatic half step smaller than a minor interval? one chromatic half step larger than a major interval?
5. What is the interval called that is one chromatic half step smaller than a perfect interval? one chromatic half step larger than a perfect interval?
6. Name as many enharmonically equivalent intervals to C♯–E as you can.
7. Examine the melodic intervals between pitches in a phrase of a piece you perform. Which interval size appears most often? What is the largest interval?
8. What qualities do intervals share that are in the same interval class?

CHAPTER 7

Triads

Outline of topics

Chords and triads

- Triads above a scale
- Triad qualities in major keys
- Triad qualities in minor keys

Spelling triads

- Spelling scale-degree triads from C major
- Spelling isolated triads by interval
- Spelling isolated triads by key signature

Scale-degree triads in a tonal context

- Roman numerals for scale-degree triads
- Triad inversion
- Triads in popular-music notation

Figured bass

Overview

In this chapter, we combine intervals to form triads. We will identify triad types and consider how they function in musical contexts.

Repertoire

Johann Sebastian Bach
"Er kommt" ("He Comes"), from Cantata 140, *Wachet auf*
"O Haupt voll Blut und Wunden" ("O Head, Full of Blood and Wounds")

Barry Gordy, Hall Davis, Willie Hutch, and Bob West, "I'll Be There"

George Frideric Handel, Chaconne in G Major

William "Smokey" Robinson and Ronald White, "My Girl"

Chords and Triads

Listen to the theme (mm. 1–8) of Handel's keyboard Chaconne while following the score in your anthology (p. 180). Beginning in measure 9, there is a series of **variations**, which are based on the theme but vary the rhythmic patterns, melody, and other features to create a satisfying succession of eight-measure variants. In each of the first four variations, identify which hand performs the melody and which plays mostly simultaneous collections of intervals, or chords.

KEY CONCEPT A **chord** is a group of pitches that forms a single harmonic idea. The pitches in a chord usually sound all at once, but they may also sound in succession.

The Handel piece includes left-hand chords in the theme and Variations 1 and 3, and right-hand chords in Variations 2 and 4. Example 7.1, drawn from the right hand of Variation 4, shows the type of chord that is the main topic of this chapter: the triad. The chord shaded in measure 33, the triad G-B-D, is made of two simultaneous thirds, one above the other.

EXAMPLE 7.1: Handel, Chaconne in G Major, Variation 4, mm. 33–36

KEY CONCEPT Three-note chords that can be represented as two thirds, one above the other, are called **triads**. When they are written in this spacing, you can recognize triads easily by their position on the staff as line-line-line or space-space-space.

Triads stacked in thirds in the left hand of Variation 1 are marked in Example 7.2: on the downbeats of measures 9 (G-B-D, with another G at the top), 11 (E-G-B, plus an "extra note," D), 12 (D-F♯-A, with another D at the top), 13 (G-B-D), and 14 (C-E-G). The extra notes in measures 9 and 12 are typical octave doublings, while the D of measure 11 forms a seventh chord, the topic of Chapter 8.

Example 7.2: Handel, Chaconne, Variation 1, mm. 9–16

KEY CONCEPT When triads are spelled in thirds, the interval between the lowest pitch (the **root**) and the highest pitch (called the **fifth**) is a fifth. The middle member, the **third**, is a third above the root. When the root is the lowest pitch of the chord, the chord is in **root position**.

We speak of the root, third, and fifth of a triad even when the triad is *not* arranged in thirds. All chords marked with arrows in Example 7.2 are in root position. We will return to the Handel variations later in this chapter to analyze non-root-position chords.

Triads Above a Scale

Since the Chaconne is in G major, we can anticipate which triads Handel is likely to include by writing triads above each note of the G major scale (Example 7.3). In musical practice, triads built on some scale degrees (such as $\hat{1}$, $\hat{2}$, $\hat{4}$, and $\hat{5}$) appear much more frequently than others.

Example 7.3: Triads above each scale degree in G major

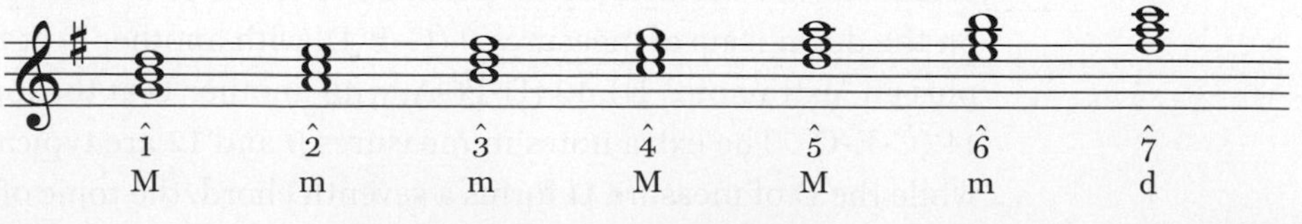

Try it #1

Compare the triads in Example 7.3 with the root-position chords identified in Example 7.2. Write the scale-degree number for the root of each of Handel's chords in the corresponding blank below.

m. 9: $\hat{1}$ m. 11: ______ m. 12: ______ m. 13: ______ m. 14: ______

Triad Qualities in Major Keys

As seen in Example 7.3, in major keys, **major triads** are built on scale degrees $\hat{1}$, $\hat{4}$, and $\hat{5}$: the bottom third of the triad is major and the top third is minor (Example 7.4a). **Minor triads** are built on $\hat{2}$, $\hat{3}$, and $\hat{6}$: the bottom third of the triad is minor and the top third is major (part b). The triad built on $\hat{7}$, a **diminished triad**, has a diminished fifth between the root and fifth, and both of its thirds are minor (part c). The triad type—major (M), minor (m), or diminished (d)—is known as its **quality**.

EXAMPLE 7.4: Triad qualities in major

(a) Major triads on $\hat{1}$, $\hat{4}$, and $\hat{5}$ (b) Minor triads on $\hat{2}$, $\hat{3}$, and $\hat{6}$ (c) Diminished triad on $\hat{7}$

Try it #2

Write the appropriate triad above each scale degree in E♭ major, in whole notes. Write the accidentals next to the note as needed. Label each triad's quality in the blank provided: M, m, or d.

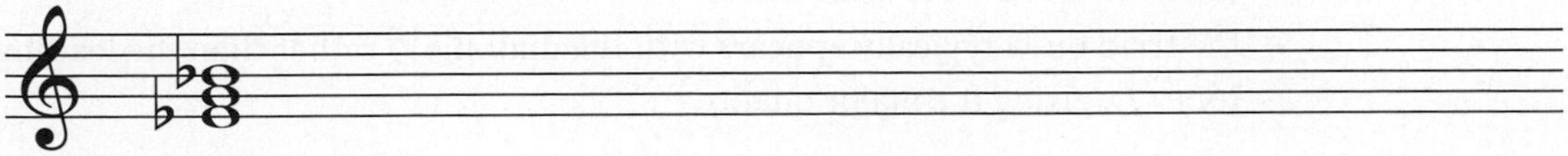

E♭ major: M ______ ______ ______ ______ ______ ______ ______

Triad Qualities in Minor Keys

If you build triads above the scale degrees of a natural minor scale, as shown in Example 7.5a, the triads on $\hat{1}$, $\hat{4}$, and $\hat{5}$ are minor, those on $\flat\hat{3}$, $\flat\hat{6}$, and $\flat\hat{7}$ are major, and the triad on $\hat{2}$ is diminished. But when the seventh scale degree is raised to create a leading tone as often happens in minor keys, the triads on $\hat{5}$ and $\hat{7}$ become major and diminished in quality, respectively (part b).

Example 7.5: Triads above each scale degree in G minor

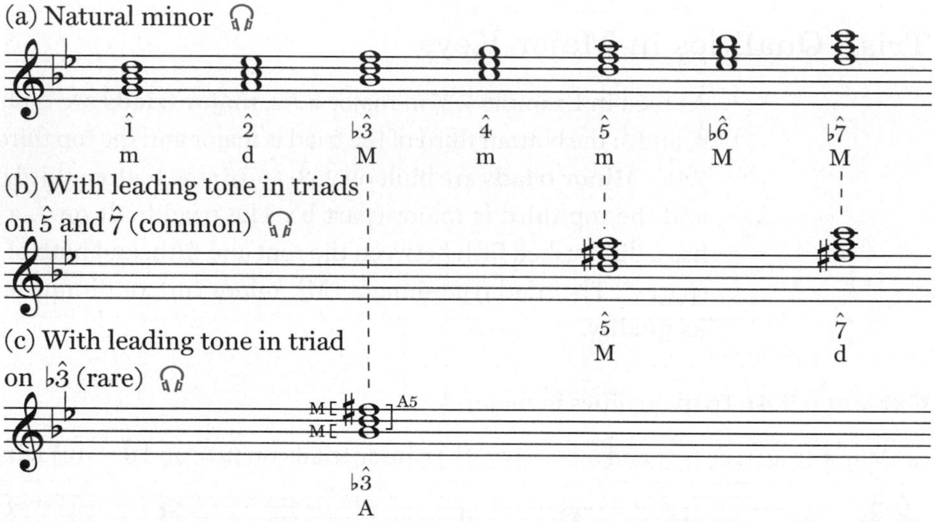

SUMMARY

In major keys,

- triads on scale degrees $\hat{1}$, $\hat{4}$, and $\hat{5}$ are major;
- triads on $\hat{2}$, $\hat{3}$, and $\hat{6}$ are minor;
- the triad on $\hat{7}$ is diminshed.

In minor keys (harmonic form),

- triads on scale degrees $\hat{1}$ and $\hat{4}$ are minor;
- triads on $\hat{5}$ and $\flat\hat{6}$ are major;
- triads on $\hat{2}$ and $\hat{7}$ are diminshed;
- the triad on $\flat\hat{3}$ typically appears with the diatonic $\flat\hat{7}$ rather than the leading tone ($\hat{7}$), giving it a major quality.

If you write a triad on $\hat{5}$ or $\hat{7}$ in a minor key, you will almost always add a ♯ or ♮ to create a leading tone and change the quality. Remember, to determine the key of a new piece, scan it quickly for the presence of an accidental on the seventh scale degree (here, an F♯ in a key signature with two flats) to determine whether it is minor.

What happens to the triad on scale degree $\flat\hat{3}$ when $\flat\hat{7}$ is raised? Look back at Example 7.5c. When $\flat\hat{7}$ is raised in minor keys, the triad built on $\flat\hat{3}$ contains major thirds both between the root and third and between the third and fifth. Since the interval between the root and fifth is an augmented fifth, this type of triad (rarely encountered) is called an **augmented triad** (labeled A). In music analysis, you will occasionally find other altered degrees of the minor scale (for example, the raised sixth). In such cases, pay careful attention to triad quality.

Try it #3

Write the appropriate triad above each scale degree in C minor. Add the accidentals before each note as needed. On the first staff, write all the triads in natural minor; on the second, add the appropriate accidental to spell a major triad on $\hat{5}$ and a diminished one on $\hat{7}$. Write the triad qualities (M, m, or d) in the blanks provided.

Natural minor:

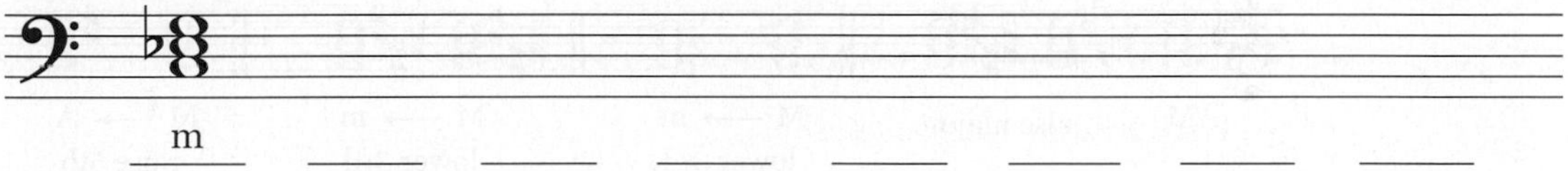

With leading tone:

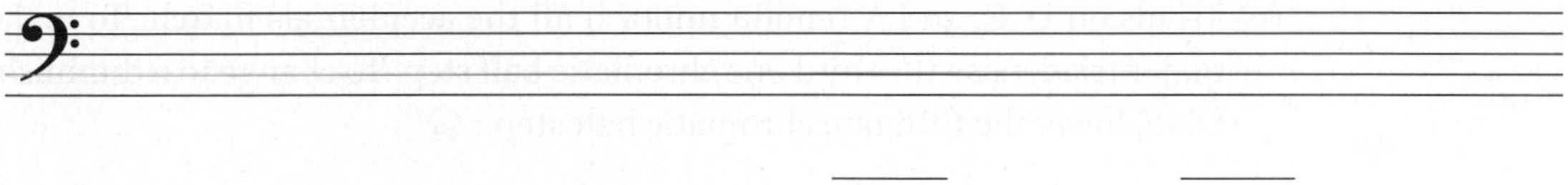

Spelling Triads

You will improve the speed with which you analyze and sight-read music by learning to spell and identify triad qualities quickly. For this reason, we provide several methods; choose the one that works best for you.

Method #1: Spelling Scale-Degree Triads from C Major

Many musicians are visual learners or naturally picture concepts in relation to their instruments. If you like to visualize triads on the keyboard or staff, you can use these images to spell any isolated triad. First learn the qualities of each triad in C major, as the piano white keys or plain note heads on the staff (Example 7.6a).

Example 7.6: Spelling isolated triads from C major qualities

(a) White-key triads

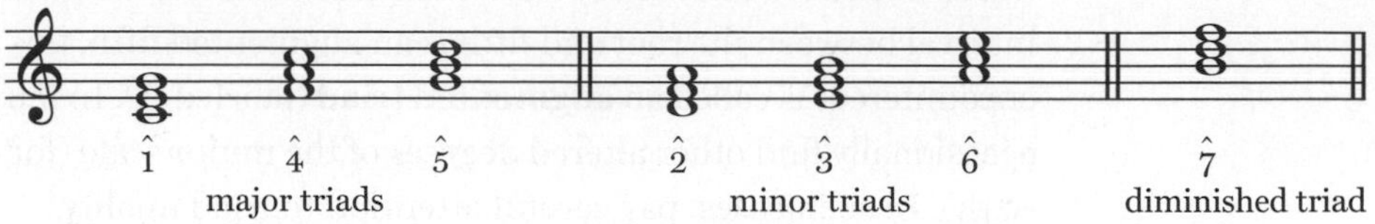

Now use this information to build the other types of triads.

(b) Triads on C, F, and G remain major if all the accidentals match. To change to a minor triad, lower the third one chromatic half step (without changing the letter name). To change to an augmented triad, raise the fifth one chromatic half step.

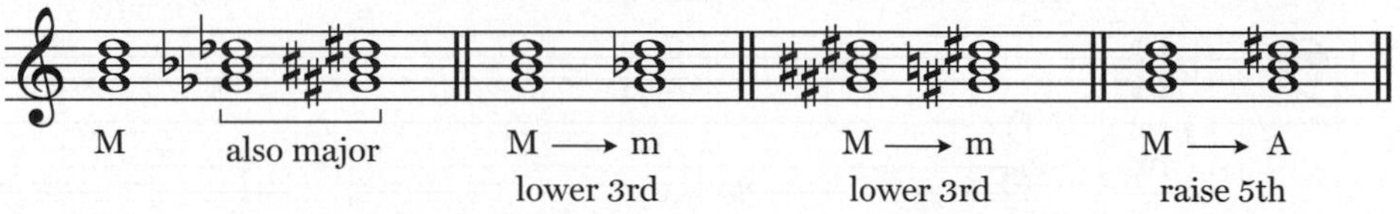

(c) Triads on D, E, and A remain minor if all the accidentals match. To make a major triad, raise the third one chromatic half step. To change to a diminished triad, lower the fifth one chromatic half step.

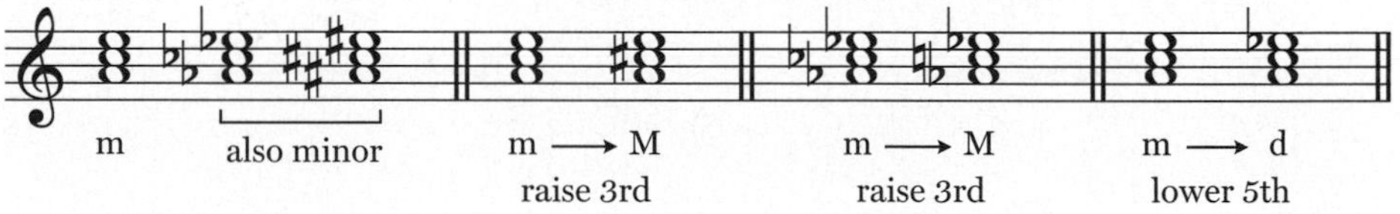

(d) Triads on B remain diminished if all the accidentals match. To make a minor triad, raise the fifth one chromatic half step. To make a major triad, raise both the third and fifth one chromatic half step.

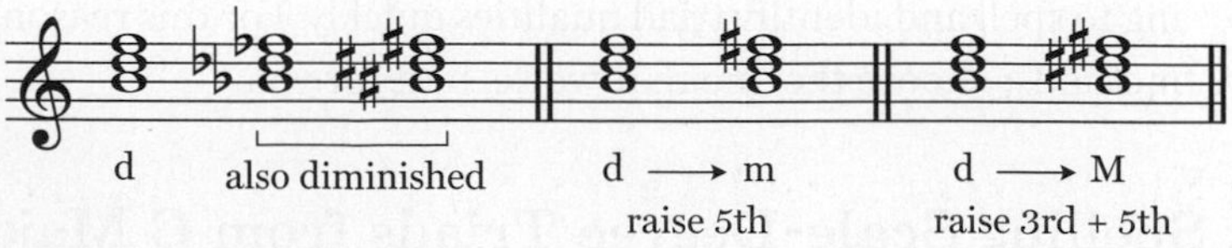

Method #2: Spelling Isolated Triads by Interval

Example 7.7a illustrates the steps for spelling a triad by the quality of its fifth and third.

1. Write the root of the triad.
2. Write a fifth above the root. For a major or minor triad, write a P5 above the root. For a diminished triad, write a d5, and for an augmented triad an A5.
3. Write a third above the root. For a major or augmented triad, make it a M3. For a minor or diminished triad, make it a m3.

Example 7.7: Spelling isolated triads by interval

(a) Spelling triads as fifths and thirds

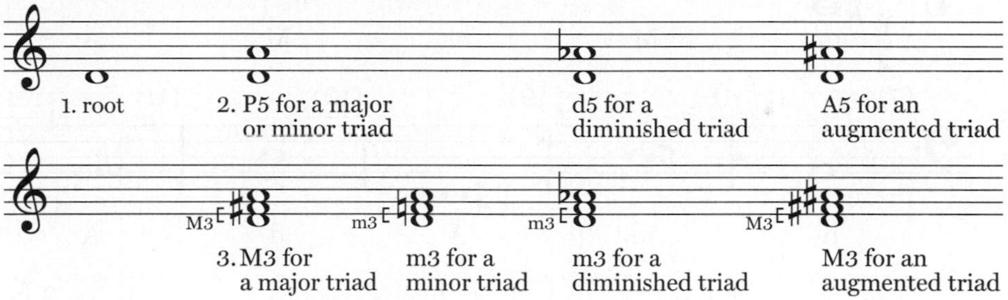

(b) Spelling triads as stacked thirds

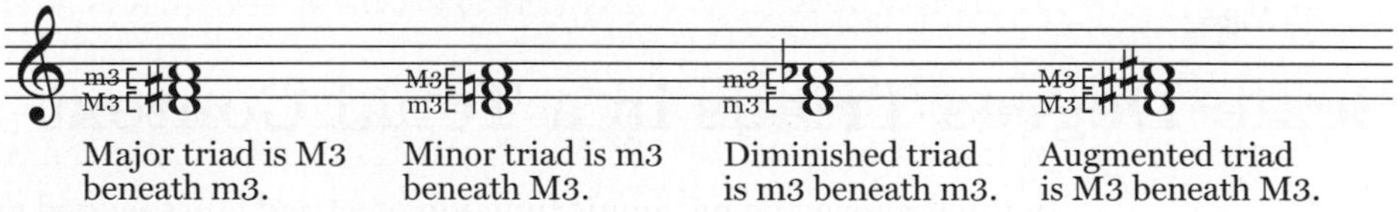

Part (b) shows another way to spell triads by interval: by the quality of their thirds.

- A major triad is a major third beneath a minor third.
- A minor triad is a minor third beneath a major third.
- A diminished triad is two minor thirds.
- An augmented triad is two major thirds.

Method #3: Spelling Isolated Triads by Key Signature

A third way to spell triads is by thinking of key signatures. Imagine a major or minor triad in a key: the root is the tonic, and the upper notes lie in the scale.

- For a major triad, think of the major key signature of the root and write $\hat{1}$, $\hat{3}$, and $\hat{5}$.

- For a minor triad, think of the minor key signature of the root and write $\hat{1}$, $\flat\hat{3}$, and $\hat{5}$.
- Spell a diminished triad by lowering the fifth of a minor triad one chromatic half step.
- Spell an augmented triad by raising the fifth of a major triad one chromatic half step.

Try it #4

Spell the following triads.

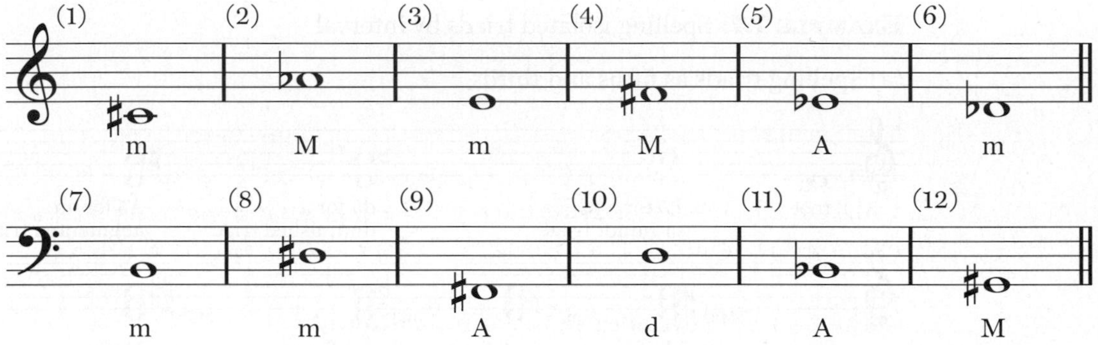

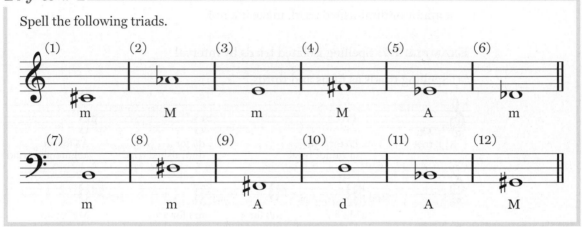

Scale-Degree Triads in a Tonal Context

In tonal music, the harmonic function of a triad is associated with the scale degree on which it is built. For example, in a piece in G major, the triad built on $\hat{1}$ (G) is the **tonic** harmony: the harmony that serves as a "home base" in that key. Each triad built on the other scale degrees is similarly referred to by the name of its root, as in Example 7.8. When referring to triads in the context of a key, we call them "scale-degree triads." Keep in mind that not all triads carry the same functional weight in tonal music, and some (such as I and V) appear much more often than others. Not all scale-degree triads are equal!

Example 7.8: Scale-degree triads in G major

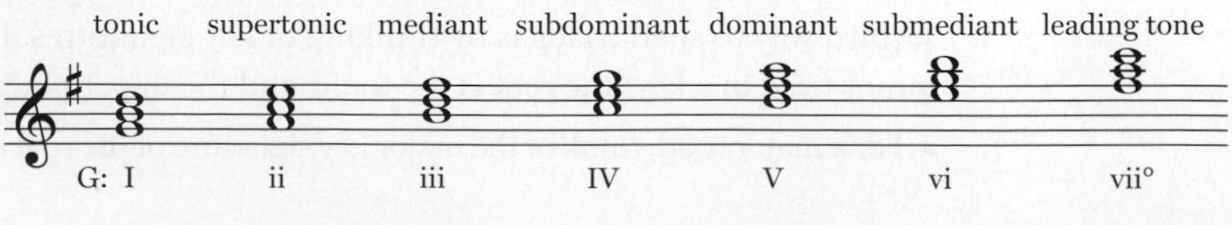

Roman Numerals for Scale-Degree Triads

As you learn more about the harmonic structure of music, you'll want to take advantage of a helpful label that indicates both the quality of the triad and its placement within a key: the Roman numeral.

KEY CONCEPT To label harmonies:

- Write capital Roman numerals (I to VII) for major triads.
- Write lowercase Roman numerals (i to vii) for minor triads.
- For diminished triads, add a small raised circle to a lowercase numeral (vii°).
- For augmented triads, add a small raised plus sign to an uppercase numeral (III^{+}).

The Roman numerals for each triad in G major and G minor are shown in Examples 7.8 and 7.9, along with the scale-degree names. When analyzing music with Roman numerals, indicate the key at the beginning of your analysis, as in the examples: an uppercase letter for major keys, a lowercase letter for minor.

Example 7.9: Scale-degree triads in G minor

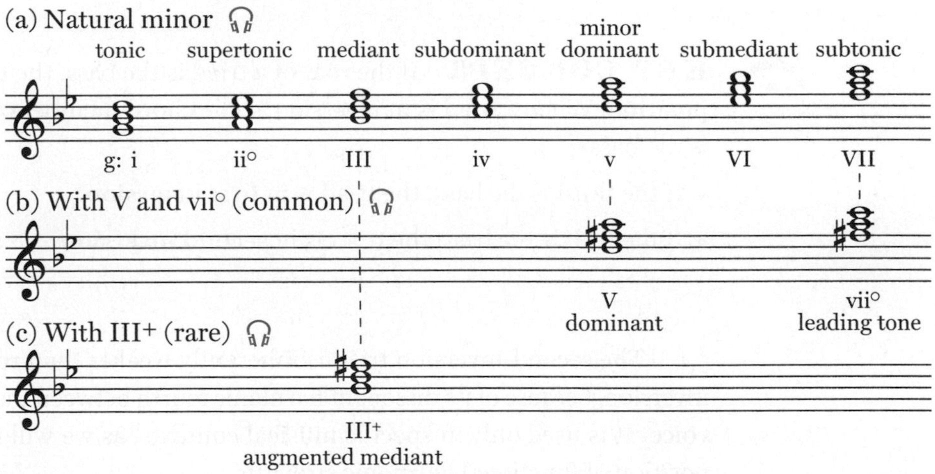

Triad Inversion

Though it is convenient to think of triads as stacked in thirds above their root, they often appear in other arrangements in music, with a note other than the root in the lowest part. Let's return now to the Handel Chaconne—the end of Variation 1, reproduced in Example 7.10.

Example 7.10: Handel, Chaconne, Variation 1, mm. 13–16

In measure 13, beat 1, the root of the bass-clef triad appears in the bass. On beat 2, the chord tones G-B-D are the same, but now B2, the third, is the lowest voice. This triad—no longer in root position—is **inverted**. Be careful not to confuse the terms "root" and "bass": any member of a triad—root, third, or fifth—may sound in the bass (lowest) voice.

KEY CONCEPT If the root of a triad is the bass, the triad is in **root position**. When a triad is in inversion, some chord member other than the root is the bass.

- If the third is the bass, the triad is in **first inversion**.
- If the fifth is the bass, the triad is in **second inversion**.

The second-inversion triad is inherently weaker than root position or first inversion, because of its dissonant harmonic fourth between the bass and an upper voice. It is used only in specific musical contexts, as we will see, and never in a position of functional harmonic strength.

For an example of triads in all three positions, look at measure 9 from Bach's "O Haupt voll Blut und Wunden" (Example 7.11). Although the chorale begins and ends in F major, this short passage is firmly in C major (every B has a natural sign, and the bass line begins with $\hat{1}$ and ends with $\hat{5}$–$\hat{1}$ in C). Since beats 1 and 2 of measure 9 express a C major harmony, with C in the bass (root position), label both with the Roman numeral I (disregard for now the shaded eighth-note offbeats). Beat 3 is an F-A-C harmony, with the A (the third of the chord) in the bass: a IV chord in first inversion. Another C major chord appears on beat 4, but this time with the fifth, G, in the bass: the I chord in second inversion.

Example 7.11: Bach, "O Haupt voll Blut und Wunden," mm. 9–10a

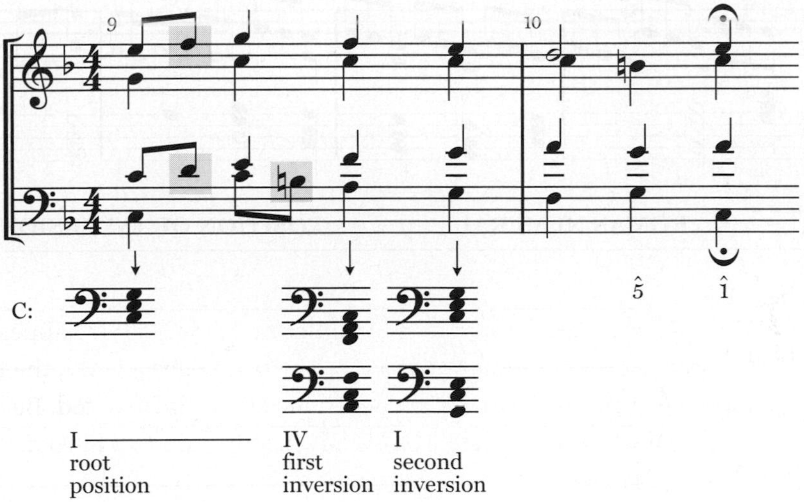

To help identify inverted triads, think about how the pitches of the chords would be notated if they were in root position. (This was the method of French composer Jean-Philippe Rameau, who is often given credit for the idea of chord inversion.) You might write the pitch classes on a separate staff and stack them in thirds, as in Example 7.11, to identify their root and Roman numeral. Eventually, you'll be able to do this quickly in your head.

KEY CONCEPT To identify the root of an inverted chord, look for the interval of a fourth. The upper note of the fourth is the root.

Look, for instance, at the F-A-C chord in measure 9, beat 3, of Example 7.11. The two treble-clef pitches are C-F; the F (at the top of the fourth) is the root of this chord.

Try it #5

Identify the Roman numeral and inversion for each left-hand triad specified below. Be sure that the Roman numeral shows the correct chord quality (major, minor, or diminished).

Handel, Chaconne, Variation 3, mm. 29–32

	ROMAN NUMERAL	POSITION OR INVERSION
1. m. 30, beat 1	________	____________________
2. m. 30, beat 2	________	____________________
3. m. 30, beat 3	________	____________________
4. m. 31, beat 1	________	____________________
5. m. 32, beat 1	________	____________________

Triads in Popular-Music Notation

In popular music, harmonies are commonly notated with chord symbols above the melody line. This type of notation, often called **lead-sheet notation**, is read by keyboard, bass, and other pop or jazz combo players. On lead sheets, the capital letter name of the root is used for all triad types, with added symbols or abbreviations for other qualities. For example:

TRIAD TYPE	LEAD-SHEET NOTATION
F major	F
F minor	Fm, Fmin, or F-
F augmented	F+ or F(♯5)
F diminished	F°, Fdim, or Fmin(♭5)

Often a lead sheet will show both the chord type and a guitar symbol known as a TAB. These guitar diagrams are a type of **tablature**, a traditional method of notation for lute and guitar that depicts the strings and shows the performer where to place fingers to produce each harmony. When playing from music with only chord symbols, players may choose any fingering or chord spacing above the specified bass note. Compare the accompaniment in Example 7.12, from Smokey Robinson's "My Girl," with the chord symbols and TABs.

Example 7.12: Robinson and White, "My Girl," mm. 27–30

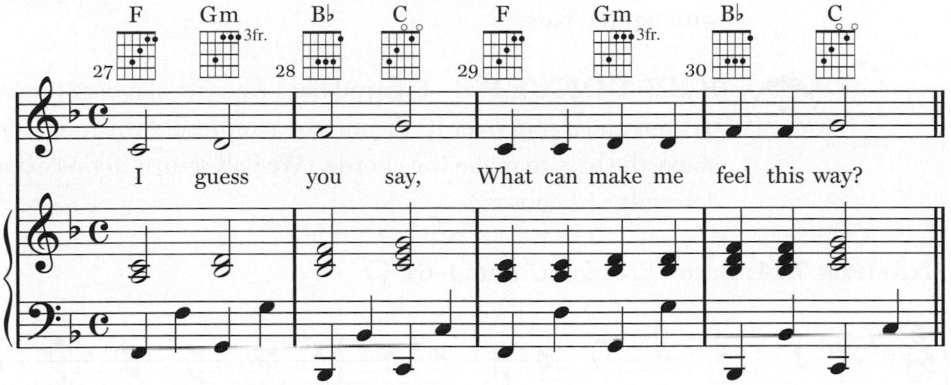

To notate an inverted triad, first write the triad type followed by a slash, then the letter name of the pitch that appears in the bass. Example 7.13 features first-inversion triads on alternate measures to create a bass line that descends by scale step. Here, a first-inversion C major triad (m. 6) is notated C/E, and a first-inversion A minor triad (m. 8) as Am/C. "Slash notation" can also be used when a note outside the triad appears in the bass, such as G/C: a G major chord with a C in the bass.

Example 7.13: Gordy, Davis, Hutch, and West, "I'll Be There," mm. 5–8

Figured Bass

Look at the opening of Bach's tenor recitative "Er kommt" in Example 7.14. A **recitative** in the Baroque era (1600–1750) usually features quick-moving pitches approximating speech (in the singer's part) over a chordal accompaniment notated with figured bass.

KEY CONCEPT **Figured bass** consists of a bass line with numbers written under it or over it; the numbers represent the intervals to be played above the bass to make the chords. (We will return to this example later to determine its chords.)

EXAMPLE 7.14: Bach, "Er kommt," mm. 1–6a

In figured-bass notation, chords in root position are indicated with the numerals 5 and 3, written one over the other below the bass note (see Example 7.15a). In a musical context, the fifth and third might be played in various ways: spaced as compound intervals, with either a major or minor third, or with one of the pitches played in two different octaves (doubled) to make four parts (part b). Such details are not specified in the basic label for the chord, but are determined by the performer and by stylistic conventions.

When a triad is in first inversion, the intervals above the bass are a sixth and a third; the figured-bass representation is thus a 6 and 3 written beneath the bass note. If the fifth is in the bass (second inversion), the intervals are a sixth and a fourth, represented by 6 and 4. The second inversion is the least common and the least stable chord position because of the dissonant fourth above the bass (here, G–C).

EXAMPLE 7.15: Figured bass for triads

(a) Triads and inversions in three voices

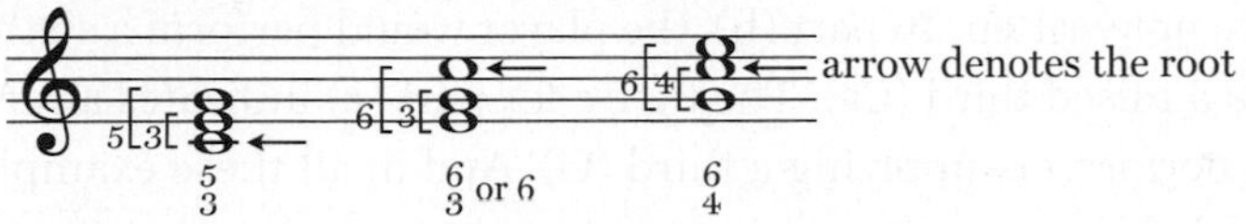

(b) Triads and inversions in four voices

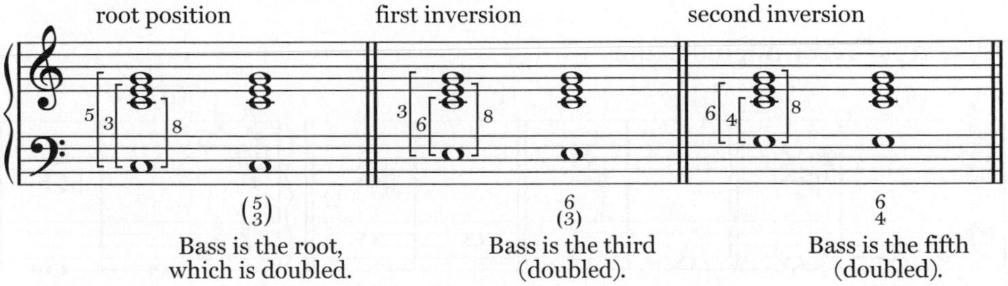

Figured bass was employed in the Baroque era in much the same way as lead-sheet notation is today: keyboard players studied the bass line and figures and knew from them which intervals (and therefore which chords) to play in the upper parts. The figures were made as simple as possible to allow musicians to read them quickly. For example, since the $^{5}_{3}$ figure was the most common, it was often left out; when performers saw a bass note without a figure (or with just ^{5}), they assumed $^{5}_{3}$. The figure $^{6}_{3}$ was frequently shortened to just ^{6} (with 3 understood to be the remaining interval). For second inversion, though—$^{6}_{4}$—which was less usual and contained the dissonant interval of a fourth above the bass, the full figure was given to avoid confusion with $^{6}_{3}$.

When reading a figured bass, play or write chord tones that are diatonic in the key, unless an accidental is given.

KEY CONCEPT Accidentals may appear in figured bass alone or next to a number.

- By itself, an accidental always refers to the note a third above the bass (not necessarily the third of the chord).
- Next to a number, an accidental tells you to alter the note lying that interval above the bass (e.g., ♯6 means to raise the note a sixth above the bass a chromatic half step; ♭3 means to lower the note a third above the bass a chromatic half step).
- A slash through a number (6̸) means the same thing as a sharp next to it (♯6).

In part (a) of Example 7.16, for instance, the lone sharp says to raise the third above the bass (making the C♯ the leading tone of the D minor key); the 5 and 3 in parentheses in the next measure are the figures that a performer would assume, if they were not written. In part (b), the player would perform a sixth above the bass (F) plus a raised third (C♯). The figure for part (c) indicates a raised sixth (C♯), with the performer supplying a third (G). And in all these examples, the bass note is doubled in an upper voice to create a four-voice texture. Parts (d) and (e) show a single accidental, each of which *lowers* the third above the bass.

EXAMPLE 7.16: Altered figures

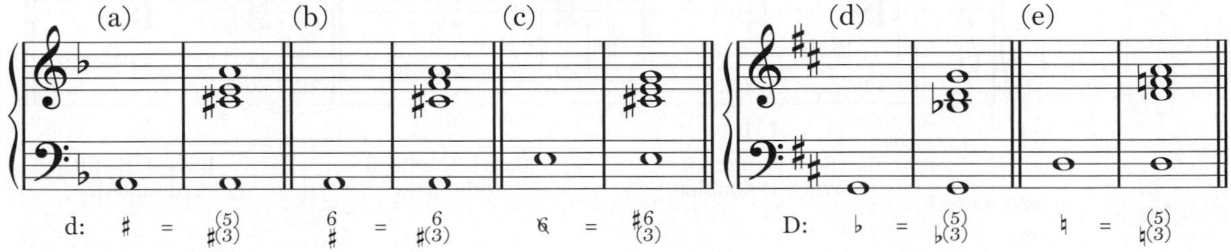

Try it #6

In the treble-clef staff, write the three notes (in whole notes) of the triad indicated by the bass and figures. Write all three notes of the triad (line-line-line or space-space-space) plus any accidentals specified.

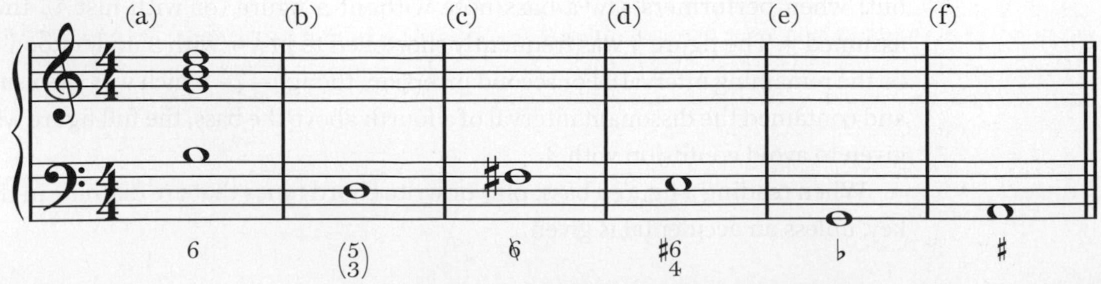

You will sometimes use figures the way Baroque musicians did—to represent intervals over a bass line. But you will also often write figures to represent inversions of chords—$^{5}_{3}$ (or nothing) for root position, $^{6}_{3}$ or ^{6} for first inversion, and $^{6}_{4}$ for second inversion. When these figures are combined with Roman numerals, they identify the chord's scale degree, quality, and inversion—providing a lot of information in one space-saving label.

Look back now at Example 7.11, Bach's recitative, to interpret some of the figured bass. The passage is in C minor. The opening figures, ^{5} and $^{6}_{4}$, represent C minor (C-E♭-G) and F minor (F-A♭-C, with C as the bass): i and iv$^{6}_{4}$.

Try it #7

In the blank provided, write the triad types (e.g., F minor) designated by the figured bass in Example 7.14.

(a) m. 5, beat 1 ____________________

(c) m. 5, beat 4 ____________________

(b) m. 5, beat 2 ____________________

(d) m. 6, beat 1 ____________________

Did You Know?

The idea of the invertible triad, with its three forms—root position, first inversion, and second inversion—first appears in writings about music in the early seventeenth century (the early Baroque era), but was not widely accepted among musicians until the mid-eighteenth century (at the end of the Baroque and beginning of the Classical era). The invertible triad is described by Otto Siegfried Harnish (c. 1568–1623) in 1608, and the term *trias harmonica* (harmonic triad) is used by Johannes Lippius (1585–1612) in 1610. Lippius, a theologian and musician, characterized the triad as being like the Holy Trinity: three elements but also one.

The French composer Jean-Philippe Rameau (1683–1764) is often credited with the idea of chord inversion, because his controversial writings (published between 1722 and 1760) brought this idea to the forefront at a time when the music being composed was increasingly built on chords rather than independent lines. Rameau labeled the chords with a separate bass-clef staff underneath the music, where he wrote in the roots of each chord; this practice was called "fundamental bass," not to be confused with figured bass. Roman numerals were not used for analysis until after Rameau's death.

TERMS YOU SHOULD KNOW

chord
- root
- third
- fifth

figured bass

inversion
- first inversion
- second inversion

lead-sheet notation

tablature (TABs)

triad
- major
- minor
- augmented
- diminished

QUESTIONS FOR REVIEW

1. Describe two different ways of spelling each of these triad types from a given root: major, minor, diminished, and augmented.
2. Given the same root, which interval or intervals differ in the following pairs of triads? Major and minor, major and augmented, minor and diminished, minor and augmented.
3. What are the differences between the following ways of labeling triads: chord quality, figured bass, Roman numeral, lead sheet?
4. How does figured bass show first inversion? second inversion? a raised third? a lowered sixth?
5. Find a piece in your repertoire with a fairly simple rhythm (preferably chordal) and no accidentals. Choose four measures to analyze three ways: (a) chord root, quality, and inversion; (b) Roman numeral and inversion; (c) lead-sheet symbols.

CHAPTER 8

Seventh Chords

Outline of topics

Seventh chords

- Diatonic seventh chords in major keys
- Seventh chords in inversion
- Diatonic seventh chords in minor keys
- Spelling isolated seventh chords

Seventh chords in popular styles

- Less common seventh chords
- Arpeggiated triads and seventh chords
- Seventh chords and musical style

Overview

This chapter explains how to spell seventh chords and several ways to label them. We consider different musical contexts for seventh chords, and look at how triads as well as seventh chords are arpeggiated in these settings.

Repertoire

Johann Sebastian Bach, Prelude in C Major, from *The Well-Tempered Clavier*, Book 1

Gerry Goffin and Michael Masser, "Saving All My Love for You"

Edward Heyman and Victor Young, "When I Fall in Love"

Wolfgang Amadeus Mozart
- Piano Sonata in C Major, K. 545, second movement
- "Voi, che sapete" ("You Who Know"), from *The Marriage of Figaro*

Seventh Chords

Listen to Example 8.1a, the opening measures of a prelude for keyboard by J. S. Bach. The beauty of this piece, composed of common triads and seventh chords, comes from the ordering of the chords, the artful way they are connected, and the delicate way the individual notes are brought out in the texture. Each measure consists of only one type of chord, which is repeated.

EXAMPLE 8.1: Bach, Prelude in C Major

(a) Mm. 1–11

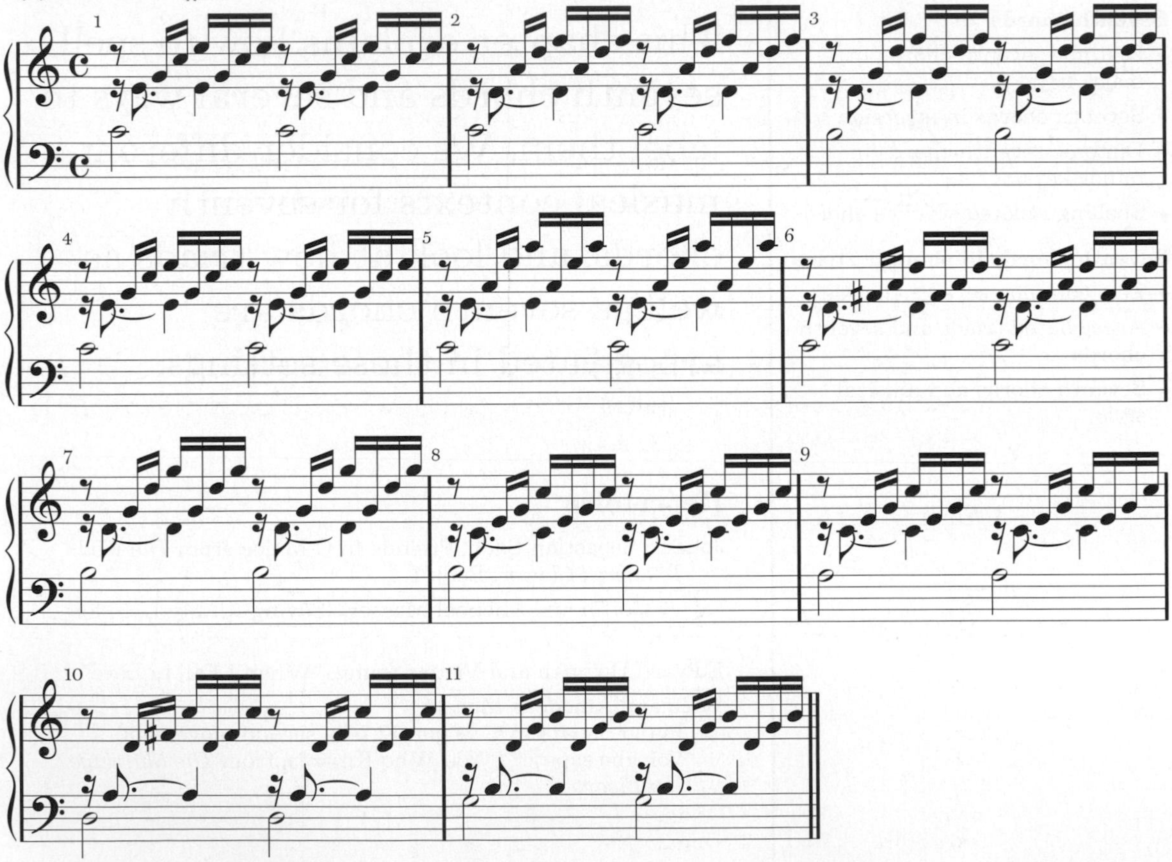

(b) Root-position chords in mm. 1–11

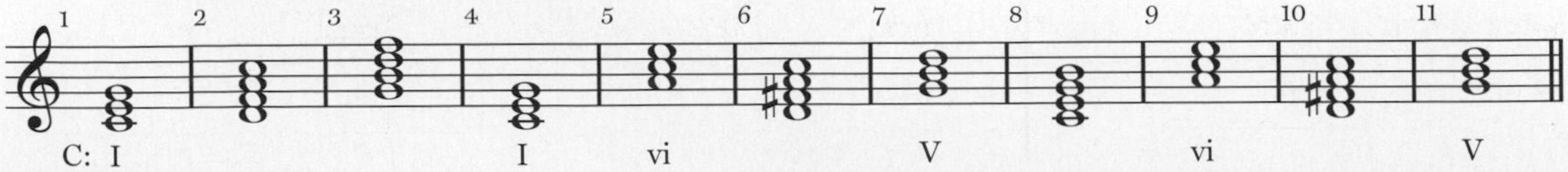

The chords from measures 1–11 are notated in root position in part (b). The triads in measures 1, 4, 5, 7, 9, and 11 should be familiar: they are C major, A minor, and G major triads, or the tonic, submediant, and dominant chords in the key of C major. The other chords (without Roman numerals) contain four pitches—an additional third has been added on top of the triad. These are called seventh chords, because the distance from the root to the top note is a seventh.

KEY CONCEPT **Seventh chords** are named by the quality of the triad plus the quality of the seventh measured from the root. A major-major seventh chord (MM7), for example, has a major triad and a major seventh.

There are several qualities of seventh chords in the Bach passage. For example, the chord in measure 2 has a D minor triad plus the note C, which forms a minor seventh from the root (D-C). The minor triad plus minor seventh makes a **minor-minor seventh** chord (mm7), or **minor seventh** for short. The chord in measure 3 has a G major triad plus the note F, a combination of a major triad and a minor seventh (G-F): this is a **major-minor seventh**, or **dominant seventh**, chord (Mm7).

Diatonic Seventh Chords in Major Keys

Seventh chords are built above each note in a major scale by adding a third above each scale-degree triad (refer to Examples 8.2 and 8.3). Here we consider all the possibilities in the key of G major.

EXAMPLE 8.2: Seventh chords built above the G major scale

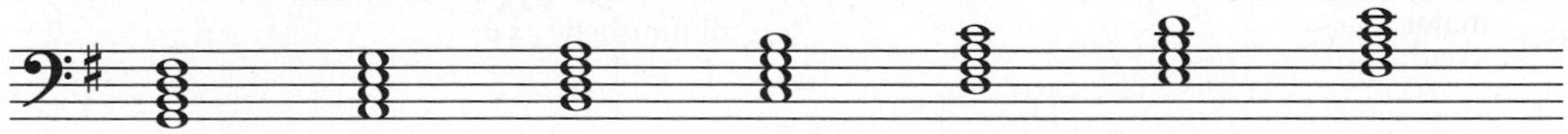

	$\hat{1}$	$\hat{2}$	$\hat{3}$	$\hat{4}$	$\hat{5}$	$\hat{6}$	$\hat{7}$
Triad quality:	M	m	m	M	M	m	d
7th quality:	M	m	m	M	m	m	m
Full name:	major-major 7th	minor-minor 7th	minor-minor 7th	major-major 7th	major-minor 7th	minor-minor 7th	diminished-minor 7th
Common name:	major 7th	minor 7th	minor 7th	major 7th	dominant 7th	minor 7th	half-diminished 7th
Abbreviation:	MM7	mm7	mm7	MM7	Mm7	mm7	ø7
Roman numeral:	I7	ii7	iii7	IV7	V7	vi7	viiø7

The seventh chords built on $\hat{1}$ and $\hat{4}$ are major triads with a major seventh (see Example 8.3a): **major-major seventh** chords, or **major seventh** chords for short (MM7). Chords built on $\hat{2}$, $\hat{3}$, and $\hat{6}$ are minor triads with a minor seventh: minor seventh chords (part b). Only one seventh chord has a major triad and a minor seventh: the chord built on $\hat{5}$ (part c). Its name is major-minor seventh, but it is usually called a dominant seventh because it is built on the dominant scale degree.

The remaining seventh chord to consider in major keys is that built on the leading tone (part d): a diminished triad and a minor seventh, called a **diminished-minor** or **half-diminished seventh** chord ("half" because there is a diminished triad but no diminished seventh). This is abbreviated with a small circle with a slash through it ($^{ø}7$): the slash divides the diminished symbol in half. As Examples 8.2 and 8.3 show, seventh chords may also be labeled with Roman numerals to indicate their scale-degree placement (and function) in the key. For example, the dominant seventh chord on $\hat{5}$ is labeled V7, and the leading-tone seventh chord vii^{ø7}.

EXAMPLE 8.3: Scale-degree seventh chords in major keys

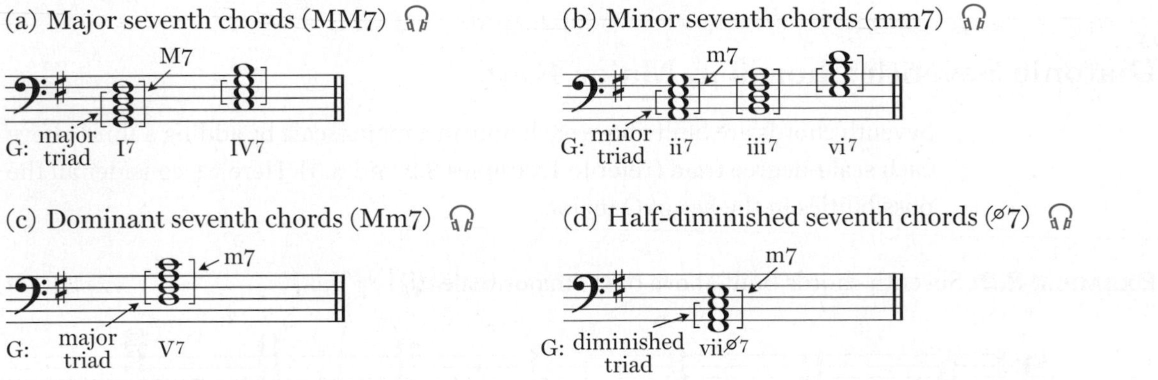

SUMMARY

In major keys:

- Seventh chords on $\hat{1}$ and $\hat{4}$ are major sevenths (MM7)—I7 and IV7.
- Seventh chords on $\hat{2}$, $\hat{3}$, and $\hat{6}$ are minor sevenths (mm7)—ii7, iii7, and vi7.
- The seventh chord on $\hat{5}$ is a dominant seventh (Mm7)—V7.
- The seventh chord on $\hat{7}$ is half diminished ($^{ø}7$)—vii^{ø7}.

Try it #1

A. Label each seventh chord with a Roman numeral that reflects the correct chord quality in the key.

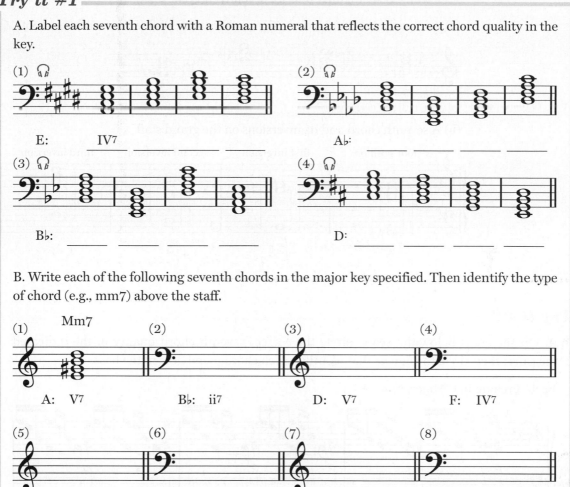

(1)

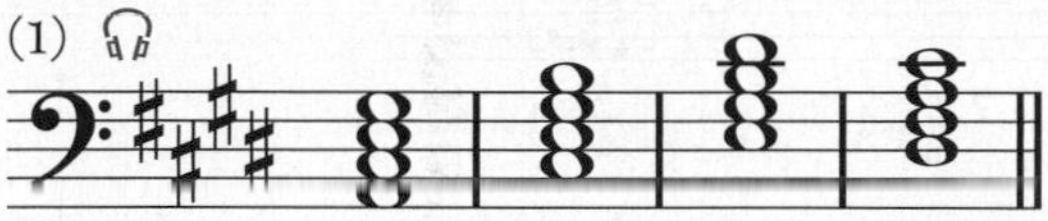

E: IV7 ______ ______ ______

(2)

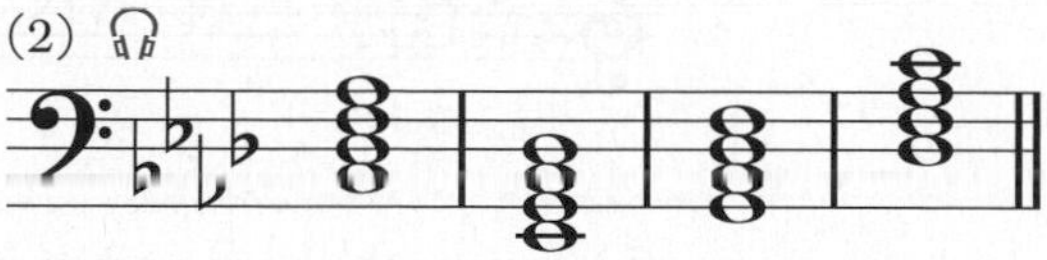

A♭: ______ ______ ______ ______

(3)

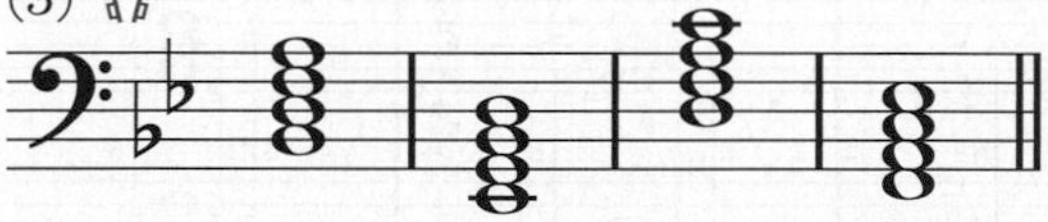

B♭: ______ ______ ______ ______

(4)

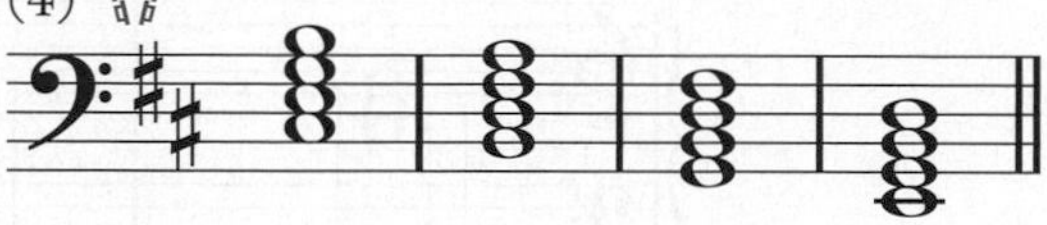

D: ______ ______ ______ ______

B. Write each of the following seventh chords in the major key specified. Then identify the type of chord (e.g., mm7) above the staff.

(1) Mm7 (2) (3) (4)

A: V7 B♭: ii7 D: V7 F: IV7

(5) (6) (7) (8)

E: V7 G: ii7 E♭: viiø7 B: I7

Seventh Chords in Inversion

Like triads, seventh chords can appear in root position or in an inversion (see Example 8.4), and like figured-bass symbols for triads, the figures are usually simplified: ^{7} for root position, $^6_5$ for first inversion, $^4_3$ for second inversion, and $^4_2$ or ^{2} for third inversion. These abbreviated figures always show the location of the second: to locate the root of an inverted seventh chord, find the upper note of the second.

EXAMPLE 8.4: Figured bass for seventh chords

(a) A seventh chord and its inversions on the treble staff (arrow marks the root)

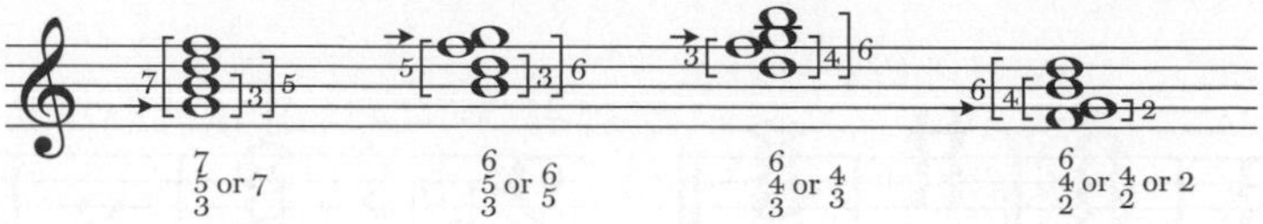

(b) A seventh chord and its inversions on the grand staff

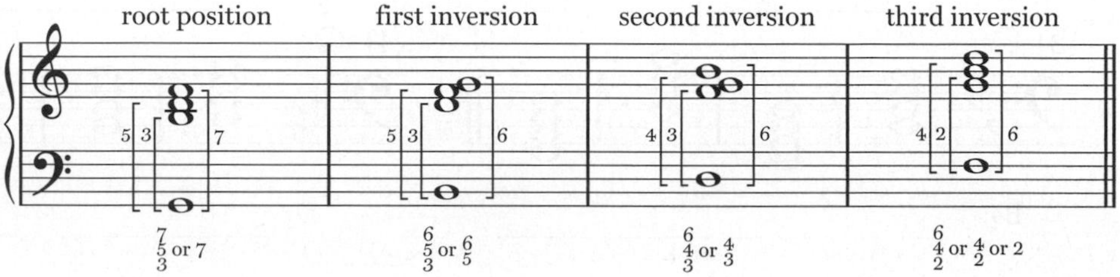

Try it #2

A. On the chart below the score, circle the correct seventh chord quality in the indicated measure; then circle the figures that identify which chord member is in the bass.

Bach, Prelude in C Major, mm. 1–6

	QUALITY				BASS AND FIGURES		
m. 2	MM7	mm7	Mm7	ø7	third $\binom{6}{5}$	fifth $\binom{4}{3}$	seventh $\binom{4}{2}$
m. 3	MM7	mm7	Mm7	ø7	third $\binom{6}{5}$	fifth $\binom{4}{3}$	seventh $\binom{4}{2}$
m. 6	MM7	mm7	Mm7	ø7	third $\binom{6}{5}$	fifth $\binom{4}{3}$	seventh $\binom{4}{2}$

B. For each key and chord specified, write the key signature and then the seventh chord in root position and inversion, as specified by the figures.

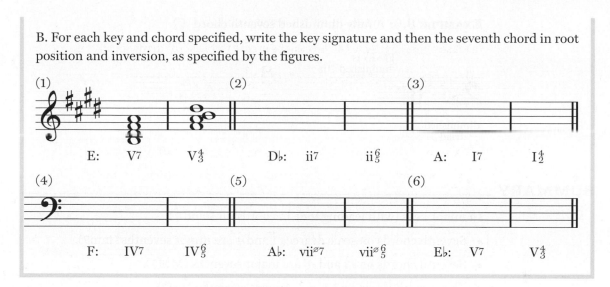

(1) (2) (3)

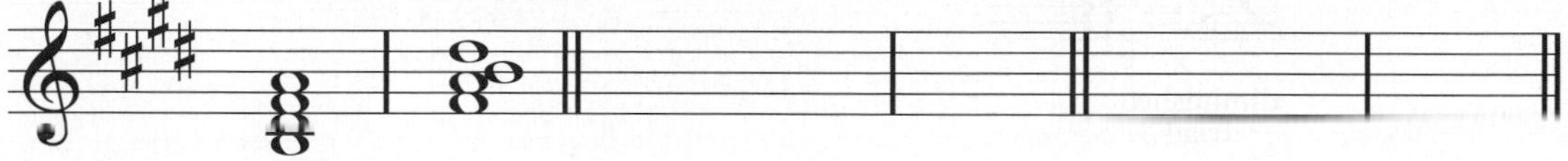

E: V7 V$^4_3$ D♭: ii7 ii$^6_5$ A: I7 I$^4_2$

(4) (5) (6)

F: IV7 IV$^6_5$ A♭: vii^{ø}7 vii$^{ø}{}^6_5$ E♭: V7 V$^4_3$

Diatonic Seventh Chords in Minor Keys

The seventh chords built from a minor scale (G minor) are given in Example 8.5. Since scale degree ♭$\hat{7}$ is typically raised in minor, the seventh chords on $\hat{5}$ and $\hat{7}$ are written here with an F♯. The seventh chord built on the leading tone thus introduces another seventh-chord type: a diminished triad plus a diminished seventh. This chord is called a **fully diminished seventh** chord, or **diminished seventh** for short, and is labeled vii°7 (see Example 8.6). In minor keys, then, both half-diminished and fully diminished sevenths are typically found: ii^{ø}7 and vii°7. Together, Examples 8.2 and 8.5 list all the commonly used diatonic seventh chords.

EXAMPLE 8.5: Seventh chords built above the G minor scale

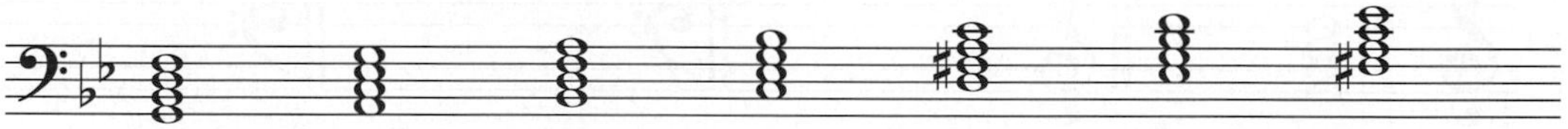

	$\hat{1}$	$\hat{2}$	$\hat{3}$	$\hat{4}$	$\hat{5}$	$\hat{6}$	$\hat{7}$
Triad quality:	m	d	M	m	M	M	d
7th quality:	m	m	M	m	m	M	d
Full name:	minor-minor 7th	diminished-minor 7th	major-major 7th	minor-minor 7th	major-minor 7th	major-major 7th	diminished-diminished 7th
Common name:	minor 7th	half-diminished 7th	major 7th	minor 7th	dominant 7th	major 7th	fully diminished 7th
Abbreviation:	mm7	ø7	MM7	mm7	Mm7	MM7	°7
Roman numeral:	i7	iiø7	III7	iv7	V7	VI7	vii°7

Example 8.6: A fully diminished seventh chord

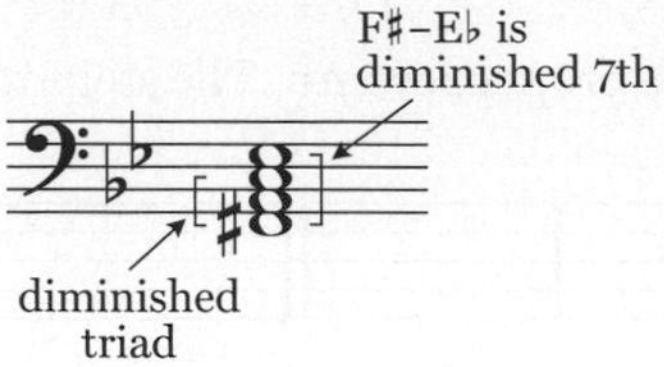

SUMMARY

In minor keys (with leading tone in chords on $\hat{5}$ and $\hat{7}$):

- Seventh chords on scale degrees $\hat{1}$ and $\hat{4}$ are minor sevenths (mm7).
- Seventh chords on $\flat\hat{3}$ and $\flat\hat{6}$ are major sevenths (MM7).
- The seventh chord on $\hat{5}$ is a dominant seventh (Mm7).
- The seventh chord on $\hat{2}$ is half diminished (ø7).
- The seventh chord on $\hat{7}$ is fully diminished (°7).

Try it #3

Spell each of the following seventh chords in the given minor key. Use the leading tone for chords on $\hat{5}$ and $\hat{7}$. Then identify the type of seventh chord above the staff.

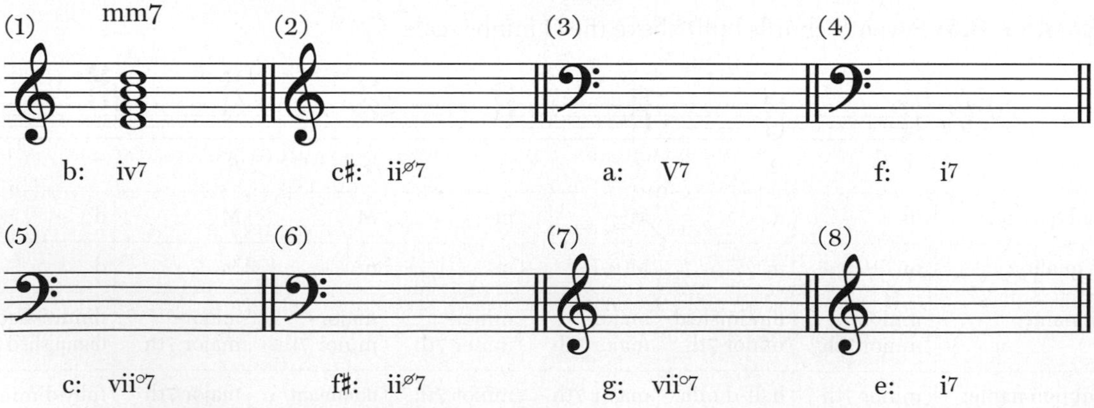

Spelling Isolated Seventh Chords

To spell a specific quality of seventh chord above a given root, first spell the correct quality triad and then add the proper seventh. The steps to spell a mm7 chord above F follow.

KEY CONCEPT To write a mm7 chord above F:

1. Spell the proper-quality triad: F-A♭-C (Example 8.7a).
2. Write the seventh by drawing a note head a third above the triad's fifth (E).
3. Check the interval quality between the root and seventh. Since F to E is a major seventh, add a flat to the E to make a minor seventh.

Example 8.7: Spelling a minor seventh chord

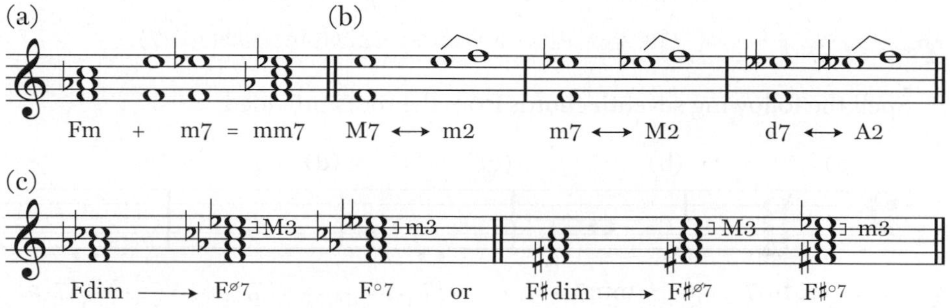

It may be easier to check the quality of the seventh by inverting the interval (part b). Imagine the root of the seventh chord up an octave, making a second. If the second is minor (half step), the seventh is major; if the second is major (whole step), the seventh is minor; if the second is augmented, the seventh is diminished.

To make a diminished seventh chord, write a diminished triad first, then add a third on top (part c): for a half-diminished seventh the third is major; for a fully diminished seventh the third is minor. In fact, all thirds in the fully diminished seventh are minor.

SUMMARY

To spell seventh chords in isolation,

(1) Write three thirds on the staff (line-line-line-line or space-space-space).

(2) Check the quality of the triad and add accidentals as needed:

- MM7 and Mm7 have major triads,
- mm7 has a minor triad,
- °7 and ø7 have diminished triads.

(3) Check the quality of the seventh and add accidentals as needed:

- MM7 has a major 7th,
- Mm7, mm7, and ø7 have a minor 7th,
- °7 has a diminished 7th.

Try it #4

Spell the following seventh chords from the roots provided.

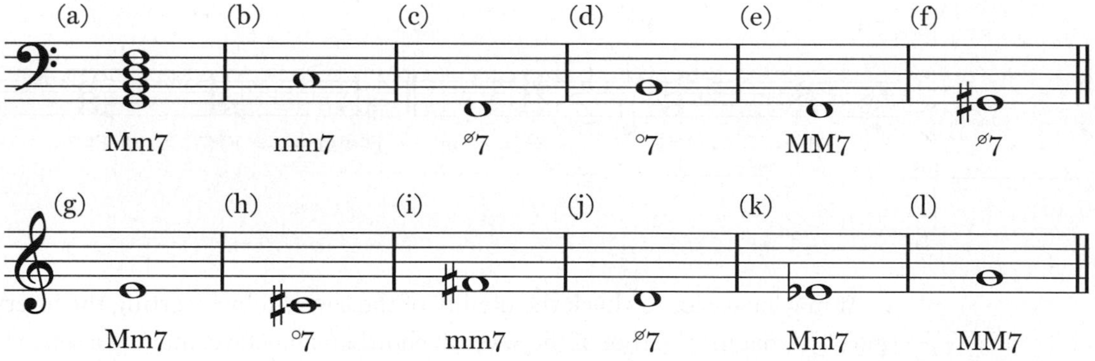

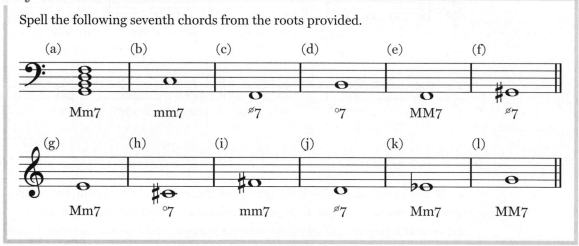

Seventh Chords in Popular Styles

If you play in studio, rock, or jazz bands, you may be familiar with another labeling system for seventh chords. This system is found in lead sheets and may be combined with guitar-chord TABs, as in Example 8.8, from "Saving All My Love for You."

As mentioned in Chapter 7, chord symbols in popular music designate a capital letter for the chord's root, and a capital letter alone indicates a major triad (for example, D). A letter name plus 7 assumes a Mm7 (dominant seventh) quality, and other seventh chord types are specified with abbreviations or other annotations.

EXAMPLE 8.8: Goffin and Masser, "Saving All My Love for You," mm. 44b–48a

The melody in this passage is harmonized almost entirely with seventh chords. The Dmaj^7 chord in measure 45 is a D major seventh (D-F♯-A-C♯); it could be labeled Dmaj^7 as here, D$^{\Delta 7}$, DM^7, or D^{+7} (the system is not completely standardized, and these symbols are used interchangeably). The next two chords are minor seventh chords built on C♯ (C♯-E-G♯-B) and B (B-D-F♯-A), labeled C♯m^7 and Bm^7. This three-chord pattern appears three times in the passage (for variety, the piano arrangement slightly changes the C♯m^7 in m. 46). The excerpt closes with D/E (a D major triad with an E in the bass), and an arrival on Amaj^7 (A-C♯-E-G♯).

Example 8.9 shows various seventh chords in C major and C minor, with some of their possible labels. Half-diminished seventh chords are often notated as minor sevenths with a ♭5.

EXAMPLE 8.9: Seventh chords in C major and C minor, with lead-sheet labels

(a) C major

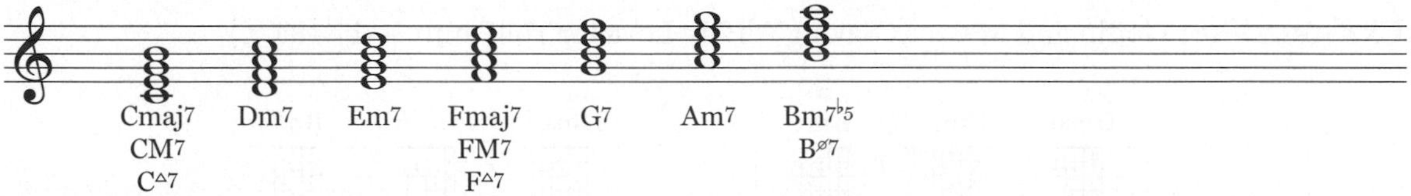

(b) C minor

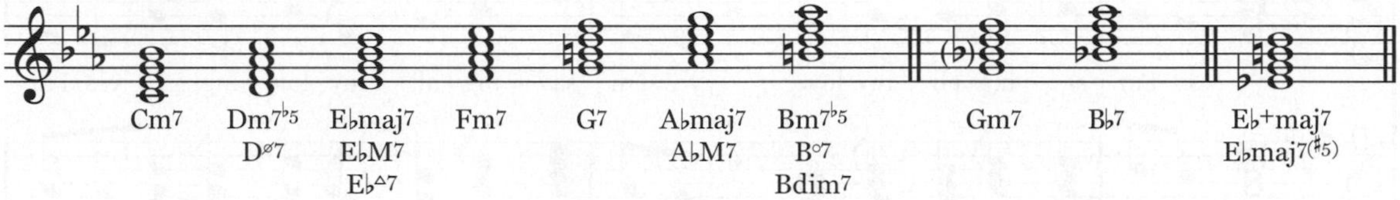

Less Common Seventh Chords

You may have noticed that Examples 8.2 and 8.5 do not exhaust *all* the possible combinations of triads and sevenths. For example, you could write an augmented triad with a major or minor seventh, or a minor triad with a major seventh. Although these seventh chords are not found in common-practice tonal music, they add harmonic richness in some styles of jazz as substitutes for diatonic seventh chords. As an illustration, listen to Example 8.10, from "When I Fall in Love." In measure 8, the B♭7 indicates a dominant seventh sonority (which sounds on beat 2, B♭-D-F-A♭), while the C7+5 in measure 10 is a seventh chord type we have not yet encountered: an augmented triad with minor seventh, C-E♮-G♯-B♭ (the G♯ is spelled A♭). The excerpt closes with an Fm7 (F-A♭-C-E♭).

EXAMPLE 8.10: Heyman and Young, "When I Fall in Love," mm. 5–11a

Try it #5

On the staves below, write the seventh chords requested. Write in all accidentals (rather than a key signature) for practice spelling these chords.

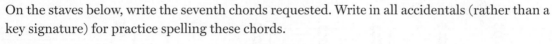

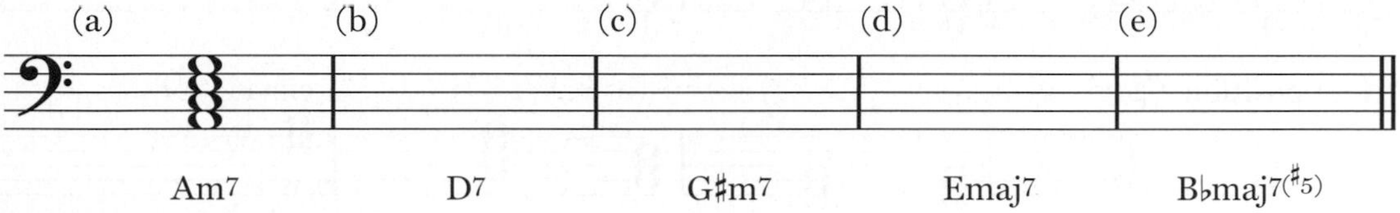

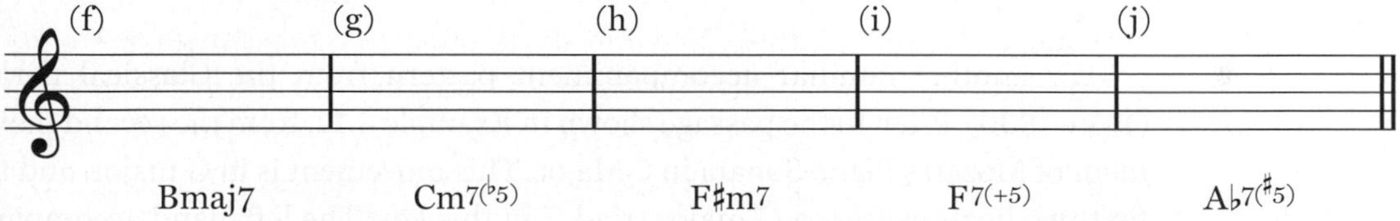

Arpeggiated Triads and Seventh Chords

In some pieces of music, all members of a chord sound at the same time. But in others, a chord may be **arpeggiated**—played one pitch at a time—as in the Bach prelude (Example 8.1) and the bass-clef part of Mozart's "Voi, che sapete," shown in Example 8.11a. (Mozart probably chose to arpeggiate the chords here because a singer onstage is pretending to accompany the aria on a guitar; the arpeggiated chords in the left hand mimic the sound of a guitar.) To analyze the left-hand chords in this B♭ major passage, first write the pitches for the whole chord in Mozart's spacing (part b) before arranging them in root position to identify the Roman numeral (part c).

In the first measure, a B♭ major triad is played one chord member at a time: B♭-D-F-B♭. In the following measure, an F major chord (V^6 in the key of B♭ major) is arpeggiated A-C-F-A. Mozart likely used a first-inversion chord here (with the A in the bass instead of the root F) to make a smooth connection between the B♭s of measures 1 and 3, instead of jumping down to the F (as in part c). The remaining chords include a ii$^6_5$ (E♭-G-B♭-C; disregard the shaded notes) and V (F-A-C).

Example 8.11: Mozart, "Voi, che sapete"

(a) Mm. 1–4

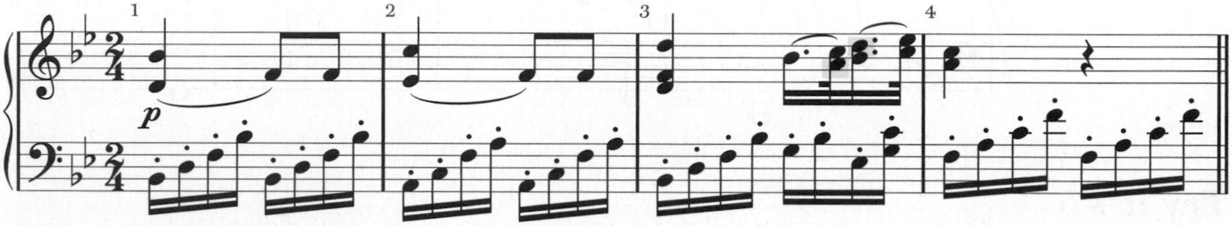

(b) Mozart's inversions

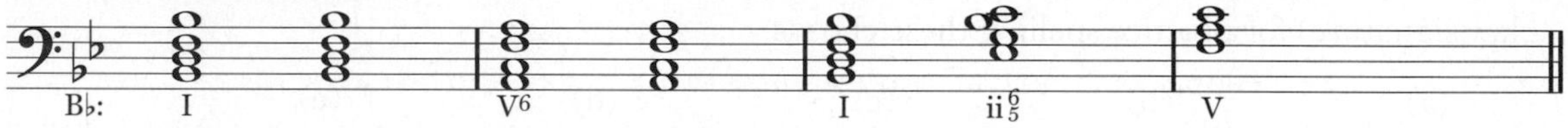

(c) Root position

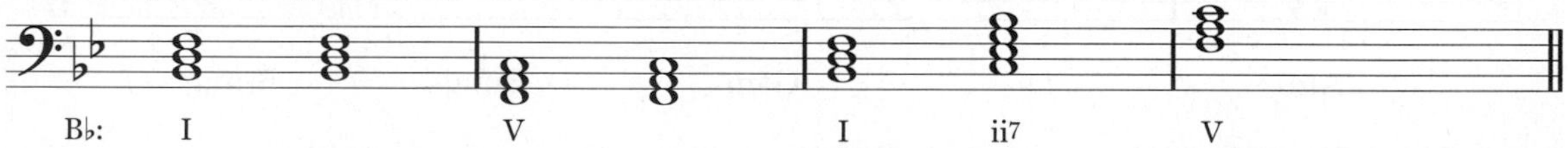

For another familiar accompaniment pattern from the Classical period (1750–1830), listen to the passage shown in Example 8.12, from the second movement of Mozart's Piano Sonata in C Major. This movement is in G major, and the first two beats express a G major triad, I in this key. The left-hand accompanimental pattern arpeggiates the harmony with a "low-up-down-up" contour that is typical of an **Alberti bass**. In this kind of pattern, the pitches at the beginning of each group of notes are typically the lowest notes of the chord (not necessarily the root) and form a bass line.

Example 8.12: Mozart, Piano Sonata in C Major, second movement, mm. 1–2

Here, the bass line is $\hat{1}$ (in a G-B-D I chord), $\hat{2}$ (in an inverted D-F♯-A-C V^4_3 chord, with the F♯ implied), and $\hat{1}$ (a return to the I chord).

The two Mozart examples represent only two of the various possible arpeggiation patterns used to set chords in tonal music; when you encounter an arpeggiated accompaniment, stack the chords in thirds to identify the root and quality.

Seventh Chords and Musical Style

The treatment of seventh chords is an important aspect of musical style. For example, only sevenths built on scale degrees $\hat{2}$, $\hat{5}$, and $\hat{7}$ appear frequently in Classical-period music; yet we find seventh chords on all scale degrees in Romantic (1830–1910), jazz, and popular styles. In some styles, the dissonant interval of a seventh must be approached and resolved down by step; in others, the seventh may be left unresolved altogether for dramatic effect, or the entire chord may simply slide up or down by step to another seventh chord. In common-practice tonal music, for example, composers typically would not end a piece with a I^7 or i^7, yet tonic chords at the end of a jazz standard *may* be embellished with an unresolved seventh. As you identify seventh chords in music you are playing, consider what type of seventh each chord is, and how the chord is connected to those around it. Later chapters on harmony and style will discuss some special uses of seventh chords.

Did You Know?

The "Alberti bass" is named for Dominico Alberti (c. 1710–1740)—an Italian singer, keyboard player, and composer—who was born in Venice and died in Rome at only thirty. Alberti was one of the first to use the left-hand arpeggiation pattern that has become associated with his name, often found accompanying a right-hand melody line in keyboard music of the Classical era. As few of Alberti's compositions are performed today, the pattern has largely become associated with keyboard works by Mozart—such as the first and second movements of the Piano Sonata in C Major, K. 545 (anthology, pp. 256, 259) and the theme of the Piano Sonata in D Major, K. 284 (p. 245).

TERMS YOU SHOULD KNOW

Alberti bass
arpeggiated chord
seventh chords
- first inversion
- second inversion
- third inversion

seventh-chord qualities
- dominant seventh (Mm7)
- fully diminished seventh ($^{\circ}7$)
- half-diminished seventh ($^{ø}7$)
- major seventh (MM7)
- minor seventh (mm7)

QUESTIONS FOR REVIEW

1. In major keys, which scale-degree seventh chords are MM7? Which are mm7? Which are Mm7? Which are $^{ø}7$ or $^{\circ}7$?
2. In minor keys (using the natural minor scale), which scale-degree seventh chords are MM7? mm7? Mm7? or $^{ø}7$ or $^{\circ}7$?
3. When the leading tone is added in minor keys, which seventh chords are usually altered? How does their quality change?
4. In the key of C minor, label each of the following sonorities three different ways—with chord quality, Roman numeral, and lead-sheet symbol: F-A♭-C-E♭, B-D-F-A♭, E♭-G-B♭-D.
5. Describe the steps you take to spell a seventh chord. How can the principle of interval inversion help?
6. What are the figures for seventh chords in each inversion?
7. How is an Alberti bass constructed?

CHAPTER 9

Connecting Intervals in Note-to-Note Counterpoint

Outline of topics

Species counterpoint

Connecting melodic intervals

Labeling harmonic intervals

- Four types of contrapuntal motion
- Consonant harmonic intervals

Writing note-to-note counterpoint in strict style

- Beginning and ending a first-species counterpoint
- Completing the middle

Overview

In this chapter, we learn how to connect melodic and harmonic intervals to make two-part note-to-note counterpoint in strict species.

Repertoire

Cantus firmi by
Johann Joseph Fux (1660–1741)
Knud Jeppesen (1892–1974)
Johann Philipp Kirnberger (1721–1783)
Heinrich Schenker (1868–1935)

Species Counterpoint

Chapters 6–8 laid the basic building blocks for tonal music: melodic and harmonic intervals, triads, and seventh chords. Here, we make the two dimensions of melody and harmony work together to form counterpoint.

KEY CONCEPT **Counterpoint** is created when two or more different melodic lines are combined so that the lines form harmonies, or when individual voices in a succession of harmonies make good melodic lines. The process of connecting harmonic and melodic intervals between triads and seventh chords is called **voice-leading**.

Composers of the eighteenth and nineteenth centuries—such as Bach, Handel, Mozart, Beethoven, and Brahms—considered counterpoint a foundation of their musical art, but the tradition of studying and writing counterpoint stretches back hundreds of years, before the tonal era, and continues as a valued component of musicians' training today. In the Baroque era (1600–1750), the **species** method of teaching counterpoint was developed: beginners would learn counterpoint in steps, beginning with the simplest style in two parts and adding complexity until they were writing in four or more parts. Like those earlier students, you will prepare to write music in four parts by learning (here and in Chapter 10) how to connect intervals in two parts.

The study of counterpoint provides a way of understanding the relationships between the underlying framework of a composition and its more elaborate musical surface. To create music, you might begin with a simple framework and add elaboration; to analyze music, you can use a knowledge of counterpoint to discover this underlying framework and see how it is embellished. While a detailed consideration of note-to-note connections may seem abstract or removed from the context of music literature, the principles involved are actually the basis of all tonal composition.

Aspiring composers and musicians traditionally begin two-voice counterpoint with a "given line"—called a **cantus firmus** (CF, or cantus, for short), a line that is not to be changed. The student then writes another voice above or below it. The simplest type of counterpoint, called **first-species** ("species" simply means "type of"), matches each note of the cantus with a note of the same duration. First-species counterpoint is also called "note-to-note," or 1:1, because both parts move at the same time to the next harmonic interval. While in traditional first-species exercises the cantus is notated in whole notes and the student provides a counterpoint in whole notes, any duration may be used to make note-to-note counterpoint as long as it is the same in both voices.

Connecting Melodic Intervals

Sing or play Example 9.1, a first-species counterpoint, to hear how each harmonic interval connects to the next. In this example, the cantus firmus is the lower part (labeled CF1), the counterpoint the upper part (CPT).

EXAMPLE 9.1: Cantus Firmus 1 (Fux, adapted) in a first-species setting

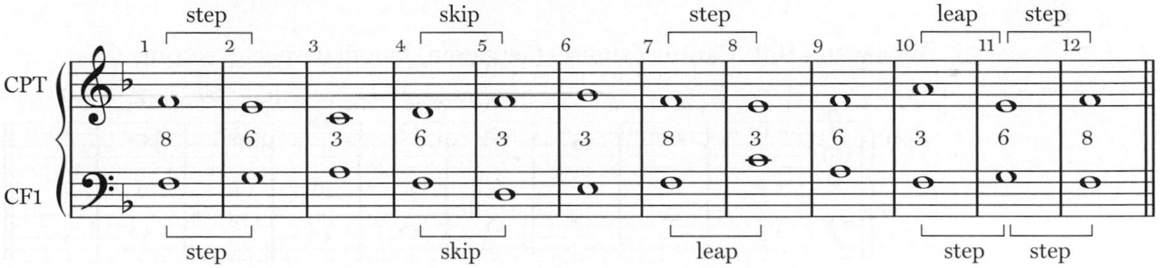

KEY CONCEPT Melodic intervals are connected by step, skip, or leap. Consider a half or whole step as a **step**, and a third as a **skip** (it "skips" between adjacent triad members). A fourth, fifth, or larger is a **leap** (it "leaps" over members of a triad).

Both upper and lower voice lines in strict counterpoint normally feature small intervals—steps and skips—as in Example 9.1. To write a good contrapuntal line in strict style, use primarily steps, with a few skips or leaps for variety. The melodic skips or leaps should be consonant: m3, M3, P4, P5, m6, M6, and P8. Dissonant melodic intervals larger than a major second, such as a m7, M7, d5, A4, or A2 (in minor), are prohibited. Aim for a line with a good shape, with one or two high or low points, and avoid repeating one or two notes excessively.

KEY CONCEPT A melodic line that moves primarily by step is **conjunct**; one that moves primarily by skip or leap is **disjunct**. Melodic lines in strict counterpoint feature mostly conjunct motion but may include a few skips or leaps (consonant intervals only).

Larger intervals create a dramatic effect and must be treated carefully. For instance, in Example 9.1 the leap from F3 to C4 in CF1 (mm. 7–8) emphasizes the climax of this melodic line.

KEY CONCEPT You may include one leap larger than a fourth in a first-species counterpont melody. Where possible, approach the leap by step in the opposite direction (for example, descending stepwise motion, then an ascending leap); after the leap, change direction and fill in the space with smaller intervals.

In CF1, for example, the leap is followed by a change of direction that fills in the leap by thirds (mm. 9–10), and in CF2 of Example 9.2, the leap in measures 1–2 is filled in by step.

EXAMPLE 9.2: Cantus firmus 2 (Jeppesen) in a first-species setting

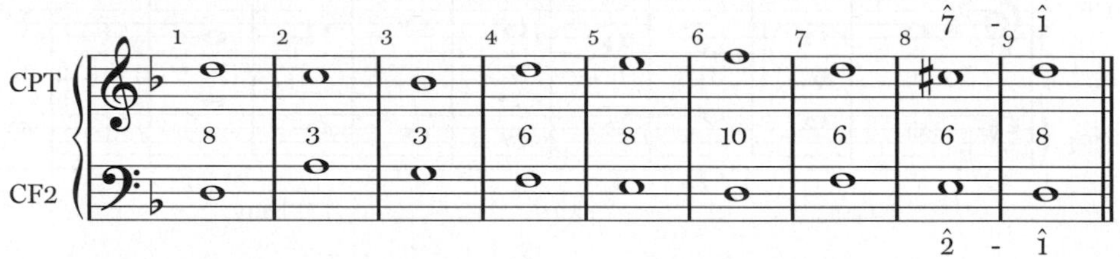

The upper line in Example 9.1 also includes a leap: the P4 in measures 10–11 from A4 down to E4. This is approached by ascending motion and followed by an ascending step (in the opposite direction of the downward leap), balancing the line and constraining its range. To preserve an overall conjunct line, avoid leaps preceded or followed by a skip in the same direction, as well as more than two skips in a row. Also avoid a mix of steps and more than one skip in the same direction.

In strict counterpoint, both the cantus and the counterpoint should begin and end on the tonic, and both voices must close with a stepwise approach to the tonic: normally $\hat{7}$–$\hat{1}$ in the counterpoint against $\hat{2}$–$\hat{1}$ in the cantus. In general, only diatonic notes of the key or mode (no accidentals) may be used in the cantus and counterpoint, with one exception at the close: in minor-mode settings like Example 9.2, raise $\flat\hat{7}$ to $\hat{7}$ in the counterpoint to create a leading tone and a firmer close. If $\flat\hat{6}$ is also present in a stepwise approach to the tonic (here, it would be B♭3), raise it as well (to $\hat{6}$, as in melodic minor), to avoid creating a melodic A2 with the leading tone. But be sure to consider the harmonic intervals that a $\flat\hat{6}$ or $\hat{6}$ would form with the cantus: neither can appear in measure 7, as each would make a dissonance with F3 in the cantus (a P4 for B♭ and an A4 for B♮, harmonic intervals not permitted in strict style; see p. 178).

If ♭$\hat{6}$ and ♭$\hat{7}$ from natural minor appear in the cantus at the approach to the close, there's the possibility of a clash between these scale degrees and the $\hat{6}$ and $\hat{7}$ (raised) in the counterpoint. This clash, called a **cross relation** (Example 9.3a), is to be avoided. (If ♭$\hat{6}$ and ♭$\hat{7}$ do not appear in the cantus, as they don't in Example 9.2, there is no potential for cross relations.) In addition, avoid following ♭$\hat{6}$ by $\hat{6}$ in the same part (part b); this makes a chromatic half step that is unacceptable in this style. A good approach to $\hat{6}$ and $\hat{7}$ is shown in part (c).

EXAMPLE 9.3: Treatment of the sixth and seventh scale degrees in minor keys

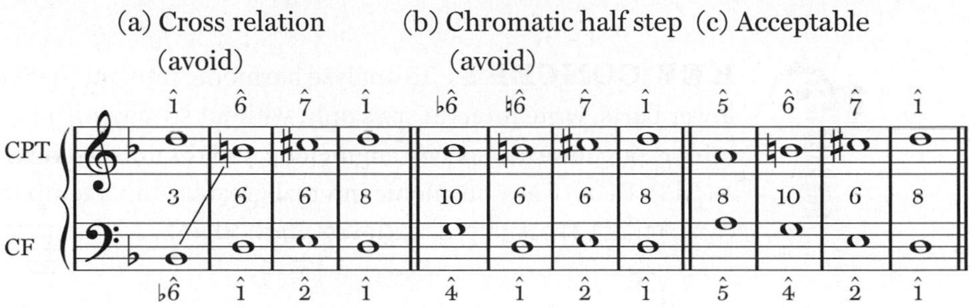

SUMMARY

Guidelines for writing a good melodic line:

- Melodic intervals larger than steps must be consonant; the intervals m7, M7, d5, A4, or A2 are prohibited.
- Create a pleasing shape, with one or two high or low points and at most one immediately repeated note; avoid too many reappearances of a single note.
- Write primarily steps and skips; normally, each line should include no more than one leap.
- Precede and follow leaps with motion in the opposite direction, stepwise where possible.
- Begin and end on $\hat{1}$, and approach $\hat{1}$ at the cadence by step.
- At the cadence in minor, raise ♭$\hat{7}$ to $\hat{7}$, but avoid a melodic A2, a cross relation, or a chromatic half step.

Connecting Harmonic Intervals

Each time you write a counterpoint exercise, label the harmonic interval sizes between the staves, as in Examples 9.1 and 9.2. Intervals larger than a tenth should get the simple rather than the compound number (4 rather than 11): in first species, the distance between the two parts is normally no larger than a tenth—the voices may occasionally move farther apart, but not for long. (Some examples in this chapter will show slightly wider spacing between the parts, to allow the cantus and counterpoint to fit on the bass and treble staves without ledger lines.)

KEY CONCEPT To analyze harmonic intervals between the upper and lower parts, write interval sizes only, without specifying perfect, major, or minor; do, however, specify augmented and diminished intervals (e.g., A4 or +4, d5). Reduce any harmonic interval greater than a tenth to within the octave (write 4, not 11). Analyze tenths as *either* 10 or 3.

Try it #1

On the example below, (1) label the harmonic intervals between the staves; (2) label any skip or leap between two melody pitches, in both parts; and (3) circle the appropriate word that describes the predominant type of motion for each part.

Cantus firmus 3 (Schenker) in a first-species setting

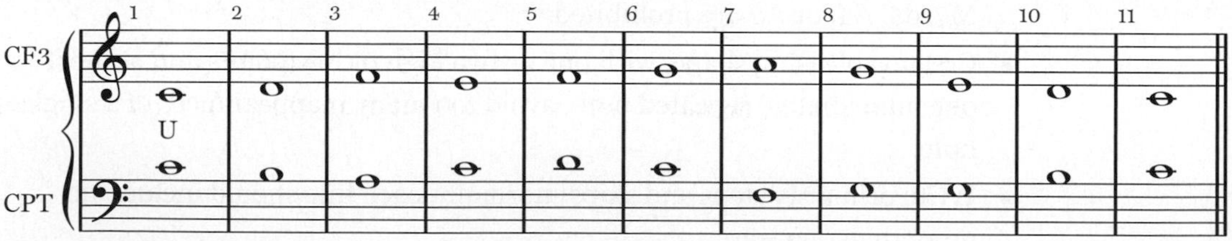

Type of melodic motion most prominent in each line:

Upper part (cantus firmus)	conjunct	disjunct
Lower part (counterpoint)	conjunct	disjunct

Four Types of Contrapuntal Motion

In writing or analyzing counterpoint, one important aspect to consider is how the voices of each harmonic interval make a linear connection with the next harmonic interval.

KEY CONCEPT There are four types of contrapuntal motion between pairs of voices.

Contrary motion (C): The two parts move in opposite directions. This is the preferred type of motion because it gives voices the most independence and balance.

Parallel motion (P): Both parts move in the same direction by the same interval; allowed between imperfect consonances, but not between perfect consonances.

Similar motion (S): Both parts move in the same direction, but not by the same interval. This type of motion may be used freely except when approaching a perfect interval, where it is acceptable only if the upper part moves by step.

Oblique motion (O): One part repeats or sustains a single pitch, the other moves by leap, skip, or step. Because oblique motion requires one part to be static, this type, though acceptable, is not as desirable.

The counterpoint from Examples 9.1 and 9.2 prominently features contrary motion; the only exceptions are parallel motion between thirds (9.1, mm. 5–6; 9.2, mm. 2–3) and sixths (9.2, mm. 7–8). Example 9.4 also features contrary motion (C) but includes parallel motion (P) twice and oblique motion (O) just before the close.

EXAMPLE 9.4: Cantus firmus 3 (Schenker) in a first-species setting

Try it #2

In the example below, write the harmonic interval numbers between the staves. Then identify the motion between these intervals as C (contrary), S (similar), O (oblique), or P (parallel) by writing the appropriate letter below the staff, between each two adjacent notes.

Cantus firmus 7 (Fux) in a first-species setting

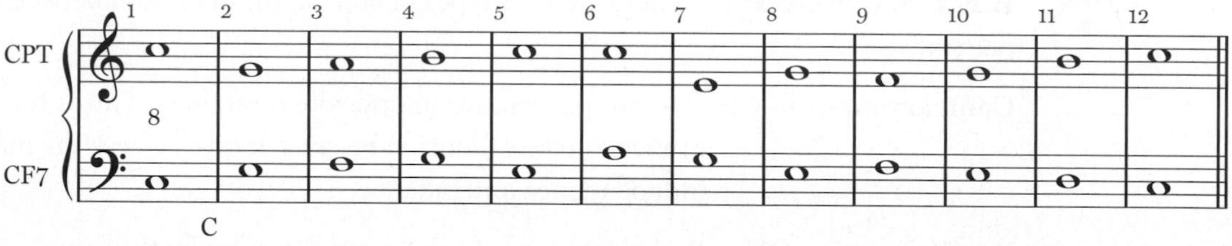

Consonant Harmonic Intervals

As discussed in Chapter 6, the consonant intervals include the PU, P5, and P8 (perfect consonances) and the M3, m3, M6, and m6 (imperfect consonances). The perfect fourth is a special case.

KEY CONCEPT The P4 is treated as a dissonance when it appears harmonically between the lowest voice and any upper voice. It is considered a consonant melodic interval, and a consonant harmonic interval between upper voices when there are three or more parts. When writing counterpoint in two parts, treat the harmonic P4 as a dissonance.

Perfect Consonances: PU, P5, P8 Of the consonant intervals, the PU is the most consonant and most stable; therefore, it appears only at the beginning or end of an exercise, as in Example 9.4, not in the middle. More frequent unisons cause two parts to sound like only one; this stops the sense of forward motion, which is undesirable except at a cadence.

The P8 is likewise very stable, and may be found at the beginning or end, but it may also occasionally be employed in the middle, since it does not have as strong a tendency to delay the forward motion. However, the P8 also sounds hollow; avoid writing it too often in a single exercise because of its open sound and relative stability.

The P5 also creates a sense of stability, but less than the P8 or PU. It implies a triad, but the quality of triad is unclear since there is no third. The P5 also has a hollow sound, and tends to stand out unless approached properly in both parts.

Because of their stability and tendency to sound open, perfect intervals must be treated carefully in contrapuntal settings.

KEY CONCEPT Moving from one perfect interval to another of the same size is prohibited in this style. If the motion is in the same direction, it results in **parallel octaves** (P8–P8; Example 9.5a), **parallel fifths** (P5–P5; part b), or **parallel unisons** (PU–PU). Contrary motion between two perfect intervals of the *same size* is likewise not acceptable (known as parallel octaves or fifths by contrary motion, or contrary octaves or fifths; parts c–d).

EXAMPLE 9.5: Hidden (or direct) octaves and fifths

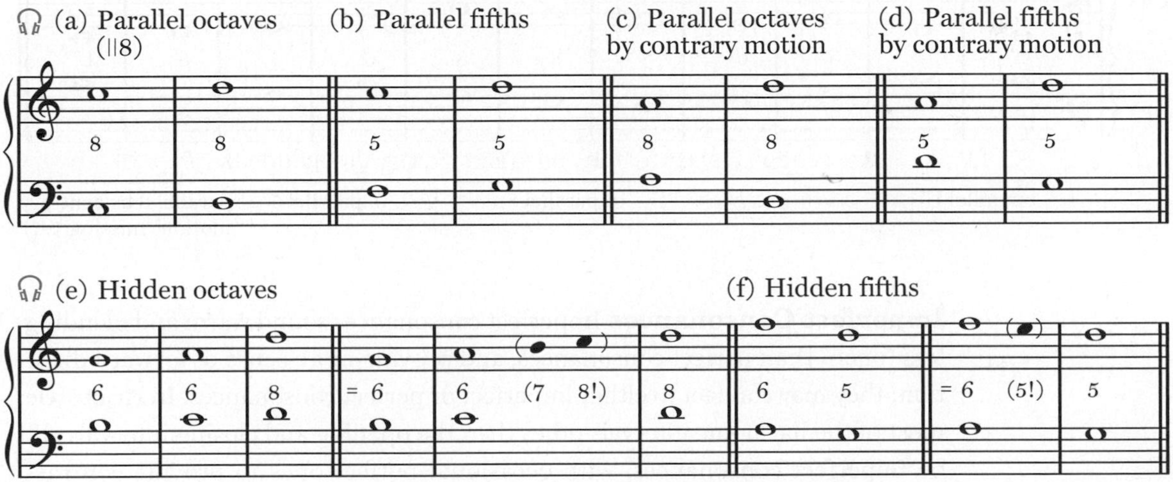

A perfect harmonic interval is normally approached by contrary motion. Often the upper voice will lead into a perfect interval by step, while the lower part may step or skip. Leaps in one or both parts into a perfect interval are not recommended, as they make the interval stand out and sound distinctively hollow. Also avoid approaches to perfect intervals by similar motion, because the motion implies parallel fifths or octaves, as illustrated in Example 9.5e–f (an approach called "hidden" fifths or octaves, sometimes "direct" fifths or octaves). When the lower part steps into the octave, as shown, the leap in similar motion in the upper part makes the P8 sound harsh because of the implied parallels. Only when the upper voice moves by step is similar motion to a perfect interval acceptable.

Example 9.6—not a model counterpoint!—illustrates several problems at once: it begins with parallel unisons, followed by a leap in the counterpoint of a P4 (m. 3) that is not balanced by contrary motion after the leap, which leads to two sets of parallel octaves (mm. 5–7). The motion from 8 to 5 (mm. 7–8) then sounds harsh, with a perfect consonance moving to another perfect consonance—even though the upper part is by step and the lower is in contrary motion. That P5 is followed by another P5, creating parallel fifths. Then the octave in measure 10 is approached from a P5 in similar motion, making hidden octaves. Finally, the close is approached by the leap of a seventh in the counterpoint—creating parallel octaves by contrary motion (8–8 *or* 8–U)—and the required formula of setting $\hat{2}$–$\hat{1}$ of the cantus with $\hat{7}$–$\hat{1}$ at the close is not followed. In this setting, nine of eleven cantus notes are set with perfect intervals—resulting in a very unsatisfying counterpoint.

EXAMPLE 9.6: Cantus firmus 3 (Schenker) in a poor first-species setting

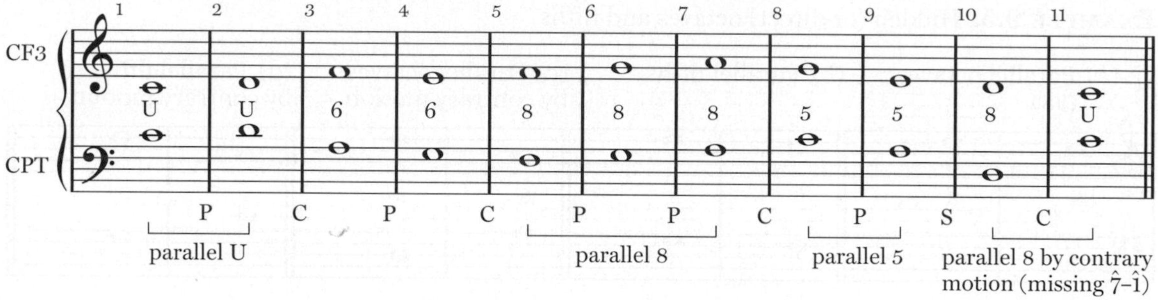

Imperfect Consonances Imperfect consonances sound warm and blending, less "open" than perfect consonances, and provide more sense of forward direction; they may connect to either imperfect or perfect consonances. In strict style, most of the harmonic intervals other than the opening and closing intervals will be imperfect consonances, with occasional perfect ones to provide contrast. Although imperfect consonances may connect to a same-size interval, making parallel thirds or sixths, such a progression should be limited to three in a row to avoid monotony and a loss of independent lines.

Now compare Example 9.7, a better setting of CF3, with Example 9.6.

EXAMPLE 9.7: Cantus firmus 3 (Schenker) in a better first-species setting

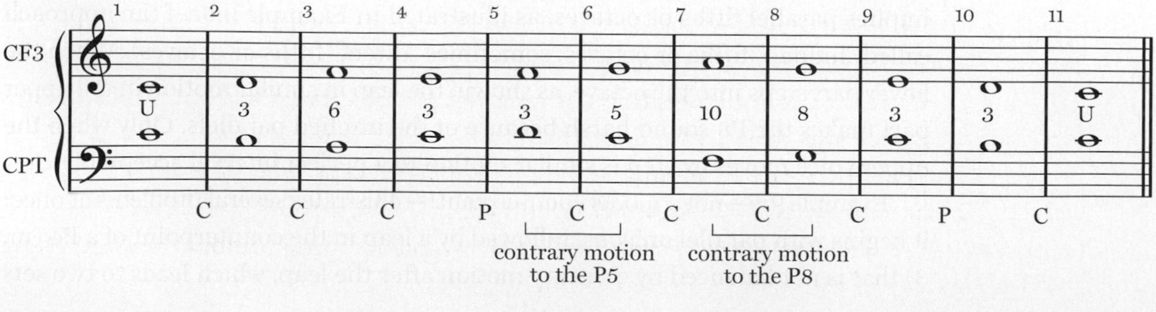

This setting features primarily contrary motion, where seven of the eleven intervals are imperfect consonances and four are perfect. The perfect consonances in measures 6 and 8 are approached and left carefully to blend gracefully into the counterpoint: they are approached by step in both voices with contrary motion. Still, although this setting is strong overall, the repetition of C4 in the counterpoint (five of the eleven notes) is a weakness.

Yet another setting of CF3 in Example 9.8 gives the same opening intervals, but sets pitches 5 to 7 of the cantus with stepwise contrary motion. This type of motion has a special name, **voice exchange**: the pitch classes F–G–A in the upper voice exchange positions with A–G–F in the lower voice. Such an intervallic pattern (6–8–10) and melodic voice exchange, characteristic in this style, are highly desirable.

Example 9.8: Cantus firmus 3 (Schenker) in another first-species setting

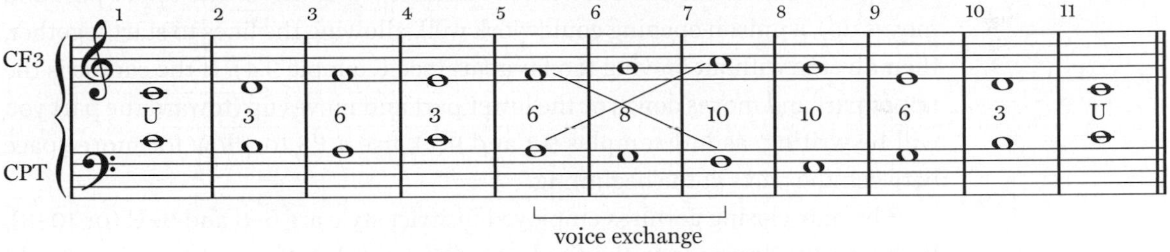

Completing a counterpoint for a cantus firmus is a process of trade-offs: choices that make an excellent setting for some portion may create challenges in others, and most good settings will include some element that could be criticized. First-species settings should follow the most essential guidelines—write the proper opening and closing gestures, watch out for parallel fifths and octaves, stick to consonant harmonic intervals, avoid dissonant melodic intervals larger than a step—but other guidelines are ideals rather than absolutes. Part of the learning process in writing counterpoint is trying out different combinations to hear their effect, while striving for a technically perfect setting.

There are two small imperfections, for instance, in Example 9.8: the counterpoint skips from A3 to C4 and back in measures 3–5, which could be considered repetitive; and while the descent to E3 after the voice exchange (m. 8) is a strong point, it necessitates two skips followed by a step to reach the cadence at the end. For alternative treatments of this same cantus, look back at Example 9.4 and *Try it #1*. Though both overall are good settings, a weakness of Example 9.4 is the contour: essentially down then up, with no other changes of direction. *Try it #1* includes a little segment C4–D4–C4 (mm. 4–6) separated by a skip on one side and a leap on the other, which breaks up the line into three distinct sections (mm. 1–3, 4–6, 7–11); the strongest lines will exhibit a flowing contour from beginning to end without any discrete segments.

Writing Note-to-Note Counterpoint in Strict Style

Beginning and Ending a First-Species Counterpoint

As a first step in writing a complete counterpoint to a given cantus firmus, set a PU or P8 against the first note of the cantus. A P5 is possible, but only if the cantus is the lower part (scale degree $\hat{1}$ should always be in the bass). To decide which opening interval to use, examine the contour of the given line, and choose the starting interval that will allow your counterpoint to stay within a tenth of the cantus, while leaving space for the lines to flow without colliding or crossing. For example, if the cantus is the lower part and moves down (or the upper part and moves up), a unison opening could work well, allowing the lines to start together, then diverge without moving too far apart (see Example 9.4). If the cantus is the upper part and moves down, or the lower part and moves up (toward the part you will be writing, as in Examples 9.1 and 9.2), use a P8 to allow for more space between the parts at the beginning.

The only closing gestures employed in strict style are 6–8 and 3–U (or 10–8). If the cantus descends to the final note (as most do), the counterpoint should ascend, with the two parts moving in contrary motion. As mentioned previously, if the cantus implies scale degrees $\hat{2}$–$\hat{1}$ in a minor mode (normally Aeolian or Dorian), ♭$\hat{7}$ in the counterpoint line should be raised to make the leading tone. And if the leading tone is preceded by ♭$\hat{6}$, then both ♭$\hat{6}$ and ♭$\hat{7}$ may be raised, as in melodic minor. These scale-degree alterations, used only at the close, should not create cross relations or chromatic half steps.

Completing the Middle

After selecting the opening and closing intervals for the counterpoint, sing through the cantus again to consider the middle—this portion will need some planning to achieve an appealing result. Take a close look at the shape of the given line: Where are the steps and skips? Is there a leap? The contour of a successful counterpoint will complement the cantus and provide contrary motion where possible.

KEY CONCEPT Set intervals as follows:

CANTUS	COUNTERPOINT
Leap	Set with a step, in contrary motion.
Steps	Can incorporate a skip or leap.
Skip	Set with either a step (preferred) or a skip.

Simultaneous skips that exchange pitch classes (e.g., an ascending E–G in the cantus, a descending G–E in the counterpoint) normally sound good as long as there are steps around them. Also, consider the overall shape of the contrapuntal line you are writing. If you use oblique motion, limit it to one or two (longer CFs only) instances, no more than one of which involves the tonic.

Try for a mix of perfect and imperfect harmonic consonances, with more imperfect consonances than perfect. At least one P5 or P8 should appear somewhere in the middle. Because perfect intervals are best approached and left by contrary motion, one typical interval sequence is 6–8–10 (or 10–8–6), making a voice exchange (as in Example 9.8). Other possible approaches to P8 and P5 are shown in Example 9.7. Remember to always approach perfect intervals by step in the upper voice, and avoid a leap into a perfect interval in either voice, even if by contrary motion. Don't write two perfect harmonic intervals in a row, even if the melodic connections are smooth.

As you complete your counterpoint, be sure that the lines generally stay within a tenth of each other and do not cross. This particular problem, **crossed voices**, can bc sccn in Example 9.9a, beat 2, where the lower voice on E4 is positioned above the upper voice's C4. (Also avoid the opposite situation, where the upper voice crosses below the lower.) In part (b), the violation of range occurs between two adjacent beats, known as **overlapping**: on beat 2, the E2 in the lower voice is higher than the beat 1 D2 of the upper voice. Similarly, in part (c), the lower voice on beat 1 is higher than the upper voice on beat 2.

Crossed or overlapping voices often appear in combination with other errors, such as the unison in part (a), or inappropriate leaps in parts (b) and (c). Also remember to avoid any melodic or harmonic dissonances (watch out for the harmonic P4!) or accidentals in the middle of the counterpoint (add an accidental only at the cadence in minor).

Example 9.9: Crossed voices and overlapping

(a) Crossed voices (b) Overlapping (c) Overlapping

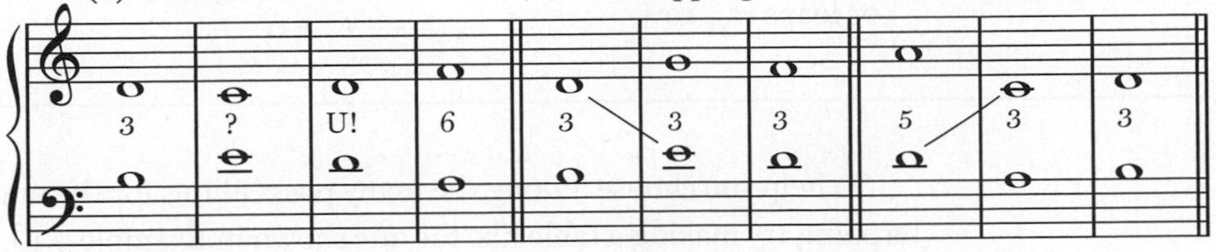

SUMMARY

Guidelines for writing first-species counterpoint:

- For the opening harmonic interval, write P8, PU, or P5 (the latter only with the cantus in the lower voice).
- For the closing harmonic intervals, write 6–8 or 3–U (10–8). In minor, raise $\flat\hat{7}$, and raise $\flat\hat{6}$ if it precedes $\hat{7}$ (to avoid an A2); but don't use $\hat{6}$ if it creates a cross relation.
- Write mostly contrary motion between the parts.
- Avoid parallel octaves or fifths (by parallel *or* contrary motion).
- Approach perfect intervals by contrary motion, or in similar motion with a stepwise upper voice.
- Don't write more than three parallel imperfect consonances (3 or 6) in a row.
- Include a mix of perfect and imperfect consonances, with more imperfect consonances than perfect.
- Avoid dissonant harmonic intervals (including P4) and accidentals other than at the cadence.
- Avoid dissonant melodic intervals (e.g., leaps of m7, M7, d5, A4, or A2 in minor).
- Write leaps sparingly, approach and leave them by step in contrary motion if possible, and set with a step in the other part (preferably in contrary motion to the leap). Don't set a leap in one voice against a leap in the other.
- Give your melodic line an interesting contour; it should not be static, repeating notes or circling around one note. Keep the ranges of the lines distinct: don't overlap or cross voices.
- Aim for primarily stepwise motion, with no more than two melodic skips or leaps in a row.

To help you choose among the many possibilities for the middle of your counterpoint, try making a table like the one shown in Example 9.10. Fill in the bottom row with the cantus letter names to show the octave-related notes. The first column at the left gives the permissible intervals 8, 3, 5, and 6. In the remaining boxes, write the note names that correspond to thirds, fifths, and sixths above each cantus note. If the cantus is the upper line, write the octave-related notes in the top row, then (top to bottom) 3, 5, and 6.

EXAMPLE 9.10: Cantus firmus 2 (Jeppesen) in a first-species setting

6	B♭	F	E	D	C	B♭	D	C♯ (LT)	B♭
5	A	E						B♭ (d5!)	A
3	F	C						G	F
8	D	A	G	F	E	D	F	E	D

Here, the shaded notes should not be used, such as the dissonant d5 and notes that do not participate in the $\hat{7}$–$\hat{1}$ motion into the cadence. Further, since the first note D3 should be set with an octave, all choices but the D have been shaded. Because this is a minor-mode cantus, the C♯ has been selected to approach the cadence on D. You may eliminate other potential intervals as you make selections, by marking any that would create parallel octaves or fifths (such as A in the second box). For the middle portion, it is essential to consider the possibilities for several notes at a time to achieve a proper balance between the cantus and counterpoint. Don't change the cantus, no matter how tempting it is to correct problems that way!

Try it #3

Complete the table and counterpoint in Example 9.10. Include at least one perfect interval in the middle of the setting. Write the harmonic interval numbers between the staves.

Since the cantus may be either the upper or lower part in strict species settings, this feature creates the possibility for **invertible counterpoint**. Invertible counterpoint is structured intervallically so that the two lines may be reversed in register (e.g., the upper counterpoint may be transposed to sound below the cantus). Example 9.11 gives an inversion of Example 9.4 (where the cantus was the upper part).

EXAMPLE 9.11: Cantus firmus 3 (Schenker) in invertible counterpoint

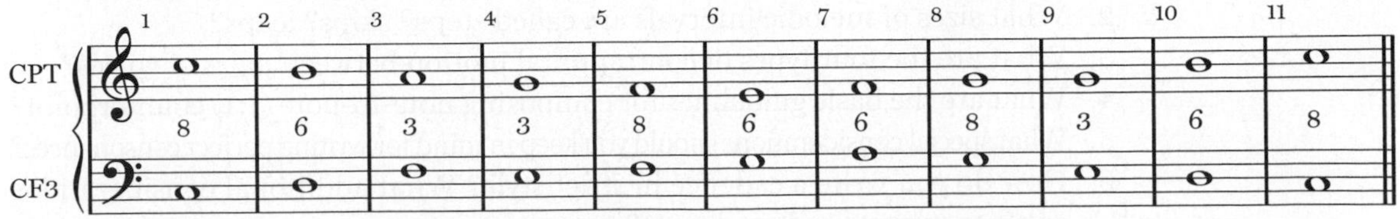

While in Example 9.4 the intervals were U–3–6–6–8–3–3–8–6–3–U, now they are 8–6–3–3–8–6–6–8–3–6–8 (recall that inverted intervals sum to 9; a P5, however, may not be used in invertible counterpoint, as the inversion is a P4). In the eighteenth century, counterpoint exercises were often written with the cantus notated in the middle stave of three, with a counterpoint above and below, which made it easy to explore inversion of the lines. In the same era, invertible counterpoint became a key element of inventions and fugues (Chapter 31).

Did You Know?

The word "counterpoint" appears in several anonymous music treatises from about 1300, although the term itself was in use much earlier. The "punctus," or point, referred to a written musical note that later became the breve (analogous to the whole note). The practice of counterpoint as a compositional technique, however, predates the term—the earliest written account is an anonymous treatise called *Musica enchiriadis* (from around A.D. 900). This textbook for musicians describes adding counterpoint to a preexisting cantus firmus by doubling the melody at a fifth to make two parts, then doubling each of those parts at the octave to get four—a practice also known as organum. Note-against-note (punctus to punctus) counterpoint gave way to florid organum, with many notes to one of the slow-moving cantus, in the twelfth century, at about the time the term "counterpoint" was coming into common use. Counterpoint was the primary compositional technique in the late Middle Ages (c. 900–1430) and Renaissance (1430–1600), and its fundamental principles remain the foundation of tonal practice up to the present day.

TERMS YOU SHOULD KNOW

- cantus firmus (or cantus)
- conjunct
- consonant
- contrary motion
- counterpoint
- cross relation
- crossed voices
- overlapping voices
- disjunct
- first species
- hidden fifths
- hidden octaves
- invertible counterpoint
- leap
- note-to-note (1:1)
- oblique motion
- overlapping voices
- parallel motion
  - parallel fifths
  - parallel octaves
- similar motion
- skip
- species
- step
- voice crossing
- voice exchange

QUESTIONS FOR REVIEW

1. Why is it important to learn counterpoint?
2. What sizes of melodic intervals are called steps? skips? leaps?
3. What are the four types of contrapuntal motion between pairs of voices?
4. What are the basic guidelines for composing note-to-note (1:1) counterpoint?
5. What special considerations should you keep in mind for writing perfect consonances?
6. How do you write a cadence in strict style? What additional considerations apply to minor-mode cadences?

CHAPTER 10

Melodic and Rhythmic Embellishment in Two-Voice Composition

Outline of topics

Melodic embellishment in second-species counterpoint
- Passing tones
- Consonant skips
- Neighbor tones

Writing 2:1 counterpoint
- Opening and closing patterns
- Melodic considerations
- Harmonic considerations

About third-species counterpoint

Rhythmic displacement in fourth-species counterpoint
- Types of suspensions
- Chains of suspensions

Writing fourth-species counterpoint

Fifth species and free counterpoint

Overview

In this chapter, we embellish two-voice note-to-note counterpoint with passing tones, neighbor tones, consonant skips, and suspensions in strict second- and fourth-species style. We also consider the embellishment types featured in the two remaining species, third and fifth.

Repertoire

Second-, third-, fourth-, and fifth-species settings of cantus firmi by Johann Joseph Fux, Johann Philippe Kirnberger, and Heinrich Schenker

Melodic Embellishment in Second-Species Counterpoint

Play or listen to the second-species counterpoint shown in Example 10.1 to consider the placement of consonances and dissonances.

EXAMPLE 10.1: Cantus firmus 4 (Fux) in a second-species setting

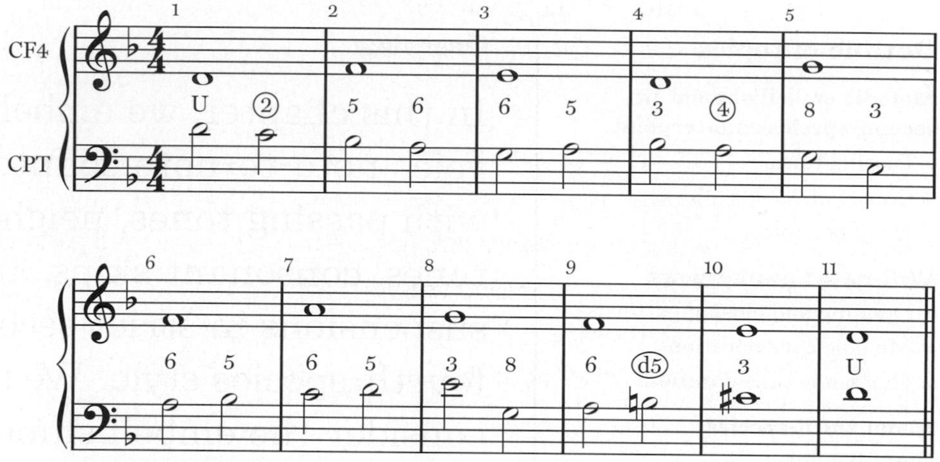

KEY CONCEPT In **second-species** (2:1) counterpoint, for each note of the cantus there are two notes in the counterpoint—one heard at the same time as the cantus note, and one that enters while the cantus note is still sounding. In strict style, the counterpoint is written as two half notes against each whole note in the cantus.

Second species introduces the concept of **metrical accent**, since the two half notes in a measure do not carry the same "weight," or emphasis: the first half note ("on the beat") is accented and the second (the "offbeat") unaccented. You can consider the metric context in two ways: as having only one beat, divided into two, or having two beats (a downbeat and an upbeat). In either case, the first half note in the measure is accented and the second unaccented. The unaccented notes are sometimes called **diminutions** because they divide the duration of the original first-species framework in half.

Second species also introduces the dissonant harmonic intervals 2, 4, A4, d5, 7, and 9.

KEY CONCEPT A dissonant harmonic interval in second-species counterpoint must fall on the unaccented second half of the measure; it is approached by step from a consonant harmonic interval (the "preparation") on the downbeat and must connect by step to a consonant harmonic interval on the following downbeat (the "resolution"). A **resolution** is motion from a dissonance to a consonance according to compositional guidelines in a particular style.

It is also possible to set two consonances against a cantus note, either by skip or leap (see Example 10.1, mm. 5 and 8) or by using 5–6 or 6–5 intervals in stepwise motion (mm. 2, 3, 6, and 7). Within each measure, the second half note's entry creates oblique motion; connections over the bar line will feature contrary, parallel, or similar motion.

SUMMARY

Second species introduces the following concepts:

- a metrical context through accented and unaccented positions in the measure;
- dissonance created by the intervals 2, 4, A4, d5, 7, and 9 in unaccented positions;
- consonant skips or leaps, and steps (5–6, 6–5).

Passing Tones

The most common type of melodically generated dissonance in 2:1 counterpoint is the passing tone.

KEY CONCEPT A **passing tone** (labeled P) is a melodic embellishment that fills in a skip by stepwise motion; it is approached by step and left by step in the same direction. Passing tones introduce the harmonic dissonances of 2, 4, and 7 on the unaccented part of the measure.

Example 10.2 includes three passing tones, in measures 2, 4, and 7, while Example 10.1 features them in measures 1 and 4. The dissonant intervals A4 (resolves to 6) and d5 (resolves to 3) may be used as passing tones only if followed by the indicated interval of resolution, as in measures 9–10 of Example 10.1. Consonant passing tones with the intervals 5–6 or 6–5 are also possible (as in mm. 2, 3, 6, and 7 of Example 10.1), but because embellishing tones are analyzed mostly to examine the treatment of dissonant intervals, consonant passing tones are usually not labeled.

EXAMPLE 10.2: Cantus firmus 5 (Kirnberger) in a second-species setting

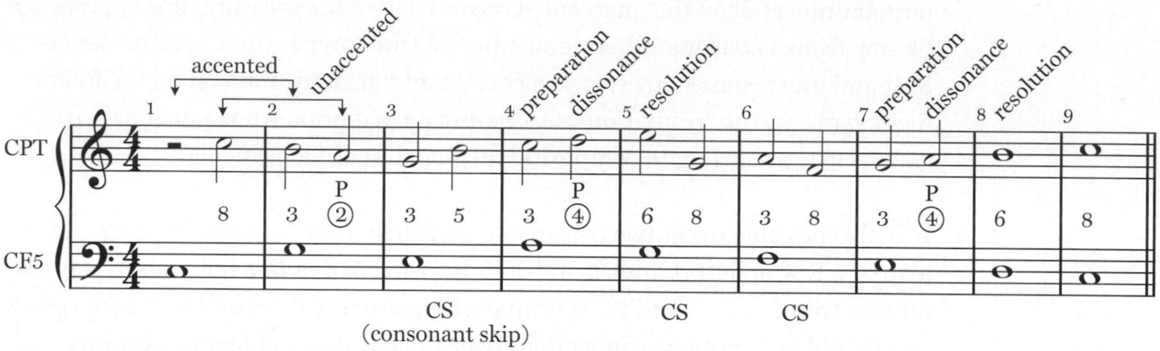

Consonant Skips

A second melodic gesture introduced in second species is the consonant skip, seen in measures 3, 5, and 6 of Example 10.2.

KEY CONCEPT **Consonant skips** (CS) or **leaps** are melodic embellishments made when both half notes of the skip or leap form a consonant harmonic interval with the cantus.

Consonant skips add melodic interest to the counterpoint by providing a contrast to the stepwise motion of passing tones. They are sometimes referred to as "chordal skips," even though the melodic intervals traversed may be a skip *or* a leap and the notes may not imply chords.

Consonant skips and leaps are employed with passing tones to provide a mix of consonant and dissonant harmonic intervals, to balance the steps, skips, and leaps provided by the cantus, and to make a pleasing shape for the contrapuntal line. But avoid using too many passing tones or consonant skips in a row, or the line will be too conjunct (P) or disjunct (CS) and therefore lacking in variety.

Neighbor Tones

A third melodic embellishment introduced in second species is the neighbor tone (Example 10.3.)

KEY CONCEPT A **neighbor tone** (N) is a melodic embellishment on an unaccented part of a measure that decorates a melody note by stepping to the note above or below it, then returning to the original note. Neighbor tones therefore are approached (prepared) and left (resolved) by step, in opposite directions.

A neighbor tone written above the melody pitch is called an **upper neighbor** (UN), while a neighbor tone below is called a **lower neighbor** (LN).

Neighbor tones temporarily displace the pitch they decorate, and may form consonant or dissonant intervals with the cantus. A consonant lower neighbor tone (LN) is shown in Example 10.3, measure 5, with dissonant neighbor tones in measures 4 (UN) and 10 (LN). Some teachers of counterpoint restrict the use of neighbor tones in second species to consonant neighbors, while others also allow dissonant ones when they help to improve the shape of the counterpoint line.

EXAMPLE 10.3: Cantus firmus 6 (Kirnberger) in a second-species setting

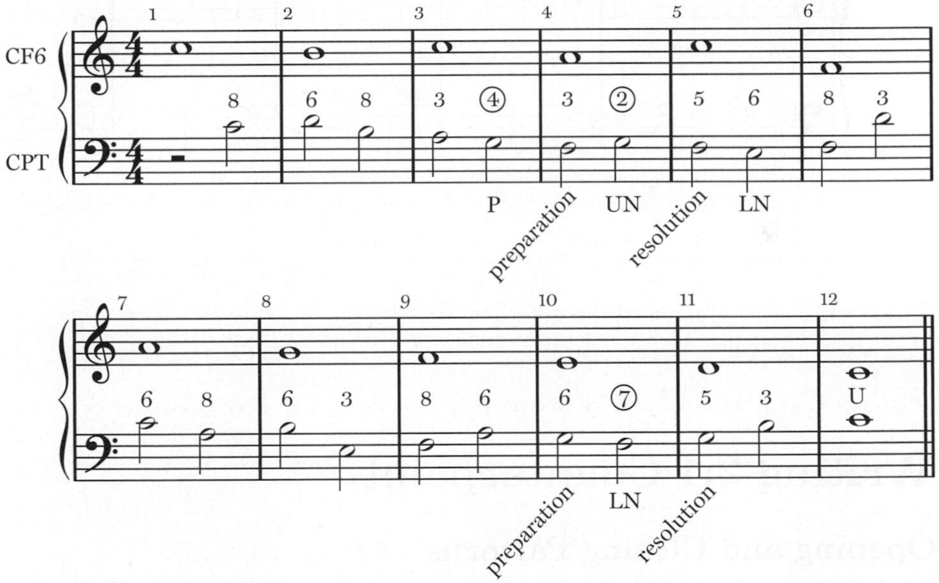

Neighbor tones are used sparingly in second-species counterpoint, and their placement in the line requires careful consideration. Because they return to the same note they left, too many will make a line static, staying on the same few pitches for too long—as happens in measures 3–6 of Example 10.3.

Try it #1

Analyze the harmonic intervals of the counterpoint below by writing the interval numbers between the staves and circling the ones that are dissonances. Locate and label one additional passing tone (P), two consonant passing tones, two neighbor tones (N), and four consonant skips or leaps (CS).

Cantus firmus 4 (Fux) in a second-species setting

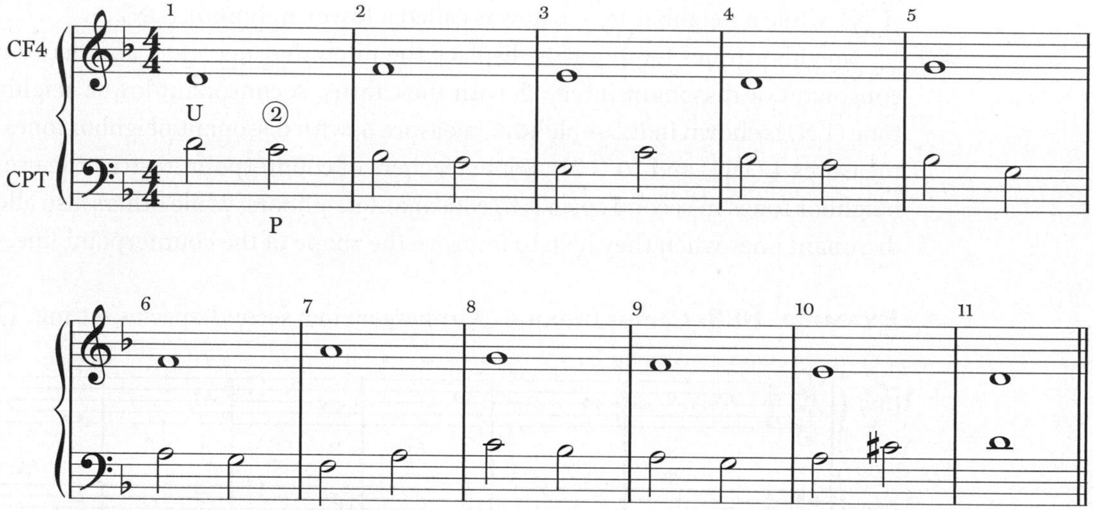

Writing 2:1 Counterpoint

Opening and Closing Patterns

To write second-species counterpoint, follow the same general procedures as in first species: compose the opening and closing measures first to ensure that they make good harmonic and contrapuntal sense, then fill in the middle section. As in first species, the opening harmonic interval in second species must be a P8 or PU (or P5 if the counterpoint is in the upper part). Rhythmically, the first note of the counterpoint may appear on the downbeat (Example 10.1), followed by another half note, or on the offbeat, preceded by a half rest (Examples 10.2 and 10.3). Starting with the half-measure rest is preferred, to allow the voices more independence.

As in first species, the final note of the counterpoint is a whole note PU or P8, and the penultimate measure may be filled with either two half notes or a whole note (see Example 10.4). In parts (a) to (c), the 3–8 or 6–8 closing gesture begins on the second half note of the penultimate measure, preceded by a 5. If the penultimate measure is a whole note, as in (d) and (e), the exercise ends as in first species. In minor, raise both the sixth and seventh scale degrees as you approach $\hat{1}$. If the leading tone is preceded by the raised $\flat\hat{6}$ in the third measure from the close, as in (d) and (e), treat the A4 or d5 as a dissonant passing tone in the last half of the measure.

EXAMPLE 10.4: Closing patterns in second species

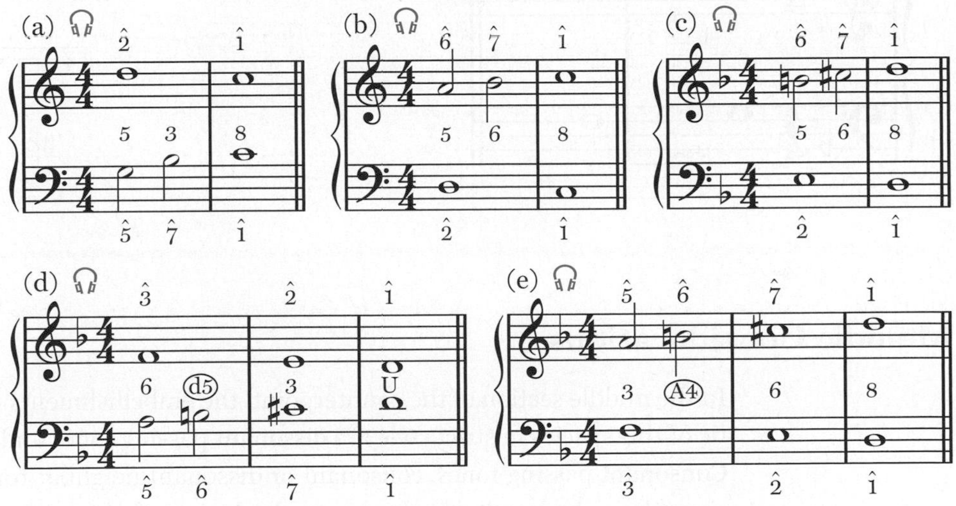

KEY CONCEPT Other than the first measure (which may begin with a rest) and the closing one or two measures, second-species counterpoint will feature two half notes per measure. Pitches may not be immediately repeated, whether within a measure or over a bar line.

Try it #2

Write a counterpoint for the following closing patterns. Use 2:1 motion in the first measure of each, and whole notes in the other measures. Label scale degrees and harmonic intervals.

(a)

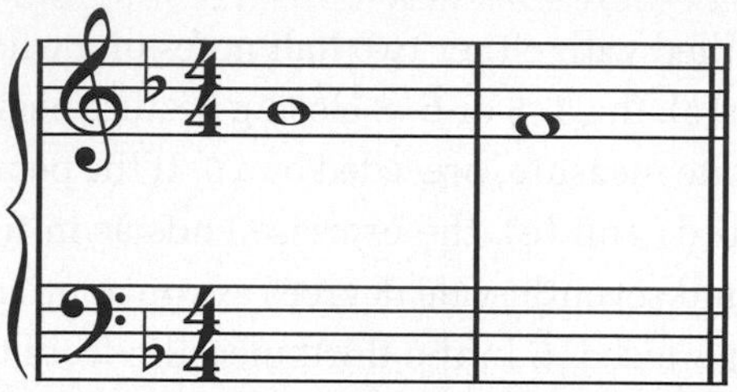

(b)

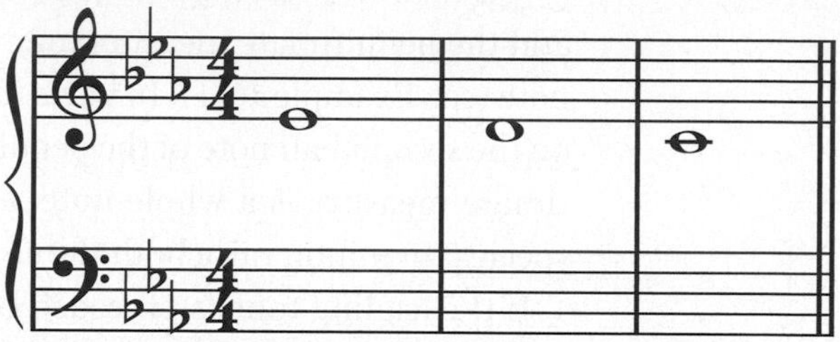

(c)

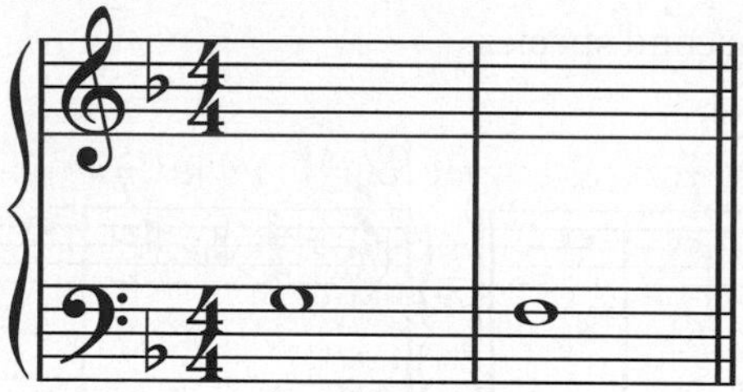

Melodic Considerations

In the middle section of the counterpoint, the embellishments most characteristic of this species in strict style are dissonant passing tones and consonant skips. Consonant passing tones, consonant or dissonant neighbor tones, and an occasional leap (as described below) may also be included to make a better line. For any of these, consider a span of at least three half notes—ideally, consider spans of two to three measures—and plan the consonant downbeats, offbeat embellishments, and contour direction for this longer stretch. As dissonant passing tones are emblematic of second species (their absence is considered an error), you may want to plan several of them as you make initial choices for the counterpoint line.

One of the challenges in writing a strong second-species setting is attending to local details (such as individual passing tones and consonant skips) while creating a line with an interesting and coherent overall shape. Consider Example 10.5, another setting of CF5. The opening (mm. 1–2) and close (mm. 7–9) are correctly executed, and the counterpoint in measures 1–7 is quite good if we examine two-

or three-measure segments: there are consonant skips, prepared and resolved dissonant passing tones, consonant passing tones (5–6) in measures 6 and 8, and mostly conjunct motion against the cantus leaps. Overall, though, the line lacks a single high point or climax, and it obsessively repeats the same few pitches: B4, C5, D5, and E5. Keep in mind the overall contour as well as attending to shorter segments.

EXAMPLE 10.5: Cantus firmus 5 (Kirnberger) in a second-species setting

Since there *is* a tendency for second-species counterpoint melodies to circle around a few pitches for too long, take advantage of the additional available notes to make a more elaborate contour than first species. Allow your line a wider range overall—spanning an octave or tenth between its highest and lowest point—and plan a subsidiary high or low point if possible, just before or after the main climax. In the middle, you may write a leap in either direction of an octave or fifth, or a leap upward of a minor sixth, if needed, to change the range (to avoid having the parts collide or move too far apart) or to add interest to the line. These larger leaps are allowed because of the additional motion available in second species, but each should be approached and left in such a way as to balance the line—preferably filling in after the leap with stepwise motion in the opposite direction. In Example 10.5, a carefully placed leap in the middle of the counterpoint or a new high point would improve the overall interest of the line.

KEY CONCEPT Leaps normally appear between the first and second half note within a measure instead of over the bar line, when the simultaneous arrival of the new cantus note would give the disjunct motion added prominence. A good rule of thumb is to skip or leap within the bar lines, but step over them.

Example 10.6 illustrates this principle. If you plan thirds on the downbeats of measures 3 and 4, there will be a melodic fourth between these accented beats, with no possibility of a stepwise connection. Use a combination of a consonant skip within measure 3 and a step over the bar.

EXAMPLE 10.6: Cantus firmus 5 (Kirnberger) in a second-species setting

Where there is too much stepwise motion in one direction or a static line, a leap of a P4 or P5 within a measure may substitute for a consonant skip of a third. Two consonant skips or a skip followed by a small leap (P4) in the same direction are also acceptable (as in mm. 4–5); they are treated as the equivalent of a leap of a fifth or sixth from downbeat to downbeat in first species. Ideally, approach any leap (or combination of skips equating to a leap) from the opposite direction, and follow the leap by motion in the opposite direction to balance it, as in measures 5–6 of Example 10.6. Whether writing steps, skips, or leaps, don't progress more than an octave in one direction before a change of direction. Neither conjunct nor disjunct motion should be used to excess: the main purpose of second species is to explore the dissonant passing tone and consonant skip, and to do that it is necessary to balance the number and placement of skips, leaps, and steps.

SUMMARY

To write a good contrapuntal line in second species:

- Use a wider range than in first species, with steps, skips, and leaps.
- Create one high point to the line, and consider a second subsidiary high point.
- Include a leap, on the offbeat, to change the range or create melodic interest.
- Consider two skips, or a skip plus small leap (P4), as equivalent to a leap.
- Ideally, after a leap, follow with stepwise motion in the opposite direction.

Harmonic Considerations

The primary harmonic consideration in second species is that the harmonic interval on the first half note of each measure must be a perfect or imperfect consonance. Write dissonant intervals only on the second half note, approached and resolved as a passing or neighbor tone. Unisons are likewise allowed only on the offbeat, and must be left by motion contrary to their approach. (An alternative is to write the counterpoint with an octave between the parts to avoid unisons, as they stop the forward contrapuntal motion.) As in first species, treat perfect intervals with special care.

KEY CONCEPT To avoid hidden (or direct) fifths and octaves, approach intervals P5 and P8 on the downbeat by step in the upper part, ideally in contrary motion. Don't approach P8 or P5 in similar motion with a skip or leap in the upper voice.

The addition of melodic embellishments in 2:1 writing provides new opportunities for forbidden parallel motion between perfect intervals. For this reason, you should evaluate the harmonic intervals in a second-species counterpoint in two ways: from the first part of one measure to the first part of the next (downbeat to downbeat) and from each note to the next. The motion from downbeat to downbeat should follow first-species guidelines. For example, perfect consonances of the same size from downbeat to downbeat will create parallel fifths or octaves (prohibited); the intervening note on the offbeat does not break up parallel motion. And no more than three consecutive downbeats should have the same imperfect consonance (3–3–3 or 6–6–6).

KEY CONCEPT Always double-check your counterpoint for parallel perfect intervals not only from downbeat to downbeat (as in 1:1, "beat-to-beat parallels"), but also from offbeat to downbeat over the bar line ("adjacency parallels").

Example 10.7 includes both kinds of prohibited motion: beat-to-beat parallels in measures 3–4 and 8–9 and adjacency parallels in 1–2 and 7–8. Perfect intervals on the offbeats of two consecutive measures are permitted (as in mm. 4–5), but not more than two in a row of the same type, as they will attract attention. Overall, the counterpoint in Example 10.7 features too many perfect intervals, with only two dissonant passing tones. Still, measures 4–7 could work with a revised opening and closing; measures 6–7 illustrate the correct resolution of the dissonant passing tone A4 to a 6. When you have finished your counterpoint, perform it (at the keyboard or with a partner) to check for parallel perfect intervals, inappropriate dissonances, or other errors.

EXAMPLE 10.7: Prohibited parallel motion in second-species counterpoint

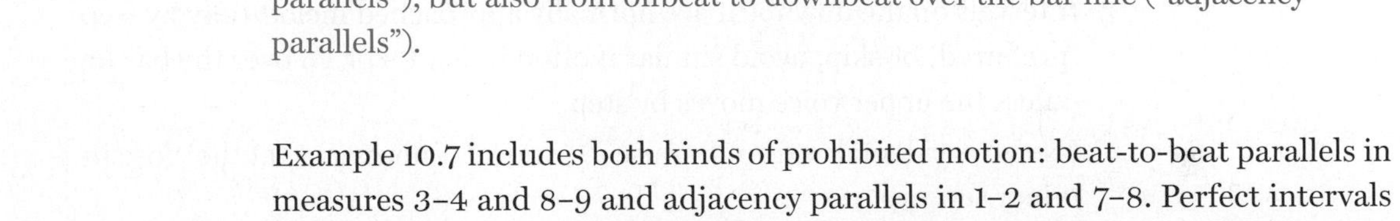

SUMMARY

To write a 2:1 counterpoint in strict style:

1. Start with either a half rest or half note on the downbeat of the first measure, followed by a half note on the offbeat; the first harmonic interval should be an 8 or U (or 5 if the counterpoint is the upper part).
2. End with a whole note in the last measure and the harmonic intervals 5–6–8 or 5–3–8 (or U); or set the last two notes with whole notes 6–8 or 3–8 (U), as in first species.
3. Other than the beginning and close, use whole notes throughout for the cantus and half notes for the counterpoint; an immediate repetition of the same pitch is not allowed within the bar or over the bar line.
4. Write consonant harmonic intervals on the beat; they also may appear on the offbeats, approached as consonant skips, steps, or leaps.
5. Include dissonant harmonic intervals (2, 4, 7, 9, and d5 and A4 if resolved correctly) on the offbeats as passing or (more rarely) neighbor tones.
6. Check from one downbeat to the next and from an offbeat to the next note for parallel fifths or octaves; perfect consonances from one offbeat to the next offbeat are allowed, but no more than two in a row.
7. Intervals on the downbeat are normally approached melodically by step (preferred) or skip; avoid similar motion into a P8 or P5 over the bar line unless the upper voice moves by step.
8. Use no accidentals except to raise $\flat\hat{7}$ (and $\flat\hat{6}$ if necessary) at the close in minor settings.
9. Continue to follow the guidelines for 1:1 counterpoint with respect to the overall motion between the parts (contrary, parallel, similar, oblique) and principles of good melodic writing.

About Third-Species Counterpoint

In **third-species** (4:1) counterpoint, the next step in Fux's method, the cantus whole note is set with four quarter notes, as in Example 10.8. Third species is a further rhythmic diminution of second species: each half note of second species is divided in two to make quarter notes. The strongest accent falls on the first of the four quarter notes (the beat, or downbeat), which enters with the cantus note. The third quarter note (offbeat, analogous to the second half note in second species) takes a lesser accent, making two levels of accents, while the second and fourth quarter notes are unaccented. The primary element to be learned in third species is how to treat elaborate embellishments of the counterpoint line, while maintaining a balanced interaction between the voices and a pleasing overall contour.

EXAMPLE 10.8: Cantus firmus 5 (Kirnberger) in a third-species setting

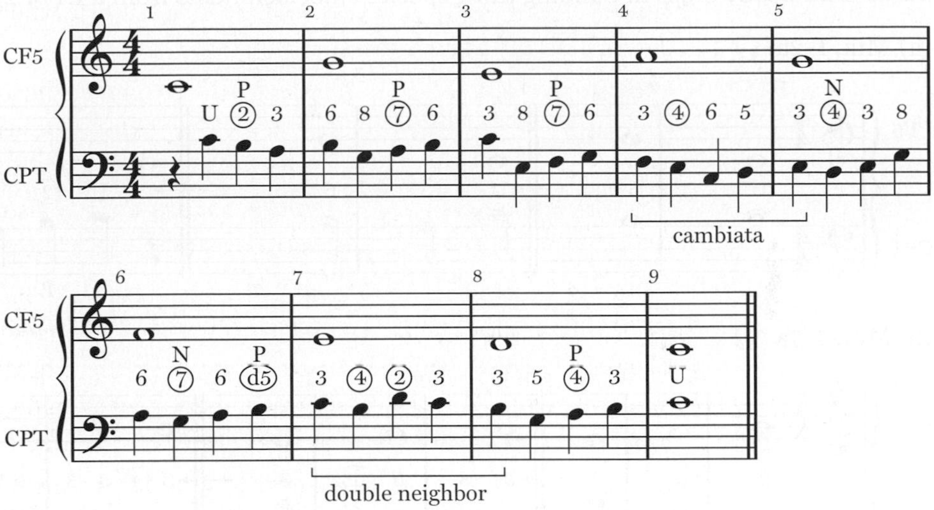

Some of the guidelines for second species apply to third as well: the harmonic interval on the first quarter notes of each measure must be consonant; those for the second, third, and fourth quarter note may be consonant or dissonant; and parallel perfect intervals are prohibited downbeat-to-downbeat or offbeat-to-downbeat. As is evident in Example 10.8, consonant skips (and especially two or more in a row) are less commonly found in third species than in second. While leaps occasionally appear in the middle of a measure to improve the distance between the lines (as in m. 3), the emphasis is on a smooth, flowing, conjunct counterpoint. To help achieve this, connections from the fourth quarter note to the first over the bar will normally be by step.

The elaborate embellishing patterns of third species are constructed from combinations of consonant skips, passing tones, and neighbor tones. Example 10.9 shows how some of Example 10.8's embellishments are created from 1:1 and 2:1 frameworks. Two new embellishments associated with third species are distinctive enough to have their own names: the cambiata and double neighbor. The **cambiata** (part c) combines passing and neighboring embellishments to make a figure with an apparent skip from a dissonance on the second quarter note. The passing tone on the second note of a cambiata resolves on the fourth note.

The **double neighbor** (DN, part d) combines successive upper and lower neighbors (in either order, but UN first is most common) around the same main pitch (here, C4). The second neighbor (D4) must resolve, and the figure must continue to the next beat in the same direction as the resolution to complete the pattern. These are only a few of the many possibilities for embellishments in third species!

EXAMPLE 10.9: Steps in building third-species embellishments from a 1:1 or 2:1 framework

(a) Mm. 1–2a

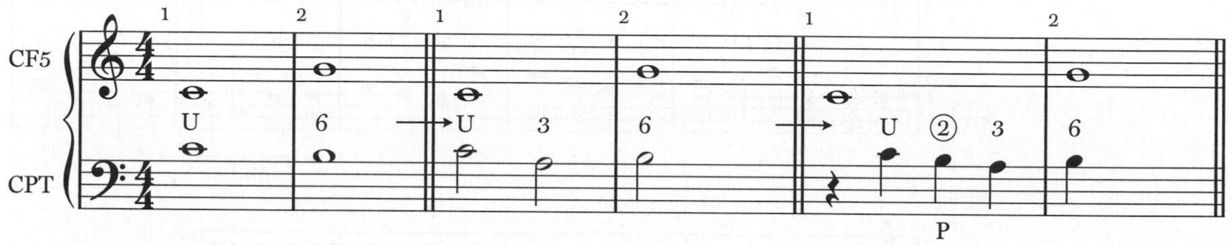

(b) Mm. 5–7a

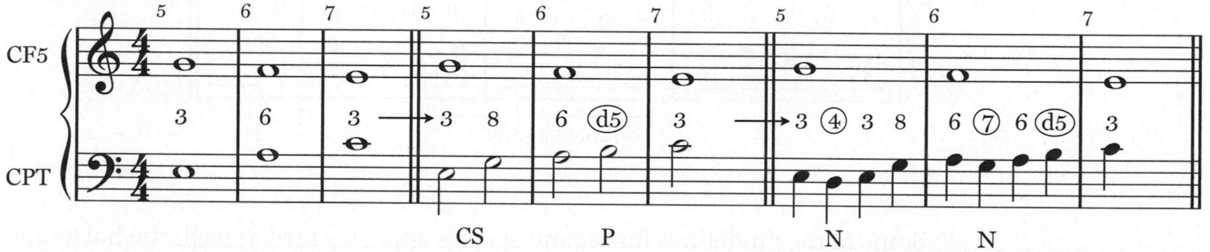

(c) Mm. 4–5a

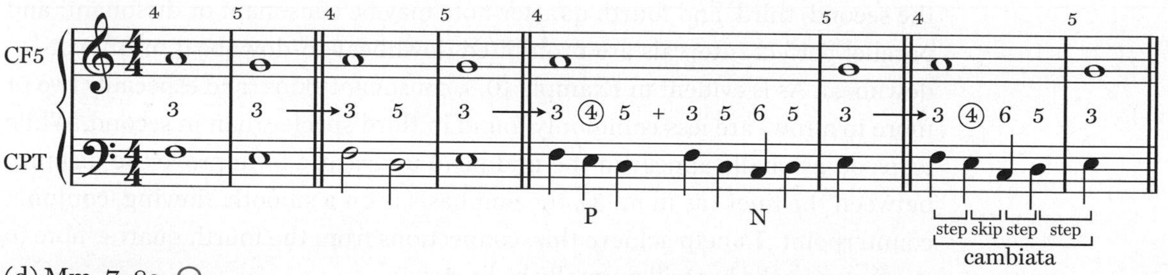

(d) Mm. 7–8a

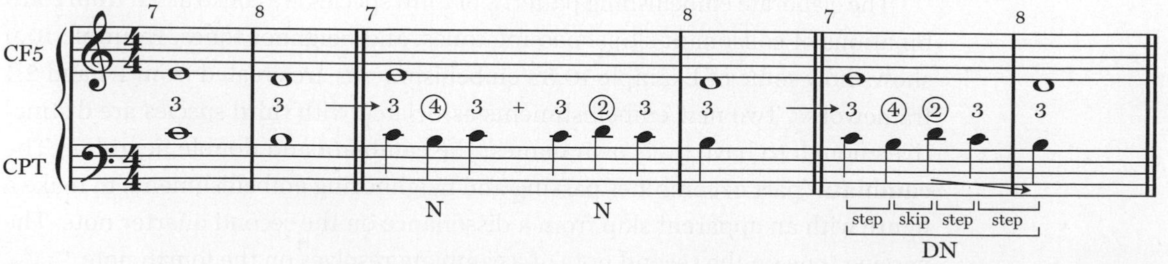

Rhythmic Displacement in Fourth-Species Counterpoint

In the species considered thus far, the basic note-to-note framework has been elaborated by adding pitches between cantus notes that create consonant or dissonant harmonic intervals and provide melodic motion. A second general category of elaboration—rhythmic displacement—involves shifting consonant pitches of the basic framework in time to create dissonant harmonic intervals; the dissonance must then resolve to complete the embellishment pattern. The most common type of rhythmic displacement is the suspension, which is studied in **fourth species** in strict style (Example 10.10).

Example 10.10: Cantus firmus 2 (Jeppesen) in a fourth-species setting

KEY CONCEPT A **suspension** is a rhythmic embellishment created when a consonant interval is held over to the first beat of the next measure, forming a harmonic dissonance until the suspended voice moves down by step to the next pitch. Suspensions consist of three parts (marked on Example 10.10):

- a consonant harmonic interval (the preparation) on the second half of the measure;
- the consonance held over to the first half of the next measure to make an accented dissonant harmonic interval (the suspension);
- the resolution of that dissonance down by step on the second half of the measure to a consonant harmonic interval (the resolution), which may itself serve as the preparation for the next suspension.

Because of these characteristic suspensions, one of the immediately recognizable aspects of fourth species is its rhythmic character: two half notes are set against a whole note, as in second species, but the second half note in most measures is tied over to the following downbeat. The parts sound in alternation, with the new cantus notes entering on the downbeat and the new counterpoint notes primarily on the offbeats. The counterpoint line begins with a half rest to start the rhythmic alternation of the parts; and the series of ties ends in the penultimate measure, whose second half note (the leading tone) is never tied over but resolves to the octave or unison as in previous species. You could think of suspensions as consonant intervals of a note-to-note first species that, rather than moving to the next pitch on time, are held so that the next pitch arrives late. The dissonant interval that results from this displacement is not melodic in nature but rhythmic.

In traditional fourth-species counterpoint, it is essential to maintain the rhythmic displacement throughout the setting, employing suspensions as much as possible. This works well with stepwise, descending portions of the cantus, as in measures 2–6 and 7–9 of Example 10.10. A consonance, however, may sometimes be tied over to another consonance, as in measures 3–4 of Example 10.11, continuing the rhythmic displacement.

EXAMPLE 10.11: Cantus firmus 6 (Kirnberger) in a fourth-species setting

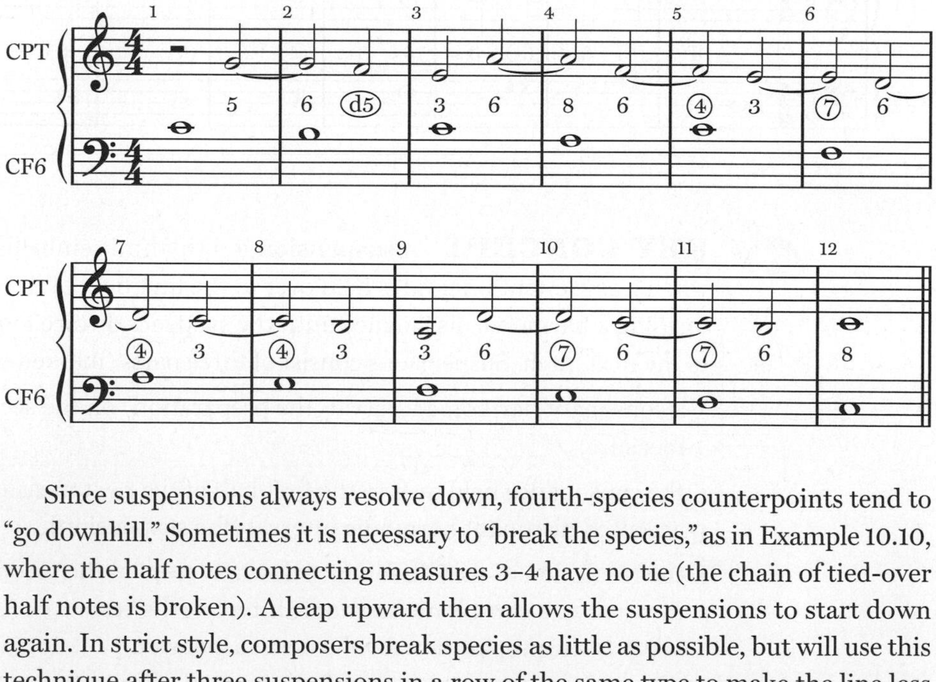

Since suspensions always resolve down, fourth-species counterpoints tend to "go downhill." Sometimes it is necessary to "break the species," as in Example 10.10, where the half notes connecting measures 3–4 have no tie (the chain of tied-over half notes is broken). A leap upward then allows the suspensions to start down again. In strict style, composers break species as little as possible, but will use this technique after three suspensions in a row of the same type to make the line less repetitive. They may also break species when there is no consonance available to tie over (Example 10.11, mm. 2–3), or to set up a particular suspension figure (especially approaching the close). Breaking species results in a short span of the exercise being written as if in second species.

The disjunct first half of the cantus in Example 10.11 makes it difficult to set measures 1–6 without breaking species somewhere. The technique applied in measures 8–9 stops the chain of 4–3 suspensions (which could continue for a total of three) and sets up a pair of 7–6 suspensions into the close. Fourth-species settings work best with stepwise, descending sections of the cantus, as in Example 10.10 or the second half of Example 10.11; cantus lines with skips or leaps or ascending steps are more challenging.

Types of Suspensions

Dissonant Suspensions There are only three types of dissonant upper-voice suspensions, labeled in Example 10.12.

KEY CONCEPT Suspensions are named by the numbers of the dissonant harmonic interval and its resolution. The most common upper-voice suspensions are 4–3 (Example 10.12a) and 7–6 (part b); both resolve to imperfect consonances. (These suspensions can also be seen in Example 10.11.) The 9–8 suspension (part c) may appear in an upper voice as well, but is less satisfactory because it resolves to a perfect consonance.

Example 10.12: Suspension types in the upper part

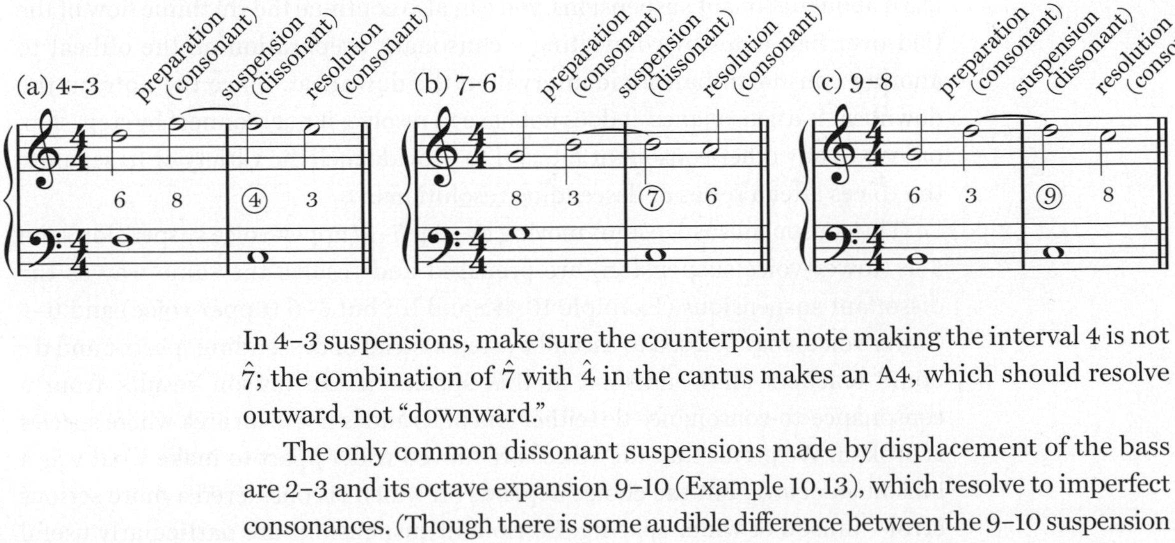

In 4–3 suspensions, make sure the counterpoint note making the interval 4 is not $\hat{7}$; the combination of $\hat{7}$ with $\hat{4}$ in the cantus makes an A4, which should resolve outward, not "downward."

The only common dissonant suspensions made by displacement of the bass are 2–3 and its octave expansion 9–10 (Example 10.13), which resolve to imperfect consonances. (Though there is some audible difference between the 9–10 suspension of m. 3 and the 2–3 suspensions in mm. 8, 10, and 11, it is customary to label all of them 2–3 as here.) Since there are fewer dissonant suspension options in the bass, preparing a good counterpoint when the cantus is in the upper part is challenging: such settings will include more consonances tied across the bar against the skips and leap in the cantus, and may require breaking species (as in mm. 1–2 and 8–9). Don't write the intervallic successions 4–5 or 7–8; or a 4–3 or 7–6 suspension with the dissonance resolving up (no matter how tempting!); these are not acceptable suspensions in the lower part.

Example 10.13: Cantus firmus 6 (Kirnberger) in a fourth-species setting

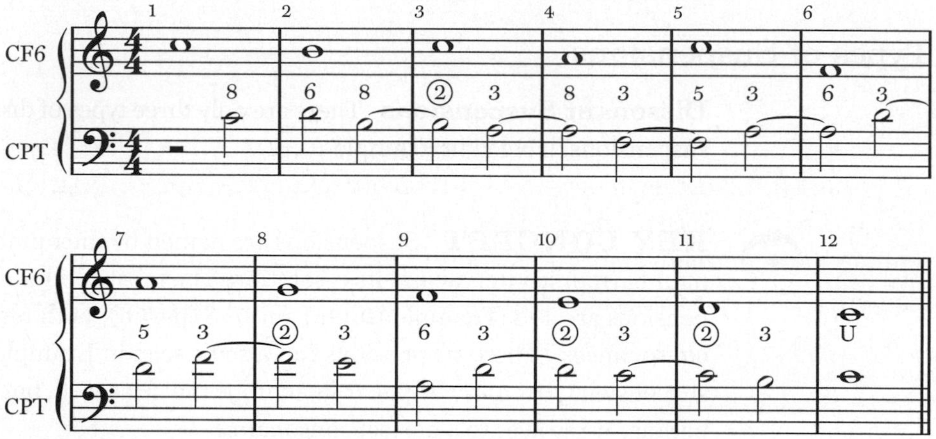

Consonant Suspensions Though the main objective of fourth species is to learn about dissonant suspensions, you can also continue the rhythmic flow of the tied-over half notes by connecting a consonant preparation on the offbeat to another consonant harmonic interval on the downbeat. Since the note on the downbeat is a consonance, it does not have to resolve; it may connect by step, skip, or leap to any other consonant interval to provide melodic variety or to separate the voices after a series of descending resolutions.

The consonant suspensions moving by step 6–5 (upper-voice suspension) and 5–6 (lower-voice suspension) are prepared and resolve the same way as the dissonant suspensions (Example 10.14a and b); but 5–6 (upper voice) and 6–5 (lower voice) may be used to ascend by step instead of descending (parts c and d). Some teachers allow unisons in this species if the unison results from a consonance-to-consonance tie (either end of it) and is not in an area where species is broken. We prefer that the voices are moved wider apart to make what was a unison an octave; but the choice depends on which is considered a more serious error—unison or wider spacing. Consonant suspensions are particularly useful when the cantus skips, leaps, or features ascending steps.

EXAMPLE 10.14: Consonant suspensions 5–6 and 6–5

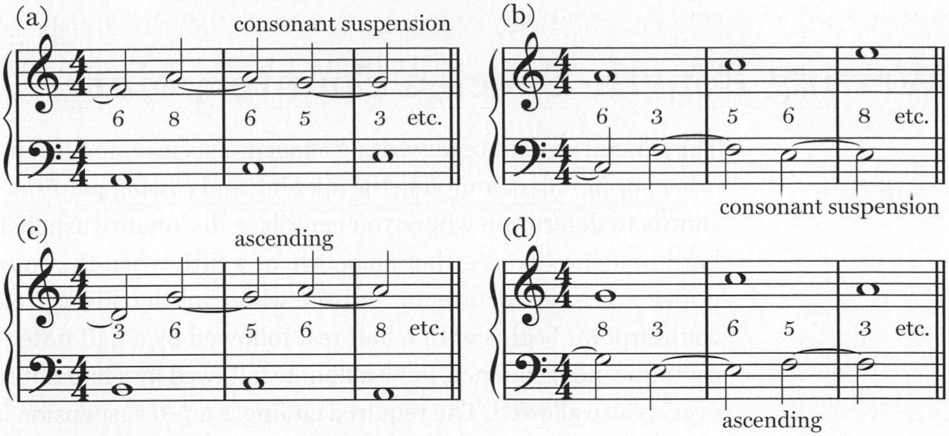

Chains of Suspensions

When the cantus features a stepwise descending line, you can follow one suspension in the counterpoint with another of the same type, creating a **chain of suspensions**. Such a chain is actually a displacement of a note-to-note series of descending parallel thirds or sixths, as shown in Example 10.15. Only 4–3, 7–6, and 2–3 suspensions are used in chains; chaining 9–8 or 5–6 or 6–5 suspensions implies parallel octaves or fifths.

EXAMPLE 10.15: Chains of suspensions

(a) Note-to-note parallel thirds and sixths

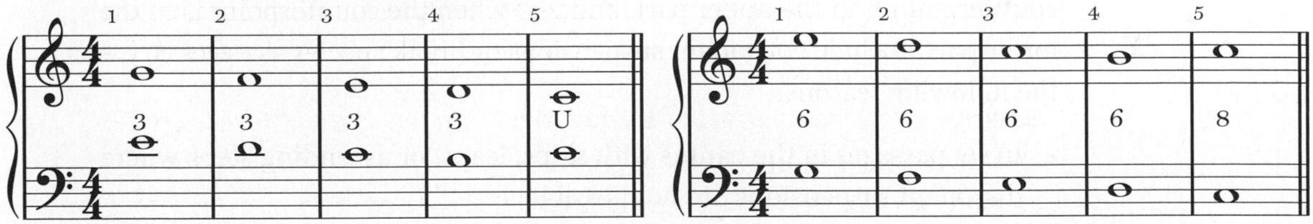

(b) Chain in the upper part

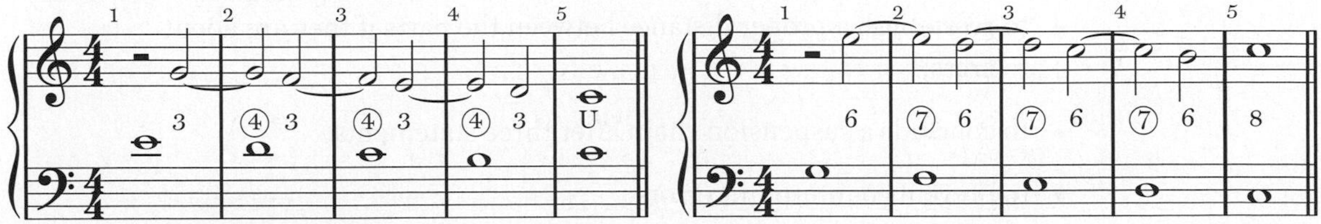

(c) Chain in the lower part

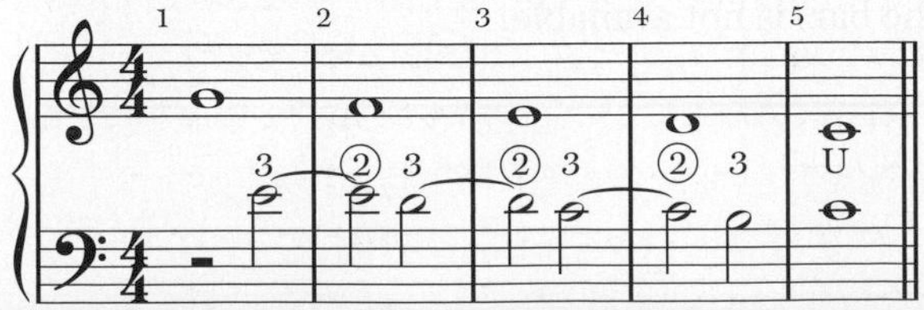

Writing Fourth-Species Counterpoint

The general procedure for writing a fourth-species counterpoint is the same as for other species: first complete the opening and closing patterns, then consider the cantus to determine where you can place dissonant suspensions. The opening harmonic interval is either an octave or a fifth when the counterpoint is in the upper voice, an octave or unison when in the lower voice. Typically, the counterpoint begins with a half rest followed by a half note to allow the voices rhythmic independence, but a half note followed by a half note (which is then tied over) is also allowed. The required ending is a 7–6 suspension if the counterpoint is in the upper voice, or a 2–3 or 9–10 if in the lower voice, leading to the final whole note P8 or U; the last note in the penultimate measure is not tied over to the final measure. In minor-mode settings, the seventh scale degree is raised to make the leading tone approaching the cadence, as in Example 10.10.

SUMMARY

In fourth species, use dissonant suspensions as much as possible. The acceptable dissonant suspensions are 7–6, 4–3, and 9–8 when the counterpoint is in the upper part, and 2–3 when the counterpoint is in the lower part. Include consonant suspensions or break species as necessary, for the following reasons:

- to set passages in the cantus with skips, leaps, or ascending steps where dissonant suspensions are not possible;
- to make a more interesting line;
- to reestablish a proper distance between the parts if they are about to cross;
- to conclude a suspension chain after three statements;
- to prevent counterpoint errors;
- to solve difficult places in the cantus where a dissonant suspension (or even any type of tie over the bar) is not available.

Try it #3

The following counterpoint is full of errors! Start by writing in the harmonic interval numbers, then check each suspension. Mark those that are good with a check in the box above that measure; mark the flawed ones with an X. Explain in the space below what type of error is in each location.

Cantus firmus 3 (Schenker) in a flawed fourth-species setting

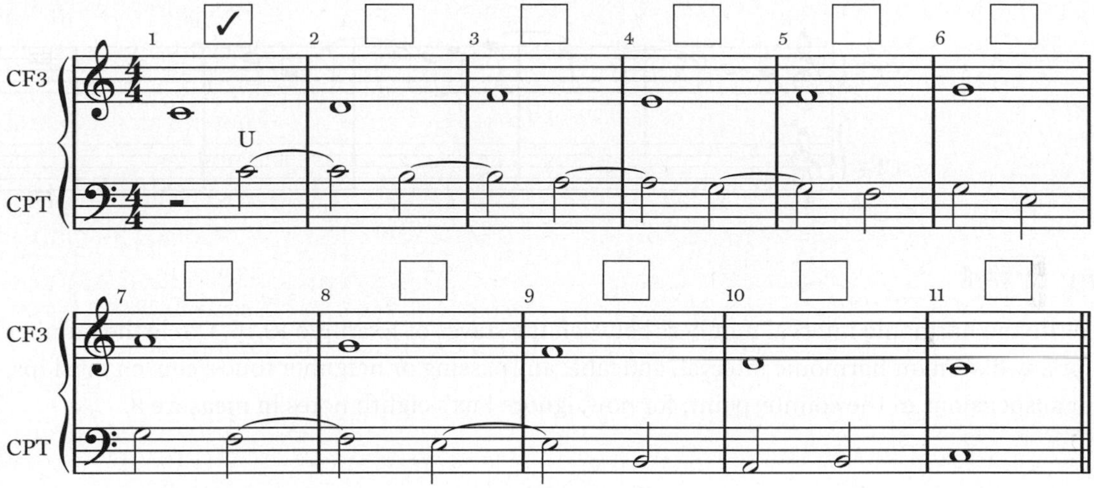

Fifth Species and Free Counterpoint

After learning fourth species, the next pedagogical step for eighteenth-century music students was to combine the individual dissonance treatment and durational patterns of all the species to create a counterpoint with varied rhythm, called **fifth species.** In fifth species (Example 10.16), the counterpoint may include quarter notes (from third species), half notes (second species), half notes tied over the bar (fourth species), and whole notes (first species) mixed together. This example, in Dorian mode (from Fux's *Gradus ad Parnassum*), is one that eighteenth-century musicians would have known. Play through or sing it with your class, then evaluate the intervals between the voices.

EXAMPLE 10.16: An example of fifth species from *Gradus ad Parnassum*

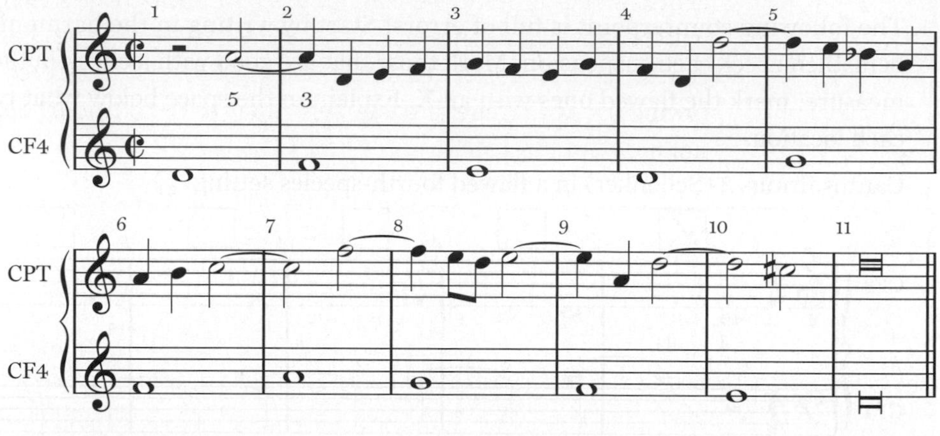

Try it #4

Write the harmonic interval numbers between the staves of Example 10.16. Circle the number for any dissonant harmonic interval, and label any passing or neighbor tones, consonant skips, or suspensions in the counterpoint; for now, ignore Fux's eighth notes in measure 8.

The opening and close of Fux's counterpoint are standard from fourth species, while measures 2–6 are based on third species. The 7–6 suspensions in measures 8–9 are ornamented as is customary in fifth species—first by a pair of eighth notes, then by a leap away to a consonance—before the dissonance resolves; the dissonant suspension and any embellishment total a half note's duration, with the resolution on the third quarter. The D5 eighth note in measure 8 may at first glance seem to be a neighbor tone, but that would imply an early arrival of the suspension's resolution; instead, the skip to a consonance from F5 to D5 is filled in with a passing tone (E5). All other tied notes are consonant suspensions. Eighth notes may only be used on the second and fourth quarters and must be approached and left by step; they typically embellish a suspension, as here. There are four places in measures 2–5 where the voices cross or touch to make a unison (which Fux's guidelines allow); dropping the entire cantus (lower part) an octave, into the bass clef, would solve these issues, but moves the voices farther apart than Fux preferred.

In most tonal music, melodic and rhythmic embellishments are not isolated in one voice—the species are mixed together in all the parts, a technique sometimes called "free counterpoint." The term may be misleading, though. It does not mean you are free to do just anything with dissonances; instead, you are free to choose where, how, and with what note values to incorporate melodic and rhythmic elaboration.

Because of the differences between strict fifth-species settings and eighteenth-century counterpoint, we will not dwell on fifth-species techniques, but instead will focus on eighteenth-century practices in the following chapters. In eighteenth-century style, you will find all the embellishments considered in this chapter, following the same general guidelines, along with additional embellishing patterns not employed in species exercises.

Did You Know?

The most famous counterpoint treatise from the seventeenth and eighteenth centuries is Johann Joseph Fux's *Gradus ad Parnassum* (Steps to Parnassus). Although Fux's approach was modeled on sixteenth-century music, this treatise was a "best-seller" in its day, and used by many eighteenth-century musicians in their studies and teaching. Fux taught counterpoint beginning with note-to-note and ending with fifth species, which is intended to approximate the use of dissonance in real music. His examples are notated with movable C-clefs, which sometimes correspond to both parts in the treble clef or both in the bass clef, whereas we have modeled soprano/bass pairings in a treble and bass clef. When musicians refer to species counterpoint today, Fux's method is what they are talking about. Portions of *Gradus ad Parnassum* are readily available in an English translation—read this best-seller for yourself! (*The Study of Counterpoint from Johann Joseph Fux's "Gradus ad Parnassum,"* trans. Alfred Mann [New York: Norton, 1943; reprinted 1965].)

TERMS YOU SHOULD KNOW

cambiata	double neighbor	neighbor tone	second species (2:1)
chains of suspensions	fifth species	passing tone	suspension
consonant skip	fourth species	preparation	third species (4:1)
diminution	metrical accent	resolution	

QUESTIONS FOR REVIEW

1. Which dissonance treatments are explored in 2:1 counterpoint?
2. What types of intervals may be used in 2:1 in the first half of the measure? in the second half?
3. How is a passing tone approached and resolved? a neighbor tone?
4. What types of embellishments are introduced in third species?
5. What are the types of suspensions used in fourth species? Which appear in the upper part? in the lower part?
6. What are the three parts of a suspension?
7. Which suspensions can be used in chains? Which are not found in chains? Why not?
8. What types of embellishments may be found in fifth species?

PART II

Diatonic Harmony and Tonicization

Soprano and Bass Lines in Eighteenth-Century Style

Outline of topics

Note-to-note counterpoint in eighteenth-century style

- Contrapuntal motion
- Chordal dissonance
- Characteristics of bass and melody lines
- Writing counterpoint with a given line

Melodic embellishment in chorale textures

- Passing tones, neighbor tones, and consonant skips
- Suspensions

Overview

In eighteenth-century style, note-to-note counterpoint incorporates dissonances made from seventh chords and features a bass line that implies tonal harmonic progressions. Here, we learn to write tonal cadences in two parts, and consider melodic embellishment in two-part chorale textures.

Repertoire

Johann Sebastian Bach, "Wachet auf" ("Awake," Chorale No. 197)

Traditional hymn settings
- "Chartres" (15th-century French melody, harmonization by Charles Wood)
- "Ein feste Burg" ("A Mighty Fortress," melody by Martin Luther, 1529; harmonization by J. S. Bach)
- "My Country, 'Tis of Thee" ("America") (Thesaurus Musicus, 1740)
- "Old Hundredth" (harmonization by Louis Bourgeois, 1551)
- "Rosa Mystica" (traditional melody, harmonization by Michael Praetorius, 1609)
- "St. George's Windsor" (harmonization by George J. Elvey, 1858)

Note-to-Note Counterpoint in Eighteenth-Century Style

Although the principles of species counterpoint underlie much of tonal music, very few pieces were written exclusively in strict style. Instead, its intervallic connections were combined with an emerging sense of harmony and functional tonality to create what we call eighteenth-century style.

Hymn settings or patriotic songs typically feature note-to-note frameworks in this style. While hymns are often set for four parts, pairs of voices, such as the soprano and the bass, form two-part note-to-note counterpoint: the soprano normally carries the traditional melody, and the bass line supplies the foundation of the harmonic progression. Such tunes are particularly appropriate for study: composers have drawn on these familiar melodies from the seventeenth century to the present with varied harmonizations and texts, and as themes for organ chorale preludes, sets of keyboard variations, and orchestral works. Though we focus on two-voice pairs in this chapter, listen to each hymn while following the anthology score to become familiar with the four-part settings.

Eighteenth-century note-to-note counterpoint differs from strict species style in several ways. A traditional first-species exercise is immediately recognizable by its whole-note durations, and because it features only consonant intervals, there is usually no strong forward momentum; only at the close is there a sense of arrival. The voices have equal roles: the cantus can be the top or bottom part, and often the counterpoint is invertible (the same counterpoint works either above or below the cantus).

In contrast, in eighteenth-century style the durations are normally half and quarter notes ("Old Hundredth," anthology p. 218) or quarter and eighth notes ("St. George's Windsor," p. 221). Composers include both consonant and dissonant harmonic intervals drawn from seventh chords to create forward motion. Further, the voices are not equal: the lowest part in each setting—the bass line—takes on a special role as the foundation of the harmonic progressions, with the melody in the highest part, the soprano; these roles are usually not invertible. In hymn settings, don't be surprised by an occasional deviation from the species guidelines, particularly with regard to dissonance. Nevertheless, the basic principle of counterpoint, including the balance between linear and harmonic motion, are the same in both styles.

Contrapuntal Motion

Some conventions of eighteenth-century counterpoint directly follow those of species counterpoint. Consider Example 11.1, note-to-note counterpoint from "St. George's Windsor": although the durations are varied, each bass note corresponds to a single soprano note in the same rhythm. As in first-species counterpoint, the intervals are a mix of perfect and imperfect consonances, the voices employ mostly contrary motion (C), and the close at the end of measure 4 features intervals 6–8. Some aspects that differ from strict style include the immediate repetition of notes in measures 1 and 3 (marked R) and repetition across the bar line in measures 2–3, resulting from repeated notes in the existing hymn melody.

Example 11.1: "St. George's Windsor," mm. 1–4 (soprano/bass)

Hymns use oblique motion more often than strict style does, to accommodate repeated notes in the melody or bass, as in Example 11.2, from a setting of "My Country, 'Tis of Thee." This example also shows a strong tonal cadence typical of eighteenth-century style: scale degrees $\hat{5}$–$\hat{1}$ in the bass and $\hat{7}$–$\hat{1}$ in the soprano.

Example 11.2: Oblique motion in "My Country, 'Tis of Thee" ("America"), mm. 1–6 (soprano/bass)

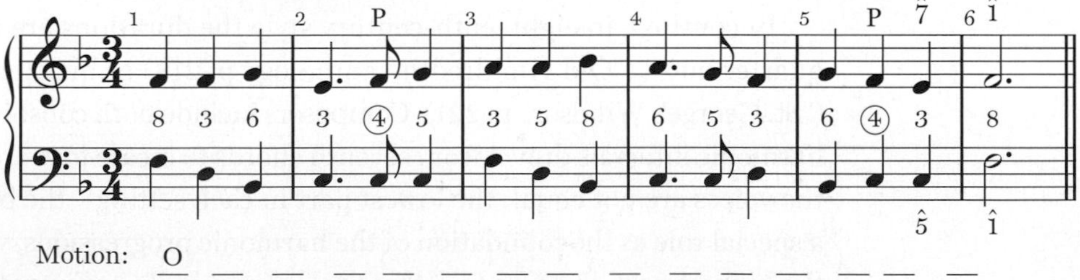

KEY CONCEPT In tonal music, a unit of musical thought that ends with a point of closure or repose is called a **phrase**. The combination of melodic, harmonic, and rhythmic elements that create a sense of closure at the end of a phrase is called a **cadence**.

The bass $\hat{5}$–$\hat{1}$ implies harmonic motion from root-position V to I. When combined with either of the typical closing gestures from strict species, $\hat{2}$–$\hat{1}$ or $\hat{7}$–$\hat{1}$ in the soprano, this motion represents the strongest type of tonal cadence.

Try it #1

In the blanks below Example 11.2, label the motion between each pair of harmonic intervals as C (contrary), O (oblique), P (parallel), S (similar), or R (repetition).

The two phrases in Example 11.3, from "Old Hundredth," feature contrary motion. Part (b) includes the voice exchange 3–8–6, while the cadence at the end of part (a) again features the strong $\hat{5}$–$\hat{1}$ bass motion—implying root position V–I in G major—but $\hat{2}$–$\hat{3}$ in the soprano. This $\hat{2}$–$\hat{3}$ motion weakens the cadence in comparison to $\hat{2}$–$\hat{1}$ or $\hat{7}$–$\hat{1}$ from strict species. We will return to cadence types typical of this style later in the chapter.

EXAMPLE 11.3: Intervals in "Old Hundredth"

(a) Mm. 1–3a feature stepwise contrary motion at the cadence.

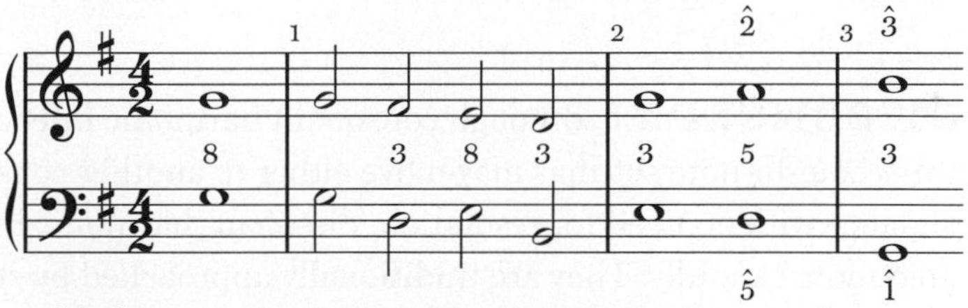

Motion: R S C S P C C

(b) Mm. 6b–9 feature contrary motion with a voice exchange.

Motion: C C C C C C S

SUMMARY

Note-to-note counterpoint in eighteenth-century style generally follows the conventions of species counterpoint in regard to contrapuntal motion and the connection of consonant intervals. Differences include

- more oblique motion or interval repetitions in eighteenth-century style, to accommodate repeated notes in a chorale melody;
- new cadence intervals (in addition to the 6–8 or 3–8 from species counterpoint) that imply stronger harmonic motion.

Chordal Dissonance

In strict counterpoint, dissonant harmonic intervals are created by melodic embellishments in second species and by rhythmic displacement in fourth species. Now we consider an additional type of dissonant interval that is essential to eighteenth-century style: **chordal dissonance**, or dissonant harmonic intervals that originate as a part of seventh chords. Like the other dissonant intervals, these harmonic dissonances need to be approached and resolved within stylistic guidelines.

KEY CONCEPT Although consonant harmonic intervals in eighteenth-century note-to-note settings may move either to another consonance or to a dissonance with no need for resolution, dissonant harmonic intervals are treated more carefully. They are traditionally approached by step in one or both voices, and must resolve to a consonant harmonic interval.

Example 11.4 shows the most significant source of chordal dissonances: the dominant seventh chord. The root and seventh of this chord ($\hat{5}$ and $\hat{4}$) form a m7 and its inversion (M2), while the third and seventh ($\hat{7}$ and $\hat{4}$) form a d5 and its inversion (A4). As shown in part (b), the root and seventh ($\hat{5}$ and $\hat{4}$) typically resolve in to a third ($\hat{1}$ and $\hat{3}$) to imply dominant-tonic motion. (Its inversion, the M2, also resolves to a third, though it is not typically found in two-voice counterpoint except as a 2–3 bass suspension.) When the dissonant tritone between the third and seventh ($\hat{7}$ and $\hat{4}$) of a dominant seventh chord is spelled as a d5, it resolves to a third; when spelled as an A4, it resolves out to a sixth. These resolutions allow $\hat{7}$ to move properly up to $\hat{1}$, and allow $\hat{4}$ (the chordal seventh) to resolve down.

EXAMPLE 11.4: Dissonant intervals of the V7 chord

(a) Harmonic dissonances

(b) Resolutions

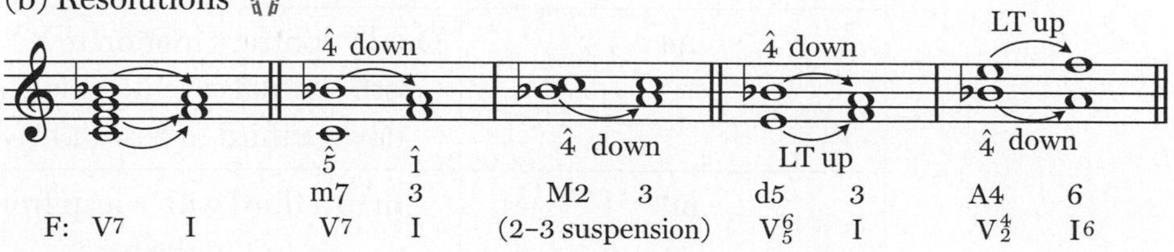

KEY CONCEPT In the dominant seventh harmony, the chordal seventh ($\hat{4}$) and the leading tone ($\hat{7}$) are **tendency tones**. Always resolve the chordal seventh down ($\hat{4}$ to $\hat{3}$) and the leading tone up ($\hat{7}$ to $\hat{1}$).

You can see the dominant seventh intervals in context in Example 11.5, from "St. George's Windsor." Part (b) isolates the chorale's A4 intervals (mm. 9 and 11) and shows how they resolve outward to a sixth, in F major (m. 10) and B♭ major (m. 12). The seventh of the chord moves down, and the third (the leading tone of the key) moves up. When the seventh is in the bass, as here, the chord is a $\frac{4}{2}$ inversion: the implied harmonies are therefore V^4_2 to I^6 as shown. Since they imply inverted seventh chords, the A4 and d5 typically fall in the middle of a phrase instead of at the end, where an implied root-position V7–I provides a stronger cadence.

EXAMPLE 11.5: Chordal dissonance in "St. George's Windsor," mm. 9–12 (soprano and bass)

(a) Soprano-bass pair

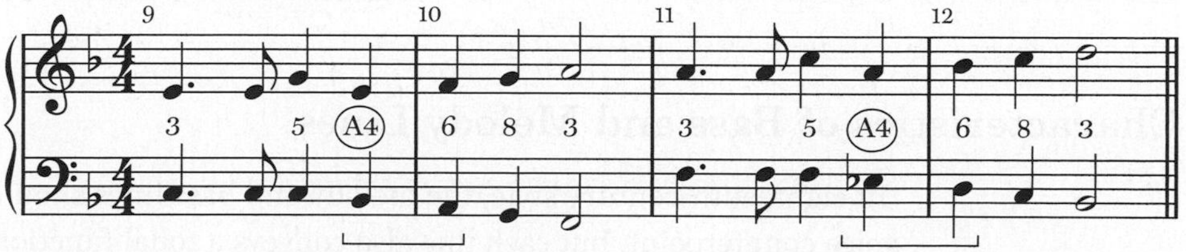

(b) Chord and interval resolutions

KEY CONCEPT The dissonant harmonic intervals of a dominant seventh chord are resolved in two parts as follows:

DISSONANT HARMONIC INTERVAL FROM V7 CHORD	DIRECTION AND INTERVAL OF RESOLUTION	CHORDS IMPLIED
d5	In by contrary motion to a third, with $\hat{7}$ resolving up to $\hat{1}$ in bass.	V^6_5 to I
A4	Out by contrary motion to a sixth, with chordal seventh resolving down a third in bass ($\hat{4}$ to $\hat{3}$).	V^4_2 to I^6
m7	In to a third with a leap from $\hat{5}$ to $\hat{1}$ in the bass.	V^7 to I

Try it #2

Identify and resolve the following chordal dissonances. Label each interval in the blanks between the staves, then write the implied harmonies (tonic or dominant) under the staff, providing both the Roman numeral and figures for inversion.

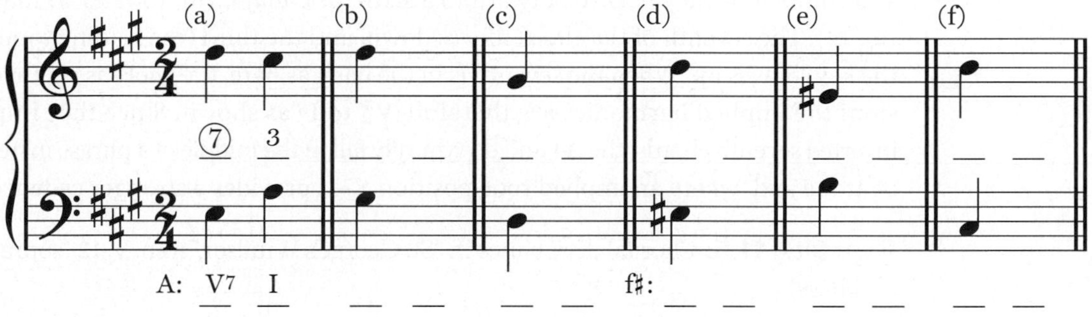

Characteristics of Bass and Melody Lines

In eighteenth-century style, the melody and bass lines should make good two-voice counterpoint, but each line also conveys a tonal function, especially at the beginning and end.

Closing the Counterpoint: Tonal Cadences Bass lines in tonal music may feature conjunct motion toward the beginning and middle of the phrase, but typically display disjunct motion toward the end, where skips or leaps feature the roots of implied chords. For this reason, when analyzing a bass line, consider its scale degrees. The beginning usually implies tonic harmony ($\hat{1}$ or $\hat{3}$) or is a V–I anacrusis ($\hat{5}$ or $\hat{7}$ moving to $\hat{1}$), while the end often features a leap of a fourth or fifth from $\hat{5}$ to $\hat{1}$ (implying root-position chords V to I), as in Example 11.6. Typical bass lines and the cadential harmonies they imply in D major and minor are given in Example 11.7.

KEY CONCEPT In two-voice eighteenth-century counterpoint, scale degrees chosen for the melody and bass line at the cadence imply particular harmonies: V or V^7 ($\hat{5}$, $\hat{7}$, $\hat{2}$, and $\hat{4}$) and I ($\hat{1}$ and $\hat{3}$).

EXAMPLE 11.6: Motion in bass lines

(a) "St. George's Windsor," mm. 1–2

(b) "Old Hundredth," mm. 1–3a

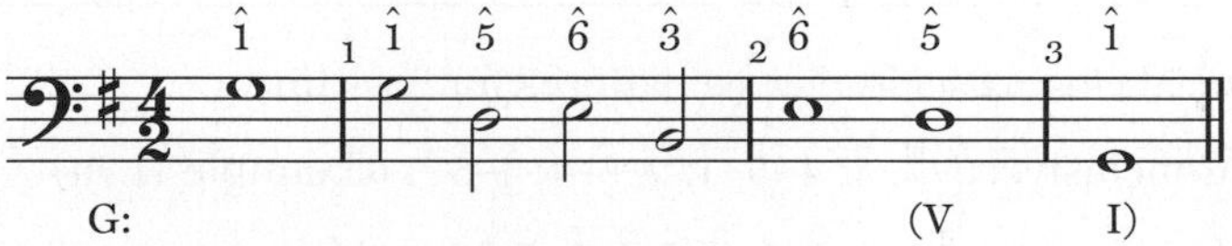

(c) "Rosa Mystica," mm. 1–4

EXAMPLE 11.7: Bass cadences in D major and D minor

(a) Conclusive

(b) Less conclusive

(c) Inconclusive: Ending on the dominant

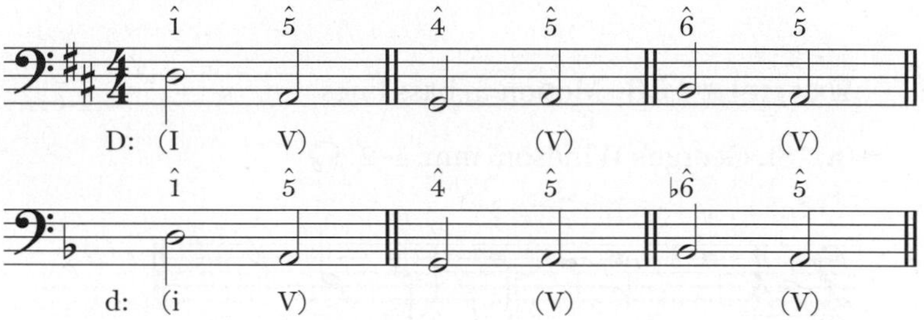

SUMMARY

Typical closing scale-degree patterns for bass lines:

- Conclusive: $\hat{6}$–$\hat{5}$–$\hat{1}$; $\hat{4}$–$\hat{5}$–$\hat{1}$; $\hat{2}$–$\hat{5}$–$\hat{1}$; $\hat{1}$–$\hat{5}$–$\hat{1}$ (Example 11.7a)
- Less conclusive: $\hat{1}$–$\hat{7}$–$\hat{1}$; $\hat{6}$–$\hat{7}$–$\hat{1}$; $\hat{5}$–$\hat{7}$–$\hat{1}$ (part b)
- Inconclusive, ending on the dominant: $\hat{1}$–$\hat{5}$, $\hat{4}$–$\hat{5}$, $\hat{6}$–$\hat{5}$ (part c), or any of the patterns above before reaching $\hat{1}$

Remember that in minor keys, the dominant harmony (V or V7) includes the leading tone; so when the bass line ascends from $\hat{7}$ to $\hat{1}$, write the correct accidental for the leading tone. If the bass line ascends from $\hat{5}$ up to $\hat{1}$, use the ascending melodic minor ($\hat{6}$ and $\hat{7}$); if it descends from $\hat{1}$ down to $\hat{5}$, use the descending form of melodic minor ($\flat\hat{7}$ and $\flat\hat{6}$).

The soprano line is typically more conjunct than the bass, but it, too, contributes to the cadence at the end of a phrase. While the strongest cadences are made from $\hat{2}$–$\hat{1}$ in the melody and $\hat{5}$–$\hat{1}$ in the bass, melodies also may close on $\hat{3}$ for a less conclusive ending on the tonic, or on $\hat{5}$, $\hat{2}$, or $\hat{7}$ for inconclusive endings on the dominant harmony, as shown in Example 11.8.

Example 11.8: Melodic cadential patterns in D major and D minor

(a) Conclusive

(b) Less conclusive

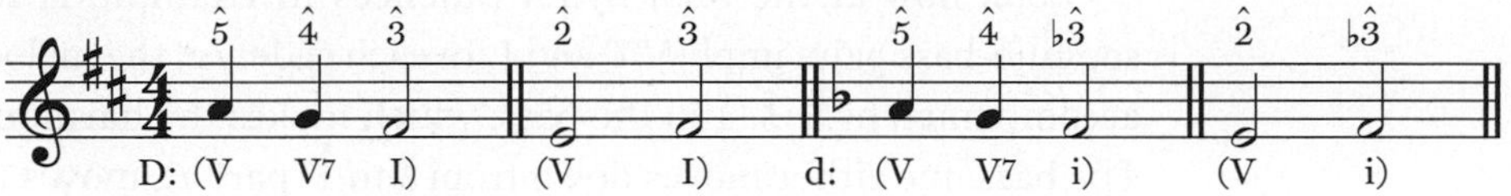

(c) Inconclusive: Ending on V

SUMMARY

Typical closing scale-degree patterns for soprano lines:

- Conclusive, ending on $\hat{1}$: such as $\hat{3}$–$\hat{2}$–$\hat{1}$; $\hat{2}$–$\hat{7}$–$\hat{1}$; $\hat{6}$–$\hat{7}$–$\hat{1}$; $\hat{2}$–$\hat{2}$–$\hat{1}$ (Example 11.8a).
- Less conclusive, ending on $\hat{3}$: such as $\hat{5}$–$\hat{4}$–$\hat{3}$; $\hat{2}$–$\hat{3}$ (part b)
- Inconclusive, ending on $\hat{5}$, $\hat{2}$, or $\hat{7}$: such as $\hat{6}$–$\hat{5}$; $\hat{4}$–$\hat{3}$–$\hat{2}$; $\hat{2}$–$\hat{1}$–$\hat{7}$ (part c).

Example 11.9 summarizes common root-position cadential patterns in two voices: part (a) shows the strongest cadence, $\hat{2}$–$\hat{1}$ in the soprano against $\hat{5}$–$\hat{1}$ in the bass, while part (b) gives another typical voicing, substituting $\hat{7}$–$\hat{1}$ in the melody. Parts (c) and (d) illustrate two weaker endings, where $\hat{5}$ to $\hat{1}$ in the bass is accompanied by $\hat{4}$–$\hat{3}$ or $\hat{2}$–$\hat{3}$ in the melody. Parts (e) and (f) show familiar cadences from strict species, also used in tonal music for less conclusive cadences. In G minor (with a change in key signature to two flats), the soprano F must be changed to F♯ in part (b) to make a leading tone.

Example 11.9: Cadences in two voices

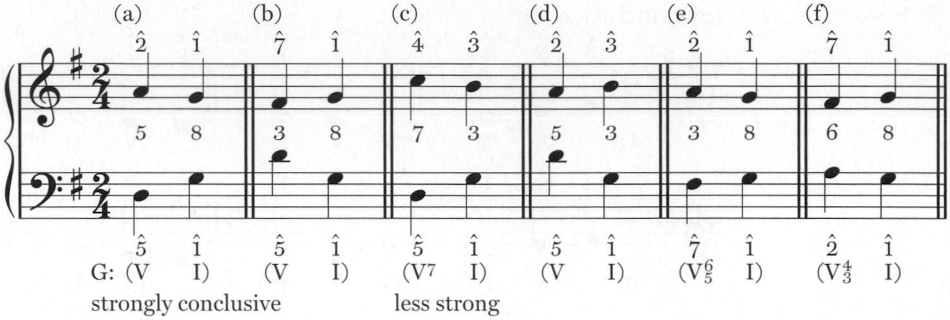

Look now at the final hymn cadences in Example 11.10 to see how their soprano-bass pairs imply V(7) and I. In each cadence, the melodic notes are $\hat{3}$–$\hat{2}$–$\hat{1}$, accompanied by $\hat{5}$–$\hat{5}$–$\hat{1}$ in the bass, which makes the harmonic intervals 6–5–8. The bass line either moves down from $\hat{5}$ to $\hat{1}$ (part a), moves up from $\hat{5}$ to $\hat{1}$ (part b), or drops an octave on $\hat{5}$ before moving up to $\hat{1}$ (part c). (Leaping up an octave, to $\hat{5}$, then down to $\hat{1}$, is unusual.)

Example 11.10: Final cadences (soprano and bass)

(a) "Old Hundredth," mm. 11–12

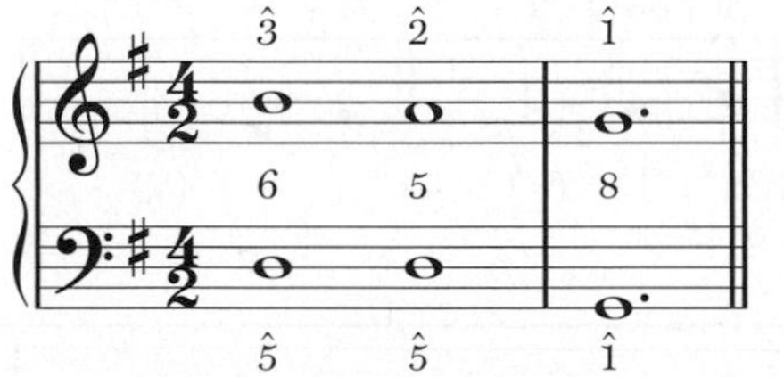

(b) "St. George's Windsor," mm. 15–16

(c) "My Country" ("America"), mm. 13–14

Try it #3

Label the following in the examples below: (1) scale-degree numbers for each note (above the melody and below the bass; (2) harmonic intervals between the parts; and (3) Roman numerals and figures for the implied chords, in the blanks provided.

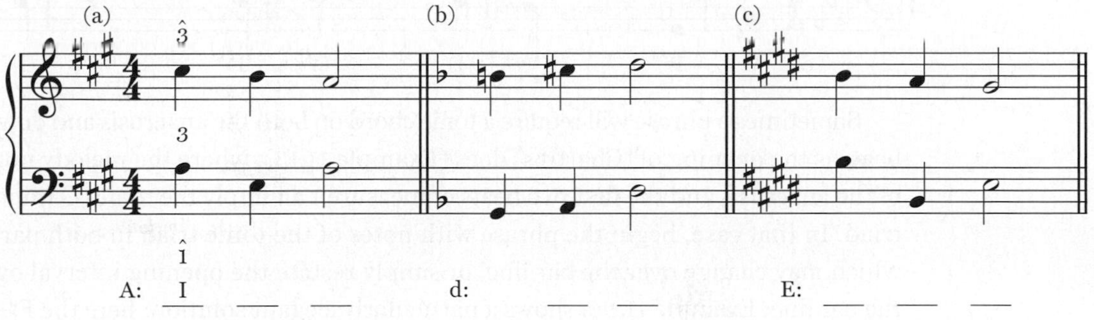

Opening the Counterpoint Melodic openings are more varied than cadences. A tonal melody often begins on $\hat{1}$ or $\hat{3}$, implying a tonic harmony, as in Example 11.11a–c. Less common are soprano-bass pairings of $\hat{5}$ and $\hat{1}$, or $\hat{5}$ and $\hat{3}$, because the harmony is ambiguous: the implied triad could be major or minor (part d); or the notes could be the third and fifth of a D major chord, or the root and third of an F♯ minor chord (part e).

EXAMPLE 11.11: Opening intervals implying tonic harmony

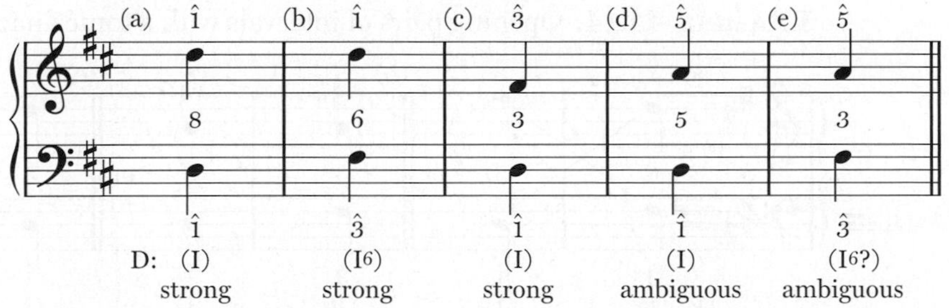

In pieces that begin with an anacrusis, the anacrusis usually implies the dominant, while the first downbeat interval establishes the tonic harmony. Some typical settings are shown in Example 11.12. These parts could be reversed: for example, the B♭–E♭ ($\hat{5}$–$\hat{1}$) of part (a) could be in the bass, with B♭–G ($\hat{5}$–$\hat{3}$) in the soprano.

EXAMPLE 11.12: Opening intervals with an anacrusis

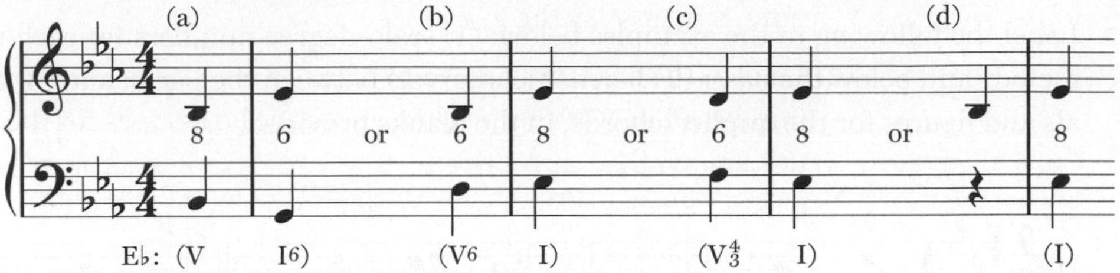

Sometimes a phrase will require a tonic chord on both the anacrusis and downbeat, as the opening of "Chartres" does (Example 11.13), where the melody notes of the anacrusis and the first two beats of measure 1 all imply the tonic (G minor) triad. In that case, begin the phrase with notes of the tonic triad in both parts, which may change over the bar line, or simply restate the opening interval over the bar line. Example 11.14a shows a particularly elegant solution: here the F♯–D in the bass is mirrored by D–F♯ in the soprano, making a voice exchange of scale degrees $\hat{3}$ and $\hat{1}$ and implying I6–I. In parts (b) and (c), the anacrusis is ambiguous, with the third and fifth of the tonic triad in (b) and only the root in (c); the arrival of the second interval clarifies that each anacrusis implies the tonic chord.

EXAMPLE 11.13: "Chartres," mm. 1–2a (soprano and bass)

EXAMPLE 11.14: Opening pairs of intervals with a tonic anacrusis

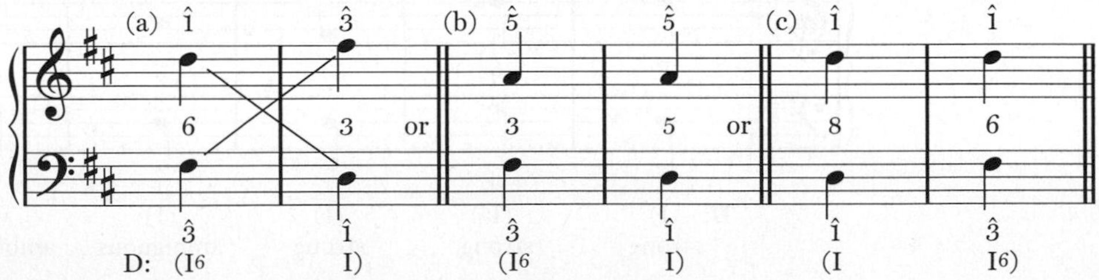

Writing Counterpoint with a Given Line

Composers in the eighteenth century often wrote counterpoint for a preexisting soprano or bass line, making new contrapuntal settings of hymn or chorale melodies or reusing a standard bass line as the starting point for creating a new melody. Follow this general procedure to write your own settings with given melodies or bass lines.

(1) Start by identifying the key and mode, then write the scale degree over each note. Sing or play the given line.

(2) Look at the beginning and end of the given line to determine where it implies a I or $V^{(7)}$ chord. Then choose scale degrees for the contrapuntal line that match the implied harmonies at the beginning and that make an appropriate cadence at the end. Fill in the first few and last few notes, and write in the intervals and implied Roman numerals.

(3) Examine the shape of the middle portion of the given part. Where there are several steps in a row, plan to include a skip or leap in the line you are writing; where there are skips or leaps, place steps in your line.

(4) Think about the contour of the given line, and how you want the contour of your melody to balance it. Choose a possible high point, with an interval that is consonant with the given line's note. Sketch out a general shape for your line.

(5) Begin filling in the middle, considering both the harmonic intervals between the two parts and the shape of your line. Label the intervals, and check every perfect interval for parallels and for the type of approach (e.g., contrary or oblique motion, or similar motion with stepwise soprano). Revise as necessary to make good contrapuntal and melodic sense.

KEY CONCEPT Always check the counterpoint you have written.

- Does it imply either tonic harmony or a V–I anacrusis at the beginning?
- Does it close with one of the standard types of cadences?
- Does it form consonant harmonic intervals or chordal dissonances (from V^7) with the given line?
- Is there a balance between perfect and imperfect consonances, with more of the latter?
- Does it avoid parallel octaves and fifths? Are perfect consonances approached by contrary or similar motion with a stepwise upper line, or oblique motion?
- And finally, does it show a pleasing overall contour that coordinates well with the shape of the given line?

Examine the opening and closing patterns in Example 11.15, a typical eighteenth-century tonal bass line, and consider how you would write a well-balanced melody, following the guidelines above. The bass line begins with an anacrusis ($\hat{5}$–$\hat{1}$ in D minor) and ends with $\hat{5}$–$\hat{5}$–$\hat{1}$.

EXAMPLE 11.15: A typical bass line in eighteenth-century style

For the opening and closing, choose a pattern that implies V or V7 to i. Example 11.16 shows one possible setting: a $\hat{5}$–$\flat\hat{3}$ opening and $\hat{5}$–$\hat{4}$–$\flat\hat{3}$ conclusion. In the first full measure, the bass line's $\hat{1}$–$\hat{7}$–$\hat{1}$ may be set in contrary motion with $\flat\hat{3}$–$\hat{4}$–$\flat\hat{3}$ to imply a i–V$^6_5$–i progression; this setting resolves the dissonant d5 correctly to a third.

EXAMPLE 11.16: Opening and closing counterpoint

The bass's D3 on beat 3 is then followed by E3 and F3. These three notes could be set with a voice exchange F4–E4–D4 in the soprano to make the intervallic pattern 3–8–6 (Example 11.17)—a strong contrapuntal gesture because it employs both imperfect and perfect consonances, and approaches and leaves the P8 stepwise in contrary motion.

EXAMPLE 11.17: One possible note-to-note setting

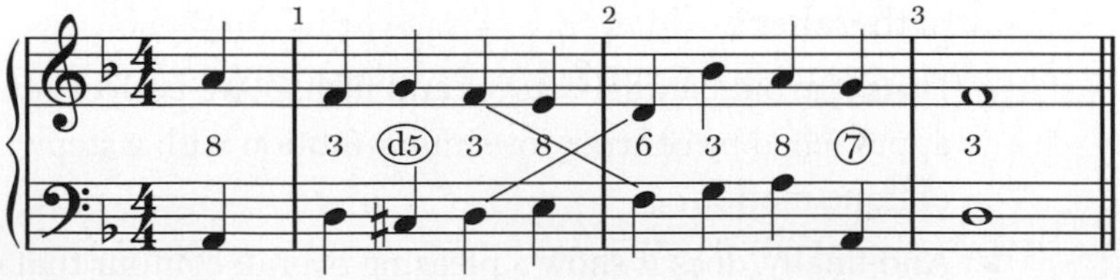

We have set the step F3–G3 in measure 2 with an upward leap D4 to B♭4, adding interest to the melody and providing a distinctive high point. The leap is approached by a series of steps in the opposite direction (G4–F4–E4–D4) and is also followed by descending steps (B♭4–A4–G4–F4). Overall, then, the contour of the soprano melody provides contrary motion with the bass, and the two parts balance each other throughout.

Try it #4

Example 11.17 is only one of many possible settings for this bass line; try out another option using the hints below. Refer to the guidelines in the Key Concepts above, and be sure to sing or play through your counterpoint when complete.

Hints: The cadence may be set with 3–3–8, 3–5–8 or 5–3–8 (don't forget to use the leading tone C♯). Explore various opening intervals: 3–8 (again, with C♯), 5–3, or 8–5. The bass's C♯3–D3–E3 in measure 1 may be set with a voice exchange, E4–D4–C♯4 (resolving to D in the next measure), as can the F3–G3–A3 in measure 2.

Melodic Embellishment in Chorale Textures

Passing Tones, Neighbor Tones, and Consonant Skips

As in second species, melodic embellishments are prevalent in eighteenth-century two-voice counterpoint—particularly unaccented passing and neighbor tones and consonant skips. But unlike species style, these embellishments may appear in different voices on different beats, creating rhythmic variety between the two lines. For an example, listen to the first phrase of "Ein feste Burg" (Example 11.18); pay particular attention to any passing tones.

Example 11.18: Bach, "Ein feste Burg," mm. 1–4a (soprano and bass)

KEY CONCEPT Three types of passing tones are permitted in eighteenth-century style: the dissonant passing tone in either an unaccented or accented position, and the unaccented consonant passing tone. The dissonant unaccented passing tone is by far the most common.

Try it #5

In Example 11.18, the intervals between the voices are labeled, along with three passing tones. Which of the remaining offbeat eighth notes also make dissonant passing tones? Circle and label them.

The bass anacrusis in Example 11.18 implies tonic harmony, with the interval 2 (9) formed by a dissonant unaccented passing tone; in measure 1, beat 2, the interval 4 from the bass's dissonant passing tone falls on the beat; and in measure 3, beat 2, the bass line maintains consonant intervals (6 and 5), by means of a consonant passing tone.

There are several places (on beats with no embellishments) where both voices move together rhythmically, making a 1:1 setting. Here, the guidelines of 1:1 counterpoint apply. If we eliminated the second note of each pair of eighth notes, for example, and adjust for accented passing tones (leave out the accented passing tone A3 in m. 1 and keep the G3), the principles of good counterpoint should be followed from beat to beat.

In addition to passing tones, both consonant and dissonant neighbor tones are also typical embellishments in this style, as are consonant skips. Listen to the soprano and bass lines of Bach's "Wachet auf," given in Example 11.19.

EXAMPLE 11.19: Bach, "Wachet auf," mm. 32b–36 (soprano and bass)

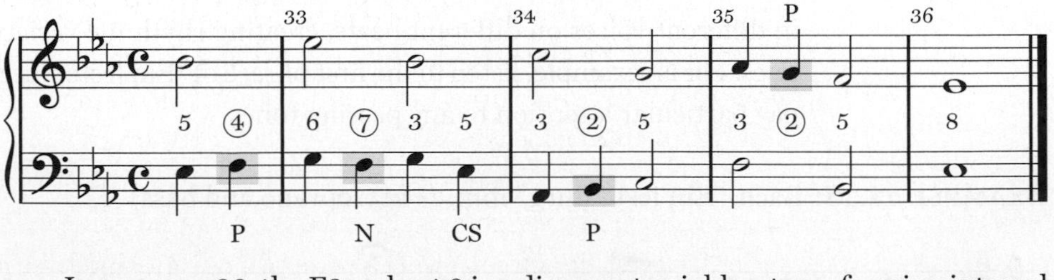

In measure 33, the F3 on beat 2 is a dissonant neighbor tone, forming interval 7 with the soprano. As in species style, the neighbor tone moves away from a consonance by step, and then returns to the pitch where it began, forming another consonant interval: 6–7–3. Neighbor tones typically appear in unaccented positions, as here. The final two beats of the measure make intervals 3 and 5, both of which are consonances and members of the E♭ major triad. In eighteenth-century style, where melody and bass lines imply harmonic progressions, a consonant skip like that on beat 4 may also be referred to as a **chordal skip** if it spans members of the same implied harmony.

Suspensions

Unlike fourth species, where there are suspensions against most notes of the given line, suspensions in eighteenth-century counterpoint are mixed with other types of embellishments or reserved to highlight a cadence. The available dissonant suspensions are the same as in strict style: 4–3, 7–6, and 9–8 in the upper part and 2–3 (or 9–10) in the lower. Less attention is paid to consonant suspensions, because they do not require preparation or resolution.

For an example of suspensions, listen to the first part of "Rosa Mystica" (soprano and bass lines are shown in Example 11.20), and focus on the intervals approaching the cadence in measures 3–4.

Example 11.20: "Rosa Mystica," mm. 1–4a (soprano and bass)

In eighteenth-century style, suspensions may be connected to their consonant preparation by a tie, as in strict style, or tied notation may be replaced with a longer duration. In measure 3, for example, the half notes G4 and F4 replace tied quarter notes for the preparation and suspension components of this 4–3 chain. Since this example is primarily note-to-note, the rhythmic interest and dissonance provided by the suspensions prove even more striking.

While we have focused primarily on soprano and bass voices in this chapter, the principles of good counterpoint also apply between the bass and each of the upper parts. In Example 11.21, for instance, the alto and bass parts from "Wachet auf," the texture is primarily 2:1, with dissonant passing tones in measures 8 and 9, and a neighbor tone in measure 7. The cadence is approached through a 7–6 suspension chain in measure 10; when the suspended note is not tied to its preparation, as in measures 9–10 across the bar line, the dissonance figure is called a **rearticulated suspension**.

EXAMPLE 11.21: Bach, "Wachet auf," mm. 6–11 (alto and bass)

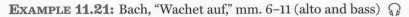

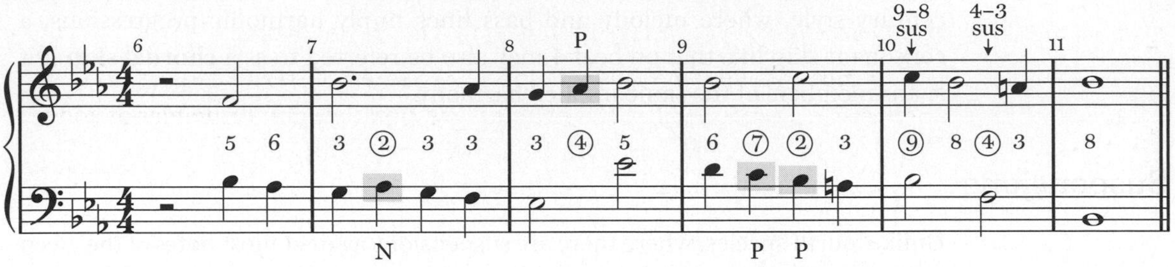

Although the durations of the consonant preparation, dissonant suspension, and resolution may vary, the suspension itself must arrive *on* the beat, as in Examples 11.20 and 11.21. In performance, musicians tend to *crescendo* slightly into the accented dissonance and pull away from the resolution; try this (subtly!) for a more expressive performance.

SUMMARY

Suspensions in eighteenth-century style, like those in strict style, consist of three parts:

(1) a consonance (the preparation), which is held over to the next beat to make

(2) an accented dissonance (the suspension), which then resolves down by step to

(3) a consonance (the resolution).

The preparation may be connected to the suspension by a tie as in strict style; the tied note may be replaced with a single note of longer duration if the preparation and suspension are in the same measure; or the tie may be missing altogether for a rearticulated suspension. Although the suspension must fall on an accented note (on the beat), the preparation and resolution may fall on the beat or offbeat.

Recognizing and labeling harmonic patterns in phrase openings and cadences, as we have done in this chapter, is the first step in learning music analysis. Be sure to identify melodic embellishments—passing tones, neighbor tones, consonant skips—and suspensions as well: they will help you understand other elements of the counterpoint.

SUMMARY

Eighteenth-century 2:1 counterpoint should do the following.

1. Continue to follow the guidelines for 1:1 counterpoint with respect to types of motion (contrary, similar, oblique, and parallel) and principles of good melodic writing. Phrase beginnings and endings will imply tonic and dominant (seventh) harmonies.
2. Incorporate chordal skips, dissonant passing tones, and neighbor tones on the offbeats, and occasionally accented passing and neighbor tones on the beat.
3. Treat the P4 as a dissonance—as a passing or neighbor tone or in a 4–3 suspension.
4. Avoid similar motion into perfect intervals unless the upper voice moves by step.
5. Avoid parallel perfect consonances (P5–P5, P8–P8) from offbeat to beat or on consecutive beats.
6. Occasionally include dissonant suspensions, especially approaching a cadence.

Did You Know?

The melodies of hymns were often composed long before the familiar SATB settings that are sung now; they also appear with different harmonizations and texts appropriate to different occasions. For example, the tune "Chartres" is a fifteenth-century French melody, but the four-part harmonization included here is by Irish composer Charles Wood, written in the nineteenth century. Our harmonization of "Old Hundredth" is by Louis Bourgeois, from the sixteenth century; one text that is often sung with this melody today is the "Doxology." The melody "St. George's Windsor," here in a nineteenth-century harmonization by George J. Elvey, is associated in the United States with the Thanksgiving hymn "Come, ye thankful people, come." All harmonizations appear in the Episcopal Hymnal 1940.

TERMS YOU SHOULD KNOW

- accented passing tone
- cadence
- chordal dissonance
- chordal skip
- phrase
- rearticulated suspension

QUESTIONS FOR REVIEW

1. What are some differences between strict first-species counterpoint and note-to-note eighteenth-century counterpoint?
2. What dissonant intervals are components of a dominant seventh chord? How should each of these dissonances resolve?
3. What types of motion are allowed when approaching a perfect interval?
4. What are typical soprano-bass patterns for openings with an anacrusis?
5. What types of conclusive cadences are used in two-part eighteenth-century style? What are the characteristic scale degrees in each part?
6. What is different about the use of passing tones, neighbor tones, and suspensions in eighteenth-century style as opposed to species style?
7. What steps should you follow to harmonize a melody in eighteenth-century style?

The Basic Phrase in SATB Style

CHAPTER 12

Outline of topics

The notation of four-part harmony

- Writing for voices: SATB
- Writing for keyboard

Parts of the basic phrase

- Defining the phrase model: T–D–T
- Establishing the tonic area
- Cadential area and cadence types

Connecting the dominant and tonic areas

- Resolving the leading tone in V and V^6
- Other voice-leading considerations

Harmonizing folk songs

- Keyboard textures

Overview

This chapter introduces the basic phrase—the harmonic foundation for most tonal music, from short phrases to entire movements. We arrange its harmonic pillars, I and V, in SATB and keyboard styles, and harmonize a melody with keyboard accompaniment.

Repertoire

Johann Sebastian Bach,
"Ach Gott, vom Himmel sieh' darein" ("O God, Look Down on Us from Heaven," Chorale No. 253)
"Wachet auf" ("Awake," Chorale No. 197)

Ludwig van Beethoven, Piano Sonata in D Minor, Op. 31, No. 2 (*Tempest*), third movement

Jeremiah Clarke, *Trumpet Voluntary* (*Prince of Denmark's March*)

Muzio Clementi, Sonatina in C Major, Op. 36, No. 1, first movement

"Clementine" (folk tune, arranged by Norman Lloyd)

Joseph Haydn, Scherzo, from Piano Sonata No. 9 in F Major

"Merrily We Roll Along"

Wolfgang Amadeus Mozart, Piano Sonata in C Major, K. 545, first movement

"My Country, 'Tis of Thee"

The Notation of Four-Part Harmony

We turn now from two-part counterpoint to four-part writing, typified by hymn style with its four distinct voices: SATB (from high to low, soprano, alto, tenor, bass). In SATB settings, individual members of triads and seventh chords are assigned to particular octaves, adding inner parts to the melody and bass-line counterpoint. These chords, as we have seen, do not always appear in root position but are voiced in different inversions to create a smooth bass melody. The principles of SATB choral writing pertain to other styles of tonal music as well, including keyboard: they all involve triads and seventh chords arranged in four voices, with smooth voice-leading connections between them.

Writing for Voices: SATB

Listen to the hymn setting of "My Country, 'Tis of Thee" ("America"), given in Example 12.1 in SATB notation, and focus on the spacing and registers (highness or lowness) that characterize the four distinct vocal parts.

Example 12.1: "My Country, 'Tis of Thee," mm. 1–6

When writing a good SATB setting, keep five basic concepts in mind: notation, range, spacing, voice crossing, and doubling. We will consider each in turn.

SATB Notation: Staff, Clefs, and Stems Notate the soprano and alto voices on the treble staff of a grand staff and the bass and tenor voices on the bass staff.

KEY CONCEPT The direction of stems, combined with the clef, indicates which note each part sings:

- The soprano part is in the treble staff with stems up.
- The alto part is in the treble staff with stems down.
- The tenor part is in the bass staff with stems up.
- The bass part is in the bass staff with stems down.

Sing or play each line (S, A, T, and B) in Example 12.1 as a melody. If the soprano and alto sing the same note in unison at the same time, the note will have two stems: one up for soprano and one down for alto, as in measure 4, beat 3. This is true for the tenor and bass as well (see Example 12.2a). When alto and tenor sing in unison, however, each voice receives its own note—one for each staff (part b). When either soprano and alto or tenor and bass sing unison whole notes, write two whole notes right next to each other (part c).

EXAMPLE 12.2: Notating unisons in SATB style

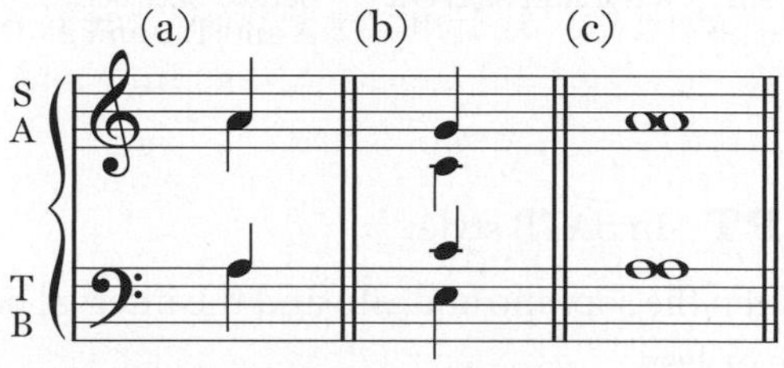

Range To make an SATB setting easy to sing, the pitches in each part need to conform to the traditional range for the singers, shown in Example 12.3. The ranges are somewhat flexible, but in general you should stay within these guidelines.

EXAMPLE 12.3: SATB vocal ranges

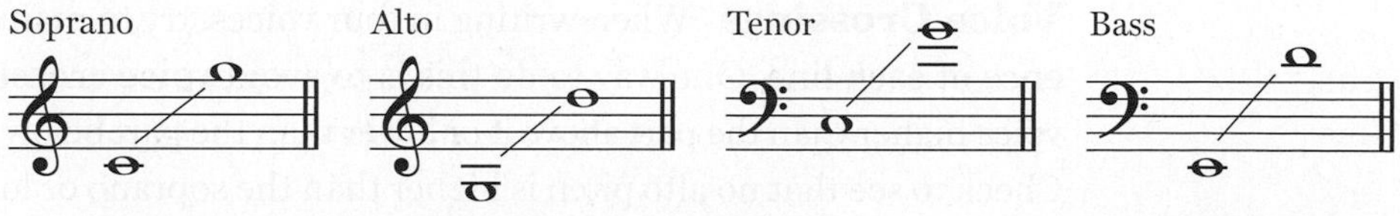

Voice ranges vary depending on the age and maturity of the singer, as well as on the type of composition. Music for children or teens, for example, requires smaller vocal ranges, and the four men's voices in a barbershop quartet have their own special ranges. Choral settings for skilled or professional adult singers may exceed the SATB range guidelines.

Spacing Four-part chords sound best if the interval between adjacent parts is an octave or less, to allow the parts to blend together with a balanced harmony. The exception is the distance between tenor and bass; these voices can sound muddy if too close in a low octave. Example 12.4a provides some guidelines for good spacing.

EXAMPLE 12.4: Spacing guidelines

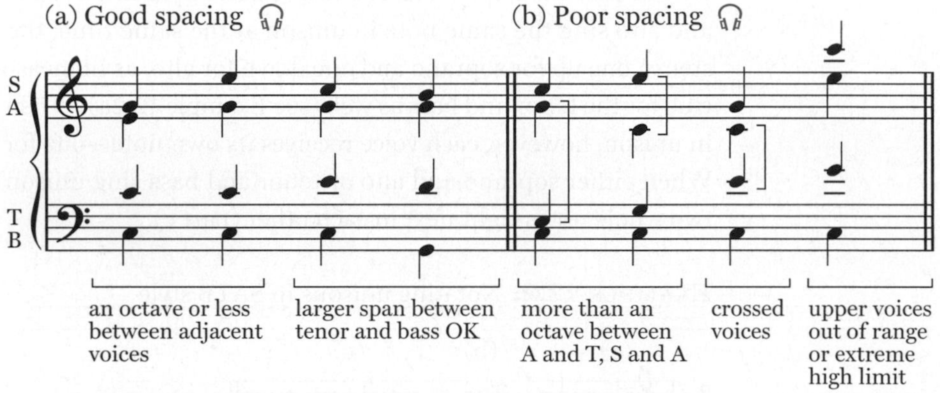

KEY CONCEPT In SATB style:

- The interval between the soprano and alto and the interval between the alto and tenor is an octave or less.
- The interval between the tenor and bass may exceed an octave, but usually remains within a twelfth.

These spacing guidelines mimic the structure of the overtone series, providing acoustic clarity.

Voice Crossings When writing in four voices, try to maintain the independence of each line. One way to do this is to avoid **voice crossings**—crossing one voice higher than the part above it or lower than the part below it (Example 12.4b). Check to see that no alto pitch is higher than the soprano or lower than the tenor, and that no tenor pitch is higher than the alto or lower than the bass.

In some Bach chorale settings, however, voice crossings are included to create a more interesting melodic line. When you find voice crossings, variations in spacing, and other departures from the guidelines given here in music you are studying, consider which concerns may have motivated the composer's choices.

Try it #1

Evaluate the range and spacing of each SATB chord below. In the blanks, write the chord's root, quality, and figure, and the letter from the list below that best describes the chord's voicing.

A. Proper range and spacing.
B. A vocal range extends beyond the recommended guidelines.
C. Spacing between soprano and alto exceeds an octave.
D. Spacing between alto and tenor exceeds an octave.
E. Voices are crossed.

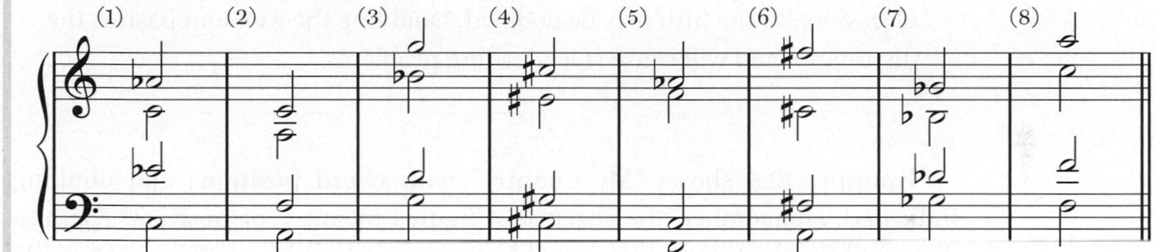

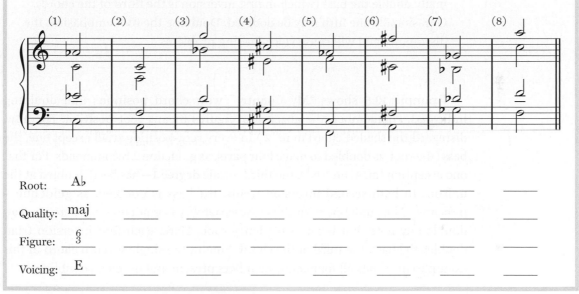

	(1)	(2)	(3)	(4)	(5)	(6)	(7)	(8)
Root:	A♭							
Quality:	maj							
Figure:	$^6_3$							
Voicing:	E							

Doubling Because triads consist of only three chord members, one of them must be represented twice, or doubled, to make four parts. Following are general guidelines for doubling in triads and seventh chords, but you will find exceptions in some pieces, where the doubling differs because of the musical context.

KEY CONCEPT Doubling guidelines for triads:

1. Never double a note with an accidental or a **tendency tone**: a scale degree or chord member that must be resolved, such as the leading tone ($\hat{7}$) and the seventh of the dominant seventh chord ($\hat{4}$).

2. For root position (major or minor quality), usually the bass (root) is doubled. Sometimes you can double the third or fifth to connect chords smoothly, but this is less common.
3. For first inversion, double any chord member that does not have an added accidental and is not a tendency tone. Doubling the soprano is one common strategy for major or minor triads; you can also double the bass.
4. For second inversion, always double the bass.
5. For diminished triads (which typically appear in first inversion), you normally double the bass (which in first inversion is the third of the chord). Occasionally, the fifth may be doubled. Doubling the root emphasizes the dissonance and will cause voice-leading problems.

Example 12.5 shows "My Country" with chord positions and doubling indicated. (Remember, the absence of figures means root position. For now, disregard the shaded chord in m. 2.) In every root-position triad except one, the bass (the root) is doubled to make four parts, as guideline 2 recommends. For that one exception (m. 4, on "-ty"), the third—scale degree $\hat{1}$—has been doubled at the unison. In both second-inversion triads, the bass is doubled, as guideline 4 indicates. The guideline with the most variability is guideline 3, where you can double any note that is not a tendency tone. Here, each first-inversion triad doubles the bass, the third of the chord. Finally, the single seventh chord in this example (m. 4) has all four chord members present and needs no doubling.

EXAMPLE 12.5: Doubling in "My Country, 'Tis of Thee," mm. 1–6

Try it #2

A. For each triad and inversion specified, write an SATB chord with the proper doubling.

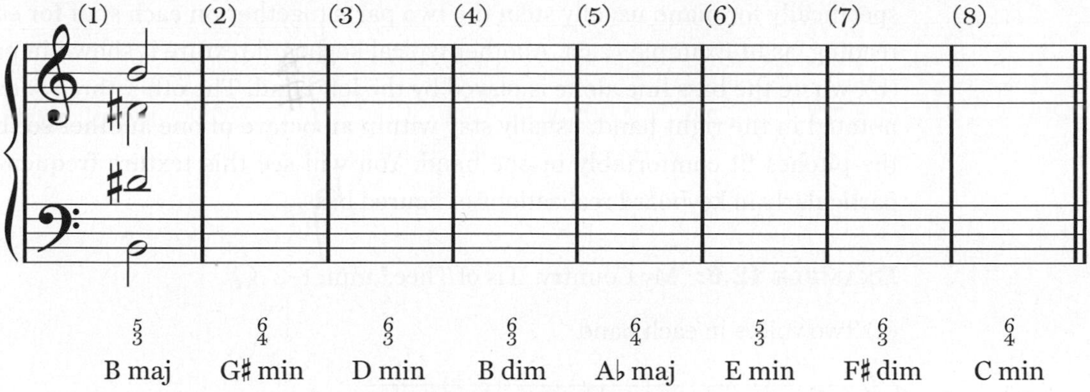

B. Now write an SATB chord with the proper doubling for each bass note and figured bass symbol. Reminder: An accidental with no number applies to the third above the bass, and a slash through a number raises that pitch (the same as a ♯).

Writing for Keyboard

When you write for the keyboard, you can take advantage of ten fingers and a large range. That means numerous types of settings are possible, some with more than four voices. We will examine a wide variety of keyboard styles in the course of this book, but for now we look at those most closely linked to four-part harmonization, where the concerns are assigning the four voices to the two hands, the spacing within each hand, and the spacing between the hands. Of course, when writing specifically for keyboard, you can include pitches higher or lower than the ranges suggested for (sung) voices.

Dividing Four Voices Between Two Hands Keyboard players can play from SATB hymn settings like "My Country" (Example 12.5)—church musicians and chorus accompanists do this frequently—but four-part textures written specifically for piano usually stem the two parts together on each staff for easy reading, as in Example 12.6a. Another typical keyboard texture is shown in part (b), where the bass line alone is played by the left hand. The other three voices, notated in the right hand, usually stay within an octave of one another so that the pitches fit comfortably in one hand. You will see this texture frequently, particularly in keyboard realizations of figured bass.

EXAMPLE 12.6: "My Country, 'Tis of Thee," mm. 1–2

(a) Two voices in each hand

(b) Three voices in the right hand, one in the left

One additional distribution of voices appears frequently in keyboard works—three parts in the left hand and one in the right. This voicing, often taught in keyboard harmony classes, can provide chordal accompaniments to a melody in the right hand, as in Example 12.7.

EXAMPLE 12.7: "Merrily We Roll Along," mm. 1–4

Left-hand chords also serve as a model for arpeggiated accompaniments, such as Alberti bass. Listen to the passage shown in Example 12.8a, the opening measures of Mozart's Piano Sonata in C Major. Here, the Alberti bass accompaniment is based on the underlying chordal model shown in part (b).

EXAMPLE 12.8: Mozart, Piano Sonata in C Major, first movement

(a) Mm. 1–4

(b) Reduction of mm. 1–4, left-hand part

Spacing When you assign pitches to each hand in a keyboard setting, be sure they fall within a hand's reach—usually an octave (although some pianists with large hands may reach a tenth or more). You should limit the number of pitches per hand to three (possibly four) to allow the player a comfortable hand position and simultaneous attack. Avoid writing a single chord for the two hands with empty space between the hands (e.g., more than a tenth between the lowest pitch in the right hand and the highest in the left). This spacing would create the effect of two different chords, one in each hand, instead of a single chord.

Parts of the Basic Phrase

Having considered the ways a single chord may be voiced in four parts, we turn now to chord connections within the context of a musical phrase. A **phrase** is a basic unit of musical thought, similar to a sentence in language, and like most sentences it has a beginning, a middle, and an end. As discussed in Chapter 11, the end is marked by a cadence: the harmonic, melodic, and rhythmic features that make a phrase sound like a discrete thought. Phrases may end conclusively (like a sentence punctuated with a period) or inconclusively (like a clause punctuated with a comma or semicolon).

Listen to the Haydn Scherzo and Clementi Sonatina excerpts in Examples 12.9 and 12.10. The Haydn passage expresses two complete four-measure phrases, while the Clementi comprises one. Which of these three phrases sounds least conclusive, as though the music must continue? Consider first the melodic scale degree with which each phrase ends. Haydn's phrases end on $\hat{3}$ and $\hat{1}$, respectively; Clementi's ends on $\hat{5}$.

EXAMPLE 12.9: Haydn, Scherzo, from Piano Sonata No. 9 in F Major, mm. 1–8

EXAMPLE 12.10: Clementi, Sonatina in C Major, first movement, mm. 1–4a

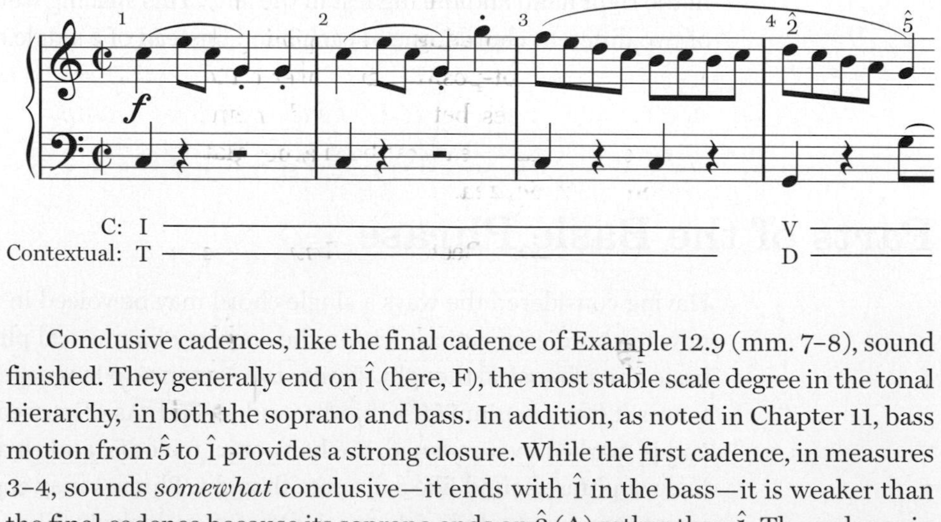

Conclusive cadences, like the final cadence of Example 12.9 (mm. 7–8), sound finished. They generally end on $\hat{1}$ (here, F), the most stable scale degree in the tonal hierarchy, in both the soprano and bass. In addition, as noted in Chapter 11, bass motion from $\hat{5}$ to $\hat{1}$ provides a strong closure. While the first cadence, in measures 3–4, sounds *somewhat* conclusive—it ends with $\hat{1}$ in the bass—it is weaker than the final cadence because its soprano ends on $\hat{3}$ (A) rather than $\hat{1}$. The cadence in

Example 12.10 sounds the most inconclusive, as though the music needs to continue further; it does not end with $\hat{1}$ in either the soprano or the bass.

Recognizing phrase types can help you shape a performance by thinking of the musical phrase as motion toward the cadence. You can use expressive timing techniques (rubato) to emphasize the sense of arrival on the tonic in a conclusive phrase, or to bring out the suspense of avoiding the tonic in an inconclusive phrase.

Defining the Phrase Model: T–D–T

Conclusive phrases include at least three tonal areas, which form the harmonic structure of the **basic phrase**: an opening tonic area (T), a dominant area (D), and tonic closure (T). The T–D–T basic phrase governs both large- and small-scale harmonic motion in much tonal music. An inconclusive phrase begins with the tonic and then may cadence in the dominant area, T–D, or on a chord substituting for the tonic. These harmonic areas are marked in Examples 12.9 and 12.10 as the lower analytical layer.

KEY CONCEPT In two-level analyses, the top level gives Roman numerals for each chord. The lower level supplies the **contextual analysis**—indicating how these harmonies function within the basic phrase model T–D–T.

Establishing the Tonic Area

The tonic at the beginning of the basic phrase establishes a stable home base. Typically, a root-position tonic triad will begin the phrase, then the tonic area will be expanded by repeating or arpeggiating the tonic triad (Example 12.9, mm. 1–2), by combining root-position and inverted tonic triads, or by adding passing tones or neighbor tones between chord members. Example 12.11, drawn from a Beethoven sonata, features both arpeggiation of the tonic and passing tones to extend the tonic area.

EXAMPLE 12.11: Beethoven, *Tempest* Sonata, third movement, mm. 1–3

d: i

Contextual: T

Example 12.12, from Bach's SATB setting of a chorale melody, expands the tonic by motion to first inversion and back. Here, you need not repeat the Roman numeral I in measure 33, but simply show the change in inversion. Passing and neighbor tones in parallel tenths between the bass and alto voices add contrapuntal interest.

EXAMPLE 12.12: Bach, "Wachet auf," mm. 32b–33

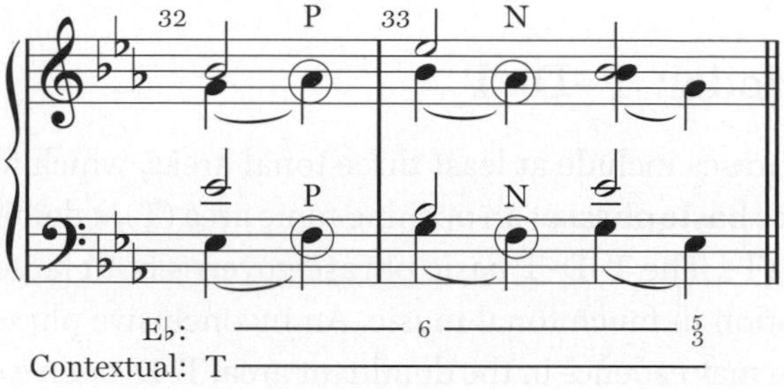

The dominant chord can also be used to expand the tonic area. One familiar technique is to precede the initial downbeat by a dominant or dominant seventh anacrusis. This chord, with its tendency tones (the leading tone and chordal seventh), has the effect of actually strengthening the initial tonic, as in the first phrase of Bach's setting "Ach Gott, vom Himmel sieh' darein" (Example 12.13). Sing this phrase as a class or play it at a keyboard to hear how the dominant anacrusis functions within the tonic area.

EXAMPLE 12.13: Bach, "Ach Gott, vom Himmel sieh' darein," mm. 4b–6a

Bach's chorale phrase also illustrates another way that V may serve to expand I. Within the tonic area, there may be embedded small I–V–I motions, which are subsidiary to the overall tonic harmony and also subsidiary to the arrival on a strong dominant at the cadence. The cadence, incidentally, is marked in chorale style by a **fermata**, or pause (𝄐). In the example, chords 2–4 and 5–7 are small i–V–i motions that prolong the tonic area. Sing or play the phrase again to hear how these early dominants sound much weaker than the V at the cadence. Embedded V chords often, though not always, appear in inversion. The $^6_4$ position is particularly weak in function and serves a more contrapuntal role; we will return to this chord in Chapter 14.

SUMMARY

The tonic area may be expanded by various means:

- simple repetition or arpeggiation,
- motion into and out of inversions,
- a dominant anacrusis,
- embedded I–V–I (or i–V–i) progressions, with or without inversions,
- embellishing tones added to any of the techniques above.

Cadential Area and Cadence Types

Authentic Cadences The cadential area of a conclusive phrase comprises the dominant-to-tonic portion of the basic T–D–T phrase. Two types of cadences may conclude such phrases, both known as authentic cadences.

KEY CONCEPT An **authentic cadence** (AC) is formed when V moves to I to end a phrase.

This type of cadence is most definitive when the harmonies are in root position and the soprano line moves from $\hat{2}$ or $\hat{7}$ to $\hat{1}$, as in Example 12.14a: a **perfect authentic cadence** (PAC). "Authentic" refers to the progression V–I, and "perfect" indicates that the soprano and bass are in their strongest positions: root-position harmonies ending with $\hat{1}$ in the soprano. Because motion between root-position V or V7 and I has such a pronounced cadential sound, this chord sequence is usually reserved for final cadences and used less often mid-phrase.

EXAMPLE 12.14: Cadence types in SATB voicing

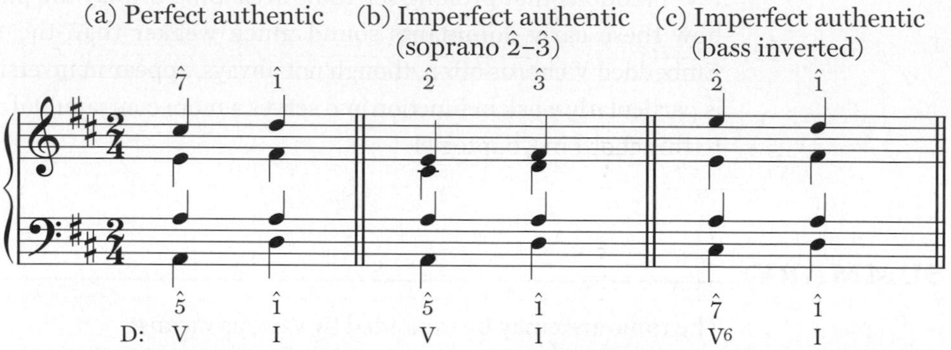

It is possible to weaken an authentic cadence by ending the soprano line on a scale degree other than $\hat{1}$ (part b) or, even more, by placing either harmony in inversion (part c). These are called **imperfect authentic cadences** (IAC). They are still "authentic" because of the progression V–I, but are no longer "perfect." Inverting the dominant in an IAC (part c) results in a cadence that is more contrapuntal, because it is the product of bass-line voice leading. It is substantially weaker than the IAC shown in part (b), which retains the strong root motion in the bass. Use IACs to end a phrase with less finality—for example, in the middle of a piece.

Look back at the two phrases from Haydn's sonata in Example 12.9: the first cadence (mm. 3–4) is an IAC (V^7–I, ending with $\hat{3}$ in the melody); the second (mm. 7–8) is a PAC (V^7–I, ending with $\hat{1}$ in the melody). As is typical in paired phrases, the first cadence is weaker than the more conclusive second.

Half Cadence An inconclusive cadence that ends on V, as in Example 12.10 or 12.13, is called a **half cadence** (HC). Here the basic phrase model is incomplete or interrupted; the phrase ends in the dominant area without moving on to the tonic.

KEY CONCEPT Authentic cadences are defined by two chords (V–I), but half cadences are identified only by their final chord; the chord that precedes the V could be one of several. Half cadences typically end on a root-position dominant, and often (though not always) feature $\hat{2}$ in the soprano.

Half cadences typically function like a comma in a sentence, where an inconclusive phrase (ending with a HC) is followed by a conclusive one (ending with an AC), as in Example 12.15.

EXAMPLE 12.15: Clarke, *Trumpet Voluntary*, mm. 1–8

Listen to these two phrases. At measure 4, the melody repeats $\hat{5}$, the harmony comes to rest on a V chord, and the forward motion is briefly suspended. Measure 5 initiates a new beginning, with the melody almost identical to measure 1. Therefore, although V (m. 4) does move on to I (in m. 5), it does not create an authentic cadence—rather, harmonic, melodic, and rhythmic factors divide the music into two distinct phrases at measure 4, each with its own cadence.

SUMMARY

The musical role of a phrase is defined in part by its cadence.

- A half cadence (HC) ends on V, with the melody often on $\hat{2}$; an inconclusive phrase ending.
- An imperfect authentic cadence (IAC) ends with V–I; the melody ends on $\hat{3}$ or $\hat{5}$, and/or either V or I is weakened by inversion; usually a less conclusive phrase ending.
- A perfect authentic cadence (PAC) ends with root-position V–I, the melody ending $\hat{2}$–$\hat{1}$ or $\hat{7}$–$\hat{1}$; the strongest conclusive phrase ending.

Try it #3

Listen to a portion of the introduction to Handel's "Rejoice greatly" (mm. 5b–9a), shown below. Identify the measure numbers of one IAC and one PAC.

IAC: ______________ PAC: ______________

Connecting the Dominant and Tonic Areas

Resolving the Leading Tone in V and V6

Connecting V and I, with strong voice-leading in an SATB texture, provides in a microcosm many concepts you will draw on when composing in freer textures. As mentioned earlier, the active ingredient in dominant triads is the leading tone, $\hat{7}$: a tendency tone with a strong linear pull upward toward the tonic. When V resolves to I, $\hat{7}$ will almost always resolve up to $\hat{1}$ by half step. This is true whether the key is major or minor: in minor, remember to raise $\flat\hat{7}$ to $\hat{7}$ so that it functions as a leading tone.

KEY CONCEPT Minor-key authentic and half cadences always need an accidental to create a leading tone and a major-quality V chord.

Look at Example 12.16 to see how different SATB voicings of the dominant and tonic are resolved in D major and D minor. First, in each case, $\hat{7}$ resolves up by half step to $\hat{1}$ (C♯ to D). Second, because I and V share one note ($\hat{5}$), this pitch is often retained as a common tone in the same voice: here, the A is kept in either the alto or tenor. The remaining voices, meanwhile, move the smallest possible distance to another chord tone, for smooth voice-leading. Although the dominant triad provides the strongest resolution to tonic when in root position, first inversion (V^6) is common as well, since the bass line will feature the upward resolution of the tendency tone: $\hat{7}$–$\hat{1}$.

EXAMPLE 12.16: Resolution of V–I(i) and V^6–I(i)

(a) D major (b) D minor

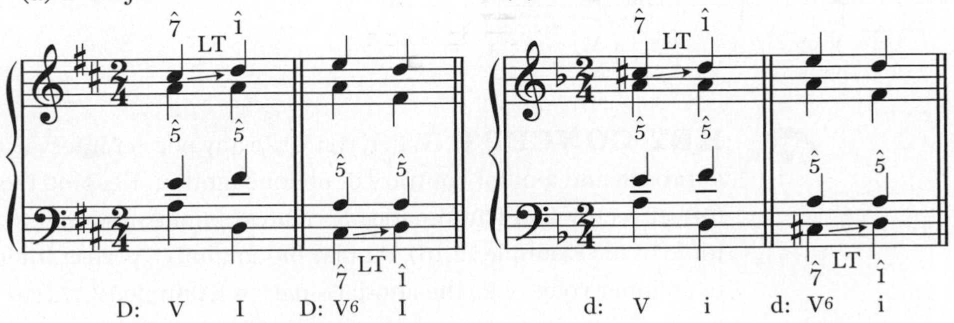

Other Voice-Leading Considerations

In SATB style, the principles of chord connection—connecting melodic lines in four voices—are intimately related to those for writing counterpoint in two voices. For example, in both two- and four-voice writing, parallel motion between imperfect consonances like sixths and thirds is usual (Example 12.17), provided that it does not continue so long that the voices lose their independence. On the other hand, parallel motion between perfect octaves or fifths (parts b and c) is not found in most common-practice compositions, though parallel fifths do appear as a "doubling" of the melody in some rock and folk music. A simple repetition of fifths or octaves, though, is fine (part d). Finally, even contrary motion from P8 to P8, or P5 to P5, is not permitted. This is known as parallel octaves or fifths by contrary motion, or simply **contrary octaves** (part e) or **contrary fifths** (part f).

Example 12.17: V–I voice-leading guidelines

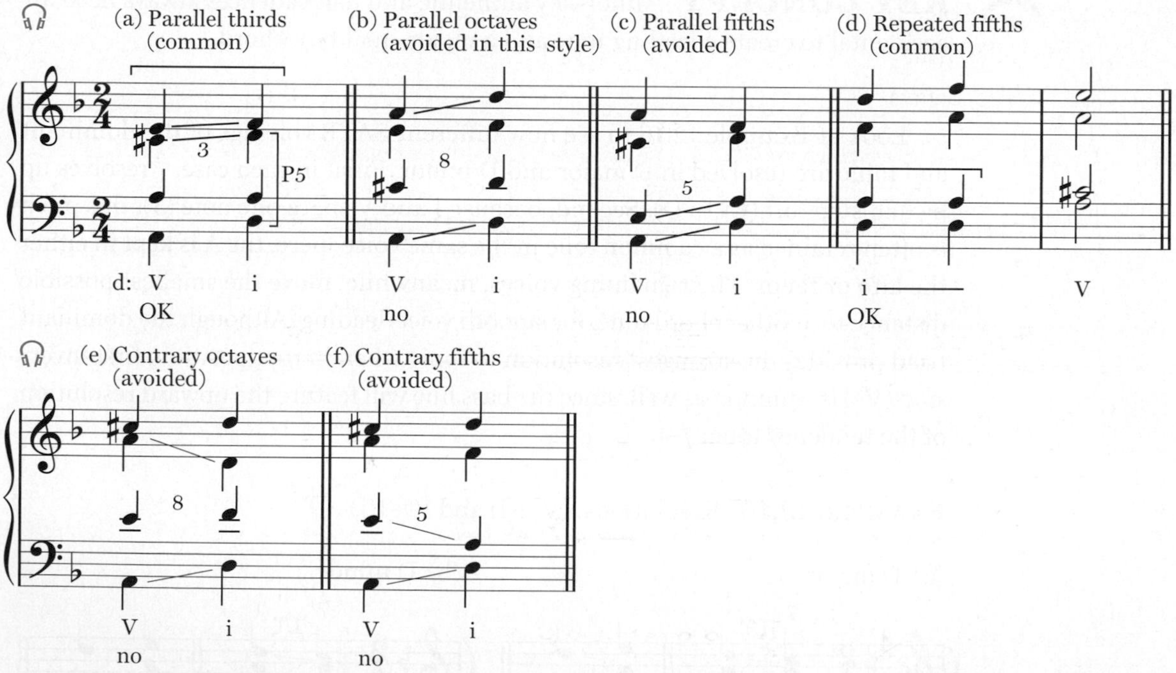

KEY CONCEPT When you write any perfect interval, consider its approach and aim for contrary or oblique motion. Keeping the common tone ($\hat{5}$) between V and I automatically creates oblique motion into the P5 of the tonic triad (Example 12.16). Similar motion into a perfect interval is permitted in an inner voice (e.g., the alto-bass pair in Example 12.17a) or in the outer voices if the soprano moves by step (Example 12.17e).

SUMMARY

When connecting V and I:

- Resolve the leading tone up to the tonic.
- Keep the common tone ($\hat{5}$) in the same voice, and move the other voices to the closest possible chord member.
- Approach perfect intervals by contrary or oblique motion (similar motion is acceptable in an inner voice only, or if the soprano moves by step).
- Follow other principles of good spacing, doubling, and voice-leading.

Try it #4

Write the key and Roman numerals for each V–I (or V–i) chord connection below. In the blank below the staff, write the letter that best describes the voice-leading between chords.

A. Proper voice-leading
B. Parallel fifths
C. Parallel octaves
D. Unresolved leading tone
E. Contrary octaves or fifths

B♭: V ___ ___ ___ ___ ___ ___ ___ ___ ___ ___ ___ ___ ___ ___ ___

A ___ ___ ___ ___

Harmonizing Folk Songs

When selecting harmonies for a melody of any type, first determine what the **harmonic rhythm** should be: how quickly the harmony needs to change to fit with the melody. This is an important element of musical style. In folk songs and some dance forms, for example, a typical harmonic rhythm is one chord per measure; pitches that do not belong to the harmony of the measure may be interpreted as passing, neighbor, or other embellishing tones. Once you have established a harmonic rhythm, keep it fairly consistent throughout. The one exception is at the cadence, where the harmonic rhythm often speeds up, then comes to rest with a longer duration on the final chord.

Many simple folk songs may be harmonized with just the tonic and dominant chords. The opening phrases of the folk tune "Clementine" are given in Example 12.18. How might you write an accompaniment to this melody? First identify the key and mode, then sing the melody with scale-degree numbers or solfège syllables, and let the numbers or syllables guide decisions about which phrases should end on I or V. Choose one harmony per measure for the accompaniment, then write the Roman numerals below or popular-music chord symbols above each measure.

EXAMPLE 12.18: "Clementine" (melody), mm. 1–8a

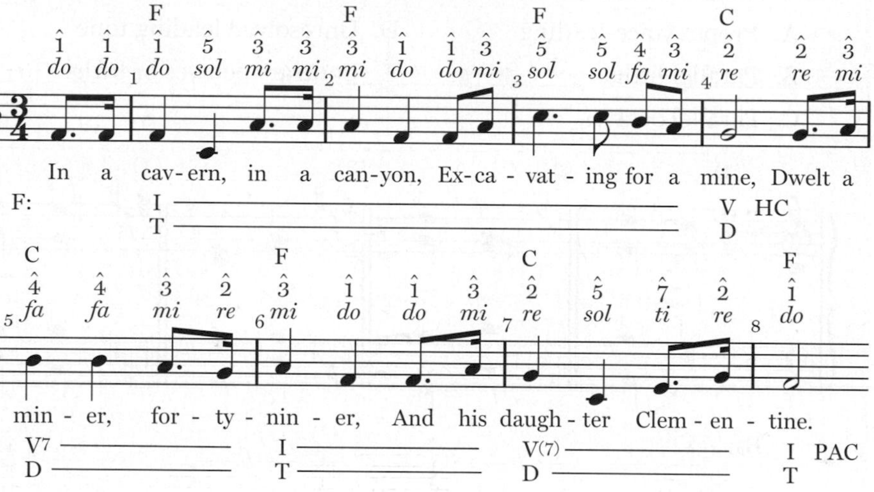

As a next step, determine the cadences: phrase 1 ends in measure 4 on $\hat{2}$ ("mine") and implies a HC: a C major chord (V in the key of F major). Phrase 2 ends in measure 8 on $\hat{1}$ ("-tine"), implying a PAC. Measures 1–3 basically arpeggiate F major, heading for the half cadence in measure 4; the B♭ in measure 3, beat 3, is a passing tone. (While m. 3 could possibly be set with a V7 chord, with the B♭ as its seventh [C–E–G–B♭], we prefer for V to arrive on the half cadence in m. 4 instead of a bar earlier.) Another passing tone is the A in measures 4 and 5. In two-phrase pairs, like this one, the first will often end on V (T–D) for a half cadence, while the second completes the T–D–T basic phrase. Here, the second phrase begins where the first ended, on V, before concluding with a final I–V–I (T–D–T).

Now play through the piano accompaniment given in Example 12.19. The arranger has chosen root-position tonic chords for the first phrase through the half cadence (now in m. 6, with the addition of a two-measure introduction). Phrase 2 begins in measure 7 with a V^4_3 moving to I, a weaker V–I progression than the strong root-position chords of the PAC (mm. 9–10). This piano arrangement doubles the melody in the right hand, while the left hand mimics the sound of a guitar arpeggio.

Example 12.19: "Clementine," mm. 1–10a, with piano accompaniment

Keyboard Textures

An SATB harmonization can be made into a piano accompaniment by adding rhythmic figuration. We'll look at several simple keyboard textures that conform to the T–D–T model.

KEY CONCEPT **Texture** refers to the number and alignment of individual voices or instrumental lines in a composition. You are already familiar with three types. (1) Contrapuntal textures combine quasi-independent melodic lines (as in species counterpoint). (2) **Homophonic** textures are chordal, with most voices moving together rhythmically (as in SATB or hymn-style writing). (3) Melody-and-accompaniment textures feature a rhythmically independent melody plus its harmonic support, which may include chordal arpeggiation or other types of figuration.

Listen to the first phrase of "Merrily We Roll Along" (Example 12.20), a melody-and-accompaniment texture, in class, while someone plays the SATB block-chord accompaniment.

EXAMPLE 12.20: "Merrily We Roll Along," mm. 1–4 with SATB accompaniment

Example 12.21 illustrates five different piano textures that can be derived from this SATB model. Part (a) is a chordal pattern with the roots in the bass on the downbeat, and the other parts in the right hand delayed to beat 2. Part (b) is a rhythmic variant, where the upper parts come on the offbeats; the downbeat is either the root of the tonic (D) or the fifth of the dominant (E), and beat 2 sounds scale-degree $\hat{5}$—similar to a Sousa march. The next two patterns are arpeggiated accompaniments, often chosen for lyrical settings. In part (c), the block chords of (a) are arpeggiated as even eighth notes, and in (d) as sixteenths. Part (e) doubles the melody in the right hand and realizes the chords as an Alberti bass in the left hand.

For a triple-meter melody, try a waltz bass—follow pattern (a), with the bass note on the downbeat and upper voices on beats 2 and 3. Play each of these to see what a different effect the accompaniment has on the character of the melody.

Example 12.21: "Merrily We Roll Along," mm. 1–4, with keyboard accompaniment patterns

(a) With chords displaced to beat 2

(b) With Sousa-style accompaniment

(c) With eighth-note arpeggiated accompaniment

(d) With sixteenth-note arpeggiated accompaniment

(e) With Alberti bass

The study of species counterpoint has served us well as a preparation for the V–I voice-leading at an authentic cadence, including the resolution of $\hat{7}$ to $\hat{1}$ and the treatment of perfect intervals, particularly avoiding parallel (or contrary) perfect octaves and fifths. In the coming chapters, which explore expansions of the basic phrase, we will see how principles of contrapuntal writing for both the soprano and bass lines add to the musical integrity of these phrases.

Did You Know?

The melody that we know as "My Country, 'Tis of Thee," or "America," is also sung in England as "God Save the Queen" (or "King," depending on the current monarch). The origin of the melody is a mystery. It was first published in England in 1744, and became popular after a version of the song with words by Thomas Arne was performed in the Drury Lane and Covent Garden Theaters in London the following year. Arne's lyrics rallied support for King George II and decried the Scots, led by "Bonnie Prince Charlie," George's Stuart rival for the throne. Both Beethoven and Haydn incorporated this melody into their own compositions.

Several different politically oriented lyrics were set to this tune in the American colonies and in the early days after the Revolution. The text beginning "My country, 'tis of thee" was written by Samuel Francis Smith, and was first performed with the tune on July 4, 1831. On August 28, 1963, Martin Luther King quoted Smith's lyrics in his "I have a dream" speech from the steps of the Lincoln Memorial, as he called on the nation to "let freedom ring."

TERMS YOU SHOULD KNOW

- basic phrase (T–D–T)
- cadence
  - half (HC)
  - imperfect authentic (IAC)
  - perfect authentic (PAC)
- contextual analysis
- contrary octaves or fifths
- dominant area
- doubling
- keyboard spacing
- parallel octaves or fifths
- resolution
- SATB
  - soprano
  - alto
  - tenor
  - bass
- spacing
- tendency tones
- tonic area
- tonic closure
- vocal range
- voice crossing

QUESTIONS FOR REVIEW

1. In general, how are stems used to show voice parts in an SATB setting? Which stems go up and which go down?
2. What is the standard range for soprano voices? alto? tenor? bass? When can you exceed these ranges?
3. What is the standard spacing between adjacent voices in SATB settings? How does this differ from keyboard spacing?
4. What chord member is usually doubled in triads in root position? in first inversion? in second inversion?
5. What elements make up the basic phrase? Name and define three possible cadences with which the phrase might conclude.
6. Within the dominant area, how do you treat the leading tone when doubling? What must you remember about the seventh scale degree in minor keys?
7. What principles of species counterpoint come into play when you approach perfect fifths or octaves?
8. What are the steps for harmonizing a folk melody?
9. How is an SATB harmonization converted into a keyboard accompaniment?
10. In music for your own instrument, find at least one example of each cadence type considered in this chapter.

Dominant Sevenths, the Predominant Area, and Melody Harmonization

Outline of topics

V^7 and its inversions

- Resolving the leading tone and chordal seventh
- Approaching perfect intervals

Realizing figured bass

Expanding the basic phrase: T–PD–D–T

- Predominant function: Subdominant and supertonic chords
- Predominant seventh chords

Harmonizing chorale melodies

- Soprano-bass counterpoint and chord choice
- Completing the inner voices
- Checking your work

Overview

In this chapter, we add sevenths to dominant harmonies, and expand the basic phrase model to include predominant harmonies: T–PD–D–T. We learn how to resolve dominant sevenths and to connect the predominant and dominant areas in SATB style, then apply this knowledge to harmonizing a chorale melody.

Repertoire

Johann Sebastian Bach
- "Ach Gott, vom Himmel sieh' darein" ("O God, Look Down on Us from Heaven," Chorale No. 253)
- "Aus meines Herzens Grunde" ("From My Inmost Heart," Chorale No. 1)

Jeremiah Clarke, *Trumpet Voluntary* (*Prince of Denmark's March*)

Wolfgang Amadeus Mozart
- Piano Sonata in C Major, K. 545, first movement
- "Voi, che sapete" ("You who know"), from *The Marriage of Figaro*

V^7 and Its Inversions

Listen to Example 13.1, the concluding measures of a Mozart piano sonata. Here, the dramatic trill in the right hand of measure 70 signals the end of the final phrase, with a V^7–I cadence. The following measures reiterate the V^7–I motion twice more with cadential flourishes, expanding the final tonic harmony.

EXAMPLE 13.1: Mozart, Piano Sonata in C Major, first movement, mm. 70–73

Resolving the Leading Tone and Chordal Seventh

When you add a seventh to the dominant chord, as in measure 70 (G-B-D-F), two new voice-leading considerations arise. First, the chordal seventh (scale degree $\hat{4}$; in this example, F in the left hand) creates a dissonance with the chord's root (G). In common-practice style, a chordal seventh almost always resolves down by step—as here, F to E. Second, good voice-leading requires the harmony's dissonant diminished fifth ($\hat{7}$-$\hat{4}$, B-F) to resolve to a consonant third ($\hat{1}$-$\hat{3}$, C-E).

KEY CONCEPT When V^7 moves to I, two tendency tones resolve stepwise, within the key: the chordal seventh resolves down ($\hat{4}$–$\hat{3}$), and the leading tone resolves up ($\hat{7}$–$\hat{1}$).

When a root-position V^7 moves to root-position I, one chord must be incomplete (missing the fifth) in order to avoid parallel fifths. Mozart's solution in measure 71 is to leave out the fifth of the tonic triad. Example 13.2 shows the correct resolution of the tendency tones for V^7–I progressions in four voices. When the tonic chord is incomplete, it is typically written with three roots and one third, (part a). When the V^7 chord is incomplete, the root is usually doubled and the fifth left out (part b).

EXAMPLE 13.2: SATB resolutions of V^7 to I

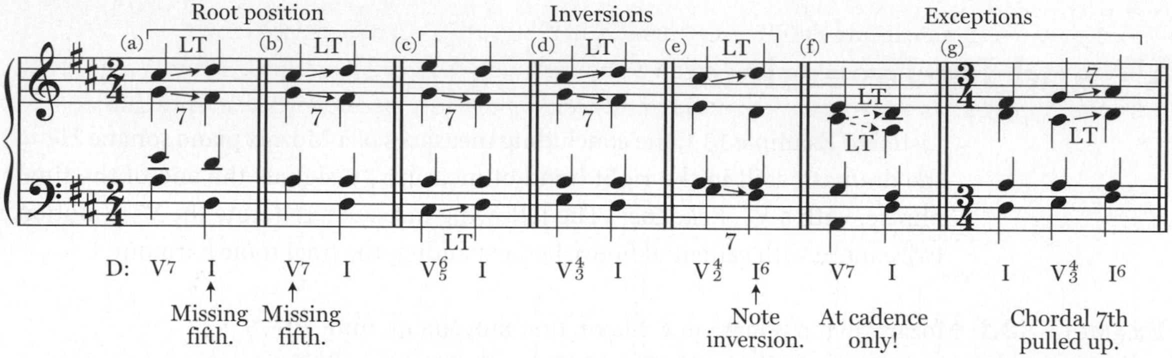

Although the V^7 can appear in any inversion, as in parts (c) to (e), the root-position V^7 creates the strongest progression, and V^6_5 the next strongest. Use second and third inversions when you want to write weaker progressions—for example, at the beginning or the middle of a phrase. Part (e) shows the only correct resolution of V^4_2: to a I^6. Since the chordal seventh ($\hat{4}$) here is in the bass, its resolution down to $\hat{3}$ creates a first-inversion tonic triad.

Two common voice-leading "exceptions" are given in parts (f) and (g). Part (f) represents a resolution of the root-position V^7 to root-position I that may be used only at the cadence in chorale style, where complete chords (including the fifth) are desired to close the phrase: here, $\hat{7}$ does not resolve to $\hat{1}$ but instead skips down to $\hat{5}$. Use this type of resolution only when $\hat{7}$ appears in an inner voice. (It works in part because we hear the $\hat{7}$ in the alto voice resolving up to $\hat{1}$ in the soprano.) When V^4_3 appears between I and I^6 (part g), with the soprano and bass voices moving in parallel tenths, the chordal seventh (here, G4) is pulled up: the voice-leading pattern of parallel tenths overrides the tendency of the chordal seventh to resolve down. Chapter 14 will delve further into expanding I to I^6.

You have already learned not to double the leading tone in the dominant harmony, because of its function as a tendency tone. Example 13.3 illustrates the two voice-leading problems that would result: either (a) both leading tones (C♯) will resolve correctly, resulting in parallel octaves (labeled ||8); or (b) one of the leading tones will resolve incorrectly.

EXAMPLE 13.3: Voice-leading problems caused by incorrect doubling

Try it #1

Provide a key signature and SATB voice parts (in half notes) for each root-position V7–I (or V7–i) progression. Where a harmony is marked with an asterisk, write an incomplete chord (omit the fifth). Draw arrows to show the resolution of the leading tone up and chordal seventh down.

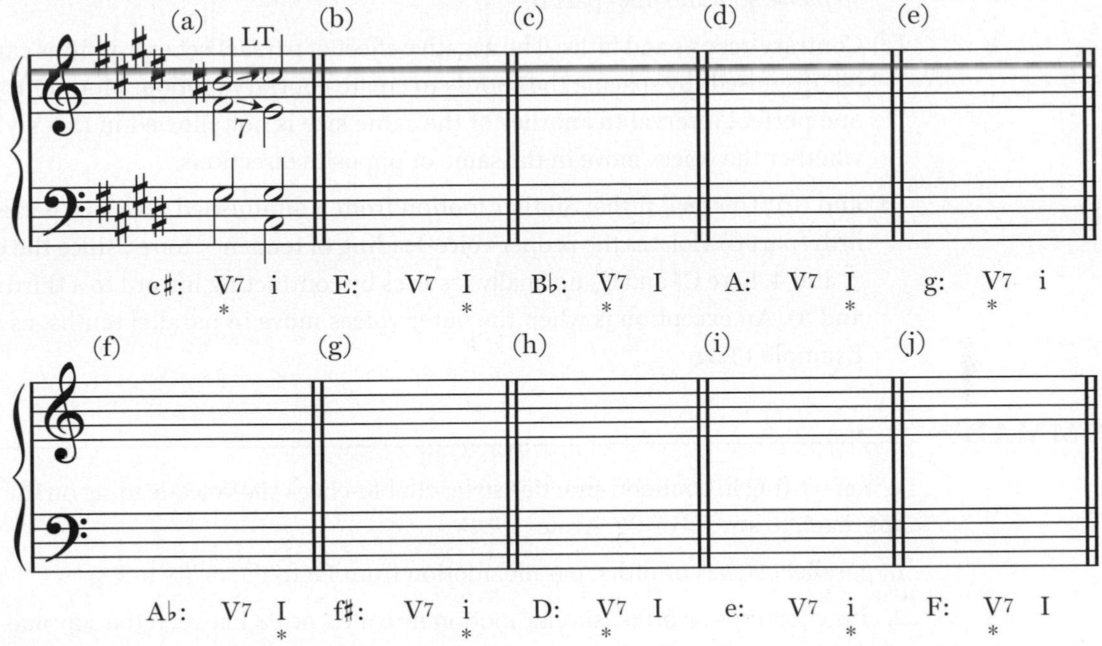

Approaching Perfect Intervals

As mentioned in earlier chapters, common-practice composers treated voice-leading into and out of perfect intervals with care. When you resolve dominant sevenths in this style, watch for the voice-leading problems shown in Example 13.4a, c, and d. To avoid them, you can change a chord's doubling or spacing.

Example 13.4: Motion into perfect intervals

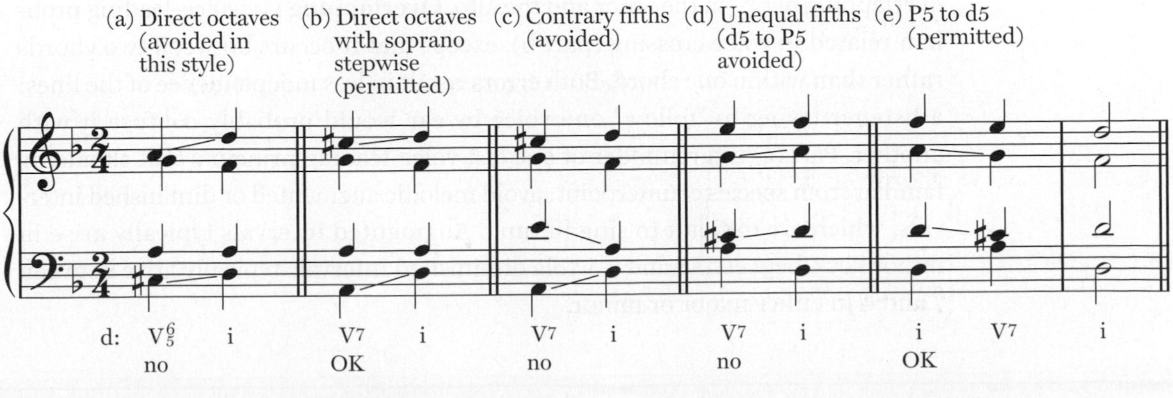

(a) and (b) Direct octaves and fifths: When perfect intervals are approached by similar motion, "direct" (or "hidden") octaves or fifths result. In common-practice style (drawing on species counterpoint), these are avoided in the outer voices (part a), but allowed in the inner voices, or in any voice paired with a *stepwise* soprano line (part b).

(c) Contrary octaves and fifths: The negative effect of parallel octaves or fifths can't be "disguised" by spacing the chords to create contrary motion. Motion from one perfect interval to another of the same size is not allowed in this style, whether the voices move in the same or opposite directions.

(d) and (e) Unequal fifths: Similar motion from a diminished fifth to a perfect fifth (part d) violates the proper voice-leading of tendency tones, since the d5 ($\hat{7}$ and $\hat{4}$, here C♯ and G) normally resolves by contracting inward to a third ($\hat{1}$ and $\hat{3}$). An exception is when the outer voices move in parallel tenths, as in Example 13.2g.

SUMMARY

When writing in common-practice style, double-check the voice-leading on the approach to any P5 or P8. Avoid

1. parallel octaves or fifths: parallel motion from P5 to P5, or P8 to P8;
2. direct octaves or fifths: similar motion into a P5 or P8 between the soprano and bass (unless the soprano moves by step);
3. contrary octaves or fifths: contrary motion from P5 to P5, or P8 to P8;
4. unequal fifths: motion from d5 to P5, especially between the soprano and bass (unless these outer voices move in parallel tenths).

Be aware that one voice-leading error can create others along with it. In Example 13.5a, the contrary fifths between the alto and bass are compounded by overlapping between the tenor and the alto. **Overlapping** is a voice-leading problem related to voice crossing (part b), except that it occurs between two chords rather than within one chord. Both errors result in less independence of the lines: a listener trying to "follow" one voice by ear would probably confuse it with another. Part (c) is a reminder of one last voice-leading principle that should be familiar from species counterpoint: avoid melodic augmented or diminished intervals, which are difficult to sing in tune. Augmented intervals typically arise in minor keys, between ♭$\hat{6}$ and $\hat{7}$, while diminished intervals typically arise between $\hat{7}$ and $\hat{4}$ in either major or minor.

Example 13.5: Some voice-leading errors

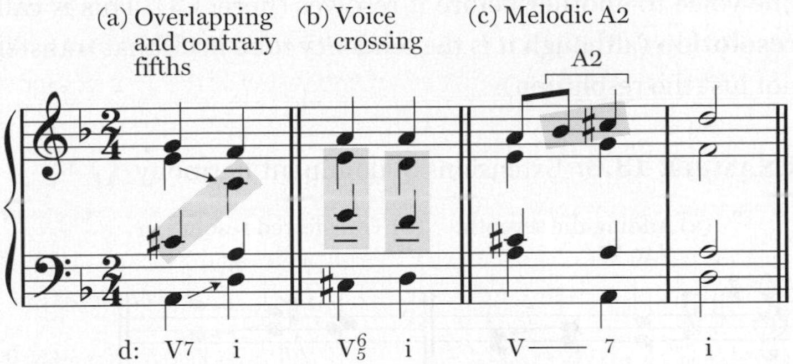

Try it #2

Check your understanding of voice-leading guidelines by examining the chorale phrase below. Sing or play through the phrase, circle and label the (numerous) mistakes, and then rewrite the phrase with correct voice-leading.

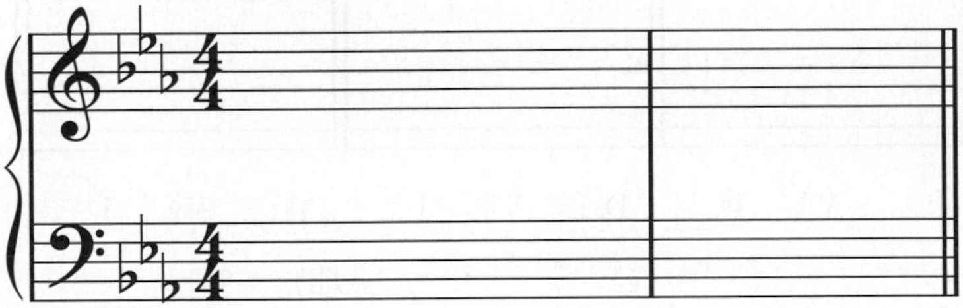

When you write harmonic progressions, you may include more than one dominant chord in the dominant area, as in Example 13.6, by writing different inversions and spacing to maintain musical interest. Place the strongest dominant chord (usually root-position V7) just before the resolution to tonic harmony. When V moves to V7 (part a), the added seventh typically acts like a passing tone, creating 8–7 motion above the bass, as here (labeled V8–7). When you extend the harmony by changing inversion (part b), a tendency tone may move from one voice to another before it resolves (here, C♯). This is called a **transferred resolution** (although it is the tendency tone itself that transfers to a new octave, not just the resolution).

Example 13.6: Extensions of dominant harmony

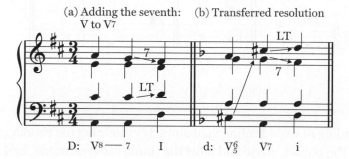

(a) Adding the seventh: V to V7 (b) Transferred resolution

D: V8 — 7 I d: V$^6_5$ V7 i

Try it #3

Write the following progressions in SATB voicing with half notes. Provide the appropriate key signatures, and add accidentals as needed. Draw arrows to show the resolution of leading tones up and chordal sevenths down.

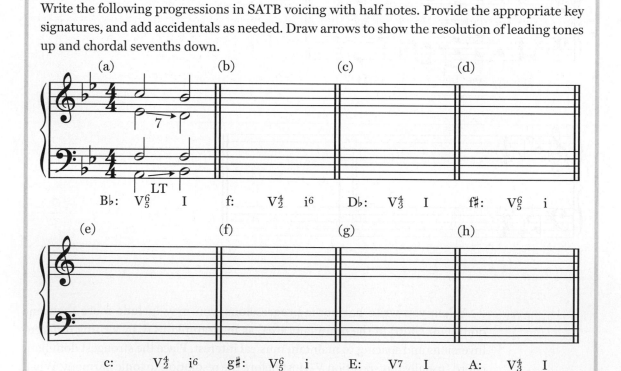

(a) (b) (c) (d)

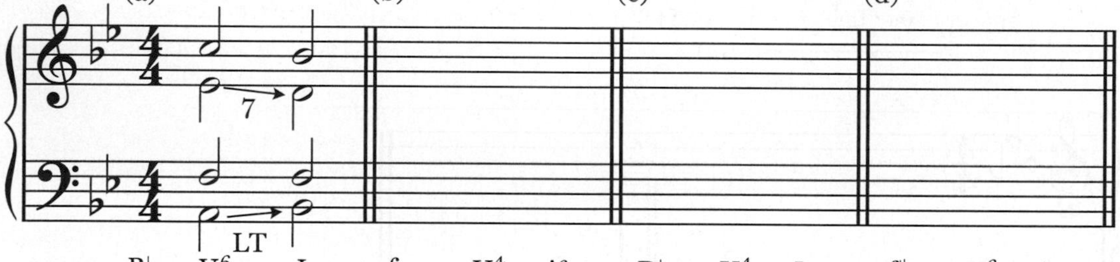

B♭: V$^6_5$ I f: V$^4_2$ i6 D♭: V$^4_3$ I f♯: V$^6_5$ i

(e) (f) (g) (h)

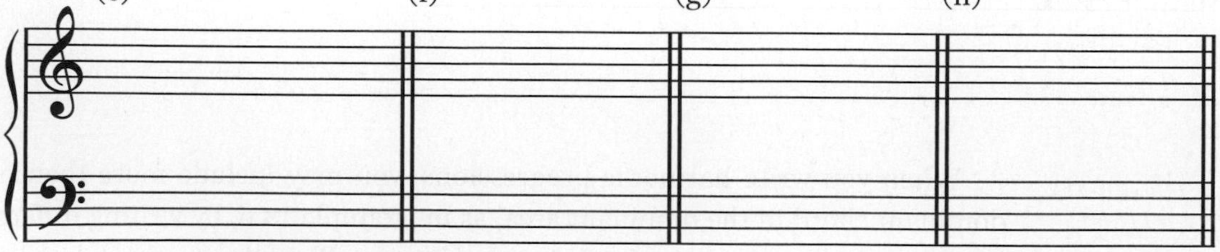

c: V$^4_2$ i6 g♯: V$^6_5$ i E: V7 I A: V$^4_3$ I

Realizing Figured Bass

Creating a full musical texture from a figured bass—**realizing** a figured bass—was an everyday part of performance in the Baroque and Classical eras. Performers on keyboards, lutes, and other harmony instruments were expected to improvise harmonic progressions from a given bass line with figures. Figured bass was also used to teach the principles of harmony and voice-leading: players would practice standard figures in various keys to become familiar with conventional chord sequences and the usual voice-leading possibilities. In realizing a figured bass, you demonstrate an ability to link chords as musically as possible within the guidelines of common-practice style, without having to make the chord choices yourself; you also internalize principles of voice-leading and dissonance treatment that can inform your own interpretation and composition. For these reasons, this text will use figured bass as well as Roman numerals (which came into use only at the end of the eighteenth century) in discussions of harmony and voice-leading.

A few basic figures are realized in Example 13.7; recall that figures indicate diatonic intervals above the bass, as well as chromatic alterations (accidentals). Melodic embellishing tones other than suspensions are not indicated in the figures because they are not part of the main harmonic framework. Musicians realizing the bass would be expected to add them according to their taste.

Example 13.7: Realization of common figures

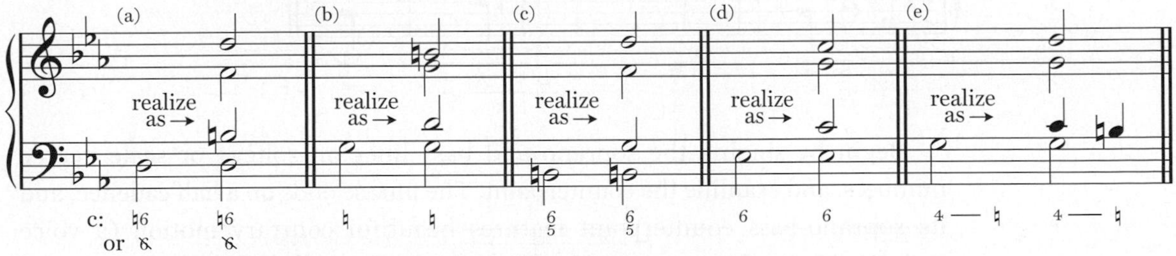

KEY CONCEPT When realizing a figured bass:

- Sing the given line(s) with scale-degree numbers or solfege.
- If there is an accidental next to a number, raise or lower the pitch associated with that number by one chromatic half step; for a slash through a number, raise the pitch a half step (Example 13.7a).
- If there is an accidental by itself, raise or lower the third above the bass (b)—not necessarily the third of the chord.

- Place pitches above the bass in an appropriate octave (of your choosing) with the intervals given in the figured-bass symbols (c).
- Use pitches diatonic in the key (d), unless an accidental is specified.
- To realize a dash between two numbers (or between a number and an accidental), place those intervals in the same voice-leading strand, as in a 4–3 suspension (e).
- Remember that accidentals in the figure apply only to that single chord, and that figured bass does not list *all* intervals above the bass—some, like octaves and thirds, may be implied by the figures.
- Follow doubling and voice-leading guidelines for the style when voicing or connecting chords; these are not specified by the figures.

The melody and bass of one of Bach's chorale hamonizations is given in Example 13.8 (the melody was written in 1524 by German Protestant reformer Martin Luther), with the figured bass below. We will complete the alto and tenor parts based on the figures.

EXAMPLE 13.8: Bach, "Ach Gott, vom Himmel sieh' darein," mm. 1–2a, melody and figured bass (adapted)

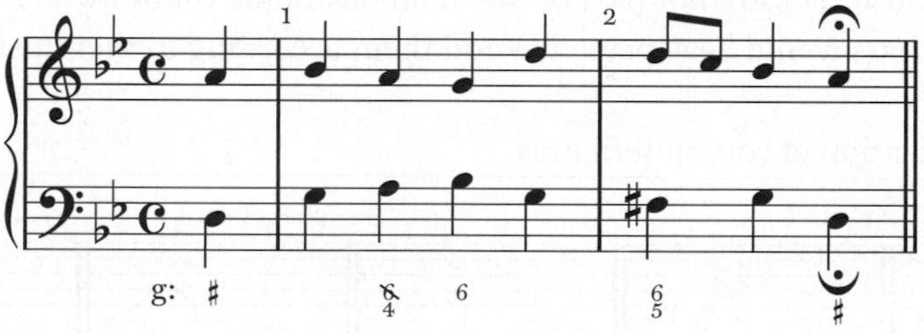

Begin by singing the soprano and bass lines on solfège or scale-degree numbers, and examine the counterpoint. The phrase ends on a half cadence, and its soprano-bass counterpoint features beautiful contrary motion (a voice exchange) in the first measure. Now consider the figures. The ♯ below the first and last bass notes indicates that the third above the bass is to be raised (from F to F♯). (Remember that the absence of other figures implies a $^5_3$ chord.) In both chords, write an F♯4 in the alto and double the root (D4) in the tenor. This spacing between bass and tenor allows room for the bass ascent that follows the anacrusis. Since the initial chord in measure 1 has no figures, this is another $^5_3$ chord.

For the second chord of measure 1, place a sixth and fourth (F and D) above this bass note, then raise the sixth to F♯. The third chord of the measure implies

$^6_3$: place a sixth and third (G and D) above this pitch. Because the sixth above the bass is also the melody note (and the root of the triad), double it in the alto by drawing stems above and below the G4. Now compose the inner voices for the next few beats on your own, according to the common-practice voice-leading guidelines.

Example 13.9 offers one possible realization, with Roman numeral and contextual analyses. The figured bass by itself is different from an analysis: it only shows intervals above the bass to be played (or written). You will see slight variations between the figures and the Roman numeral inversion symbols, since figures indicate chromatic alterations. The contextual analysis shows how the tonic area may be extended by the dominant. In this example, dominant harmonies in measures 1 and 2 are inverted, which weakens their harmonic function and strengthens their contrapuntal role. We will return to this idea in Chapter 14.

Example 13.9: Bach, "Ach Gott, vom Himmel sieh' darein," mm. 1–2a, SATB realization (adapted)

Expanding the Basic Phrase: T–PD–D–T

Predominant Function: Subdominant and Supertonic Chords

Having considered the D–T motion that completes the basic phrase, we now turn to the tonal area that typically precedes the dominant: the predominant area (PD). In Example 13.10, from Clarke's *Trumpet Voluntary*, the tonic area is expanded for over two measures by alternating tonic and dominant harmonies. (Circled embellishing tones decorate the basic harmonies.) Then in measure 7, the cadential dominant on beat 3 is prepared by a predominant (PD) harmony: ii$^6_5$.

EXAMPLE 13.10: Clarke, *Trumpet Voluntary*, mm. 5–8

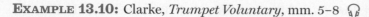

KEY CONCEPT Predominant harmonies—ii and IV (and their minor-key equivalents)—are so named because they generally lead to the dominant. Predominant triads share scale degrees $\hat{4}$ and $\hat{6}$.

The predominant area (sometimes called the "dominant preparation area" or "subdominant area") expands the basic phrase model to four parts: **T–PD–D–T**. This type of phrase is even more common than the simple T–D–T type, and its many possible variations shape most of common-practice tonal music. Following are typical Roman numerals for the T–PD–D–T basic phrase. In minor keys, the diminished triad ii°, like the vii° in major keys, generally appears in first inversion rather than in root position.

- In major keys: I — (ii, ii^6, or IV) — (V or V7) — I
  T — PD ——— D —— T
- In minor keys: i — (ii°^{6} or iv) — (V or V7) — i
  T — PD ——— D —— T

Example 13.11 shows how the predominant and dominant connect in SATB texture. Parts (a) and (c) follow the same progression, but with IV in (a) and ii^6 in (c). These two chords differ by only one note (here, in the alto) and can substitute for each other: they both have $\hat{4}$ in the bass, which accounts in part for the frequency with which the ii chord appears in first inversion.

Example 13.11: Typical voice-leading into the dominant, with upper voices in contrary motion to the bass

(a) With IV (b) In minor

(c) With ii6 (d) In minor

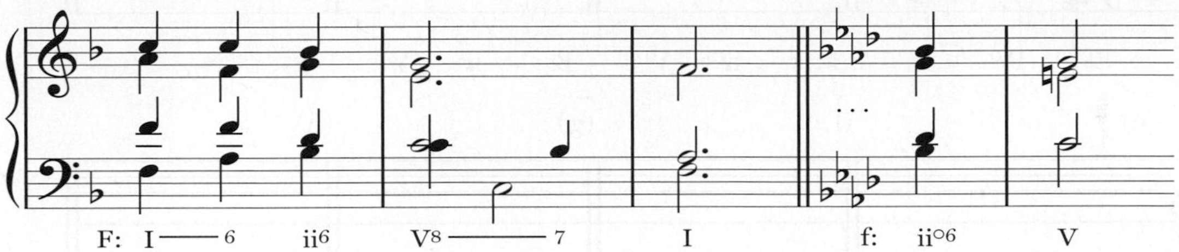

KEY CONCEPT When root-position IV moves to root-position V, write the upper the voices in contrary motion with the bass to avoid parallel fifths or octaves.

In both progressions (a) and (c), all three of the upper voices move down to the closest possible chord tone, while the bass moves up by step from $\hat{4}$ to $\hat{5}$.

KEY CONCEPT In minor keys, iv is minor (part b) and ii° diminished. For ii°6, the normal doubling is the third of the chord (part d), so that the dissonant interval (G–D♭) is not emphasized. Avoid root-position ii° for the same reason.

Try it #4

Write the following progressions in SATB voicing, with half notes. Provide the appropriate key signatures, and add accidentals as needed. Move the upper three voices in contrary motion to the bass where possible.

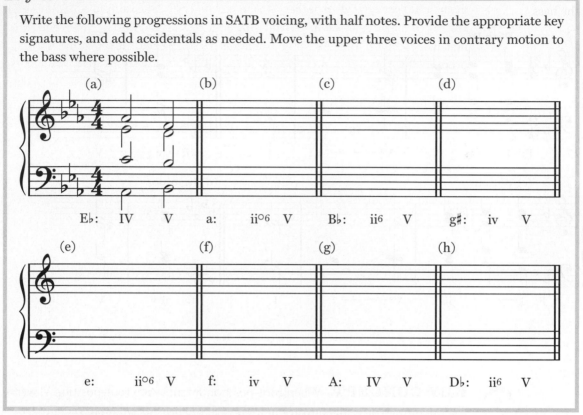

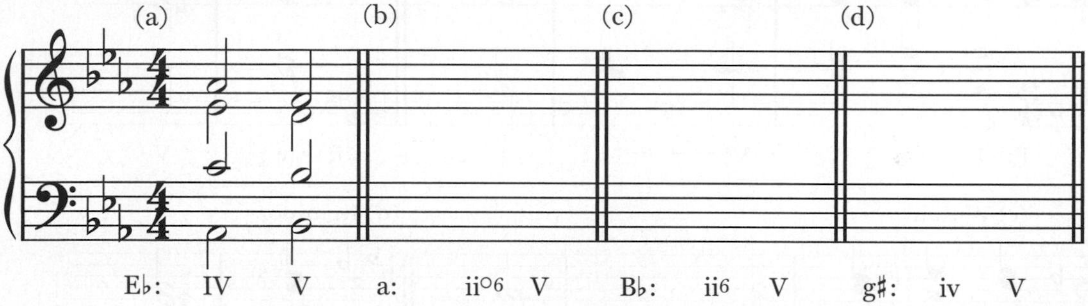

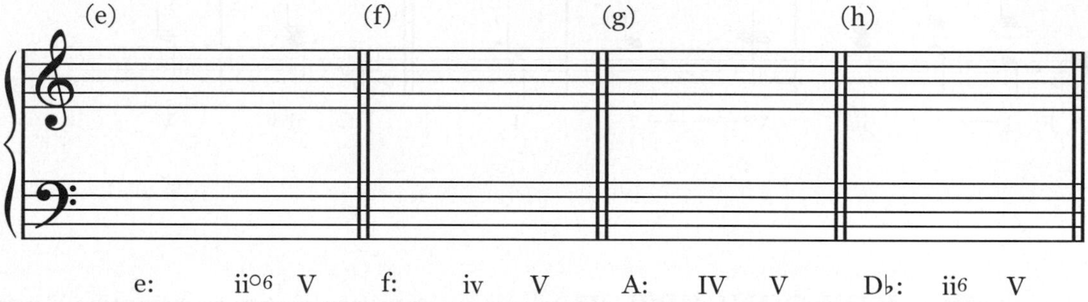

Predominant Seventh Chords

Thus far, the only seventh chord included in the basic phrase has been the dominant seventh, but you may also find predominant sevenths—like the one in measure 7 of Example 13.10 and measure 11 of 13.12.

EXAMPLE 13.12: Mozart, "Voi, che sapete," mm. 9–12

Although any predominant chord may include a seventh, ii7 and ii$^{\varnothing}$7 (and their inversions) are typical, especially ii$^6_5$ (in minor, ii$^{\varnothing 6}_{5}$). In Example 13.13, an SATB voicing, two voices move in contrary motion to the bass from ii$^6_5$ to V, with $\hat{2}$ (G) held as a common tone. As with dominant seventh chords, the seventh is normally prepared by common tone in ii7 and ii$^{\varnothing}$7.

Example 13.13: Writing a predominant seventh chord

Harmonizing Chorale Melodies

It is possible to harmonize many chorale melodies with the tonic, dominant, and predominant harmonies considered in this chapter. Follow the general procedure for harmonizing a melody from Chapter 11: select an appropriate cadence, and compose a bass line that makes good counterpoint with the melody. Then evaluate the functional areas (T–PD–D–T), which provide additional information about harmonic choices for the middle section. For chorale melodies, the typical harmonic rhythm is usually one chord per beat; if the same chord is needed for two or more beats, usually the soprano note or bass inversion of the chord will change to provide melodic or harmonic variety. After selecting the harmonic progression and composing a bass line, complete the inner parts to make an SATB setting.

Soprano-Bass Counterpoint and Chord Choice

Consider the melody excerpt in Example 13.14, which we will harmonize in SATB style. Begin by singing the melody or thinking of its solfège or scale-degree numbers in G major: *mi-sol-fa-mi-re-do*, or $\hat{3}$–$\hat{5}$–$\hat{4}$–$\hat{3}$–$\hat{2}$–$\hat{1}$. Use the scale degrees to plan the harmonies, with mostly an even quarter-note rhythm until the final chord. Because the melody ends with $\hat{2}$–$\hat{1}$, plan a perfect authentic cadence here; sketch D3 to G2 in the bass and the Roman numerals V (or V7) to I below the bass line.

Now look at the two notes at the beginning of the phrase, $\hat{3}$–$\hat{5}$; you could harmonize both with a tonic triad, or with I moving to V. Choose the latter because of the anacrusis: a change of harmony over the bar line articulates the rhythm well.

EXAMPLE 13.14: Bach, "Aus meines Herzens Grunde," mm. 4b–7 (melody)

KEY CONCEPT When you write a bass line and select harmonies for a given melody, you need not work "left to right." One way is to start with the cadence, then go back to the beginning to write the tonic opening. Finally, fill in the middle of the phrase.

You now need a bass line in counterpoint with the melody—one that supports the harmonies chosen thus far, completes a good basic-phrase progression, and includes inversions to create a singable bass line. Beginning with the tonic harmony on the anacrusis, choose the low G2 to allow the bass line to rise in measures 5–6 in counterpoint with the soprano line. On the downbeat of measure 5, write a dominant harmony, which could extend for the entire bar since the melody's $\hat{5}$–$\hat{4}$ could represent the root (D) and seventh (C) of a V^7 chord. You could place a root-position V (D) here, but you might want a V^6 instead, saving the stronger root position for the cadence. A dotted-half F♯2 (first inversion) is possible; we will return to this spot after deciding on a bass line for the next measure.

Measure 6 sets up the cadence: $\hat{3}$ (B) on the downbeat should be set with a tonic harmony. Although you could move directly from I to the cadential V to support $\hat{2}$ (A) in the melody, try a predominant (the supertonic) here first, followed by the dominant, to create the full basic phrase: T–PD–D–T. Since the melody descends by step to the cadence, craft a bass line that moves first in contrary motion, then D3 down to G2, as shown in Example 13.15.

Example 13.15: Bach, "Aus meines Herzens Grunde," mm. 4b–7 (soprano and bass)

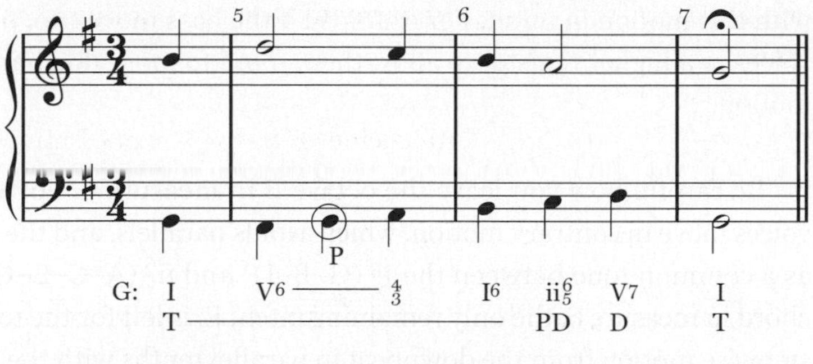

This bass line is Bach's own. The first-inversion tonic on the downbeat of measure 6 allows the bass to move up by step, $\hat{3}$–$\hat{4}$–$\hat{5}$, to the dominant; this makes C3 the bass note for the supertonic chord (beat 2), typically a first inversion (either ii^6 or ii^6_5). From measure 5, Bach leads the bass line into measure 6 with another stepwise ascent, and so creates in these two measures stepwise motion from $\hat{7}$ all the way up to $\hat{5}$. Roman numerals are given for one possible harmonization below the staff.

KEY CONCEPT Write the soprano-bass counterpoint first before filling in the inner voices. Make sure both parts have singable melodic lines, and that they make good contrapuntal and harmonic sense.

Completing the Inner Voices

The next step is to add alto and tenor lines, keeping in mind the voice-leading guidelines. First, scan the soprano-bass counterpoint to see whether there are places that might present special challenges (for example, places where the outer voices are particularly close together, or where they form fifths or octaves that need to be approached with care). In this setting, there is one octave on the downbeat of measure 6, followed by two seventh chords that may take some special attention to prepare and resolve. For this reason, it would be good to begin part-writing near the cadence, and then fill in the beginning of the phrase.

Begin with the approach to the cadence, at the downbeat of measure 6, a I^6 chord with doubled B. There are only two notes left to complete the chord (G and D), and either voicing is possible: G3 in tenor and D4 in alto, or D4 in tenor and G4 in alto. For now, pick the second alternative, and write it in Example 13.15: the higher register of the voices will allow them to move downward in contrary motion with the bass if so desired.

KEY CONCEPT Before voicing the first chord in a progression, scan the soprano and bass lines for motion up or down, and plan the chord's spacing with this motion in mind. For example, if the bass moves up, place the other voices in a higher register to allow them room to move down in contrary motion.

Be careful how you leave the octave B in measure 6. Fortunately, the outer voices move in contrary motion, which avoids parallels, and the alto G can remain as a common tone between the I^6 (G–B–D) and ii^6_5 (A–C–E–G). For the second chord in measure 6, the only remaining pitch, E, is left for the tenor voice, making stepwise motion from the downbeat in parallel tenths with the bass and contrary motion with the soprano.

Remember when connecting the predominant and dominant areas to move in contrary motion with the $\hat{4}$–$\hat{5}$ bass, if possible. This works perfectly here, with A in the soprano kept as a common tone on beat 3 (when the chord changes to D-F♯-A-C), and the remaining voices moving downward. (Bach adds 8–7 motion above the dominant for a stepwise tenor line; see Example 13.16.) Finally, when connecting V^7 to the cadential I chord, resolve the chordal seventh down (C4 to B3 in the tenor). Bach has chosen to make the final I chord a complete triad, and therefore the leading tone (F♯, in the alto) leaps down to the fifth of the chord (D) rather than resolving upward. This is his solution in most chorales, and is perfectly acceptable in our writing as well—but only at the cadence. Now listen to the passage shown in Example 13.16: a harmonization of the entire phrase.

EXAMPLE 13.16: Bach, "Aus meines Herzens Grunde," mm. 4b–7 (adapted)

Checking Your Work

When you finish a melody harmonization or figured-bass realization, always go back and proofread your work. One of the easiest ways to do this is at a keyboard—often your ear will pick out mistakes that your eye may not. Read through your work slowly, and listen and look for specific types of errors; for example, scan through once for the resolution of every tendency tone (leading tone and chordal seventh). You might want to label the tendency tones with arrows (an up arrow for leading tones and a down arrow for chordal sevenths) to remind yourself not to change those resolutions once you have checked them. When writing in a minor key, be sure that $\flat\hat{7}$ is raised to make a leading tone. Locate each perfect fifth or octave, and check the voice-leading into and out of it. Sing each line to yourself on scale degrees or solfège to check again for the resolution of tendency tones, for awkward leaps, and for a musical line.

SUMMARY

Keep in mind the following guidelines when connecting SATB chords.

1. Above all, write musically:
   - Listen to what you write, by playing or singing each line.
   - Avoid static harmonic progressions; create interest over an unchanging harmony by changing the soprano pitch, the inversion, and/or the spacing of the chord.
   - Write melodies with stepwise motion and skips between chord members; avoid large leaps (except in the bass) and melodic motion by augmented or diminished intervals.
   - Write passing or neighbor tones to create a smooth line and add melodic interest.
2. Work to achieve smooth voice-leading:
   - Resolve tendency tones correctly, and never double them.
   - If two chords share a common tone, keep that common tone in the same voice if possible.
   - Move each voice to the closest possible member of the following chord (without creating parallel perfect intervals).
   - Approach chordal sevenths from below by skip or step, or from above by step.
3. Aim for independence of the four voices:
   - Keep each voice within its own characteristic range. No pitch in one part should cross above or below that of an adjacent part—either within a single chord (voice-crossing) or between two consecutive chords (overlapping).
   - Balance parallel or similar motion with contrary and oblique motion. Avoid moving all four voices in the same direction.
   - Write in contrary or oblique motion when you approach and leave any perfect interval to avoid parallel fifths, octaves, or unisons.

Although this chapter has focused on chorale-style writing, with its simplified texture, you might be surprised to discover how many composers of different genres and eras have followed these principles to control their use of dissonance, make harmonic choices, plan voice-leading, and compose pleasing melodies and bass lines. Such common features between musical styles will be pointed out in later chapters as they arise.

Did You Know?

Composers and performers in the Renaissance (1430–1600) did not talk about chords as invertible harmonies stacked in thirds above a root as we do today. Instead, they described music by the way the intervals were prepared and resolved. At first, the interval of a seventh appeared only on the offbeats, approached by a perfect octave and resolving down by step on the next beat. Some composers of the early Baroque era (1600–1750) liked the dramatic sound made when the chordal seventh was placed in an accented position, but that treatment was not permitted in the strict style of church music, and was only deemed appropriate for theatrical or dramatic music, like opera. Over time, the seventh began to be accepted as a dissonance that could appear on the beat as a complete V^7, instead of entering with $^{8-7}$ motion after the beat. It continued to resolve down by step in common-practice tonal music, but in twentieth-century and more recent popular styles the seventh can simply be considered part of a sonority and remain unresolved.

TERMS YOU SHOULD KNOW

- contrary motion
- direct octaves and fifths
- overlapping
- predominant area
- realization
- tendency tones
- T–PD–D–T phrase
- transferred resolution
- unequal fifths

QUESTIONS FOR REVIEW

1. What tendency tones in a V^7 must resolve? Do they resolve differently when the dominant appears in an inversion? If so, how? Do they resolve differently at the cadence? If so, how?
2. What principles of species counterpoint come into play when a progression approaches perfect fifths or octaves?
3. Name several chords that might appear in the predominant area of the basic phrase. Are particular inversions more typical than others? Why or why not?
4. Which is the most common predominant seventh chord (and inversion)?
5. What voice-leading principle must be kept in mind when moving between root-position IV and V?
6. What are the steps for harmonizing a chorale melody?

Expanding the Tonic and Dominant Areas

CHAPTER 14

Outline of topics

Expanding harmonic areas with $^{6}_{4}$ chords

- The cadential $^{6}_{4}$
- The neighboring or pedal $^{6}_{4}$
- The arpeggiating $^{6}_{4}$
- The passing $^{6}_{4}$
- The four $^{6}_{4}$ types

Other expansions of the tonic area

- The subdominant in tonic expansions
- The dominant in tonic expansions
- The submediant in tonic expansions
- Embedding T–PD–D–T within a larger phrase

Overview

This chapter explores some ways the dominant and tonic areas may be expanded in the basic phrase, and considers the special contexts for $^{6}_{4}$ chords.

Repertoire

Johannes Brahms, *Variations on a Theme by Haydn*

Wolfgang Amadeus Mozart

Piano Sonata in B♭ Major, K. 333, first movement
Piano Sonata in C Major, K. 545, first movement
Piano Sonata in D Major, K. 284, third movement
Sonata for Violin and Piano, K. 296, second movement

"My Country, 'Tis of Thee" ("America")

Richard M. Sherman and Robert B. Sherman, "Feed the Birds," from *Mary Poppins*

John Philip Sousa, "The Stars and Stripes Forever"

"Wayfaring Stranger" (arranged by Norman Lloyd)

Expanding Harmonic Areas with $^6_4$ Chords

While the basic phrase model T–PD–D–T is a shared feature of all types of tonal music, the ways that composers elaborate, expand, and embellish this fundamental framework vary. Although each functional area may be expanded or embellished, here we focus on the tonic and dominant areas—in particular, expansions by means of $^6_4$ chords, some of which may be applied to the predominant area as well.

The Cadential $^6_4$

In the Classical style—the music of Mozart, for example—a typical cadence often includes a brief expansion of the dominant area by a **cadential** $^6_4$. Listen to the opening of the third movement of Mozart's Piano Sonata in D Major (Example 14.1), which features this voice-leading chord.

Example 14.1: Mozart, Piano Sonata in D Major, third movement, mm. 1–4

In this very typical-sounding Mozart cadence (m. 4), the dominant triad (A-C♯-E) is preceded by what appears to be a tonic harmony in second inversion, A–D–F♯. This chord, however, does not *function* as the tonic; rather, it displaces and embellishes the V chord by simultaneous 6–5 (F♯ to E) and 4–3 (D to C♯) motions above the sustained bass note A. The chord of resolution is V$^5_3$.

The 6 and 4 represent intervals above the bass that displace the chord tones 5 and 3, and the dashes in the 6–5 and 4–3 indicate that the figures represent voice-leading above a repeated or sustained bass note. Don't write V$^6_4$ alone as a symbol for the cadential $^6_4$, since that implies pitches of the dominant triad. Think instead of V$^{6-5}_{4-3}$ as a single analytical symbol that shows voice-leading above a dominant harmony. Likewise, it's best not to write I$^6_4$—even though many older textbooks do—because that symbol obscures the chord's dominant function.

KEY CONCEPT The cadential $^6_4$ has a dominant function, even though it is built of tones from the tonic triad. Its $^{6-5}_{4-3}$ motion expands the dominant area of the basic phrase, with the dissonant $^6_4$ on the strong beat and its resolution on a weaker beat.

If you doubt the dominant function of the cadential $^6_4$, try singing the chord roots as you listen to Example 14.1. Chances are, you will sing $\hat{5}$ on both beats of measure 4. The F5 and D4 are approached as passing tones from the previous chord, a ii^6, labeled PD in the contextual analysis.

Cadential $^6_4$s may be found in many styles of tonal music, including hymns and patriotic songs such as "My Country, 'Tis of Thee" (Example 14.2). The first full phrase of this song includes two cadential $^6_4$s: the one marked in measure 5 moves to a decisive PAC cadence (m. 6), but the one in measure 4 resolves evasively to vi (more about this Chapter 15). Both are preceded by ii^6 chords, as is typical. The $^6_4$ in measure 4 is labeled $\mathrm{V}\begin{smallmatrix}8-7\\6-5\\4-3\end{smallmatrix}$ to account for the octave C moving down to the chordal seventh, B♭.

EXAMPLE 14.2: "My Country, 'Tis of Thee," mm. 1–6

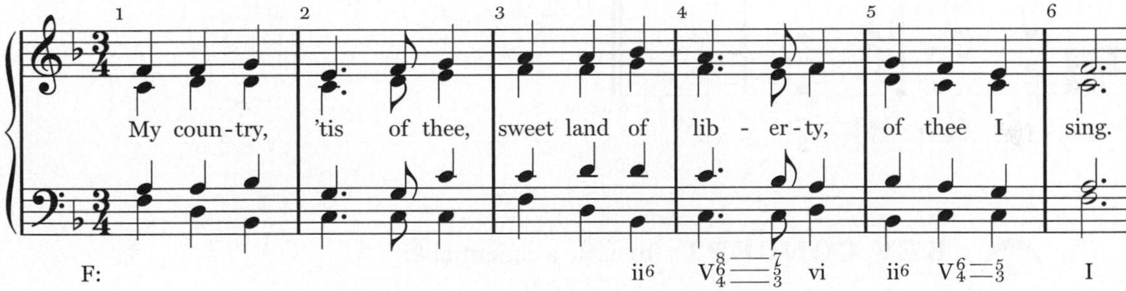

Like most embellishing chords, the cadential $^6_4$ could be removed from the cadence without changing the general harmonic plan of the phrase, but it provides smooth voice-leading from the predominant area. Cadential $^6_4$s are almost always preceded by a predominant harmony, as in Examples 14.1 and 14.2; rarely by the tonic harmony. For now, approach them with ii, ii^7, or IV (in minor, ii$^{\circ 6}$, ii$^{\varnothing 7}$, or iv) or other inversions of these chords.

Writing Cadential $^6_4$ Chords Typical progressions with a cadential $^6_4$ chord are given in Example 14.3. The voice-leading for all of these is the same in the parallel minor (part b). In minor, remember to raise $\flat\hat{7}$ to create a leading tone in the V or V^7.

EXAMPLE 14.3: Resolutions of the cadential $^6_4$

KEY CONCEPT To write a cadential $^6_4$:

1. Always double the bass. Any other doubling will result in voice-leading problems and will not be idiomatic.
2. Approach the cadential $^6_4$ from a predominant harmony: usually ii, ii7, or IV (ii°6, iiø7, or iv in minor) or other inversions. Keep common tones, if any, between the predominant chord and the $^6_4$, and move other voices the shortest distance.
3. Write the chord on a strong beat in the measure; it displaces the V or V7, which would normally occupy a strong beat. In triple meter, the cadential $^6_4$ sometimes appears on beat 2, resolving to V or V7 on beat 3.
4. Resolve the "suspended" tones of the $^6_4$ downward: the sixth above the bass moves to a fifth, and the fourth moves to a third ($^{6-5}_{4-3}$).
5. Typical soprano parts for the V$^{6-5}_{4-3}$–I progression are $\hat{1}$–$\hat{7}$–$\hat{1}$ (Example 14.3a–c) or $\hat{3}$–$\hat{2}$–$\hat{1}$ (parts d and e) over the bass $\hat{5}$–$\hat{1}$, creating a PAC.

6. If the cadential $^6_4$ resolves to a dominant seventh, the doubled bass note ($\hat{5}$ in the soprano, alto, or tenor part) moves to the seventh of the V7 chord ($\hat{4}$), making an 8–7 motion above the bass (parts d and e).

Try it #1

Complete the authenic cadences indicated by the Roman numerals below. Write the melody notes as $\hat{4}$–$\hat{3}$–$\hat{2}$–$\hat{1}$. Use quarter notes and, for the final chord, half notes.

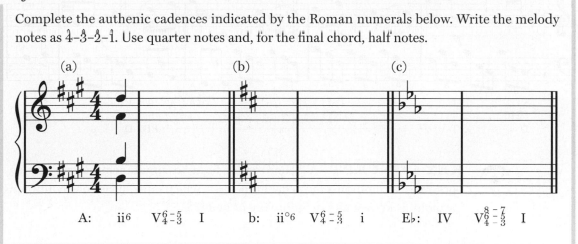

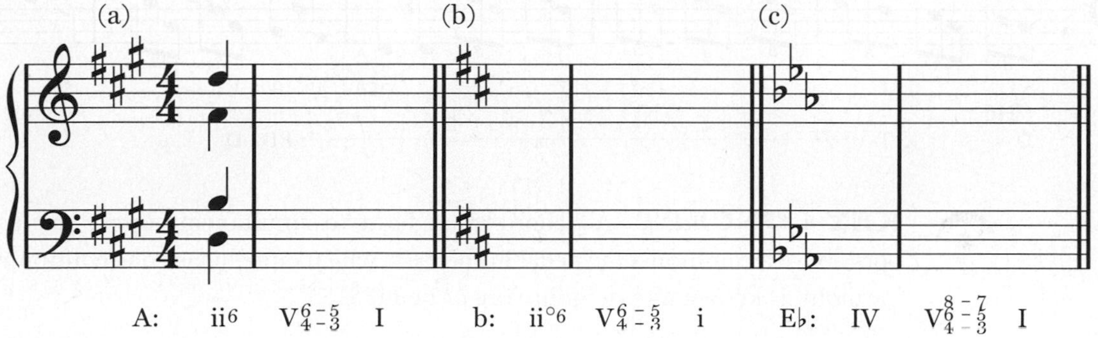

The Neighboring or Pedal $^6_4$

Listen to Example 14.4 to hear another type of $^6_4$. At the beginning of each of the two phrases in this example, the opening tonic is expanded in the triplets of the piano bass clef by neighboring motion: A–B♭–A (mm. 1–2) and C–D–C (mm. 5–6). This voicing takes advantage of the common tone between I and IV, F, by holding it in the bass, placing the IV chord in the $^6_4$ position (F–B♭–D). This bass-line common tone, which mimics a sustained low organ pedal with moving voices above, is called a **pedal point**.

Example 14.4: Mozart, Sonata for Violin and Piano, K. 296, second movement, mm. 1–8

KEY CONCEPT A $^6_4$ chord created by two simultaneous upper neighbors above a common-tone pedal in the bass, which embellishes one continuing harmony, is known as a **neighboring** or **pedal** $^6_4$.

The analysis given in measures 1–2, I$^{5-6-5}_{3-4-3}$, highlights the neighboring motion of the upper voices and emphasizes its function as a tonic expansion. Neighboring or pedal $^6_4$ chords are typically labeled this way, and usually prolong the chord for which they are a neighbor. Alternatively, you could write a IV$^6_4$, but with (N$^6_4$) or (ped$^6_4$) written below to show its function (see m. 5).

Although this type of $^6_4$ usually appears in a weak metric position, as in the example, it can sometimes be found on the strong beat of a measure, as in Example 14.5. Here, Mozart expands the tonic harmony across the bar line in measure 3, placing the $^6_4$ in a relatively strong metric position. Again, the upper voices of the $^6_4$ act as neighbors to the tonic chord tones, with the characteristic pedal point in the bass. Because it expands the tonic and does not proceed to V, this type of $^6_4$ does not carry either the IV or PD label, and the basic phrase expresses T–D–T only.

Example 14.5: Mozart, Piano Sonata in C Major, first movement, mm. 1–4

SUMMARY

The neighboring or pedal $^6_4$

- embellishes and prolongs a root-position triad;
- is typically metrically unaccented;
- shares its bass note with the harmony it embellishes, while two upper voices move in stepwise neighboring motion above that bass.

The same technique may be applied to a root-position triad in the dominant area, as in Example 14.6, or (less often) the predominant area as well.

EXAMPLE 14.6: $^6_4$ chords expanding the tonic and dominant areas

KEY CONCEPT

To write a neighboring or pedal $^6_4$:

1. Decide which harmony you want to prolong (T, D, or PD). Write that chord in root position twice with the same voicing, leaving a space between chords for the neighbor tones (Example 14.7a).
2. Fill in the bass of the $^6_4$ chord first—the same bass as the chords on either side—and double it in the same voice as the other chords (part b).
3. Write upper neighbors to decorate the other two voices (part c).

EXAMPLE 14.7: Steps in writing a neighboring or pedal $^6_4$ chord

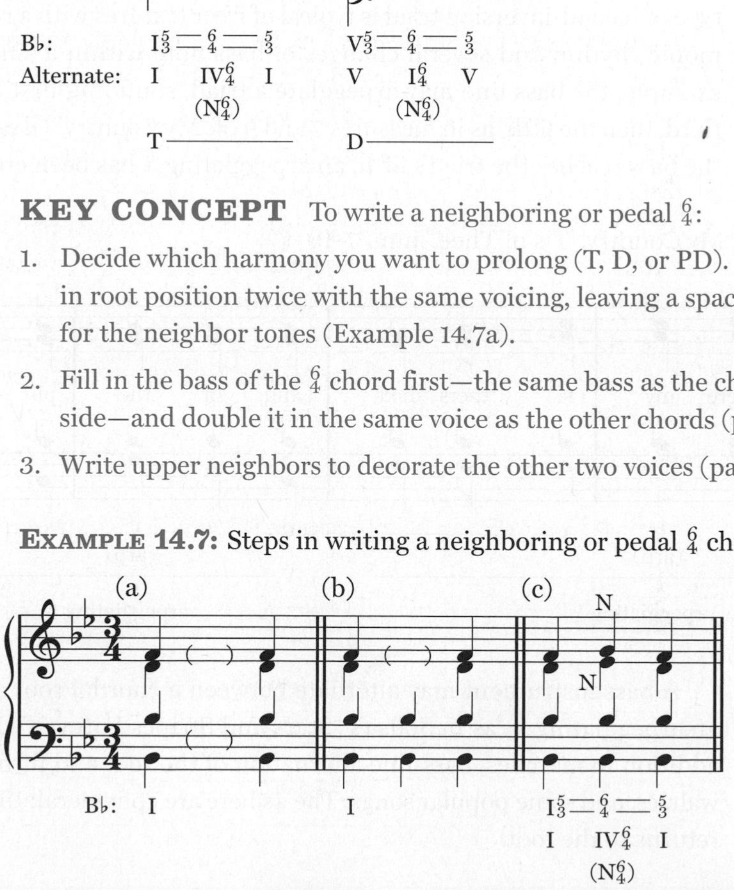

Try it #2

Write a neighboring or pedal $^6_4$ between the two tonic triads given.

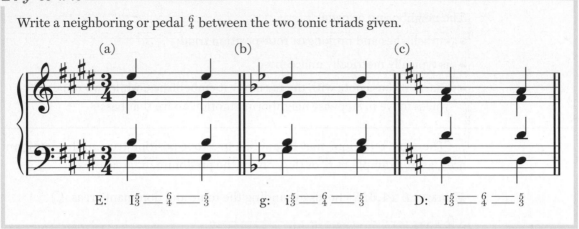

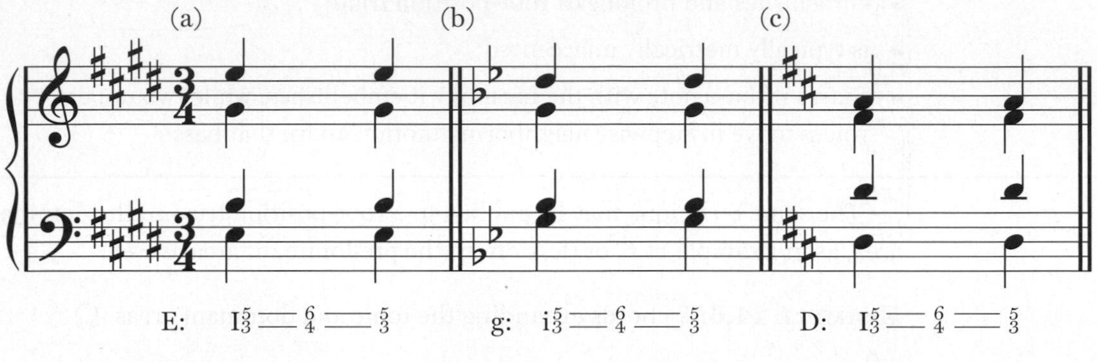

The Arpeggiating $^6_4$

The **arpeggiating** $^6_4$ prolongs a single harmony by changing its bass note. This type of second-inversion triad is typical of freer textures with a relatively slow harmonic rhythm and several changes of bass note within a single harmony. For example, the bass line may arpeggiate a triad, sounding first the root, then the third, then the fifth, as in measures 7 and 9 of "My Country" (Example 14.8). When the bass reaches the triad's fifth, an arpeggiating $^6_4$ has been created.

Example 14.8: "My Country, 'Tis of Thee," mm. 7–10

A bass instrument may alternate between a chordal root and fifth to create an arpeggiating $^6_4$, as in Sousa's "Stars and Stripes Forever" (Example 14.9). In addition to marches, bass-line alternation of the root and fifth is typical in rags, waltzes, and some popular songs. The $^6_4$s here are ephemeral: the bass line quickly returns to the root.

EXAMPLE 14.9: Sousa, "The Stars and Stripes Forever," Trio, mm. 37–40a

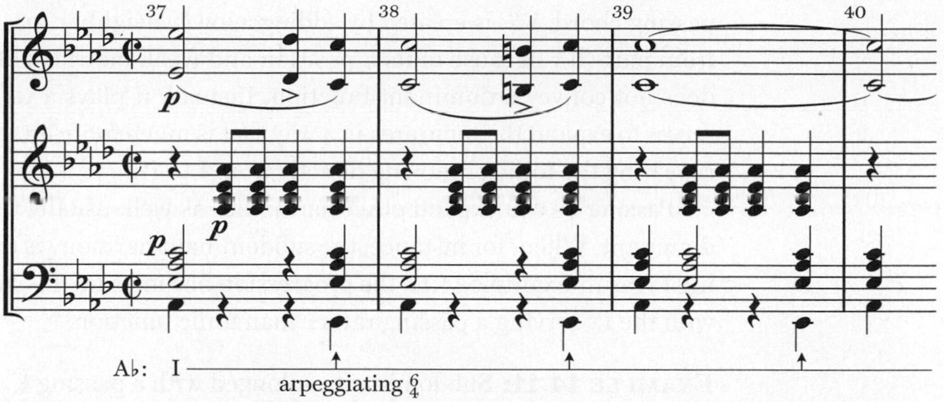

There are no special voice-leading rules for writing an arpeggiating $^6_4$, other than the recommendation that it be placed on a weak beat in a context where the primary bass note of the chord (something other than the fifth) is clear. When analyzing with Roman numerals, consider what the main bass note of the measure is—usually the lowest-sounding chord tone—and examine the progression with that note in mind. Label the chord with its Roman numeral and $^6_4$, with (arp) written beneath the $^6_4$ to show its type (Example 14.8).

The Passing $^6_4$

A common strategy for expanding the tonic area is to move from root-position I to I^6 or the reverse. This motion may involve a voice exchange between $\hat{1}$ and $\hat{3}$. Look at Example 14.10a to see a soprano-bass voice exchange, similar to those in first-species style. Part (b) shows a voice exchange embellished with passing tones (these are generally found in metrically unaccented positions), producing counterpoint in contrary motion: $\hat{1}$–$\hat{2}$–$\hat{3}$ in the bass and $\hat{3}$–$\hat{2}$–$\hat{1}$ in the soprano. The passing tone here can be harmonized, as in part (c), with a **passing** $^6_4$ chord.

EXAMPLE 14.10: Voice exchanges between I and I^6 that expand the tonic area

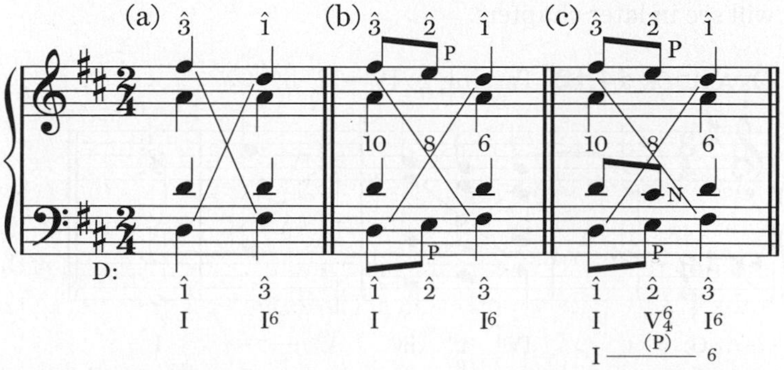

Passing $^6_4$ chords are defined by their bass-line passing motion. In part (c), the passing chord, V$^6_4$, is created by adding a lower neighbor tone to the tenor voice from part (b). Because of its $^6_4$ position and weak metric context, the passing V does not convey a dominant function. Instead, it plays a voice-leading role: it serves to expand the tonic area in a way that is much more interesting than merely repeating the tonic or moving directly from I to I^6.

Passing $^6_4$s can expand other harmonies as well, usually the subdominant or dominant. When, for instance, the subdominant harmony is expanded by a passing I$^6_4$, as in Example 14.11, the progression becomes IV–I$^6_4$–IV^6 (or IV–P$^6_4$–IV^6), with the I$^6_4$ serving a passing rather than tonic function.

EXAMPLE 14.11: Subdominant prolonged with a passing $^6_4$

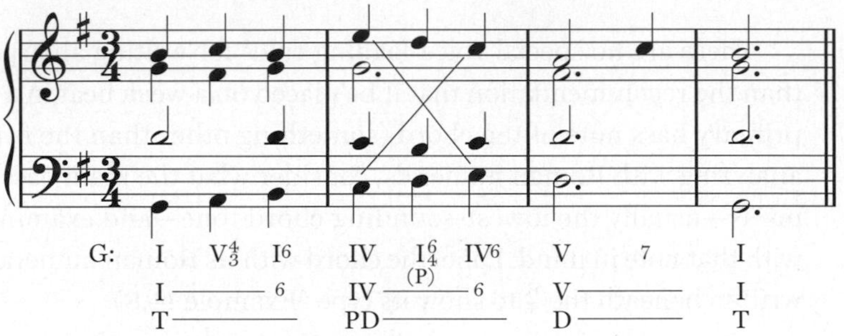

Progressions featuring passing $^6_4$s are usually "reversible": the root-position harmony can come first or last. Unlike cadential $^6_4$s, passing $^6_4$s typically occur on relatively unaccented positions in the measure. Analyze with a P beneath the chord, and in the contextual analysis simply write a long dash after the functional label (e.g., T or PD), as in Example 14.11.

The passing $^6_4$ may also connect two different chords as long as the chords serve the same function. For example, in the progression IV^6–I$^6_4$–IV, the last chord may be replaced with ii^6—a triad with the same function and the same bass as the IV chord (Example 14.12). This type of progression, sometimes with chromatic chords substituted for the diatonic ones, is a mainstay of Romantic-era harmony, as we will see in later chapters.

EXAMPLE 14.12: Passing $^6_4$: IV^6–I$^6_4$–ii^6

KEY CONCEPT To write passing $^6_4$s:

1. Decide which harmony you want to prolong (normally tonic, dominant, or subdominant).
2. Set up root-position and first-inversion chords of that harmony, with a voice exchange between the bass and one of the upper parts, often the soprano (Example 14.13a).
3. Fill in skips of a third with stepwise motion in both voices; this automatically doubles the fifth of the $^6_4$, the correct doubling (part b).
4. Complete the other voices. All parts should connect by common tone or by step, making neighboring or passing patterns (part c).

EXAMPLE 14.13: Steps in writing a passing $^6_4$

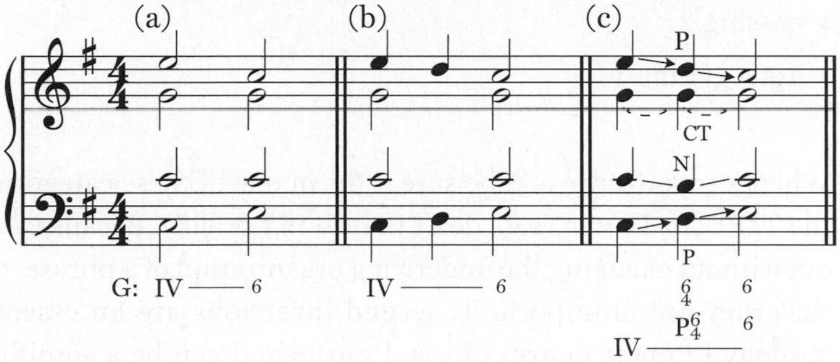

Try it #3

Fill in the space between the I and I6 (or i and i6) with a passing $^6_4$, from the bass and figures provided. Include a voice exchange with the soprano, and write a Roman numeral analysis.

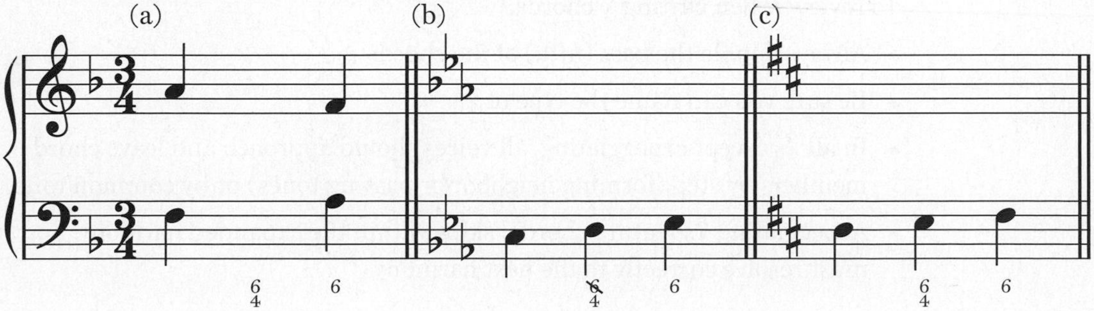

The Four $^6_4$ Types

When a root-position chord is replaced with a first-inversion chord, the inverted chord creates a weaker sense of progression, but the general function of the progression stays the same. We might infer that triads in $^6_4$ position are also interchangeable with other inversions. But $^6_4$ chords have always been treated specially in tonal music: they are considered harmonically very weak, and are used only in a few specific contexts.

KEY CONCEPT Each $^6_4$ chord you write must be one of the following types:

- cadential $^6_4$
- neighboring or pedal $^6_4$
- passing $^6_4$
- arpeggiating $^6_4$

Whenever you write a $^6_4$, be sure it fits in one of these categories, and lies within the T, PD, or D area (e.g., don't write a iii$^6_4$ or vi$^6_4$). Because $^6_4$ chords can be left out without changing the underlying organization of a phrase, this does not mean that they are unimportant: second inversions are an essential voice-leading strategy in many genres of tonal music and can be a significant indication of musical style.

SUMMARY

To review, when writing $^6_4$ chords:

- Always double the bass (fifth) of the chord.
- Be sure you can name the type of $^6_4$.
- In all $^6_4$s except arpeggiating, all voices should approach and leave chord members by step (forming neighbor or passing tones) or by common tone.
- Arpeggiating $^6_4$s feature chordal skips within the expanded harmony, but must resolve correctly to the next harmony.

Other Expansions of the Tonic Area

The Subdominant in Tonic Expansions

As we have seen, when the subdominant, in any inversion, appears between two tonic chords, it does not serve a predominant function, as it does not progress to a dominant harmony. Examples 14.14 and 14.15, showing i–iv–i and I–IV–I in folk and popular styles, illustrate this principle. (Circled notes are embellishing tones.)

Example 14.14: "Wayfaring Stranger," mm. 1–4a

Example 14.15: Sherman and Sherman, "Feed the Birds," mm. 1–4

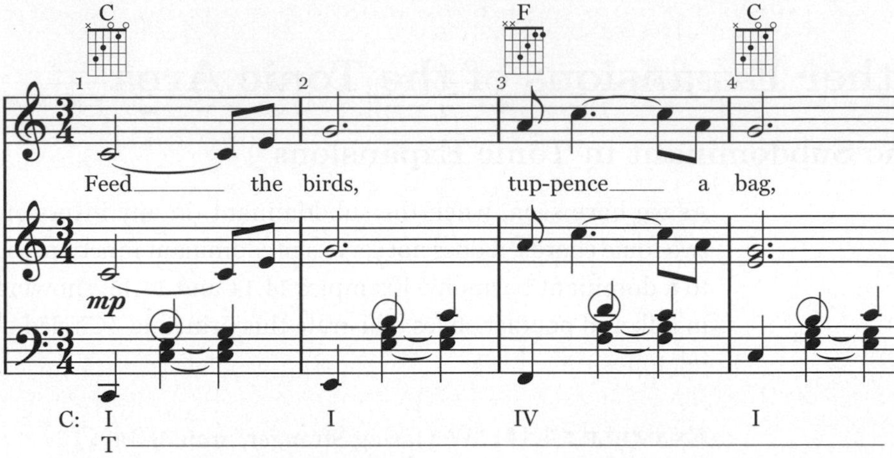

Measures 1–2 of Example 14.16 also feature a tonic expansion with root-position I–IV–I chords, as marked. In measure 1, however, the same chords appear, but with the IV as a neighboring $^6_4$ and lasting only one sixteenth note.

Example 14.16: Brahms, *Variations on a Theme by Haydn*, mm. 1–5a

The $^6_4$ in measure 1 is so fleeting that we could simply circle and label the G and E♭ as neighbor tones above a stationary bass; but the repetition of the same gesture in measure 2 with the root of the IV (E♭) in the bass draws the listener's attention to both statements.

The Dominant in Tonic Expansions

As the dominant triad can expand the tonic area, so can the dominant seventh and its inversions. These chords produce a number of outer-voice patterns that fit well within the guidelines of species counterpoint. In Example 14.17, for instance, tonic expansions with neighboring or passing motion in the soprano and/or bass produce the outer-voice intervals 8–6–8 and 10–10–10.

EXAMPLE 14.17: Tonic expansions with neighboring and passing motion

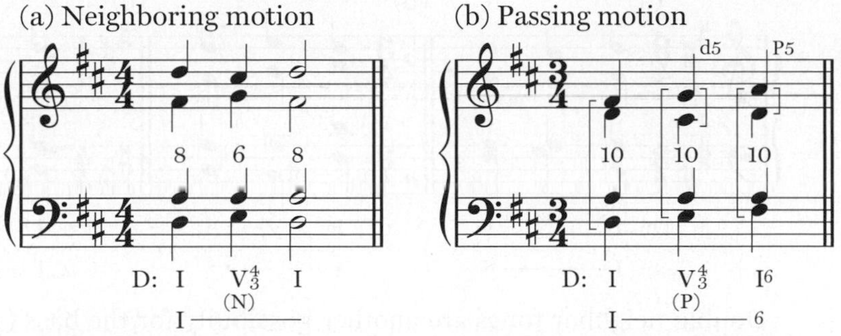

In part (b), the passing dominant is analogous to the passing $^6_4$, but now with a seventh chord. As mentioned in Chapter 13, this voice-leading pattern (10–10–10) overrides the normal resolution of the chordal seventh.

KEY CONCEPT When the soprano moves $\hat{3}$–$\hat{4}$–$\hat{5}$ against a bass line of $\hat{1}$–$\hat{2}$–$\hat{3}$, they move in parallel motion: 10–10–10. In this context, the chordal seventh of the V$^4_3$ moves upward ($\hat{4}$ to $\hat{5}$ in the soprano, G4 to A4 in the example), and the d5 may move to a P5 without creating parallel fifths.

Outer-voice patterns that imply a tonic expansion include stepwise motion between members of the tonic triad (e.g., $\hat{1}$–$\hat{2}$–$\hat{3}$, $\hat{3}$–$\hat{2}$–$\hat{1}$, $\hat{3}$–$\hat{4}$–$\hat{5}$, or $\hat{5}$–$\hat{4}$–$\hat{3}$ in either soprano or bass), or neighboring motion above or below a member of the tonic triad (e.g., $\hat{1}$–$\hat{2}$–$\hat{1}$, $\hat{1}$–$\hat{7}$–$\hat{1}$, $\hat{3}$–$\hat{2}$–$\hat{3}$, $\hat{3}$–$\hat{4}$–$\hat{3}$, or $\hat{5}$–$\hat{4}$–$\hat{5}$). Combine these patterns with contrary motion in the other voice, or with parallel motion between voices in tenths. You may also combine passing motion in one voice with neighboring motion in the other. Avoid soprano-bass patterns that result in parallel perfect intervals or a poor resolution of tendency tones.

Although we have focused on stepwise motion, bass-soprano combinations that include a bass-line skip are also possible. For example, the bass might skip from a member of the tonic triad to an inverted dominant chord before resolving, as in Example 14.18a and b. The bass note G3 in part (a) could have been approached by step from the chord tone F♯, had the initial tonic chord been in first inversion; this implied stepwise connection is what makes the bass line work. In part (b), the bass line skips a diminished fourth; although such a skip is normally avoided in common-practice voice-leading, here it makes sense because there is an implied stepwise connection from the tonic triad, had the first chord been in root position. Use skips like this only in the bass, and only where the function of the skip (here, as a tonic expansion) is clear.

EXAMPLE 14.18: Tonic expansions with skips in the bass line

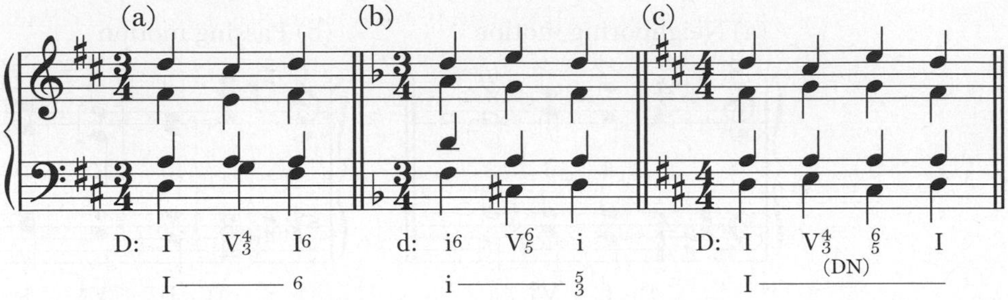

Double neighbor tones are another possibility for the bass (part c), especially if moving from one inversion of the dominant to another, as in the progression I–V^4_3–V^6_5–I (shown here), or I–V^6_5–V^4_3–I.

Try it #4

What three chords best harmonize the following patterns? Work out each solution at the keyboard or on staff paper until you are satistied with the voice-leading and chord choice.

KEY	SOPRANO	BASS	HARMONIZATION
major	$\hat{3}$–$\hat{2}$–$\hat{1}$	$\hat{1}$–$\hat{2}$–$\hat{3}$	I–V^6_4–I^6
major	$\hat{1}$–$\hat{2}$–$\hat{1}$	$\hat{1}$–$\hat{7}$–$\hat{1}$	________
minor	$\hat{1}$–$\hat{7}$–$\hat{1}$	$\hat{1}$–$\hat{4}$–$\hat{3}$	________
major	$\hat{3}$–$\hat{4}$–$\hat{5}$	$\hat{1}$–$\hat{2}$–$\hat{3}$	________
minor	$\hat{3}$–$\hat{4}$–$\hat{5}$	$\hat{1}$–$\hat{7}$–$\hat{1}$	________

The Submediant in Tonic Expansions

Since the submediant triad shares two scale degrees with the tonic triad ($\hat{1}$ and $\hat{3}$), it often serves as a a tonic expansion or substitute. The two types of tonic expansions presented here—by 5–6 motion and the progression I–vi (or i–VI in minor)—typically appear at phrase beginnings in many styles of tonal music.

With 5–6 Motion Consider the first phrase from Mozart's B♭ Major Sonata (Example 14.19), where the tonic chord in the first half of measure 1, arpeggiated in the left hand, is subtly transformed in the second half of the measure as F4 moves to G4 (G5 appears in the right-hand melody as well). This F–G motion above the bass, B♭3, forms the intervals 5–6. A Roman numeral analysis might label the second half of the measure a vi^6; however, this "submediant" is so brief that we hardly hear it as a new chord. The 5–6 linear motion allows I to move smoothly to ii (m. 2), and prevents the parallel fifths that would otherwise occur between the root-position triads.

Example 14.19: Mozart, Piano Sonata in B♭ Major, first movement, mm. 1–4a

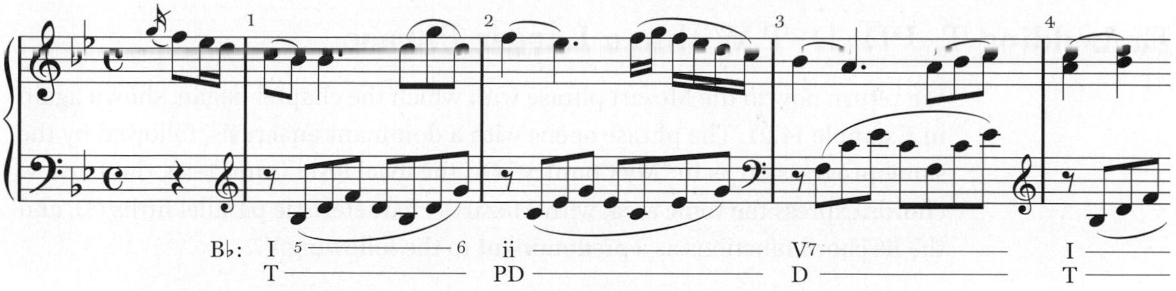

KEY CONCEPT The tonic area may be expanded by 5–6 intervallic motion above scale degree $\hat{1}$. This motion is generally labeled I^{5-6} rather than $I–vi^6$, though either is correct.

I–vi (i–VI in Minor) A phrase opening with root-position tonic and submediant harmonies creates an effect similar to the linear 5–6, but the bass movement down a third adds emphasis to the change of chord color from major to minor (I–vi) in major keys, and from minor to major (i–VI) in minor keys. This expansion of the tonic area is usually labeled with separate Roman numerals, as in measures 1 and 3 of "My Country" (Example 14.20). In the contextual analysis, the vi chord expands the tonic area in measures 1 and 3, but in measure 4 it is labeled a "Ts" (tonic substitute) in keeping with the basic phrase model. (Here the vi chord substitutes for the expected resolution to I in a PAC.) A second level of contextual analysis shows how measures 3–4 expand the tonic area of the phrase, before moving to the cadence in measures 5–6.

Example 14.20: "My Country, 'Tis of Thee," mm. 1–6

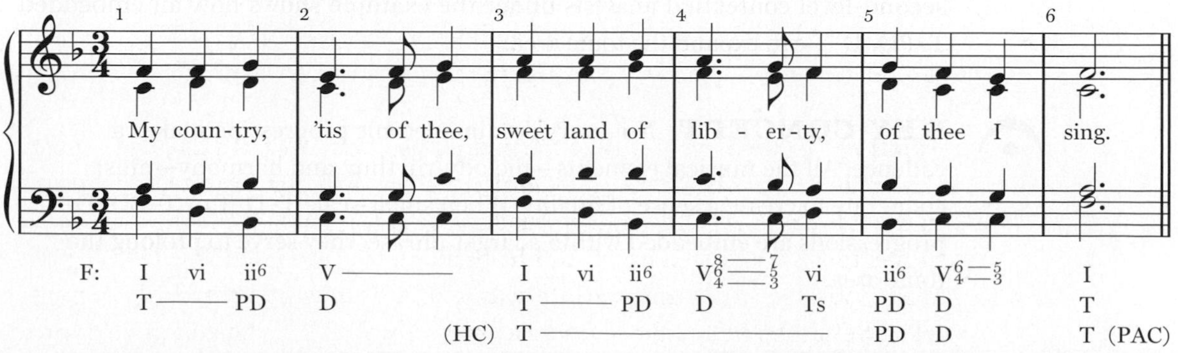

Look now at the voice-leading. In general, to connect the tonic and submediant harmonies, follow the voice-leading shown in measures 1 and 3 (beats 1 and 2): hold the common tones ($\hat{1}$ and $\hat{3}$) in two parts, move $\hat{5}$ to $\hat{6}$ in another, and move the bass down a third from $\hat{1}$ to $\hat{6}$, doubling the root of the vi chord.

Embedding T–PD–D–T Within a Larger Phrase

We return now to the Mozart phrase with which the chapter began, shown again in Example 14.21. The phrase opens with a dominant anacrusis, followed by the same progression as in "My Country." On the local level (mm. 1–2), the I and vi chords express the tonic area, with Mozart's characteristic parallel fifths (!), and the ii^6 chord functions as a predominant to the following V^7.

EXAMPLE 14.21: Mozart, Piano Sonata in D Major, third movement, mm. 1–4

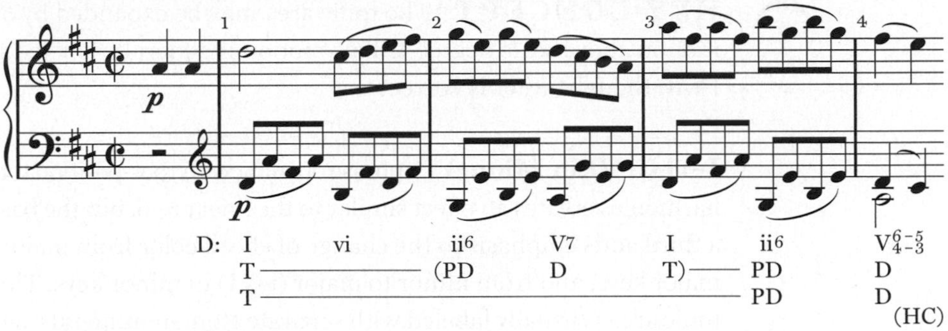

But we also need to consider what this progression means in terms of the phrase as a whole. Although the V^7 in measure 2 moves to I, it does not create a phrase-ending cadence here. While the left hand sets up a cadence, with the root motion $\hat{5}$ to $\hat{1}$, the melody refuses to cooperate—it comes to a resting place only in measure 4 at the half cadence. We can therefore hear a tonic expansion from measure 1 through the first half of measure 3, followed by predominant (ii^6) and dominant (m. 4) harmonies at the cadence, expanded by a cadential $^6_4$. The second-level contextual analysis under the example shows how an embedded T–PD–D–T can expand the tonic area.

KEY CONCEPT Not every dominant-tonic progression makes a cadence. All the musical elements—melody, rhythm, and harmony—must cooperate to create a sense of finality. When small-scale T–D–T or T–PD–D–T progressions are embedded within a larger phrase, they serve to prolong the tonic area.

Did You Know?

Johannes Brahms's *Variations on a Theme by Haydn*, consisting of a theme in B♭ major, eight variations, and a finale, was composed in 1873 and published in two versions: for two pianos (written first but designated Op. 56b) and for orchestra (Op. 56a). Recent scholarship, however, has revealed that the theme is not likely by Haydn after all. In 1870, Brahms's friend Carl Ferdinand Pohl, librarian of the Vienna Philharmonic Society, who was working on a Haydn biography at the time, showed the composer a transcription he had made of a piece attributed to Haydn titled Divertimento No. 1. The second movement bore the heading "St. Anthony Chorale"; and while current usage still prefers the original title, *Variations on the St. Anthony Chorale* is the name favored by those who object to perpetuating a misattribution. Even that name, however, tells us very little: to date, no other mention of the so-called St. Anthony Chorale has been found.

Just before the end of the piece, in the coda of the finale, Brahms quotes a passage that really is by Haydn. In measures 463–464, the violas and cellos echo the cello line from measure 148 of the second movement of Haydn's *Clock* Symphony, one of the finest examples of his pioneering work in the symphonic variation form. This fragmentary allusion may be the music's sole remaining link to Haydn.

TERMS YOU SHOULD KNOW

- 5–6 motion
- arpeggiating $^6_4$
- cadential $^6_4$
- dominant expansion
- embedded T–PD–D–T
- neighboring or pedal $^6_4$
- passing $^6_4$
- pedal point
- tonic expansion
- voice exchange

QUESTIONS FOR REVIEW

1. Why are cadential $^6_4$s labeled V^{6-5}_{4-3}? Discuss the pros and cons of other possible labeling systems.
2. What is the function of a neighboring or pedal $^6_4$? Where is it found?
3. What is the function of an arpeggiating $^6_4$? Where is it found?
4. What type of $^6_4$ is associated with the voice exchange?
5. What chords (in inversions) typically pass between I and I^6?
6. In music for your own instrument, find an example of three of the four $^6_4$ types.
7. Under what circumstances do the tendency tones of a passing dominant chord not resolve as usual?
8. What are two ways in which a submediant triad may expand the tonic area?
9. In a contextual analysis, how do you show brief T–D–T or T–PD–D–T progressions that prolong the tonic at the beginning of a phrase?

CHAPTER 15

Diatonic Harmonies and Root Progressions

Outline of topics

New cadence types

- The deceptive cadence: V–vi (or V–VI)
- The plagal cadence and plagal extension: IV–I (or iv–i)
- The Phrygian cadence: iv^6–V

Basic root progressions

- Root motion by descending fifth
- Root motion by descending third
- Root motion by second

About mediant triads

The mediant and minor dominant in minor keys

Parellel $\begin{smallmatrix}6\\3\end{smallmatrix}$ chords

Overview

This chapter introduces three additional cadence types and voice-leading for specific root progressions. We also consider uses of the mediant and minor-dominant triads.

Repertoire

Johann Sebastian Bach,
  Chaconne, from Violin Partita No. 2 in D Minor
  "Wachet auf" ("Awake," Chorale No. 197)

Archangelo Corelli, Preludio, from Sonata in D Minor, Op. 4, No. 8

Stephen Foster, "Camptown Races"

George Frideric Handel, "Hallelujah!" from *Messiah*

John Lennon and Paul McCartney, "Nowhere Man," from *Rubber Soul*

Don McLean, "Vincent"

Wolfgang Amadeus Mozart, Piano Sonata in D Major, K. 284, third movement

Modest Mussorgsky, "The Great Gate of Kiev," from *Pictures at an Exhibition*

"My Country, 'Tis of Thee" ("America")

"Wayfaring Stranger" (arranged by Norman Lloyd)

New Cadence Types

The Deceptive Cadence: V–vi (or V–VI)

Thus far, we have considered how to end phrases with a half cadence (HC), an imperfect authentic cadence (IAC), or a perfect authentic cadence (PAC). Listen to two phrases from Bach's chorale "Wachet auf," given in Example 15.1, to hear another option. Bach repeats the same melody in each phrase, but his harmonization creates a very different effect at the two cadences.

EXAMPLE 15.1: Bach, "Wachet auf," mm. 17b–24

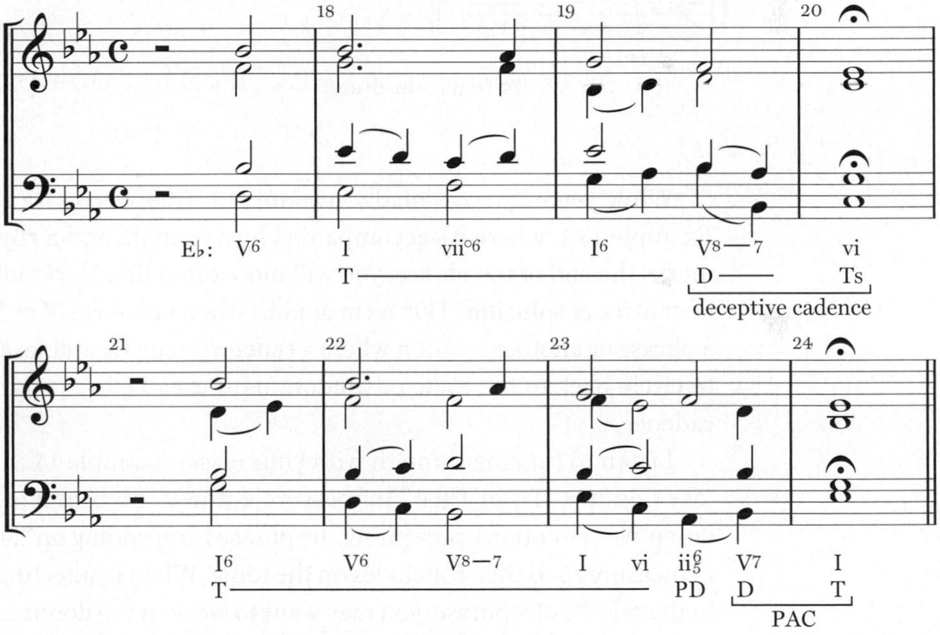

At the end of the first phrase (m. 20), Bach replaces the expected final tonic harmony with a tonic substitute (Ts), the submediant triad, to make a **deceptive cadence**: V7–vi. The name is appropriate, since the drama of this harmonic "deception" can be striking. (Typically, the following phrase will complete the thought that was interrupted by the deception.) The most effective deceptive cadences are voiced just like PACs: for the strongest deceptive effect, use V or V7 in root position, leading to a root-position vi (or VI), as in Example 15.2. Resolve the V or V7 normally, with $\hat{7}$ moving up to $\hat{1}$, and $\hat{4}$ (if present) down to $\hat{3}$. This voice-leading usually results in a doubled third ($\hat{1}$) in the vi (or VI) chord. Although the deceptive cadence with the submediant is the most typical, other resolutions of V7 at the cadence, such as V–IV6 (or other chords that share scale degrees with I or vi), can create a similar effect.

Example 15.2: Deceptive cadence model

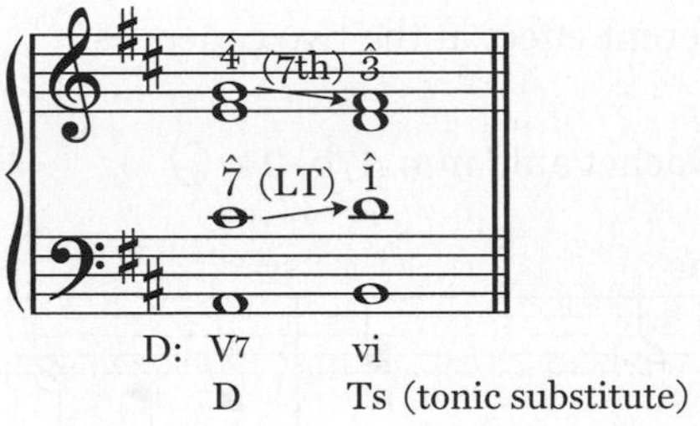

While you may occasionally encounter a "true" deceptive cadence like that in Example 15.1, where it's accompanied by a fermata and a rhythmic setting that marks the end of the phrase, you will more often find V–vi motion employed as a **deceptive resolution.** This term applies when vi follows V or V7 in the middle of a phrase or another location where a cadence is not desirable, allowing the phrase to circle back to the tonic or predominant area before progressing to the final cadence.

Listen to (or sing through with your class) Example 15.3, the first phrase of "My Country, 'Tis of Thee." In measure 4, the V7 on beat 2 is followed by a vi (a deceptive resolution), preventing the phrase from ending on "liberty"; the cadence in measures 5–6 then concludes on the tonic. When connecting V or V7 to vi or VI in the middle of a phrase, you may want to weaken the dominant chord by inverting it or by placing it in a weaker metrical position to make the progression less likely to sound like a firm cadence.

Example 15.3: "My Country, 'Tis of Thee," mm. 1–6

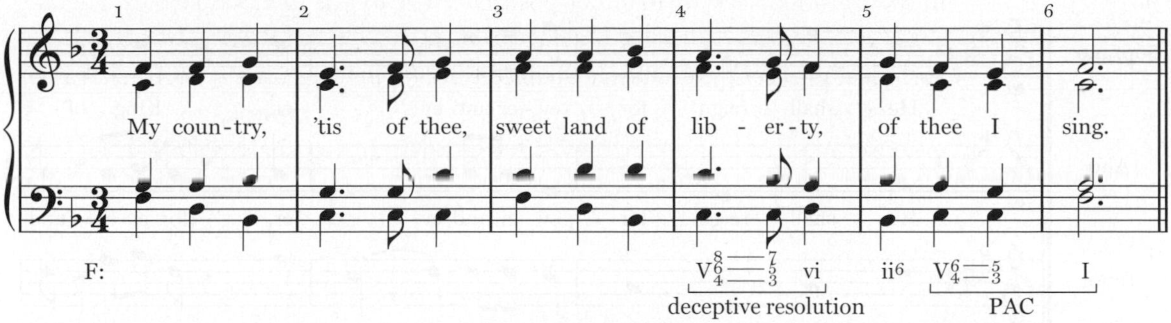

The Plagal Cadence and Plagal Extension: IV–I (or iv–i)

Now sing the final measures of "My Country" (Example 15.4) with your class. This setting includes an "Amen," as is typical in some American hymnbooks. The word is set with the root-position chords IV–I; these chords form a **plagal cadence**. Because of their association with hymns, plagal cadences are in fact sometimes called "Amen" cadences.

Example 15.4: "My Country, 'Tis of Thee," mm. 13–14

You know from earlier chapters that the progression I–IV–I prolongs the tonic area; plagal motion at the end of a composition (after the final dominant-tonic cadence) can also be interpreted as an expansion of the final tonic (some musicians speak of a "plagal resolution" or "plagal expansion of the tonic" rather than "cadence"). A famous instance is shown in Example 15.5, from the end of Handel's "Hallelujah Chorus." The final PAC arrives in measures 87–88, but the choir continues to sing I–IV–I repeatedly in a closing section that ends with a forceful plagal cadence on the final "Hallelujah!" Some conductors interpret this structure musically with a sense of arrival at the PAC in measure 88, before launching into the plagal extension. The extension allows the rhythmic energy of the piece to unwind while reaffirming the tonic with the repeated D5s in the soprano.

Example 15.5: Handel, "Hallelujah!" from *Messiah*, mm. 86–94

Examine the opening of Lennon and McCartney's "Nowhere Man" in Example 15.6. In some rock and blues styles, the progression I–V–IV–I is a basic ingredient of the harmonic structure. While this progression is rare in music of the eighteenth century, it makes a familiar and distinctive chord succession in popular styles. In "Nowhere Man," you might hear the first four measures (chord symbols E–B–A–E, or I–V–IV–I) as prolonging the tonic. Measures 5–7 then end with a plagal cadence (iv–I). Although plagal cadences may be used freely when writing in a contemporary or popular style, when composing in common-practice style, write an authentic cadence first, and then expand the final tonic with plagal motion.

Example 15.6: Lennon and McCartney, "Nowhere Man," mm. 1–7

The Phrygian Cadence: iv⁶–V

Another type of half cadence, typically found in Baroque-era music, features a iv⁶ chord in a minor key as the predominant to V; this is called a **Phrygian cadence**. This cadence, always iv⁶–V in minor, is named for its characteristic bass line: the half-step descent from $\flat\hat{6}$ to $\hat{5}$. Such a descent evokes the Phrygian mode, with its half step from $\flat\hat{2}$ to $\hat{1}$.

Listen to Example 15.7, from Corelli's Preludio in D Minor. The expressive opening of the movement, part (a), features 9–8 suspensions and a cadence on V (A major). The predominant to V is a G minor chord in first inversion, iv⁶, forming a Phrygian cadence in measure 7. At measures 37–38, part (b), the prelude also ends with a Phrygian cadence. This inconclusive "conclusion" on V sets up expectations on the part of the listener for the lively second movement.

EXAMPLE 15.7: Corelli, Preludio, from Sonata in D Minor

(a) Mm. 1–7a

(b) Mm. 32b–38

When you write a Phrygian cadence, don't move from ♭$\hat{6}$ (in an inner voice) to the leading tone $\hat{7}$ (*le* to *ti*), because that motion creates a melodic augmented second. A common voicing is to place ♭$\hat{6}$ to $\hat{5}$ in the bass and $\hat{4}$ to $\hat{5}$ in the soprano, as in parts (a) (violin 1) and (b) (violin 2).

SUMMARY

New cadence types:

- The deceptive cadence (V–vi or V–VI) avoids the expected tonic resolution.
- The plagal cadence (IV–I or iv–i; "Amen" cadence) prolongs the tonic area.
- The Phrygian cadence (iv6–V) is a special type of half cadence.

Try it #1

Part-write each of the following two-chord cadences from the Roman numerals given. In the blank below the staff, write the name of the cadence (deceptive, Phrygian, or plagal).

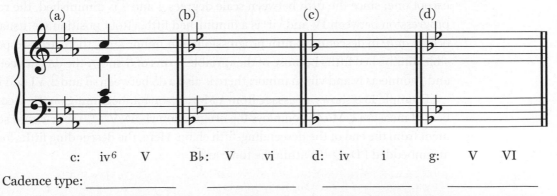

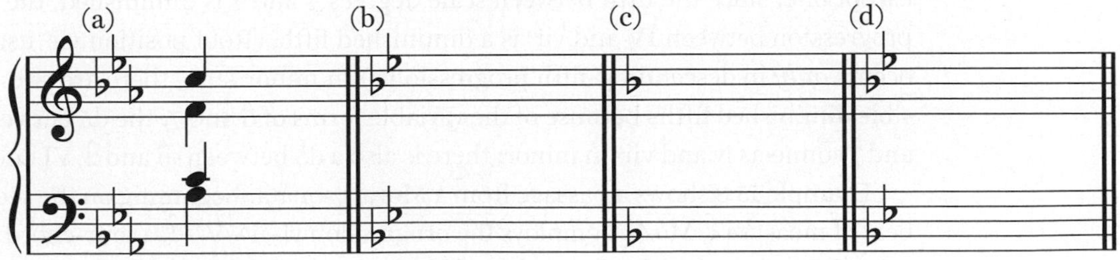

c: iv6 V   B♭: V vi   d: iv i   g: V VI

Cadence type: ____________ ____________ ____________ ____________

Basic Root Progressions

In tonal music, most of the connections between chords involve one of three basic root movements: **descending fifth**, **descending third**, or **ascending second**. For example, authentic cadences (V to I or i) show a root motion from $\hat{5}$ to $\hat{1}$ (descending fifth); even though the roots of these chords may not necessarily be in the bass, authentic cadences as a group can be thought of as descending-fifth root progressions. The descending-third root progression we have seen in the tonic expansion I to vi, but it may be found in the predominant area of a phrase as well (IV to ii). Connections between IV and V and between I and ii are examples of ascending-second root progressions, which typically connect two functional areas: predominant and dominant, or tonic and predominant, for example.

Root Motion by Descending Fifth

The strongest root motion in tonal music is by descending fifth (or ascending fourth—you can think of those as interchangeable). This root motion underlies the cadences introduced in Chapter 12 and many other typical progressions.

KEY CONCEPT The descending-fifth root progression may connect two chords, may form a chain of three or four, or may circle through all the diatonic chords in a key:

- I–IV–vii°–iii–vi–ii–V–I in major keys,
- i–iv–vii° (or VII) –III–VI–ii°–V–I in minor.

All the fifths between the roots of chords in the major-key chain are perfect except one: since the fifth between scale degrees $\hat{4}$ and $\hat{7}$ is diminished, the root progression between IV and vii° is a diminished fifth. (Root position vii° usually occurs *only* in descending-fifth progressions.) In minor keys, there are two possible diminished fifths because of the variable forms of $\hat{6}$ and $\hat{7}$: the d5 between $\hat{4}$ and $\hat{7}$ connects iv and vii° in minor; there is also a d5 between $\flat\hat{6}$ and $\hat{2}$, VI and ii°.

Example 15.8 shows a passage from a Mozart sonata; beginning on the second beat of measure 1, Mozart employs the progression vi–ii^6–V^7–I, a four-chord segment from the end of the descending-fifth chain. Here, the descending fifths form an embedded PD–D–T within the tonic area.

EXAMPLE 15.8: Mozart, Piano Sonata in D Major, third movement, mm. 1–4a

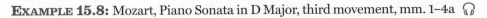

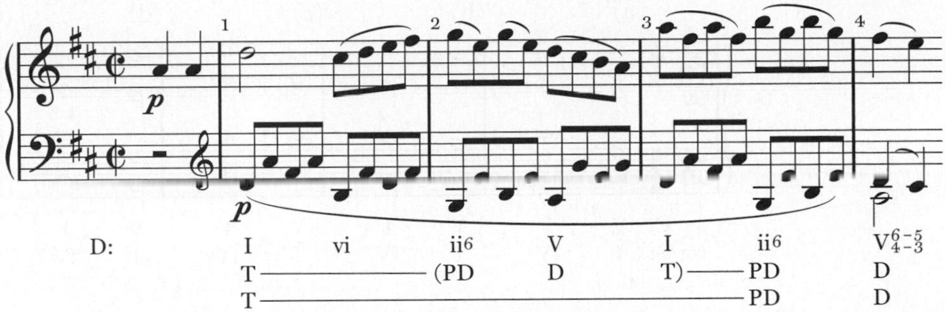

Not all the links in the descending-fifth chain are equally strong: for example, connections involving either the leading-tone or mediant triad rarely appear without the rest of the chain. We do not typically find root motion by *ascending* fifth in tonal music, other than between tonic and dominant.

KEY CONCEPT Some of the most common descending-fifth progressions:

- I–IV (or i–iv)
- vi–ii (or VI–ii°)
- ii–V (or ii°–V)
- V–I (or V–i)

Descending-fifth root motion can connect the tonic and predominant areas (as in I–IV or vi–ii, where vi is a tonic substitute), the predominant and dominant areas (ii–V), and the dominant and final tonic areas (V–I). These progressions are ubiquitous in all styles of tonal music.

Part-Writing Descending-Fifth Progressions Triads with roots a fifth apart share one chord member; for example, G–B–D and C–E–G share pitch class G. Example 15.9 illustrates how to connect these two chords. They could be functioning as V–I in the key of C major, as here, but they could also be I–IV in G major: the basic voice-leading connections are the same because of the root progression of a descending fifth.

EXAMPLE 15.9: Connecting chords a fifth apart

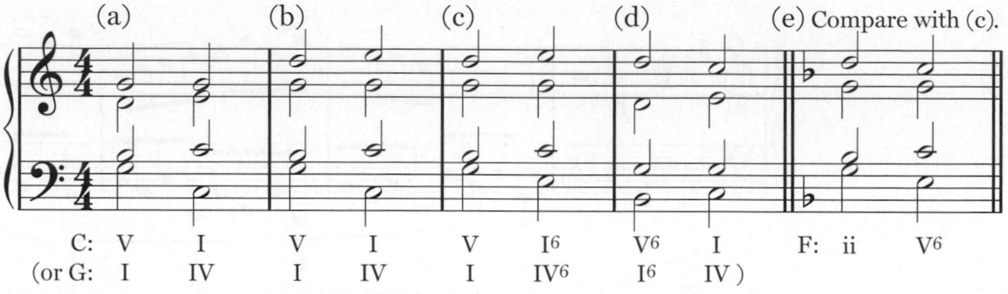

If we added a B♭ to the key signature to make the key of F major, the same voice-leading and doubling would apply for ii–V (G minor to C major) except in part (c), where you need a different doubling for the first-inversion C major chord (so that you don't double the leading tone, E, for V6 in F major; see part e). As always, observe the guidelines for doubling and resolution of tendency tones within the key.

KEY CONCEPT A typical method of connecting triads with roots a fifth apart is to hold the common tone in the same voice and move all the other parts to the closest possible chord member.

In some descending-fifth progressions, seventh chords may substitute for some of the triads: ii7 (or iiø7) and its inversions instead of ii (or ii°), or V7 and its inversions instead of V, as in Example 15.10.

EXAMPLE 15.10: Descending-fifth progressions featuring seventh chords

While it is possible to substitute the subdominant or submediant seventh chords in place of their triads, these are much less prevalent in eighteenth- and nineteenth-century music outside of descending-fifth chains. In part-writing nondominant seventh chords (such as ii7, IV7, and vi7), the chordal seventh should be approached by common tone or by step, and must be resolved down. Since V7 has both a chordal seventh and leading tone to resolve, the root-position V^7 may be incomplete, as in Example 15.10.

KEY CONCEPT Resolve the seventh of a predominant seventh chord down by step, then move the other two upper parts the shortest distance to members of the next chord. Check for parallels, doubling, and spacing.

Root Motion by Descending Third

While root motion by fifth occurs almost exclusively in descending progressions, root motion by third is possible both ascending and descending, with the latter the most typical.

KEY CONCEPT Root motion by descending third can also be repeated to make a chain:

- I–vi–IV–ii–vii°–V–iii–I in major keys,
- i–VI–iv–ii°–vii° (or VII)–V–III–i in minor.

You will encounter some parts of this chain frequently: I–vi (to expand the tonic area, for example), vi–IV–ii, and ii–$vii^{\circ 6}$. Bach includes the first three chords of the chain near the beginning of his Chaconne in D Minor (Example 15.11). Seventh chords are not typically found in descending-third progressions.

EXAMPLE 15.11: Bach, Chaconne in D Minor, mm. 3–4

Since leading-tone chords $vii^{\circ 6}$, $vii^{ø7}$, and $vii^{\circ 7}$ and their inversions share $\hat{7}$, $\hat{2}$, and $\hat{4}$ with V^7, they can act as dominant substitutes (Ds), but with a weaker sense of closure. Replacing V with vii° in the descending-fifth progression ii–V, for example, creates a descending-third approach to the cadence. (Later chapters will consider progressions involving leading-tone triads and seventh chords in more detail.)

The last parts of the chain, centered around the mediant chord (V–iii and iii–I), are rarely heard in common-practice music: instead, when the phrase reaches the dominant area, a cadence usually follows. The progression vii°–V is also rarely found if the texture of the music is chordal and the harmony changes on each chord. In pieces with a freer texture, you may encounter a dominant area that begins with vii° (or vii^{ø7} or vii$^{\circ 7}$), then brings in $\hat{5}$ to make V or V^7. If all members of V^7 and vii$^{\circ 7}$ are present, the result is a V^7 with an additional third on top—a V^9 chord. In that case, the entire dominant area may be given one label: V^7 or V^9, as appropriate.

Part-Writing Third Progressions Triads whose roots are a third apart share two pitch classes; for example, C–E–G and A–C–E share C and E. Third progressions are usually voiced with the root of the chord doubled in the bass and in an upper part to maximize the common tones between each pair, as in Example 15.12.

EXAMPLE 15.12: Connecting chords by thirds

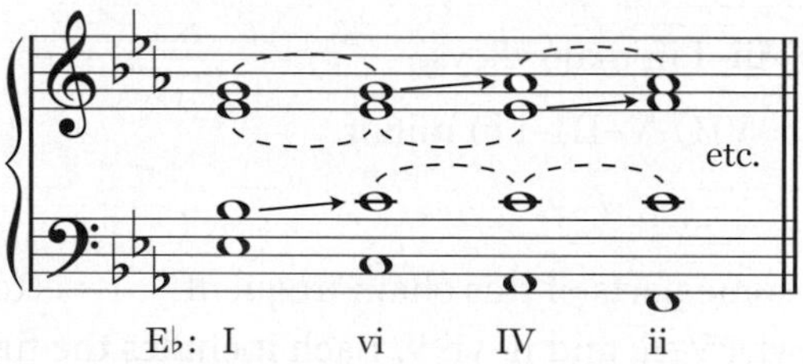

KEY CONCEPT When connecting chords with roots a third apart, hold the common tones and move the other parts to the next-nearest chord member.

The chains made by ascending-third motion are

- I–iii–V–vii°–ii–IV–vi–I in major keys,
- i–III–V–vii° (or VII)–ii°–iv–VI–i in minor.

Only a few of these connections are typical in tonal music, and each plays a special role. I–iii may be employed as a tonic expansion (discussed later in the chapter), as may vi–I; and V–vii° is usually found in freer textures where the root of the V drops out temporarily during a dominant expansion. The others may appear in contemporary tonal pieces, such as the verse of "Vincent" (Example 15.13), which expands the predominant area with the rising third ii to IV.

EXAMPLE 15.13: McLean, "Vincent," mm. 4–11a

Try it #2

Part-write each of the two-chord pairs below. Label the root motion type, then circle the common tones between chords: one common tone for descending fifth, two for descending third.

(a) (b) (c) (d)

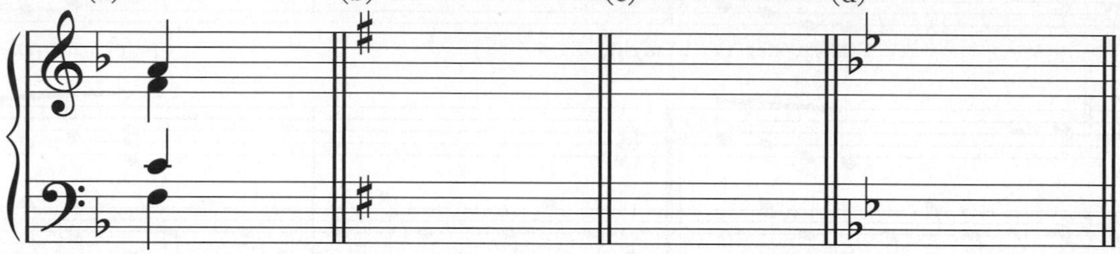

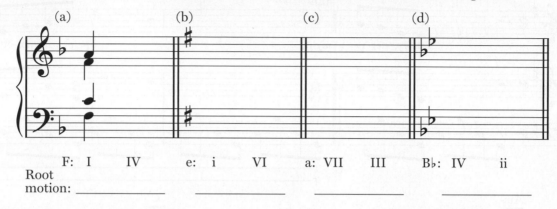

F: I IV e: i VI a: VII III B♭: IV ii

Root motion: ____________ ____________ ____________ ____________

Root Motion by Second

Root movement by second (most often by ascending second) typically connects functional areas in the basic phrase.

KEY CONCEPT Common second progressions connecting functional areas are:

Major		Minor	
• I–ii	or	i–ii°	connecting T and PD areas,
• IV–V	or	iv–V	connecting PD and D areas,
• I–vii°	or	i–vii°	connection T and D areas (omitting the PD area),
• vii°–I	or	vii°–i	connecting D and T areas (with a dominant substitute),
• V–vi	or	V–VI	connecting D and T areas (with a tonic substitute).

The most direct way to connect chords with roots a second apart is simply to shift the entire chord up or down a step. While this type of connection is sometimes found in twentieth-century music, folk-style accompaniments, and popular music, common-practice composers usually avoided it because it creates parallel fifths and octaves between the two chords, as in Example 15.14. With these parallels, it is possible to hear only one melodic line, doubled by triads, rather than four fully independent voice-leading strands.

Example 15.14: Chord progressions with parallel fifths and octaves

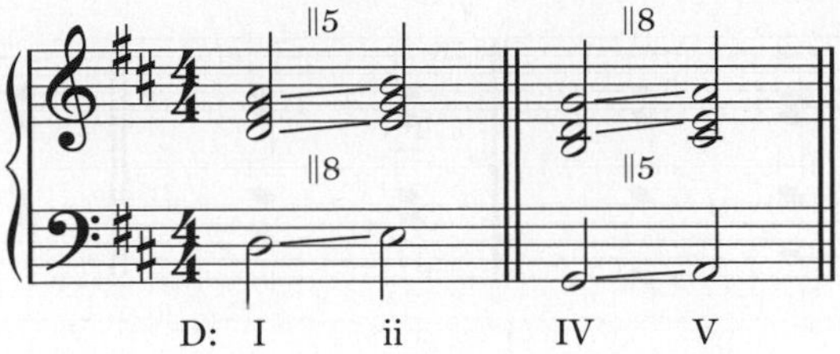

KEY CONCEPT Chords with roots a second apart are responsible for most parallel-fifth and parallel-octave errors in part-writing. Move the upper parts in contrary motion to the bass line (Example 15.15) to avoid them.

Example 15.15: Voice-leading for chords with roots a second apart

Inverting one or more of the chords also makes it easier to avoid parallels, but check the voice-leading carefully. If you have written parallels in a progression with inversions, changing the doubling in one of the chords may correct the problem.

Try it #3

Provide Roman numerals and figures for the two-chord pairs below. Identify the root motion in the blanks provided. Below the blanks, add a contextual analysis showing the role of the submediant in each pair: tonic function (T), tonic subsitute (Ts), or predominant (PD).

A.

A: I vi

Root motion: desc. 3rd ________ ________ ________ ________

T______

B.

B♭:

Root motion: __________ __________ __________ __________

About Mediant Triads

The mediant triad consists of $\hat{3}$, $\hat{5}$, and $\hat{7}$, sharing two scale degrees with the tonic ($\hat{3}$ and $\hat{5}$) and two with the dominant ($\hat{5}$ and $\hat{7}$). Mediant triads don't often appear in tonal music as freestanding chords; they don't fit cleanly into either the tonic- or dominant-function areas because they sound a little like both.

Root progressions connecting a mediant triad to a dominant-function chord (V^7 or vii°) are relatively rare. Sometimes when engaged in close, chord-to-chord analysis, you may come across what seems to be one of these progressions; in most cases, however, additional inspection reveals that the apparent mediant triad is not a "real" chord, but a dominant-function harmony where not all of the chord tones sound at the same time.

Look at the opening of Bach's Chaconne in Example 15.16. All the chords are readily accounted for by root progressions and functional areas except those with question marks. The i to $ii^{ø4}_{2}$ (mm. 0–1, 4–5) is a root progression by ascending second. The $ii^{ø4}_{2}$ to V^{6}_{5} to i (mm. 1–2, 5–6) progress by descending fifth. (Within the slightly larger context of the phrase, the opening i–$ii^{ø4}_{2}$–V^{6}_{5}–i can be considered an expansion of the tonic, with an embedded PD–D–T; the inversions give these chords a linear function.) The i–VI–iv (mm. 2–3) is by descending third.

The chord on beat 2 in measure 3 may seem at first to be a III, progressing to vii° on the next beat. But a consideration of the context reveals otherwise: this piece is based on a four-measure repeating harmonic pattern that starts with an anacrusis (a chaconne always involves a repeated harmonic progression). If you compare the corresponding measures (compare m. 3, beats 2–3, with m. 7, beats 2–3), it becomes clear that the apparent III–vii° is really a V^7 in which all the chord members simply arrive at different times. Some listeners may also hear beat 2 in measure 3 as a cadential $^{6}_{4}$ (without scale degree $\hat{1}$), expanding the dominant area.

Example 15.16: Bach, Chaconne in D Minor, mm. 1–8a

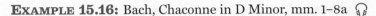

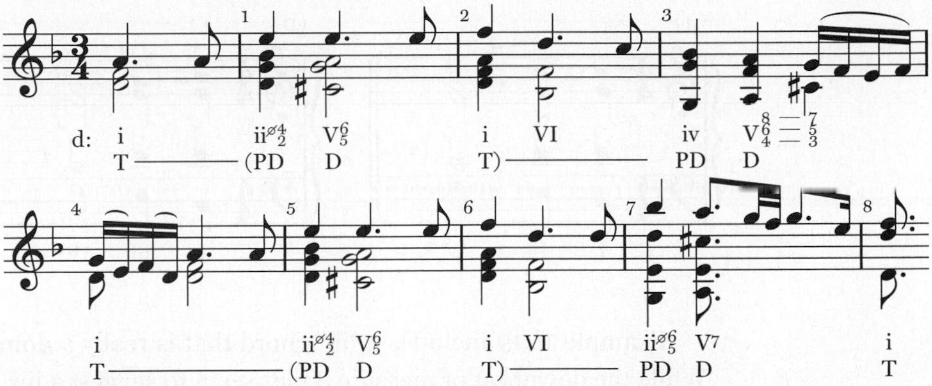

Mediants may appear in modal, folk, or popular styles. They also sometimes function as dominant substitutes in late nineteenth-century Russian nationalistic music, which draws on the modal scales of the Russian Orthodox chant tradition. For example, in the "Great Gate of Kiev" movement from Mussorgsky's *Pictures at an Exhibition* (Example 15.17), iii stands in for V in the progression ii$^6_5$–iii–I.

Example 15.17: Mussorgsky, "The Great Gate of Kiev," mm. 18–22

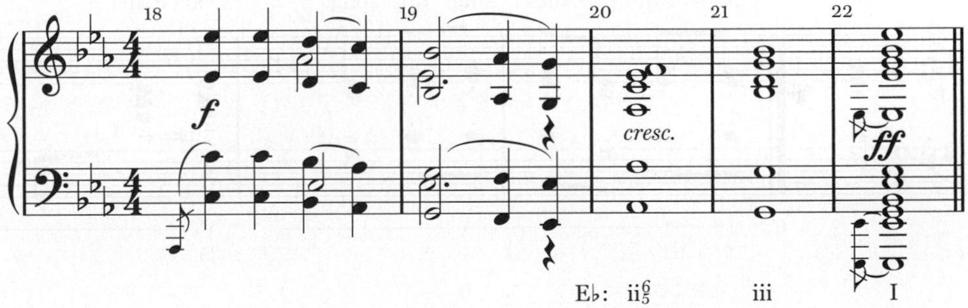

The mediant may serve as part of a tonic expansion at the beginning of a phrase: I–iii (or i–III); but because it does not share $\hat{1}$ with the tonic, it is less effective as a tonic substitute than the submediant. The progression I–iii may in fact be considered a variation of I–I^6 (Example 15.18). Here the mediant triad results from linear motion from $\hat{1}$ to $\hat{7}$ in an upper part, accompanied by a bass motion from $\hat{1}$ to $\hat{3}$—the tonic note "disappears" temporarily because of these simultaneous activities. Any predominant chord that can follow a I^6 may follow the apparent iii, but take care to avoid parallel octaves or fifths (as the example does).

Example 15.18: Voice-leading for I–iii–IV

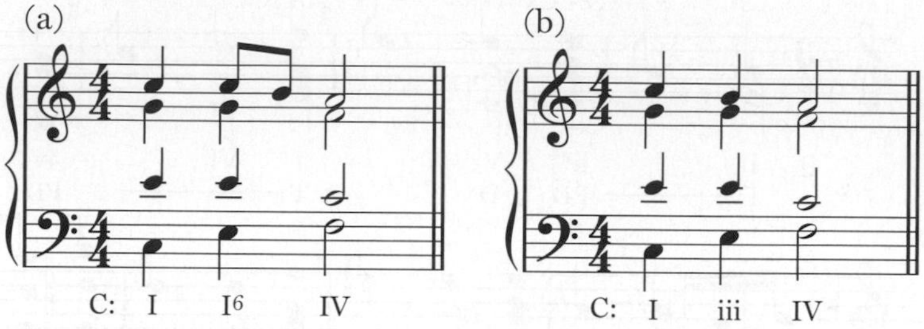

Example 15.19 includes a "iii" chord that is really a dominant in folk style. While the downbeat of measure 3 may seem to suggest a iii^6 (E–G–B), since the harmonic rhythm is one chord per bar, think of the whole measure as a single chord: its bass note is G, and its function is V^7. The "Doo-dah!" exclamation is consonant 6–5 motion above the bass, and should not be analyzed as iii^6–V.

Example 15.19: Foster, "Camptown Races," mm. 1–4a

The Mediant and Minor Dominant in Minor Keys

In minor keys, III forms a special relationship with VI (submediant) and VII (subtonic): the three possess the same qualities as I, IV, and V in the relative major key (for example, in A minor, the triads on C, F, and G sound like I, IV, V in C major). These minor-key harmonies are sometimes combined in progressions that temporarily evoke the relative major key.

One of the progressions, the descending-fifth III–VI, appears in the modal folk tune "Wayfaring Stranger," which also features another harmonic possibility for this style. Listen to Example 15.20, and examine the Roman numeral analysis. The first four measures express a i–iv–i tonic expansion, while the cadence (mm. 7–8) is iv–v–i, enlisting the minor dominant. The two chords in measures 5–6, III–VI, follow a descending-fifth pattern.

Example 15.20: "Wayfaring Stranger," mm. 1–8a

KEY CONCEPT Minor dominant chords (v) are used in folk song settings or in popular styles with a modal or folk sound. In common-practice style, they are occasionally found in the middle of a phrase, where they temporarily evoke the sounds of modal composition and serve a predominant function, but not at cadences, where the leading tone is a necessary ingredient.

Parallel $^6_3$ Chords

Another way that the minor dominant and mediant triads may appear in music literature is in a stream of parallel $^6_3$ chords. In passages like these, the contrapuntal motion of parallel sixths and thirds, rather than principles of root motion, controls the chord succession. Example 15.21 (m. 129) shows an example of the mediant in a stepwise descent of $^6_3$ chords (the $\flat$II^6 chord will be discussed later in connection with chromatic harmony.)

EXAMPLE 15.21: Mozart, Piano Sonata in D Major, third movement, Variation VII, mm. 127b–131a

Minor-key parallel $^6_3$ chord successions including the minor dominant are i–v^6–iv^6–III^6 and i–v^6–iv^6–V, where V replaces III^6. Both are employed to harmonize the bass line $\hat{1}$–$\flat\hat{7}$–$\flat\hat{6}$–$\hat{5}$ of the melodic and natural minor scales. To analyze a passage with parallel $^6_3$ chords, you can assign Roman numerals only to the beginning and end of the chord succession and write $^6_3$ figures in between, rather than giving each chord a Roman numeral. Parallel $^6_3$ chords are also used in major keys, where V^6–IV^6 is typically followed by V instead of iii^6.

Did You Know?

Musicians first began describing chord connections by root motion in the mid-eighteenth century. Jean-Philippe Rameau, who brought the ideas of the invertible triad and seventh chord to the fore, also had a theory of how chords were connected. He thought of all chords as being connected in "cadences" by the root motion of a fifth; the chord progression of our authentic cadences fit this model. But he did not limit the idea of cadence to the ends of phrases as we do now: *all* chord connections with roots a fifth apart were cadences to Rameau. When a chord connection did not fit his model—for example, the connection between I and ii^6—he theorized that the $\hat{4}$ in the bass of the ii^6 was the "real" root, and that the connection was a descending fifth from $\hat{1}$ to $\hat{4}$. From Rameau's attempts to make all progressions conform to the strong descending-fifth root motion, later theorists such as Hugo Riemann developed the idea of chord substitutes—for example, the idea that ii^6 can substitute for IV.

TERMS YOU SHOULD KNOW

- ascending-second progression
- deceptive cadence
- deceptive resolution
- descending-fifth progression
- descending-third progression
- dominant substitute
- parallel $^6_3$ chords
- Phrygian (half) cadence
- plagal cadence
- root progression

QUESTIONS FOR REVIEW

1. Where are deceptive cadences typically found? How do they differ from deceptive resolutions? What type of effect do they create?
2. Where are plagal cadences typically found? What type of effect do they create?
3. How does a Phrygian cadence differ from other types of half cadences? What gives it its distinctive sound (and name)?
4. What are the chords in a descending-fifth chain? Where are the "weak links"?
5. What are the chords in a descending-third chain? Where are the "weak links"?
6. Why are root progressions by second not generally found in chains? Where might you see them?
7. What part-writing guidelines should you follow for descending-fifth progressions? descending-third? ascending-second?
8. How are mediant triads used? How can you distinguish an apparent mediant from a real one?
9. In what contexts may minor dominant chords appear in common-practice style? In what other styles might you hear them?

Embellishing Tones in Four Voices

Outline of topics

Embellishing tones
- Writing passing and neighbor tones in chorale textures

More on suspensions
- Writing suspensions in four parts
- Suspensions with change of bass
- Combining suspensions
- Embellishing suspensions
- Retardations

More on neighbor and passing tones
- Chromatic neighbor and passing tones
- Incomplete neighbors
- Double neighbors
- Passing tones and chordal skips

Other types of embellishments
- Anticipations
- Pedal points

Embellishing tones in popular music

Overview

Here, we revisit embellishing tones to adapt concepts learned in species counterpoint to four-part writing. We also explore chromatic versions of familiar embellishments and learn several new types.

Repertoire

Johann Sebastian Bach
- "Aus meines Herzens Grunde" ("From My Inmost Heart," Chorale No. 1)
- "Christ ist erstanden" ("Christ Is Risen," Chorale No. 197)
- "Heut' ist, o Mensch" ("This Day, O Mankind," Chorale No. 168)
- "Liebster Jesu" ("Dearest Jesus," Chorale No. 131)
- "O Haupt voll Blut und Wunden" ("O Head Full of Blood and Wounds," Chorale No. 74)
- Organ Sonata No. 5 in C Major, first movement
- Prelude in E♭ Major for Organ (*St. Anne*)

Johannes Brahms, *Variations on a Theme by Haydn*, Op. 56b

George Frideric Handel, Chaconne in G Major

Alan Menken and Tim Rice, "A Whole New World," from *Aladdin*

Wolfgang Amadeus Mozart
- Piano Sonata in D Major, K. 284, third movement
- *Variations on "Ah, vous dirai-je Maman"*

Henry Purcell, "Music for a While"

Andrew Lloyd Webber and Tim Rice, "Don't Cry for Me Argentina," from *Evita*

Embellishing Tones

Despite the emphasis placed on simple chordal textures when you learn about four-part harmony, very few pieces rely solely on a succession of block chords. Indeed, much of the beauty and inventiveness of musical composition lies in how composers embellish melodic lines or chord successions. Because the pitches that embellish a musical line are usually not members of the underlying harmony, some textbooks call them "nonharmonic" or "nonchord" tones. The term "embellishing tone," on the other hand, focuses on their musical function.

Embellishing tones have expressive potential for performance: you can add accents or subtle changes in timing, for example, to emphasize the tension of a dissonant embellishment. Identifying them can also clarify a harmonic analysis: you may find it difficult to supply a Roman numeral to a harmony that includes unexplained extra pitches. Indeed, some "chords" are simply collections of embellishing tones. For this reason, beware of analyzing harmonies by taking vertical "snapshots" of each beat, stacking the pitches in thirds, and then applying a Roman numeral. This procedure can be misleading and not very musical. Instead, spend some time listening to the passage to decide which pitches are structural and which are embellishing. If in doubt, leave out the pitch in question to see if the chord makes sense—embellishing tones can be omitted without damaging the harmonic logic of a phrase.

Listen now to the last two vocal phrases of Bach's "Aus meines Herzens Grunde" (Example 16.1), and examine the circled embellishing tones: passing tones, neighbor tones, and suspensions in a chorale setting.

Example 16.1: Bach, "Aus meines Herzens Grunde," mm. 14b–21

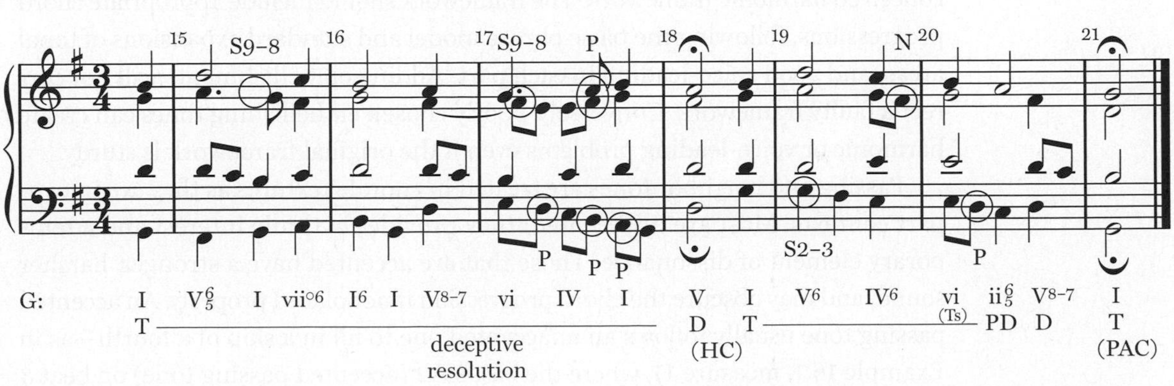

Sometimes only one part of the SATB texture includes an embellishing tone (as in mm. 19 and 20); in such cases, the harmonic progression is clear and the embellishments relatively easy to identify.

In measure 17, however, both the bass and alto feature them. The chord on beat 1 is a vi (E-G-B), but the alto has an F♯ tied over from the previous beat to make a 9–8 suspension. The following chord on beat 2 is a IV (C-E-G), with unaccented passing tones on the second half of the beat in the soprano, alto, and bass connecting to the tonic chord (G-B-D) on beat 3. The soprano and alto parts move here as simultaneous passing tones in parallel thirds, following the principles of good counterpoint. The bass part provides contrary motion, traveling from C3 (the root of the IV chord) down to G2 (the root of the I chord), requiring an *accented* passing tone on beat 3 to complete this span.

Other places may appear to feature embellishing tones—such as measure 20, beats 2 and 3, where the rhythmic pattern appears to indicate a pair of suspensions—but all these notes are chord members. Sometimes it takes a little detective work to identify the embellishing tones. For example, in measure 15, the D4 in the tenor is repeated from the previous chord; at first glance, it looks like it might be a rearticulated suspension, which resolves downward to C4. Alternatively, the C4 might be a passing tone, coming between D4 and B3. Yet a consideration of the harmonic context indicates that both the D and C are part of the chord, a V^6_5 in G major, where the seventh of the chord enters after the beat. The following chord is a I (G-B-D), with an alto A4 hanging over from beat 1, making a 9–8 suspension.

Writing Passing and Neighbor Tones in Chorale Textures

The most important step in writing passing tones, neighbor tones, and suspensions does not involve the embellishments at all: it is establishing a strong and well-conceived harmonic framework. The framework should include appropriate chord progressions, following the basic phrase model and standard expansions of tonal areas, and good voice-leading in each part. Adding embellishments will not correct a faulty framework. Conversely, poorly chosen embellishing tones can create harmonic or voice-leading problems even if the original framework is sturdy.

Passing and neighbor tones are treated in chorale textures as they are in two-part contexts. Most are unaccented: they provide rhythmic interest and a temporary element of dissonance. Those that are accented have a stronger, harsher sound, and may obscure the chord progression if not placed properly. An accented passing tone usually follows an unaccented one to fill in a skip of a fourth—as in Example 16.1, measure 17, where the bass's A2 (accented passing tone) on beat 3 together with the preceding B2 (unaccented passing tone) fills in the fourth from C3 to G2. This type of accented passing tone will not appear on the downbeat.

Passing or neighbor tones may appear at the same time in two voices in parallel sixths or thirds, as in measure 3 of Example 16.2, where there are neighbor tones (alto-tenor) and passing tones (soprano-alto) in thirds. Simultaneous passing tones in contrary motion, as at the end of the measure (alto-soprano-bass), are also possible. Such simultaneous embellishing tones may create an "embellishing chord": the F♯-A-C in measure 3 on the "and" of beat 2 could be heard as a vii°6, or simply labeled as linear embellishments leading to the tonic that precedes the half cadence.

EXAMPLE 16.2: Bach, "Aus meines Herzens Grunde," mm. 1–4a

KEY CONCEPT Passing and neighbor tones can be written in any voice and are commonly unaccented, but four-voice textures offer opportunities for accented passing or neighbor tones as well.

More on Suspensions

Writing Suspensions in Four Parts

Many of the guidelines for suspensions in two voices apply also in fuller textures, including the three-step process for writing them: (1) write a consonant preparation of the tone to be suspended, (2) retain that tone as a dissonance on a strong beat, and (3) resolve the tone down by step to a consonant interval. As in two-voice writing, the suspended note may be tied to its preparation or rearticulated (without the tie).

In music with more than two voices, the intervals specified by the suspension suggest the appropriate resolutions and inversions. For example, the 7–6 suspension usually resolves to a first-inversion chord (hence the "6" in the name), as in Example 16.3a. The 4–3 and 9–8 usually resolve to a root-position chord (parts b and c), though first inversion is also possible (here, replace the G in either chord of resolution with an A).

EXAMPLE 16.3: Two-voice suspension frameworks converted to four voices

(a) 7–6 suspensions resolve to a first-inversion triad.

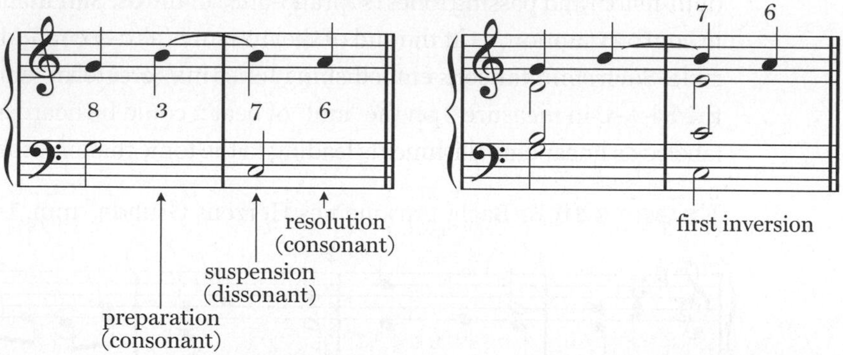

(b) 4–3 suspensions usually resolve to a root-position triad.

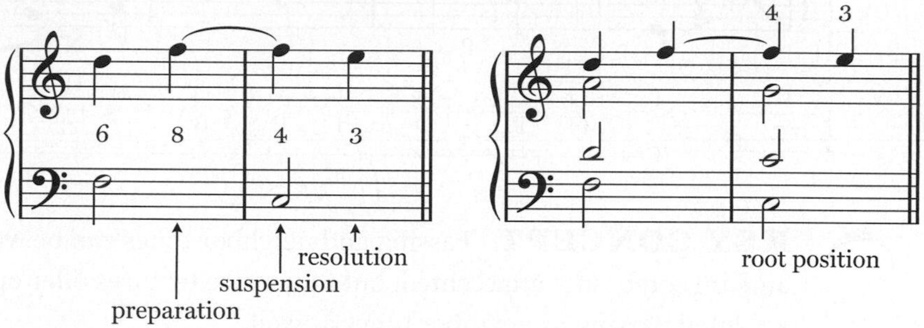

(c) 9–8 suspensions usually resolve to a root-position triad.

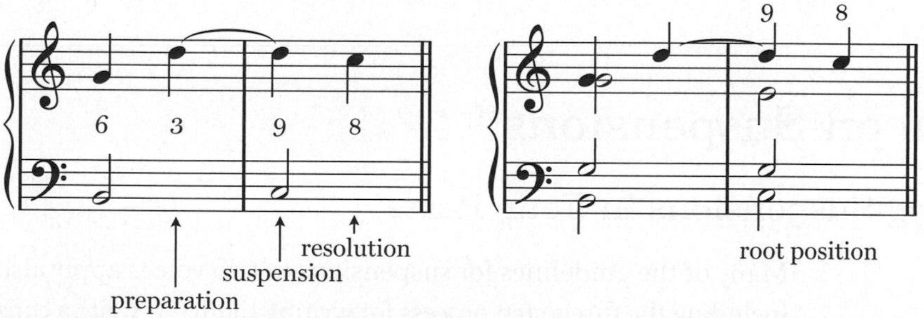

The 4–3 suspension is frequently placed over the dominant harmony in authentic cadences, where it temporarily displaces (and thus draws attention to) the leading tone (for an illustration, look ahead to Example 16.9). In all suspensions except the 9–8, the chord member to which the suspension resolves is not included elsewhere in the chord (e.g., in a 4–3, the third above the bass does not appear elsewhere in the chord—this is especially important when that note is the leading tone!). With the 9–8, however, the note of resolution (the 8) will normally be in the bass, and may appear in another voice as well.

In most dissonant suspensions, one of the upper voices is suspended and resolves to its chord tone after the bass and other voices have changed, but the opposite is also possible: the bass may be suspended against the upper voices of a chord, then resolve (late) to its chord tone. The most common bass suspension is a 2–3 (or 9–10) suspension, shown in Example 16.4, which may resolve to either a first-inversion or root-position triad.

Finally, although we consider only dissonant suspensions here, consonant suspensions above the bass, such as the 6–5, may also be found in four voices. In such cases, analyze with the Roman numeral of the triad of resolution (the 6 is not a chord member).

Example 16.4: Bass suspension framework converted to four voices

KEY CONCEPT When writing a suspension in three or more voices, plan the doubling in the chord of resolution first, so that the dissonant suspension does not sound simultaneously with its tone of resolution. The one exception is the 9–8 suspension, where the resolution of the suspension is doubled by the bass.

Suspensions with Change of Bass

In Baroque-era compositions with an active bass line, sometimes the bass note changes before a suspension in an upper part resolves. Listen to Example 16.5, paying close attention to the tenor part in the first two beats of measure 3.

Example 16.5: Bach, "O Haupt voll Blut und Wunden," mm. 2b–4

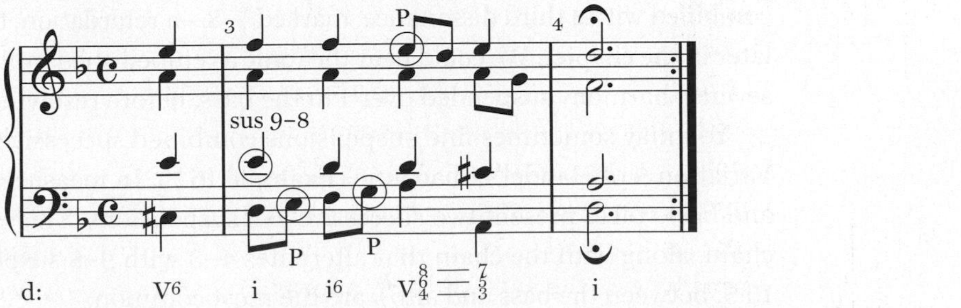

The suspended tone in the tenor, E4, is prepared by the dominant anacrusis, of which it is a member, and is suspended into the tonic harmony on the downbeat. On beat 2, when this 9–8 suspension resolves, the supporting tonic harmony changes inversion: the bass moves from D3 via passing tone to F3. The tone of resolution is present in the bass on beat 1 (D3), which is typical of 9–8 suspensions, but the change of bass results in a doubled third in the chord of resolution and the interval of a 6 instead of 8 with the bass. Such a change of bass happens often in music with an active bass line, but it does not disrupt the effect of the suspension.

For this type of suspension, Baroque musicians, who read each chord as intervals above the bass, would have seen the figures 9 6: 9 stands for the suspended dissonance, and 6 represents the interval between the tone of resolution and the new bass note.

Combining Suspensions

The opening of Bach's *St. Anne* Prelude is characterized by dotted rhythms and prominent suspensions, as you can see from Example 16.6.

Example 16.6: Bach, *St. Anne* Prelude, mm. 1–4

The accented dissonance in measure 4 is a double suspension: simultaneous 9–8 and 4–3 suspensions. In fact, the 9–8 suspension may appear in combination with either the 4–3 or 7–6 in a **double suspension**; the suspended pitches will move in parallel sixths or thirds above the bass. In this case, the double suspension is combined with a third dissonance, marked 7–8—a retardation, to which we return later in the chapter. We could hear the tonic as embellished by an entire dominant seventh harmony suspended over $\hat{1}$ in the bass, before resolving on beat 2.

You may sometimes find suspensions combined successively in chains, as in Variation 9 of Handel's Chaconne (Example 16.7). In measures 74–75, the tenor and bass voices present two successive 7–6 suspensions. This type of suspension chain, along with the chain that alternates 4–3 with 9–8 suspensions (Example 16.8, between the bass and alto), are the most common.

Example 16.7: Handel, Chaconne in G Major, Variation 9, mm. 73–76

Example 16.8: Bach, "Heut' ist, o Mensch," mm. 3b–6a

Embellishing Suspensions

Some suspensions are embellished before their resolution, as in Example 16.9, drawn from one of many Bach chorales with a 4–3 suspension above the dominant harmony at the cadence. In measure 14, Bach embellishes the suspended tone, G4 in the alto, by skipping down to E4 before resolving on F♯4.

Example 16.9: Bach, "Liebster Jesu," mm. 11–15

Measures 9–10 of "Christ ist erstanden" (Example 16.10) present a cadence highly embellished with suspensions. In measure 10, Bach employs a double suspension: a dissonant 4–3 in the tenor and a consonant 6–5 in the alto, resulting in parallel thirds between these two voices. The suspended tones resolve on beat 3, not beat 2, just as they would in fourth-species counterpoint. (Imagine the resolution as if beat 2 were missing.) The eighths on beat 2, preceding the resolution, embellish and intensify the suspension.

Example 16.10: Bach, "Christ ist erstanden," mm. 9–10

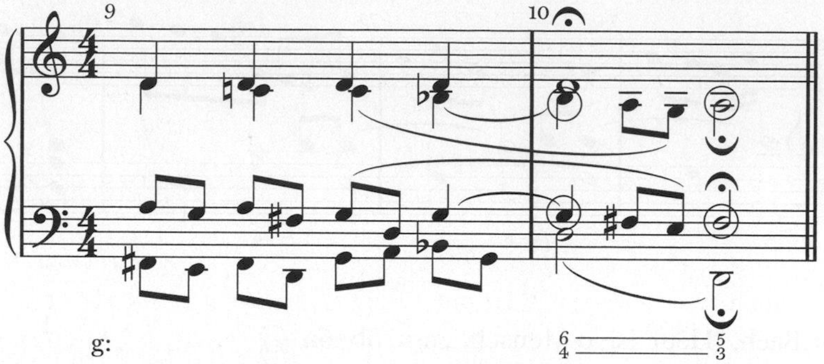

KEY CONCEPT When embellishing a suspension, decorate the dissonant suspended tone rather than the tone of resolution.

Try it #1

Circle each of the rearticulated suspensions in the vocal part of this example, and label it below the staff as a 7–6, 9–8, or 4–3. The chord of resolution (assuming the lowest note in each half measure is bass) in each case is (circle one):

root position   first inversion   second inversion

Purcell, "Music for a While," mm. 12b–14a

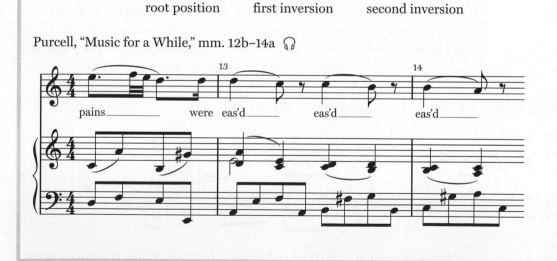

Retardations

In eighteenth-century music, you may encounter a rhythmic embellishment that looks and sounds like a suspension, but resolves *up* by step instead of down. This is called a retardation.

KEY CONCEPT A **retardation**, like a dissonant suspension, begins with a consonance that is held over—tied or rearticulated—to the next beat, creating a dissonance in the new chord. The dissonance then resolves up by step. The most common retardation is a 7–8, with scale degrees $\hat{7}$ and $\hat{8}$ above the tonic pitch in the bass.

Retardations are usually found at an authentic cadence: the tonic arrives in the bass, but part of the dominant harmony is sustained or rearticulated in one or more of the upper voices before resolving to the tonic, as in Example 16.11 (m. 205, the D4 in the top voice). Retardations are often combined with a descending suspension: here, a 4–3 suspension (A♭3–G3).

EXAMPLE 16.11: Bach, *St. Anne* Prelude, mm. 204–205 (final cadence)

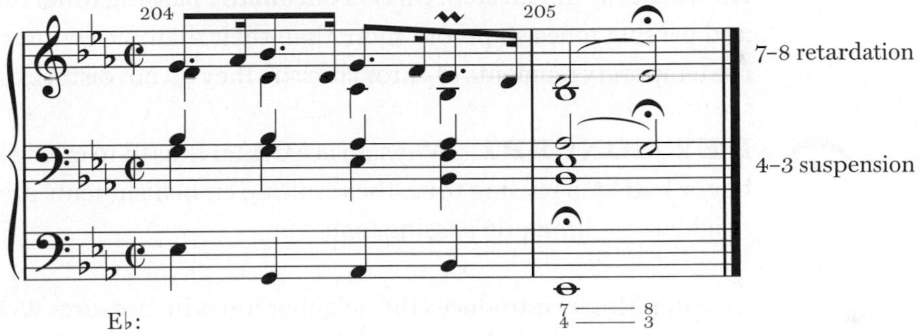

More on Neighbor and Passing Tones

Chromatic Neighbor and Passing Tones

Classical-period variations are excellent for the study of melodic and harmonic embellishments because we know from the theme what the composer considered a starting point. Mozart's *Variations on "Ah, vous dirai-je Maman,"* for example, includes a variety of melodic embellishments and draws on several contrapuntal techniques to elaborate the familiar theme. Listen to the first variation (mm. 25–48): the melody is based on the "Twinkle, Twinkle, Little Star" tune, but some additional pitches have been added (Example 16.12).

Example 16.12: Mozart, *Variations on "Ah, vous dirai-je Maman,"* mm. 25–28a

On beat 1 of measures 25 and 26, added dissonances circle around the pitches C5 and G5 of the theme: each melody pitch is preceded by the diatonic pitch a step above (an embellishing tone to which we will return), then decorated with a lower neighbor a half step below. The F♯5 in measure 26, a half step lower than the G5 it embellishes, is a **chromatic neighbor tone**. Likewise, the G♯5 on the downbeat of measure 27 serves a familiar function as a passing tone between G and A, but it passes chromatically by half step: this is a **chromatic passing tone**. Chromatic neighbor and passing tones stand out more than their diatonic counterparts; but as they are temporary moments of chromaticism, they do not disturb the sense of the key.

KEY CONCEPT When an accidental is used to create a half-step neighbor or half-step passing tone, the resulting embellishments are called chromatic neighbor or chromatic passing tones.

After Mozart introduces the neighbor tones in measures 25 and 26, he repeats them to fill out the full measure. The lower neighbors on the "and" of beats 1 and 2 are unaccented, but the lower neighbor at the beginning of beat 2 is accented. Similarly, the chromatic passing tone on the downbeat of measure 27 is accented. Accented embellishing tones generally produce a more striking aural effect because of the strong-beat dissonance, and performers may sometimes add a slight rhythmic or dynamic stress for expressive effect.

Incomplete Neighbors

As stated earlier, complete neighbor-note patterns involve three notes: the main melody pitch (a consonance that fits with the harmony), the upper or lower neighbor a step away (usually a dissonance), and the return to the main melody pitch. If one of the consonant elements is left out, the resulting embellishment is called an **incomplete neighbor** (abbreviated IN). An IN may take one of two forms: it may leap or skip to the dissonance and then resolve like a neighbor tone by step (this is sometimes called an **appoggiatura**), or it may begin by step and then skip or leap away (sometimes called an **escape tone** or **échappée**). The downbeats of measures 25 and 26 in Example 16.12 are both incomplete neighbors.

In Example 16.13, drawn from later in the Mozart *Variations*, the ascending C major scale passage in measures 169–170 is followed in measure 171 with an accented passing tone (B5) and chromatic lower neighbor (G♯5). Then the melodic line takes a dramatic leap up to D6, a tone not in the C major harmony: this is an accented incomplete neighbor to C6.

EXAMPLE 16.13: Mozart, *Variations on "Ah, vous dirai-je Maman,"* mm. 169–172a

The other type of IN (step-skip or step-leap) is shown in measure 9 of Example 16.14. Here the C5 in the melody is the chord tone in the predominant harmony. The melody steps up to the dissonant D5, an unaccented IN, then skips to resolve in the cadential V^{6-5}_{4-3}. The final tonic in measure 10 is also embellished with accented incomplete neighbors on the downbeat.

EXAMPLE 16.14: Brahms, *Variations on a Theme by Haydn*, mm. 6–10 (piano 1)

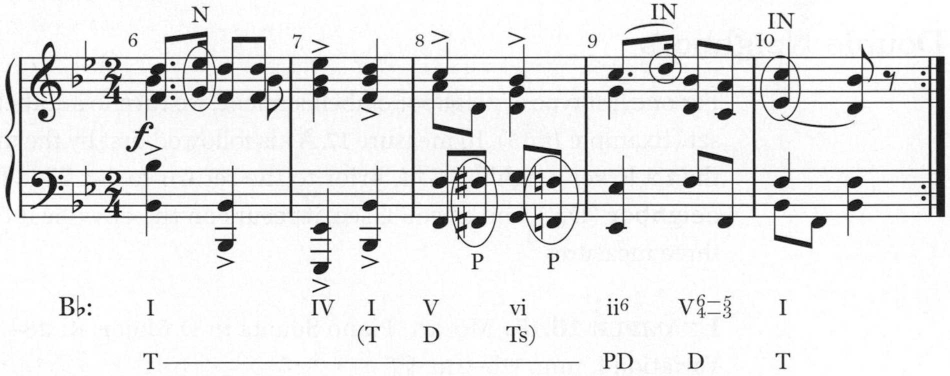

KEY CONCEPT To write an incomplete neighbor:

- skip or leap to the dissonant neighbor tone, then resolve to the main melody pitch a step away (usually in the opposite direction from the approach); or
- approach the dissonant neighbor tone by step, then leave it by skip or leap in the opposite direction.

Try it #2

Copy each chord pair in the measure to its right, and add the specified embellishing tones.

(a) Add a 7–6 suspension.

(b) Add a chromatic passing tone.

(c) Add an incomplete neighbor.

(d) Add a 4–3 suspension.

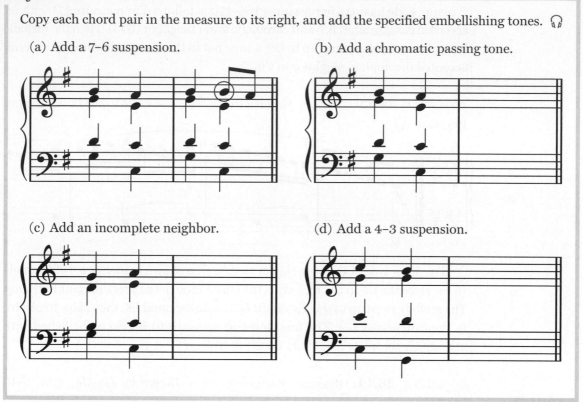

Double Neighbors

For one last type of neighbor embellishment, we turn to another Mozart variation set (Example 16.15). In measure 17, A4 is followed first by the upper neighbor B4, then a lower neighbor G♯4, prior to the return to A4. This figure is a **double neighbor** (DN), and as you'll see, it recurs on the downbeat of each of the next three measures.

Example 16.15: Mozart, Piano Sonata in D Major, K. 284, third movement, Variation I, mm. 17b–21a

KEY CONCEPT The combination of successive upper and lower neighbors (in either order) around the same main pitch is called a double neighbor. This embellishment typically skips from one neighbor to the other before returning to the chord tone.

A different DN pattern can be seen in Example 16.16, where the figuration continues throughout each measure. Here, the upper and lower neighbors in measures 49–52, left hand, are separated by the chord tone C4. There are also "single" diatonic and chromatic lower neighbors in measures 53–55.

EXAMPLE 16.16: Mozart, *Variations on "Ah, vous dirai-je Maman,"* mm. 49–56

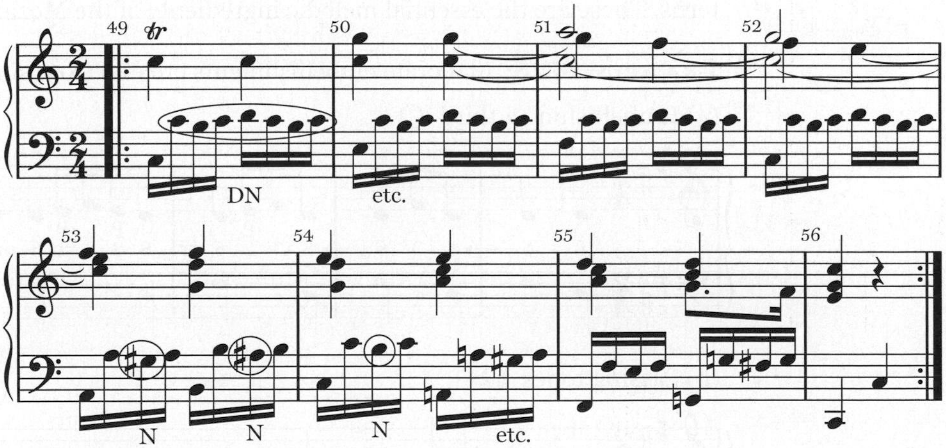

Passing Tones and Chordal Skips

When scales appear in tonal compositions, they often represent chordal (consonant) skips filled in with passing tones. In Variation VII of *"Ah, vous dirai-je Maman,"* for example, the first two measures expand the tonic harmony with a C major scale (Example 16.17a), which can be considered an arpeggiation of a C major triad, filled in with passing tones (part b). (The slurs here are simply analytical symbols to show how pitches embellish the triad.) Sometimes two passing tones are needed to fill in between skips of a fourth, as between G4 (m. 169) and C5 (m. 170, beat 1).

Example 16.17: Mozart, *Variations on "Ah, vous dirai-je Maman,"* Variation VII

(a) Mm. 169–170

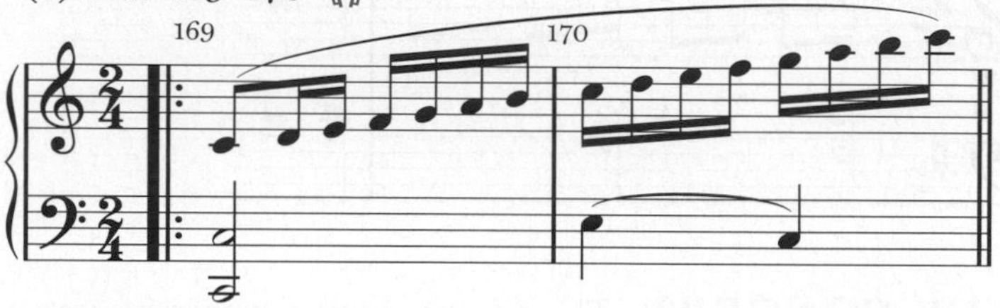

(b) Reduction of mm. 169–170, showing arpeggiation with passing tones

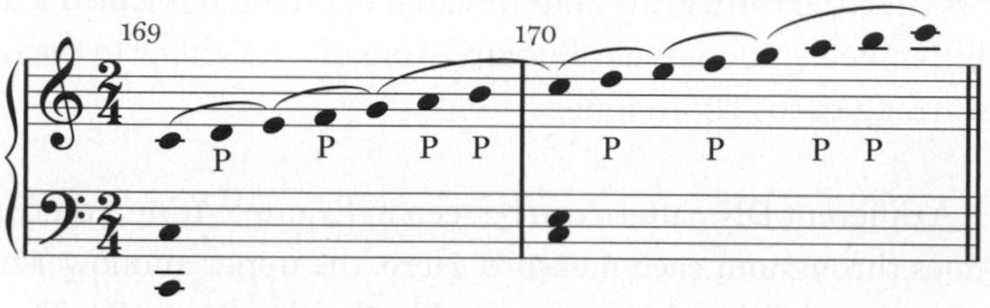

Example 16.18 shows how simple embellishments such as consonant skips, passing tones, and neighbor tones can be combined to make elaborate 4:1 patterns. These are the essential melodic ingredients of the Mozart *Variations*.

Example 16.18: Elaborate embellishments created from simple ones

(a) Embellishing a third

(b) Passing tones

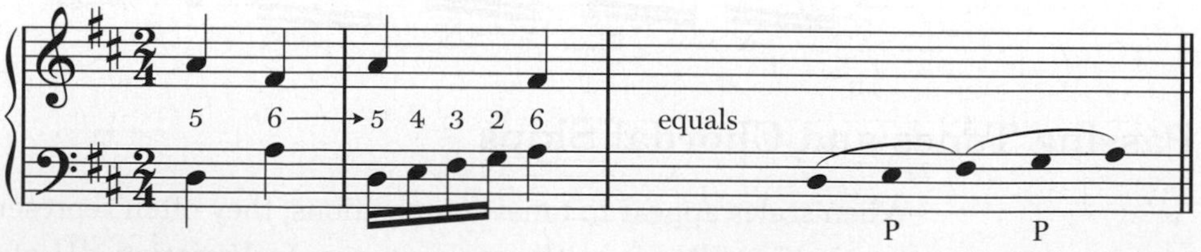

(c) Neighbor tones

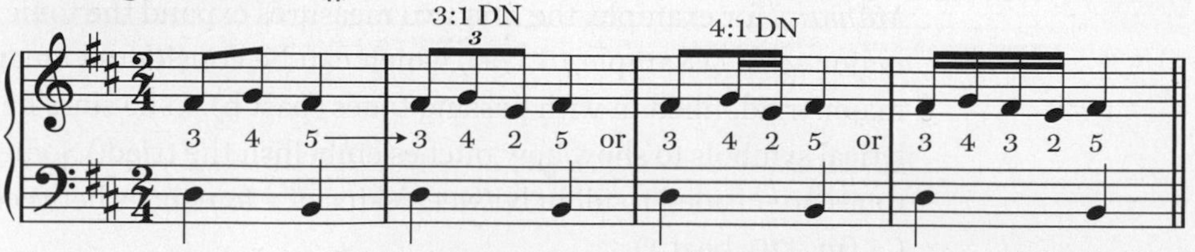

(d) Passing and neighbor tones combined

Other Types of Embellishments

Anticipations

In the case of suspensions and retardations, the embellishment is created when one part of a two-voice framework is delayed and resolves "late." With an **anticipation** (ANT), the opposite happens: one part of the framework arrives "early." Anticipations are unaccented—they appear on the offbeat or a weak beat of a measure—and are usually dissonances. They do not need to resolve; they are simply repeated on the next beat, where they "belong" in the counterpoint. Anticipations are not included in strict species counterpoint, but they are frequently used by eighteenth-century composers to decorate cadences.

Listen to the final measures of Purcell's "Music for a While" to hear anticipations in the vocal line (Example 16.19). When the soprano sings the word "beguile" (mm. 38–39), she arrives on the A4 tonic pitch one sixteenth note ahead of the tonic chord, anticipating the resolution of $\hat{2}$ to the tonic.

Example 16.19: Purcell, "Music for a While," mm. 37–39 (final cadence)

This song also features remarkable embellishments in the accompaniment, including chromatic lower neighbor tones and ornamented suspensions. In measure 37, beat 3, for example, the underlying chord is D minor, but the E4 tied across from the previous beat creates a 9–8 suspension. Rather than resolving directly by step, however—E4 to D4—the suspension is ornamented with a skip to C♯4 that resolves as an IN to D.

Try it #3

Provide labels for the circled embellishing tones in measures 4–7a of "Music for a While."

Pedal Points

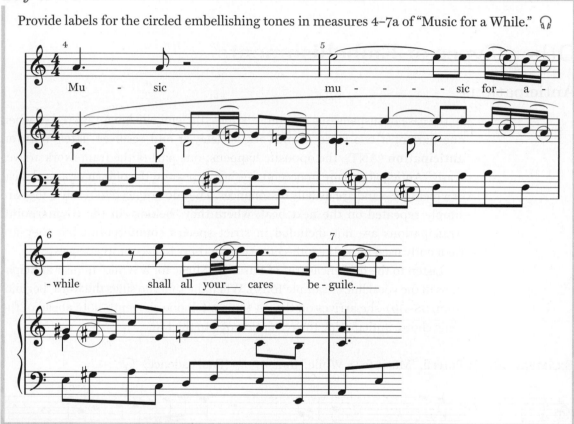

Pedal points get their name from passages in organ music, like Example 16.20, in which the organist's foot rests on a single pedal for measures at a time while the harmonies change above the sustained tone. Pedal points do not decorate a musical line in the way that passing or neighbor tones do, but they are familiar embellishments that you will come across in the literature. Like suspensions, pedal points may be sustained or rearticulated.

Example 16.20: Bach, Organ Sonata No. 5 in C Major, first movement, mm. 35–38

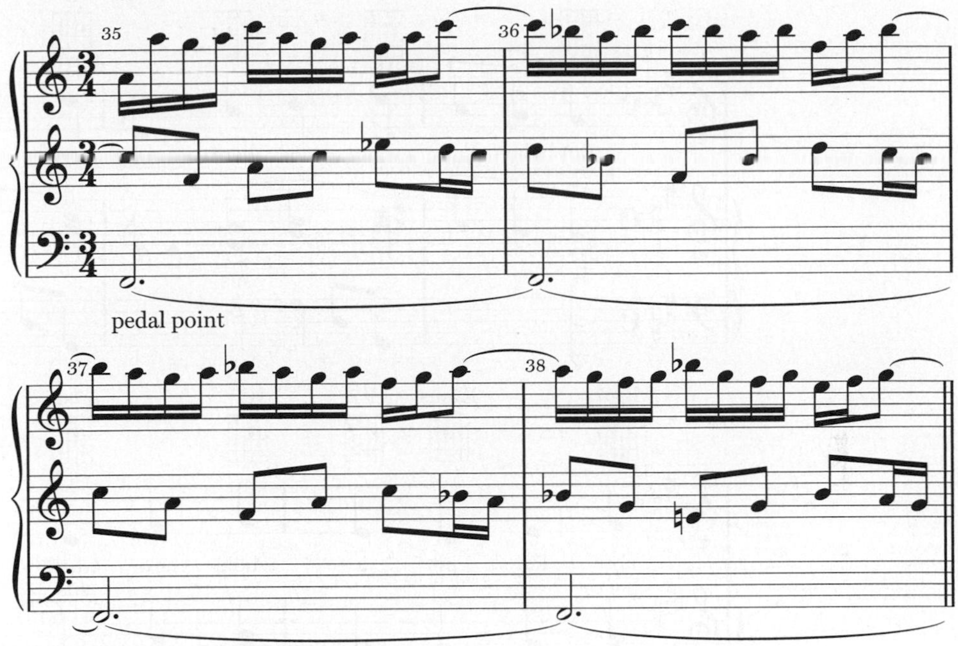

When you encounter a pedal point in music, consider carefully the larger context. Most often, the pedal prolongs a single harmony (usually tonic or dominant), and the voices above it are embellishing. Sometimes the upper harmonies are functional and can be analyzed with Roman numerals. Because the pedal point sounds below the chordal bass, some analysts omit inversion symbols for these harmonies. Others retain them, opting instead to disregard the "nonharmonic" pedal tone in their analysis. Pedal points are not limited to the bass line, but may appear in any voice; when in upper voices, they are sometimes called "inverted pedals."

Embellishing Tones in Popular Music

Suspensions and other embellishing tones are found in popular music as well, though some of the guidelines for preparation and resolution are more relaxed in this repertoire. Listen to the passage from "A Whole New World" given in Example 16.21.

Example 16.21: Menken and Rice, "A Whole New World," mm. 32b–37a

The phrase opens with a triplet whose middle note is a passing tone between D7 chord members. The downbeats of measures 33 and 34 then feature dissonant incomplete neighbors (A4 and C♯5), which add expressive accents to the text at these points. The "sus" chords in measures 35 and 36 (E7sus and A7sus) are lead-sheet notation for 4–3 suspensions. Look first at the piano realization of the E7sus chord in measure 35, beat 3. The dissonant fourth here (A3 in the alto line of the piano accompaniment) is prepared by a chord tone on beat 2, and resolves down by step to G♯3 in the following chord, but the A3 of beat 2 is not a consonance—it is the dissonant seventh of the Bm7. The A7sus in measure 36 includes no consonant preparation for the dissonant fourth, D4; however, it does resolve down by step to the chord tone, as we would expect. In popular music, suspended tones may add a dissonance that never resolves.

In lead-sheet notation, a pedal point is indicated with slash notation, as in Example 16.22 from "Don't Cry for Me Argentina." The C3 in the bass line of the piano arrangement is maintained throughout the entire excerpt through several arpeggiated chord changes; this is indicated in the chord symbols by "/C" in measures 5 and 7. In essence, the lead-sheet notation analyzes the chords above the pedal, instructing the performer which notes to place in the accompaniment, then indicates the bass note separately. The cadence provides an example of an ornamented suspension, similar to that in Bach's "Christ ist erstanden" (Example 16.10): the main bass note is C3, with a 4–3 suspension above it (F4–E4).

Example 16.22: Lloyd Webber and Rice, "Don't Cry for Me Argentina," mm. 3–10

Try it #4

Circle and label all embellishing tones in the chorale excerpt below. Then provide a Roman numeral and contextual analysis below.

Bach, "Jesu, der du meine Seele," mm. 1–3a

SUMMARY

EMBELLISHMENT	ABBREVIATION	CATEGORY	BRIEF DESCRIPTION
passing tone	P	melodic embellishment	• Dissonance approached by step and left by step in the same direction (up-up or down-down). • Fills in a consonant skip. • May be accented or unaccented; unaccented is more common. • A chromatic passing tone fills in a step with chromatic half steps.
neighbor tone	N	melodic embellishment	• Dissonance approached by step and left by step in the opposite direction (up-down or down-up). • Decorates a repeated note. • May be accented or unaccented; unaccented is more common. • May be diatonic or chromatic.
incomplete neighbor tone	IN	melodic embellishment	• A neighbor figure with either the approach or resolution omitted. • Skip (leap) then step—or step then skip (leap)—usually in opposite direction. • May be accented or unaccented; accented is more common. • May be diatonic or chromatic.
double neighbor	DN (circle both notes)	melodic embellishment	• Combination of upper and lower neighbor. • Either step up, skip 3rd down, step up to starting point, or reverse direction. May include the consonant note in the middle as well. • Usually unaccented.
suspension	S or sus (label the type: 4–3, 7–6, 9–8; bass 2–3)	rhythmic displacement	• Prepared by consonant chord tone. • That tone is held over to make a strong-beat dissonance when the chord changes. • Resolves down by step on weak part of beat.
retardation	R	rhythmic displacement	• Prepared by consonant chord tone. • That tone is held over to make a strong-beat dissonance when the chord changes. • Resolves up by step on weak part of beat (usually 7–8).
anticipation	ANT	rhythmic displacement	• One voice arrives early (making a dissonance) before the chord changes. • Dissonance is on a weak beat; repeats on a strong beat as a consonance. • Usually in the highest voice.
pedal point	PED		• Usually in the bass. • Holds through under changes of chords.

Did You Know?

Textbooks and analysts differ in how they label embellishing tones. Double neighbors are sometimes called "changing tones." As mentioned in the chapter, an incomplete neighbor may be called an appoggiatura (if it first leaps up, then resolves down by step), or échappée or escape tone (if it is approached by a step, then left by a leap). In some traditions, any embellishing tone—other than a chordal skip or suspension—that falls on an accented beat is called an appoggiatura. This term, from the Italian *appoggiare* ("to lean"), accurately describes the tendency to stress or lean on the dissonant pitch in performance. Appoggiaturas may be notated by the composer or added by the performer for expressive purposes. Suspensions also provide an opportunity for expressive interpretation: performances often add a slight *crescendo* from the preparation to the dissonance, and then a relaxation and *diminuendo* into the resolution.

TERMS YOU SHOULD KNOW

- anticipation
- appoggiatura
- chordal (consonant) skip
- chromatic neighbor tone
- chromatic passing tone
- double neighbor tone
- double suspension
- échappée (escape tone)
- incomplete neighbor tone
- neighbor tone
  - lower neighbor
  - upper neighbor
- passing tone
- pedal point
- retardation
- suspension
- suspension chain
- suspension with change of bass

QUESTIONS FOR REVIEW

1. What are the three steps necessary to write a suspension?
2. What are the most common suspension types? How might they be ornamented?
3. What embellishments are available in four voices that are not used in two voices?
4. Find an example of an ornamented suspension, an anticipation, and a pedal point in music literature that you know.
5. Which intervals above the bass are most typical for retardations?
6. Which embellishing tones appear in chromatic variants?
7. What is "incomplete" about an incomplete neighbor? What are the two IN types?
8. How are pedal points written in lead-sheet notation? How are suspensions?

CHAPTER 17

The $\text{vii}^{\circ 6}$, $\text{vii}^{\circ 7}$, $\text{vii}^{\varnothing 7}$, and Other Voice-Leading Chords

Outline of topics

Dominant substitutes: Leading-tone chords

- Doubling in and resolving $\text{vii}^{\circ 6}$
- Doubling in and resolving $\text{vii}^{\varnothing 7}$, $\text{vii}^{\circ 7}$, and their inversions
- Contexts for $\text{vii}^{\circ 6}$, $\text{vii}^{\varnothing 7}$ and $\text{vii}^{\circ 7}$

Other voice-leading chords

- Neighboring and passing $^4_2$ chords

Overview

This chapter considers voice-leading patterns that expand the tonic area of the basic phrase with $\text{vii}^{\circ 6}$, $\text{vii}^{\circ 7}$, $\text{vii}^{\varnothing 7}$, and other voice-leading chords, such as ii^4_2.

Repertoire

Johann Sebastian Bach

"Aus meines Herzens Grunde" ("From My Inmost Heart," Chorale No. 1)

"O Haupt voll Blut und Wunden" ("O Head Full of Blood and Wounds," Chorale No. 74)

Prelude in C Major, from *The Well-Tempered Clavier*, Book I

Jeremiah Clarke, *Trumpet Voluntary* (*Prince of Denmark's March*)

Dominant Substitutes: Leading-Tone Chords

The vii° triad (usually found in first inversion, vii$^{\circ 6}$) and the seventh chords vii^{ø7} and vii$^{\circ 7}$ serve as substitutes for the stronger dominant harmonies V and V^7. In particular, they often function to expand the tonic area, just as a V chord can. As an example, listen to the opening of Clarke's *Trumpet Voluntary* (Example 17.1). Locate each dominant and leading-tone harmony, and consider its role within the basic phrase.

EXAMPLE 17.1: Clarke, *Trumpet Voluntary*, mm. 1–4

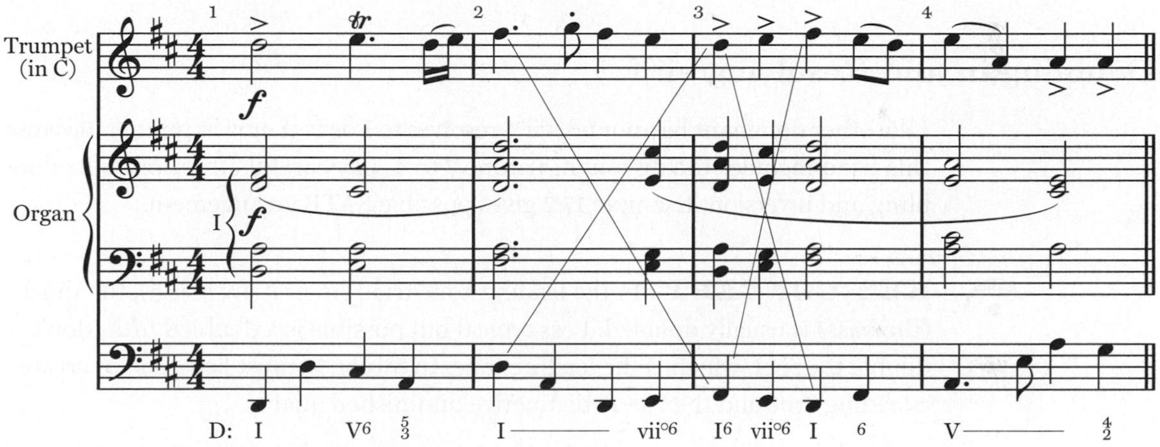

In this phrase, measures 2 and 3 contain vii$^{\circ 6}$ chords, while measures 1 and 4 feature V and V^7 chords.

KEY CONCEPT Since contain vii° triad and the seventh chords vii^{ø7} (in major) and vii$^{\circ 7}$ (in minor) are built on the leading tone—the essential active ingredient for dominant harmonies—they can substitute for V or V^7. The leading-tone triad typically appears in first inversion (vii$^{\circ 6}$) in order to soften the dissonance of the d5 from root to fifth.

The V^7 and vii$^{\circ 6}$ chords, sharing scale degrees $\hat{7}$, $\hat{2}$, and $\hat{4}$, are roughly equivalent in function, but vii$^{\circ 6}$ conveys less harmonic strength than the V^7, since it is missing $\hat{5}$. In the example's opening phrase, both vii$^{\circ 6}$ chords function in a similar way: as part of a tonic-expanding voice exchange between a root-position and first-inversion tonic chord. Write leading-tone triads and seventh chords at the beginning and middle of phrases, or in other places where a weaker dominant function is desired.

The active bass line in Example 17.1 may raise questions regarding when to specify inversions in your analysis. For example, the arpeggiating $^6_4$s that prolong the tonic harmony in measure 2 and the dominant in measure 4 are not labeled with Roman numerals because the root-position bass note overrides the weaker $^6_4$. In measure 4, if we consider the A2 to be the controlling bass note for the full measure, the final figure could be 7 rather than $^4_2$. This is a matter for individual judgment. Generally, when a chord is repeated immediately in a new inversion, it is not necessary to supply a new Roman numeral; simply provide figures for the inversion.

Doubling in and Resolving vii°6

Like other dominant harmonies, vii°6 resolves to I or I6 (i or i6 in minor). Because this triad includes the dissonant tritone $\hat{7}$ to $\hat{4}$, pay careful attention to its doubling and inversion. Example 17.2 gives possible SATB arrangements.

KEY CONCEPT In the leading-tone triad (in first inversion), the third (the bass) is usually doubled. Less typical but possible is a doubled fifth; don't double the root, which is the leading tone. In minor, $\flat\hat{7}$ must be raised to create a leading tone and the triad's distinctive diminished quality.

EXAMPLE 17.2: Voicings and spacings for vii°6

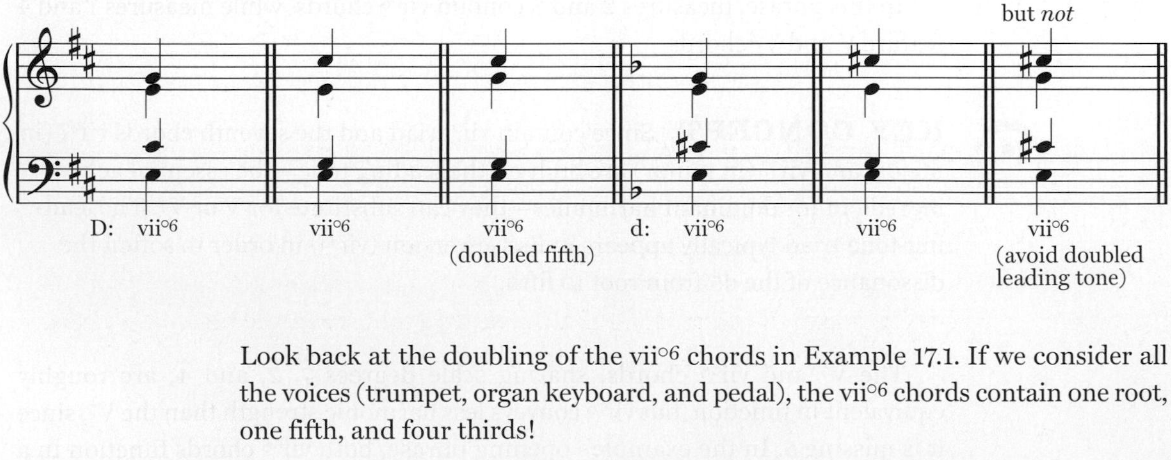

Look back at the doubling of the vii°6 chords in Example 17.1. If we consider all the voices (trumpet, organ keyboard, and pedal), the vii°6 chords contain one root, one fifth, and four thirds!

Since V7 and vii°6 share the tendency tones $\hat{7}$ and $\hat{4}$, their normal resolutions follow the same principles: $\hat{7}$ resolves up to $\hat{1}$, and $\hat{4}$ typically down to $\hat{3}$. These resolutions often lead to a tonic triad with missing fifth. The resolution of $\hat{4}$ can vary, depending on the chord's spacing and context. Example 17.3 gives several correct resolutions.

KEY CONCEPT When resolving vii°6:

- If the tritone is spelled as a augmented fourth—$\hat{4}$ below $\hat{7}$—it may move in similar motion to a perfect fourth, $\hat{5}$–$\hat{1}$ (Example 17.3a).
- If the tritone is spelled as a diminished fifth—$\hat{7}$ below $\hat{4}$—it normally resolves inward to a third: $\hat{7}$ up to $\hat{1}$, and $\hat{4}$ down to $\hat{3}$ (part b).
- The standard resolutions of $\hat{4}$ and $\hat{7}$ in the A4 are outward to a sixth (part c).
- With a d5, resolve $\hat{4}$ up to $\hat{5}$ in only one context: when the soprano-bass counterpoint moves upward in parallel tenths (part d). The strength of the parallel motion overrides the voice-leading tendency of $\hat{4}$ to resolve down.

Example 17.3: Resolutions of vii°6

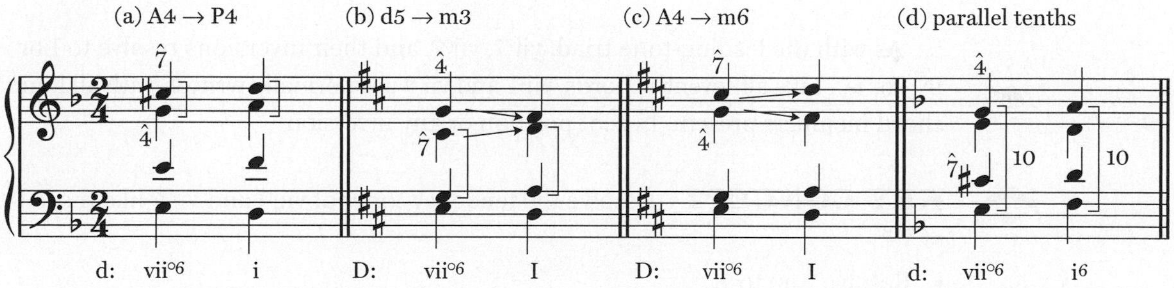

Doubling in and Resolving viiø7, vii°7, and Their Inversions

The seventh chords viiø7 and vii°7 have the same active ingredients as the diminished triad, but with the added sixth scale degree (Example 17.4). Since $\hat{6}$ is one of the modal scale degrees, the quality of the diminished seventh chord will change depending on the form of the scale used. In a minor key, the root of the chord is the raised seventh scale degree—it will require an accidental.

EXAMPLE 17.4: Spelling vii$^{\varnothing 7}$ and vii$^{\circ 7}$ in major and minor keys

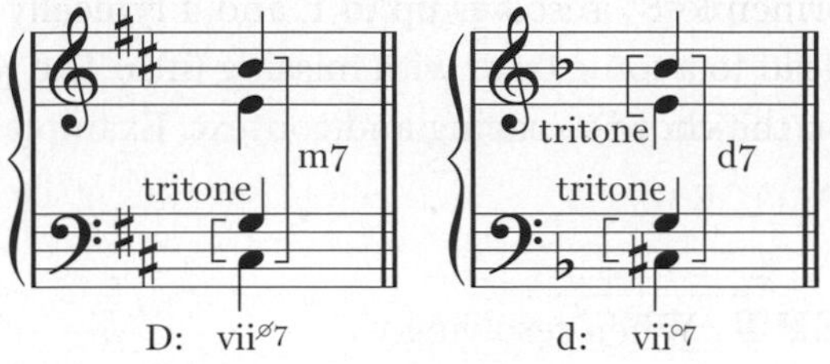

Try it #1

Spell the leading-tone seventh chord in the following keys.

KEY	SPELLING	ROMAN NUMERAL
G minor	F♯-A-C-E♭	vii$^{\circ 7}$
B major		
D minor		
F♯ minor		
E♭ major		

As with the leading-tone triad, vii$^{\varnothing 7}$, vii$^{\circ 7}$, and their inversions resolve to I or I^6 (i or i^6). Like all seventh chords, vii$^{\varnothing 7}$ and vii$^{\circ 7}$ are normally written with all four chord members present, in root position or any inversion.

KEY CONCEPT Resolve the tendency tones of vii$^{\varnothing 7}$ and vii$^{\circ 7}$ like those of V^7:

- Resolve $\hat{7}$ up to $\hat{1}$.
- Resolve $\hat{4}$ down to $\hat{3}$.
- Resolve the chordal seventh down ($\hat{6}$ to $\hat{5}$ or ♭$\hat{6}$ to $\hat{5}$).
- Move $\hat{2}$ to either $\hat{1}$ or $\hat{3}$. If the vii$^{\varnothing 7}$ or vii$^{\circ 7}$ resolves to a triad in root position, use a doubled third when $\hat{6}$ is above $\hat{2}$ to avoid parallel or unequal fifths; or put $\hat{2}$ above $\hat{6}$ to create parallel fourths (A4–P4) instead.

Example 17.5a shows a typical resolution of a root-position vii$^{\circ 7}$ to tonic, with $\hat{2}$ moving down to $\hat{1}$ in a complete tonic triad and the other tones resolving by their tendency: $\hat{7}$ up to $\hat{1}$, $\hat{4}$ down to $\hat{3}$, and ♭$\hat{6}$ down to $\hat{5}$. In part (b), the resolution of a root-position vii$^{\varnothing 7}$ to tonic (in a major key), all the tendency tones resolve correctly: here, $\hat{2}$ moves up to $\hat{3}$. This is a common voice-leading and doubling:

because the vii^{ø7} contains a P5 between its third and seventh (E and B), $\hat{2}$ (E) can't resolve down to $\hat{1}$ when $\hat{6}$ (B) is above it; this invariably leads to parallel fifths.

Example 17.5: Resolutions of root-position vii^{o7}–i and vii^{ø7}–I

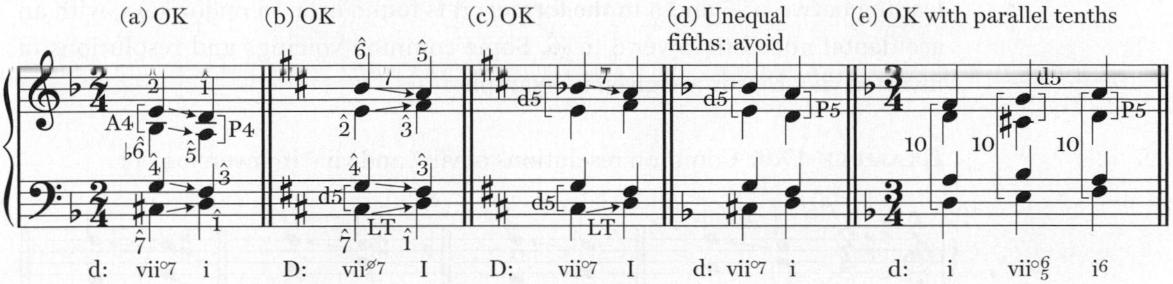

In addition to the familiar tritone between $\hat{7}$ and $\hat{4}$, the vii^{o7} (parts a and c–e) contains a second tritone between $\hat{2}$ and $\flat\hat{6}$ (here, E and B♭), which introduces the potential for unequal fifths: similar motion from d5 to P5.

KEY CONCEPT In resolving vii^{o7} and its inversions:

- When $\hat{2}$ is higher than $\flat\hat{6}$, $\hat{2}$ may resolve down to $\hat{1}$ (part a). The resulting A4 to P4 is permitted in this style.
- Resolve the d5, $\hat{2}$–$\flat\hat{6}$, inward to a third, $\flat\hat{3}$–$\hat{5}$. This results in a tonic triad with a doubled third (part c).
- Avoid unequal fifths (d5 to P5, part d). Such motion *is* allowed when the soprano voice moves $\flat\hat{3}$–$\hat{4}$–$\hat{5}$ in parallel tenths with a $\hat{1}$–$\hat{2}$–$\flat\hat{3}$ bass line (part e).

Try it #2

Spell the resolutions of $\hat{7}$ up to $\hat{1}$ and $\hat{4}$ down to $\hat{3}$ (or $\flat\hat{3}$) in the following keys.

KEY	$\hat{7}$–$\hat{1}$	$\hat{4}$–$\hat{3}$ (or $\flat\hat{3}$)
F minor	E♮–F	B♭–A♭
C minor		
A major		
B minor		
E minor		
A♭ major		

Leading-tone seventh chords are typically found in root position, first inversion, and second inversion. Third inversion is rare, as the normal resolution of the tendency tones results in a second-inversion tonic triad. The vii$^{\circ 7}$ appears more often in music literature than the vii$^{\varnothing 7}$, possibly because of the half-step voice-leading between $\flat\hat{6}$ and $\hat{5}$ in the former; it is found even in major keys, with an accidental added to lower $\hat{6}$ to $\flat\hat{6}$. Some common voicings and resolutions of inverted vii$^{\circ 7}$ chords are given in Example 17.6.

Example 17.6: Common resolutions of vii$^{\varnothing 7}$ and vii$^{\circ 7}$ in inversion

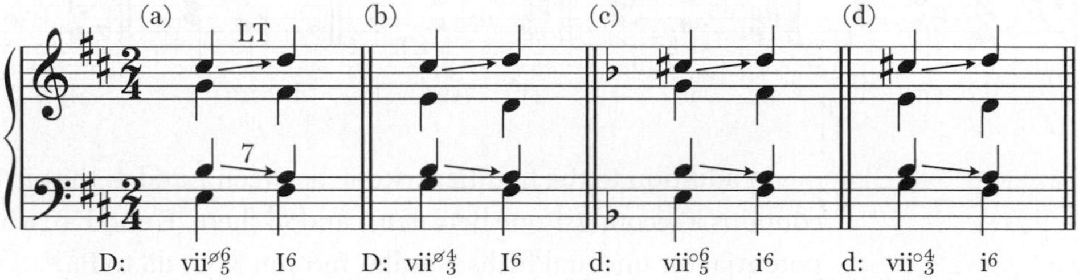

Example 17.7 shows the less common third inversion. Here, because the chordal seventh is in the bass, the bass must resolve down to $\hat{5}$, usually to a second-inversion tonic triad, which resolves as either a cadential or passing $^{6}_{4}$.

Example 17.7: Resolutions of vii$^{\varnothing 4}_{2}$ and vii$^{\circ 4}_{2}$ to cadential $^{6}_{4}$

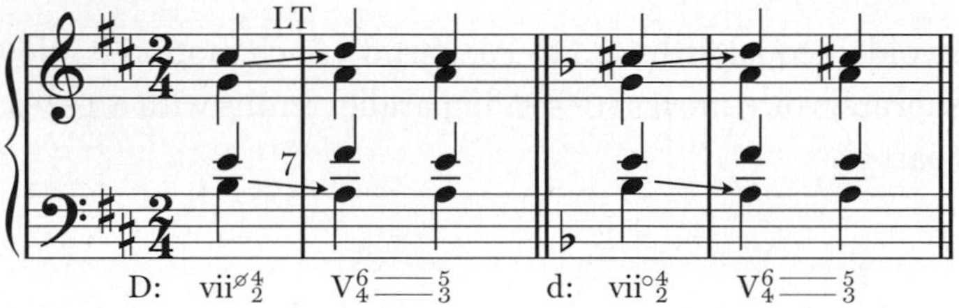

Contexts for vii$^{\circ 6}$, vii$^{\varnothing 7}$, and vii$^{\circ 7}$

Leading-tone triads and seventh chords often appear in tonic expansions as substitutes for the dominant. Expansions like those in Examples 17.8 and 17.9 produce a number of outer-voice patterns that fit well within the guidelines of species counterpoint. Example 17.8a and b show a tonic expansion moving from root position to first inversion, featuring a voice exchange in soprano and bass and the outer-voice intervals 10–8–6, first with a V$^{6}_{4}$ as the middle chord, then with vii$^{\circ 6}$. Only one note is different—A4 in part (a) becomes G4 in part (b). This same progression can also be used with a soprano line of $\hat{1}$–$\hat{7}$–$\hat{1}$ by moving the soprano and alto parts down an octave, as in parts (c) and (d). The outer-voice intervals now are 8–6–6, creating good outer-voice counterpoint, and the voice exchange is between the bass and alto parts.

EXAMPLE 17.8: Tonic expansions with a voice exchange

(a) With passing V$^6_4$, outer voices 10–8–6 (b) With vii$^{\circ 6}$, outer voices 10–8–6

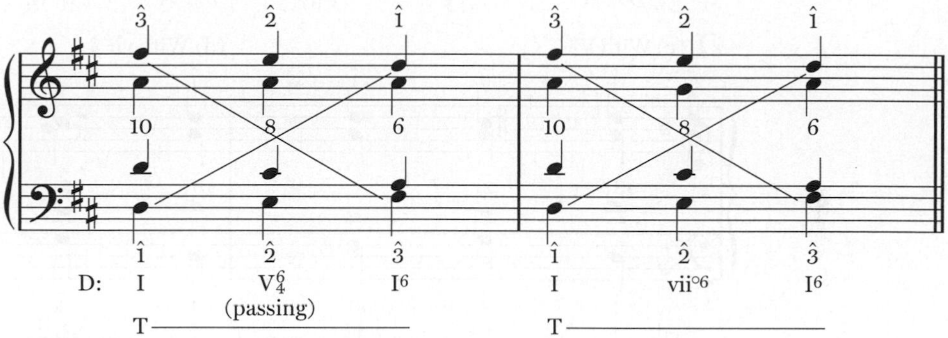

(c) With passing V$^6_4$, outer voices 8–6–6 (d) With vii$^{\circ 6}$, outer voices 8–6–6

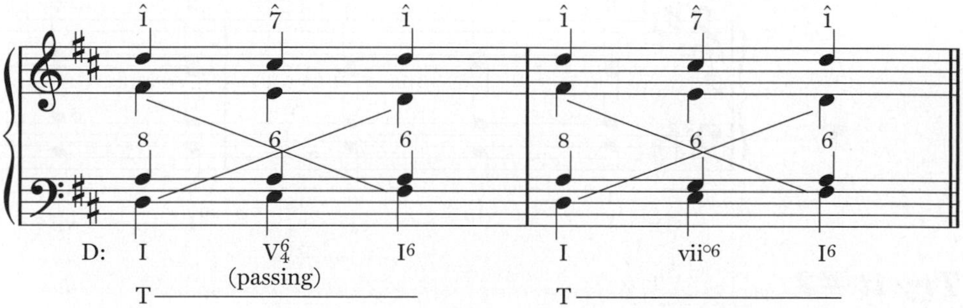

In parts (a) and (b) of Example 17.9, V$^4_3$ is replaced with vii$^{\circ 6}$. Here, the soprano and bass move up in tenths (10–10–10), and the alto and soprano have unequal fifths (d5–P5). Again, the unequal fifths are acceptable because the parallel tenths pull $\hat{4}$ up to $\hat{5}$. In parts (c) and (d), V$^4_2$ is replaced with vii$^{\circ 4}_{3}$, and in (e) and (f) V$^6_5$ is replaced with vii$^{\circ 7}$. In all of these progressions, the soprano, alto, and tenor parts may be rearranged to make any of them the soprano line, and the progression still produces good counterpoint between the soprano and bass. Part (f) shows a typical alteration in major keys, where $\hat{6}$ is changed to $\flat\hat{6}$ (B to B♭) in order to create a fully diminished sonority.

Example 17.9: Tonic expansions with neighboring and passing motion

(a) With passing V^4_3, outer voices 10–10–10 (b) With vii°6, outer voices 10–10–10

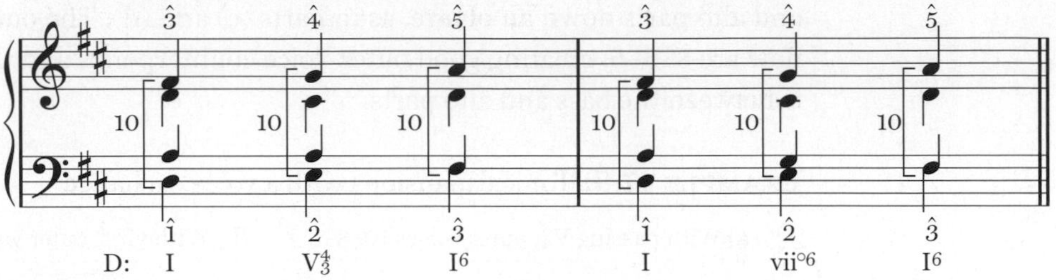

(c) With V^4_2 (d) With vii°$^4_3$

(e) With V^6_5, and neighbor motion (f) With vii°7, and neighbor motion

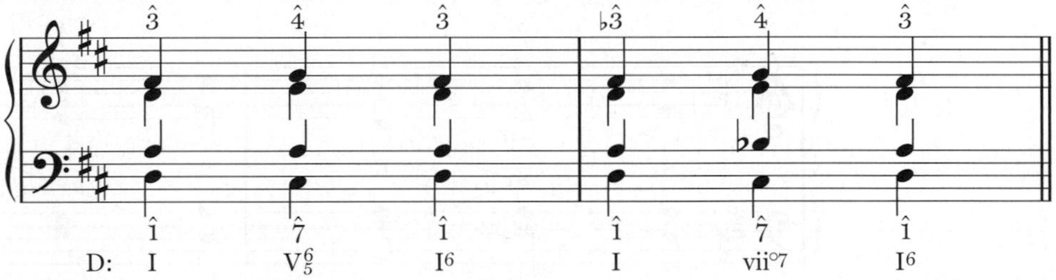

Try it #3

A good exercise to prepare for harmonizing melodies is to plan various soprano-bass contrapuntal patterns, then imagine possible Roman numerals for their harmonization. For each soprano-bass pattern below, provide two harmonizations: V or V^7 and its inversions, and vii°6 or vii°7 and its inversions.

KEY	SOPRANO	BASS	HARMONIZATION 1	HARMONIZATION 2
major	3̂–2̂–1̂	1̂–2̂–3̂	I–V^6_4–I^6	I–vii°6–I^6
major	1̂–2̂–1̂	1̂–7̂–1̂		
minor	1̂–7̂–1̂	1̂–4̂–♭3̂		
major	3̂–4̂–5̂	1̂–2̂–3̂		
minor	♭3̂–4̂–♭3̂	1̂–7̂–1̂		

You will often find leading-tone harmonies as anacrusis chords to the tonic and as voice-leading chords to prolong the tonic. For an example of the first, listen to the beginning of "O Haupt voll Blut und Wunden" (Example 17.10). Here, Bach chooses to harmonize $\hat{2}$—the dominant-function anacrusis—with $vii^{\circ 6}$ instead of V.

EXAMPLE 17.10: Bach, "O Haupt voll Blut und Wunden," mm. 2b–4

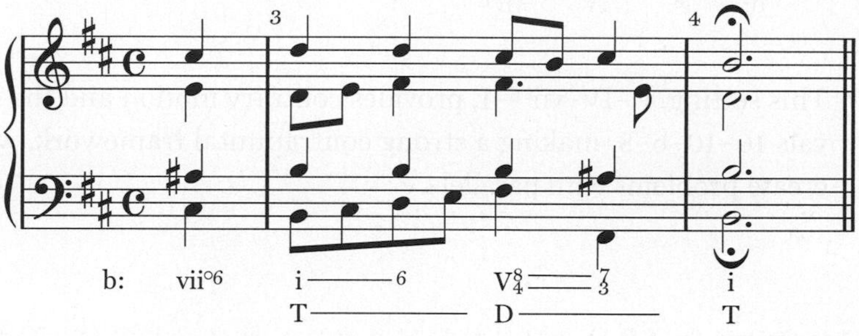

Example 17.11, from Bach's setting of "Aus meines Herzens Grunde," shows $vii^{\circ 6}$ in a tonic expansion. Here, the strong counterpoint of the soprano-bass parallel tenths in measure 8 overrides the tendency of $\hat{4}$ to resolve down to $\hat{3}$. The second beat of measure 8 could be analyzed as $vii^{\varnothing 6}_{5}$, but the seventh of the chord (E4) does not resolve down as expected. A better analysis is ii (A-C-E) to $vii^{\circ 6}$ (A-C-F♯), as part of an embedded I–ii–$vii^{\circ 6}$–I^6 (T–PD–D–T) progression expanding the tonic. If you were tempted to analyze this progression as I–ii–I^6 (T–PD–T), take another look at the F♯4—what at first appears to be a passing tone instead provides the expected dominant function.

EXAMPLE 17.11: Bach, "Aus meines Herzens Grunde," mm. 7b–10a

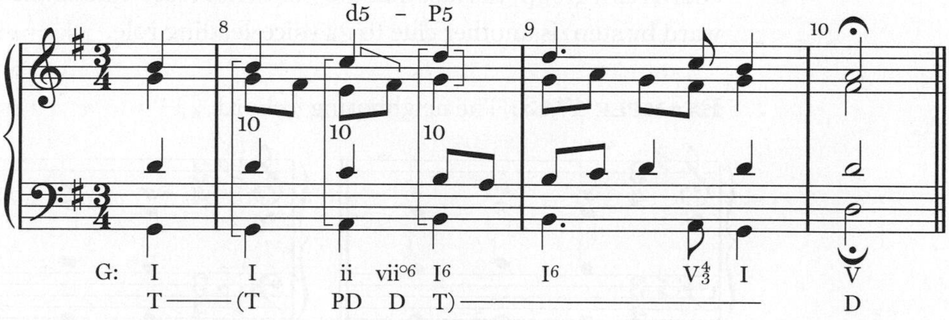

There is one progression typical in minor keys (but also possible in major keys) where leading-tone chords work well, but V or V^7 does not. This occurs when the melody ascends through $\hat{5}$, $\hat{6}$, $\sharp\hat{7}$, and $\hat{1}$, as in Example 17.12.

EXAMPLE 17.12: Use of vii$^{\circ 6}$ in minor to set $\hat{5}$–$\hat{6}$–$\sharp\hat{7}$–$\hat{1}$

This setting, i^6–IV–vii$^{\circ 6}$–I, provides contrary motion and the outer-voice intervals 10–10–6–8, making a strong contrapuntal framework, where IV–V would create problems with parallels.

Other Voice-Leading Chords

Neighboring and Passing $^4_2$ chords

The tonic-expansion chords discussed thus far are not the only ones that can fulfill a neighboring or passing function. For example, the neighboring $^4_2$ chord can expand the tonic, as I–ii$^4_2$–I. Although other diatonic chords may also be decorated with a neighboring $^4_2$ chord, the tonic harmony is most common. This tonic expansion is perhaps best understood as neighbor tones in all three upper parts above a pedal point (Example 17.13); we could therefore also call the ii$^4_2$ a "pedal $^4_2$" chord. Its function becomes clear only when taking the voice-leading of all three chords as a group; the fact that the $^4_2$ does not resolve its seventh properly (downward by step) is another clue to its voice-leading role.

EXAMPLE 17.13: The neighboring $^4_2$ chord

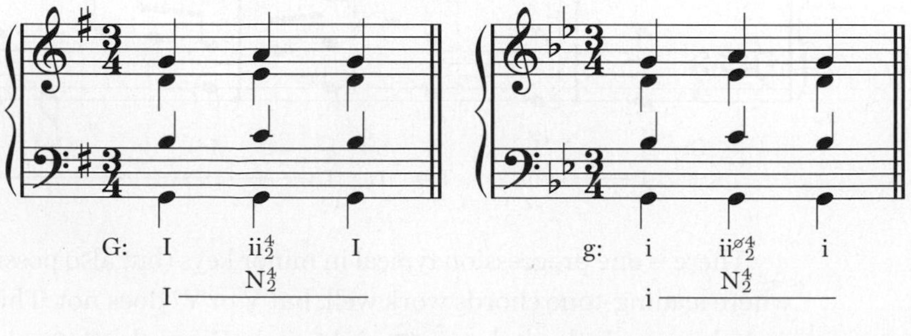

A $^4_2$ chord can also have a passing function, as I–I$^4_2$–IV^6 (Example 17.14). The $^4_2$ is created when a passing tone fills in between $\hat{1}$ and $\hat{6}$ in the bass, and the chords move from I to IV^6 (or, less often, vi). Some musicians analyze the passing chord as I$^4_2$, especially if it lasts as long as the chords surrounding it. Alternatively, you could simply label the bass note as passing, without a new Roman numeral, to show the function of this chord as a tonic expansion. Chords in $^4_2$ position are generally fairly unstable; they serve well in a contrapuntal fashion to effect smooth voice-leading between functional harmonies.

Example 17.14: The passing $^4_2$ chord

Bach's Prelude in C Major makes beautiful use of chords in $^4_2$ position. It begins with I–ii$^4_2$–V^6–I as an opening tonic expansion. Later, in the passage shown in Example 17.15, the E3 is held in the bass across the bar line from measure 15 to 16. Here the E3 acts like a bass suspension, resolving down to D3. If we were to give measure 16 a Roman numeral analysis, it would be IV$^4_2$, but we might instead simply think of this as a voice-leading $^4_2$ without Roman numeral.

Example 17.15: Bach Prelude in C Major, mm. 15–19

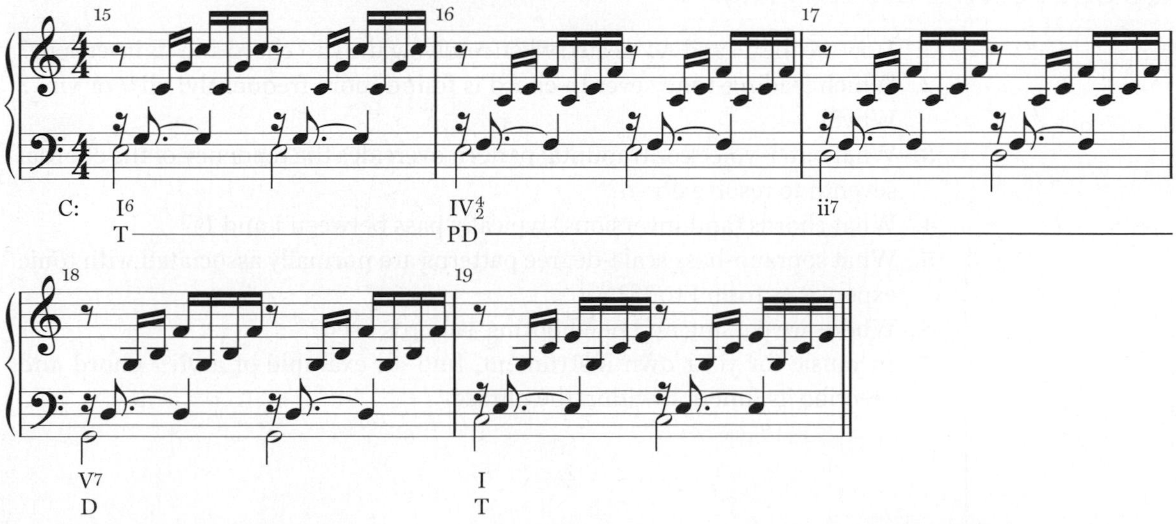

Did You Know?

Compositions from the Baroque and Classical eras offer two ways to think of leading-tone triads and seventh chords. During the early eighteenth century (the end of the Baroque era), composers considered harmony from the viewpoint of counterpoint: the music they wrote features many chords that were conceived linearly, made from melodies in each of the SATB parts. Leading-tone chords were frequently used this way, as tonic expansions, in Baroque chorales.

In the late eighteenth century, composers continued to pay careful attention to counterpoint, but some began to think of chords as thirds and fifths above a root. As a result, they chose chords to make particular harmonic progressions. Although linear leading-tone chords can be found in Classical compositions, they were less suited to the Alberti bass and slower harmonic rhythm than they were to chorales. Instead, Classical composers tended to employ leading-tone chords as dominant substitutes.

Some textbooks from the 1940s–1970s describe leading-tone triads as dominant substitutes, or dominant seventh chords without a root, labeled V$^{\circ 7}$ (see Walter Piston, *Harmony* [New York: Norton, 1941/1987]). While this view led to jokes about whether or not to double the missing root, there is a grain of truth to it—the leading-tone chord often appears in progressions where a V or V^7 could have been used instead. The idea of vii$^{\circ 6}$ as a V^7 without a root is an old one, dating back to Jean-Philippe Rameau's theories of chord progressions in the early eighteenth century. When Rameau wrote a fundamental bass (an analytical bass line written on a staff under the music's bass line, indicating the roots of each chord), for vii$^{\circ}$, he showed the root as $\hat{5}$.

TERMS YOU SHOULD KNOW

dominant substitute	half-diminished seventh	neighboring $^4_2$
fully diminished seventh	leading-tone chord	passing $^4_2$

QUESTIONS FOR REVIEW

1. How are the d5 and A4 treated when resolving the vii$^{\circ 7}$ chord and its inversions?
2. Which leading-tone seventh chord is found more frequently: vii$^{\varnothing 7}$ or vii$^{\circ 7}$? Why?
3. What outer-voice contrapuntal pattern overrides the tendency of the chordal seventh to resolve down?
4. What chords (and inversions) typically pass between I and I^6?
5. What soprano-bass scale-degree patterns are normally associated with tonic expansions from I to I^6?
6. Where are passing and neighboring $^4_2$ chords used?
7. In music for your own instrument, find an example of a vii$^{\circ 7}$ chord and describe its function within the phrase.

Phrase Structure and Motivic Analysis

Outline of topics

Phrase and harmony
- Phrase analysis

Subphrases and motives
- Transformation of motives
- Sentence structure

Phrases in pairs: The period
- Parallel and contrasting periods
- Expanded period structures

Phrase rhythm
- Phrase structure and hypermeter
- Hypermetric disruptions

Overview

In this chapter, we consider how phrases may be grouped, and how motivic and phrase analysis can inform musical interpretation.

Repertoire

Ludwig van Beethoven
- Piano Sonata in C Minor, Op. 13 (*Pathétique*), third movement
- Sonatina in F Major, Op. Posth., second movement

Muzio Clementi, Sonatina in C Major, Op. 36, No. 1, first movement

Stephen Foster, "Oh! Susanna"

Wolfgang Amadeus Mozart
- Piano Sonata in B♭ Major, K. 333, first movement
- Piano Sonata in C Major, K. 545, first and second movements
- Piano Sonata in G Major, K. 283, first movement
- "Voi, che sapete," from *The Marriage of Figaro*

Meredith Willson, "'Till There Was You," from *The Music Man*

Phrase and Harmony

In your instrument or voice lessons, you may have discussed "phrasing" with your teacher. An important part of preparing a piece for performance is determining how it divides up, where the goals are, and how to perform it with directed motion toward these goals. For our purposes, the word "phrase" will not be used as a verb—we will not consider how to "phrase" a melody (at least not in those terms). Instead, the word will be used as a noun, one with a distinct meaning.

As stated earlier, a phrase is the smallest musical gesture that ends with a cadence. It expresses a musical idea and moves toward a goal. Phrases are often two, four, or eight measures long, but these units make a phrase only when concluded with a cadence. Listen to the first sixteen measures of the beautiful love song from Meredith Willson's *The Music Man*, "Till There Was You" (Example 18.1), and determine where the phrases end.

Example 18.1: Willson, "Till There Was You," mm. 1–16a (anthology)

You may be tempted to answer that the first phrase ends in measure 4, with "ringing"; after all, a sentence of text ends there, and the singer will take a breath. But what type of cadence would this phrase ending represent? This first sentence of text extends from an E♭ major tonic triad to $\mathrm{F}^{\varnothing 7}$ in measure 4, but there is no true cadence there; the first phrase ending arrives instead in measure 8, with a B♭7 chord representing a half cadence.

The second phrase begins the same as the first, with only a slight change in text. As before, there is no cadence at measure 12 ("winging"); rather, the phrase continues to measure 16, with a PAC on "till there was you." These long, soaring phrases are almost operatic in their eloquence and may symbolize the character's admission that she has indeed fallen in love at long last.

Phrase Analysis

When analyzing phrases, it is customary to label them with lowercase letters, generally from the beginning of the alphabet. Phrases that sound different are assigned different letters—**a**, **b**, **c**, and so on—while those identical in every regard are labeled with the same letter. Phrases that are similar—that begin the same but end with different cadences, or that are based on the same musical ideas but not identical—receive the same alphabet letter with a prime mark (′): **a** and **a′**, for example. When you use a prime mark, be sure to indicate what is alike about the phrases and also what is different. Because the first two phrases of "Till There Was You" begin identically but end differently, we have labeled them **a** and **a′**. (You may also analyze similar phrases with superscripts, as $\mathbf{a}^1$, $\mathbf{a}^2$, $\mathbf{a}^3$, etc.)

The chart in Figure 18.1, for the first sixteen measures, represents the phrase structure concisely, showing the measures spanned, thematic repetitions, and cadence types.

FIGURE 18.1: Phrase structure of "Till There Was You," mm. 1–16a

	a			**a′**	
m. 1	8 mm.	8	9	8 mm.	16
E♭:		HC			PAC

Phrase analysis can help in preparing a performance. The singer might consider the interaction of text and harmony, knowing that even though a sentence of the text ends in measure 4, the harmony continues to move the line forward. Singer and pianist should agree on points of motion and repose. Even interpreting the half cadence at the end of the first phrase is somewhat tricky, since the singer's line arrives on scale degree $\hat{5}$ in measure 7, while the piano does not reach the dominant harmony until midway through measure 8. At this first vocal cadence, the performers will probably want to take some time as the singer arrives on "you," then let the pianist push the tempo forward a bit on the way to the dominant harmony.

In interpreting the second phrase, performers may want to keep a hierarchy of cadence strength in mind: the arrival on the PAC in measure 16 should be stronger than the arrival on the HC in measure 8. From the beginning of the song, they should already be thinking forward to measure 16 as the first big harmonic and formal goal.

Subphrases and Motives

Shorter musical units, like measures 1–4 of the Willson song, are **subphrases**: musically coherent gestures smaller than a phrase that complete only a portion of the basic phrase progression, without ending with a cadence. Even smaller than a subphrase is a motive.

KEY CONCEPT A **motive** is the smallest recognizable musical idea. Motives may be characterized by their pitches, contour, and/or rhythm, but they rarely contain a cadence. For a musical segment to qualify as a motive, it must be repeated either exactly or in varied form (for example, transposed or embellished).

Try it #1

Write two motives from the Willson song on the staves below.

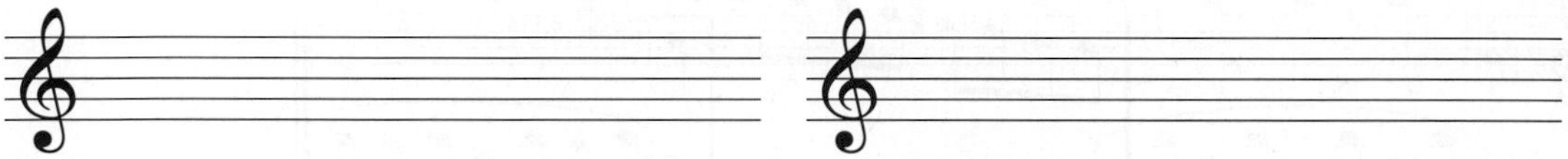

In "Till There Was You," you probably identified the opening three vocal pitches of the song as a motive: they appear in similar rhythmic contexts (♫ pickups to a downbeat ♩ or 𝅗𝅥.) three times in measures 1–3. Further, they appear in a transposed and embellished form at the anacrusis to measure 5: beginning on E♭ and embellished by the incomplete neighbor A♭ to G ("No, I never"). Although this version shares both rhythm and contour with the statements that preceded it, some motives share only one of these features, as we will see. The song also includes a striking rhythmic motive: the quarter-note triplet (mm. 5–6 and 13–14). Even though the pitches and contour differ, the repetition of the triplet defines this pattern as a motive.

In music analysis, label motives with lowercase letters from the end of the alphabet—w, x, y, z—or give them a meaningful name: the scale motive, the arpeggiated motive, the neighbor-note motive, the weeping motive, and so on. Look now at melodic motives from the beginning of Clementi's Sonatina in C Major. Begin by listening to the opening measures (Example 18.2).

Example 18.2: Clementi, Sonatina in C Major, first movement, mm. 1–11

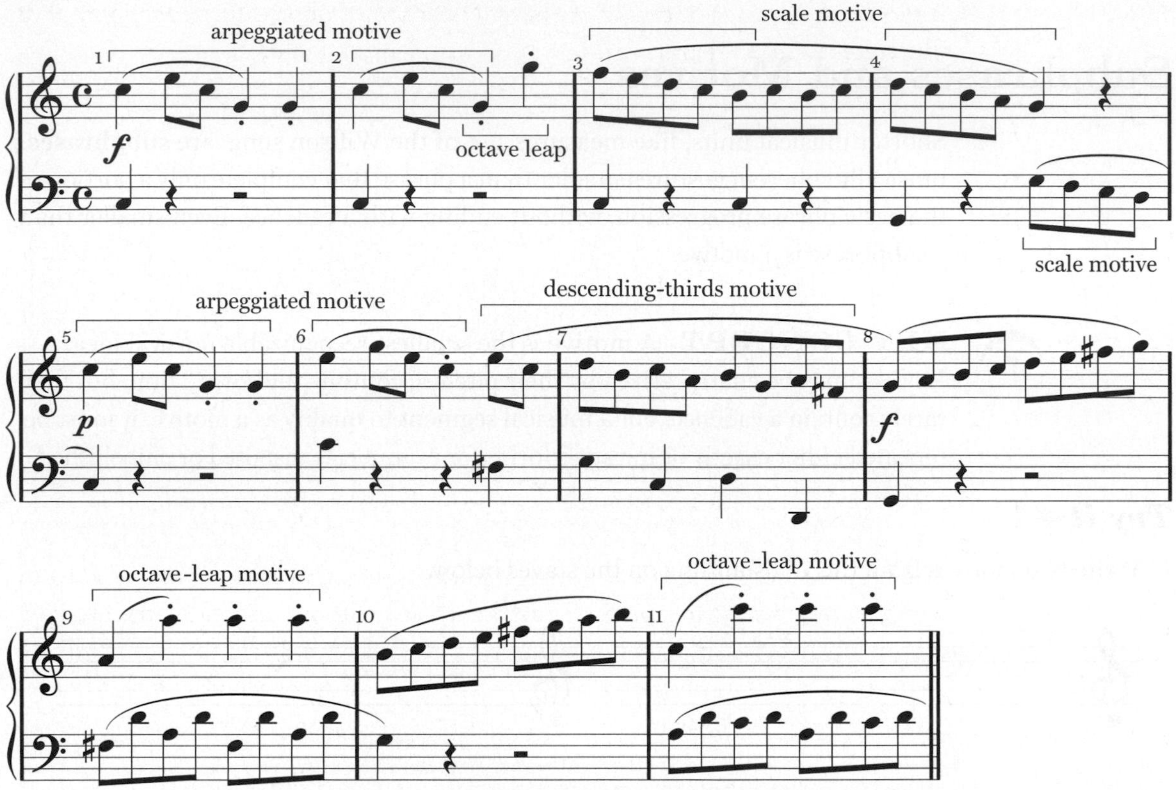

The first two phrases (mm. 1–4 and 5–8) are related by their use of the same opening motive: the "arpeggiated motive" (mm. 1–2 and 5–6). The five-note descending scale that begins measure 3 ("scale motive") reappears in measure 4. The repeated two-note pattern that permeates measure 7, the "descending-thirds motive," comes from the second and third pitches of the arpeggiated motive (a descending third), and the repeated octave leaps in measures 9 and 11 come from measure 2's octave leap.

In addition to melodic motives, composers may include motives that are purely rhythmic or that consist simply of a melodic contour (shape). A rhythmic motive maintains its rhythm but might change its contour and intervals. A contour motive maintains its shape but changes its intervals and possibly its rhythm.

Transformation of Motives

Although motives may be repeated exactly, they are usually transformed by changes in their contour, rhythm, transposition level, or intervals. When transposed, as in the Clementi sonatina, motives usually retain their rhythm, contour, and basic interval structure—that is, a third remains a third, but the interval may change in quality from major to minor or vice versa. Example 18.3 illustrates Clementi's transformations of the arpeggiated motive.

Example 18.3: The arpeggiated motive in Clementi Sonatina

When Clementi transposes the original motive, its major third (C5–E5) becomes a minor third in measure 6. In 16–17, this initial interval is likewise altered to a minor third, not by transposition but by a shift to the minor mode. The motive's final interval, originally a perfect fourth, becomes a major third in 6 and 16, but returns to a perfect fourth in 17—all without disrupting the motive's identity. Since this identity rests heavily on contour and rhythm, these slight changes in interval size or quality do not disrupt our recognition of it.

The phrase in measures 28–31 (Example 18.4) begins with the arpeggiated motive, but here its contour is turned upside down, like a reflection in a mirror: such a transformation is called **inversion**. The phrase ends with an inversion of the scale motive from 3–4. Measure 30 is derived from the descending-thirds motive of 7, but with the thirds stacked as quarter notes instead of successive eighth notes.

Example 18.4: Inversion of motives in Clementi Sonatina, mm. 28–31

KEY CONCEPT To invert a motive, keep the order of interval sizes the same, but reverse each interval in direction—for example, an ascending third becomes a descending third, and a descending fifth becomes an ascending fifth. To invert a contour, reverse the direction of each step, skip, or leap as for a motive, but the interval size may change.

True mirror inversions retain all the exact intervals of the original, but reverse their direction. In tonal music, however, inversions are typically altered so their pitches remain within the key or harmony of the passage; the quality of some intervals will change (or their size will be adjusted slightly, such as a P5 to P4). In measure 28 of Example 18.4, Clementi retains the tonic harmony through a tonal inversion: the original ascending third becomes a descending fourth so that the harmony stays tonic (not submediant).

Try it #2

Listen to the passage from Foster's "Jeanie with the Light Brown Hair" shown below. In the blanks provided, describe how x, y, and z are related to the original motive.

x: ______________________________

y: ______________________________

z: ______________________________

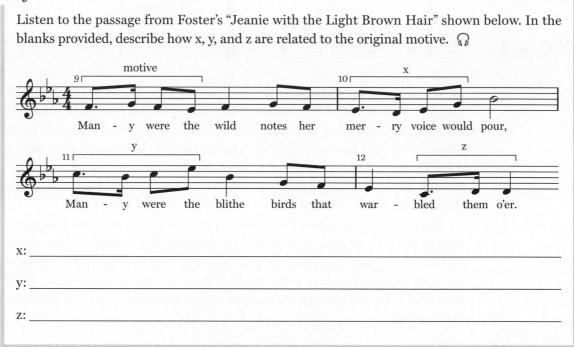

Sometimes motives are treated to rhythmic transformations that either lengthen or shorten them. This process is employed in a later passage in the sonatina, with transformations of motives from measures 1–11 (Example 18.5).

Example 18.5: Clementi, Sonatina, mm. 16–23a

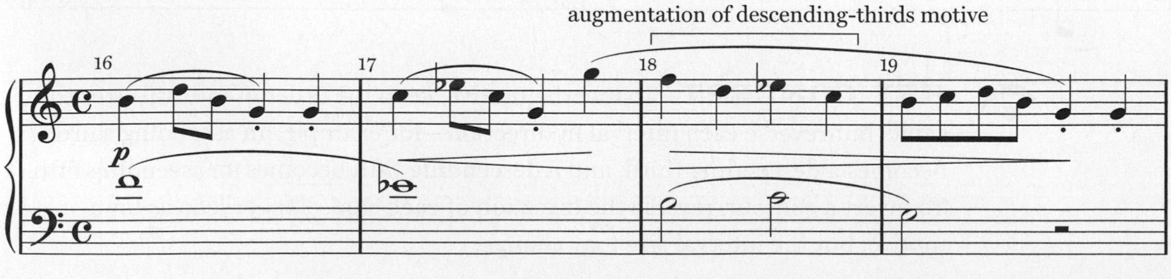

Measure 18 is a transposition of the descending-thirds motive of measure 7, but each rhythmic duration has been doubled from eighth notes to quarter notes. This type of transformation is known as **augmentation**. The right-hand octaves in 20–21 are derived from the octave leaps in 9 and 11, now inverted, but each duration has been halved: from quarter notes to eighth notes. This transformation is called **diminution**.

KEY CONCEPT To transform motives by augmentation or diminution, change each note's duration proportionately to the original: an augmentation doubles or quadruples each duration, while a diminution halves or quarters each duration. This will make the transformation easier to hear.

Another way to lengthen or shorten a motive is to extend, truncate, or fragment it. Consider the scale motive in Examples 18.2 and 18.4. When first heard in measure 3, the motive is five notes long, but when it reappears in measure 8, it is inverted and also extended to eight notes. The octave-leap motive from 9 and 11 (Example 18.6) includes repeated notes: A4–A5–A5–A5 in 9 and C5–C6–C6–C6 in 11. When it reappears in 20–21 (Example 18.5), the repeated pitches at the end have been cut off, and only the octave leap remains—the motive itself has been truncated, then the shortened version is extended. Finally, the descending-thirds motive in 6–7 (Example 18.2) includes five pairs of thirds, but in 18 (Example 18.5) only two pairs of thirds—a small section of the original motive. This motive has been fragmented as well as augmented.

EXAMPLE 18.6: Clementi, Sonatina, mm. 8–11

KEY CONCEPT To **extend** a motive, repeat elements of the motive to make it longer. To **truncate** a motive, cut off the end to make it shorter. To **fragment** a motive, use only a small (but recognizable) piece of the original.

In analysis, first identify motives by their characteristic shape and repetition, then look for possible transformations in rhythm, contour, or intervals that help to unify the passage. Above all, use your ears!

Sentence Structure

Listen now to a Beethoven sonatina to hear how motives may be combined and developed into larger structures. The opening eight measures are given in Example 18.7.

EXAMPLE 18.7: Beethoven, Sonatina in F Major, second movement, mm. 1–8

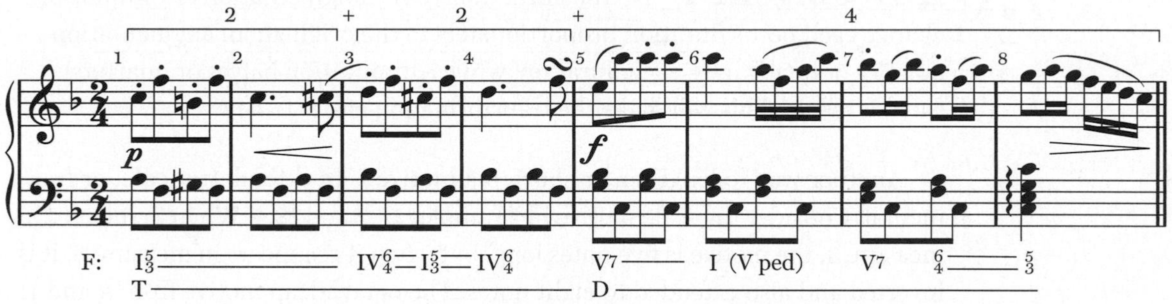

The passage opens with a chromatic neighbor-tone motive (C5–B♮4–C5), with a tonic pedal in the highest and lowest voices. This motive is repeated a step higher in measures 3–4 (D5–C♯5–D5). Each statement lasts two measures, and they are followed by a four-measure continuation and cadence (mm. 5–8). This design is so common in Classical-era melodies that it has a name: the sentence.

KEY CONCEPT A **sentence** structure consists of eight measures in a 2 + 2 + 4 design, or four measures in a 1 + 1 + 2 design. In the first unit, a motive is stated, typically over tonic harmony; in the second unit, the motive is restated, usually varied or transposed, often over a dominant harmony or progression that expands the tonic area. In the third unit, the motive is broken up and developed with an accelerated harmonic rhythm as the phrase moves toward the cadence, typically a HC or PAC.

The opening motive plus its restatement can be considered the "presentation" phase of the sentence, with the four-measure unit constituting "continuation" and cadential functions. These first two units do not close with a cadence, but require the third portion for closure. The continuation phase typically begins with some element of the introductory motive, such as its rhythm, before moving toward the cadence. In Example 18.7, for example, the continuation begins with staccato eighths derived from the opening motive.

For a slightly expanded example of a sentence, listen to the opening of Mozart's G Major Sonata, given in Example 18.8. Here, the continuation takes the rhythmic motive from the opening and develops it by expanding its interval from second to third to fourth before moving to the cadence. Mozart then expands the cadence with a flourish of scalar passages, extending the continution/cadence unit from its typical four measures to six.

EXAMPLE 18.8: Mozart, Piano Sonata in G Major, first movement, mm. 1–10a

Motivic analysis is a topic that has fascinated music analysts and composers for generations. Further analysis of the Clementi, Beethoven, and Mozart movements discussed thus far reveals remarkable compositional economy and unity, generating complete and satisfying larger forms from a handful of motives. Motivic analysis can also help in memorization for performance, since it shows how the piece develops over time. You may want to pursue motivic analysis on your own in the pieces you perform. Knowing where a motive is located (especially when it appears in an inner voice or in the bass line) can help you articulate it more clearly to your audience.

Phrases in Pairs: The Period

We now consider how phrases combine to make larger musical structures. Listen to "Oh! Susanna" (Example 18.9), then examine its phrase structure.

Example 18.9: Foster, "Oh! Susanna," mm. 1–8

This melody has a harmonic structure that is common in music from the Classical era and some American folk songs: motion in the first phrase from I to V (HC), followed by motion in the second phrase from I to V–I (AC).

KEY CONCEPT When the first phrase of a pair of phrases ends with a harmonically weak cadence (HC or IAC) and the second with a stronger cadence, they form **antecedent** and **consequent** phrases. The two together form an antecedent-consequent pair, or **period**. Typical cadences for the two phrases are HC–PAC (most common), HC–IAC, and IAC–PAC.

The melodic structure of "Oh! Susanna" is typical: the first phrase comes to rest on scale degree $\hat{2}$ over a HC (m. 4), and the second concludes with $\hat{2}$–$\hat{1}$ in a PAC (m. 8). Other folk tunes with this melodic structure include "Home on the Range," "Clementine," and "Red River Valley." Some musicians restrict the label "antecedent-consequent" to the HC–PAC relationship as in "Oh! Susanna."

Look back at Example 18.2, which also features antecedent and consequent phrases. The first phrase (mm. 1–4) ends with a half cadence (with the melody on $\hat{5}$); and the second (mm. 5–8) begins with a repetition of material from the first (as the Foster song does), but it changes key. The cadence in measures 7–8 is a PAC in G major. We will further investigate phrases that change key in later chapters on modulation, but for now you should know that this is a possibility in antecedent-consequent pairs. In the sonatina, the first phrase is known as the antecedent and the second as the "modulating consequent," forming a **modulating** period.

In the periods examined thus far, both phrases are the same length—either four or eight measures long—making a period that spans eight or sixteen measures. This is not always the case, however. When the phrases are the same length, the period is called **symmetrical**; when they are different lengths, it is **asymmetrical**.

Parallel and Contrasting Periods

Besides their harmonic structure, thematic elements of the melody work to shape periods as well. When the two phrases begin identically, or when the second phrase is audibly a variant of the first, the structure is called a **parallel period** (**a a′**). The first eight measures of Example 18.2 constitute a parallel period, as do the sixteen measures in Example 18.1.

When the two phrases begin differently from each other, as in the Beethoven sonata theme shown in Example 18.10, they form a **contrasting period** (**a b**). In contrasting periods, the phrases normally share some characteristics to make continuity between them—they are not contrasting in every way—but their beginning and overall shape and sound will differ. In this example, the varied return of the bracketed melodic idea from the beginning of phrase 1 at the end of phrase 2 makes an audible connection between the contrasting phrases.

EXAMPLE 18.10: Beethoven, *Pathétique* Sonata, third movement, mm. 1–8a

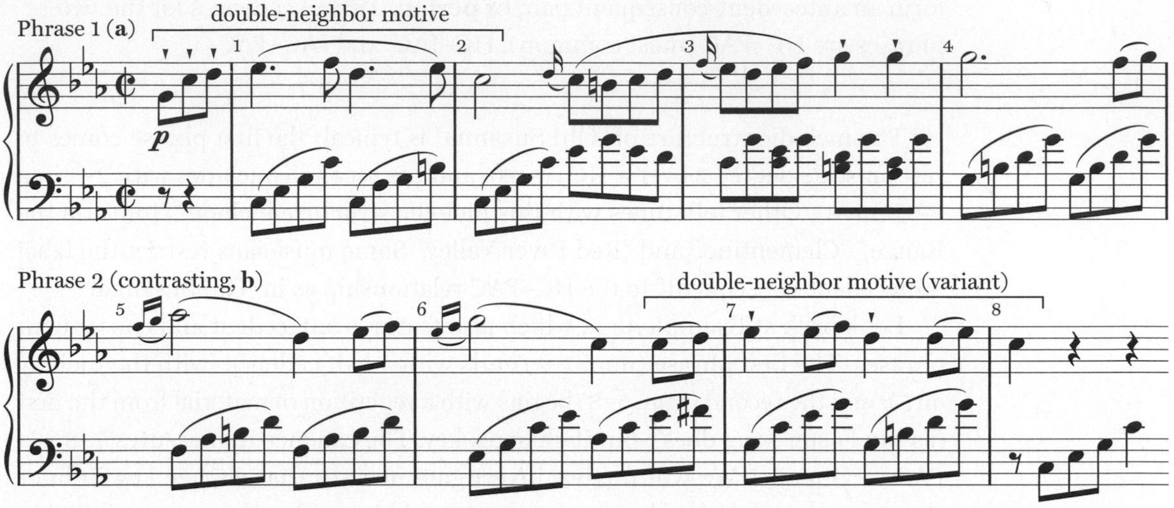

You may also encounter periods in which a sentence structure is embedded. The Beethoven phrase from Example 18.7 is the first part of a parallel period, as shown in Example 18.11: the first phrase ends on a HC and the second on a PAC. Both have parallel 2 + 2 + 4 sentence designs. Figure 18.2 gives a phrase diagram for this passage.

EXAMPLE 18.11: Beethoven, Sonatina in F Major, second movement, mm. 1–16

FIGURE 18.2: Phrase diagram for Beethoven Sonatina, mm. 1–16

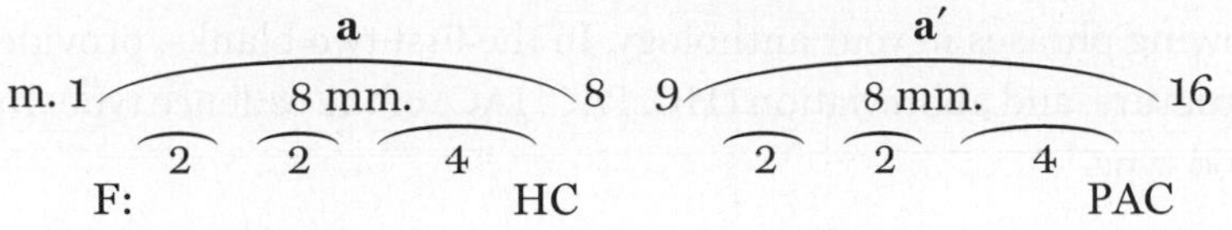

KEY CONCEPT To write a Classical-style antecedent-consequent pair of melodic phrases:

1. Begin by mapping out eight blank measures on two lines of staff paper—four on the top line and four more aligned beneath them on the second line.
2. Sketch an approach to each cadence: one that ends on $\hat{3}$–$\hat{2}$ at the end of the first line to suggest a HC, and one that ends on $\hat{2}$–$\hat{1}$ or $\hat{7}$–$\hat{1}$ on the second line for a PAC.
3. Start measure 1 on a member of the tonic triad ($\hat{1}$, $\hat{3}$, or $\hat{5}$). If you want to include an anacrusis, write one that suggests a dominant harmony.
4. Compose a melody in the first four measures whose outline implies an incomplete phrase model (T–PD–D). Plan your progression with a harmonic rhythm of one to two chords per measure. Melodies often begin with a slower harmonic rhythm that speeds up near the cadence.
5. Now write a melody that expresses your progression by including arpeggiation or passing and neighboring embellishments around chord tones. Create at least two memorable motives: melodic, rhythmic, or contour. If rhythmic, repeat the rhythm more than once. You may also want to try a sentence structure.
6. To make a parallel period, copy one or two measures of your first phrase into the beginning of the second phrase; where possible, continue developing one of the motives as you complete the phrase. To make a contrasting period, create a different but compatible melodic idea for the start of the second phrase. Complete the second phrase by writing a continuation that ends with a cadence on the tonic.
7. Most melodies feature one high point, or climax. Build yours so that its highest note is stated only once—probably in the second phrase.

Try it #3

Study the following phrases in your anthology. In the first two blanks, provide a letter to show the melodic structure, and abbreviation (HC, PAC, IAC) of the cadence type. In the third blank, name the period type.

EXCERPT	MM. 1–4	MM. 5–8	PERIOD TYPE
(a) Clarke, *Trumpet Voluntary* (p. 130)	**a** (HC)	________	________
(b) "Greensleeves" (p. 178)	________	________	________
(c) Mozart, Sonata, K. 284 (p. 245)	________	________	________

What elements make the Mozart example different from the others? What formal ambiguity is present?

Expanded Period Structures

Listen now to the opening of Mozart's aria "Voi, che sapete" (mm. 9–20 are given in Example 18.12), and consider the phrase structure.

EXAMPLE 18.12: Mozart, "Voi, che sapete," mm. 9–20

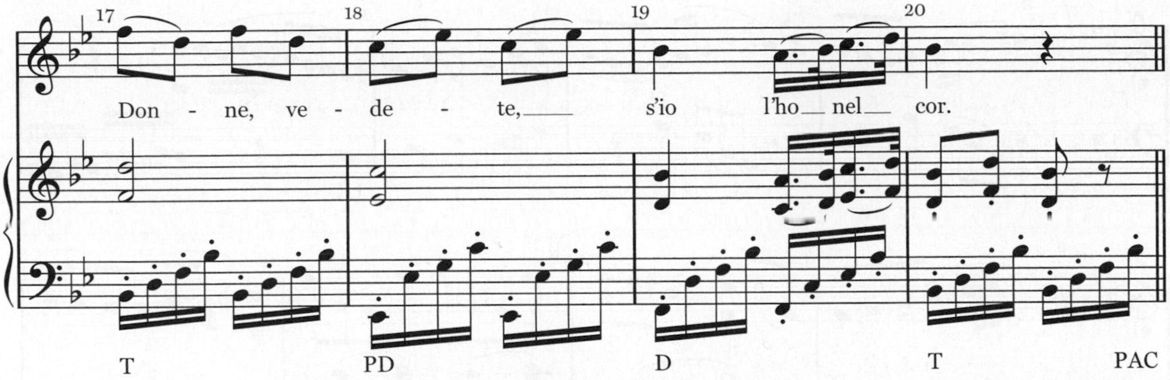

Here are three phrases that clearly form a unit: the first ends with a half cadence (m. 12); the second (mm. 13–16) prolongs the tonic for two bars and then the dominant for two bars, also ending with a half cadence; and the third states the complete basic phrase model (T–PD–D–T) to bring the passage to a tonal close. In addition, the third phrase ends with a cadential motive (♩ ♫♫ | ♩) that originated in the first (compare mm. 11–12 with 19–20), and ties the unit together. Three phrases that belong together, with cadences in a harmonically weak-weak-strong pattern as here, are called a **three-phrase period**. The thematic design for a three-phrase period varies; some possibilities are **a a b**, **a b b′**, **a b a′**, and **a b c**.

A **double period** is a group of four phrases in which the only PAC appears at the conclusion of the fourth phrase, following three inconclusive cadences. Examine Example 18.13 and the phrase diagram (Figure 18.3) below. Though the main key of the movement is B♭ major, this passage is in F major. These four four-measure phrases have cadences making the pattern IAC–HC, IAC–PAC and a thematic design of **a b a′ b′**. Because phrases 1 and 3 are similar, this passage can be labeled a parallel double period; if phrases 1 and 3 were not similar, it would be a contrasting double period. Several other cadential patterns are possible, such as HC–IAC, HC–PAC.

Example 18.13: Mozart, Piano Sonata in B♭ Major, first movement, mm. 23–38a

FIGURE 18.3: Double period in Mozart, K. 333

	a		b		a′		b′	
m. 23	4 mm.	26 27	4 mm.	30 31	4 mm.	34 35	4 mm.	38
F:		IAC		HC		IAC		PAC

Before labeling a four-part sixteen-measure unit a double period, check the pattern of cadences, since other structures are possible. As was the case in the Willson song (Example 18.1), four four-measure "phrases" may actually constitute a two-phrase period if the first and third only expand the tonic and do not conclude with a cadence. A group of four phrases melodically structured as **a b a′ b′** (or **a b a b**), with the cadences arranged HC–PAC, HC–PAC, is known as a **repeated period** because of the strong PAC at the end of phrase 2 as well as 4.

When two, three, or more phrases group together as a unit but *each* phrase ends with an inconclusive cadence, these comprise a **phrase group**. Phrase groups often repeat a phrase to create **a b a**, **a a′ b**, **a b b′**, or other patterns, or may be united by shared motives.

Phrase Rhythm

Phrase Structure and Hypermeter

Listen to the opening of the second movement of Mozart's Sonata in C Major, shown in Example 18.14. Harmonies and cadences are marked. What exactly defines a phrase and subphrase in this musical context, where melodic units seem to form clear two-measure groups? How can performers give the musical line a direction without the performance sounding choppy?

EXAMPLE 18.14: Mozart, Piano Sonata in C Major, second movement, mm. 1–16

The initial four measures divide into two two-measure subphrases. The first prolongs the tonic by a I–V^4_3–I succession; the next continues the prolongation by means of a neighboring $^6_4$ chord. The first true cadence, a HC, arrives in measure 8, ending this first phrase inconclusively. The next eight measures are then a varied repetition of the first eight, concluding with a PAC. Measures 1–16 therefore constitute a parallel period.

In performing such a piece, remember that measures 1–16 form one large unit with two parts; too much attention to the shaping of two-measure subphrases could disrupt the perception of the larger design. There are two general strategies for projecting this design, one harmonic and one metric. The harmonic approach views this piece as continuous motion toward cadences. Locate the cadences before you begin, then move through the harmonies in the middle of the phrase toward the harmonic goal. The metric strategy requires you to focus on the metric structure as it occurs at larger hypermetric levels. Hypermeter, as discussed in Chapter 2, interprets groups of measures as though they were beats within a single measure. Just as you hear four beats as strong-weak-strong-weak within a measure, you can also interpret four measures as strong-weak-strong-weak.

While other hypermeters are possible, four-bar hypermeters are by far the most common. Since Classical-era music is often structured from small one-, two-, or four-measure units that combine to make four- or eight-measure phrases and then combine into eight-, sixteen-, or thirty-two-measure sections, it is not surprising that some of these larger structures replicate the accent pattern of the smaller ones. This "nesting" of smaller structural units in similarly structured larger ones helps give Classical-era music its feeling of balance and unity.

When analyzing the hypermetric structure of a phrase, first determine whether the music suggests four-measure groups. Then number the measures 1–4, again 1–4, again 1–4, and so on, as in Example 18.14. Here, the first eight-measure phrase includes two four-measure units (mm. 1–4: strong-weak-strong-weak; mm. 5–8: strong-weak-strong-weak), with the phrase ending coinciding with the end of the second unit.

The interaction of hypermetric structure with phrase structure is known as **phrase rhythm**. In examining phrase rhythm, consider how harmonic, melodic, and motivic aspects of the musical phrase fit (or do not fit) within the context of its hypermeter. You might notice, for example, that a phrase has been expanded beyond its four-measure norm, or that measures have been added between phrases. If you are performing the piece, hypermetric analysis might translate into "thinking in one"—one large beat per measure—which can help give your performance a broad sweep and sense of direction. This strategy is particularly helpful for movements in fast tempi, where musicians can get bogged down in all the fast passagework and lose the sense of metrical flow. As you play or sing, try thinking of the strong-weak metric alternation from bar to bar. Don't simply accent the strong bars, however, a practice that could make the performance ungraceful. Rather, create a gentle ebb and flow of alternating strong and weak, as within a single measure.

SUMMARY

There are two aspects to an analysis of phrase rhythm: phrase analysis and hypermetric analysis. "Phrase" refers to the harmonies and melodies that conclude with a cadence. "Hypermeter" refers to the regular metric alternation of strong and weak measures. Typically, hypermeter and phrase structure are aligned with each other, as shown in Figure 18.4: a consistent four-bar hypermeter, aligned with four-bar phrases.

FIGURE 18.4: Phrase and hypermeter in alignment

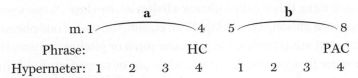

	a				b			
m.	1			4	5			8
Phrase:				HC				PAC
Hypermeter:	1	2	3	4	1	2	3	4

Hypermetric Disruptions

Not all phrases extend for exactly four or eight bars or fall into a regular four-measure hypermeter. They may be truncated or extended; there may be measures between phrases that serve as transitions or introductions to new ideas. Such alterations may disrupt the hypermeter in ways that are worthy of further analysis. As an example, turn again to the opening section of Clementi's sonatina (anthology, p. 000). The first section spans fifteen measures rather than the sixteen you might expect (four phrases of four measures each). Conduct along while listening to this passage, one beat per bar, to see whether your intuitions about metrically strong and weak measures line up with the conducting pattern. The source of the hypermetric disruption is measure 8 (Example 18.15).

page xref

EXAMPLE 18.15: Clementi, Sonatina in C Major, Op. 36, No. 1, first movement, mm. 5–11

As we have seen, the sonatina opens with a parallel period. As the first period ends on the downbeat of measure 8, another phrase begins simultaneously—indeed, on the same pitch (G), which does double duty as the end of one phrase and the beginning of the next. When one phrase ends and another begins at the same time, this is called **phrase elision** or **overlap**. (Some musicians distinguish between elision and overlap. With elision, the end of one phrase and beginning of the next are articulated by the same pitch or pitches, as here. With overlap, there is more than one musical layer: while one or more parts finish the first phrase, one or more other parts begin another.) To diagram elided phrases, draw the end of the first phrase so that it overlaps with the beginning of the next, as in Figure 18.4. Compare this diagram with the anthology score.

FIGURE 18.5: Metric reinterpretation in Clementi, mm. 1–15

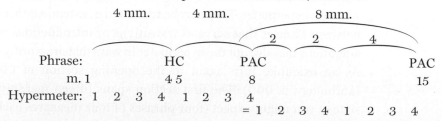

4 mm. 4 mm. 8 mm.
2 2 4
Phrase: HC PAC PAC
m. 1 4 5 8 15
Hypermeter: 1 2 3 4 1 2 3 4
= 1 2 3 4 1 2 3 4

If you follow this diagram while listening for metrically strong and weak bars, you will hear that measure 8 "should" be metrically weak, but the elision reinterprets its role in the phrase, making it the strong initiator of a new four-measure unit. This type of elision, where a disruption of the hypermeter causes a weak measure to become strong, is sometimes called **metric reinterpretation**. Not all elisions involve metric reinterpretation: for example, if phrase 1 were extended to five measures, its overlap with phrase 2 (Figure 18.6) would not disrupt the strong-weak alternation.

FIGURE 18.6: Elided phrases without metric reinterpretation

	5 mm.				4 mm.			
Phrase:					IAC			PAC
	m. 1				5			8
Hypermeter:	1	2	3	4	1	2	3	4

Sometimes a phrase is preceded by introductory material, which may or may not cause a disruption to the hypermeter. Example 18.16 begins with the conclusion of one phrase (on a half cadence in C major, mm. 11–12), ending a four-measure hypermetric unit, and continues with the beginning of the next, in G major. While the second phrase proper begins in measure 14, an inserted measure (13) precedes the theme and delays the hypermetric downbeat; for this reason, the inserted measure is given no hypermetric number. This type of insertion is known as a **lead-in**.

EXAMPLE 18.16: Mozart, Piano Sonata in C Major, first movement, mm. 11–17

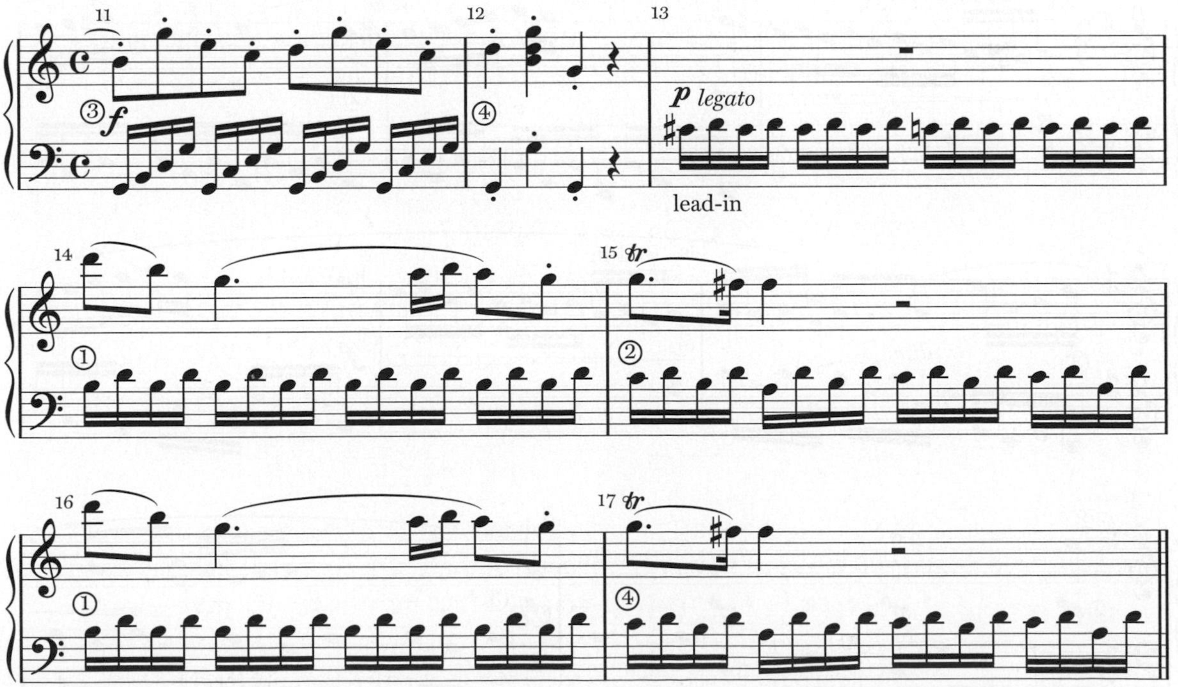

Look back at Example 18.13 for an example of a lead-in that does not disrupt the hypermeter. In measure 30, the arrival at a half cadence on the downbeat is followed by a flourish of sixteenth notes that fills out the measure and leads to the return of the **a** phrase in measure 31. This lead-in, filling out an existing measure (one that does receive a hypermetric number), provides a link to the beginning of the next phrase.

A phrase may be expanded at the beginning (as above), the middle, or the end to make it longer than four or eight measures. There are many way to expand a phrase; only a few examples will be given here. Expansions at the end of a phrase are known as **cadential extensions**. These often, but not always, coincide with an elision. In measure 65 of Example 18.17, for instance, Mozart introduces a four-measure phrase that is repeated with alterations in 69–72. Each phrase is introduced by a lead-in (in mm. 64 and 68), which does not disrupt the hypermeter. The end of the second phrase, however, is elided with a cadential extension that begins in measure 72 and lasts for three measures. This cadential extension simply repeats the cadential harmonies V7–I, echoing the PAC of 71–72 to make a codetta (a small coda) that disrupts the four-measure hypermeter and slows the momentum to end this movement.

EXAMPLE 18.17: Mozart, Piano Sonata in C Major, second movement, mm. 64–74

KEY CONCEPT A **coda** is a section of music at the end of a movement, generally initiated after a strong cadence in the tonic, that extends the tonic area or the final cadence and brings the work to a close. Codas sometimes consist of energetic cadential flourishes; alternatively, they may dissipate energy and end quietly. The term **codetta** is sometimes used for a coda only lasting a few measures, or coming at the end of a section rather than the end of a movement.

Listen to the conclusion of the first movement of the same Mozart sonata (Example 18.18), which is similar in construction. In this case, though, the last phrase spills over beyond the four-bar norm, ending in measure 71. This five-measure phrase is an example of phrase expansion. Here, the expansion is accomplished by drawing out the dominant area for two measures (mm. 69–70). Such internal expansions result most frequently from immediate repetitions of material or a prolongation of one or more harmonies, but they may also be achieved by inserting new material within the phrase. After the cadence on the downbeat of measure 71, there follows a cadential extension in the form of a codetta that brings the movement to a rousing close.

EXAMPLE 18.18: Mozart, Piano Sonata in C Major, first movement, mm. 67–73

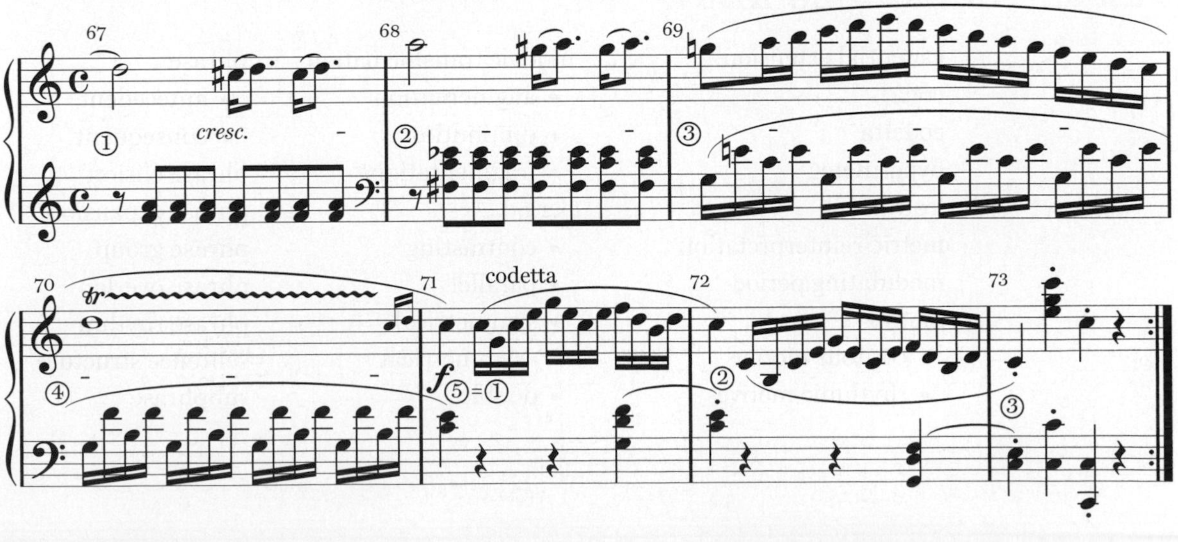

To find phrase expansions, simply count four-measure units and determine whether the phrases coincide with them or not (as in the Mozart examples). Most Classical themes fall into four-bar hypermeter, but less stable musical passages generally do not. In fact, a departure from the four-bar norm in this repertoire is one way listeners can tell that the primary thematic material has ended and a transitional passage or coda has begun. In music of the Baroque era, four-bar hypermeter is much less common; it occurs most frequently in small binary forms and dance movements. Other Baroque genres employ a technique of "spinning out" that will be covered in more detail in Chapter 23. In music from the Romantic era, composers expanded the four-bar model to create much longer melodies.

Did You Know?

Perhaps the most famous motives named for their symbolic associations are the leitmotivs used by Richard Wagner (1813–1883) in his operas. Each leitmotiv represents a character, idea, or object in the opera. For example, in the four-opera cycle *Der Ring des Nibelungen* (*The Ring of the Nibelung*), specific motives represent the ring, the giants, the Valkyries, the sword, the Tarnhelm (a magic cloak), fire, fate, and Valhalla (residence of the gods), among others. Wagner himself did not coin this term—it was popularized by a friend of his—but it has become closely associated with his music. While locating statements of each leitmotiv is only one part of an analysis of these masterworks, learning to identify them by ear can add greatly to your enjoyment of the operas. To learn more about Wagner's musical style, read the essays in the Norton Critical Score *Prelude and Transfiguration from "Tristan and Isolde,"* edited by Robert Bailey (New York: Norton, 1985). To learn more about Wagner's life, consult Ernest Newman's *Life of Richard Wagner* (London: Cassell, 1933–47; reprinted 1976).

TERMS YOU SHOULD KNOW

- cadential extension
- coda
- codetta
- hypermeter
- lead-in
- metric reinterpretation
- modulating period
- motive
  - contour motive
  - rhythmic motive
- motivic transformation
  - augmentation
  - diminution
  - fragmentation
- period
  - contrasting
  - parallel
  - symmetrical
  - asymmetrical
  - double
- phrase
  - antecedent
  - consequent
- phrase elision
- phrase expansion
- phrase group
- phrase overlap
- phrase rhythm
- sentence structure
- subphrase

QUESTIONS FOR REVIEW

1. Name three different ways motives may be transformed.
2. What type of information might be gained from phrase analysis? How might this information impact performance interpretations?
3. How do antecedent and consequent phrases differ?
4. In how many different ways might phrases be paired to form periods? What cadences may be found in a period? How can more than two phrases be grouped together?
5. What is the difference between a parallel period and a contrasting period? between a symmetrical and asymmetrical period?
6. Describe how elided phrases may or may not disrupt hypermeter.
7. What is the purpose of a coda? Where is a coda located?
8. In music for your own instrument, find an example of (a) an antecedent-consequent pair, (b) a rhythmic motive, (c) a contrasting period, (d) four-measure hypermeter.

CHAPTER 19

Diatonic Sequences

Outline of topics

Sequences

Harmonic sequences based on root progressions

- Descending-fifth sequences
- Descending-third sequences

Sequences based on seconds

- Parallel $^6_3$ chords
- 7–6 and 5–6 motion

Sequences in context

Overview

This chapter looks at the relationship between basic root movements and harmonic and melodic sequences. We also learn how linear and harmonic elements interact in sequences.

Repertoire

Johann Sebastian Bach
 Invention in D Minor
 Invention in F Major
 Prelude, from Cello Suite No. 2 in D Minor

Archangelo Corelli, Allemanda, from Trio Sonata in A Minor, Op. 4, No. 5

George Frideric Handel, Chaconne in G Major

Fanny Mendelssohn Hensel, "Neue Liebe, neues Leben"

Jerome Kern and Oscar Hammerstein II, "All the Things You Are," from *Very Warm for May*

Wolfgang Amadeus Mozart
 Dies irae, from *Requiem*
 Rondo in E♭ Major for Horn and Orchestra, K. 371

Johann Pachelbel, Canon in D Major

Sequences

Listen to the opening of Bach's Invention in D Minor, shown in Example 19.1. The first two measures introduce a musical idea, or motive, whose transformation and reappearance are essential to the work. As you listen, pay special attention to the bracketed motive as it appears in either the right or left hand, even if transposed or slightly varied. Compare each bracketed motive with the original in measures 1–2. If it has been transposed, identify by what interval (called the **level of transposition**); if it is varied, consider what has been changed.

EXAMPLE 19.1: Bach, Invention in D Minor, mm. 1–18a

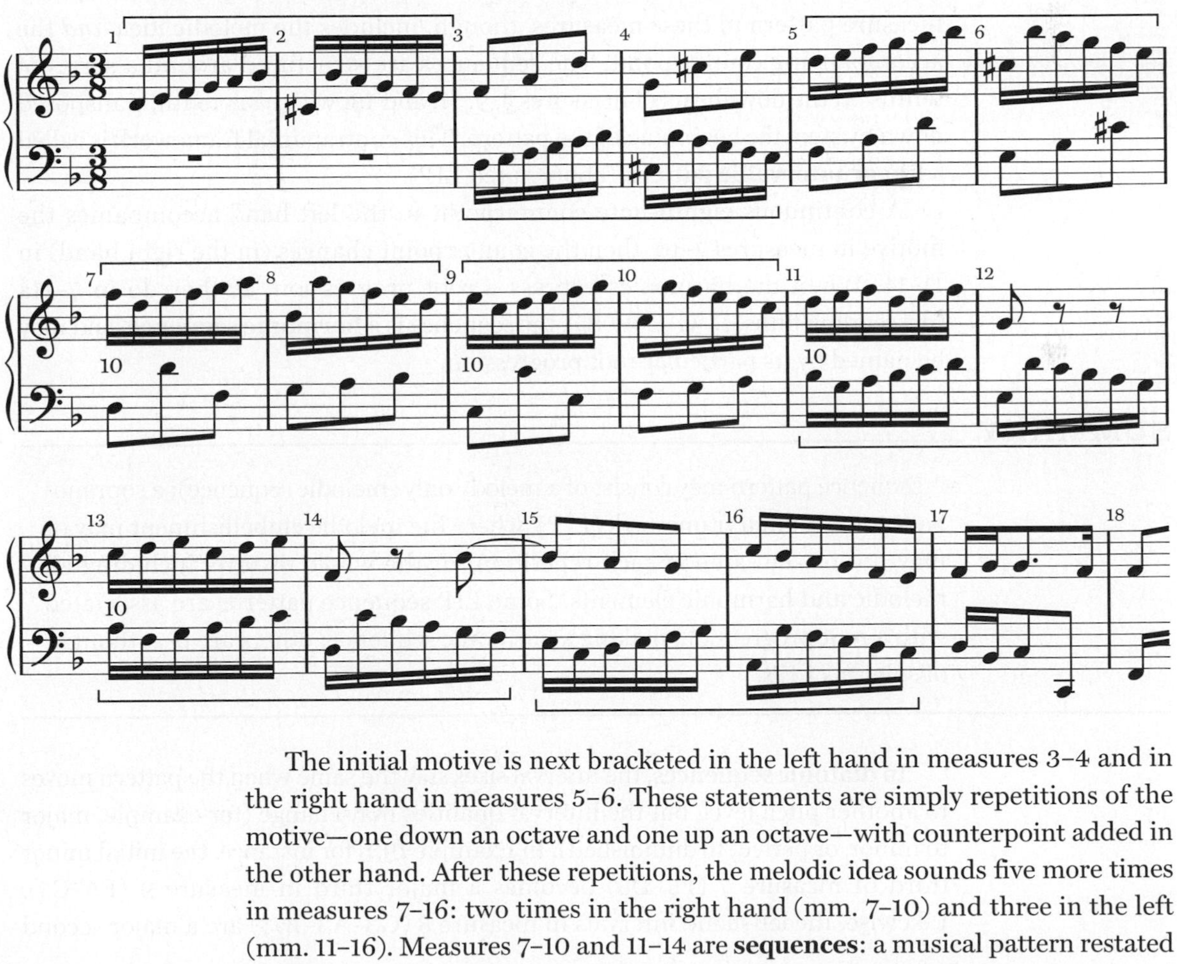

The initial motive is next bracketed in the left hand in measures 3–4 and in the right hand in measures 5–6. These statements are simply repetitions of the motive—one down an octave and one up an octave—with counterpoint added in the other hand. After these repetitions, the melodic idea sounds five more times in measures 7–16: two times in the right hand (mm. 7–10) and three in the left (mm. 11–16). Measures 7–10 and 11–14 are **sequences**: a musical pattern restated at different pitch levels—here, transposed down a step each time. (Octave-related repetitions as in mm. 3–4 and 5–6 are not considered sequences.) If you listen to the rest of the invention, you will hear that this main motive appears many more times, as in measures 15–16.

KEY CONCEPT A sequence is made when a musical idea is expressed, then restated immediately one or more times, with each restatement transposed up or down from the previous one by a consistent interval. The basic idea—normally a half measure, a full measure, or two (sometimes four) measures—is the **sequence pattern**, marked on the score with a bracket.

In Example 19.1, the rhythm and contour of the invention's main melodic idea remain consistent, for the most part, in each restatement. Measures 7–10 in the right hand and 11–14 in the left are examples of **melodic sequences**. The two-measure pattern in these measures, though, includes the melodic idea *and* the accompanying counterpoint. The sequences are structured around a series of tenths on the downbeats of measures 7, 9, 11, and 13, with each tenth, transposed down by step, the beginning of the pattern. This contrapuntal framework is called a **linear intervallic pattern** (abbreviated LIP).

A continuous eighth-note counterpoint in the left hand accompanies the motive in measures 7–10, then the counterpoint changes (in the right hand) in 11–14. When the harmonies express a root progression, as they do in 7–11a (descending fifths, D–G–C–F–B♭), the sequence is a **harmonic sequence**, and may be named by its particular root progression.

SUMMARY

A sequence pattern may consist of a melody only (melodic sequence); a soprano-bass contrapuntal framework (LIP), where the melodic embellishment may or may not be the same in each repetition; or the whole texture, including all melodic and harmonic elements. Some LIP sequence patterns are associated with a root progression, making a harmonic sequence; others are best thought of solely as LIPs.

In **diatonic sequences**, the interval sizes stay the same when the pattern moves to another pitch level, but the interval qualities may change (for example, major to minor, or perfect to diminished). In Example 19.1, for instance, the initial minor third of measure 7 (F5–D5) becomes a major third in measure 9 (E5–C5). Likewise, the left-hand intervals in measure 8 (G3–A3–B♭3) are a major second followed by a minor second, but in measure 10 the corresponding intervals (F3–G3–A3) are both M2s. In the overall tonal organization of the invention, these sequences lead from one tonal area to another: for example, from the opening D minor in measures 1–6 to a cadence in F major in 17–18.

While a melodic sequence or LIP may appear on its own, they most often appear in combination: melodic sequence, LIP, and root progression, as is the case here. Listen now to measures 18–29 (Example 19.2).

Example 19.2: Bach, Invention in D Minor, mm. 18–29a

Try it #1

In Example 19.2, draw a bracket over the motivic pattern each time you hear it (even if transposed or varied). Compare each reappearance with the original in measures 1–2, and label the level of transposition or other changes.

The melodic sequence in the left-hand part, measures 18–21 of Example 19.2, is a diatonic sequence with the pattern transposed up a third, here in the key of F major. Beginning in measure 22, though, the pattern is inverted and accidentals are introduced that are not a part of either D minor or F major, indicating harmonic motion to another key area; this is a **chromatic sequence**. In 22–25, the pattern is transposed down by a step.

Although sequences like those in the Bach examples include motivic repetitions that make it easy to hear and follow the pattern, others may not be so clear.

KEY CONCEPT To analyze a sequence, you need to determine

- what pattern it is based on (a melodic idea, a root progression, an LIP, or a combination), and
- the intervals of restatement (both the interval of the transposition and the time interval between statements).

This chapter focuses on harmonic sequence frameworks with root progressions and/or linear intervallic patterns, but in an analysis it is important to notice whether each musical example features a melodic sequence as well, since melodic patterns make sequences easier to hear.

Harmonic Sequences Based on Root Progressions

Chapter 15 discussed the use of root progressions within the basic phrase, where normally no more than three or four chords of a progression appear successively in the phrase. The "weak links" in the chains, those chord connections that tend not to be included, center around diminished triads (vii°) and triads whose function is ambiguous (iii).

When root-progression chains are found in a sequence, however, the pattern of repetition smooths over these weak harmonic links with strong voice-leading, making it possible to travel through the entire chain or at least through long sections of it. The descending-fifth root progression is by far the most common source of harmonic sequences; it is well suited to repetitive patterns both in the outer-voice framework and in the entire musical texture. Root progressions by third and second do not generate good outer-voice frameworks for sequences because they easily lead to parallel fifths and octaves, but these progressions can be adapted, by means of LIPs or multichord chains, to make acceptable sequences.

Descending-Fifth Sequences

Throughout music of the common-practice era, you will find descending-fifth sequences—the strongest progression in tonal music—with root-position triads, with alternating root-position and first-inversion triads, and with seventh chords. Such sequences may include longer segments of the chain—four or five chords, or even the entire chain from an initial tonic to an ending one—and may combine the root progression with a soprano-bass LIP.

KEY CONCEPT Descending-fifth sequences share the following characteristics:

- The harmonies follow a descending-fifth root progression or a contiguous segment of it.
- The upper-voice pattern typically groups root-progression chords into pairs: I–IV, vii°–iii, vi–ii, V–I; or I, IV–vii°, iii–vi, ii–V, I (in major keys).
- The first and second chords in each pair may have different inversions (e.g., $\substack{5\\3}$ $\substack{6\\3}$), making possible a variety of bass lines without changing the root progression.
- The recommendation against root-position vii° chords is relaxed, as are doubling guidelines.
- The bass line and upper voices of the chord pairs form repeated intervallic patterns (often LIPs of 10–10 or 10–6, for example).

Memorize the Roman numerals in the chain (I–IV–vii°–iii–vi–ii–V–I) and some of the LIPs typically associated with them, as you will encounter them often.

Example 19.3 shows voice-leading frameworks for basic descending-fifth sequences, both root position and with alternating $\substack{6\\3}$ chords, labeled with the outer-voice LIPs (10–10, 10–6, or 6–10). The progression is the same in minor keys (i–iv–VII–III–VI–ii°–V–i); the leading tone is typically raised only in the V chord. The brackets above the staff indicate the repeated pattern; the ties highlight common tones between the chords. Although the examples give the entire course of a sequence, only a portion may appear in a piece—as few as two or three chords. If the chain is complete, it expands the tonic area, as shown by the contextual analysis.

EXAMPLE 19.3: Descending-fifth sequence frameworks

(a) All root position (10–10 LIP)

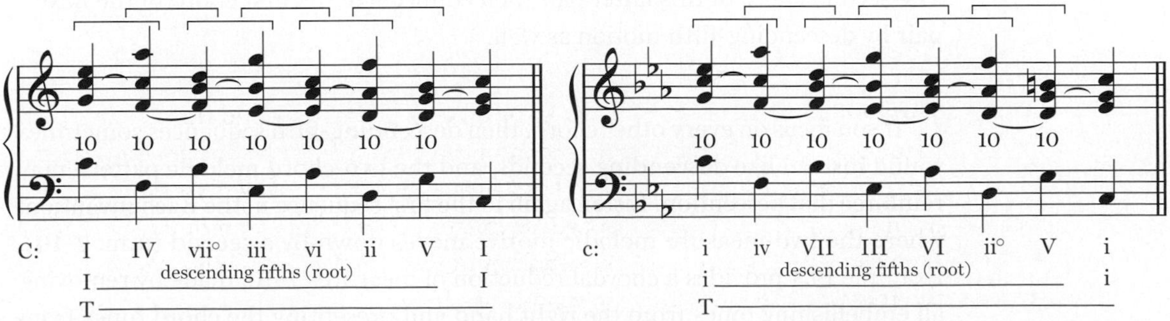

(b) Alternating root position and first inversion (10–6 LIP)

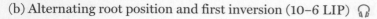

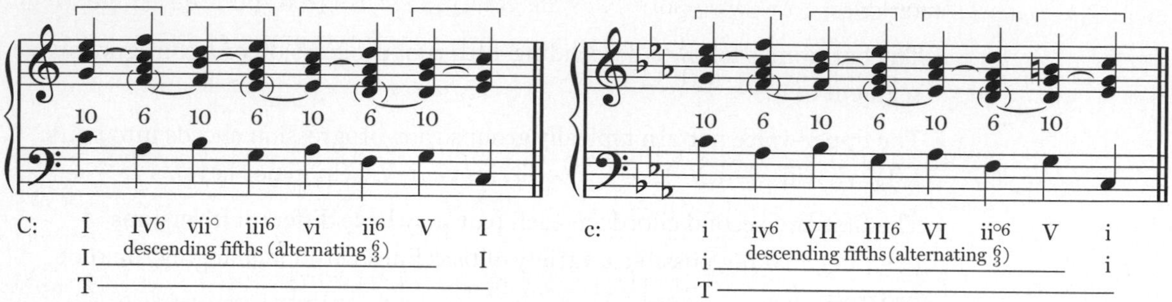

(c) Alternating first inversion and root position (6–10 LIP)

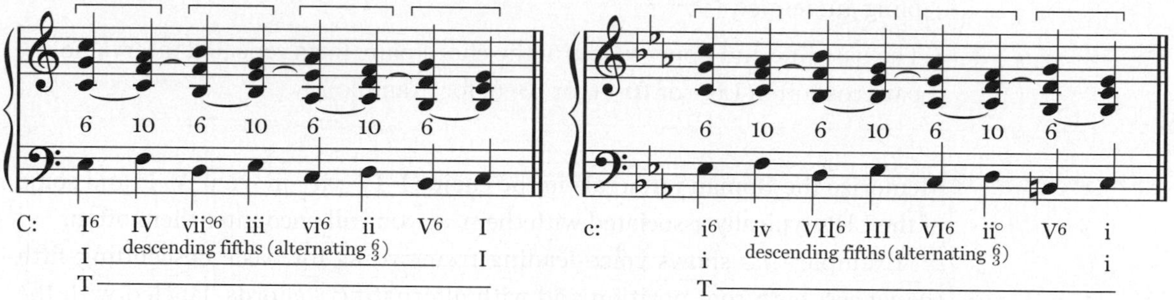

For each framework, any of the upper-voice strands could be the soprano line in an SATB setting; your choice will determine which LIP is created by the soprano and bass. In music literature, you may also encounter sequences with one of the upper parts omitted to make three voices, or with doubling to make five; sequence patterning may supersede doubling guidelines in these cases, though parallel fifths and octaves should be avoided.

KEY CONCEPT A pair of chords connected by descending-fifth root motion usually constitutes the repeated pattern. This pairing may link the first two chords of the chain, or the second and third (bracketed in Example 19.3a). The second chord of this latter pair then connects to the first chord of the next pair by descending-fifth motion as well.

If you focus on every other chord, then descending-fifth sequences sometimes sound instead like descending seconds, and the two-chord melodic pattern may reinforce that perception. Listen again to the first sequence in the Bach invention, where the two-measure melodic motive moves down by a second (mm. 7–10). Example 19.4 provides a chordal reduction of measures 7–10, made by removing all embellishing tones from the right hand and presenting the chord tones from the beginning of each measure. The bass line here consists of the lowest-sounding chord tone of each measure. Now the descending-fifth (root-position) progression is clear: roots D–G–C–F, or chords i–iv–VII–III. This example illustrates another typical descending-fifth LIP: 10–8.

EXAMPLE 19.4: Bach, Invention in D Minor

(a) Mm. 7–10: melodic pattern descends by second

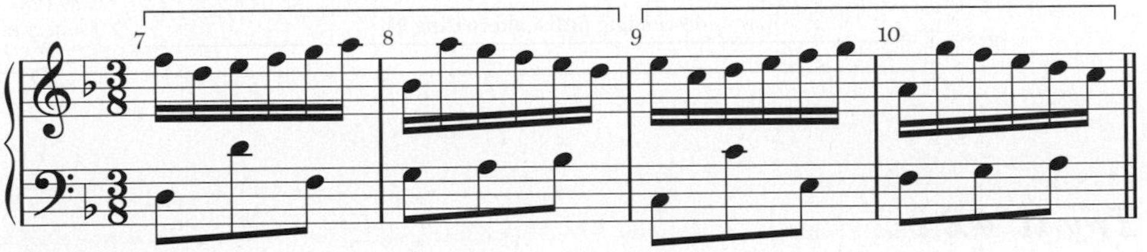

(b) Reduction of mm. 7–10: root progression descends by fifth

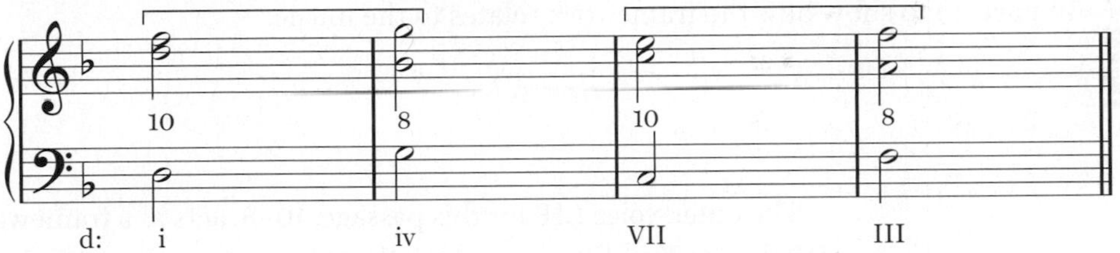

Listen to Variation 11 from Handel's Chaconne in G Major, the beginning of which is given in Example 19.5a. This variation, from the middle of the set of twenty-one variations, is in the parallel minor. The SATB framework in part (b) reveals how these measures are based on a descending-fifth root progression with alternating $\frac{6}{3}$ chords. Here, the harmony changes on the first and third beats, and the sequence pattern extends for the full measure (every two chords), moving down one step with each restatement.

EXAMPLE 19.5: Handel, Chaconne in G Major, Variation 11

(a) Mm. 89–92

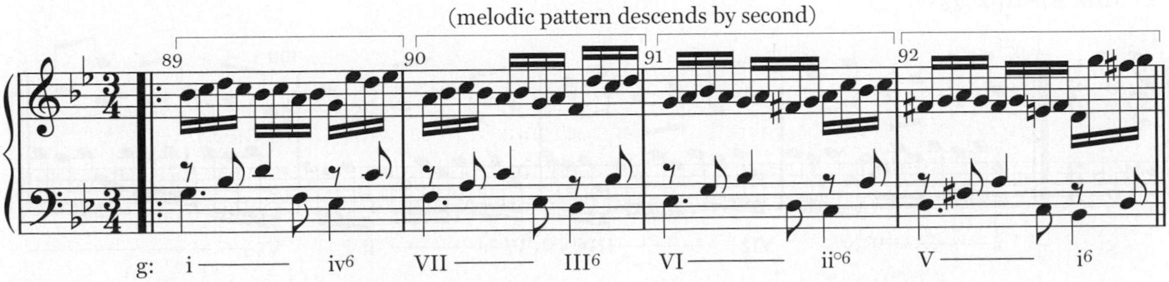

(b) Framework for mm. 89–92

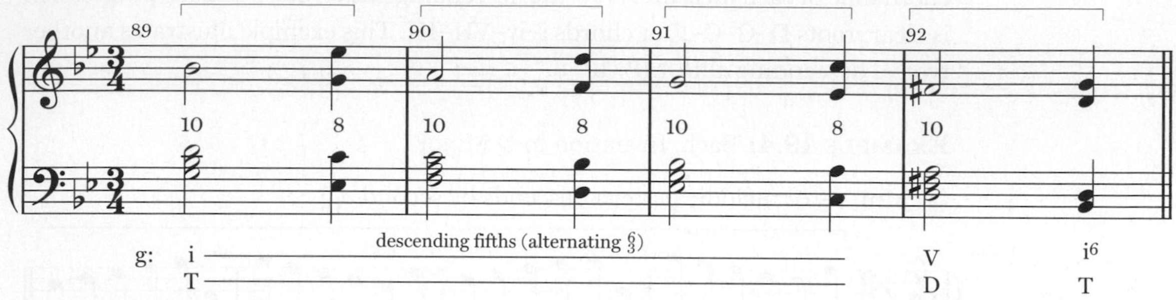

Try it #2

Compare measure 89 in parts (a) and (b) of Example 19.5: circle and label the embellishing tones in part (a) to show how the framework relates to the music.

The outer-voice LIP for this passage, 10–8, acts as a framework in many pieces with descending-fifth sequences that alternate root-position and first-inversion triads. As with most of the sequence frameworks in this chapter, you can place any of the upper-voice strands in the soprano part. While moving an inner voice to the soprano part does not change the basic root progression, it *will* change the LIP.

Listen now to Variation 12 of the Chaconne (Example 19.6). This variation, also in the parallel minor key, is built from the same framework as Example 19.5, but elaborates it with different melodic motives. Here the LIP on beats 1 and 3 is 10–10, embellished by chordal skips and neighbor tones. It is derived from moving the alto line of Example 19.5b to the soprano.

Example 19.6: Handel, Chaconne in G Major, Variation 12

(a) Mm. 97–100

(b) Framework for mm. 97–100

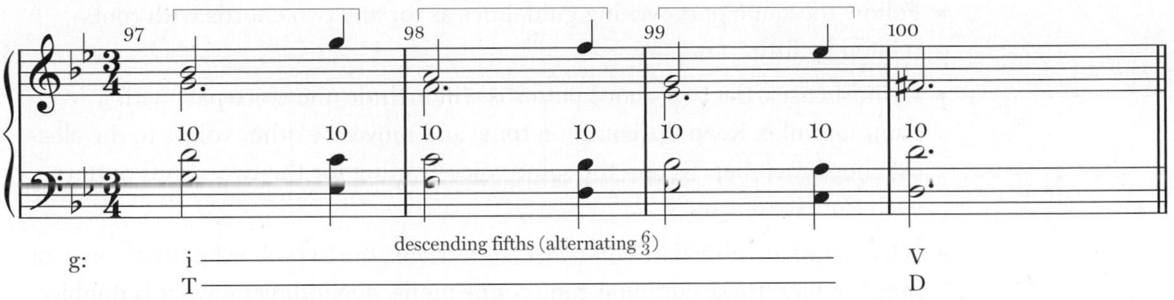

Finally, listen to Variation 13 (Example 19.7). This passage continues with elements of the previous two variations, but the chords in the descending-fifth sequence are now all in root position. One of the compositional problems of this root-position sequence in minor is how to treat the dissonant tritone in the ii° chord. Handel sets up the figuration on the third beat of measure 105 in order to avoid the problem in measure 107, where the ii° triad would appear: his solution is that none of the triads on beat 3 includes the fifth. By placing the beat 3 triads in root position, with their thirds in the soprano, he maintains the 10–10 LIP with a changed outer-voice framework.

Example 19.7: Handel, Chaconne in G Major, Variation 13

(a) Mm. 105–108

(b) Framework for mm. 105–108

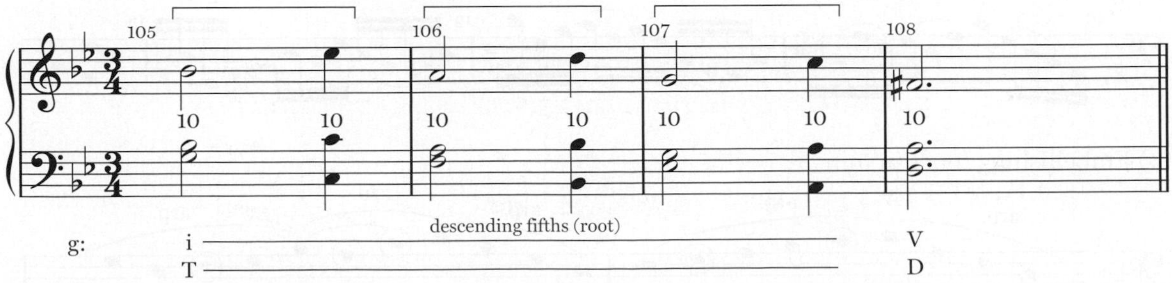

KEY CONCEPT When you write descending-fifth sequences:

- Follow the same part-writing guidelines as for any two chords with roots related by fifth.
- In most cases, the two-chord patterns will include one voice part with a common tone. Keep the common tone, and move the other voices to the closest chord member. Retain the same voice-leading for the two-chord pattern each time it appears.
- If the sequence alternates first-inversion triads, the two-chord patterns may or may not have these common-tone connections, depending on what is doubled.
- Keep the sequence pattern and LIP consistent as you move through the harmonic progression, so its sequential nature is clear to listeners.

With Seventh Chords In addition to triads, descending-fifth sequences may include seventh chords: all seventh chords, alternating triads and seventh chords, or alternating inversions of seventh chords. Example 19.8a, the opening of the Prelude from Bach's Cello Suite No. 2, provides one instance. Listen to the passage. The two-measure pattern is marked with brackets (the dotted line in m. 9 indicates that the pattern breaks off there).

EXAMPLE 19.8: Bach, Prelude, from Cello Suite No. 2 in D Minor

(a) Mm. 1–13a

(b) Embellishing tones in mm. 5–6

(c) Reduction of mm. 5–9

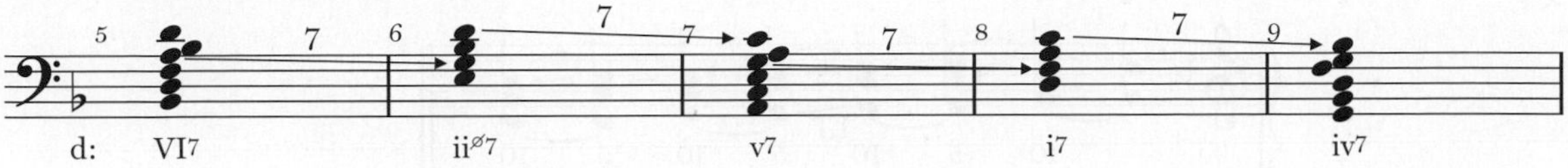

The first measure (m. 5) of the two-measure long sequence pattern is based on an arpeggiation of the chord up, then down, with passing tones C4 and G3 (part b); the second measure (m. 6) is also based on an arpeggiation of the chord, but with double neighbors C4 and A3 and a passing tone F3. Part (c) shows the underlying harmonic progression, with arrows identifying the resolution of the chordal sevenths A3, D4, G3, and C4 down by step to a chord member of the following harmony.

Some basic frameworks for descending-fifth sequences with seventh chords are illustrated in Example 19.9a–d. Study them for their treatment of the chordal seventh and use of complete (C) or incomplete (I) seventh chords.

Example 19.9: Frameworks for descending-fifth sequences featuring seventh chords

(a) All root-position chords; alternating complete (C) and incomplete (I) (10–7 LIP)

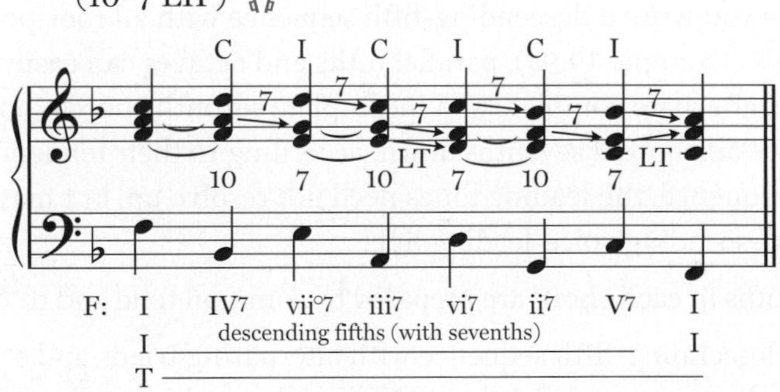

(b) Alternating triads and root-position seventh chords, all complete (10–5 LIP)

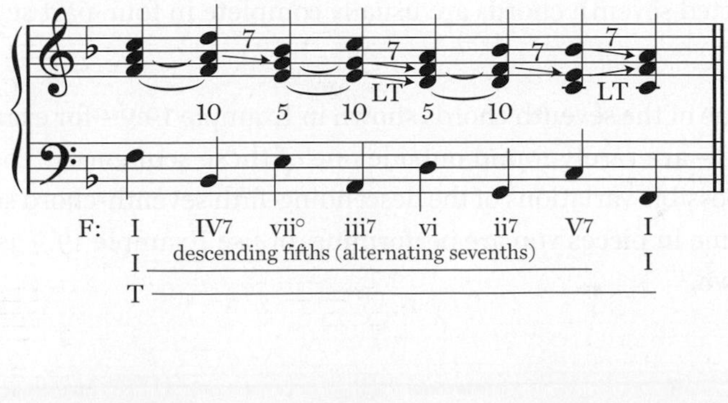

(c) Alternating triads and first-inversion seventh chords, all complete (10–5 LIP)

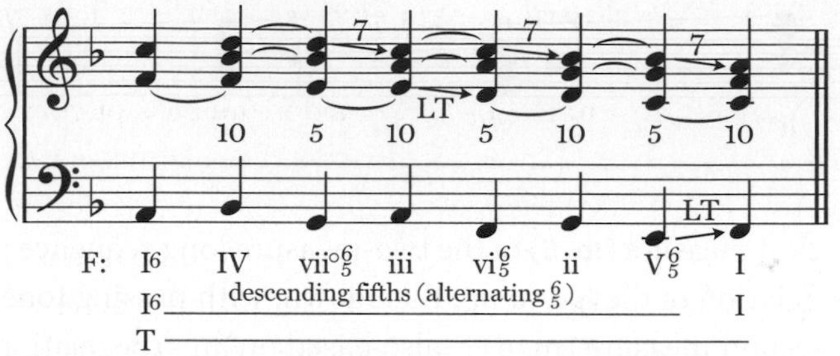

(d) Alternating first- and third-inversion seventh chords, all complete (10–5 LIP)

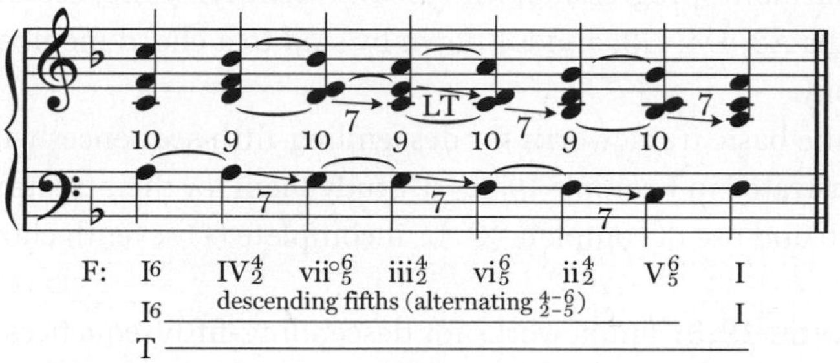

KEY CONCEPT In common-practice style:

- When you write a descending-fifth sequence with all root-position seventh chords (Example 19.9a), parallel fifths and octaves can easily result. To avoid them, alternate complete and incomplete seventh chords (omit the fifth) and resolve all chordal sevenths down, according to their tendency. In the middle of a sequence, the leading tones need not resolve up, but may be pulled down by a descending voice-leading line.
- Sevenths in each chord are prepared by common tone and resolve down by step.
- In a descending-fifth sequence with alternating triads and seventh chords (parts b–d), every chord should be complete, with standard doubling.
- Seventh-chord sequences may alternate between two inversions (part d). Inverted seventh chords are usually complete in four-part settings.

Some of the seventh chords shown in Example 19.9—for example, iii^7, IV^7, vi^6_5, and iii^4_2—are rarely found outside one of these sequences. There are, however, other possible variations of the descending-fifth seventh-chord sequence; you may find some in pieces you are performing, or use Example 19.9 as a model to write your own.

Now listen to another typical setting of the descending-fifth sequence in an excerpt from a Corelli trio sonata (Example 19.10). This passage presents a sequence with seventh chords, as the figured bass clearly shows, all in root position like the model in Example 19.9a. (Consider the bass pitches on each beat to be the primary bass line.) The chordal sevenths are prepared by common tone and resolved as a string of 7–6 suspensions, alternating between first and second violin: for example, the seventh of the chord on beat 1 of measure 23, C5, is prepared by a consonant tenth in measure 22 and resolves down by step to B4 on beat 2. These preparations and resolutions are built in to the framework, demonstrating the close link between sequences—even those associated with a strong root progression like this one—and the resolution of dissonant intervals in counterpoint.

EXAMPLE 19.10: Corelli, Allemanda, from Trio Sonata in A Minor, mm. 22b–24

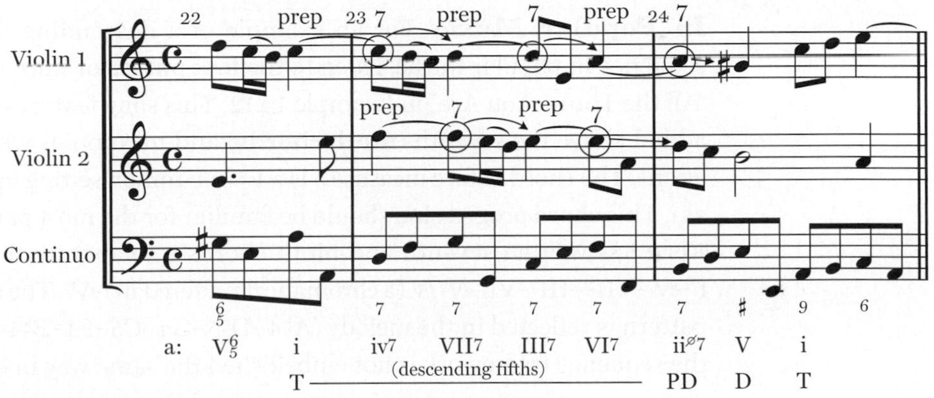

Occasionally with a sequence in a transitional passage, where Roman numerals (or a stable tonic key) are hard to determine, chord symbols or other shorthand notation can help you identify the chord roots and qualities. In Example 19.11, drawn from Bach's Invention in F Major, the two-chord pattern takes place within a single measure, with a change of chord on the second beat. If you mark each repetition of the pattern with brackets and add the chord roots and qualities, your analysis might look something like the one below. From this analysis, you can identify the sequence by its root motion down by fifths and by the pattern of alternating seventh chords, without assigning Roman numerals. You would then need to consider a larger musical context to determine the role of this sequence in the work as a whole.

Example 19.11: Bach, Invention in F Major, mm. 21–24

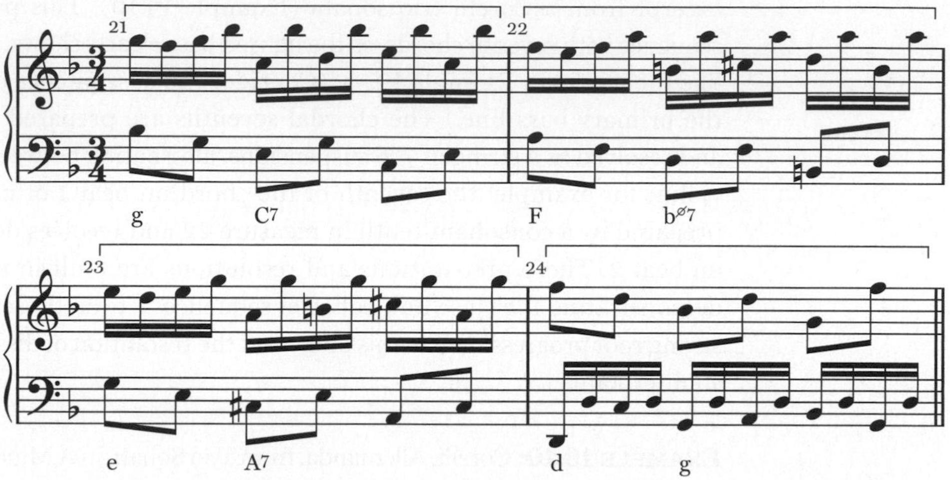

In Popular Music For an example of a descending-fifth seventh-chord sequence in popular music, listen to the first phrase of Kern and Hammerstein's "All the Things You Are" in Example 19.12. This song features chords with a third added above the seventh (**ninth chords**) and harmonies with chromatic alterations. The chord before measure 5 is a V^7 in F minor, setting up the F minor chord as i. This chord progression should be familiar for the most part: instead of triads, Kern has written seventh and ninth chords to elaborate the root progression i^7–iv^7–VII^9_7–III^7–VI^7–V^7/V (a chromatically altered ii^7)–V^7. The two-chord sequence pattern is reflected in the melody (A♭4–D♭5–G4–C5–F4–B♮4–E♮4). In this piece, the sequence framework is not embellished the same way in each pattern.

Example 19.12: Kern and Hammerstein, "All the Things You Are," mm. 5–12 (descending-fifth sequence with seventh chords)

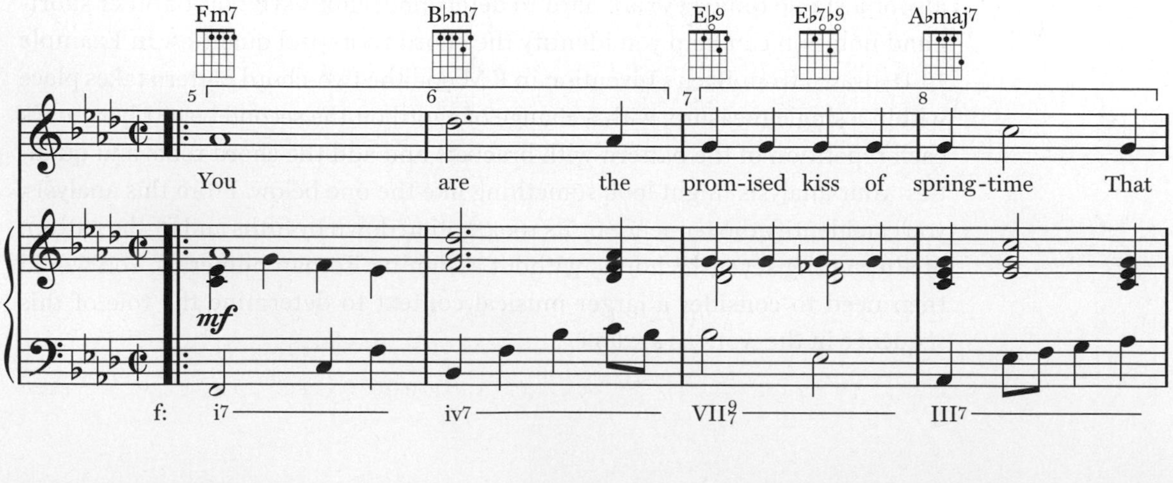

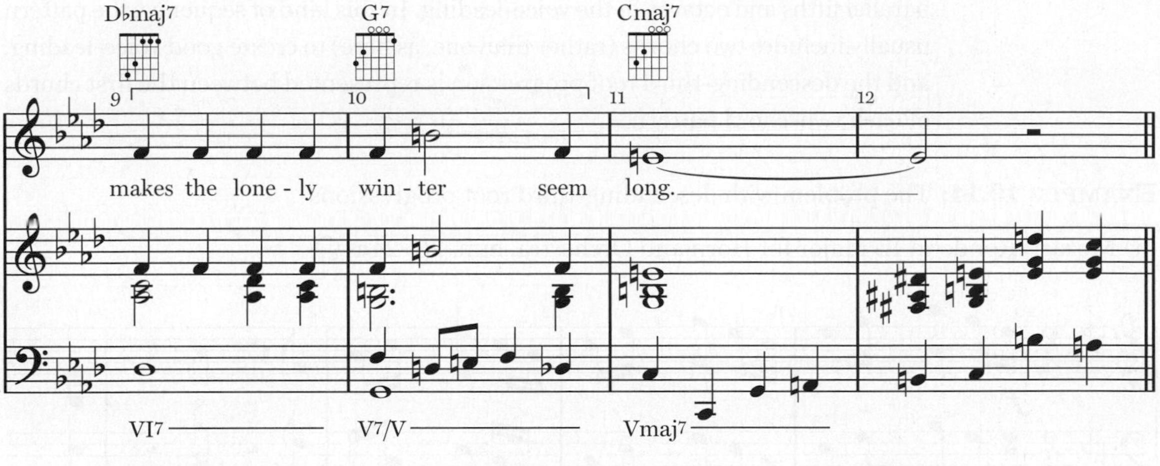

Try it #3

In Example 19.12, where do you hear differences from the expected diatonic sequence? Circle on the example the chord symbols for the nondiatonic chords. Which diatonic chord does each replace?

While possible, ascending-fifth sequences (see Example 19.13) are much less common than descending-fifth. All the root progressions in this type of sequence, except these at the beginning and end, are atypical of common-practice harmony.

Example 19.13: Framework for an ascending-fifth sequence

Descending-Third Sequences

Example 19.14a, from Mozart's Horn Rondo in E♭ Major, features a melodic sequence where the pattern is transposed down by thirds. If the arpeggiated chords that are implied by the sequence pattern are stacked up in thirds, there are parallel fifths and octaves in the voice-leading. In this kind of sequence, the pattern usually includes two chords (rather than one, as here) to create good voice-leading, and the descending-third root progression is represented between the first chords of each two-chord pattern.

Example 19.14: The problem with descending-third root progressions

(a) Mozart, Rondo in E♭ Major for Horn and Orchestra, mm. 20–24a

(b) Reduction of mm. 20–24a

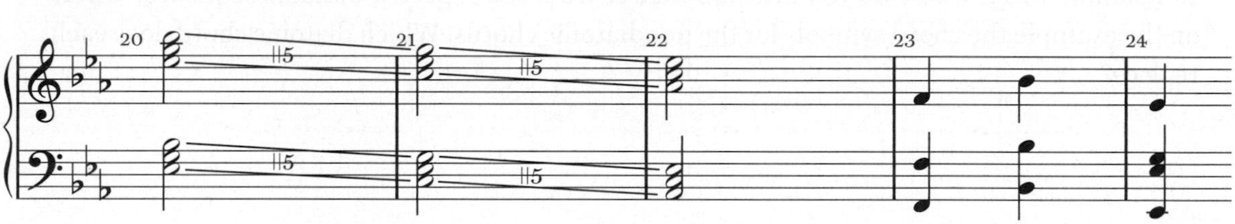

In music literature, you sometimes find these sequences with a stepwise descending bass line. This progression alternates root-position chords with interpolated first-inversion chords—usually I–V6–vi–iii6–IV–I6–ii, where the descending thirds are I–vi–IV–ii, and ii serves as a predominant to prepare the cadence. Since this pattern is two chords long, the underlying progression (I–vi–IV–ii) is somewhat concealed.

Listen, for an example, to the opening of Hensel's "Neue Liebe, neues Leben" (Example 19.15a), which employs a descending-third sequence with a stepwise bass. The entire texture—melody, bass line, and accompaniment upper voices—follows a sequential pattern, repeating down a third each measure, and breaking off after the third statement of the pattern, just before the half cadence in measures 3–4. Part (b) gives the underlying voice-leading framework for the song. Like many sequences, this one expands the tonic before the arrival on a half cadence at the end of the phrase, as indicated by the contextual analysis.

EXAMPLE 19.15: Hensel, "Neue Liebe, neues Leben"

(a) Mm. 1–4a

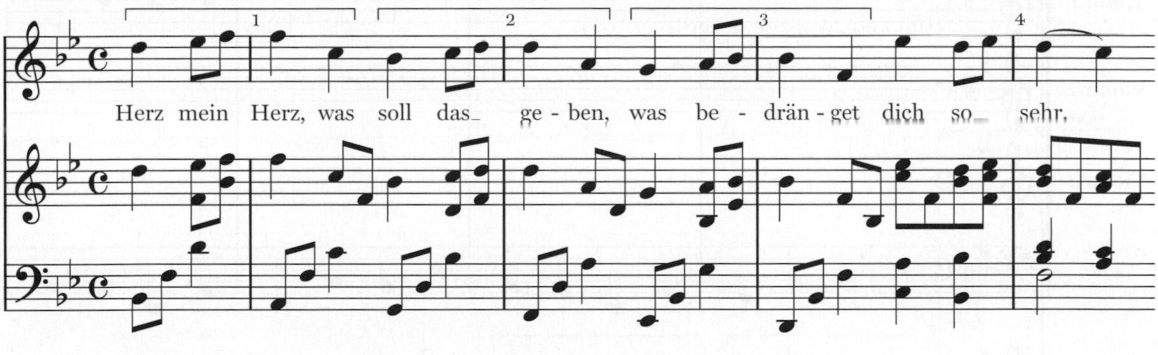

(b) Framework: Descending-third sequence with stepwise bass

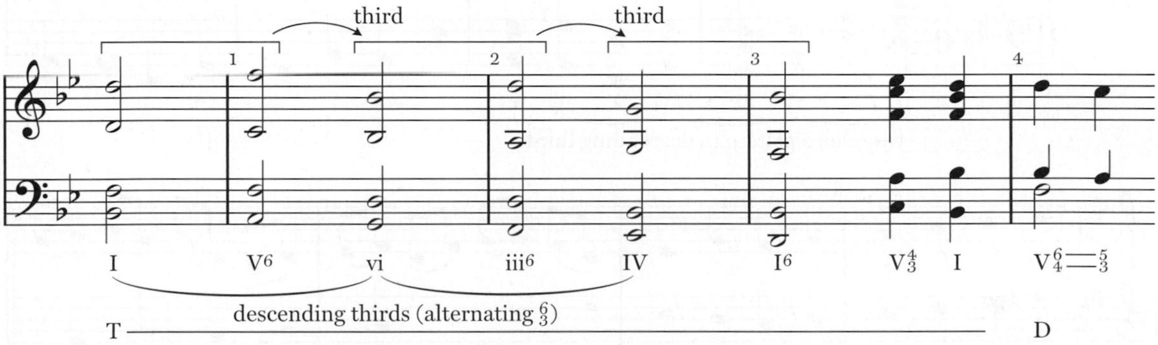

Listen now to one of the most famous harmonic-sequence-based pieces of all—Pachelbel's Canon in D (Example 19.16). Chord-to-chord analysis of the continuo part in measures 1–2 reveals a root-progression pattern of down a fourth, then up a second, until just before the cadence: I–V–vi–iii–IV–I–ii$^6_5$–V^7–I. (In this realization, entire voice-leading strands are doubled at an octave, so there are no forbidden parallels. With the soft dynamic level of a harpsichord, the player might choose a fuller texture like this one before the violin enters in m. 3.) This is a descending-third sequence because alternate chords participate in the progression: it takes two chords to complete the repeated harmonic pattern. Like descending-fifth sequences, descending-third sequences may also include sevenths on some or all of the chords.

EXAMPLE 19.16: Pachelbel, Canon in D Major, mm. 1–8

Pachelbel's progression is quite amenable to sequential melodic patterning. The bass line stays the same throughout the piece, as does the harmonic progression (with slight changes in voicing). The upper parts, however, explore the many possible melodic lines that can be generated from these chords, beginning with scalar patterns and becoming increasingly elaborate. As in the example, violin 1 introduces each new strand, which is answered after two measures by violin 2, then two measures later by violin 3.

Sequences Based on Seconds

Parallel $\frac{6}{3}$ Chords

As mentioned in Chapter 15, a chain of root progressions by second can easily result in parallel fifths and octaves. While this voice-leading problem is more of a concern in common practice than popular styles, most root progressions a second apart feature some sort of intervallic pattern to avoid the fifths and octaves—such as a parallel series of $\frac{6}{3}$ chords (ascending or descending), as shown in Example 19.17. The LIP for this kind of sequence is usually identified 6–6, though the middle voice makes 10–10 (or 3–3) with the bass; both contrapuntal gestures were examined in Chapter 9.

Example 19.17: Parallel $\frac{6}{3}$ chord sequences by descending and ascending second

(a) Descending seconds with parallel $\frac{6}{3}$ chords

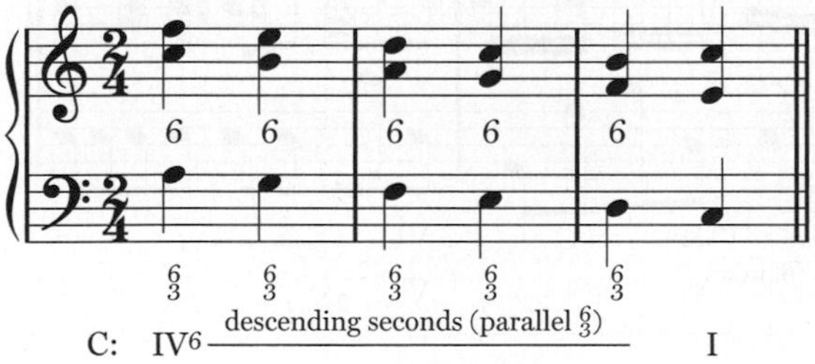

(b) Ascending seconds with parallel $\frac{6}{3}$ chords

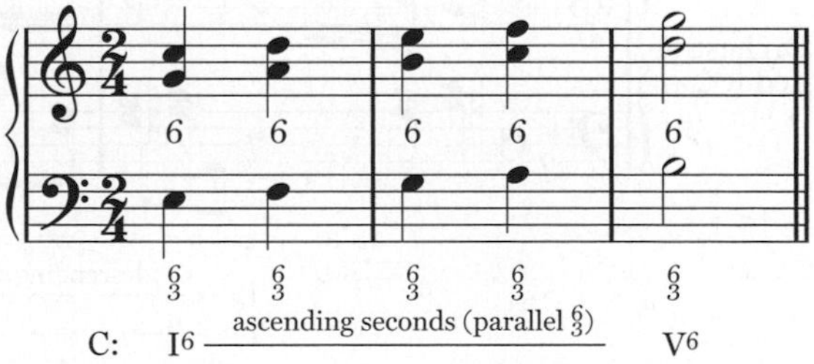

This type of root progression by seconds was not considered in Chapter 15, because in music literature, parallel $\frac{6}{3}$ chords work more like sequences than harmonic progressions: a series of first-inversion triads functions as a linear succession, spanning harmonic pillars, without a strong sense of root motion. In fact, a succession of first-inversion triads is more closely related to doubling a melody in thirds and sixths than it is to independent voice-leading. Further, if you add Roman numerals under this progression, they will not conform to the familiar phrase or root-progression models.

Look, for example, at the passage from Mozart's *Requiem* given in Example 19.18. Beginning with the last beat of measure 27, Mozart employs a succession of $^{6}_{3}$ chords: v6–iv6–III6–♭II6 (first-inversion triads e–d–C–B♭), preceding the half cadence in measure 29. (This altered form of the ii chord will be discussed in Chapter 26.) This progression clearly does not "make sense" according to the principles of harmonic progression presented thus far; however, the linear pattern of parallel $^{6}_{3}$ chords makes it perfectly acceptable, even typical, in common-practice style.

EXAMPLE 19.18: Mozart, Dies irae, from *Requiem*, mm. 27–29 (parallel $^{6}_{3}$ chords)

Translation: As foretold by David and the Sibyl.

7–6 and 5–6 Motion

One way to break up parallel motion when writing sequences of first-inversion triads by step is to delay the arrival of one of the chord members with a suspension or retardation. We have already observed that descending-fifth sequences feature linear patterns such as 7–6 suspensions; these same intervals can be used with a series of $^{6}_{3}$ chords moving down by step as well, as shown in Example 19.19 (a variant on the framework of Example 19.17a) and in Example 19.20, from Handel's Chaconne.

Example 19.19: Descending seconds with parallel $^6_3$ chords (7–6 LIP)

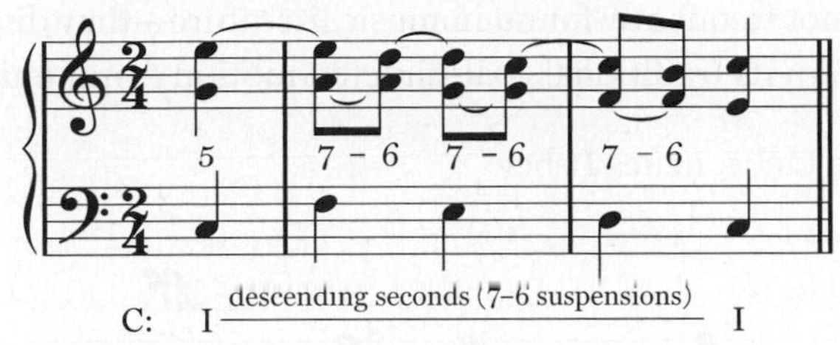

Again, if you analyze the "chords" here with Roman numerals, the root progression does not make much sense; the interval succession does, however, because of the resulting linear sequence, which is drawn from contrapuntal rather than harmonic models. The chain of 7–6 suspensions is often prepared by a 5–6 intervallic motion to set up the first suspension, as in measure 73 of the Handel variation. Listen to this passage to hear how the 7–6 suspensions break up potential parallel motion. As with the other sequences, the 7–6 motion may appear between the bass and any upper voice.

Example 19.20: Handel, Chaconne in G Major, Variation 9, mm. 73–76

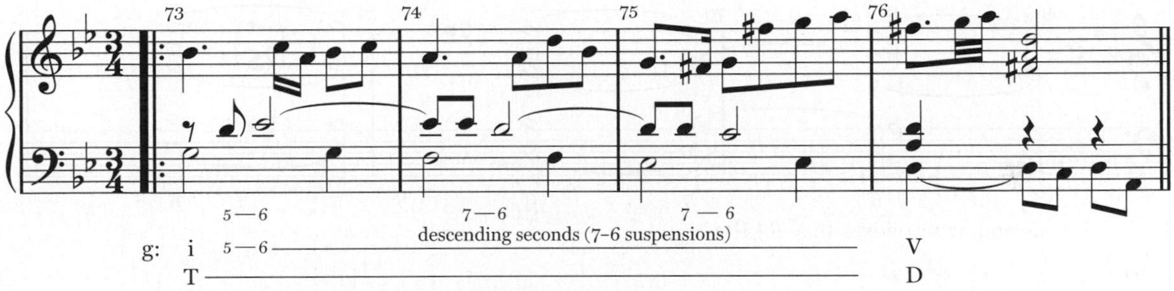

Another sequence framework based on root motion by second is shown in Example 19.21. Here, a series of first-inversion triads moves up by step, but the arrival of the sixth above the bass is delayed a half beat, making a 5–6 LIP.

Example 19.21: Ascending seconds (5–6 LIP)

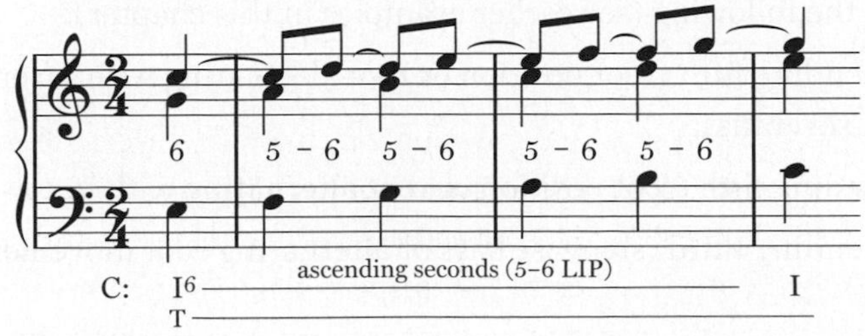

Listen to measures 69–71 of "Neue Liebe, neues Leben" (Example 19.22a) to hear this pattern; again, the 5–6 motion may be between the bass and any upper part.

Ascending sequences like this one, along with the ascending-fifth sequence, though beautiful, are not frequently found in music literature—they divert the harmonic progression from its traditional goal-directed motion from tonic to dominant.

EXAMPLE 19.22: Hensel, "Neue Liebe, neues Leben"

(a) Mm. 69–71 (anthology)

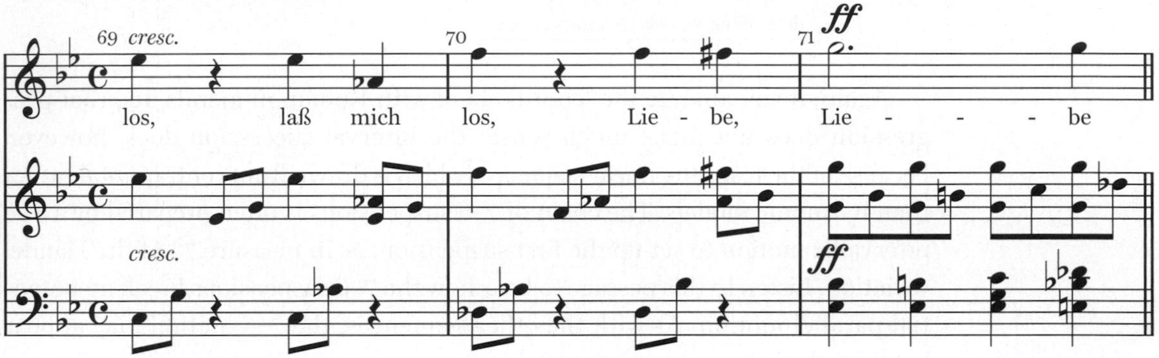

(b) Reduction of mm. 69–71

ascending seconds with 5–6 LIP

SUMMARY

When you encounter a sequence in a piece of music, write a contextual analysis below the Roman numerals to clarify the harmonic function and goal of the passage. You might substitute for beat-by-beat Roman numerals a label on the first and last chord, plus a label that describes the sequence type from among the following (see earlier examples in this chapter):

- descending fifth (root position or root alternating with inversions, possibly with sevenths);
- ascending fifth (root position or root alternating with $^6_3$);
- descending third (stepwise bass or alternating root movements);

- parallel $^6_3$ chords (roots moving by seconds, ascending or descending);
- 7–6 motion (roots descending by seconds);
- 5–6 motion (roots ascending by seconds).

You can also label sequences with brackets to show the pattern, and numbers to show the LIP: 6–6, 10–10, 7–6, and so on.

Finally, remember, that chords within sequences have a weak harmonic function on their own. They serve either to prolong a single harmony (usually in a complete sequence) or to move from one harmonic area to another (when the sequence breaks off in midstream). In performance, focus on broad goals and motion between the harmonic pillars at the beginning and end.

Sequences in Context

Any of the sequence types discussed in this chapter may take on different functions in musical contexts. Sequences are like subways, buses, or trains: you get on at one location, ride for a while, and get off when you reach your destination. Sequences are usually preceded by a chord or harmonic progression that sets up the tonic and key of the starting location, and they usually connect at their termination to a harmonic progression that reestablishes the key. Some "travel" within one key area (like a bus within a city), while others may move from one key to another (like a train that runs between cities), as those in the Bach examples do.

Some sequences, especially harmonic sequences based on the descending-fifth root progression, may be composed of progressions that make sense when analyzed with Roman numerals. Others seem to suspend the sense of progression from the point at which they begin until they connect to a regular harmonic progression at their end. You could think of these as acting like suspension bridges: there are pillars at both ends holding up the bridge, but taut cables strung between them supporting the middle. The sequence patterns with no clear sense of root progression typically have strong intervallic progressions underlying their voice-leading.

Sequences may also serve to expand melodies and phrases (reflected in a contextual analysis). While phrases in many compositions tend to be of a consistent length—such as four measures—sequences tend to subvert these regular subdivisions. Their placement depends on the style of the piece. In Classical-period pieces with regular four-measure phrases, sequences are often found in transitions between groups of regular phrases and in passages where the key area is unstable. A Baroque-era piece may be composed of a series of sequences rather than four-measure phrases. In nineteenth- and twentieth-century works, entire sections may be based on harmonic sequences. We will learn more about each of these uses as we study musical form in later chapters.

Did You Know?

Though basic principles of reduction and embellishment of a framework were known from the early eighteenth century, the concept of linear intervallic patterns underlying sequences stems from the work of Austrian music theorist Heinrich Schenker (1868–1935). Through graphic analysis of Classical- and Romantic-era works, made by reducing out embellishing tones such as passing and neighbor tones to identify the underlying intervallic framework, Schenker demonstrated that the principles of species counterpoint apply as an underlying principle in many passages of common-practice-era music that may not, at first, seem to be contrapuntally based. The term "linear intervallic pattern" and the numerical representations (10–10, 10–7, etc.) for sequence frameworks were popularized in the 1980s by American theorists Allen Forte and Steven Gilbert, in their textbook *Introduction to Schenkerian Analyis* (New York: Norton, 1982).

TERMS YOU SHOULD KNOW

level of transposition
linear intervallic pattern (LIP)
- 5–6 LIP
- 7–6 LIP

parallel $^6_3$ chords

sequence
- diatonic
- chromatic
- harmonic
- melodic
- ascending fifth
- descending fifth
- descending third

sequence pattern

QUESTIONS FOR REVIEW

1. What are sequences? Where will you find them?
2. What do you look for in analyzing a sequence pattern?
3. Which root progressions work well in sequence frameworks?
4. What aspect of harmonic sequences was discussed in a previous chapter?
5. What aspects of dissonance resolution must be retained in sequences?
6. What steps would you take to write a descending-third sequence? How does this sequence type differ from others?
7. In an embellished sequence, how can you tell whch sequence framework (e.g., descending fifth, ascending 5–6) is being used?
8. In music for your own instrument, find two different sequences and label their types.

Secondary Dominants and Leading-Tone Chords to V

Outline of topics

Intensifying the dominant

Secondary dominants to V

- Spelling secondary dominants
- Tonicization and modulation
- Secondary dominants to V in the basic phrase
- Writing and resolving secondary dominants to V
- Cross relations

Secondary leading-tone chords to V

- Writing and resolving secondary leading-tone chords to V

Secondary-function chords in dominant expansions

Overview

This chapter explains how to write and analyze chromatic chords that intensify motion toward the dominant.

Repertoire

Johann Sebastian Bach
"Ermuntre dich, mein schwacher Geist" ("Take Courage, My Weak Spirit")
"Wachet auf" ("Awake," Chorale No. 179)

Scott Joplin, "Pine Apple Rag"

Wolfgang Amadeus Mozart, Rondo in E♭ Major for Horn and Orchestra, K. 371

Elvis Presley and Vera Matson, "Love Me Tender"

Intensifying the Dominant

Listen to a phrase from Bach's setting of "Wachet auf," given in Example 20.1.

EXAMPLE 20.1: Bach, "Wachet auf," mm. 6b–11

The phrase begins with a prolonged tonic (mm. 7–8) and ends with a half cadence in measure 11. The two A♮s, marked with arrows, in measures 9 and 10 represent a raised $\hat{4}$. Write this scale degree as $\sharp\hat{4}$, to symbolize the chromatic inflection of $\hat{4}$ up by half step, even in flat keys (as here) where the score notation calls for a natural rather than a sharp.

This $\sharp\hat{4}$ changes the function of the last chord of measure 9: F-A♮-C-E♭ in first inversion (the B♭ on beat 3 is an accented passing tone). Although this chord is built on $\hat{2}$ in E♭ major, it is not a ii^6_5 chord, because its bass is the nondiatonic pitch A♮ instead of A♭. The quality of the chord reveals its local function: it is a dominant seventh chord. Dominant sevenths—whether built on $\hat{5}$ or not, whether diatonic or not—generally function like dominants, even if only in a localized way.

If you found this dominant seventh (F-A♮-C-E♭) written without a key context, you could determine its implied tonic in one of two ways:

- count a P5 down (or P4 up) from its root, or
- move a m2 up from the chord's third (A♮, the leading tone).

Both methods reveal that this V^7 should resolve to either B♭ major or B♭ minor as its tonic. In fact, both F-A♮-C-E♭ chords in measures 9–10 resolve to B♭ major (V in E♭) on the next beat; they function like "temporary dominants" to the V chord.

KEY CONCEPT Chords that act like dominants in their spelling and resolution, but resolve to a scale degree and harmony other than the tonic, are called **secondary dominants**. They are analyzed as V/V (read "V of V").

Secondary dominants are sometimes called "applied dominants" (a type of **applied chord**, because they are "applied" to a chord other than the tonic) or "secondary-function" chords. In Roman numeral analysis, applied dominants are sometimes notated with arrows that point to their chord of resolution, rather than the "slash" notation used here.

Look again at Example 20.1. We can now provide all the Roman numerals for measures 9 and 10: V^6 V^6_5/V | V V/V, ending with a half cadence on V (m. 11). Each A♮ ($\sharp\hat{4}$) functions as a "temporary" leading tone to $\hat{5}$, intensifying the arrival on the half cadence. Measures 9–11 prolong the dominant harmony. The chorale, however, clearly stays in E♭ major, with the next phrase beginning on the tonic and concluding with a PAC.

Secondary Dominants to V

Spelling Secondary Dominants

To understand secondary dominants to V, first think of V as a temporary tonic key rather than a chord, and then imagine what the dominant (or dominant seventh) chord would be in that temporary key. For example, in C major, the temporary tonic key would be G major, and *its* dominant harmony D major. So V/V in C major is a D major chord (D-F♯-A); the F♯ in G major's key signature is crucial in spelling the secondary dominant correctly. In music literature, though, you are more likely to find secondary dominant seventh chords (V^7/V) rather than thirds, since their Mm7 chord quality marks them unambiguously as having a dominant function (D-F♯-A-C). In either case, the music has not left the primary key; the idea of imagining a temporary new tonic is a simple aid in spelling the secondary dominant correctly.

Another way to think of the secondary dominant in major keys is as an altered predominant chord: raise the third of the diatonic ii chord to give it a major or dominant seventh quality (II or II^7). The chord quality resulting from this chromatic alteration, together with the voice-leading and resolution of the chord, define it as a secondary dominant (which we will label V/V or V^7/V).

All V7/V or V/V chords are spelled by raising $\hat{4}$ to $\sharp\hat{4}$, which functions as the leading tone to V. To spell a secondary dominant in a minor key, however, two chromatic alterations are necessary: $\hat{4}$ is raised to $\sharp\hat{4}$, and $\flat\hat{6}$ is raised to $\hat{6}$. Imagine, for example, C minor (three flats) and the temporary minor-dominant key of G minor (two flats). The change in key signatures provides the raised $\flat\hat{6}$ (A♭ to A♮), and changing $\hat{4}$ to $\sharp\hat{4}$ (F to F♯) creates the temporary leading tone and the dominant seventh (Mm7) quality. In sum, V7/V in C minor is spelled D-F♯-A♮-C, just as in C major.

KEY CONCEPT To spell a secondary dominant to V, double-check that

- the chord is built on $\hat{2}$ (a fifth above $\hat{5}$),
- the triad quality is major (with $\sharp\hat{4}$; in minor, also raise $\flat\hat{6}$ to $\hat{6}$), and
- the chordal seventh (if present) is minor, creating a Mm7 chord.

Secondary dominants to V may be found in many styles, including rock music, popular songs, and show tunes. Example 20.2 shows the opening phrase of "Love Me Tender." The dominant seventh chord in measure 7 is intensified by an A7 chord, V7/V, in measure 6; the C♯ here acts as a temporary leading tone to D, the dominant. (You can get a snapshot of the harmonic motion from the chord symbols above the staff. The D7sus in m. 7 accounts for the 9–8 and 4–3 suspensions.)

EXAMPLE 20.2: Presley and Matson, "Love Me Tender," mm. 5–8

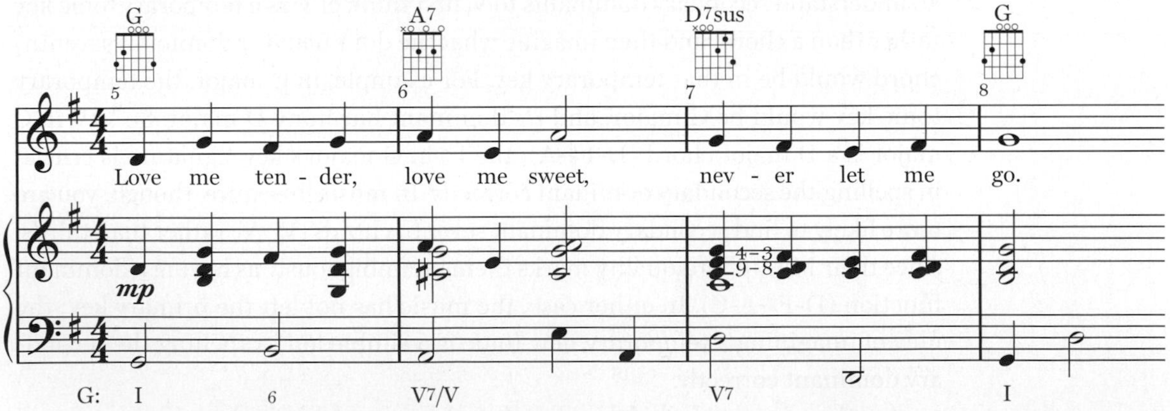

The secondary dominant to V is one of the most common chromatic chords—often found at phrase endings, preceding the dominant of an authentic or half cadence, or in other passages where the dominant harmony is prolonged. Practice spelling V7/V in various keys, and look for it in pieces you play (the presence of $\sharp\hat{4}$ is an important clue).

SUMMARY

To spell V7/V in any key:

(a) • Imagine the dominant harmony as a temporary tonic key (in A major, imagine E major as the tonic; in A minor, imagine E minor as the tonic).
• Using that key signature and key, spell its dominant seventh chord (in E major or minor, V7 is B-D♯-F♯-A).

(b) Or build a dominant seventh chord on $\hat{2}$ of the primary key (in E major or E minor, B-D♯-F♯-A).

With either method, double-check that the chord has the appropriate accidentals to create a Mm 7 quality.

Try it #1

For each of the keys below, build a secondary dominant seventh chord by imagining first the V chord as a temporary key area, and then finding the dominant of this key area. (You can double-check your answer by means of the altered ii chord method.) Where pitches are already given, supply the name of the key.

KEY	V KEY AREA	V7/V	KEY	V KEY AREA	V7/V
(a) B♭ major	F major	C-E♮-G-B♭	(f) D major	A major	______
(b) E minor	B minor	______	(g) ______	B♭ major	F-A-C-E♭
(c) ______	G minor	D-F♯-A-C	(h) ______	F♯ major	C♯-E♯-G♯-B
(d) A major	E major	______	(i) G minor	D minor	______
(e) ______	E♭ major	B♭-D-F-A♭	(j) ______	C♯ minor	G♯-B♯-D♯-F♯

Tonicization and Modulation

When a secondary dominant resolves, making its chord of resolution seem like a temporary tonic, the effect is called **tonicization**. When a harmony like V is tonicized, the key of the passage does not change except in a very temporary sense. The temporary tonic then returns to its normal functional role in the primary key and progresses as usual.

Tonicizations of greater structural significance are called **modulations**. To identify a modulation, look for such musical indications as a continuation of the passage in the new key, or the presence of a predominant harmony in the new key.

Example 20.3 shows another of Bach's chorale settings, an example of tonicization. Phrase 1 ends in measure 4 with V/V (including a 4–3 suspension), tonicizing V (D) at the half cadence. Immediately after the fermata, phrase 2 begins clearly in G major with a tonic chord. The Roman numerals illustrate another way to analyze secondary dominants, with "bracket notation": the tonicized chords are labeled briefly as though in the key of V, with a bracket labeled with the Roman numeral of the tonicized key. Be careful not to confuse the "I" chord under the fermata (in the dominant key) with the I chord after the fermata (in the tonic key). Bracket notation is particularly appropriate if there is more than one secondary dominant in a row, or if the V/V is embellished with a cadential $^6_4$ or a suspension, as here.

EXAMPLE 20.3: Bach, "Ermuntre dich, mein schwacher Geist," mm. 1–8

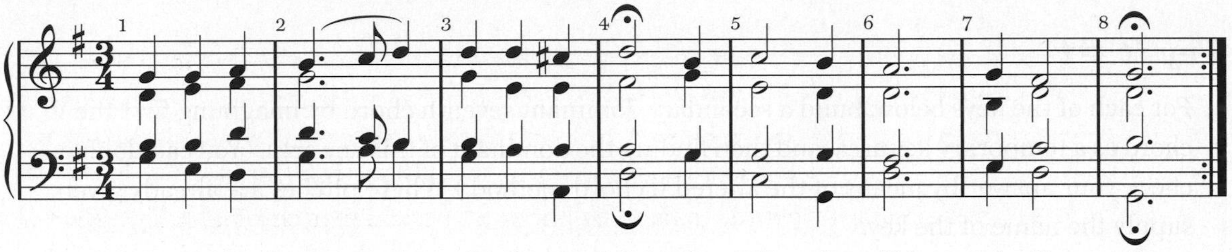

Secondary Dominants to V in the Basic Phrase

The most common role for V^7/V or V/V in the basic phrase is to replace or follow a predominant-function harmony, as in Example 20.4. You could think of V^7/V as a supercharged ii^7: the raised $\hat{4}$ combined with the descending-fifth root progression (already present between ii^7 and V) makes a very strong pull toward V—as though the V^7/V were functioning as a predominant. Because the V^7/V "belongs to" the dominant, its temporary key, place it in the dominant area of the phrase.

EXAMPLE 20.4: Typical contexts for a secondary dominant

(a) Preceded by IV

(b) Preceded by ii

(c) Preceded by IV

(d) Preceded by ii6

As in progressions from V to I, you can control the strength of the harmonic progression between the secondary dominant and temporary tonic by the choice of inversion and whether to include the seventh. The V$^6_5$/V, for example, is a typical inversion choice because it can allow a chromatic ascent to V in the bass line $\hat{4}$–♯$\hat{4}$–$\hat{5}$ (parts c and d).

One way to produce a strong and smooth connection between the predominant harmony and V7/V is by writing a **chromatic voice exchange**. Typically, the voice exchange occurs between the bass and an inner voice, as in Example 20.5. Part (a) shows a diatonic version of the voice exchange (with $\hat{6}$ and $\hat{4}$), embellished by a passing I$^6_4$ chord. In part (b), the voice exchange is chromatically inflected between $\hat{6}$ and ♯$\hat{4}$. For a voice exchange to be considered chromatic, at least one pitch must appear in both its diatonic form and its chromatically inflected form (here, D♭ and D♮).

Example 20.5: Diatonic and chromatic voice exchange

(a) Diatonic

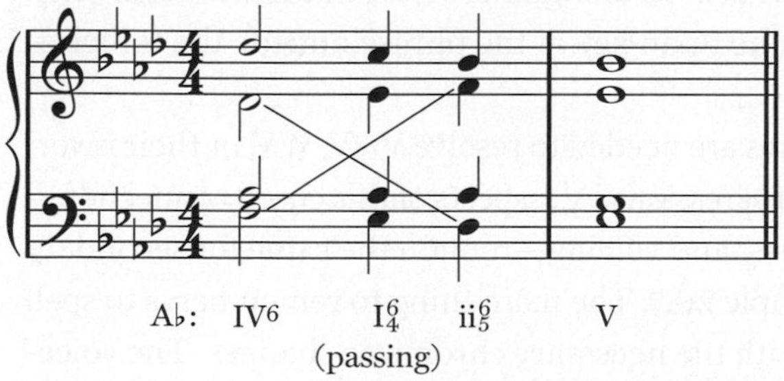

(b) Chromatic

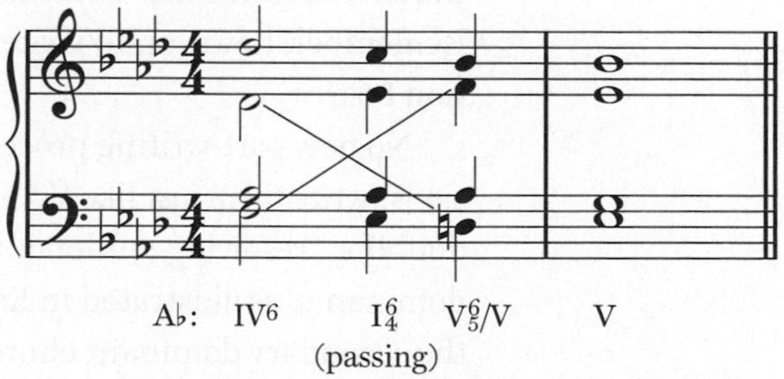

The V7/V may also be expanded by a cadential $^6_4$ in the tonicized key, as in Example 20.6. In measure 11, the voice-leading of the cadential $^6_4$ in the tonicized dominant key (F major) is the same as it would be in the tonic key, and the bracket notation makes this voice-leading clear. The secondary dominant (C-E♮-G-B♭) then resolves to V in measure 12, making a half cadence. This is only a half cadence and not a modulation to F major, as the phrase that begins in measure 13 starts out the same as the first one, firmly in the key of B♭ major.

Example 20.6: Joplin, "Pine Apple Rag," mm. 5–12

Writing and Resolving Secondary Dominants to V

Since you already have written dominant-to-tonic progressions, you may find it helpful to think of the two-chord secondary-dominant progression as being in a temporary key for just those two chords. Imagine that the two chords have a box around them, representing the boundary for the temporary key. Spell and resolve the chords inside this "tonicization box" as though they were in the temporary key. Remember, however, to write in the main key of the phrase outside the tonicization box.

No new part-writing procedures are needed to resolve V7/V, V/V, or their inversions; write them just like V(7)–I progressions. All aspects of this chord connection—doubling, resolving tendency tones, and voicing—remain the same for secondary dominants, as illustrated in Example 20.7. The main thing to remember is to spell the secondary dominant chord with the necessary chromatic changes. The voice-leading guidelines below are identical for major and minor keys.

KEY CONCEPT Writing and resolving a V7/V in common-practice style:

- Avoid doubling the $\sharp\hat{4}$ (because of its leading-tone function).
- Resolve the temporary leading tone up ($\sharp\hat{4}$ resolves up to $\hat{5}$).
- Resolve the chordal seventh down ($\hat{1}$ resolves down to $\hat{7}$).

Resolving root-position chords:

1. When moving from a V/V to a V, both chords are complete and resolve normally (Example 20.7a).
2. When moving from a complete root-position V7/V to a root-position V, the V will be incomplete (with three roots and a third) if you resolve all the tendency tones correctly (part b).
3. If you want to resolve a root-position V7/V to a complete V chord, as for a HC,
   - use an incomplete V7/V (missing its fifth; part c); alternatively,
   - let the temporary leading tone skip instead to the fifth of the V (part d). The note to which the leading tone *should* resolve is usually in another voice (as shown by the dotted arrow).
4. The V chord to which the secondary dominant resolves may be embellished by a cadential $^6_4$ (part e).

EXAMPLE 20.7: Resolutions of V/V and V7/V

C = complete chord; I = incomplete chord

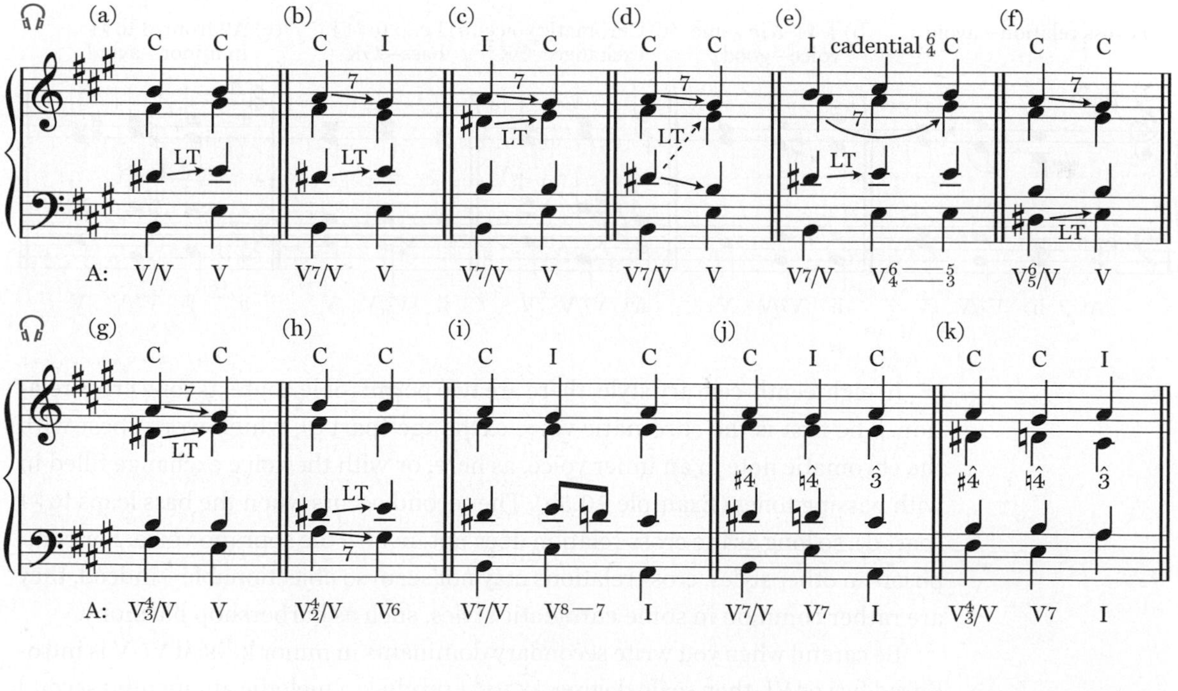

If the V7/V is inverted, this chord and the V chord to which it resolves are usually both complete (parts f–h). Often, the resolution to V is embellished by 8–7 motion before a cadence on I (part i): the ♯$\hat{4}$ moves to $\hat{5}$ first, then down to ♮$\hat{4}$.

When V^7/V resolves directly to a dominant seventh chord, one important voice-leading guideline changes: the $\sharp\hat{4}$ shifts downward (not up to $\hat{5}$) to become the seventh of V^7 (parts j and k). Here, as the V^7 resolves to I, the downward pull of $\sharp\hat{4}$–$\natural\hat{4}$–$\hat{3}$ overcomes the upward tendency of the temporary leading tone.

Cross Relations

When a secondary dominant is preceded by one of the predominant chords, IV or ii, then the chromatic alteration of $\hat{4}$ to $\sharp\hat{4}$ should be handled carefully.

KEY CONCEPT The sudden introduction of $\sharp\hat{4}$ in one voice right after the diatonic $\hat{4}$ sounds in another voice, called a **cross relation** (Example 20.8a), is generally avoided in common-practice music. Keep the diatonic pitch in the same voice as the chromatically altered pitch (part b): $\hat{4}$–$\sharp\hat{4}$–$\hat{5}$.

EXAMPLE 20.8: Avoiding voice-leading problems

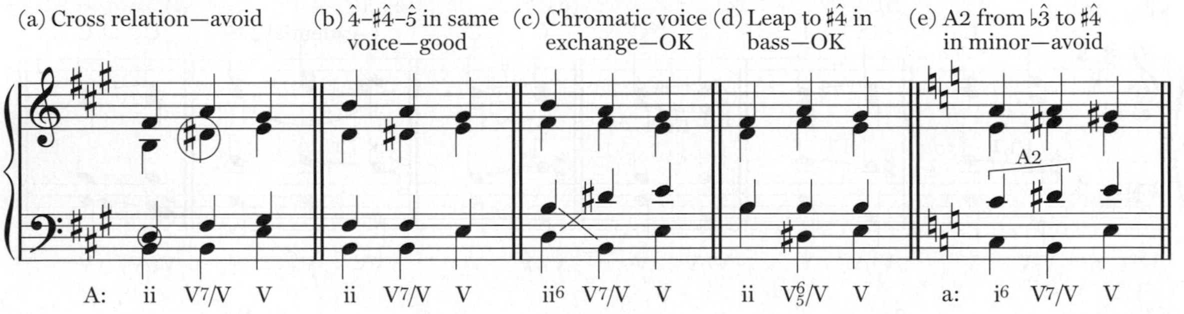

In eighteenth-century style, there are two permissible contexts for a cross relation. The first is the chromatic voice exchange (part c), which works best with the chromatic note in an inner voice, as here, or with the voice exchange filled in with passing tones (Example 20.5b). The second occurs when the bass leaps to $\sharp\hat{4}$ (part d), so long as the cross relation does not involve the soprano voice. For composers in other styles, cross relations may not seem so objectionable—indeed, they are rather common in some chromatic styles, such as barbershop harmony.

Be careful when you write secondary dominants in minor keys: if V^7/V is introduced by i or VI, then scale degrees $\flat\hat{3}$ to $\sharp\hat{4}$ produce a melodic augmented second (part e). You can avoid this by approaching the chromatic tone from above (e.g., $\hat{5}$ to $\sharp\hat{4}$).

Secondary Leading-Tone Chords to V

Since leading-tone chords can substitute for V chords as a dominant function in many progressions, secondary leading-tone chords to V can likewise substitute for secondary dominants to V, in any progression where a weaker sense of the dominant is desired. Most common of the secondary leading-tone chords is the fully diminished vii$^{\circ 7}$/V and its inversions $^6_5$ and $^4_3$; less common are the vii$^{\circ 6}$/V and vii$^{\varnothing 7}$/V.

KEY CONCEPT To spell a vii$^{\circ 7}$/V chord in any key:

1. Begin on the pitch a diatonic half step below $\hat{5}$ (on $\sharp\hat{4}$).
2. Spell a fully diminished seventh chord (all minor thirds above the root).

Try it #2

For each key below, build a vii$^{\circ 7}$/V chord by imagining first the V chord as a key area, and then finding the seventh chord built on its leading tone.

KEY	V KEY AREA	vii$^{\circ 7}$/V	KEY	V KEY AREA	vii$^{\circ 7}$/V
(a) C minor	G minor	F♯-A♮-C-E♭	(f) F major	C major	
(b) E♭ major	B♭ major		(g)	F major	E-G-B♭-D♭
(c)	C minor	B♮-D♮-F-A♭	(h) D♭ major	A♭ major	
(d) A minor	E minor		(i) G minor	D minor	
(e) E major	B major		(j)	F♯ major	E♯-G♯-B-D

Writing and Resolving Secondary Leading-Tone Chords to V

All aspects of the connection between the secondary leading-tone chord and its temporary tonic (V)—doubling, resolving the tendency tone(s), and voicing—are the same as for vii$^{\circ 7}$ to I. The one element requiring close attention is spelling. Make $\sharp\hat{4}$ (the temporary leading tone) the root of the chord, then be sure that the chord has a fully diminished seventh quality (most typical), or half-diminished quality (less common, used to tonicize major triads only). To write a secondary vii$^{\circ}$7, spell the chord as a stack of minor thirds above $\sharp\hat{4}$ (in major keys, $\hat{3}$ needs to be lowered a half step); for vii^{ø}7, the top third will be a major third. Example 20.9 gives some characteristic resolutions.

KEY CONCEPT When you resolve secondary leading-tone chords to V:

- Resolve $\sharp\hat{4}$ (the temporary leading tone) up to $\hat{5}$ (Example 20.9a–f, i–j).
- Resolve the chordal seventh down (from $\hat{3}$ or $\flat\hat{3}$ to $\hat{2}$, as in parts b–h and j).
- Avoid d5 to P5 unless you can place them in the inner voices (parts a, f, and h), or unless you can write parallel tenths between the soprano and bass (part i); A4 to P4 is okay.
- Be careful not to double the third in the chord of resolution (V)—it's the leading tone in the primary key.

In Example 20.9, part (b) shows the half-diminished version of the seventh chord, while the remaining parts feature the more typical fully diminished version. Parts (e) through (h) give short progressions to the tonic, with stepwise bass lines and the secondary leading-tone chord in inversion. As was the case with secondary dominants, the resolution to a V7 chord involves one change in the voice-leading guidelines: $\sharp\hat{4}$ resolves down through $\natural\hat{4}$ to $\hat{3}$ (g and h); or it moves to $\hat{5}$ first, introducing 8–7 motion (j).

Example 20.9: Resolutions of the secondary leading-tone seventh chord

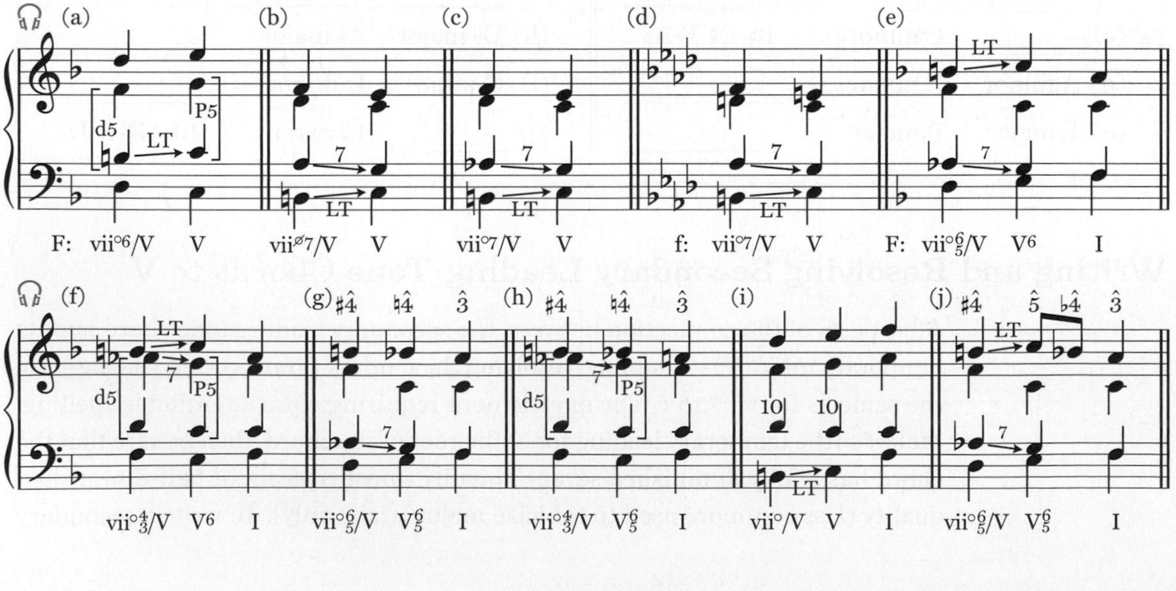

Secondary-Function Chords in Dominant Expansions

As the tonic area can be expanded with V or vii chords, so can the dominant area be expanded with secondary dominant or leading-tone chords. Write these progressions with the same voice-leading, but replace I prolonged by V with V prolonged by $V^{(7)}$/V or $vii^{\circ(7)}$/V.

The excerpt in Example 20.10, a dominant expansion from Mozart's Horn Rondo in E♭ Major, begins with a strong E♭ major tonic arpeggiation, followed by the dominant. Then in measure 90, with the introduction of $\sharp\hat{4}$ (A♮), V^7/V chords begin to alternate with V chords; this dominant expansion continues until measure 96. At that point, the dominant harmony becomes V^7 and is arpeggiated until its eventual resolution to the tonic in measure 101, where the rondo's first theme is restated. (To read the horn's pitches [scored in E♭]: when the player sees a notated C, the horn produces the E♭ a major sixth below. For example, the G5–E5 in m. 88 will sound as B♭4–G4.)

Example 20.10: Mozart, Rondo in E♭ Major for Horn and Orchestra, mm. 88–104a

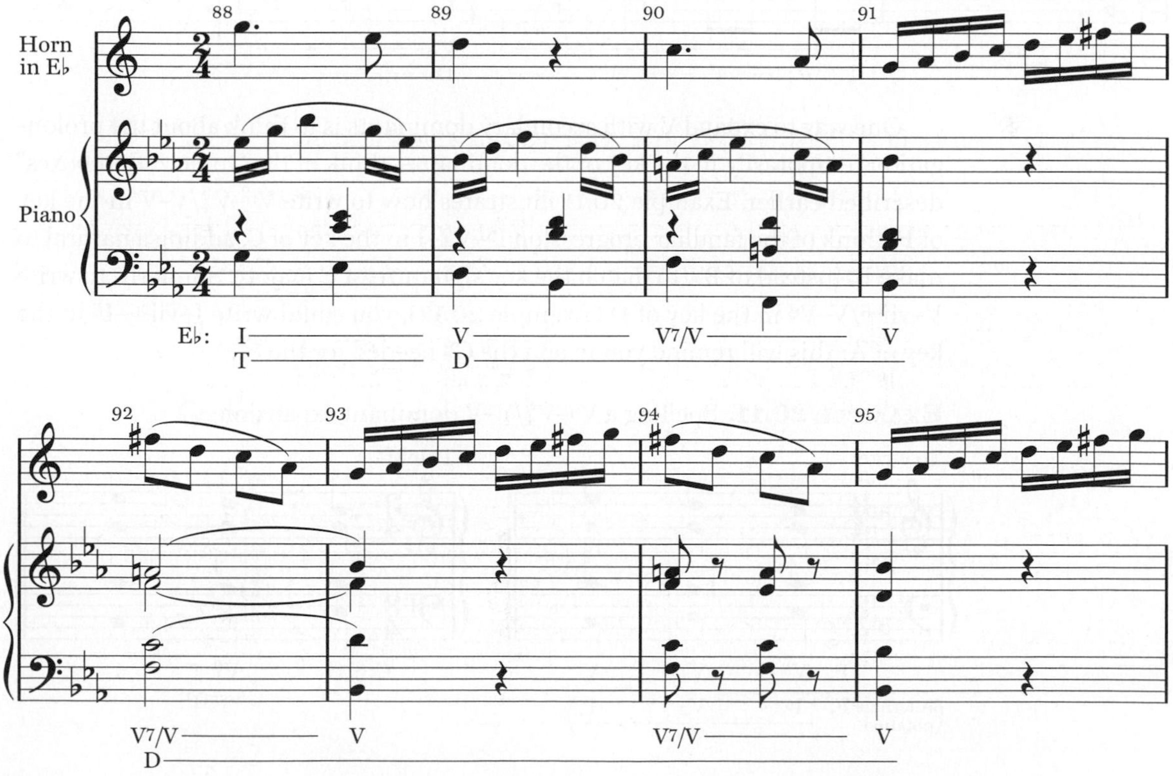

One way to expand V with secondary dominants is to think about the prolongation temporarily in the key of the dominant—think of the "tonicization boxes" described earlier. Example 20.11 illustrates how to write V^6–V^6_4/V–V in the key of F: think of the familiar progression I^6–V^6_4–I in the key of C, adding a natural to make B♮ instead of B♭ (to match the key signature of C major). Similarly, to write V–$vii^{\circ 6}$/V–V^6 in the key of D (Example 20.12), you could write I–$vii^{\circ 6}$–I^6 in the key of A: this will remind you to add the G♯ needed for the ♯$\hat{4}$.

EXAMPLE 20.11: Spelling a V^6–V^6_4/V–V dominant expansion

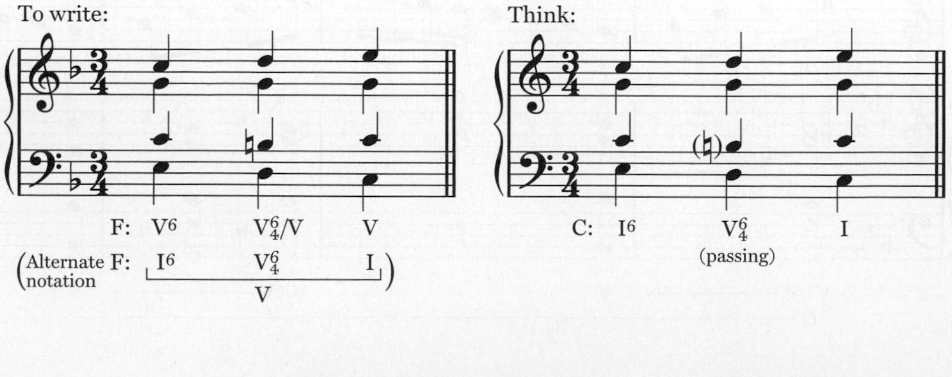

Example 20.12: Spelling a V–vii°6/V–V6 dominant expansion

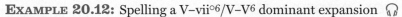

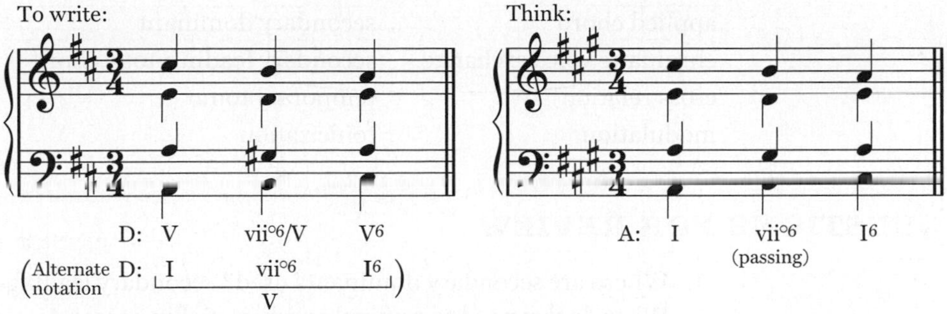

Secondary dominant and leading-tone chords to V possess distinctive features that will help you identify them quickly when you prepare a harmonic analysis. The first is their location within the phrase: V/V and vii°7/V often appear immediately after the predominant area, followed by the dominant or cadential $\frac{6}{4}$. As we've seen, they may also be found between two dominants as voice-leading chords expanding the dominant area.

A second clue is the chromatically altered ♯$\hat{4}$: if you spot this scale degree, check for its resolution to $\hat{5}$. Then check the quality and resolution of the chord—a V7 or vii°7 that is not diatonic may be functioning as a secondary dominant or leading-tone chord.

Did You Know?

J. S. Bach wrote an entire cantata based on the "Wachet auf" chorale—Cantata No. 140, scored for choir, soloists, and small orchestra and written for the twenty-seventh Sunday after the liturgical season of Trinity begins. The hymn text, from about 1731, was written by Philipp Nicolai:

> Wake up! the voice calls to us; the watchman very high on the walls calls, Wake up, you city of Jerusalem! Midnight this hour is called, they call us with bright voices, Where are you, clever young women? Wake up, the bridegroom comes, stand up, take up the lamps! Halleluia! Make yourselves ready for the wedding. You must go out to meet him.

This text draws on the ancient Christian symbolism of Jesus as the bridegroom and the wedding as the joining of Jesus with people on earth. The chorale, exhorting humanity to wake up and prepare for Christ's coming, is now often associated with Advent, the weeks immediately preceding Christmas.

TERMS YOU SHOULD KNOW

applied chord	secondary dominant
chromatic voice exchange	secondary leading-tone chord
cross relation	temporary tonic
modulation	tonicization

QUESTIONS FOR REVIEW

1. Where are secondary dominants used? secondary leading-tone chords?
2. What do you need to remember when spelling secondary dominants? secondary leading-tone chords?
3. What are the special voice-leading guidelines for resolving secondary dominant chords? secondary leading-tone chords?
4. Under what circumstances are cross relations permitted in common-practice style?
5. In music for your own instrument, find two examples of secondary dominants (in two different pieces or keys). What guidelines can help you scan the score and find them quickly?

Tonicizing Scale Degrees Other Than V

Outline of topics

Secondary-function chords within the basic phrase

- Identifying secondary dominant and leading-tone chords

Secondary-function chords in musical contexts

- Tonicizing harmonies within a phrase
- Providing a temporary harmonic diversion
- Creating forward momentum
- Evading an expected resolution
- Text painting

Spelling secondary dominant and leading-tone chords

Resolving secondary dominant and leading-tone chords

- Embellished resolutions
- Irregular resolutions

Secondary dominants in sequences

Overview

In this chapter, we examine secondary dominants and secondary leading-tone chords that tonicize harmonies other than V. We also consider how these chords fit within the basic phrase model and how to interpret them in performance.

Repertoire

Johann Sebastian Bach
- "Es ist gewisslich an der Zeit" ("It Is Certainly the Time," Chorale No. 260)
- Prelude in C Major, from *The Well-Tempered Clavier*, Book I

Ludwig van Beethoven, Piano Sonata in C Minor, Op. 13 (*Pathétique*), second movement

Fanny Mendelssohn Hensel, "Neue Liebe, neues Leben"

Scott Joplin, "Solace"

Alan Menken and Tim Rice, "A Whole New World," from *Aladdin*

Wolfgang Amadeus Mozart
- Piano Sonata in D Major, K. 284, third movement
- *Variations on "Ah, vous dirai-je Maman"*

John Philip Sousa, "The Stars and Stripes Forever"

Secondary-Function Chords Within the Basic Phrase

As you analyze secondary dominants and secondary leading-tone chords in the sections that follow, remember that although Roman numerals will distinguish between them, these chords serve the same purpose: to intensify the chords to which they resolve.

Listen to measures 5–8 of "The Stars and Stripes Forever," and consider the function of the chromatic tones. Are they embellishing tones, or do they change the chord qualities?

Example 21.1: Sousa, "The Stars and Stripes Forever," mm. 5–8

You probably identified the E♮5 in measure 7 as a chromatic neighbor tone, which has no effect on chord quality or function. Likewise, you may have heard the B♮4 in the alto voice of measure 5 as a chromatic passing tone, but this inflection of B♭ to B♮ changes the chord quality: it creates a dominant seventh (G-B♮-D-F), rather than the diatonic mm7. As you know from studying V7/V, dominant sevenths built on scale degrees other than $\hat{5}$ usually signal a secondary dominant function. Here the B♮ acts as a temporary leading tone to C ($\hat{6}$), and the harmony functions as V^4_3/vi.

The secondary dominants in the Sousa example elaborate the basic progression I–vi–ii–V without changing the harmonic direction of the phrase: the V^4_3/vi in measure 5 provides a temporary tonicization of vi within the tonic area, and the V^4_3/V in measure 7 strengthens the half cadence (m. 8) by prolonging the dominant area. The A♮3 in measure 7 serves as temporary leading tone to B♭ ($\hat{5}$); its voice-leading is like a chromatic lower neighbor tone to the repeated B♭3s in the tenor. The V^4_2 at the end of measure 8 prevents V from sounding too strong—confirming that V has been tonicized only temporarily. Both secondary dominants in this passage (mm. 5 and 7) appear in second inversion, which allows a smooth descending bass line and stepwise connections in most voice parts. Stepwise voice-leading is typical of chromatic chords and, in particular, of inverted secondary dominants.

Secondary dominants can prolong any major or minor harmony. Listen to Example 21.2, the third phrase of Bach's "Es ist gewisslich an der Zeit," or sing it with your class, and consider the role of the chromatic tone, F♯4 in measure 5.

EXAMPLE 21.2: Bach, "Es ist gewisslich an der Zeit," mm. 4b–6a

As you might expect, the F♯ signals a secondary-function chord: the F♯, which confers a diminished quality to the triad, functions as a temporary leading tone to G, the submediant in B♭. Bach expressively embellishes the chord with a 7–6 (G–F♯) suspension. Its function within the basic phrase is to expand the submediant harmony (a tonic substitute) within the tonic area: vi–vii°6/vi–vi. In sum, the tonic area of the phrase moves from I to the prolonged vi and back to I6, before moving to the dominant area—a single V chord that ends the phrase with a half cadence.

For performers, this short phrase illustrates an important point: two chords with identical Roman numerals may require strikingly different contextual analyses. For example, the root-position V chord with which the phrase ends carries considerably more structural weight than the root-position V chord in measure 5, beat 2. The first V appears in the midst of the tonic area and passes between I6 and vi; its function is only embellishing. In performance, aim for the cadential arrival on V, and focus on the voice-leading role of the first dominant as a connector between I and vi.

The most common role of a secondary dominant or leading-tone chord is to highlight an individual harmony within a basic phrase progression, while leaving the overall direction of the phrase unchanged.

KEY CONCEPT Any major or minor triad other than the tonic may be tonicized. In major keys, these are ii, iii, IV, V, and vi (iii is less common than the others). In minor keys, they are III, iv (or IV), V (or v), VI, and VII (VII is less common). Diminished or augmented triads cannot be tonicized.

As discussed in chapter 20, the presence of secondary dominant or leading-tone chords in a passage does not indicate a change of key (modulation). The chords create a temporary sense of dominant-tonic motion in a different key, but that key disappears as soon as the two-chord connection is complete.

Identifying Secondary Dominant and Leading-Tone Chords

If you recognize the sound of dominant-to-tonic motion, it should be easy to locate a secondary dominant or leading-tone chord by ear. It will simply sound like a dominant-function harmony moving to a temporary I or i. In particular, you will hear half-step voice-leading, as the temporary leading tone moves to its temporary tonic.

KEY CONCEPT One quick way to spot secondary dominant or secondary leading-tone chords in a score is to scan for chromatically raised pitches. A raised third in a minor triad or seventh chord can indicate a temporary leading tone, as can a raised root that transforms a major triad into a diminished one. Confirm your analysis by checking the chord's quality and resolution.

As Example 21.3a illustrates, in major keys ♯$\hat{1}$ can function as a leading tone to ii, ♯$\hat{2}$ can function as a leading tone to iii, and so on. The altered tone can also be employed as the third of a secondary dominant chord (part b), or as the root of a secondary leading-tone chord (part c). Although the example shows only dominant sevenths and fully diminished sevenths, remember that secondary dominant triads (without the seventh) are possible as well, as are secondary leading-tone triads and (less often) half-diminished sevenths.

EXAMPLE 21.3: Spelling secondary-function chords

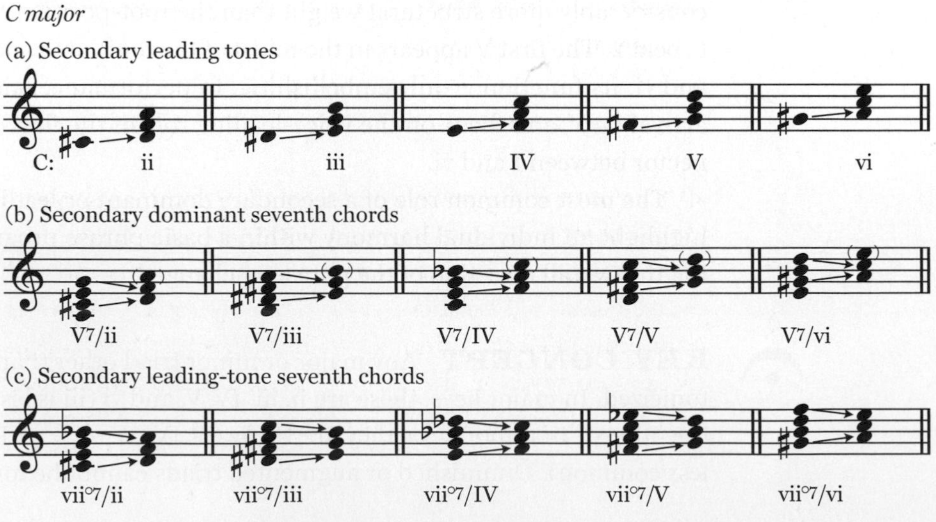

C minor

(d) Secondary leading tones

(e) Secondary dominant seventh chords

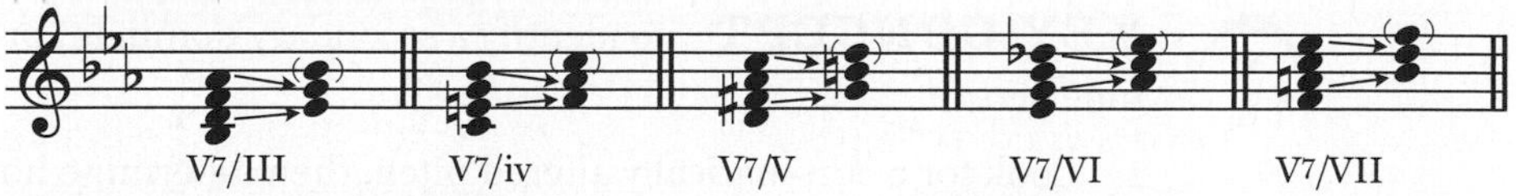

(f) Secondary leading-tone seventh chords

In major keys (parts b–c), all secondary dominant seventh chords include at least one chromatically altered pitch, typically the raised third to make the triad major. Only one secondary dominant triad is already major in its diatonic form: V/IV (C-E-G in C major). Since C-E-G is the tonic in C major, it won't function as a secondary dominant without an added minor seventh. This seventh makes V^7/IV the only secondary dominant in major keys with a chromatically lowered pitch; it is spelled like a I^7 chord with a lowered $\hat{7}$. So when you write a secondary dominant to IV, use a seventh chord rather than a triad; otherwise V/IV–IV (C-E-G to F-A-C in C major) will simply sound like I–IV. Analyze this chord pair as as I–IV if there is no seventh chord.

Part (c) of the example shows secondary leading-tone seventh chords, which may require two chromatic alterations to achieve the correct chord quality. In fact, to spell some fully diminished seventh chords, you must include two different accidentals: a sharp or natural (usually on the root) and a flat (usually on the seventh), as for the vii$^{\circ 7}$/ii and vii$^{\circ 7}$/V. There is no secondary dominant or secondary leading-tone chord to vii°, as that triad has a diminished quality and cannot be tonicized.

In minor keys (parts d–f), secondary dominants and leading-tone chords cannot tonicize ii° or vii°, since these triads are also diminished. Secondary dominant triads to III and VI are diatonic in minor keys and do not require any accidentals. Like V/IV in major keys, their secondary dominant function becomes clear only when the minor seventh is added to the triad (part e). In analysis, if there is no seventh, these chord pairs are usually labeled with their diatonic Roman numerals: III–VI (rather than V/VI–VI) and VII–III (rather than V/III–III).

Occasionally you will see a secondary leading-tone chord that is half-diminished. This chord imitates the type of chord found in the diatonic progression vii^{ø7}–I, and is only used to tonicize a major-quality triad. Since fully diminished seventh chords are more common, however, we will focus on them in this chapter.

KEY CONCEPT To identify a secondary dominant or secondary leading-tone chord:

1. Look for a chromatically altered pitch, then determine how it changes a chord's quality.
2. If the altered chord is a major triad or dominant seventh, check the following chord. If its root is a perfect fifth below (or a perfect fourth above) the root of the altered chord, you have identified a secondary dominant.
3. If the altered chord is a diminished triad or fully diminished seventh (or, less often, a half-diminished seventh), check the following chord. If its root is a half step above the root of the altered chord, you have identified a secondary leading-tone chord.
4. Occasionally, a secondary-function chord (such as V7/III in minor) will not include a chromatically altered pitch. In that case, follow steps 2 and 3 to determine the chord's function.

Secondary-Function Chords in Musical Contexts

Secondary dominant and leading-tone chords typically (1) appear within a phrase to intensify the harmony, (2) provide a temporary harmonic diversion, (3) create forward momentum in a passage, (4) evade an expected resolution, or (5) contribute to text painting. When you prepare a piece for performance, you may want to identify which role each such chord plays in order to help shape your performance.

Tonicizing Harmonies Within a Phrase

Listen to the excerpt from Beethoven's *Pathétique* Sonata given in Example 21.4. Here, the predominant area in this T–PD–D–T phrase has been expanded by a secondary dominant seventh chord. The A♮ in the melody creates a striking F-A♮-C-E♭ sonority that functions as secondary dominant to the predominant ii.

Example 21.4: Beethoven, *Pathétique* Sonata, second movement, mm. 5–8

Another way to indicate the tonicized ii is with bracket notation, where measures 6–8 would be analyzed as

I^6 ⌊V7 i⌋ V7 I
ii
T PD— D T.

Now listen to the Mozart variation shown in Example 21.5.

Example 21.5: Mozart, *Variations on "Ah, vous dirai-je Maman,"* Variation VII, mm. 169–176

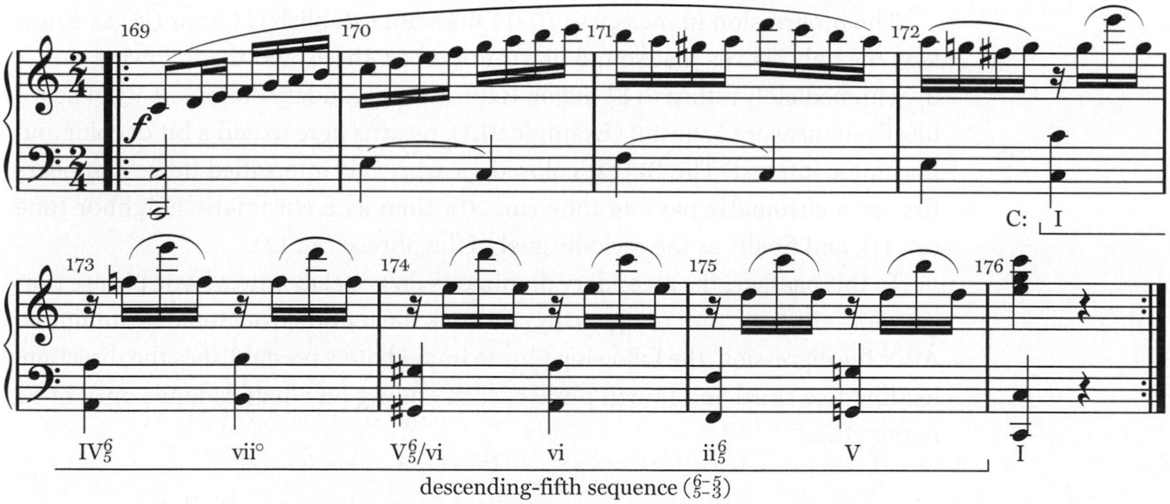

Here, the predominant portion of the phrase (mm. 172–175) features a descending-fifth sequence, alternating seventh chords (in $^6_5$ position) and triads. The diatonic version of the sequence in root position would be I–IV7–vii°–iii7–vi–ii7–V–I. Although multiple secondary dominants can embellish a sequence, only one of the chords here has been altered: the iii7 in measure 174 (beat 1) has been converted to a V$^6_5$/vi by changing the chord quality to Mm7. The tonicization of a triad within a sequence does not interrupt the sequence's motion, and can in fact intensify its effect.

Providing a Temporary Harmonic Diversion

Listen again to the beginning of "The Stars and Stripes Forever" to hear another use of secondary-function chords. The second phrase (Example 21.6), a continuation of the music in Example 21.1, begins by confirming I in E♭ major with a I^6–V$^4_3$–I progression, then ends with a HC in measure 12—but not in the primary key of the piece. The cadence tonicizes vi (C minor), though only briefly.

Example 21.6: Sousa, "The Stars and Stripes Forever," mm. 9–12

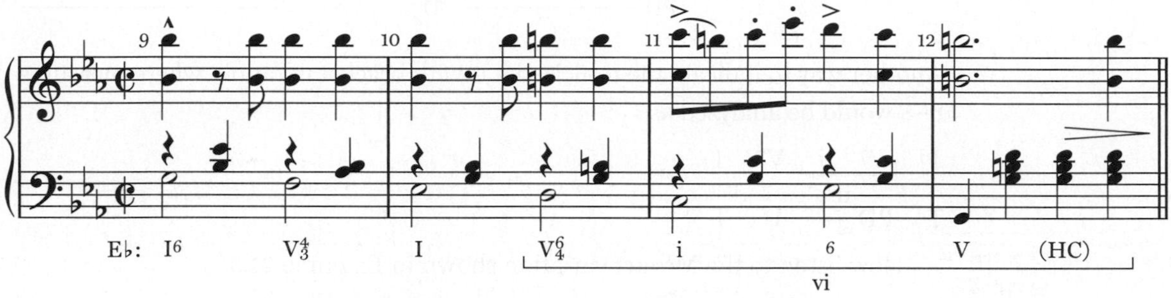

The progression in measures 10–12 does not establish C minor (vi) as a new key; the only chords that sound like C minor are these, and the following measures immediately return to E♭ major. Rather, the secondary dominant V$^4_3$/vi heard briefly in measure 5, beat 2 (Example 21.1), returns here to add a bit of color and harmonic interest. The B♮ that colored measure 5 is intensified here: it appears first as a chromatic passing tone (m. 10), then as a chromatic neighbor tone (m. 11), and finally as the melodic goal of the phrase (m. 12).

In this passage, the secondary dominants do not elaborate a basic phrase progression—instead, they temporarily sidetrack the motion from tonic to dominant. After the digression, the following phrase immediately reestablishes the direction, leading to a third and fourth phrase, each ending on a half cadence on V of E♭ major (B♭).

Creating Forward Momentum

Secondary dominants are a typical feature of Scott Joplin's ragtime piano pieces. Listen to two similar phrases from "Solace" while following Example 21.7. You will hear that the phrases are identical except for their final chords. Both demonstrate the basic progression I–vi^7–ii$^6_5$–V^7–I (T–Ts–PD–D–T), excluding the final (shaded) chords of measures 56 and 64.

Example 21.7: Joplin, "Solace"

(a) Mm. 53–57a

(b) Mm. 61–65

The first phrase cadences on the tonic in measure 56 (IAC). The shaded chord serves as an anacrusis to the next phrase, with the fermata creating harmonic tension and heightening anticipation before V7 resolves to I in measure 57.

The last chord in measure 64 is likewise an anacrusis (part b). The chord beginning the next phrase, however, is not tonic, but instead IV6 (B♭-D-F). The shaded F-A-C-E♭ chord is a secondary dominant to IV, in this case in third inversion ($^4_2$) and resolving in typical fashion down to a first-inversion triad. The resolution of the temporary leading tone (A4) upward, and the seventh of the chord (E♭3) downward, highlights the IV6 that follows by intensifying motion toward this tonicized chord.

Try it #1

Write a Roman numeral analysis in F major beneath the excerpt below.

What are the tendency tones? ______________ and ______________

Do they resolve correctly? ______________

Joplin, "Solace," mm. 72–73

How might such an analysis of secondary dominants influence your interpretive decisions? Throughout Joplin's rag, focus on the intensity of the dominant seventh and secondary dominant harmonies found at the end of many four-bar units. Be sure to follow Joplin's performance indications, lengthening the sonorities that are notated with fermatas, and observing the *a tempo* indications that usually follow. (Continue *a tempo* after each fermata, even when it is not marked.) This will propel each basic phrase forward to its cadence, in preparation for the next dominant seventh anacrusis. You may also want to experiment with "voicing out" the tendency tones. Try playing each anacrusis in such a way that you really hear the (temporary) leading tone resolving up and the chordal seventh resolving down.

Evading an Expected Resolution

We have already looked at ways of evading or weakening a cadence after a strong V or V7: for example, by using a deceptive cadence or resolving to an inverted tonic (or I7). Secondary-function chords may also be called on to evade an expected cadence or temporarily redirect a phrase. As an example, listen to a passage from Bach's C Major Prelude (Example 21.8), focusing on measures 11–12.

Example 21.8: Bach, Prelude in C Major, mm. 8–15

In measure 11, there is a strong arrival on a G major chord (preceded by its own dominant): we would expect either a continuation in the key of G major or a new phrase beginning on the tonic. Instead, while the chord in measure 12 shares two pitch classes with a tonic resolution—G and E—it also includes a C♯ and B♭. It is a diminished seventh chord—vii$^{\circ 4}_{3}$/ii—which provides a surprising harmonic shift to tonicize the supertonic. Although the V in measure 11 would not normally progress to the ii of measure 13, the progression Bach has written sounds smooth and logical, while still providing a sense of surprise. The same progression then appears in measures 14–15, transposed down a step (vii$^{\circ 4}_{3}$ to I^6), creating a sequence that leads back to the tonic.

In performance, you need do nothing to bring out the harmonic surprise, but you might try focusing on the voice-leading aspects that make this progression work. In the upper voice, hear the connection between the pitches at the top of each arpeggio—they move in stepwise motion upward from measure 11 to 13: B4, C♯5, D5. The bass line of almost the entire composition to measure 19 is a slow stepwise descent from the initial C4 tonic down to C3. You might think of the arrival in measure 19 (anthology, p. 48) as a large-scale goal: aim for it, without getting bogged down in small details.

Text Painting

In songs and choral works, secondary-function chords sometimes play a role in text painting, the musical depiction of images found in the words. Listen to the excerpt from "A Whole New World" given in Example 21.9. Here, the character Jasmine sings about the "whole new world" she is discovering. Which words seem most important in this passage? Take a close look at the settings of "never knew" in measures 31–32 and "whole new world" in measure 36.

EXAMPLE 21.9: Menken and Rice, "A Whole New World," mm. 30–37a

Try it #2

Label the shaded chords in measures 31–35 of Example 21.9 with Roman numerals and figures in the blanks.

The words "never knew" (m. 31) are highlighted by secondary leading-tone and dominant seventh chords to vi, which arrives on beat 1 of measure 32, making a deceptive cadence that brings out the foreignness of the world the character is now seeing. The secondary dominant in measure 32 (on "But when I'm") combines with the rhythmic impetus of the quarter-note triplets to push forward harmonically, emphasizing that she's "way up here," and on the highest note she has sung yet in the phrase.

The final text-painting touch in this passage is the setting of "whole new world" in measure 36. The chord on the downbeat is preceded by a V7/V ("in a"), and followed by V7 ("world with," with a 4–3 suspension)—a typical resolution for a V7/V. Yet the first chord in measure 36 temporarily evades the expected dominant. You will learn more about this harmonic choice—a ♭VII chord—in Chapter 25. For now, observe how combining the V7/V with the unusual resolution to ♭VII highlights this "whole new world."

Spelling Secondary Dominant and Leading-Tone Chords

Now that you have seen and heard what secondary dominant and leading-tone chords can do, it is time to write some.

KEY CONCEPT To spell a secondary dominant seventh chord:

1. First, write the triad it tonicizes. For example, if you want to write a V7/ii in the key of D major, first write the ii chord (E-G-B), leaving a space before it for the V7/ii (Example 21.10a).
2. Imagine a box around the ii chord and the empty space before it. Imagine that the chords in that box are in the key of ii, or E minor, with one sharp (F♯) in the key signature (b).
3. What chord is V7 in E minor? Remember that in minor keys you need to raise $\flat\hat{7}$ to create a leading tone and give the dominant harmony its major quality: V7 in E minor is B-D♯-F♯-A. Write this chord, remembering that the F♯ is already provided in the key signature of D major (c).

To spell a secondary leading-tone chord:

Follow the same procedure, but write vii°7–i in the tonicized key instead (parts d–f).

You can adapt these guidelines for triads, omitting the seventh, or for the viiø7 (presuming that this chord precedes a major triad) by altering the quality of the seventh.

EXAMPLE 21.10: Procedure for writing secondary dominant and leading-tone chords

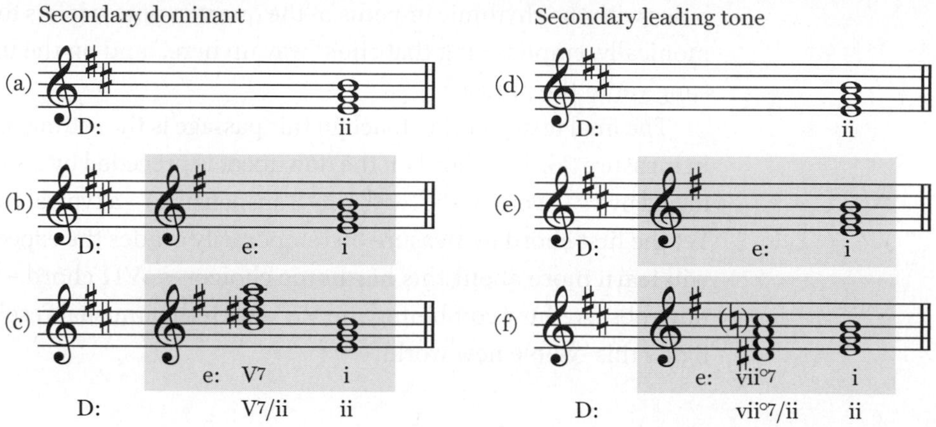

Another way to spell secondary chords is illustrated in Example 21.11. First write the tonicized triad, as before (a). Then in the space to the left, move up a P5 from the root of the tonicized chord (in this case, ii), and write the note heads for a seventh chord: B-D-F♯-A (b). Be sure to include any accidentals from the key signature, in this case F♯. Now check the chord's quality—is it a dominant seventh (Mm7) chord? If not, alter the pitches with the necessary accidentals (c). Here, change D to D♯ to get B-D♯-F♯-A.

For a vii°7 chord, again begin by writing the tonicized triad (d). Then move down a half step from the root of the tonicized chord, and write the note heads for a seventh chord (retaining any accidentals from the key signature): D♯-F♯-A-C♯ (e). Now check the chord's quality—is it a fully diminished seventh chord? If not, add the accidentals required (f). In this case, you would need to change C♯ to C♮.

EXAMPLE 21.11: Alternate procedure for writing secondary dominant and leading-tone chords

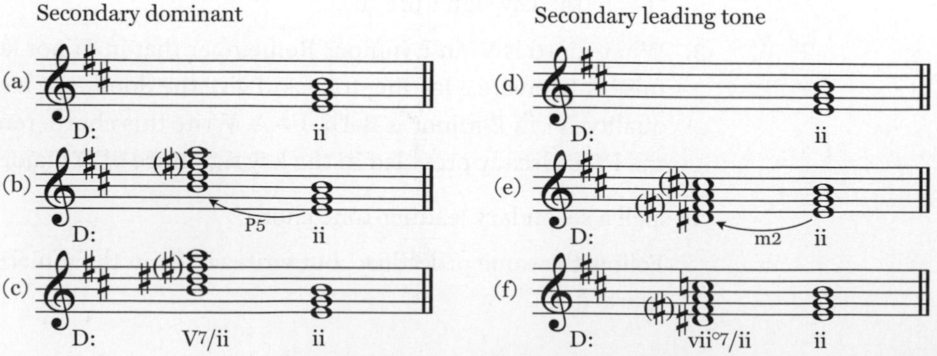

Another Way

Another way to spell secondary dominants quickly is to imagine them as "altered" diatonic chords, following the chart below (in C major). Add whatever accidentals are necessary to create a Mm7 quality.

TO MAKE A . . .		START WITH . . .		ALTER QUALITY TO Mm7
V7/IV	→	I7 (C-E-G-B)	→	I7 (C-E-G-B♭)
V7/V	→	ii7 (D-F-A-C)	→	II7 (D-F♯-A-C)
V7/vi	→	iii7 (E-G-B-D)	→	III7 (E-G♯-B-D)
V7/ii	→	vi7 (A-C-E-G)	→	VI7 (A-C♯-E-G)
V7/iii	→	viiø7 (B-D-F-A)	→	VII7 (B-D♯-F♯-A)

Try it #3

A. For each key below, write the tonicized chord in the first measure, then the secondary dominant in the second measure. Use whole notes.

KEY	ROMAN NUMERAL	TONICIZED CHORD / SECONDARY DOMINANT
(1) B♭ major	V7/IV	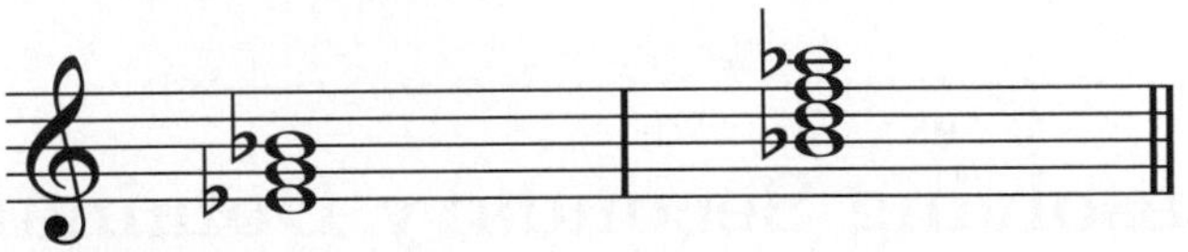
(2) F♯ minor	vii°7/III	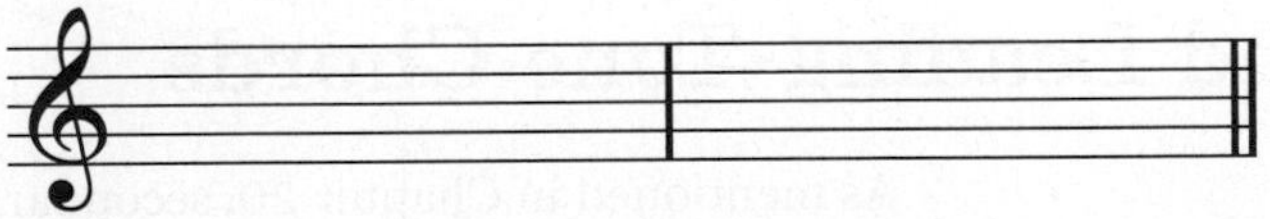
(3) A major	V7/ii	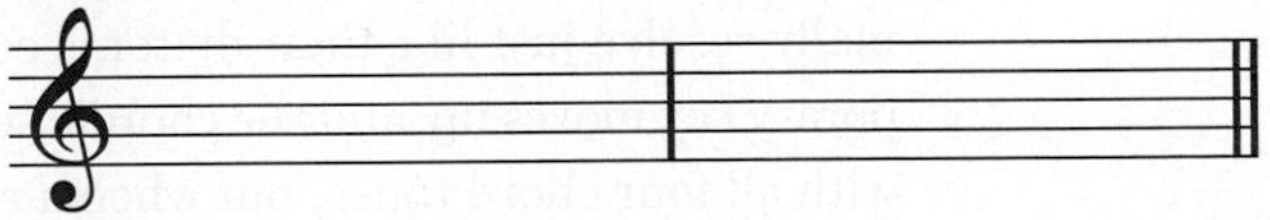
(4) G major	vii°7/vi	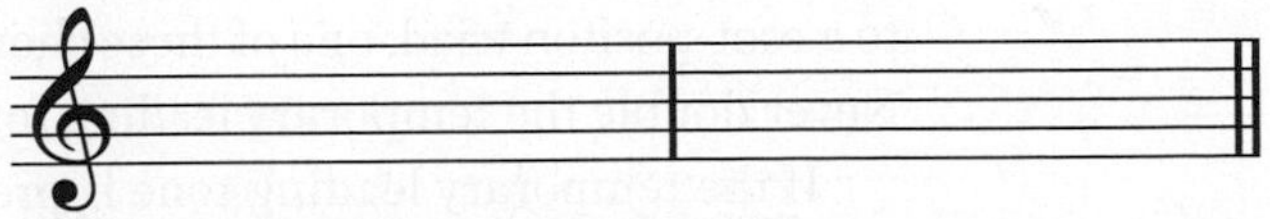
(5) E♭ major	V7/vi	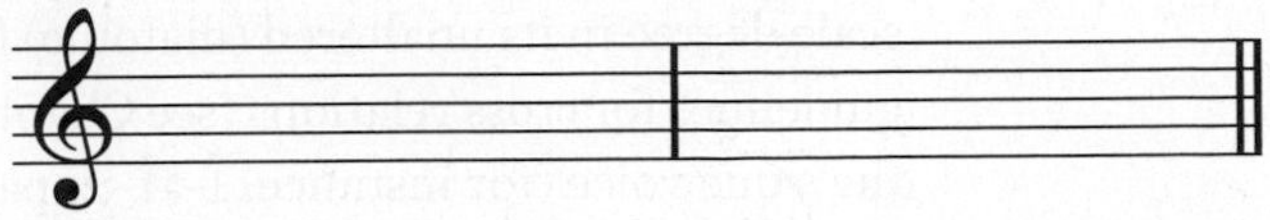
(6) C minor	V7/V	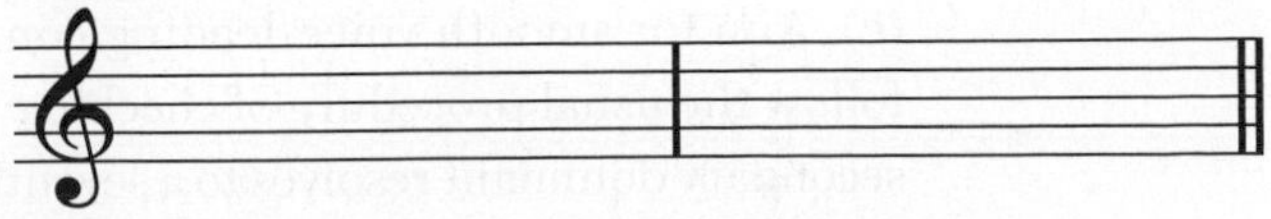

B. Provide the correct Roman numerals in the key specified, for each chord spelled below.

		KEY	ROMAN NUMERAL
(1)	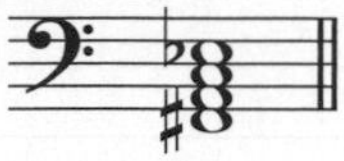	D major	vii°7/IV
(2)		G major	______
(3)		F major	______
(4)		C♯ major	______
(5)	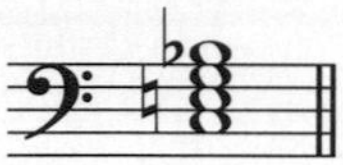	C minor	______
(6)		F minor	______

Resolving Secondary Dominant and Leading-Tone Chords

As mentioned in Chapter 20, secondary dominant and leading-tone chords normally resolve just like their diatonic counterparts: the leading tone of the temporary key moves up, and the chordal seventh down. These chords usually appear with all four chord tones, but when a root-position secondary V7 chord resolves to a root-positon triad, one of those chords will be incomplete (leave out the fifth). Never double the temporary leading tone or the seventh of the chord.

If the temporary leading tone is preceded by a chord that contains the same scale degree in its unaltered (diatonic) form, as in example 21.12a, remember the guidelines for cross relations (see Chapter 20)—either keep the chromatic tone in the same voice (for instance, $\hat{1}$–♯$\hat{1}$–$\hat{2}$; part b) or write a chromatic voice exchange (c). Aim for smooth voice-leading connections (by step or common tone), and follow the usual procedure of checking for parallel fifths and octaves. Finally, if a secondary dominant resolves to a seventh chord, its leading tone may resolve down (see Example 21.15, m. 245).

Example 21.12: Voice-leading guidelines

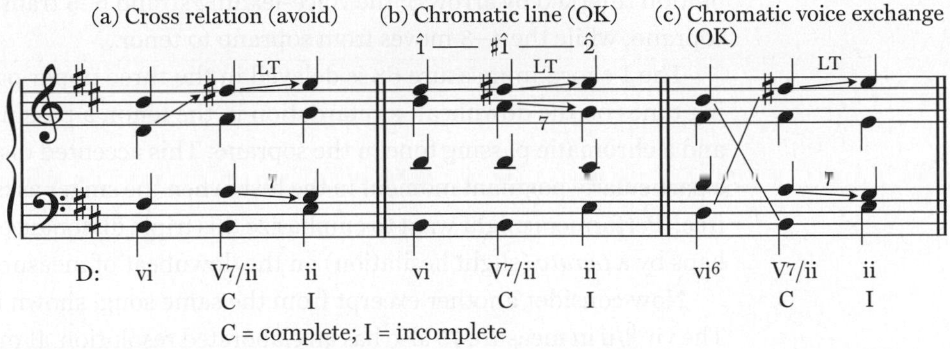

Embellished Resolutions

Because secondary chords frequently appear in elaborate, highly chromatic Romantic-period music, you may encounter embellished resolutions of these harmonies. For example, listen to the passage from "Neue Liebe, neues Leben" analyzed in Example 21.13. The chords on the first three beats of measure 66 express I6 in B♭ major, and the last beat of the measure has D-B♮-A♭-F: vii°$^{6}_{5}$/ii. We expect this chord to resolve to a ii chord (C-E♭-G) in measure 67, and it does, but the resolution is delayed by suspensions in the soprano and alto and a retardation in the tenor. The ii6 chord is also embellished by a voice exchange from the "and" of beat 1 to the "and" of beat 2.

Example 21.13: Hensel, "Neue Liebe, neues Leben," mm. 66–68a (anthology)

The voice exchange in the ii^6 chord is followed by V$^{6-5}_{4-3}$, with a transferred resolution (marked by arrows): the voice-leading strand 6–5 transfers from tenor to soprano, while the 4–3 moves from soprano to tenor.

The I chord in measure 68 is delayed in the three upper parts by embellishing tones on the downbeat: a retardation in the tenor, a passing tone in the alto, and a chromatic passing tone in the soprano. This accented dissonance comes at a particularly poignant moment in the text, when the singer asks a lover to "let me free." Performers might want to emphasize this triple dissonance in some way, perhaps by a *tenuto* (slight hesitation) on the downbeat of measure 68.

Now consider another excerpt from the same song, shown in Example 21.14. The vii$^{\circ 6}_{5}$/ii in measure 75 also has an elaborated resolution. It moves to a ii^6 chord as it should, but the tendency tones do not resolve in the correct octave until the voice exchange in the soprano and tenor parts from beats 3 to 4.

EXAMPLE 21.14: Hensel, "Neue Liebe, neues Leben," mm. 75–77 (anthology)

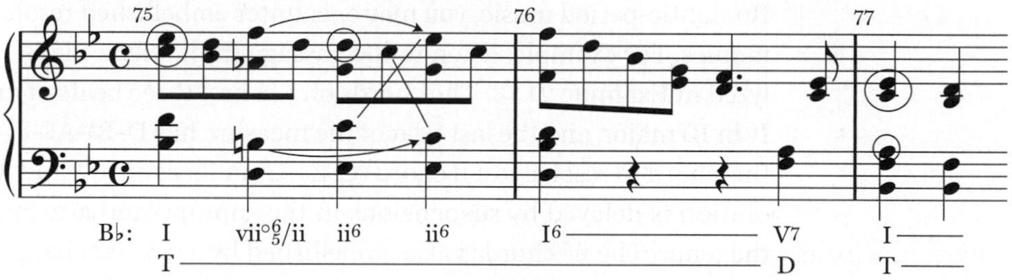

KEY CONCEPT To recognize embellished resolutions:

1. Listen carefully for the point of resolution (this particularly helps when resolutions are delayed in multiple voices by suspensions, passing tones, or retardations).
2. Know what the expected resolution is, and look ahead a little if you don't find it where you expect it.

Irregular Resolutions

Although the quality of secondary dominant and leading-tone chords strongly implies a particular resolution, sometimes composers do not resolve these chords exactly as you expect. Instead, they write an **irregular resolution.**

Listen to the Mozart Variation in Example 21.15, then focus on the passage in measures 244b–248.

Example 21.15: Mozart, *Variations*, Variation X, mm. 241–248

Try it #4

Provide a contextual analysis for Example 21.15. In the secondary-function chords, mark the resolution of all tendency tones with an arrow.

In measure 245, the expected ii on beat 1 is replaced with V/V (a triad with the correct root but an altered chord quality), and the expected V on beat 2 is replaced by vii°7 (a chord with the same function that shares three common tones with V7, but not the expected root). The F♯5 (temporary leading tone) in the V/V resolves down, pulled down by the descending chromatic line in the piano melody. Both the vii°7 and vii°7/V chords in measures 245 and 246 resolve as expected, to I and V respectively, and in each case there are strong voice-leading connections that make these chord choices work.

Passages like this one are fairly common in highly chromatic voice-leading. To analyze, carefully determine each chord's quality, then compare the actual resolution in the music with the expected one. With that information, you should be able to explain each chord's resolution. Your Roman numerals will show irregular resolutions automatically. For example, if you write V7/IV–ii6, it's clear that the expected IV chord is replaced with a ii6 instead.

Secondary Dominants in Sequences

You might also find secondary-function chords elaborating a sequence: in alternation with triads or as dominant seventh harmonies in a descending-fifth sequence (creating a **chromatic sequence**). Composers may take a short portion of the elaborated sequence to move between functional areas or use a complete sequence to prolong the tonic area. As an example of the former, listen to the portion of Mozart's Piano Sonata in D Major shown in Example 21.16, here in A major. The basic root progression in measure 9 is labeled: descending fifths.

EXAMPLE 21.16: Mozart, Piano Sonata in D Major, third movement, mm. 8b–10

If this were a diatonic sequence in A, the progression would be ii^7–V–I^7–IV, a descending-fifth sequence. Here, Mozart has changed the ii^7 chord to a dominant seventh quality (B-D♯-A, leaving out F♯). This sets up a pattern of alternating secondary dominant sevenths, a chromatic descending-fifth sequence.

KEY CONCEPT In the most common type of chromatic sequence, dominant-seventh-quality chords are substituted for all or some (usually every other chord) of the chords in a descending-fifth sequence. The sequence typically features root-position chords, but may also include inversions.

The voice-leading for descending-fifth sequences with root-position dominant seventh chords alternating with triads is the same as for any secondary dominant resolution. In a chain of *all* root-position seventh chords, however, every other chord is incomplete (to avoid parallels). The chordal sevenths resolve down by step as expected, but the leading tones also resolve down—pulled downward by the stepwise chromatic line—to become the seventh of the following chord.

Did You Know?

There are a number of systems for analyzing secondary dominant and leading-tone chords. You have already seen "bracket notation," where the key of the tonicization is given below a horizontal bracket:

$$\underbrace{\text{ii}^{6}_{5}\ \text{V}^{6-5}_{4-3}\ \text{I}}_{\text{V}}$$

Other systems you may encounter are those used by Allen Forte in *Tonal Harmony in Concept and Practice*, and by Edward Aldwell and Carl Schachter in *Harmony and Voice Leading*. Forte simply encloses the secondary-function chord within vertical square brackets: V/V would be [V]. Aldwell and Schachter use a small curved arrow beneath the secondary dominant that points to the chord of resolution V$\curvearrowright$V.

German music theorists use an analytical symbol invented by nineteenth-century music theorist Hugo Riemann, two Ds (for "dominant") interlocked, one above and to the left of the other: DD. Our symbol V/V represents the same concept shown by this "D of D" (dominant of the dominant).

TERMS YOU SHOULD KNOW

- cross relation
- embellished resolution
- irregular resolution
- secondary dominant
- secondary leading-tone chord
- temporary tonic
- tonicization

QUESTIONS FOR REVIEW

1. Which diatonic chords may be tonicized in a major key? in a minor key? What chords (which quality) may not be tonicized?
2. What roles do secondary dominants typically play in a harmonic progression?
3. What are the steps for finding the root and adding the proper accidentals to spell a secondary dominant chord? to spell a secondary leading-tone chord?
4. What tendency tones need to be resolved in a secondary dominant or leading-tone chord? When may the temporary leading tone resolve down?
5. What are two ways that cross relations can be avoided when a secondary dominant is preceded by its diatonic counterpart?
6. How can you identify irregular resolutions of secondary dominant and leading-tone chords in their Roman numeral analysis?
7. What part-writing guidelines are important to remember when secondary dominants appear in sequences of seventh chords?
8. In music for your own instrument, find two examples of secondary dominants other than V/V or V^7/V (in two different keys). For each one, examine the context—does it fit within one of the typical uses of secondary dominants considered in this chapter? How might understanding its role and resolution in the phrase influence your performance of the passage?

PART III

Chromatic Harmony and Form

Modulation to Closely Related Keys

Outline of topics

Common pivot-chord modulations

- Modulation or tonicization?
- Modulation from a major key to its dominant
- Modulation from a minor key to its relative major
- Closely related keys

Other pivot-chord modulations

- From a major key to its submediant
- From a minor key to its minor dominant
- From a major key to its supertonic, mediant, or subdominant
- Writing a pivot-chord modulation

Direct modulations

- Modulations introduced by secondary dominants

Locating modulations

Modulations in musical contexts

- Harmonizing modulating melodies

Overview

This chapter focuses on modulation, changing from one key to another. We learn to change keys by means of pivot chords, and to determine which keys are closely related. We will also harmonize a melody that changes keys.

Repertoire

Anonymous, Minuet in D Minor, from the *Anna Magdalena Bach Notebook*

Johann Sebastian Bach
"Er kommt"("He Comes"), from Cantata No. 140, "Wachet auf"
"O Haupt voll Blut und Wunden" ("O Head, Full of Blood and Wounds")

Muzio Clementi, Sonatina in C Major, Op. 36, No. 1, first movement

Archangelo Corelli
Allemanda, from Trio Sonata in A Minor, Op. 4, No. 5
Prelude, from Trio Sonata in D Minor, Op. 4, No. 8

Wolfgang Amadeus Mozart, Piano Sonata in D Major, K. 284, third movement

Franz Schubert, "Nur wer die Sehnsucht kennt (Lied der Mignon)" ("Only One Who Knows Longing [Mignon's Song]")

Common Pivot-Chord Modulations

Most tonal compositions include passages that prolong a harmonic area other than the tonic. Many common-practice forms, such as binary and sonata forms, rely on these harmonic changes to create contrast between sections. Indeed, composers show their ingenuity and artistry by how and where they move between key areas. Some analysts view these different harmonic areas as large-scale tonicizations of harmonies within a single key, the tonic; this approach emphasizes the overall harmonic coherence of the work. Other analysts, however, view structurally significant tonicizations as **modulations**, or changes of key. This approach focuses on how chords function within the local context of a new key and how the new key relates to the tonic key. For purposes of this chapter, we will take the latter approach and look at specific ways composers move between harmonic areas.

Listen to the opening of the third movement of Mozart's Piano Sonata in D Major, while examining the score in Example 22.1. Chapters 14 and 15 analyzed the basic phrase model in measures 1–4. Now look at the phrase that follows (mm. 5–8), to see how the cadences in measures 4 and 8 differ.

EXAMPLE 22.1: Mozart, Piano Sonata in D Major, third movement, mm. 1–8

While both cadences end on an A major triad, the first is a half cadence in the tonic key (D major); but the second so strongly tonicizes A that it sounds like a PAC in A major, making a modulation to the key of the dominant. The change is so smooth, you may not hear the shift of harmonic focus until the return to D major when measures 1–8 are repeated.

Look carefully at measures 5–6. Measure 5 begins with I^6 in D major, followed by vi^6; then in measure 6, a G♯ is introduced. This ♯$\hat{4}$ could simply indicate a secondary dominant, V^7/V, except that the G♯ appears three more times in 6 and 7, and the remainder of the phrase functions according to the basic phrase model in the key of A major: measures 7–8 are I–ii^6–V$^{8-7}_{\substack{6-5\\4-3}}$–I in A (Example 22.2).

EXAMPLE 22.2: Mozart, Piano Sonata in D Major, third movement, mm. 4b–8

D: I^6 | vi^6
A: ii^6 | V^7 —— | I | ii^6 | V$^{8-7}_{\substack{6-5\\4-3}}$ | I
(V)

When a modulation is composed this smoothly, there often are one or more transitional chords that function diatonically in both keys. The vi^6 (in D major) on the second half of measure 5 is such a chord: it also functions as ii^6 in A major, preparing the entrance of the V^7 in A in measure 6 and the subsequent cadence in that key. A chord like this one—which has "full membership" in both keys—is called a **pivot chord**, and this type of modulation is called a **pivot-chord**, or **common-chord, modulation**. It is the most common means of modulation between two keys.

Notate this type of modulation by writing the first key and Roman numerals in the normal way, then the second key and Roman numerals underneath. Label the pivot chord (or chords), with the two Roman numerals right on top of each other and enclosed in a bracket or box, as in Example 22.2. Indicate the relationship between the primary key and the new one by writing a Roman numeral in parentheses below the new key label. In the example, the (V) below the A indicates that A major is the dominant of the composition's overall key, D major.

Modulation or Tonicization?

The decision whether to analyze a passage as a tonicization or modulation is not always clear-cut, and different analysts may hear the passage in different ways. When making this decision, use the guidelines below to inform your choice, and be ready to defend it with concrete musical reasons.

KEY CONCEPT To determine whether a passage has modulated, look for at least one of the following:

- a PD–D–T progression in the new key;
- a firm cadence (usually a PAC or an IAC) in the new key, preceded by a predominant-function harmony and/or followed by music that continues in the new key;
- an extended progression in the new key (not just dominant-tonic).

Keep in mind that this "establishment of a new key" may only be a temporary emphasis on a harmonic area within the context of the larger harmonic structure. There is some latitude here: what may seem like a modulation on the small scale may be reinterpreted as a tonicization when you consider the entire composition. Occasionally, extended progressions (especially in Romantic-era music) may focus on a temporary tonic without a cadence or clear PD–D–T motion. In such a case, consider how long the progression lasts: does it seem to establish a new key because of its length, even without a cadence? If so, label it a modulation.

Modulation from a Major Key to Its Dominant

Return now to the Mozart phrase in Example 22.2 to determine whether it fulfills one or more of the modulation criteria listed above. It does, because the progression in the new key, ii^6–V^7–I–ii^6–$\text{V}\begin{smallmatrix}8-7\\6-5\\4-3\end{smallmatrix}$–I, includes two predominants preceding the cadential dominant-tonic (one of which also serves as the pivot). The pivot chord here—vi in the primary key = ii in the key of the dominant—is one of the most common means of modulating from a tonic key to its dominant.

Pivot Chords Between Tonic and Dominant Keys in Major The first step in writing a modulating progression is to choose a pivot chord. Compare the diatonic chords in D and A major (Figure 22.1) to find possibilities for moving between a tonic key and its dominant (these are boxed). You cannot use a chord built on E as the pivot, for example, because this triad has a minor quality in D major (ii) but a major quality A major (V).

FIGURE 22.1: Comparison of chords in D major and A major

D major							
Roman numerals:	I	ii	iii	IV	V	vi	vii°
Chords:	D	e	f♯	G	A	b	c♯°
A major							
Chords:	D	E	f♯	g♯°	A	b	c♯
Roman numerals:	IV	V	vi	vii°	I	ii	iii

KEY CONCEPT Pivot chords are diatonic in both keys and must have the same quality in both keys.

Some pivot chords are more typical than others. The pivot vi = ii makes a smooth progression because the triad can serve a predominant function in both keys, and both vi and ii are triads frequently found in major-key progressions. Other the other hand, iii = vi is less common since the mediant triad, iii, does not often appear in common-practice progressions. When iii = vi acts as a pivot, it usually appears in a pivot area with several chords. The pivot I = IV is also less effective: it is not easy to convince the ear that the tonic triad no longer has a tonic function, but instead is functioning as IV in a new key. For this reason, I^6 is not marked as a pivot chord (IV^6 in the dominant key) in Example 22.2 (m. 5)—you are unlikely to hear this chord functioning as IV^6 in A major.

Although the chords V = I are boxed in Figure 22.1 as a possible pivot, this pairing is also rarely found. The V chord tends to sound like V in the tonic key unless it is preceded by other chords in the new key—in which case *they* are the pivot chords. In addition to pivot chords, chords that are not shared by the two keys play an important role in establishing a modulation. Their appearance, and the accidentals that usually accompany them, signal that the key has changed.

When performing a phrase that contains a pivot-chord modulation, you might want to aid in the "deception" of the pivot chord's dual nature by playing or singing it as though nothing unusual has happened. Then once the new key has emerged, aim toward the cadence in the new key, attending to the resolution of the new leading tone with expressive timing, to emphasize the new tonal goal.

Try it #1

Construct a chart of pivot chords for the pair of keys given below, using Figure 22.1 as a model. Draw a box around pivot chords that are diatonic in both keys.

(a) *A♭ major*

Roman numerals:	I	ii	iii	IV	V	vi	vii°
Chords:	A♭	b♭	____	____	____	____	____

(b) *E♭ major*

Chords:	A♭	B♭	____	____	____	____	____
Roman numerals:	IV	V	____	____	____	____	____

Modulation from a Minor Key to Its Relative Major

Listen now to the opening measures of the Minuet in D Minor, shown in Example 22.3 (the staves below each line of the minuet make clear the implied harmonies in this two-voice texture). The cadence in measure 4 is an authentic cadence in D minor, but by measure 8 the piece has modulated to F major, the relative major, which is confirmed by a PAC. To identify the location of the modulation, you need to know what pivot chords would work for modulations between these relative keys.

Example 22.3: Anonymous, Minuet in D Minor, mm. 1–8

Pivot Chords Between Tonic and Mediant Keys in Minor Compare the chords in common between D minor and its relative major (or mediant), F major, given in Figure 22.2. The figure shows all typical chords in D minor, including most of those built from the natural and harmonic minor versions of the scale.

FIGURE 22.2: Comparison of chords in D minor and F major

D minor:	i	ii°	III	iv	v	V	VI	VII	vii°
Chords:	d	e°	F	g	a	A	B♭	C	c♯°
F major:	vi	vii°	I	ii	iii		IV	V	

As this chart shows, there are several potental pivot chords between relative keys; the most frequently used are i = vi, III = I, iv = ii, and VI = IV. As in modulations from I to V in a major key, pivot chords from minor keys to the relative major are most effective when they fall into the predominant-function area of the phrase (for example, iv = ii). The tonic chord in one of the keys can also serve as a pivot, particularly if paired with a predominant to form a two-chord pivot area.

The dominant-function chords in minor keys, V and vii°, are distinctive because of their altered leading tone—they do not appear as diatonic harmonies in F major and therefore cannot function as pivot chords. However, the analogous dominant-function chords in the major key, V and vii°, *are* diatonic chords in the relative minor (VII and ii°) and occasionally serve as pivots.

Try it #2

Construct a chart of pivot chords for each pair of keys given below, using Figure 22.2 as a model. Draw a box around pivot chords that are diatonic in both keys.

C♯ minor:	i	ii°	III	iv	v	V	VI	VII	vii°
Chords:	c♯	d♯	____	____	____	____	____	____	____
E major:	vi	vii°	____	____	____	____	____	____	____

Now return to measures 5–7 of the minuet (Example 22.4). When the phrase begins, the first chord is i in D minor, the tonic key, followed by v^6 (decorated by an incomplete upper neighbor)—a typical use of minor v at the beginning of a phrase, where a strong dominant function is not desired. Although these chords function as vi and iii^6 in F major, it is unlikely that we would hear the first chord (the tonic triad in D minor) as vi in F major. We choose instead v^6 = iii^6 (beat 2 of m. 5) as the pivot chord. (Though the iii^6 chord is not typical in major keys, here it is approached smoothly by one of the standard root progressions, descending fifth.) From measure 6 to the end of the phrase, the harmonies are clearly in F major: I^6–V^6_5–I–I^6–V–I.

EXAMPLE 22.4: Anonymous, Minuet in D Minor, mm. 5–8

We have neglected the last chord in measure 5 thus far, because it is ambiguous. If the D5 is part of the chord, it is VI in D minor and IV in F major; if the C5 is the chord tone (decorated by an incomplete upper neighbor), the chord is V$^4_2$ in F major, which resolves as expected to a I^6 in the next measure. In this two-part counterpoint, both harmonies are implied, but the V$^4_2$ seems to capture better the impetus toward the new key, and in performance it makes sense to treat both the B♭4 and the D5 as incomplete upper neighbors (appoggiaturas) by stressing them slightly before sinking into the chord tone. This embellishing tone pattern in Baroque music is sometimes referred to as a "sigh" motive and is typically performed with emphasis on the downbeat dissonance.

Finally, surely you noticed the luxuriant harmony in measure 3 (Example 22.3). The arpeggiated chord sounds like a combination of V^7 (A-C♯-E-G) and vii^{o7} (C♯-E-G-B♭). This dominant-function harmony, which may be labeled V$^9_7$, represents a typical "ninth chord" in Baroque music. The B♭4, the ninth above the bass A3, though approached by arpeggiation as a chord tone, immediately resolves to the octave (A4), then passes through the seventh of the chord (G4) as the chord resolves to the tonic. Another way to interpret this ninth is as part of a 9–8 suspension. If you hear the top note of the arpeggio as the "soprano voice," then it connects back to the B♭4 of measure 2 as the suspension's consonant preparation. The suspended tone then resolves down by step (B♭–A) as expected. The rich sound of this rising arpeggiation makes a truly magical moment in this brief, deceptively simple-looking composition.

Closely Related Keys

The concept of closely related keys can help you determine other modulation possibilities.

KEY CONCEPT The most typical modulations in common-practice tonal music are from the primary key to a **closely related key**, effected by means of a pivot chord. Closely related keys are those whose tonic chords are diatonic in the primary key.

A closely related key to any given major key is represented by the triad on ii, iii, IV, V, or vi. Figure 22.3 gives the closely related keys for D major: E minor (supertonic, ii), F♯ minor (mediant, iii), G major (subdominant, IV), A major (dominant, V), and B minor (submediant, vi, or the relative minor).

FIGURE 22.3: Closely related keys to a major key

D major:	I	ii	iii	IV	V	vi	(vii°)
	D	e	f♯	G	A	b	(c♯°)

Since the chord built on the leading tone is diminished, it cannot serve as a goal of modulation—the tonic must be a major or minor chord. Therefore, each key can claim five closely related keys. Practice naming closely related keys from any given tonic, so that you are aware of the possibilities for pivot-chord modulation when you compose.

Another Way

Closely related keys may also be identified by their key signatures. Those with the same key signature (relative major or minor) or with a signature that differs by one accidental are closely related. You might think of movement along the circle of fifths (clockwise or counterclockwise). For example, closely related keys to D major are B minor (same key signature); A major and F♯ minor (add one sharp), and G major and E minor (remove one sharp). For E♭ major, the closely related keys are C minor (same key signature), B♭ major and G minor (remove one flat), and A♭ major and F minor (add one flat).

Try it #3

Name five keys that are closely related to each of the following major keys.

GIVEN KEY	CLOSELY RELATED KEYS
F major	______________________
E major	______________________
A major	______________________
G major	______________________
B♭ major	______________________

A closely related key to any given minor key is represented by the triad on III, iv, v, VI, or VII. The five closely related keys for A minor (Figure 22.4) are C major (mediant, III, or the relative major), D minor (subdominant, iv), E minor (minor dominant, v), F major (submediant, VI), and G major (subtonic, VII).

FIGURE 22.4: Closely related keys to a minor key

A minor:	i	(ii°)	III	iv	v	VI	VII
	a	(b°)	C	d	e	F	G

Closely related keys are calculated from scale-degree triads in the natural minor scale. The major dominant key, E major, is therefore not considered closely related, and is not typically a goal of modulation from A minor. (Its key signature, 4 sharps, is too different from 0 sharps to be considered a "close" relation.)

Another Way

Since relative major and minor keys share the same set of closely related keys, another way to locate the closely related keys for A minor is to consider those for C major.

C major:	I	ii	iii	IV	V	vi	(vii°)
	C	d	e	F	G	a	(b°)

Closely related keys for both C major and A minor are D minor, E minor, F major, and G major; the fifth closely related key is the relative major or minor key, C major or A minor.

Try it #4

Name five keys that are closely related to each of the following minor keys.

GIVEN KEY	CLOSELY RELATED KEYS
E minor	
G minor	
C♯ minor	
F minor	
B minor	

Other Pivot-Chord Modulations

From a Major Key to Its Submediant

As we have seen, in major-key compositions, modulation to the dominant is the most common tonal motion, while in minor-key compositions, modulation to the relative major is the most common. From a major key, modulation to the submediant (or relative minor) is another typical destination. In minor-key pieces, this type of modulation frequently serves to return from a foray into the relative major. Figure 22.5 shows the possible pivot chords. (Compare Figure 22.2, where the pairs are the same but the roles are reversed.)

FIGURE 22.5: Comparison of chords in C major and A minor

C major:	I	ii	iii		IV	V		vi	vii°
Chords:	C	d	e	E	F	G	g♯°	a	b°
A minor:	III	iv	v	V	VI	VII	vii°	i	ii°

The modulation from a major key to its relative minor is relatively easy to write because of the large number of shared diatonic triads between these keys: I = III, ii = iv, iii = v, IV = VI, V = VII, vi = i, and vii° = ii°. Again, typical pivot choices are those where both chords have a predominant function, in this case, ii = iv and IV = VI.

Pieces in minor keys sometimes move freely between the tonic and its relative major. One example of this is seen in Example 22.5, a passage from the opening of a Corelli trio sonata movement. Measures 1–2 express A minor, the main key of the movement, then measure 3 moves toward C major, with a ii^6_5–V–I motion in C in measures 3–4. A pivot area is designated here since two successive chords are diatonic and make good progressions in both keys: i = vi and $iv^6_5 = ii^6_5$.

EXAMPLE 22.5: Corelli, Allemanda, from Trio Sonata in A Minor, mm. 1–7

Measures 4–5 center on C major, but in measure 6, F♯ and G♯ signal a return to A minor. The pivot here is I = III on beat 1 of measure 6. It is not possible to use a more typical pivot, like ii^6 = iv^6, on beat 3 because of the need for F♯ in the bass ($\hat{6}$ in A minor) to connect to the leading tone G♯; the chord here is a major IV$^6_5$ instead.

From a Minor Key to Its Minor Dominant

In minor keys, the other frequent destination of pivot-chord modulation is the minor dominant (v), a modulation often found in Baroque-period compositions. Listen to the opening of the Corelli prelude given in Example 22.6. The movement begins in D minor. The first phrase reaches a Phrygian half cadence in D minor in measure 7, followed by a dominant anacrusis to the tonic in measure 8 to start the second phrase in D minor. The second phrase, however, ends with a PAC in A minor. The possible pivot chords are shown in Figure 22.6.

EXAMPLE 22.6: Corelli, Prelude, from Trio Sonata in D Minor, mm. 1–14 (anthology)

FIGURE 22.6: Comparison of chords in D minor and A minor

D minor											
Roman numerals:	i	ii°		III	iv		v	V	VI	VII	vii°
Chords:	d	e°		F	g		a	A	B♭	C	c♯°
A minor											
Chords:	d	e	E	F	G	g♯°	a		b°	C	
Roman numerals:	iv	v	V	VI	VII	vii°	i		ii°	III	

This pairing of keys yields few workable pivot chords. The most typical is i = iv. The III = VI and VII = III pivots may look promising, but they are not as common. One possible reason is that they are associated with relative-major and relative-minor key relations, and do not make as clean a modulation from a minor key to its minor dominant.

In Example 22.6, the pivot chord is indeed i = iv. Some listeners may hear the point of modulation as early as measures 9–10, where v is tonicized; others may hear that use of minor v as remaining in D minor, as the phrase moves immediately back to a D minor triad in measure 11. In measure 12, an E dominant seventh chord (V^7 in A minor) resolves to an F major triad; this progression clearly sounds like a deceptive resolution in A minor. We therefore identify the pivot as i = iv in measure 11.

From a Major Key to Its Supertonic, Mediant, or Subdominant

While pivot modulations from a major key to its supertonic, mediant, or subdominant are possible, each of these pairings is problematic in ways we will see below. Here is a good chance to practice identifying pivot chords.

Try it #5

For each of these key relationships—I to ii, I to iii, and I to IV—complete the chart of pivot chords, using previous figures as models. Draw a square around viable pivot chords. For minor keys, use diatonic chords from the natural minor (no leading tone).

(a) *D major*

Roman numerals:	I	ii	iii	IV	V	vi	vii°
Chords:	D						
E minor							
Chords:	D						
Roman numerals:	VII						

(b) *D major*

Roman numerals:	I	ii	iii	IV	V	vi	vii°
Chords:							
F♯ minor							
Chords:							
Roman numerals:							

(c) *D major*

Roman numerals:	I	ii	iii	IV	V	vi	vii°
Chords:	____	____	____	____	____	____	____
G major							
Chords:	____	____	____	____	____	____	____
Roman numerals:	____	____	____	____	____	____	____

Check your answers before reading further.

The pivot choices from a major key to the key of its supertonic are limited: two of the pairings involve the tonic in one of the keys (I = VII and ii = i), one includes the mediant chord (IV= III), and one involves minor v (vi = v). Modulation to ii is often accomplished by tonicizing ii with V7/ii or vii°7/ii, then continuing in the key of ii, or by sequence.

Modulation from a major key to its mediant is not a popular choice of Baroque or Classical composers, possibly because making vii° (C♯-E-G in D major) into V of the mediant (C♯-E♯-G♯) means altering two chord members. The pivot choices are I = VI, iii = i, V = III, and vi = iv. Of these, I = VI and vi = iv work best.

The problem with modulating from a major key to its subdominant is that to be a convincing modulation, I of the original key has to stop sounding like the tonic and take on the role of the dominant. But if it starts sounding too convincingly like the dominant of IV, then we lose the sense of tonic as the home key. Modulations to IV in common-practice music are typically brief, or they occur well into a longer composition, so that the sense of home key is already well established. There are several good pivot chords, however, including I = V, ii = vi, IV = I, and vi = iii. The best of these is ii= vi, which often appears in a pivot area with vi = iii or IV = I.

SUMMARY

When planning a modulation between closely related keys, you may want to make a chart like those above to help you choose a pivot chord. The smoothest pivots are chords that occur in the predominant-function area in both keys. When you construct a chart, pay careful attention to the two key signatures in determining chord quality; don't try to use a "pivot" that has a different chord quality in the two keys.

Writing a Pivot-Chord Modulation

KEY CONCEPT To create a pivot-chord modulation:

1. Establish the first key, by writing one or more phrases in the initial key or a progression that firmly establishes a sense of tonic.
2. Examine the possible pivot chords. Compare the diatonic chords in the two keys, and determine which chords can function in both.
3. Write a progression in the first key through the pivot chord(s).
4. Continue from the pivot chord with a normal progression in the new key.
5. Write a cadence in the new key.

The music that follows the modulation may continue in the new key or return to the old. All voice-leading guidelines that are relevant to the progressions in each key apply: follow normal guidelines for doubling and parallels, resolve leading tones according to the prevailing key at that moment, and don't forget to resolve sevenths and other tendency tones.

Direct Modulations

Not all modulations to closely related keys involve pivot chords. Sometimes a new phrase simply begins in the new key; or a new key may be introduced midphrase, without a pivot chord, by dominant-to-tonic motion in that key. These **direct modulations** are typical in chorale settings, but may also be found in other contexts. Depending on how sudden and unexpected the change of key is, some writers refer to direct modulations as **abrupt modulations**. Others may refer to phrases that begin in the new key without preparation or transition as **phrase modulations**.

Listen, for example, to the first two phrases from Bach's "O Haupt voll Blut und Wunden" (Example 22.7).

EXAMPLE 22.7: Bach, "O Haupt voll Blut und Wunden," mm. 1–4

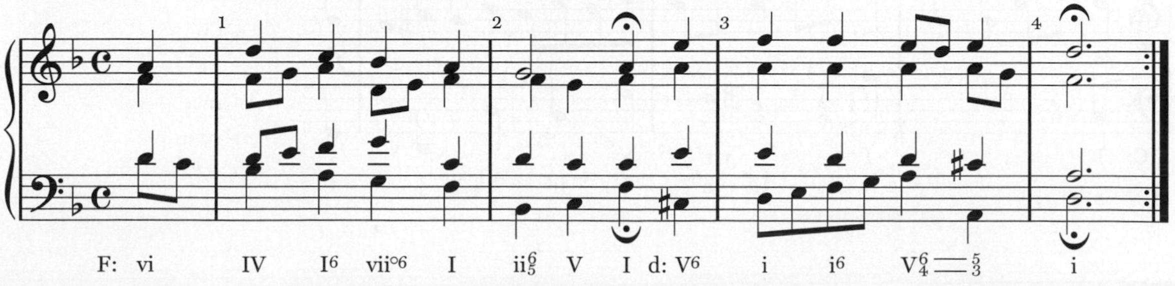

The first phrase cadences in F major, the primary key of this setting, with the progression (beginning in m. 1, beat 4) I–ii$^6_5$–V–I. The next phrase starts right out in the new key of D minor, with V^6–i. If those two chords were immediately followed by chords in F major, we would label them V^6/vi–vi and consider them a tonicization of vi. Instead, the phrase continues in D minor and cadences in that key, confirming a modulation to D minor. The direct modulation in this chorale setting is less abrupt than it could be because the arrival of D minor is prepared by the beginning of the first phrase. The first two chords of this phrase could be labeled i–VI in D minor instead of vi–IV in F major, although the rest of the first phrase confirms that the F major analysis is the preferred one. Still, without this opening emphasizing a D minor triad, the shift to D minor at the beginning of the second phrase might seem more sudden.

Modulations Introduced by Secondary Dominants

It is possible to introduce a direct modulation anywhere within a phrase with a secondary-dominant-function chord. Write the progression with a secondary dominant as though a tonicization, then continue the progression in the new key. Be sure to include predominant-function chords and a cadence in the new key to confirm the modulation. While this type of modulation is not as seamless as a pivot-chord modulation, it does not have to sound abrupt.

For an example of this type of modulation, listen to the first eight measures of Clementi's Sonatina in C Major, shown in Example 22.8.

EXAMPLE 22.8: Clementi, Sonatina in C Major, mm. 1–8a

The first phrase (mm. 1–4) establishes the main key of the piece, C major. Measures 7–15, though, are in the secondary key of G major. Clementi moves from one key to the next by what may seem at first to be a tonicization: a secondary leading-tone chord, vii^{ø7}/V, resolving to V in measure 7. This secondary-dominant resolution is followed, however, by a typical phrase-model conclusion (T–PD–D–T) in G major: I–ii^6–V$^{6-5}_{4-3}$–I. The G major key area then continues to measure 15.

Locating Modulations

The procedure for locating modulations is similar to the one followed in Chapters 20 and 21 to find secondary dominants. First, determine the tonic key. Then scan for accidentals to locate a dominant-function chord that resolves to a new, temporary tonic. Remember that dominant-function chords may include both dominant sevenths (Mm7) and leading-tone seventh chords (usually fully diminished). You may also scan the score for the characteristic $\hat{5}$–$\hat{1}$ bass motion associated with dominant-to-tonic progressions. In many cases where there is a modulation, the dominant-to-tonic motion falls at the end of a phrase, making it easy to spot.

To find the pivot chord, back up from the point of the cadence or the first appearance of chromatic alterations: the chord will usually be located just before the chromatic alteration and may be a predominant-function harmony. Keep in mind that there may be more than one chord that makes sense in both keys. In that case, choose one or label the whole pivot area in both keys.

If the modulation is made by a secondary dominant and continuation in the new key, the first accidental of the new key may be in the secondary dominant harmony; look for a continuation in the new key, including a PD–D–T progression. If there is only a dominant-to-tonic cadence (without a predominant), check to see whether the next phrase continues in the new key. If so, the cadence may be interpreted as a modulation; if not, it should be labeled with a secondary dominant (a tonicization).

Modulations in Musical Contexts

Listen to the opening of "Er kommt," a tenor solo from Bach's Cantata No. 140. To analyze this modulatory passage, begin by determining the opening and closing keys, then find the pivot chord that shifts the tonal center from the first key to the second. As marked in Example 22.9, the passage begins in C minor, with a tonic triad expanded by a neighboring ii$^{\varnothing 4}_{2}$ and leading-tone triad above a tonic pedal, and closes with a T–PD–D–T progression in G minor. Where does the key shift?

EXAMPLE 22.9: Bach, "Er kommt," mm. 1–6a

Look for specific new accidentals: for a modulation from C minor to G minor, the A♭ of the key signature should shift to A♮, and the C minor leading tone (B♮) will disappear in favor of the new F♯ leading tone of G minor. Find the measure in which these accidentals begin to appear consistently—the pivot chord should come right before, in this case measure 3. Either chord in that measure is a potential pivot: i = iv (beat 1) and III^6 = VI^6 (beat 2). Choose one, or include both for a pivot area, then write Roman numerals for measures 3–4 to complete the analysis. Follow this procedure when analyzing modulatory passages, and the choice of pivot chord should be clear.

Harmonizing Modulating Melodies

The principles of pivot-chord and direct modulations may be applied to the harmonization of melodies as well.

KEY CONCEPT To harmonize a melody with an implied change of key, start by making a harmonic plan.

1. Write the scale degrees for the first few pitches of the melody. Harmonize these pitches with chords that clearly establish the primary key.
2. Divide the melody into phrases. A period will require two phrases, while a chorale-style melody will have several short phrases.
3. Examine the melodic cadence at the end of each phrase to see what key it suggests. For phrases whose accidentals and/or melodic cadence imply a change of key, write scale degrees for the cadence in the new key, and select chords that make an effective cadence in that key.
4. In the middle of a modulating phrase, pick a spot for the pivot chord or direct modulation before any accidentals appear in the new key, then write the scale degrees for the entire melodic phrase, indicating the change of key.
5. Choose the remaining harmonies to make a good phrase progression. Remember to add all the necessary accidentals for the new key.

If just the phrase ending indicates a cadence in a new key, you may be able to set the cadence with either a tonicization (V^7–I in the new key) or a full modulation. Think about how firmly you want the new key to be established, and choose progressions to make the effect you want. If the entire new phrase seems to be in a new key (most typical in chorales), you may use a direct modulation. These modulations are easy to write—simply think of the melody pitches for the whole second phrase in the new key, and set them in the normal fashion. Phrases with direct modulations often begin with a dominant-tonic anacrusis.

We now apply these principles to a melody by Schubert, "Nur wer die Sehnsucht kennt" (Example 22.10a).

Example 22.10: Schubert, "Nur wer die Sehnsucht kennt"

(a) Mm. 7–14 (vocal line)

Translation: Only one who knows longing knows what I suffer.

Begin by singing both phrases. The first begins and ends (in m. 10) in the primary key of E minor, with $\hat{2}$ implying a half cadence at the end of the phrase. Although there are no accidentals to point toward a modulation, the second phrase ends on $\hat{3}$ (G), and seems to focus more on $\hat{3}$ than on $\hat{1}$. If you sing the second phrase by itself, it has a G major sound and could be set in G major by means of a direct modulation. Schubert, however, provides a modulation in the midst of the phrase to make the transition more subtle.

Measures 13 and 14 end the phrase with $\hat{1}$–$\hat{7}$–$\hat{6}$–$\hat{7}$–$\hat{2}$–$\hat{1}$ in G major, which can be set with V^{6-5}_{4-3}–I. Therefore, if you begin with a tonic in E minor in measure 11a, you need to modulate between 11b and 12b. There are several ways to do this. Two are shown in Example 22.10b.

(b) Mm. 11–14 (vocal line)

Measures 11–12, beginning in E minor, could be set i iv^6 | V i iv = ii (in G major). Alternatively, i V7/III | III = I (in G major) ii would work (with a suspension in the melody, beat 2 of m. 12, in both harmonizations). Schubert's setting is shown in Example 22.11.

You may be able to think of other possibilities as well. To complete other settings, compose the bass line, using inversions where needed to make a good counterpoint with the melody, then part-write the inner voices as usual. When setting song melodies, give your piano accompaniment a keyboard figuration.

EXAMPLE 22.11: Schubert, "Nur wer die Sehnsucht kennt," mm. 7–15a

Did You Know?

Austrian theorist and composer Joseph Riepel, writing in 1775 in the second volume of his *Anfangsgründe der musikalischen Setzkunst* (*Elements of Musical Composition*), described the relationship between closely related keys as being like the relationships between workers on an estate. In the key of C major, for example, C major is the steward (*Meyer*) of the estate, who appears frequently to keep everything in order; G major is the overseer (*Oberknecht*), second in command; A minor is the head maid (*Obermagd*); E minor is the assistant maid (*Untermagd*); F major is a hired day laborer (*Taglöhner*); and D minor is one of the female household workers who run errands (*Unterläufferin*).

Riepel also describes the key of C minor (again, in relation to C major) as Black Gredel (*schwarze Gredel*)—a woman of a neighboring manor who sometimes lends a hand and therefore is welcome on occasion on the estate, but, as implied by her name, is rather exotic.

TERMS YOU SHOULD KNOW

closely related keys
modulation
- abrupt modulation
- direct modulation
- phrase modulation
- pivot-chord (common-chord) modulation

pivot area
pivot chord
tonicization

QUESTIONS FOR REVIEW

1. What is a modulation?
2. What is the difference between a tonicization and a modulation? What criteria do you use to identify a modulation?
3. What is the most common key to modulate to from a major key? from a minor key?
4. How do you locate the possible pivot chords between two keys?
5. In music for your own instrument, find a modulation from a major key to its dominant. What clues will you look for to locate this modulation?
6. In music for your own instrument, find a modulation from a minor key to its relative major. What clues will you look for to locate this modulation?
7. What are the steps for harmonizing a melody that modulates from one key to another?
8. How would identifying a modulation help you perform a passage?

CHAPTER 23

Binary and Ternary Forms

Outline of topics

Binary form

- Binary form in a major-key piece
- Binary form in a minor-key piece
- Phrase design in binary form
- Tonal structures in binary form
- Types of binary form
- Writing binary-form pieces

Ternary form

- Simple ternary

Binary forms as part of a larger formal scheme

- Composite ternary
- Marches and ragtime

Overview

In this chapter, we consider how musical elements covered thus far contribute to the overall structure of a composition. Specifically, we learn how to recognize two common forms: binary form and ternary form.

Repertoire

Anonymous, Minuet in D Minor, from the *Anna Magdalena Bach Notebook*

Joseph Haydn, String Quartet in D Minor, Op. 76, No. 2, third movement

Wolfgang Amadeus Mozart, Piano Sonata in D Major, K. 284, third movement

Dominico Scarlatti, Sonata in G Major, L. 388

Robert Schumann, "Trällerliedchen" ("Humming Song"), from *Album for the Young*, Op. 68, No. 3

John Philip Sousa, "The Stars and Stripes Forever"

Binary Form

Earlier chapters focused on details of musical construction: intervals, chords, progressions, counterpoint, phrases, and cadences. While we have sometimes considered extended passages, we have not yet addressed **musical form**: the overall harmonic and thematic organization of a composition. One of the most common musical forms, **binary form**, is comprised of two sections, each of which is usually repeated. Two pieces discussed in Chapter 22—Mozart's Piano Sonata in D Major, K. 284, and the Minuet in D Minor from the *Anna Magdalena Bach Notebook*—demonstrate two common ways binary form may be expressed.

Binary Form in a Major-Key Piece

Listen to the theme (mm. 1–17) of the third movement of Mozart's sonata (a theme and variations movement), while following Examples 23.1 and 23.2. You previously examined the harmonic organization of measures 1–8, a modulation from the main key of D major to the key of the dominant, A major, by means of a pivot chord.

Example 23.1: Mozart, Piano Sonata in D Major, third movement, mm. 1–8

Try it #1

Examine the phrases and cadences in Example 23.1. Circle any labels that apply to this phrase structure:

parallel period   phrase group   contrasting period   modulating consequent

Since Mozart's theme divides into two parts, each of which is repeated, it is a binary form. The two phrases in measures 1–8 form the first part. This section is a modulating parallel period, with the phrases labeled **a** (mm. 1–4) and **a′** (mm. 5–8); as it is customary to use capital letters to name sections, this first section is designated **A**.

KEY CONCEPT When the first large section of a binary form ends with a cadence that is not on the tonic harmony, the form is called **continuous binary**, indicating that the piece must continue to a cadence on the tonic. When the first section does end with a cadence on the tonic, the form is called **sectional binary**, indicating that this section is tonally complete and could stand on its own.

Now look at the second half of Mozart's theme (mm. 8b–17) in Example 23.2, and examine its phrase structure. This section, **B**, also divides into two four-measure phrases. While listening to this piece, you may have noticed that measures 13–17 are similar in motivic and harmonic design to the two phrases in section **A**. Compare these three phrases to determine how they are alike and how they differ.

Example 23.2: Mozart, Piano Sonata in D Major, mm. 8b–17

The final (fourth) phrase of the theme (mm. 13–17) encapsulates the melodic and harmonic ideas of the earlier **A**-section phrases, **a** and **a′**. Measures 13b–15 are identical to 0b–2, and 16–17 are a transposition of 7–8 into the key of D major. This phrase can be labeled **a″** to indicate both the similarity to the first two phrases and the differences.

The third phrase of the theme (mm. 8b–12) shares some motivic connections to the other phrases, but it sounds different and forms a contrast to what came before. It is labeled with a small **b** to show its contrasting role. What key or keys do you hear in this phrase? The anacrusis emphasizes the pitch A5, which suggests A major. On the other hand, measure 9 features a short descending-fifth sequence, alternating dominant seventh chords and triads, so that it is hard to hear the tonic. Measure 10 doesn't determine the key either, as the scalar motives do not imply a clear harmony. The tonal ambiguity here is intentional. This phrase ends in measure 12 with a half cadence in D major, but Mozart interprets measures 11–13 quite differently in the various variations of this set. In some cases, the progression seems clearly in A major; in others, D major.

When the initial melody (or the first part of the melody) from the first phrase returns at the end of a binary piece, the form is called **rounded binary**: the return of material from the beginning "rounds out" the formal plan. The overall design of rounded binary is represented by ‖: **A** :‖: **B A** (or **A′**) :‖, with the symbols ‖: :‖ indicating that the music between them is to be repeated. The final section is labeled **A** if the section returns unchanged, and **A′** if the material is shortened or altered (changed to remain in the tonic key, for example). When you write a prime (′) with a letter designation in your analyses, be sure to indicate what is changed to merit the prime.

KEY CONCEPT The term "thematic design" refers to a piece's melody, figuration, texture, and musical characteristics other than harmony. "Harmonic structure" describes the harmonic plan. Even though the thematic design of rounded binary suggests three sections (**A B A′**), its harmonic structure (and, usually, its framing repeat signs) defines a two-part form.

The form of Mozart's theme is diagrammed in Figure 23.1, with the thematic design elements on top and the harmonic structure, with Roman numerals, below. The form is rounded continuous binary: rounded because of its design (the last phrase is **a″**), and continuous because of its harmonic structure (the first section does not cadence on the tonic).

FIGURE 23.1: Rounded continuous binary in the Mozart K. 284 theme

		A		B	A′
Thematic design	𝄆	a	a′ 𝄇𝄆	b	a″ 𝄇
Harmonic structure	D:	I–V (HC)	I modulates to V	sequence (ending with HC in I)	I–I
	mm.	1–4	5–8	9–12	13–17

Binary Form in a Minor-Key Piece

In Chapter 22, you examined measures 1–8 of the Minuet in D Minor, which modulate from the tonic key to F major, the relative major. Listen to the piece again, then consider the phrase design of the opening section of this binary-form piece (Example 23.3).

EXAMPLE 23.3: Anonymous, Minuet in D Minor, mm. 1–8 🎧

Unlike the Mozart example, the first eight measures of this minuet (**A**) consist of contrasting phrases, labeled **a** (mm. 1–4) and **b** (mm. 5–8). The two phrases form a contrasting period. Because section **A** does not cadence in the tonic key, the form is continuous binary.

Now consider the harmonic structure of the second half of the piece, shown in Example 23.4.

Try it #2

Analyze the chords in measures 13–16 of Example 23.4 with Roman numerals.

(a) Measures 13–14 prolong what harmony? ______

(b) The basic progression in measures 15–16 consists of Roman numerals

______ ______ ______ ______.

EXAMPLE 23.4: Anonymous, Minuet in D Minor, mm. 9–16

While the last phrase (mm. 13–16) is firmly in the key of the tonic, D minor, from beginning to end, measures 9–12 feature a melodic sequence. The two phrases, which are contrasting (with each other, as well as with those of the first section) can be labeled **c** (mm. 9–12) and **d** (13–16).

Although all four phrases of this minuet share enough motivic similarity to sound as though they are from the same composition, no two are similar enough to merit the same label. The melodic or motivic materials from the opening section do not return at the end. This type of form, called **simple binary**, is represented by the diagram ‖: **A** :‖: **B** :‖; a formal diagram is shown in Figure 23.2. This minuet is simple continuous binary: simple because thematic elements of the first phrase do not return in the fourth, and continuous because the first section does not cadence in the tonic key.

FIGURE 23.2: Simple continuous binary form in the D Minor Minuet

		A			**B**	
Thematic design	‖:	**a**	**b**	:‖: **c**	**d**	:‖
Harmonic structure	d:	i–i	i modulates to III	melodic sequence (III, i)	V–i	
	mm.	1–4	5–8	9–12	13–16	

Phrase Design in Binary Form

Repeat signs, like those in Examples 23.3 (m. 8) and 23.4 (m. 16), are often the first visual clue that a piece is in binary form. The minuet includes repeat signs, and also first and second endings (which differ in the left-hand part), for each section. The first ending in measure 8 smooths the return to D minor as measures

1–8 are repeated, and the second allows for more finality at the cadence. In some editions of this piece, and in other binary-form movements, the repeats are written out, but the formal organization is unchanged.

KEY CONCEPT The two sections of a binary form may be the same length, or the second may be somewhat longer than the first. The first section consists of at least one four- or eight-measure phrase; it is often a two-phrase parallel or contrasting period. Other typical lengths for the first section are sixteen or thirty-two measures, but it may be longer, and its length need not divide evenly into four-measure phrases.

Because binary form originated in dance movements, individual phrases in many binary-form pieces are four or eight measures long. In binary pieces written for concert performance rather than dancing, there may be some variation in phrase lengths in the second section, often created by phrase extensions or elision.

As already mentioned, the first section of the Mozart theme (Example 23.1) is a parallel period made of two four-measure phrases. There is one unusual element, however, in the second half of the theme (Example 23.2): it is nine measures long rather than eight, with the extra measure formed by the three-and-a-half-beat silence from 12b to 13a. When the theme is performed, this silence simply sounds as though the performer is taking some time between the third and fourth phrases for expressiveness and to heighten anticipation of the concluding phrase. In the other variations, however, Mozart fills this silent span in different ways. Both sections of the minuet, on the other hand, are eight measures long. You could dance to this minuet!

Tonal Structures in Binary Form

KEY CONCEPT The first section in a binary form begins in the main key of the piece.

- In sectional binary forms, the first section stays in the tonic.

Major keys: ‖: I to I (PAC) :‖	Minor keys: ‖: i to i (PAC) :‖

- In continuous binary forms, the first section typically modulates, or it may end on a half cadence.

Major keys: ‖: I modulates to V :‖	Minor keys: ‖: i modulates to III :‖
‖: I to tonicized V :‖	‖: i modulates to v :‖
‖: I to HC (V) :‖	‖: i to tonicized III :‖
	‖: i to HC (V) :‖

The most common modulation goal in major-key pieces is the key of the dominant, and in minor-key pieces the mediant (relative major) or the minor dominant (in Baroque-era works). In some brief and uncomplicated binary forms, a tonicization of V (major keys) or III (minor keys) may substitute for the full modulation, or the first section may remain in the tonic and cadence there, with either a PAC (sectional) or a HC (continuous). In both pieces we have examined, the **A** sections follow the usual modulatory plan: the Mozart theme modulates to the dominant, and the minuet to the relative major.

After the first section's mild foray into new harmonic territory, the second section begins with relative harmonic ambiguity or instability. This instability may be expressed by a sequence or a modulation to another key (usually one of the closely related keys). In the case of sectional binary forms, the second half may begin with a prolongation of the dominant (major-key pieces) or a modulation to the relative major (minor-key pieces). The dramatic instability of the beginning of the **B** section is followed by a reassuring return to the tonic, with a phrase (or at least a strong cadential pattern) reestablishing harmonic stability in the home key.

KEY CONCEPT The organization of the second section of a binary form depends, in part, on the harmonic plan of the first section. Following are some typical harmonic plans for second sections in brief binary pieces.

	1st portion	*2nd portion*		*1st portion*	*2nd portion*
Major keys:	‖: sequence	I–I :‖	Minor keys:	‖: tonicized III	i–i :‖
	‖: tonicized V	I–I :‖		‖: tonicized iv	i–i :‖
	‖: tonicized ii	I–I :‖		‖: tonicized v	i–i :‖
	‖: tonicized vi	I–I :‖		‖: sequence	i–i :‖

In each case, the chart above shows the final portion of the second section entirely in the tonic key. While this is the most common ending, it is also possible for the last phrase or phrases to modulate back to the tonic from some previous "wandering." Occasionally, in slightly longer binary forms (those with a second section sixteen measures or longer), more than one sequence or tonicization may be completed before the main key is reestablished. As we have seen, the second sections of both the Mozart theme and the minuet begin with relative harmonic instability and ambiguity, including a sequential passage, before the tonic key returns.

Types of Binary Form

The minuet and the Mozart theme represent the two main types of binary form: simple and rounded binary. The rounded binary design is the most common in late eighteenth- and nineteenth-century compositions; the material that returns (**A′**) is usually a shortened version of the initial **A**, made from the opening few measures, with a cadence in the tonic key attached. (The cadence pattern may be similar to the cadence at the end of the **A** section, transposed into the tonic key, or not.) This design, **‖: A :‖: B A′ :‖**, is also the basis for sonata form, as you will see in Chapter 32.

The simple binary design, **‖: A :‖: B :‖**, is prevalent in Baroque-era composition. Sometimes, however, the melodic motives of the two sections are quite similar; in these cases, a formal outline of **‖: A :‖: A′ :‖** is more appropriate. Listen to the Sonata in G Major by Dominico Scarlatti, while following the score in your anthology (p. 324), for an example of this design. In simple continuous binary movements like this one (either **‖: A :‖: A′ :‖** or **‖: A :‖: B :‖**), material from the end of the first section sometimes returns at the end of the second section, transposed to the tonic key. In such cases, we say that the two sections are **balanced**. In the Scarlatti sonata, the first section modulates from G major to D major (the ending of the first section is shown in Example 22.5a); this material returns only slightly varied at the end of the second section, transposed to G major (part b).

EXAMPLE 23.5: Scarlatti, Sonata in G Major

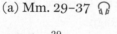

(a) Mm. 29–37

(b) Mm. 69–78

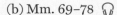

This design can be diagrammed as **‖: A** (x) **:‖: B** (x) **:‖**, or **‖: A** (x) **:‖: A′** (x) **:‖**, where x represents the material that returns. Balanced sections are typically found in Baroque simple continuous binary pieces, as here, where the return of this material can be quite memorable, and can engage a substantial passage of music instead of only a cadential pattern.

SUMMARY

Binary forms are compositions in two parts. They are labeled according to their harmonic structure and thematic design.

If the first half

- ends on the tonic, the binary type is sectional;
- ends on a HC, modulates, or tonicizes a harmony other than the tonic, the binary type is continuous.

If the thematic design of the second half

- contrasts with the first half, the binary type is simple (**‖: A :‖: B :‖**);
- varies or develops material from the first half, the binary type is also simple (**‖: A :‖: A′ :‖**);
- brings back opening (phrase 1) melodic material from **A** in the final phrase, the binary type is rounded (**‖: A :‖: B A′ :‖**);
- brings back material from the end of the first half, the two sections are balanced (**‖: A** (x) **:‖: B** (x) **:‖**).

Writing Binary-Form Pieces

You have already learned most of the techniques needed to compose short binary-form pieces: in Chapter 22, you wrote opening sections that modulate, and you are by now familiar with basic phrase progressions, which typically form the final phrase of the second section. We now focus on how to compose the harmonically unstable beginning of the second section.

To help his students learn how to write this part of a short binary-form piece, Austrian theorist and composer Joseph Riepel (writing in 1755) suggested three progressions, and gave them rhyming Italian names to help his students remember them. These are not the only possible progressions, but they suit our purposes nicely, as well as his.

1. *Ponte* (bridge): main key: V | V | V^{8-7} | I |

   Works well when the first section closes in the tonic key (sectional).

2. *Monte* (mountain): main key: V^7/IV | IV | V^7/V | V |

   Works well when the first section closes in the dominant key, on the tonicized dominant (continuous), or in the tonic key.

3. *Fonte* (fountain): main key: V^7/ii | ii | V^7 | I |

   Works well when the first section closes in the dominant key, on the tonicized dominant, or in the tonic key.

The first progression is called *Ponte*, the bridge, because it spans the measures with a prolonged dominant harmony. Since it is not very interesting harmonically, you would need to revoice the chords or provide melodic interest. This phrase is followed with a final phrase that begins and ends in the tonic.

The second progression is called *Monte*, the mountain, because it sounds like a hiker gradually climbing a steep incline. In composing *Monte* settings, include a melodic sequence to highlight the climbing effect. Here, too, you would follow this phrase with a final phrase that begins and ends in the tonic. You can recognize a *Monte* by its two-chord pattern (a triad preceded by its own dominant) and the pattern's sequential repetition—up a step (from IV to V). It may also be transposed to other pitch levels within the key—for example, V/V | V | V/vi | vi, or V | I | V/ii | ii. This progression does not work as well in minor keys, because of the two alternations needed to turn i into V^7/iv.

The third progression is called *Fonte*, the fountain, because it sounds like water bubbling from one level of a fountain down to another. In composing *Fonte* settings, include a melodic sequence to highlight the bubbling-down effect. As in *Ponte* and *Monte*, you would follow this phrase with a final phrase that begins and ends in the tonic. You can recognize *Fonte* by its two-chord pattern (a triad preceded by its own dominant) and the pattern's sequential repetition—down a step (from ii to I). The progression ii to I is not found in minor keys, because the supertonic chord in minor is diminished (ii°) and cannot be tonicized. This progression may appear transposed to other pitch levels, however, such as V/iv | iv | V/III | III.

In minor-key pieces, the opening of the second section may be a phrase in the relative major or minor dominant. The area of relative harmonic instability may end with a modulation back to the tonic with a half cadence on V, or with a cadence in the temporary key followed by a direct modulation to the tonic at the beginning of the next phrase.

Ternary Form

Simple Ternary

Another common musical form, comprising three sections, is called **ternary form**. Listen to Schumann's "Trällerliedchen," while following the score in Example 23.6. This little piece is part of a collection Schumann composed for children to play, like the *Anna Magdalena Bach Notebook*. Brief ternary-form pieces like this one are sometimes called **simple ternary**.

Example 23.6: Schumann, "Trällerliedchen"

In ternary form (**A B A** or **A B A′**), the first large section, **A**, usually begins and ends in the tonic, with a conclusive cadence at the end. Here, **A** spans measures 1–8, a parallel period (**a** = mm. 1–4; **a′** = mm. 5–8) beginning and ending in C major. The middle section, **B**, is normally in a contrasting key, usually closely related. Schumann's **B** section (mm. 9–16) is also a parallel period (**b** = mm. 9–12; **b′** = mm. 13–16), in the key of G major. As with binary form, the most popular contrasting keys are the dominant in major-key pieces and the relative major in minor-key pieces.

The middle section in a ternary piece often contrasts with the **A** section in at least one way other than key—in its motives, texture, harmonic complexity, or other features. Here, the **B** section shares melodic and harmonic elements with the **A** section, but the roles of the two hands are reversed: in **A**, the right hand has the melody, while in **B** the left hand does. Sometimes the middle section ends with a conclusive cadence in the contrasting key, as this work does in measure 16 (G major). When this happens, the form is said to be sectional—both **A** and **B** are harmonically "closed" and complete in themselves.

When the **B** section ends inconclusively, on the other hand—either with some sort of inconclusive cadence or by connecting without a stop to the return of **A**—the form is said to be continuous: **B** cannot stand alone, and must continue into **A** to reach a harmonic conclusion. The **A** section may be repeated exactly as the third part of a ternary form, as in the Schumann piece, or it may be varied a little (**A′**). In all cases, the return of the **A** section begins and ends in the tonic key as before. The phrase design and tonal structure of "Trällerliedchen" are shown in Figure 23.3.

FIGURE 23.3: Ternary form in Schumann's "Trällerliedchen"

	A		**B**		**A**	
	‖ **a**	**a′**	‖ **b**	**b′**	‖ **a**	**a′** ‖
C:	I		V		I	
mm.	1–4	5–8	9–12	13–16	17–20	21–24

Individual sections in ternary form may be brief—as little as two phrases—or quite long. The three sections are usually balanced in length, as they are in the Schumann piece, but they don't have to be: sometimes the **A** sections are longer, sometimes the **B** sections. Sections may be repeated (with or without first and second endings or written-out repeats), but often, as here, they are not.

KEY CONCEPT Simple ternary form may be distinguished from rounded binary by observing

- the repetition pattern: in ternary form, **B** and the return of **A** (or **A′**) are never repeated together as a pair; if either section is repeated, it is repeated by itself.
- the character of the **B** section: the beginning **B** in binary form is often unstable, sequential, or modulatory; in ternary form, **B** is usually more stable, in its own contrasting key.
- the length of the **B** section: **B** is often longer in ternary forms than in rounded binary.

Sometimes when the **A** section returns after **B**, unchanged from its original appearance, it is not written out but instead indicated by the words *Da capo al Fine*, written at the end of the **B** section. This marking tells the performer to play from the "head" (*capo*), or beginning of the piece, to the word *Fine* (end) at the end of the first **A** section. Another indication, *Dal segno al Fine*, is written if there is an anacrusis or introduction at the beginning of the **A** section that should be skipped on the repeat (*segno* means "sign"). These indications were such a common way of saving paper in opera scores that ternary arias (solo songs within operas) are referred to as *da capo arias*, a song form to be covered in more detail in Chapter 27.

Binary Forms as Part of a Larger Formal Scheme

Composite Ternary

Although a binary form can be complete and freestanding, it can also function as part of a larger work. For example, themes for sets of "sectional variations" are often written in rounded binary form (see Chapter 31).

Sometimes two binary forms in contrasting keys are combined to make a large ternary design: an example is a minuet and trio (or scherzo and trio) movement in a sonata, string quartet, or other multimovement work. This design is called "composite ternary": ternary because of the large three-part form, and composite because it combines shorter binary forms. In Figures 23.4 and 23.5, the highest-level letters are boxed to distinguish them from the letters on the next level, the **A** and **B** sections of the individual binary forms.

(anthology)

Listen to the Menuetto and Trio from Haydn's String Quartet in D Minor (anthology, p. 199) for an example. As is typical for a minuet or scherzo, the first large section ([**A**]) is a complete binary form (in this case, sectional rounded binary) and is followed by a trio (large section [**B**]), also in binary form, in a contrasting key or mode—here, a continuous rounded binary in the parallel major key. In this movement, the minuet and trio differ in style as well, with "learned" counterpoint in the minuet contrasting with a "rustic" country dance in the trio. In performance, the movement concludes with a repetition of the initial minuet, either complete ([**A**] again), or without taking the internal repeats. The indication to return to the beginning and repeat [**A**] is given at the end of the trio as M.D.C, or "Menuetto da capo."

FIGURE 23.4: Composite ternary in Haydn's Menuetto and Trio

	A (Menuetto, D minor) continuous rounded binary				B (Trio, D major) sectional rounded binary			A (Menuetto)
	‖: **A**		:‖: **B**	**A′**	:‖: **C**	:‖: **D**	**C′**	:‖ Repeat of minuet
	a	**b**	**c**	**a′***	**d**	**e**	**d′**	
mm.	1–5a	5–11a	11b–22b	22b–37	38–52a	52b–64a	64b–80	

*The **a′** section is unusual, in that it also includes thematic elements from **c**.

Marches and Ragtime

(anthology) Composite forms may also be found in marches, ragtime, and other types of pieces. Listen to "The Stars and Stripes Forever" while following the score in your anthology (p. 374). This work is typical of band marches, with an opening section (March) in the tonic key (E♭), followed by a Trio in a contrasting key (A♭). Follow the diagram below as you listen. As Figure 23.5 indicates, the March section is a simple continuous binary form and could be played as a complete piece on its own; likewise, the Trio is a rounded sectional binary form and could stand on its own. In marches, the **A**, **B**, **C**, and **D** sections are sometimes called **strains**.

FIGURE 23.5: Composite form in Sousa's march

Introduction	A (March) simple continuous binary				B (Trio) modified sectional rounded binary				
	A		**B**		**C**		**D**	**C**	
	‖: **a**	**b**	:‖: **c**	**c′**	:‖ **d**	**d′**	‖: **e**	**d**	**d′** :‖
E♭:	I–HC (on vi)	I–V	I–HC	I–I	A♭: I–HC (IV)	I–I	sequential "dogfight"	I–HC	I–I
mm. 1–4	5–12	13–20	21–28	29–36	37–52	53–68	69–92	93–108	109–124

While Sousa's March is fairly standard in its tonal and thematic design, the lengthy and elaborate Trio presents some features worth noting. First, the "repeat" in the first section (**C**) is written out because of differences in ways the phrases end. Measures 37–40 and 53–56 are identical, but 41–52 are directed toward half cadences in 44 and 51, while 57–68 diverge to tonicize the submedient (F minor) before moving toward the tonic PAC in measure 68. Second, the Trio's second section (**D**) presents an energetic chromatic and sequential texture that is typical of the beginning of the second half of binary forms. In marches and rags, this section is sometimes called the "dogfight"—a term that aptly characterizes its nature!

The usual formal schemes for marches and rags are similar to composite ternary (for example, minuet and trio), except that they have two large sections instead of three—there is no final return **A** at the end—and within the large sections, the binary forms may be modified. Occasionally, you will find a rag or march in a composite form where one of the embedded smaller forms is ternary rather than binary.

Did You Know?

In the classical era, the components of binary form were so well established that binary pieces could be composed by throwing dice (or other random procedures) to select the phrase beginnings, cadences, and sequences to "plug in" to the formal model. Composing a variety of different pieces from a few stock segments was called *ars permutoria*—the art of combination and permutation. For example, to make an eight-measure parallel period for section **A** of a binary form, a composer could

- select a two-measure phrase beginning;
- select a standard two-measure inconclusive cadence;
- repeat the two-measure opening;
- choose a standard two-measure conclusive cadence.

For a rounded binary form, the composer could choose a four-measure sequence to begin section **B**, then arrange a four-measure concluding phrase from the components of **A** to make a sixteen-measure piece—all selected by "chance."

TERMS YOU SHOULD KNOW

binary form
- balanced
- continuous
- rounded
- sectional
- simple

design
Fonte
minuet and trio
Monte
Ponte
scherzo and trio

strain
structure
ternary form
- composite ternary
- simple ternary

QUESTIONS FOR REVIEW

1. What is the basic principle of binary form?
2. What are the most common harmonic structures for the first section (**A**) in a binary form in major keys? in minor keys?
3. What are the most common harmonic structures for the second section (**B**) in a binary form in major keys? in minor keys?
4. Where are you most likely to find a sequence in a binary-form piece? Where are you most likely to find a modulation?
5. What is the difference between simple binary and rounded binary?
6. What distinguishes simple ternary and rounded binary?

7. What is the difference between simple ternary and composite ternary?
8. How are binary forms used in composite ternary pieces?
9. In music for your own instrument, find one piece in simple binary form and one in rounded binary. How can you use the date of composition to help you locate a piece of each type?
10. What larger forms incorporate smaller binary forms within them?

Invention, Fugue, and Other Contrapuntal Genres

Outline of topics

Baroque melody

- *Fortspinnung*
- Compound melody and step progressions

Invention and fugue: The exposition

- The subject
- The answer and countersubject

Episodes and later expositions

Special features

- Double and triple fugues
- Stretto
- Inversion, augmentation, diminution, and other subject alterations
- Canon
- Vocal fugues

Overview

This chapter focuses on Baroque-era inventions, fugues, and canons. We also consider melodic aspects of Baroque style, including phrase structure, motivic variation, and embellished sequences.

Repertoire

Johann Sebastian Bach
- Fugue in C Major, from *The Well-Tempered Clavier*, Book I
- Fugue in C Minor, from *The Well-Tempered Clavier*, Book I
- Fugue in D♯ Minor, from *The Well-Tempered Clavier*, Book I
- Fugue in E♭ Major for Organ (*St. Anne*)
- Invention in C Minor
- Invention in D Minor
- Prelude, from Cello Suite No. 2 in D Minor (BWV 1008)

Wolfgang Amadeus Mozart, Kyrie eleison, from *Requiem*

Baroque Melody

Fortspinnung

The previous two chapters examined the D Minor Minuet from the *Anna Magdalena Bach Notebook*, which is organized by clear four-measure phrases and antecedent-consequent pairs. While this type of phrase structure is typical of Baroque dance movements, many Baroque melodies are organized by a different strategy. Listen to the Bach's C Minor Fugue (anthology, p. 52) and consider its phrase structure. The opening musical idea, or **subject**, on which this fugue is based, is shown in Example 24.1.

EXAMPLE 24.1: Bach, Fugue in C Minor, mm. 1–3a

Compared with the binary and ternary form compositions studied in Chapter 23, the music of this fugue has no obvious breaks or stopping points. Instead it flows on, with the melody "spinning out" motives introduced in the first measures, until the final cadence. This melodic technique, called by its German name, *Fortspinnung*, is found in Baroque preludes, fantasias, and fugues, as well as in choral works and larger instrumental forms. While the opening idea is short—only two measures—the musical line doesn't stop in measure 3 but continues in sixteenth notes as the next voice is added. *Fortspinnung* passages can be quite beautiful; part of their excitement resides in their unpredictable harmonies and their development of motivic material.

KEY CONCEPT *Fortspinnung* passages are characterized by continuous motion, unequal phrase lengths, melodic or harmonic sequences, changes of key, and elided phrases. To analyze such passages, focus on identifying cadential goals and sequence types, but don't expect equal phrase lengths.

Now listen to the beginning of the Prelude from Bach's Cello Suite No. 2 (Example 24.2); listen for harmonic motion and phrase boundaries, and identify any repeated motives.

Example 24.2: Bach, Prelude, from Cello Suite No. 2 in D Minor, mm. 1–13a

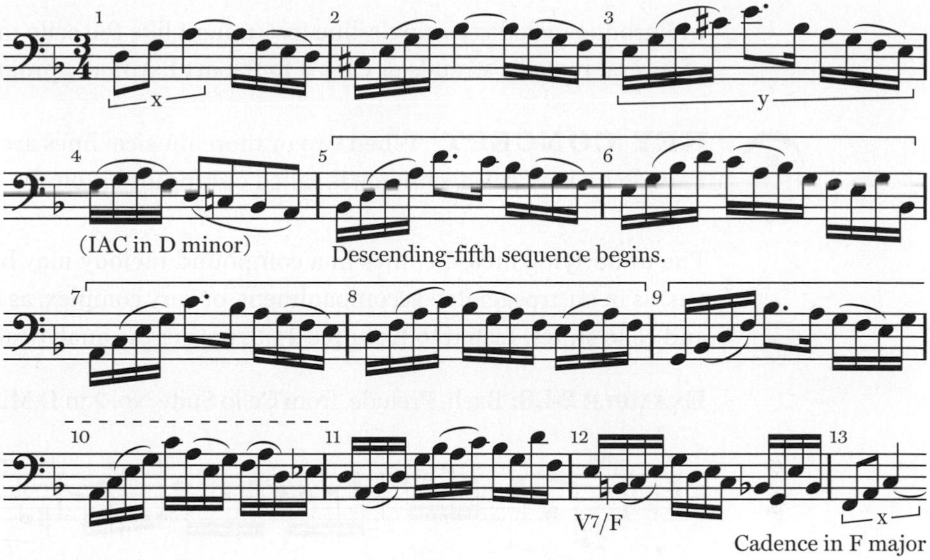

The opening motive in measure 1—we'll call it x—expresses an ascending eighth-note D minor triad, which returns in measure 13 in a new key. Measure 3 features motive y, an ascending arpeggio leading to a dotted-eighth high point, followed by descending sixteenths.

Although this movement is not divided into regular antecedent-consequent pairs, there are some audible cadences that delineate phrases. The task of identifying phrases in unaccompanied solo music like this is challenging, in part because you must infer the harmonic structure from the melody. In addition, there are few pitches of longer duration and no rests to identify phrase endings, since the rhythmic structure is mostly continuous sixteenth notes. Cadences often "rest" for only a sixteenth note—the end of one phrase is connected to the next through an elision—keeping the motion constant. Sequences also contribute to creating longer phrases.

If you judge phrases by the location of cadences, you can determine that this passage consists of a four-measure phrase followed by a nine-measure phrase, with the second phrase characterized by a descending-fifth sequence. The sequence pattern is two measures long, and features motive y in alternate measures (mm. 5, 7, 9). (Listen again to hear how sequential motion impacts the length of the second phrase.) The sequence leads to the change of key to the relative major, F, in measure 13, eliding with the beginning of the next phrase. The x motive repeated here helps make the connection. Unequal phrase lengths and phrase elision, like those here, are typical of Baroque melodies. The movement continues in the same vein: the next phrase is twelve measures in length, sequential, and cadences in yet another key (A minor).

Compound Melody and Step Progressions

In Baroque melodies, a single-line instrument like the cello may create the effect of several melodic strands or even a four-part harmonic progression.

KEY CONCEPT When two or more musical lines are expressed within a single melody, this technique is called **compound melody**.

The underlying melodic lines in a compound melody may be simple and obvious, as in an arpeggiated accompaniment, or very complex, as in Bach's solo violin and cello suites. Listen to Example 24.3, noting the analytical markings.

Example 24.3: Bach, Prelude, from Cello Suite No. 2 in D Minor, mm. 40–48

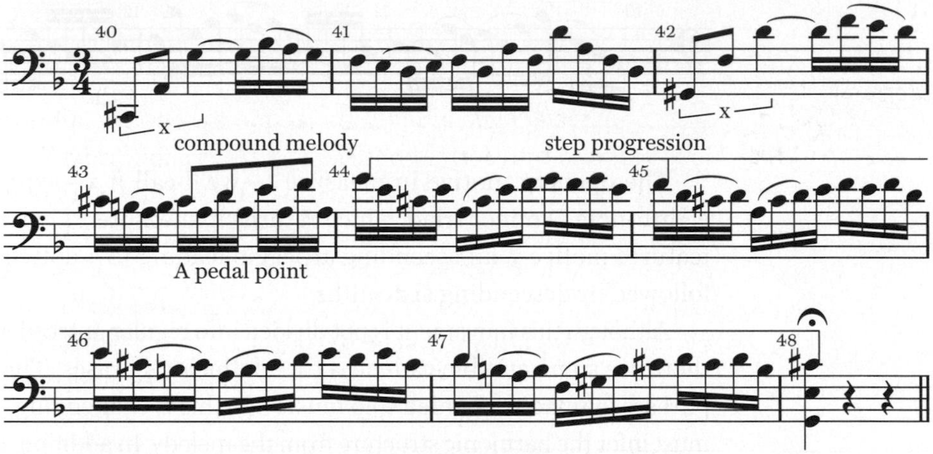

Most striking at the beginning of the example is the development of motive x, transformed from a perfect fifth (D3–F3–A3) to a diminished twelfth (C♯2–A2–G3). The registral shifts from measures 40–42 set up a clear example of compound melody in 43–44, where the cello's repeated A3 (the dominant) becomes a lower-voice pedal point on the sixteenth-note offbeats, while the upper voice climbs by step from C♯4 to G4. The two voices are clearly distinct, an effect created by leaping between two registers.

Another technique for writing compound melody is seen in measures 44 and following: the first pitch of each measure creates a stepwise line—G4, F4, E4, D4, C♯4. This technique is sometimes called a **step progression** and can be marked by stems as in the example. The entire passage between measures 43 and 48 prolongs the dominant harmony: beat 2 of 44–46 touches on a lower-voice A3. Playing the whole passage while singing an A pedal point makes the underlying harmonic framework clearly audible. Cellists who can simultaneously convey the dominant prolongation and the different voices of the compound melody will create an exciting approach to the half cadence in measure 48, which leads to the closing section.

Both of these types of melodic motion—*Fortspinnung* and compound melody—are essential to fugues, inventions, and many other types of Baroque composition. In compositions after the Baroque era, *Fortspinnung* phrase structure, with its dramatic unpredictability and usefulness in connecting key areas, may be found in sonata forms and in improvisatory pieces such as fantasias.

Invention and Fugue: The Exposition

Baroque fugues and inventions are based on the exploration of an initial melodic idea, called the **subject** (abbreviated S or Subj), which establishes the main key and mode, and provides the primary motives for the entire piece. Since part of the joy in listening to a fugue or invention is tracing the path of the subject through various keys and transformations as the counterpoint progresses, the subject is presented several times at the beginning to allow listeners to remember it, with each entry introducing one of the parts, or "voices," of the fugue. Inventions and fugues follow similar contrapuntal processes, but they have a few important differences. **Inventions** are written in two voices (three-part inventions are usually called **sinfonias**); **fugues** typically have three to five voices. The initial section, where the subject is presented in each voice, is called the **exposition**. In an invention, the exposition typically features statements of the subject an octave apart, while a fugue exposition presents statements at the fifth and octave, as described below.

The Subject

The subject of an invention or fugue must be immediately recognizable—with a distinctive contour and a memorable rhythmic pattern—and must be capable of motivic and rhythmic variation. It may be short—only a motive implying one or two harmonies—or several measures long, implying an entire basic phrase harmonic progression. The subject is normally unaccompanied in its first appearance (though there are exceptions, especially if the subject is long).

Examples 24.4 and 24.5 show subjects from an invention and fugue, respectively. They illustrate two typical compositional strategies: scalar subjects and subjects that arpeggiate the tonic triad. The simple but elegant subject from Bach's D Minor Invention (Example 24.4) features a D harmonic minor scale with a change of octave between $\flat\hat{6}$ (B♭) and the leading tone (C♯). This subject introduces the key and mode through the scale and the implied harmonic progression from tonic to dominant (m. 2) and back to tonic (m. 3), and it also displays a distinctive melodic contour with the diminished seventh leap and sixteenth-note rhythmic pattern.

EXAMPLE 24.4: Bach, Invention in D Minor, mm. 1–3a

The subject from Bach's D♯ Minor Fugue (Example 24.5) begins with a memorable ascending-fifth motive, introducing scale degrees $\hat{1}$ and $\hat{5}$. The first two measures emphasize chord tones from the tonic triad, with $\hat{3}$ on the downbeat of measure 2 and motion from $\hat{5}$ back to $\hat{1}$ to establish the initial key and mode.

EXAMPLE 24.5: Bach, Fugue in D♯ Minor mm. 1–3a

Bach also employs a striking rhythmic motive here: a quarter note tied across the beat to stepwise descending eighths. This motive is stated in measure 1 (notated with a dot instead of a tie) and again, crossing the bar line, from measure 2 to 3. We'll call this the "cascade" motive, since the eighth notes cascade down in stepwise motion after the rhythmic impetus of the tie. The motive makes the fugue subject easy to recognize when it returns later in the fugue.

Once the initial statement of the subject has been made, the exposition continues with additional statements, one for each voice. In two-part inventions, the second presentation of the subject is usually transposed up or down an octave in the other part, as in Example 24.6.

EXAMPLE 24.6: Bach, Invention in D Minor, mm. 1–5a

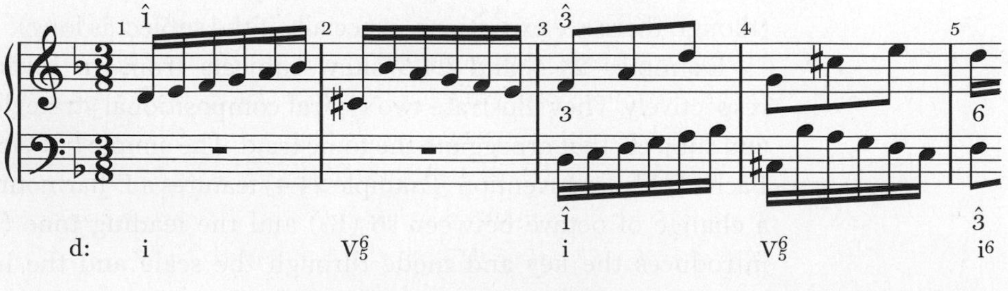

As this example shows, invention subjects often begin with $\hat{1}$ and end on $\hat{3}$; this facilitates the entry of the second part at the octave by creating the interval of a third or sixth. The harmonic implications of the unaccompanied subject become clear as it is set in counterpoint—the upper part in measures 3–4, in combination with the subject, clearly articulates i and V^6_5.

KEY CONCEPT The presentation of a melodic idea in one part, which is then answered by the melodic idea in another part, is called a **point of imitation**.

The Answer and Countersubject

Real and Tonal Answers As in inventions, a fugue exposition normally begins with the entries of the individual voices, one by one. What differs, however, is that the second entry of a fugue subject is typically transposed up a fifth or down a fourth. This transposed entry is called the **answer** (abbreviated A or Ans). In Example 24.7, the subject ends with $\hat{3}$ (E4) on beat 3 of measure 2; the answer, transposed up a fifth from C4, enters on G4.

EXAMPLE 24.7: Bach, Fugue in C Major, mm. 1–4a

If the subject is transposed exactly, as here, with no changes in the sizes of intervals (though they may change in quality), the second entry is called a **real answer**.

In fugues written for keyboard instruments, each voice is active in a specific part of the keyboard range. For four-voice fugues, use the letters SATB to label each contrapuntal line; for three-voice fugues, use S and B for the highest and lowest parts, and either A or T for the middle, depending on its range. (Five-voice fugues may be labeled S1, S2, A, T, B, or some other arrangement.) In Example 24.7, the first two voices of this four-voice fugue enter in the alto and soprano ranges, respectively. While there is no strict guideline for which voice enters first and which second, the parts often enter in pairs that occupy adjacent spans of the keyboard range: S then A, A then S, B then T, and so on. Another possible strategy in three-voice fugues is to begin in the middle voice, add the voice above, then conclude with a bass entrance (as in Example 24.8).

If the fugue subject emphasizes $\hat{1}$ and $\hat{5}$ at the beginning of the subject, it is customary for the second entry to answer with $\hat{5}$ and $\hat{1}$, as shown in Example 24.8. This adjustment, called a **tonal answer**, keeps the answer from drifting off into the dominant key by emphasizing $\hat{5}$ and $\hat{1}$ instead of $\hat{5}$ and $\hat{2}$, which would result from an exact transposition.

EXAMPLE 24.8: Bach, Fugue in D♯ Minor, mm. 1–10a

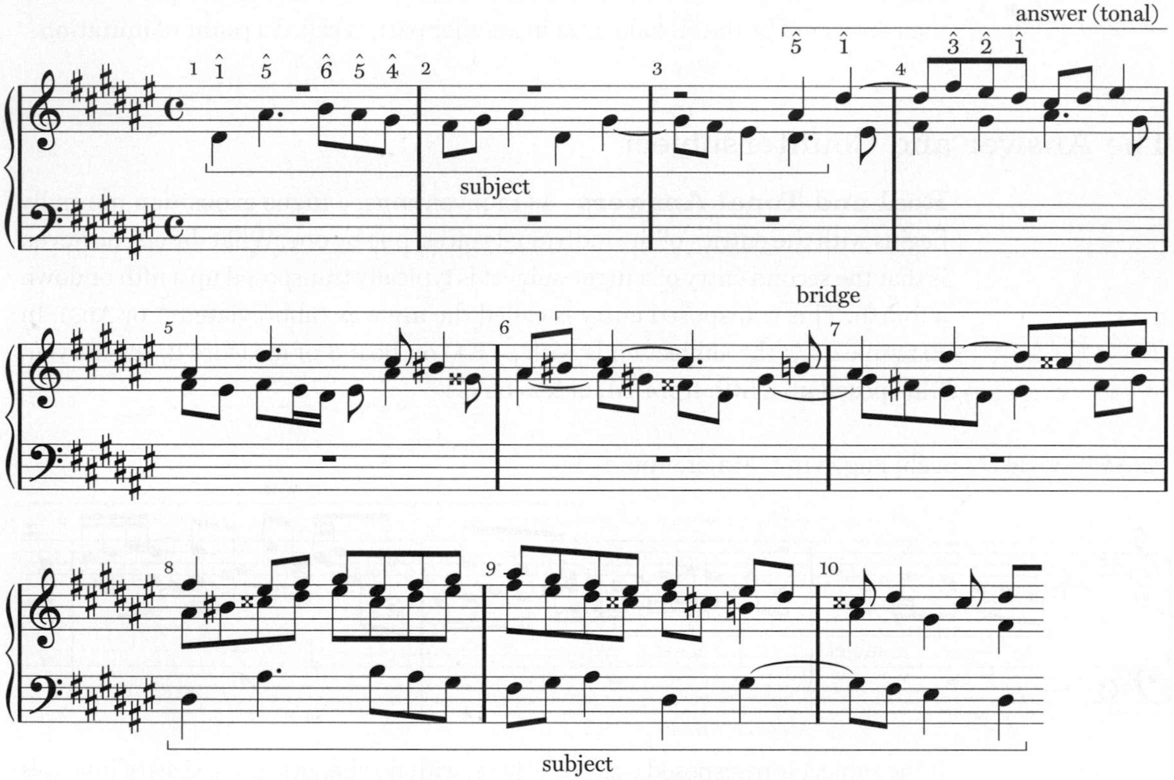

Other adjustments may be made in the tonal answer immediately after the initial ones. In Example 24.8, the second interval of the answer (m. 4) is altered: $\hat{5}$–$\hat{6}$ becomes $\hat{1}$–$\hat{3}$ to make a third instead of a step—which preserves the contour of the subject, and allows the tonal answer to begin and end on $\hat{5}$, just as the subject began and ended on $\hat{1}$. These changes make the opening motive (ascending fifth, then step) a contour motive, since its distinctive intervals change in size in the answer. After these initial adjustments, the tonal answer normally continues without alterations, except for accidentals necessary for the dominant key.

SUMMARY

1. A real answer is an exact transposition of the fugue subject up a fifth (or down a fourth).

2. A tonal answer modifies the initial intervals and scale degrees of the subject slightly so that it does not express the dominant key too strongly.

- A leap from $\hat{1}$ to $\hat{5}$ is answered by $\hat{5}$ to $\hat{1}$ (not $\hat{5}$ to $\hat{2}$).
- A subject that begins on $\hat{5}$ is answered on $\hat{1}$ (instead of $\hat{2}$).
- A subject that begins with $\hat{5}$–$\hat{6}$ is answered with $\hat{1}$–$\hat{3}$.

Try it #1

Examine the subject and answer in this excerpt of the C Minor Fugue.

Circle the answer type: real tonal

If tonal, what intervals and scale degrees are changed? ______________________

____

Look back at Example 24.8 to find the third entry of this three-voice fugue, in measure 8. The third entry normally presents the subject on the tonic again; the initial exposition ends when all voices have presented the subject or answer. Because the answer may introduce accidentals from the dominant key, a short link of a few measures may be needed to prepare metrically and harmonically for the entrance of the subject in the tonic in the third part. Such linking measures may consist of "free" counterpoint or may be derived from the subject's motives, as in Example 24.8 (mm. 6–7). These measures within the initial exposition are called a **bridge** (if more than a few beats long) or a **link** (if only a few beats). In a four-voice fugue, the fourth entry will typically present the answer immediately following the third-voice subject, to create an exposition design of subject-answer-link-subject-answer. Occasionally, the subject and answer entries may be reversed, as in Example 24.9. These measures, from the C Major Fugue, follow after those in Example 24.7. Here, the dominant answer precedes the subject as the last two entries: subject-answer-answer-subject.

EXAMPLE 24.9: Bach, Fugue in C Major, mm. 4–7a

The Countersubject In the exposition, the second entry of the subject (the answer) is set with counterpoint, which may or may not appear again in this exact form later in the work.

KEY CONCEPT The counterpoint accompanying the subject or answer is called a **countersubject** (abbreviated CS) if it appears consistently with the subject later in the piece. If it does not, it is called a **free counterpoint**.

In either case, the counterpoint normally contrasts with the subject in rhythm or contour to keep the two distinct, and the two parts must create correct intervallic and harmonic successions. In Example 24.10, a typical contrast between a subject and its accompanying counterpoint, the sixteenth-note scalar subject contrasts with eighth-note arpeggiation in the counterpoint. Later in the invention, a variety of arpeggiated patterns in eighth notes, rather than this exact counterpoint, accompany the invention subject.

Example 24.10: Bach, Invention in D Minor, mm. 1–5a

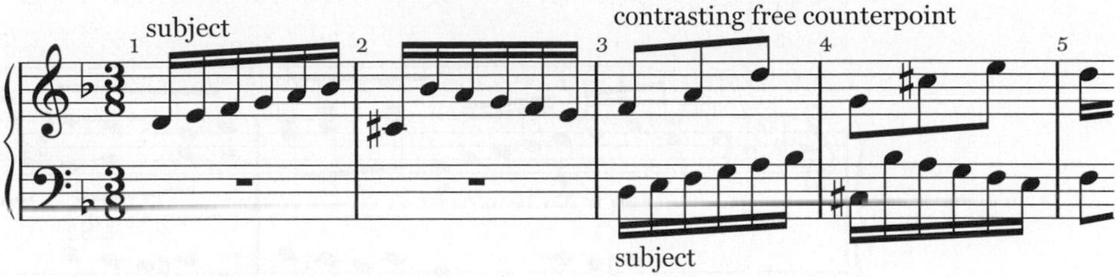

Invertible Counterpoint The subject and countersubject are often written in invertible counterpoint—that is, either the subject or countersubject may appear in the upper voice, with the other in the lower voice, and with the intervals of the counterpoint working properly in either arrangement. For an example, consider the opening of Bach's Fugue in C Minor, in Example 24.11.

Example 24.11: Bach, Fugue in C Minor, mm. 1–5a

The countersubject in measure 3 begins with the scale descending from C5. It is labeled a countersubject, because it reappears many times in the course of this fugue.

Example 24.12 shows the entrance of the third voice, in the bass. Here, the countersubject appears in the soprano part, transposed up a third, and above the subject rather than below it. This fugue is unusual in that it has two countersubjects that return consistently throughout: the new counterpoint in measures 7b–9 in the alto (CS2) also reappears with the subject and CS1 throughout the fugue. One example of this return is shown in part (b), where the soprano has CS1, the alto the answer, and the bass part CS2. When two parts are set in invertible counterpoint, it is called **double counterpoint**; three voices in invertible counterpoint, as here, are called **triple counterpoint**.

Example 24.12: Bach, Fugue in C Minor

(a) Mm. 7–9a

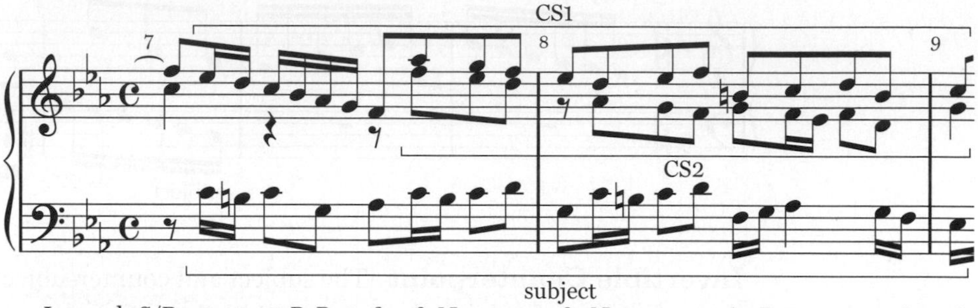

Intervals S/B: 3 3 8 P P 8 6 6 N 5 3 6 N 3 3 3 A4 P 3 4 3 P 6
(IN) (IN)

(b) Mm. 15–17a

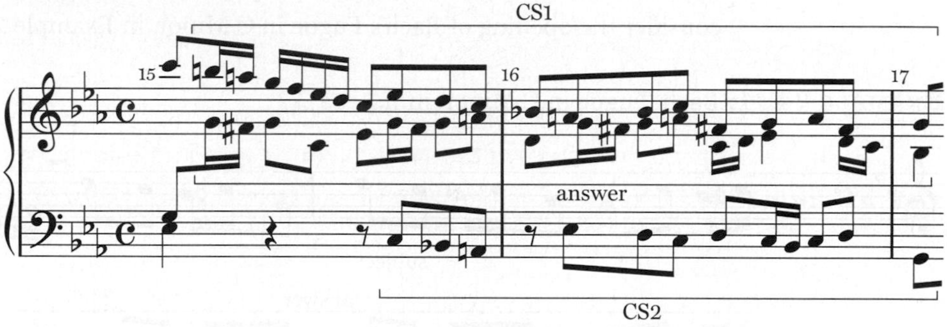

The intervals labeled in Example 24.11 reveal many thirds and sixths, with embellishing tones between them and a d5 on beat 3 of measure 4 that resolves to a third on the downbeat of measure 5. When the voices are rearranged, these intervals become inverted (Example 24.12a)—for example, the thirds become sixths and sixths become thirds. The term "invertible counterpoint" comes from the idea that when the voices are rearranged, the intervals between them invert. P4s are avoided because they are harmonic dissonances (unless they can be interpreted as embellishing tones), and P5s are likewise avoided or treated as dissonances because they become fourths when inverted.

SUMMARY

In invertible counterpoint, the pairs of voices typically feature the intervals 3 and 6 between the parts (implying triads) or the successions d5–3 and A4–6 (which imply V7–i). The P4, P5, and dissonances are employed only as embellishing tones.

Episodes and Later Expositions

Following the initial exposition in the main key, a sequential passage leads to the second key area, where the subject is again presented. The sequential passage is called an **episode** because it strays from the subject. An episode may include one or more sequence patterns (often there are two). Normally the sequence is based on melodic or rhythmic motives from the subject or countersubject. Its harmonic goal is typically the dominant (in major keys) or the relative major (minor keys). As the episode prepares to establish the new key area, several measures of nonsequential free counterpoint may be added to lead to the cadence. Once a new key has been reached, the subject appears, alone or with its answer, followed by another episode leading to a third key (also clearly related), and additional subject entries.

The fugue follows this pattern of "middle entries" of the subject and/or answer alternating with episodes, until a final entry in the tonic key closes the work. Successive entries of the subject may be called exposition 2, exposition 3, and so forth; they differ from the initial exposition, however, in that they rarely present the subject/answer pairings in all voices, and may feature the subject only once in the new key.

Example 24.13 gives the first episode of the C Minor Fugue: the sequence begins in measure 9, beat 1, with the bass clef's C4—a measure-length pattern that moves down by step in measure 10, arriving on an E♭ major chord on the downbeat of 11 to prepare for the subject and countersubjects in that key. Measures 11–13a then constitute a middle entry in E♭, or exposition 2.

EXAMPLE 24.13: Bach, Fugue in C Minor, mm. 9–13a

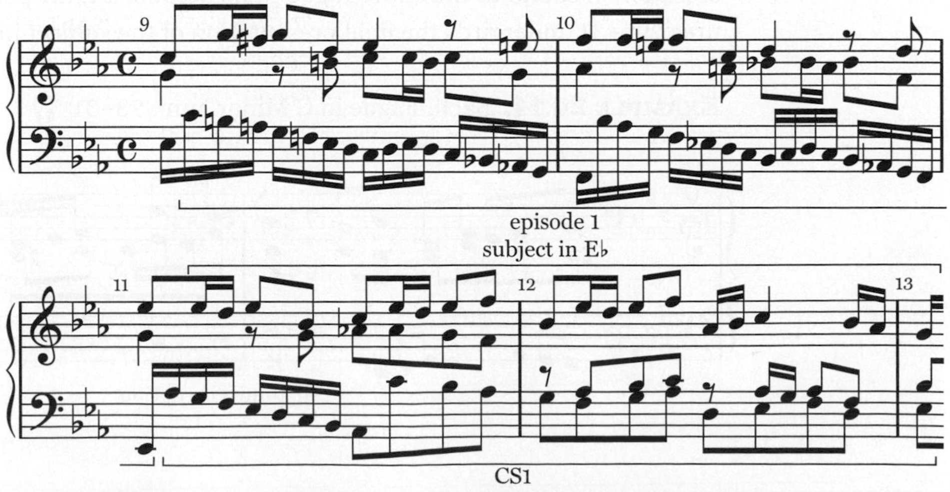

While you can mark the subjects, countersubjects, expositions, episodes, key changes, and cadences directly on the score, these elements may also be represented in a chart or graph, as in Figure 24.1.

FIGURE 24.1: Graph of the C Minor Fugue, mm. 1–16

MM.	1–2	3–4	5–6	7–8	9–10	11–12	13–14	15–16
FUNCTION	exposition	———	(bridge)	———	episode 1 (modulates to E♭ major)	exposition 2 in E♭ major (III)	episode 2 (modulates to G minor)	exposition 3 in G minor (v)
SOPRANO		tonal answer		CS1	sequence on CS1 and subject	subject	based on CS1 and CS2	CS1
ALTO	subject	CS1		CS2		CS2		subject
BASS				subject		CS1		CS2

Although expositions and episodes usually alternate, as in the C Minor Fugue, some fugues devote more measures to the subject (and fewer to episodes), while others may feature longer and more extended episodes (and briefer passages of exposition). Normally the subject and countersubject appear a final time in the tonic key before the end of the piece, in what are sometimes called the "final entries." As the invention or fugue winds down toward the final cadence, the momentum is sometimes slowed by a pedal point, deceptive cadence, or other feature that helps signal the end. Example 24.14 illustrates two of these features: first, a brief eighth-note rest interrupts the entire texture in measure 28—the only such cessation of sound in the entire fugue—and second, a tonic pedal point in measures 29b–31 undergirds the final presentation of the subject in the tonic key.

EXAMPLE 24.14: Bach, Fugue in C Minor, mm. 28–31

Special Features

Double and Triple Fugues

Longer, more elaborate fugues may be based on more than one subject; these are called **double** (two subjects) and **triple** (three subjects) **fugues**. Here, one subject is typically introduced in an exposition at the beginning and the other subject(s) introduced later, either in separate sections or in combination with the previous subject(s).

KEY CONCEPT

1. A double fugue features two subjects (not necessarily appearing at the same time); it should not be confused with double counterpoint, another term for invertible counterpoint in two parts.
2. A triple fugue features three subjects (not necessarily appearing at the same time); triple counterpoint is a rare variety of invertible counterpoint in three parts (usually S, CS1, and CS2).

Bach's *St. Anne* Fugue is a five-voice triple fugue for organ, with three subjects (Example 24.15a, b, and c) introduced in three distinct sections, each with its own character. (The first subject so resembles the hymn tune "St. Anne" [anthology, p. 220] that the fugue has come to be known by that name.) The opening section is set in a stately style, with a half-note beat unit reminiscent of earlier eras. The second section features a lilting compound duple meter (with dotted-half beat unit), and the third a spritely subject that sounds almost dance-like in its $\frac{12}{8}$ meter.

Example 24.15: Bach, *St. Anne* Fugue

(a) Mm. 1–7: Subject 1

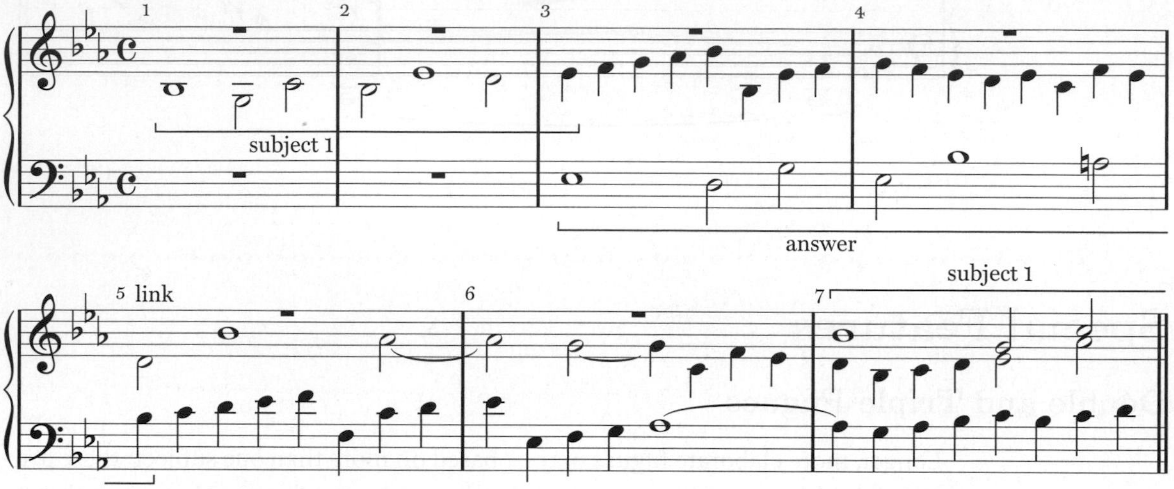

(b) Mm. 37–41a: Subject 2

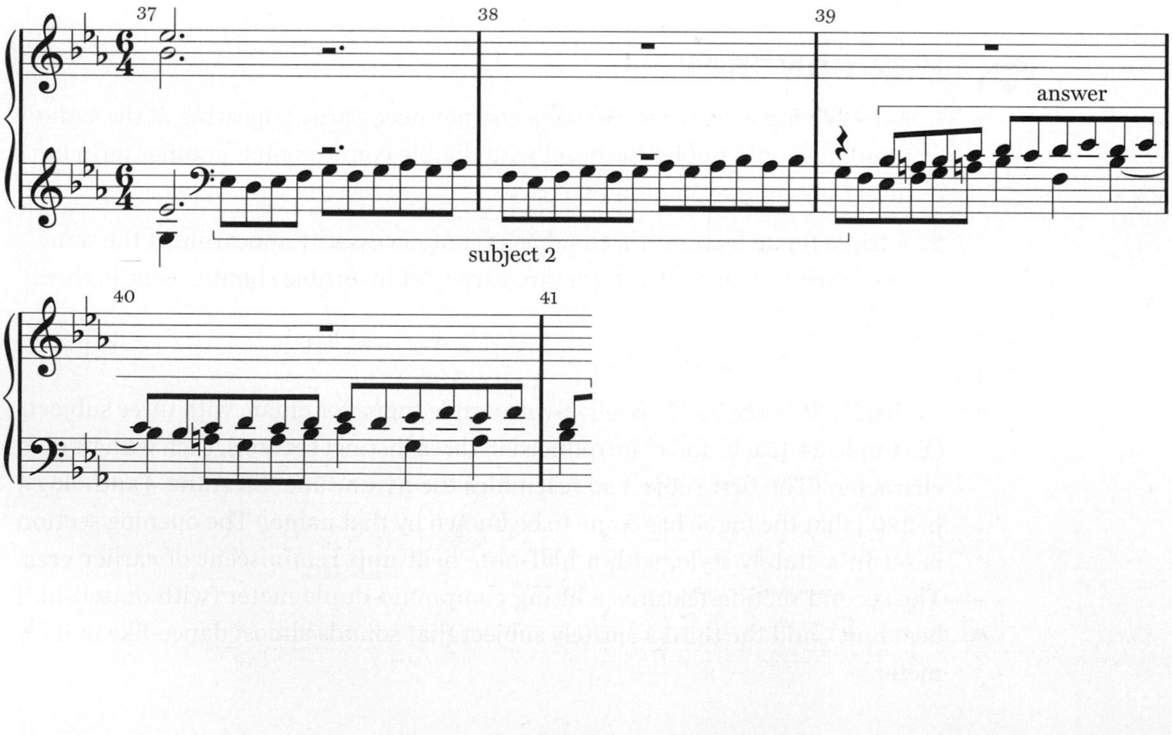

(c) Mm. 82–85: Subject 3

One thing that makes this fugue so remarkable is that Bach combines modified statements of subject 1 (*St. Anne*) with each of the other two subjects as each section drives to its climax. Example 24.16 shows the introduction of the *St. Anne* subject in parts 2 and 3 of the fugue.

EXAMPLE 24.16: Bach, *St. Anne* Fugue

(a) Mm. 59–64a: Subject 2 combined with *St. Anne* subject

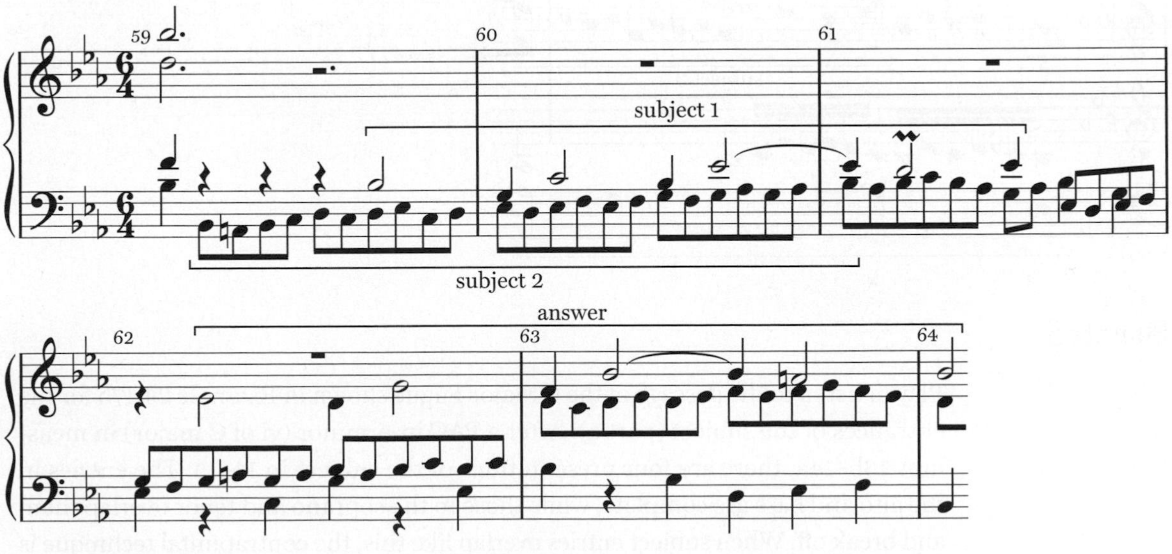

(b) Mm. 91–96a: Subject 3 combined with *St. Anne* subject

Stretto

Play or listen to the passage of the C Major Fugue shown in Example 24.17b for the entrances of the subject (part a). After a PAC in A minor (vi of C major) in measures 13b–14a, there are four presentations of the subject in 14–15. The entries in the alto and bass are complete, while those in the soprano and tenor overlap them and break off. When subject entries overlap like this, the contrapuntal technique is referred to as **stretto**. In stretto, the subject may be complete or incomplete, as here.

EXAMPLE 24.17: Bach, Fugue in C Major

(a) Mm. 1–2a

(b) Mm. 13–18

Try it #2

In measures 16–18 of Example 24.17, the subject enters in stretto in each of the four voices, beginning with the soprano. Mark the other subject entries, and complete the chart below.

Stretto entries: Fugue in C Major, mm. 16–18

MEASURE	BEAT	VOICE PART	STARTING PITCH	COMPLETE OR INCOMPLETE ENTRY?
16	2	soprano	C5	complete

Inversion, Augmentation, Diminution, and Other Subject Alterations

For some additional contrapuntal techniques featured in fugues, we return to the D♯ Minor Fugue, whose subject and answer are given again in Example 24.18. In part (b), the answer appears in stretto in measure 27 in the soprano and alto, accompanied by the cascade motive. Measure 30 introduces another form of the answer in the soprano—this time in **inversion**, accompanied by inverted and noninverted cascade motives.

EXAMPLE 24.18: Bach, Fugue in D♯ Minor

(a) Mm. 1–6a

(b) Mm. 27–34a

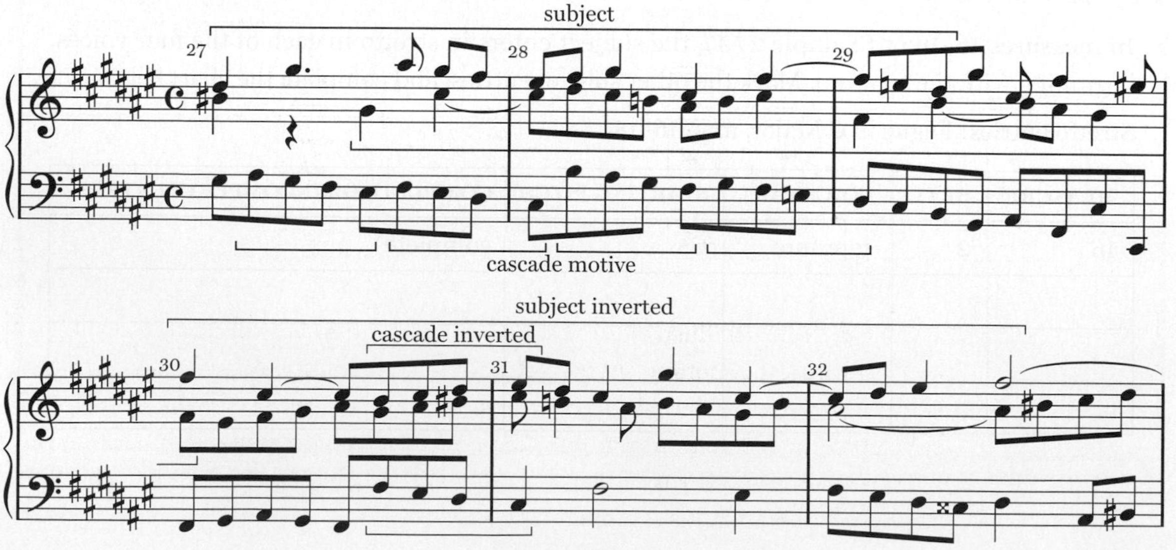

As the fugue continues, Bach also introduces **augmentation**—where the duration of each note of the subject is doubled—as shown in Example 24.19. Here, an augmentation of the answer in the bass (beginning in m. 62) is combined in stretto with an ongoing statement of the answer in the alto (which began in m. 61, and moves from treble to bass clef). After the alto answer concludes, the ongoing bass augmentation is set in stretto with an answer in inversion (beginning in m. 64), in the soprano. One of the few techniques Bach does *not* employ in this figure is **diminution**, where the subject's durations are halved.

EXAMPLE 24.19: Bach, Fugue in D♯ Minor, mm. 61–67a

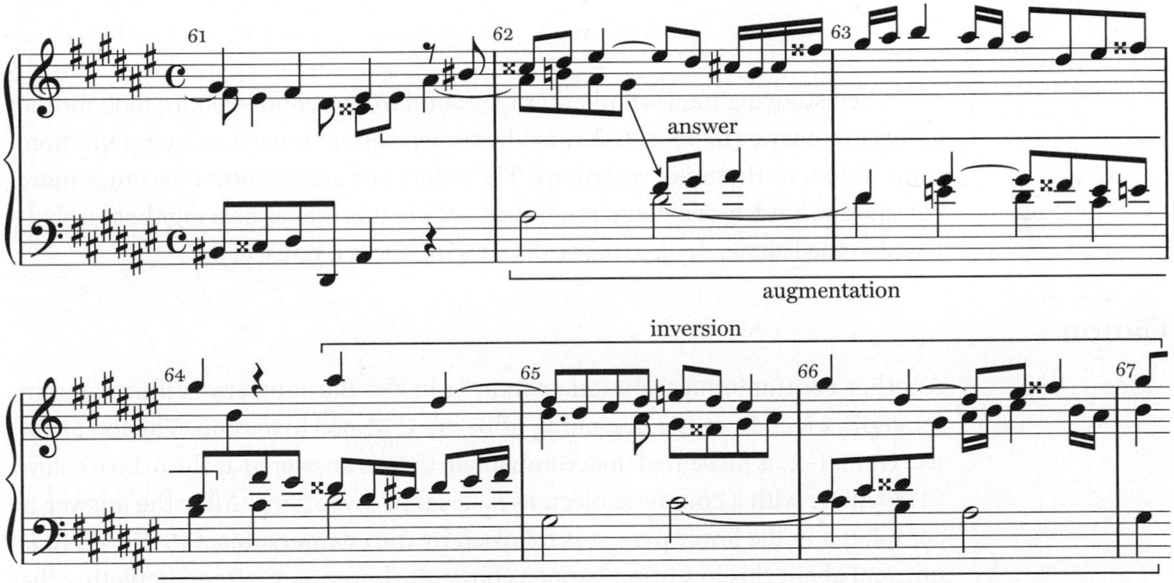

Example 24.20 illustrates one last subject alteration in this fugue: at the end of measure 47, the soprano enters with a rhythmic variation of the answer in inversion. This type of variation might at first seem too far removed from the original subject to constitute a subject entry, but because it is prominently placed in the soprano part and returns in measure 77 to accompany the augmented subject, it should be recognized as a subject variant.

EXAMPLE 24.20: Bach, Fugue in D♯ Minor, mm. 47–50

Try it #3

In Example 24.20 another answer sounds at the same time as the soprano's rhythmically altered answer. This answer enters in m. ______ beat ______, in the (circle any that apply):

soprano alto tenor bass

The answer is (circle any that apply):

inverted augmented diminished complete incomplete

When studying fugues and other types of Baroque counterpoint, look for the subject or answer to be transformed by transposition, inversion, augmentation, diminution, or rhythmic variations. The subject or answer often becomes more complex or hidden as a fugue progresses. While this makes hearing them a challenge to the listener, it also makes discovering them a musical joy.

Canon

Another contrapuntal technique common in the Baroque era is illustrated in Example 24.21, from the beginning of Bach's C Minor Invention. The long subject (mm. 1–2) is presented unaccompanied, then is answered at the octave below (3–4) along with a countersubject, as is usual in inventions. After the answer is completed in the lower part, it is followed by the countersubject (5–6). What is unusual about this invention happens next: the lower part, after completing the countersubject, presents the counterpoint (7–8) that was in the upper part in 5–6. Indeed, the lower part in 3–8 is a complete replication of the upper part's 1–6, transposed down an octave.

This passage and other large portions of the invention are set in **canon**: a contrapuntal procedure where the second part can be derived from the first by following a set of instructions (in this case, "transpose down an octave and delay by two measures"). The canon not only spans the exposition but also serves as the episode, modulating to prepare the second entrance of the subject.

EXAMPLE 24.21: Bach, Invention in C Minor, mm. 1–8

Vocal Fugues

While inventions and fugues are commonly associated with keyboard instruments such as harpsichord and organ, composers from the Baroque era onward have occasionally adapted these contrapuntal principles to vocal and other instrumental genres as well. In Classical and Romantic works, the use of a fugal texture evokes an earlier Baroque style. In Example 24.22, from Mozart's *Requiem*, the "Kyrie eleison" and "Christe eleison" texts are set as an invertible subject-countersubject pair, doubled by the orchestra. The subject and countersubject are distinctly different: an angular ♩. ♪♩ subject ("Kyrie") contrasts with a countersubject that begins with repeated eighths and continues with a long sixteenth-note run moving primarily in stepwise motion ("Christe").

EXAMPLE 24.22: Mozart, Kyrie, from *Requiem*, mm. 1–6

Translation: Lord, have mercy on us. Christ, have mercy on us.

SUMMARY

To analyze an invention or fugue:

1. Examine the subject: What are its key and mode, what harmonies does it imply? What motives does it introduce? Does it have a real or tonal answer?
2. Examine the countersubject. Does it reappear? Is it in invertible counterpoint with the subject? How does it interact rhythmically, melodically, and contrapuntally with the subject?
3. Label the entries of the subject, answer, and countersubject in the initial exposition.
4. Locate the returns of the subject and countersubject throughout the piece. Wherever the subject is present, label and number these expositions.
5. Examine the episodes: Do they include sequences, and if so, what type? Which motives from the subject or countersubject appear? If an episode modulates, how does it accomplish the modulation?
6. What key areas are presented? Where is each established, and how? How do these keys relate to the main key of the piece?
7. Are any subject or answer transformations (such as inversion, augmentation, diminution, or rhythmic variation) employed? Are there strettos?
8. How does the composer bring the invention or fugue to a close?

Did You Know?

The *St. Anne* Fugue is the concluding work of Bach's monumental *Clavierübung III*, sometimes called his *Organ Mass*. Bach wrote four different sets of works that he called *Clavierübung*—literally, "keyboard practice." Other keyboard works bearing this title include the *French* and *Italian Suites* and the *Goldberg Variations*. *Clavierübung III*, for organ, positions the E♭ Major Prelude and Fugue like bookends, on either end of a large collection of chorale preludes. These preludes are based on chorales whose texts are derived from the Lutheran mass and biblical texts, such as the Ten Commandments and Lord's Prayer. The *St. Anne* Fugue is thought to be infused with Christian symbolism of the Holy Trinity ("three in one"). For example, it is written in E♭ major, three flats. It is a triple fugue, with three subjects set in three large sections, where duple beat divisions give way to triple as the fugue progresses: the half-note beat unit of the first section divides into quarter-note threes for part two (in $\frac{6}{4}$), and then further into eighth-note threes for part three (in $\frac{12}{8}$).

TERMS YOU SHOULD KNOW

answer
- real
- tonal

augmentation
bridge
canon
compound melody
diminution
double counterpoint
double fugue
episode
exposition
Fortspinnung
free counterpoint
fugue
invention
inversion
invertible counterpoint
link
middle entries
pedal point
sinfonia
step progression
stretto
subject
triple counterpoint
triple fugue

QUESTIONS FOR REVIEW

1. How do *Fortspinnung* melodies differ from antecedent-consequent phrases?
2. What are some differences between expositions in inventions and those in fugues?
3. In what order do fugue voices typically enter?
4. What scale-degree patterns in a fugue subject require a tonal answer?
5. In what portion of a fugue is invertible counterpoint typically written?
6. What is the tonal function of an episode, and how is this accomplished?
7. How might a fugue slow its motion into the final cadence?
8. What techniques may transform the subject in the middle of a fugue to add interest?
9. In music for your own instrument, find examples of (a) a *Fortspinnung* melody, (b) a compound melody.

Modal Mixture

CHAPTER 25

Outline of topics

Harmonic color and text setting

Mixture chords in major keys

- The spelling and function of mixture chords
- Tonicizing mixture chords
- Embellishing tones
- Mixture and the cadential $^6_4$ chord
- Intonation and performance
- Mixture in instrumental music

Mixture chords in minor keys

Mixture and modulation

Overview

In this chapter, we add harmonic color to compositions by incorporating chords from the parallel major or minor key: these dramatic and unexpected chords are especially effective in music with text, where the color change may highlight important words.

Repertoire

Ludwig van Beethoven, Piano Sonata in C Minor, Op. 13 (*Pathétique*), third movement

Wolfgang Amadeus Mozart
- Piano Sonata in D Major, K. 284, first movement
- "Voi, che sapete" ("You Who Know"), from *The Marriage of Figaro*

Henry Purcell, "When I am laid in earth," from *Dido and Aeneas*

Franz Schubert
- "Du bist die Ruh" ("You Are Rest")
- "Im Dorfe" ("In the Village"), from *Winterreise* (*Winter Journey*)
- *Moment musical* in A♭ Major, Op. 94, No. 6

Robert Schumann, "Ich grolle nicht" ("I Bear No Grudge"), from *Dichterliebe* (*The Poet's Love*)

Harmonic Color and Text Setting

Begin by listening to excerpts from two contrasting vocal works: Mozart's "Voi, che sapete" and Schumann's "Ich grolle nicht." First read the text translations, given beneath Examples 25.1 and 25.2, and choose one important word or phrase that you would highlight musically if you were the composer. Then listen to see how these composers handle the texts.

EXAMPLE 25.1: Mozart, "Voi, che sapete," mm. 29–36

Translation: I feel an emotion, full of desire, which now is pleasure, now is suffering.

EXAMPLE 25.2: Schumann, "Ich grolle nicht," mm. 1–4a

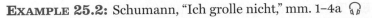

Translation: I bear no grudge, even if my heart breaks.

In Example 25.1, Mozart represents the conflicting emotions of the character Cherubino by introducing chromatic alterations that change the chord quality. The two phrases (mm. 29–32, 33–36) have a parallel structure, but compare measures 31 and 35, and the shift in the vocal line from $\hat{3}$ to $\flat\hat{3}$. This unexpected change of harmonic color makes measure 35 stand out from its surroundings and illuminates its text ("which now is . . . suffering"); the appearance of minor i instead of major I emphasizes Cherubino's state of simultaneous pleasure and pain. (The last chord in this measure combines a $\flat\hat{6}$ and a $\sharp\hat{4}$ with the $\flat\hat{3}$ to make a type of chord explored in Chapter 26: an augmented-sixth chord.)

In Example 25.2, Schumann highlights the word "Herz" with the longest-held pitch of the phrase and a striking A♭, which colors the accompanying supertonic seventh and changes it to a half-diminished sonority, depicting the singer's breaking heart. This shift from $\hat{6}$ to $\flat\hat{6}$—like Mozart's shift from $\hat{3}$ to $\flat\hat{3}$—is an example of **mixture**.

Mixture Chords in Major Keys

Modal mixture, a "mixing" of parallel major and minor modes, is a technique composers employ to enrich their melodic and harmonic language.

KEY CONCEPT Mixture is applied most often in major keys, where the modal scale degrees ♭$\hat{3}$, ♭$\hat{6}$ and ♭$\hat{7}$ are borrowed from the parallel natural minor. For this reason, mixture chords are sometimes called "borrowed chords." The most common mixture chords in major keys, aside from the minor tonic, are those that include ♭$\hat{6}$: ii°6, ii⌀$^{6}_{5}$, iv, ♭VI, and vii°7.

To analyze a mixture chord:

- Adjust the quality of the Roman numeral (uppercase for major or lowercase for minor).
- If necessary, add a ° or ⌀ to a lowercase Roman numeral for a diminished triad or seventh chord.
- If the root has been lowered, add a ♭ before the Roman numeral (for example, ♭VI is built on ♭$\hat{6}$).

For consistency, we will refer to the modal scale degrees as ♭$\hat{3}$, ♭$\hat{6}$ and ♭$\hat{7}$ and the common mixture chords created with them as ♭III, ♭VI, and ♭VII, even when they are spelled with naturals (in sharp keys) instead of flats.

Example 25.3a shows triads built on each degree of an E♭ major scale. In part (b), the triads built on an E♭ natural minor scale are labeled as though they were to appear in E♭ major as mixture chords.

EXAMPLE 25.3: Roman numeral analysis of mixture chords

(a) Triads built on the E♭ major scale

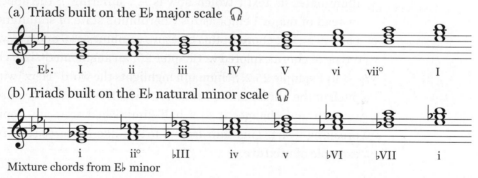

(b) Triads built on the E♭ natural minor scale

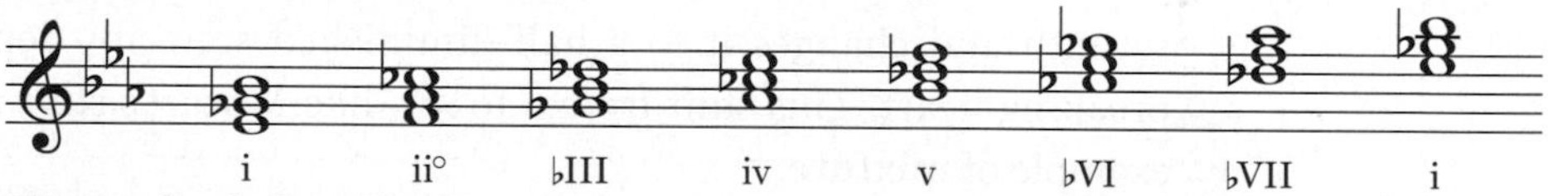

Mixture chords from E♭ minor

Try it #1

For each major key below, identify the key signature of the parallel minor (give the number of sharps or flats), and list the modal scale degrees.

KEY	PARALLEL MINOR SIGNATURE	♭$\hat{3}$	♭$\hat{6}$	♭$\hat{7}$
C major	3 flats			
E major				

KEY	PARALLEL MINOR SIGNATURE	♭$\hat{3}$	♭$\hat{6}$	♭$\hat{7}$
B♭ major				
D major				
B major				

The Spelling and Function of Mixture Chords

When writing progressions with mixture chords, treat them like their diatonic counterparts: they have the same harmonic function and follow the same common-practice voice-leading guidelines as the diatonic chords they replace. Most typical are iv, iv^6, ii$^{\circ 6}$, and ii$^{ø6}_{5}$ in the predominant area, and i, ♭VI, iv, vii$^{\circ 7}$, and their inversions to expand the tonic area. Spell mixture chords as if they appeared in the parallel minor key. For example, to spell iv in C major, imagine iv in C minor: F-A♭-C. To spell ♭VI in F major, imagine VI in F minor: D♭-F-A♭, and so on.

Try it #2

Spell the mixture chords requested in the major keys below. Begin with the key signature, then add accidentals borrowed from the parallel minor key to spell the requested chords.

KEY SIGNATURE | iv | ♭III | ♭VI | vii$^{\circ 7}$ | ii^{ø7}

F major

A major

E♭ major

G major

C♯ major

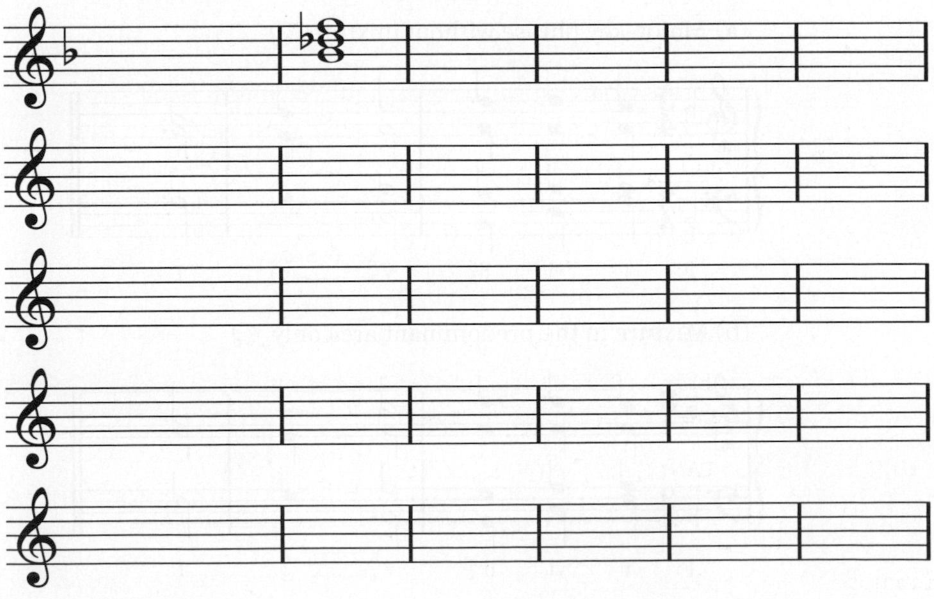

When part-writing or composing progressions with mixture chords, follow the same principles for doubling and voice-leading as in the parallel minor: (1) double the root in a root-position chord, (2) double any stable chord member in a first-inversion chord (often the soprano or bass), (3) double the bass in a second-inversion chord, and (4) double the third (usually in the bass) of a diminished chord. Treat the mixture chords exactly as you would in the parallel minor key: "borrowed" tones may be doubled, and the chords follow the basic phrase model, T–PD–D–T. For example, write iv or ii° in the predominant area, where you would expect IV or ii to precede V. Write ♭VI as a prolongation of the tonic area or for a dramatic deceptive cadence: V–♭VI. Another common progression with ♭VI descends by thirds: I–♭VI–iv. Use ♭VII as a secondary dominant to ♭III, and ♭III as a secondary dominant to ♭VI.

Examples 25.4 and 25.5 demonstrate how a standard basic phrase progression in major may be chromatically enriched by including mixture chords. In both examples, the spacing, doubling, and voice-leading of the original major-key progression is maintained, but accidentals have been added to incorporate the mixture chords. Example 25.4a shows a standard T–PD–D–T progression in F major, including a cadential $^6_4$. In (b), only the ii$^6_5$ has been altered, to iiø$^6_5$ (as in Example 25.2); in this progression, this is the most likely mixture chord. Part (c) features mixture in both the predominant and dominant areas, including a cadential $^6_4$ resolving to the minor tonic. In (d), the opening and closing tonic triads are the only chords that ground the progression in a major key.

EXAMPLE 25.4: Mixture chords in the basic phrase

(a) Major-key phrase without mixture

(b) Mixture in the predominant area only

(c) Mixture in the predominant and dominant areas

(d) Mixture permeating the phrase

Example 25.5a illustrates two common mixture chords: the fully diminished vii°7 chord and the deceptive cadence to ♭VI. This alteration of the leading-tone seventh chord (introduced in Chapter 17) softens the dissonance of the diatonic viiø7; the vii°7 may be written even in passages that do not otherwise feature mixture. Listen to the effect of the V7–♭VI cadence in part (a), rendered all the more surprising by the half-step motion in the bass and the major quality. The ♭VI chord always involves two alterations: ♭$\hat{3}$ and ♭$\hat{6}$.

Measure 2 of part (b) illustrates one potential voice-leading problem that may arise when a major triad is shifted, through mixture, to minor. A cross-relation results when a diatonic pitch (D4 in the alto) is altered chromatically in the next chord in a different voice (D♭3 in the bass). The voice-leading will be much smoother if the IV chord on beat 1 is placed in first inversion so that the bass can move chromatically down from $\hat{6}$ to ♭$\hat{6}$ to $\hat{5}$. Another alternative, shown in part (c), is to introduce mixture one beat earlier, with a root-position iv.

Example 25.5: More progressions with mixture chords

(a) Mixture chords in a tonic expansion and deceptive cadence

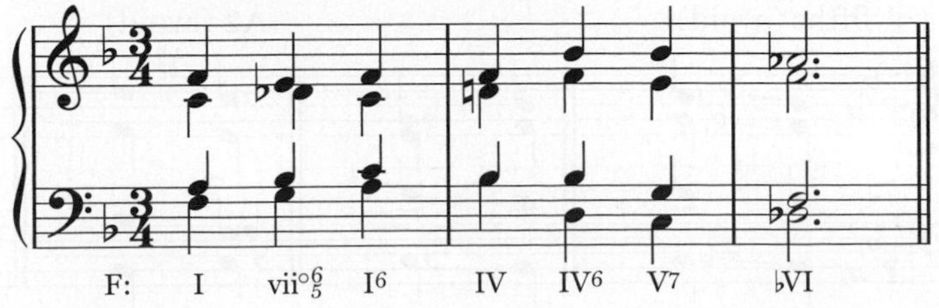

(b) Mixture chord giving rise to a cross relation (avoid)

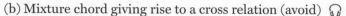

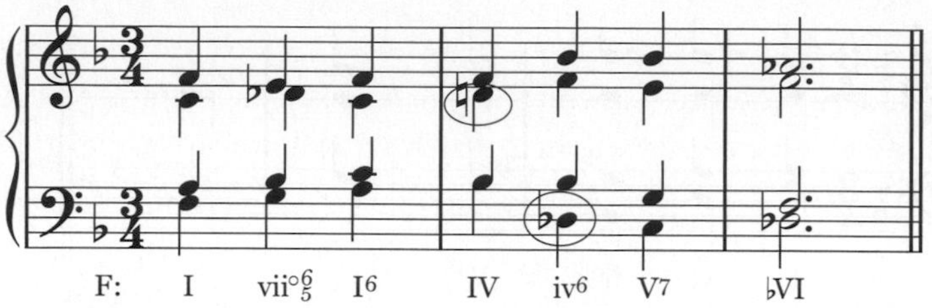

(c) Mixture chords permeating the phrase, except for tonic triads

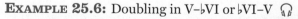

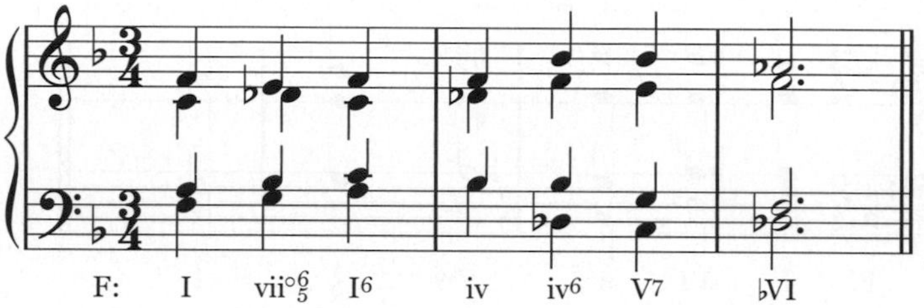

KEY CONCEPT Pay careful attention to altered tones that may create augmented seconds in any voice. Where possible, keep the chromatic semitone (half-step motion between two notes with the same letter name) in a single voice to avoid cross relations, especially between the outer voices. As a general rule, in major keys resolve chromatic tones that arise from mixture down, since they are derived from lowered scale degrees: for example, $\flat\hat{6}$–$\hat{5}$.

Occasionally you will need to change the standard doubling guidelines for smooth voice-leading or to avoid parallels (see Example 25.6). When writing the progression V–♭VI or ♭VI–V, avoid doubling $\flat\hat{6}$, since this creates parallel octaves moving $\hat{5}$–$\flat\hat{6}$ or $\flat\hat{6}$–$\hat{5}$ (part a) or a melodic augmented second $\flat\hat{6}$ to $\hat{7}$ (part c). Remember also, when setting a stepwise bass, to move the upper voices in contrary motion to the bass where possible.

EXAMPLE 25.6: Doubling in V–♭VI or ♭VI–V

(a) Doubled $\flat\hat{6}$ and parallel octaves or fifths (avoid)
(b) OK
(c) Doubled $\flat\hat{6}$ and melodic A2 (avoid)
(d) OK

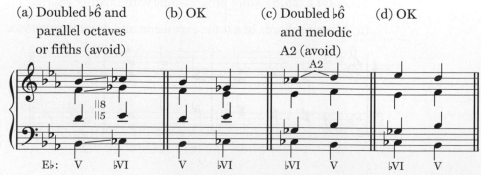

Tonicizing Mixture Chords

Secondary dominants may precede any chord with a major or minor quality, including most mixture chords. When you write secondary dominants or leading-tone chords to tonicize a mixture chord, follow the normal guidelines for spelling and resolution, but be careful to include all necessary chromatic alterations to achieve the correct chord quality (Mm7 or ø7).

Look, for example, at Example 25.7, and compare the two parts. Part (a) shows the singer's opening vocal phrase, a completely diatonic setting with a placid accompaniment that depicts the peaceful imagery of the text. Part (b), however, turns to a passionate statement of love. In measures 54–55, the expected I–vi^6 motion (alternatively labeled I$^{5-6}$) of 8–9 is transformed into I–♭VI^6. This progression highlights the word "Augenzelt" (tabernacle of my eyes) and introduces the accidentals G♭ (♭$\hat{3}$) and C♭ (♭$\hat{6}$). Although the triad in measure 56 might be labeled ♭III, a better interpretation is V/♭VI, which makes the tonicization of ♭VI clear.

EXAMPLE 25.7: Schubert, "Du bist die Ruh"

(a) Mm. 8–11

Translation: You are rest, the gentle peace.

(b) Mm. 54–65

Translation: The tabernacle of my eyes from your splendor alone is illuminated, oh fill it completely!

Consider how the harmonic analysis above can help shape a performance of this passage. First, the introduction of C♭ in the vocal line at measure 55 is an unexpected and dramatic moment. One way to interpret it is for the pianist and singer to hesitate here almost imperceptibly between measures 54 and 55, then continue in tempo—perhaps even pushing the tempo forward a bit until the climax of the phrase, lingering on the temporary tonicization of IV, setting the word "erhellt" (illuminated). This is not the end of the phrase, however: a phrase is defined by a cadence, which in this passage does not arrive until 64–65. The expectation and avoidance of a true cadence makes the silence in measure 61 even more tension-filled. You may want to lengthen this silence slightly, before continuing the phrase in measure 62 with a startling change of mood, dynamic, tessitura, and harmonies. The music concludes with gentle motion toward the diatonic PD–D–T cadence, and not a hint of the dissonance and chromaticism (suspensions, mixture chords, and secondary dominants) that shaped the first half of the phrase.

Embellishing Tones

Mixture can also be employed in melodic lines as an expressive embellishment, without necessarily borrowing whole chords from the parallel key. Sometimes melodic mixture foreshadows mixture chords or modulations occurring later in a work. Listen, for instance, to the passage in Example 25.8, an interlude that falls between verses of "Du bist die Ruh." Up to this point, Schubert's setting has been mostly diatonic, except for a secondary diminished seventh chord that introduces the chromatic element $\flat\hat{3}$ (G♭) in measure 16. In measure 26, he introduces $\flat\hat{6}$ (C♭) as a passing tone, then emphasizes this chromatic embellishment by alternating between C♮ and C♭ in the following measures. These two chromatic elements prepare the mixture chords that arrive some twenty measures later. This type of chromatic "foreshadowing" is a hallmark of Schubert's style.

Example 25.8: Schubert, "Du bist die Ruh," mm. 26–30

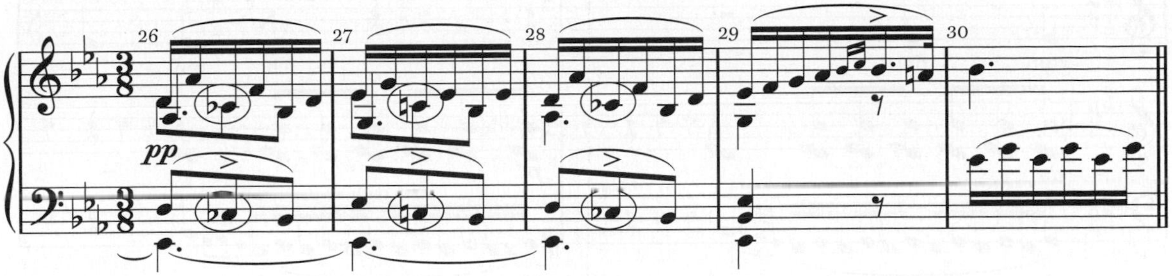

Mixture and the Cadential $^6_4$ Chord

Listen now to two final excerpts by Schubert, from "Im Dorfe," shown in Examples 25.9 and 25.10. This song is highly colored by mixture and provides a good summary and review of mixture chords in major-key compositions.

Try it #3

Example 25.9 is partially analyzed with Roman numerals. Where there is a blank below the staff, provide the appropriate Roman numeral for the mixture chord.

Example 25.9: Schubert, "Im Dorfe," mm. 31b–41a

Translation: Bark me away, you watchdogs, don't let me rest in the hour of slumber. I am finished with all dreams, why should I linger among the sleepers?

In measures 39–40, a tonic $^6_4$ chord appears with a passing function between root-position and first-inversion subdominants. In a parallel passage, measures 44–46 (Example 25.10), the passing $^6_4$ is followed by a cadential $^6_4$ colored by mixture. An analysis of V^{6-5}_{4-3} at the cadence, with uppercase V, would obscure the shift of the suspended $^6_4$ sonority to the minor. To show the change in quality in measure 45, and simultaneously indicate the dominant function of the cadential

$^{6}_{4}$, add an accidental to the figures to indicate that the sixth above the bass has been lowered: $V^{6-\flat 6-5}_{4-4-3}$.

EXAMPLE 25.10: Schubert, "Im Dorfe," mm. 43b–47a

Intonation and Performance

If you are a singer or play an instrument (such as the violin) that requires careful attention to intonation, you may find that passages with mixture are more difficult to sing or play in tune. If that is the case, you might try drawing on a sight-singing strategy for intonation.

KEY CONCEPT To sing or play passages that include mixture pitches, use altered (movable-*do*) solfège syllables to assist with tuning.

$\hat{3} \rightarrow \flat\hat{3}$: *mi* becomes *me*

$\hat{6} \rightarrow \flat\hat{6}$: *la* becomes *le*

$\hat{7} \rightarrow \flat\hat{7}$: *ti* becomes *te*

In Example 25.9, for instance, the melody of measures 36–38 is *re–me–fa–me–do* ($\hat{2}$–$\flat\hat{3}$–$\hat{4}$–$\flat\hat{3}$–$\hat{1}$); changing the syllable from *mi* to *me* can remind you of the narrow half step that mixture provides here. In contrast, in measure 39, the vocalist sings the diatonic *la*, not *le* ($\hat{6}$, not $\flat\hat{6}$) on "unter," despite the prolonged $\flat\hat{6}$ (B♭) in the piano the measure before. Careful distinction between diatonic and lowered scale degrees is essential for performing passages with mixture. Finally, to appreciate the implications of mixture for the interpretation of the text, you need to find a good translation if the song is not in English. Look for a literal, word-by-word translation rather than a "singing translation," which may move the words around or shift the meaning slightly. Then check the meaning of any words set with chromatic inflection or mixture chords. In "Im Dorfe," the use of ♭$\hat{3}$ for the words "finished" and "dreams" may foreshadow the protagonist's eventual death.

Mixture in Instrumental Music

In addition to highlighting important text in vocal music, mixture chords can create an analogous effect in instrumental music. Listen, for instance, to Example 25.11, from Beethoven's *Pathétique* Sonata. Here, parallel phrases are varied by the use of model mixture, changing the tonic triad from major to minor (compare mm. 25–26 with 29–30).

Example 25.11: Beethoven, *Pathétique* Sonata, third movement, mm. 25–33a

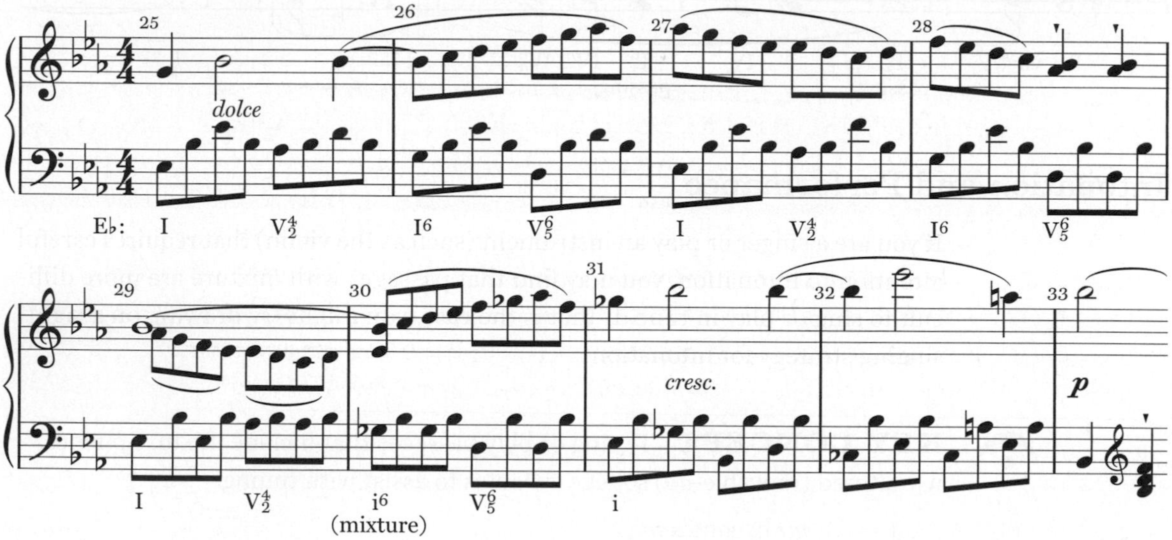

Now listen to a dramatic passage with pervasive mixture from a Mozart sonata (Example 25.12).

Example 25.12: Mozart, Piano Sonata in D Major, first movement, mm. 64–72a

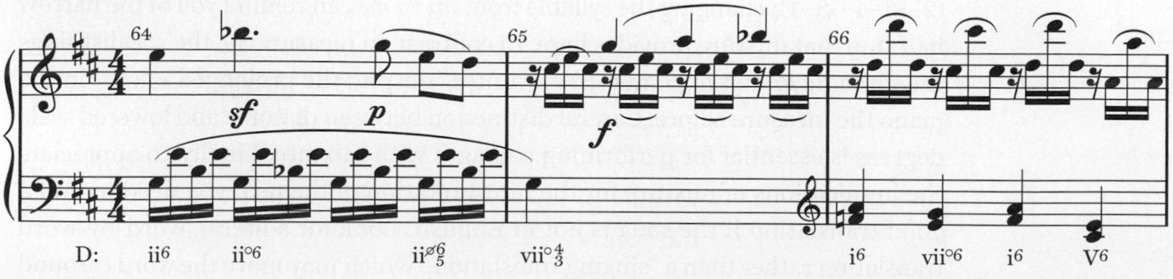

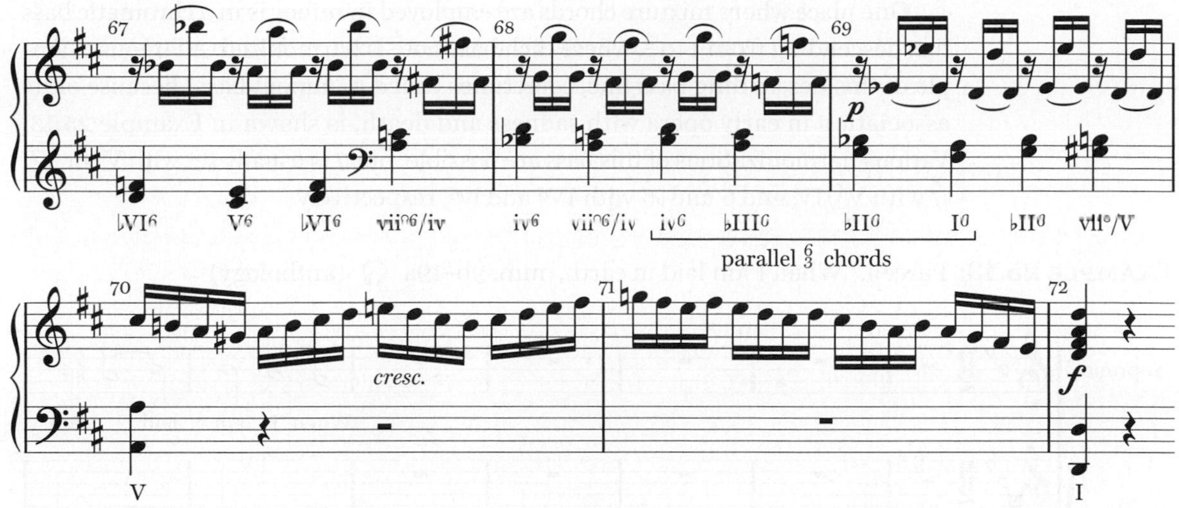

Here, as is typical, the mixture chords appear in the predominant area leading to V. In measure 64, Mozart begins with a diatonic ii^{6}, which is colored on beat 2 by B♭ (♭$\hat{6}$), derived from mixture. The predominant harmony intensifies from ii^{6} to ii$^{\circ 6}$ to ii$^{\varnothing 6}_{5}$, leading to a fully diminished vii$^{\circ 4}_{3}$ (its quality results from the B♭5 on beat 4) that resolves to a minor tonic (with the introduction of F♮, ♭$\hat{3}$). The following measures introduce ♭VI, iv, and ♭III as well. Measure 69 introduces a new harmony that will be the topic of Chapter 26: ♭II^{6}. This harmony is sometimes considered a mixture chord, even though one of its chromatic elements, ♭$\hat{2}$, does not come from the parallel minor scale. In passages that employ mixture for an extended period, as here, ♭II^{6} chords are common.

Mixture Chords in Minor Keys

If mixture chords are defined as borrowed elements from the parallel key, then some alterations to chords in minor keys can be viewed as mixture. For example, in minor keys the minor v chord typically appears as major V, and the subtonic triad VII is altered to create the leading-tone vii°. Both alterations arise from borrowing the leading tone ($\hat{7}$) from the parallel major key. Occasionally composers borrow other scale degrees from major—transforming the minor iv to IV, the major VI to vi, or the minor i to I (known as a "Picardy third" when placed at an authentic cadence)—but mixture, other than that involving the leading tone, is far less common in minor keys than in major.

One place where mixture chords are employed in minor is in a chromatic bass line descending from $\hat{1}$ to $\hat{5}$, where each bass note is harmonized. A famous example of this descending bass line, sometimes called a "lament bass" because of its association in early opera with sadness and death, is shown in Example 25.13. Various harmonizations of this bass are possible, but $\hat{7}$ is usually set with V^6 or V^6_5, $\flat\hat{7}$ with V^4_2/IV, and $\hat{6}$ and $\flat\hat{6}$ with IV^6 and iv^6, respectively.

Example 25.13: Purcell, "When I am laid in earth," mm. 9b–19a (anthology)

Mixture and Modulation

Mixture can color longer spans of music when a piece modulates to the key of a mixture chord. Typically, composers introduce elements of mixture within the primary key to prepare for such a modulation. Look, for example, at the excerpt from Schubert's *Moment musical* in Example 25.14. After the repeat sign, Schubert introduces the modal scale degrees $\flat\hat{3}$ (C♭) and $\flat\hat{6}$ (F♭) in a transitional chromatic section (mm. 17–28) that leads to a new phrase clearly in E major (in m. 29), complete with change of key signature—an enharmonic respelling of ♭VI (F♭ major). Seemingly distant key relations, especially in Romantic-era compositions, may be extended tonicizations of respelled mixture chords. Such respellings allow the performer to read the score in a more comfortable key.

Example 25.14: Schubert, *Moment musical* in A♭ Major, mm. 8b–33a

Did You Know?

The idea that composers might musically interpret the drama and meaning of a vocal text was not new with Classical- and Romantic-era music. Renaissance composers sometimes used melodic patterns and rhythms to represent bird cries or other natural sounds, or they might depict a reference to heaven or a word like "ascending" with a rising melodic line. This technique, as stated earlier, is called "text painting."

Certain Baroque composers employed chromaticism to convey pain or death (see, for example, Bach's settings of the Passion chorale, "O Haupt voll Blut und Wunden"). Their chromatic alterations typically involved inflections within a melodic line and secondary dominants or diminished seventh chords, rather than mixture chords. Bach also used suspensions and other types of accented dissonance to help portray pain and death. Another feature of Baroque composition was the use of "nontempered" tunings, in which different keys sounded distinctive; thus the key or mode used by a composer was, on its own, enough to convey an emotion. The types of rhythms and meter selected by the composer were also an important key to the "affect," or mood, of the piece. For example, long-note durations (whole and half notes, indicating a slow tempo) might represent majesty or grandeur; short-note durations (indicating a quick tempo) might represent gaiety. The interplay of text and music is a rich area for exploration as you prepare vocal music for performance.

TERMS YOU SHOULD KNOW

borrowed chord	mixture	parallel key
lament bass	modal scale degree	Picardy third

QUESTIONS FOR REVIEW

1. What does the term "mixture chord" signify? Why are such chords sometimes called "borrowed chords"?
2. What are the most common mixture chords in major keys? Where in the phrase do they typically appear?
3. What are the most common mixture chords in minor keys? Where in the phrase do they typically appear?
4. Explain how to label mixture chords with Roman numerals.
5. What part-writing guidelines apply to mixture chords?
6. What alterations are needed in solfège syllables when singing mixture chords?
7. In a major-key composition for your own instrument, find a passage that includes mixture chords and bring it to class. (Hint: Look in Romantic-era pieces, and hunt for characteristic alterations such as $\flat\hat{3}$ and $\flat\hat{6}$.) Be prepared to analyze with Roman numerals and sing the melodic line on solfège syllables.

The Neapolitan Sixth and Augmented-Sixth Chords

Outline of topics

Chromatic predominant chords

The Neapolitan sixth

- Voice-leading and resolution
- Writing Neapolitans: Spelling and voicing
- Intonation and performance
- Tonicizing the Neapolitan

Augmented-sixth chords

- Voice-leading, spelling, and resolution
- Writing augmented sixths: Italian, French, German
- Approaches to augmented-sixth chords
- Intonation and performance
- Less common spellings and voicings
- Secondary augmented-sixth chords

Overview

This chapter considers two new ways in which chromatic voice-leading can intensify motion toward the dominant. The chords created by this voice-leading—the Neapolitan sixth and several types of augmented-sixth chords—are among the most distinctive in tonal harmony. We will learn to write, recognize, and interpret them in performance.

Repertoire

Ludwig van Beethoven, Piano Sonata in C♯ Minor, Op. 27, No. 2 (*Moonlight*), first movement

Frédéric Chopin, Prelude in C Minor, Op. 28, No. 20

Fanny Mendelssohn Hensel, "Nachtwanderer" ("Night Wanderer")

Jerome Kern and Oscar Hammerstein II, "Can't Help Lovin' Dat Man," from *Show Boat*

Wolfgang Amadeus Mozart
  Dies irae, from *Requiem*
  Piano Sonata in D Major, K. 284, third movement
  String Quartet in D Minor, K. 421, third movement

Franz Schubert
  "Der Doppelgänger" ("The Ghostly Double"), from *Schwanengesang* (*Swan Song*)
  "Erlkönig" ("The Elf King")

John Philip Sousa, "The Stars and Stripes Forever"

Chromatic Predominant Chords

Among the mixture variants discussed in Chapter 25 was the replacement of $\hat{6}$ with $\flat\hat{6}$ in major keys. This substitution creates a new tendency tone, one with a strong pull to resolve down by half step: $\flat\hat{6}$–$\hat{5}$. In this chapter, we consider two new harmonies that share this $\flat\hat{6}$–$\hat{5}$ voice-leading. They are typically found in minor keys (where $\flat\hat{6}$ is the "normal" sixth scale degree) or in major-key passages that include elements of mixture. These harmonies—the Neapolitan sixth and a family of chords called augmented sixths—characteristically share the same position in the basic phrase: as chromatic predominant chords that intensify harmonic motion to V.

Listen to the minor-key Variation VII from the third movement of Mozart's Piano Sonata in D Major, and consider the chromatically altered chords (marked ??) that lead to V in the two passages excerpted below.

EXAMPLE 26.1: Mozart, Piano Sonata in D Major, third movement, mm. 119b–123a

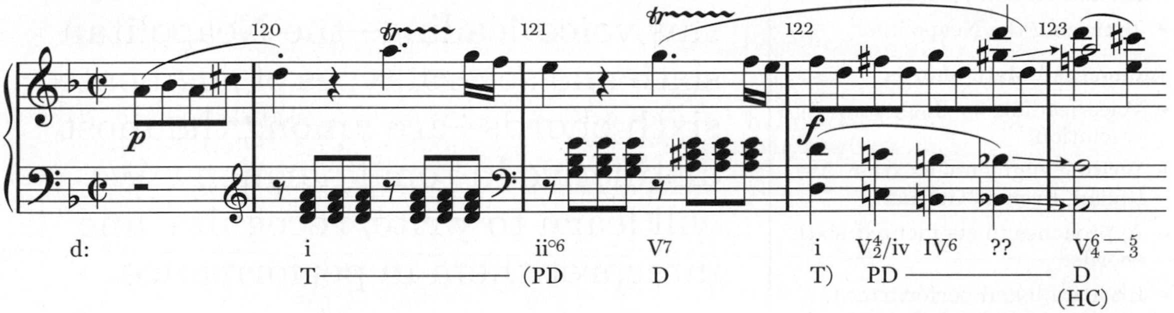

The variation opens with an expansion of the tonic area, by means of an embedded T–PD–D–T, before moving to a PD–D close. The descending chromatic bass line in measure 122 is harmonized with a secondary dominant and major mixture chord (IV^6), followed by a new chromatic chord that intensifies the motion to $\hat{5}$ in two voices: $\flat\hat{6}$–$\hat{5}$ in the left hand and $\sharp\hat{4}$–$\hat{5}$ in the right. This chord, spelled B♭–D–G♯, features the characteristic interval of an **augmented sixth** from B♭ to G♯, which resolves outward to an octave: G♯5 moves up to A5, while B♭2 (with B♭3 doubling) resolves down to A2 (and A3). The resolution, a half cadence on the dominant, is embellished by a cadential $^{6}_{4}{-}^{5}_{3}$.

Now observe a phrase from later in this binary-form variation, the harmonically unstable beginning of the second half (Example 26.2). These measures likewise feature a major mixture chord (IV in m. 128) and a new chromatic harmony in measure 129.

Example 26.2: Mozart, Piano Sonata in D Major, third movement, mm. 127b–131a

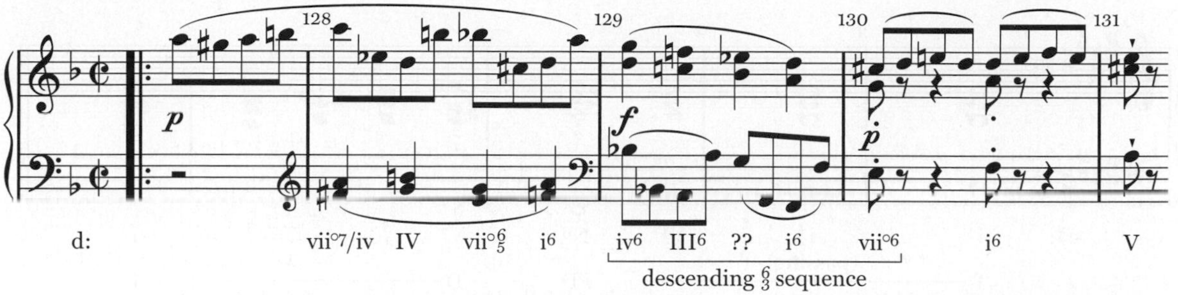

In measures 129–130, a descending $^6_3$ sequence passes from the subdominant to the leading-tone harmony. In the midst of this sequence is a nondiatonic chord that, if stacked in thirds, is an E♭ major chord: ♭II in first inversion. This triad, which includes both $\flat\hat{6}$ and $\flat\hat{2}$, is called a **Neapolitan sixth chord** ($\flat II^6$). It typically appears at a cadence as a chromatic alteration of a predominant harmony, or (as here) as a colorful variant within a descending $^6_3$ sequence.

The Neapolitan Sixth

For an example of the Neapolitan sixth as a cadential predominant, listen to the serene first movement of Beethoven's *Moonlight* Sonata. Follow Example 26.3a as you listen, watching for accidentals that signal chromaticism.

Example 26.3: Beethoven, *Moonlight* Sonata, first movement

(a) Mm. 1–5a

(b) Mm. 1–5a in block chords

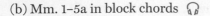

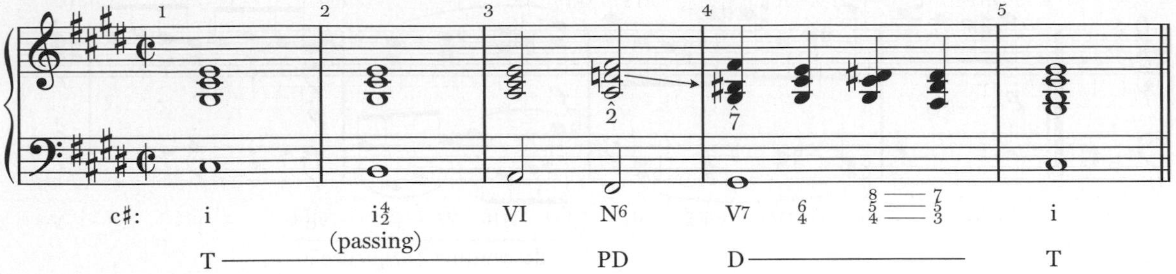

Part (b) provides a block-chord reduction of the figuration and an analysis. At the cadence (m. 4), Beethoven raises $\flat\hat{7}$ to $\hat{7}$ (B to B♯) to function as the leading tone. Preceding this chromatic alteration in measure 3 is an unexpected accidental: D♮, the lowered supertonic. This pitch supports a major-quality triad (D♮-F♯-A), which appears in first inversion—the same type of chromatic predominant chord identified in Example 26.2 as a Neapolitan sixth chord. The Neapolitan takes the place of the diatonic iv chord (F♯-A-C♯), which differs by only one pitch (F♯-A-D♮). In analysis, this chromatic harmony is often simply labeled N6 in place of a Roman numeral, although ♭II6 is also correct. (Another possible name for these chords is Phrygian II, after the distinctive half-step motion $\flat\hat{2}$ to $\hat{1}$ of that mode.) As with other mixture chords, use a flat to designate the lowered second scale degree, even in sharp keys (as in the Beethoven example), where the actual accidental is a natural sign.

Voice-Leading and Resolution

The progression in Example 26.3b clearly follows the basic phrase model, T–PD–D–T, with the Neapolitan chord filling a predominant function and moving directly to V. Follow the alto voice of the reduction to see how $\flat\hat{2}$ moves directly to the leading tone in measures 3–4, spanning the interval of a diminished third (D♮–B♯). Although augmented or diminished melodic intervals are generally avoided in common-practice voice-leading, composers will permit the diminished third in the context of a N6 resolution (see Example 26.4a). Some composers smooth the motion from $\flat\hat{2}$ to $\hat{7}$ by inserting a passing tone to soften the effect: $\flat\hat{2}$–$\hat{1}$–$\hat{7}$ (part b). The passing tone may or may not be harmonized; if harmonized, the typical choice is a cadential $^6_4$ chord (parts c and e) or vii°7/V (parts d and e).

Example 26.4: Resolutions of the Neapolitan sixth

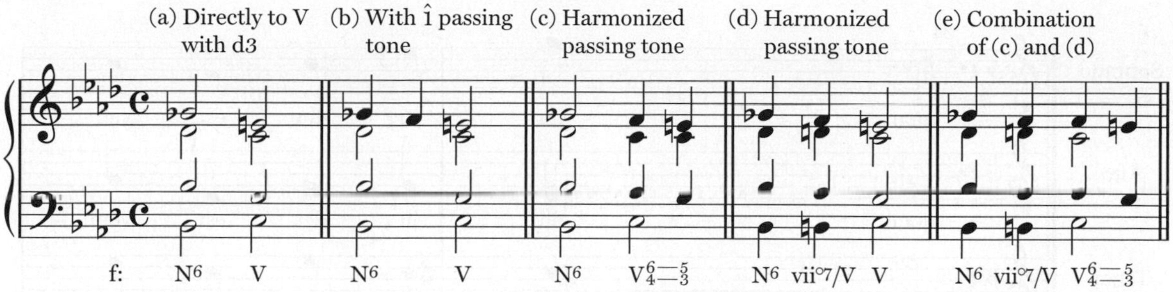

SUMMARY

The N^6 typically appears at a cadence in minor keys, or in major-key passages with mixture chords. It resolves

- directly to V,
- to V through a cadential $^6_4$, or
- to V through a vii°7/V (with or without a cadential $^6_4$).

The other possible context for N^6 is in a chromatic $^6_3$ sequence.

Now listen to the dramatic excerpt from Mozart's Dies irae shown in Example 26.5, or sing through the passage with your class. The text, taken from the Requiem Mass (Mass for the Dead), depicts a wrathful Judgment Day when, according to Christian texts, sinners will be punished and the world destroyed. Mozart represents the day of wrath with agitated string arpeggiation, full chorus, a minor key, diminished seventh sonorities, and colorful Neapolitan harmonies—with $\flat\hat{2}$ prominently voiced in the soprano line (mm. 37 and 39).

In this passage, Mozart prolongs the predominant area in measures 37–39 by means of parallel $^6_3$ chords that extend from one Neapolitan chord to the next. Since the first Neapolitan (m. 37) does not move directly to V, there is no diminished third (although there *is* an expressive augmented second in the soprano). In resolving the second Neapolitan (m. 39), Mozart harmonizes the passing tone $\hat{1}$ with a vii°7/V before the cadential V^{6-5}_{4-3}. This succession of harmonies, $\flat II^6$–vii°7/V–V^{6-5}_{4-3}, is one of the most familiar progressions associated with the Neapolitan's resolution.

EXAMPLE 26.5: Mozart, Dies irae, mm. 34–40a

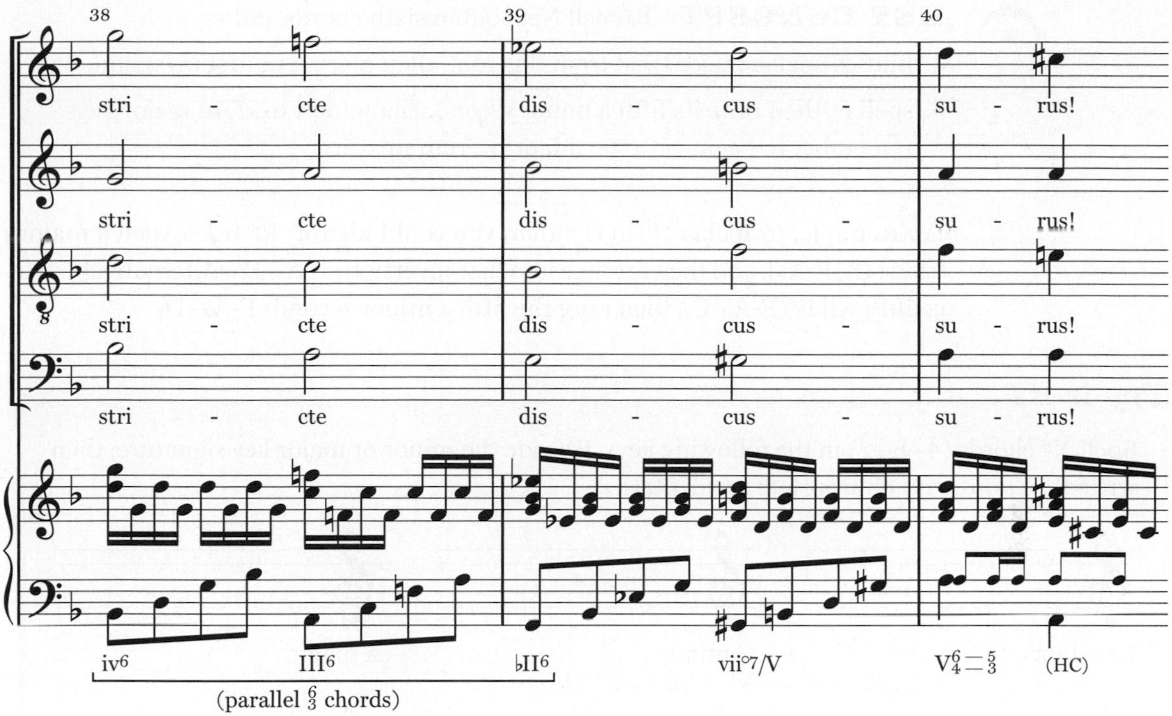

Translation: When the judge comes to adjudicate all things strictly!

Writing Neapolitans: Spelling and Voicing

As mentioned earlier, another way to think of the Neapolitan harmony is as an altered iv chord. Example 26.6 shows the D minor context for a iv chord: the lowest two voices in these chords ($\hat{4}$-$\hat{6}$, or G-B♭) are identical; the Neapolitan's ♭$\hat{2}$ (E♭) displaces $\hat{1}$. This not only changes the quality of the chord to major, it also adds an element of surprise to the harmony, since the E♭ lies outside the diatonic scale.

Example 26.6: Comparison of iv and N6

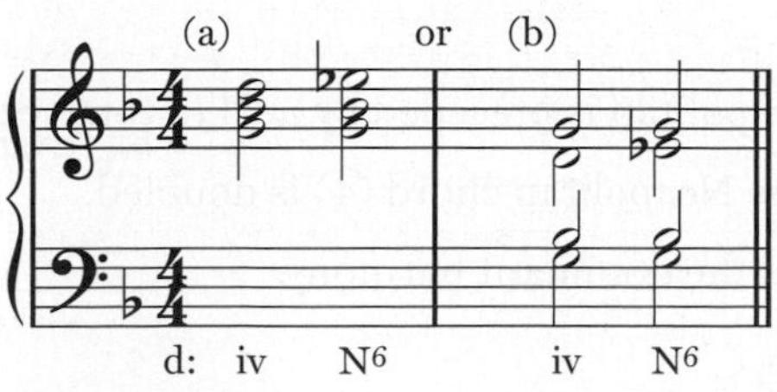

KEY CONCEPT To spell Neapolitan sixth chords, either
- find $\flat\hat{2}$, spell a major triad from this root, then place it in first inversion; or
- spell iv, then raise its fifth a minor second, changing $\hat{1}$ to $\flat\hat{2}$. In major keys, remember to begin with the minor iv, from mixture.

For example, to spell a N^6 in C minor, you could identify $\flat\hat{2}$ as D♭, spell a major triad (D♭-F-A♭), and then arrange it in first inversion: F-A♭-D♭. Alternatively, you could spell iv (F-A♭-C), then raise the fifth a minor second: F-A♭–D♭.

Try it #1

Spell N^6 chords ($\hat{4}$-$\flat\hat{6}$-$\flat\hat{2}$) in the following keys. Provide the minor or major key signature, then write the chord with appropriate accidentals.

KEY CONCEPT When writing the N^6 chord, place $\flat\hat{2}$ or $\hat{4}$ in the highest voice. Don't place $\flat\hat{6}$ there if the N^6 moves through a tonic chord before progressing to V: the resolution of $\flat\hat{6}$–$\hat{5}$ above $\flat\hat{2}$–$\hat{1}$ invariably leads to parallel fifths.

Look back at the Beethoven and Mozart examples to see how these composers handle the issues of progression, doubling, and resolution.

Example 26.3:
- In measure 3, the Neapolitan is preceded by a VI (a tonic expansion).
- The third (bass) of the Neapolitan chord ($\hat{4}$) is doubled.
- $\flat\hat{2}$ moves down to $\hat{7}$ in the dominant harmony.

Example 26.5:
- In measure 39, the Neapolitan is preceded by a string of $^6_3$ chords.

- $\flat\hat{6}$ is doubled in the choral parts (in inner voices).
- $\flat\hat{2}$ moves down, through a harmonized passing tone, to $\hat{7}$ in the dominant harmony.

From these examples, we can add the following to the list of guidelines.

KEY CONCEPT When writing N^6 chords:

1. Precede the Neapolitan with any harmony that would normally precede a predominant-function harmony. This may include another predominant harmony, a tonic harmony, tonic substitute, or tonic expansion; another possibility is a string of parallel $^{6}_{3}$ chords.
2. Double $\hat{4}$, the bass note, when the chord appears in its characteristic first inversion. If necessary, you may use another doubling; but if $\flat\hat{2}$ is doubled, it moves to $\natural\hat{2}$ in an inner voice only, not in the soprano.

Mozart's treatment of the Neapolitan in Example 26.5 differs somewhat from these guidelines, however. Look first at the final Neapolitan chord of this example (mm. 39–40). The chord is preceded by a descending string of $^{6}_{3}$ chords, but here the fifth ($\flat\hat{6}$, B♭) is doubled in the choral parts. The $\flat\hat{2}$ (E♭) resolves normally, down through a harmonized passing tone $\hat{1}$ to $\hat{7}$ in the dominant harmony, but because of the doubled $\flat\hat{6}$, Mozart must resolve one of them irregularly in order to avoid parallel octaves. His choice is to have the $\flat\hat{6}$ in the tenor leap upward by a perfect fifth.

The first Neapolitan of this passage (m. 37) shows another unconventional doubling, with $\flat\hat{2}$ in the soprano and tenor. This results in unusual voice-leading in the soprano, which moves upward by an augmented second (E♭ to F♯). Perhaps Mozart decided on these unusual doublings because he felt that the A2 in measure 37 and the tenor leap to a high F4 in measure 39 would contribute to the text's overall sense of despair and frenzy. In your own writing, conform to the guidelines for doubling and voice-leading unless you have a good reason for doing otherwise.

Intonation and Performance

When performing the Mozart *Requiem* excerpt and, by extension, other passages with Neapolitan sixth chords, keep the following performance issues in mind. Since $\flat\hat{2}$ lies outside the diatonic major and minor scales, and since the Neapolitan relies on its major quality for its identity, correct tuning should be a primary concern. If you sing the soprano line of Example 26.5 with solfège syllables, you will need to inflect three of them: *ti* for $\hat{7}$, *ra* for $\flat\hat{2}$ (*re* lowered a half step), and *mi* for $\hat{3}$.

Try it #2

Write the correct solfège syllables or scale-degree numbers for the soprano line of Example 26.5 in the blanks provided for each measure below.

m. 34	m. 35	m. 36	m. 37	m. 38	m. 39	m. 40
ti *fa*	___ ___ ___ ___	___ ___ ___	___ ___	___ ___	___ ___	___ ___
$\hat{7}$ $\hat{4}$	___ ___ ___ ___	___ ___ ___	___ ___	___ ___	___ ___	___ ___

The soprano's diminished fifth (*ti–fa*) in measure 34 can be somewhat difficult to tune, but probably more challenging is the augmented second in measure 37, *ra–mi*. It is sometimes helpful to exaggerate the altered $\flat\hat{2}$ (*ra*) very low, and think $\hat{3}$ (*mi*) very high. In tuning N6 when it resolves to V, think also of the eventual goal of $\flat\hat{2}$ (*ra*), beyond the passing $\hat{1}$ (*do*) to $\hat{7}$ (*ti*). You may even wish to employ a darker tone color for the lowered pitches and brighter for the raised pitches. Such exaggerations hold true especially in ensemble singing and playing, where this line is crucial in tuning the chord qualities.

SUMMARY

- The Neapolitan harmony appears most often in minor keys.
- Build it on $\flat\hat{2}$, with a major quality, and place it (usually) in first inversion ($\flat$II6).
- When writing the Neapolitan in major keys, be sure to include $\flat\hat{6}$ (from mixture) to make the chord major.
- Place N6 in a predominant role and resolve it to V, with both its tendency tones resolving down: $\flat\hat{6}$ to $\hat{5}$, and $\flat\hat{2}$ (usually through passing tone $\hat{1}$) to $\hat{7}$. Do not resolve $\flat\hat{2}$ to $\natural\hat{2}$, since this voice-leading conflicts with the tendency of $\flat\hat{2}$ to move downward.
- If you harmonize the passing tone $\hat{1}$ when resolving N6, choose vii°7/V or V^{6-5}_{4-3}.

Tonicizing the Neapolitan

The Neapolitan harmony can be tonicized, either by its own secondary dominant or by an extended progression in the $\flat$II key area; the secondary dominant is diatonic in minor keys (VI) or available by mixture in major keys ($\flat$VI). Listen to the passage from Schubert's "Erlkönig" given in Example 26.7, and follow the Roman numeral analysis beneath the score.

Example 26.7: Schubert, "Erlkönig," mm. 115–123a

Translation (sung by the Elf King): "I love you, I am tempted by your beautiful form; and if you are not willing, I will use force."

Measures 117–119 tonicize ♭II, with this harmonic area prolonged by the secondary vii°7. As is typical when the Neapolitan is tonicized, it appears in root position. Consider how the harmonies in this passage correspond with the meaning of the text. The Elf King is a sinister creature who tries to entice a young boy to his death, while the boy and his father ride on horseback through a dark forest.

Schubert's tonicization of the Neapolitan coincides with the otherworldly character and falsely affectionate words of the Elf King, while the return to tonic signals a return to the reality of the situation: if the boy will not go willingly, the Elf King will take him by force.

KEY CONCEPT When you tonicize ♭II:

1. Think temporarily in the ♭II key area in order to remember the correct accidentals (♭II is usually in root position when tonicized, and $\flat\hat{2}$ may be doubled).
2. Double-check that secondary dominant or secondary leading-tone chords have the correct quality (V7 or vii°7).
3. Follow the regular guidelines for part-writing and dissonance resolution.

Augmented-Sixth Chords

Listen again to Variation VII from Mozart's Piano Sonata in D Major, and pay special attention to the cadence in measures 122–123 (Example 26.8).

Example 26.8: Mozart, Piano Sonata in D Major, third movement, mm. 122–123a

With the predominant IV^6 chord on the third beat of measure 3, we expect motion from IV^6 to V—a typical half cadence. At the last moment, though, Mozart raises $\hat{4}$ to $\sharp\hat{4}$ (G to G♯), resolving in the next measure to $\hat{5}$ (A). This chromatic alteration ($\sharp\hat{4}$–$\hat{5}$) should be familiar from your study of the V7/V and vii°7/V chords. Mozart also lowers $\hat{6}$ to $\flat\hat{6}$ (B♮ to B♭)—a familiar operation from modal mixture—which then moves down by half step to $\hat{5}$.

These chromatic alterations are what define the predominant family of chords called **augmented-sixth chords**, so called because the interval from $\flat\hat{6}$ to $\sharp\hat{4}$ is an augmented sixth. The particular chromatic predominant in the Mozart example—built of $\flat\hat{6}$, $\sharp\hat{4}$, and $\hat{1}$ (*le*, *fi*, and *do*) and featuring a resolution to V by half-step motion outward ($\sharp\hat{4}$–$\hat{5}$ in an upper voice and $\flat\hat{6}$–$\hat{5}$ in the bass)—is called an **Italian augmented-sixth chord**, labeled It^6.

KEY CONCEPT To identify an augmented-sixth chord quickly, look for $\flat\hat{6}$–$\hat{5}$ in the bass, then confirm by checking for $\sharp\hat{4}$–$\hat{5}$ in an upper voice.

Try it #3

Identify the characteristic tendency tones of the augmented-sixth sonorities in the following keys.

KEY	$\flat\hat{6}$	$\sharp\hat{4}$	KEY	$\flat\hat{6}$	$\sharp\hat{4}$
A minor	F	D♯	E major	____	____
C♯ minor	____	____	B minor	____	____
F major	____	____	G♯ minor	____	____

In measures 124–127 of the Mozart variation (Example 26.9), the key has changed from D minor to A minor (the minor dominant). The chord in measure 125 contains the notes F, A, C, and D♯: $\flat\hat{6}$, $\hat{1}$, and $\sharp\hat{4}$ of the Italian augmented sixth plus $\flat\hat{3}$. This sonority is known as the **German augmented-sixth chord**, labeled Gr^6. As expected, D♯5 resolves up by half step to E5 in measure 126, and F3 resolves down by half step to E3. As in this example, the Gr^6 usually resolves to an embellished V^{6-5}_{4-3} rather than directly to V: the left-hand triad (F-A-C) would produce audible parallel fifths if it were to move directly to V (E-G♯-B). Scale degree $\flat\hat{3}$ (C) serves as a common tone between the two.

EXAMPLE 26.9: Mozart, Piano Sonata in D Major, third movement, mm. 124–127

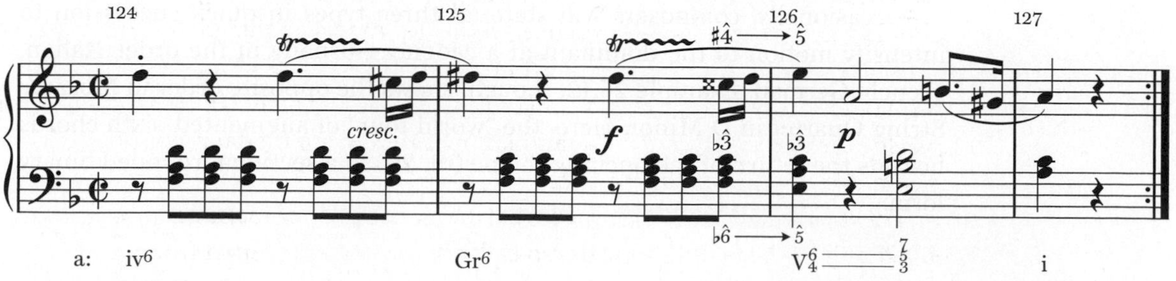

Sometimes $\hat{2}$ (*re*) is added to the $\flat\hat{6}$, $\hat{1}$, and $\sharp\hat{4}$ of the Italian sixth, making the sonority known as the **French augmented-sixth chord** (Fr⁶). Look, for example, at the excerpt from Chopin's Prelude in C Minor shown in Example 26.10.

EXAMPLE 26.10: Chopin, Prelude in C Minor, mm. 5–6

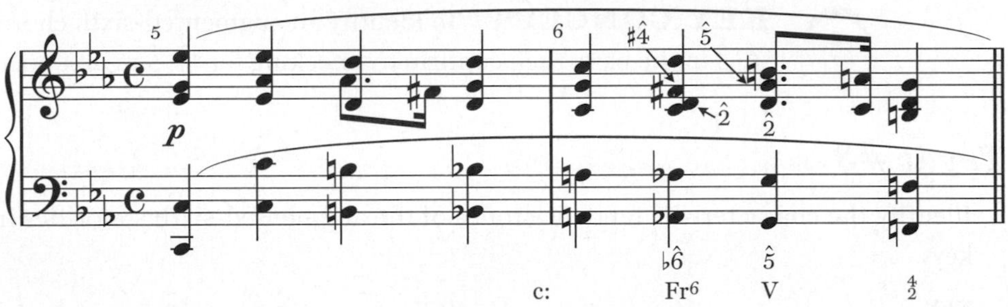

This augmented-sixth chord, on beat 2 of measure 6, is the French type. Like the augmented sixth in Example 26.1, this one is approached by a descending chromatic bass line, doubled in octaves. The chord immediately preceding the Fr⁶ is a tonic triad (with chromatic passing tone in the bass). The Fr⁶ resolves as expected to V, with F♯ in the alto moving up to G, A♭ in the bass resolving down to G, and $\hat{2}$ (D) serving as a common tone.

The three types of augmented-sixth chords are summarized in Example 26.11.

EXAMPLE 26.11: Three types of augmented-sixth chords

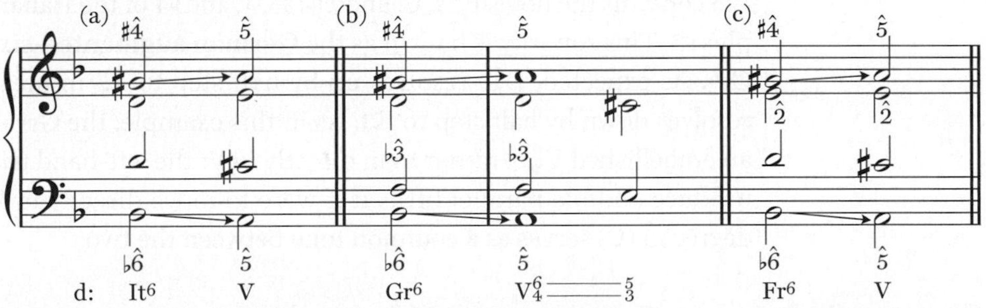

Occasionally, composers will state all three types in quick succession to intensify motion to the dominant at a cadence—usually in the order Italian, French, German. Example 26.12, though, shows the opposite order in Mozart's String Quartet in D Minor. Here, the "world tour" of augmented-sixth chords heralds the return of the opening theme (m. 29) in a sectional rounded binary form.

EXAMPLE 26.12: Mozart, String Quartet in D Minor, third movement, mm. 27–31

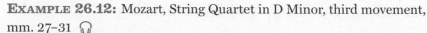

The augmented-sixth sonority is not often heard in pre-Classical-era compositions, and does not appear frequently in figured basses. In Classical style, these chords are typically positioned to emphasize the arrival of a particularly significant dominant harmony. Their dramatic sound is more freely employed in Romantic-era compositions, but even then the sound is saved for dramatic points. While augmented-sixth sonorities are less common in twentieth-century Broadway and song literature, they can be found. Look, for example, at the approach to the cadence in measure 33 of Example 26.13, an excerpt from "Can't Help Lovin' Dat Man." Measure 32 features the now-familiar tendency tones of the Gr6: the C♭ ($\flat\hat{6}$) in the bass, resolving down to B♭ ($\hat{5}$), and the A♮ ($\sharp\hat{4}$) in the alto voice. In this freer style, the $\sharp\hat{4}$ does not resolve up to $\hat{5}$, but the augmented-sixth sound is still a distinctive intensification of the motion to V. Interestingly, the chord symbol given above the staff is B♮7, an enharmonic respelling of the augmented-sixth chord.

EXAMPLE 26.13: Kern and Hammerstein, "Can't Help Lovin' Dat Man," mm. 31–33a

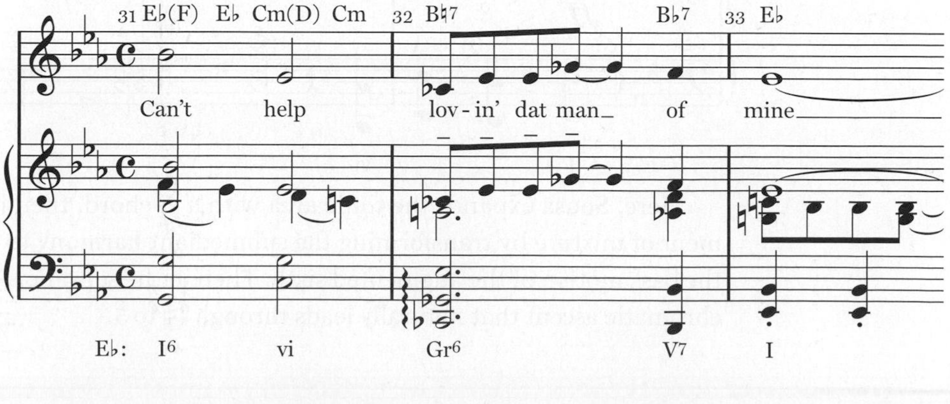

Voice-Leading, Spelling, and Resolution

All varieties of augmented-sixth chords share the same pattern of voice-leading to V: $\sharp\hat{4}$ up to $\hat{5}$ in an upper voice, and $\flat\hat{6}$ down to $\hat{5}$ in the bass (Example 26.14). In addition, these chords include $\hat{1}$, which usually resolves down to the leading tone. Think of the two tendency tones of the augmented sixth as derived from two ideas you have already studied: $\sharp\hat{4}$ up to $\hat{5}$ captures the temporary leading tone of secondary dominants to V, while $\flat\hat{6}$ down to $\hat{5}$ derives from mixture. Because of these two chromatic elements, augmented-sixth chords have the strongest tendency of any predominant harmony to move to V; they usually go directly to V (in the case of Gr^6, to V^{6-5}_{4-3}), without intervening chords.

Example 26.14: Voice-leading for augmented-sixth chords

Although augmented-sixth chords more naturally arise in minor keys, they are not uncommon in major keys, especially in passages that employ mixture. For the bass-line resolution pattern ($\flat\hat{6}$ to $\hat{5}$) to work in major keys, $\hat{6}$ must be lowered to $\flat\hat{6}$. Two accidentals are therefore necessary in major keys, whereas only one ($\sharp\hat{4}$) is added in minor keys. One familiar example of an augmented sixth in a major key is the introduction to "The Stars and Stripes Forever." Listen to Example 26.15 to hear how Sousa prepares for the $\sharp\hat{4}$ and $\flat\hat{6}$.

Example 26.15: Sousa, "The Stars and Stripes Forever," mm. 1–4a

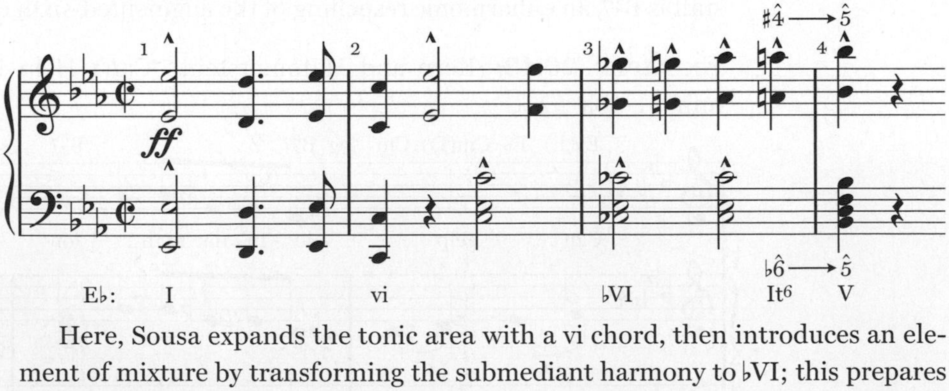

Here, Sousa expands the tonic area with a vi chord, then introduces an element of mixture by transforming the submediant harmony to ♭VI; this prepares the bass motion of the augmented sixth. Then in the soprano, Sousa introduces a chromatic ascent that naturally leads through $\sharp\hat{4}$ to $\hat{5}$.

SUMMARY

Augmented-sixth chords typically appear in minor keys, or in major-key passages with mixture chords.

- All share ♭$\hat{6}$, $\hat{1}$, and ♯$\hat{4}$, and resolve to V.
- All share the same voice-leading pattern: ♯$\hat{4}$ up to $\hat{5}$ in an upper voice, and ♭$\hat{6}$ down to $\hat{5}$ in the bass.
- Consider the ♯$\hat{4}$–$\hat{5}$ / ♭$\hat{6}$–$\hat{5}$ outer-voice pattern as the scaffold upon which to build each of the three types: Italian, French, or German.

Writing Augmented Sixths: Italian, French, German

KEY CONCEPT To write an augmented-sixth progression to V in four voices:

1. In the resolution chord, place $\hat{5}$ in the bass and an upper voice (the soprano is a characteristic voicing but not required), leaving an empty space before it for the augmented sixth (Example 26.16a).
2. In the empty space, write in the two tendency tones leading to $\hat{5}$: ♭$\hat{6}$–$\hat{5}$ in the bass and ♯$\hat{4}$–$\hat{5}$ in the upper voice. In a major key, add the correct accidental to lower $\hat{6}$ to ♭$\hat{6}$ (part b).
3. Add $\hat{1}$ to one of the inner voices (part c).
4. Add a fourth note, following these guidelines (part d):
   - For It[6], double $\hat{1}$.
   - For Fr[6], add $\hat{2}$ (an augmented fourth above the bass note).
   - For Gr[6], add ♭$\hat{3}$ (a perfect fifth above the bass note). In major keys, add an accidental to lower $\hat{3}$ to ♭$\hat{3}$.

EXAMPLE 26.16: Spelling augmented-sixth chords

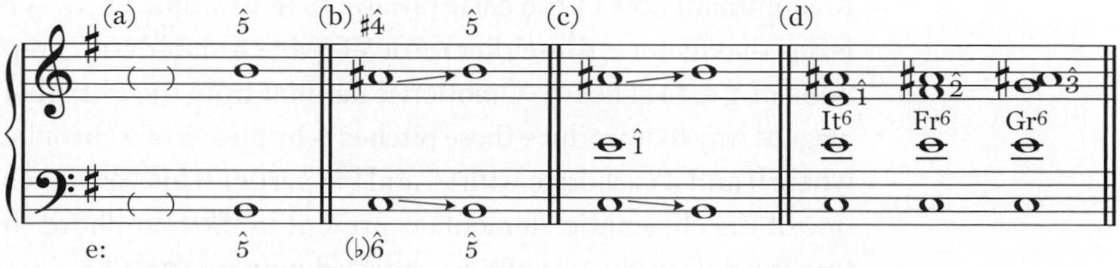

We will generally refer to augmented-sixth chords by their abbreviations: It^6, Fr^6, and Gr^6. One way to remember them is to think of the geography of these countries in relation to the scale degrees added: moving from south to north, you have Italy ($\hat{1}$), France ($\hat{2}$), and Germany ($\hat{3}$). Another way is to memorize the figured bass associated with each chord: It^6, Fr$^4_3$, and Gr$^6_5$. (Keep in mind that these numbers represent figured bass, not inversion symbols. Augmented-sixth chords function as voice-leading chords, not as inversions of an "altered chord." Don't attempt to stack the thirds to find a "root.") Figures would help remind you that the Fr$^4_3$, for example, has a third ($\hat{1}$) and a fourth ($\hat{2}$) above the bass, in addition to the augmented sixth, and that the Gr$^6_5$ has a perfect fifth.

Try it #4

Spell the specified augmented-sixth chords in three or four voices, in the keys indicated. Place $\sharp\hat{4}$ in the highest voice and $\flat\hat{6}$ in the lowest. If it helps to write the octave $\hat{5}$ after the augmented sixth, as shown below, do so.

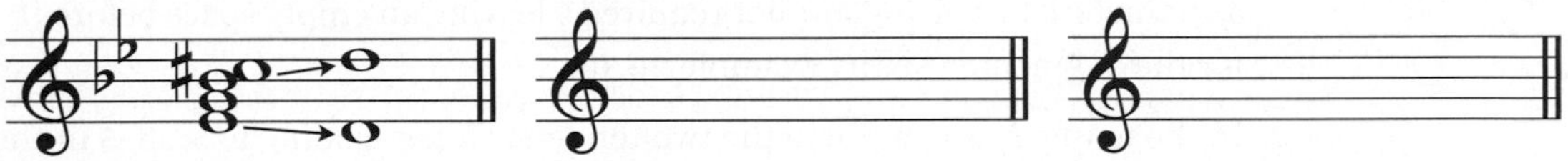

g: Gr^6 B: It^6 C: Fr^6

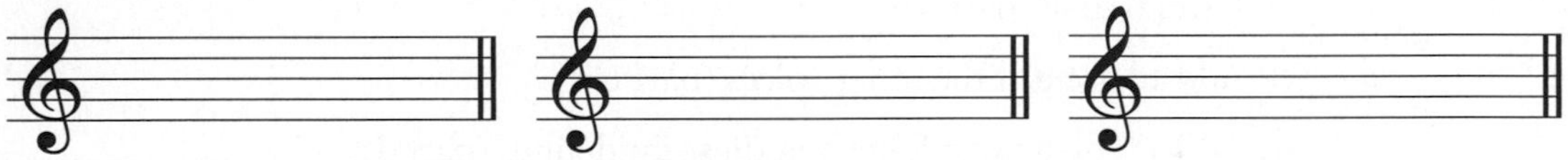

f: It^6 f♯: Gr^6 e: Fr^6

Approaches to Augmented-Sixth Chords

Augmented-sixth chords are generally preceded by harmonies from the tonic or predominant area of the basic phrase, as in Example 26.17. A common approach is one that features $\flat\hat{6}$—either iv^6 or VI (parts a and b)—accompanied by the alteration of $\hat{4}$ to $\sharp\hat{4}$. The iv^6–V motion is familiar from the Phrygian cadence. Another elegant way to introduce these pitches is by means of a chromatic voice exchange, where $\hat{6}$ and $\hat{4}$ exchange with $\flat\hat{6}$ and $\sharp\hat{4}$ (part c). This voice exchange also works if one of the chromatic elements is present in the first chord through mode mixture (part d) or the use of a secondary dominant (part e).

Example 26.17: Approaches to augmented-sixth chords

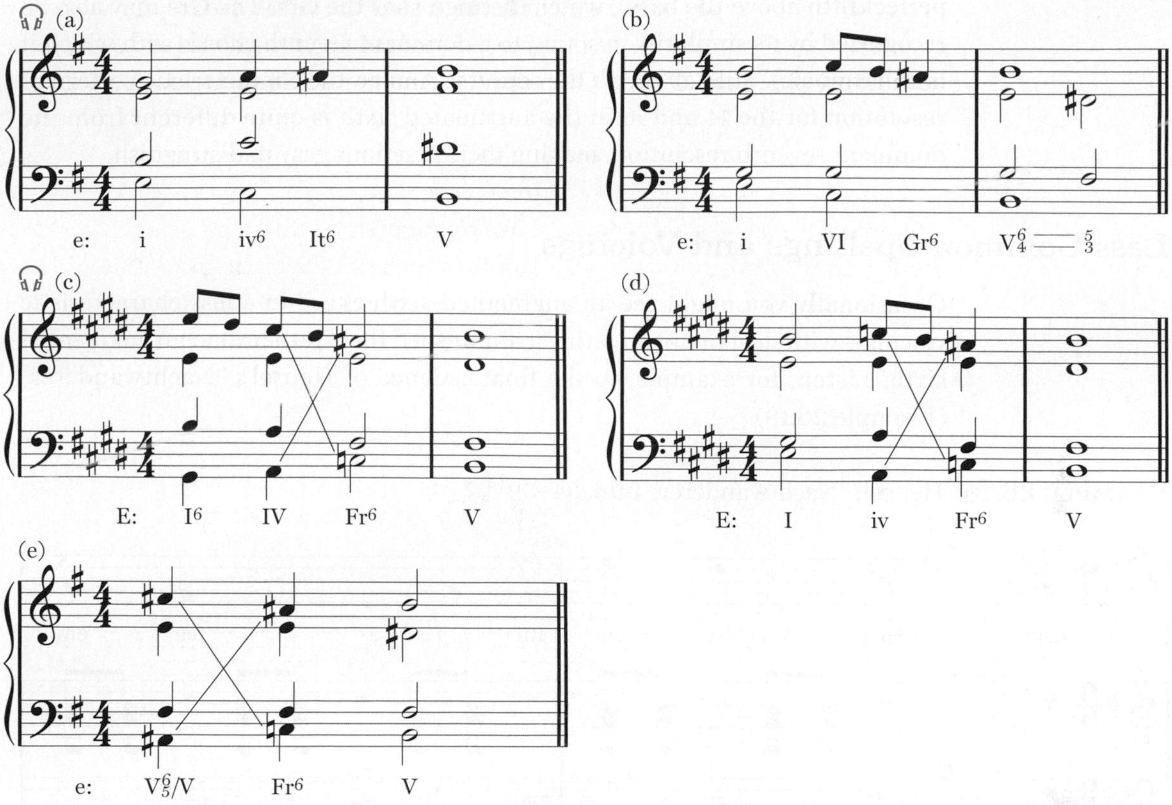

Intonation and Performance

When you perform an augmented sixth, try to make the resolution of the tendency tones clear—if appropriate, bring out the voices that carry the ♯$\hat{4}$–$\hat{5}$ and ♭$\hat{6}$–$\hat{5}$ voice-leading. You may find that singing solfège syllables helps to identify and tune these altered pitches: *fi–sol* for ♯$\hat{4}$–$\hat{5}$ and *le–sol* for ♭$\hat{6}$–$\hat{5}$. Aim high when tuning ♯$\hat{4}$ and low when tuning the ♭$\hat{6}$ on a non-keyboard instrument, so that the interval is absolutely clear.

Thinking of scale degrees and the intervals formed by these tendency tones will also help identify augmented-sixth chords aurally. Probably the easiest to identify is the Fr6, since, in addition to the augmented sixth between ♭$\hat{6}$ and ♯$\hat{4}$ and the augmented fourth (or diminished fifth) between $\hat{1}$ and ♯$\hat{4}$, you can also listen for the augmented fourth between ♭$\hat{6}$ and $\hat{2}$. Some listeners may also be able to identify the Fr6 from the whole step (or minor seventh in some voicings) between $\hat{1}$ and $\hat{2}$. In all, the Fr6 typically sounds the most dissonant.

The It^6 and Gr^6 are easier to confuse with each other: listen carefully for $\hat{3}$ (the perfect fifth above the bass), which distinguishes the Gr^6. The Gr^6 may also be recognized by its similarity in sound to a dominant seventh chord (with which it is enharmonic). Still, although the sound is similar, the characteristic pattern of resolution for the $\sharp\hat{4}$ and $\flat\hat{6}$ in the augmented sixth is quite different from the dominant seventh resolution, making their functions easy to distinguish.

Less Common Spellings and Voicings

Occasionally you might see an augmented-sixth chord in a less characteristic voicing—with $\flat\hat{6}$ above $\sharp\hat{4}$, creating a diminished third rather than an augmented sixth. Listen, for example, to the final cadence of Hensel's "Nachtwanderer" (Example 26.18).

EXAMPLE 26.18: Hensel, "Nachtwanderer," mm. 34–39

Translation: My singing is a cry, a cry only from dreams.

Since the chord in question (in m. 37) appears on the word "Träumen" (dreams), its dissonant ambiguity may be an element of text painting. The analyst who tries to stack this chord in thirds gets B♮-D♭-F-A♭—not a familiar type of seventh chord, given its diminished third from B♮ to D♭. Instead, recognize the familiar elements of the augmented sixth in this F major context to identify the chord: B♮ is $\sharp\hat{4}$, and D♭ is $\flat\hat{6}$. Since the chord also includes $\hat{1}$ and $\flat\hat{3}$, it is called a **German diminished-third chord** ($Gr^{\circ 3}$). The chord is normally approached by a chromatic voice exchange, as marked in the example. In measure 35, Hensel elegantly prepares all the chromatic elements of the diminished-third chord by introducing D♭ as a chromatic passing tone in the bass, and B♮ and A♭ as the root and seventh of a $vii^{\circ 7}/V$; she then maintains $\flat\hat{6}$ as an element of mixture in the word "Rufen" (cry) in measure 36.

Occasionally, for voice-leading purposes, composers spell the Gr^6 in major keys with a doubly augmented fourth above the bass, rather than a perfect fifth (that is, with $\sharp\hat{2}$ instead of $\flat\hat{3}$), as in Example 26.19a. In analysis, it is easier simply to call this chord a Gr^6 rather than create a new name and symbol. Another possible chord in the "augmented-sixth family" is $\flat\hat{6}$-$\hat{7}$-$\hat{2}$-$\sharp\hat{4}$—the so-called half-diminished augmented-sixth chord, where $\hat{7}$ substitutes for $\hat{1}$ of a Fr^6 (part b). In these and related chords, the augmented sixth usually resolves as expected, and the other voices move by step to members of the next chord.

EXAMPLE 26.19: Other types of augmented-sixth chords

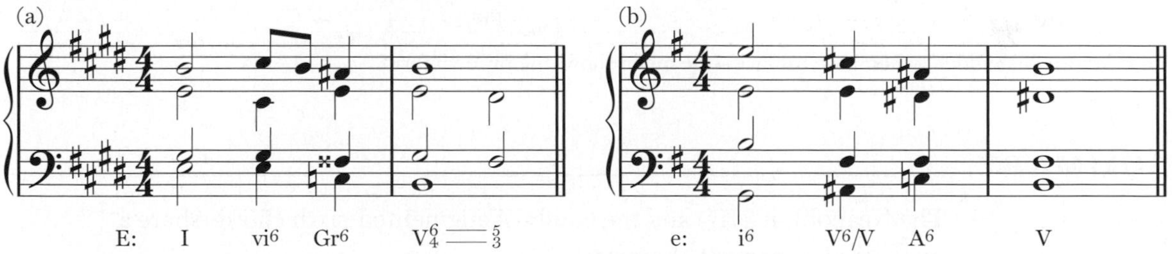

Secondary Augmented-Sixth Chords

For special effect, composers sometimes apply the voice-leading principles of the augmented sixth to $\hat{1}$ and the tonic triad, lending the A^6 a kind of secondary function. Label this type of chord as though it were a secondary dominant: for example, Gr^6/i (German sixth of i). Here, the characteristic voice-leading is $\flat\hat{2}$–$\hat{1}$ in the bass and $\hat{7}$–$\hat{1}$ in an upper voice. The interval A6, from which the chord gets its name, is now from $\flat\hat{2}$ to $\hat{7}$ rather than $\flat\hat{6}$ to $\sharp\hat{4}$. All varieties of the "secondary" A^6 (It, Fr, Gr) include $\hat{4}$; the French adds $\hat{5}$, and the German adds $\flat\hat{6}$. Look at Example 26.20, drawn from Schubert's song "Der Doppelgänger," to see how this voice-leading chord operates.

Example 26.20: Schubert, "Der Doppelgänger," mm. 36–43a

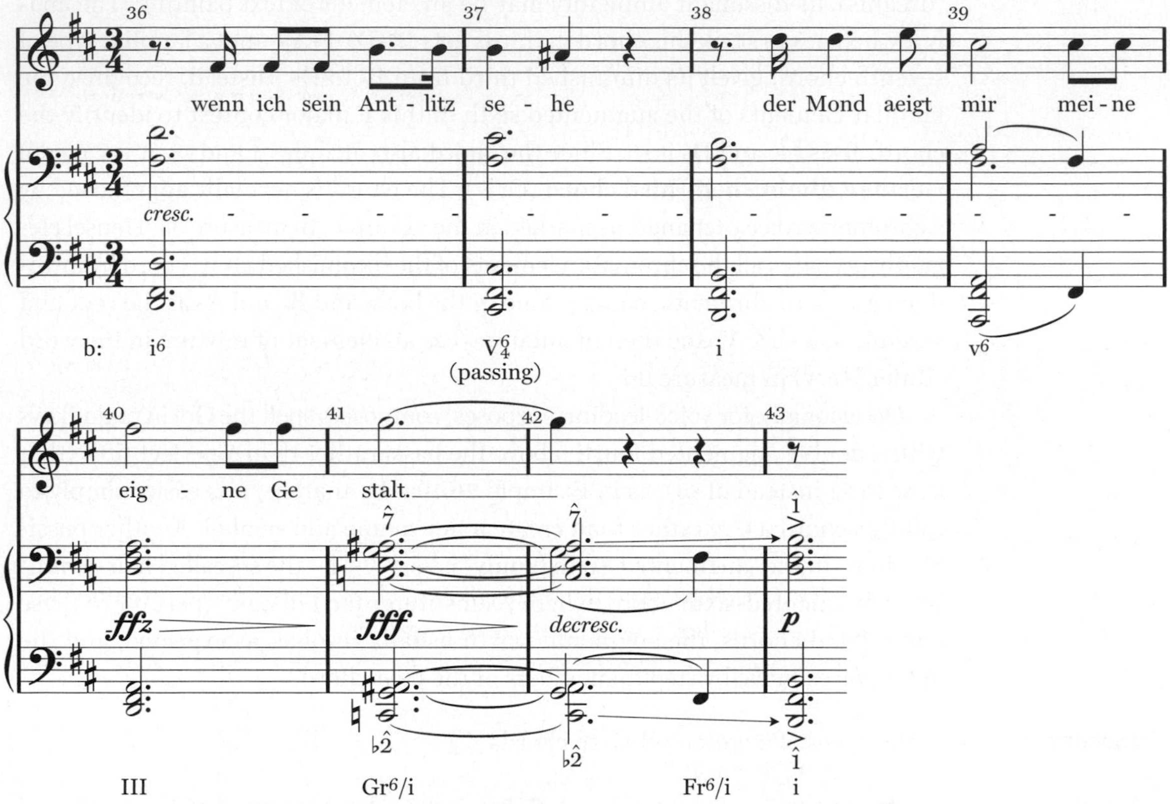

Translation: [I shudder] when I see his face—the moon shows me my own form.

SUMMARY

The Neapolitan (♭II6) and the family of augmented-sixth chords share a number of important characteristics:

- They typically appear in minor keys, or in major-key passages with mixture.
- They share $\flat\hat{6}$ as an important scale-degree component.
- They are predominant chords that intensify motion to V through chromaticism.
- In addition to $\flat\hat{6}$, N6 includes $\hat{4}$ (usually in the bass) and $\flat\hat{2}$; $\flat\hat{2}$ resolves down to the leading tone of the dominant harmony, often via a passing $\hat{1}$.
- In addition to $\flat\hat{6}$ (usually in the bass), all augmented-sixth chords feature $\sharp\hat{4}$ and $\hat{1}$; $\flat\hat{6}$ and $\sharp\hat{4}$ resolve by contrary motion to $\hat{5}$.

Did You Know?

The geographical names for augmented-sixth chords are used widely today, but until recently their origin was shrouded in mystery. These terms appear in an 1806 treatise by John Callcott called *A Musical Grammar* (London). The chords were named according to Callcott's perception of the national character of the Italians ("elegance"), French ("feebleness"), and Germans ("strength"). Most treatises from that time, however, do not refer to these terms when they describe augmented-sixth sonorities and explain how to resolve them.

TERMS YOU SHOULD KNOW

augmented-sixth chord	Fr6	It6
diminished-third chord	Gr6	Neapolitan sixth chord

QUESTIONS FOR REVIEW

1. Why are Neapolitan and augmented-sixth chords often found in minor-key pieces or major-key pieces that employ mixture?
2. Where are Neapolitan sixth chords typically found in a phrase? What is their function?
3. In what voicing of Neapolitan chords are parallel fifths a possibility, and how do you avoid them?
4. What chords may precede a Neapolitan sixth? What chords usually follow it?
5. Under what conditions might Neapolitan chords appear in root position? What is doubled if the N6 is in root position?
6. Where are augmented-sixth chords usually found in a phrase? What is their function?
7. Which elements of the augmented-sixth chords are shared with secondary-dominant-function chords to V? In major keys, which elements are shared with mixture chords?
8. Which augmented sixth may lead to parallel fifths, and how are they avoided?
9. What chords may precede an augmented sixth? What chords usually follow it?
10. In music for your own instrument, find one Neapolitan sixth chord and at least two different types of augmented-sixth chords (solo-line instrumentalists will need to consider both melody and accompaniment). How does the chord color the passage in question? How might you play the passage to bring out this unusual chord color?

CHAPTER 27 Vocal Forms

Outline of topics

Text and song structure

- Strophic form
- Text painting
- Analysis and interpretation

Other vocal forms

- Modified strophic form
- Through-composed form
- Three-part song forms
- Recitatives
- French mélodie

Overview

We now consider how chromatic harmonies are employed in art song, opera, and oratorio. We examine standard formal designs for solo vocal works, and see how composers use harmony and motivic development to realize their interpretation of the text.

Repertoire

Johann Sebastian Bach, "Schafe können sicher weiden" ("Sheep may safely graze"), from Cantata No. 208

Gabriel Fauré, "Après un rêve" ("After a Dream")

George Frideric Handel, "Thy rebuke hath broken his heart," from *Messiah*

Wolfgang Amadeus Mozart
"Quanto duolmi, Susanna" ("How I grieve, Susanna," recitative) and "Voi, che sapete" ("You Who Know," aria), from *The Marriage of Figaro*

Franz Schubert
"Erlkönig" ("The Elf King")
"Morgengruss" ("Morning Greeting"), from *Die schöne Müllerin*

Clara Schumann, "Liebst du um Schönheit" ("If You Love for Beauty")

Robert Schumann, "Im wunderschönen Monat Mai" ("In the Lovely Month of May"), from *Dichterliebe*

Text and Song Structure

Consider the poem "Im wunderschönen Monat Mai," by nineteenth-century German poet Heinrich Heine, set to music by Robert Schumann.

Im wunderschönen Monat Mai,	a	In the lovely month of May,
Als alle Knospen sprangen,	b	When all the buds were bursting,
Da ist in meinem Herzen	c	Then within my heart
Die Liebe aufgegangen.	b	Love began to blossom.
Im wunderschönen Monat Mai,	a	In the lovely month of May,
Als alle Vögel sangen,	b	When all the birds were singing,
Da hab' ich ihr gestanden	d	Then I confessed to her
Mein Sehnen und Verlangen.	b	My longing and desire.

An analysis of songs involves text as well as music, including consideration of the words in relation to a composer's harmonic and motivic choices. Begin by thinking about the imagery, story, and structure of the text, apart from its musical setting. Often the pattern of words, lines, and rhymes will suggest a particular type of musical design that may or may not be borne out in the composer's realization.

Heine's text consists of two four-line **strophes**, sometimes called "stanzas" or "verses." The letters indicate the rhyme scheme: rhyming German words at the end of each line take the same lowercase letter. The first two lines of each strophe have a parallel structure: both begin with the same six words. This structure suggests that the composer might set these parallel lines with parallel music.

Further, each group of four lines pairs into two couplets (of two lines each). The first couplet is almost entirely objective—lines written in the third person that simply describe a spring or summer day, with flowers blooming and birds singing. The second couplet focuses on the poet's subjective feelings: "within my heart love began to blossom" and "I confessed to her my longing and desire."

Listen to the first verse, while following Example 27.1, to hear how the structure of the poetry is portrayed musically. Following a piano introduction that suggests F♯ minor, the verse extends for eight measures (mm. 5–12), in two-measure units, beginning in A major. The two objective phrases are set in parallel structure (**a a**), as are the two subjective phrases (**b b′**). Here, the musical setting (**a a b b′**) parallels the meaning of the text—the shift from objective to subjective—rather than the rhyme scheme (abcb).

Example 27.1: Schumann, "Im wunderschönen Monat Mai," mm. 4–12

Strophic Form

Each two-measure grouping in measures 5–12 expresses only the PD–D–T portion of the phrase: the objective lines in A major (ii^6–V^7–I) and the subjective lines in different transpositions, tonicizing B minor and D major (iv^6–V^7–i or I). The objective couplet of each strophe also contrasts with the subjective by its lower range, stable key, and stepwise approach to the tonic: $\hat{6}$–$\hat{7}$–$\hat{1}$ over a V^7–I harmony. The shift to first person narrative in the subjective text is marked by upward transpositions, a higher vocal range, an ascending melody, and vocal skips to downbeat appoggiaturas (mm. 10 and 12)—all expressive means to depict the longing of the protagonist. As you can see in the anthology score, the second verse employs exactly the same music (mm. 16–23).

KEY CONCEPT Songs in which more than one strophe (or verse) of text is sung to the same music are called **strophic**, a term derived from the strophes of poetry.

Because strophic settings feature the same music for several verses, they may appear printed with the strophes of text aligned under a single melodic line, as in Example 27.2, with repeat or "da capo" signs indicating a return to the beginning; or each verse may be written out separately, as in Schumann's song. Verses may also be set apart by instrumental interludes as in the Schumann song, or preceded or followed by instrumental introductions or postludes, as in both examples. Other genres employing strophic structures include hymns and carols, patriotic and folk songs, and popular songs.

Example 27.2: Schubert, "Morgengruss," mm. 1–10a

SUMMARY

Poetry set to music is typically analyzed with respect to

- strophes — the division of the poem into verses;
- couplets — paired lines within the poem;
- rhyme scheme — the pattern of rhymes at the end of each line;
- parallelism of text — repeated words, or similar change in narrative voice, in two or more strophes;
- objective or subjective stance – third person narrative vs. personal reflection.

Try it #1

Provide a rhyme-scheme analysis for the poem below, set to music by Clara Schumann, by writing alphabet letters at the end of each line of German text. Does this lyric feature a shift from an objective to subjective stance? Are there parallelisms in the text that might suggest a particular musical design?

Friedrich Rückert, "Liebst du um Schönheit"

Liebst du um Schönheit, o nicht mich liebe!	___	If you love for beauty, oh do not love me!
Liebe die Sonne, sie trägt ein goldnes Haar!	___	Love the sun; she has golden hair!
Liebst du um Jugend, o nicht mich liebe!	___	If you love for youthfulness, oh do not love me!
Liebe den Frühling, der jung ist jedes Jahr!	___	Love the springtime; it is young every year!
Liebst du um Schätze, o nicht mich liebe!	___	If you love for wealth, oh do not love me!
Liebe die Meerfrau, sie hat viel Perlen klar!	___	Love the mermaid; she has many fair pearls!
Liebst du um Liebe, o ja—mich liebe!	___	If you love for love itself, oh yes, love me!
Liebe mich immer, dich lieb ich immerdar!	___	Love me always, and I will love you forever!

Text Painting

Heine's "Im wunderschönen Monat Mai" seems to express the joys of spring and first love, which might best be represented by an exuberant major-key setting. Yet Schumann's song instead seems uneasy and restless: his choice of harmonies suggests that all is not well—perhaps the poet's love is not returned. This uneasiness begins with the piano introduction (Example 27.3), which implies F♯ minor ambiguously through a series of Phrygian resolutions (iv6–V7), without ever expressing a complete phrase or tonic harmony; the leading tone (E♯) is left dangling in the piano's melodic line (mm. 2 and 4). Even the iv6 is clouded with a dissonant incomplete neighbor, A♯3. Further obscuring the harmony is the initial C♯5, part of a dissonant 7–6 suspension, that emerges in measures 4–5 as the first pitch of the vocal line. Only with the entrance of the voice does the C♯5 finally lead unambiguously into A major, setting the first phrase of the text.

EXAMPLE 27.3: Schumann, "Im wunderschönen Monat Mai," mm. 1–6a

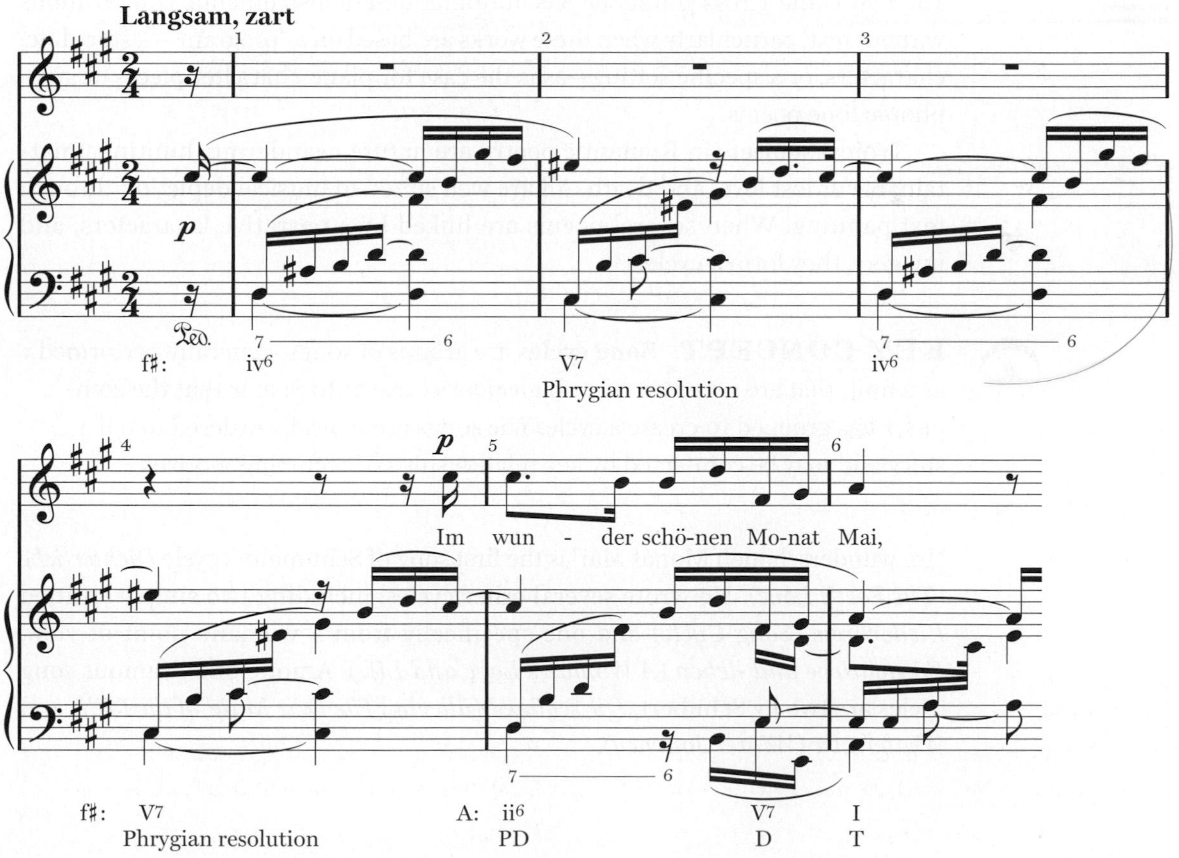

The conflict between the F♯ minor introduction and the A major start of the verse raises questions regarding the main key of the song. The tonality continues to be unstable throughout, perhaps indicating doubt that the poet's ardor is returned. The postlude does not bring resolution—the song ends on an unstable V7 chord in F♯ minor. This unstable harmonic setting could foreshadow the state of this lover's relationship as the group of songs continues; as such, the setting is an example of text painting.

KEY CONCEPT **Text painting** is a means of depicting images or ideas from a text through music. Examples in piano accompaniments include the rustling of trees, the babbling of a brook, the thunder of horse hooves, or the cooing of a dove. Text painting in vocal lines may include rising passages or upward leaps to depict joy or heaven, and dissonances, downward leaps, or descending semitones to depict sadness or the grave.

You may come across similar effects in Romantic-era instrumental compositions without text, particularly when these works are based on a "program"—a story line, characters, or a specific setting—as is the case for piano character pieces or symphonic tone poems.

Typical subjects in Romantic poetry are nature, wandering, hunting, unattainable or lost love, and death. All are well suited to musical depiction through text painting. When several poems are linked by a narrative, characters, and imagery, they form a cycle.

KEY CONCEPT **Song cycles** are groups of songs, generally performed as a unit, that are set either to a single poet's cycle or to poems that the composer has grouped to create a cycle. The songs are typically ordered to tell a story and may be connected by key relationships or recurring motives.

"Im wunderschönen Monat Mai" is the first song of Schumann's cycle *Dichterliebe* (*The Poet's Love*). He wrote several other cycles, including two simply entitled *Liederkreis* (*Song Cycle*) and one specifically from a woman's point of view, *Frauenliebe und -leben* (*A Woman's Love and Life*). Among other famous song cycles are two by Schubert, *Die schöne Müllerin* (*The Fair Maid of the Mill*) and *Winterreise* (*Winter Journey*).

Analysis and Interpretation

In a performance of Schumann's song, the pianist and the singer alike might bring out its musical ambiguities, as preparation for the story of love and loss to come. For example, the pianist could hesitate on the opening C♯5 (Example 27.3), whose role is unclear, before adding the supporting harmony that explains its dissonant function. The perpetual arpeggiated texture of the piano part—perhaps representing wind blowing on the flower blossoms or some other natural image—might be played with the rhythmic freedom of nature, especially where the voice is not present. Also important for the pianist is the close of the song, with its unresolved dominant seventh harmony and incomplete iv6–V7 motion (Example 27.4).

Example 27.4: Schumann, "Im wunderschönen Monat Mai," mm. 22–26

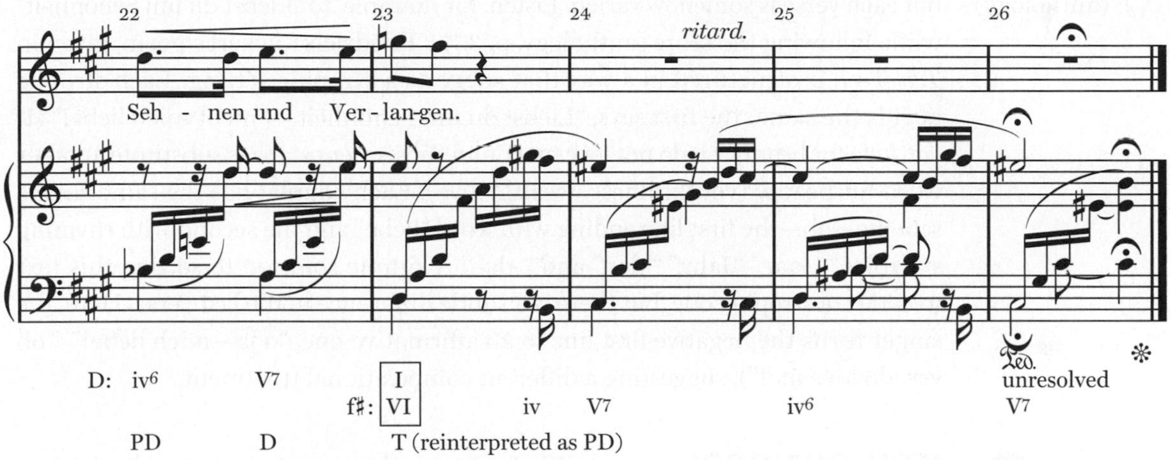

Here Schumann notates a *ritard* in measure 24 and a fermata both on the downbeat of measure 26 and on the final chord. The most active tones of this chord are left exposed in the upper voices: the leading tone in the soprano (E♯5) and the unresolved chordal seventh (B4). Performers may wish to linger on these tones before beginning the next song, which returns to A major.

The singer's role is, in part, to portray the objective-subjective duality of the poem. When he enters with the first line, the opening C♯ is a dissonant suspension against the harmony that supports it, like the initial note of the piano accompaniment. He could linger on this beautiful dissonance, which highlights the descriptive word "wunderschönen" (lovely), before proceeding. The objective lines might be sung with a vocal tone that supports the joy and beauty of the spring day; with the subjective lines, the singer may wish to change to a tone that expresses love, longing, and uncertainty of what is to come. As he climbs to the higher register, he may also want to *crescendo* and emphasize the accented dissonances, especially on "Verlangen" (desire). The singer's face and body should likewise maintain the sense of longing throughout the postlude, as the piano reinforces the mood of the text so effectively.

Other Vocal Forms

Modified Strophic Form

(anthology)

Sometimes you will encounter songs where the music basically seems strophic, but each verse is somehow varied. Listen, for example, to "Liebst du um Schönheit" while following the score (anthology, p. 357). Friedrich Rückert's poem, given in *Try it #1*, is structured in a way that suggests a strophic setting. Each strophe begins the same: the first says, "Liebst du um Schönheit, O nicht mich liebe!" (If you love for beauty, oh do not love me!), and subsequent stanzas substitute another word for beauty (youthfulness, wealth, love). Each couplet has the same rhyme scheme—ab—the first line ending with word "liebe" and the second with rhyming syllables "Haar," "Jahr," "klar," and "-dar." A simple solution to setting this text would be a strophic one, but there is a subtle difference in the last verse. Here, the singer turns the negative first line to an affirmative one, "o ja—mich liebe!" ("oh yes, do love me!"), suggesting a different compositional treatment.

KEY CONCEPT In **modified strophic form**, each verse may begin the same way but end differently, or the song may vary the verses through harmonic or melodic changes, interpolated music, or other means.

Schumann begins her setting of each stanza identically, but adds subtle differences in each continuation. The first and third stanzas are quite similar; the second and fourth end differently, and the fourth is extended with a repetition of text and its crucial "oh ja—mich liebe!" to mark the climactic shift to the affirmative.

Through-Composed Form

In a sense, the "opposite" of a strophic song is a through-composed one: here, rather than repeating the melody from stanza to stanza, the music for each stanza (or each line) is different.

KEY CONCEPT A **through-composed** song is one in which the composition develops continuously—in new, though perhaps motivically related, ways—as the song unfolds. While a through-composed song may include patterns of repetition, these patterns will not fall into typical musical forms, such as **A A′**, **A B A**, **A A B**, or **A A B A**.

Schubert's "Erlkönig" is a dramatic example of a through-composed song, united from verse to verse by a piano motive that appears as introduction, interlude, and accompaniment to some verses. You have listened to portions of this work in recent chapters, but now consider the song as a whole, to see how its text, harmony, and motivic structure work together to create a powerful musical drama. Read through Goethe's poem and translation in your anthology (p. 347) to decide which of the four characters—the narrator, the father, the son, or the Elf King—is speaking at any given moment. In your score, mark the beginning and end of each strophe, as well as who is speaking. Observe any motives or accompanimental patterns that are associated with particular characters.

Try it #2

Listen to "Erlkönig" in its entirety. (anthology)

1. Each strophe of "Erlkönig" has the same rhyme scheme. Circle the alphabet letters that best capture this design: abab abcb aabb abca

2. For each of the eight strophes, write the name of the character(s) speaking, and the corresponding measure numbers.

	Character(s)	*Measures*
Strophe 1:	______________	mm. ______________
Strophe 2:	______________	mm. ______________
Strophe 3:	______________	mm. ______________
Strophe 4:	______________	mm. ______________
Strophe 5:	______________	mm. ______________
Strophe 6:	______________	mm. ______________
Strophe 7:	______________	mm. ______________
Strophe 8:	______________	mm. ______________

Although it is through-composed, "Erlkönig" includes a number of compositional features—particularly recurring motives—that help tie the work into one unified whole. One of the most striking motives appears in the piano left hand (Example 27.5). This triplet motive (mm. 2–3, 4–5), accompanies the narrator and is heard in the interludes as well as introduction. Although this motive appears in G minor at the beginning and end of the song, it is transposed to other keys during the course of the story. Meanwhile the triplet octaves in the right hand evoke the thundering of horse hooves through the night as the boy and his father ride through the forest. (For convenience of reading, the triplet eighths are notated ♪..)

EXAMPLE 27.5: Schubert, "Erlkönig," mm. 1–5 (riding motive)

The motive most associated with the son is the half-step neighbor tone, shown in Example 27.6. This motive is often sung to the text "Mein Vater, mein Vater" (My father), and each time the son sings this plaintive plea, it appears higher in his range: compare measures 72–74 (D5–E♭5–D5) with 97–99 (E5–F5–E5) and 123–125 (F5–G♭5–F5). Further, it is sung as dissonant 7–6 motion above an arpeggiated V^6_5 of the local key (adding a minor ninth to the V^7 harmony), emphasizing the child's distress. Before the "Mein Vater" pleas, the son sings the half-step motive even in his first milder exclamation (mm. 46–47 and 48–49, C5–D♭5).

Example 27.6: Schubert, "Erlkönig," mm. 72b–76a (son's motive)

Translation: My father, my father, don't you hear?

The father's reassurances to his son often feature perfect intervals of the fourth or fifth to the text "Mein Sohn" (My son)—in staunch denial of any danger—and his vocal range lies consistently lower than the boy's. Example 27.7 shows the father's first rising P4 motive, which also climbs higher and higher as the song progresses, from measures 36–37 (D4–G4) to 80–81 (F♯4–B4) and 105–106 (G♯4–C♯5).

Example 27.7: Schubert, "Erlkönig," mm. 37–40 (father's motive)

Translation: My son, why do you hide your face, so afraid?

Both of these motives, while associated with son and father, appear in the music of the narrator and—more chillingly—the Elf King. This evil forest spirit attempts to coax the boy rather than frighten him, therefore his music is almost always in a major key. In measures 69–70, the Elf King appropriates the rising P4 from the father and sings it to the text "meine Mutter" (my mother). In 116–117, in his final appeal before snatching the boy away, the Elf King uses both the son's neighbor-tone motive and the father's perfect fourth, now descending as well as rising, as he sings "Ich liebe dich" (I love you). Example 27.8 gives this climactic moment, tonicizing the Neapolitan of the local D minor tonic.

Example 27.8: Schubert, "Erlkönig," mm. 115–119a (son and father motives sung by the Erlking)

Translation: I love you, I am tempted by your beautiful form.

Sometimes composers embed motives in their works at different hierarchical levels. That is, a motive that originally appears within a single measure may be drawn out to span many measures, in a new rhythmic and tonal context—a practice called **motivic parallelism**. There are a few instances of the left-hand G minor "riding" motive from the song's introduction (mm. 2–3) drawn out into larger statements. This motive is characterized by two parts. The first is a rising scale with half-step neighbor tone at the top, perhaps the source of the son's half-step motive: G–A–B♭–C–D–E♭–D. The second part is a descending minor triad: D–B♭–G. The rising scale helps structure the narrator's final speech (Example 27.9). Here, the narrator's melody climbs the G minor scale to place the neighbor E♭–D as a grace note on "Armen"—a large-scale replication of this motive in the vocal part, accompanied by the original version simultaneously in the piano. This subphrase ends by poignantly combining the P4 and neighbor-tone motives to "ächzende Kind" (moaning child).

Example 27.9: Schubert, "Erlkönig," mm. 135–141a

Translation: [The father] rides quickly, he holds in his arms the moaning child.

While the motivic recurrences provide unifying elements in this long and complex song, the pattern of tonicized keys likewise plays a unifying role. In a striking motivic parallelism, the large-scale succession of keys in the song also "spells out" most of the rider motive: G minor (beginning in m. 1), B♭ major (m. 58), C major (m. 87), D minor (m. 112), E♭ (briefly tonicized as a Neapolitan, m. 117), D minor (m. 123), tonicized V/B♭ (m. 124), G minor (m. 131).

Three-Part Song Forms

Most songs divide clearly into sections, usually (though not always) corresponding with the division of the text into strophes. Vocal works that are neither strophic nor through-composed often divide into three clear parts, marked by changes in accompanimental pattern, key, and/or contrasting melody. **Three-part** (or **ternary**) song forms are typically arranged **A B A′** or **A A B**. In Baroque arias, ternary design usually takes the form of a da capo aria.

KEY CONCEPT An **aria** is an art song situated within an opera, oratorio, or cantata. The Baroque **da capo aria** is an **A B A** design where the final **A** section is not written out again. Rather, performers are instructed to return "da capo" (to the beginning) or "dal segno" (to the sign) and repeat the first section until they come to a fermata marking the end. The repeat of the **A** section may be abbreviated to include only the opening instrumental introduction or only the **A**-section vocal part.

Da capo arias, especially in Bach cantatas, typically feature a solo instrument (or instruments) in the introduction and in interludes between the singer's phrases. The solo instrument often has its own thematic material, referred to as the **ritornello**, which may foreshadow the vocal line or play in counterpoint with it. The **B** section is usually in a contrasting key (the dominant or a closely related key).

Example 27.10 shows two portions of a Bach da capo aria that illustrate the opening ritornello and dal segno notation. Part (a) gives the B♭ major ritornello played by a flute or recorder duo. At measure 6, the dal segno (D.S.) sign marks the place where the performers will return at the conclusion of the **B** section; they play until the marking "fine" (end) (or until a fermata sign), indicating the end of the **A B A** design. The **B** section, in G minor, ends with a modulation to F (part b), to prepare for the return to the B♭ major opening section. The entire score appears in the anthology (p. 5).

EXAMPLE 27.10: Bach, "Schafe können sicher weiden" (in a modern realization)

(a) Mm. 1–6, opening ritornello

Translation: Sheep may safely graze.

(b) Mm. 36b–41, end of **B** section and return of **A**

Translation: [One can] feel peace and tranquility, and that which makes countries fortunate. Sheep may [safely graze].

We turn now to an example of ternary form in a vocal work from the Classical era: Mozart's "Voi, che sapete" (anthology, p. 233). Listen to the whole aria to determine the measure numbers in each formal unit (the **A** section should be familiar from previous chapters).

Try it #3

Write the measure numbers spanned for each section of "Voi, che sapete." (anthology)

	Introduction	**A**	**B**	**A′**
Measures:	________	________	________	________

As is the case here, the three parts of a ternary form may not be equal in length: the return of **A** may be extended at the end or shortened, and the contrasting **B** section may be either shorter or longer than **A**. Section **B** typically explores a contrasting tonal area or may be tonally unstable. In Mozart's aria, the **A** section is a tonally stable three-phrase period in B♭ major. **B**, longer and less stable, moves first to F major (m. 21) and then is modally inflected to F minor (m. 35) as a means to tonicize A♭ major (m. 37) before passing through C minor to cadence in G minor (mm. 51–52). This section ends with a sequential passage (Example 27.11) that leads to the tonic B♭ and the **A′** section.

EXAMPLE 27.11: Mozart, "Voi, che sapete," mm. 52b–63

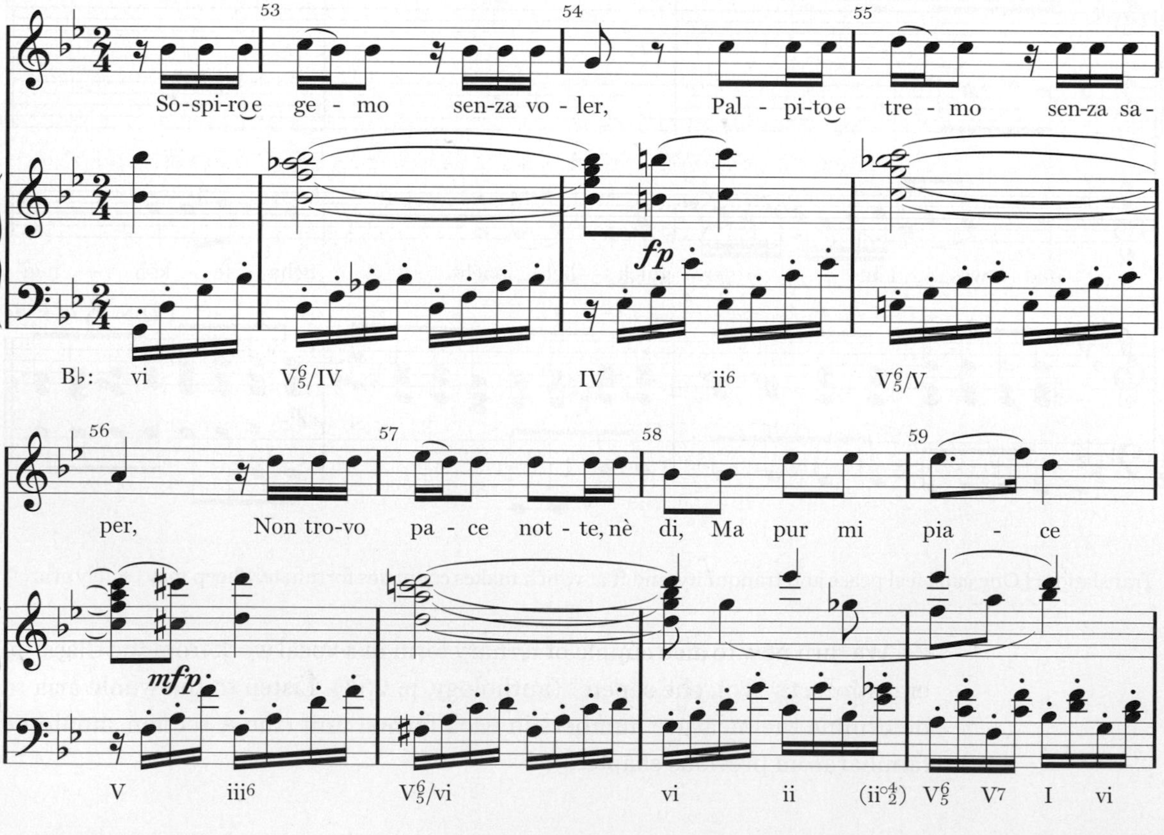

Translation: I sigh and moan without wanting to, throb and tremble without knowing why, I find no peace night or day, yet I enjoy languishing this way.

Turn to the libretto—the opera's text—to see how Lorenzo da Ponte's words for the character Cherubino might suggest this aria's form (anthology, p. 239) and musical interpretation. While the libretto consists of rhyming couplets (aabbccdd, etc.) and no return of the opening text, Mozart made the decision to repeat the opening "Voi, che sapete" to create this rounded form, a typical compositional strategy. The first two lines of text are set in the **A** and **A′** sections, with the remaining twelve lines forming the **B** section. As in the Schumann song, there is a change in voice in the text: the first two lines are addressed to the other characters ("You who know what love is, ladies . . ."), and the remaining lines are a first-person description of Cherubino's tremulous feelings ("I freeze," "I sigh," "tremble," etc.). These agitated lines set the context for the modulatory **B** section and its sequential ending (Example 27.11), which climbs ever higher as his excitement grows. Text painting is abundant here with the rising line, sixteenth-note rapid-fire text, and short subphrases to suggest breathlessness, and the poignant D♭ on "languir" (languishing) over a fully diminished seventh chord. In sum, three-part song forms vary quite a bit in terms of the dimensions, variation, tonal stability, and degree of contrast between sections—much of this hinges on the text and, of course, the composer's interpretation.

Recitatives

Cherubino's aria in *The Marriage of Figaro* is preceded by a recitative sung by a trio of characters (the Countess, Susanna, and Cherubino) as a conversation.

KEY CONCEPT A **recitative** is a relatively short vocal movement, typically paired with an aria, written in a style intended to simulate speech. Recitatives feature a quick declamation of text over sustained chords, and often modulate—sometimes rapidly and repeatedly—to underscore the drama of the text or to provide a transition to the key of the aria.

Recitatives normally serve to advance the story in operas, oratorios, and cantatas. Example 27.12 shows an excerpt of the Mozart recitative, in which Susanna asks Cherubino to sing the song he has written. The recitative begins in C major and modulates to B♭ major, the key of the following aria ("Voi, che sapete"). Recitatives of this type are sung with considerable rhythmic freedom, in imitation of speech (*parlando* style), and rhythms notated here only approximate what would be heard in a performance. This type of recitative, accompanied by sustained chords on a continuo instrument (like harpsichord), is known as **recitativo secco** (dry recitative). In contrast, **recitativo accompagnato** (accompanied recitative) employs, as the name implies, a fully notated orchestral accompaniment, and is performed more closely to the notated rhythms.

EXAMPLE 27.12: Mozart, "Quanto duolmi, Susanna," mm. 22b–29

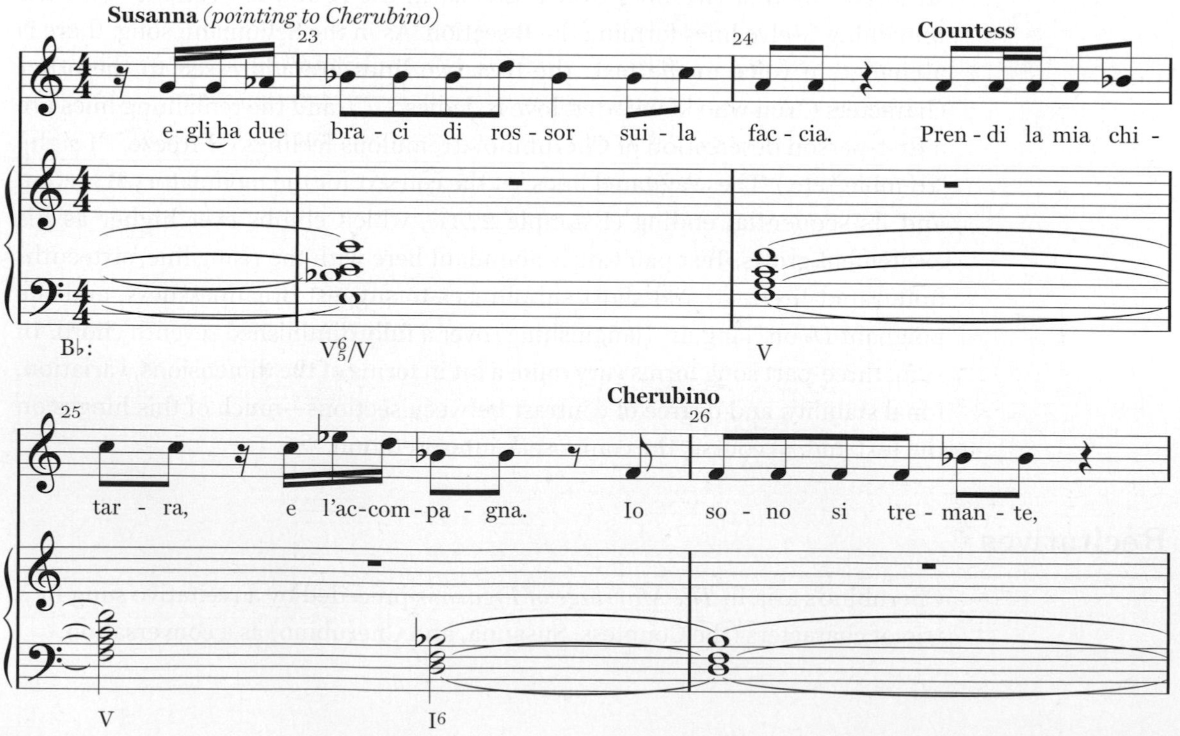

Translation: (Susanna) Look, he has two blushing embers on his face. (Countess) Take my guitar and accompany him. (Cherubino) I am trembling, but if Madame wishes. (Susanna) She wishes, yes she wishes—no more talk.

Baroque-era recitatives tend to be highly expressive and tonally less stable than the Mozart recitative. Look, for example, at a passage from "Thy rebuke hath broken his heart," a tenor recitative from Handel's *Messiah*. The recitative as a whole modulates from F minor to B minor, but ends on a B major triad (with a Picardy third), which functions as V of the following E minor movement. Within the recitative's short eighteen measures are numerous brief tonicizations of other keys (see Example 27.13). In analyzing the shifting tonality, the best strategy may be to listen for cadential formulas, such as V7–i and V^{6-5}_{4-3}, which clearly articulate the tonal arrivals in measures 8–10 and 13, then work backward from those points. Expect sudden direct modulations, without pivot chords. Some abrupt key juxtapositions may be prepared by the same series of harmonies previously heard in another key; for example, the distinctive progression of measures 11–13 in D minor, which reappears in 16–18 in B minor.

Example 27.13: Handel, "Thy rebuke hath broken his heart," mm. 8–18

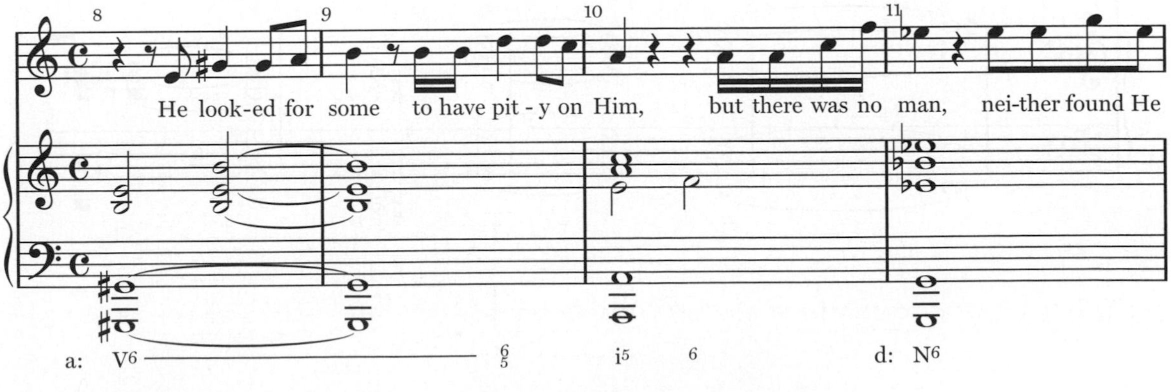

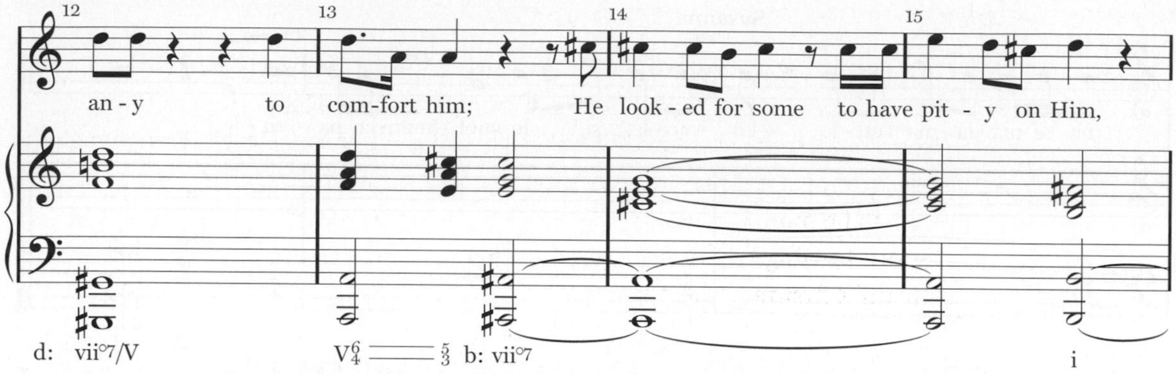

Try it #4

Provide a Roman numeral analysis for measures 4–7 of the Handel recitative.

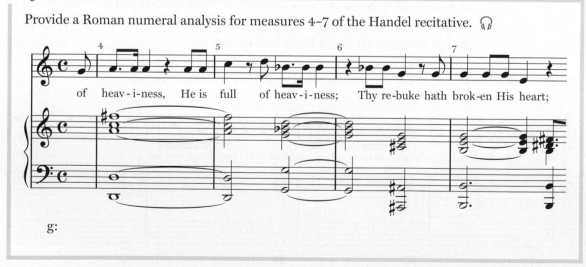

French Mélodie

Romantic-era songs in the French tradition are called **mélodie**, and principal composers include Charles Gounod, Jules Massenet, Henri Duparc, and Gabriel Fauré (and, somewhat later, Claude Debussy and Maurice Ravel). French mélodie typically fall into two- or three-part forms, as do German Lieder, but the forms tend to be more concise and the harmonic language enriched in different ways. Before turning to the harmonic language of Fauré's "Après un rêve" ("After a Dream"), first read the poem by Romain Bussine.

Dans un sommeil que charmait ton image	In a sleep that your image charmed,
Je rêvais le bonheur, ardent mirage,	I dreamed of happiness, ardent mirage,
Tes yeux étaient plus doux, ta voix pure et sonore,	Your eyes were softer, your voice pure and sonorous,
Tu rayonnais comme un ciel éclairé par l'aurore;	You shone like a sky lit by the dawn;
Tu m'appelais et je quittais la terre	You called me and I left the earth
Pour m'enfuir avec toi vers la lumière,	To run away with you toward the light,
Les cieux pour nous entr'ouvraient leurs nues,	The skies parted their clouds for us,
Splendeurs inconnues, lueurs divines entrevues,	Splendors unknown, divine light glimpsed,
Hélas! Hélas! triste réveil des songes	Alas! Alas! sad awakening from the dreams,
Je t'appelle, ô nuit, rends moi tes mensonges,	I call you, O night, give me back your lies,
Reviens, reviens radieuse,	Return, return radiant,
Reviens, ô nuit mystérieuse!	Return, O mysterious night!

Each strophe has an aabb rhyme scheme, with the last two couplets set apart from the rest of the poem by their repeated words: "Hélas! Hélas!" and "Reviens, reviens." There is also a shift from dreaming to wakefulness: the first two verses speak of rapturous love taking place in a dream, but the last describes a sad awakening and a plea to return to pleasant dreams. This poetic structure suggests an **A A B** song form, which Fauré indeed follows in his setting (anthology, p. 180).

Look at the opening of the mélodie, in Example 27.14. The dreamlike mood is established at the beginning by the *pianissimo* dynamic level, placid reiterated chords, and languid descending triplets in the vocal line. The harmonies, even in the first measures, already differ from the Germanic music discussed previously by the absence of a leading tone in minor: for example, the minor dominant of measure 2 and subtonic ninth chord (a product of 9–8 motion above the stationary bass) in measure 4. The leading tone appears only at the half cadence in measures 7–8 (not shown). Similar alterations of diatonic harmonies color the entire song, which never modulates from its C minor tonality.

EXAMPLE 27.14: Fauré, "Après un rêve," mm. 1–4

When you prepare a song for performance, consider well the structure and meaning of the text, as well as whether it fits one of the forms discussed in this chapter. In strophic settings, think about how to create a sense of the story's development despite the literal repetition of music—perhaps by inflecting particular words, selecting contrasting dynamic levels, making subtle changes in tempo, or through other expressive means. In ternary songs, the same strategy applies for the repeated **A** sections, while the **B** sections need to be set apart through interpretive choices—changes in color, articulation, or tempo, for example. In Baroque da capo arias, performers often ornament the return of **A** to create variety and a graceful close to the work.

In any song form, think about the distinction between a phrase of text and a phrase of music. Look for the cadence to determine musical phrase endings, and examine the harmonic (as well as poetic) structure to determine points of arrival, where to take a breath, and where not to breathe if possible. Think about the effect of unexpected harmonies or mixture chords and how these relate to crucial words. Above all, the singer and accompanist should study the text and music together to make collaborative decisions in service of the poetry and song.

Did You Know?

Oratorios, like operas, are extended works for vocal soloists and chorus accompanied by orchestra. They are intended for concert performance and typically recount religious or historical stories (as does Handel's *Messiah*). Cantatas are similar—especially in their mature form in eighteenth-century Germany—in that they also feature soloists, choir, and small orchestra, but they were originally composed as religious service music with texts appropriate to their position in the church year. (Earlier cantatas, in the seventeenth century, featured only one or two solo voices and often secular texts.) The sacred cantatas of J. S. Bach incorporate chorale settings, other choral movements, recitatives, and arias with religious texts. The performance of sacred cantatas in church settings allowed people who would not normally have an opportunity to hear opera or oratorios to enjoy the latest art music styles. Bach wrote secular cantatas as well, including Cantata No. 208, which features pagan gods Diana, Endymion, Pan, and Pales, and depicts pastoral images of sheep and shepherds and the joys of the hunt.

TERMS YOU SHOULD KNOW

- aria
  - da capo aria
- cantata
- couplet
- libretto
- mélodie
- objective-subjective stance
- oratorio
- recitative
  - accompagnato
  - secco
- ritornello
- song cycle
- song forms
  - strophic
  - modified strophic
  - ternary (three part)
  - through-composed
- strophe (or verse or stanza)
- text painting
- textual analysis

QUESTIONS FOR REVIEW

1. How might an analysis of the text help determine the form of a song? How might it influence analysis of the music? of the performance?
2. What formal designs are commonly found in song settings?
3. How might a composer create unity or continuity in a through-composed song?
4. How do da capo arias differ from other arias? from other ternary forms?
5. What strategies might an analyst use to interpret rapidly shifting keys in recitatives?

6. What differences in harmonic choices are found in French mélodie in comparison with German Lieder?
7. In music for your own instrument, find a piece that uses text painting. (Instrumentalists: Examine pieces with titles that imply a story line or other programmatic element; consider ensemble works as well.) What types of motives represent the ideas in the text or program? How might you perform those motives to express the meaning of the text or program?

CHAPTER 28

Popular Music

Outline of topics

Early twentieth-century popular song

- Broadway and Tin Pan Alley
- Quaternary and verse-refrain forms
- Chord extensions: Added-sixth and ninth chords
- Mixture chords and diminished sevenths
- Suspensions and rhythmic displacement
- Chords with altered fifths

The twelve-bar blues

- Pentatonic and blues "scales"
- Blues harmonic progressions and phrase structure

Post-1950 popular song

- New elements of form
- Harmony and melody

Overview

In this chapter, we look at the harmonic features and formal organization typical of Broadway show tunes, Tin Pan Alley songs, jazz standards, and the blues—all twentieth-century popular song styles originating in America. We then touch on more recent popular styles that incorporate some of their features.

Repertoire

Count Basie, "Splanky"

George Gershwin and Ira Gershwin, "I Got Rhythm," from *Girl Crazy*

Brian Holland, Lamont Dozier, and Edward Holland Jr., "Baby Love"

Carole King, "You've Got a Friend"

Jerry Leiber and Mike Stoller, "Hound Dog"

John Lennon and Paul McCartney, "Eleanor Rigby," from *Revolver*

Freddy Mercury, "Crazy Little Thing Called Love"

James Myers and Max Freedman, "Rock Around the Clock"

Vicki Sue Robinson, "Turn the Beat Around"

Liz Rose and Taylor Swift, "You Belong with Me"

Meredith Willson, "Till There Was You," from *The Music Man*

Brian Wilson and Mike Love, "Help Me, Rhonda"

Early Twentieth-Century Popular Song

Broadway and Tin Pan Alley

The American popular song literature is expansive—from minstrel songs and parlor ballads of the late nineteenth century to Tin Pan Alley and Broadway show tunes and the blues in the early twentieth century, and ongoing adaptations of these tunes as "standards" to be improvised on by jazz musicians. Rock and roll emerged mid-century to become a worldwide phenomenon, followed by progressive rock, punk, metal, hip-hop, rap, emo, and other genres prevalent today.

In some ways, early twentieth-century popular songs can be viewed as a continuation of the art song tradition: text setting and text painting are important elements of analysis of this repertoire, as is consideration of form. The form of popular songs is usually different from that of art songs, however. Listen to Meredith Willson's "Till There Was You," while following the score in your anthology (p. 401). In Chapter 18, you analyzed the opening phrases; now listen to the entire song, mark each phrase ending and cadence type, then identify similar and contrasting phrases with lowercase letters.

(anthology)

The song begins with a parallel period, with the antecedent phrase (**a**) ending on a half cadence in measures 7–8, and the consequent phrase (**a′**) ending on an authentic cadence in 15–16. The following phrase, shown in Example 28.1, is contrasting (**b**): here, the harmonic rhythm speeds up, and the melody soars into a higher register, to a climax on "music" and "wonderful," before slowly descending to a HC on "dew" in measure 24. The opening melody then returns with the upbeat to measure 25, rounding out a four-part **a a′ b a′** formal scheme.

EXAMPLE 28.1: Willson, "Till There Was You," mm. 16b–24a (**b** section) (anthology)

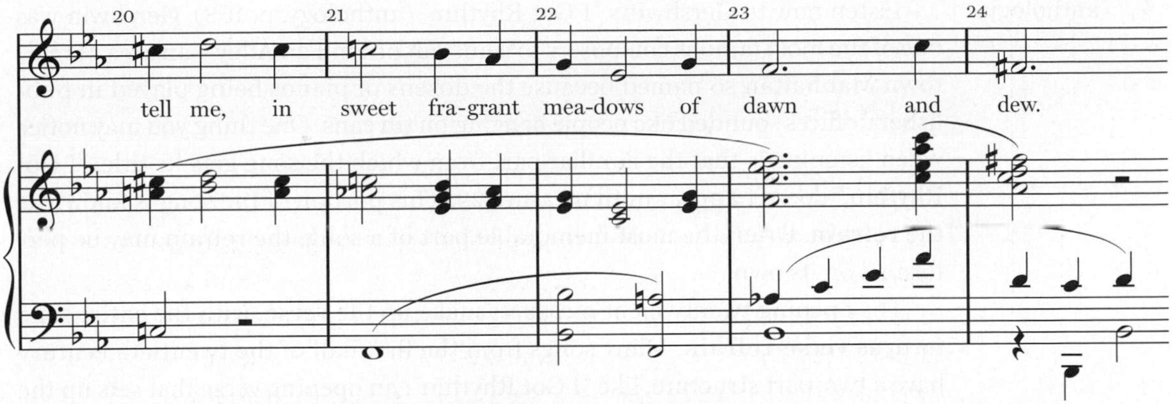

Quaternary and Verse-Refrain Forms

A song with four phrases is in **quaternary form**. Each phrase is typically four or eight measures long, often with an **a a b a** design. (If each phrase is eight measures long, as in "Till There Was You," the form may be referred to as **thirty-two-bar form**.) The first two phrases begin the same—they may be identical (**a a**) or may differ at the cadence (**a a′**)—then are followed by a contrasting section and a return to the opening material.

KEY CONCEPT In quaternary (**a a b a**) song form, the contrasting section (**b**) is known as the **bridge**. The bridge section may temporarily tonicize another key, and may end harmonically open (on a HC or with no cadence) to prepare the return of the **a** section.

Quaternary songs may also be written with other phrase designs, most commonly **a b a c**, with a contrasting period instead of a parallel one, and no bridge. Other possibilities are **a b c b** (or **b′**) or **a b c a** (or **a′**), where **c** is the bridge.

Try it #1

Write in the phrases (measure numbers and letters) for measures 1–32 of "Till There Was You" on the graph below. Identify any period structures. (anthology)

Measures: 1–8a ______ ______ ______ ______

Phrase letters: a ______ ______ ______ ______

Period structures? ______________________________

(anthology) Listen now to Gershwin's "I Got Rhythm" (anthology, p. 168). Gershwin was one of the most famous composers to come out of Tin Pan Alley—an area of midtown Manhattan so named because the dozens of pianos being played in publishers' offices sounded like people banging on tin cans. One thing you may notice when listening is that the familiar part from which the song gets its title, "I Got Rhythm," doesn't appear until measure 29. This portion of the song is known as the **refrain**. Often the most memorable part of a song, the refrain may be performed on its own.

The opening twenty-eight measures make up the **verse**, with the entire song form as **verse-refrain**. Many songs from the first half of the twentieth century have a two-part structure, like "I Got Rhythm": an opening verse that sets up the story, followed by a refrain (typically in quaternary form) that includes the song's "hook" (usually the title idea). The verse in Broadway show tunes may be performed only once, playing a similar role to the recitative in an opera's recitative-aria by setting the scene and telling a story. In that case, the verse may display a less predictable harmonic structure than the refrain, and may modulate, as recitatives often do. In other songs, the verse may be repeated two or more times, with the same music but different texts. The refrain normally returns with the same music *and* text.

SUMMARY

The design of a verse-refrain song generally follows this model:

verse: like recitative, may modulate
refrain: like aria, **a a b a**

Each time the refrain is repeated, it has the same music and text; if a verse is repeated, the music will be the same, but the text is different.

Chord Extensions: Added-Sixth and Ninth Chords

The formal elements of early twentieth-century popular songs are not the only aspect that distinguishes them from their art song predecessors: these songs also may employ an expanded harmonic palette. For an example, listen again to measures 3–10 of Gershwin's verse (Example 28.2).

EXAMPLE 28.2: Gershwin, "I Got Rhythm," mm. 3-10 (anthology)

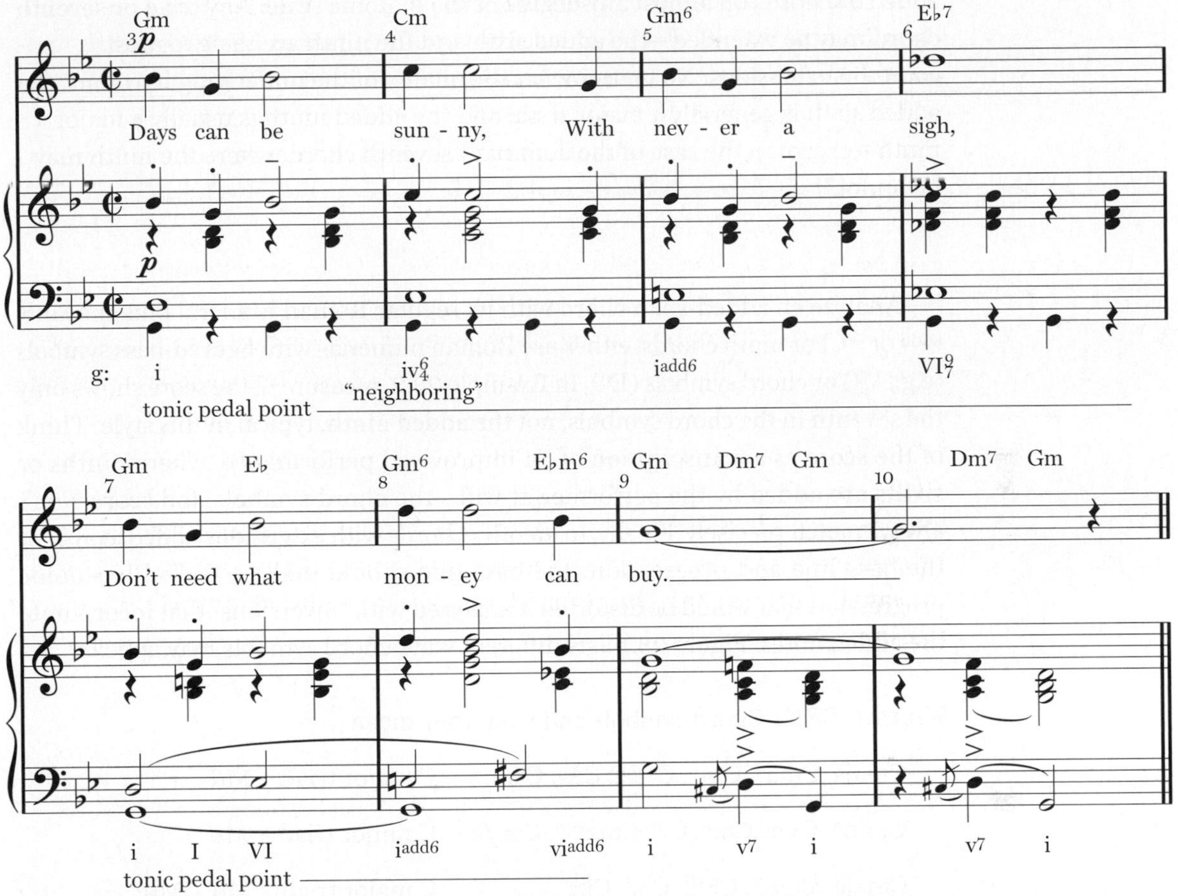

The first three measures express a typical harmonic phrase opening, with a neighboring $^6_4$ chord prolonging the tonic harmony i$^{5-6-5}_{3-4-3}$, yet the tonic harmony of measure 5 is "clouded" by an additional pitch, E♮3, a major sixth above the bass note. Pitches added to triads or seventh chords are sometimes called **extensions** (or "tensions" by jazz musicians). The sonority here is an added-sixth chord (its chord symbol could be Gm^{add6} or Gm^{+6}, as well as Gm^6). Don't confuse the numeral 6 with an inversion symbol—it would be a strange chord indeed if stacked in thirds above the E♮ "root," and would not correctly identify the chord's tonic function. The next chord (m. 6) consists of E♭-G-B♭-D♭-F. These pitches create a **ninth chord**, an E♭ dominant seventh chord plus a major ninth (F) above the root.

KEY CONCEPT In popular styles, major or minor sevenths may be added to chords on almost any degree of the diatonic scale. Any triad or seventh chord may be extended—the added sixth and the ninth are the two most common extensions. No matter what the quality of the underlying harmony, the added sixth is generally a major sixth, and the added ninth is usually a major ninth—except in the case of the dominant seventh chord, where the ninth may be minor.

Analyze an added-sixth chord with its regular Roman numeral plus the label ^{add6} or $^{+6}$. For ninth chords, either use Roman numerals with figured-bass symbols (e.g., V$^{9}_{7}$) or chord symbols (E^{9}). In Example 28.2, measure 6, the score shows only the seventh in the chord symbols, not the added ninth, typical in this style. Think of the score as a transcription of an improvised performance, where ninths or sixths are added by the performer at will—the chord symbols and score won't always match precisely. Finally, to identify chords with extensions added, consider the bass line and progression: the bass line should make a logical harmonic progression that would be distorted if analyzed with "inversions" that incorporate the added notes. Figure 28.1 lists different ways chord symbols may appear.

FIGURE 28.1: Chord symbols and what they mean

Cmaj^{6}, Cma^{6}, CM^{6}, C^{add6}, CΔ^{6}, C^{6}:	C major triad + M6
Cmin^{6}, Cmi^{6},Cm^{6}, C-^{6}, Cm^{add6}, Cm^{+6}:	C minor triad + M6
Cmaj$^{9}_{6}$, Cma$^{9}_{6}$, CM$^{9}_{6}$, CΔ^{9}_{6}, C$^{9}_{6}$:	C major triad + M6 + M9
Cmin$^{9}_{6}$, Cmi$^{9}_{6}$, Cm$^{9}_{6}$, C-$^{9}_{6}$, c$^{9}_{6}$:	C minor triad + M6 + M9
Cmaj^{9}, Cma^{9}, CM^{9}, CΔ^{9}:	Cmaj^{7} + M9 (MM7 + M9)
Dmin^{9}, Dmi^{9}, Dm^{9}, d^{9}, d-^{9}:	Dm^{7} + M9 (mm7 + M9)
G$^{7(\flat 9)}$:	G^{7} + m9 (Mm7 + m9)
G^{9}:	G^{7} +M9 (Mm7 + M9)

Try it #2

Locate a ninth chord and an added-sixth chord (not indicated in the chord symbols) in the passage below. Circle the appropriate measure and beat.

Gershwin, "I Got Rhythm," mm. 15–18 (anthology)

	Measure	*Beat*
Ninth chord:	15 16 17 18	1 & 2 &
Added-sixth chord:	15 16 17 18	1 & 2 &

Mixture Chords and Diminished Sevenths

Mixture chords appear often in popular songs, as in art songs. Some show tunes, such as "I Got Rhythm," also include ♭$\hat{5}$ in a type of extended mixture, prominently featured in Example 28.2 on the word "sigh." Here, ♭$\hat{5}$ creates the minor seventh of the VI^9_7. This note is accentuated by its position at the top of the musical phrase and the end of a vocal subphrase, as well as by its coloring of "sigh." Listen now to Example 28.3; consider whether each accidental is the product of modal mixture and what its effect is on the harmony.

EXAMPLE 28.3: Gershwin, "I Got Rhythm," mm. 37–44 (anthology)

Mixture notes are circled in measures 39, 42, and 44. The G♭ in 42 creates a minor subdominant by mixture, and the A♭ in 44 is a brief chordal embellishment ($\flat\hat{7}$) that initiates the lead-in to the bridge. The E♮ in 43 is a passing tone. The E♮ in measure 39 is $\sharp\hat{4}$, which together with the D♭ create a fully diminished seventh chord built on E♮. In common-practice style, fully diminished seventh chords on scale degrees other than $\hat{7}$ usually function as secondary diminished sevenths. In this case, we might expect a vii°7/V, where the E♮ would resolve up to F and the D♭ would resolve down to C. But the chord does not resolve this way, and should therefore be considered a voice-leading chord (CT°7) without a Roman numeral.

KEY CONCEPT In popular styles, fully diminished and half-diminished seventh sonorities may appear on any scale degree, and need not function as secondary diminished seventh chords.

Suspensions and Rhythmic Displacement

Suspensions that conform to common-practice voice-leading may also be found in popular styles; see, for example, the 4–3 suspensions (B♭ to A) in measures 40 and 43 of Example 28.3. We also sometimes find "4–3 suspensions" with no resolution: an added fourth above the bass displaces the third but never resolves. Such harmonies are called **sus chords** and labeled sus or sus^4.

Other sonorities may result from a rhythmic displacement of pitches—for example, pitches that are "held over" like suspensions from one chord to the next, or pitches that "arrive early" before the rest of a harmony. Look, for instance, at the first harmony of measure 39 in Example 28.3. Here, the chord symbol implies a B♭ root, yet no B♭ is notated. Instead, the C5 from the previous chord is held over across the bar, displacing the B♭, which returns at the end of the measure. Jazz soloists intuit these "missing" pitches; they know the notes will be supplied by bass or piano in the rhythm section (bass, drums, piano).

Analyze chords with rhythmic displacement as though the chord tone were present, rather than including the displaced pitch (in m. 39, I^{add6}). Alternatively, you may hear the C as creating a ninth chord above the missing pitch—this implies an analysis of I^9_7. You may also find in some textbooks or lead sheets indications for eleventh or thirteenth chords. To interpret these chord symbols, simply add the specified interval (4 for an eleventh chord or 6 for a thirteenth chord) above the bass.

Chords with Altered Fifths

Listen now to a final excerpt from "I Got Rhythm," this one drawn from the bridge (Example 28.4). Listen especially to the chromatic voice-leading in the lower notes of the right hand. We will analyze the harmonies in these measures for chord quality rather than with Roman numerals.

EXAMPLE 28.4: Gershwin, "I Got Rhythm," mm. 45–52a (bridge) (anthology)

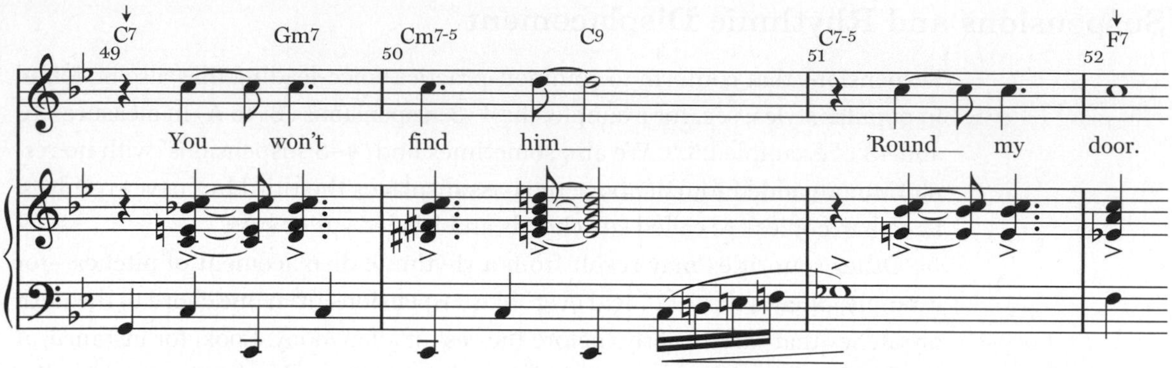

The bridge begins with a D dominant seventh chord and articulates a descending fifth pattern: D^7–$G^{(7)}$–C^7–F^7. In measure 45, the right hand's lower voices begin a chromatic ascent in parallel thirds, prolonging a ninth chord at the end of 46. In measure 47, the parallel thirds reach their high point and begin to descend chromatically. You can see one harmonic by-product of Gershwin's voice-leading by looking at the chord symbols: the Dm^7 chord of measure 46 has its fifth lowered by a half step (shown as Dm^{7-5}), and the last sonority of 47 has its fifth raised by a half step (D aug^5). Triads and seventh chords with altered fifths are a typical harmonic feature of popular song, and may also be found in common-practice music of the nineteenth century.

KEY CONCEPT Triads or seventh chords may be colored and intensified by lowering or raising the fifth of the chord by a half step, thereby altering the quality of the interval between the root and fifth.

When analyzing harmonies with altered fifths, add traditional symbols ($^{\circ 7}$ or ^{ø7}) to Roman numerals for those that create diminished or half-diminished seventh sonorities. Major triads or dominant sevenths with raised fifths are labeled with Roman numeral plus either $^{+5}$ or $^{\sharp 5}$, and lowered fifths with either $^{-5}$ or $^{\flat 5}$; they often function as secondary dominants (e.g., $V^{7\flat 5}$/IV). (Alternatively, you may see "aug5" or "dim5" attached to chord symbols.)

Try it #3

Find two additional triads or seventh chords with altered fifths in measures 49–52 of Example 28.4. What are their chord qualities? What Roman numeral would you assign each harmony, assuming a B♭ tonic key?

	Measure	Quality	Roman numeral
(a)	________	________	________
(b)	________	________	________

The Twelve-Bar Blues

Another early twentieth-century song style that has influenced subsequent popular music is a genre known as the **blues**. While this style originated in the Mississippi Delta among African American musicians, it has spread worldwide, and was an essential influence on rock and roll in the 1950s. Blues songs normally feature a minor-sounding vocal melody, accompanied by chords in the parallel major key.

Pentatonic and Blues "Scales"

Listen to the beginning of Count Basie's "Splanky" while following Example 28.5, a transcription of the melody.

EXAMPLE 28.5: Basie, "Splanky," mm. 1–12 (includes an introduction)

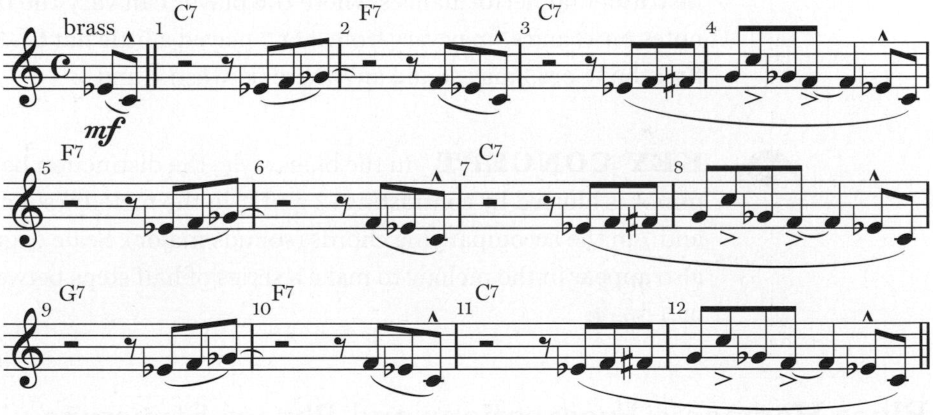

This melody has C as its tonic—evident from both the shape of the tune and the chord progression in C major—but it also includes $\flat\hat{3}$, lending it a minor quality, as well as $\hat{4}$, $\sharp\hat{4}$ or $\flat\hat{5}$ (the spelling is based on the direction the line is moving), and $\hat{5}$. Example 28.6a shows the notes in "Splanky" written as a scale—the so-called **blues scale**—plus $\flat\hat{7}$, a note not played in this melody but heard as part of the C7 accompanying chord. Part (b) shows the C minor pentatonic ($\hat{1}$–$\flat\hat{3}$–$\hat{4}$–$\hat{5}$–$\flat\hat{7}$, or *do-me-fa-sol-te*) on which this scale is based; $\sharp\hat{4}$ and $\flat\hat{5}$ are added to the minor pentatonic to make the blues scale.

EXAMPLE 28.6: Blues and minor pentatonic scales

(a) Blues scale on C

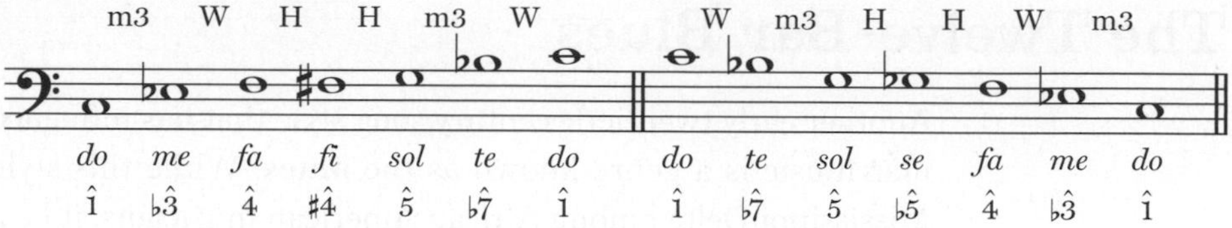

(b) C minor pentatonic

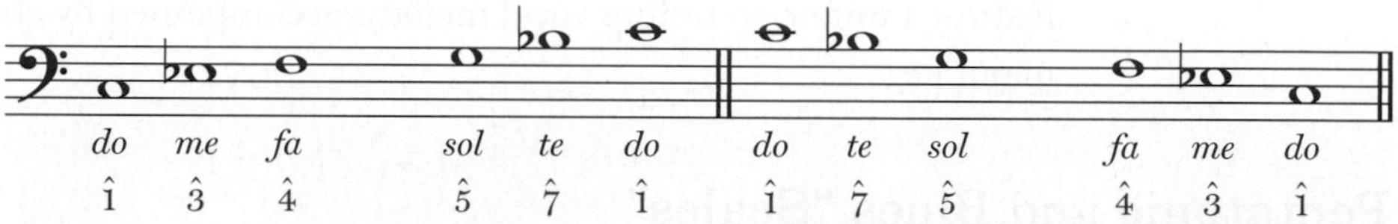

The blues scale is not a scale proper, but rather a collection of notes from which selections are made when improvising a melody. The $\flat\hat{3}$, $\flat\hat{7}$, and $\sharp\hat{4}$ or $\flat\hat{5}$ are sometimes called **blue notes** because they lend a hint of sadness to the melodic line that contrasts with the major-key accompaniment. When sung, and in instrumental performances where the player can vary the intonation, the blue notes on $\flat\hat{3}$ and $\flat\hat{7}$ may vary from $\hat{3}$ or $\hat{7}$ played a little flat to $\flat\hat{3}$ or $\flat\hat{7}$ played a little flat; the $\sharp\hat{4}$ or $\flat\hat{5}$ may sound anywhere between $\hat{4}$ and $\hat{5}$.

KEY CONCEPT In the blues style, the distinction between major and minor is blurred by contrasting $\flat\hat{3}$ and $\flat\hat{7}$ in the melody (sounds minor) with $\hat{3}$ and $\hat{7}$ in the accompanying chords (sounds major). Scale degrees $\sharp\hat{4}$ and $\flat\hat{5}$ may also appear in the melody to make a series of half steps between $\hat{4}$ and $\hat{5}$: $\hat{4}$–$\sharp\hat{4}$–$\hat{5}$ or $\hat{5}$–$\flat\hat{5}$–$\hat{4}$.

Blues Harmonic Progressions and Phrase Structure

One of the most striking aspects of blues compositions is a characteristic repeated harmonic progression in the accompaniment known as the **twelve-bar blues**. The basic progression (Figure 28.2) consists of three subphrases, each four measures long: (1) four measures of tonic harmony, followed by (2) two measures of IV and two of I, then (3) V–IV–I–I. Minor sevenths may be added to any of these chords to make a dominant seventh quality, as in "Splanky" (Example 28.5). The last measure may serve as a "turnaround," with the addition of a V7 leading back to the beginning and a repeat of the progression. These harmonies, as well as other harmonic progressions in popular styles, are often referred to as the **changes**, short for chord changes.

FIGURE 28.2: Twelve-bar blues progression

mm. 1–4				mm. 5–8				9–12			
I	I	I	I (or V7/IV)	IV	IV	I	I	V	IV	I	I

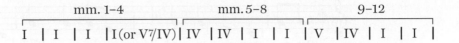

In blues-style songs, the phrases of the vocal part usually conform to those of the harmonic progression, with one subphrase every four measures and the only conclusive close when tonic returns in measures 11–12. The texts typically describe hard times, lost love, and other sorrows, expressed in simple colloquial language that may take on added meaning through metaphor. The first two subphrases (mm. 1–4 and 5–8) normally present a "problem," with the third offering a consequence of that problem, as in Leiber and Staller's "Hound Dog" as sung by Willie Mae "Big Mama" Thornton. In the context of Big Mama's performance, it is clear that the "hound dog" is two-legged instead of four-legged. In Elvis Presley's performance, however, the lyrics are changed to make the meaning ambiguous. (See "Did you know?" for more details.) This example and others in the remainder of this chapter are available online; listen to them while reading the discussions.

‖: You ain't nothin' but a hound dog,
Been snoopin' round my door. :‖
You can wag your tail,
But I ain't gonna feed you no more.

In a performance of "Hound Dog," "Splanky," or any other blues tune, two or more presentations of the melody (with text if sung) and harmonies are followed by additional repetitions of the harmonic progression with improvised instrumental solos over it. After these improvisations, the original melody returns. In jazz settings, the clearly recognizable melody—whether sung or instrumental—is called the **head**. This practice of playing solos in the middle of a performance, showcasing members of the ensemble, is a common feature in jazz and post-1950s popular music as well (where the solo instrument is typically lead guitar), whether the music is based on the blues progression, a quaternary song form, or some other form.

The twelve-bar blues progression was adopted by rock musicians in the 1950s, and appears in songs of various styles after that time. One typical example, from "Rock Around the Clock," is given in Example 28.7.

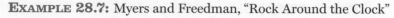

Example 28.7: Myers and Freedman, "Rock Around the Clock"

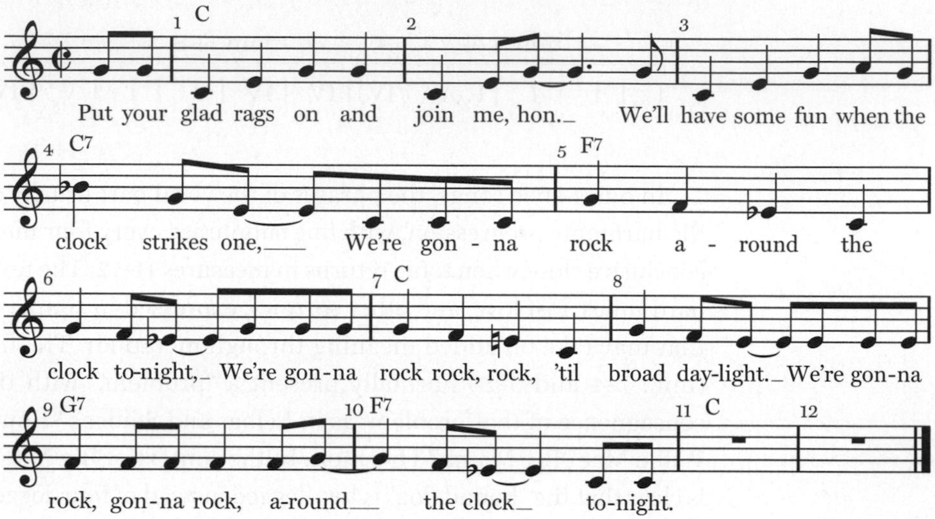

Try it #4

Play through the progression in Example 28.7 in block chords while singing the melody.

(a) Is this a blues progression? YES NO

(b) Blue notes appear in mm. _______, _______, _______, and _______.

Listen to various performances online to hear where performers place blue notes.

Post-1950 Popular Song

New Elements of Form

After 1950, the terminology for labeling sections of songs shifted. **Verse** came to designate a musical section that might appear in a song multiple times with the same music but a different text. A verse may be based on quaternary or twelve-bar blues design, or may follow some other formal plan. It normally carries the story-line for the song, and may consist of one sentence, with the conclusion of the thought at the verse's end. **Chorus** refers to a section of music that is repeated, each time with the same (or a similar) text. The chorus often includes the song's "hook"—a musical setting of a few words or a phrase, usually including the title, that is the most "catchy" or memorable part of the song.

Many popular songs from the 1950s and 1960s are made of only these two elements. A song with only verses is in **simple verse form** (a comparable art song would be called strophic). Examples of simple verse songs include Elvis Presley's "Heartbreak Hotel" (six repetitions of the verse; the fifth is instrumental), Bob Dylan's "Blowin' in the Wind," and "Baby Love" by the Supremes (Figure 28.3). The hook for this song, "baby love," appears in various places in the verse.

FIGURE 28.3: Simple verse form in "Baby Love"

Intro: Ooh, ooh-hoo (4 measures in $\frac{4}{4}$)

Verse 1: "Baby love . . . I need you, oh how I need you . . ." (12 measures)

Verse 2: "'Cause baby love . . . been missing ya, miss kissing ya . . ." (12 measures)

Verse 3: "Need ya . . . Baby love . . ." (12 measures; 4 vocal + 8 instrumental)

Verse 4: "Baby love . . . why must we separate . . ." (12 measures)
(modulates up a whole step, 2 measures like intro, "Ooh, ooh")

Verse 5: "Need to hold you . . ." (12 measures)

Verse 6: "Me my love . . . I need ya." (12 measures)

Verse 7: "Till it's hurtin' me . . . don't throw our love away." (partial verse with fade out)

Songs that alternate verse and chorus are in **verse-chorus form**: both verse and chorus may be sung to the same or similar music (**simple verse-chorus**), or they may be contrasting sections (**contrasting verse-chorus**). An example of simple-verse chorus is Little Richard's "Tutti Frutti"—both verses ("Got a girl named . . .") and the chorus ("Tutti-frutti, oh Rudy") are sung to the same music. Chuck Berry's "Rock and Roll Music," Deep Purple's "Smoke on the Water," and the Beach Boys' "Help Me, Rhonda," whose form is outlined below, are contrasting verse-chorus.

FIGURE 28.4: Contrasting verse-chorus form in "Help Me, Rhonda"

Verse 1: "Since she put me down . . ." (16 measures)

Chorus: "Help me, Rhonda . . ." (16 measures)

Verse 2: "She was gonna be my wife . . ." (16 measures)

Chorus: "Help me, Rhonda . . ." (16 measures)

Verse 3: Instrumental (16 measures)

Chorus: "Help me, Rhonda" (6 measures + 2 instrumentals to fade)

In post-1950 popular music, **refrain** refers to a line or pair of lines that normally appear at the end of each verse with the same music and words. A familiar example is the line "All the lonely people . . ." that appears at the end of each verse of the Beatles song "Eleanor Rigby." The refrain differs from a chorus in that it is not a full-length independent section; rather it is a repeated line that completes the verse. Occasionally a refrain will appear on its own without being a part of the verse, but it remains only one or two lines long—shorter than a chorus normally would be.

SUMMARY

- Verse: same music reappears later in the song with different text(s).
- Chorus: same music reappears later in the song with the same text.
- Refrain: one- or two-line text at the end of the verse that reappears with the same music.
- Simple verse form: a song with only verses (no chorus or other sections).
- Verse-chorus: a song that alternates verses and choruses.
- Simple verse-chorus: both verse and chorus are sung to the same music.
- Contrasting verse-chorus: verse and chorus have different music.

In "Rock Around the Clock," the music shown in Example 28.7 serves as the main harmonic-melodic material for the entire song. The music to measures 1–4a reappears with different words ("When the clock strikes two, three and four, if the band slows down we'll yell for more") in other verses. The words and music of 4b–10 are consistently the same throughout the song (a refrain). While these measures could constitute a chorus, this entire example is based on the twelve-bar blues progression, and the thought expressed in the text is not concluded until the end of the harmonic progression. Both "Rock Around the Clock" and "Eleanor Rigby" are in simple verse form.

"Rock Around the Clock" begins, as do many popular songs, with an eight-measure introduction ("intro"), to the words "One, two, three o'clock, four o'clock, rock . . ." An introduction is usually instrumental, but may also include text, as does this one, or a repeated syllable, such as "Oh" or "Ooh" (as in "Baby Love"). It may be based on music later associated with the verse or chorus, or on a chord progression or a **riff** (a repeated instrumental motive); sometimes the intro fades in, or instruments may join in to build up the sound for the entry of the main part of the song.

Many songs also end with music known as an "outro," or coda, often instrumental. The outro may fade out, or it may repeat the hook. For example, the last verse in "Baby Love" is incomplete, repeats the hook, and fades out, while "Help

Me, Rhonda" has an instrumental outro that fades out. The length of the intro and outro (their proportion relative to the rest of the song) and their content can be a marker of a particular group or musician's style. The term "coda" is more likely to be used if it follows the last substantial cadence of the song, similar to common-practice music.

After the introduction and two verses of "Rock Around the Clock," as performed by Bill Haley and the Comets, there is an instrumental passage based on the verse but without a sung text. An instrumental section in the middle of a song is referred to as an **instrumental break** (if several instruments are featured) or a **solo break** (one instrument). Instrumental breaks may be based on the melody and chord progression of the verse and/or chorus or may include improvisation over a harmonic progression only. In hip-hop or rap songs, a "rap break"—a passage with a rhythmic, inflected spoken solo, usually accompanied by background instruments—may substitute for the verse (or chorus, though rap breaks normally replace the verse and are followed by the chorus).

KEY CONCEPT Beginning in the mid-1960s, **bridge** came to refer to a section of music with text that contrasts with the verse and/or chorus. The bridge typically appears only once in a song, and serves to heighten anticipation of the return of the verse or chorus.

For an example, consider "You've Got a Friend," a Grammy-winning song written by Carole King in 1971, and popularized by James Taylor. (If you are unfamiliar with this song, download either performance and listen to it.)

FIGURE 28.5: Form in "You've Got a Friend"

Intro

Verse 1: "When you're down and troubled . . ."

Chorus: "You just call . . . "

Verse 2: "If the sky above you . . ."

Chorus: "You just call . . ."

Bridge: "Now ain't it good to know . . ."

Chorus: "You just call . . ."

Outro

In songs where the verse and chorus are strongly contrasting, or when the verse ends without harmonic closure, there may be a **prechorus**: a short passage of music with text that comes between the verse and the chorus. "City of Blinding Lights" by U2 illustrates this element. The song opens with two verses ("The more you see the less you know . . ." and "Neon heart dayglo eyes . . ."), followed by a prechorus ("And I miss you when you are not around . . .") and then the chorus ("Oh . . . Oh you look so beautiful tonight . . .").

Some songs include an instrumental **interlude**, a passage with new music that serves as transition between or change of pace from other sections. A short instrumental **link** may be used to connect two musical sections.

SUMMARY

- Prechorus: short passage of music that usually comes between the verse and the chorus.
- Bridge: music with text that contrasts with the verse and chorus; usually appears once in the song to prepare a final return of the chorus or verse.
- Instrumental break: a section in the middle of a song (usually based on one of its harmonic progressions) played only by instruments.
- Instrumental interlude: a passage with new music connecting other sections of a song.

An award-winning song from 2009, "You Belong with Me," by Taylor Swift and Liz Rose, illustrates how these formal elements—verse, chorus, prechorus, instrumental break, bridge, intro, outro—may be employed in recent songs. Here, two different sets of lyrics are sung with the chorus melody and harmonies. While this song, and the others included in this chapter, is made up of four- and eight-measure units, combining to form sixteen-measure sections, and stays in the same meter throughout, meter and phrase length are parameters that can be varied in popular songs.

Figure 28.6: Form in "You Belong with Me"

Intro: (4 measures)
Verse 1: "You're on the phone . . ." (8 measures)
Verse 2: "I'm in the room . . ."
Prechorus: "But she wears short skirts . . ." (8 measures)
Chorus 1: "If you could see . . ." (8 measures)
(Refrain: "You belong with me . . .")
Link (2 measures, like intro)
Verse 3: "Walking the streets . . ."
Verse 4: "And you've got a smile . . ."
Prechorus: "She wears high heels . . ."
(Refrain: "You belong with me . . .")

Chorus 1: "If you could see . . ."

Chorus 2 (same music, different lyric): "Standing by and waiting . . ."

Instrumental break (8 measures)

Bridge: "Oh, I remember you driving . . ." (8 measures)

Verse 5: "Can't you see . . ."

(Refrain: "You belong with me . . .")

Chorus 2: "Standing by and waiting . . ."

Outro (based on refrain): "You belong with me . . ."

Harmony and Melody

Many popular songs written after 1950 continue to employ the harmonic conventions of earlier tonal music—the basic phrase progression and principles of voice-leading—though they may include chord extensions, mode mixture, sus chords, added sixths, secondary dominants, and other chromatic harmonies. In some songs that are guitar-based instead of keyboard-based, common-practice voice-leading has been replaced by chord connections easier to make on a guitar fretboard. For songs clearly in a major or minor key that follow basic phase progressions, we can provide a Roman numeral and contextual analysis (T–PD–D–T), even though the voice-leading may not follow earlier practice. Songs based on the twelve-bar blues progression also can be labeled with either chord symbols or Roman numerals, though a contextual analysis will not conform to the basic phrase design because of the V–IV–I progression in the last four bars and the underlying pentatonic framework.

While some songs include four- or eight-bar units ending with typical common-practice cadence types—PAC, IAC, and HC—others may feature melodic phrases with no harmonic or melodic cadence. For an example, look at the opening of the verse of "Eleanor Rigby" (Example 28.8); the five measures that follow have the same melody and harmonies.

Example 28.8: Lennon and McCartney, "Eleanor Rigby," mm. 9–13

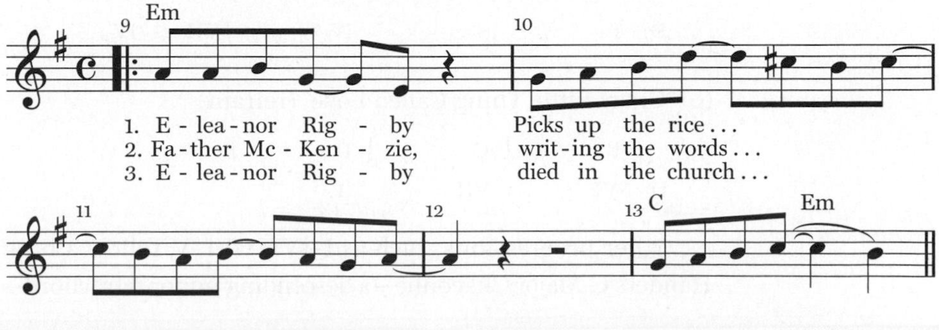

These five-measure groupings constitute a melodic thought, but neither the melody nor harmonies follow a traditional progression—the chords are Em to C (is this e: i–VI?). The introduction to the song starts with a C major triad, but then moves to Em, and back again, C–Em (is this C: I–iii?). The refrain ("All the lonely people") is also based on Em and C, and the song ends on an E minor triad, with the melody on the third (G) of the chord. In deviating from a common-practice progression, the harmonies reflect the loneliness and the repetitive life of the characters described in the lyrics. When analyzing popular songs, such as this one, don't be surprised to find progressions that are not based on the basic-phrase progressions—instead consider what chords are being used, how they are connected, and what their possible relation might be to the lyrics or genre.

Many other options are explored in post-1950 popular styles. Some songs retain voice-leading conventions, but not the harmonic progressions typical of earlier styles. With electric guitars, new types of chord voicing and doubling came into use, including the "power chord" with only root and fifth (no third, which leaves its quality ambiguous). When combined with amplification and distortion and played in the middle register of the guitar, "power chords" generate overtones that increase the volume and richness of the sound. They are typically connected by shifting the hand in a parallel motion, rather than with traditional voice-leading. The minor pentatonic scale and the chords available to it generate root progressions that include the triads I or i, ♭III, IV, V, or ♭VII in various combinations, as in Example 28.9.

Example 28.9: Examples of progressions from the minor pentatonic

(a) Robinson, "Turn the Beat Around" (chorus)

(b) Mercury (Queen), "Crazy Little Thing Called Love" (repeated figure throughout song)

	D	D	G	C	G
D:	I	I	IV	♭VII	IV

(c) "Crazy Little Thing Called Love" (refrain)

	B♭	C	D
D:	♭VI	♭VII	I

Other progressions, such as I–♭VII–♭VI–V, follow a bass line familiar from Handel's G Major Chaconne—a descending minor tetrachord—but the chords may now be connected with parallel motion that was not typical of the earlier style. While these chords may be identified with Roman numerals, the progressions may bear little or no connection to common-practice progressions or voice-leading—instead, the Roman numerals simply represent the motion between roots. Chord symbols may be used instead, especially if there is not a clear sense of which chord is the tonic.

The chord progressions explored in the rock era (post-1950) are rich and varied—to study them in the same detail as we have the progressions of Baroque, Classical, and Romantic music would require as many pages as have been devoted to those styles. For now, listen with an open mind—don't expect the progressions to follow earlier norms. When you encounter a progression you like, analyze it: What are the chords? How do they connect? How are they used in this song? And how do they relate to the meaning of the song's lyrics or to its style?

Did You Know?

The 1956 remake of "Hound Dog" by Elvis Presley, with changed lyrics, is the best-known version of the song; it ranked as #19 on *Rolling Stone*'s list of "500 Greatest Songs of All Time" and is heard in several movie soundtracks, including *Forrest Gump*, *Lilo & Stitch*, and *Indiana Jones and the Kingdom of the Crystal Skull*. The original version, written by Jerry Leiber and Mike Stoller, was recorded in 1952 by Willie Mae "Big Mama" Thornton, and the following year held the #1 spot on the Billboard Rhythm and Blues charts for seven weeks. Like many songs achieving popularity on the R&B charts (which at that time were intended for a primarily African American audience), "Hound Dog" was released in cover versions almost immediately by various country singers, expanding its audience. A version with revised lyrics—"snoopin' round my door" was replaced with "cryin' all the time," and "You can wag your tail, but I ain't gonna feed you no more" was replaced by "You ain't never caught a rabbit, and you ain't no friend of mine"—by Freddie Bell and the Bellboys (also used by Presley), was intended to appeal to a broader radio audience by removing the sexual innuendo typical of blues songs. "Hound Dog" (with both sets of lyrics) has since been covered by artists performing in a variety of styles, including Jimi Hendrix, Jerry Lee Lewis, John Lennon, the Rolling Stones, Eric Clapton, Jeff Beck, and James Taylor.

TERMS YOU SHOULD KNOW

- added-sixth chord
- altered fifth
- blue notes
- blues scale
- bridge
- changes
- chorus
- extensions
- head
- hook
- instrumental break
- interlude
- intro
- link
- ninth chord
- outro
- prechorus
- quaternary song form
- refrain
- riff
- simple verse form
- thirty-two-bar song chorus
- twelve-bar blues
- verse
- verse-chorus form
- verse-refrain form

QUESTIONS FOR REVIEW

1. What are some phrase designs typical of early twentieth-century popular songs?
2. What added notes might you find in the chords used to harmonize early twentieth-century popular songs?
3. Which scale degrees may be altered to create blue notes?
4. When jazz combos play a jazz standard, how do solos alternate with ensemble playing, and improvised music with notated music?
5. What changes have taken place in the use of the terms "verse," "refrain," and "chorus"?
6. What other formal designs are found in post-1950 song settings?
7. Find a piece with added notes in chords, altered fifths, or blue-note alterations. (Hint: Look in music of the twentieth century, especially by jazz composers or those who have been influenced by jazz.)

CHAPTER 29

Chromatic Harmony and Voice-Leading

Outline of topics

Chromatic elaboration of diatonic frameworks

- Chromatic sequence patterns
- Descending chromatic bass lines
- Chromatic voice exchanges
- Common-tone diminished seventh and augmented-sixth chords
- The raised chordal fifth

Chromatic mediants and submediants

Overview

In this chapter, we consider harmonies and voice-leading characteristic of Romantic-era chromaticism, and learn how to write chromatic progressions by embellishing familiar diatonic ones.

Repertoire

Johannes Brahms, Intermezzo in A Major, Op. 118, No. 2

Gabriel Fauré, “Après un rêve” (“After a Dream”)

George Frideric Handel, Chaconne in G Major

Fanny Mendelssohn Hensel, “Neue Liebe, neues Leben” (“New Love, New Life”)

Jerome Kern and Otto Harbach, “Smoke Gets in Your Eyes,” from *Roberta*

Wolfgang Amadeus Mozart, String Quartet in D Minor, K. 421, third movement

Franz Schubert
“Am Meer” (“By the Sea”), from *Schwanengesang* (*Swan Song*)
“Der Wegweiser” (“The Sign Post”). from *Winterreise*

Robert Schumann, “Ich grolle nicht” (“I Bear No Grudge”), from *Dichterliebe*

Hugo Wolf, “In dem Schatten meiner Locken” (“In the Shadow of My Tresses”), from *Spanisches Liederbuch* (*Spanish Songbook*)

Chromatic Elaboration of Diatonic Frameworks

Chromatic Sequence Patterns

The most ubiquitous sequences in tonal music are descending-fifth sequences, whose basic framework may include all root-position chords, all seventh chords, or an alternation of the two, either with roots in the bass or with inversions.

KEY CONCEPT The most common type of **chromatic sequence** is a descending-fifth sequence in which dominant-seventh-quality chords are substituted for all or some (usually every other chord) of the chords in the diatonic pattern. Sequence patterns typically include root-position seventh chords (like diatonic sequences) but may also include inversions.

For one example, listen to the Menuetto of the Mozart String Quartet in D Minor, and focus on measures 22–29, the end of the **B** section of this binary form (Example 29.1).

Example 29.1: Mozart, String Quartet in D Minor, third movement, mm. 22–29

The bass line (cello part) reveals the harmonic foundation of the passage. In this progression, based on a descending-fifth sequence, each triad's quality has been altered to make a dominant seventh chord—the V7 of the chord that comes next. Example 29.2a shows a reduction of this chromatic sequence, while part (b)

gives a diatonic descending-fifth progression with root-position seventh chords for comparison. The voice-leading in (b) is typical of this kind of sequence in that the chordal sevenths all resolve down by step as expected; in the chromatic version (part a), the leading tones also resolve down—pulled downward in a stepwise descending chromatic line.

You can analyze this type of sequence with V7 and Roman numerals, as here, or with V7 and letter names (V7/G, V7/C, V7/F, etc.). The former is preferred if the key context for the sequence is obvious, as in Example 29.1, where the sequence begins and ends in the same key. The latter is helpful if the key context of the sequence is not clear, or if the sequence is used to modulate.

EXAMPLE 29.2: Comparison of chromatic and diatonic descending-fifth sequences

(a) Reduction for Mozart string quartet movement, mm. 22–29

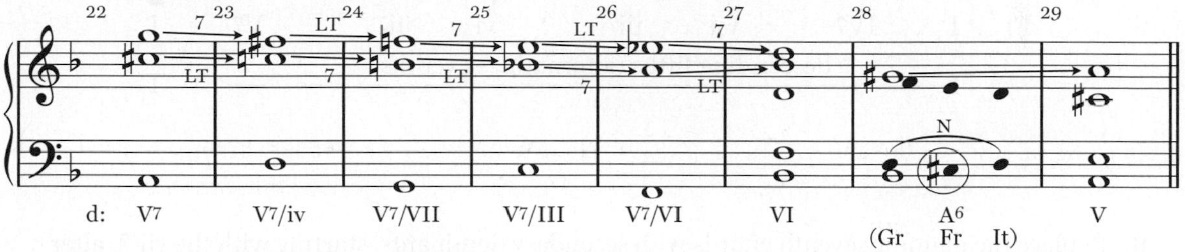

(b) Diatonic descending-fifth sequence framework with root-position seventh chords

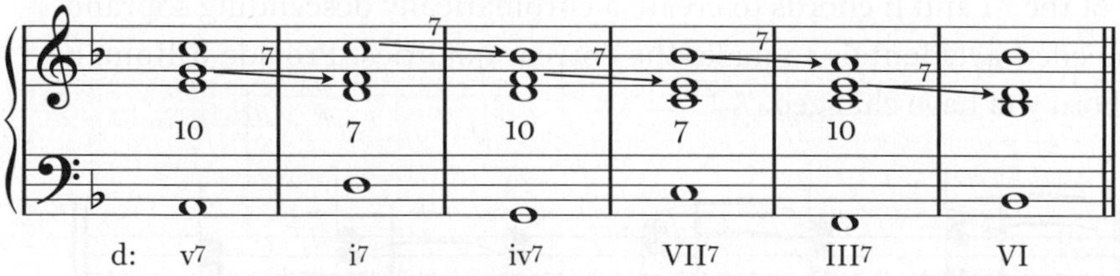

KEY CONCEPT To transform diatonic sequences into chromatic sequences,

- substitute chromatic harmonies for similar diatonic ones (e.g., a dominant seventh for a diatonic chord, or a mixture chord for a same-function diatonic chord); or
- embellish the diatonic framework with chromatic passing or neighbor tones.

When chromatic descending-fifth sequences include inversions, the bass line may skip by an augmented or a diminished interval.

Try it #1

A. Replace the diatonic seventh chords below (every other chord) with secondary dominants by adding accidentals, starting with the IV7: add an A♭ to make it V7/E♭ (V7/♭VII). This sequence will accumulate flats as each secondary dominant resolves. When you reach the ii7, use mode mixture instead of a secondary dominant to connect it into the cadence (otherwise it will head toward F♭ major). Write a Roman numeral below any chord you have changed. 🎧

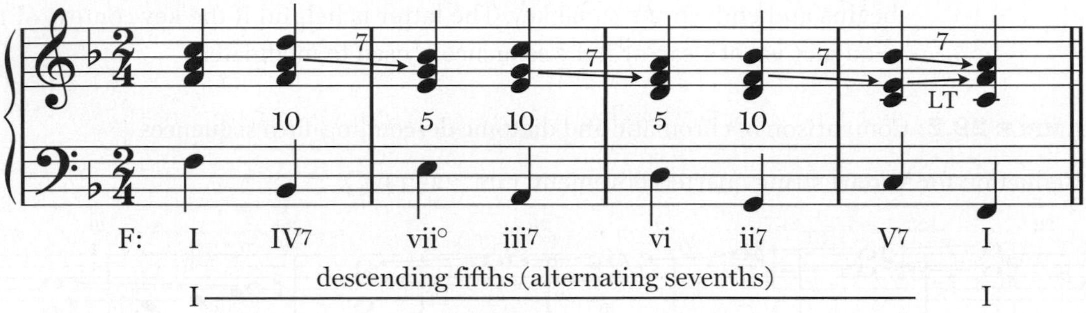

B. Replace the diatonic seventh chords with secondary dominants, starting with the vii$^{\circ 6}_{5}$: alter it to make it V$^{6}_{5}$/A. This sequence will acquire sharps in the bass line to create leading tones. Change the qualities of the iii and ii chords to create a chromatically descending soprano line. Watch out for needed accidentals to make the correct qualities. Provide a Roman numeral below any chord you have changed. 🎧

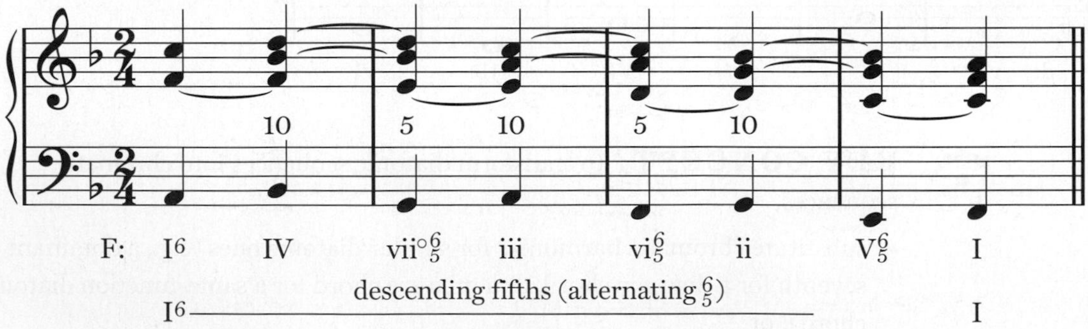

Descending Chromatic Bass Lines

Chromatic sequences with chords in inversion may be used to create a descending chromatic bass line. Listen to the excerpt from "Neue Liebe, neues Leben" shown in Example 29.3. After a repetition of the opening parallel period (mm. 1–8) in measures 17–24, and a two-measure extension that cadences in B♭, the character of the song begins to change—with a new vocal line and accompanimental texture, and a chromatic descent in the bass line. Undoubtedly, this change is sparked by the unrest of the text, which speaks of quickly fleeing away. Because of the sequence with secondary dominants and the lack of a cadence to confirm the key, the key in this passage could be read as B♭ major (the key of the previous phrase) or G minor (the key of the following phrase); both analyses have been provided.

Example 29.3: Hensel, "Neue Liebe, neues Leben," mm. 26–31 (anthology)

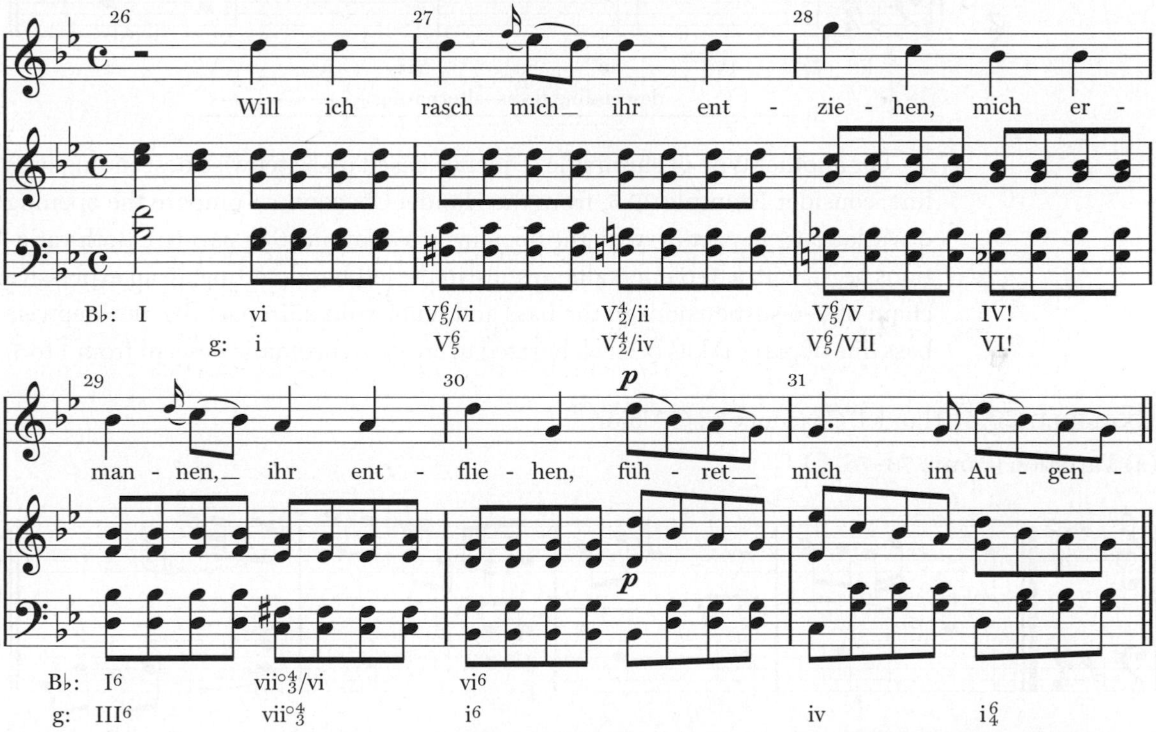

Translation: If I swiftly run away from her, to take courage, to flee from her, at that moment, ah, my way leads me back to her.

The chords in measures 27–28 are based on a descending-fifth root progression from D to G to C, with alternating $^6_5$ and $^4_2$ inversions, a chromaticized version of the pattern shown in Example 29.4. The second chord in measure 28 is not a

V^4_2 (or V^4_2/III in G minor) as expected, but IV (or VI). If the pattern had been continued, the chord here would have been F-A-C-E♭, with the E♭ in the bass, which would have resolved normally to the chord in measure 29. Instead, Hensel holds two common tones, B♭3 and G4, and moves the other two voices by step—E3 to E♭3, and C5 to B♭4—breaking the sequence. The key of G minor is not confirmed until measures 33–34 (with an IAC). Perhaps Hensel chose to reflect the indecisiveness expressed by the text in the harmonic progression.

EXAMPLE 29.4: Diatonic descending-fifth sequence with seventh chords alternating $^6_5$ and $^4_2$ inversions

For another type of chromatic sequence based on a stepwise descending bass line, consider Example 29.5, from the Handel Chaconne. Compare the opening of Variation 9 in part (a) with the opening of Variation 16 in part (b). Both variations begin with a 5–6 intervallic gesture in the left hand, setting up an expressive chain of 7–6 suspensions in the bass and tenor voices. In part (b), the stepwise bass line of part (a) has been elaborated to create a chromatic descent from $\hat{1}$ to $\hat{5}$.

EXAMPLE 29.5: Handel, Chaconne in G Major

(a) Variation 9, mm. 73–76

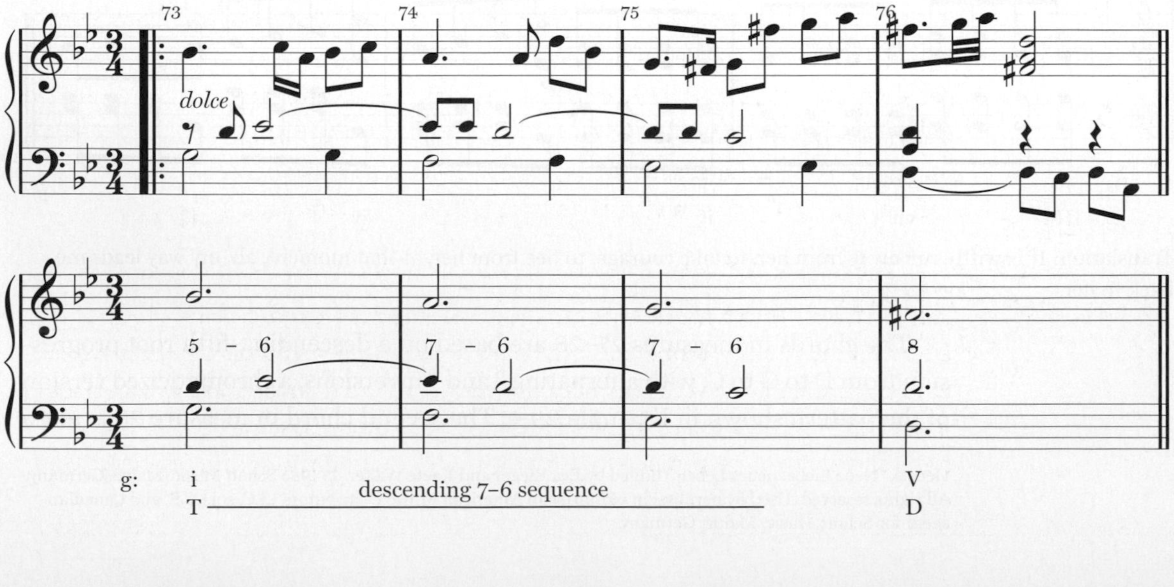

(b) Variation 16, mm. 129–132

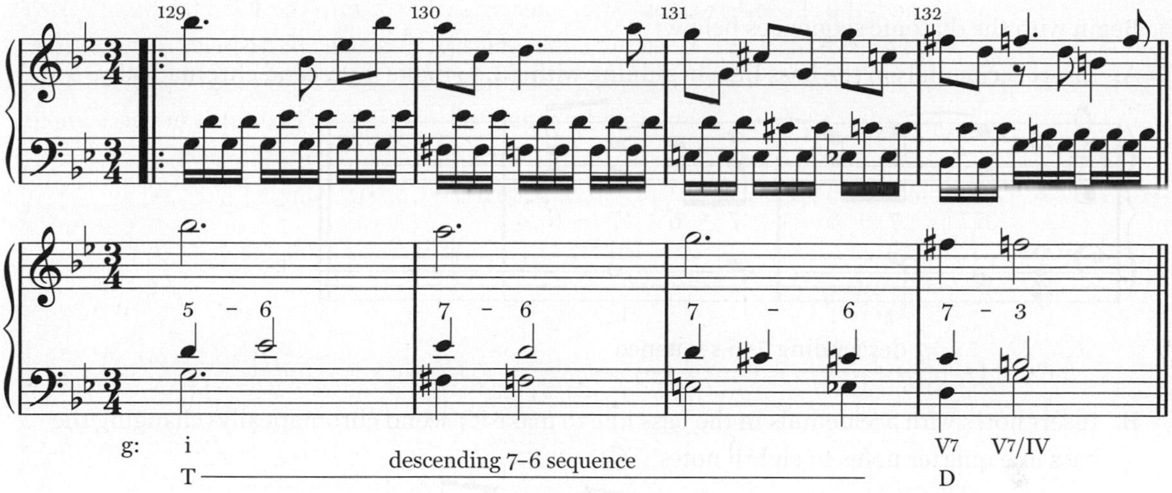

An attempt to apply Roman numerals to measures 130–132 would be an exercise in futility; this passage is strongly linear, and is not based on a root progression. These simultaneities can be stacked in thirds to spell diminished seventh chords followed by triads, and the chordal sevenths of the diminished seventh chords do resolve downward, following the 7–6 linear pattern of previous variations. However, the roots F♯3 and E3 of the apparent diminished seventh chords on the downbeats of measures 130 and 131 move downward by half step as part of the chromatically embellished bass line that created them in the first place. These voice-leading chords are best analyzed as a chromaticized 7–6 sequence. Descending 7–6 and ascending 5–6 sequences are linear, and therefore are not analyzed with a root progression; their chromaticized variants are treated the same way. In measure 131, beat 2, the C♯-E-G sonority is a diminished triad produced by chromatic embellishment. Although it could be given a Roman numeral (a vii°6/V that resolves irregularly), this "chord" is best labeled simply by identifying the C♯s as chromatic passing tones.

The Mozart, Hensel, and Handel examples illustrate how familiar diatonic sequences may be embellished chromatically by substituting secondary dominant and leading-tone chords for diatonic ones. They also show how chromatic pitches can be inserted between whole steps in the basic 7–6 framework.

SUMMARY

Any sequence that features stepwise voice-leading is a candidate for chromatic embellishment. The embellishment can be as simple as filling in whole steps chromatically in one voice (usually the bass), or it may involve elaborate chromaticism in several voices. In descending-fifth sequences, some or all of the seventh chords may be replaced with chromatic secondary-dominant-function chords in root position or inversions.

Try it #2

Begin with the diatonic sequences below.

A. Insert accidentals in the bass line, beginning with E3, to make it descend chromatically.

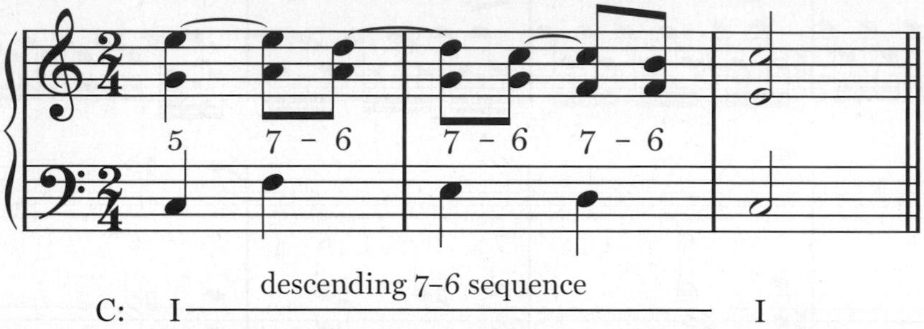

B. Insert notes with accidentals in the bass line to make it ascend chromatically (changing the bass line quarter notes to eighth notes).

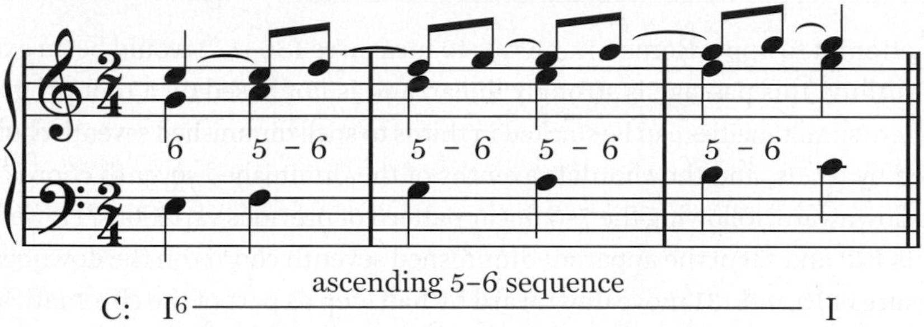

Chromatic Voice Exchanges

Listen to Example 29.6, a chromatic introduction. In this progression, the inner voices (D4 and F4) stay the same throughout, while the outer voices move in contrary motion from G2 (bass) and B4 (soprano) to B2 and G4 and back again—making a voice exchange, filled in with half steps. As is typical with a voice exchange, the chord with the interval that is exchanged, in this case a V7 chord, is prolonged; the "chords" in between are not strong functional harmonies but rather by-products of voice-leading.

EXAMPLE 29.6: Chromatic introduction

Example 29.7 demonstrates a number of ways that voice exchanges may be filled in chromatically. Previous chapters considered voice exchanges filled in with a diatonic passing chord—usually a second-inversion triad or seventh chord, as in part (a). They also described the chromatic voice exchange; for example, a progression between ii7 and V$^6_5$/V (part b), where $\hat{2}$ and $\hat{4}$ in the ii7 chord change places with $\hat{2}$ and $\sharp\hat{4}$ in the V$^6_5$/V. In Romantic-era compositions, voice exchanges provide a framework for elaborate chromatic progressions: a relatively simple elaboration of the basic voice exchange of part (a), for example, can be made by filling in the half steps between the notes that are exchanged, as in part (c). This sequence of pitches may then be immediately reversed to return chromatically to the beginning point, as in Example 29.6.

EXAMPLE 29.7: Voice exchanges and their chromatic elaborations

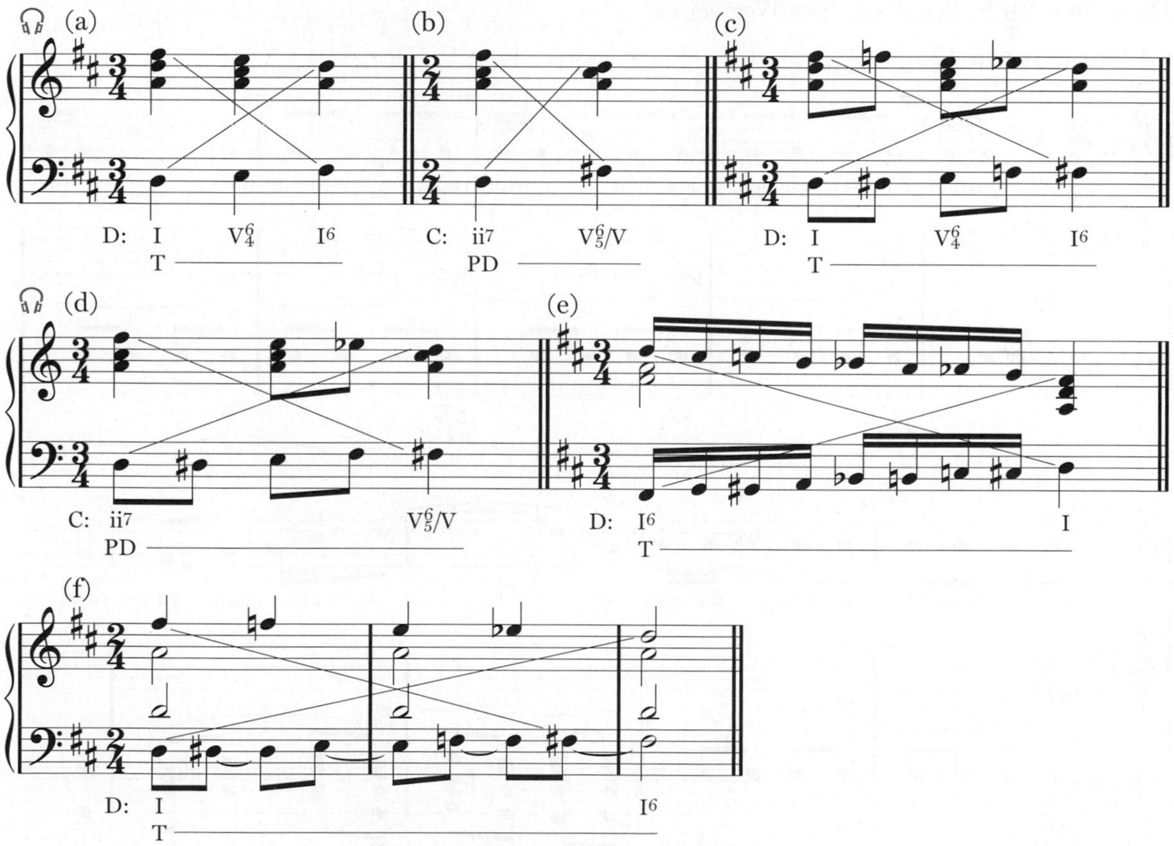

In part (b), the soprano descends by a m3, while the bass ascends a M3. To chromaticize this voice exchange requires a repeated pitch (or a longer note value) in the upper voice to match the duration of the lower (part d). There are many possible variants of the chromatically filled voice exchange: the frameworks here can be inverted to begin with outer voices spanning a sixth rather than a third (part e), the chromatic motion can be offset between the parts (compare part f with c), and so on. While it is sometimes possible to analyze the chords between the "ends" of the voice exchange with Roman numerals, these labels do not make sense functionally; rather, these chromatic successions serve to prolong the chords at either end.

Now listen to Example 29.8a, an excerpt from Schubert's "Der Wegweiser." In measures 68b–75, two voices move in contrary motion by half step. The upper voice spans G4 (supplied by the vocal anacrusis to m. 69 and continuing in the piano part) down to B♭3 (beat 2 of m. 75), while the bass line spans B♮1 to G2 (m. 76)—a chromatic voice exchange. Part (b) clarifies how each voice progresses chromatically, with the held root of the G chord filling in an inner voice.

EXAMPLE 29.8: Schubert, "Der Wegweiser"

(a) Mm. 68b–77a

Translation: One sign I see standing, unmoving before my gaze; one street must I go down, from which no one has come back.

(b) Reduction of mm. 68b–75

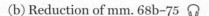

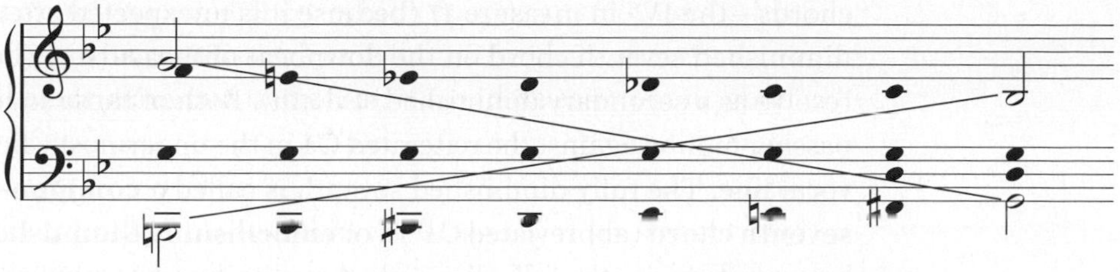

An analysis of these sonorities with Roman numerals does not make sense: you would end up with a series of secondary dominants and augmented-sixth chords (even a diminished third chord!), with their implied resolutions unfulfilled. Better simply to label the chord that is prolonged, and not worry about the simultaneities in between.

Listen to the excerpt again to hear how Schubert interprets the words "unverrückt" (unmoving) and "keiner" (no one) musically. The phrase begins with the vocal line literally unmoving, a repeated G4 unremitting above the accompaniment's chromatic lines. These repeated notes might be sung with a fairly uninflected "straight" interpretation to portray the unmoving sign. The high point of the line in terms of register, duration, and emotional content falls on "keiner," and Schubert's use of the lowered $\hat{2}$ and Neapolitan harmony on the last syllable all work to create a sense that this is a road from which no one returns. Singer and pianist alike can intensify this foreboding through tone color and timing decisions.

Common-Tone Diminished Seventh and Augmented-Sixth Chords

Turn now to two contrasting songs to learn additional ways to embellish harmonies chromatically. Listen first to Schumann's poignant "Ich grolle nicht," while following the score in your anthology; an excerpt is shown in Example 29.9.

Example 29.9: Schumann, "Ich grolle nicht," mm. 16b–19a

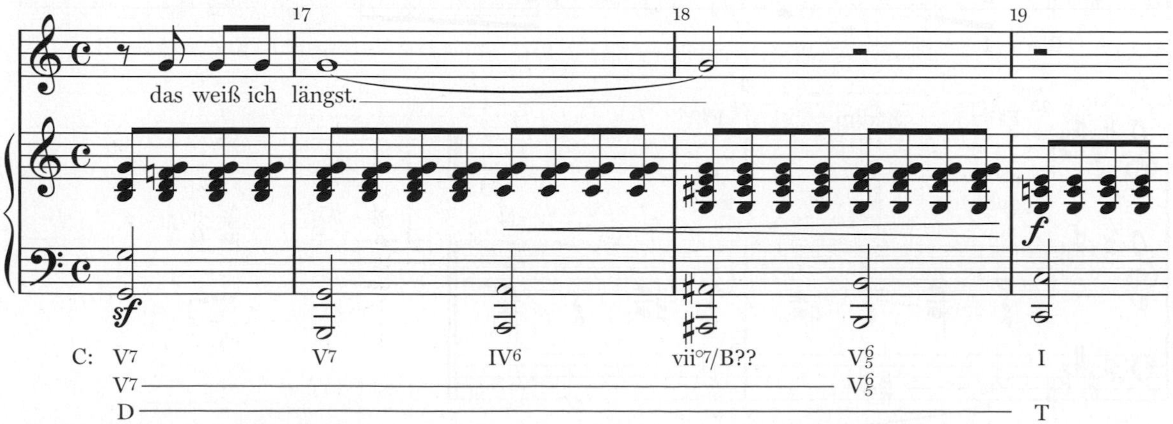

Translation: That I have known for a long time.

The harmonic analysis of this passage is fairly straightforward except for two chords—the IV^6 in measure 17 (because it is unexpected after V^7) and the fully diminished seventh chord on the downbeat of measure 18 (because it does not resolve as a secondary diminished seventh). Both of these sonorities result from passing motion against the reiterated G4 in the uppermost voice of the piano and vocal line. The fully diminished seventh is called a **common-tone diminished seventh chord** (abbreviated CT^{o7}), or **embellishing diminished seventh chord**, because it carries the fully diminished quality, but does not function as a diatonic or secondary diminished seventh chord. These types of embellishing chords function in the same way as passing or neighboring $^6_4$, $^4_2$, or other chords, but with additional chromaticism.

Look now at another fully diminished seventh chord, from Kern and Harbach's famous song "Smoke Gets in Your Eyes" (Example 29.10). Listen to the passage, concentrating on the diminished seventh chord in measure 23, beat 3 (D♯-F♯-A-B♯ [C♮]). As in the Schumann example, the diminished seventh here embellishes the dominant harmony, and the common tone of the CT^{o7} is in the uppermost voice.

EXAMPLE 29.10: Kern and Harbach, "Smoke Gets in Your Eyes," mm. 21–24

KEY CONCEPT Common-tone diminished seventh chords are collections of chromatic and diatonic neighbor or passing tones that happen to make a fully diminished seventh sonority. They always share one pitch with the chord that precedes or follows them. They do not resolve as dominant-function chords, but have an embellishing role in the progression.

It is also possible to find similar collections of chromatic neighbors that make a so-called **common-tone German augmented sixth** (CT A^6). This chord typically prolongs the tonic harmony, as in Example 29.11, from the beginning of Schubert's "Am Meer"; both pitches of its distinctive augmented sixth still resolve outward to $\hat{5}$—though in this context, to the fifth of the tonic harmony. Here, the $\flat\hat{3}$ of the CT A^6 is spelled $\sharp\hat{2}$ (D♯ rather than E♭). A French version of the CT A^6 is also possible, with $\hat{2}$ instead of $\flat\hat{3}$.

EXAMPLE 29.11: Schubert, "Am Meer," mm. 1–6a

Translation: The sea sparkled in the distance in the last light of the evening.

KEY CONCEPT To write a common-tone diminished seventh chord:

1. Find a position for the chord between two harmonies that share one or more common tones (it may be the same harmony, possibly with change of voicing).
2. Write the first and third chords, leaving a space in the middle.
3. Choose a common tone to share with the first or third harmony (typically the soprano or bass note); build a diminished seventh chord with that common tone as one element and stepwise motion in the other voices.
4. Remember that CT$^{\circ 7}$ chords have an embellishing function. In Example 26.12a, the bass line features a chromatic neighbor tone, in part (b) a chromatic passing tone, and in part (c) a pedal.
5. Because the $\frac{4}{2}$ inversion is typical for CT$^{\circ 7}$ chords, you may keep the common tone in the bass and build a $^{\circ 7}$ chord in $\frac{4}{2}$ position by raising the fourth and second above the bass (part c).

Example 29.12: Common-tone embellishing chords

(a) Neighboring

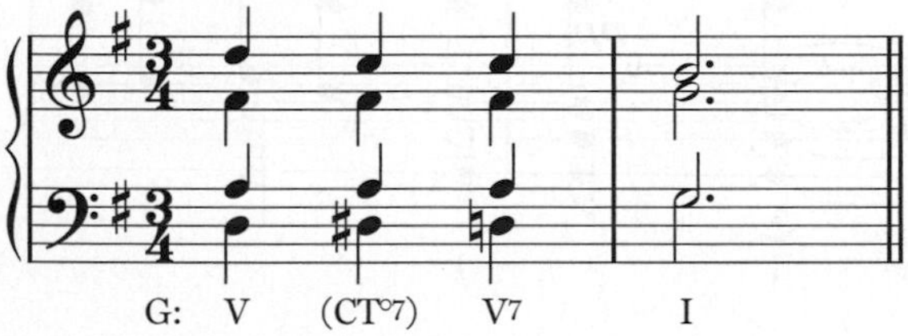

(b) Passing

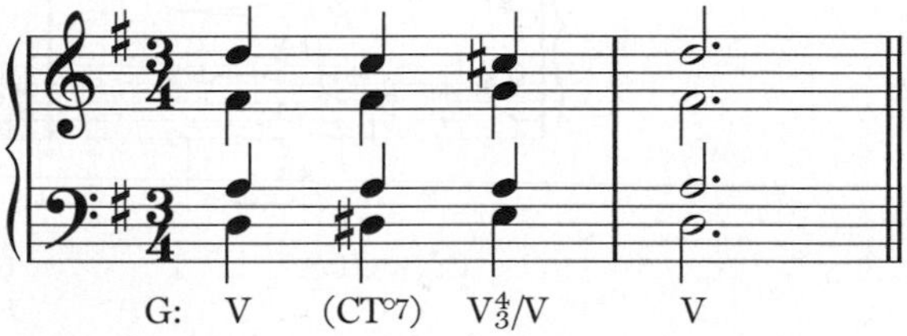

(c) CT$^{\circ 7}$ in $\frac{4}{2}$ position

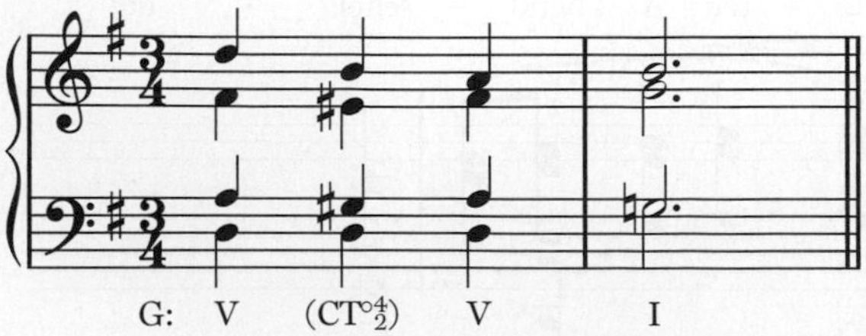

(d) CT A^6 (German)

Try it #3

Write a CT$^{\circ 7}$ that departs from and returns to the given chord, first using model (a) in Example 29.12 (neighboring motion in the bass), then model (c) (common tone in the bass).

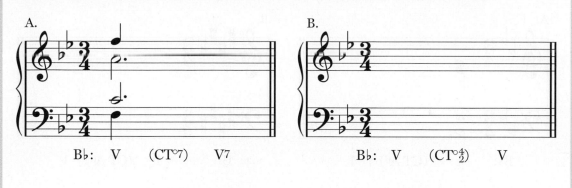

A.

B♭: V (CT$^{\circ 7}$) V7

B.

B♭: V (CT$^{\circ 4}_{2}$) V

KEY CONCEPT To write a progression with a common-tone augmented-sixth chord:

1. Write the root-position tonic chord as the first and third chords of the progression. In both tonic chords, double the fifth instead of the root (see Example 26.12d; the CT A^6 may also appear without a tonic chord preceding it).

2. For the CT A^6, write a note a half step below the upper $\hat{5}$ to make ♯$\hat{4}$, and a note a half step above the lower $\hat{5}$ to make ♭$\hat{6}$; these should resolve to the doubled fifth in the third chord.

3. Fill in the remaining pitches of the A^6 chord. The common tone ($\hat{1}$) is usually maintained in the bass. The missing element is ♭$\hat{3}$ for a German A^6 (the most frequently used CT A^6). Because it lies a chromatic half step below the third ($\hat{3}$) of the tonic chord, ♭$\hat{3}$ is sometimes spelled ♯$\hat{2}$, as a chromatic neighbor tone. In minor keys, the ♭$\hat{3}$ and ♭$\hat{6}$ are already in the key signature; the only note with an accidental will be ♯$\hat{4}$.

Try it #4

Write three chords in each measure below. The first and third should be the tonic chord in the given key: for the second, write a CT A^6.

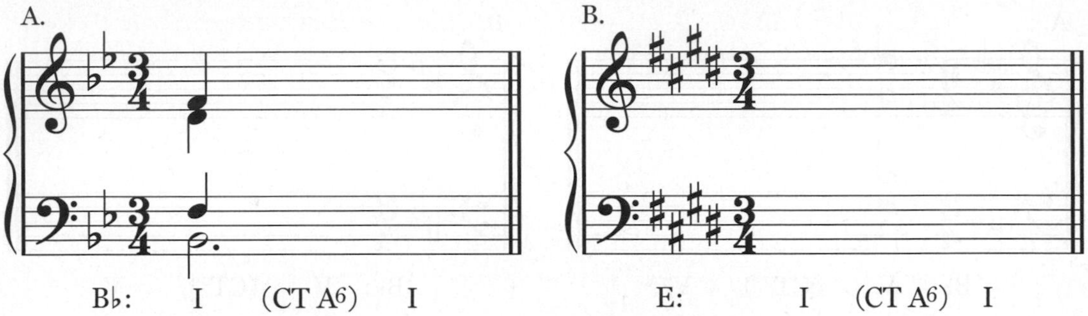

The Raised Chordal Fifth

Another typical chromatic alteration of a diatonic harmony—one you have already seen in a popular-music context—is the inflection of a chordal fifth up a half step to create an augmented triad. This occurs frequently in the dominant or dominant seventh harmony, and in secondary dominants, but may also appear in the tonic triad (sometimes as a variant of $5\text{–}6$ motion to $5\text{–}\sharp5\text{–}6$) or chromatically embellish other diatonic harmonies. One way to analyze these chords is by identifying the embellishing tones that create the augmented triad; alternatively, analyze them with Roman numerals and figures such as $I^{\sharp5}$, $V^{\sharp5}$ or $V^{7}_{\sharp5}$.

Example 29.13 shows both a secondary dominant (m. 5) and a diatonic triad with raised chordal fifth (m. 6). The excerpt ends with a dominant seventh expanded by a CT^{ø7} (less typical than the fully diminished CT$^{\circ7}$).

Example 29.13: Fauré, "Après un rêve," mm. 1–8

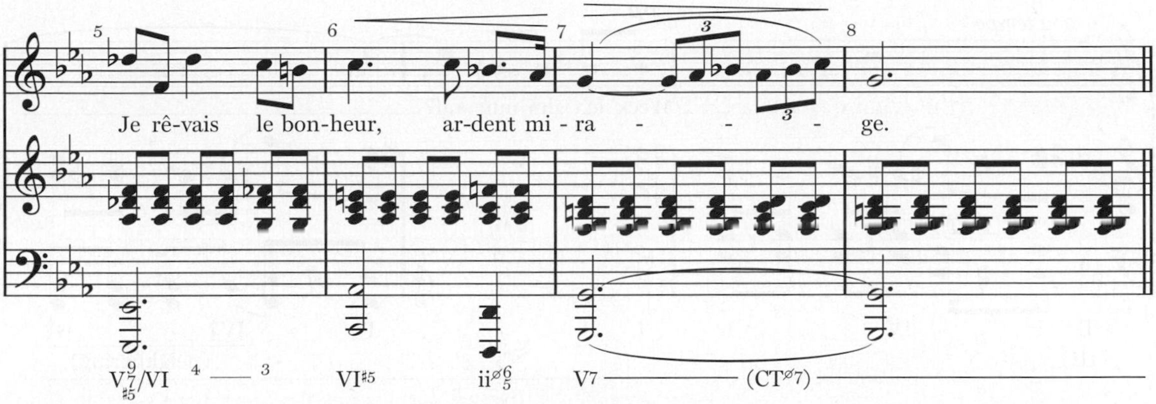

Translation: In a sleep that your image charmed, I dreamed of happiness, ardent mirage.

Chromatic Mediants and Submediants

Nondiatonic chords related to the tonic by a third, above or below, whose qualities cannot be attributed to modal mixture, are called **chromatic mediants** or **submediants**. A chromatic mediant to B♭ major, for example, is D major (III): the root is diatonic, but the chord's quality has been changed from minor to major. (Contrast this tonal relation with ♭III, D♭ major, which is a mixture chord; it requires no chromatic adjustment other than the "borrowing" from the parallel key.)

The first two phrases of Wolf's "In dem Schatten meiner Locken" (Example 29.14) provide an example of chromatic mediant relations. The first phrase begins with an expansion of the tonic area by IV, with chromatic embellishments (and an inflection of IV to iv through mixture); it ends with a tonicization of V (m. 4). The second phrase begins with a D major triad (m. 5), the major chromatic mediant (III), by direct modulation. Another direct modulation, to G♭ major (♭VI, a tonicized mixture chord) in measure 9, ends phrase 2 in the lowered submediant key.

Example 29.14: Wolf, "In dem Schatten meiner Locken," mm. 1–10a

Translation: In the shadow of my tresses my beloved has fallen asleep. Shall I wake him up now? Ah, no!

This sequence of keys—B♭ to D to G♭, and eventually back to B♭—spans a cycle of major thirds. Tonicizations that span the entire octave by some equal interval are called **symmetrical divisions of the octave**. Most typical of the Romantic era are symmetrical designs that divide the octave by major third, as here, or by minor third. It takes three modulations to bring a major-third cycle back to the tonic (e.g., C–E–A♭–C) and four modulations to bring a minor-third cycle back to the tonic (e.g., C–E♭–G♭–A–C).

In major keys, you might encounter such chords as ♭iii, III, and ♭III (by mode mixture), and VI, ♭vi, and ♭VI (by mode mixture)—all are considered "chromatic mediants" because of their position a third above or below the tonic. Such chords make possible a variety of unexpected harmonic colors in minor keys, which enjoy few mixture possibilities when limited to chords borrowed from the parallel major. You might also find chromatic chords that do not fall into the chromatic mediant or submediant category: for example, the D♭ minor chord in C major, ♭ii.

KEY CONCEPT When analyzing chords that have been chromatically altered:

- Use uppercase Roman numerals for major and augmented chords and lowercase for minor and diminished chords.
- Include $^+$ or $^\circ$ for augmented and diminished chords.
- Check whether seventh chords need $^\varnothing$ or $^\circ$ designations.
- Place an accidental before the Roman numeral only if the root has been altered.

Remember: With Roman numerals or scale-degree numbers, use flat for lowered and sharp for raised regardless of the key signature. For example, the lowered-submediant root in A major is spelled with a natural sign, F♮, but the chord is still designated ♭VI.

Chromatic mediants and submediants, while not common as individual chords, frequently serve as key areas in Romantic-era pieces. When analyzing such chords, first check to see whether the alterations in chord quality and resolution may be attributed to a temporary tonicization (or secondary-dominant function). In the Wolf song, the second phrase begins as a sequential repetition of the first (transposed up a major third), though it ends with a phrase extension (making it a six-measure phrase) and a cadence in G♭ major. The G♭s in measures 1–2 and the F♯s in measures 5–8 prepare the listener for this abrupt shift in key; this preparation is typical of late-Romantic harmonic practice.

Three brief snapshots from Brahms's Intermezzo in A Major demonstrate how Brahms likewise prepares the listener for the chromatic-mediant relation he explores later in the work. The piece in begins in A major (Example 29.15a), with a phrase that ends in a half cadence preceded by a cadential $^6_4$; the melody is then repeated and varied in the first large section. In contrast, a second large section begins with the music shown in part (b); this passage is in F♯ minor (vi), the relative minor of A major. The excerpt in part (c), which follows shortly after the F♯ minor passage, is in F♯ major (VI), a chromatic mediant. The modulations in each case are direct—a new section of the piece simply begins in the new key—but Brahms reaches this relatively distant key by first "traveling" through a closely related key, then by modal coloration.

Example 29.15: Brahms, Intermezzo in A Major

(a) Mm. 1–4a

(b) Mm. 49–52

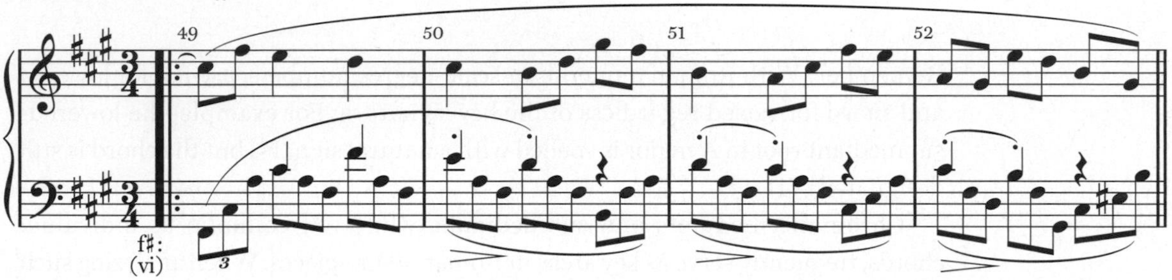

(c) Mm. 57–61a

You have now learned all the common diatonic and chromatic triads and seventh chords employed in common-practice tonal music. These chords, and the relationships between them, are summarized in Example 29.16—a master table of diatonic and chromatic chords. The table illustrates the chords related to C major / C minor, but the same relationships hold in all other keys. The diatonic triads for C major and C minor are given in parts (a) and (b), marked by a bracket. The diatonic sevenths are given in (c) and (d). Their respective secondary dominants are shown in (e) and (f), and the chromatic mediants, submediants, and other related chords in (g) and (h). (Everything above part a applies to major keys, everything below to minor keys.) At the bottom of the table (i) are the augmented-sixth chords associated with both major and minor keys.

Example 29.16: Master table of diatonic and chromatic chords related to C major and C minor

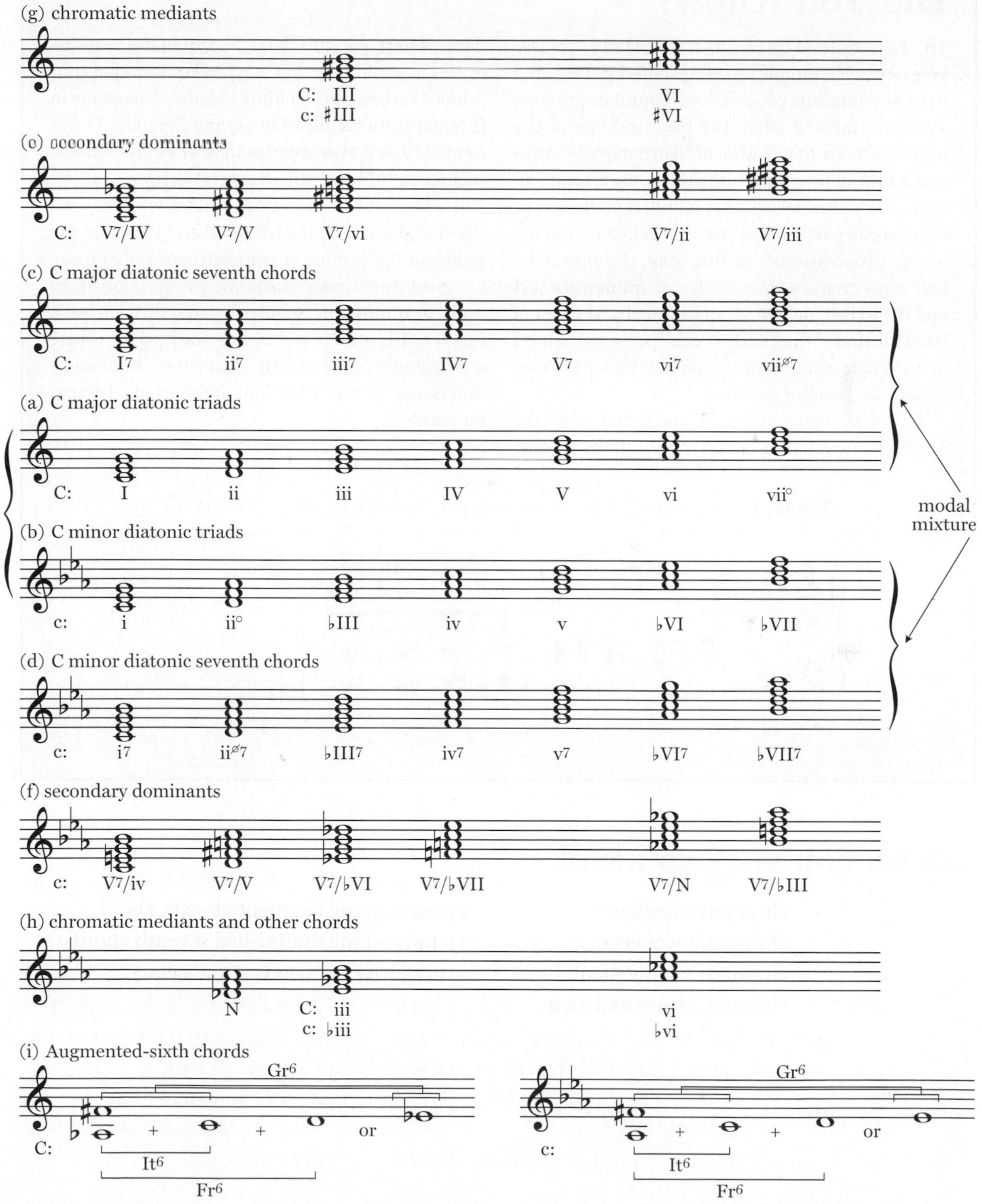

Did You Know?

The harmonic progression from Schubert's "Der Wegweiser" (Example 29.8a) is sometimes referred to as an "omnibus progression." Omnibus progressions are formed when the bass and one of the upper parts (soprano, alto, or tenor) move by chromatic half steps in opposite directions, creating an outer voice framework that is "filled in" by one or more static parts. (They are also called chromatic wedge progressions.) In this song, the chromatic half steps create a voice-exchange framework (G4 and B♮1 to B♭3 and G2, Example 29.8b). The pair of voices forming the "wedge" can span a tetrachord or as much as an octave, and the bass part may ascend (as here) or descend.

Theorist Paula Telesco has found that the omnibus originated in harmonizations of the "lament bass"—a chromatic descent in the bass line from $\hat{1}$ to $\hat{5}$ in minor that is typical of Baroque continuous variations (including Handel's Chaconne in G Major from Example 29.5a, and Purcell's "Dido's Lament"), but also appears in later compositions, such as the Mozart sonata excerpt below.

In Mozart's chromatically filled wedge (mm. 122–123: D3–A2 in the left hand and F5–A5 in the right hand), the inner voices form chords that make a logical, functional harmonic progression from tonic to dominant. Schubert takes this one step further: his inner voices are static, and create a harmonic progression that does not make functional sense when analyzed with Roman numerals.

Mozart, Piano Sonata in D Major, K. 284, third movement, mm. 121–123a

TERMS YOU SHOULD KNOW

- chromatic mediant
- chromatic sequence
- chromatic submediant
- chromatic voice exchange
- common-tone augmented-sixth chord
- common-tone diminished seventh chord
- symmetrical divisions of the octave

QUESTIONS FOR REVIEW

1. What are some ways that diatonic sequence frameworks may be embellished chromatically?
2. What are some standard harmonizations for descending chromatic bass lines?
3. Which diatonic progressions may be enhanced through chromatic voice exchanges?
4. What is the function of common-tone diminished seventh and augmented-sixth chords?
5. What are the chromatic mediants and submediants for E♭ major? How do they relate to other chords in the key, such as mixture chords?
6. In music for your own instrument, find examples of (a) a chromatic sequence, (b) a chromatic voice exchange, and (c) a chromatic mediant key area. (Hint: Think first about the time period when each technique was widespread.)
7. How might the function of chromatic elements affect the way they should be interpreted in performance?

CHAPTER 30

Chromatic Modulation

Outline of topics

Chromatic modulation

- Modulation by common tone
- Modulation by chromatic inflection
- Modulation through mixture
- Modulation by descending-fifth sequence
- Modulation by other chromatic sequences
- Enharmonic modulation with augmented-sixth chords
- Enharmonic modulation with diminished seventh chords

Linear chromaticism

- Chromaticism and voice-leading chords
- Intentional harmonic ambiguity
- Analyzing and performing chromatic passages

Overview

This chapter introduces new ways to modulate that are characteristic of Romantic-era compositions. We also consider linear harmonic practices of late-Romantic chromaticism.

Repertoire

Ludwig van Beethoven
- Piano Sonata in C Minor, Op. 13 (*Pathétique*), first and second movements
- Piano Sonata in C Major, Op. 53 (*Waldstein*), first movement

Frédéric Chopin
- Prelude in C Minor, Op. 28, No. 20
- Prelude in E Minor, Op. 28, No. 4

Jerome Kern and Otto Harbach, "Smoke Gets in Your Eyes," from *Roberta*

Wolfgang Amadeus Mozart
- Piano Sonata in D Major, K. 284, third movement
- String Quartet in D Minor, K. 421, first movement

Richard Wagner, Prelude to *Tristan und Isolde*

Chromatic Modulation

In the Romantic era, composers began to explore distant key relationships. For example, from C major, instead of modulating to the closely related keys of G major (V), A minor (vi), F major (IV), or D minor (ii), they might modulate to A♭ major (♭VI), A major (VI), E♭ major (♭III), E major (III), or D♭ major (Neapolitan ♭II), or even to such distant keys as C♯ minor (♯i), F♯ major (♯IV), or B♭ major (♭VII). While pivot chords may sometimes aid in these modulations, fewer pivot choices are available, and distant keys may share no harmonies that are diatonic in both keys. Direct modulations to keys that are not closely related may be effected by means of a secondary dominant or simply by starting a phrase in a new key, but the change may sound quite abrupt if it occurs suddenly within a phrase, without preparation or transition. Composers have devised a wide range of methods to facilitate less abrupt modulations.

KEY CONCEPT There are several techniques for writing a seamless transition between two distantly related keys: modulation by common tone, chromatic inflection, mixture, sequence, and enharmonic reinterpretation.

Modulation by Common Tone

Composers in the Romantic era continued to use pivot- (or common-) chord modulation where two keys were closely related. For pairs of keys that did not share an entire triad but had triads or seventh chords with one, two, or three pitches in common, the common tones were held and the other pitches shifted up or down, usually by half step. This type of modulation is called a **common-tone**, or **pivot-tone, modulation** if only a single pitch is held between the two keys, and **common-dyad**, or **pivot-dyad, modulation** if two pitches are held between the keys.

A single shared pitch is enough to make a smooth modulation, to either a closely related or a more distant key. Listen to the short passage from the second movement of Beethoven's *Pathétique* Sonata shown in Example 30.1. Here, the C4 from the cadence in A♭ major in measure 16 becomes an anacrusis for the melody in measure 17, accompanied by a repeated C in the left hand. This isolation of a single pitch smooths the transition to F minor (vi in A♭), tonicized in 18–19.

Example 30.1: Beethoven, *Pathétique* Sonata, second movement, mm. 16–19

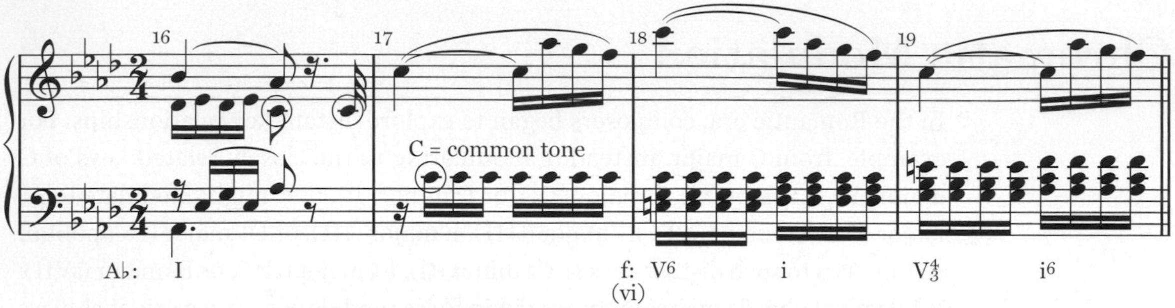

Common-tone modulations are particularly helpful in moving to distantly related keys. For an example, look at the excerpt from “Smoke Gets in Your Eyes” shown in Example 30.2. The first verse of the song cadences in measures 19–20 in E♭ major; the key for the following phrase is B major (the excerpt ends with a half cadence in m. 24), spelled as a ♯V (an enharmonic spelling of the chromatic submediant ♭VI, C♭ major). The connection is made by the melody pitch E♭4 of measures 19–20, which seamlessly becomes D♯4 in the following measure, making the move to a distant key sound not so distant. In addition, Kern introduces the pitch class B (the new tonic) as a prominent embellishing tone in measure 16, foreshadowing the modulation.

Example 30.2: Kern and Harbach, “Smoke Gets in Your Eyes,” mm. 16b–24 (mm. 18b–24 recorded)

Modulation by Chromatic Inflection

(anthology) Listen to measures 18–30 of Beethoven's *Waldstein* Sonata, following the score in your anthology. This passage is part of a transition from the first key area, C major, to the second, E major—a chromatic mediant, quite a distant tonal area from C major. In measures 20–23 (Example 30.3), the harmonic reference point moves from C major to V in E major. The A minor first-inversion chord in 20–21 (C-E-A) is a vi^6 chord in C major. In measure 22, it moves to C-E-A♯, an Italian sixth in the key of E major, which resolves normally to the B-D♯-F♯ chord in 23. The A minor triad and the augmented-sixth chord share two pitches in common, C and E, which connect the two harmonies while the A moves to A♯. Because the modulation is activated by the shift of one pitch by a half step, this type is sometimes called modulation by **chromatic inflection**, though it also involves a pivot dyad. The chromatic motion here does not sound abrupt; rather, it seems an intensification of the drama already unfolding. The blurring of the key by the sequence in measures 14–21 helps make this striking modulation seamless.

EXAMPLE 30.3: Beethoven, *Waldstein* Sonata, first movement, mm. 20–23

Modulation Through Mixture

Sometimes it is easier to modulate to a distantly related key by shifting to the parallel major or minor key through mode mixture. In retrospect, we can understand the A minor chord in measures 20–21 of Example 30.3 as a pivot, if we consider the palette of mixture chords available in the new key: the vi^6 chord in C major could be heard as iv^6, a mixture chord in E major that leads to the augmented sixth in measure 22.

KEY CONCEPT When a mixture chord acts as a pivot between two distantly related keys, one of the two keys will be closely related to the key of the mixture chord.

In the Beethoven example, C major, although distantly related to E major, *is* closely related to E minor, from which the A minor mixture chord comes. Modulations that include a chromatic pivot chord—typically a mixture chord such as i, ♭III, or ♭VI, or possibly a secondary dominant or leading-tone chord—are sometimes called **altered common-chord**, or **altered pivot-chord, modulations**.

The second movement of the *Pathétique* Sonata modulates from A♭ major to E major, an enharmonically respelled ♭VI through mixture, but not with ♭VI as a pivot. Listen to the excerpt in Example 30.4, which begins in A♭ minor, a direct shift from the parallel major key that preceded it. Measure 41 starts to repeat the motive from 37–40 when something unusual happens—look at all the sharps in measure 42! The chord on the downbeat of 42 is B-D♯-F♯-A, or V^4_2 in E major; it resolves to a first-inversion E major chord on beat 2, leading to a cadence in measures 43–44 in E major. The move first to the parallel minor (A♭ minor) through mixture allowed for the common-dyad (enharmonically respelled: C♭-E♭ = B-D♯) modulation, thereby making the distance between A♭ major and its chromatic submediant, F♭ major (= E major), much easier to negotiate.

EXAMPLE 30.4: Beethoven, *Pathétique* Sonata, second movement, mm. 39–44

Modulation by Descending-Fifth Sequence

(anthology) Listen now to the theme from the third movement of Mozart's Piano Sonata in D Major; measures 8b–10 are given in Example 30.5. In measure 9, the brief descending-fifth sequence with secondary dominants (B^7–E–A^7–D) could be labeled in A as V^7/V–V–V^7/IV–IV, since the previous section ended in A major; or the last three chords could be interpreted in D major as V/V–V^7–I .

EXAMPLE 30.5: Mozart, Piano Sonata in D Major, third movement, mm. 8b–12

This sequence is ambiguous without further study of its context: it can serve equally well to connect A major and D major or to stay in either. (Measure 10 does not clarify the situation—it is also sequential, but the underlying chord progression is less clear.) Sequences like the one in measure 9 may function as pivot chords, in that they are at home in two or more keys. The multiple possibilities mask the point of modulation until after the clear arrival in the new key.

While any type of sequence may be used to modulate—the sequence stops when it arrives at the new tonic—descending-fifth sequences with secondary dominants work particularly well. A dominant seventh chord at any point in a descending-fifth sequence may resolve to a triad that can be established as a new key by a cadence, a continuation in the new key, or both. Measures 112–125, from the first movement of the *Waldstein* Sonata, provide an example; the initial pattern for this descending-fifth sequence is shown in Example 30.6.

EXAMPLE 30.6: Beethoven, *Waldstein* Sonata, first movement, mm. 112–116

The four-measure sequence pattern begins with an arpeggiated C major triad and ends (in m. 115) with a C dominant seventh chord (with an added flatted ninth, D♭). This $C^{\flat 9}_{7}$ is a secondary dominant that resolves down by fifth as expected, to an F major triad in measure 116, then the entire four-measure pattern is repeated in 116–119, transposed to F major (with a very slight alteration in the arpeggiation in m. 118). The third and final statement of the sequential pattern—again transposed down a fifth, this time to B♭—begins in measure 120 and ends in 124–125 with the resolution of the B♭ dominant harmony to E♭ minor, a chromatic mediant not closely related to C major. E♭ minor is tonicized for only two measures (124–125) before moving on.

Modulation by Other Chromatic Sequences

Now listen to the opening of the sonata to hear how a sequence can be transposed to a distantly related key without sounding jarring. The opening four measures (Example 30.7) are transposed down a whole step in measures 5–8, creating a "distantly related" phrase in B♭ major. This type of modulation by sequential transposition is like a direct modulation, yet the repetition of the melodic pattern makes the effect seem less abrupt. Such modulations often function as tonicizations when considered in the larger musical context. In this case, the B♭ might be heard as a passing tonicization in a C major context with much mode mixture.

Example 30.7: Beethoven, *Waldstein* Sonata, first movement, mm. 1–8

Enharmonic Modulation with Augmented-Sixth Chords

How a composer spells a chord has implications for how we expect it to resolve. For example, when played without its chord of resolution, the German augmented-sixth chord sounds exactly like a dominant seventh chord. This ambiguity between functions is especially valuable in modulations, because the Mm7 sonority can be resolved two or more ways depending on how it is spelled. It may be approached with one spelling, yet resolve as though spelled another way, and that "deceptive" resolution will suddenly introduce a new key area. The effect is like an aural sleight of hand.

Look back at Example 30.3. Another way to hear the modulation from C major to E major in this passage is to think of the harmony in measure 22 through the lens of the old key (C major). If you weren't looking at the spelling of the chord but only listening to the passage, you might expect the chord to resolve as V7/IV in C, as though spelled C-E-(G)-B♭ (a dominant seventh chord). But Beethoven's spelling, C-E-A♯ (an augmented-sixth chord), and the chord's resolution move toward the new tonal area of E major.

Look now at the passage in Example 30.8a, an excerpt from the first movement of Mozart's String Quartet in D Minor. The key in measure 42 is E♭ major, the Neapolitan of D minor. This passage is heavily colored by mixture chords, including the minor subdominant and tonic, as shown in the reduction in part (b). We would expect the V7/V in E♭ major (m. 45) to resolve to a B♭ dominant harmony, yet it resolves instead to a cadential $\frac{6}{4}$–$\frac{5}{3}$ in A minor.

EXAMPLE 30.8: Mozart, String Quartet in D Minor, first movement

(a) Mm. 42–46

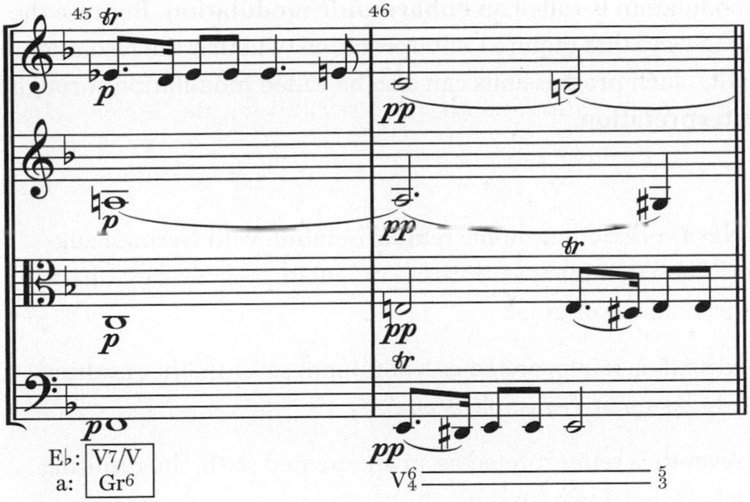

(b) Reduction of mm. 42–46

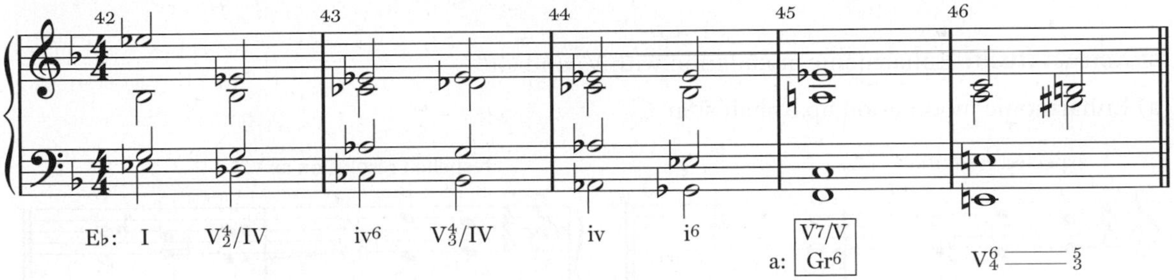

(c) Resolutions of mm. 44b–45

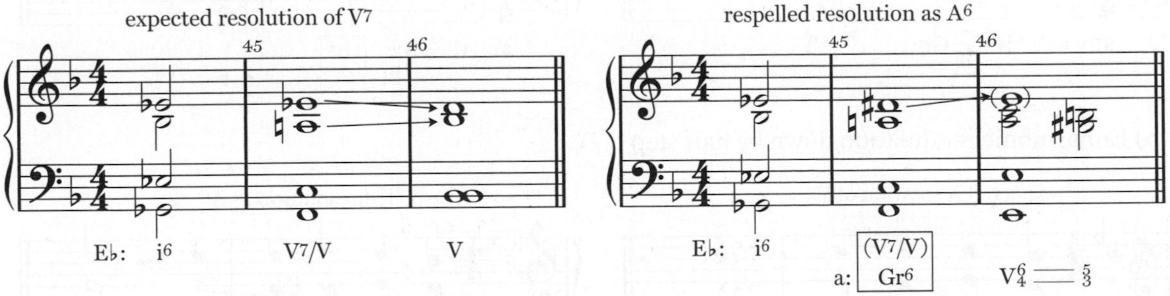

Although this resolution sounds a bit surprising, it makes sense in retrospect. Part (c) shows the chords from measures 44b and 45 with the resolution we expect, then the measure 45 chord respelled to indicate its augmented-sixth function—with D♯ instead of E♭. The resolution to a cadential $^6_4$ rather than directly to V (E major, V of A minor) is customary with any German A6 chord. The modulation to A minor is confirmed when the passage continues in that key through measure 53.

This type of modulation is called an **enharmonic modulation**. Because the harmonies resolve in ways that require reinterpretation (whether the resolutions are respelled or not), such progressions can also be called modulation through **enharmonic reinterpretation**.

KEY CONCEPT Use enharmonic reinterpretation with German augmented-sixth chords and dominant sevenths to modulate to a new key a half step higher or lower than the original.

- If an augmented sixth is reinterpreted as a dominant seventh, the resulting modulation is a half step up (Example 30.9a).
- If a dominant seventh is reinterpreted as an augmented sixth, the resulting modulation is a half step down (part b).

EXAMPLE 30.9: Enharmonic modulation with V7 and Gr6

(a) Enharmonic modulation up by half step

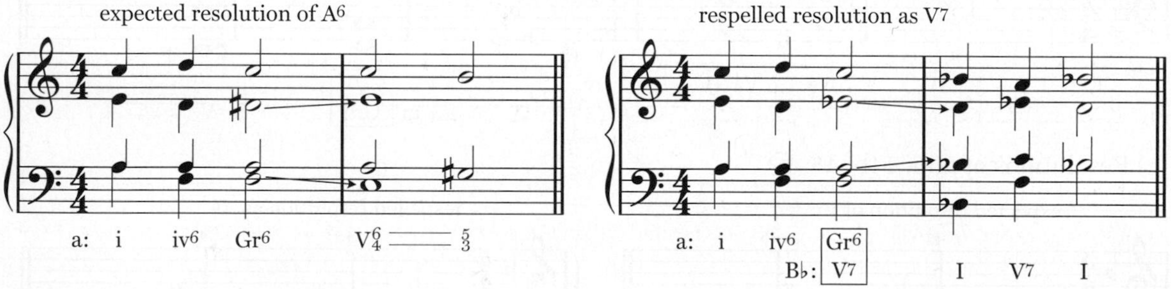

(b) Enharmonic modulation down by half step

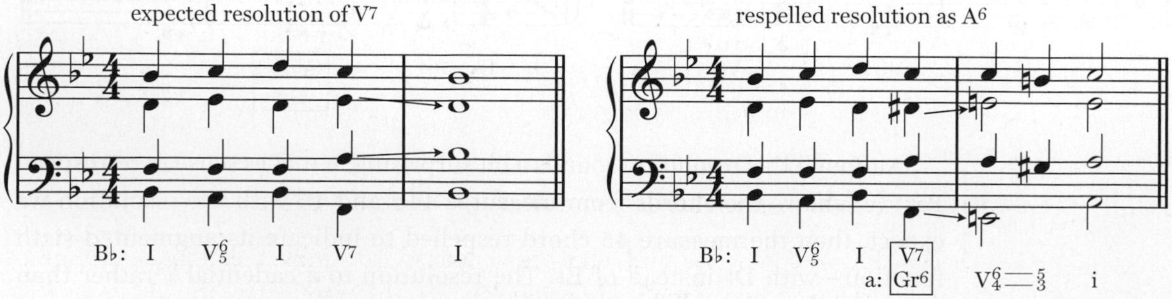

Try it #1

Write the requested V7 or Gr6 chord in each progression, and resolve it normally. Then respell the chord as requested in the given key, and resolve it normally. Use half and whole notes. Avoid parallel fifths in resolving the Gr6.

A.

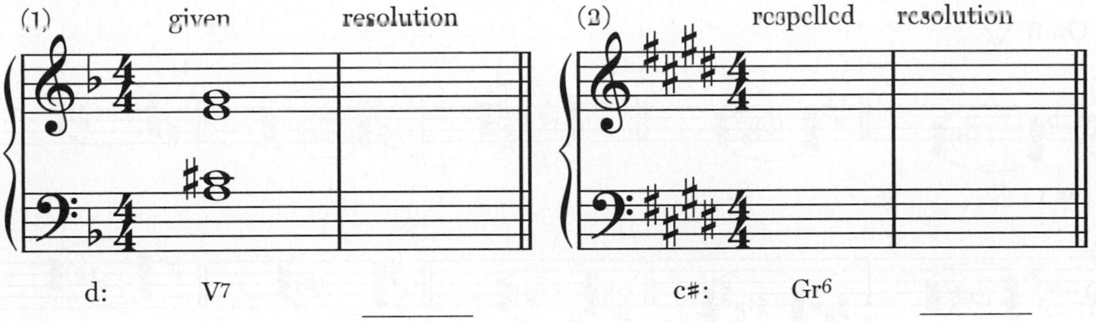

B.

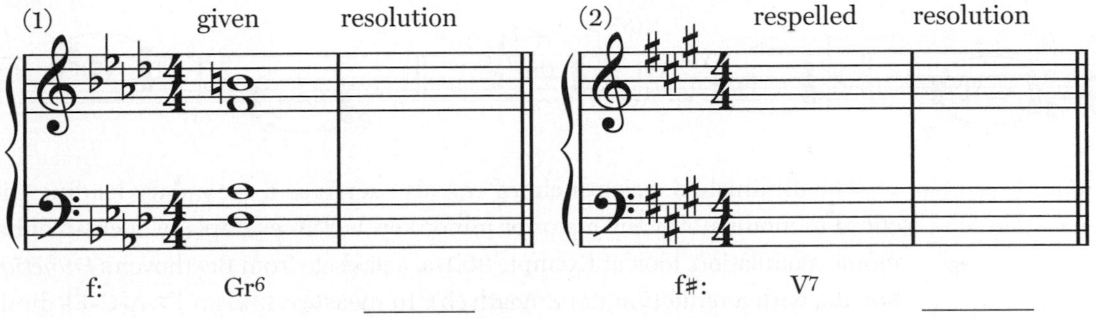

As in the Mozart example, it is possible to use a secondary dominant reinterpreted as an augmented sixth to modulate to other distant keys—here, a tritone apart, E♭ major and A minor—instead of a half step. When you write enharmonic modulations, pay careful attention to accidentals in the new key, since the half-step tonal relation requires several chromatic alterations to establish the new tonic. Play these examples to hear how the harmonic "deception" sets up the new tonic.

Enharmonic Modulation with Diminished Seventh Chords

The fully diminished seventh chord is an even more flexible means of enharmonic modulation. It may potentially resolve in four different ways (to either a major or minor "temporary tonic"), depending on how it is spelled, since the spelling determines both the root and resolution of the chord. A B diminished seventh, for example, if spelled with B as the root (Example 30.10A, part 1), can resolve to either C major or C minor; if spelled with D as the root (A, part 2), it resolves to either E♭ major or E♭ minor, and so on. In addition, in music of the Romantic era you may see a voice-leading shift from one diminished seventh chord up or down a half step to a second diminished seventh chord before the chord resolves to a new key.

EXAMPLE 30.10: Fully diminished seventh chords and their possible resolutions

A. On B

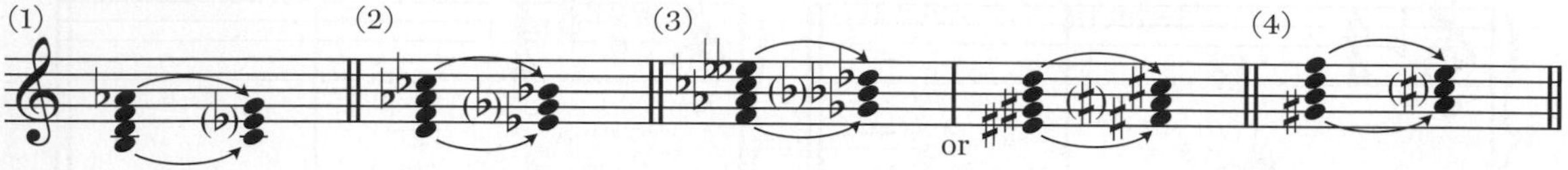

B. On C

C. On C♯

The diminished seventh chord can also serve as a secondary leading-tone chord to modulate to any major or minor key. For an example of such an enharmonic modulation, look at Example 30.11a, a passage from Beethoven's *Pathétique* Sonata, with a reduction underneath (b). In measure 134, an F♯-A-C-E♭ diminished seventh chord resolves to G-B♭-D after a voice exchange involving C and E♭ in the highest and lowest parts, filled in with passing-tone Ds. The motive is repeated in measure 135, but the F♯-A-C-E♭ is respelled D♯-F♯-A-C on the third beat, and now resolves to a cadential $^6_4$ in the key of E minor—the chromatic submediant of G minor (the key of mm. 133–134). Play through part (b) several times to hear the effect of the different resolutions of the diminished seventh chord.

EXAMPLE 30.11: Beethoven, *Pathétique* Sonata, first movement

(a) Mm. 133–136

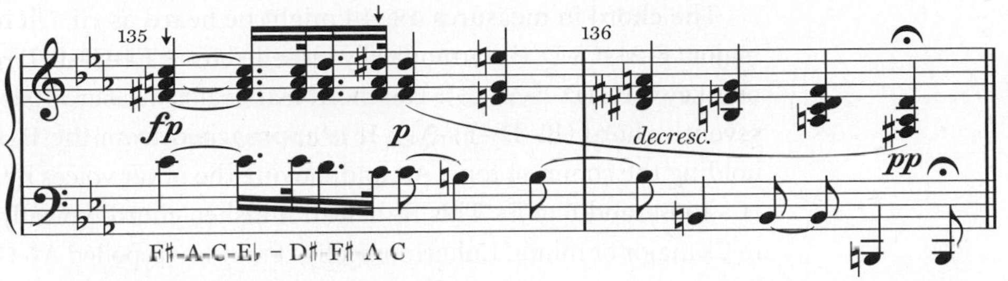

(b) Reduction of mm. 134–136a

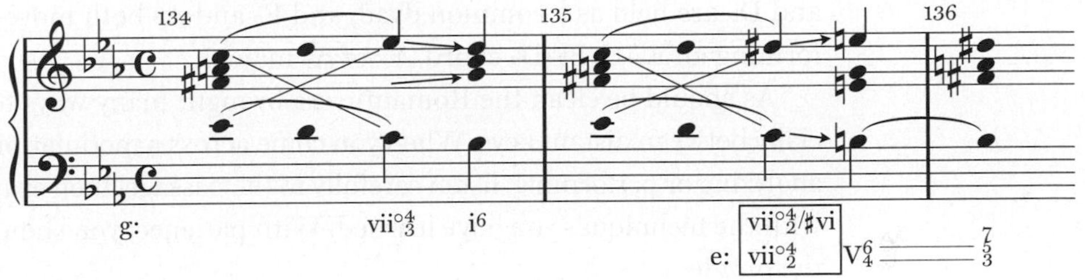

KEY CONCEPT An enharmonic pivot chord can be spelled as it functions in the first key or as it functions in the second key. It may also appear twice, spelled once each way (Example 30.11).

Sometimes modulations involve a combination of techniques. Listen to the modulation in measures 49–50 of the second movement. The passage shown in Example 30.12 is the transition back from E major (F♭ major) to A♭ major. The chord in measure 47, an E major triad, is followed by a fully diminished seventh chord (D-F-A♭-C♭) in measures 48–49.

Example 30.12: Beethoven, *Pathétique* Sonata, second movement, mm. 47–51

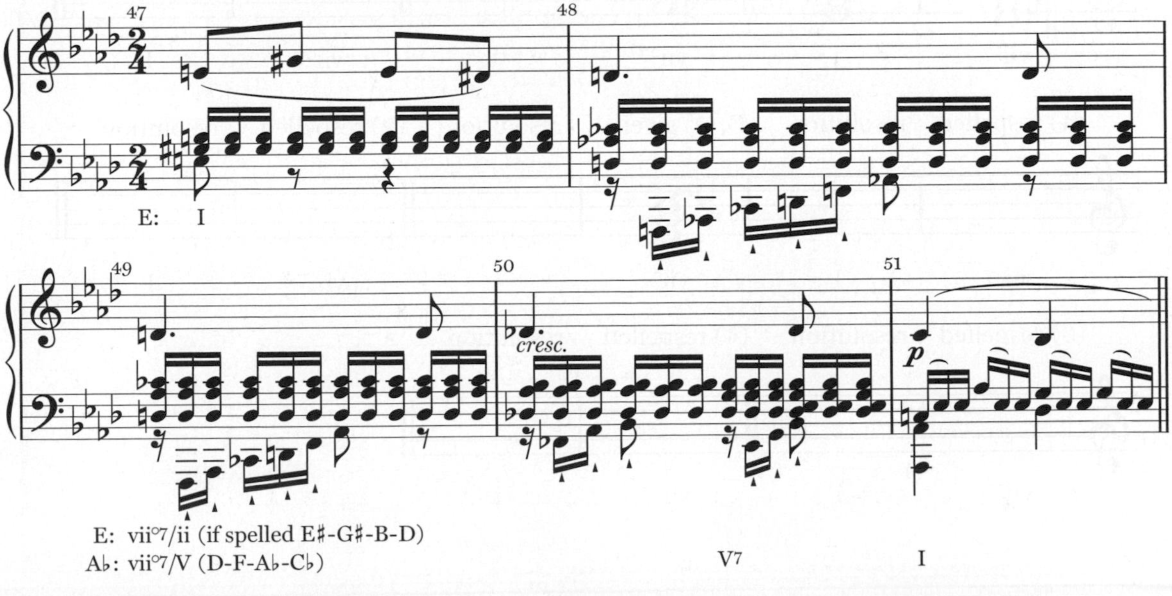

The chord in measures 48–49 might be heard as $vii^{\circ 7}$/ii in the old key of E major (F-A♭-C♭-D, enharmonically respelled from E♯-G♯-B-D) or as $vii^{\circ 6}_{5}$/V in the new key of A♭ (D-F-A♭-C♭). The chord that begins measure 50 is a half-diminished seventh chord (B♭-D♭-F♭-A♭). It is approached from the D-F-A♭-C♭ chord by holding the common tone, A♭, and moving the other voices by half step: D to D♭, C♭ to B♭, and F to F♭. This B♭ half-diminished chord typically functions as $vii^{ø7}$ in C♭ major or minor. Enharmonically, it may be respelled A♯-C♯-E-G♯, or $vii^{ø7}$ in B major or minor. Here, it does not resolve in either of those ways; instead, the B♭ and D♭ are held as a common dyad, and F♭ and A♭ both move down a half step, forming an E♭-G-B♭-D♭ chord (V^7 of A♭ major).

As should be clear, the Romantic era brought many ways to modulate, especially between distant keys. When you come across a modulation in music you are analyzing or performing, listen carefully to the passage, then examine the evidence with the techniques you have learned. With patience, you should be able to solve the puzzle.

Try it #2

Resolve each given diminished seventh chord in (1) to i or I. Then invert the chord and respell it enharmonically in (2)–(4) so that each note of the original chord is the root. Resolve each chord to its tonic (i or I). In the blanks, write the key of the tonic to which each respelled chord resolves.

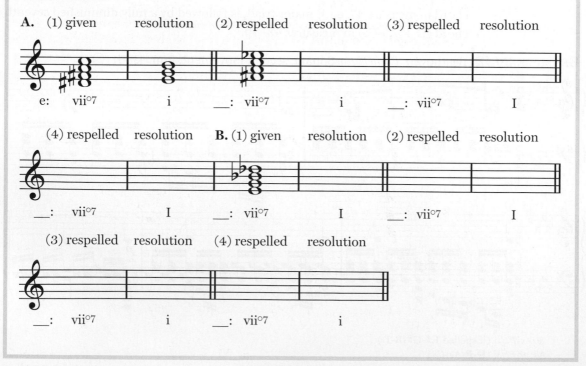

A. (1) given resolution (2) respelled resolution (3) respelled resolution

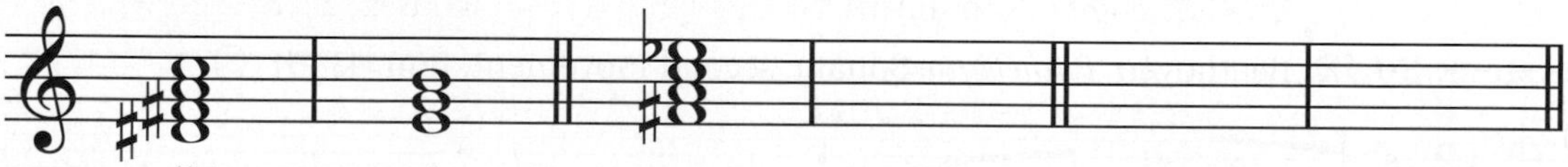

e: $vii^{\circ 7}$ i ___: $vii^{\circ 7}$ i ___: $vii^{\circ 7}$ I

(4) respelled resolution **B.** (1) given resolution (2) respelled resolution

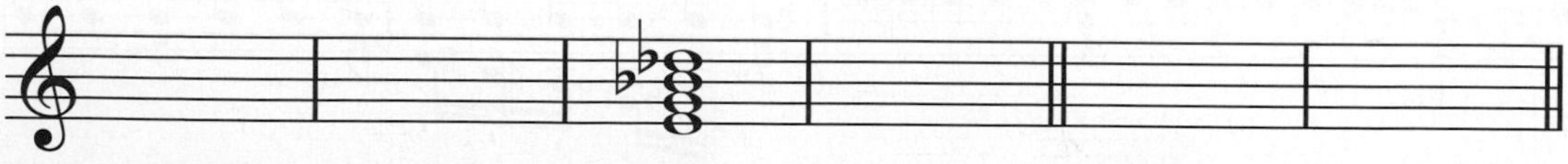

___: $vii^{\circ 7}$ I ___: $vii^{\circ 7}$ I ___: $vii^{\circ 7}$ I

(3) respelled resolution (4) respelled resolution

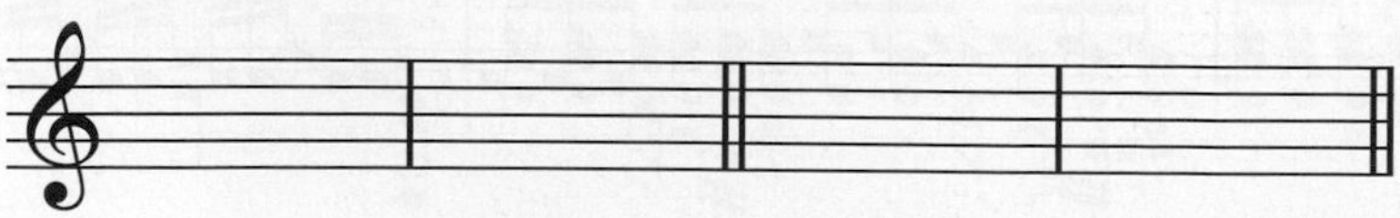

___: $vii^{\circ 7}$ i ___: $vii^{\circ 7}$ i

Linear Chromaticism

Chromaticism and Voice-Leading Chords

Many types of passing and neighboring chords may be created by combining embellishing tones vertically into **voice-leading chords** (VL) that expand a functional harmony. Since there are too many possible chords of this type for each one to have a specific name, we refer to them as a category by this term, but you may also see then called linear chords, apparent chords, or embellishing chords. There are times when it makes sense simply to label the individual embellishments, instead of considering the "chord" they make—particularly if the duration of the embellishments is less than the prevailing harmonic rhythm, or if the embellishments are metrically unaccented. Identify harmonic elements of the basic phrase through a contextual analysis, to understand the musical contexts for these sonorities.

For an example of linear chromaticism, we turn to a voice-leading chord from Chopin's Prelude in C Minor, given in Example 30.13. The chords on beats 1, 2, and 4 in measure 5 are i^{5-6} and v^6 (or alternatively, i–VI^6–v^6). But what is the third chord? We can best explain it by considering the relationship of each of its pitches to those of the chords on either side. The bass is an octave-doubled chromatic passing tone. The soprano and tenor parts are shared with the chord that follows, and the alto skips from A♭ (a pitch in the previous chord) to F♯, making a kind of double neighbor around the G to which it resolves on beat 4. Each individual voice makes sense in the context, but if we stack this simultaneity in thirds, we get B-D-F♯-A♭, a very bizarre seventh chord. Another interpretation of the chord is to hear the embellished motion from A♭ to G in the alto as a 7–6 suspension with a chromatic change of bass.

Example 30.13: Chopin, Prelude in C Minor, mm. 5–6

The first chord in measure 6 is also linear in origin, and can be interpreted as a tonic chord with a passing tone in the bass. Harmonic analysis with Roman numerals in these cases may not provide much useful information beyond what is gleaned from analyzing the embellishments. If you like, write "linear" (or VL) in the analysis, and then label the embellishments in the score.

Voice-leading chords like these are particularly prevalent in the chromatic harmony of Romantic-era compositions: the incorporation of chromatically altered scale degrees opens up many additional possibilities for passing tones, neighbor tones, and other embellishments. There are too many passing and neighboring chord types to cover all of them here. Still, with persistence and careful consideration of the context, you should be able to determine "What is that? And what is it doing there?" for voice-leading chords in music you are performing and studying.

Some Romantic composers took the voice-leading idea even further, writing pieces where long spans of music consist of linear chords held together by their smooth, chromatic voice-leading without much, if any, sense of progression or root motion. For a famous example, listen to Chopin's Prelude in E Minor, whose opening phrase is given in Example 30.14. The beginning and end of the phrase are the only places with clearly functional harmonic progressions.

EXAMPLE 30.14: Chopin, Prelude in E Minor, mm. 1–12

Try it #3

Write the chords in measures 1–4 of Example 30.14 on the staff below. Determine their quality and inversion. Include pitches from the right-hand melody only where they seem to fit in the chord; the others should be considered embellishing tones. What chord qualities can you identify? Do any resolve correctly?

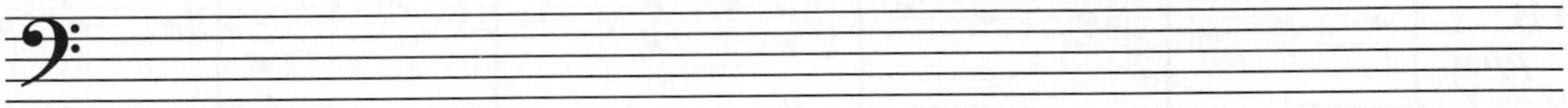

While providing a Roman numeral analysis is good practice for identifying chord types, such an analysis does not explain much about this passage other than the general qualities of the sounds. Concentrate rather on the linear motion. The melody in the right hand prolongs a B4 with a neighboring C5 in measures 1–4, then descends via a passing-tone B♭4 to prolong A4 in measures 5–8 with a neighboring B4. A skip from A4 in measure 8 to F♯4 in measure 10 is embellished in measures 8–9 and reiterated in 10–11. The basic strategy for both the melody and accompanying harmonies seems to be a gradual descent from the i chord at the beginning to the V^7 in measure 12. While the descent in the melody is primarily diatonic, the descent in the left hand is primarily chromatic, with voices taking turns moving chromatically downward.

This book has tried to draw a balance between discussing "strength of progression" (that is, passages with strong root-movement-based chord progressions) and "strength of line" (passages with less strong root movement, but smooth linear connections between chords). The chord patterns in the Chopin prelude do not make much sense from a root-progression standpoint, yet the strength of line—in particular, voice-leading based on chromatic half-step motion—makes this phrase work musically.

Intentional Harmonic Ambiguity

Pieces like the Chopin prelude demonstrate intentional harmonic ambiguity. Although the prelude is written for piano and is not associated with a specific programmatic idea, harmonic ambiguity is often called on in songs to express multiple meanings of the text, and is an important element in Romantic-era opera. Perhaps the most famous intentionally ambiguous passage in Romantic-era music is the opening of the Prelude to Richard Wagner's opera *Tristan und Isolde*, shown in a piano reduction in Example 30.15. Examine this passage for clues regarding key areas.

EXAMPLE 30.15: Wagner, Prelude to *Tristan und Isolde*, mm. 1–17a

Measures 1–3 and 4–7 form a sequence, with the entire texture transposed up a minor third except for the anacrusis (perhaps to make the first two pitches in mm. 4–5 match the B-G♯ in m. 3). Since the work begins with A3 and measure 3 ends with an E dominant seventh chord, the opening could imply A minor, with a $\flat\hat{6}$-$\hat{5}$-$\sharp\hat{4}$ encircling $\hat{5}$ (but continuing chromatically downward to introduce $\hat{4}$ in the V^7). As sequences often function as "traveling music," this opening is quite ambiguous—by measure 7, no key has been established as a point of departure.

The third presentation of the sequence pattern, in measures 8–11, is not an exact transposition. It begins with the anacrusis transposed up a minor third from the previous pattern, again matching pitch classes in the last chord of measure 7. But the next portion is expanded, with notes added as it strives forward and upward. Measures 12–15 then simply reiterate 10–11 in a truncated form. In measures 16–17, the first standard cadence, an E dominant seventh resolves deceptively to an F major triad. Does that mean the piece is in A minor? Clearly the ambiguity of harmony and key is a musical depiction of unfulfilled desire or longing, and it prepares the listener beautifully for the drama between two lovers that follows.

Analyzing and Performing Chromatic Passages

When you find chromaticism in pieces you are analyzing or performing, think about which type it represents. Can the chromatic pitches be attributed to embellishing tones, mixture, sequential transpositions, applied chords? If you identify chromatic melodic embellishments (passing tones and neighbor tones), remember that they are basically a surface event—a flourish or decoration within a diatonic context. The chromatic "additions" do not usually imply harmonic function or need resolution beyond the completion of the embellishment pattern. These chromatic pitches may often be circled and labeled N or P. Even if they make "chords," sonorities may not need a Roman numeral if their origin in voice-leading is clear. In performance, however, chromatic embellishments need to be considered carefully; they often lend a sense of direction or help to establish the music's character. It is vitally important to this sense of direction and character that chromatic alterations be performed in tune.

You might also identify chromatic chords within the basic phrase that serve as substitutes for diatonic chords with a similar function. These include secondary dominant and leading-tone chords, mixture chords, and Neapolitan and augmented-sixth chords. Chromatic descending-fifth sequences fall within this category as well. Substituting a chromatic chord for a diatonic one often intensifies the sense of forward motion in a progression; for this reason, the resolutions of chromatic tendency tones need to be considered carefully in performance, as do changes of tone color that might highlight the composer's use of mixture.

Passages that are in their very essence chromatic and linear can present quite a challenge to the analyst and performer. These vary from passages whose beginning and end are firmly functional to passages where voice-leading chords permeate the harmonies throughout. In studying a chromatic passage, determine the harmonic points of arrival and shape your performance toward them. Establish which embellishments affect the underlying harmonic progression and which are ornamental. Identify the quality of each sonority, and determine whether dominant-function seventh chords or A^6 chords resolve as expected, resolve deceptively, tonicize scale degrees, or initiate new keys. Locate sequences and transitory or modulatory passages. All this information will help you identify a hierarchy of musical function. Remember that not all sonorities carry equal weight, and only after you have determined the musical function of each can you convey your vision effectively to an audience.

Finally, when analyzing pieces that include chromatic voice-leading, don't forget to listen. In pieces like the Chopin prelude, there are some progressions that sound (and are) functional—label those first, then listen attentively to the rest. Careful analysis of some chromatic musical surfaces may reveal a relatively simple underlying diatonic progression, which you can convey through performance; other passages may rely almost entirely on harmonic ambiguity. It is your job as musical interpreter to determine which view of the materials to present.

Did You Know?

The opera *Tristan und Isolde* was composed in the years 1865–69 by Richard Wagner, but the story of Tristan and Isolde dates back to the Middle Ages and the Renaissance, when it was a well-known and often-retold romance. For his setting, Wagner relied on Gottfried von Strassburg's poetic retelling of the story, with the traditional characters placed in a courtly setting. For other operas—including the *Ring of the Niebelungen* cycle and *Parsifal*—Wagner based his librettos on tales set in poetry by medieval Germanic poets. The rediscovery of these early poems was influential on the German Romantic movement, but also in the early twentieth century on the young Adolf Hitler, who, in the development of Nazism, seized on Wagner's ideas as expressed in his operas and writings.

The story of *Tristan und Isolde* is one of intense love and passion, but each time there is an opportunity for the lovers to be together, they are separated. To represent the theme of unfulfilled love, Wagner composed progressions that repeatedly lead toward a cadence that is evaded at the last moment, with the dissonant intervals instead moving linearly to form another dissonant chord; only with the musical conventions of tonality was Wagner able to represent the intensity of the characters' striving and lack of fulfillment. It becomes clear in the course of the opera that Tristan and Isolde will only be permanently united in their deaths; during the "Liebestod" (the "love-death"), a final aria that Isolde sings over the body of Tristan just before dying of grief herself, the series of dissonances set in motion at the very beginning of the overture (Example 30.15) finally finds resolution.

TERMS YOU SHOULD KNOW

chromatic inflection
chromatic modulation
- altered common-chord
- altered pivot-chord
- common-dyad
- common-tone
- enharmonic
- pivot-dyad
- pivot-tone

enharmonic reinterpretation
intentional harmonic ambiguity
voice-leading chord (VL)

QUESTIONS FOR REVIEW

1. How may the principle of diatonic pivot-chord modulations be expanded to modulate to distant keys?
2. How can mixture smooth a modulation to a distant key?
3. How may a chromatic descending-fifth sequence be used to modulate?
4. Chords of what quality are suitable for enharmonic reinterpretation?
5. List as many ways to modulate from C major to A♭ major as you can.
6. In music for your own instrument, find a Romantic-era piece with one of the following: (a) common-tone or -dyad modulation, (b) a modulation with an altered pivot chord, (c) a modulation with enharmonic reinterpretation. If this proves difficult for your instrument, check the piano repertoire.
7. How does the function of chromatic elements affect the way they should be interpreted in performance?

CHAPTER 31 Variation and Rondo

Outline of topics

Sectional variations
- Variation themes
- Organization in variation sets
- Figural variations
- Chromatic variations
- Character variations
- Textural and timbral variations

Continuous variations
- Formal organization

Performing variations

Rondo
- Five-part rondo
- Refrains and episodes
- Transitions and retransitions

Overview

This chapter considers three formal designs from the Baroque and Classical eras: sectional variation, continuous variation, and rondo.

Repertoire

Johann Sebastian Bach, Chaconne, from Violin Partita No. 2 in D Minor

Ludwig van Beethoven
- Piano Sonata in C Minor, Op. 13 (*Pathétique*), second movement
- *Variations on "God Save the King"*

John Barnes Chance, *Variations on a Korean Folk Song*

Wolfgang Amadeus Mozart
- Piano Sonata in C Major, K. 545, third movement
- *Variations on "Ah, vous dirai-je Maman"*

Henry Purcell, "Music for a While"

Sectional Variations

Previous chapters looked at several theme-and-variations movements and pieces, including Mozart's *Variations on "Ah, vous dirai-je Maman"* and Chance's *Variations on a Korean Folk Song*. We now return to these works to learn how their melodies are varied and how they are organized formally.

(anthology) Listen to the Mozart and Chance variations while following the scores in your anthology. Among other features, these variations share a sectional design. That is, each variant is clearly articulated from the next by a strong conclusive cadence (and even by double bars) and sometimes by a striking change in style or timbre. Since each variation could be played as a brief but complete stand-alone section, these sets are called **sectional variations**.

Variation Themes

Both sets of variations are based on a melody that serves as a **theme**—the main idea to unify the set. While the length may vary, melodies are usually sixteen measures or more. Like the two themes here, the melodies typically show a clear phrase structure and end with a definitive cadence.

Sectional variation themes also often make up a complete formal unit, such as the rounded binary of the Mozart theme. They are long enough that a single setting of the theme can make a complete short piece in itself. Many are based on a preexisting melody—such as "God Save the King" or "Twinkle, Twinkle, Little Star." Folk songs, patriotic songs, and other types of familiar melodies work particularly well: when the melody is familiar, listeners can more easily follow its outline even when it is transformed as a part of the variation process. Variations, however, may also be based on a newly composed melody.

Organization in Variation Sets

Mozart's theme is a melody he knew as a French folk song, "Ah, vous dirai-je Maman." Listen to the theme, given in Example 31.1, to review its phrase structure and formal organization.

EXAMPLE 31.1: Mozart, *Variations on "Ah, vous dirai-je Maman,"* theme, mm. 1–24

In this piece, the variations are numbered in the score, a convention that is typical of sectional variations. If they were not indicated, as in the Chance set, the next step would be to locate the starting point for each new variation. If you glance through the rest of Mozart's score, you will see that most variations follow the rounded binary form of the theme: **‖: a :‖: b a :‖**, or **‖: a :‖: b a′ :‖**.

Take a close look at the last variation: the first section is eight measures long as before, and the first ending of the second section cadences as expected, but the second ending adds eleven measures. These added measures, which help bring the piece to a close, constitute a coda. Codas are common in longer pieces, such as variation sets, rondos, and sonata-form movements.

Now listen to the entire piece. As you listen, think about what has been changed in each variation compared with the theme and also how the variations work together as a set.

KEY CONCEPT When you analyze variation movements, keep the following questions in mind.

- Does the variation you are analyzing differ in key, mode, meter, phrase structure, length, or character from the theme?

- Is a melodic or rhythmic figure or a specific embellishment pattern featured? If so, what is it?
- Does the variation form a pair with another, or a unit with several others?
- Is chromaticism used? If so, is the chromaticism surface embellishment, or does it change the harmonic function?
- Are the harmonies more complex than the theme or previous variation? Are they simplified?

Try it #1

In the Mozart *Variations*, the key, meter, and form are consistent in almost every variation. Identify one variation that differs from the others with respect to the following:

Changed element	*Which variation?*	*Changed how?*
form	XII	adds a coda
mode		
meter		

Figural Variations

Most of the variations in this piece are **figural**: they feature a specific embellishment pattern or figure throughout. Figural variations are often grouped in pairs. In the Mozart set, the first and second variations share sixteenth-note motion in one hand against quarter-note motion in the other; this rhythmic relationship reverses hands from Variation I to II. The third and fourth variations share triplet motion in one hand against primarily quarter-note motion in the other. Variations VIII and IX both feature imitative textures and suspensions in the upper voices (suspensions first appeared in Variation II). Rounding out the piece is a return in Variation XII of the sixteenth-note accompanimental pattern heard in Variation II, now adapted for triple meter.

Compare Example 31.2a with measures 8–12 of the theme to see how the melody is embellished in Variation I. The embellishment figure consists first of a step above the melody pitch (upper neighbor, or UN), then the melody pitch, a lower neighbor (LN), melody pitch, LN, melody pitch, UN, and melody pitch. This type of pattern, with slight alterations, appears frequently in this variation. A second figure with a leap and a scale appears in measures 28–30 (part b).

Example 31.2: Mozart, *Variations on "Ah, vous dirai-je Maman,"* Variation I

(a) Mm. 33–36

(b) Mm. 28–30

Variation V is built on a rhythmic figure—𝄾♬♩—that is applied to both the melody and accompaniment (Example 31.3). In other variations, such as VI (Example 31.4), each hand is characterized by a different figure. Some figures embellish and disguise the melody, while others appear in the accompanimental voice, with the melody floating above.

Example 31.3: Mozart, *Variations*, Variation V, mm. 121–124

Example 31.4: Mozart, *Variations*, Variation VI, mm. 145–148

Chromatic Variations

Several of Mozart's variations feature chromaticism. When you find chromaticism, check to see whether it is embellishing a melodic line or represents a change in harmony. In Example 31.2a, the F♯5, D♯5, and C♯5 are all chromatic neighbors—the chromaticism embellishes the melodic figure.

For an instance of chromaticism that changes the harmonic progression, listen to Example 31.5. In measure 68, the C♯3 and B♭4 on beat 2 transform the original C major tonic into a fully diminished seventh chord that resolves in the next measure. The addition of A♭4 on beat 2 of measure 69 creates another diminished seventh chord that resolves in measure 70. In both cases, the chromatic pitches are part of secondary leading-tone chords. The C♯4 and A♯3 in measure 69, in contrast, are simply chromatic neighbors.

Example 31.5: Mozart, *Variations*, Variation II, mm. 68–69

In variation sets built on a major-key theme, you may also find chromaticism in passages that include modal mixture or a complete change of mode. Listen, for instance, to measures 197–198 of Variation VIII (Example 31.6). Minor-mode variations, like this one, are normally in the parallel rather than the relative minor, to retain the same key center. This gives the effect of modal mixture and allows the opportunity for expressive chromaticism. Here, the accidentals indicate the melodic minor. Elsewhere in minor-mode variations, composers often substitute dramatic chromatic harmonies such as the Neapolitan and augmented-sixth chords.

Example 31.6: Mozart, *Variations*, Variation VIII, mm. 193–200

Character Variations

Some variations are designed to represent a particular style or "character," as are several from Beethoven's *Variations on "God Save the King."* Listen to Example 31.7, an excerpt from Variation VI. Here, the tempo, meter, and rhythmic patterns are all typical of march style; there are even "trumpet flourishes" in the last measure of the excerpt. The march strongly contrasts with the previous variation, a lyrical, minor-mode serenade. Although a character variation may feature a repeated melodic or rhythmic figure, the figure is not itself the driving impetus.

Example 31.7: Beethoven, *Variations on "God Save the King,"* Variation VI, mm. 1–6

Textural and Timbral Variations

In most variation sets, one of the elements that is varied is texture. In a general sense, we might refer to a "thin" texture when there are only a few voices and/or simple rhythmic patterns—as in the theme for the Mozart variations—and a "thick" texture when there are many voices and/or a lot of rhythmic activity. Remember that lines may be doubled in octaves, doubled by other instruments, or sometimes doubled in thirds or sixths; while this may create a somewhat thicker texture, doubling does not create additional independent lines.

In general, variations tend to be organized texturally from the simplest to the most complex, but sometimes composers include a variation with a thin texture or reduced harmonic palette in the middle of a set for contrast. Variation VII is an example (an excerpt is shown in Example 31.8); this type is sometimes called a **simplifying variation**. Another relatively common textural variant, a **polyphonic variation**, may include imitative entries, as several of the Mozart variations do, or a change from a harmonically based setting to one with independent voices. Refer back to Example 31.6 for an example of imitative entries.

Example 31.8: Mozart, *Variations*, Variation VII, mm. 169–172

The Mozart and Beethoven variation sets call for the same instrumentation, a keyboard instrument, throughout. The Chance variations, on the other hand, offer a wide range of timbral combinations. Listen to the opening theme (Example 31.9). This statement sounds quite different in the rich, low range of the clarinets than it does when it returns in the saxophones and baritone (mm. 17–24) and in the horns and clarinets (mm. 25–32).

Example 31.9: Chance, *Variations on a Korean Folk Song*, mm. 1–8

Perhaps the most unusual variation is at the "Con Islancio" marking, beginning in measure 199 and featuring the percussion section (anthology, p. 116). The snare drum starts a rhythmic pattern, soon joined by cymbal and gong. Then in measure 208, the temple blocks layer on a figure that was introduced in a previous figural variation (beginning at m. 128). Three measures later (m. 211), the vibraphone enters with the theme's melody, answered in imitation by the flutes and piccolos. In the rest of the variation, Chance passes the melody to every section of the band.

This variation thus explores both timbre and texture by changing timbral colors and building up layers.

As in the "Con Islancio" variation, which combines textural, timbral, figural, and contrapuntal elements, composers may freely combine variation procedures that we have looked at in isolation—and usually this is the case. When analyzing variations, feel free to combine the labels as needed. If none of the labels fits, come up with your own to describe what you are hearing.

Continuous Variations

While sectional variations were the standard type of variation movement in the Classical era, when clear phrase and sectional organization was prized, some variations from the Baroque era show a different design. Rather than divisions articulated by authentic cadences and double bar lines, these **continuous variations** feature a continuous flow of musical ideas and *Fortspinnung* phrase structure. Listen to Bach's Chaconne and Purcell's "Music for a While," while following the scores in your anthology. Examples 31.10 and 31.11 reproduce the opening two statements of the theme for each work.

(anthology)

EXAMPLE 31.10: Bach, Chaconne in D Minor, mm. 1–8a

EXAMPLE 31.11: Purcell, "Music for a While," mm. 1–7a (anthology)

Try it #2

For Examples 31.10 and 31.11:

A. Give the measure numbers for the first complete statement of the theme.

Bach: ____________________

Purcell: ____________________

B. What aspect of the theme's final cadence is shared in both pieces?

____

C. How do these themes differ from those of the sectional variations studied?

____

The repeated element—the basis for the variations—in continuous sets is typically a bass line or a chord progression, rather than a melody with accompaniment as in many sectional variations. In addition, the themes are usually shorter, and the repetitions of the theme tend to be elided at the cadence to maintain the continuous structure. The rhythmic flow throughout the variations is likewise continuous. Where phrases are not connected by elision, a lead-in (or connecting idea) typically links one variation with the next.

Some of the names associated with Baroque continuous variations are "passacaglia," "chaconne," and "ground bass." As you study compositions in this genre, you will discover some inconsistency in how the terms are applied; this is because the musical characteristics associated with each term (especially "chaconne" and "passacaglia") varied depending on the time and place of composition.

KEY CONCEPT There are two types of continuous variation.

- A **ground bass** or **passacaglia** has a repeated bass line that remains constant while the upper voices are varied. The variations in a passacaglia may reharmonize the bass line and may include phrase lengths that differ from, and overlap with, the statements of the ground bass.
- A **chaconne** has a harmonic progression that is repeated and varied. While the bass line may remain unchanged for several successive variations, it is usually altered as the piece progresses—rhythmically, harmonically, or through inversion.

It is helpful to differentiate between these two types of compositional methods—ground bass versus repeated harmonic progression—even if, historically, their labels may have varied.

Formal Organization

Chaconnes and passacaglias may include as many as sixty or more variations. These variations are typically grouped into pairs or sets that are linked by a shared figure or other musical characteristic; for example, the first and second variations might form a pair, as well as the third and fourth, fifth and sixth, and so on. Paired variations help keep the movement from sounding choppy or heavily segmented.

The first forty measures of the Bach Chaconne illustrate a large-scale rhythmic process that often structures portions of variation movements: the work begins with predominantly quarter-note motion, then moves gradually through shorter note values to sixteenth notes in measures 27 and following. This is known as **rhythmic acceleration**, or **rhythmic *crescendo***. Another rhythmic acceleration begins in measure 56 with mostly eighth-note motion, gradually moving to sixteenth notes and culminating in thirty-second notes in measures 65 and following.

Try it #3

Listen to measures 1–41 of the Bach Chaconne while following the anthology score. In your score, number the statements of the chaconne theme. (anthology)

A. How many times is the theme stated in this passage? ______________

B. Statements 1–6 form pairs. What do these pairs share?

Statements 1–2: ______________________________

Statements 3–4: ______________________________

Statements 5–6: ______________________________

In addition to the variation process, most continuous variations also exhibit a large-scale structure, often some type of **A B A′**. In many cases, the contrasting section is achieved by motion to the parallel key. Bach's Chaconne is no exception: measures 132–207 are in D major (Example 31.12). The passage is not a simple transcription of the beginning measures into the parallel major key, yet it does share some features with the opening, including the initial rhythmic motives and a similar (though not identical) harmonic progression.

Example 31.12: Bach, Chaconne in D Minor, mm. 132–136a

In passacaglias, another way to create contrast is to move the repeated bass-line theme out of the bass voice temporarily, into an upper voice. This practice can be particularly effective in an organ passacaglia, since it means moving the theme out of the distinctive pedal register and timbre.

Purcell's "Music for a While" illustrates yet another way to help keep a continuous variation set from sounding too sectional and repetitive. Two presentations of the ground bass were given in Example 31.11. Listen to the entire song now, while following the score in your anthology, and focus on the bass line. This line is repeated exactly, note for note, three times in measures 1–12, but then is altered to modulate to new keys. It passes briefly through E minor (m. 15, with the ground bass now shifted to begin mid-measure), G major (m. 18), and C major (m. 22). The ground bass returns to A minor briefly in measure 23, and passes once more through E minor (m. 28) before settling in the tonic key for the remainder of the piece. Throughout these tonal changes, the bass line never loses its characteristic rhythm, contour, or prominence as the organizing principle behind the piece, even when transposed or extended.

(anthology)

Listen to the song one last time, now focusing on the vocal melody and large-scale design. You should hear an **A B A′** structure superimposed on the continuous variation. This organization is most clear when the **A** section returns in measure 29: at this point, the text and a substantial part of the melody from the song's opening return (nearly six measures of the opening melody are repeated exactly), and the ground bass returns to its downbeat metrical position. The beginning of the **B** section (Example 31.13) is more difficult to determine, but it surely includes the modulatory statements of the ground bass and introduction of new text. We can therefore begin the **B** section in measure 10, with the new text.

EXAMPLE 31.13: Purcell, "Music for a While," mm. 9–15a (anthology)

Although ground bass 3 and the vocal phrase conclude together at the beginning of measure 10 (on "beguile"), this is not the case for the rest of the example. The next vocal phrase ("Wond'ring") begins on the third beat of ground bass 4 and continues right through the beginning of ground bass 5 in measure 13 ("were eas'd"). The two are then back in alignment at the cadence in E minor in measure 15. Places where the vocal melody and ground bass pattern do not align help create a more seamless (and more interesting) piece than complete alignment of the two would provide.

Performing Variations

In the centuries before recorded music, variation movements were an ideal format for listeners who might hear a piece of music only one time. They would listen to the initial idea—perhaps a typical chord progression or a familiar tune—then follow the transformation of the idea through a series of variations without having to hear the work several times to perceive its organization. When performing variations, however, you need not "bring out" the subject or theme each time you play it. Instead, shape the music in a way that is appropriate to the style, being aware of the repeated theme but not overemphasizing it.

A first step in preparing a variation set for performance might be to locate each presentation of the theme to make sure you can find it in the midst of the embellishment, transposition, or other type of technique present. In the case of continuous variations, you may want to choose an articulation for the bass line that remains consistent so that the beginning of each repetition is clear without being emphasized. In sectional variations, be careful that you don't "miss the forest for the trees"—that is, that you don't overemphasize the embellishments and lose the theme. It is then the listeners' task to discern the increasingly disguised melody, the repeated bass line, or the varied harmonic progression as the set progresses—if they wish to listen that way.

To further prepare for performance, identify the phrase and sectional form, the type of melodic or harmonic embellishment, and the elements of continuity (to help with memorization), and determine the style or character of individual variations. Understanding the role of overall form—especially paired or grouped variations, rhythmic acceleration, contrasting sections, and the dramatic shaping of the set—will help you achieve the sweep and grace of a well-designed variation movement in performance.

Rondo

Five-Part Rondo

(anthology) Listen to the lyrical second movement of Beethoven's *Pathétique* Sonata, played on a fortepiano, a predecessor of the modern piano—first without the score to get an idea of how this movement is organized, then again while following along in your anthology. Label the first sixteen measures **A**, the first large section. Find and label each cadence in measures 1–8 (Example 31.14), then use this information to determine the phrase organization of the entire sixteen-measure **A** section.

Example 31.14: Beethoven, *Pathétique* Sonata, second movement, mm. 1–8a

The **A** section is divided into two periods—measures 1–8 and 9–16—each of which is made up of two phrases; the second period (9–16) is a varied repetition of the first. The first phrase ends with a tonicized HC (m. 4), the second with a PAC (m. 8). You may have thought that the first eight measures were a single phrase, since the inner-voice accompaniment does not pause and the melody and bass lines are elided over the phrase break. If so, try listening to the first four measures again and stopping before beat 2 in measure 4, to hear the resolution of the V^4_3/V (B♭-D♮-F-A♭) to V. You should hear a clear point of repose at the half cadence.

As a first step in charting the form of this movement, listen again and mark any return of the **A** material in your score. If the section is altered when it returns, add prime marks (**A′** or **A″**); if you hear any changes of key, mark these. Label the measures between the **A** sections with other letters, as shown below. This formal design is called a **five-part rondo**. (The arrows indicate tonal instability.)

A	B	A′	C	A″	Coda
mm. 1–16	16b–28	29–36	36b–50	51–66	66b–73
A♭	f–E♭ →	A♭	a♭ → E →	A♭	A♭

KEY CONCEPT **Rondo** form is characterized by a repeated section (called a **refrain**, or **ritornello**) alternating with sections that contrast in key, mode, texture, harmonic complexity, thematic content, and/or style. The contrasting sections are called **episodes**. Although other designs are possible, the two most common are

- five-part rondo: **A B A C A** (plus optional coda) and
- seven-part rondo: **A B A C A B** (or **D**) **A** (plus optional coda; see Chapter 32).

After their initial presentation, the restatements of **A** and **B** may be varied.

Refrains and Episodes

As the Beethoven example shows, the rondo's refrain is usually harmonically closed—it ends with a conclusive cadence—and it returns each time in the tonic key. Its phrase structure is typically balanced and symmetrical. The first episode, **B**, does not exhibit four-measure phrase lengths or regular hypermeter. It is harmonically unstable: the section begins by touching on F minor (vi of A♭), then drifts to E♭ major (V of A♭, m. 23). The cadence at the end of the section elides with the beginning of the **A′** section. In addition, the melody of the **B** section, with its leaps, contrasts with the lyrical **A** melody.

Section **C** likewise does not exhibit regular four-measure phrase lengths or regular hypermeter, but is instead chromatic and dramatic. The initial key is A♭ minor, followed by a modulation to E major (the enharmonically respelled chromatic submediant, F♭ major). The **C** section introduces triplet sixteenth notes, which will reappear in the **A″** section. It also elides with the refrain's return in measure 51.

The episodes in this movement are typical of episodes in general: they present contrasting keys and are often harmonically open. Episodes may include modulations or end in a key different from that in which they began, and they may elide with the refrain that follows without achieving harmonic closure. While the refrain often consists of four- or eight-measure phrases organized in period structure with a regular hypermeter, the episodes tend to fall into irregular phrases with irregular hypermeter. The diagram below is a typical design for five-part rondos.

Refrain	Episode	Refrain	Episode	Refrain	
A	**B**	**A**	**C**	**A**	(optional coda)
I–I	V* →	I–I	i* →	I–I	
i–i	III or v* →	i–i	I* →	i–i	

*or other contrasting key

Now consider the music that concludes the Beethoven movement. A PAC elides the conclusion of the **A″** section with the beginning of the final section—a coda. The remaining music has the character of an extended cadence with repeated dominant-tonic chord successions. This coda fulfills multiple functions: it reminds listeners of the motives of the piece, "closes out" each of the registers (in mm. 66–68 and 68–70), and slows down the action by shortening the length of melodic ideas (mm. 70–73a) until all that remains is a repeated chord (m. 73) to end the movement.

Transitions and Retransitions

The end of an episode typically provides cues for the listener that the **A** section is about to return. For example, both contrasting sections in the Beethoven movement end with a modulation back to the **A** section's key, A♭. In addition, the **B** section also ends with a short dominant pedal (mm. 27–28), while the **C** section closes with an acceleration of the harmonic rhythm.

KEY CONCEPT The end of an episode, where the music begins to turn back toward the **A** section's return, is called a **retransition**. Most retransitions prolong the dominant harmony, in preparation for the return of the refrain's tonic key. Refrains in turn may be linked to episodes by **transitions**, modulatory passages that move toward the key of the new section.

Both transitions and retransitions usually consist of repetitions of short motives (possibly transposed) and irregular hypermeters, rather than balanced four- or eight-measure phrases.

(anthology) Listen now to the final movement of Mozart's Sonata in C Major, while following the score in your anthology (p. 262). The refrain is given in Example 31.15a. As you listen, label the large formal sections with letters; mark any change of key in the score as well. Determine whether the refrain and first episode are separated by a transition, and whether you hear a retransition after the first episode to prepare for the return of the refrain.

The **A** section, repeated, is an antecedent-consequent period with a HC in measure 4 and PAC in measure 8. After the double bar, the **B** section begins immediately in a new key, G major, without a transition. The eight-measure **B** section stays in G throughout, again with antecedent-consequent phrases. Interestingly, the consequent phrase takes motives from the **A** section and states them in the new key. In cases like this, think of the key (rather than theme) as the stronger identifier of the formal section—don't be fooled into thinking that the refrain has returned.

Example 31.15: Mozart, Piano Sonata in C Major, third movement

(a) Mm. 1–8

Look now at part (b), drawn from the end of the **B** section. The passage in measures 16b–20a provides a clear example of a retransition. As the key moves away from the G major of the **B** section, Mozart prolongs the G chord, transforming it via the F♮ into a dominant seventh of the tonic key, C major. The entire four bars prolong V7 of C in preparation for the refrain's return.

(b) Mm. 15–24a

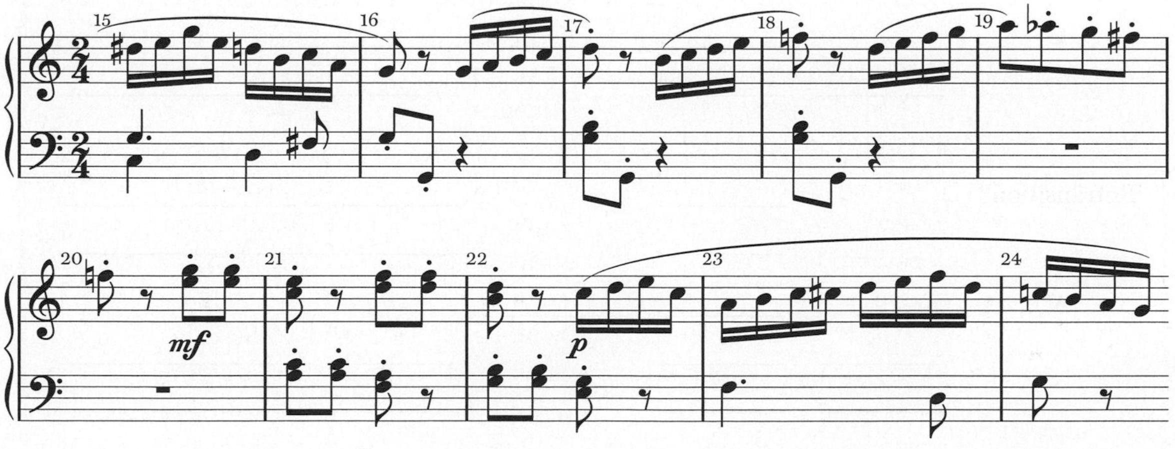

Try it #4

The chart below is a partial summary of the form of the Mozart rondo. Listen to the movement again, and then complete the chart. Be sure to include any transitions or retransitions. Use the "Comments" section to note cadence types, motivic recurrences, unusual key relationships, or any other musical feature you find striking. (When a theme begins on an upbeat, start counting measures with the first downbeat of the phrase.) What is unusual about the **C** section? Are there any unexpected tonal areas, based on what you have learned about rondos thus far?

SECTION	PHRASES	MEASURES	KEY/MODE	COMMENTS
A		1–8	C major	Section repeated.
	a	1–4		Ends with a HC.
	a′	5–8		Ends with a PAC.
B		9–16	G major	No transition.
	b	9–12		HC.
	a″	13–16		PAC; motives from **A**.
Retransition		17–20		Prolongs V^7 of C.
A		21–28	C major	Same as 1–8.
	a	21–24		Same as 1–4.
	a′	25–28		Same as 5–8.
C		________	________	________
	________	________		________
	________	________		________
Retransition?		________		________
		________		________
A′		________	________	
	________	________		________
	________	________		________
Coda?		________		________

Did You Know?

John Barnes Chance (1932–1972) was a popular composer of band music. He studied at the University of Texas at Austin and served as an arranger for the Fourth and Eighth U.S. Army Bands before taking a faculty position at the University of Kentucky. His *Variations on a Korean Folk Song*, his most well-known composition, won the prestigious Oswald Award from the American Bandmasters Association in 1966. Other often-performed band works include *Incantation and Dance* (1962) and *Elegy* (1972). Chance's life was tragically cut short by accidental electrocution in his own backyard, when he was forty years old.

TERMS YOU SHOULD KNOW

chaconne
coda
episode
five-part rondo
ground bass
passacaglia
refrain
retransition
rhythmic acceleration (rhythmic *crescendo*)
ritornello
rondo
transition
variation
- character
- chromatic
- continuous
- figural
- polyphonic
- sectional
- simplifying
- textural
- timbral

QUESTIONS FOR REVIEW

1. In what ways may a theme be varied?
2. What are some types of larger structural organization in variation movements?
3. How do continuous variations differ from sectional variations?
4. In what ways may analysis inform a performance of variations?
5. In a rondo, how do the non-refrain sections typically contrast with the refrain?
6. In music for your own instrument, find an example of one of the following: (a) a continuous variation movement, (b) a sectional variation movement, (c) a rondo.

CHAPTER 32 Sonata and Related Forms

Outline of topics

Classical sonata form

- The first large section
- The second large section

Sonata form in the Romantic era

- Increasing length and complexity
- Key areas and the organization of the exposition
- The development section
- The recapitulation and coda

Related forms

- Concerto form
- Large ternary form
- Seven-part rondo and sonata-rondo

Performing and listening to sonata-form movements

Overview

The focus of this chapter is sonata form. We consider the roles of melody and harmony in shaping a sonata-form movement, and observe how sonata form changed from the Classical to the Romantic era. We also look at sonatina and concerto and two other forms of the Classical and Romantic eras: large ternary and sonata-rondo.

Repertoire

Ludwig van Beethoven, Piano Sonata in C Major, Op. 53 (*Waldstein*), first movement

Wolfgang Amadeus Mozart, Piano Sonata in G Major, K. 283, first movement

Classical Sonata Form

🎧 (anthology) Listen to the first movement (*Allegro*) of Mozart's three-movement Sonata in G Major, while following the score in your anthology. Think about the overall formal organization, and mark in your score where you hear sections beginning or ending. Label any material that reappears later in the movement, and write in measure numbers to indicate where you first heard these themes or motives. (As you read this chapter, keep your score and recording at hand to see and listen to each new element under discussion.)

While you were listening, you may have noticed some musical hints indicating formal boundaries. One obvious cue is the repeat signs—at measure 53 to indicate a repeat of measures 1–53a and at the end to indicate a repeat of 53b–120. The movement seems to be organized like a large-scale continuous rounded binary form.

The First Large Section

The first section is fifty-three measures long. Its first phrase (Example 32.1) is a sentence (2+2+6) that establishes the key of G major. The second half of the phrase (the continuation-cadential portion) has been extended beyond the expected cadence in measure 8, with scalar flourishes in the right hand that lead to a PAC in measure 10. This second part is then repeated with slight variations, completing a sixteen-measure opening idea in the tonic key.

In sonata form, this opening musical idea in the tonic is sometimes called the **first theme**, or **primary theme**. Because there may be more than one melodic idea expressed in the opening, however, some musicians instead call it the "first tonal area" or "first theme group." We will generally speak of the **first theme group**, understanding that it may consist of more than one thematic idea but expresses the tonic key throughout.

Example 32.1: Mozart, Piano Sonata in G Major, first movement. mm. 1–10a (first theme group) 🎧

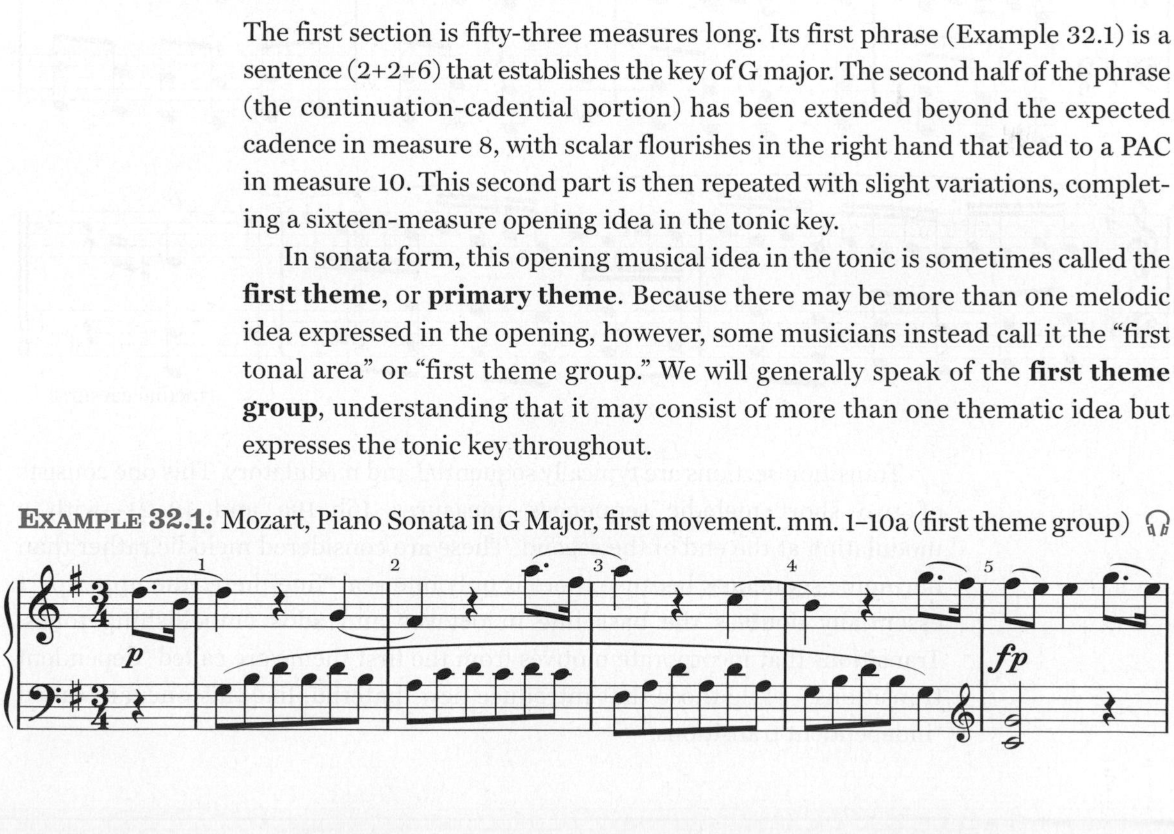

The next significant cadence comes in measure 22 (Example 32.2). This cadence could be interpreted as a HC preceded by a secondary-dominant-function chord, but the music continues in the new key of D major, as shown by the consistent presence of C♯ in the following measures and by cadences through measure 53. Measures 16b–22 therefore have a transitional function: they lead from the first theme group to a cadence that prepares a second key area. For this reason, they are called the **transition**.

EXAMPLE 32.2: Mozart, Sonata in G Major, first movement, mm. 16b–22 (transition)

Transition sections are typically sequential and modulatory. This one consists of two short melodic sequences—measures 16b–19a and 19–21—with a modulation at the end of the second. These are considered melodic rather than harmonic sequences because there is only one real "line" here: the upper part essentially doubles the bass line in octaves and adds embellishing tones. Transitions that incorporate motives from the first theme are called "dependent transitions," while those that introduce new material, like this one, are called "independent transitions."

With a dependent transition, it may be difficult to decide where the first theme group ends and where the transition begins—after all, they use the same thematic material. Listen for tonal function: if the passage sounds like it is leaving the tonic key, it is transitional. Independent transitions can be identified by the change in melodic material and by sequential activity, even when the modulation is delayed until the very end. The end of the transition may be marked by an abrupt silence, called a **medial caesura** ("caesura" means "pause"), sometimes preceded by a dramatic chord or octave leap, as in measure 22.

Measures 23–53, in the key of D major, constitute the "second tonal area," or **second theme group**. (Other possible terms include "secondary theme" or "subordinate theme.") The word "group" is especially apt here because the second theme group typically divides into a number of themes that may seem unrelated, except for the fact that they are united by a single key area: usually the dominant. Perhaps the best way to explore the organization of measures 23–53 is to look at their constituent motives, sequences, and phrases.

SUMMARY

The first large section of a major-key sonata form typically has two main parts, defined primarily by their key relationship: the first theme group expresses the tonic and the second theme group (usually) the dominant. The first theme group is usually shorter than the second, and the second may be subdivided into several thematically distinct units. The transition section modulates between the two groups.

Mozart's second theme group shows how many short thematic ideas—some stable melodies, others more transitional in nature—can work together in a single unified key area. Measures 23–31a present a syncopated melody that is clearly in D major, the second key area. The first phrase of this theme, measures 23–26 (Example 32.3), ends with a half cadence; then the phrase is repeated and varied in 27–30, also ending with a HC.

EXAMPLE 32.3: Mozart, Sonata in G Major, first movement, mm. 23–26 (second theme group)

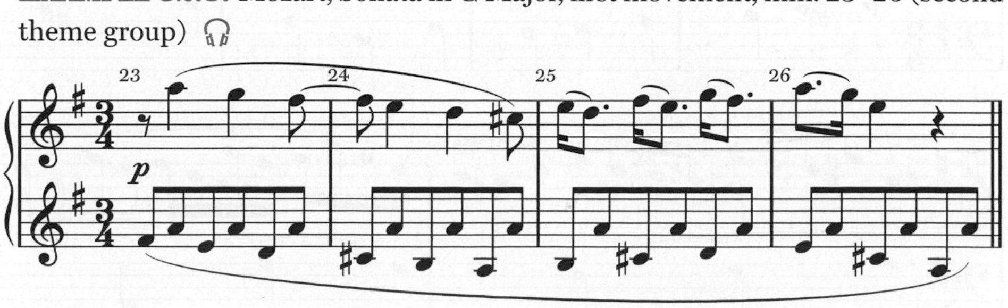

Measures 31–34 (Example 32.4) have a transitional character, because of the repeated motive and secondary leading-tone chords, but they do not modulate. They are followed by a harmonically stable progression in D major in 35–38a. Measures 38–43a are then a varied repetition of 33–38a.

Example 32.4: Mozart, Sonata in G Major, first movement, mm. 31–38a (second theme group)

Measures 43–44, based on a motive from the transition (mm. 16–18), connect to a final theme in 45–51a (Example 32.5). Some analysts call this another secondary theme; others refer to it as a **closing theme**, since it comes just before the close of the section. We will use the latter term, but with the understanding that the closing theme is really part of the second theme group when it expresses the same harmonic area (in this case, the dominant).

Example 32.5: Mozart, Sonata in G Major, first movement, mm. 45–51a (closing theme)

In sonata-form movements of the Romantic era, the closing theme may appear in a third key area, and it may include more than one distinct melody. In that case, it may be called the "third theme group," "closing theme group," or simply "closing group." The closing theme often contrasts in its motives or character with the second theme group. In this movement, however, the theme in measures 45–47 and 48–51a is reminiscent of the syncopated melody of 23–31, making a connection back to the beginning of the D major key area (compare Examples 32.3 and 32.5).

Finally, what is the function of measures 51–53 (Example 32.6)? There is a strong PAC on D in measure 51, but stopping the section there would seem abrupt. Measures 51–53 form a codetta that extends and repeats the cadence in D major.

Example 32.6: Mozart, Sonata in G Major, first movement, mm. 51–53 (codetta)

Although this first large section is similar to a continuous binary-form first section in its key areas, it is much longer and includes transitional passages and a codetta. In addition, it features three harmonically stable melodies (mm. 1–16a, 23–30a, and 45–51a), one in the tonic key and two in the dominant. This organization is typical of a sonata-form movement's first large section, called the **exposition** (in which the themes and motives for the entire movement are "exposed" for the first time).

SUMMARY

Typical Classical-era sonata-form expositions in major keys consist of the following sections:

First theme group	*Transition*	*Second theme group (optional codetta)*
Key: I	Modulates to V.	V (may include a closing theme, still in V)

The exposition is usually repeated. The first and second theme groups always contrast in key, and may present themes with contrasting moods. In some early sonata-form movements, particularly those of Haydn, the first and second themes are quite similar, differing primarily in their keys.

Minor-Key Expositions Sonata-form movements in minor keys follow a similar course, except that the second key area is usually the relative major (III) or, less often, the minor dominant (v).

KEY CONCEPT Typical Classical-era expositions in minor keys consist of the following sections:

First theme group	*Transition*	*Second theme group (optional codetta)*
Key: i	Modulates to III (or v).	III (or v) (may include a closing theme in the same key)

The Second Large Section

Before proceeding to the second large section of Mozart's sonata, you may want to listen again to the entire movement, while following the score. Listen for the return of the first and second theme groups (including the closing theme) in the second large section (pay close attention to measures 71b–120). This return of earlier material is another similarity between sonata form and rounded binary form, but the way the two forms treat the returning material is not identical: in rounded binary, sometimes only part of the music from the first section returns; in sonata form, the entire contents of the first section usually reappear, with some alterations.

The Return of Opening Material Compare measures 1–53 with 71b–120: what is alike and what is different? The return of the exposition in the second large section of a sonata form is called the **recapitulation** (meaning "return to the head," or beginning). When the exposition's material returns, however, some changes are customary: the recapitulation traditionally presents *all* of the exposition materials in the tonic key. The first theme, already in the tonic in the exposition, can usually be restated in the recapitulation with little or no alteration. What about this sonata? Compare the first theme group, measures 1–16, with the corresponding passage, shown in Example 32.7.

Example 32.7: Mozart, Sonata in G Major, first movement, mm. 71b–83a (recapitulation)

The first four measures of the first theme group return unchanged in the recapitulation, but the second half (4b–10a in the exposition) has been replaced with a variant; this passage tonicizes A minor (ii) by means of its secondary dominant (represented by the G♯s). The only part of the original that remains here is the rhythm of measures 79b–80, which corresponds to that of 12b–13.

The transition from the first to the second theme group, which modulates in the exposition, is usually modified in the recapitulation to stay in the original key. In this case, however, the transition passages are identical (compare mm. 16–22 with 83–89). Recall that in the exposition, the end of the transition could have been analyzed as a HC with V tonicized, except that the movement continued in the key of D. Here the cadence *is* treated as a HC—there is no modulation—and the movement continues in the tonic key, G. Perhaps, in retrospect, the changes to the second phrase of the first theme (mm. 75b–83a) were intended to balance the reappearance of the transition exactly as before.

In a typical sonata-form movement, the second theme group and codetta (if any) are transposed from the key of the dominant (in the exposition) to the original tonic for the recapitulation. We would therefore expect measures 90–120, corresponding to 23–53, to appear in G major—and they do.

Composers also generally make some slight changes in the second theme group when transposing it to the tonic key for the recapitulation. For example, a melody and its accompaniment, two contiguous phrases, or even repetitions of sequence patterns may be transposed up a fourth or down a fifth.

Try it #1

Compare the components of the second theme in the recapitulation with those in the exposition. What has been transposed up? What has been transposed down? Has anything been changed other than by transposition?

Harmonic Instability In a rounded binary form, we would expect the beginning of the second large section to display harmonic instability through a modulation or through sequences that touch on different keys; the same is true for Classical-era sonata-form movements. A quick glance at measures 54–71a reveals several chromatically inflected pitches.

Try it #2

Listen carefully to measures 54–71a again. Are there any places that seem to establish a temporary key? Do you hear a sequence or modulation or both? Is the musical material similar to anything you heard in the exposition?

The beginning of the second large section in a sonata-form movement is often called the **development**, because in sonatas by Beethoven and later Romantic-era composers, this section was devoted to the development and exploration of motives and themes from the exposition. A close examination of measures 54–62, though (Example 32.8), reveals few connections to the motives of the exposition. Instead, the dominant is prolonged through its own dominant (hence the C♯s). Mozart's treatment of the "development" is typical for sonata-form movements of his time. In essence, this section is simply an expanded version of the same type of harmonic instability and sequential material that would be found in a rounded binary form.

EXAMPLE 32.8: Mozart, Sonata in G Major, first movement, mm. 54–62a (development)

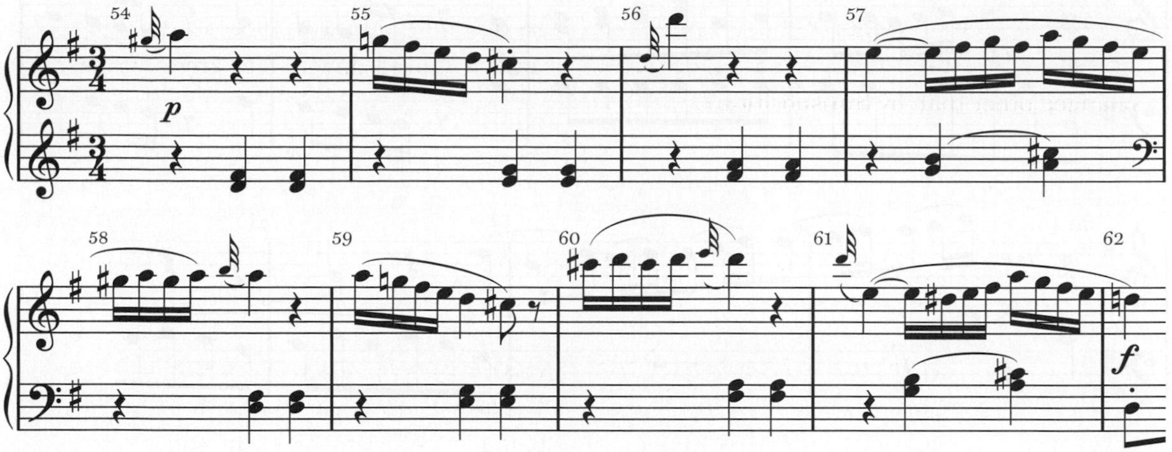

The Retransition After the harmonic instability of the development section, there are a few measures that perform a special task: preparing for the return of music from the opening of the piece. This part of the development, called the **retransition**, serves as a connector between the development and recapitulation sections. It sets up the return of the first theme harmonically—by establishing and often prolonging the V^7 chord of the tonic key. The retransition also sets the mood for the first theme's return. In some sonata-form movements, it builds tension, making the listener anticipate the first theme's triumphant return; in others, it brings back the first theme almost as a surprise—the listener does not even hear it coming. Other dramatic roles for the retransition are possible, but the harmonic function of this passage is consistent: to establish the dominant seventh chord of the tonic key.

In Mozart's sonata, the retransition features a long dominant pedal, extending from measure 62 to 68 (Example 32.9). This rearticulated pedal point, with a melodic sequence above it, builds tension but does not immediately connect to the return of the first theme. Instead, Mozart inserts two ascending pentachords (68–70a), each ending with a brief rest, as if to say, "Not yet, not yet." Then, in 70–71, a descending scalar pattern brings back the first theme.

EXAMPLE 32.9: Mozart, Sonata in G Major, first movement, mm. 62–73a (retransition)

Listen to this retransition in several different performances: in some, the pianist will slow measures 68 and 69 noticeably, perhaps extending the rests, to heighten anticipation of the resolution in measure 72; in others, the performer maintains a consistent tempo throughout. How would you perform this passage?

SUMMARY

The second large section of Classical-era sonata-form movements includes the development and recapitulation sections. This section is usually repeated, and may end with a coda.

Development sections may explore thematic material from the exposition or may simply represent an area of harmonic instability. In early sonata forms, the development section is usually brief compared with the exposition and recapitulation.

Typical Classical-era recapitulations consist of the following sections:

First theme group	*Transition*	*Second theme group*
Key: I (or i)	Altered to stay in tonic.	I (or i) (may include a closing theme still in tonic) optional codetta and/or coda

Sonata Form in the Romantic Era

(anthology) The rise of the Romantic style brought changes and new developments to sonata form. We will consider some of these changes as they appear in the first movement of Beethoven's *Waldstein* Sonata. Listen to the entire movement while following the score in your anthology. While listening, mark any formal elements you notice—themes, transitions, phrases, cadences, key areas, and so on—and try to identify the main parts of the form. Some Romantic-era sonata forms also add a slow introduction and lengthy coda—does this one?

Increasing Length and Complexity

Some differences between the Mozart and Beethoven movements that are immediately apparent are the length—302 measures for the Beethoven, 120 for the Mozart—and the later sonata's chromatic and exuberant Romantic character. Scan through the score to find the repeat signs marking the end of the exposition (with a first and second ending, mm. 86 and 87). After you have identified the first theme as beginning in measure 1 (there is no slow introduction), mark the beginning of the recapitulation (m. 156). In the Romantic era, the development grew to balance the exposition in length and complexity, overlaying a ternary element—exposition (**A**), development (**B**), recapitulation (**A′**)—on the formerly binary-based organization.

On hearing this work for the first time, you may have noticed the complexity of the harmonic choices, particularly as compared with the Mozart movement: mode mixture, embellishing and harmonically functional chromaticism, and sequences associated with Romantic-era harmony are all present.

Key Areas and the Organization of the Exposition

Listen again to the exposition of the *Waldstein*'s first movement, and consider these questions: Are the themes and transitions located where you would expect, based on the Mozart sonata model? Are the key areas what you would expect?

The first idea of the first theme group is four measures long (like the Mozart sonata's first phrase), ending on a tonicized half cadence (see Example 32.10). In an earlier Classical-era sonata, the first phrase probably would have been followed by a phrase of similar length and character that ended with a conclusive cadence, making a period structure to firmly establish the tonic key. Here, however, the initial idea is abruptly transposed down a whole step to B♭ major (♭VII). This dramatic shift in harmony brings in elements of mode mixture, E♭ and B♭, which are present through the C minor half cadence in measures 11–13. Measures 1–4, 5–8, and the elaboration in 9–13 of the first theme group display elements of a sentence structure, but with Romantic-era modification and Beethovian innovation: here, the harmony of the second phrase is ♭VII rather than the more typical V, and the length of the third phrase is an asymmetrical five measures. There is no strong cadence in C major in the first theme group; the movement's first PAC in C major appears only at the end of the exposition, measures 85–86, to prepare the exposition's repeat.

Example 32.10: Beethoven, *Waldstein* Sonata, first movement, mm. 1–13 (first theme group)

On first listening, measures 14–17 sound like a rhythmic variation of 1–4, but in 18 the passage begins to veer in a new harmonic direction—to D minor (ii) rather than B♭ major—and with a chromatic inflection in 22, the passage decisively moves away from the first key area, leading toward the second key (see Example 32.11). (Two layers of Roman numerals show two possible harmonic readings of this passage.) Measure 14 is the beginning of the transition—a "dependent transition" because it sounds so much like a variant of the opening phrase. Measures 23–30 continue the transition section with a prolonged B major (and B dominant seventh) chord expanded by an E minor $\substack{6\\4}$, chromatically embellished, which implies a move to E minor (iii in C major). It dissipates into a B major arpeggiation in 29–30, then connects to an ascending scale fragment (doubled in octaves) in 31–34, which leads to E major (not minor!) on the downbeat of measure 35.

EXAMPLE 32.11: Beethoven, *Waldstein* Sonata, first movement, mm. 14–23 (dependent transition, first part)

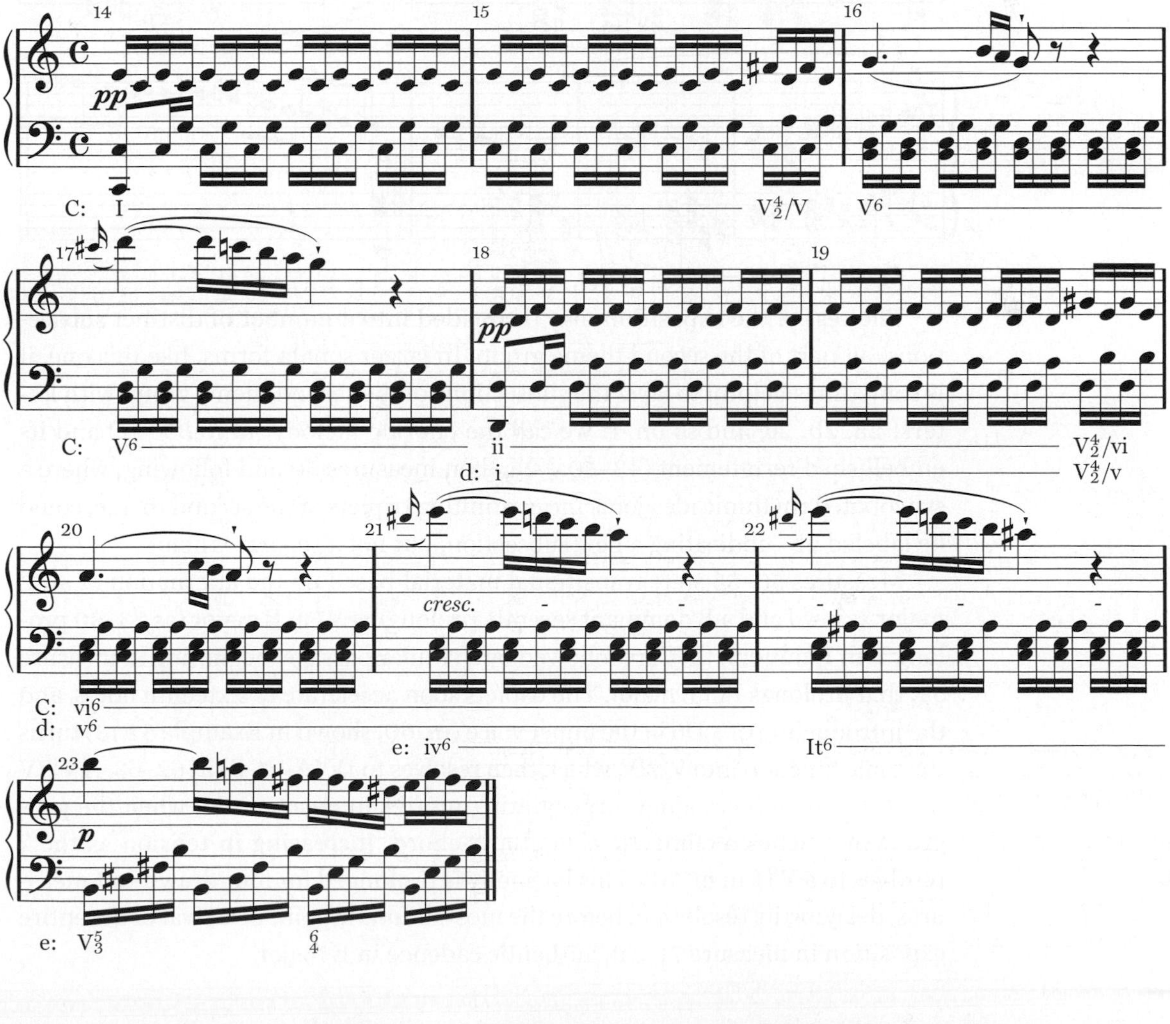

The E major theme that begins in measure 35 initiates the second theme group (Example 32.12), identified by its harmonic stability, regular phrase lengths, and chorale-style voicing. The key here is the chromatic mediant, not the expected G major (dominant) of the Classical-era movement. This type of harmonic innovation is a hallmark of Romantic sonatas. The eight-measure second theme is then followed immediately by a variation (mm. 43–50a), with the chorale decorated by a triplet melody in the highest part.

EXAMPLE 32.12: Beethoven, *Waldstein* Sonata, first movement, mm. 35–42a (second theme)

The rest of the exposition may be divided into a number of distinct subsections, all part of the second theme group. In larger sonata forms, like this one, it is sometimes helpful to label the subsections of the second theme group with letters: 2a, 2b, 2c, and so on. If we call the chorale melody (mm. 35–42) and its embellished restatement (43–50a) 2a, then measures 50 and following, where a syncopated rhythmic idea joins the continuing triplets of the second theme, could be labeled 2b—indicating a new subsection, but not a separate theme.

Measures 50–53 state transitional material based on the alternation of an E major $^6_4$ chord and a B dominant seventh, prolonging V^7 in E major (as 23–30 prolong V in E minor); they are followed by a similar passage, beginning in measure 54, that prolongs I in E major. The triplets soon accelerate to sixteenth notes, and the introduction of a D6 in the upper voice (m. 60, shown in Example 32.13) turns the tonic function into V^6_5/IV, which then resolves to IV (A-C♯-E) in 62–63. A V^6_5/V in 64–65 introduces a new arpeggiating motive in measure 66, when the progression reaches a climactic cadential $^6_4$ chord, increasing in tension as the $^6_4$ resolves to a V^9_7 (in m. 70). This harmony is prolonged for four drawn-out measures, delaying its resolution, before the most dramatic point of arrival of the entire exposition in measure 74—an authentic cadence in E major.

EXAMPLE 32.13: Beethoven, *Waldstein* Sonata, mm. 59–74

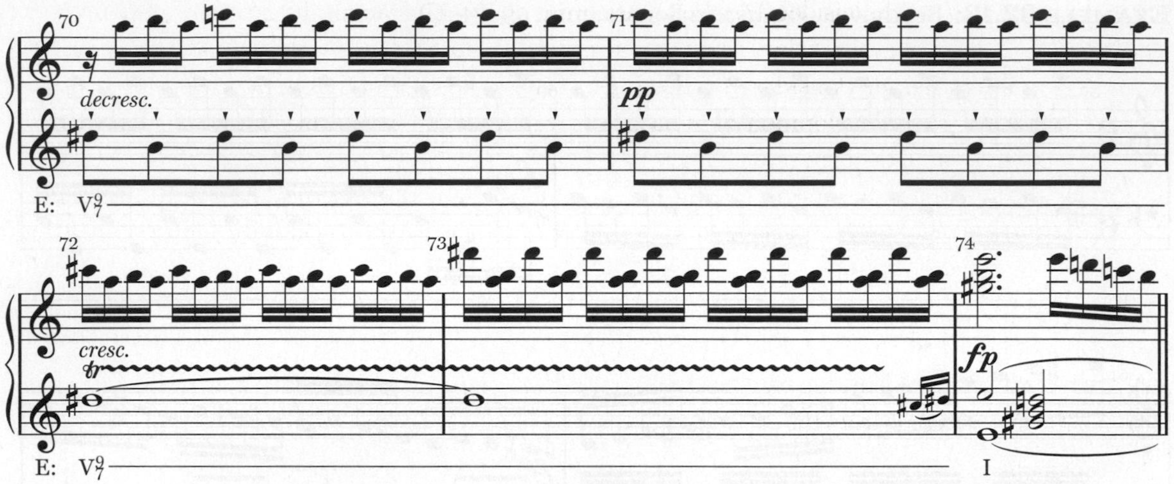

The cadence initiates a new subsection in measure 74, which we could call 2c. This passage might be labeled the closing theme (still part of the E major second key area), but a better term would be codetta, since it follows harmonic closure in E major and since it serves a dual role—as preparation for the repetition of the exposition and for the sequence that connects to the development section.

Try it #3

There are many motivic links between themes in this movement. Where, for example, have you heard the upper part of measures 74–76a before? What is the origin of the left-hand material here?

Mm. 74–76, right hand, are similar to mm. ________________.

Mm. 74–77, left hand, are drawn from mm. ________________.

The Development Section

In a typical Classical-era sonata-form movement, the development section is easy to locate: it begins after the repeat markings, usually following the exposition's definitive final cadence. For this Romantic-era sonata, the situation is much less clear-cut. Listen again to this movement through measure 90 to identify the beginning of the development. The sequence in 80b–89 is what makes locating it difficult. This sequence, the first time through, modulates from E minor back to C major for the repeat of the exposition; yet the second time through, the same music keeps spinning on past C to cadence in measure 90 (on F major), with a motion so smooth that it is hardly noticeable.

To consider this question more broadly, think about the developmental aspects of the exposition: what are measures 14–22 if not a "development" of the primary theme? Consider also the "variation" of the second theme in 43–50a; that activity is developmental in nature as well. One of Beethoven's innovations in writing sonata-form movements was the incorporation of the principle of development into all aspects of the movement, not just the development section. Other Romantic era composers to a greater or lesser extent followed his lead. Here, the development section is measures 90–156a.

Try it #4

Which of the materials in the exposition does Beethoven explore in the development section? Identify three elements from the exposition and where they are developed (give measure numbers).

	Element	*Measures*	*Where developed*
(a)	______________________	__________	______________
(b)	______________________	__________	______________
(c)	______________________	__________	______________

Now locate the harmonic goal of the development: the retransition, which normally prolongs a V7 of the primary key (here G7), preparing for the key's return in the recapitulation. The first G7 comes in measure 136, but the texture and rhythm of this passage connect it to the sequential passage that came before. A better location for the retransition is measure 142, where the texture and rhythm change and a new section clearly begins. This retransition is quite long and dramatic, beginning with the introduction of a "rumbling motive" and G pedal point in the bass. The development process continues through the retransition, with the continued exploration of the sixteenth-note motive that originated from measure 3 of the first theme.

Of the many motives developed in measures 90–156, we will focus on two especially prominent ones, shown in Example 28.14: the skip up a third with a stepwise return (the "skip motive"), and the descending five-note scale (the "scale motive"). The derivation of these motives from the first theme should be obvious; the variants and repetitions in 94–111 are numerous and also fairly obvious. Now think about their role in the retransition: the "rumble" in the left hand in measure 142 might be considered a combination of the skip motive and the scale motive. The ascending fragments in the right hand in 146–156a also feature rhythms that are reminiscent of the skip motive's sixteenths without the opening dotted quarter, and the contour of those fragments is that of the skip motive inverted; other fragments seem related to the scale motive, again ascending instead of descending.

EXAMPLE 32.14: Two motives from Beethoven's *Waldstein* Sonata, first movement

The harmonic activity in the development is interesting as well. Most of the development is composed of descending-fifth sequences. A glance at the accidentals indicates that the mode mixture of the exposition is featured here as well. Some of the tonal areas briefly tonicized include G minor (v in C major; mm. 96–99a), C minor (i; 100–103), F minor (iv; 104)—a pattern of descending fifths. Then beginning in measure 112, Beethoven initiates another extended descending-fifth sequence, including tonicizations of C major (I; 112–113), F major (IV; 116–117), B♭ major (♭VII; 120–121), E♭ minor (♭iii; 124–125), and B minor (vii; 128–129). While these tonicizations are brief, each may be identified by the presence of at least a dominant seventh chord and its resolution to the temporary tonic. In addition, some of these sequences include a chain of secondary dominants, a particularly common type of chromatic sequence.

The Recapitulation and Coda

In the recapitulation, beginning in measure 156, we expect each of the main parts of the exposition to return in order, all in the tonic key. The first theme does return essentially unchanged, as measures 156–168, with one unusual and striking difference: the arpeggiated C minor triad (m. 167, shown in Example 32.15) is followed by with a deceptive move to A♭, instead of the expected G. Another arpeggiation in measure 169 spans a D♭ major chord, then ends on B♭ (a surprising change from the Classical tonic return). Measures 167–173 explore more deeply the modal mixture only hinted at in the first theme of the exposition.

EXAMPLE 32.15: Beethoven, *Waldstein* Sonata, first movement, mm. 166–176

Try it #5

Write in a Roman numeral analysis for measures 167–174 in Example 32.15. For measures with only one member of a chord, assume it is the root of a triad.

After three measures (171–173) of new material, measures 14–21 return as 174–181; measure 22 is expanded and altered as 182–183; and measures 23–34 reappear as 184–195. Since the transition section in a recapitulation no longer needs to serve a modulatory function, it is usually altered, often extended, so that its sequential motion will return to the tonic key. Here, however, the chorale theme (the first part of the second theme group, originally mm. 35–50a) extends from 196 to 211a in A major, the chromatic submediant—or is it A minor (look at 200–203)? The transition in 184–195 is altered to move toward A major instead of staying in C major.

In measure 200, the mode shifts to A minor, in part to bring back the expected key of C major for the triplet variation (204–211a), followed by the return of 50–74a, now in C major (211–235a). The codetta starts off in measure 235 in C major, incorporating elements of mixture even more, as evidenced by all the flats. Measures 241b–249a present the sequence that connected the exposition and the development. Compare 245–249 with 86 (second ending)–90a: both statements suggest motion toward F major by transforming the C major tonic to a C^7: V^7/IV.

The second time, however, the passage is colored through mixture to F minor, and the V7 resolves deceptively, to ♭VI (D♭ major, m. 249), to begin the coda. Though surprising and quite far afield from C major, this D♭ arrival is prepared by the ♭II (Neapolitan) in the extension to the first theme in the recapitulation (m. 169), and also briefly in the development section (m. 134).

There are now almost three pages of music left, indicating that this coda is longer than some entire sonata-form movements. Uncharacteristically, there was no PAC in C major to initiate the coda. Further, the second theme has yet to reappear in the tonic key. This coda has the character and structure of another development section—it is a Beethovenian innovation, the "developmental coda." Measures 249–277 precede another retransition in 278–283 that ends on a strong and convincing V7 in the key of C major (Example 32.16). The resolution of the V7 in 284 forms a PAC that is elided with the "missing" second theme in C major. At the cadence in 295, all the tasks of the recapitulation are completed. A brief codetta based on the main theme finally brings the movement to an end.

Example 32.16: Beethoven, *Waldstein* Sonata, first movement, mm. 281–292

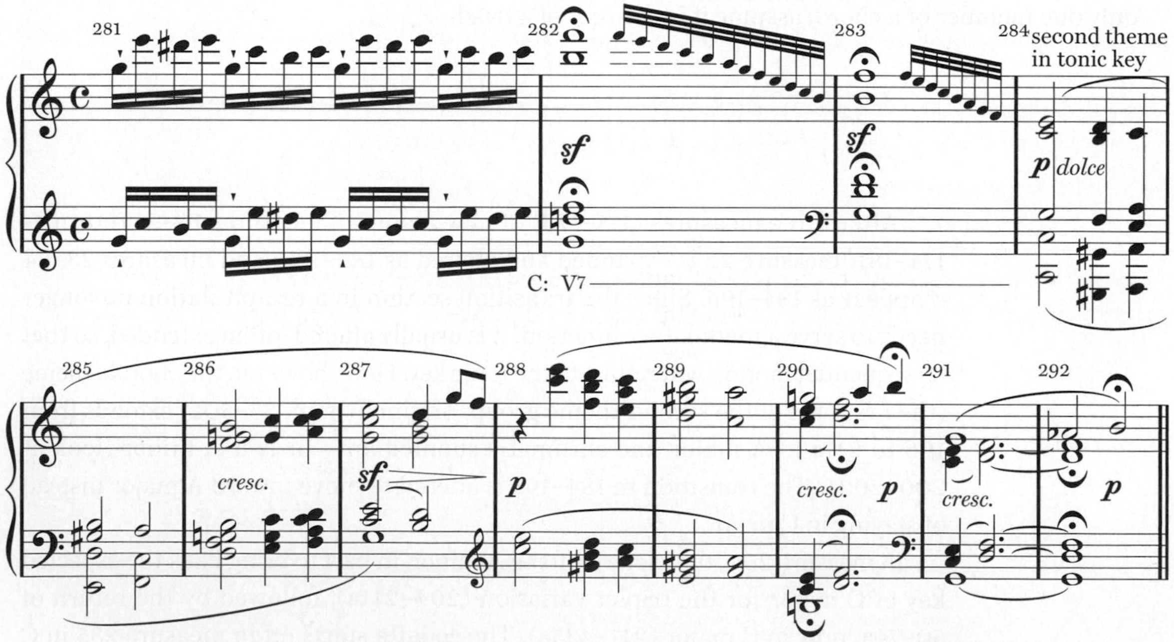

SUMMARY

The exposition section of Romantic-era sonata forms usually includes several distinct contrasting themes. The two key areas are typically tonic and dominant (major key) and tonic and relative major (minor key), but contrasting keys (including distant keys) may also be explored. In late Romantic movements, a third key is sometimes introduced in the closing theme. The exposition in Romantic (and some Classical) movements may be preceded by an introduction, possibly in a contrasting tempo and/or key area. The exposition may be repeated.

The development and recapitulation of Romantic-era sonata forms are sometimes paired as a section and repeated, as in Classical sonatas, but often constitute separate sections that are near-equal in length. The movement may end with a substantial coda, which includes additional development of the themes.

Typical development sections explore thematic material or motives from the exposition and may feature sequences, modulation to distant keys, harmonic instability, or even a new theme. The retransition normally follows the pattern of Classical sonatas by prolonging V7.

Related Forms

The term "sonata" technically refers to a multimovement composition for piano, or a solo-line instrument (such as the violin) and piano. Sonatas typically comprise three or four movements. The first is almost always in sonata form, sometimes called "sonata-allegro form" after the typical tempo marking for such movements. Mozart's Sonata in C Major (anthology p. 256) is an example of a three-movement sonata: the first movement is sonata-allegro, the second a slow movement (*Andante*), and the third a rousing rondo. The last movement may also be in sonata form.

A **sonatina** is simply what it sounds like—a little sonata. The first movement is usually in an abbreviated sonata form. Sonatinas may have a very short development section (about the same scope as the **B** section in a rounded binary) or no development at all. Their first and second themes are also typically compact (often four to eight measures), without long transitions. Sonatina form is distinguished from rounded binary by the presence of themes, transitions, development, and other elements of sonata form—only on a reduced scale. Sonatinas are associated with Classical-era composers, but these "little sonatas" were written in the Romantic era as well, usually composed for children or beginning players.

Concerto Form

Concertos—compositions for a solo instrument and orchestra—often consist of three movements, arranged fast-slow-fast, that follow a formal pattern similar to the three-movement sonata. Concerto first movements are usually based on sonata form, but alternate sections featuring the orchestra and the soloist. In early Classical-era concertos, often the first movement is written with a "double exposition." That is, the orchestra begins the movement by playing both the first and/or second theme group in the tonic key, without the soloist. Then the ensemble plays material from the exposition a second time, this time featuring the solo instrument (with the orchestra playing an accompanimental role) and with the standard modulation to the dominant or relative-major key. The double-exposition format is not maintained in the recapitulation, however, where the orchestra and soloist share thematic material more equally. In later Romantic-era concertos, the double exposition was less favored; indeed, some concertos begin with the solo performer.

Concertos are showcases for virtuosic performers. Nowhere are their talents more evident than in the **cadenza**, a solo passage that features rapid passagework and technical challenges. It is generally positioned between the end of the recapitulation and the beginning of the coda, and is prepared harmonically by a cadential $^6_4$ chord played by the orchestra, which the soloist expands. The cadenza's end is signaled in the solo instrument by a prominent scale degree $\hat{2}$ (often with a trill or other ornamentation) over a dominant-function harmony, which resolves to the tonic with the beginning of the coda (and the entrance once again of the orchestra).

In Classical concertos, it was expected that the soloist would improvise the cadenza (or prepare it in advance): here, performers could showcase both their technical and compositional skills. In later concertos, cadenzas were more often composed. Today, most concerto editions include a cadenza written out by the composer, a different composer, a reputable soloist, or the editor after the style of a particular performer.

Large Ternary Form

The **large ternary form** is an extended movement with three large sections, usually **A B A′**. As in simple and composite ternary, the **A** sections are normally harmonically closed—beginning and ending in the tonic key—but the **B** section may be modulatory and unstable, and may end in a different key; in Romantic works, it may explore different keys. The sections may be connected by a transition and a retransition, though, as in rondo forms, the latter is more common. Like other large movements, the large ternary movement typically ends with a coda. Second movements of multimovement works may take a large ternary form, with a slow tempo and ornamentation like that in an instrumental da capo aria (another ternary design), but this formal plan is also used for free-standing pieces, such as Brahms's Intermezzo in A Major.

Seven-Part Rondo and Sonata-Rondo

Seven-part rondos are generally extended movements, with longer refrains and episodes than the five-part rondo. A typical design for a seven-part rondo is shown below. The **C** section is often much longer than the other sections; it is usually developmental but may be in a small, self-contained binary or ternary form. The transitions and retransitions between sections are not shown on the chart, but typical locations are given with arrows. These sections are generally more extended in seven-part than five-part rondos. When a seven-part rondo includes a developmental center section, and extended transitions and retransitions between the refrain and contrasting sections, it is generally considered a **sonata-rondo**—a movement that exhibits elements of both sonata form and rondo.

	Exposition			Development	Recapitulation			
	A	**B**	**A**	**C**	**A**	**B′** (or **D**)	**A**	**Coda**
Major key:	I–I	V* ⟶	I–I	i* ⟶ dev ⟶	I–I	I (or i)	I	
Minor key:	i–i	III or v* ⟶	i–i	I* ⟶ dev ⟶	i–i	i (or I)	i	

*or other contrasting key

As in some Romantic-era sonata forms, the sections may group into an overall tripartite design corresponding to an exposition, development, and recapitulation: the initial **A B A** (exposition) might express the tonal areas I–V–I (or i–III–i), with the **C** section (development) providing large-scale contrast through its key area(s) and developmental character, and the final **A B′A** (recapitulation) typically returning in the tonic key. The sonata-rondo differs from sonata form in that the "exposition" ends with a return of the **A** section (refrain) in the tonic key, instead of staying in the second key area and presenting a closing or codetta theme; the **A** section likewise returns at the end of the "recapitulation." The entire movement typically ends with a coda, as do most sonata and larger ternary form movements.

Performing and Listening to Sonata-Form Movements

When you perform or listen to a movement in sonata form, your familiarity with its expected structure should help you to understand, convey, and remember the movement better. Here are some questions you might ask as you prepare or listen.

Which passages exhibit a stable key area? Where are there clear phrases? What is the character of each theme—is it stolid, humorous, energetic, lyrical? What musical clues help you decide? Which passages are transitional? What is the intended effect of a transition—do the harmonies and melodic patterns indicate increasing tension that is released with the arrival of the new key, or is the section designed to flow to the new key area without the listener even noticing?

In the development section, are there motives that should be brought out by the performer? What is the affect of the development: mysterious, agitated, seemingly aimless, joyous? Which keys are visited and where? At what point do the harmonies begin to turn toward the home key by reestablishing the dominant? Is the retransition intended to build tension, to be released as the first theme reappears? Or does the return come as a surprise?

When the music from the exposition returns in the recapitulation, what has changed? Are there coda and codetta passages? Do the closing sections bring the piece to a gentle end, or do they end with a flourish?

Finally, consider the date of composition and the style of the movement; that information will provide important clues to the form. Classical-era pieces need to be played cleanly, with lightness, precision, and grace. In the Romantic era, on the other hand, the overt expression of emotion was valued and encouraged, and your performance can bring such emotions to the fore.

Think also about the drama that unfolds in the sonata you are playing. If you are a listener, ask what the performer is trying to convey. Music is about so much more than simply "music"—it expresses the emotion and flow of life. A musician who only plays the correct notes and the durations is like an actor who reads a text accurately, but without feeling. If you are the performer, enjoy the dramatic aspects of this extended form, and your audience will, too.

Did You Know?

Beethoven's *Waldstein* Sonata gets its name from its dedicatee, Count Ferdinand Ernst Gabriel von Waldstein, a German count and patron of the arts. Count Waldstein recognized the young composer's talent and in 1787 accompanied Beethoven on a visit from Bonn to Vienna, the city he would make his home (five years later) and where he would achieve his fame. Waldstein also arranged for Beethoven to meet Mozart on that first visit, and later recommended him to Joseph Haydn. Though Waldstein is primarily known today as an early admirer, patron, and personal friend of Beethoven, he led an extraordinary life as a diplomat. He expended much of his fortune raising an army in an attempt to defeat Napoleon in the Napoleonic Wars, then traveled to London in 1796 and joined the British army, before finally returning to Vienna and his estates in 1809. After depleting his wealth in unwise expenditures, he died in poverty in 1823.

TERMS YOU SHOULD KNOW

- cadenza
- closing theme
- coda
  - developmental coda
- codetta
- concerto
- development
- exposition
  - double exposition
- first theme group
- large ternary
- medial caesura
- recapitulation
- retransition
- second theme group
- seven-part rondo
- sonata
- sonata (sonata-allegro) form
- sonata rondo
- sonatina
- transition

QUESTIONS FOR REVIEW

1. What key areas are expected in the exposition of a sonata-form movement in a major key? in a minor key?
2. What characteristics distinguish the first theme group from the second theme group?
3. Where are you likely to find a codetta? What are the characteristics of a codetta?
4. What are some typical elements of a development? How do you identify where a development section starts? How do you locate the retransition?
5. How is the material from the exposition typically changed when it reappears in the recapitulation? Where are changes expected? Why?
6. How is Classical-era sonata form like a continuous rounded binary form? How are the two forms different?
7. What are some differences between Romantic- and Classical-era sonata form?
8. How do you identify themes? transitional passages? In performance, how might you differentiate between themes and transitional passages?

9. What characteristics are common to sonata form and large ternary form? sonata form and sonata-rondo form?
10. How might knowing that a piece is in sonata form save you time in preparing and memorizing the music? Which sections might you compare as you prepare the work for performance?
11. In music for your own instrument, or for a symphony or string quartet, find an example of one of the forms described in this chapter. How does the movement correspond to the description presented in the chapter?

PART IV

The Twentieth Century and Beyond

CHAPTER 33 Modes, Scales, and Sets

Outline of topics

Listening to twentieth-century compositions

Pitch-class collections and scales revisited

- Analyzing mode and scale types
- Sets and subsets
- Composing with diatonic modes
- Pentatonic scales

Other types of scales

- Whole-tone scales
- Octatonic scales

Scale analysis and formal design

Overview

This chapter focuses on scales and pitch-class collections other than major and minor, and introduces the terminology musicians have developed to discuss the motives, chords, and compositional techniques heard in twentieth-century music.

Repertoire

Béla Bartók
- "Five-Tone Scale," from *Mikrokosmos* (No. 78)
- "Song of the Harvest," for two violins

Claude Debussy, "Voiles," from *Preludes*, Book I

Maurice Ravel, "Aoua!" from *Chansons madécasses*

Igor Stravinsky, "Lento," from *For the Five Fingers*

Anton Webern, String Quartet, Op. 5, third movement

Listening to Twentieth-Century Compositions

In this chapter, you will listen to works by five prominent composers of the early twentieth century: Béla Bartók, Claude Debussy, Maurice Ravel, Igor Stravinsky, and Anton Webern. Although their works are very different, these composers employ some of the same compositional techniques. None of the pieces follow the conventions of functional tonality discussed thus far. Here and in the following chapters, we will learn new ways composers organize musical ideas in the absence of functional tonality.

Listen first to two works for strings, Bartók's "Song of the Harvest" and the third movement of Webern's String Quartet, Op. 5—first without the music, then following your anthology scores. As you listen, consider the following, and be ready to discuss your responses in class:

- Can you hum a tonic at any point in the piece?
- How is musical form articulated? Can you identify phrases or distinct sections, changes in motive, texture, or mood?
- Can you hear familiar compositional techniques (transposition, imitation, inversion)?
- What musical features contribute to your emotional reaction to the piece?

Mark on your score any of these aspects you notice.

When you analyze music of the twentieth or twenty-first century, don't make the mistake of working solely from the score. Always take time to listen, preferably several times through, then use your musical intuitions to make basic observations about form, phrase, imitation, variation, contrast, and other elements. Such observations will inform your more detailed analysis and give you a deeper appreciation for the music.

Pitch-Class Collections and Scales Revisited

Many stylistic features make the Bartók and Webern pieces sound different from each other. Webern's features shorter motives and fuller instrumentation than Bartók's; it also covers a wider range and calls for numerous string effects—for example, *pizzicato* (plucking rather than bowing the strings) and *col legno* (playing with the wood, rather than the hair, of the bow). Bartók employs longer melodic lines and easily perceived patterns of imitation between the two violin parts. He incorporates tempo and meter changes, as well as the transposed repetition of melodies, to distinguish between musical sections. The collections of pitch classes (or pcs) these composers choose also give the works their distinct sounds.

Remember that a pitch class represents all the pitches that sound exactly one or more octaves apart—for example, C4, C6, C3, B♯2, and D𝄫5. The term invokes both enharmonic equivalence (C and B♯) and octave equivalence (C4 and C6).

KEY CONCEPT The word "collection" refers to a group of pitch classes that serves as a source of musical materials for a work or a section of a work. Examine the pitch-class materials of a piece by "collecting" them and writing them in ascending order, without repetitions.

Listen to the two short works excerpted below. Beneath each example, the pitch-class collection is given. Consider how the collections differ, and whether there is one pitch class that seems more important than the others.

Example 33.1: Webern, String Quartet, Op. 5, third movement, mm. 6–7 (anthology)

Pitch-class collection: C♯ D E♭ E♮ F F♯ G G♯ A B♭ B♮ C♮ (C♯)

Example 33.2: Bartók, "Song of the Harvest," mm. 30–33 (anthology)

Pitch-class collection: E♭ F G♭ A♭ B♭ C♭ D♭ (E♭)

Were you able to hum a tonic while listening to the Webern movement? Probably not, since Webern features all twelve pcs in this composition—a complete chromatic collection—without strongly emphasizing any one pc over the others. Music that does not establish a tonic or tonal hierarchy is called **nontonal** (or **atonal**) music to distinguish it from music that does, or **post-tonal** to signal that this style emerged after the era of tonal music.

KEY CONCEPT Recall that tonal music is characterized by

- melodies built from major and minor scales, whose scale-degree functions point toward the tonic (for example, $\hat{7}$ resolves to $\hat{1}$);
- harmonies that relate to each other in functional progressions leading toward a tonic harmony;
- identifiable embellishing tones (dissonant suspensions, neighbor or passing tones) that resolve, or imply a resolution.

Music lacking one or more of these organizational conventions is nontonal music.

In contrast with pitches in the Webern movement, Bartók's E♭4 (the first and last pitch of Example 33.2) does seem to provide a strong starting and ending point for the excerpt. This E♭ serves a similar function to the tonic in a tonal piece, even though "Song of the Harvest" is not built on functional harmonies. The other pitches of the phrase seem to expand outward from the E♭4 and converge back to form a cadence. We will therefore use the terms "phrase" and "cadence" when they seem musically appropriate, even in nontonal contexts. When you apply these terms, be sure to indicate what musical features lead you to hear a nontonal passage as a complete musical thought, or phrase, with a close at the end.

KEY CONCEPT A pitch or pc that appears pervasively in a work (or section) and establishes a sense of hierarchy is called a **center**, and music that features it **centric** music. Traditional tonal music technically falls within the centric category.

Nontonal music may be centric *or* noncentric. In noncentric nontonal music, the pervasive chromaticism, symmetrical interval patterns, and absence of familiar scale segments make it difficult to identify a "tonic" pitch class or hierarchy. In centric nontonal music, you can sense a hierarchy that is different from that of common-practice tonality; list this type of pc collection as a scale, starting and ending with the pc center.

Even in fully chromatic nontonal works such as the Webern movement, some pitch classes may be more prominent than others in a portion of the piece because of repetition, registral placement, duration, or other means. All pitch classes need not be treated equally in nontonal music. Look, for example, at the complete score of the Webern movement in your anthology. Consider the pitch class C♯, which begins and ends the movement in the cello, and functions as an ostinato. (An **ostinato** is a rhythmic or melodic motive that is repeated successively, to tie a passage together.) This C♯ helps provide cohesiveness to the opening section of the movement and some measure of closure when it returns at the end; but it is emphasized only through repetition. It does not function as a pitch-class center here because there is no sense of hierarchy between the C♯ and the other pcs.

KEY CONCEPT Pitches or pcs that are emphasized through repetition or motivic use, but that do not establish a functional hierarchy, are called **focal pitches** or **pcs**. Focal pitches or pcs are not tonics because they do not imply a functional system of scale degrees in any key or mode. And they are not centers because they do not imply any hierarchy among the remaining pitches of the collection.

Analyzing Mode and Scale Types

Look back now at Example 33.2, the end of "Song of the Harvest," and its pc collection. If you begin on E♭ (the cadential resting point) and list all the pitch classes, you get the familiar scale E♭ natural minor. But because the piece does not speak the familiar melodic and harmonic functional language of tonal music, the modal name is used for this pitch-class collection: E♭ Aeolian.

KEY CONCEPT

1. When analyzing a piece of nontonal music, first identify the collection of pitch classes from which it is composed, by listing each pc in ascending order, without repetitions.
2. Listen to determine whether the pitches or pcs relate hierarchically to a stable center. If they do, then rewrite your list in ascending order beginning with the centric pc.
3. A nontonal piece may have no pc center: all pcs may be treated equally, or one or more may be emphasized as focal pitches or pcs (but without a sense of centric hierarchy).

Sets and Subsets

The study of nontonal compositions requires some additional terminology to identify meaningful musical relationships.

KEY CONCEPT The term **set** refers to a group of pitches (pset) or pitch classes (pcset). The pitches or pcs in a set are called its **elements**. List elements of a set only once. While "set" and "collection" may be used interchangeably, collections are generally considered to be sets of five elements or more. It is sometimes useful to refer to only some of a set's elements; in that case, the smaller grouping is called a **subset**.

The Bartók excerpt in Example 33.2 includes only seven pitches of the chromatic scale; they make up a subset of the chromatic collection. These seven pitches are divided between the two violin parts so that each part consists of a four-element subset (a tetrachord) of the larger seven-element collection.

KEY CONCEPT A group of pitches or pcs is often referred to by a single word that specifies its number of elements, or **cardinality**. Among the terms you should know:

two elements—interval, or dyad
three elements—trichord
four elements—tetrachord
five elements—pentachord
six elements—hexachord
seven elements—heptachord, or heptad
eight elements—octachord, or octad
nine elements—nonachord, or nonad

A trichord has a cardinality of 3, a hexachord has a cardinality of 6, and so on.

Composing with Diatonic Modes

In the twentieth and twenty-first centuries, composers have discovered new possibilities for the diatonic modes. For one thing, unlike their predecessors, modern composers typically transpose modal materials to begin on any pitch class; the Aeolian mode, for instance, need not begin and end on A. The E♭ Aeolian of Example 33.2 is a good example, and its unconventional key signature (different for each violin) is also characteristic of Bartók's musical notation. Contemporary composers are more likely to draw on all possible modal rotations of the diatonic scale, including the **Locrian mode** (the B-to-B rotation of the C major scale), which was avoided in Renaissance works because of its prominent tritone. Some composers create mixed modes by combining a distinctive portion of one diatonic mode with another. For example, the **Lydian-Mixolydian mode** (C D E F♯ G A B♭ C) is derived from the lower pentachord of the Lydian mode and the upper tetrachord of the Mixolydian. Jazz musicians also call this mode the "Lydian-dominant," or "overtone scale." The Lydian-Mixolydian mode is not a diatonic mode, however, since it is not a rotation of the major scale.

KEY CONCEPT When you analyze modal passages, use your ear to decide whether the third scale degree is major or minor. Then refer to this chart to determine which mode you hear.

Modes with $\hat{3}$:

- Ionian —identical to major
- Mixolydian —like major, but with $\flat\hat{7}$
- Lydian —like major, but with $\sharp\hat{4}$
- Lydian-Mixolydian —like major, but with $\sharp\hat{4}$ and $\flat\hat{7}$

Modes with $\flat\hat{3}$:

- Aeolian —identical to natural minor
- Dorian —like natural minor, but with $\sharp\hat{6}$
- Phrygian —like natural minor, but with $\flat\hat{2}$
- Locrian —like natural minor, but with $\flat\hat{2}$ and $\flat\hat{5}$

Try it #1

Write each of the following modes, starting with the given pc center, on the staves.

MODE	PC CENTER
Mixolydian	F
Dorian	C♯
Lydian	B♭
Aeolian	F♯
Phrygian	G
Locrian	E
Ionian	A♭
Lydian-Mixolydian	A

As in tonal repertoire, it is common in twentieth-century music for a mode, scale, or collection to be represented by only some of its members. Listen now to Stravinsky's short piano piece "Lento," from *For the Five Fingers*, while following the score (anthology, p. 387), and determine which musical elements distinguish one section from another.

Example 33.3 reproduces the opening measures. While the key signature suggests D minor (or F major), and the pc center is clearly D, a list of the pitch classes in the opening measures produces no scale or mode that we know of: D E F F♯ G A. This collection corresponds to the combined lower pentachords of the D Ionian (D E F♯ G A) and Aeolian (D E F G A) modes—one mode in each hand. (Stravinsky's emphasis on pentachords surely relates to the *Five Fingers* of the title.)

EXAMPLE 33.3: Stravinsky, "Lento," mm. 1–4a (anthology)

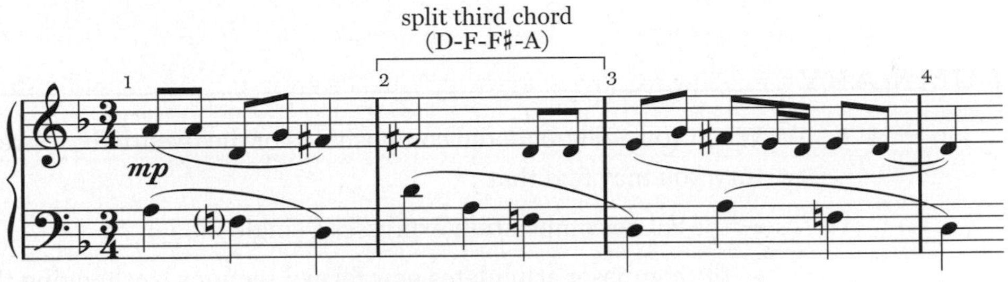

Right hand: D E F♯ G A (Ionian pentachord)
Left hand: D (E) F♮ (G) A (Aeolian pentachord)

Different analysts may focus on different aspects of Stravinsky's compositional choices. Some might examine the harmony created by the two simultaneous modes: the arpeggiated four-note chord (D-F-F♯-A) that spans these measures. Because this sonority sounds like a triad with both a major and a minor third above the root, it is sometimes called a **split-third chord**, or a **major-minor tetrachord**. Other analysts might focus on the linear aspects of the two contrapuntal melodies (in the right and left hand), and on the subsets in each. They would label this composition **bimodal**, or **polymodal**, with one musical stream (or layer, or stratum) based on one mode and another stream based on another. If the passage features two or more pc centers simultaneously, you may also see the terms "bitonal" and "polytonal" applied to this technique.

Indeed, one hallmark of Stravinsky's musical style is a **stratification** of musical materials. This piece shows linear, or horizontal, stratification, while others (such as *The Rite of Spring*) show vertical stratification—sudden short juxtapositions of register, rhythm, texture, timbre, and/or pc collection. Stravinsky's use of bimodality is even more prominent in the **B** section of this piece (Example 33.4), where the right hand implies F Ionian while the left continues with a subset of D Aeolian.

EXAMPLE 33.4: Stravinsky, "Lento," mm. 9–13 (anthology)

RH: F G A B♭ C D (E) F (subset of F Ionian)
LH: D E (F G A) B♭ (C) D (subset of D Aeolian)

SUMMARY

When you analyze modal compositions of the twentieth or twenty-first century, you may find that

- the entire composition expresses a single mode;
- the composer articulates new formal sections by changing the pc center and/or mode;
- the composer presents two modes (bimodality) or more than two modes (polymodality) simultaneously in different musical layers, or strata (stratification).

For an example that brings together several of these techniques, listen to an excerpt from a work by Maurice Ravel (Example 33.5). Like "Song of the Harvest," this song shows different key signatures in different parts: six sharps in the vocal part and piano right hand, but no sharps or flats in the remaining parts. Like "Lento," it has a stratified texture, and like Webern's string quartet, the passage features ostinati.

EXAMPLE 33.5: Ravel, "Aoua!," mm. 8–12a

Translation: In the times of our fathers, white men descended to this island; they said to them: "Here is some land."

Try it #2

Listen again to Example 33.5, then answer the following questions.

(a) What are the pitch classes of the vocal line?

____

(b) What pitch class is missing that would make this a seven-note diatonic scale?

____

(c) What two diatonic modes are combined in this scale?

________________ ________________

(d) What is the pc center?

____

(e) Choose three instrumental ostinato layers to describe. For each layer, specify the instrument, types of harmonic intervals featured, and the pitch class. If the layer you choose has no harmonic intervals, give melodic intervals.

Instrument	*Intervals featured*	*Pc list*
flute	__________	____________________
cello	__________	____________________
piano RH	__________	____________________
piano LH	__________	____________________

Pentatonic Scales

Now play through measures 1–8 of Bartók's "Five-Tone Scale," given in Example 33.6. In this excerpt, E is the apparent pc center, since the passage ends on an octave doubling, E3 and E4, and the melody begins with a characteristic skip up a fourth to E5. List the pcs beneath the example.

Example 33.6: Bartók, "Five-Tone Scale," mm. 1–8

Pc collection: ______________________________

You should have found only five distinct pitch classes (as the title implies): E G A B D. This collection is a minor pentatonic scale, familiar as the $\hat{1}$–$\flat\hat{3}$–$\hat{4}$–$\hat{5}$–$\flat\hat{7}$ (*do-me-fa-sol-te*) pentachord from Chapter 5. The major pentatonic scale, the $\hat{1}$–$\hat{2}$–$\hat{3}$–$\hat{5}$–$\hat{6}$ (*do-re-mi-sol-la*) pentachord, is actually a rotation of the minor pentatonic: that is, E G A B D can be rotated to G A B D E. You can therefore think of both scales as representing the pentatonic collection. You will sometimes see pentatonic collections written as scales, with the first pitch class repeated (in parentheses) at the end: E G A B D (E).

SUMMARY

The pentatonic collection is a subset of the diatonic collection: the major pentatonic scales C D E G A, F G A C D, and G A B D E are all subsets of the major scale C D E F G A B. The minor pentatonic scale E G A B D is also a subset of C D E F G A B, and consists of the same pitch-class set as G A B D E (in rotation).

One easy way to remember the interval pattern that makes up the pentatonic collection is to think of the black keys on the piano: C♯ D♯ F♯ G♯ A♯ (C♯). These pitch classes are a subset of the C♯ major scale, missing E♯ and B♯. The black-key pentatonic collection combined with the white-key diatonic collection make a chromatic collection.

KEY CONCEPT The white-key diatonic collection and the black-key pentatonic collection are considered **literal complements**, because they share no common elements and combine to make a complete chromatic collection. When literal complements appear together—for example, with each set in a different hand or layer—they make an **aggregate**, a collection with all twelve pitch classes.

The pentatonic collection is **symmetrical**, because its pitch classes can be ordered so that the intervals between adjacent scale steps—m3, M2, M2, m3 in the E G A B D collection—are the same going forward and backward. While we do not often think of it this way, the diatonic collection is also symmetrical in one of its rotations (Dorian): the intervals in D E F G A B C D (W H W W W H W) read the same way forward and backward. Some twentieth-century composers explore this symmetrical property in their works.

Because of the symmetry of the pentatonic scale, and its lack of the major scale's $\hat{4}$ and $\hat{7}$ tendency tones, you may find it difficult to decide which pitch class is functioning as center in a pentatonic passage. It often doesn't matter, since any of the pitch classes in the set can be made to sound stable by the musical context. Bartók's pentatonic collection, for example, might be realized in another composition as D E G A B (D), with D as its center, or in the major pentatonic ordering G A B D E (G), with G as its center.

Now look at Example 33.7, the next section of Bartók's piece. Play through the excerpt, then list the pcs beneath the example. Here the composer introduces a new pitch class (F♯), in the left hand only; a pc list reveals another pentatonic collection, A B D E F♯. If you compare the pentatonic set of Example 33.6 (E G A B D) with this one, you can see and hear that the two share a four-note subset, A B D E. (This set is sometimes called the "I Got Rhythm" tetrachord, after the first four notes in Gershwin's famous song.) The change from G in the opening section to F♯ in the second creates an effective contrast, while maintaining the pentatonicism that characterizes the work. In the final section, Bartók returns to the opening collection to end the piece.

Example 33.7: Bartók, "Five-Tone Scale," mm. 9–19

Pc collection: ______________________________

Other Types of Scales

Whole-Tone Scales

Whole-tone scales are made up of six distinct pitch classes that, when listed in scale order, are a whole step apart. Consider the excerpt shown in Example 33.8, from Debussy's prelude "Voiles." List the pitch classes in measures 33–37 as a scale, beginning with B♭, which is emphasized by its constant presence as a pedal tone.

EXAMPLE 33.8: Debussy, "Voiles," mm. 33–40

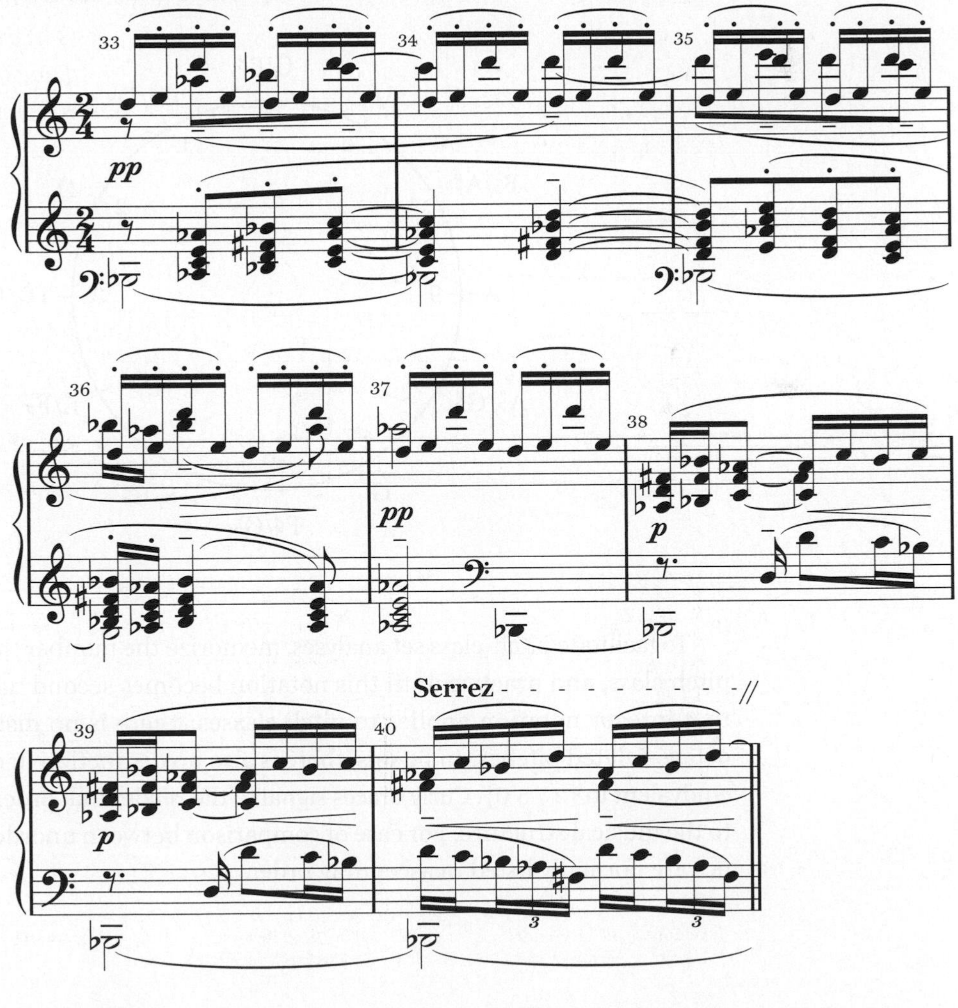

Pc collection: ______________________________

You should have found B♭ C D E F♯ A♭ (B♭). Each element of the scale is a whole step from the next, but some whole steps are obscured by their spellings (for example, F♯ and A♭). Music theorists have devised an analytical tool to reveal such relationships more clearly: they translate the pitch classes to numbers, with enharmonic pcs receiving the same number. This technique is called **integer notation**. For uniformity, most theorists adopt C as the reference pitch class: C = 0, C♯ or D♭ = 1, D = 2, D♯ or E♭ = 3, and so on. To avoid confusing 1 and 0 with the two-digit 10 and 11, you can substitute the letters t for ten and e for eleven.

KEY CONCEPT It is sometimes helpful to think of the pitch classes around a clock face, with 0 (C) at the top and (F♯/G♭) at the bottom.

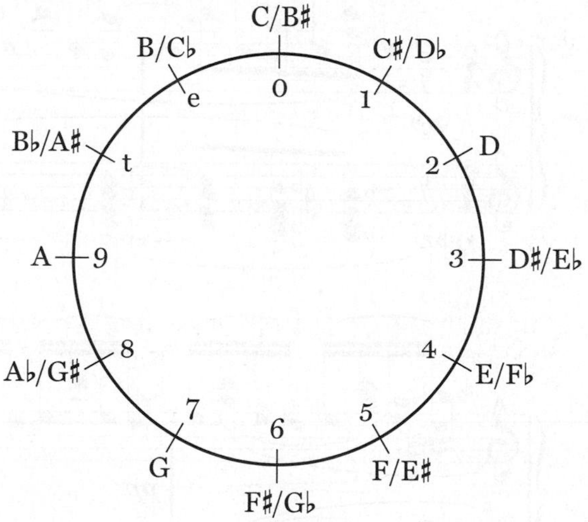

To facilitate pitch-class set analyses, memorize the number that goes with each pitch class, and practice until this notation becomes second nature. Remember that integer notation applies to pitch classes; there is no distinction between octave-related pitches. In pc sets, there is also no distinction in order: {0 2 5 7} is equivalent to {2 7 5 0}. Curly braces signal to the reader that order is not important to the musical structure. For ease of comparison between unordered sets, though, pcs are normally listed in ascending order.

Try it #3

Write each sonority below in integer notation. In the second column, maintain the ordering of the original chord. In the third column, rewrite in ascending order with curly braces.

SONORITY	INTEGER NOTATION	ASCENDING ORDER
Dominant seventh chord on A	9147	{1479}
Half-diminished seventh chord on D		
Do-re-mi-fa-sol on E		
Augmented triad on F♯		
Fully diminished seventh chord on C♯		
Major-major seventh chord on A♭		

Using integer notation, we can identify the collection B♭ C D E F♯ A♭ from Example 33.8 as t 0 2 4 6 8, or {0 2 4 6 8 t}. Such notation makes the whole steps between the pcs readily apparent: from each integer to the next is two half steps. It thus gives us a handy way to identify whole-tone collections.

KEY CONCEPT There are only two possible whole-tone collections: WT0 {0 2 4 6 8 t} and WT1 {1 3 5 7 9 e}; they are literal complements of each other, sometimes referred to as the "even" and "odd" whole-tone collections. Whole-tone collections may be written as a scale, starting with any of their pitch classes.

In major and minor scales, diatonic modes, and pentatonic scales, there are at least two types of intervals between adjacent scale members: half steps, whole steps, or minor thirds. In a whole-tone scale, however, there are only whole steps (or their enharmonic equivalents) between adjacent scale members—it is not possible to discern any aural landmarks from the scale itself. This scale is completely symmetrical: from any starting pitch class, the intervals between scale members read the same forward and backward (M2 M2 M2 M2 M2).

A close examination of Example 33.8 reveals that within the whole-tone texture of measures 33–37 there are several layers of activity. For example, as observed earlier, there is a pedal point: B♭1. There are also triads in the left-hand part that connect in parallel motion. The lowest note of each chord is doubled at the octave and in the right-hand octaves above. If you write out those triads as stacks of pc integers, as in the diagram below, you can quickly determine their qualities—all are augmented triads {0, 4, 8} or {2, 6, t}, two subsets of the even whole-tone collection—and you can see how they connect. Play these chords (leaving out the octave doublings) to hear how the passage works.

FIGURE 33.1: Parallel voice-leading in Debussy's "Voiles"

M. 33	**M. 34**	**M. 35**	**M. 36**	**M. 37**
4 6 8	t	0 t 8	6 4 6 4	4
0 2 4	6	8 6 4	2 0 2 0	0
8 t 0	2	4 2 0	t 8 t 8	8

KEY CONCEPT The type of chord connection where a line is doubled in several voices, resulting in parallel motion, is called **planing** and is associated particularly with Debussy's style.

An ostinato—D5 E5 D6 E5—in an upper voice, based on the dyad {2 4}, repeats throughout this passage. The texture is clearly stratified in three layers (both rhythmically and registrally), with the bass pedal point, the sixteenth-note treble ostinato, and the inner-voice planed augmented triads moving in eighth, quarter, and sixteenth notes.

Octatonic Scales

The beginning of Bartók's "Song of the Harvest" is shown in Example 33.9. What is the scale or mode of this example? A pitch-class list yields the collection D♯ E♯ F♯ G♯ A B C D, with A D C B in the first violin and G♯ F♯ E♯ D♯ in the second. The pc content in integer notation, beginning with 0, is {0 2 3 5 6 8 9 e}, revealing a clear pattern of alternating whole and half steps. This type of symmetrical scale in called an **octatonic scale**. The scale is remarkable for its versatility. Among its subsets are the following sonorities: major, minor, and diminished triads; Mm7, mm7, and fully and half-diminished seventh chords.

Example 33.9: Bartók, "Song of the Harvest," mm. 1–5 (anthology)

Pc collection: D♯ E♯ F♯ G♯ A B C D

KEY CONCEPT The octatonic collection consists of eight pitch classes that alternate whole step and half step. There are three possible octatonic collections, beginning on pc 0, 1, or 2: {0 1 3 4 6 7 9 t}, {1 2 4 5 7 8 t e}, and {2 3 5 6 8 9 e 0}. They are referred to by their initial two pcs: OCT 01, OCT 12, and OCT 23. These can be arranged into scales beginning with any pc and with either a half or whole step first.

Try it #4

Spell each of the following scales, starting with the given pitch class. Then rewrite each answer in integer notation.

SCALE TYPE	STARTING PC	LETTER NAMES	INTEGER NOTATION
Octatonic 01	F♯	F♯ G A B♭ C D♭ E♭ E♮ (F♯)	6 7 9 t 0 1 3 4 (6)
Whole tone	E♭		
Minor pentatonic	D		
Octatonic 23	E♭		
Major pentatonic	B		
Whole tone	B♭		

Compare the focal pitches and mode in Examples 33.9 and 33.10. The first example is somewhat ambiguous: either the first violin's focal pitch, A4, or the second violin's repeated lowest pitch, D♯4, could be interpreted as the beginning pc of the scale or mode. In either case, the collection is OCT 23: {2 3 5 6 8 9 e 0}.

Example 33.10: Bartók, "Song of the Harvest," mm. 6–15 (anthology)

Pc collection: ______________________________

The collection in Example 13.10 is {1 2 4 5 7 8 t e} (OCT 12). While both passages are octatonic, they are not the same set. Neither are they are complementary sets (like the two whole-tone collections), since they have four pcs in common: {2 5 8 e}. This common subset is a familiar chord type—the fully diminished seventh chord B-D-F-A♭. Each octatonic collection shares one diminished seventh subset with each of the other two collections. Further, any two different diminished seventh chords may be combined to make an octatonic collection (for example, {0 3 6 9} plus {2 5 8 e} equals {2 3 5 6 8 9 e 0}), and the literal complement of that collection will always be the third diminished seventh chord (in this case, {1 4 7 t}). In fact, octatonic scales are saturated with diminished seventh chords—you can build one on every degree of the scale. For this reason, jazz musicians call the octatonic the **diminished scale**.

Try it #5

In the two examples below, spell each fully diminished seventh chord with integer notation. Then combine the diminished sevenths into an octatonic scale (also in integers).

1. Diminished seventh on C: ______________________

   Diminished seventh on G: ______________________

   Combine to form which octatonic scale? ______________________

2. Diminished seventh on D♭: ______________________
   Diminished seventh on E♭: ______________________
   Combine to form which octatonic scale? ______________________

How are the two octatonic scales related? ______________________

Scale Analysis and Formal Design

Listen once again to "Song of the Harvest" while following the score in your anthology. Listen for changes indicating formal divisions; make a notation when you hear motivic, rhythmic, dynamic, tempo, and other changes that distinguish one section from the next.

Try it #6

What features recur from section to section? On the score, identify one or more focal pcs in each section, and write the pcs in scale order beneath the staff. Then fill in the chart below.

SECTION	A	B	A′	B′	Coda
MEASURES	1–5				
SCALE TYPE	OCT 23				
FOCAL PCS	A/D♯				

One thing that makes this short piece so interesting is that although its motivic and rhythmic structure divides into a clear **A B A′ B′** form, plus coda, the changes in scale type and focal pcs do not coincide with this form. The pc structure instead is rounded, with OCT 23 in the beginning and ending sections (excluding the coda) and the contrasting OCT 12 in the middle two sections. The focal pcs in each section are tritone-related between the two violins, but the **B′** section brings back the initial pair {D♯ A} as a kind of tonal closure, though respelled enharmonically and reversed between the two instruments. As another reversal, in the first two sections violin 1 is the leader while violin 2 follows in imitation, but in the second half of the piece violin 2 becomes the leader and violin 1 follows, until the coda.

As for the motivic structure, the two **B** sections are simply transpositions of each other, up a half step, but the relationship between **A** and **A′** is more complex. **A′** not only swaps the melodic lines between violins 1 and 2, it also inverts each of these lines. The opening violin melody begins with an upward leap of a P4, followed by a descending whole-step, half-step, whole-step sequence. Violin 2 in measure 16 does the opposite: it makes a downward leap of a P4, followed by an ascending whole step, half step, and whole step. The other part is inverted as well.

Finally, how do we account for the pitch structure of the coda, the only non-octatonic measures of the duet? Although we have focused on octatonicism in this piece, the individual melodies for each instrument are tetrachords *shared* by the diatonic and octatonic collections. In the opening measures, for example, violin 1 has the diatonic tetrachord A B C D, while violin 2 has the diatonic tetrachord D♯ E♯ F♯ G♯. Only when the tetrachords are combined do we hear the full octatonic collection. The coda takes one tetrachord from each octatonic collection—E♭ F G♭ A♭ from the OCT 23 collection, and A♭ B♭ C♭ D♭ from the OCT 12 collection. Together they make the E♭ Aeolian collection.

How might an understanding of the octatonic structure help in performing the duet? Knowing that the octatonic collections will change from section to section may help the violinists prepare for key signature changes and avoid playing incorrect accidentals. Assuming that they practice their parts alone first, they will probably be surprised to hear how the two parts sound together. In particular, they may find it difficult to tune the focal pitches, which are a tritone apart. Hearing the underlying octatonic scale in advance (perhaps playing or singing the full scale in preparation for the duo rehearsal), and learning to expect its characteristic diminished sonorities, should help the violinists stay in tune.

Did You Know?

Composer Arnold Schoenberg objected strongly to the term "atonal," preferring instead "pantonal." Here is how he put it in a 1923 essay called "Hauer's Theories," from *Style and Idea* (1984):

> I find . . . that the expression "atonal music" is most unfortunate—it is on a par with calling flying "the art of not falling," or swimming "the art of not drowning." . . . This expression is wrong: with tones only what is tonal, in keeping with the nature of tones, can be produced . . . an opposite, "atonal," can no more exist among tones and tone-relationships than can an opposite "aspectral" or "acomplementary" among colors and progressions of color.

Unfortunately for Schoenberg, his preferred term did not catch on, but his music was highly influential on generations of composers.

TERMS YOU SHOULD KNOW

- aggregate
- atonal
- bimodal
- cardinality
- center
- centric
- collection
- diminished scale
- element
- focal pitch
- integer notation
- literal complement
- Locrian mode
- Lydian-Mixolydian mode
- major-minor tetrachord
- nontonal
- octatonic
- ostinato
- pentatonic
- planing
- polymodal
- post-tonal
- set
  - subset
  - superset
  - symmetrical set
- split-third chord
- stratification
- whole-tone scale

QUESTIONS FOR REVIEW

1. Trichords include three elements, tetrachords include four. What word best describes a set with five elements? with six? with seven? with eight?
2. Name the diatonic modes. Explain how to use your knowledge of major and minor key signatures to spell each mode.
3. What is the purpose of integer notation?
4. What is the difference in the pattern of adjacent intervals between the Aeolian/Ionian modes and the whole-tone/octatonic scales? How does this difference impact your ability to hear a tonic pitch class?
5. Name three symmetrical scales, and describe how they are constructed.
6. In music for your own instrument, find an example written by Debussy, Ravel, Stravinsky, or Bartók in any diatonic mode or symmetrical scale. Identify the mode or scale. (Consult with your teacher, if necessary.)
7. How can analysis of modes or scales in a piece you are performing help you to learn, interpret, and/or memorize the work?

CHAPTER 34

Music Analysis with Sets

Outline of topics

Relationships between sets

- Listing the elements of a pitch-class set
- Pitch-class set transposition and mod12 arithmetic
- Pitch-class intervals
- Pitch intervals
- Interval classes and the interval-class vector

The inversion of pitch sets and pitch-class sets

- The inversion of pitch sets
- The inversion of pitch-class sets
- Identifying transposition and inversion

Overview

In this chapter, we focus on a single work by Bartók in order to learn how to transpose and invert pitch sets and pitch-class sets.

Repertoire

Béla Bartók, "Bulgarian Rhythm," from *Mikrokosmos* (No. 115)

Relationships Between Sets

(anthology) Listen to Bartók's "Bulgarian Rhythm" while following the score in your anthology. Do you hear a pitch class center? As you listen, mark phrase endings and formal divisions in your score. Write alphabet letters to indicate which sections you hear as contrasting or similar. In this part of the book, "phrase" will refer, as before, to a complete musical thought that ends with a cadence—but the definition of cadence is no longer limited to authentic, half, or other familiar types.

KEY CONCEPT A "cadence" in nontonal music is a point of musical repose, which may be designated by a longer pitch or sonority, phrase markings, the return to a pitch or pitch-class center, or the completion of a musical process.

"Bulgarian Rhythm" divides primarily into four-bar phrases (usually with two-bar subphrases) that articulate a large-scale ternary form, **A B A′**, as shown in the diagram below. The **B** section is distinguished from **A** by its change of texture (from two-part counterpoint to a single motive spread between the two hands), its new melodic material, and the move away from G and D as centric pitch classes.

A		**B**		**A′** (extended)	
a	**a′**	**b**	**b′**	**a″**	**a‴**
mm. 1–4	5–8 (melodic inversion of **a**)	9–12	13–16 (melodic inversion of **b**)	17–24 (canonic and transposed to D)	25–32 (imitation ends)

In the **A** and **A′** sections, the primary center is G—the soprano and bass lines begin and end the work on G, and many of the melodic phrases and subphrases end on G (for example, in mm. 6, 8, 26, 28, 30, and 32). We also hear a secondary emphasis on D, with several phrases and subphrases beginning on D (mm. 5, 7, 17, 19, 22, and 25). In addition, a cadential gesture at the end of the piece evokes dominant-tonic motion from D to G in the bass. But this is not a work built on common-practice tonality, and for that reason it is called a centric nontonal composition.

If you make a list of the pitch classes in this piece, you'll find that all twelve are included, though some phrases draw on only part of the chromatic collection. Simply analyzing the collection, however, does not capture the many interesting features of the piece. you also need to consider other musical details—such as chords, motives, and melodic ideas—to get a more complete sense of how the piece is structured. A good way to begin is by looking at some characteristic motives. Listen again to measures 5–8 (Example 34.1), or play through them at a keyboard.

Example 34.1: Bartók, "Bulgarian Rhythm," mm. 5–8 (anthology)

Now look at the circled trichords. This basic first step, choosing groups of pitches to analyze, is called **segmentation**. Thoughtful and musical segmentation is crucial for the success of your analysis. The sets circled in the Bartók example were chosen because they are clearly defined as units by such features as rhythmic patterns, rests before or after the grouping, and changes of contour in a melodic line. Other segmentation factors might include repetition, articulation as a chord, or the grouping of a melody note together with the chord that harmonizes it. While your segmentation will normally focus on pitches that are adjacent, you can also group nonadjacent pitches if some feature such as similar register, timbre, or articulation groups them aurally. When in doubt, trust your ears!

Listing the Elements of a Pitch-Class Set

Play or sing the circled pitch sets in Example 34.1; you will find that they sound very similar, although you may not know how to describe their relationships. The first step is to write out the pitch classes of the sets—in a uniform order, so that you can compare the sets more easily. Remember that to analyze tonal triads, the first step was to take out octave doublings and pitch duplications, and then rewrite the triad in its simplest form: root-third-fifth. Reordering of pcs in a set serves a similar function: to make the set easier to recognize and compare with others. Chapter 35 will explain how sets are named.

KEY CONCEPT The elements of a pitch-class set are listed as integers in ascending order. Arrange the ascending elements with the smallest possible gaps between pcs.

A clock face like the one in Figure 34.1 can help you find the most compact ordering with the smallest gaps. As an example, look at the first three pitches in the Bartók excerpt and find them on the clock face: pcs 2, 1, and e. You might list them in ascending order as {1 2 e}, but this order on the clock reveals a large gap (clockwise) between 2 and e. Much more compact is the ordering {e 1 2}, which wraps around the top of the clock with no large gap at all. Think of an "ascending" order as one that proceeds in a clockwise direction.

FIGURE 34.1: Clock-face diagram

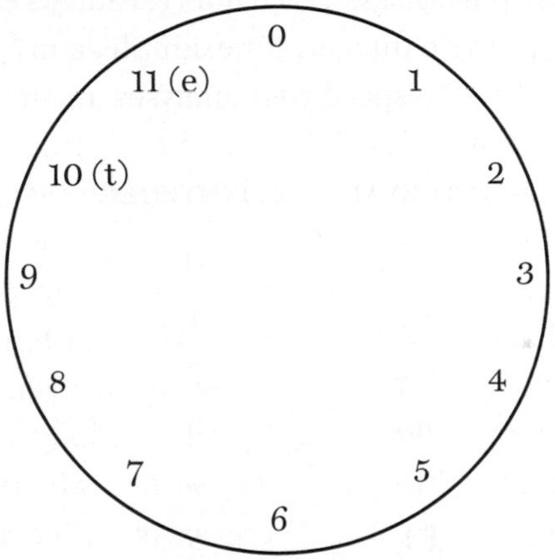

Try it #1

For each set below, write out the pcs in ascending (clockwise) order, in the most compact form with fewest gaps.

B E♭ C♯ A	{9 e 1 3}	E C♯ A	{____________}
F♯ D B	{____________}	F A♭ D A	{____________}
D A E♭ C♯ E	{____________}	D C F♯ A	{____________}
B E♭ A C♯ E♮	{____________}	G D E A♭ E♭	{____________}

Now write the pc integers for each circled set in Example 34.1. Place the pcs of each set in ascending order, referring to the clock face to find the most compact arrangement. You should have written {e 1 2} under the identical sets in the right hand in measures 5 and 7, and in the left hand spanning measures 7–8. In addition, you should have written {9 e 0} under the sets in the right hand in measures 6 and 8, and {1 3 4} under the set spanning 5–6 in the left hand. You probably noticed that the left-hand set in measures 7–8 is an octave transposition (and rhythmic augmentation) of the first set in the right hand; the other pcsets are related by transposition as well. For small sets like these, the transpositions are easy to hear and identify. For larger sets, we need a procedure to identify transpositions accurately.

Pitch-Class Set Transposition and mod12 Arithmetic

Like pitch classes, each interval and its enharmonic equivalents can be represented by a single integer: for example, a m7 and an A6 are both **pitch-class interval** (pci) 10. To speed your analyses, memorize the pci integers in the chart below.

INTERVAL	PCI INTEGER	INTERVAL	PCI INTEGER
unison	0	tritone	6
m2	1	P5	7
M2	2	m6	8
m3	3	M6	9
M3	4	m7	10 (t)
P4	5	M7	11 (e)

When pcsets are represented in integer notation, you can transpose them by adding to each pc one of the pitch-class intervals given above. For example, to transpose {3 5 7} by a minor third, or pci 3, add 3 to each element. You will get {6 8 t}; that is, {E♭ F G} becomes {G♭ A♭ B♭}. Sometimes it is helpful to refer to the clock face when you transpose. For example, if you wanted to transpose {e 1 2} by pci 2, imagine the clock face again (Figure 34.1). Think of the original set circled on a transparent overlay, fastened with a thumbtack in the middle of the clock, so that the overlay can spin around. Then spin the overlay clockwise the number of "clicks" you want to transpose the set. Transpose the set {e 1 2} up two semitones by circling e, 1, and 2 on the overlay, then rotating it two positions to the right, so that the circle that was around e is now over 1. The other circles will be over 3 and 4, yielding the transposition of {e 1 2} by pci 2: {1 3 4}.

You can get the same result with **mod12** arithmetic, which converts a number greater than 11 to an integer between 0 and 11. We already rely on this system when reading twenty-four-hour clocks: when we see a time like 16:00, we convert it to 4:00 p.m.

KEY CONCEPT To convert a large integer to a pc number between 0 and 11, divide the number by 12 and take the remainder (this is mod12 arithmetic). Shortcut: For integers between 12 and 23, simply subtract 12.

Integers that differ by a multiple of 12 are "equivalent mod12"; you can add 12 to any integer and get its mod12 equivalent. For example, 7 = 19 mod12, and 11 = 23 mod12.

If you add 2 to each element of {e 1 2} using mod12 arithmetic, you also get {1 3 4}. This is because 11 + 2 = 13, which is converted to pc 1 by mod12 (shortcut: 13 − 12 = 1). For another example, transpose the same set by pci 7, as shown below.

Transposition by 7:

$$\begin{array}{rrrr} & 11 & 1 & 2 \\ + & 7 & 7 & 7 \\ \hline & 18 & 8 & 9 \end{array}$$

9, which converts mod12 to {6 8 9}.

Another Way

You can transpose pitch-class sets without resorting to clock faces, arithmetic, or integer numbers simply by working at the keyboard or other instrument. To transpose pcset {2 4 8} by a tritone, or pci 6: (1) play the set in any pitch realization—for example, {D4 E4 G♯4}; (2) listen for the succession of intervals (up a M2, up a M3); (3) find the first note of the transposed set, a tritone away (A♭); then, (4) play the same succession of intervals beginning on that pitch: {A♭ B♭ D}. The same transposition in mod12 arithmetic is: {2 4 8} + 6 = {8 t 2}.

Some advantages of integer notation and arithmetic are precision, speed, the elimination of enharmonic spelling problems and octave placement questions, and the ability to do transpositions quickly in your head. Some advantages of the keyboard realization are the connection with your ear (which can detect mistakes) and the kinesthetic reinforcement of the process in your fingers. Try all of these methods, and tailor an approach that works best for you.

Try it #2

Translate each trichord on the left into integer notation, then transpose it by the designated interval.

TRICHORD	INTEGER NOTATION	TRANSPOSE BY	TRANSPOSED SET IN INTEGER NOTATION
{D F A}	{2 5 9}	minor third	{5 8 0}
{B C C♯}	______	minor second	______
{C♯ D F♯}	______	major second	______
{E F♯ A♯}	______	pci 5	______
{C E G♯}	______	pci 7	______
{G♭ A♭ B♭}	______	pci 4	______
{C D F}	______	pci 6	______

Pitch-Class Intervals

Another way to compare sets in a piece of music is to examine their intervals: you can look at the intervals between pcs within each set, and then compare the results. Listen again to the Bartók passage in Example 34.2, or play it at the piano. For now, we will analyze pitch classes rather than pitches, using **ordered pitch-class intervals** and subtraction mod12 to discover the intervals of a pcset.

EXAMPLE 34.2: Bartók, "Bulgarian Rhythm," mm. 5–8 (anthology)

KEY CONCEPT To find the ordered pitch-class interval between two pitch classes, a and b, subtract (b – a) mod12. For example, the ordered pci between pc 2 and pc 7 is (7 – 2), or 5.

To practice subtraction mod12, find the ordered pcis for the dyads D–F♯ and F♯–D. Will they be the same or different? For the first dyad, subtract 2 from 6 and get 4. For the second dyad, where you must subtract 6 from 2, you need to use mod12 arithmetic: add 12 to the smaller number (2 becomes 14), then subtract: 14 – 6 = 8. The ordered pci from D to F♯ is 4, while the ordered pci from F♯ to D is 8. These intervals, 4 and 8, are in a complementary relationship—together they span the entire octave (twelve half steps).

KEY CONCEPT The ordered pitch-class intervals (a – b) and (b – a) always sum to 12. Pcis in this relationship are called **inverses**, or complementary intervals. Inverses appear directly across the clock face from each other (for example, 3 and 9, 2 and 10).

To compute ordered pcis on a clock face, count the number of moves around the clock (clockwise) from the first integer to the second. If you take the dyad D to F♯, count each move from 2 to 6: 2 to 3, 3 to 4, 4 to 5, and 5 to 6—four moves, so the ordered pci is 4. If you are looking for the ordered pci between 6 and 2, you still proceed in a clockwise direction—6 to 7, 7 to 8, and so on—arriving at the ordered pci of 8. Incidentally, with pitch-class intervals, there is no "up" or "down"—these intervals have size but not direction, since pcs belong to no particular octave. To consider interval direction, analyze pitch intervals, which show direction up and down by means of positive and negative integers.

Pitch Intervals

To measure the distance between pitches (not pitch classes), simply count semitones; for example, the interval from D4 to F♯5 is sixteen semitones. Intervals between ordered pitches are written with a plus or minus sign to show direction: D4 up to F♯5 is +16, F♯5 down to D4 is –16. This distance is called an **ordered pitch interval**. If the two pitches occur simultaneously, or if you don't care to specify an order or direction (up or down), the distance is an **unordered pitch interval**. For example, if D4–F♯5 were set in a chord, where order didn't matter, you would label the unordered pitch interval 16.

Ordered pitch intervals represent both direction (plus or minus sign) and size (integer). Pitch intervals thus accurately represent compound intervals; pitch-class intervals do not, because of octave equivalence. It is useful to calculate both pitch and pitch-class intervals when analyzing music of the twentieth and twenty-first centuries.

Interval Classes and the Interval-Class Vector

To determine why some pcsets sound similar to each other and others sound different, make a list of all the intervals in one pcset and compare it with a list of intervals in another set. The list will also give you a rough idea of the sound of a pcset, since a set with several minor seconds, for example, will sound different from one with several perfect fourths. To make the lists general enough to apply to any musical realization of the set, use **unordered pitch-class intervals**.

KEY CONCEPT Find unordered pitch-class intervals by subtracting both (b – a) and (a – b) mod12 and taking the smaller of the two differences.

Return to the dyads D–F♯ and F♯–D, and calculate both intervals: (2 – 6) = 8 and (6 – 2) = 4. The lower number, 4, is the unordered pci between pcs 6 and 2. You can also compute unordered pcis on a clock face: mark the two pc integers, 2 and 6, then move the shortest distance (not always clockwise) between them and count the number of moves. The distance from pc 2 to pc 6 is four moves clockwise, but eight moves counterclockwise. The unordered pci is therefore 4, the shortest distance.

KEY CONCEPT Another name for an unordered pitch-class interval is an **interval class** (ic). Each interval class represents one ordered pc interval and its inverse. There are six interval classes.

INTERVAL CLASS	PCIS	SOME TONAL INTERVAL NAMES
ic 1	1, e	m2, M7, d8
ic 2	2, t	M2, m7, A6
ic 3	3, 9	m3, M6, A2
ic 4	4, 8	M3, m6, d4
ic 5	5, 7	P4, P5
ic 6	6	A4, d5

To memorize ic numbers, remember that a pc interval and its inverse always sum to 12 (so ic 3 consists of pci 3 plus its inverse, 9). Interval class 6 is its own inverse. Even pc 0 fits this guideline, since pc 0 is equivalent to 12 mod12.

Now construct a list of interval classes in a pcset, to compare sets and get an idea of their sound. Look back at the Bartók passage in Example 34.2. What are the interval classes of the trichord with which the passage begins, {e 1 2}? There is ic 2 between the elements in {e 1}, ic 1 between those in {1 2}, and ic 3 between those in {e 2}: one instance each of ic 1, 2, and 3, but no ic 4, 5, or 6. To summarize the analysis, represent each interval class with a box, and write in each box the number of times you found that particular ic in the set.

1	2	3	4	5	6	= interval classes
1	1	1	0	0	0	

This tally is called an **interval-class vector** (or **ic vector**), often written within square brackets without commas or spaces: [111000]. The ic vector shows at a glance that pcs in this trichord can be paired to make one half step, one whole step, and one minor third (or compounds or inverses of these)—but no other intervals.

Now try calculating the ic vector for a larger pcset: {0 1 2 4 8}. First, find the interval class from every pc to every other pc. You could realize the set as pitches at the keyboard or on staff paper, then make a hand tally of the interval classes you find. A quicker method involves subtraction and a triangular chart of ordered pc intervals, as shown below.

0	1	2	4	8	
	1	2	4	8	(subtract 0 from each pc after the first: 1 – 0, 2 – 0, 4 – 0, 8 – 0)
		1	3	7	(subtract 1 from each pc after the second: 2 – 1, 4 – 1, 8 – 1)
			2	6	(subtract 2 from each pc after the third: 4 – 2, 8 – 2)
				4	(subtract 4 from the remaining pc: 8 – 4)

Next, convert each pci above 6 into an interval class (for example, 8 becomes 4), and count how many of each interval class appear in the triangle. Write the count in the appropriate box, as shown.

1	2	4	4	
	1	3	5	
		2	6	
			4	

2	2	1	3	1	1

The result is two ic 1s, two ic 2s, one ic 3, three ic 4s, one ic 5, and one ic 6. The ic vector is [221311]. As you may have noticed, larger pcsets have higher numbers in the ic vector. Specifically, $\frac{n^2 - n}{2}$, where n is the number of elements in the set. With five elements, $\frac{25 - 5}{2}$ = ten intervals. Look back at the ic vector to check: 2 + 2 + 1 + 3 + 1 + 1 = 10.

Try it #3

Calculate the ic vector for the following pcsets.

(a) (1) {1 4 8} [001110]

(2) {1 3 4 7} ______

(3) {0 2 4 6 9} ______

(4) {0 1 3 5 7 8} ______

(b) Which set has the fewest tritones? ______

(c) Which set has the most P4s or P5s? ______

SUMMARY

Measure the intervals between pitches and pitch classes in the following ways.

1. Pitches: Count the semitones between pitches; show direction with + or –.
   - Ordered pitch interval: B♭3 to C5 = +14
     C5 to B♭3 = –14
   - Unordered pitch interval: B♭3 and C5 = 14
2. Pitch classes: For two pitch classes, a and b, subtract (b – a) mod12; if order is unimportant, subtract both (a – b) and (b – a) and take the lower number.
   - Ordered pci: B♭ to C (t to 0) = 2
     C to B♭ (0 to t) = t
   - Unordered pci (also called interval class): B♭ to C or C to B♭ = 2
   - Pcis 2 and t are complements; they sum to 12.

The Inversion of Pitch Sets and Pitch-Class Sets

Passages of music saturated with repetitions of the same type of sets create a different effect from passages that feature diverse or contrasting sets. One task in music analysis is to point out similarities and differences between sets and relate these to observations about form, motives, text, or other musical features. What features make sets "the same"? Some early theories of nontonal music considered any two sets that shared the same ic vector to be equivalent. For example, {C E G} and {A C♯ E} would be equivalent because their pcs span the same three interval classes: one ic 3, one ic 4, and one ic 5 (pci 7 becomes 5), for an ic vector of [001110]. As you will see, two sets sharing the same ic vector are usually related by transposition (as are {C E G} and {A C♯ E}) or by inversion, and it is this relationship that defines set equivalence.

KEY CONCEPT Equivalent sets are related by either transposition or inversion.

The Inversion of Pitch Sets

You know how to invert pitch intervals and how to invert triads and seventh chords, but what is **inversion** in relation to pitch sets? It is not so different from the melodic inversion of motives.

Listen again to the opening of "Bulgarian Rhythm" (Example 34.3), focusing on the circled pentachords A and B. How are they related? Play or sing them, then write the ordered pitch intervals for each pentachord beneath the staff, with positive and negative integers to show direction up and down.

EXAMPLE 34.3: Bartók, "Bulgarian Rhythm," mm. 1–2 (pentachords A and B)

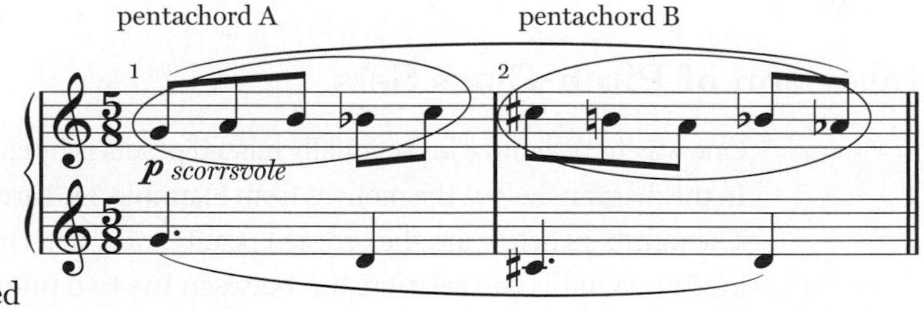

Ordered
pitch intervals: ____________________ ____________________

The ordered pitch-interval sequence for pentachord A is +2, +2, −1, +2. The sequence for pentachord B is −2, −2, +1, −2. Pentachords A and B are inversions of each other because they share the same ordered sequence of pitch intervals, with the directions reversed. At the keyboard, try playing additional transpositions and inversions of the motive by beginning on different random pitches and following the ordered pitch-interval sequence to determine the remaining pitches. Listen carefully to hear the aural links between inversionally related sets.

KEY CONCEPT To write or play the inversion of an ordered pitch set:

1. Analyze its ordered pitch intervals.
2. Choose a beginning pitch for your inverted set.
3. Write or play the remaining pitches from the ordered pitch-interval sequence, but with the direction of each sign reversed.

Try it #4

Sing or play the motive below, and analyze the ordered pitch intervals. Then write or play an inverted set for this motive, beginning on E4, in the empty measure.

Bartók, "Bulgarian Rhythm," m. 9

Ordered
pitch intervals: ______________________ Inverted: ______________________

Where, after measure 9, does Bartók use this inverted set? mm. ______________________

The Inversion of Pitch-Class Sets

One way to recognize inversionally related pcsets is by comparing their ordered pcis. In the diagram below, the motives from Example 34.3 are written in integer notation. The numbers below are the ordered pc intervals, determined by subtracting (b – a) mod12. What is the relationship between the two interval sequences?

	pentachord A	pentachord B
	7 9 e t 0	1 e 9 t 8
pc intervals:	2 2 e 2	t t 1 t

Each pc interval in pentachord A is replaced by its inverse in B: pci e becomes 1, and pci 2 becomes t. (Remember: An ordered pci and its inverse always sum to 12.) You can write the inversion of a given pcset, however, without first calculating the pcis.

KEY CONCEPT To find the inversion of a pcset, replace each pc of the set with its inverse. To find the transposed inversion of a pcset, always *invert* first, then transpose.

Now use integer notation to find the precise relationship between Bartók's pentachords A and B. (List these pcs in the order they appear in the melody, rather than in the most compact ascending order.) First, find the inversion of pentachord A: 7 9 e t 0. Replacing each pc with its inverse yields 5 3 1 2 0. You then need to transpose by eight semitones to get pentachord B: 1 e 9 t 8. When comparing sets, it is helpful to rearrange the pcs in ascending order: pentachord A becomes {7 9 t e 0}. To invert and place pcs in ascending order in a single step, use the "rainbow method":

Another way to invert pcsets is to represent them on a clock face, as shown in Figure 34.2. Circle the pcs of the set you want to invert, then draw an arrow from each pc to its opposite number on the clock. Try it with set A: 7 9 e t 0. First circle each pc integer, then draw arrows from 7 to 5, from 9 to 3, from 11 to 1, and from 10 to 2; 0 stays 0. That yields unordered set 5 3 2 1 0. Then transpose this set by eight semitones (by spinning a transparency eight clicks clockwise or four counterclockwise) to get Bartók's unordered set B: 8 9 t e 1 (see Figure 34.3).

FIGURE 34.2: Clock-face diagram (pcset inversion)

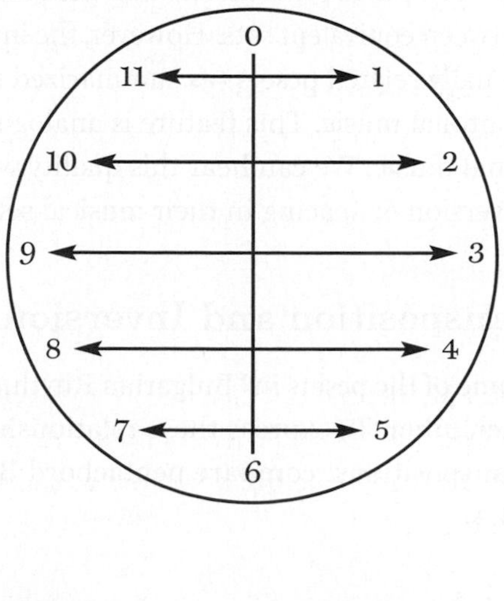

FIGURE 34.3: Pcset inversion and transposition

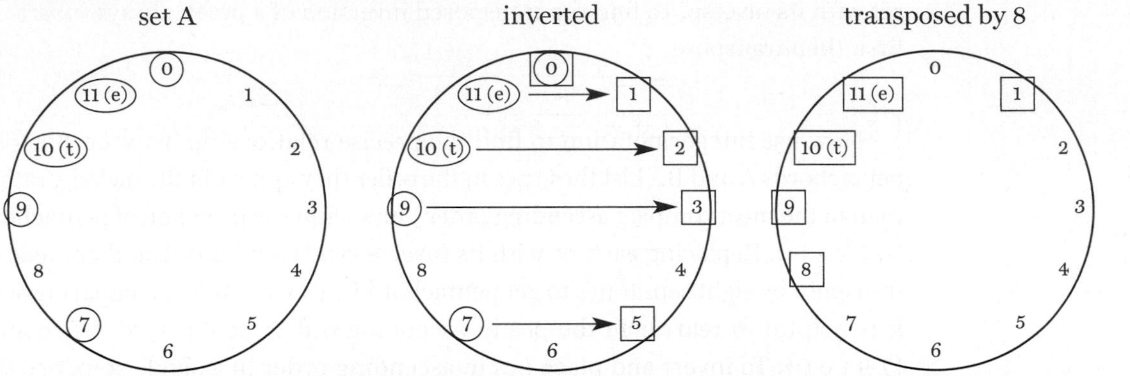

Try it #5

For each pcset below, write out the inversion by substituting for each pc its inverse.

{e 1 4} { 1 e 8 } {3 6 8 9} { ________ }

{9 t 2 3} { ________ } {e 1 2 3 5} { ________ }

{e 2 5} { ________ } {6 9 0 1} { ________ }

Pitch-class transpositions and inversions may not be as easily recognized by ear as pitch transpositions and inversions. Composers can place pcs from a pcset into any octave, without disturbing the transpositional or inversional relationship between pcsets; this means that the musical contour and effect may differ greatly between equivalent sets. However, the interval classes in transpositionally or inversionally related pcsets (as summarized in the ic vector) are an audible feature of nontonal music. This feature is analogous to our recognition of chord quality in tonal music. We can hear this quality whether or not the chords share the same inversion or spacing in their musical setting.

Identifying Transposition and Inversion

Some of the pcsets in "Bulgarian Rhythm" are transpositions and/or inversions of each other. To express these relationships accurately and succinctly, start with transpositions: compare pentachord B with pentachord D, shown in Example 34.4.

Example 34.4: Bartók, "Bulgarian Rhythm"

(a) Mm. 1–2 (pentachords A and B)

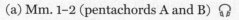

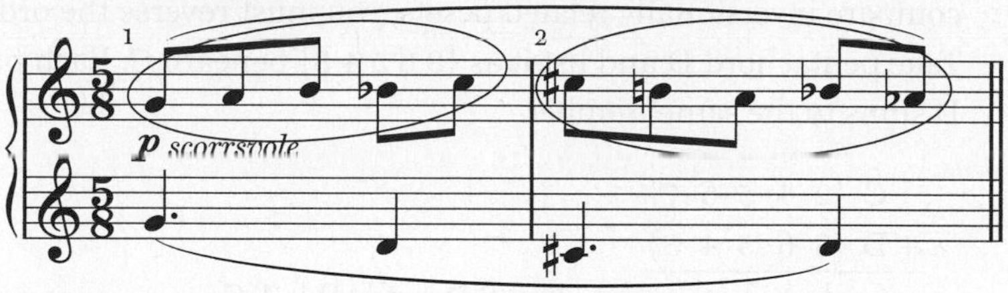

(b) Mm. 17–18 (pentachords C and D) (anthology)

First, place the pentachords in their most compact ascending order (around the clock) and line them up, one beneath the other, for comparison. You can show their transpositional relationship by subtracting the pc integers of one set from the other, mod12:

B {8 9 t e 1}
– D {3 4 5 6 8}
5 5 5 5 5 ⟶ B = T_5D

We express this relationship as follows: B = T_5D (where T stands for "transposition" and the subscript 5 represents the pci 5 between the two pcsets). To interpret B = T_5D, think right to left: D transposed by T_5 yields B.

Now look at pentachord C in part (b) of the example. If you compare pentachords A and C, the results are similar: A = T_5C.

A {7 9 t e 0}
– C {2 4 5 6 7}
5 5 5 5 5 ⟶ A = T_5C

Recall that these are ordered pc intervals. The order in which you arrange the pcsets matters. Pcset A minus C reveals a T_5 relationship, but C minus A yields the complement, a T_7 relationship:

C {2 4 5 6 7}
– A {7 9 t e 0}
7 7 7 7 7 ⟶ C = T_7A

To express the "distance" between inversionally related sets, look at pentachords C and D, which are inversionally related (as are A and B). First, list the pcs in ascending and most compact order: C is {2 4 5 6 7}, and D is {3 4 5 6 8}. To compare inversionally related pcsets, you must reverse the order of one of them. Take pentachord D and list it as {8 6 5 4 3} beneath C. Each pair of pcs in C and D sums to the same number.

```
  C {2 4 5 6 7}
+ D {8 6 5 4 3}
-----------------
     t t t t t  →  C = TtD  and  D = TtC
```

If you *add* (mod12) the pcs that are vertically aligned, you consistently get 10 (t). We call 10 the **index number** between the two inversionally related sets, and represent their relationship as follows: C = T_tI D, and also D = T_tI C (where I stands for "inversion" and the subscript t stands for the index number 10).

Try it #6

Look back at Example 34.4, and write out the pcs for pentachords B and C in ascending order. Use the space provided to calculate their inversional relationships. (Hint: Reverse the order of one set and add.)

(a) Pentachord B: ________________

(b) Pentachord C: ________________

(c) What is the index number? __________

(d) Fill in the blank: C = T____I B.

For composition or analysis with pcsets, you may want a quick way to produce T_nI-related sets. Given Bartók's pentachord A {7 9 t e 0}, find T_4I. Because two T_nI-related sets will sum to a consistent index number—in this case, 4—you can simply subtract each pc from 4:

```
  4 4 4 4 4
– 7 9 t e 0
-----------
  9 7 6 5 4  (ascending order {4 5 6 7 9})
```

To check your work, add the pcs of the original set to the new T_4I version. They should consistently sum to 4.

pentachord A:	7	9	t	e	0
T_4I of A:	+9	7	6	5	4
	4	4	4	4	4

In "Bulgarian Rhythm," it is easy to observe that some of the pentachords are transpositionally or inversionally related because of their musical context: Bartók uses specific pitches, contours, and rhythms to make the relationships stand out. Further, if you calculate the ic vectors for pentachords A, B, C, and D, you find that they have the exact same interval classes between pcs, which gives them a similar sound. As with other musical details identified in previous chapters, you may not choose to bring out these relationships when playing the piece, but knowing about them helps you understand why and how the music sounds the way it does, and what factors make the piece cohesive. More about relationships between sets will be discussed in Chapter 35.

Did You Know?

Bartók's *Mikrokosmos* is a six-volume collection of piano pieces of progressive difficulty, ranging from simple compositions for children to masterful mature compositions. Biographer Halsey Stevens, in *The Life and Music of Béla Bartók* (Oxford University Press, 1993), describes the origins of this massive work:

> In 1926, spurred by the necessity of providing new material for his concert tours, Bartók wrote a large number of works for the piano: the Sonata, the set of pieces called *Out of Doors*, the Nine Little Piano Pieces, and the (first) Piano Concerto. At around the same time he began work on a collection of piano pieces, eventually called *Mikrokosmos*, designed to introduce young pianists to the technique and musical problems of contemporary writing. The first two volumes are dedicated to Bartók's second son, Péter; the later ones—especially Nos. 5 and 6—make severe demands upon the performer, and Péter Bartók has said that the set rapidly outgrew his performing abilities.

These are wonderful study pieces for the music theorist, as well as for the pianist, since they beautifully demonstrate many of Bartók's compositional techniques.

TERMS YOU SHOULD KNOW

index number
interval class
interval-class vector
inversion
mod12
pitch interval
- ordered
- unordered

pitch-class interval (pci)
- ordered
- unordered

segmentation

QUESTIONS FOR REVIEW

1. How are the terms "cadence" and "phrase" adapted for nontonal music?
2. What musical factors do you focus on when choosing pitch or pitch-class sets for analysis?
3. What are the steps to construct ic vectors, and how can they be helpful in analysis?
4. What are the steps to transpose pcsets? pitch sets?
5. What are the steps to invert pcsets? pitch sets?
6. Describe how a clock face can be helpful for calculating (a) transposition and (b) inversion.
7. What are the steps to find the transpositional relationship between two pcsets? the inversional relationship?

Sets and Set Classes

CHAPTER 35

Outline of topics

Set classes and their prime forms

- Finding prime form (on the keyboard, from pcs in integer notation, on a clock face)
- Set-class labels

Characteristic trichords of familiar scales and modes

- Whole tone
- Pentatonic
- Octatonic
- Chromatic

Reading set-class tables

- Complementary sets
- Using ic vectors

Overview

In this chapter, we group sets into set classes, and learn how to recognize some of the most distinctive set classes in twentieth-century compositions.

Repertoire

Béla Bartók

"Bulgarian Rhythm," from *Mikrokosmos* (No. 115)

Sonata for Two Pianos and Percussion

"Whole-Tone Scales," from *Mikrokosmos* (No. 136)

Claude Debussy, "La cathédral engloutie," from *Préludes*

Olivier Messiaen, "Liturgie de crystal," from *Quartet for the End of Time*

Anton Webern, String Quartet, Op. 5, third movement

Set Classes and Their Prime Forms

(anthology) Listen once again to Bartók's "Bulgarian Rhythm," while following the score in your anthology. As you listen, keep in mind the form, centricity, and transpositionally and inversionally related sets identified in Chapter 34.

Now look at the left-hand melody in measures 1–2, labeled in Example 35.1 as trichord x. This set is the trichord {1 2 7}. (Remember: When a segment repeats a pitch, as with D4, list it only once.) Compare trichord x with trichord y in measure 9. Trichord y's elements are {4 9 t}. The sets are inversionally related, by T_eI. To express the relation precisely, reverse the order of one set and add:

$$\begin{array}{rccc} & 1 & 2 & 7 \\ + & t & 9 & 4 \\ \hline & e & e & e \end{array}$$

Example 35.1: Bartók, "Bulgarian Rhythm," mm. 1–9 (anthology)

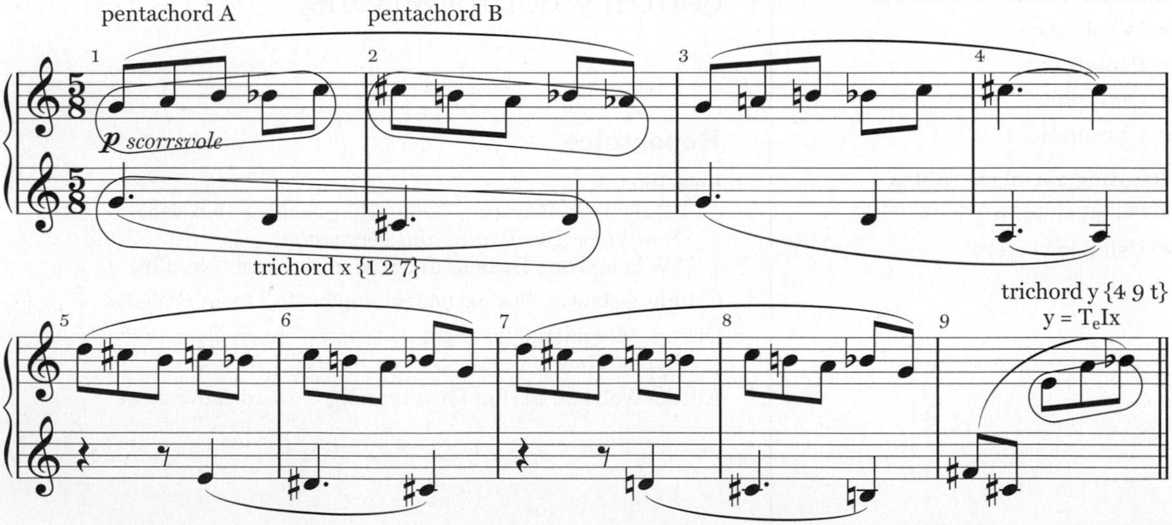

Within the work's first few measures, there are other transpositionally and inversionally related sets. For example, look at the left-hand parts in measures 5–6 and 7–8. These sets, {1 3 4} and {e 1 2}, are related by T_t. You may also have heard pcsets that are simply repeated. Pentachord A is an example: it appears in the right hand in measures 1, 3, 6, 8, 24, 26, and 27. Sets that are repeated, that are related by some operation, or that share identical interval classes lend coherence to nontonal works. Sets that differ provide contrast, just as motion to a new key provides contrast in tonal music. If you prepared a thorough analysis of this piece, you could identify many different sets to discuss. To keep this number of sets a manageable size, theorists consider transpositionally and inversionally related sets to be equivalent, and group them together into set classes.

KEY CONCEPT A **set class** (SC) contains all possible distinct transpositions of a pcset, as well as all distinct transpositions of its inversion. Pcsets in the same set class share the same ic vector.

Consider pentachord B from Example 35.1: {8 9 t e 1}. To find all members of the set class for pentachord B, follow the three steps shown below. (1) Write B with its eleven transpositions. Next, (2) find the inversion of {8 9 t e 1} by replacing each pc with its inverse: {4 3 2 1 e}. Rearrange these pcs into the most compact ascending order around the clock face: {e 1 2 3 4}. Then (3) write out this inversion's eleven transpositions as well.

Step 1: {8 9 t e 1}, {9 t e 0 2}, {t e 0 1 3}, {e 0 1 2 4}, {0 1 2 3 5}, {1 2 3 4 6}, {2 3 4 5 7}, {3 4 5 6 8}, {4 5 6 7 9}, {5 6 7 8 t}, {6 7 8 9 e}, {7 8 9 t 0}

Step 2: {4 3 2 1 e}, reverse order to {e 1 2 3 4}

Step 3: {e 1 2 3 4}, {0 2 3 4 5}, {1 3 4 5 6}, {2 4 5 6 7}, {3 5 6 7 8}, {4 6 7 8 9}, {5 7 8 9 t}, {6 8 9 t e}, {7 9 t e 0}, {8 t e 0 1}, {9 e 0 1 2}, {t 0 1 2 3}

Most set classes, like pentachord B's, have twenty-four distinct members, representing each transposition and (transposed) inversion. However, there are some SCs with fewer members; when you transpose or invert some pcsets, they "reproduce themselves." For an example, transpose the augmented triad, {0 4 8}, by T_4 or T_8: you get {4 8 0} and {8 0 4}. The number of operations that will reproduce the elements of the original set is the set's "degree of symmetry." For {0 4 8}, the degree of symmetry is 6; the set reproduces itself when transposed by pci 0, 4, or 8 (three operations), or when it is inverted and then transposed by 0, 4, or 8 (another three). The augmented triad's set class has only four distinct members; other common sets with fewer than twenty-four members include the diminished seventh chord (three members), the octatonic collection (three members), and the whole-tone collection (only two members). We will return to this property later in the chapter.

Try it #1

(a) Write out the three possible diminished seventh chords in integer notation.

{0 3 6 9} ____________ ____________

(b) These are the operations under which the set reproduces itself.

Transpositions: T_0 T_3 T_6 T_9

Inversions: T_0I T_3I T_6I T_9I

What is the degree of symmetry? ____________

Finding Prime Form

With pcsets grouped into set classes, a single pcset represents the entire group. This representative pcset, called **prime form**, is written in a standard ordering and transposition. Pcsets in prime form always begin with a zero and are written with ascending pcs between square brackets [ ]. Remember that a pcset in prime form is a "token" that represents all the transpositions and inversions that belong to that single set class. In music analysis, finding the prime form of pcsets allows us to compare two pcsets that may look different in the score (different contour, timbre, pitch classes, rhythm) and discover that they are actually members of the same set class.

From Pitches on the Keyboard or Staff Playing pitches at the keyboard and writing them on a staff can help you get to know the process of finding prime form informally, and see and hear how it works.

KEY CONCEPT To find a pitch set's prime form:

1. Reorder the pitches, substituting octave displacements as needed, so that they all fall within a single octave (for example, between C4 and C5). Play or write them in ascending order like a scale.
2. Now play or write each rotation of the scale by moving the lowest pitch to the top (like playing successive inversions of a triad). Look for the most compact rotation—the one that spans the smallest interval from the lowest to highest note.
3. This most compact rotation is called the **normal order**. (See also the "tie-breaker" instructions below.)
4. If your set in normal order has smaller intervals (usually half and whole steps) near the bottom and wider intervals near the top, transpose your set so

that the first pitch is C. (Move your hand to C and play the same succession of intervals.)

5. If your set in normal order has larger intervals near the bottom and smaller intervals near the top (for example, F4 G4 A4 B♭4 B♮4), you'll need to invert it. Beginning on any pitch (for now, F4), play the set's ordered pitch-interval sequence (+2 +2 +2 +1 +1) going down instead of up (-2 -2 -2 -1 -1, or F4 E♭4 D♭4 C4 B3). Reverse the order of pitches so they ascend (B3 C4 D♭4 E♭4 F4), then transpose to C: C4 C♯4 D4 E4 F♯4.

If you find a "tie" between two compact rotations of the set, with equally small spans, look for the "best" normal order—the one with the smallest intervals toward the bottom. Compare the interval between the first and second pcs in both rotations, and choose the one with the smaller interval. If that also results in a tie, then compare the interval between the first and third pcs, and so on, until you break the tie. (This method is based on that of theorist Allen Forte, from *The Structure of Atonal Music*; other methods are possible.)

Return now to the opening of "Bulgarian Rhythm" (Example 35.1) to find the prime form of the work's opening pitch sets. Sing or play each pentachord several times to get its sound in your ears, beginning with pentachord B.

Example 35.2 shows the pitches of pentachord B written in ascending order: A♭4 A♮4 B♭4 B♮4 C♯5. A♭4 to C♯5 is pitch interval 5. Now play the rotations. Which rotation is the most compact—which spans the smallest interval from bottom to top?

EXAMPLE 35.2: Bartók, "Bulgarian Rhythm," m. 2

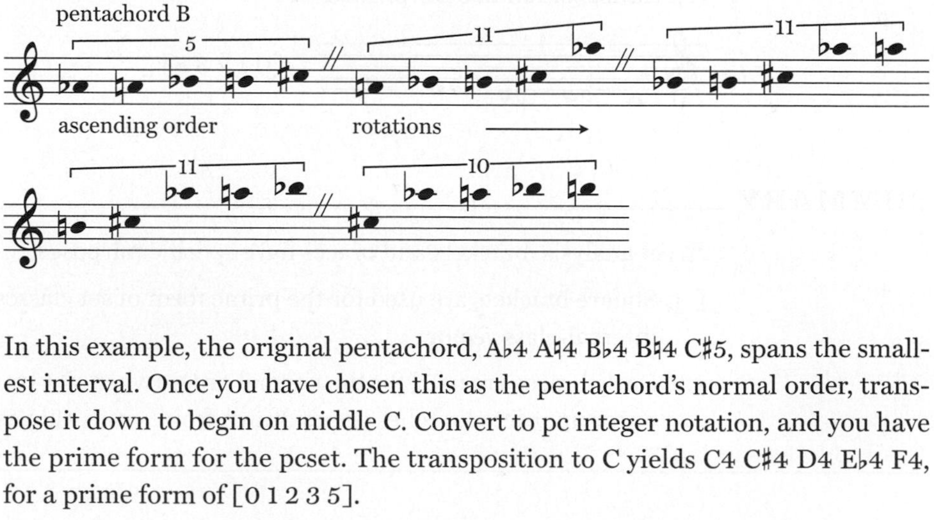

In this example, the original pentachord, A♭4 A♮4 B♭4 B♮4 C♯5, spans the smallest interval. Once you have chosen this as the pentachord's normal order, transpose it down to begin on middle C. Convert to pc integer notation, and you have the prime form for the pcset. The transposition to C yields C4 C♯4 D4 E♭4 F4, for a prime form of [0 1 2 3 5].

Use the same procedure for pentachord A (Example 35.1). Play or write out the rotations, then choose the normal order. The normal order for pentachord A (Example 35.3a) has the largest interval near the bottom (whole step) and smaller intervals near the top (half steps); you therefore need to invert it. Say you choose G4 (arbitrarily) as the beginning pitch. First play (or write) the original pitch-interval sequence: +2 +1 +1 +1. Then reverse the direction of each interval, beginning on G4 (−2 −1 −1 −1), as in part (b). Now find the normal order and prime form for the inverted set (part c). You will discover that pentachords A and B are equivalent (by inversion); they belong to the same set class.

Example 35.3: Bartók, "Bulgarian Rhythm," m. 1

(a) Normal order

(b) Inversion on G4

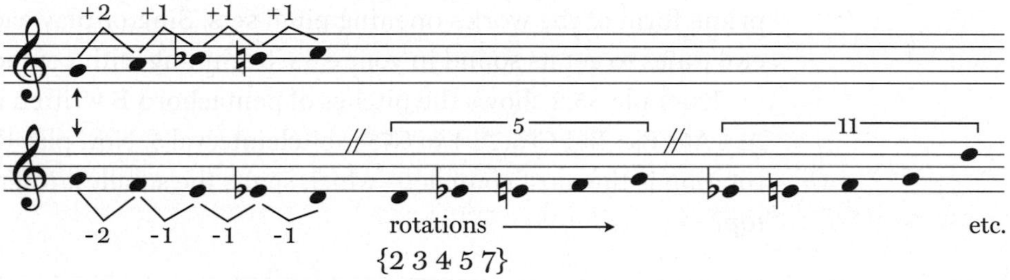

(c) Transposition to 0 for prime form

SUMMARY

In set analysis, brackets and braces have specific purposes.

[ ]: Square brackets are used for the prime form of set classes and the interval-class vector.

{ }: Curly braces are used for the normal order (when not transposed to 0), or for unordered pitches or pcs drawn from a musical passage.

From PCs in Integer Notation You can also calculate prime form with integer notation. Order the pcs by placing the integers in ascending order, and calculate interval distance with subtraction mod12. Taking pentachord A as an example, {9 t e 0 7}, write out each rotation and then calculate the interval spanned by subtracting the first pc from the last, as shown below:

{9 t e 0 7} ⟶ {9 t e 0 7} interval spanned = t (7 – 9) = (19 – 9) = t
{t e 0 7 9} interval spanned = e (9 – t) = (21 – t) = e
{e 0 7 9 t} interval spanned = e (t – e) = (22 – e) = e
{0 7 9 t e} interval spanned = e (e – 0) = e
{7 9 t e 0} interval spanned = 5 (0 – 7) = (12 – 7) = 5

The normal order is {7 9 t e 0}, since it spans the smallest "outside" interval: pci 5. Since a larger interval is at the bottom (to the left), the set needs to be inverted. Replace each pc with its inverse: {7 9 t e 0} becomes {5 3 2 1 0}. Then reverse the order of the pcs so they ascend, and you have the prime form: [0 1 2 3 5]. Or use the rainbow method:

Try it #2

For each set of pcsets below, find the prime form.

{E A♭ A}	[0 1 5]	{D C F♯ A}	[ ]
{G C♯ D}	[ ]	{F♯ D B C E}	[ ]
{F A♭ D A}	[ ]	{D A E♭ C♯ E}	[ ]
{B E♭ C♯ A}	[ ]		

On a Clock Face The now-familiar clock face can help you find the shortest span and normal order without writing out all the rotations. Take the pcset {9 t e 0 7} and circle the numbers on a clock face (see Figure 35.1). Determine the interval between each pair of adjacent pcs. Look for the *largest* interval: 0 to 7. The second pc of the largest interval will be the first pc of the set in normal order: {7 9 t e 0}. To find the prime form, you must invert. Draw an arrow from each pc to its inverse, and draw a box around the inverse. Write in ascending order, then transpose to 0.

FIGURE 35.1: Clock-face diagram (prime form)

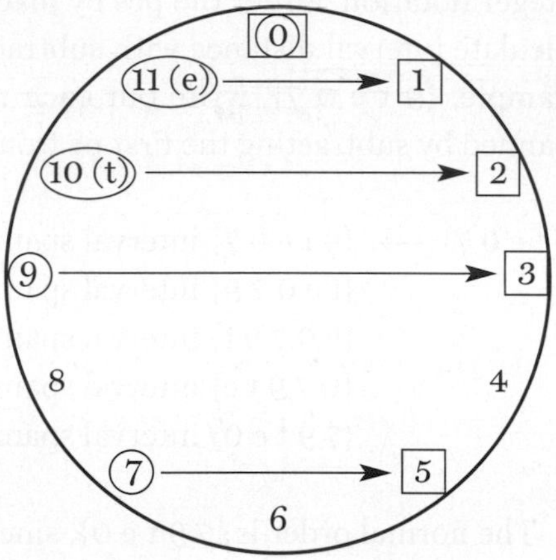

Another Way

Remember, when a set is in normal order, you can invert and transpose it in one step using the principle of index numbers. Take the last normal order in *Try it #2*, {9 1 2 3 4}. Begin with the last pc and subtract every pc from this number:

```
  4 4 4 4 4
- 9 1 2 3 4
-----------
  7 3 2 1 0  →  prime form: [0 1 2 3 7]
```

This works because 4 is the index number (T_4I) between the normal order and its inversion-transposition to 0.

(anthology) Now listen to the **A′** section of "Bulgarian Rhythm," measures 17 to the end. Use integer notation to find the prime form of pcsets in this passage, and determine whether they belong to the same set class as pentachords A and B or to a different one. Begin by placing pentachord C (Example 35.4) in integer notation in ascending order: {2 4 5 6 7}. If you imagine each of the rotations, you will see that this ordering spans the smallest outside interval. Since the larger interval is to the left and semitones are to the right, replace each pc with its inverse, {t 8 7 6 5}, and reverse the order so that the integers ascend: {5 6 7 8 t}. Transpose to the 0 level to find the prime form: [0 1 2 3 5]. Pentachord C has the same prime form as A and B; the three pentachords are equivalent, and are members of the same set class.

Further, we know from Chapter 34 that pentachords C and D are inversionally related (C = T_tI D). Pentachord D thus belongs to the same set class as A, B, and C, helping to give Bartók's piece its consistent sound.

EXAMPLE 35.4: Bartók, "Bulgarian Rhythm," mm. 17–18 (anthology)

Try it #3

Find the normal order and prime form for the two pentachords in the example below. One of them is not equivalent to pentachords A–D. Which one?

Bartók, "Bulgarian Rhythm," mm. 25–26 (anthology)

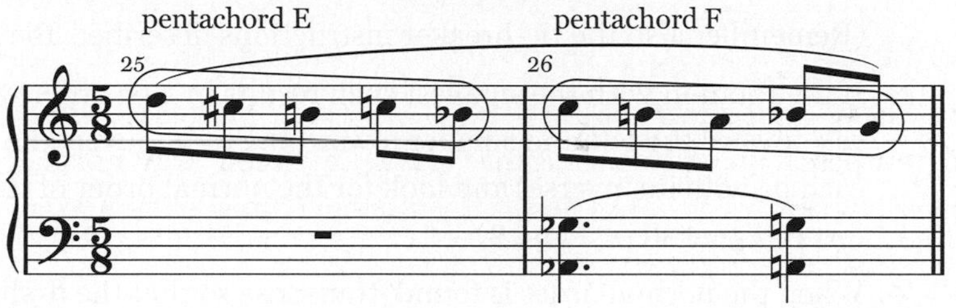

Normal order: ____________________ ____________________

Prime form: ____________________ ____________________

Finally, look at one last "Bulgarian Rhythm" pentachord, shown in Example 35.5, and apply the tie-breaker instructions to find the prime form. The pcs in ascending order are {1 4 6 9 t}. Looking for the rotation with the smallest span reveals a three-way tie: {9 t 1 4 6}, {1 4 6 9 t}, and {4 6 9 t 1}; all span pci 9. To find the best normal order, check the interval between the first and second pcs (or, in case the pcset needs to be inverted, the next-to-last and last pcs). This eliminates {4 6 9 t 1}, which has gaps at both ends. Pcset {9 t 1 4 6} transposed to 0 produces {0 1 4 7 9}. The other choice, {1 4 6 9 t}, needs to be inverted: {e 8 6 3 2}. Reorder so that the integers are in ascending order, {2 3 6 8 e}, and transpose to 0: {0 1 4 6 9}. Of these two choices—{0 1 4 7 9} and {0 1 4 6 9}—the prime form is the latter. If you compare the intervals between each pc and the first, you get one interval {0 6} that is smaller in the second part than in the first {0 7}.

Example 35.5: Bartók, "Bulgarian Rhythm," m. 9 (anthology)

SUMMARY

To find a pcset's prime form:

1. Reorder the pcs so that they ascend numerically, and consider each rotation.
2. Look at the interval from first to last pc in each rotation, and choose the rotation with the smallest possible span. This is the normal order. (Remember also the tie-breaker instructions described above.)
3. If the rotation with the smallest span results in a pc order with larger intervals toward the left and smaller toward the right, invert the set (replace each pc with its inverse) and look for the normal order of this inverted form (repeat steps 1 and 2).
4. When the normal order is found, transpose so that the first pc is 0. That is prime form.

Set-Class Labels Each set class can be identified with a label, just as the labels "augmented triad," "Mm7," and "fully diminished seventh" identify three- and four-note sets in tonal music. We will borrow labels derived from Allen Forte's complete set-class list. Forte grouped together pcsets with the same number of elements (or cardinality) and then ordered them by ic vector. To each set class, he gave a hyphenated number (for example, 5-35). The number before the hyphen represents the cardinality of the pcset, and the number after represents the pcset's position on the list; thus, 5-35 is a pcset of five elements that appears thirty-fifth on the list. These numbers are sometimes called "Forte numbers." Forte's complete table, helpful for set-class analysis, is given in Appendix 5. When analyzing a nontonal work, first identify musical segments of interest, find the prime form, and then look up the set-class label. The labels will allow you to discuss sets without having to write out and compare all the pcs each time. Some analysts use the prime form to label the set class ([0 2 4 7 9] for 5-35).

Characteristic Trichords of Familiar Scales and Modes

You will find it easier to analyze nontonal music as well as understand it aurally if you learn to recognize the trichords. One effective way to do this is to associate them with the collections studied in Chapter 33: whole-tone, diatonic, pentatonic, octatonic, and chromatic. If you look at the set-class table in Appendix 5, you will see that there are only twelve three-element set classes; try to learn them all. Many of these you already know—for example, triad types. Spend some time at the piano, playing through the excerpts below; identify as many trichords as you can. Sing them back after playing them; try to find and play their inversions as well. When you can recognize the twelve trichord types, you will have a strong foundation upon which to build your appreciation of and skill in performing nontonal repertoire.

Whole Tone

Listen to Example 35.6, drawn from Bartók's "Whole-Tone Scales." The circled sets belong to the set classes [0 2 4], [0 2 6], and [0 4 8]. These are the only trichords closely associated with the whole-tone collection. You can identify them by their whole steps, major thirds, and tritones, the only intervals in these trichords, as their ic vectors show.

Example 35.6: Bartók, "Whole-Tone Scales," mm. 1–3

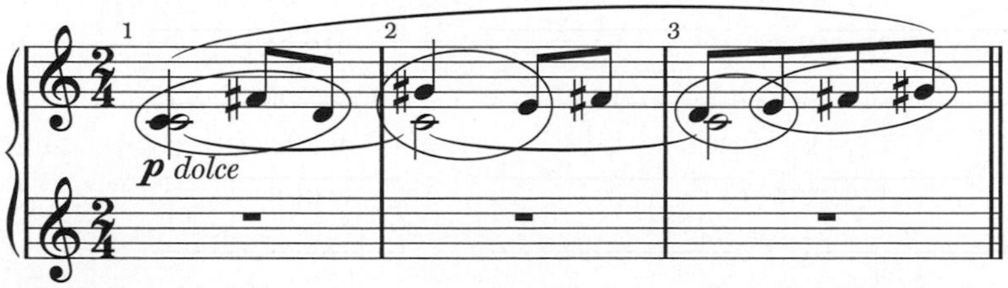

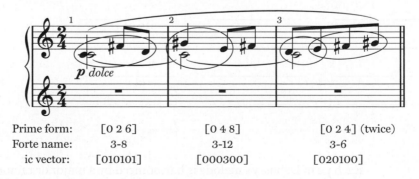

Prime form:	[0 2 6]	[0 4 8]	[0 2 4] (twice)
Forte name:	3-8	3-12	3-6
ic vector:	[010101]	[000300]	[020100]

Pentatonic

The most characteristic trichords of the pentatonic collection are [0 2 5] and [0 2 7], but pentatonic compositions also share [0 2 4] with the whole-tone and diatonic collections, and [0 3 7] with the diatonic collection. Example 35.7, from the Debussy piano prelude "La cathédral engloutie," includes all of these.

Example 35.7: Debussy, "La cathédral engloutie," mm. 72–75

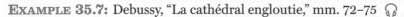

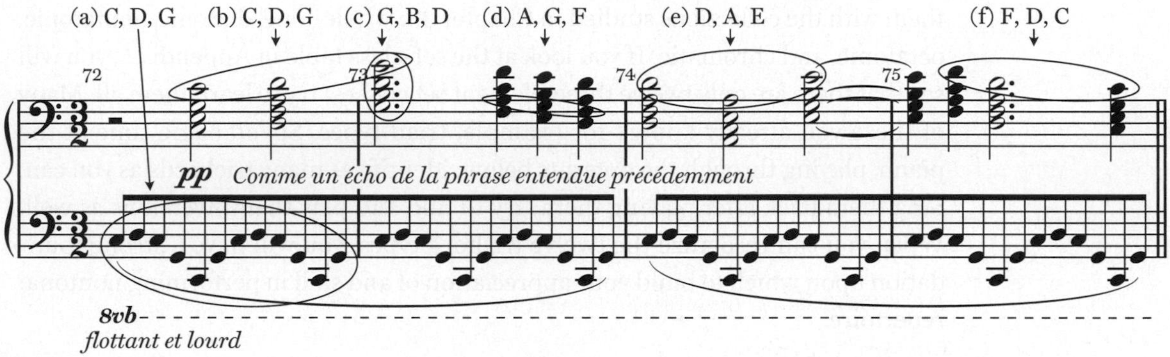

Try it #4

Provide the prime form for each trichord circled in Example 35.7. Then find the Forte number and ic vector in Appendix 5.

	Prime form	*Forte number*	*ic vector*
(a)	[0 2 7]	3-9	[010020]
(b)			
(c)			
(d)			
(e)			
(f)			

Each pc in Debussy's melody is harmonized by a major or minor triad. The prime form for each triad in measure 73 is [0 3 7]; major and minor triads are equivalent by inversion.

Octatonic

We turn now to the octatonic collection to discover its characteristic trichords. Look first at one form of the scale in pc integer notation—{0 1 3 4 6 7 9 t }—to see how diminished, major, and minor triads are embedded in it. The diminished triad [0 3 6] can be built on any degree of the octatonic scale: {0 3 6}, {1 4 7}, {3 6 9}, and so on. Pcs 0, 3, 6, or 9 can support either a major or minor triad: {0 3 7} and {0 4 7}, {3 6 t} and {3 7 t}, {6 9 1} and {6 t 1}, and so on. These scale degrees can also support the "split-third" chord [0 3 4 7].

Just as characteristic of the octatonic scale, but new to our study, are the subsets that begin with a semitone: [0 1 3], [0 1 4], and [0 1 6]. Example 35.8 shows two primary themes of Bartók's *Sonata for Two Pianos and Percussion*. Listen to the melody line (top voice) in each, then determine the set class to which each group of circled pitches (labeled x, y, or z) belongs: each features a semitone.

Example 35.8: Bartók, *Sonata for Two Pianos and Percussion*

(a) Mm. 1–2 (piano 1)

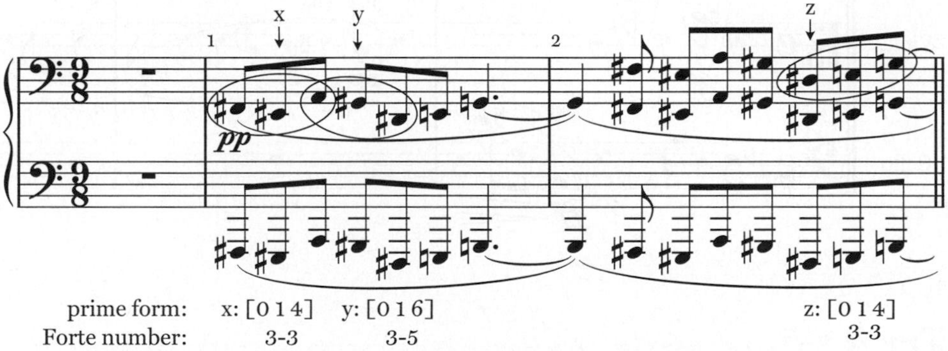

(b) Mm. 33–34 (piano 1)

Chromatic

We complete our study of trichords by looking at a passage from the third movement of Webern's String Quartet, Op. 5 (Example 35.9). This passage includes almost the entire chromatic collection and is saturated with SCs [0 1 2], [0 1 4], and [0 1 5]. Listen to the passage, then play individual lines or chords at the keyboard to identify the sound of the trichords.

EXAMPLE 35.9: Webern, String Quartet, Op. 5, third movement, mm. 8–10 (anthology)

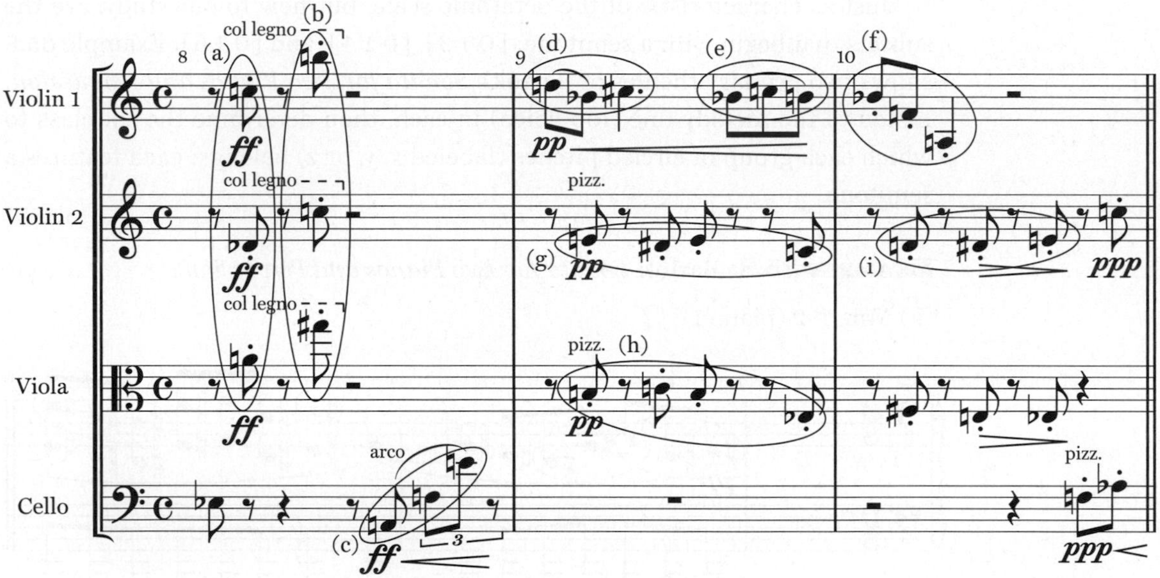

Try it #5

Provide the prime form and Forte number for each circled trichord in Example 35.9.

	Prime form	*Forte number*		*Prime form*	*Forte number*
(a)	________	________	(f)	________	________
(b)	________	________	(g)	________	________
(c)	________	________	(h)	________	________
(d)	________	________	(i)	________	________
(e)	________	________			

SUMMARY

There are only twelve distinct trichords. Learn them as characteristic subsets of familiar collections.

- Subsets of the whole-tone collection: [0 2 4], [0 2 6], [0 4 8].
- Subsets of the pentatonic and diatonic collections: [0 2 4], [0 2 5], [0 2 7], [0 3 7].
- Subsets of the octatonic and diatonic collections: [0 3 6], [0 3 7].
- Subsets of the octatonic and chromatic collections: [0 1 3], [0 1 4], [0 1 6].
- Subsets of the chromatic collection: [0 1 2], [0 1 5], and others.

(All trichords can be considered subsets of the chromatic collection.)

Your teacher may ask you to memorize the Forte set-class numbers for the trichords, listed below for quick reference. In practice, it is helpful to list both the Forte number and prime form for each set class: write SC 3-3 [0 1 4], or SC 5-35 [0 2 4 7 9].

SUMMARY

The twelve trichords with their Forte numbers, prime forms, and interval-class vectors:

3-1 [0 1 2]	icv [210000]	3-7 [0 2 5]	icv [011010]
3-2 [0 1 3]	icv [111000]	3-8 [0 2 6]	icv [010101]
3-3 [0 1 4]	icv [101100]	3-9 [0 2 7]	icv [010020]
3-4 [0 1 5]	icv [100110]	3-10 [0 3 6]	icv [002001]
3-5 [0 1 6]	icv [100011]	3-11 [0 3 7]	icv [001110]
3-6 [0 2 4]	icv [020100]	3-12 [0 4 8]	icv [000300]

Reading Set-Class Tables

Look for a moment at the table in Appendix 5. The first column gives Forte's set-class number. The number in parentheses shows how how many distinct sets belong to that set class, if other than twenty-four. (The set class for the augmented triad, for example, 3-12, gives the number 4 in parentheses to show that there are only four distinct augmented triads.) The second column lists the pcs for the prime form of that set class, and the third column lists the interval-class vector. For visual clarity, all brackets are omitted in the table.

The remainder of this chapter discusses further properties of sets and set classes that can be learned from reading the set-class table. In particular, we focus on properties of set classes that can be revealed by studying the interval-class vector.

Complementary Sets

Sets listed directly across from each other on Forte's table are **complements**.

KEY CONCEPT Complementary sets, when combined in the proper transposition or inversion, form an **aggregate** (one set completes the aggregate of all twelve tones begun by the other). Complementary sets have parallel set-class numbers: 3-12 and 9-12 are complements, as are 4-28 and 8-28, 5-35 and 7-35, and so on.

As an example of complementation, look at one pair of set classes: SC 4-28 [0 3 6 9] and SC 8-28 [0 1 3 4 6 7 9 t]. These should be familiar to you as the fully diminished seventh chord and the octatonic scale. In their prime forms, the sets don't necessarily show their complementary relation, since {0 3 6 9} is actually a literal subset of {0 1 3 4 6 7 9 t}. But if you transpose 4-28 by T_2 to {2 5 8 e}, you find the literal complement of {0 1 3 4 6 7 9 t}; that is, the pcs {2 5 8 e} are "literally" missing from the larger set. When two set classes—such as [0 3 6 9] and [0 1 3 4 6 7 9 t]—are related by complementation in some transposition, though not necessarily the transposition you see in the score, they are called **abstract complements.**

The ic vectors of complementary set classes are related in a particular way: the difference between entries is the same as the difference in cardinality between the two sets. The only exception is in the last ic position, 6 (because 6 is its own complement). For example, the ic vector of 4-28 is [004002] and that of 8-28 is [448444]: each entry in the 8-28 vector except the last is four more than the corresponding entry in the 4-28 vector; the last entry is only two more.

$$\begin{array}{r} 4\ 4\ 8\ 4\ 4\ 4 \\ -\ 0\ 0\ 4\ 0\ 0\ 2 \\ \hline 4\ 4\ 4\ 4\ 4\ (2) \end{array}$$

While the larger set creates more intervals, the two complementary set classes share a similar distribution of interval classes, which is part of the reason they tend to sound like each other. Because a pcset's interval-class content (as represented in the ic vector) does not change as it is transposed, any representatives of 4-28 and 8-28 have this relationship.

KEY CONCEPT When you analyze nontonal music, make note of repeated set classes, subset relationships, and complementary sets. These set relationships often correspond to a consistent sound within a section of music.

Using ic Vectors

To get a quick profile of the sound of a set class, examine its ic vector. For example, the ic vector of SC 6-35 [0 2 4 6 8 t], the whole-tone scale, is [060603]. This vector clearly gives the picture of a set class completely saturated with major seconds (6 in the ic 2 position), major thirds (6 in the ic 4 position), and tritones (3 in the ic 6 position). Similarly, the ic vector of SC 7-35 [0 1 3 5 6 8 t], the diatonic collection, is distinctive for the fact that no two entries in its vector are the same: [254361]. Another ic vector of interest is that for 4-15 [0 1 4 6] and 4-29 [0 1 3 7]: [111111]. These two tetrachords are often called the "all-interval" tetrachords, since their pcs span one each of every interval class. They also share a special relationship: although they have the same ic vector, they are not related by transposition or inversion; such set classes are said to be Z-related. Forte lists these as 4-Z15 and 4-Z29.

Composer Olivier Messiaen was fascinated by what he called the "charm of impossibilities" in various musical dimensions. For example, some modes and scales can be transposed only a limited number of times before they repeat the same pcs again. Messiaen called set classes with this property "modes of limited transposition," and ic vectors can predict which set classes have it.

KEY CONCEPT The number in each position of the ic vector also tells how many common tones will be generated between a pcset and its transposition by that interval class. For example, 1 in the ic 3 position means that when the set is transposed by 3, there will be one common tone. This property is sometimes called the **common-tone theorem**. The only exception is that the number in the ic 6 position must be doubled.

To see how the common-tone theorem works, consider a mode of limited transposition and its ic vector. The whole-tone set class, 6-35, exists in only two distinct forms: {0 2 4 6 8 t} and {1 3 5 7 9 e}. Any transposition (or inversion) reproduces one of these two collections. In its ic vector, [060603], there are two entries of 6. These 6s indicate that when you transpose either of these pcsets by ic 2, the transposition will yield six common tones with the original pcset—because there is a 6 in the ic 2 position of the vector. Similarly, when you transpose either pcset by ic 4, you will also find six common tones—because there is a 6 in the ic 4 position.

The common-tone theorem also means that transposing the whole-tone scale by ic 1, 3, or 5 yields no common tones with the original pcset, because there are zeros in the 1, 3, and 5 vector positions. What about the 3 in the ic 6 position? Double this entry and get another 6; therefore, transposition by ic 6 also yields six common tones. The 3 is doubled because while every other interval class represents two intervals—for example, ic 3 represents both pci 3 and 9—ic 6 is its own inverse; you need to "count" it twice.

To sum up, transposition of {0 2 4 6 8 t} by ic 2, 4, or 6 yields exactly the same pcset back again. On the other hand, transposition by ic 1, 3, or 5 produces no common tones; it produces the other whole-tone collection: {1 3 5 7 9 e}. This is an example of Messiaen's "charm of impossibilities"—that all possible transpositions produce only two distinct forms of the set.

Messiaen identified seven modes of limited transposition. Three of them we already know: his mode 1 is SC 6-35 (the whole-tone collection); mode 2 is SC 8-28 (the octatonic collection); and mode 3 is SC 9-12 (the complement of the augmented triad). Example 35.10 gives a passage from one of Messiaen's compositions—the "Liturgie de cristal," from *Quartet for the End of Time*—featuring two modes of limited transposition.

Example 35.10: Messiaen, "Liturgie de crystal," mm. 5–9

Try it #6

Identify the circled passages (a) and (b) as Messiaen's mode 1, 2, or 3.

	Mode	*Prime form*	*Forte number*
(a)	________	________	________
(b)	________	________	________

Did You Know?

You will find a complete list of Messiaen's modes of limited transposition in his book *The Technique of My Musical Language*, translated by John Satterfield (Paris: A. Leduc, 1956). Messiaen wrote the *Quartet for the End of Time* while incarcerated in a prisoner-of-war camp during World War II. He chose his text from the Revelation of St. John. Messiaen says this about the instrumental ensemble, all fellow prisoners:

> The unusual group for which I wrote this quartet—violin, clarinet, cello and piano—is due to the circumstances surrounding its conception. I was a prisoner-of-war (1941), in Silesia, and among my fellow prisoners were a violinist . . . a clarinetist . . . and a cellist . . . myself being the pianist. . . . Why this choice of text? Perhaps because, in these hours of total privation, the basic forces which control life reasserted themselves. (From the liner notes to Angel/EMI recording S-36587.)

It is remarkable that an artwork of such power was composed in such dire circumstances—a testament to the human spirit.

TERMS YOU SHOULD KNOW

- aggregate
- common-tone theorem
- complement
  - abstract complement
- Forte number
- mode of limited transposition
- normal order
- prime form
- set class

QUESTIONS FOR REVIEW

1. What properties do pcsets belonging to the same set class share?
2. What purpose does prime form serve in music analysis? Describe the process for finding prime form.
3. What is true of the ic vectors for sets related by transposition or inversion?
4. Which trichords are common subsets of the whole tone scale? of the pentatonic scale? of the octatonic scale?
5. What characteristic of complementary sets is revealed by comparing their ic vectors?
6. In twentieth-century music for your own instrument, or a piece specified by your teacher, find a passage that seems to fall naturally into pc groupings of threes (in chords, motives, and so on). Analyze the trichords; find their prime forms. If applicable, show transposition or inversion levels of sets belonging to the same set class.

Ordered Segments and Serialism

CHAPTER 36

Outline of topics

Serial composition

- Ordered pitch segments
- Labeling pitch-class segments
- Operations on pitch classes

Twelve-tone rows

- Labeling rows
- Choosing row forms
- Hearing row relationships
- Realizing twelve-tone rows

Overview

This chapter explores how composers use ordered pitch and pitch-class segments in their works, and suggests strategies for listening to serial music.

Repertoire

Luigi Dallapiccola, "Die Sonne kommt!" from *Goethe-lieder*
John Tavener, "The Lamb"

Serial Composition

Listen to the opening verse of John Tavener's 1982 composition "The Lamb" without a score. Would you call this work nontonal, centric, tonal? You might decide on more than one answer. Here Tavener beautifully contrasts tonal passages with centric ones that feature transformations of ordered pitch segments. Since medieval times, musicians have experimented with ordered pitch and rhythmic segments in their works. In the twentieth and twenty-first centuries, this method of composition reached its pinnacle.

KEY CONCEPT **Serial** music is composed with ordered segments of musical elements—typically pitch or pitch-class segments. Other elements, such as durations, dynamics, and articulations, may also be ordered.

Ordered Pitch Segments

Look at the first phrase of "The Lamb," given in Example 36.1. The tender opening melody sung by the sopranos sounds at first like G major. When the altos join them in measure 2, however, their melodic line creates dissonant intervals with the sopranos in unexpected ways. Sing each line, then calculate the ordered sequence of pitch intervals in the soprano melody (using pluses and minuses). Compare this sequence with that of the alto melody to discover their relationship.

EXAMPLE 36.1: Tavener, "The Lamb," mm. 1–2 (anthology)

Soprano pitch intervals: ______________________

Alto pitch intervals: ______________________

KEY CONCEPT The distinction between sets and segments is an important one in nontonal and serial music analysis.

The term **set** refers to an *unordered* collection.

- Write the elements of sets in curly braces: {0 5 6}.
- Write the prime form of sets and set classes in square brackets: [0 1 6].

The term **segment** refers to an *ordered* collection.

- Write the elements of segments in angle brackets: <7 e 9 6>.

The term **element** may refer to pitches, pitch classes, intervals, interval classes, durations, dynamics, or other musical features.

In Example 36.1, intervals <+4 –2 –3 +1> in the soprano line become <–4 +2 +3 –1> in the alto. The two melodies are pitch **inversions** (I) of each other—that is, they share the same ordered sequence of pitch intervals, but the direction (+ or –) is reversed. How are the melodic segments of the next two measures, Example 36.2, related to each other?

Example 36.2: Tavener, "The Lamb," mm. 3–4 (anthology)

The soprano melody in measure 4 is identical to that of measure 3, only it appears in reverse order. This relationship, called **retrograde** (R), is easiest to see and hear if you attend to the pcs (rather than the intervals). When you retrograde a pitch segment, its intervals will reverse order and change direction (up or down) as well, as the analysis below the staff shows.

Now look at Example 36.3, the third phrase of this piece. The soprano's melody in measure 5 is the same as in measure 3. Take this soprano segment (m. 3 or 5) as the standard—the **prime** segment (P), from which the other melodies are derived. The melody of measure 1 would not work as the standard because it is only a fragment; the melody in measure 3 is repeated numerous times in the piece.

EXAMPLE 36.3: Tavener, "The Lamb," mm. 5–6 (anthology)

Try it #1

Write the sequence of pitch intervals for each voice part in Example 36.3 in the blanks below. Then circle the appropriate word, if any, that applies to each sequence.

(a) m. 5 soprano ___<+4 -2 -3 -3 +2 +3>___ prime inversion retrograde

(b) m. 5 alto ________________ prime inversion retrograde

(c) m. 6 soprano ________________ prime inversion retrograde

(d) m. 6 alto ________________ prime inversion retrograde

(e) How do the m. 6 alto intervals compare with the prime?

____

In Example 36.3, the sopranos sing P followed by R. The altos sing I, followed by a new transformation: the **retrograde inversion** (RI) of P. The alto's pitches here (m. 6) are identical to the inversion sung in reverse order (in retrograde); its intervals are identical to the prime, but in reverse order.

SUMMARY

The first complete ordered segment in a piece is usually designated the prime (P), and later segments are compared with it, using one of four transformations: T (transposition), R (retrograde), I (inversion), or RI (retrograde inversion).

Listen again to "The Lamb," while following the score in your anthology. Try to hear the relationships between P and each of its transformations (I, R, and RI) in measures 1–6 by listening for the relations between the pitch-interval sequences. Listen also to hear how the composer artfully alternates serial passages with tonal ones.

KEY CONCEPT One way to begin hearing relationships between ordered pitch segments is to listen for transformations of their interval sequences.

Transpositions (T): The pitch-interval sequences are identical.

Inversions (I): The direction of each pitch interval is inverted (+ becomes – and vice versa).

Retrograde (R): The pitch-interval sequence is in reverse order.

Retrograde inversion (RI): The pitch-interval sequence is in reverse order and inverted.

Labeling Pitch-Class Segments

You can represent relationships between segments in a precise way with labels based on the first pc integer of the segment's P or I form. In Example 36.3, the P segment (m. 5, soprano) begins with pc 7; we therefore call the segment T_7P. Add an R to the prime label to show the retrograde form (m. 6, soprano): RT_7P. The inversion of P (m. 5, alto) also begins with pc 7; call it T_7IP. Add an R to the inverted segment's label to show retrograde inversion (m. 6, alto): RT_7IP. Write these labels in Example 36.3.

While the labels are accurate and precise, many people prefer a shorthand notation: P_7 (or T_7) instead of T_7P, R_7 instead of RT_7P, and so on. We will use the shorthand labels here, but be aware of one common source of confusion: while P and I labels match the first pc integer of the segment, R and RI labels do not. For example, R_7 does not begin with pc 7. Its more precise label makes this clear: RT_7P is the retrograde of T_7P. Since P_7 starts with pc 7, R_7 *ends* with pc 7. The same principle holds for RI_7, which also ends with pc 7 (check the alto line in m. 6 of Example 36.3 to confirm this).

SUMMARY

P_7: a segment P that begins with pc 7

R_7: a retrograde form of P that ends with pc 7

I_7: an inverted form of P that begins with pc 7

RI_7: a retrograde of P's inversion that ends with pc 7

Another Way

There are two main systems for labeling segments. The first system (P_7, R_7, and so on) you have just read about. But some analysts label the first appearance of the segment as T_0P, or P_0, to show that it is the first and "original" form, on which others are based. Each subsequent transposition is then calculated from this original. (That is, transposition up a whole step would be labeled P_2.) The two systems are akin to fixed *do* and movable *do*. The system that labels each segment by the number of its first pc is a fixed-*do* system; the system that labels the original P_0 and the others by the interval of transposition is a movable-*do* system. Because the fixed-*do* system is most common, we will follow it here.

Operations on Pitch Classes

Given a pitch-class segment, P, how do you calculate its R, I, and RI forms? Look again at Example 36.3, which shows all four forms. The integer notation for P_7, in the soprano's measure 5, is <7 e 9 6 3 5 8>. The R_7 form, which follows in measure 6, is the same sequence in reverse order: <8 5 3 6 9 e 7>. To find the inversion of <7 e 9 6 3 5 8>, substitute for each pc its inverse: <5 1 3 6 9 7 4>. Then, since Tavener chose the form beginning on pc 7 for the alto line of measure 5, transpose this segment by adding 2 to each element: <7 3 5 8 e 9 6>.

KEY CONCEPT Always invert *first* before transposing pcs or retrograding the order of pcs. Performing these operations in the opposite order will result in a different set of pcs.

Finally, find the retrograde inversion by running the pcs of the inverted form backward: <6 9 e 8 5 3 7>, the same as the alto melody of measure 6.

SUMMARY

Following are the four classic operations for pitch classes in a prime segment (P).

Transposition (T): Add a constant integer (mod12) to each pc in P.

Retrograde (R): Reverse the pc order of P (so the pcs run backward).

Inversion (I): Replace each pc in P with its inverse (mod12), and then transpose as needed.

Retrograde inversion (RI): Reverse the pc order of I.

Remember: When these operations are combined, always invert first, then transpose, then retrograde.

Another Way

You can use index numbers as a shortcut for inverting a segment. Given a segment <7 e 9 6 3 5 8>, if you want to write its inversion on pc 7, determine the index number by adding the first pc of each row (7 + 7 = 14 = 2): the index is 2. Now subtract all pcs of the original segment from 2 to get the inverted segment:

	2	2	2	2	2	2	2
-	7	e	9	6	3	5	8
<	7	3	5	8	e	9	6> = inversion.

Twelve-Tone Rows

Serial music composed with twelve-pc segments is called **twelve-tone**, or **dodecaphonic**, music (from the Greek for "twelve sounds").

KEY CONCEPT When an ordered segment consists of twelve distinct pcs, one from each pitch class, it is called a **twelve-tone row**.

Dodecaphonic composition originated with Arnold Schoenberg and his students Anton Webern and Alban Berg in Vienna in the 1920s. Later, many other composers—even Igor Stravinsky and Aaron Copland, whose nonserial music may be more familiar to you—wrote some twelve-tone works. Elsewhere in Europe, composers such as Pierre Boulez and Luigi Dallapiccola wrote music with twelve-tone rows, as did Milton Babbitt and Elliott Carter in the United States.

Listen to Dallapiccola's "Die Sonne kommt!" for soprano and E-flat clarinet, while following the translation below. Watch for text painting around the words "comes up," "crescent," "such a pair," "riddle," and any other significant words.

Die Sonne kommt! Ein Prachter scheinen!	The sun comes up! A glorious sight!
Der Sichelmond umklammert sie.	The crescent moon embraces her.
Wer konnte solch ein Paar vereinen?	Who could unite such a pair?
Dies Rätsel, wie erklärt sich's? wie?	This riddle, how to solve it? How?

Probably most obvious associations are the ways the melody's contour fits the words: for example, the broad ascending intervals to which the composer sets "sun comes up!" and the twisting of the musical line around "crescent." "Moon" is set to broad descending intervals, perhaps to contrast with the sun's ascent. "Such a pair" refers to the sun and moon, but Dallapiccola provides additional associations by scoring the piece for voice and clarinet duo, and by basing the primary pitch material on two transpositions of a twelve-tone row. We will return to the question of the riddle!

EXAMPLE 36.4: Dallapiccola, "Die Sonne kommt!" mm. 1–9a (voice) (anthology)

Try it #2

There are two complete rows in Example 36.4. The second is an inversion of the first.

(a) Write out the pcs to see where each row begins and ends. In measure 6, omit the two repeated notes.

Row 1: < 8 9 7 5 ________ > Label: P_8

Row 2: < ________ > Label: ____

(b) Divide P_8 into trichords, and provide the prime form for each.

Row 1: < 8 9 7 5 __ __ __ __ __ __ __ __ >

Trichords: [0 1 2] [____] [____] [____]

The first row in Example 36.4 (mm. 1–5) is the prime row. Label it P8, since it begins with pc 8. The row divides into set classes 3-1 [0 1 2], 3-5 [0 1 6], 3-4 [0 1 5], and a repetition of 3-5 [0 1 6]. Compare the normal orders of the two statements of 3-5 [0 1 6] within the row to discover their relation: they are {e 4 5}, and {0 1 6}, related by T_5I. Set-class identification remains an important tool for the analysis of serial music; if you had any difficulty identifying the set-class labels for these trichords or the relation between equivalent trichords, work through the review that follows (otherwise, skip ahead to "Labeling Rows").

SUMMARY

When you list the trichord pcs in the order they appear in the score, enclose them in angle brackets to show they are *ordered* segments: <8 9 7>, <5 e 4>, <2 3 t>, <1 0 6>. To find the set-class labels for these segments, rearrange the pcs (in ascending order, around the clock face) into a normal order that no longer represents their order in the composition. They are now considered *unordered* sets, written with curly braces. The normal orders for the Dallapiccola trichords (not yet transposed to prime form) are {7 8 9}, {e 4 5}, {t 2 3}, and {0 1 6}.

To find prime form and the set-class label: first determine whether any trichord needs to be inverted (because the larger intervals lie to the left rather than to the right), and then transpose so that the first pc is 0. The first trichord of the row, {7 8 9}, can be transposed by T_5 to begin on 0; it belongs to SC 3-1 [0 1 2]. The second trichord, {e 4 5}, must be inverted to {1 8 7}, reordered around the clock to {7 8 1}, and transposed (also by T_5); it belongs to SC 3-5 [0 1 6], as does the last trichord. The third trichord, {t 2 3}, must also be inverted, to {2 t 9}, then reordered to {9 t 2} and transposed by T_3. It belongs to SC 3-4 [0 1 5]. The two 3-5 trichords—{e 4 5} and {0 1 6}—are T_5I related, because the pcs when aligned properly (when one trichord is reversed) sum to 5:

$$\begin{array}{rrr} \text{e} & 4 & 5 \\ +6 & 1 & 0 \\ \hline 5 & 5 & 5 \end{array}$$

Labeling Rows

Listen to phrase 2 of "Die Sonne kommt!" (beginning "Der Sichelmond," mm. 6–9a). You might initially be confused because Dallapiccola repeats pitches here: <9 8 t 9 8>. While a twelve-tone row itself does not repeat pcs, composers may repeat one or more pcs when they set the row in a piece of music, just as a motive might be repeated; simply disregard the repetition when labeling rows.

Example 36.5 gives phrases 2 and 3, including the entrance of the clarinet. Does the clarinet line sound familiar? It should, since the melody is an exact repetition of the opening vocal line (mm. 1–5). It is unusual—and not characteristic of most twelve-tone music—that Dallapiccola repeats not just the original row's pcs, but its exact original pitches, with the same contour and rhythm.

Example 36.5: Dallapiccola, "Die Sonne kommt!" mm. 6–12 (anthology)

Now compare the ordered pc intervals of the "Sichelmond" phrase with those of the original row. Use the ordered pci succession to determine the row form. Remember that ordered pcis need to be calculated *clockwise* around the clock face, or subtracted (b – a) mod12.

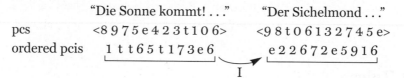

	"Die Sonne kommt! . . ."		"Der Sichelmond . . ."
pcs	<8 9 7 5 e 4 2 3 t 1 0 6>		<9 8 t 0 6 1 3 2 7 4 5 e>
ordered pcis	1 t t 6 5 t 1 7 3 e 6	→ I	e 2 2 6 7 2 e 5 9 1 6

KEY CONCEPT When rows are related by inversion, each ordered pc interval in one row corresponds with its inverse in the other row.

The two rows are inversionally related. We can label the "Sichelmond" row I_9—because it begins with pc 9.

Another Way

If you were using the movable-*do* system of row labeling, you would have labeled the initial row P_0. Since the original row began on G♯ as P_0, the I form beginning on A (m. 6) would be labeled a half step above that: I_1.

Try it #3

Add row labels in the blanks below for the rows in Example 36.5.

m. 6 (voice): ______ m. 8 (clarinet): ______ m. 9 (voice): ______

The only "new" row in this passage, not heard previously in the song, is ______ .

KEY CONCEPT Sometimes composers make a row's construction, or relationships between row forms, clear by the musical context: by the rhythm, contour, register, or correspondence to motives or phrases. They may also obscure rows in various ways, such as setting them as chords where the ordering may be difficult to discern.

As you probably noticed, the repeated B5 in measure 9 signals the beginning of a retrograde—the same melody (pitch, contour, and rhythm) as measures 6–8. It is therefore labeled RI_9. The rest of the song continues in the same vein, with exact repetitions of previous row forms and exact retrogrades, including contour and rhythm. When a segment of music is followed by a repetition entirely in retrograde (pitch, rhythm, and so on), the two segments together are called a **palindrome**. Perhaps the palindrome represents the poem's "riddle." Dallapiccola builds an entire work out of simple repetition and transformation, in the same way that Renaissance and Baroque composers wrote "riddle" canons whose solutions involved performing the canonic melody backward or upside-down.

Choosing Row Forms

The internal structure of a row has a great deal to do with larger decisions composers make about their twelve-tone pieces, just as a small-scale motive in a tonal work might foreshadow a change of key or large-scale tonal design. Look, for example, at Dallapiccola's row choices in light of the T_5I relationship between the two statements of SC 3-5 [0 1 6]. Because these two trichords are related by index number 5, any two rows whose T_nI numbers sum to 5 will reproduce the pcs of these two trichords as a unit within the row. More advanced study of twelve-tone theory can explain why this is so. For our purposes, we can simply observe that Dallapiccola has chosen row pairs—P_8 and I_9, plus their retrogrades—that sum to 5. You will find these pc duplications, called **invariant pcs**, or **invariant sets**, between each pair of rows related by T_5I.

KEY CONCEPT **Invariance** means "kept the same," or "does not vary." Composers use pitch, pitch-class, or segment invariance to make connections between rows, sets, or segments. These invariant elements are often audible features of a work, and may contribute to its musical coherence.

To see invariance at work, look at the underlined trichords below. The two rows in measures 8–12 are P_8 (clarinet, beginning in m. 8) and RI_9 (voice, m. 9b). These transposition levels, 8 and 9, sum to index number 5 (mod12). Study the rows below to see how trichords {e 4 5} and {0 1 6} reappear though their order varies. They too are related by T_5I.

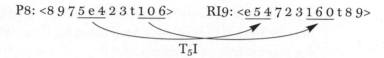

P8: <8 9 7 5 e 4 2 3 t 1 0 6>   RI9: <e 5 4 7 2 3 1 6 0 t 8 9>

T_5I

Pcs {8 9} and {2 3} also appear consecutively in the two rows. This too is a predictable feature, since 8 + 9 and also 2 + 3 sum to 5.

Now look at Example 36.6 to see how Dallapiccola features some of these pc recurrences in his musical setting. The circles mark instances where the composer has placed these invariant pcs in close proximity. His choice to realize many of them in the same pitch register makes audible the pc correspondences between rows, and the text painting of "such a pair" played out by paired statements of {e 4 5}, {2 3}, and {0 1 6}.

EXAMPLE 36.6: Dallapiccola, "Die Sonne kommt!" mm. 6–12 (showing invariant pcs) (anthology)

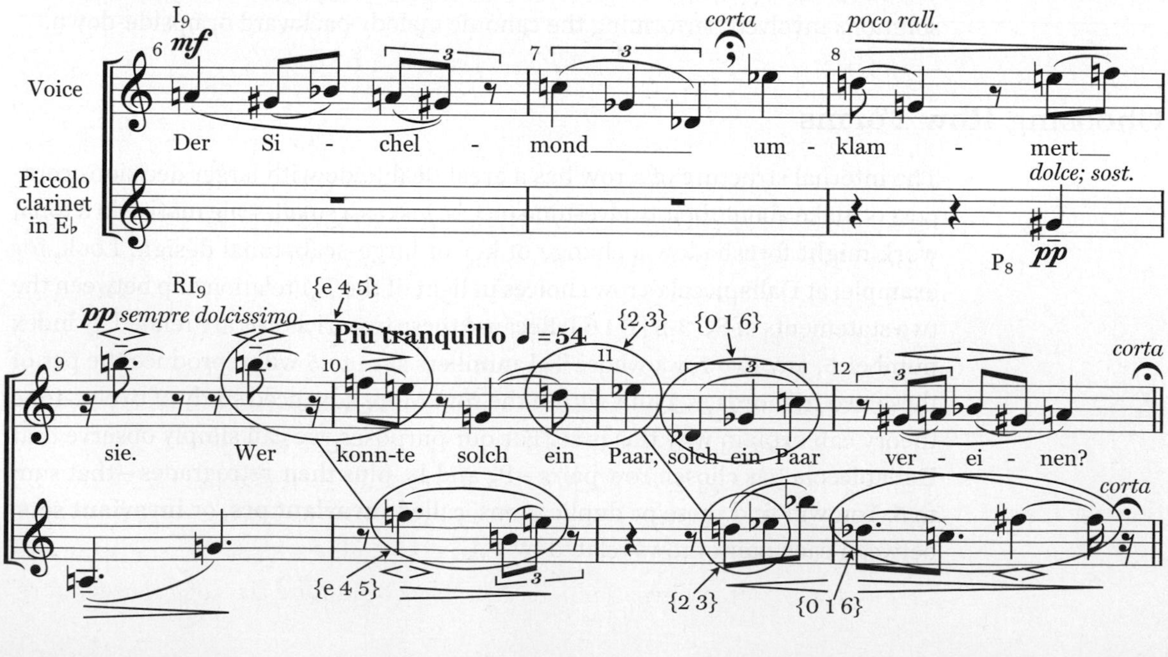

Hearing Row Relationships

You need no special abilities, other than patience and practice, to hear how rows are related. The first step is to analyze aurally the ordered pci sequence of a row. Write down this sequence as you hear it: often it will contain distinctive intervals or trichords at the beginning and end that will help you determine which row form is being used. Dallapiccola's row begins with the [0 1 2] trichord: listen for opening chromaticism or leaps of major sevenths. It ends with a distinctive interval: a tritone. If you hear a row beginning with chromaticism, it must be a P or I form, but if you hear a row beginning with a tritone, it must be an R or RI form.

If the beginning and end of the row are highly similar, then you will want to write down the entire sequence of intervals as you hear them. It is often easier to take ordered pitch intervals in dictation than it is to take pc intervals. Write down these pitch intervals, and then convert them to pc intervals. When you hear the next row, compare its pci sequence with the one you have written down. With time and practice, you can learn to do this. While such dictation helps you appreciate one dimension of the composition, don't forget to listen for other musical aspects: form, phrase, harmony or distinctive set classes, motivic repetition, and so on. The early twelve-tone composers saw their innovation as an outgrowth of motivic development and variation technique in Western music—not as a rejection of the earlier tradition but as a continuation and enrichment of that tradition.

Realizing Twelve-Tone Rows

A row is a precompositional idea—a sequence of pitch classes that composers then realize musically in various ways, just as Baroque composers could realize figured bass in different ways. The repetitions of a row might involve an entirely different contour and sequence of pitches (the same pitch classes, but different pitches), or a different rhythm or tempo. Some pcs may be repeated before proceeding to the next pcs of the row, and the row may be presented linearly (in a melody or voice-leading strand), harmonically, or with melody and harmony together. The row may be performed by one instrument or shared among a group of instruments. More than one form of the row (or even two or more different rows) may be heard at the same time.

The row, or a segment of it, may be rotated—with elements of the ordered segment moved from the end to the beginning, or vice versa. This allows composers great flexibility in creating contrasting musical sections, by any number of musical means, while still maintaining the order of intervals in the row. Schoenberg was convinced that a composer's craft included the ability to work with material from a row. He wrote: "The time will come when the ability to draw thematic material from a basic set of twelve tones will be an unconditional prerequisite for obtaining admission into the composition class of a conservatory"

(*Style and Idea*, 1948). Musical unity in a serial composition is created both by the row and by its realization through the compositional process.

Did You Know?

Just as the musical palindromes that structure Dallapiccola's song may have intrigued you, linguistic palindromes have charmed readers for many years. Some examples include "Doc, note; I diet on cod" and "Able was I, ere I saw Elba."

Anton Webern was fascinated with what is called the Sator Square, made of the Latin words SATOR AREPO TENET OPERA ROTAS written in a square so that they may be read top-to-bottom, bottom-to-top, left-to-right, and right-to-left:

S A T O R
A R E P O
T E N E T
O P E R A
R O T A S

Webern cited this square as inspiration for his serial compositions. The earliest known appearance of the square was in the ruins of Pompeii, preserved by being buried in the ash of Mt. Vesuvius in A. D. 79. The saying translates as "The farmer Arepo has work [with] wheels [i.e., a plow]."

TERMS YOU SHOULD KNOW

- dodecaphonic
- invariance
    - invariant pcs
    - invariant sets
- inversion (I)
- palindrome
- prime (P)
- retrograde (R)
- retrograde inversion (RI)
- row
- serial
- twelve tone
- twelve-tone row

QUESTIONS FOR REVIEW

1. What is serialism? What elements other than pitches can be ordered?
2. How does the pattern of pitch-class intervals change from P to I forms of the row? from P to R? from P to RI?
3. What are some characteristics to look for in studying the row for a serial piece?
4. The row numbers for R and RI forms come from which pc of the row (first or last)?
5. If a row contains two equivalent sets related by T_nI, what happens when the entire row is transformed by that same T_nI?
6. How can properties of the row be brought out (or not) in its musical realization?
7. Are all serial works twelve tone? Explain, citing examples from this chapter.

Twelve-Tone Rows and the Row Matrix

CHAPTER 37

Outline of topics

The row matrix

- Hexachordal combinatoriality
- Finding combinatorial row pairs

Serialism and compositional style

Overview

This chapter introduces advanced twelve-tone techniques, including how composers choose which row forms to combine. We will see and hear how twelve-tone compositions may differ in style by examining two contrasting piano works.

Repertoire

Arnold Schoenberg, *Klavierstück*, Op. 33a
Anton Webern, *Variations for Piano*, Op. 27, second movement

The Row Matrix

(anthology) To learn how composers might create contrasting material from a single row, we turn now to a more extended work: Schoenberg's *Klavierstück*, Op. 33a. Listen to the piece while following the score in your anthology (p. 326). This piano work is sometimes described as a twelve-tone sonata form: listen for an expository first theme and lyrical second theme; then mark where those two themes return in the "recapitulation." Of course, without tonality this cannot be a true sonata, since the form by definition hinges on the tension between contrasting keys. Nevertheless, Schoenberg's composition alludes to sonata form, even in this nontonal context. This is acknowledged by Anton Webern, who once said in a lecture (later published as *The Path to the New Music*), "We too are writing in classical forms, which haven't vanished."

Example 37.1a gives the opening of the work. In this chordal texture, it is not possible to determine the row's order; we need to look for a melodic statement of the row, where the ordering is clearer. One possibility is the return of this first theme in the "recapitulation," shown in part (b). Here, the right hand brings back the chordal opening in measures 32–33, after the fermata, but now in arpeggiated form. When you have determined the order of the row pcs, label their placement in the chords by giving them **order numbers**—counting out the elements of the row from 1 to 12.

Example 37.1: Schoenberg, *Klavierstück*, Op. 33a

(a) Mm. 1–2

(b) Mm. 32–34

Try it #1

Write out the ordered pcs for the first row in Example 37.1b (above the score), beginning in the right hand of measure 32, after the fermata.

(a) Copy the pcs below, and write the corresponding order numbers beneath.

Row pcs: < t 5 0 e ______________

Order numbers: 1 2 3 4 ______________

(b) Write the order numbers for the three chords in measure 1 of Example 37.1a next to the notes, then copy them here, arranged from low to high.

Chord 1: 1 2 3 4 (from top to bottom: 1, 2, 3, 4) ______ Chord 2: ______ Chord 3: ______

SUMMARY

When the first row in a piece is presented chordally, look for a later appearance of the row as a melody to determine the pc order. Label individual row elements in the score with order numbers from 1 to 12, to show where they appear in the musical context.

The distinctive set classes or intervals that lie at either end of this row (<t 5 0 e 9 6 1 3 7 8 2 4>) help make the row relationships audible. P and I forms begin with an ic 5, and the first trichord is the pentatonic subset 3-9 [0 2 7]. The R and RI forms begin with an ic 2, and the whole-tone subset 3-8 [0 2 6]. Listen for these different sounds to identify the row forms.

To label other row forms in this piece, take Schoenberg's row and build a **row matrix**—a 12 x 12 chart that displays all possible P, I, R, and RI forms of a row, and a convenient aid to musical analysis. Complete the matrix with either letter names or pc integers; use integers for this matrix for now, to make calculating T and I forms easier.

KEY CONCEPT To build a row matrix:

1. Write the P form of the row across the top, transposed to begin with 0.
2. Write the I form of the row—found by taking the inverse of each pc in the row—down the left-hand column.
3. Consider each pc in the left-hand column as the first pc in each P form (transpose the original P form to begin on this pc).

If you transpose the initial row to begin on 0, then the main diagonal from the upper left- to lower right-hand corner will contain all zeros. This is a helpful property, since you can judge from the diagonal of zeros whether you have calculated correctly.

The matrix on the opposite page is partially completed. Read P forms left to right; in this matrix, the first row is P_0, the second is P_5, the third is P_t, and so on. To find R forms, read the rows backward, right to left. The first row is R_0, the second is R_5, the third is R_t, and so on. (Remember, R forms are named by the first pc of their related P form.) Read the I forms top to bottom as columns: the first column is I_0, the second is I_7, the third is I_2. Finally, read the RI forms as columns bottom to top: the first column is RI_0, the second is RI_7, the third is RI_2. (Remember, RI forms are named by the first pc of their related I form.)

Try it #2

Fill in the remaining positions in the matrix on your own. (You may find the task easier if you complete the matrix in this order: P_0, P_1, P_2, P_3, and so on. This way you only have to add 1 each time.) Complete the labels along each side of the matrix in the blanks provided.

I ↓ P → ← R

	I_0	I_7	I_2	I_1	I_e								
P_0	0	7	2	1	e	8	3	5	9	t	4	6	R_0
P_5	5	0	7	6	4	1	8	t	2	3	9	e	R_5
P_t	t	5	0	e	9	6	1	3	7	8	2	4	Rt
P_e	e	6		0			2						R_e
P_1	1	8			0		4						R_1
	4	e				0	7						
	9	4					0						
	7	2					t	0					
	3	t					6		0				
	2	9					5			0			
	8	3					e				0		
	6	1	8	7	5	2	9	e	3	4	t	0	
	RI_0	RI_7	RI_2	RI_1	RI_e								

↑ RI

When you have completed the matrix, refer to it as you label the remaining rows in the Schoenberg examples.

Try it #3

Fill in the requested row labels.

Example 37.1a:

m. 1: P_______ m. 2: RI_______

Example 37.1b:

mm. 32–33a, right hand: P_______ mm. 33b–34a, right hand: RI_______

left hand: I_______ left hand: R_______

Hexachordal Combinatoriality

Listen to the second theme of Schoenberg's piece, given in Example 37.2. This theme has a slower "harmonic rhythm"—that is, it takes longer for each row to be completed. Label the row forms, one in the right hand and one in the left, from the matrix you completed. Interestingly, Schoenberg uses the same transpositions of the row as earlier in the composition, but to very different musical effect.

EXAMPLE 37.2: Schoenberg, *Klavierstück*, mm. 14–18 (anthology)

If you had not been tipped off to look for one row in each hand, you might have had difficulty identifying rows in this passage. This is because Schoenberg completes an aggregate in measures 14–16, before either row concludes. To understand this concept, notate the passage in pc integers. Divide the row in each hand into two hexachords, just as Schoenberg does in measure 16, by means of rests and changes in register. Remember that pitches can be repeated, but they will maintain row order.

		mm. 14–16a	mm. 16b–18
right hand:	P_t	<t 5 0 e 9 6	1 3 7 8 2 4>
left hand:	I_3	<3 8 1 2 4 7	0 t 6 5 e 9>
		aggregate	aggregate

Look at the first hexachord of each row. When they are performed in combination, you hear all twelve pcs—an **aggregate**. Likewise, the second hexachords of each row, when combined, make a complete aggregate.

KEY CONCEPT **Hexachordal combinatoriality** occurs when two forms of the same row are paired so that the rows' initial hexachords, when combined, complete an aggregate. Similarly, the rows' second hexachords, when combined, complete an aggregate.

When aggregates are created by pcs from more than one row form, they are sometimes called **secondary sets** (from the old naming of rows as "sets"). Hexachordal combinatoriality may help create variety in the pcs and intervals in the counterpoint between voices. It can also contribute to a faster harmonic rhythm—that is, the frequency with which a row or aggregate is completed and the next one begins.

You can diagram the combinatorial relationship as follows, where A represents the unordered pc content of one hexachord, and B the content of the other.

row:	A	B
transformation of row:	B	A
	aggregate	aggregate

In the Schoenberg example, hexachord A is {5 6 9 t e 0} and hexachord B is {1 2 3 4 7 8}.

There are four types of combinatoriality: P-, I-, R-, and RI-combinatoriality. We have already seen an example of I-combinatoriality, where a row is paired with its inversion, in the Schoenberg example (P_t paired with I_3). In P-combinatoriality, a row is paired with another P form (a transposition of the original). In R- or RI-combinatoriality, a row is paired with a retrograde or retrograde-inversion form. A hexachord that can generate all four types of combinatoriality is called an **all-combinatorial hexachord.**

There are only six all-combinatorial hexachords:

6-1	[0 1 2 3 4 5]	6-20	[0 1 4 5 8 9]
6-7	[0 1 2 6 7 8]	6-32	[0 2 4 5 7 9]
6-8	[0 2 3 4 5 7]	6-35	[0 2 4 6 8 t]

Finding Combinatorial Row Pairs

If you wanted to compose a twelve-tone work that featured combinatorial row pairs, you would need to know how to "find" pairs that work.

The easiest way to determine whether a row is combinatorial is by examining its row matrix. As an example, consider the row matrix for Webern's *Variations for Piano*, since this row happens to feature an all-combinatorial hexachord (although, as we will see, the movement analyzed here does not employ combinatoriality at all). To find a combinatorial pair of rows, first divide the matrix into four quadrants, as shown below. This isolates the hexachords for comparison. If you wanted to find a P-combinatorial pair for P_5, whose first hexachord is <5 1 0 4 3 2>, you would circle this collection on the left side of the matrix and hunt for the same unordered collection, {0 1 2 3 4 5}, on the right side of the matrix; the content of the A hexachord should appear in the second (B) hexachord of the new row. Once you have found it, you can see that P_5 and P_e are P-combinatorial.

	0	8	7	e	t	9	3	1	4	2	6	5
	4	0	e	3	2	1	7	5	8	6	t	9
P_5	**5**	**1**	**0**	**4**	**3**	**2**	8	6	9	7	e	t
	1	9	8	0	e	t	4	2	5	3	7	6
	2	t	9	1	0	e	5	3	6	4	8	7
	3	e	t	2	1	0	6	4	7	5	9	8
	9	5	4	8	7	6	0	t	1	e	3	2
P_e	e	7	6	t	9	8	**2**	**0**	**3**	**1**	**5**	**4**
	8	4	3	7	6	5	e	9	0	t	2	1
	t	6	5	9	8	7	1	e	2	0	4	3
	6	2	1	5	4	3	9	7	t	8	0	e
	7	3	2	6	5	4	t	8	e	9	1	0

P_5: <5 1 0 4 3 2 8 6 9 7 e t>
P_e: <e 7 6 t 9 8 2 0 3 1 5 4>
aggregate   aggregate

Try it #4

Follow the same procedure to find other P-combinatorial rows.

(a) What row is P-combinatorial with P_9? _____

(b) What row is P-combinatorial with P_7? _____

To find an I-combinatorial pair, again begin by circling the first hexachord of the P form on the left side of the matrix, as shown. This time, hunt for the equivalent content of this unordered hexachord anywhere on the bottom half, as part of a column. Look at columns rather than rows, because you are looking for I forms; and the bottom half because you want to find an I row whose second (B) hexachord is equivalent in content to hexachord A.

												I_6	
	0	8	7	e	t	9	3	1	4	2	6	5
	4	0	e	3	2	1	7	5	8	6	t	9
P_5	**5**	**1**	**0**	**4**	**3**	**2**	8	6	9	7	e	t
	1	9	8	0	e	t	4	2	5	3	7	6
	2	t	9	1	0	e	5	3	6	4	8	7
	3	e	t	2	1	0	6	4	7	5	9	8
	9	5	4	8	7	6	0	t	1	e	**3**	2
	e	7	6	t	9	8	2	0	3	1	**5**	4
	8	4	3	7	6	5	e	9	0	t	**2**	1
	t	6	5	9	8	7	1	e	2	0	**4**	3
	6	2	1	5	4	3	9	7	t	8	**0**	e
	7	3	2	6	5	4	t	8	e	9	**1**	0

Again, once you have found it, simply read the row forms from the matrix: P_5 and I_6 are I-combinatorial.

P_5: <5 1 0 4 3 2 8 6 9 7 e t>
I_6: <6 t e 7 8 9 3 5 2 4 0 1>
aggregate aggregate

Try it #5

Follow the same procedure to find other I-combinatorial rows.

(a) What row is I-combinatorial with P_9? _____

(b) What row is I-combinatorial with P_7? _____

You can use an analogous procedure to find RI-combinatoriality. The R-combinatorial pair in this row is P_5 and R_5. Any row paired with its own retrograde will produce R-combinatoriality.

P_5: <5 1 0 4 3 2 8 6 9 7 e t>
R_5: <t e 7 9 6 8 2 3 4 0 1 5>
aggregate aggregate

Serialism and Compositional Style

Together, the centric serialism of Tavener's "The Lamb," the riddle canons of the Dallapiccola song, and the sonata-like Schoenberg piano work demonstrate that not all serial music sounds alike. Indeed, there is a greater resemblance between Schoenberg's later twelve-tone works and his early, "free" nontonal (nonserial) compositions than there is between the twelve-tone music of Schoenberg and Webern, or between Webern and Berg. Twelve-tone compositional technique is independent of musical style and genre, and it can be difficult to determine aurally whether a work is serial or more freely nontonal. Webern's *Variations for Piano* demonstrates a few musical features that are typical of this composer's serial works.

Listen to the second movement, at first without a score, as an introduction to the composer's style. Webern is much less likely than Schoenberg to write long, lyrical melodies. Instead, he opts for short movements with a succession of brief melodies, creating a tapestry of sound. One thing that stands out on a first hearing is that the movement sounds repetitive in ways that extend beyond the repeat signs of the binary form. Why, for instance, do we keep hearing the A4—a repeated pitch in the midst of so much other varied pitch activity? Other pitches stand out because of their extreme high register: the same high notes, G6 and E6, appear here and there. Listen again while following the score in your anthology, then we will begin a row analysis to see if we can find the reasons for these choices.

Webern's row for the entire three-movement composition is the same, and we have already seen the row matrix in the discussion of combinatoriality above. Refer to the matrix (p. 776) to analyze the row forms in Example 37.3. Here are some hints. First, there is one row in each hand. Second, the row placement switches from one hand to the other midway through the phrase. Third, Webern employs a technique similar to phrase overlap, or elision, in this composition—that is, he chooses row forms where the last pc in one row is the same as the first pc in the next. These shared pcs he states only once, so you'll need to "count" them twice. This technique is sometimes called **row elision** (or "row linkage").

EXAMPLE 37.3: Webern, *Variations for Piano*, second movement, mm. 1–11 (anthology)

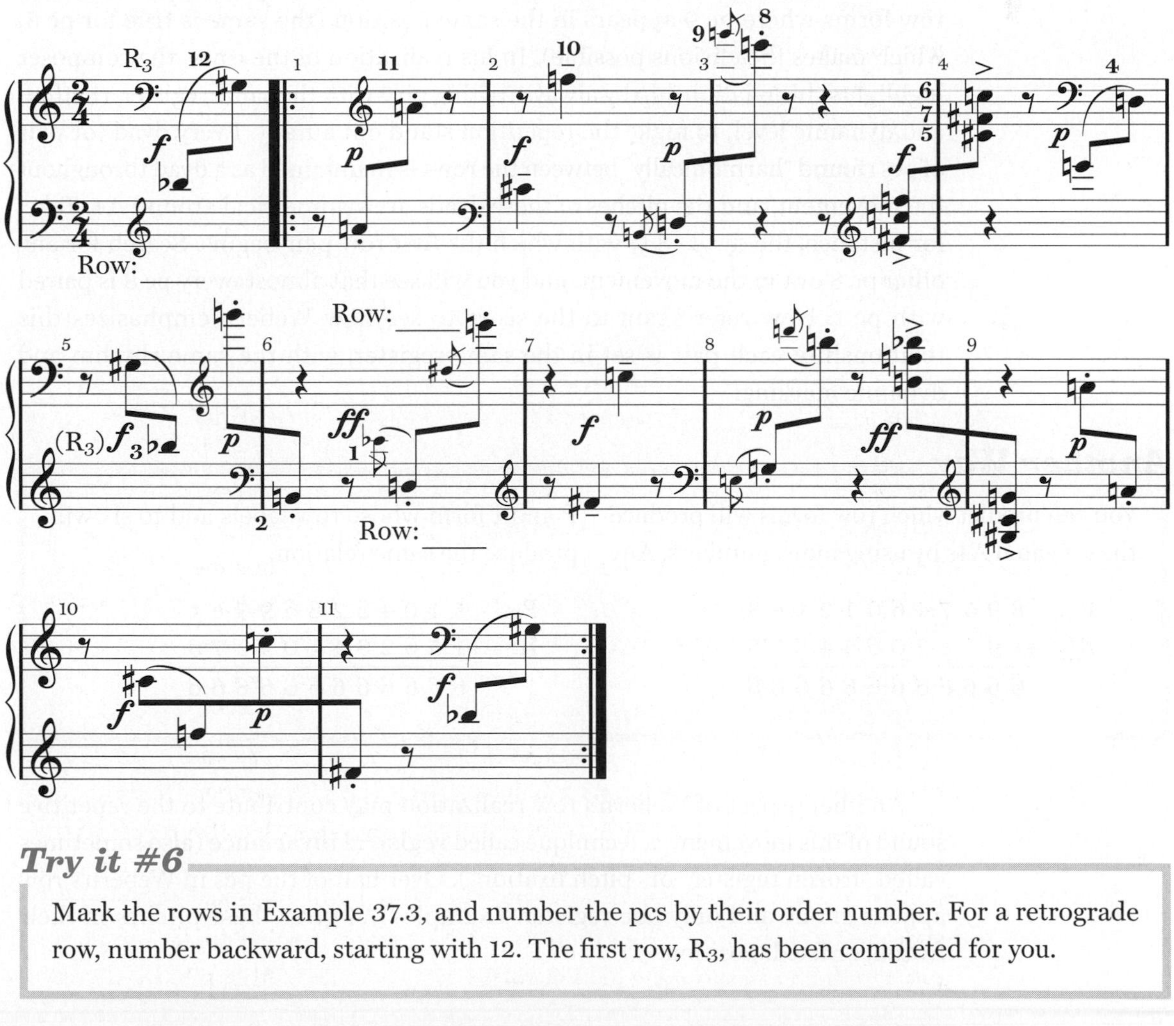

Try it #6

Mark the rows in Example 37.3, and number the pcs by their order number. For a retrograde row, number backward, starting with 12. The first row, R_3, has been completed for you.

Think of the texture in this movement as a canon between hands. The rhythms, articulations, and dynamics are identical from the left hand (the **dux**, or leader) to the right (the **comes**, or follower). This relationship swaps within the row (m. 5), which helps identify the point at which the rows switch from one hand to the other. The dux/comes relationship continues to swap throughout the piece, and can help you locate the rows.

It is sometimes helpful to write out the row pairs in integer notation to consider relationships of interest, just as you did for the combinatorial pairs. The rows in the first half of the movement are listed below (with the pcs that are elided in parentheses):

R_3:	<8 9 5 7 4 6 0 1 2 t e 3>	R_t:	<(3) 4 0 2 e 1 7 8 9 5 6 t>
RI_3:	<t 9 1 e 2 0 6 5 4 8 7 3>	RI_8:	<(3) 2 6 4 7 5 e t 9 1 0 8>

Begin by exploring those repeated A4s, circled above. Webern specifically chose row forms where pc 9 appears in the same position (the same is true for pc 3, which makes the elisions possible). In his realization of the rows, the composer highlights this relationship by always writing pc 9 with the same register, rhythm, and dynamic level, to make the repetition stand out aurally. Every dyad (or pair of pcs) found "harmonically" between the rows is maintained as a dyad throughout the movement, and the pitches of these dyads are symmetrical around A4. Take, for instance, the dyad {8 t} with which the first row pair begins. Search for any other pc 8 or t in the movement, and you will see that almost every pc 8 is paired with pc t. Now refer again to the score to see how Webern emphasizes this relationship: each pair is set in the same register, with the same rhythm and dynamic marking.

Another Way

You can predict which row forms will produce the repeated A4s by using index numbers. Any P and I form whose row labels add to six will produce the same relation.

R_3:	8 9 5 7 4 6 0 1 2 t e 3
RI_3:	+t 9 1 e 2 0 6 5 4 8 7 3
	6 6 6 6 6 6 6 6 6 6 6 6

P_5:	5 1 0 4 3 2 8 6 9 7 e t
I_1:	+1 5 6 2 3 4 t 0 9 e 7 8
	6 6 6 6 6 6 6 6 6 6 6 6

Another aspect of Webern's row realization may contribute to the repetitive sound of this movement: a technique called **registral invariance** (also sometimes called "frozen register" or "pitch fixation"). Over half of the pcs in Webern's row appear in one and only one register. Example 37.4 gives these pitches in their frozen, or fixed, position.

Example 37.4: Seven pitches from Webern, Variations for Piano, second movement

To hear how registral invariance works, play these pitches on a piano (all together or as a rolled chord) while listening to the movement; they will stand out from the rest of the texture because of their repetition as pitches (rather than pitch classes).

In *The Path to the New Music,* Webern hints that he composed rows according to certain guiding principles he was reluctant to share: "Now I'm asked, 'How did I arrive at this row?' Not arbitrarily, but according to certain secret laws." Perhaps he is referring to a system for predicting which row forms will produce the types of relationships discussed in this chapter. On the other hand, later in the same passage, Webern attributes his row composition to "inspiration."

Did You Know?

Anton Webern held a doctorate in musicology. His dissertation dealt with the polyphonic music of Flemish Renaissance composer Heinrich Isaac, who uses canonic imitation and other contrapuntal features Webern favored. Webern's writings express an evolutionary view of music history that leads from Renaissance polyphony to nontonal composition—through Bach, Beethoven, and Mahler to his teacher Schoenberg. In 1932–33, he gave a series of lectures later published as *The Path to the New Music* (edited by Willi Reich and published by Universal Edition in 1960; English translation by Leo Black in 1975). In these lectures, Webern expressed this historical line clearly (p. 42): "We must know, above all, what it means: 'twelve-note composition.' Have you ever looked at a work of that kind? It's my belief that ever since music has been written, all the great composers have instinctively had this before them as a goal."

In another lecture, Webern again alludes to this evolutionary vision of music history (p. 35):

> So the style Schoenberg and his school are seeking is a new inter-penetration of music's material in the horizontal and the vertical: polyphony, which has so far reached its climaxes in the Netherlanders and Bach, then later in the classical composers. There's the constant effort to derive as much as possible from one principal idea. It has to be put like this, for we too are writing in classical forms, which haven't vanished. . . . It's not a matter of reconquering or reawakening the Netherlands, but of re-filling their forms by way of the classical masters, of linking these two things.

In Webern's mind, all of music history was building toward the pivotal moment when the horizontal (melody) and vertical (harmony) were united in a new way through twelve-note composition.

TERMS YOU SHOULD KNOW

- aggregate
- all-combinatorial hexachord
- comes
- dux
- hexachordal combinatoriality
- order number
- registral invariance
- row elision
- row matrix
- secondary set

QUESTIONS FOR REVIEW

1. Describe how to construct a row matrix. What goes along the top? down the side? What does the main diagonal reveal?
2. What is combinatoriality? What does it allow the composer to do in the music?
3. How is the term "harmonic rhythm" used in a twelve-tone context?
4. Is it always possible to tell by listening if a work is serial or freely nontonal?
5. After consulting your teacher, find one twelve-tone work for your own instrument. Try to identify the row and at least one transformation. Does the composer align phrase structure with row forms?
6. What are some ways different composers use rows to make their compositions sound distinctive in style? (Hint: Compare the pieces by Webern, Schoenberg, Dallapiccola, and Tavener in this chapter and the previous one.)

CHAPTER 38

New Ways to Organize Rhythm, Meter, and Duration

Outline of topics

Rhythm and meter in early twentieth-century music

- Perceived and notated meter
- Changing meter and polymeter
- Asymmetrical meter
- Ametric music
- Additive rhythm

Rhythm and meter in post-1945 music

- Nontraditional rhythmic notation
- Serialized durations
- The Fibonacci series
- Metric modulation

Analyzing and performing contemporary rhythm and meter

Overview

Here, we review new kinds of rhythms and metrical frameworks explored by composers of the twentieth and twenty-first centuries.

Repertoire

Béla Bartók
- From *Mikrokosmos*: No. 115, 133, 148
- "Song of the Harvest," for two violins

Luciano Berio, *Sequenza III*, for voice

Pierre Boulez, *Structures Ia*, for two pianos

John Cage, *4'33"*

Elliott Carter, String Quartet No. 2

John Corigliano, "Come now, my darling," from *The Ghosts of Versailles*

György Ligeti
- *Continuum*
- *Hungarian Etudes*, third movement

Olivier Messiaen, "Danse de la fureur," from *Quartet for the End of Time*

Luigi Nono, *Il canto sospeso*

Igor Stravinsky
- "Bransle Gay," from *Agon*
- *Les noces*, Tableau II

Edgard Varèse, *Density 21.5*

Anton Webern, *Variations for Piano*, Op. 27, second movement

La Monte Young, *Composition 1960*, No. 5

Rhythm and Meter in Early Twentieth-Century Music

In common-practice style, rhythmic patterns and notated meter reinforce each other—with a few notable exceptions, such as syncopations and hemiola, which contrast with the regular beat to achieve their intended effect. There are also hierarchical levels of meter, including hypermeter, that work together to reinforce the measurement of time into regular units. In the twentieth century, however, while some pieces of music conform to common-practice rhythmic and metrical conventions, others explore new ways of organizing durations.

Perceived and Notated Meter

Listen to the second movement of Webern's *Variations for Piano*, without the score, and conduct along with the music. Which conducting pattern did you select? Now look at measures 1–4, in Example 38.1. Although this movement is notated in $\frac{2}{4}$, most listeners would not select that pattern to conduct. What they tend to hear is a series of evenly spaced beats, with downbeats on the second note of each group of two (the G♯3 of the anacrusis, the second A4 of m. 1, the F5 of m. 2, and so on). Some listeners group these stronger pulses into measures of $\frac{3}{8}$; others may choose $\frac{6}{8}$ or another meter—but rarely $\frac{2}{4}$ as notated. This piece thus illustrates a distinction between the notated meter, $\frac{2}{4}$, and the perceived meter.

Example 38.1: Webern, *Variations for Piano*, second movement, mm. 1–4 (anthology)

In common-practice compositions, the notated and perceived meter are usually one and the same (with brief exceptions). In twentieth-century music, on the other hand, the notated and perceived meter may not correspond at all. In some cases, pieces carefully notated in traditional ways may not convey a meter of any sort, while other pieces not notated in a traditional meter may have a regular perceptible beat or meter created by the rhythmic patterns. With twentieth-century scores, what you see is not always what you hear. While the performer must attend to the music as notated, the primary metrical framework of the piece is the one perceived by the listener.

Changing Meter and Polymeter

Several sections of Stravinsky's ballet *Agon* are based on old dance patterns. Listen to an excerpt from "Bransle Gay" twice without looking at Example 38.2: the first time, conduct along with the castanet; the second time, with the wind parts (flutes and bassoons). Is there always a clear meter? Did you pick the same conducting pattern for the castanet as for the winds?

Now look at measures 1–6 below. Stravinsky notates the first measure in $\frac{3}{8}$, matching the castanet. The castanet part provides a rhythmic ostinato (a repeated pattern), which continues to sound in three-beat groups throughout the passage. Then, beginning in measure 2, Stravinsky notates measures of $\frac{7}{16}$ and $\frac{5}{16}$ to match the rhythmic patterns of the wind parts.

EXAMPLE 38.2: Stravinsky, "Bransle Gay," mm. 1–6

KEY CONCEPT Shifting between different notated meters is called **changing meter.**

Listeners can hear changing meters if the rhythms clearly articulate the metrical organization. On the other hand, the changes may simply be a notational feature for the convenience of the players and conductor, and may be difficult for listeners to perceive. Other terms for this kind of notation include "mixed meter," "variable meter," and "multimeter."

In Example 38.2, the castanet and wind parts imply at least two different meters: the continuing $\frac{3}{8}$ in the castanet and the changing patterns in the winds.

KEY CONCEPT **Polymeter** occurs when two or more different metric streams are heard at the same time.

Example 38.3: Stravinsky, *Les noces*, Tableau II, mm. 54–59

Translation: And to whom do you belong now, beautiful round curls? To the girl with red cheeks, with a name like [Natasia]

The Stravinsky example illustrates both changing meter in the wind parts and polymeter in the relation between the castanet and the winds. Polymetrical passages are easiest to identify when the music is notated in two or more meters, but they may be perceived even when notated in one meter throughout all the parts. Look, for instance, at Example 38.3, from Stravinsky's *Les noces*. All parts are notated in $\frac{2}{4}$, but the strongly accented entrances of the ostinato pattern in pianos 2 and 4 and the percussion sound like downbeats in $\frac{3}{4}$. This type of polymeter occurs when the metrical accents in different lines of a composition are not aligned.

Example 38.4 summarizes four different types of polymeter: (a) same beat unit but different measure lengths; (b) same beat unit but nonaligned measures; (c) same beat unit but different beat divisions; and (d) same beat division but different beat unit. In Example 38.5, from Bartók's "Song of the Harvest," the possibilities of 38.4a and b are combined. In measures 11–12, one part is notated in $\frac{3}{4}$ followed by $\frac{2}{4}$, while the other part has the reverse. The different metrical strands in measure 11 lead to offset measures of $\frac{3}{4}$, when the lower part begins a new measure on beat 3 of the upper part's measure. Bartók helps us perceive this polymeter by placing accents on the downbeats of many measures. These should be carefully articulated when performing the piece.

EXAMPLE 38.4: Four types of polymeter

(a) Same beat unit but different measure lengths

(c) Same beat unit but different beat divisions

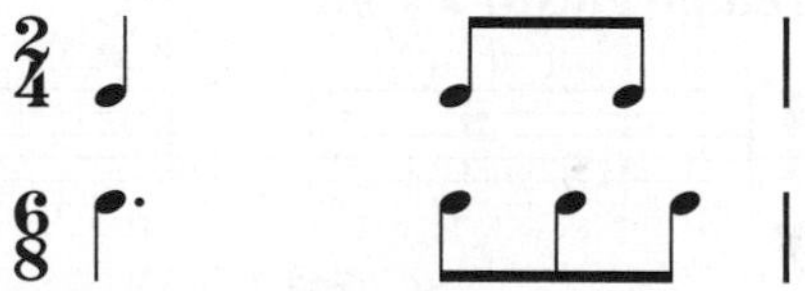

(b) Same beat unit but nonaligned measures

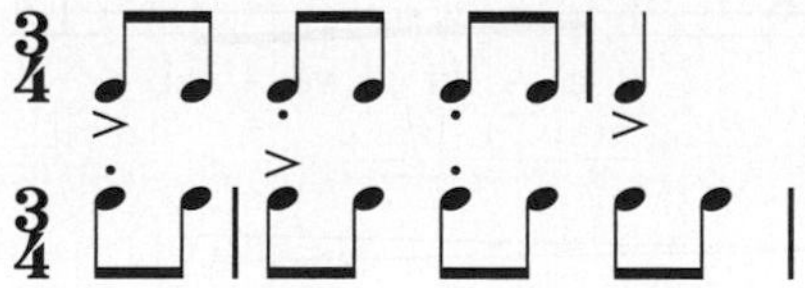

(d) Same beat division but different beat unit

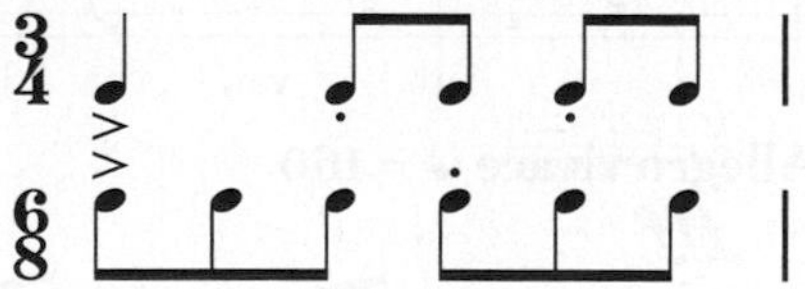

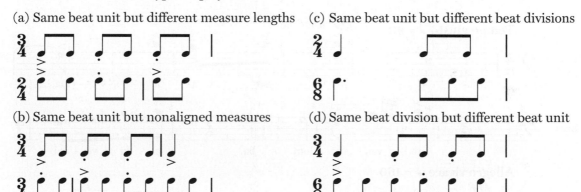

EXAMPLE 38.5: Bartók, "Song of the Harvest," mm. 11–15 🎧 (anthology)

In Example 38.4c, the beat divides in twos (simple meter) in one line and divides in threes (compound meter) in the other, with the same beat duration for the dotted-quarter note in $\frac{6}{8}$ as for the quarter note in $\frac{2}{4}$. In part (d), the polymetric structure results in a different number of beats: three beats in simple meter against two beats in compound meter. Here, $\frac{3}{4}$ is placed against $\frac{6}{8}$, with the eighths the same duration in each meter. There are six eighth notes in each measure, but the grouping of eighths and the accent patterns differ (2 + 2 + 2 vs. 3 + 3). In contrast, the eighths in part (c) have different durations.

Finally, polymeter may also be created by assigning different tempi to individual parts, as in the third movement of Ligeti's *Hungarian Etudes*. In this composition, all five choir parts are notated in $\frac{4}{4}$, but in five different tempi—♩ = 90, 110, 140, 160, and 190. Example 38.6 is drawn from the opening of the third movement, with the entrances of the choir 1 bass section at ♩ = 90 and the altos at ♩ = 160. (Each part has its own tempo markings and measure numbers. Your class may want to discuss strategies a conductor might consider to keep the choir together!)

EXAMPLE 38.6: Ligeti, *Hungarian Etudes*, third movement, mm. 1–7

Translation:

Bass: Cheap apples! Here they are in a heap. Who buys them, eats them. Cheap apples!

Alto: The dog sled runs, it races truly, truly. I am the sled master.

Asymmetrical Meter

All the common-practice meters we have studied feature beats grouped into twos, threes, or fours; the beats are divided into two or three parts, and subdivided into four or six parts. These meters are considered **symmetrical** because the primary beats within each measure are equally spaced and each beat has a consistent number of divisions.

Listen to the opening of Bartók's "Bulgarian Rhythm" (Example 38.7a). Conduct the meter as you listen. Is this a symmetrical meter? Do you conduct in equally spaced beat units? The meter signature is $\frac{5}{8}$ and a measure lasts for five eighth notes, but the primary beat unit is not the eighth note. This meter divides into two unequal "halves": the first half has three eighths, the second half only two. The beat unit is not consistent; as the left-hand part shows, the beat unit shifts between dotted-quarter and quarter notes. Later in the same piece, part (b), the division reverses: $\frac{5}{8}$ is grouped into two eighths, then three.

Example 38.7: Bartók, "Bulgarian Rhythm" (anthology)

(a) Mm. 1–4

(b) Mm. 9–12

KEY CONCEPT **Asymmetrical meters** are compound meters with beat units of unequal duration. These "irregular" beat lengths are typically created by measures with five or seven eighth notes or quarter notes at the beat-division level, which cannot group into evenly spaced beats.

For example, the five eighths of $\frac{5}{8}$ may be divided 3 + 2 or 2 + 3 (♩. ♩ or ♩ ♩.), 2 + 2 + 1 (♩ ♩ ♪), or some other combination of 2 and 1. The meter $\frac{5}{4}$ works the same way (for example, 𝅗𝅥 𝅗𝅥. or 𝅗𝅥 𝅗𝅥 ♩). Like other compound meters, these meters are typically conducted at the beat level, or possibly at the beat-division level if the tempo is slow. Other common asymmetrical meter signatures are $\frac{7}{4}$ and $\frac{7}{8}$, which may divide 2 + 2 + 3, 3 + 2 + 2, 2 + 2 + 2 + 1, and so on. Less common signatures include $\frac{11}{8}$, $\frac{13}{8}$, $\frac{5}{16}$, and $\frac{7}{16}$.

Sometimes, when the same groupings run through several measures, the composer will indicate the subdivisions in the meter signature, as in Example 38.8. Play these measures at the keyboard to hear the grouping. In this meter signature, the upper numbers indicate the subdivisions within the measure: $\frac{4+2+3}{8}$. The signature could have read $\frac{9}{8}$ (the sum of 4 + 2 + 3), but that would not have shown the groupings and subdivisions, which differ from the expected 3 + 3 + 3.

Example 38.8: Bartók, "Six Dances in Bulgarian Rhythm," mm. 1–2

Asymmetrical meters can be heard as transformations of symmetrical meters—that is, listeners may interpret $\frac{5}{8}$ as a $\frac{6}{8}$ that is missing an eighth, or as a $\frac{2}{4}$ with a "hiccup." When performing these meters, observe the groupings carefully and place a slight stress at the beginning of groups. When meters include an upper number of 5 or 7, avoid holding the last note in the measure too long, making $\frac{5}{8}$ sound like $\frac{6}{8}$, or $\frac{7}{8}$ like $\frac{4}{4}$. You may need to practice counting the beat divisions in groups, beginning each group with an accented number 1 ($\overset{>}{1}$-2-3, $\overset{>}{1}$-2 or $\overset{>}{1}$-2, $\overset{>}{1}$-2, $\overset{>}{1}$-2-3) until the patterns are familiar and you can feel the proper accentuation.

Meters that are usually considered symmetrical may be divided asymmetrically, as in Example 38.8. Example 38.9 shows several measures of another Bartók piece from *Mikrokosmos*, "Syncopation." This passage features a changing meter pattern alternating $\frac{5}{4}$, an asymmetrical meter, with $\frac{4}{4}$, usually a symmetrical meter. How are the beats divided in each measure? In this example, the $\frac{4}{4}$ meter is treated like the $\frac{5}{4}$, with asymmetrical groupings in each. (In some pieces with such rhythms, you see a signature of $\frac{8}{8}$ instead of $\frac{4}{4}$.) Other meters, such as $\frac{3}{4}$, $\frac{9}{8}$, and $\frac{12}{8}$, may also be treated like asymmetrical meters.

Example 38.9: Bartók, "Syncopation," mm. 1–3

Try it #1

Play Example 38.9 at the piano, then continue to mark the groupings of eighth notes below the score in measures 1 and 2, as shown.

Ametric Music

Listen now to Varèse's *Density 21.5* without the score, and conduct along. Is there a clear, even beat? Look at measures 1–17 (Example 38.10), notated in a regular common-time (**c**) meter. Although the piece sounds as if it is played with a lot of rubato, or flexibility in the tempo, the performer is given the following instructions: "Always [play] strictly in time—follow metronomic indications."

How do the rhythms in this piece avoid articulating a clear, consistent meter? And how does Varèse achieve the sense of tempo variation through a score that is so precisely notated? Explore these questions by marking the example with the location of each beat, then conducting in a quadruple meter while listening to the music again, this time following the score. Circle the places where the beginning of a rhythmic idea lines up with a notated beat.

Example 38.10: Varèse, *Density 21.5*, mm. 1–17 (anthology)

Several prominent rhythms do line up with beats; for example, the initial motive (F4–E4–F♯4) and its repetition in measures 3, 9, and 15 fall on notated beats. They do not reinforce a sense of meter, however, since the first presentation begins on beat 1 and the repetition starts on beat 4. Two additional statements, in measures 9 and 15, appear on beat 1, like the original motive.

While common-practice composers tend to limit the number of different rhythmic patterns in a piece, we see no such limitation here. Many of the rhythms in this piece do not line up neatly with the notated beats. Some notes are tied over to the following beat or through several beats, with a new pitch entering in the middle of a beat unit. If there were a strong sense of beat in an accompaniment or other instrumental part, or if the solo flute had established a clear, regular pulse, these tied-over notes would sound syncopated. But because there is no regular pulse in this music—or perhaps because there are too many implied meters not corresponding to a consistent beat unit, each lasting only a brief time—the effect is one of no perceived meter.

KEY CONCEPT In some twentieth-century music notated in the traditional manner, rhythmic patterns may conflict with the notated meter and resist alignment into regular beat and accent patterns. If there is no meter perceived, the music is said to be **ametric**. Ametric music may also be notated in nontraditional ways.

Additive Rhythm

One method of generating a series of durations that sounds ametrical is by **additive rhythm**. That is, instead of conceiving of rhythm in terms of a beat unit with divisions and subdivisions, you begin with a small unit (often a sixteenth note or smaller) and add these small durations together to create larger, ametric rhythm patterns. This type of rhythm is typically notated without a meter.

One composer who is well known for his additive rhythms is Olivier Messiaen. Look now at the rhythm in Example 38.11, drawn from "Danse de la fureur" ("Dance of Fury"), a movement scored for piano, cello, B♭ clarinet, and violin from the *Quartet for the End of Time*. Most obvious are the absence of a meter signature and the irregular durations of the melody notes (doubled in octaves). Among the elements that help Messiaen to achieve this rhythmic structure are ties and what the composer calls "dots of addition." For example, in measure 27, the durations—♪., ♩‿𝅘𝅥𝅯, 𝅗𝅥., ♩‿𝅘𝅥𝅯, and ♪.—keep the rhythm from falling into metric regularity. Tap the rhythm of this passage, or chant it on a neutral syllable like "tah." When you first read it through, you may need to count in sixteenth notes: for measure 27, 1-2-3, 1-2-3-4-5, 1-2-3-4-5-6-7-8, and so on. After it becomes familiar, you should be able to feel the durations in larger note values.

EXAMPLE 38.11: Messiaen, "Danse de la fureur," mm. 27–31

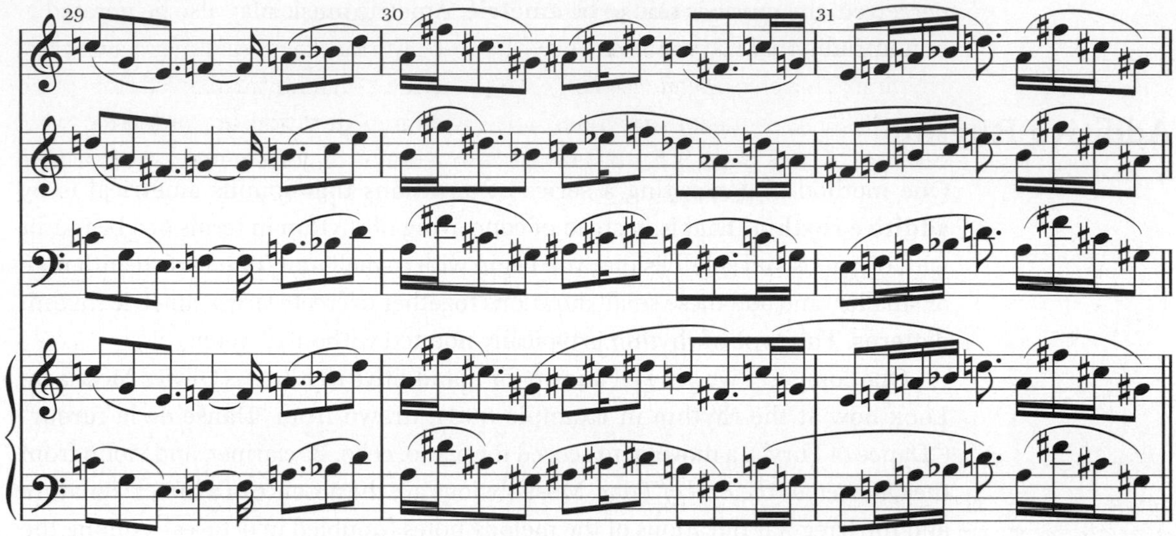

Another interesting rhythmic technique is at work in this excerpt as well. Consider each measure a one-bar unit. Compare the first duration of the measure with the last, then the second with the next-to-last, until you reach a single duration that stands at the center. Every measure of this excerpt is a palindrome—the same going backward and forward. Rhythms like these are another example of Messiaen's delight in the "charm of impossibilities"—it is impossible to run this rhythm in reverse order, since the result is the same as the original rhythm.

Rhythm and Meter in Post-1945 Music

In the early twentieth century, there was a tendency toward precise notation of every musical parameter: durations were indicated exactly, with as many ties or dots as needed, dynamic markings were abundant (in some cases provided for individual notes), articulations were carefully specified. While conveying the composer's intention, however, these practices when taken to an extreme made scores difficult to perform because of the need to pay attention to so many details.

Nontraditional Rhythmic Notation

The two decades after World War II were marked by an intense exploration of compositional methods, including new approaches to rhythm, meter, durations, and their notation. Example 38.12, a score for solo voice by Luciano Berio, is an example of **time-line notation**. In this system, the passing of time is measured by the number of seconds elapsed between markers (10 seconds, 20 seconds, and so on), and the musical events take place between the markers, resulting in ametrical rhythms. This piece, *Sequenza III* (1966), illustrates an innovative notation of pitch as well. Score notation in which both pitch and duration are indicated with nonstandard symbols is called **graphic notation**. It may seem to be an imprecise method of communicating musical information to the performer, but a comparison of performances of the Berio score reveals remarkable consistencies—results almost as similar as performances generated by scores with detailed traditional notation.

EXAMPLE 38.12: Berio, *Sequenza III*, for voice, first staff

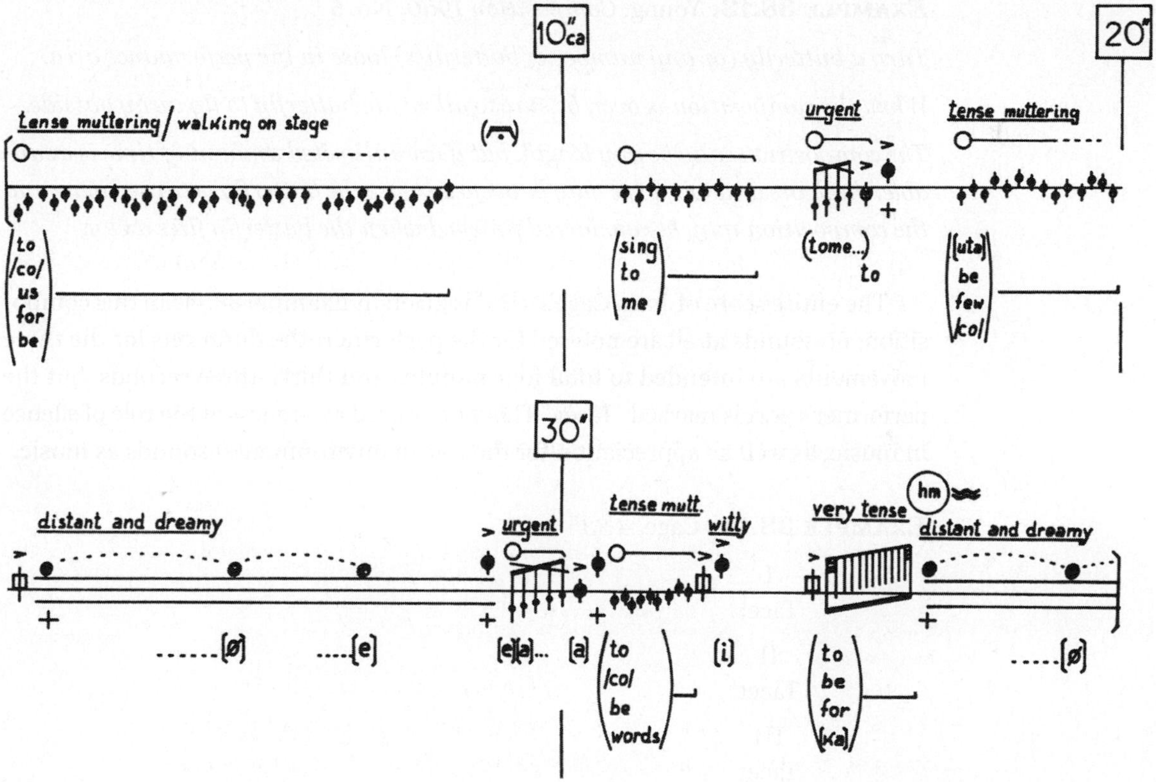

In other works, you may see pitches specified exactly, but without precise durations. For example, a group of pitches may be notated in a box, with instructions to play them in any order and as fast as possible or with durations of the performer's choosing. Another variation of this idea is Witold Lutosławski's aleatoric counterpoint, which gives the ordering of pitches but leaves the durations of individual pitches to the performer. Other scores, including works by Morton Feldman, show note heads with horizontal lines extending from them to indicate that the pitch is held for a long time.

Some pieces composed during the second half of the twentieth century are characterized by **text notation** (or "text scores"): instructions for performing the piece are written out in prose or poetry, without any traditional musical notation. Some of these pieces explore the edges of musical performance—extremes of dynamics or instrument ranges, elements of noise, even dance or drama. Some indicate that a passage or a rhythmic pattern is to be played "as fast as possible" or a pitch is to be sustained "as long as possible." Sometimes the sounds produced in such compositions are very soft, like the sounds butterflies make in La Monte Young's *Composition 1960*, No. 5 (Example 38.13).

EXAMPLE 38.13: Young, *Composition 1960*, No. 5

Turn a butterfly (or any number of butterflies) loose in the performance area.

When the composition is over, be sure to allow the butterfly to fly away outside.

The composition may be any length, but if an unlimited amount of time is available, the doors and windows may be opened before the butterfly is turned loose and the composition may be considered finished when the butterfly flies away.

The entire score of John Cage's *4'33"* is given in Example 38.14; in this composition, no sounds at all are notated for the performer; the durations for the three movements are intended to total four minutes and thirty-three seconds, but the performer's part is marked "Tacet." This work raised awareness of the role of silence in music, as well as appreciation for the role of environmental sounds as music.

EXAMPLE 38.14: Cage, *4'33"*

I
Tacet

II
Tacet

III
Tacet

You may also encounter variants on traditional rhythmic notation—for example, meter signatures with a duration symbol rather than a lower number (such as 4 over ♩. instead of $\frac{12}{8}$). Other pieces, such as Ligeti's *Continuum* (1967), stick with simple and traditional notation but create new effects nevertheless. Look at the opening of *Continuum* in Example 38.15. Here, all durations are eighth notes, but they combine to produce complex and detailed rhythmic interactions, which gradually change as the piece progresses. There are no traditional bar lines, but Ligeti does provide dotted lines as a visual reference.

Play through this passage slowly at the keyboard (Ligeti's tempo is "extremely fast, so that individual tones can hardly be perceived, but rather merge into a continuum"). You will hear that the work opens with a two-note minor-third pattern in both hands. In measure 10, the pattern changes in the right hand, enlarged to a three-note set spanning a perfect fourth. The interplay of a three-note pattern against a two-note creates an unsettling rhythmic effect. The next change comes in measure 15: now each hand plays a three-note pattern, but the patterns are offset by one eighth note. Play the rest of the passage again, and listen for the remaining changes. Mark these in your score.

As the work proceeds, the length and starting point of patterns continue to change and occasionally become aligned again. In measures 21–22, for example, the patterns are realigned—now in five-note sets in contrary motion. Where patterns align like this, we hear clear accents.

EXAMPLE 38.15: Ligeti, *Continuum*, "measures" 1–22 (mm. 8–15 recorded)

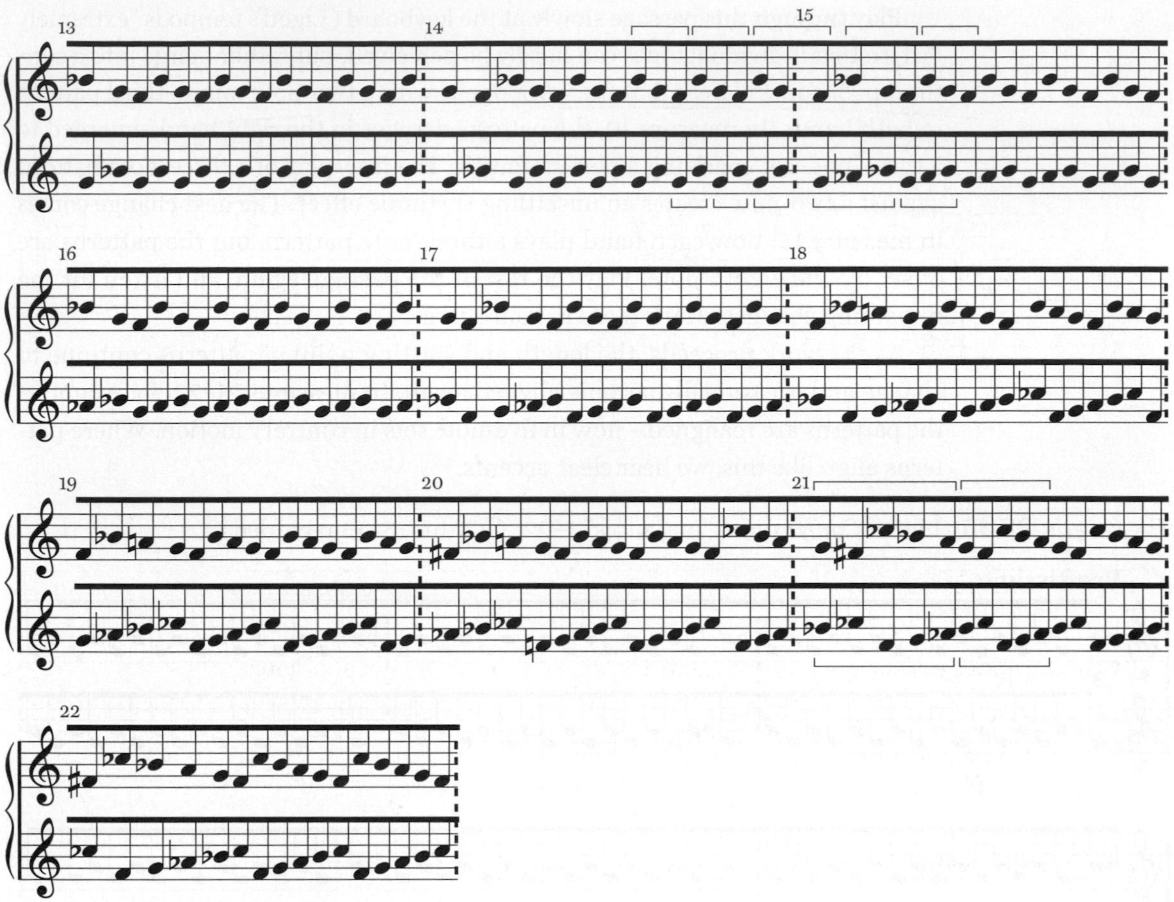

Serialized Durations

At the same time that graphic notation and text scores were being explored by some composers—as a way to make rhythmic notation more flexible or to reduce the composer's control over the duration of sounds—other composers who wanted precise control of durations, articulations, and dynamics continued the trend toward extreme detail in traditional notation. One significant development in the 1950s and early 1960s was the extension of serial procedures to dimensions other than pitch—a procedure referred to as **total serialism**, or **integral serialism**. In a groundbreaking experimental piece from the 1950s, *Structures Ia* (for two pianos), Pierre Boulez serialized not only pitch classes, but also durations, articulation, and dynamics. Pitch-class rows were paired with duration rows, and each section of the work was assigned a dynamic level and articulation type from an ordered series of dynamics and articulations.

Example 38.16: Boulez, *Structures Ia*

(a) Mm. 24–31 (piano 2)

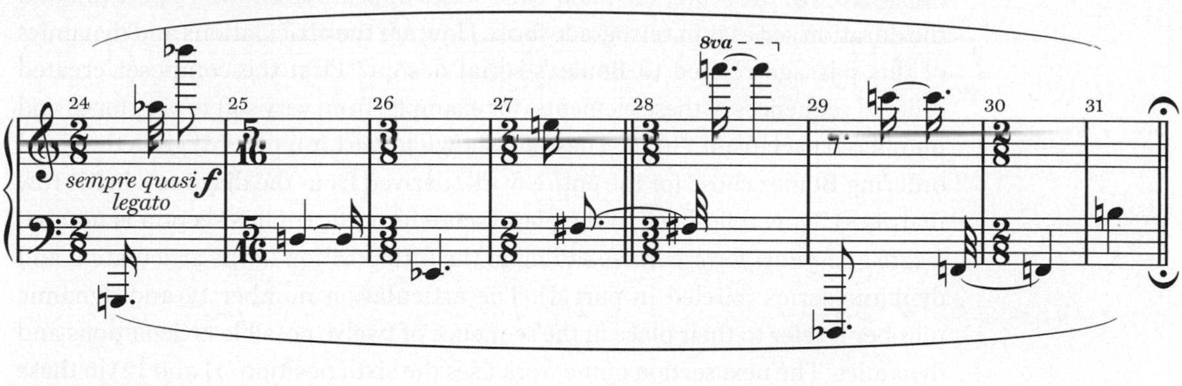

(b) Pitch-class series

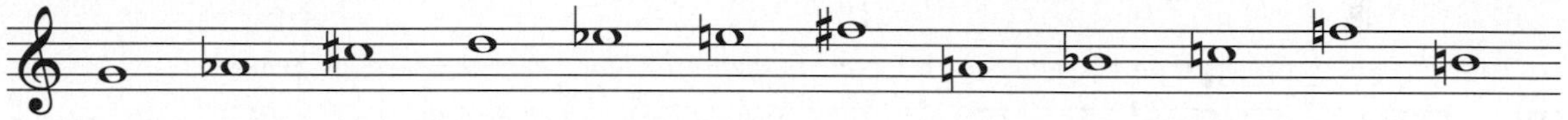

Duration series (each number represents the duration in thirty-second notes)

(c) Articulation sequence

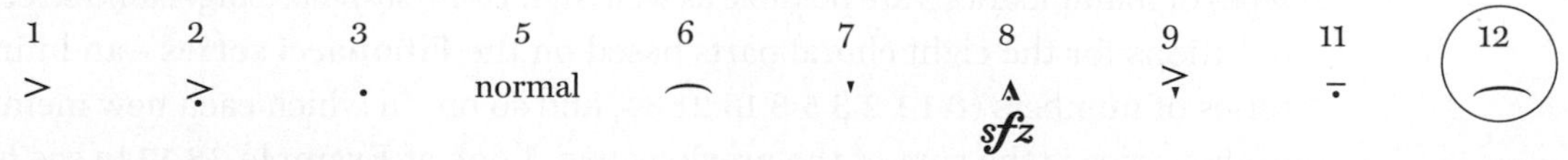

Dynamic sequence

1	2	3	4	5	6	7	8 (circled)	9	10	11	12
pppp	***ppp***	***pp***	***p***	*quasi* ***p***	***mp***	***mf***	*quasi* ***f***	***f***	***ff***	***fff***	***ffff***

(d) Articulations (one level per section)

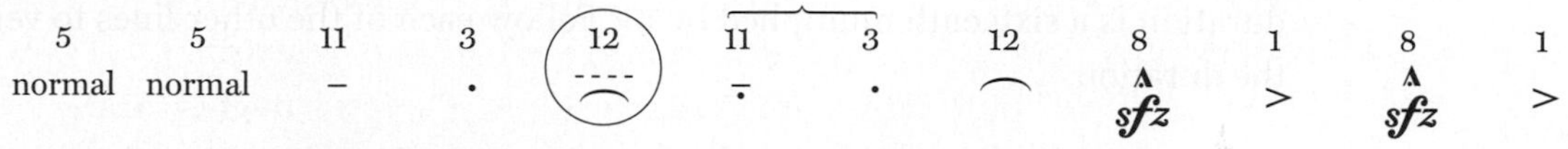

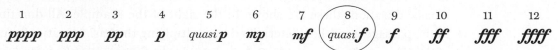

Dynamics (one level per section)

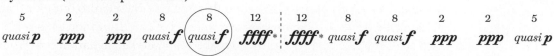

5	2	2	8	8 (circled)	12 ¦	12	8	8	2	2	5
quasi ***p***	***ppp***	***ppp***	*quasi* ***f***	*quasi* ***f***	***ffff**** ¦	***ffff****	*quasi* ***f***	*quasi* ***f***	***ppp***	***ppp***	*quasi* ***p***

Look at the excerpt in Example 38.16a, drawn from the fourth section of the work. Only piano 2 is playing here, from the pitch-class and duration series shown in part (b). In the score, the pitch-class series appears as shown in part (b), and the duration series is in retrograde form. How are the articulations and dynamics of this passage related to Boulez's serial design? First the composer created ordered sequences of these elements (for example, from very soft to very loud) and numbered each from 1 to 12. These are shown in part (c); part (d) gives the serial ordering Boulez chose for the entire work (derived from the diagonals in his row matrices). Now refer back to the piano score in part (a). This section is notated *legato* and *quasi forte*, corresponding to the fifth position in the articulation and dynamic series (circled in part d). The articulation number 12 and dynamic number 8 refer to their place in the sequence of twelve possible articulations and dynamics. The next section of the work uses the sixth position (11 and 12) in these series.

The Fibonacci Series

Boulez's duration series (Example 38.16b) illustrates one way composers can create ametric rhythms: by adding up small durations, like thirty-second notes or sixteenths, into a series of longer note values. Composers generally decide in advance how to structure such rhythms.

In *Structures Ia*, Boulez's durations were achieved by serial principles. Other types of manipulations are possible as well. In *Il canto sospeso*, Luigi Nono selected durations for the eight choral parts based on the **Fibonacci series**—an infinite series of numbers (0 1 1 2 3 5 8 13 21 34, and so on) in which each new member of the series is the sum of the previous two. Look at Example 38.17 to see how this works in a short passage for sopranos and altos. Nono assigned each part a basic duration; these are shown to the right of the example. All durations in the passage were then determined by multiplying the basic duration by one of the Fibonacci numbers: 1, 2, 3, 5, 8, or 13. In the first soprano line, for example, the first duration (a dotted eighth) is a sixteenth multiplied by 3; the second duration is a sixteenth multiplied by 13. Follow each of the other lines to verify the duration.

Example 38.17: Nono, *Il canto sospeso*, mm. 108–109 (soprano and alto parts)

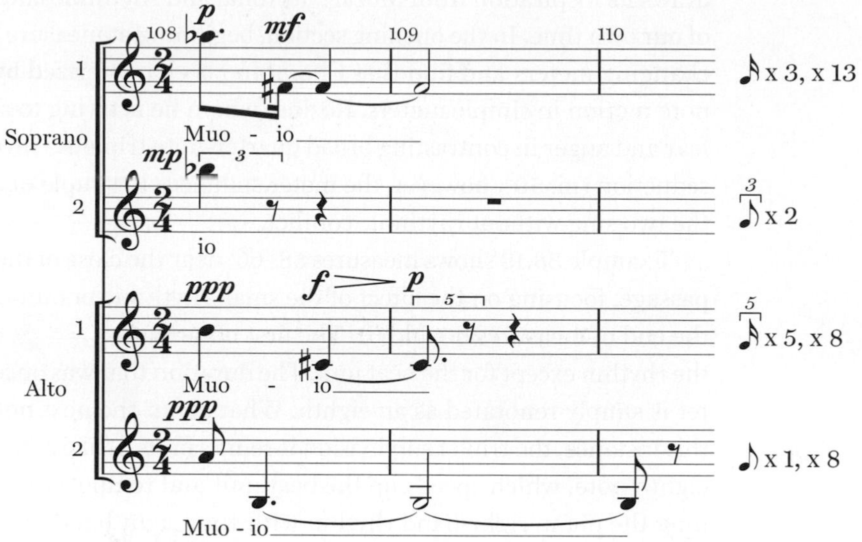

Translation: I am dying.

Musical applications of the Fibonacci series are not limited to the post–1945 time period—analysts have drawn on the series to locate significant events in several Bartók pieces (see, for example, the first movement of *Music for Strings, Percussion, and Celeste*, where important events enter in measures that match Fibonacci numbers). Bartók was also fond of using asymmetrical meters with Fibonacci numbers as the upper value, such as $\frac{5}{8}$, $\frac{8}{8}$, and $\frac{13}{8}$. The Fibonacci series may determine the length of phrases or sections or the placement of climactic moments in a piece. There is a connection to music of even earlier eras as well. Pairs of adjacent Fibonacci numbers converge (as the infinite series continues) toward a proportion that has been associated with balance in artworks since Greek antiquity, known as the **golden section.** This proportion, about 62 percent (.618) of the total length of a piece or section, has been shown to be significant in music of previous centuries. For example, in many Classical sonatas, the recapitulation begins about 62 percent of the way through the movement.

Metric Modulation

(anthology)

We turn now to a recent composition, John Corigliano's 1991 opera *The Ghosts of Versailles*. Listen to the duet "Come now, my darling," sung by mezzo-soprano Cherubino and soprano Rosina—characters borrowed from Mozart's *The Marriage of Figaro*. (Corigliano's work features an "opera within an opera.") While this duet draws its inspiration from Mozart, its tonal and rhythmic language are decidedly of our own time. In the opening section, beginning at measure 19, we see and hear changing meters and find that Cherubino is characterized by primarily eighth-note motion in simple meters. Rosina (whom he is trying to seduce) sings of her fear and anger in contrasting broad quarter-note triplets. Once she gives in to the seduction (m. 50), however, the meter stabilizes in simple quadruple meter, and the two sing without rhythmic conflict.

Example 38.18 shows measures 58–66, near the close of the duet. Listen to the passage, focusing on the effect of the small rhythmic notations above the staff at the end of measures 60 and 61. The first notation, ⌐3¬♩ = ⌐3¬♪, changes nothing in the rhythm except for the beat unit. The duration that was once notated as a quarter is simply renotated as an eighth. What about the next notation, ⌐3¬♪ = ♪? In this instance, the triplet subdivision is reinterpreted (like a "pivot" duration) as an eighth note, which speeds up the beat unit and tempo. (In mm. 60–62, try tapping the piano right-hand rhythm with your right hand and the beat unit with your left, to feel the tempo change.) This type of rhythmic change is called a **metric modulation**. Metric modulation is more accurately a tempo modulation—a means of smoothing what would otherwise be abrupt changes of tempo by introducing subdivisions or groups of beats in the first tempo that match durations in the new one. The new tempo is recognized in retrospect, much like a modulation by pivot chord.

EXAMPLE 38.18: Corigliano, "Come now, my darling," mm. 58–66 🎧 (anthology)

The composer most often associated with metric modulation is Elliott Carter. Example 38.19, from his String Quartet No. 2, illustrates the technique in a characteristic way. The quartet begins with a tempo of ♩ = 105. In measure 9, performers need to think about the cello's sixteenth-note subdivisions of the beat as though they are grouped into threes, to make accurate dotted-eighth durations (violin 2) in measure 10. This dotted-eighth pulse is then renotated in the next section at a tempo of ♩ = 140. Between measures 9 and 10, the ♪. = ♪. indicates that the dotted eighths in measure 10 should be equal in duration to three sixteenths, with no change (yet) in the duration of those sixteenths. The dotted eighths become a pivot duration; since there are only three sixteenths per beat instead of four, the beat sounds faster. Then the notation between measures 10 and 11, ♪. = ♩, indicates that the duration formerly notated as a dotted eighth is now to be represented as a quarter note, restoring the division of each beat into four sixteenths. This makes the ♩ = 140 tempo in measure 11 faster by one-third than the ♩ = 105 in measure 9, but smooths the change from one to the other.

EXAMPLE 38.19: Carter, String Quartet No. 2, mm. 7–13

The pieces presented above represent only a small sampling of the variety of treatments of rhythm, meter, and duration in post–1945 avant-garde composition. Tape-recording equipment, synthesizers, computers, and MIDI sequencers have made it possible for composers to execute levels of rhythmic complexity and exact control over durations, articulations, and dynamics that would not be possible with human performers. On the other hand, performances of **indeterminate** pieces—compositions including graphic notation, text notation, and other methods that rely on the performer's choices—may vary substantially in their rhythmic and durational details from performance to performance. Interestingly, to the listener who does not know what the scores look like, the pieces with extremely detailed traditional notation or precise electronic control of pitch, durations, articulation, and dynamics often sound similar in their rhythm to those with indeterminate notation.

Analyzing and Performing Contemporary Rhythm and Meter

When considering rhythm and meter in an unfamiliar piece of contemporary music, begin by listening to determine whether there is a regular underlying pulse. If you perceive one, consider whether the beats fall into any sort of regular groupings. Listen to determine whether individual strata of the music have different metrical implications. Remember that the notated meter may not correspond to the perceived meter.

An important way that listeners relate to music is to move to it: tap their feet, clap their hands, conduct along, dance, or otherwise feel the beat in their bodies. Listeners new to contemporary music may be frustrated by the lack of a regular beat and metrical organization, perhaps even more than by the lack of functional tonality. But if you listen to an ametrical piece until it becomes familiar, you may learn to feel more comfortable with the treatment of time in absence of a continuous beat or regular metrical organization.

When you perform contemporary music that uses traditional notation, you should execute the rhythms as precisely as possible. You may have to work carefully with a sequence of durations to get the timing exactly right, and also with the meter (if present) to get the metric accents correct. Familiarity and careful practice are key. Passages in a piece without a clear metrical framework may have to be practiced longer than a similarly difficult passage in a metrical piece before it feels secure. For post-1945 pieces with unusual notation, composers often provide an explanation of the notation in "Notes for Performance" either in the individual parts or in the score. As with any piece of music you are preparing for performance, it is essential to understand all the score notation to realize the piece correctly. These pieces can be very interesting to play—don't let unfamiliar notation keep you from learning a new work!

Did You Know?

Among the compositions you will consider in the homework to this chapter is *Stripsody* by Cathy Berberian (1925–1983). Berberian was a renowned American singer who premiered a number of works written expressly for her by composers such as John Cage, Igor Stravinsky, Darius Milhaud, William Walton, and Luciano Berio, whom she married. She was well known for her vocal versatility and theatricality, and was a tireless proponent of new music. In 1966, she composed her first piece, *Stripsody*, which you can hear on her website: http://www.cathyberberian.com/. According to the site, this work was "an exploration of the onomatopoeic sounds of comic strips, which she used to convey an amusing succession of vignettes, illustrated by Roberto Zamarin." Berberian died of a heart attack at age fifty-seven, one day before she was scheduled to perform at a commemoration of Karl Marx, where she planned to "sing a rendition of the Communist Party national anthem 'Internationale' in 'Marilyn Monroe' style."

TERMS YOU SHOULD KNOW

additive rhythm	graphic notation	symmetrical meter
ametric	indeterminate	text notation
asymmetrical meter	integral serialism	time-line notation
changing meter	metric modulation	total serialism
Fibonacci series	polymeter	

QUESTIONS FOR REVIEW

1. What are typical characteristics of common-practice meters?
2. How do rhythmic patterns reinforce the perception of a meter? What is the role of metrical accent in the perception of a meter?
3. Is it possible to have changing meter and polymeter at the same time?
4. How are asymmetrical meters similar to traditional compound meters? How are they different?
5. How do durations, rhythm, and notated meter interact to make a piece that sounds ametric?
6. How would you recognize a passage that features additive rhythms? With which composer is this technique associated?
7. How does metric modulation work? With which composer is this technique associated?
8. In music for your own instrument, find one piece with changing meter, one with an asymmetrical meter, and one with polymeter. How can the date of composition help you locate a piece of each type?
9. In music for your own instrument, find one piece with graphic notation or text notation. How can the date of composition help you locate a piece of each type? (Ask your teacher for help with questions 8 and 9 if necessary.)

New Ways to Articulate Musical Form

CHAPTER 39

Outline of topics

Form in post-common-practice music

- Sectional forms
- Form and register
- Substitutes for tonal function

New approaches to traditional musical forms

- Repetition forms in nontonal music
- Canon and imitation

New developments in musical form

- Form as process
- Moment form and mobile form
- Indeterminacy and chance

Analyzing form in recent music

Overview

This chapter examines approaches to musical form after the common-practice era. We will listen for phrases and sections in pieces that lack functional tonality, and discover how to represent new types of form in analyses.

Repertoire

Béla Bartók, *Bagatelle*, Op. 6, No. 2

György Ligeti
Ten Pieces for Wind Quintet, ninth movement
"Wenn aus der Ferne" ("If from the Distance"), from *Three Fantasies on Texts by Friedrich Hölderlin*

Kenneth Maue, *In the Woods*

Krzysztof Penderecki, *Threnody for the Victims of Hiroshima*

Steve Reich, *Piano Phase*

Terry Riley, *In C*

Karlheinz Stockhausen, *Klavierstück XI*

Anton Webern, String Quartet, Op. 5, fourth movement

Form in Post-Common-Practice Music

In many compositions written after the common-practice era, musical elements that play supporting roles in defining form in tonal pieces—contrasts in range, register, timbre, dynamics, motivic content, articulation, and duration—play a stronger role in creating musical form. Collections, sets, rows, and nontriadic chords may also take the place of tonal keys, modulation, and triads to help define formal sections. In recent works, older compositional methods like canon and imitation find a place, and new structural elements, such as symmetry, are helping to articulate form.

We will examine formal processes on several levels, from the organization of materials into phrases and sections to the overall structure of a work. While most common-practice works have a hierarchical formal organization, not all recent music does. Each piece you study will have to be approached on its own terms.

Sectional Forms

Listen to the first large section (up to rehearsal number 25) of a piece by Krzysztof Penderecki, originally called simply *Piece for 52 Strings* but best known as *Threnody for the Victims of Hiroshima*. Listen several times without the score, and think about where you hear formal divisions. How does Penderecki create subsections and closure at the end of the excerpt?

Now look at the score in your anthology from the beginning to rehearsal number 10. This piece is written with graphic notation developed by Penderecki (similar to the time-line notation described in Chapter 38). The number of seconds between rehearsal numbers (the dotted vertical lines, like bar lines) is provided at the bottom of the score. The string parts are notated with symbols explained in a key on the first page: the little triangles pointing up mean to play the highest note possible on the instrument, and the wavy lines indicate the presence and intensity of vibrato. The other symbols seen after rehearsal 6 indicate sound effects, as listed on the first page. After the imitative entrances at the beginning of the piece, the effect is of one large mass of sound, rather than of individual instruments. The sound quality up to rehearsal 10 changes smoothly, with one type of sound eliding to the next.

Try it #1

Listen to the Penderecki excerpt again. How does the music to rehearsal 10 connect to the music that follows? Where do you hear the next division?

Consider rehearsal numbers 10–18. The graphic notation here depicts what the music sounds like, with the black pitch clusters expanding and then contracting. The outer boundaries of the clusters are notated exactly, but the players must listen carefully to fill in their portion of the space in between and to create the musical shape. In 15–16, the score specifies the pitches for each player within the cluster. Many listeners will hear each of these clusters as an individual phrase—with a starting point, midpoint, and close—even though each cluster is elided with the entry of the next. The subsection is unified and characterized by these elisions and by the sonic similarity of the clusters. Closure at the end of the section is achieved by the *glissandi* in opposing directions, which make a cadential gesture, and by the entrance of the next contrasting subsection.

The third subsection begins with individual, pointillistic entrances at rehearsal 18. The score indicates the exact pitches and order of entry for each instrument with an "arrowhead" notation.

Try it #2

Listen again to rehearsal numbers 18–25. List three ways Penderecki creates the sense of an ending in 25.

(a)

(b)

(c)

The close of this first large section draws on elements that, in tonal music, would typically support a tonal cadence: a closing of range, a thinner texture, softer dynamics, arrival on a point of rest, and silence. When these elements are combined in contemporary pieces, they can create closure as definitive as any in tonal music, even without functional harmony. The end of this section is also confirmed by the entrance of contrasting music at 26 (not shown), the beginning of the second large section.

The challenge in identifying formal divisions in nontonal music is that there is no standard system of "markers" such as tonal cadences. The key is listening. Become familiar with the piece, and then decide whether it has some sort of sectional structure. If you followed the instructions above carefully, you should have listened to the first section of *Threnody* five or more times, enough to begin hearing its sectional form. If, after repeated listening to a nontonal composition, you hear a musical gesture that creates a phrase, cadence, or sectional division—trust your ears! Then take the next step: try to explain how and why the gesture conveys that musical function.

Form and Register

In *Threnody*, range and register play important roles in creating form: sections open with an expansion of range, while phrases and sectional closure are created when that range shrinks to a unison or when string clusters *glissando* in opposing directions. Composers writing in a variety of styles use similar techniques to make formal divisions. Listen now to Bartók's *Bagatelle*, Op. 6, No. 2, while following the score in your anthology. Mark in the score where you hear sectional divisions, and consider why you hear a division there.

This little piece begins with an ostinato A♭4-B♭4 in the right hand, as shown in Example 39.1. The left hand moves outward by half steps from the pitches of the ostinato, making a wedge shape. Most listeners hear this first section as ending on the downbeat of measure 7—because of the resolution of the A♭4-B♭4 dyad outward to G4-B4, the expansion of the left-hand wedge downward to C4, then B3 (joining the chord in the right hand), the slowing of the tempo, and the softer volume. A change of motive, dynamic level, and tempo in measure 7 confirms the perception of a section ending here. Call measures 1–7a section **A**.

EXAMPLE 39.1: Bartók, *Bagatelle*, mm. 1–7a

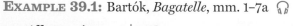

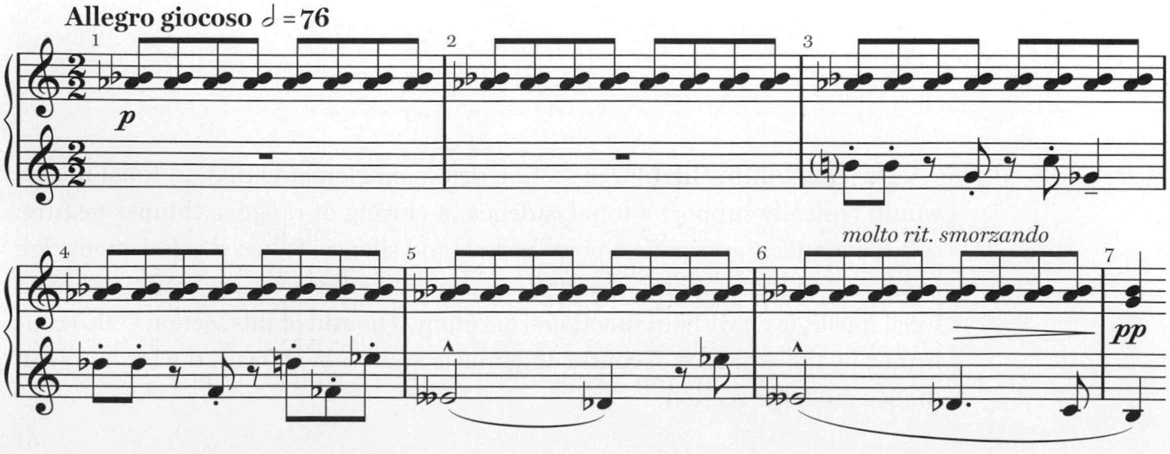

Perhaps the wedge and the relationship between the hands was easier to hear than to see; the traditional notation disguises the hands' overlapping range and half-step voice-leading. In contrast, Penderecki's graphic score for *Threnody* clearly shows the expansions and contractions in range and register. It is sometimes helpful when analyzing pieces in traditional notation to transcribe the work into a graph, to see how how range and texture work together to shape musical form.

One example is a **pitch-time graph**. This is easy to construct, either by using the piano-roll notation on a MIDI sequencing program or by hand on graph paper. On a piece of graph paper, plot pitches on the y-axis (vertically, to show the pitch range from high to low) and the passage of time on the x-axis (horizontally). Example 39.2 shows an analytical graph of measures 1–7a of the *Bagatelle*. Each square on the vertical axis represents one pitch of the equally tempered chromatic scale; each square on the horizontal axis represents one eighth note duration (the smallest duration in this passage). The shading represents the "voices": the right-hand ostinato is lighter, while the pitches of the left-hand wedge are darker. The **pitch symmetry** around the silent A4 (the note in between the A♭4 and B♭4 of the ostinato) and the interaction of the hand parts are clearly visible in the graph.

EXAMPLE 39.2: Pitch/time graph of Bartók, *Bagatelle*, mm. 1–7a

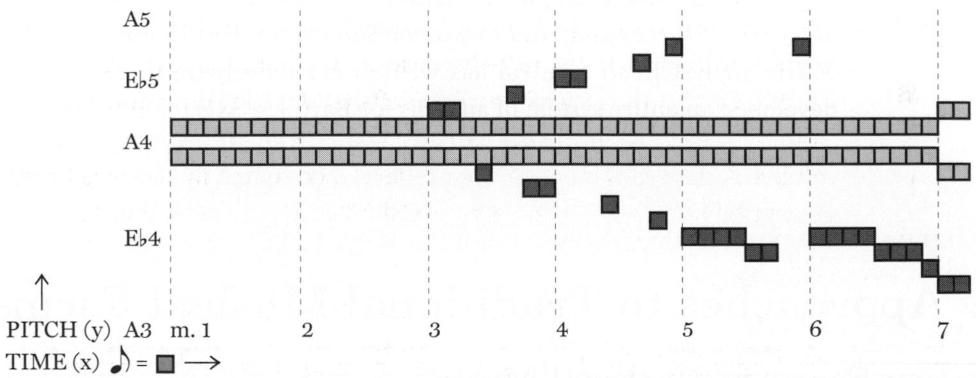

Substitutes for Tonal Function

The section **A** material returns later in the *Bagatelle*, in measures 18–23. Listen to the piece again while following your anthology score. In measures 18–20, the repeated dyad is now D4-E4 (with E♭4 as its center), and the wedge is centered on a silent E♭5: the ostinato has moved down a tritone, while the wedge has moved up a tritone. Call measures 18–23 **A′** to show its relation to the opening section.

In measures 24–30, A returns as the center of the symmetries, but now in three octaves. The wedge appears in the left hand, symmetrical around A3, and we hear the A♭-B♭ dyad with A5 as its center. The center of these two symmetries is A4. Because of the octave duplications, this is a pitch-class center. Label measures 24–30 **A″**; they feature a return of the original pitch-class center, but the range has expanded outward a tritone from the E♭4/E♭5 of the previous section.

The overall form of this *Bagatelle* is **A B A′ A″**. In some ways, however, it also resembles a ternary form: the first section (mm. 1–7) and the last (18–30) are similar in material, while the middle section (mm. 7–18) is contrasting, with 15–18a serving as a retransition to **A′**.

In some nontonal music, composers treat the tritone interval in a way that may be analogous to the tonic-dominant perfect fifth of tonal pieces. In the *Bagatelle*, the motion from A4 as a center of symmetry to pitch-class E♭ and back to pitch-class A can be thought of as replacing the traditional motion from tonic to the key of the dominant and back to tonic. This use of the tritone is called a **tritone axis** (as the traditional motion is called the "tonic-dominant axis"). In Bartók's music, a primary tritone axis may be supplemented by a secondary axis. For an A–E♭ primary axis, the secondary axis would be C–F♯, dividing the octave into four equal parts by minor thirds: C–A–F♯–E (D♯). The relationships between this type of axis and other materials in his music, such as the octatonic collection, should be readily apparent. For good examples of a tritone axis in a larger work, see Bartók's *Music for Strings, Percussion, and Celeste* or *Sonata for Two Pianos and Percussion*. Music analyst Erno Lendvai has written extensively on these two pieces and developed an entire system of analysis for Bartók's "axis tonality."

New Approaches to Traditional Musical Forms

Repetition Forms in Nontonal Music

Nontonal materials that may substitute for familiar elements of tonal form, in addition to the tritone axis, include contrasting sets or collections—or contrasting transpositions of scales. An example is found in the fourth movement of Webern's String Quartet, Op. 5. Listen to this movement at least twice, and take note of the form. As you listen, keep in mind the ways other twentieth-century composers have structured pieces. In particular, try to hear how Webern creates a contrasting section by means of timbre and texture, and also by means of contrasting set classes.

(anthology)

The movement opens with two shimmering *am Steg* (on the bridge) *tremolo* chords played by the violins (set classes 4-8 [0 1 5 6] and 4-9 [0 1 6 7]), set off by a cello "foghorn" (Example 39.3). The *pizzicato* chord in measure 2, which has the same pitch content as the first "shimmer" chord, also belongs to SC 4-8. The second shimmer chord is arpeggiated into a melody in measure 3, which is passed in canonic fashion first to violin 2 (transposed down a perfect fifth), then to the cello (down three octaves) in measure 4. The cello then continues in measures 5–6 with a canonic imitation of the first violin. Listen again to hear these features.

EXAMPLE 39.3: Webern, String Quartet, Op. 5, fourth movement, mm. 1–6 🎧 (anthology)

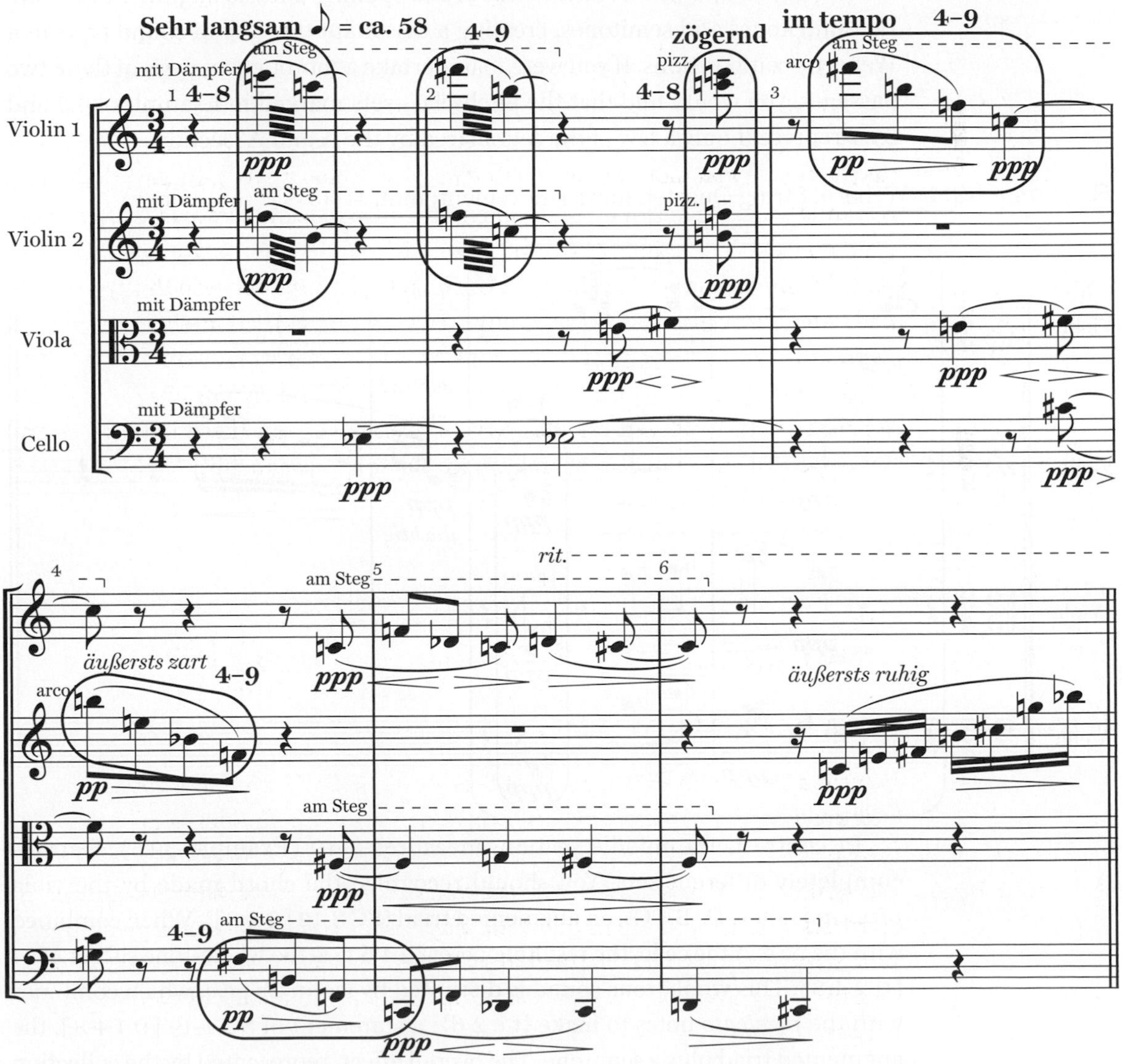

The texture of the opening returns in measures 11–13, as do many of the pitch-class sets (see Example 39.4) and even a melody. The first violin's ordered pcset <0 5 1 0> of measures 4–5 also returns in 11–12, transposed up an octave in the viola and two octaves in violin 2. If we label the opening section (mm. 1–6) **A**, we could label measures 11–13 **A′**. The entire texture in measures 11–13 (pcs 0, 1, 2, 5, 6, 7, 8, 9) forms SC 8-8 [0 1 2 3 4 7 8 9], the abstract complement of the **A** section's SC 4-8. (Remember, abstract complements are those that demonstrate literal complementation only after they are transposed: SC 4-8 [0 1 5 6] when transposed to {5 6 t e} is the literal complement of SC 8-8 [0 1 2 3 4 7 8 9].) The pizzicato chord in measure 12 belongs to SC 4-9, circled and labeled in the example. These set classes—4-8, 4-9, 8-8, and others of the opening and closing measures—are rich in tritones and semitones, creating a dissonant tapestry of sound typical of Webern's compositions. If you were to undertake a thorough analysis of these two passages, you would find that the pitch-class sets marked in Examples 39.3 and 39.4 represent only a few of the sets shared by the **A** and **A′** sections.

Example 39.4: Webern, String Quartet, fourth movement, mm. 11–13 (anthology)

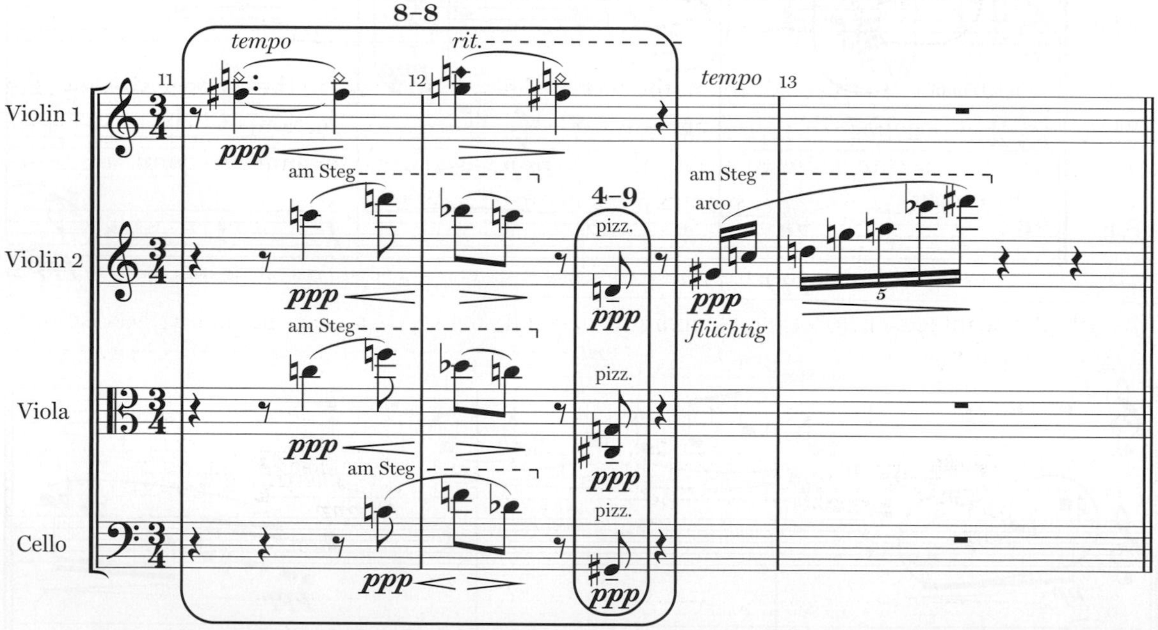

In contrast, the middle section, measures 7–10 (Example 39.5), features completely different sets. You should recognize the chord made by the viola *pizzicato* notes: D–B♭–G♭, an augmented triad (SC 3-12 [0 4 8]). When combined with the pc 4 in the cello, the resulting pcset {2 4 6 t} is the whole-tone subset 4-24 [0 2 4 8]. This whole-tone sound is disrupted by violin 2's pc e, which combines with the *pizzicato* notes to make {t e 2 6}: a statement of SC 4-19 [0 1 4 8], the augmented triad plus a semitone. The overall effect, represented by the collection of all the pcs in measures 7–10—{0 2 3 4 6 8 t e}, a member of SC 8-24—includes a strong whole-tone component, in contrast to the sets of the opening.

Example 39.5: Webern, String Quartet, fourth movement, mm. 7–10 (anthology)

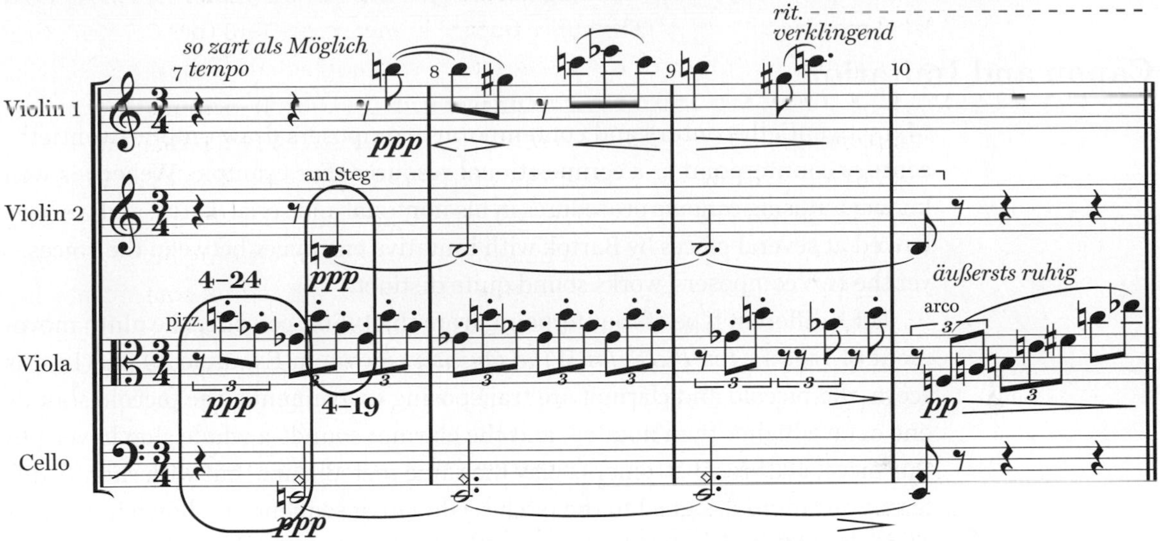

In this movement, the sectional divisions shown in the set analysis above are reinforced by the contrasting texture of the middle section, melody over ostinato accompaniment, and by the return of melodic and textural elements in measures 11–12. The movement is a ternary form: **A B A′**.

Try it #3

Write the pc integers below each ascending seven-tone figure, then describe their relationship. What is their function in the form?

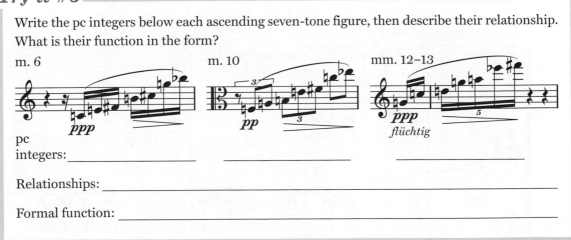

m. 6

m. 10

mm. 12–13

pc integers: ____________________ ____________________ ____________________

Relationships: ____

Formal function: ____

Examples from earlier chapters also demonstrate that pitch-class relationships, rather than tonal keys, can define form in twentieth-century pieces. In Bartók's

"Song of the Harvest" (Chapter 33), different versions of the octatonic collection help establish the form. In Webern's *Piano Variations* (Chapter 37), rows and repetition patterns articulate a simple binary form. In both works, range and register also play a key role in defining form.

Canon and Imitation

Many twentieth-century and contemporary composers draw on pre-twentieth-century counterpoint as a compositional resource. For example, Webern is well known for using canonic procedures in his nontonal and serial works, and we have looked at several pieces by Bartók with imitative entrances between the voices—yet the two composers' works sound quite distinct.

For a different type of counterpoint, from the 1960s, consider the ninth movement of Ligeti's *Ten Pieces for Wind Quintet*, shown in Example 39.6a. (In this score, the piccolo and clarinet are transposing instruments: the piccolo sounds one octave higher than notated, and the clarinet sounds a whole step lower.) In this piece, all three instruments play the same melodic line, but with slightly different durations assigned to the pitches (the pitch sequence is shown in part b). The form of this piece is represented in the pitch-time graph in part (c). Its beginning and end are similar to a description in one of the earliest written sources of information about counterpoint, the *Musica enchiriadis* from around 900: it opens with a unison and ends with a gradual close to an octave.

EXAMPLE 39.6: Ligeti, *Ten Pieces for Wind Quintet*

(a) Ninth movement

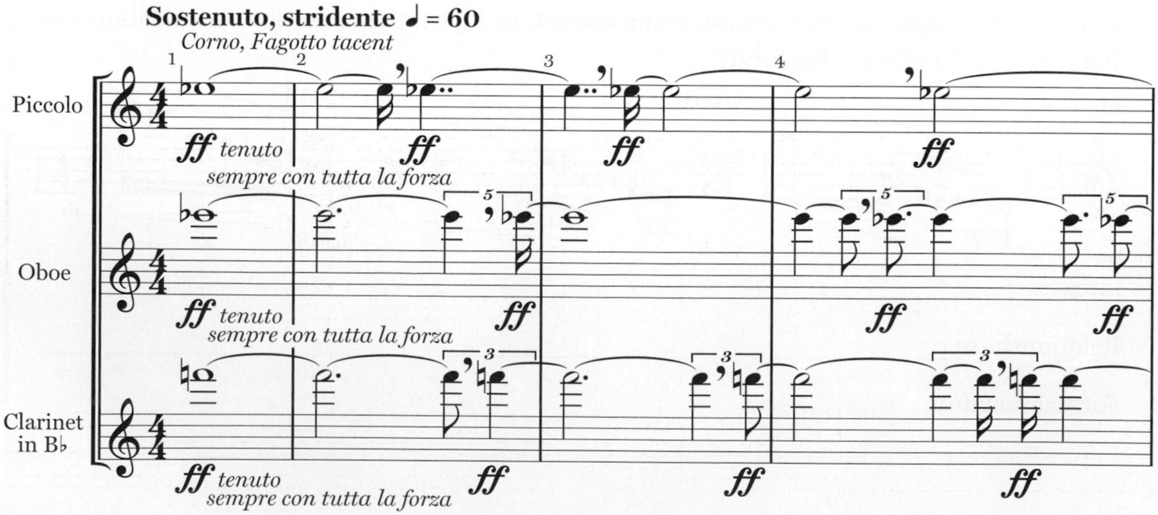

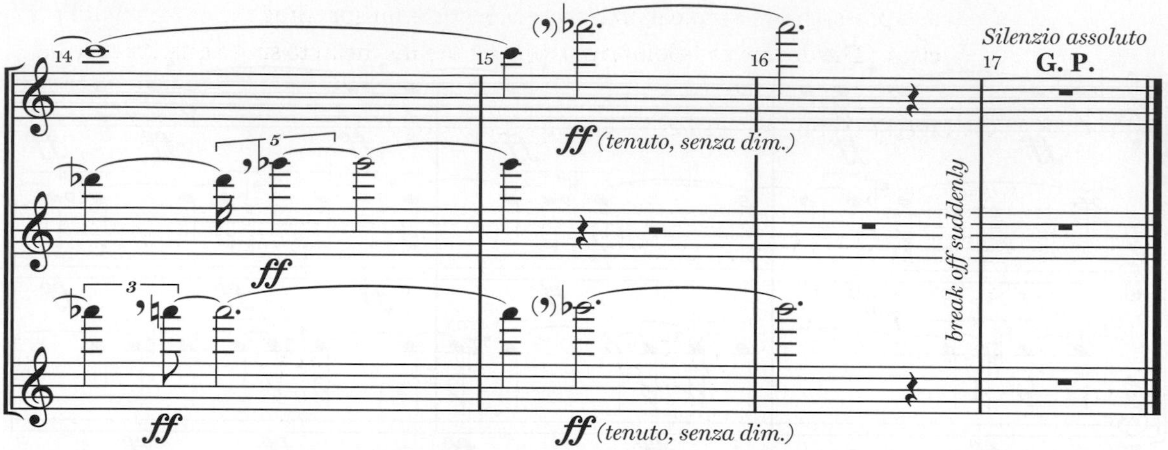

(b) Pitch sequence for ninth movement

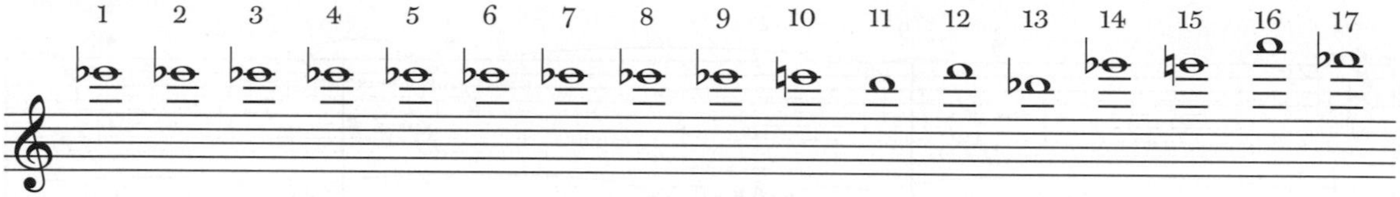

(c) Pitch/time graph for ninth movement

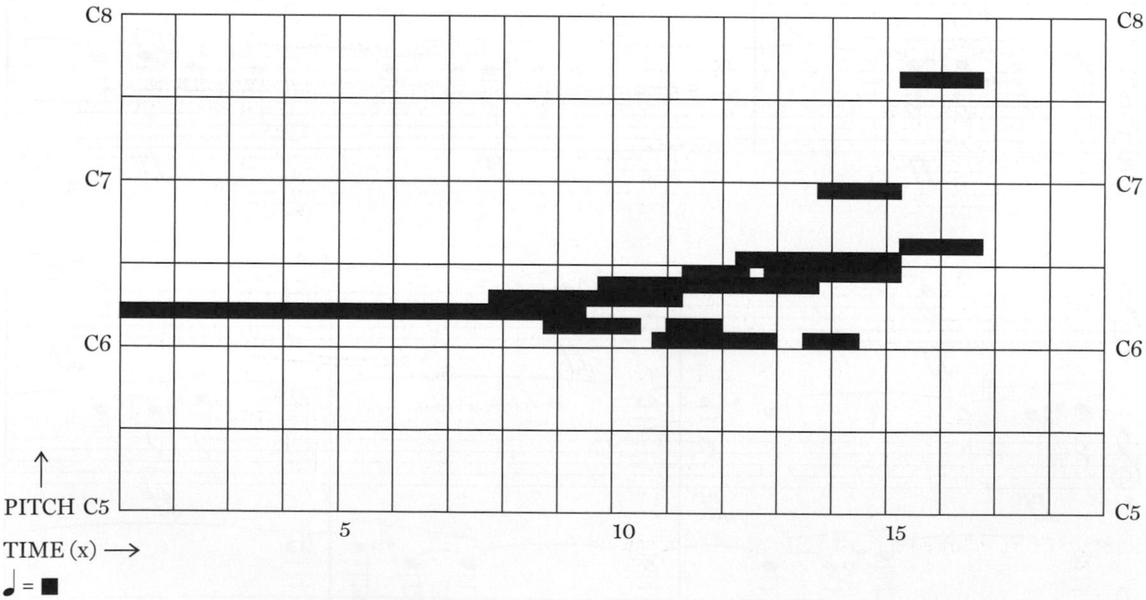

Ligeti employs other types of imitation in his compositions as well. Look at Example 39.7, measures 19–23 of the second song from *Three Fantasies on Texts by Friedrich Hölderlin* (composed in the 1980s). This passage, consisting of the alto parts, shows a typical imitative entry at the unison. Sing the passage with your class. (The downward-pointing arrows on the B♭s mean to sing a quarter tone flat.)

EXAMPLE 39.7: Ligeti, "Wenn aus der Ferne," mm. 19–23 (alto parts)

Translation: How flowed the lost hours, how calm was my soul.

For another example of imitation, listen again to the beginning of Penderecki's *Threnody* while following the score, to see how the entrances of sound effects are organized. Example 39.8 shows the patterns for the four entrances in the cellos at rehearsal number 6, labeled A, B, C, and D. How do these entrances compare with those in the violas, violins, and basses (from there to rehearsal 10)? Mark those entrances in your score with the same labels. The individual parts enter in a kind of imitation. Although this portion of the *Threnody* follows strict contrapuntal procedures, you probably did not hear it this way; instead, it sounds like a swirling insect ostinato. The choice of imitative entries is significant to the sound of this passage, however: it allows Penderecki to balance the diverse string effects and thus achieve an even blending.

Example 39.8: Penderecki, *Threnody for the Victims of Hiroshima*, cello entrances at rehearsal number 6 (anthology)

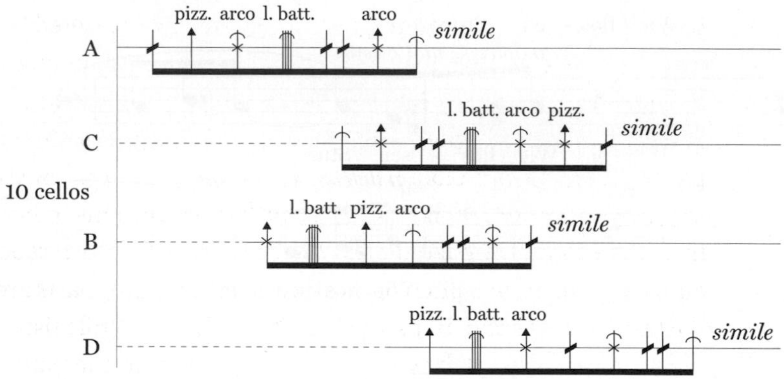

New Developments in Musical Form

Form as Process

Beginning in the 1960s, some composers reacted to the extremes of integral serialism by composing pieces in a style known as **minimalism**, in which each piece was created from a "minimum" of musical materials. Some minimalist pieces are notated in scores, like La Monte Young's *Composition 1960*, No. 5, discussed in Chapter 38. Other minimalist pieces feature the incessant repetition of a series of pitches (usually drawn from a diatonic collection) that change gradually over time. In these latter pieces—preferred in the 1960s by composers Terry Riley, Philip Glass, and Steve Reich—the gradual change of pitches involves a process that, once started, must run to completion. For example, Riley's *In C* requires a group of players to move through a set of fifty-three melodic patterns, repeating each one for a while before proceeding to the next. (The first four patterns are shown in Example 39.9.) Each player chooses when to start a new pattern and how long to repeat the old one, but must stay with the group, so that all players move through the score within a few patterns of each other, making a gradually changing musical kaleidoscope.

Example 39.9: Riley, *In C*, first four patterns

Several of Steve Reich's compositions from the 1960s draw on the idea of **phasing**: patterns moving in and out of alignment, creating additional sounds and patterns not visually present in the score. Reich discovered this effect by accident, when trying to get two reel-to-reel tape players to play copies of the same tape in synchronization (nearly impossible with the equipment he had). His composition *Piano Phase*, an excerpt of which is given in Example 39.10, begins with one pianist playing a repeated melodic pattern. A second pianist joins with the same pattern, in synchronization, then gradually accelerates until his or her part is one pitch off from the original aligned pairing. The process of pattern repetition, acceleration, and realignment one pitch off continues until the two parts are once more aligned.

Listen now to the first section of *Piano Phase*. While listening, concentrate on the rhythmic and pitch patterns that emerge from the pairings of the two parts. Can you hear the approach of the alignment at the end of the section? In a piece like this one, when the process is complete, the section (or whole composition) is also complete—the process defines the overall form.

Example 39.10: Reich, *Piano Phase*, first three patterns (anthology)

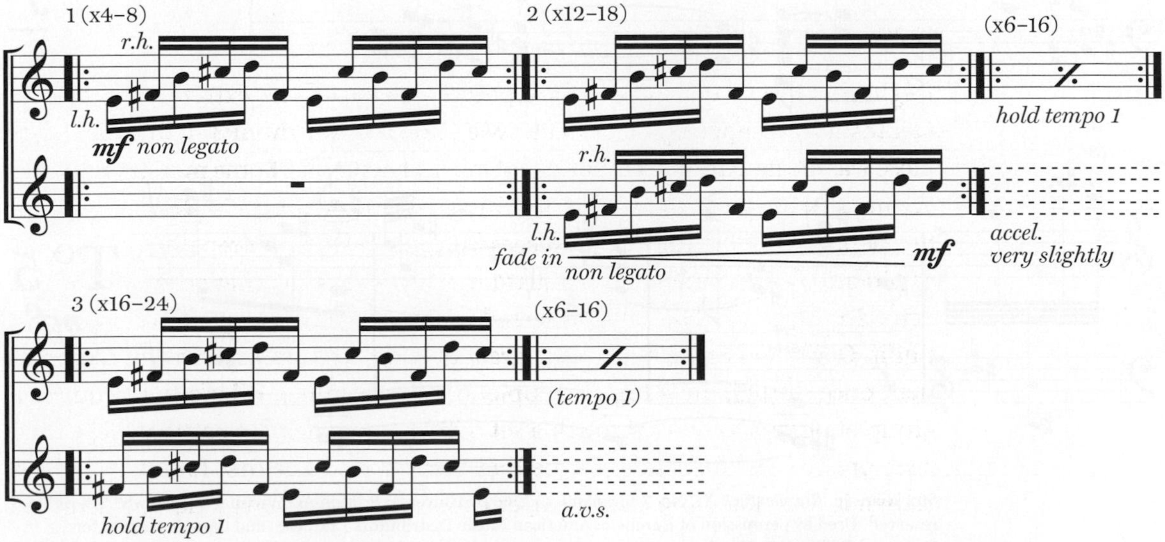

Moment Form and Mobile Form

One of the new developments in form in the second half of the twentieth century was the idea that formal sections of a piece did not have to connect in some logical way or in a predetermined order. Compositions featured abrupt changes from one style of music to another, without any interest in making a logical connection. Rather than hearing a piece as a structured and unified whole, listeners were to hear and enjoy whatever music was sounding at a particular time "in the moment"; hence the term **moment form**. This type of piece is said to have a **nonteleological form** (as opposed to the **teleological**, or goal-directed, forms of traditional tonal music).

A famous example of nonteleological form is Stockhausen's *Klavierstück XI*, which consists of nineteen different independent musical fragments in (for the most part) traditional music notation. Two of the fragments are shown in Example 39.11. Tempo, dynamics, and articulation for any given segment are specified at the end of the previous segment. (For example, the end of the first segment specifies tempo 2, *forte*, and a sustained articulation, —.) In performance, any one of the fragments may follow any other; the pianist chooses the order according to where his or her eye falls next on the score. (This is Stockhausen's instruction. However, many pianists select their order of segments initially at random, then practice the segments in that same order to prepare the performance. The piece is just too difficult to make formal decisions at sight!)

Example 39.11: Stockhausen, *Klavierstück XI*, two segments

Pieces like *Klavierstück XI*, where segments, sections, or movements may be played in varying orders, have what is called a **mobile form**, after artist Alexander Calder's mobile sculptures, whose parts may move into different positions relative to each other, perhaps as a result of the wind or a mechanical action. In analyzing a piece with a mobile form, keep in mind the possible permutations of sections or segments. While the contents of segments may remain consistent from one performance to another, the overall organization of the piece will not.

Indeterminacy and Chance

Indeterminate pieces, composed primarily after 1950, incorporate some elements that are either not specified by the composer, selected by a random procedure (such as throwing dice or flipping coins), or selected by **chance** (such as turning on a radio and including whatever sounds it happens to be making at the time, whether tuned to a station or not). Mobile form compositions also typically include some degree of indeterminacy.

Indeterminacy is not really new in the twentieth century—in Mozart's time, musicians played dice games in which music was composed by a random selection of phrase beginnings and endings (indeterminacy of composition). Further, any realization of a figured bass required choices on the part of the performer that could result in different voicings of chords (indeterminacy of performance). Indeed, all music has an element of indeterminacy: performers must make many choices as they bring the notated music to life. You can think of indeterminacy on a continuum, with indeterminate compositions from the post–World War II era actually focusing on relinquishing control as an organizing feature.

Compositions in graphic scores or text notation often include a degree of indeterminacy in their performance. Some graphic scores, like Penderecki's *Threnody*, represent the tasks of the performer as accurately as (or even more accurately than) a traditionally notated piece; others leave much room for interpretation. Consider the piece *In the Woods*, by Kenneth Maue, reproduced in Example 39.11.

Example 39.12: Maue, *In the Woods*

Begin in the morning. Bring some lunch, four large discs of day-glo paper, some thumbtacks, and some tape. Choose a roughly rectangular or circular area of solid woods.

Enter the woods at different locations along the periphery. Start walking in any direction. Sometimes move toward specific locations; sometimes just wander here and there; sometimes follow streams or paths, sometimes bushwhack; sometimes just sit.

As you walk around, find places to tack or tape your day-glo discs, in such a way that they can be seen by other players as they walk by. And be on the lookout for other players' discs. When you come across one, take it down, carry it for a while, then put it in a new location for someone else to find.

In the middle of the day, find each other by making noises. Make noise by any available means. Make sounds and listen. Move toward sounds you hear. When everyone has gathered together, have lunch. Then set out again, each in a different direction. This time, when you find a disc, take it down and keep it. After the day seems to be ending, make your way to the periphery, and wait to be picked up by a car.

Try it #4

What elements of *In the Woods* are indeterminate? Which would be the same in every performance that follows the score closely?

Indeterminate *Same each time*

What is the form of *In the Woods*? Would it be consistent in every accurate performance? The piece, surprisingly enough, does have a consistent form that is comparable to traditional forms. There is a setting out (the first section), which lasts all morning; a span of time where performers are making noises to assemble (the middle section), which concludes with the eating of lunch together; and a return to the periphery (a final section), which takes all afternoon and is similar to the beginning section in many respects. The piece thus has an overall ternary form, **A B A′**. *In the Woods* reminds us that each piece must be approached on its own terms. A score's appearance does not always indicate the presence or absence of form.

Surely by this point some of you are arguing, "This isn't music." A definition of music contemporaneous with this piece is "Music is organized sound." Indeed, there are sounds in this piece, and they are organized in such a way that any accurate performance should be recognizable as *In the Woods*. Musicians must choose for themselves how to define "music." You will have an opportunity to make that decision in the workbook exercises for this chapter.

Analyzing Form in Recent Music

The basic form-defining element in the musics we have studied is contrast. In common-practice-era music, the contrast might involve key areas, motives, themes, or even types of musical activity (exposition, transition, or development). In more recent music, the contrast may be found in timbre, texture, dynamics, collections or rows or sets, or other features. As we have seen, it is possible to create formal closure in music without functional tonality by drawing on other elements that help make a point of repose: a slowing of musical activity, a stop on a longer duration than normal, a rest that breaks the musical flow, a contrapuntal close to a unison or octave or some other stable interval or harmony.

One of the problems with analyzing form in recent music is that there is such a wide range of possibilities. If you examine the first movement of a Beethoven sonata, you have a good idea of what form to expect. On the other hand, music of the twentieth and twenty-first centuries tends to be less predictable. The starting point for any formal analysis is listening to the piece enough times that you can clearly hear it in your head—then attempting to explain what you hear. As you study and perform more repertoire from the twentieth and twenty-first centuries, you will become better able to predict which elements of style and form a composer will choose. While comparing form in nontonal pieces with tonal conventions is sometimes useful, be cautious in making these comparisons. Consider which elements of the piece are traditional in some way, but also the effect of nontraditional elements. Treat the examples in this chapter as an introduction, then move on to discover the formal processes in the contemporary pieces that you play or study.

Did You Know?

The 1950s to mid-1970s were a time of great experimentation in composition and performance of new music. In the years immediately following World War II, a new generation of European and American composers and performers—including Milton Babbitt, Luciano Berio, John Cage, György Ligeti, Olivier Messiaen, Luigi Nono, and Karlheinz Stockhausen—gathered at the Internationale Ferienkurse für Neue Musik, Darmstadt (Darmstadt International Summer Courses for New Music) to study new and early twentieth-century compositions (among them works of Webern and Schoenberg), and receive instruction in serialism and atonal composition. Though the instruction focused on the modernist styles prevalent in Europe prior to the war, composers from this group also were innovators in the development of electronic music, indeterminacy, and other postwar styles.

During the 1960s, American composers explored text or graphic representations, phasing and minimalism, and chance procedures. Other areas of innovation included the development and widespread distribution of electronic instruments (synthesizers, electric organs and pianos, electric guitars), which made possible a range of sounds never before heard or even imagined, and new recording technologies, from reel-to-reel tape to digital media. The explosion of new compositional ideas and resources led to a profusion of musical styles in the second half of the twentieth century, and with them, a need for new theories and analytical methods to explain their new musical structures.

TERMS YOU SHOULD KNOW

- chance
- indeterminate
- minimalism
- mobile form
- moment form
- nonteleological form
- ostinato
- phasing
- pitch symmetry
- pitch-time graph
- teleological form
- time-line notation
- tritone axis

QUESTIONS FOR REVIEW

1. What are typical characteristics of common-practice forms?
2. How have composers adapted common-practice forms in the posttonal era? What are some substitutes for the relationship of tonic and dominant in nontonal works?
3. How are formal units defined without tonal cadences? What features may create closure without functional harmony?
4. What are some elements that help establish sections in nontonal works?
5. How is closure achieved in pattern-repetition pieces?
6. If a piece contains indeterminate elements, is its form also indeterminate? Explain.
7. In music for your own instrument, find one piece that does not use functional tonality but has clearly audible formal divisions.
8. In music for your own instrument, find one piece that incorporates indeterminacy. (Ask your teacher for assistance, if needed, with questions 7 and 8.)

Recent Trends

Outline of topics

Contemporary composers and techniques of the past

- Materials from the pretonal era
- Materials from the Baroque, Classical, and Romantic periods
- Materials from the twentieth century

A look ahead

Overview

Twenty-first century composers have many compositional methods at their disposal. This chapter considers works that illustrate materials in use at the end of the twentieth century and the beginning of the twenty-first.

Repertoire

John Corigliano, "Come now, my darling," from *The Ghosts of Versailles*

György Ligeti, "Désordre," from *Piano Etudes*, Book I

Arvo Pärt, *Magnificat*

Steve Reich
City Life
Proverb

Contemporary Composers and Techniques of the Past

For most of the recorded history of Western music (or any music, for that matter), specific styles were associated with composers of any particular location and time. The styles typically included (1) slightly older compositional methods (practiced by traditionalists and the somewhat old-fashioned composers) that formed the bulk of what composers were taught; (2) the current style, practiced by those in vogue; and (3) the beginnings of a new style—whatever came next. For example, when J. S. Bach (1685–1750) was young, he was trained in the old-fashioned styles of the late seventeenth century, including modal counterpoint and traditional church music styles. As his career progressed, he incorporated newer ideas and developed his mature style, which included complex tonal counterpoint and pieces written in all twelve keys. Late in his life, his own compositions were considered old-fashioned by his sons and others writing in the new "galant" style.

From the early twentieth century through the 1970s, particular art-music styles came to be in vogue and others (such as functional tonality) were rejected, even though some composers still wrote in these older styles. The conflict of the **modernist** aesthetic—espoused by composers such as Schoenberg, Stravinsky, Bartók, and later Stockhausen and Babbitt—was to reject the past while at the same time venerating it. Modernist composers adopted the novel, scientific, mathematical, and revolutionary, yet wished to be considered the successors to the great musical masters of the past.

In the last fifteen years of the twentieth century, this tendency changed. Both popular and art music began to draw more freely on earlier musical languages, creating a new style from the combination of materials originating from different times. This style is sometimes referred to as **postmodernism**, a term borrowed from literary and art criticism. At the end of the twentieth century and today, the composer's materials include everything known from previous eras. In the 1970s, composers began to rediscover tonal materials: triads, melody and melodic development, regular beat and meter, consonant sonorities, diatonic scales and resources. Of course, those materials were present through the entire century in a wide variety of popular and folk musics, and in the works of some art-music composers, but they had been out of fashion in the mainstream modernist community since the early part of the century. The resurgence of interest in older materials did not mean a wholesale return to writing music that could be mistaken for that of an earlier century. The music produced at the end of the twentieth century is, for the most part, clearly "contemporary"—bearing the mark of the experimentation of the previous fifty years even when it draws on materials from earlier eras.

Our fast-paced, information-age society is reflected in **style juxtaposition**: elements strongly associated with one style or musical culture appear side by side with another type of music without a transition between the two, or any attempt to reconcile the differences. Some compositions include literal quotations or **stylistic allusions** to works of other composers (both contemporaneous and from previous centuries) that are intended to be recognized by the listener; others employ **parody** (where previous ideas are distorted by such means as unexpected timbres or rhythms, or changes in mode). Quotation, allusion, and parody are not new techniques, but recent compositions take them to extremes, juxtaposing radically different musical styles.

In this chapter, we examine excerpts from works inspired by compositional styles of the past. The chapter is too brief to be more than an overview; consider it an introduction and a stimulus to further study. After all, the meaning and significance of many of the techniques considered here, especially those of the past quarter century, will not be fully understood until more time has passed and historical distance has clarified them.

Materials from the Pretonal Era

In the medieval and Renaissance eras, limited communications, a lack of printing facilities, and difficult travel conditions restricted musicians' knowledge of music to what was available in their native locales. Musicians today are not so restricted; in fact, by the end of the twentieth century, more was known about Western music composed before 1650 than at any previous time, including the time when the music was originally composed. Partly as a result, the last century saw an upsurge of interest in historically accurate performance practice. This interest was backed by detailed research into traditions of composition and performance, the restoration of old instruments and the production of new "historical" instruments, as well as the publication of editions, translations, and treatises that describe "how it was done at the time." New recording technology has made it possible for pieces preserved in centuries-old manuscripts to be performed and distributed worldwide, and for today's listeners to appreciate their beauty. Who would have thought that one of the best-selling CDs of art music in the 1990s would be a recording of monks singing medieval chant? Yet that was the case.

One piece that draws on pretonal compositional ideas is Steve Reich's *Proverb*, a work from 1995 for three sopranos, two tenors, two vibraphones, and two samplers or electronic organs, based on a text from the twentieth-century philosopher Ludwig Wittgenstein. The piece begins with a single soprano voice singing, "How small a thought it takes to fill a whole life . . . how small a thought" (Example 40.1). This melody, in a modal-sounding B minor, captures the haunting spirit of plainchant. The soprano is soon joined by a second soprano, singing the same melody in canon with a delay of only one beat. Perform the passage with your class or listen to a recording.

Although the spirit of medieval chant continues to be present in the counterpoint, the clashing half-step harmonic intervals, produced by the time-delayed canonic voice and the changing asymmetric meters in which it is notated, clearly mark this piece as a product of the twentieth century. The entire work combines contrapuntal techniques and an *a cappella* singing style that are almost a thousand years old with a text that is not much more than fifty years old, electronic organs (a typical sound of the 1960s), and vibraphones (a percussion instrument invented in the first quarter of the twentieth century).

EXAMPLE 40.1: Reich, *Proverb*, mm. 1–22a (sopranos 1 and 2)

A second piece that evokes the sounds of an earlier era is Arvo Pärt's *Magnificat*, written in 1989. The opening two phrases are shown in Example 40.2. Listen to or sing each passage in class.

EXAMPLE 40.2: Pärt, *Magnificat*, opening two phrases 🎧 (mm. 5–12 recorded)

Translation: My soul doth magnify the Lord, and my spirit hath rejoiced in God my savior.

Try it #1

(a) The passage in Example 40.2 divides into two phrases:

mm. 1 to ______, and mm. ______ to ______.

(b) How do the phrases correspond to the text? What marks the end of each phrase?

(c) What determines the placement of the dashed measure divisions?

(d) Are there tonal centers or scales or triads that you recognize?

(e) How is the ametric rhythm structured?

This composition is intended as contemplative religious music—a type of sounding icon. It is written in Pärt's *tintinnabuli* style, which he developed in the late 1970s: that is, it is built on a modal scale, is homophonic, does not modulate, and does not feature functional harmony. Instead, the piece draws on the resonance available in the triad. The primary melodic line is diatonic and generally moves stepwise, with occasional skips emphasizing accented words; the accompanying lines fill in the chord members of the primary triad of the work, F minor (F-A♭-C), or provide stepwise motion between members of the triad. (Look at measures 5–12 to see how F minor is articulated.) The only dissonances are those occasionally created between a melody pitch and the triad, and they are not "resolved" in a traditional fashion, but dissipate as the melody moves to a chord tone.

Both pieces call for the "pure," vibratoless singing style revived in the twentieth century for the performance of early music. In the *Magnificat*, the singers are to listen carefully, blending to make pure triadic intervals—the resonant triads of the overtone series—not the slightly adjusted intervals of the equal-tempered chromatic scale. This blending gives Pärt's works their characteristic bell-like sound. Both the Reich and Pärt selections are "minimalist" in their use of a limited palette of compositional materials, but are very different in sound from the pattern-repetition minimalist compositions examined in previous chapters.

Elements of pretonal styles that recent composers have adopted include modal scales and counterpoint from the Renaissance and the oldest types of contrapuntal cadences, such as closing in to a unison or expanding out to an octave. Chant and monophonic techniques have been borrowed, and compositional details like **isorhythm** (a repeated series of durations combined with a repeated melodic idea, usually of a different length; see Nono's *Il canto sospeso* in Chapter 38) and **quodlibet** (multiple texts, usually not all in the same language) appear in some compositions as early as the 1960s.

The idea of writing a piece without specifying the precise instrumentation (for example, Riley's *In C*, from Chapter 39) has also been adapted from earlier practice. Tunings other than equal temperament found their way into pieces from mid-century on, influenced by both non-Western and Western sources. At first these works were performed with handmade instruments or with altered fingerings or performance techniques on traditional instruments, but later synthesizers and electronic means were used to create variant tunings.

Materials from the Baroque, Classical, and Romantic Periods

In the last few decades, some composers have incorporated quotations of older pieces or even newly composed fragments intended to capture the style of an older composer. One example is John Corigliano's opera *The Ghosts of Versailles*, which blends newly composed "faux Mozart" with characters and plot elements drawn from operas by Mozart and Rossini (and references to quite a few other styles) into a work that clearly sounds like the late twentieth century. Listen to measures 1–72 of the duet "Come now, my darling," while following the score in your anthology.

(anthology)

If you know Mozart's *The Marriage of Figaro*, to which this scene refers, the characters will be familiar. The setting is a flashback to the seduction of Rosina by Cherubino. As we saw in Chapter 38, Cherubino, a young man of the Count's household (actually the singer is a mezzo-soprano, in a "pants" role), is seducing Rosina, the Count's wife. Two excerpts from this scene are given in Example 40.3 and 40.4.

Example 40.3: Corigliano, "Come now, my darling," mm. 10–13 (anthology)

Try it #2

(a) How do the the tonal harmonies in Example 40.3, including the key and mode, express Rosina's reluctance? Consider the key Cherubino is singing in at the beginning of the excerpt, and the key in which Rosina enters, then identify the harmonies.

(b) What rhythmic and metrical aspects of Rosina's music indicate her internal conflict?

Now listen to a second excerpt, measures 38–41 (Example 40.4). This passage exhibits many features that are associated with Mozart's music, including two-measure symmetrical subphrases, melodic style, chord choices, and keyboard right-hand figuration patterns; in fact, the melody bears a striking resemblance to the beginning of Mozart's "Voi, che sapete," also sung by Cherubino. Yet this duet could not be mistaken for one from Mozart's time. The changes of key and meter that come later in the passage are too extreme.

EXAMPLE 40.4: Corigliano, "Come now, my darling," mm. 38–41 (anthology)

In addition to references to Mozart's operas, *The Ghosts of Versailles* includes "ghost music" reminiscent of Penderecki, an aria with Middle Eastern influences, and elements of musical stage productions from Rossini to Wagner to Broadway. In some ways, the scope and scale of this contemporary work resembles the grand operas of the Romantic period more than those of Mozart.

Elements of Romantic style—from lush orchestration to the use of recurring motives like Wagner's leitmotivs (to represent a person, action, idea, or place)—have appeared throughout the twentieth century in pieces that are not in a Romantic style overall. For example, Berg, in his nontonal opera *Wozzeck* (1922), includes leitmotivs, much like those of Wagner, but made from pitch-class sets and without the tonal harmonies. In addition to extended chromatic harmony and the adaptation of traditional forms, the Romantic period offered expanded orchestral resources and colorful orchestration. Art song, opera, and programmatic orchestral works flourished in the expression of the Romantic ideal: love and loss on an epic scale.

In the last quarter century, composers have shown a resurgence of interest in incorporating elements from Baroque, Classical, and Romantic styles into their own works. Among the materials they have borrowed are traditional forms (binary, ternary, and sonata) and genres (concertos, sonatas, symphonies, and variation sets); traditional phrase structure and cadences; tonal counterpoint, including fugue and canon; symmetrical meters and rhythms that reinforce them; motivic development and melodic embellishment; and functional tonal harmony and dissonance treatment.

Today's composers will usually pick and choose among the older elements. For example, Chapter 39 discussed pieces with traditional formal structures but no tonal harmony or phrase structure, as well as minimalist pieces that draw on a diatonic collection, repeated motives, and motivic development but lack scale-degree function. In some compositions, functionally tonal passages combine with other sections employing newer techniques. For example, Tavener's "The Lamb" juxtaposes serial techniques with functional tonal sections.

Materials from the Twentieth Century

The composer's materials from the first half of the twentieth century include many of the techniques covered in Chapters 33–39: octatonic, pentatonic, whole-tone, and other nondiatonic scale materials; nonfunctional harmonies built on intervals other than thirds; pitch-class sets and serialism; and rhythmic innovations such as changing meter, asymmetrical meters, and ametrical music. At the same time, they also include the innovations of early jazz, the song forms of the Broadway musical, elements of post-1950s popular music, and a variety of world music resources.

The second half of the century saw an increasing emphasis on timbre and rhythm as compositional materials—some pieces require a stage full of percussion instruments. Such timbres as environmental noises, speech, and electronically produced sounds were considered fair game. World music influences have brought new ways of considering time and rhythm, from the patterns of the Balinese gamelan to those of West African drumming. After their absence in avant-garde music for much of the century, a regular beat and traditional meter found their way back into art music in the 1980s and 1990s, along with metrical and rhythmic practices of the earlier twentieth century.

"Désordre," from Ligeti's *Piano Etudes*, is an example of this rhythmic eclecticism (Example 40.5). At the time the piece was written, Ligeti was very interested in the cross rhythms created in various styles of African drumming. His music also draws on the rhythmic and metrical practices of Bartók and on mimimalist pattern repetition from the 1960s.

EXAMPLE 40.5: Ligeti, "Désordre," mm. 1–9a

Minimalism continued as an active style to the end of the twentieth century, but with some changes; this style, once associated with highly restricted materials, became more "maximal," with larger ensembles and increased levels of activity. A recent piece by Steve Reich, *City Life*, illustrates this change. In the first movement—scored for two flutes, two oboes, two clarinets, two pianos, two samplers (which play digitized snippets of recorded sounds), percussion, string quartet, and string bass—a recording of a New York street vender saying "Check it out" provides the primary rhythmic idea. Other movements bring in car horns, sirens, door slams, heartbeats, a pile driver, and speech samples from the New York City Fire Department's field communications on February 26, 1993, the day the basement of the World Trade Center was bombed—all treated as musical sounds and incorporated into the texture. Pattern repetition is a significant element in this piece, as in Reich's pieces from the 1970s, but the texture is much thicker, with a variety of event layers combining to make a wall of sound. The excerpt in Example 40.6 includes "Check it out" and some of the instrumental motives derived from that spoken rhythm.

Example 40.6: Reich, *City Life*, first movement, mm. 30–35

In many pieces written at the end of the century, the materials are so well integrated that their origin is not easy to determine. One composer who successfully crosses stylistic boundaries is the Japanese composer Toru Takemitsu. While primarily trained in Western compositional techniques, Takemitsu incorporates some elements of Japanese aesthetics. His works are often evocative of Debussy, Ravel, and Messiaen, yet bring to mind images of a Japanese garden—nature, balance, and calmness. His music is nontonal but also motivic, with repetition at times reminiscent of the minimalists, though his materials are not minimal. Like many end-of-century works, his resist labeling as belonging to any one compositional practice.

A Look Ahead

It is impossible for us to know what changes will take place in music composition, performance, recording, and score production in the current century. One thing that seems clear is that performers, composers, conductors, and music teachers will be expected to know more than ever about music of the past. That includes music of the common-practice era—our primary focus in this book—and of the twentieth century. All the styles of music discussed in this book are continuing to be studied and performed, a state of affairs that is unlikely to change. Musicians are expected to know the conventions of each period represented in their repertoire, and to apply these conventions in a stylistic and musical performance.

Your studies have just begun. The process of becoming a musician is a life's task, not something accomplished in one semester or year, or even in an undergraduate course of study. What you should have acquired now, though, is a firm foundation for continuing your studies. Be curious, take more courses, and above all, perform and investigate music of many styles and periods. We are lucky to live, and to be able to make music, in the twenty-first century—everything is open to us. Enjoy and explore!

Did You Know?

For American composers, the Pulitzer Prize for Music is a coveted recognition of achievement. Only since 1983 have any women won this prestigious prize, and the number of active female composers is a fraction of the number of male composers, as reflected in these chapters. Why is this the case? Before the twentieth century, women who were composers typically learned their craft growing up in a musical household, where siblings and/or parents were musicians. For example, Clara Schumann began learning piano and music composition at an early age from her father, Friedrich Wieck, who also taught her future husband Robert Schumann; and Fanny Mendelssohn Hensel studied with the same musical tutors as her younger brother Felix. Even when educational opportunities were available, women were not expected to work as composers or performers, and most who succeeded against societal pressures had both self-determination and the strong support of either a father or husband who encouraged their musical aspirations.

As educational opportunities expanded for women in the twentieth century, additional paths into composition and performance became available. It became possible for women to take composition lessons at women's colleges and universities in the early part of the century, and later they studied in the same classes as men. Though still outnumbered by men, there are many women composers of the late twentieth century who have had very successful careers, including Ellen Taaffe Zwilich, the first woman to receive the Pulitzer Prize (1983). Other women whose work has been recognized by the Pulitzer board include winners Shulamit Ran (1991), Melinda Wagner (1999), and Jennifer Higdon (2010), and finalists Vivian Fine (1983), Joan Tower (1993), Chen Yi (2006), Augusta Read Thomas (2007), and Julia Wolf (2010). Two composers featured in this chapter, Steve Reich (2009) and John Corigliano (2001), have also won this award. Visit individual composers' websites to hear samples of their works.

TERMS YOU SHOULD KNOW

isorhythm
modernism
parody
postmodernism
quodlibet
style juxtaposition
stylistic allusion

QUESTIONS FOR REVIEW

1. For each piece discussed in this chapter, make a list of the elements in the music that are based on older styles, and a list of elements that indicate the piece is contemporary.
2. What aspects of counterpoint do you find in these compositions?
3. How would you determine if a piece that features triads has functional tonality?
4. What are some characteristics of twentieth-century rhythm and meter?
5. What elements of minimalism are found in works in this chapter?
6. Find a piece of contemporary music for your own instrument that draws on stylistic elements of an earlier era. (Confer with your instrumental teacher for ideas.)

Appendixes

APPENDIX 1

Try it Answers

Chapter 1

Try it #1

A. (1) F; (2) D; (3) E; (4) F; (5) A; (6) D; (7) G; (8) B; (9) B; (10) C; (11) G; (12) F; (13) C; (14) F; (15) D.

B. (1) G: B–D–F–A; (2) D: F–A–C–E; (3) A: C–E–G–B; (4) B: D–F–A–C; (5) C: E–G–B–D.

Try it #2 (1) F♯; (2) C; (3) B♭; (4) C♯; (5) C♭; (6) G♯; (7) F; (8) A♯; (9) E♭; (10) F♭; (11) G♭; (12) E♯.

Try it #3

A. (1) G♯ or A♭; (2) C or B♯; (3) F or E♯; (4) A; (5) D♯ or E♭; (6) E or F♭; (7) G; (8) G.

B. (1) W; (2) H; (3) W; (4) W; (5) H; (6) W; (7) N; (8) W.

Try it #4

A. (1) F♯; (2) D; (3) E♭; (4) B; (5) G♯; (6) A♭; (7) D; (8) C♯; (9) G; (10) D♯.

B.

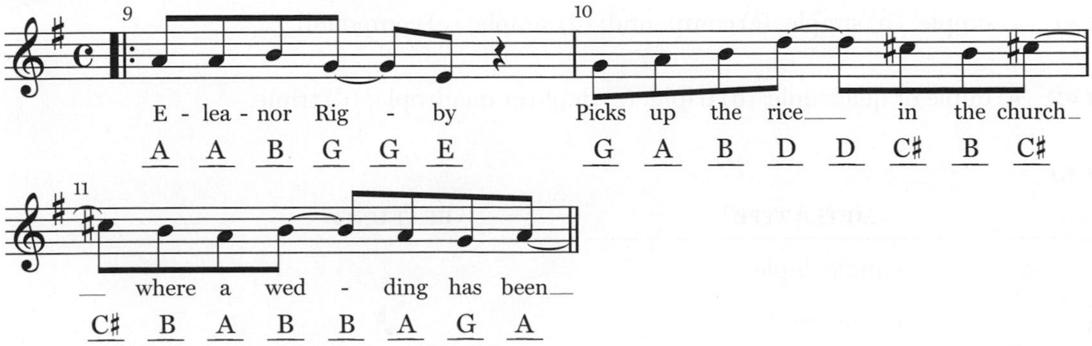

C. (1) H; (2) H; (3) W; (4) W; (5) H; (6) W; (7) N; (8) W; (9) W; (10) H; (11) W; (12) W; (13) H; (14) H.

Try it #5

A. (1) F♯; (2) G; (3) D♭; (4) B; (5) F♯; (6) A♭; (7) C; (8) G; (9) F; (10) E♯.

B.

C. (1) W; (2) H; (3) H; (4) W; (5) W; (6) H; (7) H; (8) H; (9) H; (10) H; (11) N; (12) W; (13) N; (14) W.

Try it #6

A. Clef: alto; (1) A; (2) F♯; (3) E; (4) E♭; (5) C; Clef: tenor; (6) B♭; (7) D; (8) F♯; (9) G; (10) C.

B.

C. (1) W; (2) H; (3) H; (4) W; (5) H; (6) W.

Try it #7

A. (1) G♯4; (2) B5; (3) A♭3; (4) E5; (5) D♭3; (6) F♯2; (7) E4; (8) B2.
(1) D4; (2) C5; (3) F3; (4) G♭4; (5) E4; (6) C♯3; (7) B♭4; (8) B3.

B. (1) G3; (2) F3; (3) G1; (4) C2; (5) F1.

Chapter 2

Try it #1 (a) simple; (b) simple; (c) compound; (d) simple; (e) compound.

Try it #2 (a) duple or quadruple; (b) triple; (c) duple or quadruple; (d) triple.

Try it #3

	METER TYPE	BEAT UNIT
(a) $\frac{2}{2}$	simple duple	𝅗𝅥
(b) $\frac{3}{16}$	simple triple	𝅘𝅥𝅯
(c) $\frac{3}{8}$	simple triple	𝅘𝅥𝅮
(d) $\frac{4}{2}$	simple quadruple	𝅗𝅥

Try it #4

(a)

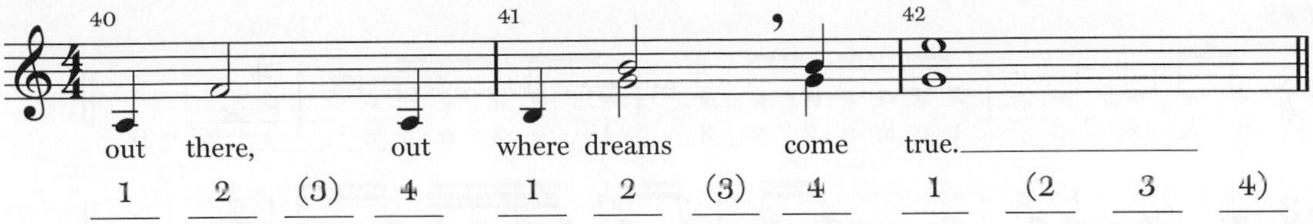

(b)

(c)

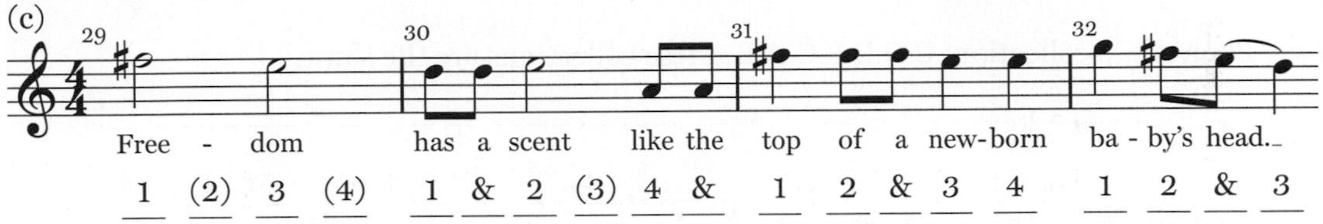

Try it #5

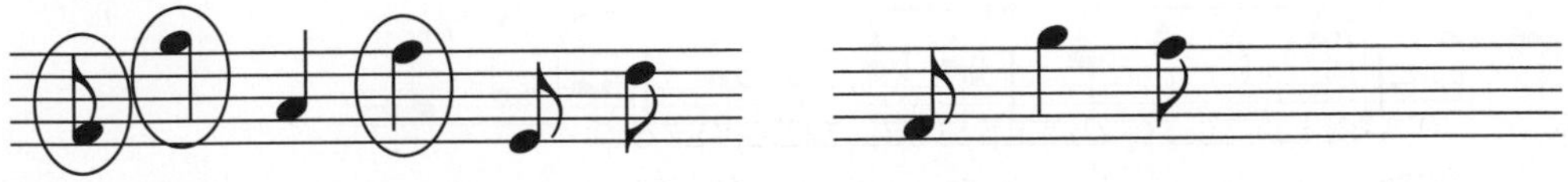

Try it #6

(a)

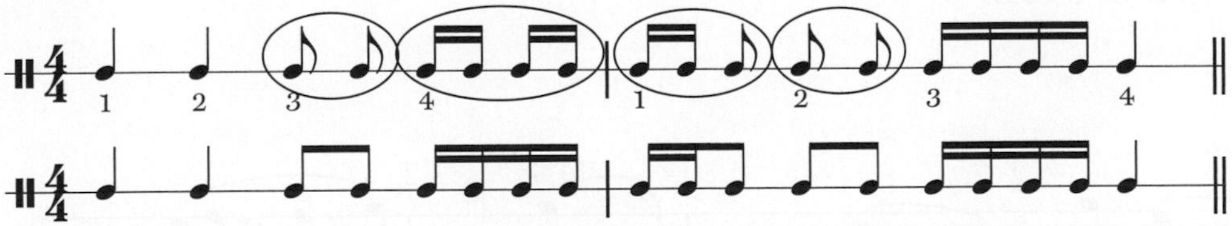

(b)

(c)

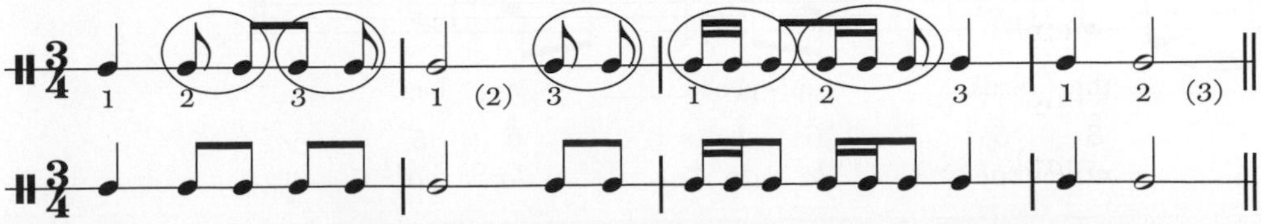

Try it #7 (a) 𝅗𝅥. or 𝅗𝅥 𝄽; (b) 𝅗𝅥 or ♩ 𝄽.

Try it #8

(a)

(b)

(c)
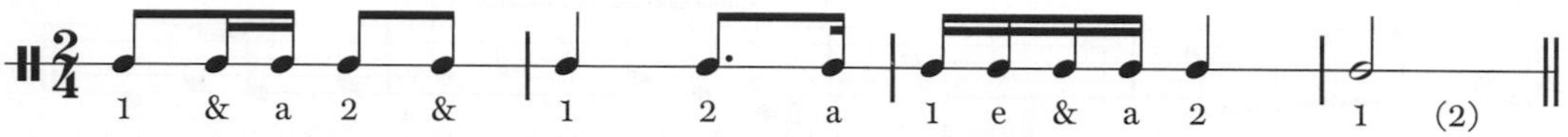

Chapter 3

Try it #1 Pitch-class collection: C D E F G A B; these collections are the same.

Try it #2

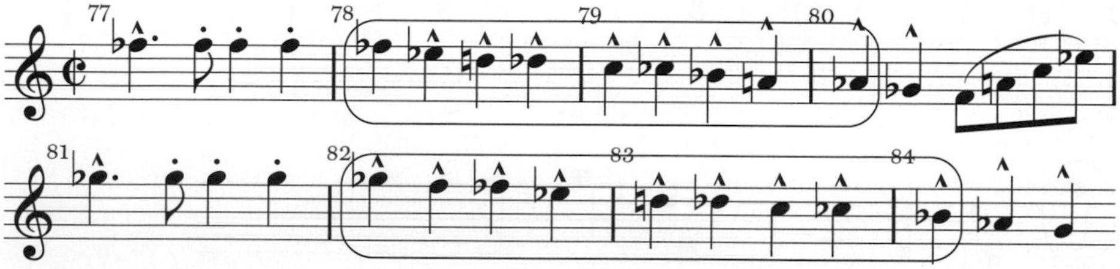

(a) F♭ E♭ D D♭ C C♭ B♭ A A♭

(b) G♭ F F♭ E♭ D D♭ C C♭ B♭

Try it #3

(a)

(b)

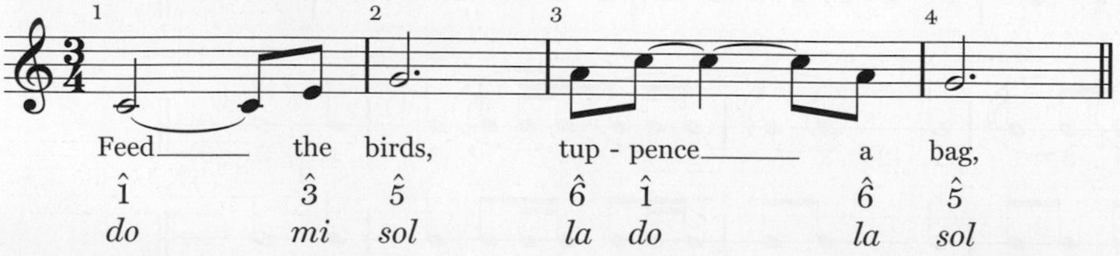

(c) The two melodies share a similar contour and scale-degree underpinning. $\hat{1}$–$\hat{3}$–$\hat{5}$–$\hat{6}$–$\hat{1}$–$\hat{5}$ (*do-mi-sol-la-do-sol*). Mozart's melody intersperses decorative tones.

(d) "Are You Sleeping?": $\hat{1}$–$\hat{2}$–$\hat{3}$–$\hat{1}$, $\hat{1}$–$\hat{2}$–$\hat{3}$–$\hat{1}$, $\hat{3}$–$\hat{4}$–$\hat{5}$, $\hat{3}$–$\hat{4}$–$\hat{5}$, $\hat{5}$–$\hat{6}$–$\hat{5}$–$\hat{4}$–$\hat{3}$–$\hat{1}$, $\hat{5}$–$\hat{6}$–$\hat{5}$–$\hat{4}$–$\hat{3}$–$\hat{1}$, $\hat{1}$–$\underline{\hat{5}}$–$\hat{1}$, $\hat{1}$–$\underline{\hat{5}}$–$\hat{1}$. *do-re-mi-do, do-re-mi-do*, mi-fa-sol, *sol-la-sol-fa-mi-do, sol-la-sol-fa-mi-do, do-<u>sol</u>-do, do-<u>sol</u>-do.*

"Happy Birthday": $\underline{\hat{5}}$–$\underline{\hat{5}}$–$\underline{\hat{6}}$–$\underline{\hat{5}}$–$\hat{1}$–$\underline{\hat{7}}$, $\underline{\hat{5}}$–$\underline{\hat{5}}$–$\underline{\hat{6}}$–$\underline{\hat{5}}$–$\hat{2}$–$\hat{1}$, $\underline{\hat{5}}$–$\underline{\hat{5}}$–$\hat{5}$–$\hat{3}$–$\hat{1}$–$\underline{\hat{7}}$–$\underline{\hat{6}}$, $\hat{4}$–$\hat{4}$–$\hat{3}$–$\hat{1}$–$\hat{2}$–$\hat{1}$. *<u>sol</u>-<u>sol</u>-<u>la</u>-<u>sol</u>-do-<u>ti</u>, <u>sol</u>-<u>sol</u>-<u>la</u>-<u>sol</u>-re-do, <u>sol</u>-<u>sol</u>-sol-mi-do-<u>ti</u>-<u>la</u>, fa-fa-mi-do-re-do.*

Try it #4

(a) A major

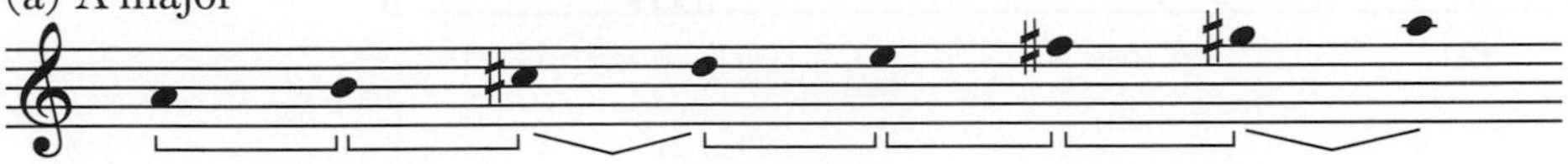

(b) A♭ major

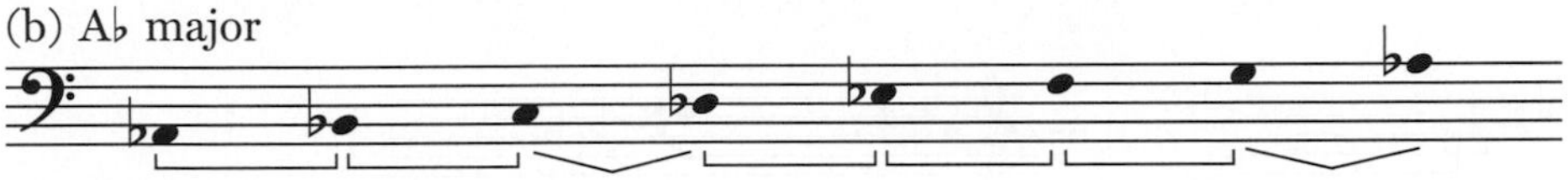

(c) G major

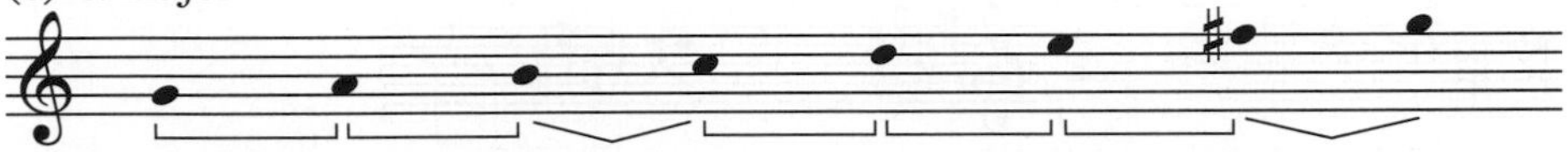

(d) B major

Try it #5

(a)

(b)

(c)

(d)

Try it #6

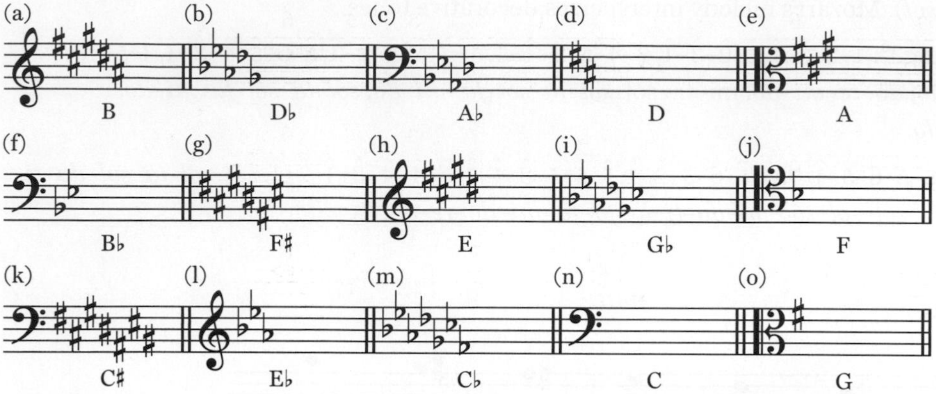

Try it #7

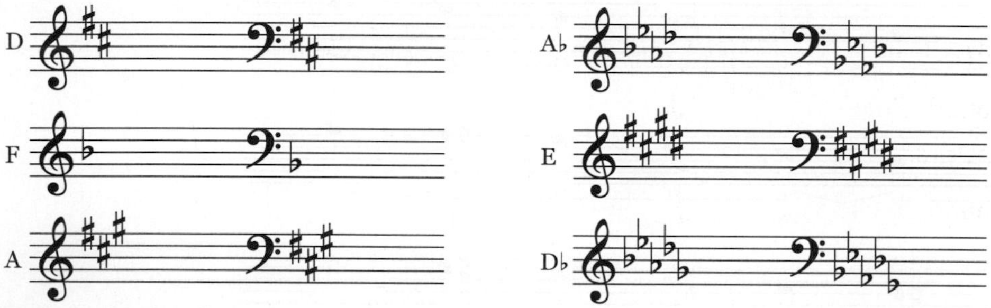

Try it #8 Key signature suggest what key?: A♭ major; First two scale degrees?: $\hat{5}$–$\hat{1}$ in A♭ major; Last scale degree?: $\hat{1}$; Key of piece: A♭ major.

Try it #9

SCALE	SCALE DEGREE	LETTER NAME
F major	$\hat{4}$	B♭
G major	leading tone	F♯
A♭ major	$\hat{5}$	E♭
E major	mediant	G♯
B major	supertonic	C♯
D♭ major	$\hat{6}$	B♭

Try it #10

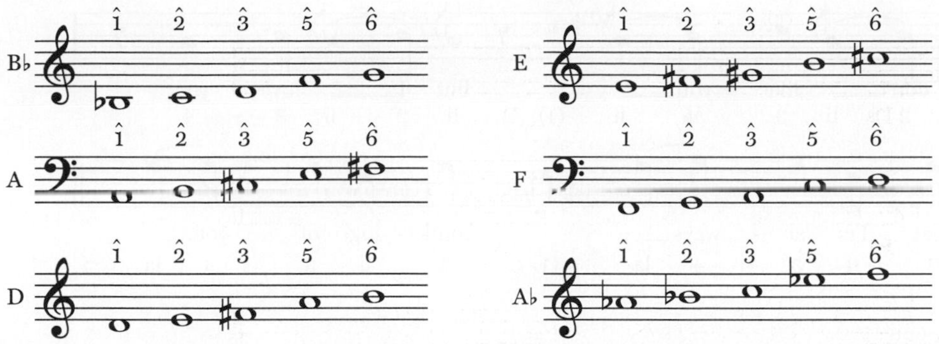

Chapter 4

Try it #1

METER	METER TYPE	BEAT UNIT	BEATS PER MEASURE
9/8	compound triple	♩.	3
2/2	simple duple	𝅗𝅥	2
12/8	compound quadruple	♩.	4
4/8	simple quadruple	♪	4
3/2	simple triple	𝅗𝅥	3
2/4	simple duple	♩	2
6/8	compound duple	♩.	2

Try it #2

(a)

(b)

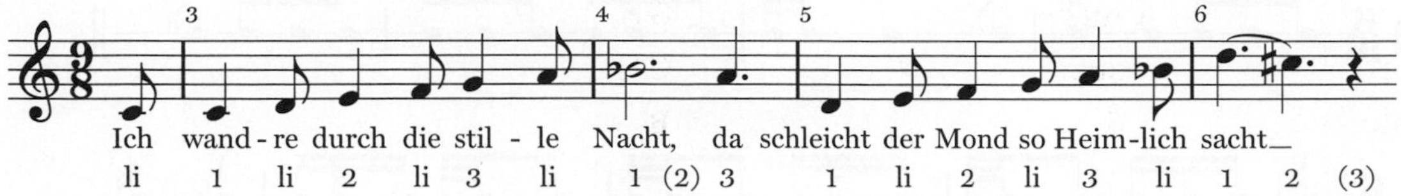

(c)

Try it #3

A.

B.

Try it #4

(a)

(b)

Chapter 5

Try it # 1

(a)

KEY	RELATIVE MINOR	KEY	RELATIVE MINOR
E major	C♯ minor	A♭ major	F minor
D major	B minor	E♭ major	C minor
B major	G♯ minor	F major	D minor

(b)

KEY SIGNATURE	MINOR KEY	KEY SIGNATURE	MINOR KEY
	G♯ minor		F♯ minor
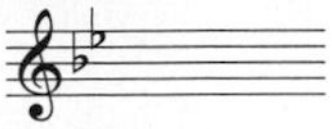	G minor	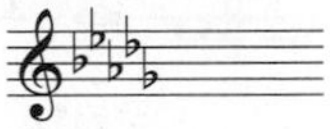	B♭ minor
	E♭ minor	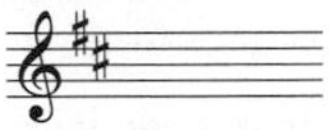	B minor

Try it # 2

KEY	RELATIVE MAJOR	KEY	RELATIVE MAJOR
A minor	C major	C♯ minor	E major
G♯ minor	B major	F minor	A♭ major
C minor	E♭ major	E minor	G major
D minor	F major	B♭ minor	D♭ major

Try it #3 (a) B♭ major; (b)F minor; (c) A minor; (d) D♭ major; (e) G minor.

Try it #4

	SIGNATURES		SIGNATURES
B major–B minor	5♯–2♯	F♯ major–F♯ minor	6♯–3♯
B♭ major–B♭ minor	2♭–5♭	A major–A minor	3♯–0♯
C major–C minor	0♭–3♭	C♯ major–C♯ minor	7♯–4♯

Try it #5

m. 41

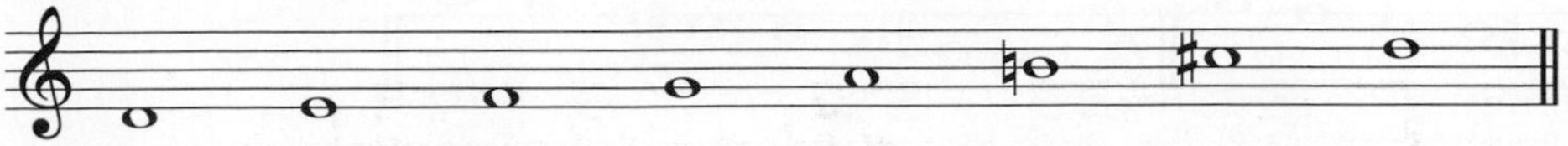

m. 45

Try it #6 Natural signs are optional (only relevant if you are imagining a key signature).

(a) C harmonic minor

(b) B♭ melodic minor

(c) F melodic minor

(d) G♯ melodic minor

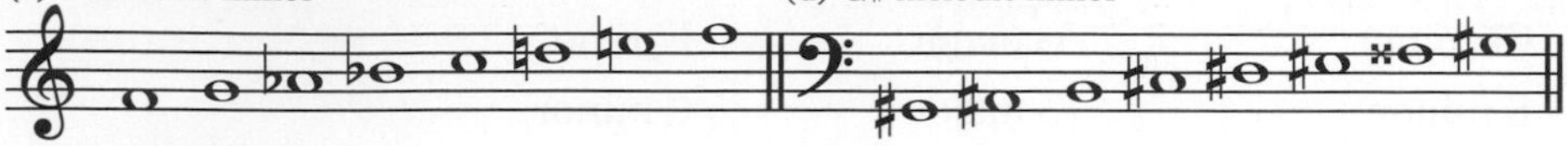

(e) B harmonic minor

(f) C♯ melodic minor

(g) F♯ harmonic minor

(h) E harmonic minor

Try it #7

(a) E major pentatonic

(b) E minor pentatonic

(c) B major pentatonic

(d) B minor pentatonic

(e) F♯ major pentatonic

(f) F♯ minor pentatonic

(g) B♭ major pentatonic

(h) B♭ minor pentatonic

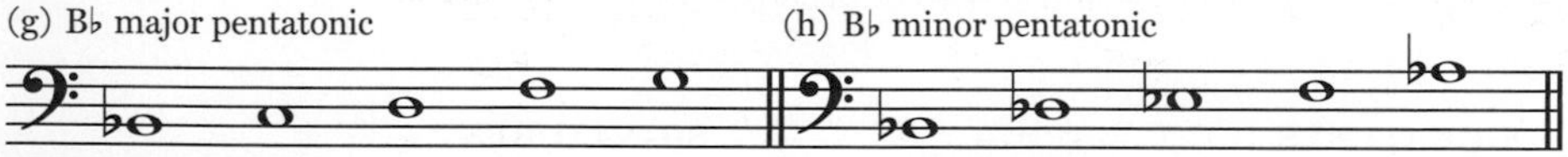

Try it #8

(a) E Dorian

(b) B♭ Lydian

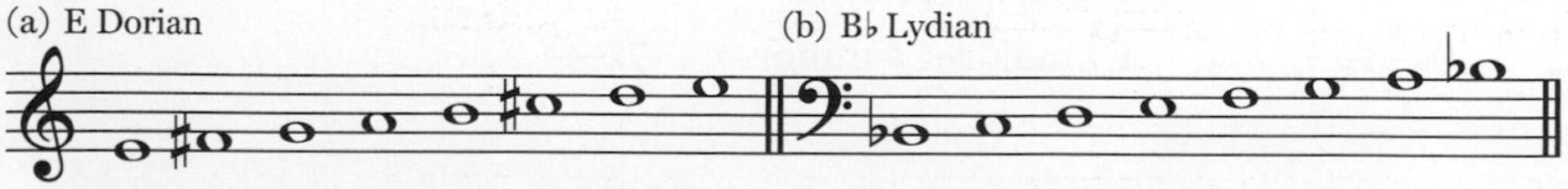

(c) B Aeolian

(d) A Mixolydian

(e) F♯ Phrygian

(f) E♭ Ionian

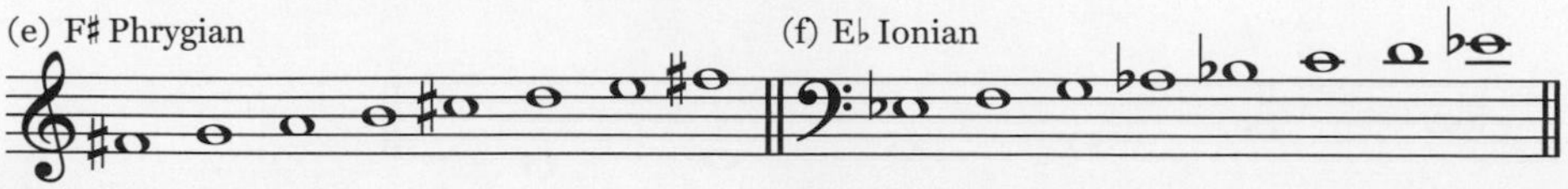

Chapter 6

Try it #1

(a)

2 3 4 5 6 7 6

(b)

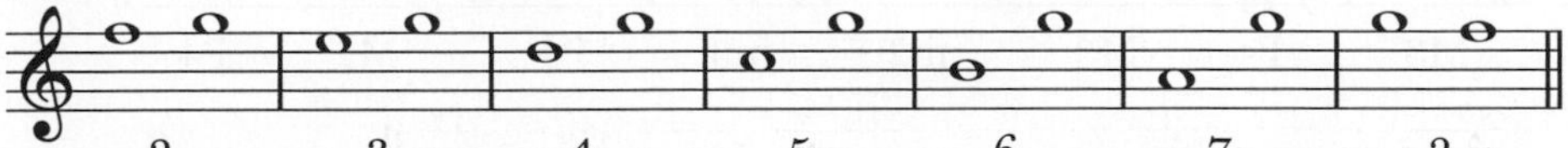

2 3 4 5 6 7 2

(c)

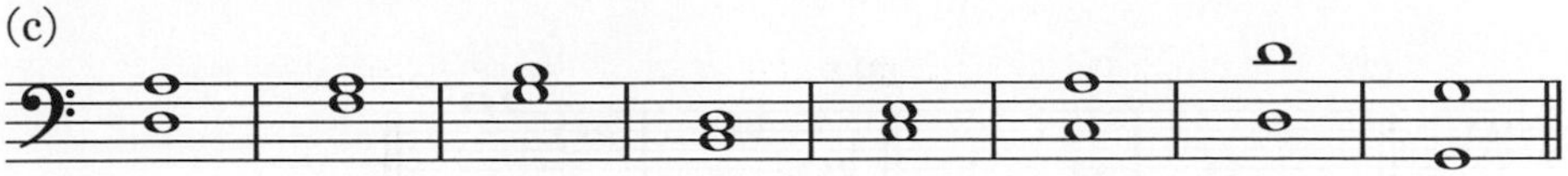

5 3 3 3 3 6 8 8

Try it #2

(1) 7; (2) 13 (6); (3) 8; (4) 13 (6); (5) 13 (6); (6) 12 (5); (7) 8; (8) 9 (2); (9) 10 (3); (10) 10 (3).

Try it #3

(a)

A♭ major

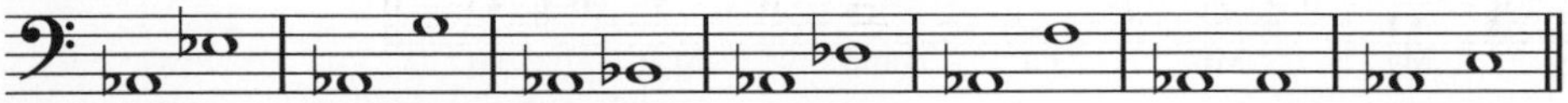

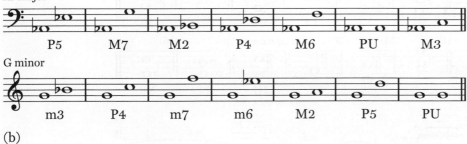

P5 M7 M2 P4 M6 PU M3

G minor

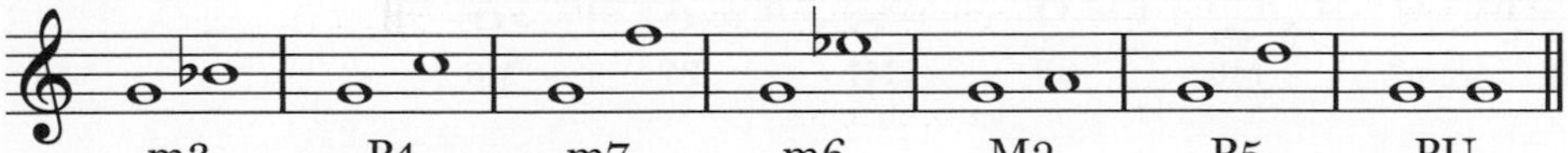

m3 P4 m7 m6 M2 P5 PU

(b)

E major

M6 P5 M7 PU M3 P4 M2

F minor

P4 m3 m7 P5 P8 m6 PU

Try it #4

(a)

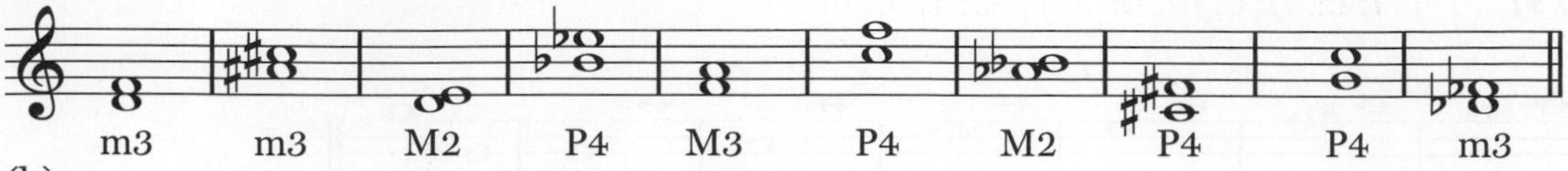

(b)

Try it #5

(a)

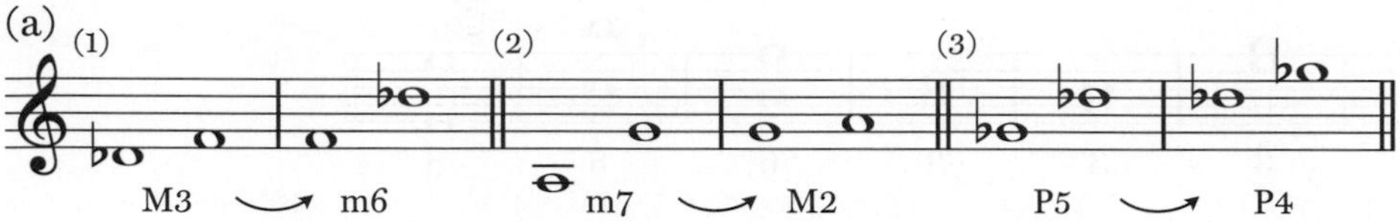

(b)

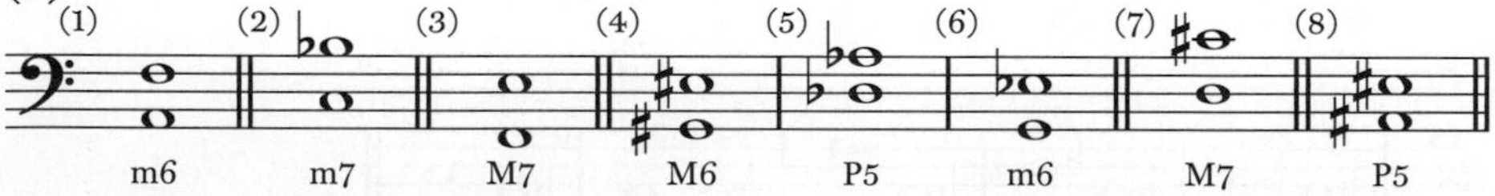

Try it #6

Chapter 7

Try it #1 m. 9: $\hat{1}$; m. 11: $\hat{6}$; m. 12: $\hat{5}$; m.13: $\hat{1}$; m. 14: $\hat{4}$.

Try it #2

E♭ major: M m m M M m d M

Try it #3

Natural minor:

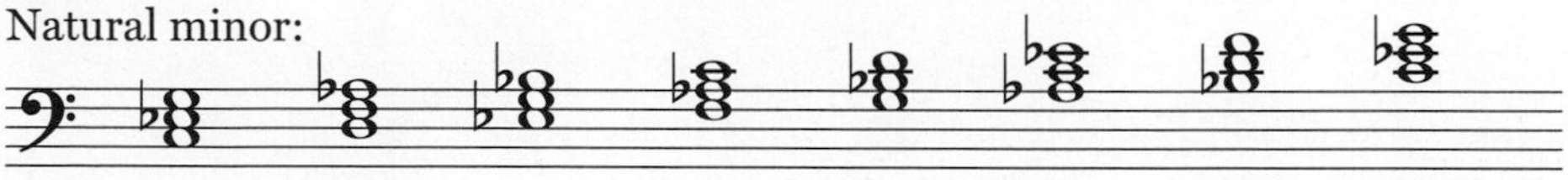

m d M m m M M m

With leading tone:

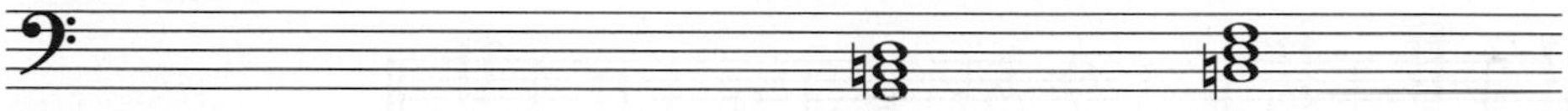

M d

Try it #4

m M m M A m

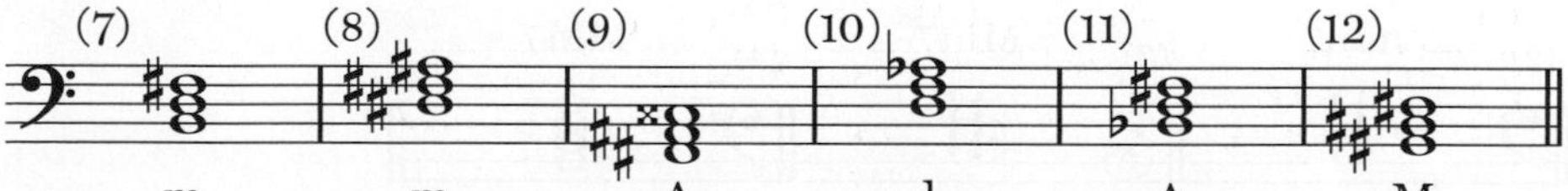

m m A d A M

Try it #5

	ROMAN NUMERAL	POSITION OR INVERSION
1. m. 30, beat 1	IV	root position
2. m. 30, beat 2	vii°	first inversion
3. m. 30, beat 3	I	first inversion
4. m. 31, beat 1	ii	first inversion
5. m. 32, beat 1	I	root position

Try it #6

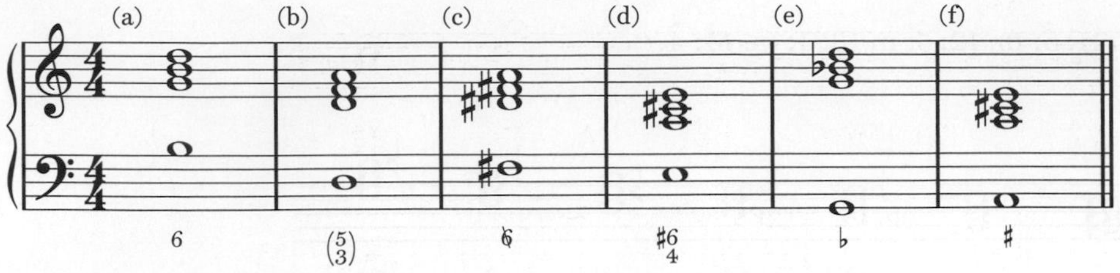

Try it #7 (a) m. 5, beat 1: G minor; (b) m. 5, beat 2: C minor; (c) m. 5, beat 4: D major; (d) m. 6, beat 1: G minor.

Chapter 8

Try it #1

A.

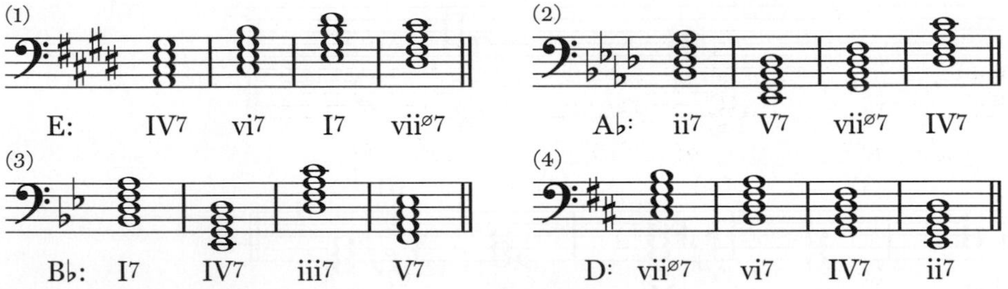

B.

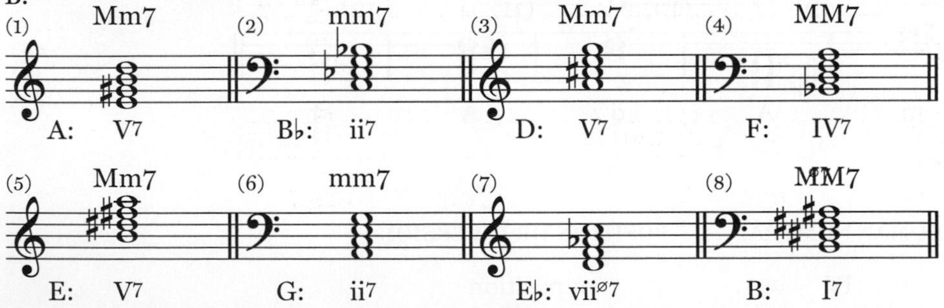

Try it #2

A.	QUALITY	BASS AND FIGURES
m. 2	mm7	seventh ($^4_2$)
m. 3	Mm7	third ($^6_5$)
m. 6	Mm7	seventh ($^4_2$)

B.

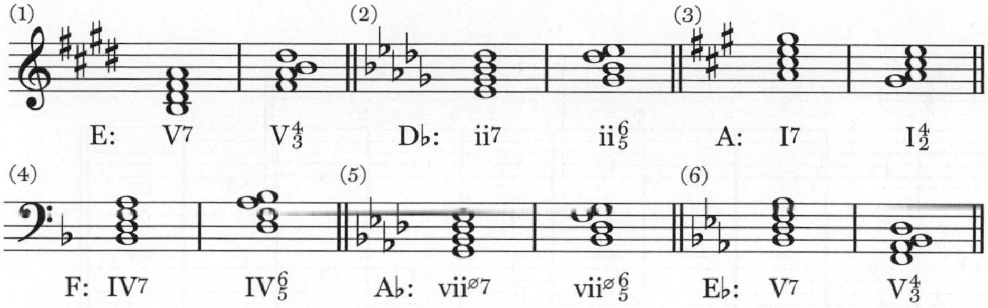

Try it #3

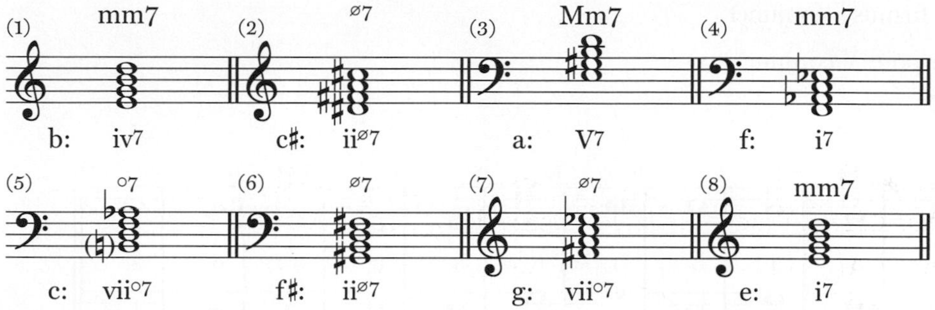

Try it #4

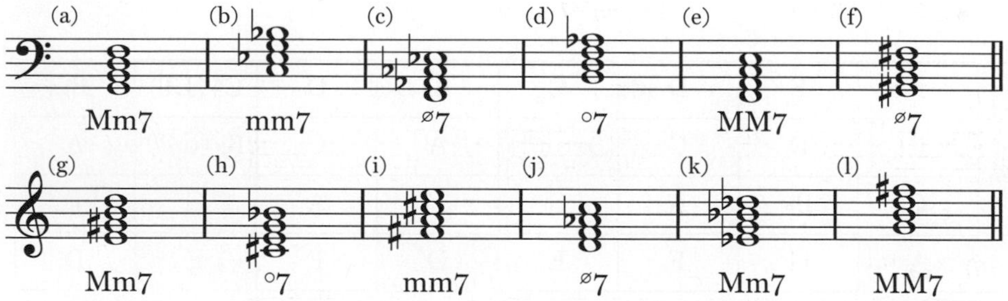

Try it #5

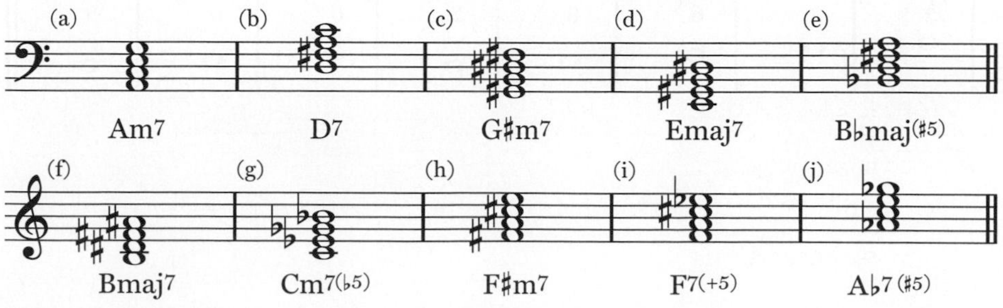

Chapter 9

Try it #1

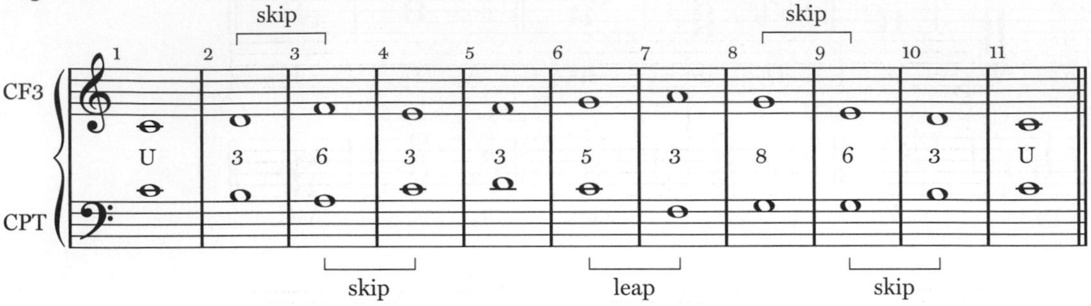

Upper part (cantus firmus): conjunct

Lower part (counterpoint): conjunct

Try it #2

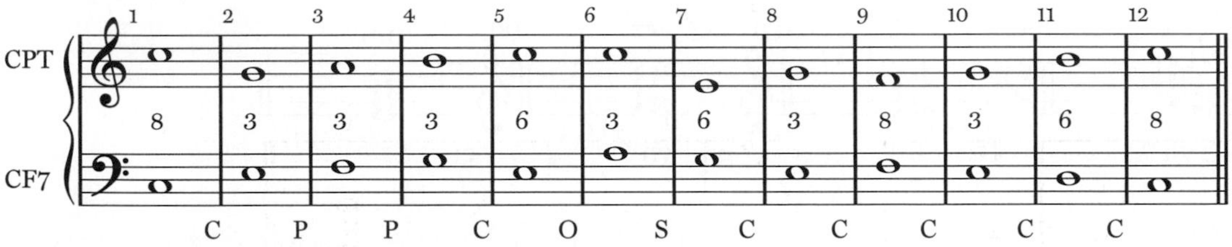

Try it #3

6	B♭	F	E	D	C	B♭	D	C♯ (LT)	B♭
5	A	E	D	C	B♭ (d5!)	A	C	B♭ (d5!)	A
3	F	C	B♭	A	G	F	A	G	F
8	D	A	G	F	E	D	F	E	D

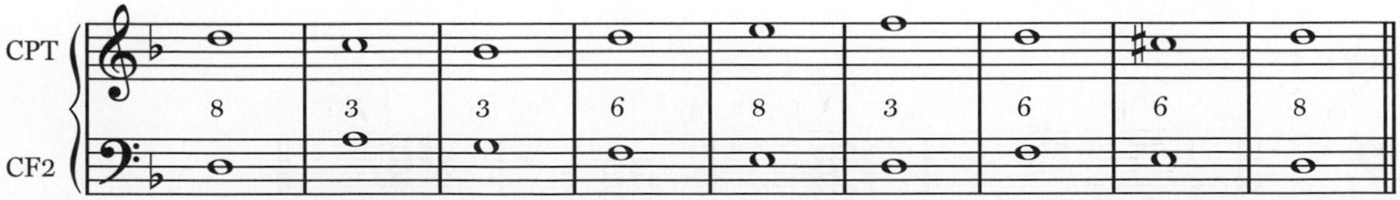

Chapter 10

Try it #1

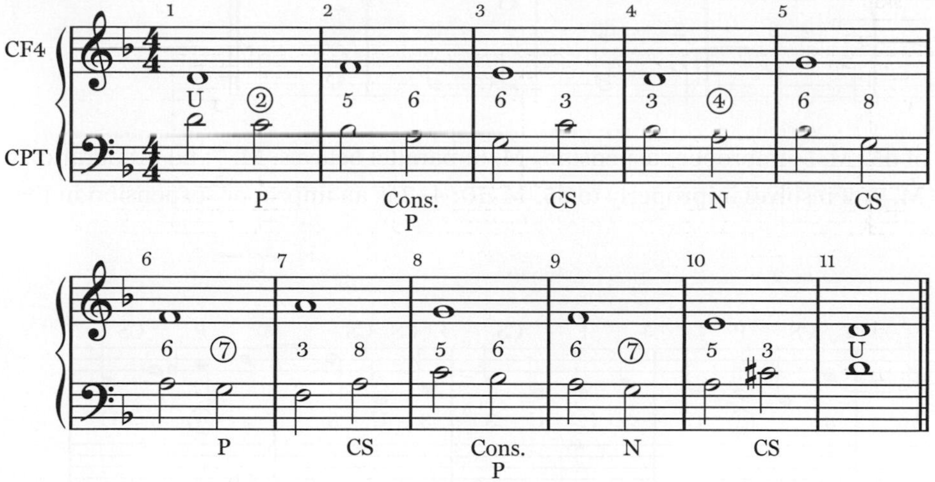

Try it #2

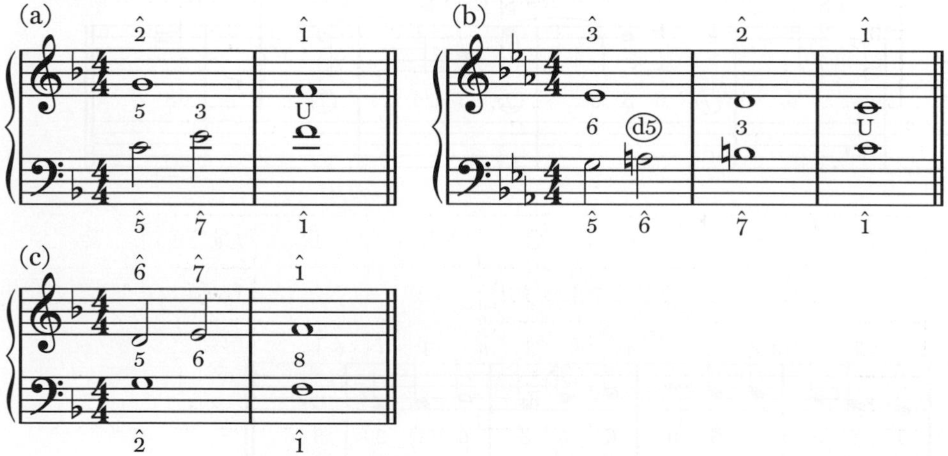

Try it #3

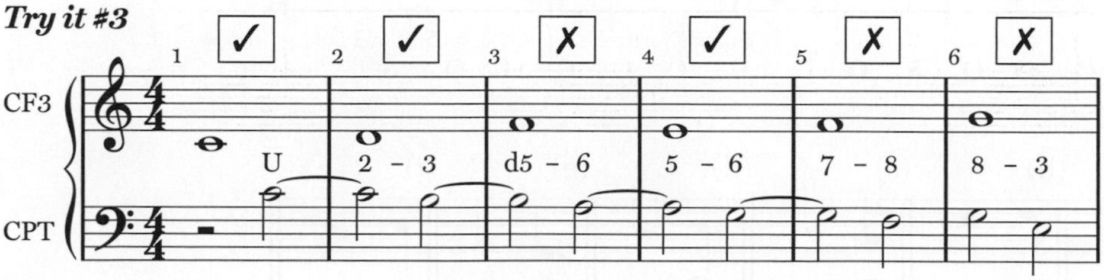

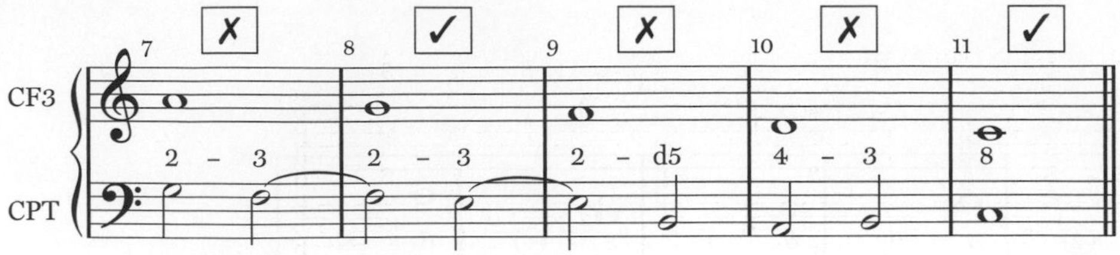

M. 3: incorrect use of d5. M. 5: improper suspension. M. 6: parallel octaves. M. 7: no preparation for the suspension. M. 9: 2 resolves improperly to d5. M. 10: 4–3 is an improper suspension in the lower voice.

Try it #4

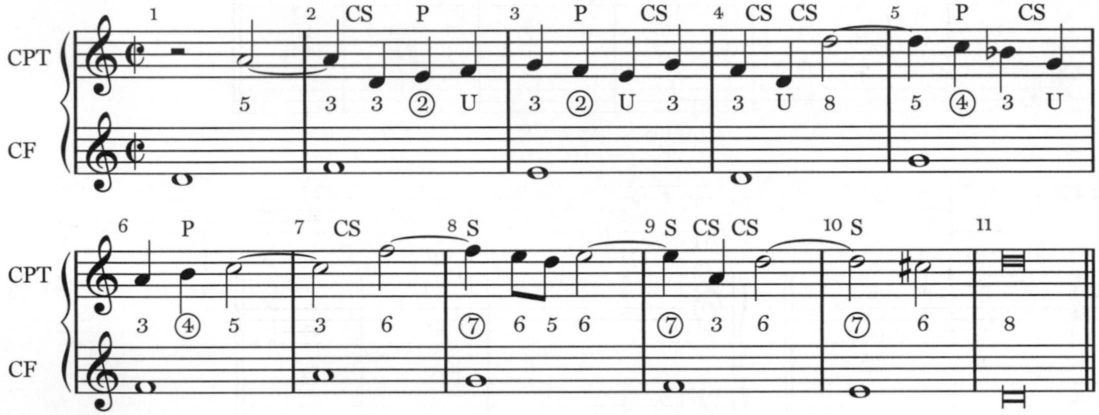

Chapter 11

Try it #1

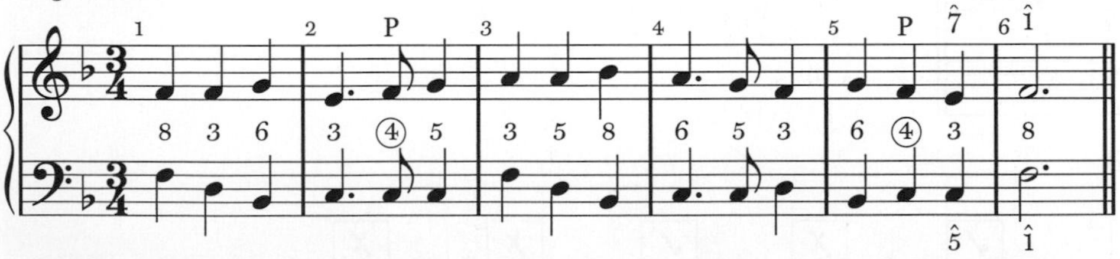

Motion: O C C O O S O C C O C C C O S

Try it #2

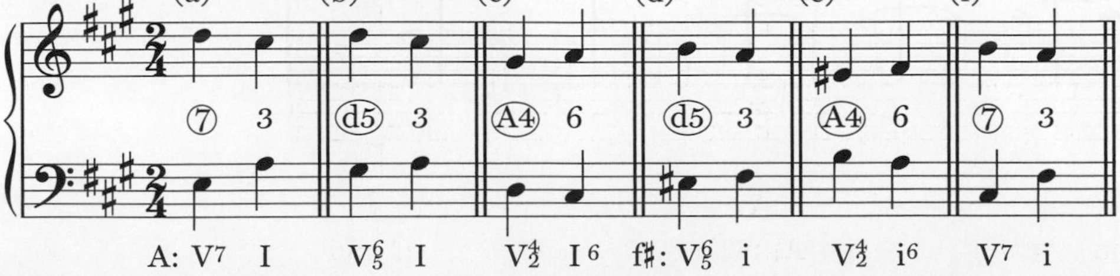

Try it #3

Try it #4

Try it #5

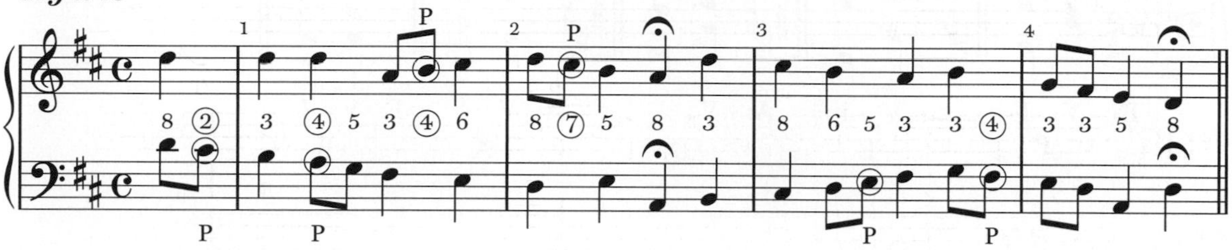

Chapter 12

Try it #1

	(1)	(2)	(3)	(4)	(5)	(6)	(7)	(8)
Root:	A♭	F	G	C♯	F	F♯	G♭	F
Quality:	maj	maj	min	maj	min	min	maj	maj
Figure:	6 3	6 3	5 3	5 3	5 3	6 3	5 3	5 3
Voicing:	E	B	A	A	D	C	E	B

Try it #2

A.

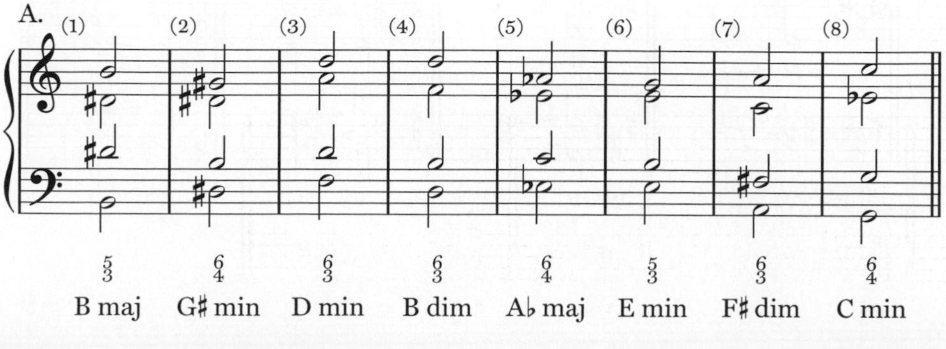

B.

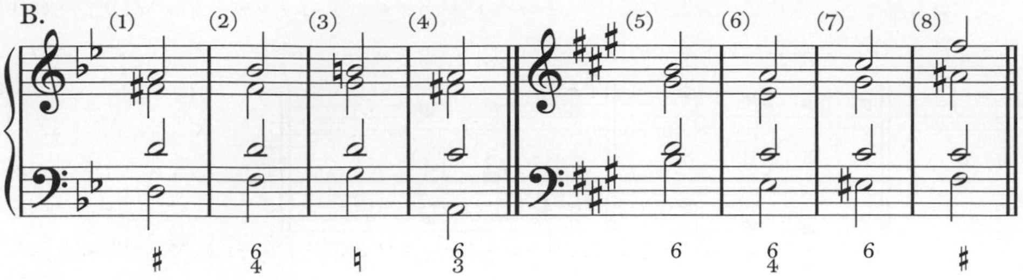

Try it #3 IAC: 6–7; PAC: 8–9.

Try it #4

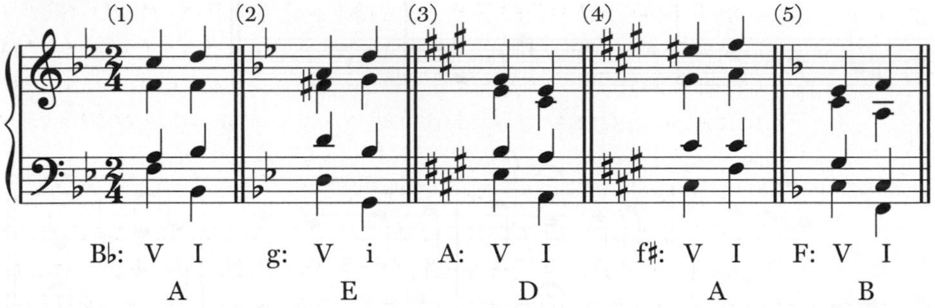

Chapter 13

Try it #1

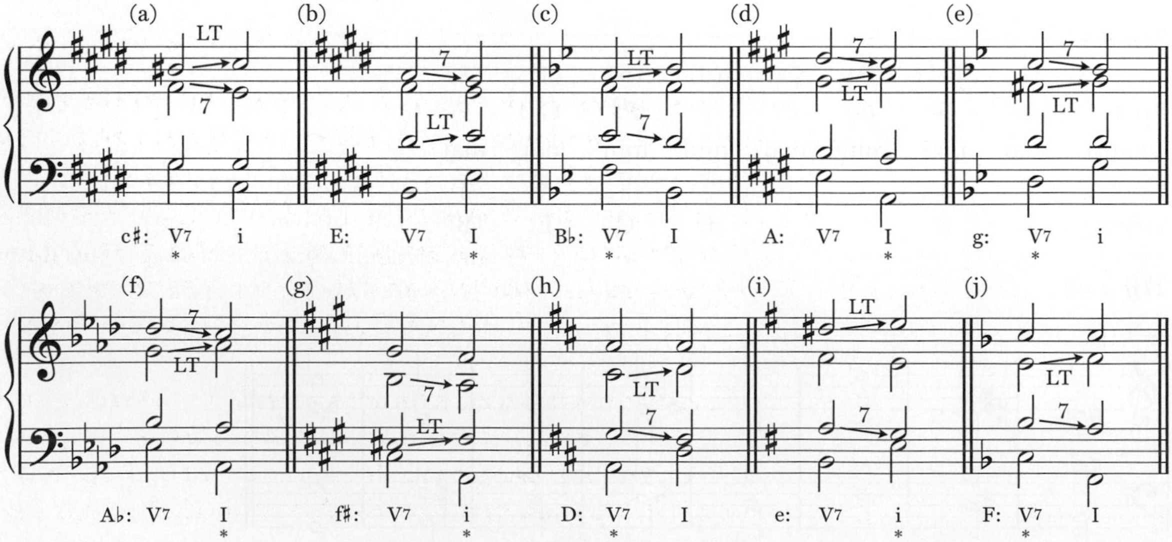

Try it #2

With mistakes labeled:

With corrections:

Try it #3

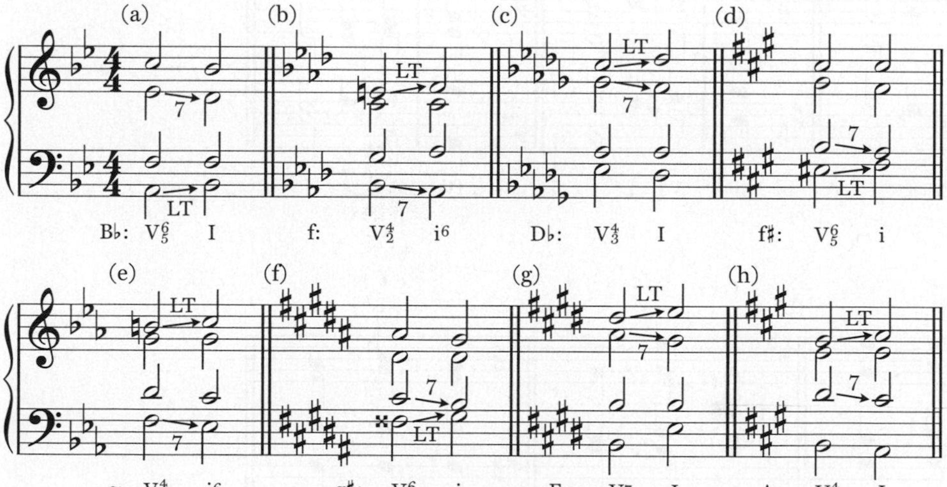

Try it #4

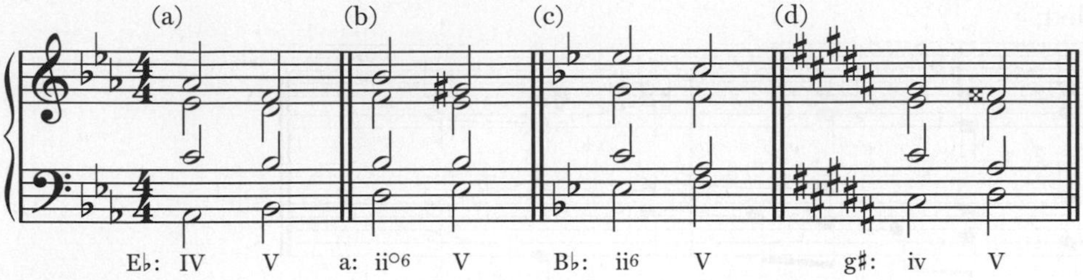

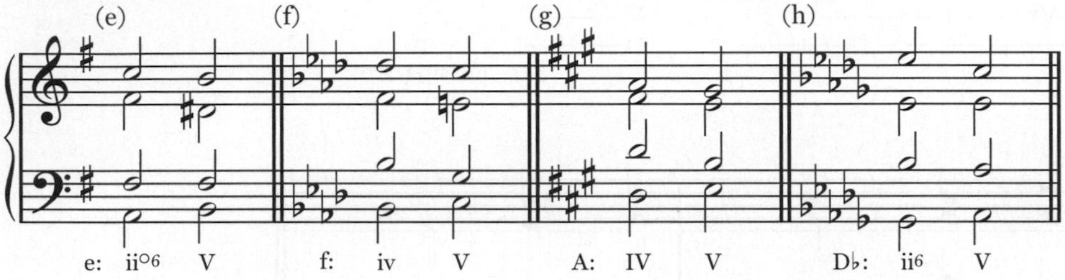

Chapter 14

Try it #1

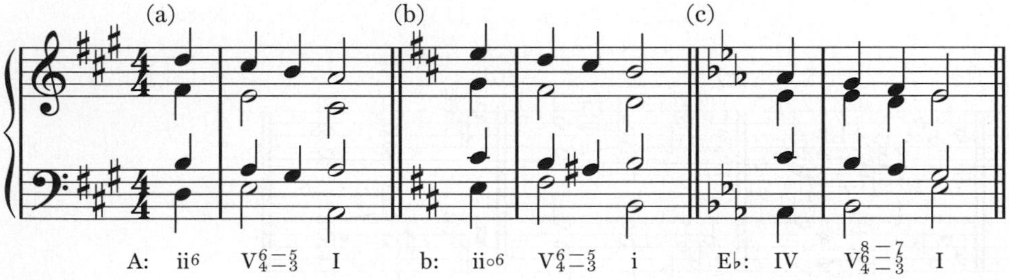

Try it #2

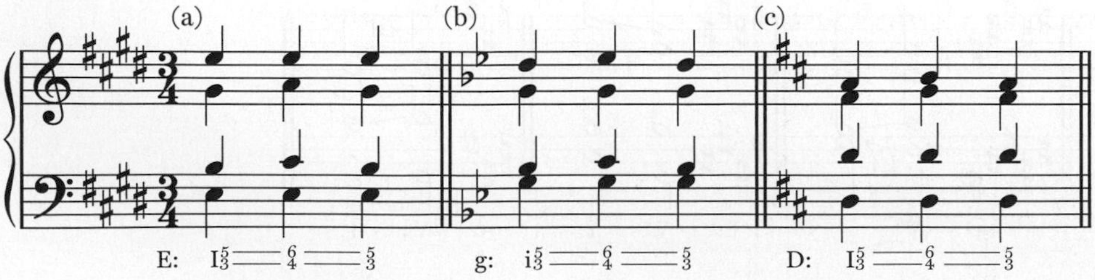

Try it #3

(a) F: I V^6_4 (P) I^6 (b) c: i V^6_4 (P) i^6 (c) D: I V^6_4 (P) I^6

Try it #4

KEY	SOPRANO	BASS	HARMONIZATION
major	$\hat{3}$–$\hat{2}$–$\hat{1}$	$\hat{1}$–$\hat{2}$–$\hat{3}$	I–V^6_4–I^6 or I–V^4_3–I^6
major	$\hat{1}$–$\hat{2}$–$\hat{1}$	$\hat{1}$–$\hat{7}$–$\hat{1}$	I–V^6–I or I–V^6_5–I
minor	$\hat{1}$–$\hat{7}$–$\hat{1}$	$\hat{1}$–$\hat{4}$–$\hat{3}$	i–V^4_2–i^6
major	$\hat{3}$–$\hat{4}$–$\hat{5}$	$\hat{1}$–$\hat{2}$–$\hat{3}$	I–V^4_3–I^6
minor	$\hat{3}$–$\hat{4}$–$\hat{5}$	$\hat{1}$–$\hat{7}$–$\hat{1}$	i–V^6_5–i

Chapter 15

Try it #1

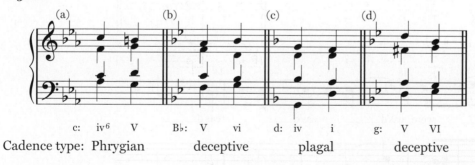

c: iv^6 V B♭: V vi d: iv i g: V VI

Cadence type: Phrygian deceptive plagal deceptive

Try it #2

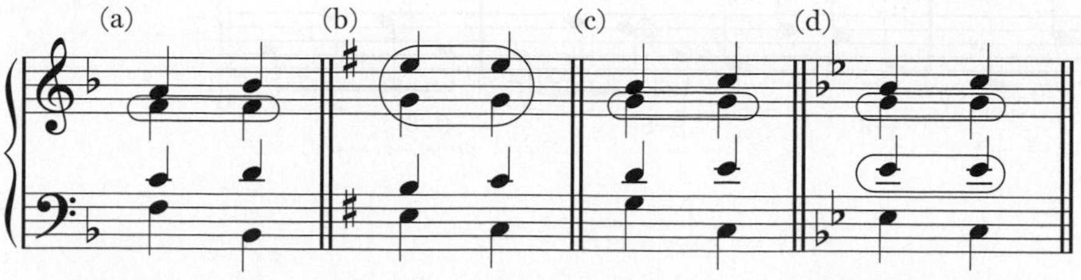

F: I IV e: i VI a: VII III B♭: IV ii

Root motion: desc. 5th desc. 3rd desc. 5th desc. 3rd

Try it #3

A.

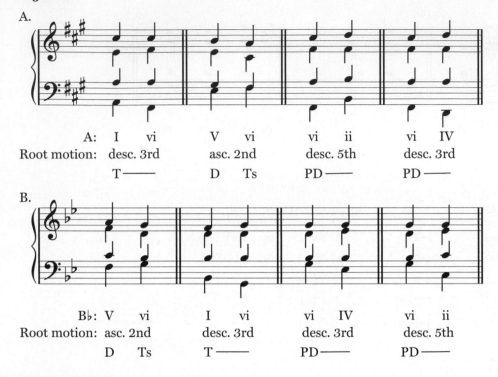

A: I vi | V vi | vi ii | vi IV

Root motion: desc. 3rd | asc. 2nd | desc. 5th | desc. 3rd

T—— | D Ts | PD—— | PD——

B.

B♭: V vi | I vi | vi IV | vi ii

Root motion: asc. 2nd | desc. 3rd | desc. 3rd | desc. 5th

D Ts | T—— | PD—— | PD——

Chapter 16

Try it #1

Try it #2

(a) (b) (c) (d)

Try it #3

While the chromatic embellishments in the bass line of mm. 4 and 5 (F♯, G♯, and C♯) may at first appear to function as incomplete neighbor tone, you could also interpret them as chromatic passing tones. The bass line in 4–5 seems to split into two separate lines, one in the lower register, and one in the upper. This type of melodic line is a **compound melody**; it expresses two distinct musical lines embedded within a single melody (renotated below). When viewed as elements of a compound melody, the chromatic pitches would be interpreted as chromatic passing tones.

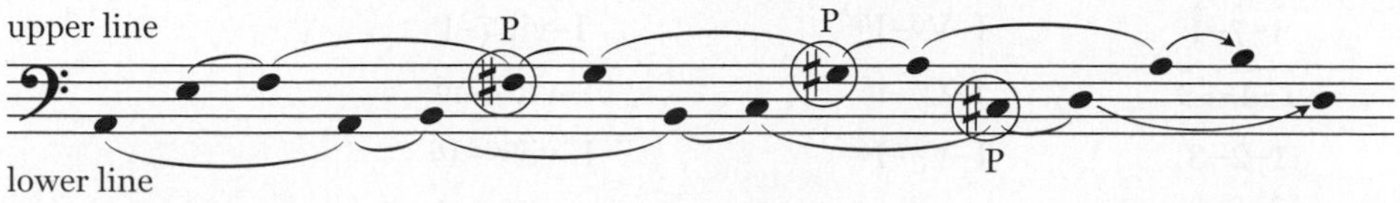

Try it #4

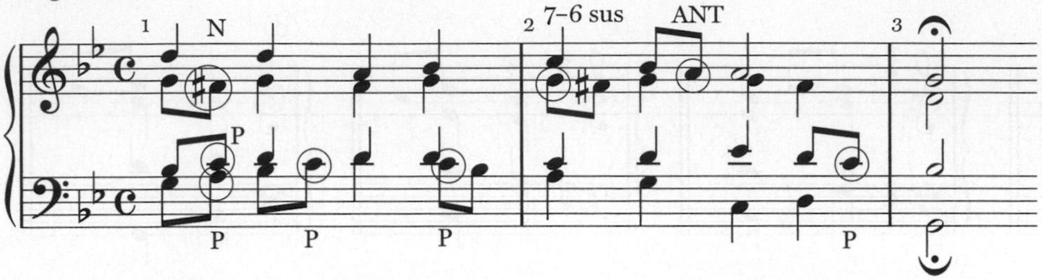

g: i i^6 V i^6 vii°6 i $ii^{ø6}_{5}$ V^{8-7} i

T———————————— PD D T(PAC)

Chapter 17

Try it #1

KEY	SPELLING	ROMAN NUMERAL
G minor	F♯-A-C-E♭	vii°7
B major	A♯-C♯-E-G♯	viiø7
D minor	C♯-E-G-B♭	vii°7
F♯ minor	E♯-G♯-B-D	vii°7
E♭ major	D-F-A♭-C	viiø7

Try it #2

KEY	$\hat{7}$–$\hat{1}$	$\hat{4}$–$\hat{3}$ (or ♭$\hat{3}$)
F minor	E♮–F	B♭–A♭
C minor	B♮–C	F–E♭
A major	G♯–A	D–C♯
B minor	A♯–B	E–D
E minor	D♯–E	A–G
A♭ major	G–A♭	D♭–C

Try it #3

KEY	SOPRANO	BASS	HARMONIZATION 1	HARMONIZATION 2
major	$\hat{3}$–$\hat{2}$–$\hat{1}$	$\hat{1}$–$\hat{2}$–$\hat{3}$	I–V^6_4–I^6	I–vii°6–I^6
major	$\hat{1}$–$\hat{2}$–$\hat{1}$	$\hat{1}$–$\hat{7}$–$\hat{1}$	I–V^6–I^6	I–vii°7–I
minor	$\hat{1}$–$\hat{7}$–$\hat{1}$	$\hat{1}$–$\hat{4}$–♭$\hat{3}$	i–V^4_2–i^6	i–vii°$^4_3$–i^6
major	$\hat{3}$–$\hat{4}$–$\hat{5}$	$\hat{1}$–$\hat{2}$–$\hat{3}$	I–V^4_3–I^6	I–vii°6–I^6
minor	♭$\hat{3}$–$\hat{4}$–♭$\hat{3}$	$\hat{1}$–$\hat{7}$–$\hat{1}$	i–V^6_5–i	i–vii°7–i

Chapter 18

Try it #1

Try it #2

x: inversion (last interval expanded)
y: inversion (last interval expanded); y is also a transposition of x.
z: rhythmic motive only (shortened)

Try it #3

EXCERPT	MM. 1–4	MM. 5–8	PERIOD TYPE
(a) Clarke, *Trumpet Voluntary* (p. 130)	**a** (HC)	**a′** (PAC)	parallel
(b) "Greensleeves" (p. 178)	**a** (HC)	**a′** (PAC)	parallel
(c) Mozart, Sonata, K. 284 (p. 245)	**a** (HC)	**b** (PAC)	contrasting

The Mozart piece includes a modulating consequent. In addition, the second phrase begins the same as the first but only for three notes, before it continues with contrasting material.

Chapter 19

Try it #1

a = transposed down an octave plus a 6th
b = transposed down an octave plus a 4th
c = inverted and modified (the interval over the bar line is a 6th, not d7th)
d = inverted and modified
e = same as original but transposed up a P5

Try it #2 Look first at the left hand of the Handel variation. The first triad is arpeggiated (G3–B♭3–D4), divided between the bass and the tenor parts. Then a passing tone (F3) connects the bass line G3 to E♭3. The C4 at the end of the measure is the tenor part in the iv6 chord.

Now for the right-hand part. The B♭4 in measure 89 is decorated first by a consonant skip to D5, then passing tones are added to make B♭4–C5–D5–B♭4. The B♭4 is then ornamented with a double neighbor. The G4 on the third beat is a chord tone in an inner voice, and the chord tone E♭5 is decorated by a lower neighbor.

Try it #3 In m. 10 of the Kern song, the expected gm7 (ii7) is replaced with G7 (a dominant seventh chord on G), and the expected C7 (the C dominant seventh that is V7 in F minor) in m. 11 is replaced with Cmaj7 (a major seventh chord on C). These replacements set up a cadence in m. 11 on the word "long." Incidentally, the G7 in m. 10 is a "secondary dominant" to C (marked V7/V) (to be discussed in Chapter 20).

Chapter 20

Try it #1

KEY	V KEY AREA	V7/V	KEY	V KEY AREA	V7/V
(a) B♭ major	F major	C-E♮-G-B♭	(f) D major	A major	E-G♯-B-D
(b) E minor	B minor	F♯-A♯-C♯-E	(g) E♭ major	B♭ major	F-A-C-E♭
(c) C minor	G minor	D-F♯-A-C	(h) B major	F♯ major	C♯-E♯-G♯-B
(d) A major	E major	B-D♯-F♯-A	(i) G minor	D minor	A-C♯-E♮-G
(e) A♭ major	E♭ major	B♭-D-F-A♭	(j) F♯ minor	C♯ minor	G♯-B♯-D♯-F♯

Try it #2

KEY	V KEY AREA	vii°7/V	KEY	V KEY AREA	vii°7/V
(a) C minor	G minor	F♯-A♮-C-E♭	(f) F major	C major	B♮-D-F-A♭
(b) E♭ major	B♭ major	A♮-C-E♭-G♭	(g) B♭ major	F major	E-G-B♭-D♭
(c) F minor	C minor	B♮-D♮-F-A♭	(h) D♭ major	A♭ major	G♮-B♭-D♭-F♭
(d) A minor	E minor	D♯-F♯-A-C	(i) G minor	D minor	C♯-E♮-G-B♭
(e) E major	B major	A♯-C♯-E-G♮	(j) B major	F♯ major	E♯-G♯-B-D

Chapter 21

Try it #1

The tendency tones in the V^6_5/ii chord, F♯2 (LT) and C5 (7) do resolve correctly.

Try it #2

Try it #3

A.

	KEY	ROMAN NUMERAL	TONICIZED CHORD / SECONDARY DOMINANT
(1)	B♭ major	V7/IV	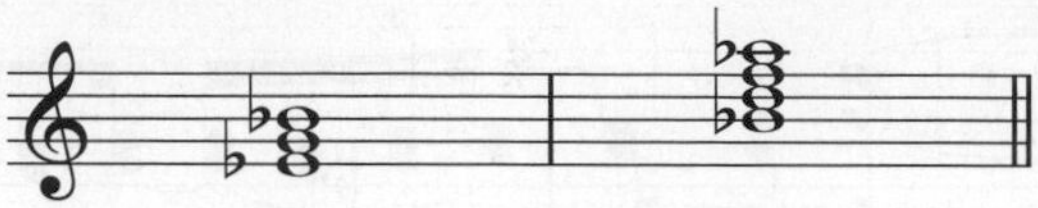
(2)	F♯ minor	vii°7/III	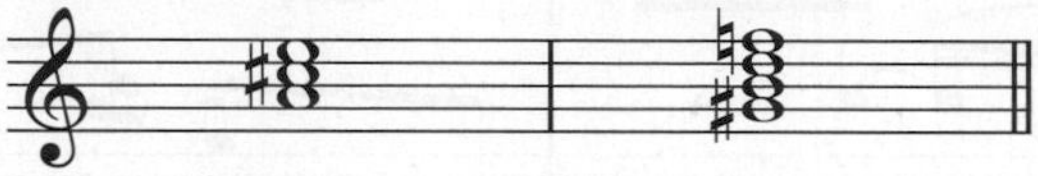
(3)	A major	V7/ii	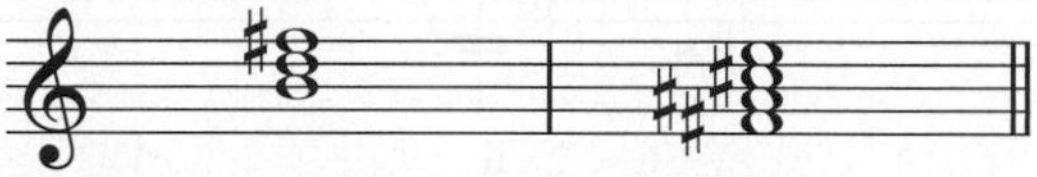
(4)	G major	vii°7/vi	
(5)	E♭ major	V7/vi	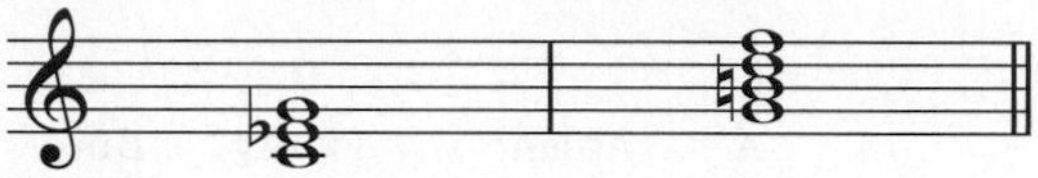
(6)	C minor	V7/V	

B.

		KEY	ROMAN NUMERAL
(1)		D major	vii°7/IV
(2)		G major	V7/vi
(3)		F major	vii°7/iii
(4)		C♯ major	vii°7/IV
(5)		C minor	V7/IV
(6)		F minor	vii°7/III

Try it #4

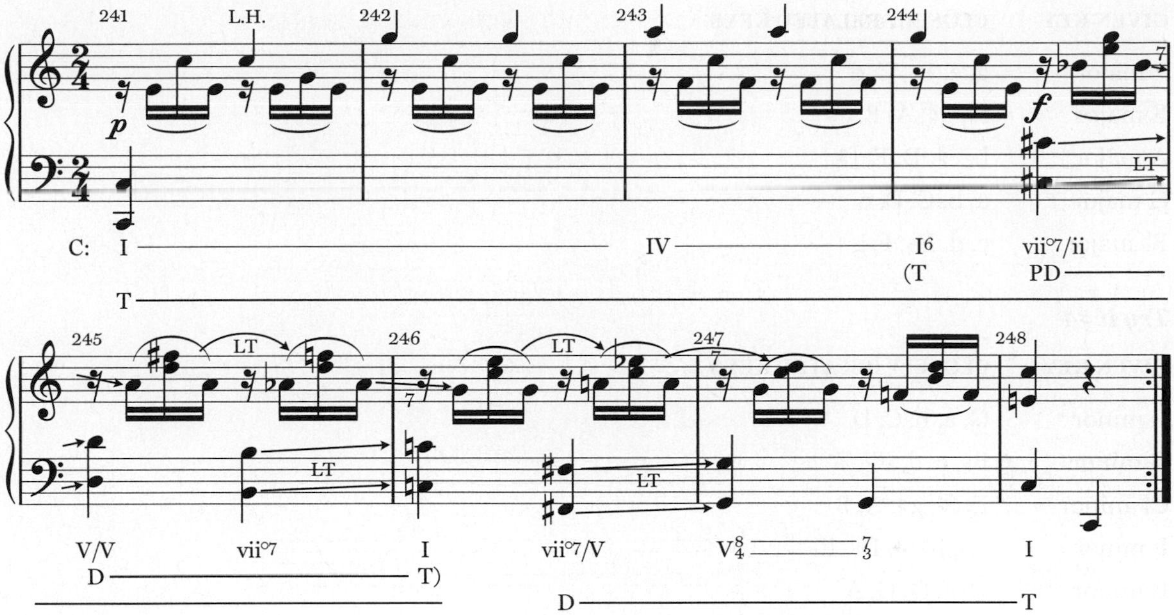

Chapter 22

Try it #1

(a) *A♭ major*

Roman numerals:	I	ii	iii	IV	V	vi	vii°
Chords:	A♭	b♭	c	D♭	E♭	f	g°

(b) *E♭ major*

Chords:	A♭	B♭	c	d°	E♭	f	g
Roman numerals:	IV	V	vi	vii°	I	ii	iii

Try it #2

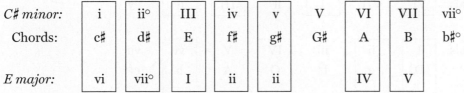

C♯ minor:	i	ii°	III	iv	v	V	VI	VII	vii°
Chords:	c♯	d♯	E	f♯	g♯	G♯	A	B	b♯°
E major:	vi	vii°	I	ii	ii		IV	V	

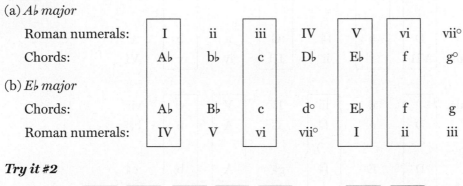

Try it #3

GIVEN KEY	CLOSELY RELATED KEYS
F major	g, a, B♭, C, d
E major	f♯, g♯, A, B, c♯
A major	b, c♯, D, E, f♯
G major	a, b, C, D, e
B♭ major	c, d, E♭, F, g

Try it #4

GIVEN KEY	CLOSELY RELATED KEYS
E minor	G, a, b, C, D
G minor	B♭, c, d, E♭, F
C♯ minor	E, f♯, g♯, A, B
F minor	A♭, b♭, c, D♭, E♭
B minor	D, e, f♯, G, A

Try it #5

(a) *D major*

Roman numerals:	I	ii	iii	IV	V	vi	vii°
Chords:	D	e	f♯	G	A	b	c♯°

E minor

Chords:	D	e	f♯°	G	a	b	C
Roman numerals:	VII	i	ii°	III	iv	v	VI

(b) *D major*

Roman numerals:	I	ii	iii	IV	V	vi	vii°
Chords:	D	e	f♯	G	A	b	c♯°

F♯minor

Chords:	D	E	f♯	g♯°	A	b	c♯
Roman numerals:	VI	VII	i	ii°	III	iv	v

(c) *D major*

Roman numerals:	I	ii	iii	IV	V	vi	vii°
Chords:	D	e	f♯	G	A	b	c♯°

G major

Chords:	D	e	f♯°	G	a	b	C
Roman numerals:	V	vi	vii°	I	ii	iii	IV

Chapter 23

Try it #1 parallel period, modulating consequent

Try it #2 (a) V7; (b) i–ii°6–V–i.

Chapter 24

Try it #1 The answer is tonal: the P4 leap from C5 to G4 ($\hat{1}$ to $\hat{5}$) of the subject is transformed to a P5 leap, G5 to C5 ($\hat{5}$ to $\hat{1}$), in the answer; the interval following is also changed, so that ♭$\hat{6}$ of the subject is answered with ♭$\hat{3}$.

Try it #2

MEASURE	BEAT	VOICE PART	STARTING PITCH	COMPLETE OR INCOMPLETE ENTRY?
16	2	soprano	C5	complete
16	3	alto	G4	complete
17	1	tenor	A3	complete
17	3	bass	D3	complete; first note enlongated

Try it #3 There is an inverted answer entry in the alto on beat 3 of m. 47, which is missing the last note.

Chapter 25

Try it #1

KEY	PARALLEL MINOR SIGNATURE	♭$\hat{3}$	♭$\hat{6}$	♭$\hat{7}$
C major	3 flats	E♭	A♭	B♭
E major	1 sharp	G♮	C♮	D♮
B♭ major	5 flats	D♭	G♭	A♭
D major	1 flat	F♮	B♭	C♮
B major	2 sharps	D♮	G♮	A♮

Try it #2

KEY SIGNATURE | **iv** | **♭III** | **♭VI** | **vii°7** | **iiø7**

F major

A major

E♭ major

G major

C♯ major

Try it #3

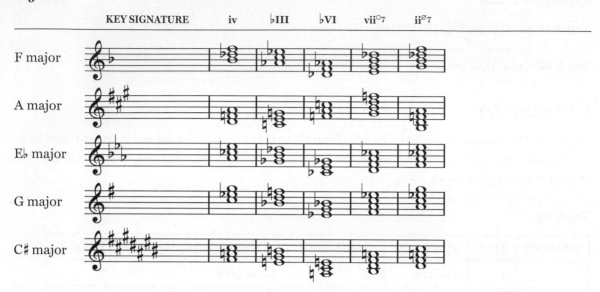

Chapter 26

Try it #1

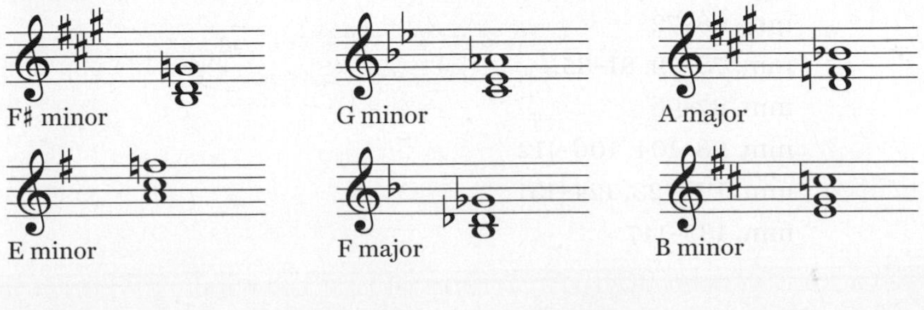

Try it #2

m. 34	m. 35	m. 36	m. 37	m. 38	m. 39	m. 40
ti fa	*re ti sol ti*	*ti do do*	*ra mi*	*fa me*	*ra do*	*do ti*
$\hat{7}$ $\hat{4}$	$\hat{2}$ $\hat{7}$ $\hat{5}$ $\hat{7}$	$\hat{7}$ $\hat{1}$ $\hat{1}$	$\flat\hat{2}$ $\hat{3}$	$\hat{4}$ $\flat\hat{3}$	$\flat\hat{2}$ $\hat{1}$	$\hat{1}$ $\hat{7}$

Try it #3

KEY	$\flat\hat{6}$	$\sharp\hat{4}$	KEY	$\flat\hat{6}$	$\sharp\hat{4}$
A minor	F	D♯	E major	C♮	A♯
C♯ minor	A	F𝄪	B minor	G	E♯
F major	D♭	B♮	G♯ minor	E	C𝄪

Try it #4

g: Gr6

B: It6

C: Fr6

f: It6

f♯: Gr6

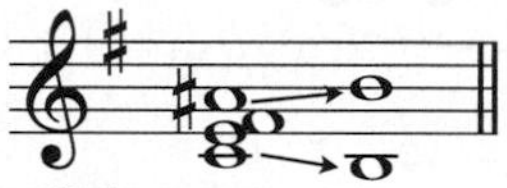
e: Fr6

Chapter 27

Try it #1

The rhyme scheme is ab ab ab ab. Each stanza is only two lines long, and each has the same rhyme scheme: ab. Rather than an objective-subjective contrast for the lines, this poem features a first-person speaker throughout. In line 1 of strophes 1–3, she begs her partner not to love her if it's for the wrong reason; in line 2, he is directed to love other things instead. In the final stanza, "nicht" (no) turns to "ja" (yes), if he loves for love. The musical setting might be strophic, given the parallel structure of text.

Try it #2

	Character(s)	*Measures*
Strophe 1:	narrator	mm. 16–32
Strophe 2:	father, son, father	mm. 37–40, 42–50, 52–54
Strophe 3:	elf king	mm. 58–72
Strophe 4:	son, father	mm. 73–79, 81–85
Strophe 5:	elf king	mm. 87–96
Strophe 6:	son, father	mm. 98–104, 106–112
Strophe 7:	elf king, son	mm. 117–123, 124–131
Strophe 8:	narrator	mm. 133–147

Try it #3

	Introduction	**A**	**B**	**A′**
Measures:	1–8	9–20	21–61	62–79

Try it #4

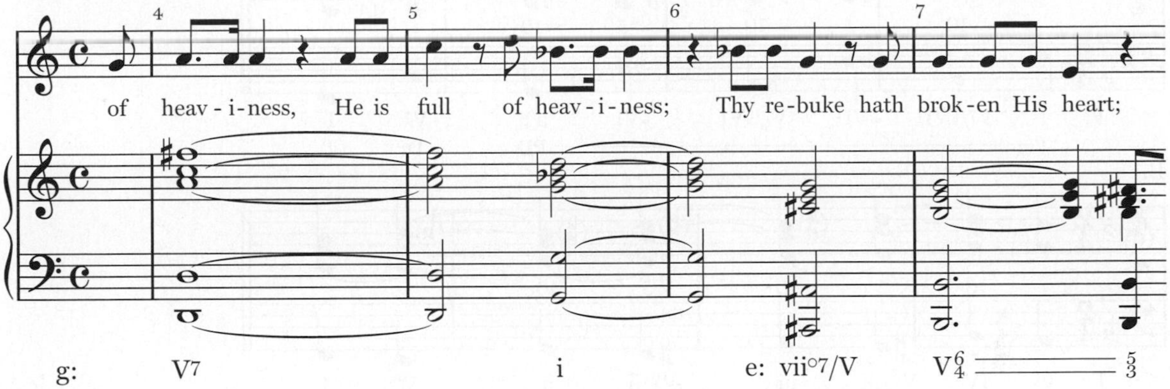

Chapter 28

Try it #1

Measures:	1–8a	8b–16a	16b–24a	24b–32a
Phrase letters:	**a**	**a′**	**b**	**a**
Period structures?	parallel period			

Try it #2

	Measure	*Beat*
Ninth chord:	16	(1) &
Added-sixth chord:	16	(2) &

Try it #3 M. 50, downbeat, is a Cm$^{7\text{-}5}$, ii^{ø7} (a half-diminished seventh chord in an enharmonic respelling: C–E♭–G♭–B♭). M. 51, downbeat, is a C$^{7\text{-}5}$: C–E♮–G♭–B♭(a dominant seventh chord with lowered fifth), V$^{7♭5}$/V.

Try it #4 The chord progression follows the typical twelve-bar blues progression; the melody includes the blue notes E♭ and B♭.

Chapter 29

Try it #1

A.

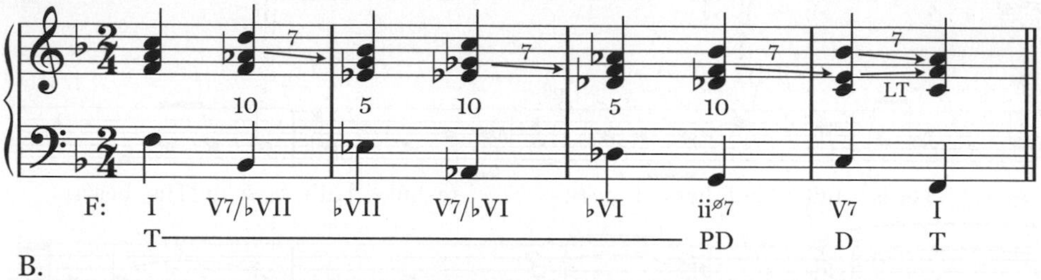

B.

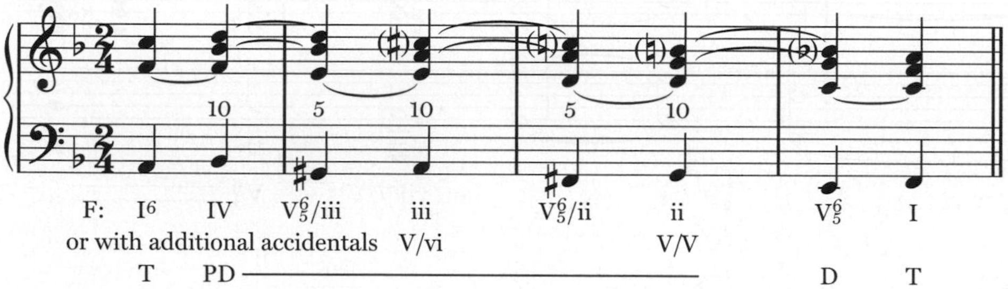

Try it #2

A.

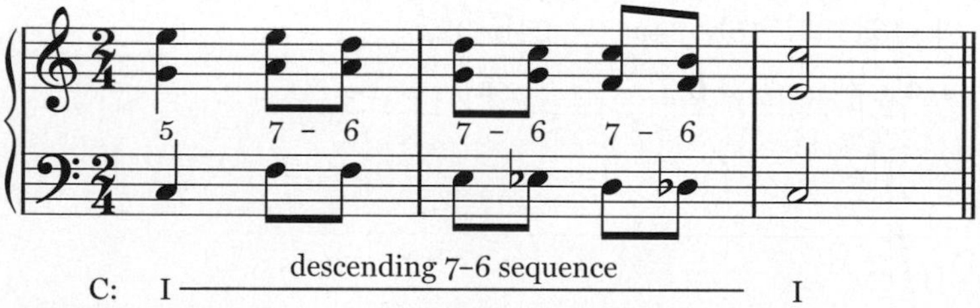

B.

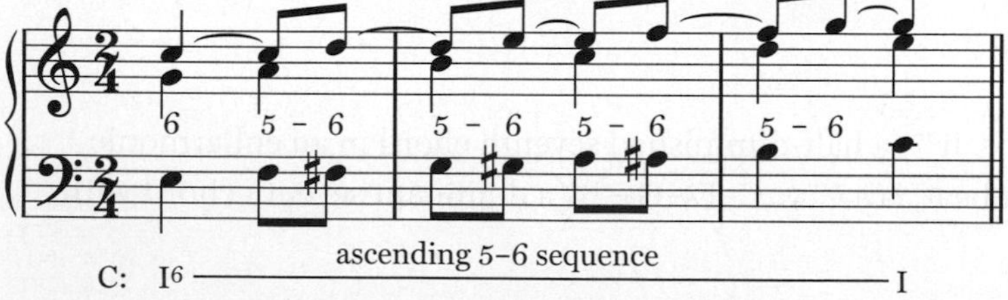

Try it #3

A.

B.

Try it #4

A.

B.

Chapter 30

Try it #1

A.

(1)

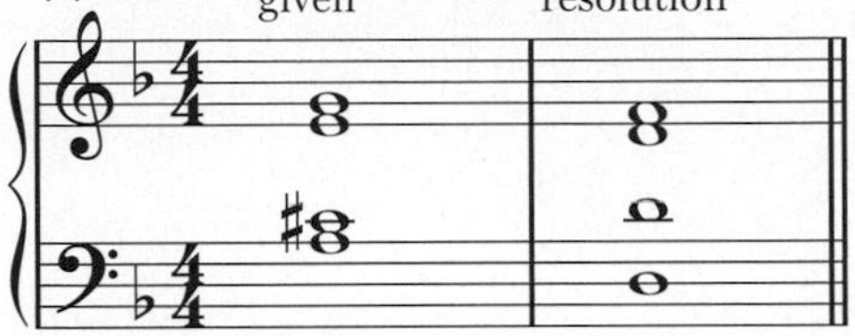

(2)

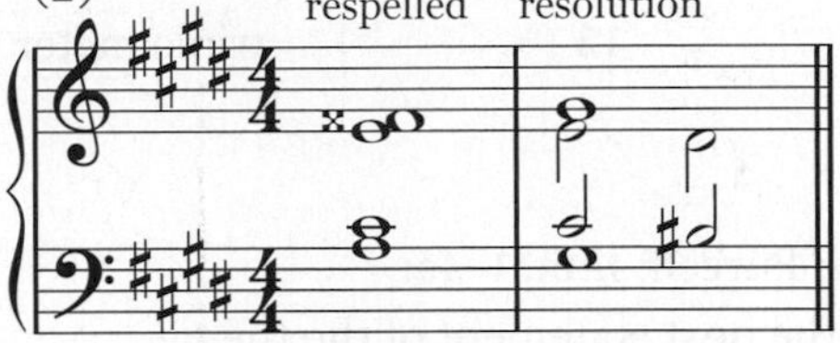

B.

(1)

(2)

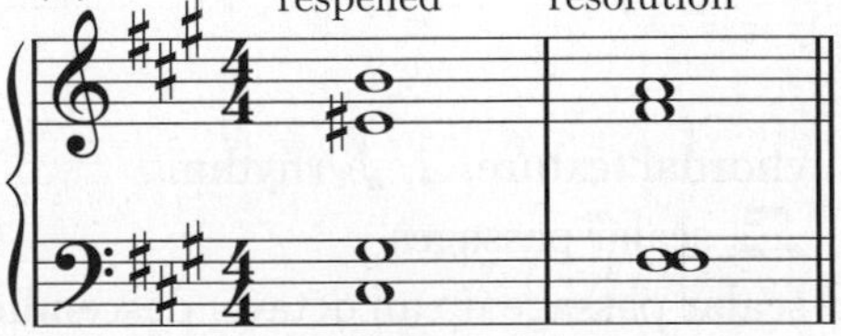

Try it #2

A.

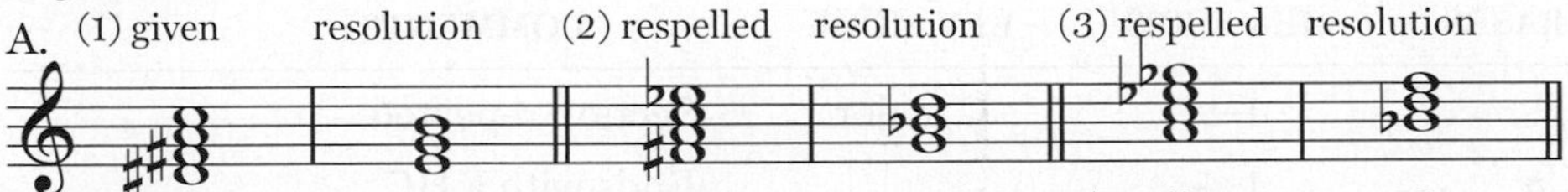

B.

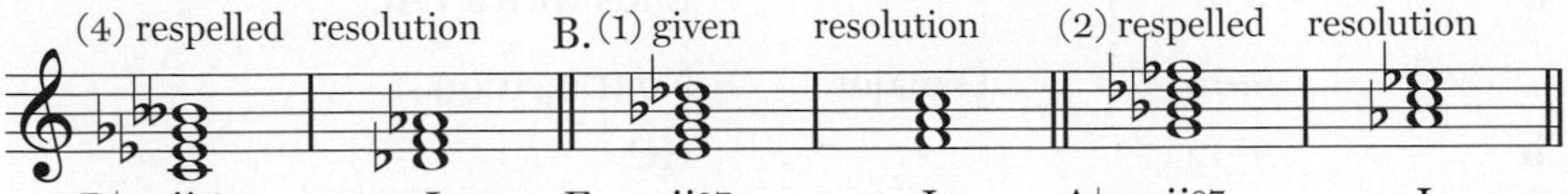

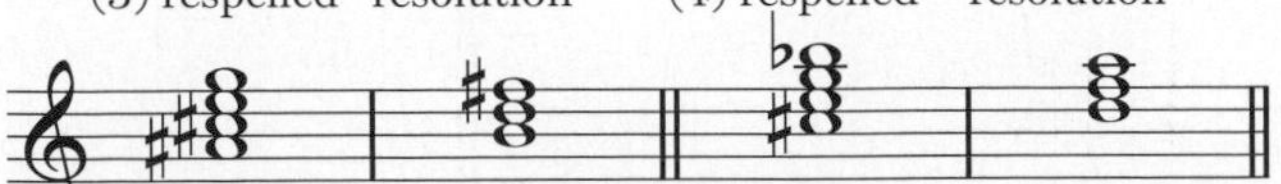

Try it #3

e: i^6 $\text{vii}^{ø7}$/G? vii^{o7}/G V^7/B♭? d^6 or $\text{vii}^{ø4}_{3}$/C $\text{vii}^{ø4}_{2}$/A V^7/A e^7 vii^{o6}_{5}/D

None of the chords resolve exactly as expected.

Chapter 31

Try it #1

Changed element	*Which variation?*	*Changed how?*
form	XII	adds a coda
mode	8	parallel minor
meter	12	triple meter

Try it #2

A. Bach: mm. 1–5a; Purcell: mm. 1–4a.
B. It is elided into the next statement of the theme.
C. They are much shorter and do not express complete small forms (e.g., binary).

Try it #3

A. 10
B. Statement 1–2: chordal texture, ♩. ♪ rhythm
Statement 3–4: ♩.♬, scalar passages
Statement 5–6: scalar passage up an octave; descending chromatic line

Try it #4

SECTION	PHRASES	MEASURES	KEY/MODE	COMMENTS
A		1–8	C major	Section repeated.
	a	1–4		Ends with a HC.
	a′	5–8		Ends with a PAC.
B		9–16	G major	No transition.
	b	9–12		HC.
	a″	13–16		PAC; motives from **A**.

SECTION	PHRASES	MEASURES	KEY/MODE	COMMENTS
Retransition		17–20		Prolongs V7 of C.
A		21–28	C major	Same as 1–8.
	a	21–24		Same as 1–4.
	a′	25–28		Same as 5–8.
C		29–48	A minor	Relative minor; no transition; longer section; developmental.
	a‴	29–40		HC; 4-bar suffix (mm. 36–40) prolongs V.
	a⁗	41–48		PAC; exchanges voices in comparison with mm. 29ff.
Retransition?		49–51 52		Stays in A minor until last bar. Ends with dramatic fermata to meet 4-bar hypermeter expectation.
A′		53–60	C major	
	a	53–56		Like mm. 1–4.
	a′	57–60		Like mm. 5–8.
Coda		61–73		Cadential flourishes.

The **C** section includes motives from the refrain and treats them developmentally. This section is longer, proportionally, than the rest and includes more chromatic harmonies (including Neapolitans in mm. 33 and 47). The first half of the **C** section ends with a four-bar suffix that extends the dominant. The key area (relative minor) is a closely related key, and thus not unexpected.

Chapter 32

Try it #1 The phrase of the second theme from mm. 23–26 is transposed down a perfect fifth in 90–93, while the following phrase, mm. 27–31, is transposed up a perfect fourth in 94–98, altering the registral relationship between the phrases. The same transposition pattern is followed for the two phrases of 45–51 (and 112–118).

Try it #2 This section establishes a temporary key, the dominant, similar to the beginning of the second large section in some binary-form movements; and there are sequences, especially in mm. 62–70. However, the motivic materials are not immediately recognizable as related to the exposition's themes.

Try it #3

Mm. 74–76, right hand, are similar to mm. 9–10.

Mm. 74–77, left hand, are drawn from mm. 35–38.

The right hand is reminiscent of the upper line in mm. 9–10, which are themselves an expansion of the melodic upper part in m. 4. Compare also m. 23, and the contour (although it is much slower-moving) of the second theme. The left hand is drawn from the chorale (second) theme.

Try it #4 Some of the elements include the main theme from measures 1–4 (see mm. 90–95 especially, though motives from the main theme persist through m. 111); the accompaniment pattern from 14–22 (in 96–103); the arpeggiation accompaniment from 23–28 (in 104–110); subsection 2b, with its syncopation and triplets, from 50–56a (in 112–141).

Try it #5

Chapter 33

Try it #1

MODE	PC CENTER
Mixolydian	F
Dorian	C♯
Lydian	B♭
Aeolian	F♯
Phrygian	G
Locrian	E
Ionian	A♭
Lydian-Mixolydian	A

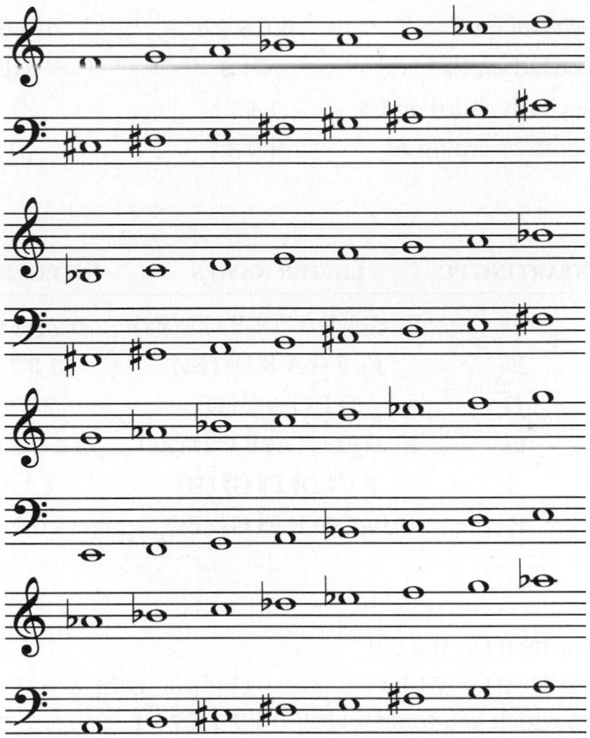

Try it #2

(a) D♯ E F♯ G♯ A♮ C♯

(b) B

(c) Aeolian; Locrian (♭$\hat{5}$)

(d) D♯

(e)

Instrument	*Intervals featured*	*Pc list*
flute	semitones	C♯ D D♯ E F (chromatic subset)
cello	P4 and P5	D G A (subset of the major pentachord)
piano RH	P5ths	D♯ F♯ A♯ C♯ (mm7 chord)
piano LH	M7 (also P5)	D F♯ G A (subset of the major pentachord)

Try it #3

SONORITY	INTEGER NOTATION	ASCENDING ORDER
Dominant seventh chord on A	9 1 4 7	{1 4 7 9}
Half-diminished seventh chord on D	2 5 8 0	{0 2 5 8}
Do-re-mi-fa-sol on E	4 6 8 9 e	{4 6 8 9 e}
Augmented triad on F♯	6 t 2	{2 6 t}
Fully diminished seventh chord on C♯	1 4 7 t	{1 4 7 t}
Major-major seventh chord on A♭	8 0 3 7	{0 3 7 8}

Try it #4

SCALE TYPE	STARTING PC	LETTER NAMES	INTEGER NOTATION
Octatonic 01	F♯	F♯ G A B♭ C D♭ E♭ E♮ (F♯)	6 7 9 t 0 1 3 4 (6)
Whole tone	E♭	E♭ F G A B D♭ (E♭)	3 5 7 9 e 1 (3)
Minor pentatonic	D	D F G A C (D)	2 5 7 9 0 (2)
Octatonic 23	E♭	E♭ F F♯ G♯ A♮ B C D (E♭)	3 5 6 8 9 e 0 2 (3)
Major pentatonic	B	B C♯ D♯ F♯ G♯ (B)	e 1 3 6 8 (e)
Whole tone	B♭	B♭ C D E F♯ G♯ (B♭)	t 0 2 4 6 8 (t)

Try it #5

1. Diminished seventh on C: 0 3 6 9
   Diminished seventh on G: 7 t 1 4
   Combine to form which octatonic scale? 0 1 3 4 6 7 9 t
2. Diminished seventh on D♭: 1 4 7 t
   Diminished seventh on E♭: 3 6 9 0
   Combine to form which octatonic scale? 0 1 3 4 6 7 9 t

How are the two octatonic scales related? They are the same.

Try it #6

SECTION	A	B	A′	B′	Coda
MEASURES	1–5	6–15	16–20	21–29	30–33
SCALE TYPE	OCT 23	OCT 12	OCT 12	OCT 23	Aeolian
FOCAL PCS	A/D♯	D/G♯	B♭/E	E♭/A	E♭

Chapter 34

Try it #1

B E♭ C♯ A	{9 e 1 3}	E C♯ A	{9 1 4}
F♯ D B	{e 2 6}	F A♭ D A	{2 5 8 9}
D A E♭ C♯ E	{9 1 2 3 4}	D C F♯ A	{6 9 0 2}
B E♭ A C♯ E♮	{9 e 1 3 4}	G D E A♭ E♭	{2 3 4 7 8}

Try it #2

TRICHORD	INTEGER NOTATION	TRANSPOSE BY	TRANSPOSED SET IN INTERGER NOTATION
{D F A}	{2 5 9}	minor third	{5 8 0}
{B C C♯}	{e 0 1}	minor second	{0 1 2}
{C♯ D F♯}	{1 2 6}	major second	{3 4 8}
{E F♯ A♯}	{4 6 t}	pci 5	{9 e 3}
{C E G♯}	{0 4 8}	pci 7	{7 e 3}
{G♭ A♭ B♭}	{6 8 t}	pci 4	{t 0 2}
{C D F}	{0 2 5}	pci 6	{6 8 t}

Try it #3

(a) (1) [0 0 1 1 1 0]
(2) [1 1 2 1 0 1]
(3) [0 3 2 2 2 1]
(4) [2 3 2 3 4 1]

(b) {1 4 8}

(c) {0 1 3 5 7 8}

Try it #4

Ordered pitch intervals: -5 +3 +5 +1 Inverted: +5 -3 -5 -1

Bartók uses this inverted set in mm. 13–15.

Try it #5

{e 1 4}	{1 e 8}	{3 6 8 9}	{9 6 4 3}
{9 t 2 3}	{3 2 t 9}	{e 1 2 3 5}	{1 e t 9 7}
{e 2 5}	{1 t 7}	{6 9 0 1}	{6 3 0 e}

Try it #6

(a) {8 9 t e 1}
(b) {2 4 5 6 7}
(c) 3
(d) C = T_3I B.

```
 8 9 t e 1
+7 6 5 4 2
----------
 3 3 3 3 3
```

Chapter 35

Try it #1 (a) {0 3 6 9}, {1 4 7 t}, {2 5 8 e}; (b) 8.

Try it #2

{E A♭ A}	[0 1 5]	{D C F♯ A}	[0 2 5 8]
{G C♯ D}	[0 1 6]	{F♯ D B C E}	[0 1 3 5 7]
{F A♭ D A}	[0 1 4 7]	{D A E♭ C♯ E}	[0 1 2 3 7]
{B E♭ C♯ A}	[0 2 4 6]		

Try it #3

Normal order: {t e 0 1 2} {7 9 t e 0}
Prime form: [0 1 2 3 4] [0 1 2 3 5]

Try it #4

	Prime form	*Forte number*	*ic vector*
(a)	[0 2 7]	3-9	[010020]
(b)	[0 2 7]	3-9	[010020]
(c)	[0 3 7]	3-11	[001110]
(d)	[0 2 4]	3-6	[020100]
(e)	[0 2 7]	3-9	[010020]
(f)	[0 2 5]	3-7	[011010]

Try it #5

	Prime form	*Forte number*		*Prime form*	*Forte number*
(a)	[0 1 4]	3-3	(f)	[0 1 5]	3-4
(b)	[0 1 4]	3-3	(g)	[0 1 4]	3-3
(c)	[0 1 5]	3-4	(h)	[0 1 4]	3-3
(d)	[0 1 4]	3-3	(i)	[0 1 2]	3-1
(e)	[0 1 2]	3-1			

Try it #6

	Mode	*Prime form*	*Forte number*
(a)	mode 3	[0 1 2 4 5 6 8 9 t]	9-12
(b)	mode 2	[0 1 3 4 6 7 9 t]	8-28

Chapter 36

Try it #1

(a)	m. 5 soprano	<+4 -2 -3 -3 +2 +3>	prime
(b)	m. 5 alto	<-4 +2 +3 +3 -2 -3>	inversion
(c)	m. 6 soprano	<-3 -2 +3 +3 +2 -4>	retrograde
(d)	m. 6 alto	<+3 +2 -3 -3 -2 +4>	(none of the above!)

(d) exactly the same but backward

Try it #2

(a) Row 1: <8 9 7 5 e 4 2 3 t 1 0 6> Label: P_8
Row 2: <9 8 t 0 6 1 3 2 7 4 5 e> Label: I_9

(b) Row 1: < 8 9 7 | 5 e 4 | 2 3 t | 1 0 6 >
Trichords: [0 1 2] [0 1 6] [0 1 5] [0 1 6]

Try it #3

m. 6 (voice): I_9 m. 8 (clarinet): P_8 m. 9 (voice): RI_9
The only "new" row in this passage, not heard previously in the song, is RI_9.

Chapter 37

Try it #1

(a) Row pcs: < t 5 0 e 9 6 1 3 7 8 2 4 >
Order numbers: 1 2 3 4 5 6 7 8 9 10 11 12

(b)

	1		6		9
	2		8		12
	3		7		11
Chord 1:	4	Chord 2:	5	Chord 3:	10

Try it #2

I ↓ (top); P → (left); R ← (right); RI ↑ (bottom)

	I_0	I_7	I_2	I_1	I_e	I_8	I_3	I_5	I_9	I_t	I_4	I_6	
P_0	0	7	2	1	e	8	3	5	9	t	4	6	R_0
P_5	5	0	7	6	4	1	8	t	2	3	9	e	R_5
P_t	t	5	0	e	9	6	1	3	7	8	2	4	R_t
P_e	e	6	1	0	t	7	2	4	8	9	3	5	R_e
P_1	1	8	3	2	0	9	4	6	t	e	5	7	R_1
P_4	4	e	6	5	3	0	7	9	1	2	8	t	R_4
P_9	9	4	e	t	8	5	0	2	6	7	1	3	R_9
P_7	7	2	9	8	6	3	t	0	4	5	e	1	R_7
P_3	3	t	5	4	2	e	6	8	0	1	7	9	R_3
P_2	2	9	4	3	1	t	5	7	e	0	6	8	R_2
P_8	8	3	t	9	7	4	e	1	5	6	0	2	R_8
P_6	6	1	8	7	5	2	9	e	3	4	t	0	R_6
	RI_0	RI_7	RI_2	RI_1	RI_e	RI_8	RI_3	RI_5	RI_9	RI_t	RI_4	RI_6	

Try it #3

Example 37.1a:

m. 1: P_t m. 2: RI_3

Example 37.1b:

mm. 32–33a, right hand: P_t left hand: I_3

mm. 33b–34a, right hand: RI_3 left hand: R_t

Try it #4 (a) P_3; (b) P_1.

Try it #5 (a) I_t; (b) I_8.

Try it #6

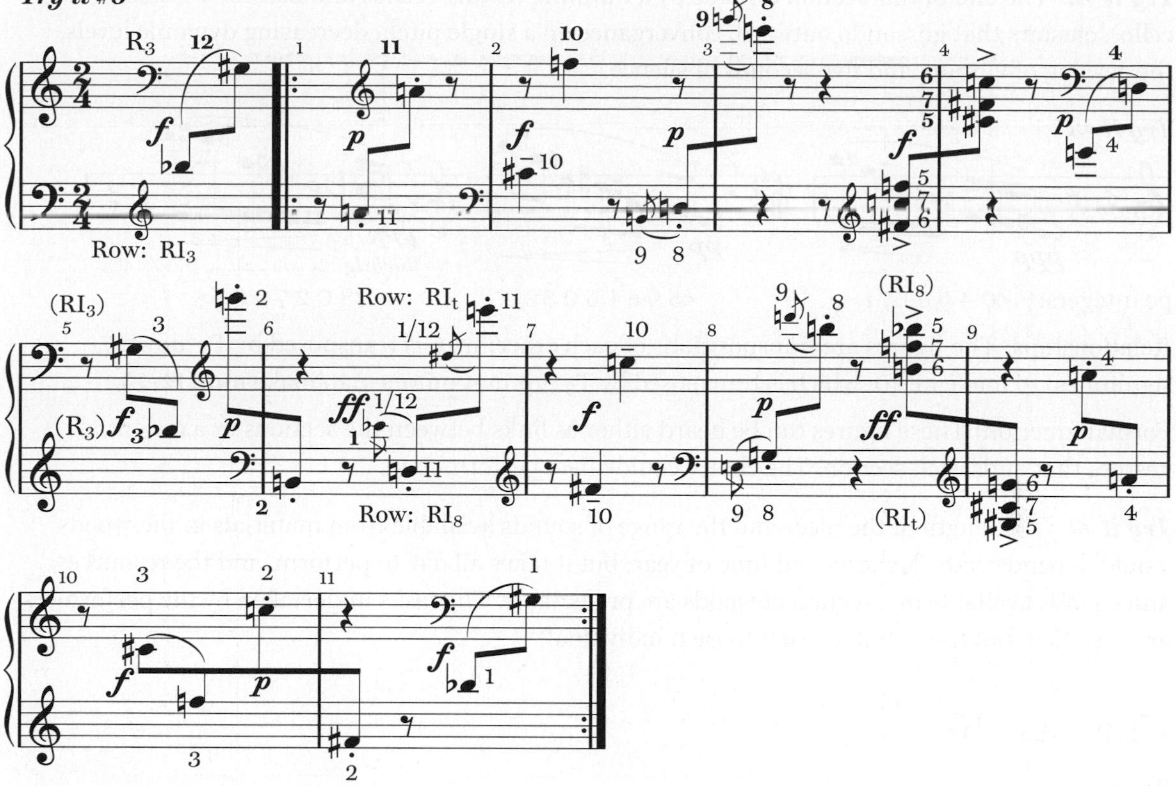

Chapter 38

Try it #1

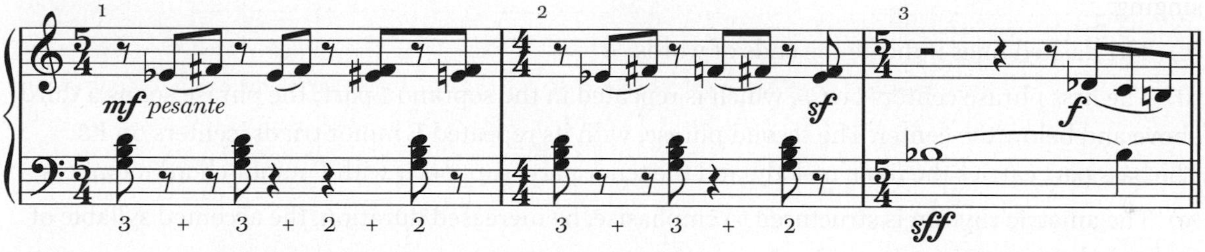

Chapter 39

Try it #1 There is a sectional division at rehearsal 10, as the "insect sounds" stop to reveal a cluster of pitches expanding, then shrinking in range. Because this connection is elided, not all listeners will hear a sectional division here. The next subsection (10–18) is marked by clusters that are sustained, then glissando up or down, sounding like fireworks rockets taking off. The division is reinforced by a change in texture to individual, pointillistic, imitative entries. You may have heard internal ideas within this section, made by individual pitch clusters expanding and then shrinking in range, similar to the way the subsection opened (at rehearsal 10).

Try it #2 The end of this section is made by a thinning texture (cellos and basses → cellos → solo cello), clusters that glissando outward, convergance on a single pitch, decreasing dynamic levels, the ceasing of vibrato, and five seconds of silence.

Try it #3

pc integers: <0 4 6 e 1 7 t> <5 9 e 4 6 0 3> <8 0 2 7 9 3 6>

Relationships: The figures are transpositions of each other: m. 6 is transposed by T_5 (down 7 semitones) to make m. 10, which is transposed by T_3 (up 15 semitones) to make mm. 12–13.

Formal function: These figures can be heard either as links between the sections or a cadential gesture that ends each section. The choice could affect performance.

Try it #4 The length of the piece and the range of sounds available from materials in the woods would depend on the location and time of year; but it takes all day to perform, and the resources and sounds available in a section of woods are predictable. The tasks undertaken by the performers are specified, but the details are left to each individual.

Chapter 40

Try it #1

(a) mm. 1 to 4 and mm. 5 to 12.

(b) Each phrase division follows a unit of text and is marked by a change in which vocal parts are singing.

(c) The dashed lines indicate the ends of words.

(d) The first phrase centers on C5, which is repeated in the soprano 1 part; the phrase spans a third above and below the center. The second phrase, with its repeated F minor triads, centers on F3. The bass part carries the main melody, and the tenor parts support it with F minor chord members.

(e) The ametric rhythm is structured to emphasize, by increased duration, the accented syllable of each word.

Try it #2

(a) The passage opens with Cherubino singing in G major. In m. 11, Rosina's entry (with a change of key signature to A major) disturbs an impending half cadence in G by introducing a B minor $^4_2$ followed by a E dominant seventh chord, which progresses to an A major chord in 13—a harmonic destination quite distant from Cherubino's key. The chords in her section are also inverted, which weakens the harmonic strength of the progression.

(b) Rosina's accompaniment includes two-beat triplets, a striking contrast to Cherubino's even quarters and eighths.

APPENDIX 2

Glossary

1:1 (one-to-one): See *first species.*
2:1 (two-to-one): See *second species.*
4:1 (four-to-one): See *third species.*
5-6 motion: Expansion of the opening tonic area with motion from a fifth to a sixth above the bass; an alternative analysis is I–vi^6.

A

a a b a: See *quaternary song form.*
A B A: See *ternary form.*
abrupt modulation: See *direct modulation.*
abstract complement: Two sets are abstract complements if they can be combined in transposition or inversion to form a complete aggregate. Forte set labels show this relationship: the numbers before the hyphen sum to 12 and the numbers after the hyphen are the same (e.g., 4-z15 and 8-z15).
accent: Stress given to a note or other musical element that brings it to the listener's attention—may be created by playing louder or softer, using a different timbre or articulation, or slightly changing rhythmic durations.
accidental: A musical symbol (♯, ♭, ♮, 𝄪, or 𝄫) that appears before a note to raise or lower its pitch.
added-sixth chord: A root-position triad that contains an extra pitch a major sixth above the bass note.
additive rhythm: An ametric rhythm created when a brief duration (often a sixteenth or smaller) is chosen as a basic element and then several are added together to form larger durations.
Aeolian mode: An ordered collection with the pattern of whole and half steps corresponding to the white-key diatonic collection starting and ending on A; the same collection as the natural minor scale.
aggregate: A collection of all twelve pitch classes. The term generally refers to the combination of two or more twelve-tone rows to generate new twelve-note collections. Aggregates may also appear in non-twelve-tone music.
Alberti bass: A common Classical-period accompaniment formed by arpeggiating triads in repeated patterns, such as root-fifth-third-fifth.
all-combinatorial hexachord: A hexachord capable of all four types of combinatoriality (P, I, R, and RI).
altered common-chord modulation: See *altered pivot-chord modulation.*
altered-fifth chord: A triad or seventh chord that has been colored and intensified by raising or lowering the fifth by a half step.
altered pivot-chord modulation: A modulation whose pivot chord is a chromatic chord (e.g., a mixture chord or secondary dominant) in one or both keys.
alto: The second-highest voice in four-part (SATB) writing, usually directly below the soprano.
alto clef: A C-clef positioned on a staff so that the middle line indicates middle C (C4).
ametric: Music for which no regular meter is perceived; may be notated in nontraditional ways.
anacrusis: Occurs when a melody starts just before the first downbeat in a meter; also called an upbeat, or pick-up.
anhemitonic pentatonic: A pentatonic scale with no half steps.
answer: The statement of a fugue subject, transposed up a fifth or down a fourth, that follows the statement of the subject in the exposition. See also *real answer* and *tonal answer.*

antecedent phrase: The first phrase of a period; ends with an inconclusive cadence (usually a half cadence).

anticipation: An unaccented embellishing tone resulting from the "early" arrival of a pitch. The embellishing tone is repeated as a consonance on the next beat.

applied chord: See *secondary dominant.*

appoggiatura: A dissonance that occurs on a strong beat and usually resolves down by step; sometimes refers to an accented dissonance approached by skip or leap, or an accented incomplete neighbor.

aria: A solo vocal movement within an opera, oratorio, or cantata.

arpeggiating $^6_4$: A $^6_4$ created when the bass line sounds each note of a triad in turn (root, third, fifth), or alternates between the root and the fifth.

arpeggio, arpeggiated: A chord played one pitch at a time.

articulation: Ways a note can be attacked and connected to other notes: played very short (*staccato*), held (*tenuto*), played suddenly and loudly (*sfzorzando*), highly connected (*legato*), or separated.

art song: A song, usually featuring a poetic text, written for performance outside the popular- and folk-music traditions.

ascending-second progression: Root motion by ascending seconds; frequently used to connect functional areas in the basic phrase.

asymmetrical meter: A compound meter with beat units of unequal duration, typically (though not always) created by five or seven beat divisions grouped into beat lengths such as 2 + 3 or 2 + 3 + 2.

asymmetrical period: A period containing two phrases of differing length.

atonal: See *nontonal.*

augmentation: The process of systematically lengthening the duration of pitches in a musical line, usually by a consistent proportion (e.g., doubling all note values).

augmented interval: An interval one half step larger than a major or perfect interval.

augmented-sixth chord: A chord featuring $\flat\hat{6}$ in the bass and $\sharp\hat{4}$ in an upper voice, creating an augmented sixth. Such chords usually resolve to V: $\flat\hat{6}$ and $\sharp\hat{4}$ resolve outward by half step to $\hat{5}$.

augmented triad: A triad with major thirds between the root and third and between the third and fifth, and an augmented fifth between the root and fifth.

B

B♭ instrument: An instrument whose sounding pitch is a whole step lower than the notated pitch.

balanced binary form: A continuous simple binary form in which material from the end of the first section returns at the end of the second section.

bar line: A vertical line that indicates the end of a measure.

Baroque era: The period in Western music dating roughly from 1600 until 1750. Some Baroque composers are Johann Sebastian Bach, George Frideric Handel, François Couperin, Antonio Vivaldi, and Henry Purcell. Genres associated with this era are the concerto grosso, oratorio, keyboard suite, and cantata.

basic phrase: A conclusive phrase that consists of an opening tonic area (T), an optional predominant area (PD), a dominant area (D), and tonic closure (T, a cadence on I). Written in contextual analysis as T–PD–D–T, beneath Roman numerals.

bass: The lowest voice in four-part (SATB) writing.

bass clef: Clef positioned on a staff to indicate F; its two dots surround the F3 line. (Also known as the F-clef.)

beat: The primary pulse in musical meter.

beat division: The secondary pulse in musical meter; the first level of faster-moving pulses beneath the primary beat.

bimodality: The simultaneous use of two modes in two different layers of music.

binary form: A composition organized into two sections. Usually each section is repeated.

bitonality: The simultaneous use of two keys in two different layers of music.

blue note: One of three pitches, derived from the blues scale, that can be altered in popular music for expressive effect: $\flat\hat{3}$, $\sharp\hat{4}$ (or $\flat\hat{5}$), and $\flat\hat{7}$.

blues scale: A collection of notes, $\hat{1}$, $\flat\hat{3}$, $\hat{4}$, $\sharp\hat{4}$ (or $\flat\hat{5}$), $\hat{5}$, and $\flat\hat{7}$, from which performers can choose when improvising a blues melody. Since it contains the minor modal scale degrees $\flat\hat{3}$ and $\flat\hat{7}$, the blues scale blurs the distinction between major and minor when it is used as the basis for improvisation against a major-key blues progression.

borrowed chord: See *mixture chord.*

bridge: (1) In a fugue exposition, music that metrically and harmonically prepares for a subject entry in the tonic after the conclusion of an answer. (2) In a quaternary song form, the contrasting b section.

C

C-clef: A movable clef that may be placed on a staff to identify any one of the five lines as middle C (C4).

C instrument: An instrument whose sounding pitch is the same as the notated pitch.

C score: A nontransposed score that shows all the parts in the concert key—i.e., all the pitches sound as notated, without transposition. Also known as concert-pitch score.

cadence: The end of a phrase, where harmonic, melodic, and rhythmic features articulate a complete musical thought.

cadential extension: An extension created by the repetition of the cadence with little new or elaborative melodic material.

cadential $^6_4$: A $^6_4$ chord that embellishes the V chord by displacing it with simultaneous 6–5 and 4–3 suspension-like motion above the sustained bass note $\hat{5}$. Usually occurs on a strong beat.

cadenza: A solo at the end of a concerto movement that features rapid passagework and other technical challenges. Can appear in any concerto movement, but is generally found in the first movement after a prominent cadential $^6_4$ harmony in the orchestra, before the beginning of the coda.

cambiata: Contrapuntal embellishment, involving an apparent skip from a dissonance, that combines passing and neighboring motion.

canon: A contrapuntal procedure where the second part can be derived from the first by following a set of instructions (e.g., transpose down a fifth and delay by a measure).

cantus firmus: The given melody against which a counterpoint is written.

cardinality: The number of elements in a collection.

center: A pitch or pitch class pervasively heard in a work or section of a work. A center does not imply a functional system of scale degrees (as would a tonic), but it can establish a sense of hierarchy.

centric: Music that focuses on a pitch or pitch-class center, but not in the sense of a conventional tonal hierarchy.

chaconne: A set of continuous variations in which the entire harmonic texture, not just the bass line, is repeated and varied. While the bass line may remain unchanged for several successive variations, it is usually altered as the chaconne progresses—through rhythmic variation, changes in inversion, or substitute harmonies.

chain of suspensions: A series of suspensions, often used in fourth-species counterpoint to set descending notes in the cantus firmus.

chance: A method of composition or performance that is determined by a random procedure, such as the toss of coins, dice, or the *I-Ching.*

change of bass suspension: A type of suspension in which the bass changes when the suspension resolves; e.g., a 9–8 suspension that becomes a 9–6 because the bass skips up a third.

changes: A chord progression in a popular style; short for "chord changes."

changing meter: In contemporary pieces, meter that changes from measure to measure.

character variation: A variation intended to reproduce a particular musical style or evoke a certain genre.

chorale: A hymn set for four voices. The voices tend to move together, creating a chordal texture. Most often, the melody is given to the soprano.

chord: A group of pitches sounded together. In common-practice harmony, chords are generally built in thirds.

chord members: The pitches that make up a chord. In tonal music, each chord member is described by the interval it forms with the lowest (or bass) pitch of the chord.

chordal dissonance: A dissonant harmonic interval that originates as part of a seventh chord.

chordal skip: A melodic embellishment made by skipping from one chord member to another.

chromatic: Pitches from outside the diatonic collection. The chromatic collection consists of all twelve pitch classes.

chromatic half step: A semitone between two pitches with the same letter name (e.g., D and D♯).

chromatic inflection: A method of modulation effected by shifting one pitch by a half step.

chromatic mediant: A nondiatonic triad related to the tonic by a third, above or below.

chromatic neighbor tone: A nondiatonic half-step neighbor that embellishes a chord tone.

chromatic passing tone: A passing tone that divides a diatonic whole step into two half steps.

chromatic sequence: A diatonic sequence transformed by substituting chromatic harmonies for diatonic ones, or by chromatic embellishment.

chromatic variation: A variation that contrasts with the original theme through increased chromaticism, embellishing the melodic line or elaborating the chord progressions.

chromatic voice exchange: The chromatic alteration of one of the pitches in a voice exchange (e.g., $\hat{2}$ and $\hat{4}$ in a ii(7) might exchange places to become $\sharp\hat{4}$ and $\hat{2}$ in a V7/V).

circle of fifths: A circular diagram showing the relationships between keys. The sharp keys appear around the right side of the circle, with each key a fifth higher. The flat keys appear around the left side, with each key a fifth lower.

Classical era: The period in Western music dating roughly from 1750 until 1830. Some Classical composers are Wolfgang Amadeus Mozart, Joseph Haydn, and Ludwig van Beethoven. Genres most associated with this era are the string quartet, the sonata, the symphony, and opera.

clef: A symbol that appears on the far left of every staff to designate which line or space represents which pitch (in which octave).

closed: Term referring to a melody or formal section that ends with a conclusive cadence on the tonic.

closely related key: Any key whose tonic is a diatonic triad (major or minor) in the original key. The key signatures of closely related keys differ at most by one accidental.

closing theme: A "third theme" that might be found near the end of a sonata-form exposition; part of the second theme group if it shares the same key.

coda: A section at the end of a piece, generally following a strong cadence in the tonic; extends the tonic area and brings the work to a close.

codetta: A "little coda" at the end of a section or piece.

coda/codetta theme: A distinctive, identifiable melody introduced in a coda or codetta.

collection: A group of unordered pitches or pitch classes that serve as a source of musical materials for a work or a section of a work; a large set.

comes: In a canon, the voice that follows.

common-chord modulation: See *pivot-chord modulation.*

common-dyad modulation: See *pivot-dyad modulation.*

common practice: The compositional techniques and harmonic language of the Baroque, Classical, and Romantic eras.

common-tone augmented-sixth chord: A collection of neighbor or passing tones that makes an augmented-sixth chord; shares one pitch with the preceding or following chord.

common-tone diminished seventh chord: A collection of neighbor or passing tones that makes a diminished seventh chord; shares one pitch with the preceding or following chord.

common-tone modulation: See *pivot-tone modulation.*

common-tone theorem: The number in each position of a pcset's ic vector tells the number of common tones that will result when that particular interval class is used to transpose the pcset.

complement: See *literal complement* and *abstract complement.*

compound duple: Any meter with two beats in a measure, with each beat divided into three (e.g., $^{6}_{8}$ or $^{6}_{4}$).

compound interval: An interval larger than an octave.

compound melody: A melody created by the interaction of two or three voices, usually separated by register. Often features large leaps.

compound meter: Meter in which the beat divides into threes and subdivides into sixes. The top number of compound meter signatures is 6, 9, or 12 (e.g., $^{12}_{8}$ or $^{6}_{8}$).

compound quadruple: Any meter with four beats in a measure, with each beat divided into three (e.g., $^{12}_{8}$ or $^{12}_{4}$).

compound triple: Any meter with three beats in a measure, with each beat divided into three (e.g., $^{9}_{8}$ or $^{9}_{4}$).

concert pitch: The sounding pitch of an instrument. For transposing instruments, this differs from notated pitch.

concerto: A composition for a solo instrument and orchestra. Concertos often consist of three movements, arranged fast-slow-fast (following a formal pattern similar to the three-movement sonata).

conclusive cadence: A cadence that makes a phrase sound finished and complete. Generally the harmonic progression is V–I, with both soprano and bass ending on $\hat{1}$.

conjunct motion: Melodic motion by step.

consequent phrase: The second phrase of a period; ends with a conclusive cadence (usually a PAC).

consonance, imperfect: The intervals of a third and sixth.

consonance, perfect: The intervals of a unison, fourth, fifth, and octave. The harmonic interval of a fourth is treated as a dissonance in common-practice style.

consonant: A relative term based on acoustic properties of sound and on the norms of compositional practice. A consonant harmonic interval—unison, third, fifth, sixth, or octave—is considered pleasing to hear.

consonant skip: See *chordal skip*.

contextual analysis: A second level of harmonic analysis, showing how passing chords (and other voice-leading chords) function to expand the basic phrase model (T–PD–D–T).

continuo: An instrumental accompaniment that is read from only a given bass line (often with figures). The continuo typically consists of a low bass instrument (cello, bass viol, or bassoon) that plays a single-voice bass line, and an instrument capable of producing chordal harmonies (harpsichord, organ, guitar, or lute). The chordal instrument realizes the bass line harmonically—from figures if given, or following principles of harmonic progression and voice-leading.

continuous: Term referring to a section of a piece that has a tonally open ending and must therefore continue into the following section for tonal completion.

continuous binary: A binary form in which the first large section ends with a cadence that is not in the tonic. The piece must continue into the following section to conclude in the tonic.

continuous variation: A variation form characterized by a continuous flow of musical ideas—as opposed to strong, section-defining cadences—and *Fortspinnung* phrase structure. Continuous variations usually feature a short bass line or harmonic progression that remains constant.

contour motive: A motive that maintains its contour, or musical shape, but changes its intervals; its rhythm may or may not be altered.

contrapuntal: A composition based on the principles of counterpoint. See *counterpoint*.

contrapuntal chord: See voice-leading chord.

contrary fifths or octaves: Motion from one perfect interval to another of the same type, in which the voices move in opposite directions.

contrary motion: Contrapuntal motion in which two voices move in opposite directions.

contrasting period: A period in which the two phrases do not share the same initial melodic material.

counterpoint: A musical texture that sets two or more lines of music together so that the independent lines together create acceptable harmony; or harmonies set one after another so that the individual voices make good, independent melodic lines.

couplet: Two paired lines of poetic text.

cross relation: The chromatic alteration of a pitch in one voice part, immediately after the diatonic version has sounded in another voice.

D

da capo aria: An **A B A** design where the final **A** section is not written out again; rather, performers are instructed to return to the beginning (“da capo”) and repeat the first section until they come to a fermata or other indication marking the end.

deceptive cadence: The cadence $V^{(7)}$–vi in major, or $V^{(7)}$–VI in minor. Generally, any nontonic resolution from V at a cadence.

deceptive resolution: A midphrase resolution to the submediant from V.

descending-fifth progression: Root motion by descending fifths (or ascending fourths), creating a segment (or all) of the chain I–IV–vii^{ø}–iii–vi–ii–V–I in major, or i–iv–VII (or vii^{ø})–III–VI–ii^{ø}–V–i in minor.

descending-third progression: Root motion by descending thirds, creating a segment (or all) of the chain I–vi–IV–ii–vii^{ø}–V–iii–I in major, or i–VI–iv–ii^{ø}–vii^{ø} (or VII)–V–III–i in minor.

design: The melodic or thematic aspects of musical form, as distinct from the harmonic structure.

development: The section of a sonata form devoted to the exploration and variation of motives and themes from the exposition. Generally features sequential and modulatory passages.

developmental coda: A coda having the character and structure of a sonata-form development; sometimes called a "second development."

diatonic: (1) The collection of seven pitch classes that, in some rotation, conforms to the pattern of the whole and half steps of the major scale. (2) Made up of pitches belonging to a given diatonic collection.

diatonic half step: A semitone between two pitches with different letter names (e.g., D and E♭).

diatonic sequence: A sequence made up of pitches belonging to the diatonic collection. When the sequence pattern is transposed, generic melodic intervals stay the same, but interval qualities change (e.g., major to minor, or perfect to diminished).

diminished interval: An interval one half step smaller than a minor or perfect interval.

diminished scale: Another name for octatonic scale, so called because of the two fully diminished seventh chords that are its subsets.

diminished seventh chord: See *fully diminished seventh chord.*

diminished triad: A triad with minor thirds between the root and third and between the third and fifth, and a diminished fifth between the root and the fifth.

diminution: (1) Unaccented notes added to a first-species framework in second- and third-species counterpoint; so called because they divide the whole-note durations of the first-species framework. (2) The process of systematically shortening the durations of pitches in a melodic line, usually by a consistent proportion (e.g., reducing all note values by half).

direct fifths or octaves: Similar motion into a perfect interval, permitted only in inner voices or if the soprano moves by step.

direct modulation: Modulation accomplished without the use of a pivot chord or pitch.

disjunct motion: Melodic motion by skip or leap.

displacement: (1) The rhythmic offsetting of a pitch so that it is "held over" like a suspension from one sonority to the next, or "arrives early" before the rest of a harmony. (2) The offsetting of a triadic pitch in a harmony by another pitch, as in a sus chord.

dissonant: A relative term based on acoustic properties of sound and on the norms of compositional practice. A dissonant harmonic interval—second, fourth (in common-practice harmony, as in a 4–3 suspension), tritone, or seventh—is considered unpleasant or jarring to hear.

dodecaphonic: See *twelve tone.*

dominant: (1) Scale degree $\hat{5}$. (2) The triad built on $\hat{5}$.

dominant area: One of the harmonic areas in a basic phrase preceding the final tonic close in a conclusive cadence.

dominant expansion: See *expansion.*

dominant seventh chord: A seventh chord consisting of a major triad and a minor seventh. Occurs on $\hat{5}$ in a major key.

dominant substitute: The harmonies vii^{ø}, vii^{ø}7, or vii °7 (built on the leading tone), which may function as substitutes for the dominant. Because they lack $\hat{5}$, dominant substitutes have a weaker dominant function than V(7).

Dorian mode: An ordered collection with the pattern of whole and half steps corresponding to the white-key diatonic collection starting and ending on D; equivalent to a natural minor scale with $\hat{6}$ raised by a half step.

dot: Rhythmic notation that adds to a note half its own value (e.g., a dotted half equals a half note plus a quarter note).

double counterpoint: Two parts in invertible counterpoint.

double exposition: A feature of sonata form in some Classical-era concertos, where material in the exposition is heard twice: once played by the orchestra without modulation to the secondary key, and then by the soloist following the standard tonal scheme (and with the orchestra playing an accompanimental role).

double flat: An accidental (𝄫) that lowers a pitch two half steps (or one whole step) below its letter name.

double fugue: A fugue with two subjects.

double neighbor: The combination of successive upper and lower neighbors (in either order) around the same pitch.

double passing tones: Passing tones that occur simultaneously in two or more voices, usually creating parallel thirds or sixths.

double period: A group of four phrases in which a PAC appears only at the end of the fourth phrase, following three inconclusive cadences.

double sharp: An accidental (𝄪) that raises a pitch two half steps (or one whole step) above its letter name.

double suspension: Simultaneous suspensions in two voices combining 9–8 with either 4–3 or 7–6.

doubling: In four-part writing, a triad member represented in two different voices.

downbeat: Beat 1 of a metrical pattern.

duple meter: Meter in which beats group into units of two (e.g., $\frac{2}{4}$, $\frac{2}{2}$, or $\frac{6}{8}$).

duplet: In compound meters, a division of the beat into two, borrowed from simple meters, instead of the expected three parts.

dyad: A collection of two distinct pitches or pitch classes.

dynamics: The degree of loudness or softness in playing. Common terms (from soft to loud) are *pianissimo, piano, mezzo piano, mezzo forte, forte*, and *fortissimo*.

E

E♭ instrument: An instrument whose sounding pitch is a major sixth lower (or minor third higher) than the notated pitch.

échappée: An embellishing tone approached by step and left by leap. Also called an escape tone.

eighth note: A stemmed black note head with one flag. In simple meters, two eighth notes divide a quarter-note beat; in compound meters, three eighth notes divide a dotted-quarter-note beat.

element: Most commonly, a pitch class in a set, segment, or collection. The elements of a set or segment may also be dynamics, durations, articulations, or other musical features.

elision: The simultaneous ending of one phrase and beginning of another, articulated by the same pitches.

embedded T–PD–D–T: A small-scale T–PD–D–T progression occurring within a larger basic phrase; used to embellish the opening tonic area.

enharmonic equivalence: The idea that two or more possible names for a single pitch (e.g., C♯, D♭, B𝄫) are musically and functionally the same.

enharmonic modulation: Modulation in which a chord resolves according to the function of its enharmonic equivalent. Chords that can be spelled (and therefore resolved) enharmonically include fully diminished sevenths, dominant sevenths, and German augmented sixths.

enharmonic pitches: Pitches with the same sound but different letter names, such as B♭ and A♯.

episode: (1) A contrasting section in a rondo; generally less tonally stable than the rondo's refrain. (2) A modulating passage in a fugue.

expansion: An extension of a function by means of contrapuntal motion and voice-leading chords.

exposition: (1) In sonata form, the first large section (often repeated), where the themes for the movement are "exposed" for the first time; features two primary key areas with a modulatory transition between them. (2) In a fugue or invention, the initial section where the subject is presented in each voice.

extension: (1) The lengthening of a motive, melody, or phrase. (2) A pitch added to a triad or seventh chord (e.g., an added sixth, ninth, or eleventh).

F

Fibonacci series: An infinite series in which each new member is the sum of the previous two (e.g., 0, 1, 1, 2, 3, 5, 8, 13, etc.). Associated with compositions by Bartók and others, and sometimes used in conjunction with time points.

fifth: (1) The distance spanned by five consecutive letter names. (2) The pitch in a triad that is five scale steps above the root.

fifth species: Counterpoint that combines the patterns of each of the other species. Sometimes known as free composition.

figural variation: A variation that features a specific embellishment pattern or figure throughout.

figuration prelude: A prelude featuring a rhythm based on a consistent arpeggiation scheme. The prelude could be notated as a series of chords, with each harmony unfolding according to the arpeggiation pattern.

figured bass: The combination of a bass line and Arabic numbers (figures), indicating chords without notating them fully; the numbers represent some of the intervals to be played above the bass line. Typically found in continuo parts.

first inversion: A triad or seventh chord voiced so that the chordal third is in the bass.

first species: Counterpoint written so that each note in one voice is paired with a single note in the other voice, using only consonant intervals. Also called note-to-note or 1:1 counterpoint.

first theme (group): The tonic-key melody (or melodies), and accompaniment, with which a sonata form begins.

five-part rondo: A rondo with the form **A B A C A** or **A B A B′ A**, plus optional coda.

flat: An accidental (♭) that lowers a pitch a half step.

focal pitch: A pitch or pitch class that is emphasized through repetition or other means, but does not establish a hierarchy with other pitches in the piece's collection.

***Fonte*:** A type of progression, identified by Joseph Riepel, that could be used at the unstable beginning of the second section of a binary form; literally, "fountain." Consists of the sequence V7/ii | ii | V7 | I.

Forte set label: A set-class-labeling system developed by Allen Forte, in which set classes are ordered by size (or cardinality) and then by ic vector. To each set class, Forte gave a hyphenated number (e.g., 5-35). The number before the hyphen represents the cardinality of the pcset, and the number after it represents the pcset's ordinal position on Forte's list; thus, 5-35 is a pcset of five elements that appears thirty-fifth on the list.

***Fortspinnung*:** A feature of Baroque-era works in which a melody is "spun out" in uninterrupted fashion. Continuous motion, uneven phrase lengths, melodic or harmonic sequences, changes of key, and elided phrases are all characteristics of *Fortspinnung* passages.

fourth species: Counterpoint in which one voice is rhythmically displaced by ties across the bar; characterized by its use of suspensions.

fragmentation: The isolation and/or development of a small but recognizable part of a motive.

French augmented-sixth chord (Fr^6 or Fr$^4_3$): An augmented-sixth chord with $\hat{1}$ and $\hat{2}$ in the upper voices. The distinctive sound of this chord is created by two dissonances above the bass: the augmented sixth and the augmented fourth.

fugue: An imitative contrapuntal composition, usually in three or four voices, that features repeated statements of a subject and its answer in various keys, with accompanying counterpoint and modulatory episodes in between.

full score: A score showing each instrumental part in the piece on a separate staff (or staves).

fully diminished seventh chord: A seventh chord consisting of a diminished triad and a diminished seventh. Because its thirds are all minor, it has no audible root. May be used as a means to modulate to distantly related keys.

fundamental bass: An analytical bass line consisting of the *roots* of a chord progression, as opposed to the sounding bass line.

G

German augmented-sixth chord (Gr^6 or Gr$^6_5$): An augmented-sixth chord with $\hat{1}$ and $\flat\hat{3}$ in the upper voices. This chord, characterized by its perfect fifth above the bass, is an enharmonic respelling of a dominant seventh chord.

grand staff: Two staves, one in the treble clef and one in the bass clef, connected by a curly brace; typically found in piano music.

graphic notation: Nonstandard symbols used to indicate pitch, duration, articulation, etc., in some nontonal scores.

ground bass: A set of continuous variations built on a repeating bass line.

H

half cadence (HC): An inconclusive cadence on the dominant.

half-diminished seventh chord: A seventh chord consisting of a diminished triad and a minor seventh.

half note: A stemmed white note head; its duration is equivalent to two quarter notes.

half step: The musical space between a pitch and the next-closest pitch on the keyboard.

harmonic ambiguity: Characteristic of highly chromatic passages in late-Romantic music. The musical coherence comes not through "strength of progression" (strong root-movement-based chord progressions) but rather through "strength of line": smooth linear connections between chords.

harmonic interval: The span between two pitches played simultaneously.

harmonic minor: See *minor scale.*
harmonic rhythm: The rate at which harmonies change in a piece (e.g., one chord per measure or one chord per beat).
harmonic sequence: A succession of harmonies based on a root-progression with a repeated intervallic pattern in an upper voice.
harmony: (1) A chord. (2) A progression of chords, usually implying common-practice principles of voice-leading.
head: In jazz, a clearly recognizable melody and harmonic progression that is the basis for improvisation over the course of the piece.
hemiola: a temporary duple-rhythmic grouping in the context of an underlying triple meter (e.g., two measures of $\frac{3}{4}$ meter heard as three measures of $\frac{2}{4}$), or a temporary two-part division of the beat in the context of an underlying three-part division (e.g., measures of $\frac{6}{4}$ heard as measures of $\frac{3}{2}$).
hexachord: A collection of six distinct pitches or pitch classes.
hexachordal combinatoriality: A compositional technique in which two forms of the same row are paired so that the rows' initial hexachords, when combined, complete an aggregate. Similarly, the rows' second hexachords, when combined, complete an aggregate. There are four kinds of hexachordal combinatoriality: P, I, R, and RI.
hidden fifths or octaves: See *direct fifths* or *octaves.*
hook: In popular songs, a musical setting of a few words or a phrase, usually including the title, that is the most "catchy" or memorable part of the song.
hypermeter: A high-level metric grouping that interprets groups of measures as though they were groups of beats within a single measure.

I

I-combinatoriality: Pairing a row and its inversion form(s) to make aggregates.
imitation: The contrapuntal "echoing" of a voice in another part.
imperfect authentic cadence (IAC): An authentic cadence weakened by (1) placing the I or V harmony in inversion, or (2) ending with the soprano on a scale degree other than $\hat{1}$.
imperfect consonance: The intervals of a third and sixth.
incomplete neighbor: A neighbor tone without either (1) the initial motion from the main pitch to the neighbor, or (2) the returning motion of the neighbor to the main pitch.
inconclusive cadence: A cadence that makes a phrase sound less complete than a PAC. Generally, either the soprano or the bass ends on a scale degree other than $\hat{1}$.
indeterminate: Some musical element or event in a score that is left to chance (either in performance or during composition).
index number: The value that measures the "distance" between two inversionally related pcsets. If pcsets A and B are inversionally related by the index number n, then A = T_nI B, and B = T_nI A. When paired correctly, every pc in one set added to the corresponding pc in the other set will sum uniformly to the index number.
instrumental break: An instrumental section in the middle of a popular song.
instrumental chorus: Chorus of a popular song performed with instrumental solos rather than vocals.
integer notation: The system of labeling pcs by number instead of letter name: C = 0, C♯ or D♭ = 1, D = 2, D♯ or E♭ = 3, and so on. The letter t substitutes for 10 (B♭ or A♯) and e for 11 (B).
interlude: A passage that serves as a transition between or a change of pace from other sections.
internal expansion: The lengthening of a phrase between its beginning and end. Results from immediate repetitions of material, an elongation of one or more harmonies, or the addition of new material within the phrase.
interval: The musical space between two pitches or pitch classes.
interval class (ic): All pitch intervals that can be made from one pair of pitch classes belong to the same interval class (e.g., M3, m6, and M10). Also called unordered pitch-class interval.
interval-class vector (ic vector): A concise summary of all interval classes within a given pcset; written as six numbers within square brackets, without commas. For example, the ic vector for the trichord {0 4 6}, [010101], shows that it contains one whole step, one major third, and one tritone.

intro: Music, usually instrumental, that introduces a popular song.

invariance: The retention of pitch classes between a pcset or row and its transposition or inversion.

invention: A contrapuntal composition, usually in two voices, that features repeated statements of a subject, imitated at the octave, with accompanying counterpoint and modulatory episodes in between.

inverse: Given a pc or pc interval, the inverse is the corresponding pc or pc interval such that the two sum to 0 (mod12). For example, the inverse of pc 5 is pc 7.

inversion (chordal): A voicing in which a chord member other than the root is the lowest-sounding pitch.

inversion (motivic): A melodic or motivic transformation in which successive generic intervals reverse direction (e.g., an ascending third becomes a descending third).

inversion (pitch): A melodic or motivic transformation in which successive ordered pitch intervals reverse direction (e.g., a +2 becomes a −2).

inversion (pitch class): A transformation in which each pc in a pcset is replaced by its inverse (e.g., the inversion of {0 1 6 7} is {0 e 6 5}). To find the transposed inversion of a pcset, always invert first, then transpose.

inversion (row): The form of a twelve-tone row in which each pc is replaced by its inverse; abbreviated I_n, where n is the pc integer of the row's first element.

inversionally related intervals (tonal): Two intervals that, when combined, span an octave (e.g., E3-G♯3, a major third; plus G♯3-E4, a minor sixth). When inverted, major intervals become minor (and vice versa), diminished become augmented (and vice versa), and perfect stay perfect. The interval numbers of inversionally related intervals sum to 9 (third and sixth, second and seventh, etc.).

invertible counterpoint: Counterpoint that is structured intervallically so that the two lines can be reversed in register.

Ionian mode: An ordered collection with the pattern of whole and half steps corresponding to the white-key diatonic collection starting and ending on C; the same collection as the major scale.

isorhythm: A repeating series of durations (which may be associated with repeating pitch materials); used in various style periods, but most prominently in the Middle Ages and twentieth century.

Italian augmented-sixth chord (It⁶): An augmented-sixth chord with (doubled) $\hat{1}$ in the upper voices.

K

key: (1) The key of a tonal piece takes its name from the first scale degree of the major or minor tonality in which that piece is written; this pitch class is the primary scale degree around which all other pitches in the piece relate hierarchically. (2) A lever on an instrument that can be depressed with a finger (like a piano key).

key signature: A sign that appears at the beginning of each line of a musical score, after the clef, showing which pitches are to be sharped or flatted consistently; helps determine the key.

L

lament bass: Chromatic bass line descending from $\hat{1}$ to $\hat{5}$; so called because of its association in early opera with sadness and death.

large ternary: A formal scheme created by joining smaller, composite forms into an **A B A** form (e.g., minuet and trio, or scherzo and trio). The **A** and **B** sections themselves may have their own form (such as rounded binary).

lead-in: A musical passage that connects the end of one melodic phrase with the beginning of the next.

leading tone: $\hat{7}$ of the major scale and harmonic or ascending-melodic minor scale; a half step below the tonic.

leading-tone chord: Harmonies built on the leading tone: vii°, $vii^{ø7}$, or vii^{o7}.

lead-sheet notation: A type of notation, commonly used in popular music, where roots are indicated by capital letters and qualities by added abbreviations or symbols (e.g., Fmin indicates an F minor triad).

leap: A melodic interval larger than a third (larger than a skip).

ledger line: Extra lines drawn through stems and/or note heads to designate a pitch above or below a staff.

libretto: The text of an opera.

Lied: German art song of the Romantic era (plural is Lieder).

linear chord: See *voice-leading chord.*

linear-intervallic pattern (LIP): The intervallic framework between outer voices. LIPs underlie all harmonic sequences, although sometimes they are hidden behind complicated surface elaborations.

link: (1) In a fugue exposition, a passage of a few beats that rhythmically and harmonically connects the end of the answer with the beginning of the subject in the tonic key. (2) In popular styles, a short instrumental passage, used to connect sections. (3) A lead-in.

literal complement: The pcset that, when combined with a given pcset, produces the complete aggregate.

Locrian mode: An ordered collection with the pattern of whole and half steps corresponding to the white-key diatonic collection starting and ending on B; equivalent to a natural minor scale with $\hat{2}$ and $\hat{5}$ lowered by half steps.

Lydian mode: An ordered collection with the pattern of whole and half steps corresponding to the white-key diatonic collection starting and ending on F; equivalent to a major scale with $\hat{4}$ raised by a half step.

Lydian-Mixolydian mode: A mixed mode created by combining the lower tetrachord of the Lydian mode with the upper tetrachord of the Mixolydian (e.g., C D E F♯ G A B♭ C); equivalent to a major scale with $\hat{4}$ raised by a half step and $\hat{7}$ lowered by a half step.

M

major interval: The quality of the intervals second, third, sixth, and seventh above $\hat{1}$ in the major scale.

major-minor seventh chord: See *dominant seventh chord.*

major-minor tetrachord: See *split-third chord.*

major pentatonic: A five-note subset of the diatonic collection that features major-key $\hat{1}$, $\hat{2}$, $\hat{3}$, $\hat{5}$, and $\hat{6}$.

major scale: An ordered collection of pitches arranged according to the pattern of whole and half steps W-W-H-W-W-W-H.

major seventh chord: A seventh chord consisting of a major triad and a major seventh.

major triad: A triad with a major third between the root and third, a minor third between the third and fifth, and a perfect fifth between the root and the fifth. Corresponds to $\hat{1}$, $\hat{3}$, and $\hat{5}$ of a major scale.

measure: A unit of music grouped by beats; generally, a measure begins and ends with notated bar lines.

medial caesura: An abrupt silence marking the end of the transition in the exposition of a sonata-form movement before the second-theme group.

mediant: (1) Scale degree $\hat{3}$. (2) The triad built on $\hat{3}$.

medieval era: The period in Western music dating roughly from 800 to 1430. Some medieval composers are Hildegard of Bingen, Pérotin, and Guillaume de Machaut. Genres associated with this era are Gregorian chants, motets, chansons, and organum.

melisma: A vocal passage that sets one syllable of text to many notes.

melodic interval: The span between two notes played one after another.

melodic minor: See *minor scale.*

melodic sequence: A motive repeated several times in successive transpositions (often up or down by step).

mélodie: Romantic-era art songs in the French tradition.

meter: A hierarchical arrangement of beats and their divisions that repeat from measure to measure and are perceived as relatively strong and weak. The first beat of each measure is perceived as strongest.

meter signature: A sign that appears at the beginning of a piece, after the clef and key signature: the upper number indicates meter type and the lower number indicates which note gets the beat; also called a time signature.

metric modulation: A means of smoothing what would otherwise be abrupt changes of tempo by introducing subdivisions or groups of beats in the first tempo that match durations in the new tempo. The new tempo is recognized in retrospect, much like a modulation by pivot chord.

metric reinterpretation: A disruption in the established hypermetric pattern at the cadence. This can occur when a measure simultaneously functions as strong and weak in the case of a phrase elision.

metrical accent: The pattern of strong and weak beats based on the "weight" of the downbeat and the "lift" of the upbeat.

Middle Ages: See *medieval era.*

middle C: C4, the C located at the center of the piano keyboard.

minimalism: A style in which music is composed through the repetition and gradual change of "minimal" musical elements.

minor interval: The quality of the intervals third, sixth, and seventh from $\hat{1}$ in the minor scale. A minor second (diatonic half step) is formed between $\hat{7}$ and $\hat{1}$ in a major, harmonic minor, or ascending melodic minor scale.

minor pentatonic: A five-note subset of the diatonic collection that features minor-key $\hat{1}$, $\flat\hat{3}$, $\hat{4}$, $\hat{5}$, and $\flat\hat{7}$.

minor scale: The natural minor scale is an ordered collection of pitches arranged according to the pattern of whole and half steps W-H-W-W-H-W-W. The harmonic minor scale raises $\flat\hat{7}$ to $\hat{7}$ (the leading tone). The melodic minor raises $\flat\hat{6}$ and $\flat\hat{7}$ ascending, but takes the natural minor form descending.

minor seventh chord: A seventh chord consisting of a minor triad and a minor seventh.

minor triad: A triad with a minor third between the root and third, a major third between the third and fifth, and a perfect fifth between the root and the fifth. Corresponds to $\hat{1}$, $\flat\hat{3}$, and $\hat{5}$ of a minor scale.

minuet and trio: The most common type of composite ternary form, generally written in triple meter. Typically the third (dance-like) movement of a Classical-era sonata, string quartet, or symphony.

Mixolydian mode: An ordered collection with the pattern of whole and half steps corresponding to the white-key diatonic collection starting and ending on G; equivalent to a major scale with $\hat{7}$ lowered by one half step.

mixture (or modal mixture): (1) Shifting temporarily from a major key to the parallel minor (or vice versa) in a musical passage. (2) "Mixing" the parallel major and minor modes, most often in major keys, where the modal scale degrees, $\flat\hat{3}$, $\flat\hat{6}$, and $\flat\hat{7}$ are borrowed from the parallel minor.

mixture chord: A chord whose spelling and chord quality are derived from the parallel mode. Most often, chords from the parallel minor mode appear in a major key. Also called borrowed chords.

mobile form: Form consisting of segments, sections, or movements that may be played in varying orders. While the contents of segments may remain consistent from one performance to another, the overall form of the piece will not.

mod12 arithmetic: Arithmetic that keeps integers in the range 0 to 11. To convert a number greater than 11, divide by 12 and take the remainder. Used to label pcs in integer notation and perform operations such as transposition or inversion.

modal scale degrees: The scale degrees that differ between major and natural minor scales: $\hat{3}$, $\hat{6}$, and $\hat{7}$.

mode: (1) Rotations of the major (or natural minor) scale (e.g., the Dorian mode is a rotation of the C major scale beginning and ending on D). (2) Term used to distinguish between major and minor keys (e.g., a piece in "the minor mode").

mode of limited transposition: Composer Olivier Messiaen's term for pc collections that can be transposed by only a few intervals; other transpositions replicate the original collection (the whole-tone and octatonic collections are examples).

modified strophic: A variation of strophic form. Rather than repeating the melody exactly, the music is slightly altered from verse to verse.

modulating period: A period whose consequent phrase modulates, leading to an authentic cadence in a different key from the antecedent phrase.

modulation: A change of key, usually confirmed by a (perfect) authentic cadence.

moment form: The concept that sections of a piece do not have to connect in some logical way or in a predetermined order, but can change abruptly from one style of music to another.

***Monte*:** A type of progression, identified by Joseph Riepel, that could be used at the unstable beginning of the second section of a binary form; literally, "mountain." Consists of the sequence V7/IV | IV | V7/V | V.

motet: A polyphonic choral work.

motive: The smallest recognizable musical idea. Motives may be characterized by their pitches, contour, and/or rhythm, but rarely contain a cadence. Generally they are repeated (exactly or varied).

musical form: The overall organization of a composition into sections, defined by harmonic structure—change of key, mode, pcset, collection, or row form—as well as by changes in (or a return to) a theme, texture, instrumentation, rhythm, or other feature.

N

natural minor: See *minor scale.*

natural sign: An accidental (♮) that cancels a sharp or flat.

Neapolitan: The major triad built on ♭II; typically occurs in first inversion (Neapolitan sixth), with $\hat{4}$ in the bass and ♭$\hat{2}$ and ♭$\hat{6}$ in the upper voices.
neighbor tone: An embellishment that decorates a melody pitch by moving to a pitch a step above or below it, then returning to the original pitch; approached and left by step in opposite directions.
neighboring $^4_2$: A $^4_2$ chord arising from neighbor tones in all three of the upper parts (e.g., in the tonic expansion I–ii$^4_2$–I).
neighboring $^6_4$: A $^6_4$ chord, usually unaccented, that shares a bass note with the harmony it embellishes, while two upper voices move in stepwise upper-neighbor motion. Also called a pedal $^6_4$.
ninth chord: A triad or seventh chord with a ninth added above the bass.
nonad: A collection of nine distinct pitches or pitch classes.
nonmetric: See *ametric.*
nonteleological form: Form, such as moment form and mobile form, in which the music lacks a sense of a goal or direction.
nontonal: Music that freely employs all twelve pitch classes. The pervasive chromaticism and absence of whole- and half-step scale patterns make a true "tonic" pitch class impossible to discern in nontonal music.
normal order: The order of consecutive pcs in a pcset that (1) spans the smallest interval and (2) places the smallest intervals toward the left.
notated meter: The way in which rhythms are notated in a score. In common-practice music, notated meter and perceived meter are usually the same. In music of the twentieth century and later, they may not be.
note-to-note: See *first species.*

O

oblique motion: Contrapuntal motion in which one part repeats the same pitch while the other moves by leap, skip, or step.
octad: A collection of eight distinct pitches or pitch classes.
octatonic scale: A scale composed of eight distinct pcs in alternating whole and half steps.
octave: The distance of eight musical steps.
octave equivalence: The concept that two pitches an octave apart are functionally equivalent.
offbeat: A weak beat or weak portion of a beat.
omnibus: A special chromaticized voice exchange, usually prolonging the dominant. The exchanged pitches form the interval of a tritone, which enables the voice exchange to continue chromatically until the exchanged voices arrive where they began (but up or down an octave). All the resulting chromatic simultaneities are *voice-leading chords.*
open: A harmonic feature of a phrase or section of a piece in which the end is inconclusive, or in a different key from the beginning.
open score: A score with a staff for every part, unlike a piano score; for example, an SATB choral score on four staves.
orchestration: Setting or composing for a large ensemble.
ostinato: A repeated rhythmic and/or pitch pattern.
outro: Music, often instrumental, that brings a popular song to its close.
overlap: A means of phrase connection in which one or more voices begin a new phrase while one or more voices simultaneously finish the previous phrase.
overlapping voices: A voice-leading error in which one voice moves into the register of an adjacent voice on an adjacent beat.

P

P-combinatoriality: Pairing a row and its transposed form(s) to make aggregates.
palindrome: A segment (of pitches, pcs, intervals, and/or rhythms) that reads the same backward and forward.
parallel fifths or octaves: Contrapuntal and voice-leading error that results from approaching a perfect fifth in parallel motion from another perfect fifth, or perfect octave from another perfect octave.
parallel keys: Keys in different modes that share the same letter name and tonic, such as F major and F minor.
parallel major: The major key that shares the same tonic as a given minor key. The parallel major raises the third, sixth, and seventh scale degrees of the minor key.

parallel minor: The minor key that shares the same tonic as a given major key. The parallel minor lowers the third, sixth, and seventh scale degrees of the major key.

parallel motion: Contrapuntal motion in which both parts move in the same direction by the same interval.

parallel period: A period in which the two phrases share the same beginning melodic material.

parody: The compositional borrowing or reshaping of another composer's materials, emphasizing particular features.

passacaglia: Continuous variations with a repeated bass line (or ground bass).

passing chord: A voice-leading "chord" arising from passing motion.

passing $^4_2$: A $^4_2$ chord created by passing motion in the bass (e.g., in the progression I–I$^4_2$–IV^6).

passing $^6_4$: A voice-leading $^6_4$ chord, usually connecting root-position and first-inversion chords of the same harmony and harmonizing a bass-line passing tone.

passing tone: A melodic embellishment that fills in the space between chord members by stepwise motion; approached and left by step in the same direction.

pc: Abbreviation of *pitch class.*

pcset: Abbreviation of *pitch-class set.*

pedal point: A note held for several measures while harmonies change above it. Chords above a pedal point do not participate in the harmonic framework.

pentachord: A collection of five distinct pitches or pitch classes.

pentatonic scale: A scale with five pcs. In Western music, the pentatonic scale is a subset of the diatonic collection. The two most common are the minor pentatonic (*do, me, fa, sol, te*) and the major pentatonic (*do, re, mi, sol, la*)

perfect authentic cadence (PAC): A strong conclusive cadence in which a root-position V$^{(7)}$ progresses to a root-position I, and the soprano moves from $\hat{2}$ or $\hat{7}$ to $\hat{1}$.

perfect consonance: The intervals of a unison, fourth, fifth, and octave. The harmonic interval of a fourth is treated as a dissonance in common-practice style.

period: A musical unit consisting (usually) of two phrases. Generally, the first phrase ends with a weak cadence (typically a HC), answered by a more conclusive cadence (usually a PAC) at the end of the second.

phasing: The compositional technique of moving musical patterns in and out of alignment, creating additional sounds and patterns that are not present in the original materials.

phrase: A basic unit of musical thought, similar to a sentence in language, with a beginning, a middle, and an end. In tonal music, a phrase must end with a cadence; in nontonal music, other musical features provide closure.

phrase group: Three or more phrases with tonal and/or thematic design elements that group them together.

phrase modulation: See *direct modulation.*

phrase rhythm: The interaction of hypermeter and phrase structure.

phrase structure: The melodic and harmonic characteristics of a phrase or group of phrases, identified by cadence type, harmonic motion, number of measures, and melodic or motivic repetition or contrast.

Phrygian cadence: The half cadence iv^6–V in minor, so called because of the half-step descent in the bass.

Phrygian mode: An ordered collection with the pattern of whole and half steps corresponding to the white-key diatonic collection starting and ending on E; equivalent to a natural minor scale with $\hat{2}$ lowered by a half step.

Phrygian II: See *Neapolitan.*

Picardy third: In a minor key, the raised third of a tonic chord (making the harmony major), typically at an authentic cadence at the end of a piece.

pitch: A tone sounding in a particular octave.

pitch class (pc): Notes an octave (or several octaves) apart that share the same name (e.g., F3, F5, and F2 all belong to pc F). Pitch-class names assume octave and enharmonic equivalence.

pitch-class interval (pci): The interval spanned by two pcs. Ordered pitch-class intervals measure the distance from pc a to b by subtracting (b – a) mod12; the distance can range from 0 to 11. Unordered pitch-class intervals measure the shortest distance between two pcs, either from the first to the second or vice versa; the distance ranges from 0 to 6. See *interval class.*

pitch interval: The musical space between two pitches, described either with tonal labels (e.g., minor second, augmented sixth, perfect fifth) or by the number of half steps from one pitch to the other. Unordered pitch intervals measure distance;

ordered pitch intervals measure distance and direction (shown with a + or −).

pitch symmetry: The spacing of pitches at equal distances above and below a central pitch.

pitch-time graph: A graph that plots pitch (the vertical axis) against time (the horizontal axis).

pivot area: In a pivot-chord modulation, a series of harmonies that function diatonically in both the old and new key.

pivot chord: In a pivot-chord modulation, a harmony that functions diatonically in both the old and new key.

pivot-chord modulation: Modulation from one key to another by means of a harmony (the pivot chord) that functions diatonically in both keys.

pivot-dyad modulation: Modulation in which two pitches of a chord function as a "pivot." Other pitches of this modulating chord may shift up or down a half step, making a chromatic connection.

pivot-tone modulation: Modulation in which only a single pitch of a chord or melodic line functions as a "pivot." Other pitches of this modulating chord may shift up or down a half step, making a chromatic connection.

plagal cadence: The cadence IV–I (iv–i in minor), sometimes called the Amen cadence.

planing: Twentieth-century technique of connecting chords via parallel motion.

polymeter: Music with two or more different simultaneous metric streams.

polymodality: Music with several modes sounding in different layers of music simultaneously.

polyphonic variation: A variation that changes from a harmonically based setting to one with independent voices; may include imitative entries.

polytonality: Music with several keys sounding in different layers of music simultaneously.

***Ponte*:** A type of progression, identified by Joseph Riepel, that could be used at the unstable beginning of the second section of a binary form; literally, "bridge." Consists of a dominant prolongation, such as V | V | V^{8-7} | I.

postmodernism: Combining materials originating from different times and styles. The term is borrowed from literary and art criticism.

post-tonal music: Music composed after 1900 that is not restricted to compositional principles of the common-practice era.

prechorus: In popular styles, a short passage of music with text that comes between the verse and the chorus.

predominant: (1) The triad or seventh chord built on $\hat{2}$, $\hat{4}$, or $\hat{6}$. (2) A category of harmonic function that includes chords that precede the dominant, typically ii and IV ($ii^{ø}$ and iv in minor keys), but also the Neapolitan sixth and augmented-sixth chords.

predominant area: A harmonic area in a basic phrase that often precedes the dominant area (T–PD–D–T).

primary theme (group): See *theme (group).*

prime (row): Row in a twelve-tone composition considered a starting point, usually the first appearance of the row; labeled P_n, where n is the first pc of the row.

prime form: The representative pcset for a set class, beginning with 0 and enclosed in square brackets; the set's best normal order (which may include the normal order for its inversion) transposed to begin with 0.

prolong: To expand the function of a harmony by means of contrapuntal motion and contrapuntal or linear chords.

pset: Abbreviation of "pitch set."

Q

quadruple meter: Meter in which beats group into units of four (e.g., $\frac{4}{4}$ or $\frac{12}{8}$).

quadruplet: In compound time, a subdivision group borrowed from simple time.

quarter note: A stemmed black note head, equivalent in duration to two eighth notes.

quaternary song form: A song form consisting of four (usually eight-bar) phrases. The first two phrases begin the same (they may be identical or may differ at the cadence). They are followed by a contrasting section (bridge) and then a return to the opening material, making the overall form **a a b a**. Also known as thirty-two-bar song form.

quodlibet: A medley, or amalgamated borrowing, of songs; may feature multiple texts, sometimes in different languages.

R

R-combinatoriality: Hexachordal combinatoriality achieved by pairing a row and its appropriate retrograde form(s) to make aggregates.

raised submediant: Raised $\hat{6}$ in melodic minor.

real answer: Exact transposition of a fugue subject up a fifth (or down a fourth); the answer directly follows the subject, with accompanying counterpoint, in a fugue exposition.

realization: (1) A full musical texture created from a figured (or unfigured) bass. (2) In pieces composed with pcsets or rows, pitch classes in a specific register and rhythm. (3) Performance of a work from a text or graphic score.

rearticulated suspension: A suspension in which the suspended voice sounds again (instead of being held over) at the moment of dissonance.

recapitulation: The final section of a sonata form (or penultimate section, if the movement ends with a coda), in which the music from the exposition is heard again, this time with the theme groups usually in the tonic key.

reduction: (1) A score transcribed so that it can be performed by fewer instrumental forces (usually by piano). (2) The underlying harmonic framework and linear counterpoint of a passage of music, revealed after embellishing tones or harmonies have been eliminated.

refrain: (1) The section of a song that recurs with the same music and text. (2) In popular-music verse-refrain form, the second portion of the song, after the verse; generally in **a a b a**, or quaternary, song form. (3) In rondo form (usually **A B A C A** or **A B A C A B (D) A**), the refrain is the **A** section, which returns with opening thematic material in the tonic key. Another word for ritornello.

register: The particular octave in which a pitch sounds.

registral invariance: A compositional technique in which certain pcs are realized as pitches only in one specific register. Also known as frozen register and pitch fixation.

relative keys: Major and minor keys that share the same key signature (e.g., C major and A minor).

relative major: The major key that shares the same key signature as a given minor key. The relative major is made from the same pitch-class collection as its relative minor, but begins on $\flat\hat{3}$ of the minor key.

relative minor: The minor key that shares the same key signature as a given major key. The relative minor is made from the same pitch-class collection as its relative major, but begins on $\hat{6}$ of the major key.

Renaissance era: The period in Western music dating roughly from 1430 until 1600. Some Renaissance composers are Josquin des Prez, Palestrina, Guillaume Dufay, and Carlo Gesualdo. Genres most associated with the era are the mass, madrigal, masque, and instrumental dances.

resolution: The way a harmony or scale step progresses to the next harmony or pitch. The term usually refers to the manner in which a dissonant interval moves to a consonant one.

rest: A duration of silence.

retardation: A rhythmic embellishment where a consonance is held over to the next beat, creating a dissonance with the new harmony. The dissonance is resolved upward by step, creating another consonant interval.

retransition: A musical passage that harmonically prepares for the return of previously heard material. In sonata form, it appears at the end of the development section and prolongs the dominant harmony in preparation for the tonic return of the recapitulation's first theme group. In rondo form, a retransition may appear before any recurrence of the refrain (**A** section).

retrograde: The form of a twelve-tone row in which the pcs are in the reverse order of the prime. Abbreviated R_n, where n refers to the last pc of the row, i.e., the first pc of the original, prime row.

retrograde inversion: The form of a twelve-tone row in which the pcs are in the reverse order of the inversion. Abbreviated RI_n, where n refers to the last pc of the row, i.e., the first pc of the inverted row.

retrogression: Progressions that reverse typical common-practice harmonic norms; common in other musical idioms (e.g., V–IV in blues and rock music).

ritornello: An instrumental section of a piece that returns. Another word for refrain.

rhyme scheme: The pattern of rhyming in a poetic verse or stanza, generally designated with lowercase letters. Repeated letters indicate lines that end with rhyming words.

rhythm: The patterns made by the durations of pitch and silence (notes and rests) in a piece.

rhythmic acceleration: The gradual move from long note values to shorter note values in a passage of music; also called a rhythmic *crescendo*.

rhythmic motive: A motive that maintains its rhythm but changes its contour and interval structure.
RI-combinatoriality: Hexachordal combinatoriality achieved by pairing a row and its appropriate retrograde-inversional form(s) to create aggregates.
Romantic era: The period in Western music dating roughly from 1830 until 1910. Some Romantic composers are Robert Schumann, Frédéric Chopin, Giuseppe Verdi, and Richard Wagner. Genres most associated with this era are the art song, program symphony, character piece, tone poem, and grand opera.
rondo: A musical form characterized by a repeated section (refrain, or ritornello) alternating with sections that contrast in key, mode, texture, harmonic complexity, thematic content, and/or style (usually **A B A C A** or **A B A C A B (D) A**). The contrasting sections are called episodes.
root: The lowest pitch of a triad or seventh chord when the chord is spelled in thirds.
root position: A chord voiced so that the root is in the bass.
rounded binary: A binary form in which melodic or motivic features in the initial phrase return at the end of the piece, "rounding out" the formal plan.
row: A specific ordering of all twelve pitch classes.
row elision: One way of connecting rows in a twelve-tone piece: the same pc or pcs are shared at the end of one row and the beginning of the next.
row matrix: A twelve-by-twelve array that displays all possible P, I, R, and RI forms of a row.

S

SATB: An abbreviation for the four main voice ranges: soprano, alto, tenor, and bass. Also indicates a particular musical style or texture: chorale style.
scale: A collection of pitch classes arranged in a particular order of whole and half steps.
scale degree: A name for each pitch class of the scale, showing its relationship to the tonic pitch (for which the key is named). Scale-degree names may be numbers ($\hat{1}$, $\hat{2}$, $\hat{3}$), words (tonic, supertonic, mediant), or solfège syllables (*do, re, mi*).
scale step: Same as scale degree.
scherzo and trio: A composite ternary form in a fast tempo, usually in triple meter. Typically the third movement of a Romantic-era sonata, quartet, or symphony.
second inversion: A triad or seventh chord voiced so that the chordal fifth is in the bass.
second species: Counterpoint written so that one voice has two notes for every single note in the other voice. Permits consonances and passing tones, according to specific rules of voice-leading; eighteenth-century style also allows neighbor tones. Another name for 2:1 counterpoint.
second theme (group): The melody (or melodies) heard at the start of the new key area in a sonata form.
secondary dominant: A dominant-function harmony (V or vii°, with or without the chordal seventh) "applied" to a chord other than tonic (may also refer only to a secondary V chord). A secondary dominant typically includes chromatic alterations (relative to the tonic key). Also called an applied dominant, or applied chord.
secondary leading-tone chord: A leading-tone chord that functions as an applied, or secondary, dominant; usually a fully diminished seventh chord.
secondary set: An aggregate formed by combining segments belonging to more than one row form.
section: A large division within a composition, usually set off by a cadence (or other elements denoting closure). May be delineated by repeat signs or a double bar.
sectional: A harmonic feature of tonal forms, in which a section is tonally closed (with an authentic cadence in the tonic key); the section could stand on its own.
sectional binary: A binary form in which the first section ends with a cadence on the tonic. The section is tonally complete and could stand on its own.
sectional variation: A variation form in which each variation is clearly distinguished from the next by a strong conclusive cadence (and often by double bars). Each variation could be played as a complete stand-alone section.
segment: An ordered sequence of pitches or pcs.
sentence: A phrase design with a 1 + 1 + 2 (or 2 + 2 + 4) motivic structure. Typically shaped by an opening idea that is repeated, then a continuation that works out the idea further and brings the phrase to a cadence.

sequence: A musical pattern that is restated successively at different pitch levels. See *harmonic sequence* and *melodic sequence*.

sequence pattern: A short (one- or two-measure) melodic or harmonic idea, transposed up or down to form a sequence.

serial music: Music composed with (ordered) pitch-class segments and ordered transformations of these segments; may also feature ordered durations, dynamics, and articulations.

set: A group of unordered pitches or pitch classes. See *collection*.

set class: The collection of pcsets that contains all possible distinct transpositions of the pcset, as well as all distinct transpositions of its inversion. Pcsets in the same set class also share the same ic vector.

seven-part rondo: A rondo whose form is **A B A C A B (D) A**, plus optional coda.

seventh chord: A chord that can be arranged as a root-position triad with another third stacked on top. This third forms a seventh with the root. There are five types of seventh chords in common-practice tonal music: major seventh, minor seventh, major-minor seventh (dominant seventh), half-diminished seventh, and fully diminished seventh.

sharp: An accidental (♯) that raises a pitch a half step.

short score: A score that shows several parts combined on each staff.

similar motion: Contrapuntal, or voice-leading, motion in which both parts move in the same direction, but not by the same generic interval.

simple binary: A binary form that generally has an **𝄆 A 𝄇𝄆 B 𝄇 or 𝄆 A 𝄇𝄆 A′ 𝄇** design.

simple duple: Any meter with two beats in a measure, with each beat divided into two (e.g., $\frac{2}{4}$).

simple meter: Meter in which the beat divides into twos and subdivides into fours. The top number of the meter signature will be 2, 3, or 4 (e.g., $\frac{4}{8}$ or $\frac{3}{2}$).

simple quadruple: Any meter with four beats in a measure, with each beat divided into two (e.g., $\frac{4}{4}$).

simple ternary: A ternary form that is relatively brief (as opposed to composite ternary), with three distinct sections, usually in the form **A B A**. The **B** section generally expresses both a contrasting key and contrasting thematic material.

simple triple: Any meter with three beats in a measure, with each beat divided into two (e.g., $\frac{3}{4}$ or $\frac{3}{8}$).

sixteenth note: A stemmed black note head with two flags. In duple beat divisions, two sixteenths divide an eighth-note beat; in triple beat divisions, three sixteenths divide a dotted-eighth-note beat.

skip: A melodic interval of a third or fourth.

slur: An arc that connects two or more different pitches. Slurs affect articulation but not duration.

solfège, fixed-*do*: A singing system in which a particular syllable is associated with a particular pitch class; e.g., *do* is always C, *re* is always D, etc., no matter what the key.

solfège, movable-*do*: A singing system in which a particular syllable is associated with a particular scale step; e.g., *do* is always $\hat{1}$, *re* is always $\hat{2}$, etc., no matter what the key.

sonata: A multimovement composition for piano or a solo-line instrument (usually with keyboard accompaniment), typically in three or four movements. The first movement is almost always in sonata form.

sonata form: A formal plan with a three-part design (exposition, development, recapitulation) and a two-part harmonic structure (the most common is 𝄆 I–V 𝄇𝄆 → I 𝄇 for major keys, with motion to III instead of V in minor keys). Sonata form can be thought of as an expanded continuous rounded binary form.

sonatina: A "little sonata." The first movement of a sonatina is usually a reduced sonata form, with compact first and second themes and a very short development section or no development at all.

song cycle: A group of songs, generally performed as a unit, either set to a single poet's cycle of poetry or set to poems that have been grouped by the composer into a cycle.

soprano: The highest voice in four-part (SATB) writing.

sounding pitch: The pitch that is heard when a performer plays a note on an instrument. For transposing instruments, this differs from notated pitch. Also called concert pitch.

spacing: The arrangement of adjacent parts in four-part writing, in which vocal range and the intervals between voices are considered.

species: A particular type of counterpoint, used as a tool for teaching composition. The various species (types) of counterpoint differ by the embellishments permitted and the rhythmic relationship between the voices. See *first species* (1:1), *second species* (2:1), *third species* (4:1), *fourth species*, and *fifth species*.

split-third chord: A four-note "triad" with both a major and a minor third above the root.

staff: The five parallel lines on which music is written.

step: The melodic interval of a half or whole step.

step progression: A technique for writing compound melody, in which nonadjacent pitches are connected by an overall stepwise motion.

strain: In marches, the sections corresponding to the **A** and **B** portions of binary (or ternary) forms.

strophe: A stanza, or verse, in a song.

strophic: A song form in which more than one strophe (verse) of text is sung to the same music.

style juxtaposition: A method of composing in which elements strongly associated with one musical style are placed side-by-side with another style without a transition between the two.

stylistic allusion: A musical passage that either literally quotes another composition, or is written in imitation of a previous style, intended to be recognized by the listener as belonging to another time or piece.

subdivision: The third level of pulse in musical meter, after beat and division.

subdominant: (1) Scale degree $\hat{4}$. (2) The triad built on $\hat{4}$.

submediant: (1) Scale degree $\hat{6}$. (2) The triad built on $\hat{6}$.

subordinate theme (group): Another name for second theme (group).

subphrase: A melodic and harmonic unit smaller than a phrase. Subphrases complete only a portion of the basic phrase progression and do not conclude with a cadence.

subset: A subgroup of a given set.

substitute chord: A harmony that can stand for another. The most common are vi for I, ii for IV, and vii^{ø} for V.

subtonic: (1) Scale degree $\flat\hat{7}$ of the natural minor scale, so called because it is a whole step below tonic. (2) The triad built on $\flat\hat{7}$ of natural minor.

supertonic: (1) Scale degree $\hat{2}$. (2) The triad built on $\hat{2}$.

sus chord: In popular music, a chord with a fourth above the bass instead of a third. The fourth does not necessarily resolve, as in a typical 4–3 suspension.

suspension: A rhythmic embellishment where a consonance is held over to the next beat, creating a dissonance with the new harmony. The dissonance is resolved downward by step, creating another consonant interval. Suspensions are designated by intervals above the bass; the most common are 7–6, 4–3, and 9–8.

suspension chain: A combined succession of suspensions, sometimes of a single type (e.g., 4–3, 4–3) or alternations of two kinds (e.g., 7–6, 4–3, 7–6, 4–3); the resolution of each suspension prepares the next.

symmetrical meter: A meter with equally spaced primary beats within each measure, each beat having the same number of divisions.

symmetrical phrase: A phrase with an even number of measures.

symmetrical set: A set whose pcs can be ordered so that the intervals between adjacent elements are the same when read left to right or right to left. The pentatonic scale, whole-tone scale, octatonic scale, and chromatic collection are all symmetrical sets.

symmetry: Having the same pattern from start to middle as end to middle.

syncopation: Off-beat rhythmic accents created by dots, ties, rests, dynamic markings, or accent marks.

T

teleological form: Form that gives the listener a sense that the music moves toward a goal; usually associated with common-practice forms.

tempo: How fast or slow music is played. Examples of tempo markings include *adagio* (slow), *andante* (medium speed), and *allegro* (fast).

temporary tonic: The chord to which a secondary dominant or secondary leading-tone harmony is applied; also known as a "tonicized harmony."

tendency tone: A chord member or scale degree whose dissonant relation to the surrounding tones requires a particular resolution in common-practice style (i.e., chordal sevenths resolve down, and leading tones resolve up).

tenor: The second-lowest voice in four-part (SATB) writing. Usually directly above the bass.

tenor clef: A C-clef positioned on a staff so that the fourth line from the bottom indicates middle C (C4); typically read by bassoons, cellos, and tenor trombones in their higher registers.

ternary form: A composition divided into three sections. The outer sections usually consist of the same musical material, while the inner section features contrasting musical qualities (including key), creating an overall **A B A** form. In some song forms, the contrasting section may occur last (**A A B**).

tessitura: The vocal or instrumental range most used by a singer or instrumentalist.

tetrachord: (1) A collection of four distinct pitches or pitch classes. (2) A segment of four consecutive members of a scale.

text notation: A musical score with instructions written in prose or poetry, without any traditional musical notation.

textural variation: A variation written in a texture that contrasts with that of surrounding variations or the original theme. Two possibilities are (1) the simplifying variation, which features only a few voices, resulting in a thin texture; and (2) the contrapuntal variation, which features imitative entries of the voices.

theme and variations: A variation set based on a given theme, in which each variation differs in melody, rhythm, key, mode, length, texture, timbre, character, style, or motive. Theme and variation sets after the Baroque era are usually sectional variations, in which each variation could be considered a brief, stand-alone piece. See also *continuous variation*.

third inversion: A seventh chord voiced so that the chordal seventh is in the bass.

third species: Counterpoint written so that one voice has four notes for every single note in the other voice; allows consonances, passing tones, and neighboring tones, according to strict rules of voice-leading. Another name for 4:1 counterpoint.

thirty-second note: A stemmed black note head with three flags; equal in duration to two sixty-fourth notes.

thirty-two-bar song form: Another term for quaternary song form.

through composed: A composition organized so that each section (e.g., each verse in a song) consists of different music, with little or no previous material recurring as the work progresses.

tie: A small arc connecting the note heads of two (or more) identical pitches, adding the durations of the notes together.

timbral variation: A variation that exploits instrumentation and/or sound color different from previous variations.

time-line notation: Music written so that the passing of time is measured out in the number of seconds elapsed between markers.

time points: Locations in a score indicating a musical event; determined by a duration series, a numerical pattern, chance, or a series of proportions.

time signature: Another term for meter signature.

tonal answer: The modified transposition of a fugue subject up a fifth or down a fourth.

tonal music: Music based on the following organizational conventions: (1) melodies built from major and minor scales using scale-degree function, in relation to a tonic (e.g., $\hat{7}$ resolving to $\hat{1}$); (2) harmonies that relate to each other in functional progressions leading toward a tonic harmony; (3) identifiable embellishing tones (dissonant suspensions, neighbors, passing tones) that resolve (or imply a resolution).

tonal plan: The progression of keys in a composition.

tonic: (1) Scale degree $\hat{1}$. (2) The triad built on $\hat{1}$.

tonic area: Usually the opening and closing area in a basic phrase (T–PD–D–T).

tonic closure: A conclusive ending that confirms the key of a musical passage, usually accomplished by means of an authentic cadence.

tonic expansion: An extension of tonic function effected by means of contrapuntal motion and voice-leading chords.

tonic substitute: A chord other than tonic (most often the submediant) that fulfills tonic function in the basic phrase model.

tonicization: The result when a chord becomes a temporary tonic by means of a secondary, or applied, dominant. The key of the passage does not really change, and the temporary tonic soon returns to its normal functional role in the primary key.

total serialism: The extension of serial procedures to musical elements other than pitch. Also called integral serialism.

transferred resolution: The movement of a tendency tone from one voice part to another prior to resolution.

transition: A musical passage that modulates from one key and establishes another, often by means of sequential treatment. In sonata form, the transition links the first and second theme groups.

transpose: (1) To notate a score for transposing instruments so that pitches will sound correctly in the concert key. (2) To rewrite a section of music at a different pitch level. (3) To add or subtract a constant to pitches or pitch classes in integer notation.

transposed score: A score that shows the pitches as notated in the performers' parts (which may be transposed for certain instruments), rather than the sounding pitches.

transposing instrument: An instrument (e.g., clarinet, saxophone, or horn) whose notated pitches are not the same as the pitches that sound when played.

transposition (row): The form of a twelve-tone row derived by transposing the prime. Abbreviated P_n, where n is the pc integer of the row's first element.

transpositional equivalence: The relationship between two sets such that each one can be transposed to make the other.

treble clef: On a staff, the treble clef (also known as G-clef) denotes the line for G4, by means of the end of its curving line; typically read by flutes, clarinets, oboes, horns, sopranos, altos, and piano right hand.

triad: A chord made from two stacked thirds.

triad quality: The description of a triad according to the quality of its stacked thirds and fifth: major, minor, diminished, or augmented.

trichord: A collection of three distinct pitches or pitch classes.

triple meter: Meter in which beats group into units of three (e.g., $\frac{3}{2}$ or $\frac{9}{8}$).

triplet: In simple meters, a division group borrowed from compound meters.

tritone: An interval made up of three whole tones or six semitones: an augmented fourth or diminished fifth. By some definitions, only an augmented fourth is a tritone, since in this spelling the interval spans three whole steps.

tritone axis: Music (in nontonal pieces) that moves from a first pitch center to a second pitch center a tritone away, and then returns; analogous to the tonic-dominant axis in tonal music.

twelve-tone: Music with a specific ordering of all twelve pitch classes, called a row. The row is musically realized by means of transformations (transposition, inversion, retrograde, or retrograde inversion) throughout a composition.

U

unequal fifths: Similar motion from a d5 to P5 or P5 to d5. d5 to P5 is prohibited in strict counterpoint, but allowable in some situations in four-part writing if not placed in the outer voices.

unison: The interval size 1, or the distance from a pitch to itself; interval 0 if measured in semitones.

upbeat: Occurs when a melody starts just before the first strong beat in a meter; named for the upward lift of the conductor's hand. Another word for anacrusis.

V

verse: (1) The section of a song that returns with the same music but different text. (2) In popular song forms, the first section of verse-refrain form; the verse is usually not repeated, and it may be tonally less stable than the refrain.

verse-refrain form: A typical form of popular songs and show tunes: an introductory verse, possibly modulatory, precedes a chorus that is often in quaternary song form (**a a b a**).

vocal range: The range of pitches (high and low) that may be sung comfortably by singers of a particular voice type (e.g., alto or tenor).

voice crossing: In four-part writing, one voice written higher than the part above it or lower than the part below it; considered poor voice-leading in common-practice SATB style.

voice exchange: The expansion of a functional area in which two voices exchange chord members (e.g., $\hat{1}$ moves to $\hat{3}$ in the bass, and $\hat{3}$ moves to $\hat{1}$ in the soprano). This skip is often filled in with a passing tone or passing chord.

voice-leading: The combination of melodic lines to create harmonies according to principles of common-practice harmony and counterpoint.

voice-leading chord: A "chord" created by combining embellishing tones in the expansion of a structural harmony. In analysis, label the individual embellishments rather than the chord, or label the chord as "voice-leading" (VL) or as a passing or neighboring chord.

W

whole note: A stemless open note head; equal in duration to two half notes.

whole step: The combination of two adjacent half steps.

whole-tone scale: An ordered collection of pcs arranged so that each scale step lies a whole step away from the next. A whole-tone scale consists of six elements and exists in two distinct forms: pcs {0 2 4 6 8 t} and {1 3 5 7 9 e}.

APPENDIX 3

Guidelines for Part-Writing

Contents

I. Vocal Ranges

Typical ranges for common-practice SATB writing:

- Soprano: C4 to G5
- Alto: G3 to D5
- Tenor: C3 to G4
- Bass: E2 to D4

II. Doubling Guidelines

- If the triad is in *root position* (and major or minor quality), double the root. Sometimes you double the third or fifth, but these doublings are much less common.
- If the triad is in *first inversion*, double any chord member that is not a tendency tone or other altered tone. Doubling the soprano is a common strategy (for major or minor triads only).
- If the triad is in *second inversion*, double the fifth (the bass).
- Never double a tendency tone. This guideline applies most frequently to the leading tone ($\hat{7}$) and to the seventh of the dominant seventh chord ($\hat{4}$), but includes any tone that must be resolved, such as a chromatic passing tone or altered tone.
- For *diminished triads* (which typically appear in first inversion), double the third. Doubling the root emphasizes the dissonance and causes voice-leading problems. Occasionally, the fifth may be doubled.
- For N^6 *chords*, double the bass (the third of the chord).
- For It^6 *chords*, double $\hat{1}$.

III. Spacing Guidelines

When writing SATB parts, check to see that

- the interval between soprano and alto, and the interval between alto and tenor, is an octave or less;
- the interval between the tenor and bass line usually remains within a tenth;
- no alto pitch is higher than soprano or lower than tenor;
- no tenor pitch is higher than alto or lower than bass.

IV. General Voice-Leading Guidelines

A. Work to achieve smooth voice-leading:

- Resolve tendency tones correctly, and never double them.

- Move each voice to the closest possible member of the following chord (without creating parallel perfect intervals or errors in doubling or spacing).
- Avoid skipping down to a chordal seventh.
- If two chords share a common tone, keep the common tone in the same voice.

B. Aim for independence of the four voices based on principles of good counterpoint:

- Keep each voice within its own characteristic range.
- Write the soprano-bass counterpoint first before filling in the inner voices.
- Avoid moving all four voices in the same direction.
- Avoid placing a pitch in one voice part so that it crosses above or below the pitch sung by an adjacent voice part—either within a single chord (voice crossing) or between two consecutive chords (overlapping).
- Avoid prolonged parallel or similar motion; balance with contrary and oblique motion.

C. Make each voice a "singable" melody:

- Write primarily stepwise motion or chordal skips, with few large leaps (except bass leaps between chord members).
- Avoid melodic motion by augmented or diminished intervals (e.g., the augmented second between scale degrees $\flat\hat{6}$ and $\hat{7}$ in harmonic minor).
- Use passing or neighboring tones to create a smooth line or add melodic interest.

D. Pay careful attention to voice-leading to and from perfect intervals:

- Choose contrary or oblique motion when you approach and leave any perfect interval (unison, octave, fifth), since parallel perfect intervals are prohibited in this style.
- Do not use
  (1) direct octaves or fifths (similar motion into a perfect interval in the soprano-bass pair)—these are permitted only in inner voices or if the soprano moves by step;
  (2) contrary octaves or fifths (contrary motion from one perfect interval to another of the same size);
  (3) unequal fifths (motion from a diminished fifth to a perfect fifth, especially in the soprano-bass pair), since they interfere with proper resolution of the tendency tones ($\hat{7}$ resolving up to $\hat{1}$ and $\hat{4}$ resolving down to $\hat{3}$); motion from a perfect fifth to a diminished fifth is acceptable.

E. Keep in mind typical voice-leading based on root progressions:

- Roots a fifth apart: hold the common tone in the same voice, and move all the other parts to the closest possible chord member.
- Roots a third apart: hold the common tones, and move the other part to the closest possible chord member.
- Roots a second apart: move the upper parts in contrary motion to the bass line.

F. Remember to write musically:

- When a harmony is repeated, create some variety by changing the soprano pitch, the inversion, and/or the spacing of the chord.
- Where possible, avoid static or repetitive melodic lines.

V. Realizing Figured Bass

- Sing the given line(s) to help orient yourself tonally.
- Place pitches above the bass in an appropriate octave according to the generic intervals written in the figured bass.
- Use pitches diatonic in the key, unless indicated otherwise by the bass or figures.
- An accidental next to a number means to raise or lower the pitch associated with that number by one half step.
- An accidental by itself means to raise or lower the third *above the bass* (not necessarily the third of the chord).
- A slash through a number means to raise the pitch associated with that number.

- Accidentals in the figure apply only to that single chord.
- A figured bass does not list all intervals above the bass; some, like octaves and thirds, may be implied by the figures.
- Follow all doubling and voice-leading guidelines when voicing or connecting chords.
- A dash between two numbers means that those intervals belong in the same voice-leading strand (like a suspension: 4–3).
- Melodic embellishing tones (other than suspensions) are not shown in the figures because they are not a part of the main harmonic framework.

VI. Voice-Leading Considerations for Specific Harmonies

A. When resolving V7 to I (or i):

- Two tendency tones resolve at once.
- The chordal seventh moves down ($\hat{4}$ moves to $\hat{3}$), and
- the leading tone resolves up by half step ($\hat{7}$ resolves to $\hat{1}$).
- When both chords are in root position, either the V7 or I will be incomplete (lacking the fifth) to avoid parallels.
- At a cadence, $\hat{7}$ in an inner voice may leap to $\hat{5}$ to complete the tonic triad.
- The same rules apply when resolving secondary dominant chords, except that scale-degree numbers refer to the "temporary" tonic.

B. When resolving the leading-tone triad or seventh chord:

- If the tritone is spelled as a diminished fifth ($\hat{7}$ below $\hat{4}$), it normally resolves inward to a third: $\hat{1}$-$\hat{3}$.
- If the tritone is spelled as an augmented fourth ($\hat{4}$ below $\hat{7}$), it may follow the voice-leading of the tendency tones and resolve outward to a sixth, or it may move in similar motion to a perfect fourth ($\hat{5}$-$\hat{1}$).
- When the tritone is spelled as a diminished fifth, resolve $\hat{4}$ up to $\hat{5}$ in only one context: when the soprano-bass counterpoint moves upward in parallel tenths ($\hat{2}$ to $\hat{3}$ in the bass, $\hat{4}$ to $\hat{5}$ in the soprano). The strength of the parallel motion in this contrapuntal pattern overrides the voice-leading tendency of $\hat{4}$ to resolve down.
- Resolve the tendency tones of vii^{ø7} and vii^{o7} like V7: resolve $\hat{7}$ up to $\hat{1}$, resolve $\hat{4}$ down to $\hat{3}$, and resolve the chordal seventh down ($\hat{6}$ to $\hat{5}$).
- The same rules apply when resolving secondary leading-tone chords, except that scale-degree numbers refer to the "temporary" tonic.

C. When writing a cadential $^6_4$:

Always double the bass.

- Hold the common tones between the chord of approach and the $^6_4$, and move other voices the shortest distance.
- Write the cadential $^6_4$ on a strong beat in the measure; it displaces the V or V7 to a weaker beat.
- Resolve the "suspended" tones of the $^6_4$ downward: the sixth above the bass moves to a fifth, and the fourth above the bass moves to a third.
- If there is a seventh in the dominant harmony that follows the cadential $^6_4$, the doubled bass note (an octave above the bass) usually moves to the seventh of the dominant seventh chord.

D. When writing other types of $^6_4$s:

- Each second-inversion triad will be one of the following types: cadential $^6_4$, passing $^6_4$, neighboring (or pedal) $^6_4$, or arpeggiating $^6_4$.
- Always double the bass (fifth) of the chord.
- In all $^6_4$s except arpeggiating (which are consonant), all voices should approach and leave chord members by step (forming neighbor or passing tones) or by common tone.
- Arpeggiating $^6_4$s may include skips within members of the chord that is arpeggiated, but must resolve correctly to the next harmony.

E. When writing N6 chords:

- Use the Neapolitan harmony most often in minor keys. Build it on $\flat\hat{2}$ with a major quality, and (usually) in first inversion ($\flat$II^6). In major keys, be sure to include ♭$\hat{6}$ (from mixture) to ensure the chord's major quality.

- Precede the Neapolitan with any harmony that would normally precede a predominant-function harmony: e.g., I, VI, iv^6, a string of parallel $^6_3$ chords.
- Double $\hat{4}$ (the bass note, when the harmony appears in its characteristic first inversion). If ♭$\hat{2}$ is doubled, it may move to ♮$\hat{2}$ in an inner voice only—never in the soprano.
- Place the N^6 in a predominant role and resolve it to V, with both its tendency tones moving down: (♭)$\hat{6}$ to $\hat{5}$, and ♭$\hat{2}$ (usually through the passing-tone $\hat{1}$) to $\hat{7}$. Note: Don't resolve ♭$\hat{2}$ to ♮$\hat{2}$ (unless it has been doubled in an inner voice), since this voice-leading conflicts with the tendency of ♭$\hat{2}$ to move downward.
- If you harmonize the passing-tone $\hat{1}$ when resolving the N^6, choose vii$^{\circ 7}$/V or V$^{6-5}_{4-3}$.
- Typically, ♭$\hat{2}$ or $\hat{4}$ appears in the highest voice. Don't place (♭)$\hat{6}$ in the highest voice if the N^6 moves through a tonic chord before progressing to V, because the resolution of (♭)$\hat{6}$–$\hat{5}$ above ♭$\hat{2}$–$\hat{1}$ invariably leads to parallel fifths in the voice-leading.

F. When writing augmented-sixth chords:

- Place $\hat{5}$ of the V chord (the chord of resolution) in the bass and an upper voice (the soprano is a characteristic but not required voicing), leaving an empty space before it for the augmented sixth.
- In the empty space, write in the two tendency tones leading by half step to $\hat{5}$: (♭)$\hat{6}$–$\hat{5}$ in the bass, and (♯)$\hat{4}$–$\hat{5}$ in the upper voice. In major keys, don't forget to add the correct accidental to lower $\hat{6}$.
- Add $\hat{1}$ in one of the inner voices.
- Add a fourth note, following these guidelines.
  (1) Italian 6 (It^6): double $\hat{1}$;
  (2) French 6 (Fr^6): add $\hat{2}$ (an augmented fourth above the bass note);
  (3) German 6 (Gr^6): add $\hat{3}$ from the minor mode (a perfect fifth above the bass note—in major keys, you will need to add an accidental).
- Resolve the tendency tones by half step to $\hat{5}$, and move the remaining tones to the closest possible chord tone in the dominant harmony.
- Resolve an It^6 or a Fr^6 directly to V; Gr^6 chords often resolve to V$^{6-5}_{4-3}$ to avoid parallel fifths.

APPENDIX 4

Ranges of Orchestral Instruments

INSTRUMENT	WRITTEN RANGE	SOUNDING RANGE
Strings		
Violin	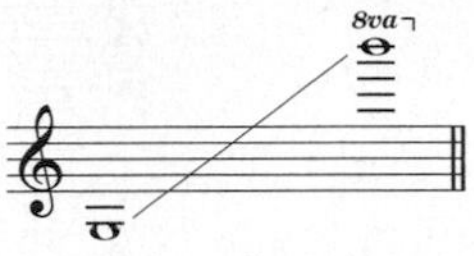	as written
Viola		as written
Cello		as written
Bass		octave lower
Harp	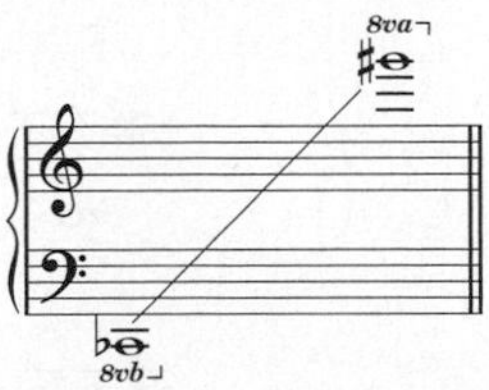	as written
Guitar	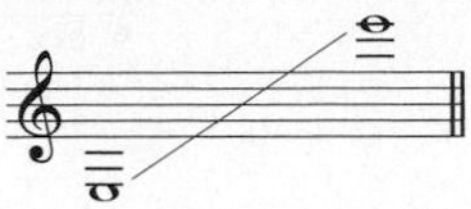	octave lower
Banjo		as written, but tenor banjo sounds an octave lower

SOURCE: Samuel Adler, *The Study of Orchestration*, 3rd ed. (New York: Norton, 2002)

INSTRUMENT	WRITTEN RANGE	SOUNDING RANGE
Woodwinds		
Piccolo	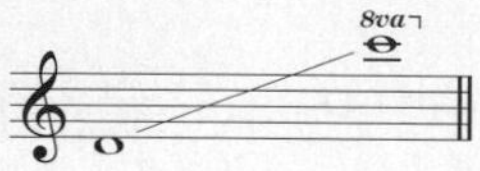	octave higher
Flute	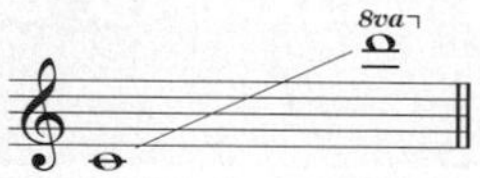	as written
Oboe	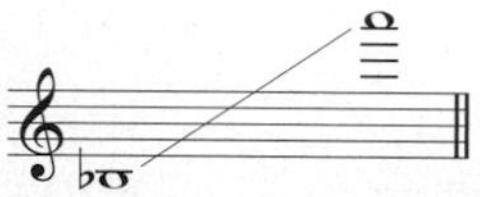	as written
English horn	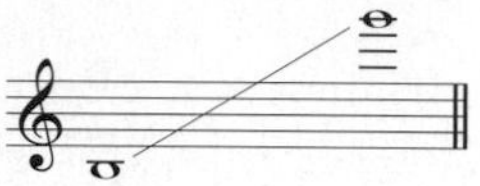	perfect fifth lower
All clarinets except bass	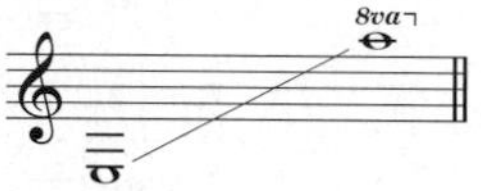	B♭: major second lower A: minor third lower D: major second higher E♭: minor third higher E♭ alto: major sixth lower
Bass clarinet	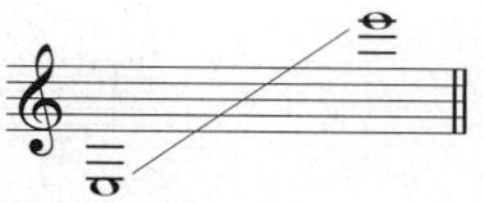	major ninth lower; if written in bass clef, major second lower
Bassoon	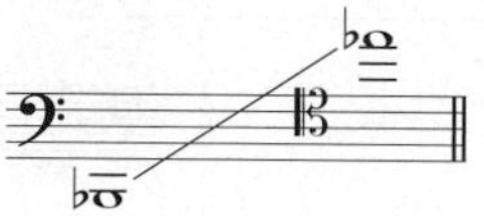	as written
Contrabassoon	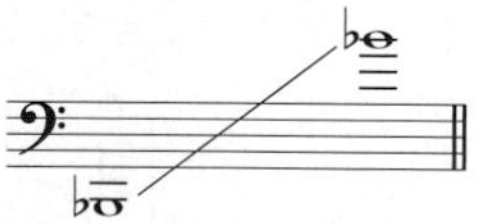	octave lower
All saxophones	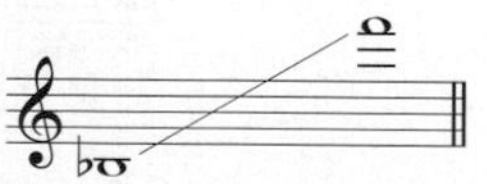	B♭ soprano: major second lower E♭ alto: major sixth lower B♭ tenor: major ninth lower E♭ baritone: octave plus major sixth lower B♭ bass: two octaves plus a major second lower

INSTRUMENT	WRITTEN RANGE	SOUNDING RANGE
Brass		
Horn (plus pedal notes)	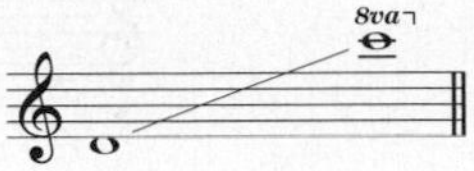	perfect fifth lower
All trumpets except E♭ and D bass	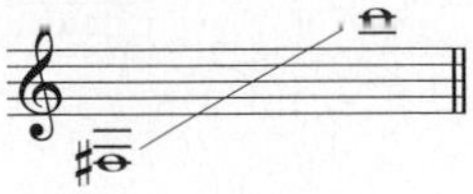	C: as written B♭: major second lower D: major second higher E♭: minor third higher B♭ cornet: major second lower C bass: octave lower B♭ bass: major ninth lower
E♭ and D bass trumpets	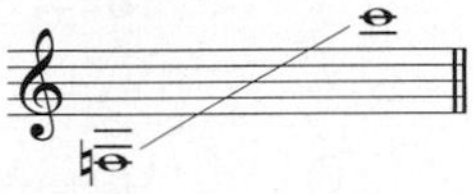	E♭: major sixth lower D: minor seventh lower
Tenor trombone	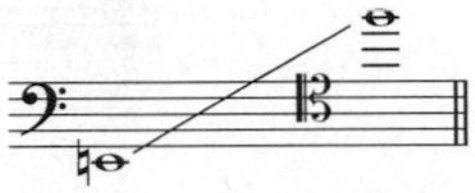	as written
Bass trombone	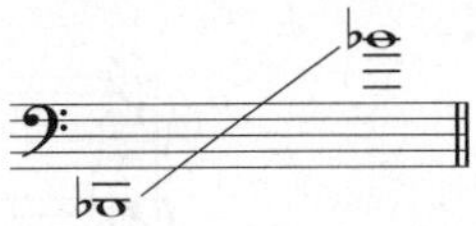	as written
Alto trombone	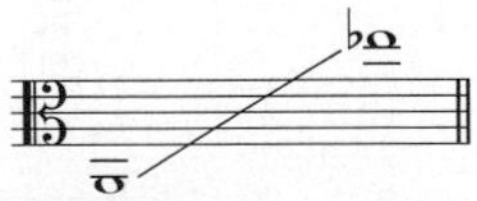	as written
Tuba	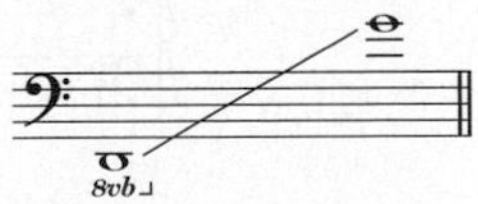	as written
Euphonium	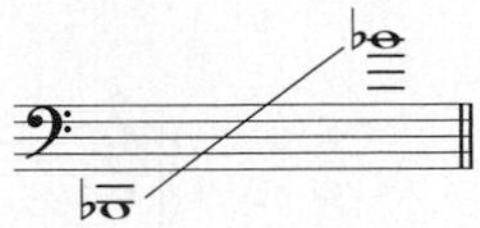	as written; if notated in treble clef, major ninth lower
Baritone	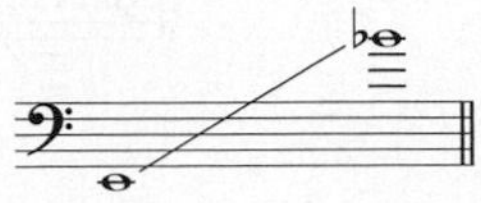	as written; if notated in treble clef, major ninth lower
Percussion		
Timpani	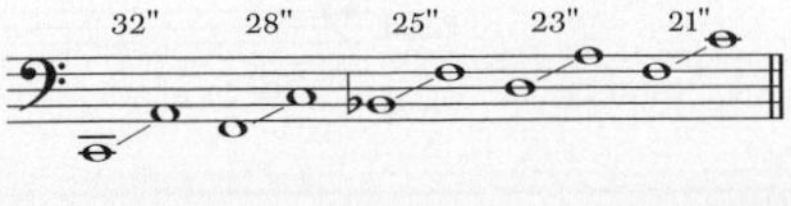	as written

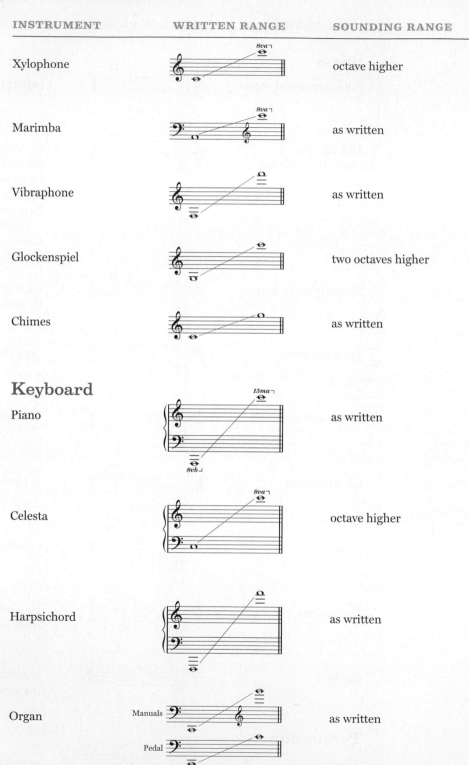

INSTRUMENT	WRITTEN RANGE	SOUNDING RANGE
Xylophone	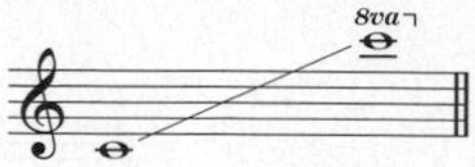	octave higher
Marimba		as written
Vibraphone	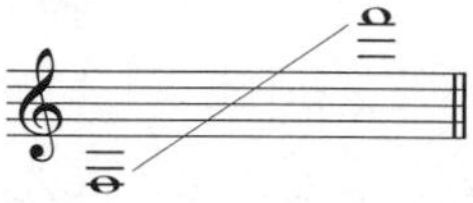	as written
Glockenspiel	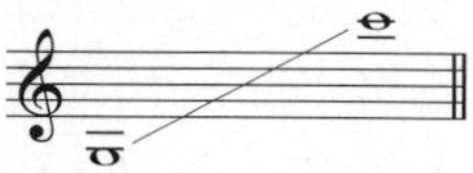	two octaves higher
Chimes	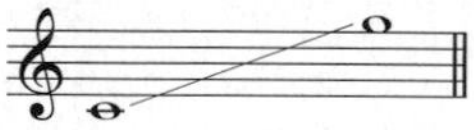	as written

Keyboard

INSTRUMENT	WRITTEN RANGE	SOUNDING RANGE
Piano	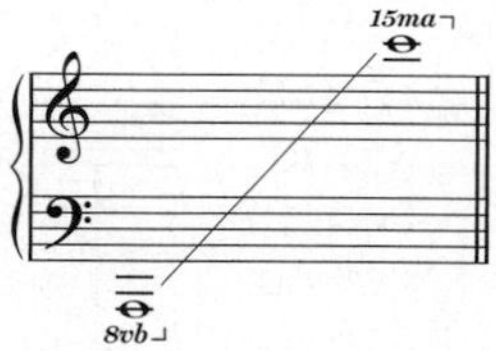	as written
Celesta	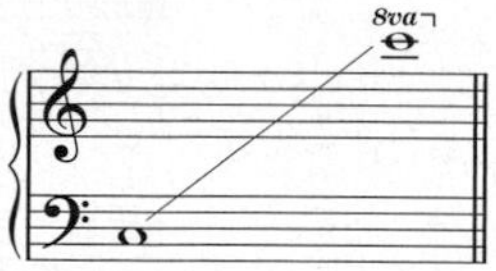	octave higher
Harpsichord		as written
Organ		as written

APPENDIX 5

Set-Class Table

NAME	PCS	IC VECTOR
3-1(12)	0,1,2	210000
3-2	0,1,3	111000
3-3	0,1,4	101100
3-4	0,1,5	100110
3-5	0,1,6	100011
3-6(12)	0,2,4	020100
3-7	0,2,5	011010
3-8	0,2,6	010101
3-9(12)	0,2,7	010020
3-10(12)	0,3,6	002001
3-11	0,3,7	001110
3-12(4)	0,4,8	000300
4-1(12)	0,1,2,3	321000
4-2	0,1,2,4	221100
4-3(12)	0,1,3,4	212100
4-4	0,1,2,5	211110
4-5	0,1,2,6	210111
4-6(12)	0,1,2,7	210021
4-7(12)	0,1,4,5	201210
4-8(12)	0,1,5,6	200121
4-9(6)	0,1,6,7	200022
4-10(12)	0,2,3,5	122010
4-11	0,1,3,5	121110
4-12	0,2,3,6	112101
4-13	0,1,3,6	112011
4-14	0,2,3,7	111120
4-Z15	0,1,4,6	111111
4-16	0,1,5,7	110121
4-17(12)	0,3,4,7	102210
4-18	0,1,4,7	102111
4-19	0,1,4,8	101310

NAME	PCS	IC VECTOR
9-1	0,1,2,3,4,5,6,7,8	876663
9-2	0,1,2,3,4,5,6,7,9	777663
9-3	0,1,2,3,4,5,6,8,9	767763
9-4	0,1,2,3,4,5,7,8,9	766773
9-5	0,1,2,3,4,6,7,8,9	766674
9-6	0,1,2,3,4,5,6,8,t	686763
9-7	0,1,2,3,4,5,7,8,t	677673
9-8	0,1,2,3,4,6,7,8,t	676764
9-9	0,1,2,3,5,6,7,8,t	676683
9-10	0,1,2,3,4,6,7,9,t	668664
9-11	0,1,2,3,5,6,7,9,t	667773
9-12	0,1,2,4,5,6,8,9,t	666963
8-1	0,1,2,3,4,5,6,7	765442
8-2	0,1,2,3,4,5,6,8	665542
8-3	0,1,2,3,4,5,6,9	656542
8-4	0,1,2,3,4,5,7,8	655552
8-5	0,1,2,3,4,6,7,8	654553
8-6	0,1,2,3,5,6,7,8	654463
8-7	0,1,2,3,4,5,8,9	645652
8-8	0,1,2,3,4,7,8,9	644563
8-9	0,1,2,3,6,7,8,9	644464
8-10	0,2,3,4,5,6,7,9	566452
8-11	0,1,2,3,4,5,7,9	565552
8-12	0,1,3,4,5,6,7,9	556543
8-13	0,1,2,3,4,6,7,9	556453
8-14	0,1,2,4,5,6,7,9	555562
8-Z15	0,1,2,3,4,6,8,9	555553
8-16	0,1,2,3,5,7,8,9	554563
8-17	0,1,3,4,5,6,8,9	546652
8-18	0,1,2,3,5,6,8,9	546553
8-19	0,1,2,4,5,6,8,9	545752

NOTE: Numbers in parentheses show the number of distinct sets in the set class if other than 48. All brackets are eliminated here for ease of reading.

NAME	PCS	IC VECTOR	NAME	PCS	IC VECTOR
4-20(12)	0,1,5,8	101220	8-20	0,1,2,4,5,7,8,9	545662
4-21(12)	0,2,4,6	030201	8-21	0,1,2,3,4,6,8,t	474643
4-22	0,2,4,7	021120	8-22	0,1,2,3,5,6,8,t	465562
4-23(12)	0,2,5,7	021030	8-23	0,1,2,3,5,7,8,t	465472
4-24(12)	0,2,4,8	020301	8-24	0,1,2,4,5,6,8,t	464743
4-25(6)	0,2,6,8	020202	8-25	0,1,2,4,6,7,8,t	464644
4-26(12)	0,3,5,8	012120	8-26	0,1,2,4,5,7,9,t	456562
4-27	0,2,5,8	012111	8-27	0,1,2,4,5,7,8,t	456553
4-28(3)	0,3,6,9	004002	8-28	0,1,3,4,6,7,9,t	448444
4-Z29	0,1,3,7	111111	8-Z29	0,1,2,3,5,6,7,9	555553
5-1(12)	0,1,2,3,4	432100	7-1	0,1,2,3,4,5,6	654321
5-2	0,1,2,3,5	332110	7-2	0,1,2,3,4,5,7	554331
5-3	0,1,2,4,5	322210	7-3	0,1,2,3,4,5,8	544431
5-4	0,1,2,3,6	322111	7-4	0,1,2,3,4,6,7	544332
5-5	0,1,2,3,7	321121	7-5	0,1,2,3,5,6,7	543342
5-6	0,1,2,5,6	311221	7-6	0,1,2,3,4,7,8	533442
5-7	0,1,2,6,7	310132	7-7	0,1,2,3,6,7,8	532353
5-8(12)	0,2,3,4,6	232201	7-8	0,2,3,4,5,6,8	454422
5-9	0,1,2,4,6	231211	7-9	0,1,2,3,4,6,8	453432
5-10	0,1,3,4,6	223111	7-10	0,1,2,3,4,6,9	445332
5-11	0,2,3,4,7	222220	7-11	0,1,3,4,5,6,8	444441
5-Z12(12)	0,1,3,5,6	222121	7-Z12	0,1,2,3,4,7,9	444342
5-13	0,1,2,4,8	221311	7-13	0,1,2,4,5,6,8	443532
5-14	0,1,2,5,7	221131	7-14	0,1,2,3,5,7,8	443352
5-15(12)	0,1,2,6,8	220222	7-15	0,1,2,4,6,7,8	442443
5-16	0,1,3,4,7	213211	7-16	0,1,2,3,5,6,9	435432
5-Z17(12)	0,1,3,4,8	212320	7-Z17	0,1,2,4,5,6,9	434541
5-Z18	0,1,4,5,7	212221	7-Z18	0,1,2,3,5,8,9	434442
5-19	0,1,3,6,7	212122	7-19	0,1,2,3,6,7,9	434343
5-20	0,1,3,7,8	211231	7-20	0,1,2,4,7,8,9	433452
5-21	0,1,4,5,8	202420	7-21	0,1,2,4,5,8,9	424641
5-22(12)	0,1,4,7,8	202321	7-22	0,1,2,5,6,8,9	424542
5-23	0,2,3,5,7	132130	7-23	0,2,3,4,5,7,9	354351
5-24	0,1,3,5,7	131221	7-24	0,1,2,3,5,7,9	353442
5-25	0,2,3,5,8	123121	7-25	0,2,3,4,6,7,9	345342
5-26	0,2,4,5,8	122311	7-26	0,1,3,4,5,7,9	344532
5-27	0,1,3,5,8	122230	7-27	0,1,2,4,5,7,9	344451
5-28	0,2,3,6,8	122212	7-28	0,1,3,5,6,7,9	344433
5-29	0,1,3,6,8	122131	7-29	0,1,2,4,6,7,9	344352
5-30	0,1,4,6,8	121321	7-30	0,1,2,4,6,8,9	343542
5-31	0,1,3,6,9	114112	7-31	0,1,3,4,6,7,9	336333
5-32	0,1,4,6,9	113221	7-32	0,1,3,4,6,8,9	335442
5-33(12)	0,2,4,6,8	040402	7-33	0,1,2,4,6,8,t	262623
5-34(12)	0,2,4,6,9	032221	7-34	0,1,3,4,6,8,t	254442
5-35(12)	0,2,4,7,9	032140	7-35	0,1,3,5,6,8,t	254361

NAME	PCS	IC VECTOR	NAME	PCS	IC VECTOR
5-Z36	0,1,2,4,7	222121	7-Z36	0,1,2,3,5,6,8	444342
5-Z37(12)	0,3,4,5,8	212320	7-Z37	0,1,3,4,5,7,8	434541
5-Z38	0,1,2,5,8	212221	7-Z38	0,1,2,4,5,7,8	434442
6-1(12)	0,1,2,3,4,5	543210			
6-2	0,1,2,3,4,6	443211			
6-Z3	0,1,2,3,5,6	433221	6-Z36	0,1,2,3,4,7	*
6-Z4(12)	0,1,2,4,5,6	432321	6-Z37(12)	0,1,2,3,4,8	
6-5	0,1,2,3,6,7	422232			
6-Z6(12)	0,1,2,5,6,7	421242	6-Z38(12)	0,1,2,3,7,8	
6-7(6)	0,1,2,6,7,8	420243			
6-8(12)	0,2,3,4,5,7	343230			
6-9	0,1,2,3,5,7	342231			
6-Z10	0,1,3,4,5,7	333321	6-Z39	0,2,3,4,5,8	
6-Z11	0,1,2,4,5,7	333231	6-Z40	0,1,2,3,5,8	
6-Z12	0,1,2,4,6,7	332232	6-Z41	0,1,2,3,6,8	
6-Z13(12)	0,1,3,4,6,7	324222	6-Z42(12)	0,1,2,3,6,9	
6-14	0,1,3,4,5,8	323430			
6-15	0,1,2,4,5,8	323421			
6-16	0,1,4,5,6,8	322431			
6-Z17	0,1,2,4,7,8	322332	6-Z43	0,1,2,5,6,8	
6-18	0,1,2,5,7,8	322242			
6-Z19	0,1,3,4,7,8	313431	6-Z44	0,1,2,5,6,9	
6-20(4)	0,1,4,5,8,9	303630			
6-21	0,2,3,4,6,8	242412			
6-22	0,1,2,4,6,8	241422			
6-Z23(12)	0,2,3,5,6,8	234222	6-Z45(12)	0,2,3,4,6,9	
6-Z24	0,1,3,4,6,8	233331	6-Z46	0,1,2,4,6,9	
6-Z25	0,1,3,5,6,8	233241	6-Z47	0,1,2,4,7,9	
6-Z26(12)	0,1,3,5,7,8	232341	6-Z48(12)	0,1,2,5,7,9	
6-27	0,1,3,4,6,9	225222			
6-Z28(12)	0,1,3,5,6,9	224322	6-Z49(12)	0,1,3,4,7,9	
6-Z29(12)	0,1,3,6,8,9	224232	6-Z50(12)	0,1,4,6,7,9	
6-30(12)	0,1,3,6,7,9	224223			
6-31	0,1,3,5,8,9	223431			
6-32(12)	0,2,4,5,7,9	143250			
6-33	0,2,3,5,7,9	143241			
6-34	0,1,3,5,7,9	142422			
6-35(2)	0,2,4,6,8,t	060603			

*Z-related hexachords share the same ic vector; use vector in the third column.

SOURCE: Allen Forte, *The Structure of Atonal Music* (New Haven: Yale University Press, 1973) (adapted)

Credits

Béla Bartók, "Bulgarian Rhythm," from *Mikrokosmos*, SZ107, No. 115. © Copyright 1940 by Hawkes & Son London Ltd. Reprinted by permission of Boosey & Hawkes Inc. **Béla Bartók, "Five-Tone Scale," from *Mikrokosmos*, SZ107, No. 78.** © Copyright 1940 by Hawkes & Son London Ltd. Reprinted by permission of Boosey & Hawkes Inc. **Béla Bartók, *Mikrokosmos*.** Published by Boosey & Hawkes Inc. **Béla Bartók, Sonata for Two Pianos and Percussion.** Published by Boosey & Hawkes Inc. **Béla Bartók, "Song of the Harvest," from *44 Duos*.** © Copyright 1933 by Boosey & Hawkes Inc. for the U.S.A. Copyright renewed. Reprinted by permission of Boosey & Hawkes Inc. **Béla Bartók, "Song of the Harvest," from *44 Duos*.** © 1933 by Universal Edition AG, Wien/UE 10452A/B. © Renewed 1960 by Boosey & Hawkes Inc., New York. All rights reserved. Used in the world excluding the U.S. by permission of European American Music Distributors LLC, U.S. and Canadian agent for Universal Edition AG, Wien. **Count Basie, "Splanky."** By Neal Hefti. © 1958 (renewed) WB Music Corp. Used by permission of Alfred Music Publishing Co. Inc. All rights reserved. **Beach Boys, "Help Me Rhonda."** Published by Hal Leonard Corporation. **Luciano Berio, *Sequenza III*, for voice.** Published by Universal Edition (London) Ltd. **Bono and U2, "Miracle Drug."** Published by Hal Leonard Corporation. **Pierre Boulez, *Structures (premier livre)*.** © 1955 by Universal Edition (London) Ltd., London/UE 12267. © Renewed. All rights reserved. Used by permission of European American Music Distributors LLC, U.S. and Canadian agent for Universal Edition (London) Ltd., London. **John Cage, *4'33"*.** Copyright © 1960 by Henmar Press Inc. (C. F. Peters Corporation). **Elliott Carter, String Quartet No. 2.** Copyright © 1961 (renewed) by Associated Music Publishers Inc. (BMI). International copyright secured. All rights reserved. Used by permission. **John Barnes Chance, *Variations on a Korean Folk Song*.** © Copyright 1967 by Boosey & Hawkes Inc. Copyright renewed. Reprinted by permission of Boosey & Hawkes Inc. **Jeremiah Clarke, *Trumpet Voluntary*.** Music: Sue Mitchell-Wallace & John Head. © 1988 Hope Publishing Company, Carol Stream, IL 60188. All rights reserved. Used by permission. **Aaron Copland, "Simple Gifts," from *Appalachian Spring*.** Published by Boosey & Hawkes Inc. **Archangelo Corelli, Sonata in D Minor, Op. 4, No. 8.** Edited by Walter Kolneder. © 1955 by Schott Music Ltd., London. © Renewed 1983, assigned to Schott Music, Mainz, Germany. All rights reserved. Used by permission of European American Music Distributors LLC, sole U.S. and Canadian agent for Schott Music, Mainz, Germany. **John Corigliano, "Come Now, My Darling."** Words by William Hoffman. Music by John Corigliano. Copyright © 1991 by G. Schirmer Inc. (ASCAP). International copyright secured. All rights reserved. Used by permission. **Luigi Dallapiccola, "Die Sonne kommt," from *Goethe-lieder*, for voice and clarinets.** © Sugarmusic S.p.A., Edizioni Suvini Zerboni, Milan (Italy). **George Gershwin and Ira Gershwin, "I Got Rhythm."** Music and Lyrics by George Gershwin and Ira Gershwin. © 1930 (renewed) WB Music Corp. Gershwin® and George Gershwin® are registered trademarks of Gershwin Enterprises. Ira Gershwin™ is a trademark of Gershwin Enterprises. Used by permission of Alfred Music Publishing Co. Inc. All rights reserved. **George Gershwin and Ira Gershwin "'S Wonderful."** Music and Lyrics by George Gershwin and Ira Gershwin. © 1927 (renewed) WB Music Corp. Gershwin® and George Gershwin® are registered trademarks of Gershwin Enterprises. Ira Gershwin™ is a trademark of Gershwin Enterprises. Used by Permission of Alfred Music Publishing Co. Inc. All rights reserved. **Gerry Goffin and Michael Masser, "Saving All My Love for You."** Published by Hal Leonard Corporation. **Gordy, Davis, Hutch, and West, "I'll Be There."** Published by Hal Leonard Corporation. **Fanny Mendelssohn Hensel, "Nachtwanderer."** © 1994 by Breitkopf & Härtel, Wiesbaden. **Fanny Mendelssohn Hensel, "Neue Liebe, Neues Leben."** Edited by Eva Rieger and Kaete Walter. © 1985 Schott Music, Mainz, Germany. All rights reserved. Used by permission of European American Music Distributors LLC, sole U.S. and Canadian agent for Schott Music, Mainz, Germany. **Edward Heyman and Victor Young,** "When I Fall in Love." Published by Hal Leonard Corporation. **Horner, Mann, and Weil, "Somewhere Out There."** Published by Leonard Corporation. **Jerome Kern and Oscar Hammerstein, "All the Things You Are," from *Very Warm for May*.** Published by Hal Leonard Corporation. **Jerome Kern and Oscar Hammerstein, "Can't Help Lovin' Dat Man," from *Show Boat*.** Published by Hal Leonard. **Jerome Kern and Otto Harbach, "Smoke Gets In Your Eyes," from *Roberta*.** Words by Otto Harbach. Music by Jerome Kern. Copyright © 1933 Universal-Polygram International Publishing Inc. Copyright renewed. This arrangement copyright © 2010 Universal-Polygram International Publishing Inc. All rights reserved. Used by permission. Reprinted by permission of Hal Leonard Corporation. **Carole**

King, "You've Got a Friend." Published by Hal Leonard Corporation. **Jerry Leiber and Mike Stoller, "Hound Dog."** Published by Hal Leonard Corporation. **John Lennon and Paul McCartney, "Eleanor Rigby."** Published by Hal Leonard Corporation. **John Lennon and Paul McCartney, "Norwegian Wood."** Published by Hal Leonard Corporation. **John Lennon and Paul McCartney, "Nowhere Man."** Published by Hal Leonard Corporation. **György Ligeti, *Continuum*.** © 1970 by Schott Music, Mainz, Germany. © Renewed. All rights reserved. Used by permission of European American Music Distributors LLC, sole U.S. and Canadian agent for Schott Music, Mainz, Germany. **György Ligeti, "Désorde," from *Piano Etudes*, Book I.** Published by Schott Music, Mainz, Germany. **György Ligeti, *Hungarian Etudes*.** Published by Schott Music, Mainz Germany. **György Ligeti, *Ten Pieces for Wind Quintet*.** © 1969 by Schott Music, Mainz, Germany. © Renewed. All rights reserved. Used by permission of European American Music Distributors LLC, sole U.S. and Canadian agent for Schott Music, Mainz, Germany. **György Ligeti, "Wenn aus die Ferne," from *Three Fantasies on Texts by Fredrich Hölderlin*.** Published by Schott Music, Mainz, Germany. **Kenneth Maue, "In the Woods," from *Water in the Lake: Real Events for the Imagination*.** Copyright 1979, Harper & Row. Reprinted by permission of HarperCollins. **Don McLean, "Vincent."** Published by Hal Leonard Corporation. **Alan Menken and Tim Rice, "A Whole New World."** Music by Alan Menken. Lyrics by Tim Rice. © 1992 Wonderland Music Company Inc. Walt Disney Music Company. All rights reserved. Used by permission. **Oliver Messiaen, *Quartet for the End of Time*.** Published by Editions Durand. **Wolfgang Amadeus Mozart, "The Marriage of Figaro."** English translation by Ruth and Thomas Martin. Copyright © 1947, 1951 (Renewed) by G. Schirmer Inc. (ASCAP). International copyright secured. All rights reserved. Used by permission. **James Myers and Max Freedman, "Rock Around The Clock."** Words and music by Max C. Freedman and Jimmy DeKnight. Copyright © 1953 Myers Music Inc. and Capano Music. Copyright renewed 1981. This arrangement copyright © 2010 Myers Music Inc. and Capano Music. All rights on behalf of Myers Music Inc. administered by Sony/ATV Music Publishing LLC, 8 Music Square West, Nashville, TN 37203. International copyright secured. All rights reserved. Reprinted by permission of Hal Leonard Corporation. **Luigi Nono, *Il canto sospeso*.** Published by Eulenburg Edition. **Arvo Pärt, *Magnificat*.** © 1989 by Universal Edition AG, Wien. All rights reserved. Used by permission of European American Music Distributors LLC, U.S. and Canadian agent for Universal Edition AG, Wien. **Dolly Parton, "I Will Always Love You."** Published by Hal Leonard Corporation. **Krzysztof Penderecki, *Thernody for the Victims of Hiroshima*.** Published by Alfred Music Publishing Co. Inc. **Elvis Presley, "Love Me Tender."** Published by Hal Leonard Corporation. **Henry Purcell, "Music for a While."** Arranged by Michel Tippett and Walter Bergman. © 1947 by Schott Music Ltd., London. © Renewed. All rights reserved. Reproduced by permission. **Henry Purcell, "When I am Laid in Earth," from *Dido and Aeneas*.** Edited and arranged by Edward J. Dent. © Oxford University Press, 1925. Extract reproduced by permission. All rights reserved. **Queen, "Crazy Little Thing Called Love."** Published by Hal Leonard Corporation. **Maurice Ravel, "Aoua!" from *Chansons madécasses*.** Published by Editions Durand. **Steve Reich, *City Life*.** Published by Boosey & Hawkes Inc. **Steve Reich, *Piano Phase*.** Published by Universal Editions (London) Ltd. **Steve Reich, *Proverb*.** © Copyright 1997 by Hendon Music Inc., a Boosey & Hawkes company. Reprinted by permission of Boosey & Hawkes Inc. **Terry Riley, *In C*. Smokey Robinson, "You've Really Got a Hold on Me."** Published by Hal Leonard Corporation. **Smokey Robinson and Ronald White, "My Girl."** Published by Hal Leonard Corporation. **Vicki Sue Robinson, "Turn the Beat Around."** Published by Hal Leonard Corporation. **Liz Rose and Taylor Swift, "You Belong with Me."** Published by Hal Leonard Corporation. **Lalo Schifrin, Theme from *Mission Impossible*.** Published by Hal Leonard Corporation. **Arnold Schoenberg, *Klavierstuck*, op. 33a.** Used by permission of Belmont Music Publishers. **Richard Sherman and Robert Sherman, "Feed the Birds."** Published by Hal Leonard Corporation. **Karlheinz Stockhausen, *Klavierstück XI*, No. 7, for piano.** © 1956 by Universal Edition AG, Vienna. © Renewed. All rights reserved. Used by permission of European American Music Distributors LLC, U.S. and Canadian agent for Universal Edition AG, Vienna. **Igor Stravinsky, "Bransle Gay," from *Agon*.** Published by Boosy & Hawkes Inc. **Igor Stravinsky, "Lento," from For the *Five Fingers*.** © Copyright 1922 Chester Music Limited, 14-15 Berners Street, London W1T 3LJ, United Kingdom. Worldwide rights except the United Kingdom, Ireland, Australia, Canada, South Africa and all so-called reversionary rights territories where the copyright © 1996 is held jointly by Chester Music Limited and Schott Music GmbH & Co. KG, Mainz, Germany. All rights reserved. International copyright secured. Used by permission. **Igor Stravinsky, *Les Noces*.** Published by Chester Music Limited. **The Supremes, "Baby Love."** Published by Hal Leonard Corporation. **John Taverner, "The Lamb."** Published by Chester Music Limited. **Edgard Varese, *Density 21.5*.** © Copyright by Universal Music Publishing Ricordi SRL. Reproduced by permission of Universal Music MGB Publications SRL, Via Liguria 4, Fraz. Sesto Ulteriano, 20098 San Giuliano Milanese (MI), Italy. **Andrew Lloyd Webber and Tim Rice, "Don't Cry for Me Argentina," from *Evita*.** Published by Hal Leonard Corporation. **Anton Webern, *Symphonie für Kammerensemble*, op. 21.** © 1929 by Universal Edition AG, Wien/PH 368. © Renewed. All rights reserved. Used by permission of European American Music Distributors LLC, U.S. and Canadian agent for Universal Edition AG, Wien. **Meredith Willson, "Till There Was You," from *The Music Man*.** © 1950, 1957 (renewed) Frank Music Corp. and Meredith Willson Music. This arrangement © 2010 Frank Music Corp. and Meredith Willson Music. All rights reserved. Reprinted by permission of Hal Leonard Corporation. **La Monte Young, *Composition 1960*, No. 5, June 1960.** Reproduced with permission from An Anthology (1963). Copyright © La Monte Young 1963, 1970.

Index of Music Examples

Note: Page numbers in italic indicate music examples.

Index of Terms and Concepts

Note: Page numbers in italic indicate music examples. Please consult the Index of Music Examples *for specific compositions.*